MW00564415

Amos

OLD TESTAMENT AND CPH EDITOR

Christopher W. Mitchell

NEW TESTAMENT EDITOR

Curtis P. Giese

CONCORDIA COMMENTARY VOLUMES

Leviticus, John W. Kleinig

Joshua, Adolph L. Harstad

Ruth, John R. Wilch

1 Samuel, Andrew E. Steinmann

2 Samuel, Andrew E. Steinmann

**1 Kings 1–11*, Walter A. Maier III

Ezra and Nehemiah, Andrew E. Steinmann

Proverbs, Andrew E. Steinmann

Ecclesiastes, James Bollhagen

The Song of Songs, Christopher W. Mitchell

Isaiah 40–55, R. Reed Lessing

Isaiah 56–66, R. Reed Lessing

Ezekiel 1–20, Horace D. Hummel

Ezekiel 21–48, Horace D. Hummel

Daniel, Andrew E. Steinmann

Amos, R. Reed Lessing

Jonah, R. Reed Lessing

Matthew 1:1–11:1, Jeffrey A. Gibbs

Matthew 11:2–20:34, Jeffrey A. Gibbs

**Matthew 21:1–28:20*, Jeffrey A. Gibbs

Mark 1:1–8:26, James W. Voelz

Luke 1:1–9:50, Arthur A. Just Jr.

Luke 9:51–24:53, Arthur A. Just Jr.

John 1:1–7:1, William C. Weinrich

Romans 1–8, Michael P. Middendorf

Romans 9–16, Michael P. Middendorf

1 Corinthians, Gregory J. Lockwood

Galatians, A. Andrew Das

Ephesians, Thomas M. Winger

Colossians, Paul E. Deterding

Philemon, John G. Nordling

Hebrews, John W. Kleinig

2 Peter and Jude, Curtis P. Giese

1–3 John, Bruce G. Schuchard

Revelation, Louis A. Brighton

For subscription information and a current list of available Concordia Commentary volumes, visit our website: cph.org/commentary.

*In preparation

CONCORDIA COMMENTARY

A Theological Exposition of Sacred Scripture

AMOS

R. Reed Lessing

Concordia Publishing House
Saint Louis

3558 S. Jefferson Avenue, St. Louis, MO 63118-3968
1-800-325-3040 • www.cph.org

The SymbolGreek II, NewJerusalem, JacobiteLS, and TranslitLS fonts used to print this work are available from Linguist's Software, Inc., PO Box 580, Edmonds, WA 98020-0580, USA; telephone (425) 775-1130; www.linguistsoftware.com.

Manufactured in the United States of America

Library of Congress Cataloging-in-Publication Data

Lessing, R. Reed (Robert Reed), 1959–
Amos / R. Reed Lessing.
p. cm. — (Concordia commentary)
Includes bibliographical references and indexes.
ISBN-13: 978-0-7586-1269-4
ISBN-10: 0-7586-1269-9
1. Bible. O.T. Amos—Commentaries. I. Title. II. Series.

BS1585.53.L47 2009
224'.8077—dc22

2008032133

---

3 4 5 6 7 8 9 10 11 12 26 25 24 23 22 21 20 19 18 17

To the honor and glory of Jesus,
the Lion of the tribe of Judah,
who has triumphed (Rev 5:5)

Contents

Editors' Preface

What may a reader expect from the Concordia Commentary: A Theological Exposition of Sacred Scripture?

The purpose of this series, simply put, is to assist pastors, missionaries, and teachers of the Scriptures to convey God's Word with greater clarity, understanding, and faithfulness to the divine intent of the original Hebrew, Aramaic, or Greek text.

Since every interpreter approaches the exegetical task from a certain perspective, honesty calls for an outline of the presuppositions held by those who have shaped this commentary series. This also serves, then, as a description of the characteristics of the commentaries.

First in importance is the conviction that the content of the scriptural testimony is Jesus Christ. The Lord himself enunciated this when he said, "The Scriptures … testify to me" (Jn 5:39), words that have been incorporated into the logo of this series. The message of the Scriptures is the Good News of God's work to reconcile the world to himself through the life, death, resurrection, ascension, and everlasting session of Jesus Christ at the right hand of God the Father. Under the guidance of the same Spirit who inspired the writing of the Scriptures, these commentaries seek to find in every passage of every canonical book "that which promotes Christ" (as Luther's hermeneutic is often described). They are *Trinitarian* and *Christological* commentaries.

As they unfold the scriptural testimony to Jesus Christ, these commentaries expound Law and Gospel. This approach arises from a second conviction—that Law and Gospel are the overarching doctrines of the Bible itself and that to understand them in their proper distinction and relationship to each other is a key for understanding the self-revelation of God and his plan of salvation in Jesus Christ.

Now, Law and Gospel do not always appear in Scripture labeled as such. The palette of language in Scripture is multicolored, with many and rich hues. The dialectic of a pericope may be fallen creation and new creation, darkness and light, death and life, wandering and promised land, exile and return, ignorance and wisdom, demon possession and the kingdom of God, sickness and healing, being lost and found, guilt and righteousness, flesh and Spirit, fear and joy, hunger and feast, or Babylon and the new Jerusalem. But the common element is God's gracious work of restoring fallen humanity through the Gospel of his Son. Since the predominant characteristic of these commentaries is the proclamation of that Gospel, they are, in the proper sense of the term, *evangelical.*

A third, related conviction is that the Scriptures are God's vehicle for communicating the Gospel. The editors and authors accept without reservation that the canonical books of the Old and New Testaments are, in their entirety, the inspired, infallible, and inerrant Word of God. The triune God is the ultimate author of the Bible, and every word in the original Hebrew, Aramaic, and Greek is inspired by the Holy Spirit. Yet rather than mechanical dictation, in the mysterious process by which the Scriptures were divinely inspired (e.g., 2 Tim 3:16; 2 Pet 1:21), God made use of the human faculties, knowledge, interests, and styles of the biblical writers, whose individual books surely are marked by distinctive features. At the same time, the canon of Scripture has its own inner unity, and each passage must be understood in harmony with the larger context of the whole. This commentary series pays heed to the smallest of textual details because of its acceptance of *plenary and verbal inspiration* and interprets the text in light of the whole of Scripture, in accord with the analogy of faith, following the principle that *Scripture interprets Scripture.* The entirety of the Bible is God's Word, *sacred* Scripture, calling for *theological* exposition.

A fourth conviction is that, even as the God of the Gospel came into this world in Jesus Christ (the Word Incarnate), the scriptural Gospel has been given to and through the people of God, for the benefit of all humanity. God did not intend his Scriptures to have a life separated from the church. He gave them through servants of his choosing: prophets, sages, evangelists, and apostles. He gave them to the church and through the church, to be cherished in the church for admonition and comfort and to be used by the church for proclamation and catechesis. The living context of Scripture is ever the church, where the Lord's ministry of preaching, baptizing, forgiving sins, teaching, and celebrating the Lord's Supper continues. Aware of the way in which the incarnation of the Son of God has as a consequence the close union of Scripture and church, of Word and Sacraments, this commentary series features expositions that are *ecclesiological* and *sacramental.*

This Gospel Word of God, moreover, creates a unity among all those in whom it works the obedience of faith and who confess the truth of God revealed in it. This is the unity of the one holy Christian and apostolic church, which extends through world history. The church is to be found wherever the marks of the church are present: the Gospel in the Word and the Sacraments. These have been proclaimed, confessed, and celebrated in many different cultures and are in no way limited nor especially attached to any single culture or people. As this commentary series seeks to articulate the universal truth of the Gospel, it acknowledges and affirms the confession of the scriptural truth in all the many times and places where the one true church has been found. Aiming to promote *concord* in the confession of the one scriptural Gospel, these commentaries seek to be, in the best sense of the terms, *confessional, ecumenical*, and *catholic.*

All of those convictions and characteristics describe the theological heritage of Martin Luther and of the confessors who subscribe to the Book of Concord (1580)—those who have come to be known as Lutherans. The editors and authors forthrightly confess their subscription to the doctrinal exposition of Scripture in the Book of Concord. As the publishing arm of The Lutheran Church—Missouri Synod, Concordia Publishing House is bound to doctrinal agreement with the Scriptures and the Lutheran Confessions and seeks to herald the true Christian doctrine to the ends of the earth. To that end, the series has enlisted confessional Lutheran authors from other church bodies around the world who share the evangelical mission of promoting theological concord.

The authors and editors stand in the exegetical tradition of Martin Luther and the other Lutheran reformers, who in turn (as their writings took pains to demonstrate) stood in continuity with faithful exegesis by theologians of the early and medieval church, rooted in the hermeneutics of the Scriptures themselves (evident, for example, by how the New Testament interprets the Old). This hermeneutical method, practiced also by many non-Lutherans, includes (1) interpreting Scripture with Scripture according to the analogy of faith, that is, in harmony with the whole of Christian doctrine revealed in the Word; (2) giving utmost attention to the grammar (lexicography, phonetics, morphology, syntax, pragmatics) of the original language of the Hebrew, Aramaic, or Greek text; (3) seeking to discern the intended meaning of the text, the "plain" or "literal" sense, aware that the language of Scripture ranges from narrative to discourse, from formal prose to evocative poetry, from archaic to acrostic to apocalyptic, and it uses metaphor, type, parable, and other figures; (4) drawing on philology, linguistics, archaeology, literature, philosophy, history, and other fields in the quest for a better understanding of the text; (5) considering the history of the church's interpretation; (6) applying the text as authoritative also in the present milieu of the interpreter; and (7) above all, seeing the fulfillment and present application of the text in terms of Jesus Christ and his corporate church; upholding the Word, Baptism, and the Supper as the means through which Christ imparts salvation today; and affirming the inauguration, already now, of the eternal benefits of that salvation that is yet to come in the resurrection on the Last Day.

To be sure, the authors and editors do not feel bound to agree with every detail of the exegesis of our Lutheran forefathers. Nor do we imagine that the interpretations presented here are the final word about every crux and enigmatic passage. But the work has been done in harmony with the exegetical tradition that reaches back through the Lutheran confessors all the way to the biblical writers themselves, and in harmony with the confession of the church: grace alone, faith alone, Scripture alone, Christ alone.

The editors wish to acknowledge their debt of gratitude for all who have helped make possible this series. It was conceived at CPH in 1990, and a couple of years of planning and prayer to the Lord of the church preceded its formal launch on July 2, 1992. During that time, Dr. J. A. O. Preus II volunteered his enthusiasm for the project because, in his view, it would nurture and advance the faithful proclamation of the Christian faith as understood by the Lutheran church. The financial support that has underwritten the series was provided by a gracious donor who wished to remain anonymous. Those two faithful servants of God were called to heavenly rest not long after the series was inaugurated.

During the early years, former CPH presidents Dr. John W. Gerber and Dr. Stephen J. Carter had the foresight to recognize the potential benefit of such a landmark work for the church at large. CPH allowed Dr. Christopher W. Mitchell to devote his time and energy to the conception and initial development of the project. Dr. Mitchell has remained the CPH editor and is also the Old Testament editor and the author of the commentary on the Song of Songs. Dr. Dean O. Wenthe served on the project since its official start in 1992 and was the general editor from 1999 until 2016; he is also the author of the commentaries on Jeremiah and Lamentations. Julene Gernant Dumit (M.A.R.) has been the CPH production editor for the entire series. Dr. Jeffrey A. Gibbs served on the editorial board as the New Testament editor from 1999 until 2012 and is the author of the commentaries on Matthew. Dr. Curtis P. Giese, author of the commentary on 2 Peter and Jude and the commentary on James, joined the board in 2011 and now serves as the New Testament editor.

CPH thanks all of the institutions that have enabled their faculty to serve as authors and editors. A particular debt of gratitude is owed to Concordia Theological Seminary, Fort Wayne, Indiana, for kindly allowing Dr. Dean O. Wenthe to serve on the editorial board and to dedicate a substantial portion of his time to the series for many years. CPH also thanks Concordia Seminary, St. Louis, Missouri, for the dedication of Dr. Jeffrey A. Gibbs during his tenure as the New Testament editor. Moreover, Concordia University Texas is granting Dr. Curtis P. Giese a reduced load to enable him to carry on as the New Testament editor of the series. These institutions have thereby extended their ministries in selfless service for the benefit of the greater church.

The editors pray that the beneficence of their institutions may be reflected in this series by an evangelical orientation, a steadfast Christological perspective, an eschatological view toward the ultimate good of Christ's bride, and a concern that the wedding feast of the King's Son may be filled with all manner of guests (Mt 22:1–14).

> Now to him who is able to establish you by my Gospel and the preaching of Jesus Christ, by the revelation of the mystery kept secret for ages past but now revealed also through the prophetic Scriptures, made known to all the nations by order of the eternal God unto the obedience of faith—to the only wise God, through Jesus Christ, be the glory forever. Amen! (Rom 16:25–27)

Author's Preface

My first academic exposure to the book of Amos was in a class taught by Dr. Paul Raabe at Concordia Seminary in June 1994. His insightful and enthusiastic presentation of Amos has motivated me over the years to dig deeper into this minor prophet who has a major message. Now, fifteen years later, it gives me great joy to record my interpretations of the sacred text in this Concordia Commentary on Amos.

To prepare himself for ministry, Amos spent time in the libraries, newsrooms, fields, forests, homes, and social gatherings of his day. He became well-informed about Israel's history, her sacred texts, events going on in the ancient Near East, social norms, and religious practices. And somewhere along the way he became a master at Hebrew poetry and rhetoric.

Anyone who writes a commentary on this prophetic book must also invest time and energy in order to appreciate, understand, and then write about the message of Amos. Many people have made it possible for me to journey back into eighth-century BC Israel to listen again to the prophetic Word of Yahweh. I am indebted to my students at Concordia Seminary who have been my God-given companions in the study of Amos. I especially thank my student research assistants Jon Furgeson, Rick Blythe, and J. Wesley Beck. Their congenial spirits, attention to detail, and academic excellence have been most helpful.

My family has been most supportive of my time spent in Amos. My children, Abi Joy, Jonathan Curtis, and Lori Beth, continue to be the loves of my life. Also supporting this labor of love, even through some of her own graduate work, has been my delightful wife, Lisa, who has learned over the years to put up with my fascination with Hebrew prophets.

Several people and institutions have made the writing of this commentary not only possible but also a most enjoyable experience. The administration at Concordia Seminary in St. Louis graciously granted me study leaves in the fall quarter of the 2005–2006 academic year as well as a sabbatical during the 2006–2007 academic year to write this book.

This is now my second commentary in the Concordia Commentary series, and I appreciate all the more the opportunity to again work with the erudite and tireless editor, Dr. Christopher Mitchell, as well as Mrs. Julene Dumit, the series production editor, whose attention to detail, precision, and clarity are great gifts to the church.

Every scholarly project is interwoven with the author's previous works. My published dissertation, *Interpreting Discontinuity: Isaiah's Tyre Oracle*, introduced me to Hebrew poetry and rhetoric as well as to the prophetic genre known as oracles against the nations. My first volume in this series, *Jonah*, introduced me to the Minor Prophets and launched me into an appreciation for this oft-neglected part of the biblical canon. Both of these studies prepared me to undertake this project. I am thankful for the opportunity to further investigate some of their themes as they appear in Amos.

One of the most famous verses in Amos is 3:8, where the prophet asks, "A lion has roared; who should not be terrified? The Lord Yahweh has spoken; who cannot prophesy?" The Lion's roar seeks to awaken the church from her apathetic slumber, from what has grown ordinary and stale and routine. Most of the prophet's preaching is radical, subversive, affrontive, and unsettling. In all likelihood, many who heard Amos considered him a fool or a maniac (cf. Hos 9:7). But I thank God for Amos because the Holy Spirit has used his words to enable me to better hear the roar of the Lion of the tribe of Judah, whom John identifies as Jesus (Rev 5:5). And it is because this Lion was dead and is alive forevermore (Rev 1:18) that this commentary was written, and it is to Christ's glory that it is dedicated.

The Resurrection of Our Lord 2009

Principal Abbreviations

Books of the Bible

Gen	2 Ki	Is	Nah	Rom	Titus
Ex	1 Chr	Jer	Hab	1 Cor	Philemon
Lev	2 Chr	Lam	Zeph	2 Cor	Heb
Num	Ezra	Ezek	Hag	Gal	James
Deut	Neh	Dan	Zech	Eph	1 Pet
Josh	Esth	Hos	Mal	Phil	2 Pet
Judg	Job	Joel	Mt	Col	1 Jn
Ruth	Ps (pl. Pss)	Amos	Mk	1 Thess	2 Jn
1 Sam	Prov	Obad	Lk	2 Thess	3 Jn
2 Sam	Eccl	Jonah	Jn	1 Tim	Jude
1 Ki	Song	Micah	Acts	2 Tim	Rev

Books of the Apocrypha and Other Noncanonical Books of the Septuagint

1–2 Esdras	1–2 Esdras
Tobit	Tobit
Judith	Judith
Add Esth	Additions to Esther
Wisdom	Wisdom of Solomon
Sirach	Sirach/Ecclesiasticus
Baruch	Baruch
Ep Jer	Epistle of Jeremiah
Azariah	Prayer of Azariah
Song of the Three	Song of the Three Young Men
Susanna	Susanna
Bel	Bel and the Dragon
Manasseh	Prayer of Manasseh
1–2 Macc	1–2 Maccabees
3–4 Macc	3–4 Maccabees
Ps 151	Psalm 151
Odes	Odes
Ps(s) Sol	Psalm(s) of Solomon

Reference Works and Scripture Versions

ABD	*The Anchor Bible Dictionary.* Edited by D. N. Freedman. 6 vols. New York: Doubleday, 1992
ACCS	Ancient Christian Commentary on Scripture
AE	*Luther's Works.* St. Louis: Concordia, and Philadelphia: Fortress, 1955– [American Edition]
ANEP	*The Ancient Near East in Pictures Relating to the Old Testament.* Edited by J. B. Pritchard. 2d ed. Princeton: Princeton University Press, 1969
ANET	*Ancient Near Eastern Texts Relating to the Old Testament.* Edited by J. B. Pritchard. 3d ed. Princeton: Princeton University Press, 1969
ANF	*The Ante-Nicene Fathers.* Edited by A. Roberts and J. Donaldson. 10 vols. Repr. Peabody, Mass.: Hendrickson, 1994
BDAG	Bauer, W., F. W. Danker, W. F. Arndt, F. W. Gingrich. *A Greek-English Lexicon of the New Testament and Other Early Christian Literature.* 3d ed. Chicago: University of Chicago Press, 2000
BDB	Brown, F., S. R. Driver, and C. A. Briggs. *A Hebrew and English Lexicon of the Old Testament.* Oxford: Clarendon, 1979
BHS	*Biblia Hebraica Stuttgartensia.* Edited by K. Elliger and W. Rudolph. Stuttgart: Deutsche Bibelgesellschaft, 1967/1977
CCSL	Corpus Christianorum: Series latina. Turnhout: Brepols, 1953–
DBI	*Dictionary of Biblical Interpretation.* Edited by J. H. Hayes. Nashville: Abingdon, 1999
DCH	*The Dictionary of Classical Hebrew.* Edited by D. J. A. Clines. Sheffield: Sheffield Academic Press, 1993–
Ep	Epitome of the Formula of Concord
ESV	English Standard Version of the Bible
ET	English translation
FC	Formula of Concord
Gesenius	Gesenius, Wilhelm. *Hebräisches und aramäisches Handwörterbuch über das Alte Testament.* 12th ed. Leipzig: Vogel, 1895

GKC	*Gesenius' Hebrew Grammar.* Edited by E. Kautzsch. Translated by A. E. Cowley. 2d ed. Oxford: Clarendon, 1910
HALOT	Koehler, L., W. Baumgartner, and J. J. Stamm. *The Hebrew and Aramaic Lexicon of the Old Testament.* Translated and edited under the supervision of M. E. J. Richardson. 5 vols. Leiden: Brill, 1994–2000
IDB	*The Interpreter's Dictionary of the Bible.* Edited by G. A. Buttrick. 4 vols. Nashville: Abingdon, 1962
IDBSup	*The Interpreter's Dictionary of the Bible: Supplementary Volume.* Edited by K. Crim. Nashville: Abingdon, 1976
Jastrow	Jastrow, M., comp. *A Dictionary of the Targumim, the Talmud Babli and Yerushalmi, and the Midrashic Literature.* 2 vols. Brooklyn: P. Shalom, 1967
Joüon	Joüon, P. *A Grammar of Biblical Hebrew.* Translated and revised by T. Muraoka. 2 vols. Subsidia biblica 14/1–2. Rome: Editrice Pontificio Istituto Biblico, 1991
KAI	*Kanaanäische und aramäische Inschriften.* Edited by H. Donner and W. Röllig. 3 vols. Wiesbaden: Harrassowitz, 1962–1964
KJV	King James Version of the Bible
LC	Large Catechism of Martin Luther
LEH	Lust, J., E. Eynikel, and K. Hauspie. *A Greek-English Lexicon of the Septuagint.* 2 vols. Stuttgart: Deutsche Bibelgesellschaft, 1992–1996
LSB	*Lutheran Service Book.* St. Louis: Concordia, 2006
LW	*Lutheran Worship.* St. Louis: Concordia, 1982
LXX	Septuagint
MT	Masoretic Text of the Hebrew Bible
NASB	New American Standard Bible
NEAEHL	*The New Encyclopedia of Archaeological Excavations in the Holy Land.* Edited by Ephraim Stern. 4 vols. Jerusalem: Israel Exploration Society & Carta, 1993
NEB	New English Bible
NIDOTTE	*New International Dictionary of Old Testament Theology and Exegesis.* Edited by Willem A. VanGemeren. 5 vols. Grand Rapids: Zondervan, 1997
NIV	New International Version of the Bible
NKJV	New King James Version of the Bible

NPNF[1]	*The Nicene and Post-Nicene Fathers.* Series 1. Edited by P. Schaff. 14 vols. Repr. Peabody, Mass.: Hendrickson, 1994
NPNF[2]	*The Nicene and Post-Nicene Fathers.* Series 2. Edited by P. Schaff and H. Wace. 14 vols. Repr. Peabody, Mass.: Hendrickson, 1994
NRSV	New Revised Standard Version of the Bible
NT	New Testament
OT	Old Testament
Payne Smith	Payne Smith, R. *A Compendious Syriac Dictionary.* Oxford: Clarendon, 1903
RSV	Revised Standard Version of the Bible
SC	Small Catechism of Martin Luther
TDNT	*Theological Dictionary of the New Testament.* Edited by G. Kittel and G. Friedrich. Translated by G. W. Bromiley. 10 vols. Grand Rapids: Eerdmans, 1964–1976
TDOT	*Theological Dictionary of the Old Testament.* Edited by G. J. Botterweck, H. Ringgren, and H.-J. Fabry. Translated by J. T. Willis et al. 15 vols. Grand Rapids: Eerdmans, 1974–2006
TWOT	*Theological Wordbook of the Old Testament.* Edited by R. L. Harris, G. L. Archer Jr., and B. K. Waltke. 2 vols. Chicago: Moody, 1980
WA	*D. Martin Luthers Werke: Kritische Gesamtausgabe.* 73 vols. in 85. Weimar: Böhlau, 1883– [Weimarer Ausgabe]
WA Br	*D. Martin Luthers Werke: Kritische Gesamtausgabe. Briefwechsel.* 18 vols. Weimar: Böhlau, 1930–1985 [Weimarer Ausgabe Briefwechsel]
Waltke-O'Connor	Waltke, B. K., and M. O'Connor. *An Introduction to Biblical Hebrew Syntax.* Winona Lake, Ind.: Eisenbrauns, 1990
Williams	Williams, R. J. *Hebrew Syntax: An Outline.* 2d ed. Toronto: University of Toronto Press, 1976

Icons

These icons are used in the margins of this commentary to highlight the following themes:

Trinity

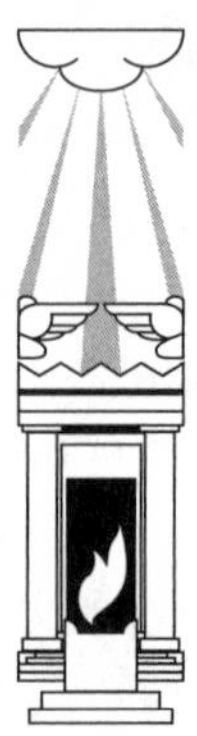

Temple, Tabernacle

Incarnation

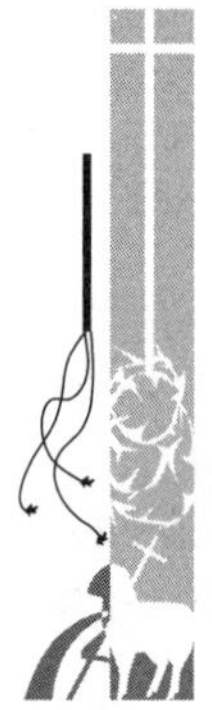

Passion, Atonement

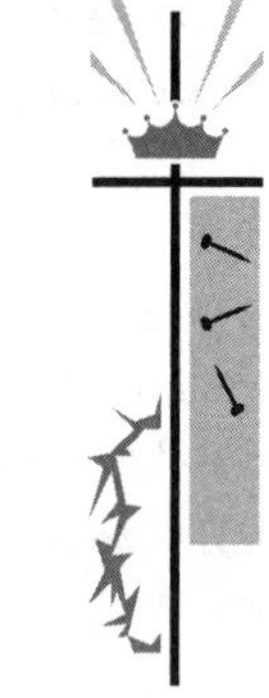

Death and Resurrection, Theology of the Cross, the Great Reversal

Christus Victor, Christology

Baptism

Catechesis, Instruction, Revelation

Lord's Supper

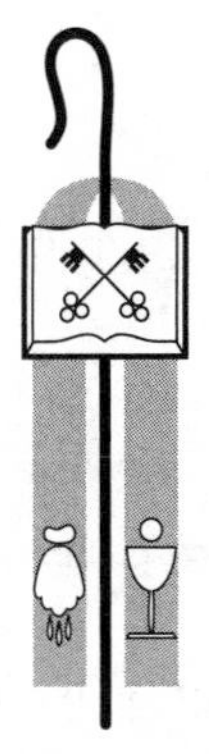

Ministry of Word and Sacrament,
Office of the Keys

The Church,
Christian Marriage

Worship

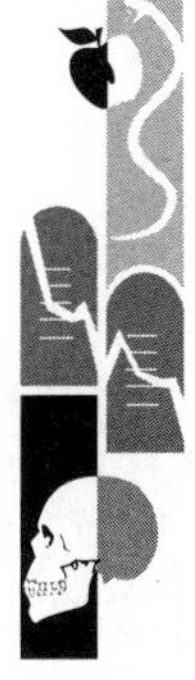

Sin, Law Breaking,
Death

Hope of Heaven,
Eschatology

Justification

Bibliography

Ackroyd, Peter R. "Isaiah I–XII: Presentation of a Prophet." Pages 16–48 in *Congress Volume: Göttingen 1977*. Supplements to Vetus Testamentum 29. Leiden: Brill, 1978.

Aharoni, Y. *The Samaria Ostraca, Eretz Israel in the Biblical Period*. Jerusalem, 1987 (in Hebrew).

Albright, William Foxwell. *Archaeology and the Religion of Israel*. 3d ed. Baltimore: Johns Hopkins Press, 1953.

———. *From the Stone Age to Christianity: Monotheism and the Historical Process*. 2d ed. Baltimore: Johns Hopkins University Press, 1957.

Alonso Schökel, Luis. *A Manual of Hebrew Poetics*. Rome: Pontifical Biblical Institute, 1988.

Alter, Robert. *The Art of Biblical Poetry*. New York: Basic, 1985.

———. "The Characteristics of Ancient Hebrew Poetry." Pages 611–24 in *The Literary Guide to the Bible*. Edited by Robert Alter and Frank Kermode. Cambridge, Mass.: Harvard University Press, 1987.

Andersen, Francis I. "Linguistic Coherence in Prophetic Discourse." Pages 137–56 in *Fortunate the Eyes That See: Essays in Honor of David Noel Freedman in Celebration of His Seventieth Birthday*. Edited by Astrid B. Beck, Andrew H. Bartelt, Paul R. Raabe, Chris A. Franke. Grand Rapids: Eerdmans, 1995.

Andersen, Francis I., and David Noel Freedman. *Amos*. Anchor Bible 24A. New York: Doubleday, 1989.

———. *Micah*. Anchor Bible 24E. New York: Doubleday, 2000.

André, Gunnel. *Determining the Destiny: PQD in the Old Testament*. Lund, Sweden: Gleerup, 1980.

Arand, Charles P., and Joel Biermann. "Why the Two Kinds of Righteousness?" *Concordia Journal* 33 (2007): 116–35.

Archer, Gleason L., Jr. *A Survey of Old Testament Introduction*. Rev. ed. Chicago: Moody, 1974.

Auld, A. G. *Amos*. Old Testament Guides. Sheffield: JSOT Press, 1986.

Balentine, Samuel E. *The Hidden God: The Hiding of the Face of God in the Old Testament*. Oxford: Oxford University Press, 1983.

Balla, Emil. *Die Droh- und Scheltworte des Amos*. Leipzig: Edelmann, 1926.

Barkay, Gabriel. "Royal Palace, Royal Portrait? The Tantalizing Possibilities of Ramat Raḥel." *Biblical Archaeology Review* 32/5 (September/October 2006): 34–44.

Barr, James. *Biblical Faith and Natural Theology*. Oxford: Clarendon, 1993.

Barré, Michael L. "The Meaning of *lʾ ʾšybnw* in Amos 1:3–2:6." *Journal of Biblical Literature* 105 (1986): 611–31.

Barstad, Hans M. *The Religious Polemics of Amos: Studies in the Preaching of Am 2, 7B–8; 4, 1–13; 5, 1–27; 6, 4–7; 8, 14*. Supplements to Vetus Testamentum 34. Leiden: Brill, 1984.

Bartelt, Andrew H. *The Book around Immanuel: Style and Structure in Isaiah 2–12*. Winona Lake, Ind.: Eisenbrauns, 1996.

———. "Dialectical Negation: An Exegetical Both/And." Pages 57–66 in *Hear the Word of Yahweh: Essays on Scripture and Archaeology in Honor of Horace D. Hummel*. Edited by Dean O. Wenthe, Paul L. Schrieber, and Lee A. Maxwell. St. Louis: Concordia, 2002.

Barth, Hermann. *Die Jesaja-Worte in der Josiazeit: Israel und Assur als Thema einer produktiven Neuinterpretation der Jesajaüberlieferung*. Neukirchen-Vlyun: Neukirchener, 1977.

Barth, Karl. *Church Dogmatics*. 4 vols. Edinburgh: T&T Clark, 1936–1962.

———. *Evangelical Theology: An Introduction*. Translated by Grover Foley. New York: Holt, Rinehart and Winston, 1963.

Bartlett, J. R. "The Brotherhood of Edom." *Journal for the Study of the Old Testament* 4 (1977): 2–27.

Barton, John. "Ethics in Isaiah of Jerusalem." Pages 80–97 in *"The Place Is Too Small for Us": The Israelite Prophets in Recent Scholarship*. Edited by Robert P. Gordon. Winona Lake, Ind.: Eisenbrauns, 1995.

———. *Reading the Old Testament: Method in Biblical Study*. Rev. ed. Louisville: Westminster John Knox, 1996.

———. *Understanding Old Testament Ethics: Approaches and Explorations*. Louisville: Westminster John Knox, 2003.

Baumgartner, Walter. *Kennen Amos und Hosea eine Heils-Eschatologie?* Zürich: Schaufelberger, 1913.

Becking, Bob. *The Fall of Samaria: An Historical and Archaeological Study*. Leiden: Brill, 1992.

Ben Zvi, Ehud. *Hosea*. Forms of the Old Testament Literature 21A/1. Grand Rapids: Eerdmans, 2005.

———. "Introduction: Writings, Speeches, and the Prophetic Books: Setting an Agenda." Pages 1–29 in *Writings and Speech in Israelite and Ancient Near Eastern Prophecy*. Edited by Ehud Ben Zvi and Michael H. Floyd. Atlanta: Scholars, 2000.

———. "Twelve Prophetic Books or 'The Twelve': A Few Preliminary Considerations." Pages 125–56 in *Forming Prophetic Literature: Essays on Isaiah and the Twelve in Honor of John D. W. Watts*. Edited by James W. Watts and Paul R. House. Journal for the Study of the Old Testament: Supplement Series 235. Sheffield: Sheffield Academic Press, 1996.

Bendor, Shunya. *The Social Structure of Ancient Israel: The Institution of the Family (Beit ʾAb) from the Settlement to the End of the Monarchy*. Jerusalem: Simor, 1996.

Benne, Robert. *Reasonable Ethics: A Christian Approach to Social, Economic, and Political Concerns.* St. Louis: Concordia, 2005.

Bentzen, A. "The Ritual Background of Amos i 2–ii 16." Pages 85–99 in Oudtestamentische Studiën 8. Edited by P. A. H. de Boer. Leiden: Brill, 1950.

Berlin, Adele. "The Prophetic Literature of the Hebrew Bible." Pages 114–19 in *Approaches to Teaching the Hebrew Bible as Literature in Translation.* Edited by Barry N. Olshen and Yael S. Feldman. New York: Modern Language Association of America, 1989.

Berry, R. J. "Christianity and the Environment: Escapist Mysticism or Responsible Stewardship." Pages 397–407 in vol. 2 of *Readings in Christian Ethics.* Edited by David K. Clark and Robert V. Rakestraw. 2 vols. Grand Rapids: Baker, 1994–1996.

Bewer, Julius A. "Critical Notes on Amos 2:7 and 8:4." *American Journal of Semitic Languages and Literature* 19/2 (January 1903): 116–17.

———. "Note on Amos 2:7a." *Journal of Biblical Literature* 28 (1909): 200–2.

Bikai, Patricia Maynor. "Phoenician Tyre." Pages 45–53 in *The Heritage of Tyre: Essays on the History, Archaeology, and Preservation of Tyre.* Edited by Martha Sharp Joukowsky. Dubuque, Iowa: Kendall/Hunt, 1992.

———. "The Phoenicians: Rich and Glorious Traders of the Levant." *Archaeology* 43/2 (March/April 1990): 22–26, 28, 30.

Biran, Avraham. *Biblical Dan.* Jerusalem: Israel Exploration Society, 1994.

———. "An Israelite Horned Altar at Dan." *Biblical Archaeologist* 37 (1974): 106–7.

Black, C. Clifton. "Keeping Up with Recent Studies XVI: Rhetorical Criticism and Biblical Interpretation." *Expository Times* 100 (1989): 252–58.

Bleibtreu, Erika. "Five Ways to Conquer a City." *Biblical Archaeology Review* 16/3 (May/June 1990): 36–44.

———. "Grisly Assyrian Record of Torture and Death." *Biblical Archaeology Review* 17/1 (January/February 1991): 52–61, 75.

Blenkinsopp, Joseph. *A History of Prophecy in Israel.* Louisville: Westminster John Knox, 1996.

Block, Daniel I. *The Book of Ezekiel.* 2 vols. New International Commentary on the Old Testament. Grand Rapids: Eerdmans, 1997–1998.

———. *The Gods of the Nations: Studies in Ancient Near Eastern National Theology.* 2d ed. Grand Rapids: Eerdmans, 2000.

Boadt, Lawrence. *Ezekiel's Oracles against Egypt: A Literary and Philological Study of Ezekiel 29–32.* Biblica et orientalia 37. Rome: Pontifical Biblical Institute, 1980.

———. "The Poetry of Prophetic Persuasion: Preserving the Prophet's Persona." *Catholic Biblical Quarterly* 59 (1997): 1–21.

———. "Reflections on the Study of Hebrew Poetry Today." *Concordia Journal* 24 (1998): 156–63.

Booth, Wayne C. *A Rhetoric of Irony*. Chicago: University of Chicago, 1974.

Bottéro, Jean. *Religion in Ancient Mesopotamia*. Translated by Teresa Lavender Fagan. Chicago: University of Chicago Press, 2001.

Bramer, Stephen J. "The Literary Genre of the Book of Amos." *Bibliotheca sacra* 156 (1999): 42–60.

Braun, Michael A. "James' Use of Amos at the Jerusalem Council: Steps toward a Possible Solution of the Textual and Theological Problems." *Journal of the Evangelical Theological Society* 20 (1977): 113–21.

Bright, John. *Covenant and Promise: The Prophetic Understanding of the Future in Pre-exilic Israel*. Philadelphia: Westminster Press, 1976.

———. *A History of Israel*. 4th ed. Philadelphia: Westminster, 2000.

Brighton, Louis A. *Revelation*. Concordia Commentary. St. Louis: Concordia, 1999.

Brongers, H. A. "Die Partikel לְמַעַן in der biblisch-hebräischen Sprache." Pages 84–96 in *Syntax and Meaning: Studies in Hebrew Syntax and Biblical Exegesis*. Oudtestamentische Studiën 18. Edited by A. S. van der Woude. Leiden: Brill, 1973.

Bronznick, Norman. "More on *HLK ʾL*." *Vetus Testamentum* 35 (1985): 98–99.

Broshi, Magen. "The Expansion of Jerusalem in the Reigns of Hezekiah and Manasseh." *Israel Exploration Journal* 24 (1974): 21–26.

Brown, Walter. "Amos 5:26: A Challenge to Reading and Interpretation." *Theological Educator* 52 (1995): 69–78.

Bruce, F. F. *The Epistle to the Hebrews: The English Text with Introduction, Exposition, and Notes*. Grand Rapids: Eerdmans, 1964.

Bruckner, James K. *Implied Law in the Abraham Narratives: A Literary and Theological Analysis*. Journal for the Study of the Old Testament: Supplement Series 335. Sheffield: Sheffield Academic Press, 2001.

Brueggemann, Walter. "Amos IV 4–13 and Israel's Covenant Worship." *Vetus Testamentum* 15 (1965): 1–15.

———. "Amos' Intercessory Formula." *Vetus Testamentum* 19 (1969): 385–99.

———. "At the Mercy of Babylon: A Subversive Rereading of the Empire." *Journal of Biblical Literature* 110 (1991): 3–22.

———. "The Book of Jeremiah: Portrait of the Prophet." *Interpretation* 37 (1983): 130–45.

———. *The Book That Breathes New Life: Scriptural Authority and Biblical Theology*. Minneapolis: Fortress, 2005.

———. *Isaiah 1–39*. Louisville: Westminster John Knox, 1998.

———. *The Land: Place as Gift, Promise, and Challenge in Biblical Faith*. 2d ed. Minneapolis: Fortress, 2002.

———. *Like Fire in the Bones: Listening for the Prophetic Word in Jeremiah*. Minneapolis: Fortress, 2006.

———. *Texts That Linger, Words That Explode: Listening to Prophetic Voices*. Minneapolis: Fortress, 2000.

Budde, C. "Das hebräische Klagelied." *Zeitschrift für die alttestamentliche Wissenschaft* 2 (1882): 1–52.

Buss, Martin J. *Biblical Form Criticism in Its Context*. Journal for the Study of the Old Testament: Supplement Series 274. Sheffield: Sheffield Academic Press, 1999.

Carroll, Robert P. "Ancient Israelite Prophecy and Dissonance Theory." Pages 377–91 in *"The Place Is Too Small for Us": The Israelite Prophets in Recent Scholarship*. Edited by Robert P. Gordon. Winona Lake, Ind.: Eisenbrauns, 1995.

Carroll R., M. Daniel. *Amos—The Prophet and His Oracles: Research on the Book of Amos*. Louisville: Westminster John Knox, 2002.

———. *Contexts for Amos: Prophetic Poetics in Latin American Perspective*. Journal for the Study of the Old Testament: Supplement Series 132. Sheffield: JSOT Press, 1992.

———. " 'For So You Love to Do': Probing Popular Religion in the Book of Amos." Pages 168–89 in *Rethinking Contexts, Rereading Texts: Contributions from the Social Sciences to Biblical Interpretation*. Edited by M. D. Carroll R. Journal for the Study of the Old Testament: Supplement Series 299. Sheffield: Sheffield Academic Press, 2000.

Carter, Charles. "Opening Windows onto Biblical Worlds: Applying the Social Sciences to Hebrew Scripture." Pages 421–51 in *The Face of Old Testament Studies: A Survey of Contemporary Approaches*. Edited by David W. Baker and Bill T. Arnold. Grand Rapids: Baker, 1999.

Carter, Charles E., and Carol L. Meyers, eds. *Community, Identity, and Ideology: Social Science Approaches to the Hebrew Bible*. Winona Lake, Ind.: Eisenbrauns, 1996.

Ceresko, Anthony R. "Janus Parallelism in Amos's 'Oracles against the Nations' (Amos 1:3–2:16)." *Journal of Biblical Literature* 113 (1994): 485–90.

Chapman, Colin. *Whose Promised Land? The Continuing Crisis over Israel and Palestine*. Grand Rapids: Baker, 2002.

Childs, Brevard S. *Introduction to the Old Testament as Scripture*. Philadelphia: Fortress, 1979.

Childs, James M., Jr. "Ethics and the Promise of God: Moral Authority and the Church's Witness." Pages 97–114, 197–200 in *The Promise of Lutheran Ethics*. Edited by Karen L. Bloomquist and John R. Stumme. Minneapolis: Fortress, 1998.

Christensen, Duane L. *Transformations of the War Oracle in Old Testament Prophecy: Studies in the Oracles against the Nations*. Missoula, Mont.: Scholars, 1975.

Clark, David K., and Robert V. Rakestraw, eds. *Readings in Christian Ethics.* 2 vols. Grand Rapids: Baker, 1994–1996.

Clements, Ronald E. *Old Testament Prophecy: From Oracles to Canon.* Louisville: Westminster John Knox, 1996.

———. *One Hundred Years of Old Testament Interpretation.* Philadelphia: Westminster, 1976. Published in Great Britain under the title *A Century of Old Testament Study.*

———. *Prophecy and Tradition.* Growing Points in Theology. Atlanta: John Knox, 1975.

———. "Prophets, Editors, and Tradition." Pages 443–52 in *"The Place Is Too Small for Us": The Israelite Prophets in Recent Scholarship.* Edited by Robert P. Gordon. Winona Lake, Ind.: Eisenbrauns, 1995.

Clifford, Richard J. "The Use of *Hôy* in the Prophets." *Catholic Biblical Quarterly* 28 (1966): 458–64.

Cogan, Mordechai. " 'Ripping Open Pregnant Women' in Light of an Assyrian Analogue." *Journal of the American Oriental Society* 103 (1983): 755–57.

Conrad, Edgar W. "Heard But Not Seen: The Representation of 'Books' in the Old Testament." *Journal for the Study of the Old Testament* 54 (June 1992): 45–59.

Cooper, Alan. "The Meaning of Amos's Third Vision (Amos 7:7–9)." Pages 13–21 in *Tehillah le-Moshe: Biblical and Judaic Studies in Honor of Moshe Greenberg.* Edited by Mordechai Cogan, Barry L. Eichler, and Jeffrey H. Tigay. Winona Lake, Ind.: Eisenbrauns, 1997.

Coote, Robert B. *Amos among the Prophets: Composition and Theology.* Philadelphia: Fortress, 1981.

Craigie, Peter C. "Amos the *Nōqēd* in the Light of Ugaritic." *Studies in Religion* 11 (1982): 29–33.

Crenshaw, James L. "Amos and the Theophanic Tradition." *Zeitschrift für die alttestamentliche Wissenschaft* 80 (1968): 203–15.

———. "Education in Ancient Israel." *Journal of Biblical Literature* 104 (1985): 601–15.

———. *Education in Ancient Israel: Across the Deadening Silence.* New York: Doubleday, 1998.

———. "The Expression *Mî Yôdēaʿ* in the Hebrew Bible." *Vetus Testamentum* 36 (1986): 274–88.

———. *Hymnic Affirmation of Divine Justice: The Doxologies of Amos and Related Texts in the Old Testament.* Missoula: Scholars, 1975.

———. "The Influence of the Wise upon Amos: The 'Doxologies of Amos' and Job 5:9–16; 9:5–10." *Zeitschrift für die alttestamentliche Wissenschaft* 79 (1967): 42–52.

———. *Joel: A New Translation with Introduction and Commentary.* Anchor Bible 24C. New York: Doubleday, 1995.

Cross, Frank Moore, and David Noel Freedman. *Early Hebrew Orthography: A Study of the Epigraphic Evidence*. New Haven, Conn.: American Oriental Society, 1952.

Crowfoot, J. W., and Grace M. Crowfoot. *Early Ivories from Samaria*. Samaria-Sebaste 2. London: Palestine Exploration Fund, 1938.

Cuddon, J. A. *A Dictionary of Literary Terms and Literary Theory*. 3d ed. Oxford: Blackwell Reference, 1991.

Cyril of Alexandria. *Commentary on the Twelve Prophets*. Translated by Robert C. Hill. 2 vols. Fathers of the Church 115–116. Washington, D.C.: Catholic University of America Press, 2007–2008.

Dahood, Mitchell. "Denominative *Riḥḥam*, 'to Conceive, Enwomb.' " *Biblica* 44 (1963): 204–5.

———. *Psalms*. 3 vols. Anchor Bible 16–17A. Garden City, N.Y.: Doubleday, 1968.

Davies, W. D. *The Gospel and the Land: Early Christianity and Jewish Territorial Doctrine*. Berkeley: University of California Press, 1974.

De Waard, Jan. "The Chiastic Structure of Amos V 1–17." *Vetus Testamentum* 27 (1977): 170–77.

———. *A Handbook on Isaiah*. Textual Criticism and the Translator 1. Winona Lake, Ind.: Eisenbrauns, 1997.

Dearman, John Andrew. *Property Rights in the Eighth-Century Prophets: The Conflict and Its Background*. Atlanta: Scholars, 1988.

Delitzsch, Franz. *Commentary on the Epistle to the Hebrews*. Translated by Thomas L. Kingsbury. 2 vols. Repr., Minneapolis: Klock & Klock, 1978.

———. *A New Commentary on Genesis*. Vol. 1. Translated by Sophia Taylor. Edinburgh: T&T Clark, 1899.

Dempster, Stephen. "The Lord Is His Name: A Study of the Distribution of the Names and Titles of God in the Book of Amos." *Revue biblique* 98 (1991): 170–89.

DeVries, Simon J. *Yesterday, Today and Tomorrow: Time and History in the Old Testament*. Grand Rapids: Eerdmans, 1975.

Diepold, Peter. *Israels Land*. Stuttgart: Kolhammer, 1972.

Dijk, H. J. van. *Ezekiel's Prophecy on Tyre (Ez. 26,1–28,19): A New Approach*. Biblica et orientalia 20. Rome: Pontifical Biblical Institute, 1968.

Dillard, Raymond. "Joel." Pages 239–313 in *The Minor Prophets: An Exegetical and Expository Commentary*. Vol. 1: *Hosea, Joel, and Amos*. Edited by Thomas E. McComiskey. Grand Rapids: Baker, 1992.

Dillenberger, John. *God Hidden and Revealed: The Interpretation of Luther's Deus Absconditus and Its Significance for Religious Thought*. Philadelphia: Muhlenberg, 1953.

Drinan, Robert F. *Cry of the Oppressed: The History and Hope of the Human Rights Revolution*. San Francisco: Harper & Row, 1987.

Driver, Samuel R. *The Books of Joel and Amos*. 2d ed. Cambridge: Cambridge University Press, 1915.

Duhm, Bernhard. *Die Theologie der Propheten als Grundlage für die innere Entwicklungsgeschichte der israelitischen Religion*. Bonn: Adolph Marcus, 1875.

Eagleton, Terry. *Literary Theory: An Introduction*. Oxford: Blackwell, 1983.

Ebeling, E. "Ein Heldenlied auf Tiglatpileser I." *Orientalia* 18 (1949): 30–39.

Eerdmans Dictionary of the Bible. Edited by David Noel Freedman, Allen C. Myers, and Astrid B. Beck. Grand Rapids: Eerdmans, 2000.

Eichrodt, Walther. *Theology of the Old Testament*. Translated by J. A. Baker. Vol. 2. London: SCM, 1967.

Eissfeldt, Otto. *The Old Testament: An Introduction*. Translated by Peter R. Ackroyd. Harper & Row, 1965.

Elat, Moshe. "Phoenician Overland Trade within the Mesopotamian Empires." Pages 21–35 in *Ah, Assyria ... : Studies in Assyrian History and Ancient Near Eastern Historiography Presented to Hayim Tadmore*. Edited by Mordechai Cogan and Israel Eph'al. Jerusalem: Magnus, 1991.

Elert, Werner. *The Structure of Lutheranism*. Vol. 1. Translated by Walter A. Hansen. St. Louis: Concordia, 1962.

Ellis, Robert R. "Are There Any Cows of Bashan on Seminary Hill?" *Southwestern Journal of Theology* 38/1 (Fall 1995): 44–48.

Enns, Peter. *Inspiration and Incarnation: Evangelicals and the Problem of the Old Testament*. Grand Rapids: Baker, 2005.

Ferreiro, Alberto, ed. *The Twelve Prophets*. Ancient Christian Commentary on Scripture, Old Testament 14. Downers Grove, Ill.: InterVarsity, 2003.

Festinger, Leo, Henry W. Riecken, and Stanley Schachter. *When Prophecy Fails*. Minneapolis, University of Minnesota Press, 1956.

Fiorenza, Elisabeth Schüssler. *Rhetoric and Ethic: The Politics of Biblical Studies*. Minneapolis: Fortress, 1999.

Fishbane, Michael. *Biblical Interpretation in Ancient Israel*. Oxford: Clarendon, 1985.

———. "The Treaty Background of Amos 1:11 and Related Matters." *Journal of Biblical Literature* 89 (1970): 313–18.

Fohrer, Georg. *Introduction to the Old Testament*. Translated by David Green. Nashville: Abingdon, 1968.

———. "Prophetie und Magie." *Zeitschrift für die alttestamentliche Wissenschaft* 78 (1966): 25–47.

Forde, Gerhard O. *Theology Is for Proclamation*. Minneapolis: Fortress, 1990.

Forell, George Wolfgang. *Faith Active in Love: An Investigation of Principles Underlying Luther's Social Ethics*. Minneapolis: Augsburg, 1954.

Fowler, Alastair. *Kinds of Literature: An Introduction to the Theory of Genres and Modes*. Cambridge: Harvard University Press, 1982.

Fox, Michael V. "The Rhetoric of Ezekiel's Vision of the Valley of the Bones." *Hebrew Union College Annual* 51 (1980): 1–15.

Fredrickson, David. "Pauline Ethics: Congregations as Communities of Moral Deliberation." Pages 115–29, 200–4, in *The Promise of Lutheran Ethics*. Edited by Karen L. Bloomquist and John R. Stumme. Minneapolis: Fortress, 1998.

Freedman, David Noel. "But Did King David Invent Musical Instruments?" *Bible Review* 1/2 (Summer 1985): 48–51.

———. "Confrontations in the Book of Amos." *Princeton Seminary Bulletin* 11 (1990): 240–52.

———. *Pottery, Poetry, and Prophecy: Studies in Early Hebrew Poetry*. Winona Lake, Ind.: Eisenbrauns, 1980.

Freedman, David Noel, and Andrew Welch. "Amos's Earthquake and Israelite Prophecy." Pages 188–98 in *Scripture and Other Artifacts: Essays on the Bible and Archaeology in Honor of Philip J. King*. Edited by Michael D. Coogan, J. Cheryl Exum, and Lawrence E. Stager. Louisville: Westminster John Knox, 1994.

Fretheim, Terence E. *God and World in the Old Testament: A Relational Theology of Creation*. Nashville: Abingdon, 2005.

———. "The Reclamation of Creation: Redemption and Law in Exodus." *Interpretation* 45 (1991): 354–65.

———. "The Repentance of God: A Key to Evaluating Old Testament God-Talk." *Horizons in Biblical Theology* 10 (1988): 10:47–70.

———. *The Suffering of God: An Old Testament Perspective*. Philadelphia: Fortress, 1984.

Galling, Kurt, ed. *Biblisches Reallexikon*. 2d ed. Tübingen: Mohr, 1977.

Gardiner, Alan. *The Kadesh Inscriptions of Ramesses II*. Oxford: Oxford University Press, 1960.

Garr, W. Randall. "The Qinah: A Study of Poetic Meter, Syntax and Style." *Zeitschrift für die alttestamentliche Wissenschaft* 95 (1983): 54–75.

Gehman, Henry S. "Natural Law and the Old Testament." Pages 109–22 in *Biblical Studies in Memory of H. C. Alleman*. Edited by J. M. Myers, O. Reimherr, and H. N. Bream. Locus Valley, N.Y.: Augustin, 1960.

Gelin, Albert. *The Poor of Yahweh*. Translated by Mother Kathryn Sullivan. Collegeville, Minn.: Liturgical, 1964.

Geller, Stephen A. "Were the Prophets Poets?" Pages 154–65 in *"The Place Is Too Small for Us": The Israelite Prophets in Recent Scholarship*. Edited by Robert P. Gordon. Winona Lake, Ind.: Eisenbrauns, 1995.

Gerhard, Johann. *On the Nature of God and on the Most Holy Mystery of the Trinity*. Theological Commonplaces. Translated by Richard J. Dinda. St. Louis: Concordia, 2007.

Gerstenberger, Erhard. "The Woe-Oracles of the Prophets." *Journal of Biblical Literature* 81 (1962): 249–63.

Gese, H. "Komposition bei Amos." Pages 74–95 in *Congress Volume: Vienna 1980.* Edited by J. A. Emerton. Supplements to Vetus Testamentum 32. Leiden: Brill, 1981.

Gibbs, Jeffrey A. *Jerusalem and Parousia: Jesus' Eschatological Discourse in Matthew's Gospel*. St. Louis: Concordia, 2000.

———. *Matthew 1:1–11:1*. Concordia Commentary. St. Louis: Concordia, 2006.

Gibson, John C. L. *Hebrew and Moabite Inscriptions*. Vol. 1 of *Textbook of Syrian Semitic Inscriptions*. Oxford: Clarendon, 1971.

———. *Language and Imagery in the Old Testament*. Peabody, Mass.: Hendrickson, 1998.

Gieschen, Charles A. "The Real Presence of the Son before Christ: Revisiting an Old Approach to Old Testament Christology." *Concordia Theological Quarterly* 68 (2004): 105–26.

Giles, Terry. "A Note on the Vocation of Amos in 7:14." *Journal of Biblical Literature* 111 (1992): 690–92.

Gitay, Yehoshua. "Deutero-Isaiah: Oral or Written?" *Journal of Biblical Literature* 99 (1980): 185–97.

———. "Isaiah and His Audience." *Prooftexts* 3 (1983): 223–30.

———. *Isaiah and His Audience: The Structure and Meaning of Isaiah 1–12*. Studia Semitica Neerlandica 30. Assen, Netherlands: Van Gorcum, 1991.

———. *Prophecy and Persuasion: A Study of Isaiah 40–48*. Forum Theologiae Linguisticae 14. Bonn: Linguistica Biblica, 1981.

———. "Reflections on the Study of the Prophetic Discourse: The Question of Isaiah I 2–20." *Vetus Testamentum* 33 (1983): 207–21.

———. "A Study of Amos's Art of Speech: A Rhetorical Analysis of Amos 3:1–15." *Catholic Biblical Quarterly* 42 (1980): 293–309.

Good, Edwin M. *Irony in the Old Testament*. Philadelphia: Westminster, 1965.

Gordis, Robert. "The Composition and Structure of Amos." Pages 217–29 in *Poets, Prophets, and Sages: Essays in Biblical Interpretation*. Bloomington: Indiana University Press, 1971.

———. "The Heptad as an Element of Biblical and Rabbinic Style." *Journal of Biblical Literature* 62 (1943): 17–26.

Gordon, Robert P. "A Story of Two Paradigm Shifts." Pages 3–26 in *"The Place Is Too Small for Us": The Israelite Prophets in Recent Scholarship*. Edited by Robert P. Gordon. Winona Lake, Ind.: Eisenbrauns, 1995.

Gottwald, Norman K. *The Tribes of Yahweh: A Sociology of the Religion of Liberated Israel, 1250–1050 B.C.E.* Maryknoll, N.Y.: Orbis, 1979.

Gowan, Donald E. *When Man Becomes God: Humanism and Hybris in the Old Testament*. Pittsburgh: Pickwith, 1975.

Graffy, Adrian. *A Prophet Confronts His People: The Disputation Speech in the Prophets*. Rome: Pontifical Biblical Institute, 1984.

Grant, Frederick C., and H. H. Rowley, eds. *Dictionary of the Bible*. Rev. ed. New York: Scribner, 1963.

Grayson, Albert Kirk. "Assyria: Ashur-dan II to Ashur-nirari V (934–745 b.c.)." Pages 238–81 in *The Cambridge Ancient History*. 2d ed. Vol. 3/1: *The Prehistory of the Balkans; and the Middle East and the Aegean World, Tenth to Eighth Centuries b.c.* Edited by John Boardman et al. Cambridge: Cambridge University Press, 1982.

———. *Assyrian Royal Inscriptions*. Vol. 2. Wiesbaden: Harrassowitz, 1976.

Greenberg, Moshe. *Ezekiel*. 2 vols. Anchor Bible 22–22A. Garden City, N.Y.: Doubleday, 1983–1997.

———. "What Are the Valid Criteria for Determining Inauthentic Matter in Ezekiel?" Pages 123–35 in *Ezekiel and His Book: Textual and Literary Criticism and Their Interrelation*. Edited by J. Lust et al. Leuven: Leuven University Press, 1986.

Greenstein, Edward L. *Essays on Biblical Method and Translation*. Brown Judaic Studies 92. Atlanta: Scholars, 1989.

Gressmann, Hugo. *Der Messias*. Göttingen: Vandenhoeck & Ruprecht, 1929.

———. *Der Ursprung der israelitisch-jüdischen Eschatologie*. Göttingen: Vandenhoeck & Ruprecht, 1905.

Gunkel, Hermann. *Creation and Chaos in the Primeval Era and the Eschaton: A Religio-Historical Study of Genesis 1 and Revelation 12*. Translated by K. William Whitney, Jr. Grand Rapids: Eerdmans, 2006.

———. "The Israelite Prophecy from the Time of Amos." Pages 48–75 in vol. 1 of *Twentieth Century Theology in the Making*. Edited by Jaroslav Pelikan. Translated by R. A. Wilson. 3 vols. New York: Harper & Row, 1969. Vol. 1 is a selection from *Die Religion in Geschichte und Gegenwart*. 2d ed. Tübingen: Mohr (Siebeck), 1927–1932.

———. "Die israelitische Literatur." Pages 51–102 in *Die orientalischen Literaturen*. Vol. 1.7 of *Die Kultur der Gegenwart*. Edited by Paul Hinneberg. Berlin: Teubner, 1906.

———. *Die Propheten*. Göttingen: Vandenhoeck & Ruprecht, 1917.

———. *Die Psalmen*: Übersetzt *und erklärt*. 4th ed. Göttingen: Vandenhoeck & Ruprecht, 1926.

———. *What Remains of the Old Testament and Other Essays*. Translated by A. K. Dallas. New York: Macmillan, 1928.

Habel, Norman C. *The Land Is Mine: Six Biblical Land Ideologies*. Minneapolis: Fortress, 1995.

Hackett, Jo Ann. *The Balaam Text from Deir ʿAllā*. Harvard Semitic Monographs 31. Chico, Calif.: Scholars, 1980.

Halpern, Baruch. "Jerusalem and the Lineages in the Seventh Century BCE: Kinship and the Rise of Individual Moral Liability." Pages 11–107 in *Law and Ideology in Monarchic Israel.* Edited by Baruch Halpern and Deborah W. Hobson. Journal for the Study of the Old Testament: Supplement Series 124. Sheffield: Sheffield Academic Press, 1991.

Hammershaimb, Erling. *The Book of Amos: A Commentary.* Translated by John Sturdy. Oxford: Basil Blackwell, 1970.

Haran, Menaḥem. "Observations on the Historical Background of Amos 1:2–2:6." *Israel Exploration Journal* 18 (1968): 201–12.

Harden, Donald B. *The Phoenicians.* London: Thames & Hudson, 1962.

Harper, William Rainey. *A Critical and Exegetical Commentary on Amos and Hosea.* Edinburgh: T&T Clark, 1905.

Harstad, Adolph L. *Joshua.* Concordia Commentary. St. Louis: Concordia, 2004.

Hasel, Gerhard F. "The Alleged 'No' of Amos and Amos' Eschatology." *Andrews University Seminary Studies* 29 (1991): 3–18.

———. *The Remnant: The History and Theology of the Remnant Idea from Genesis to Isaiah.* Berrien Springs, Mich.: Andrews University Press, 1972.

———. *Understanding the Book of Amos: Basic Issues in Current Interpretations.* Grand Rapids: Baker, 1991.

Hayes, John H. *Amos, the Eighth-Century Prophet: His Times and His Preaching.* Nashville: Abingdon, 1988.

———. "The History of the Form-Critical Study of Prophecy." Pages 60–99 in vol. 1 of *Society of Biblical Literature 1973 Seminar Papers.* Edited by George MacRae. Cambridge, Mass.: Society of Biblical Literature, 1973.

———. The Usage of Oracles against Foreign Nations in Ancient Israel." *Journal of Biblical Literature* 87 (1968): 81–92.

Hayes, John H., and Frederick C. Prussner. *Old Testament Theology: Its History and Development.* Atlanta: John Knox, 1985.

Hayes, John H., and Stuart A. Irvine. *Isaiah, the Eighth-Century Prophet: His Times and His Preaching.* Nashville: Abingdon, 1987.

Hempel, Johannes. *Das Ethos des Alten Testaments.* Beihefte zur Zeitschrift für die alttestamentliche Wissenschaft 67. Berlin : Töpelmann, 1938.

Hengel, Martin. *Crucifixion.* Philadelphia: Fortress, 1977.

Hengstenberg, E. W. *Christology of the Old Testament and a Commentary on the Messianic Predictions.* Translated by Theodore Meyer. 2d ed. Vol. 1. Edinburgh: T&T Clark, 1868.

Heschel, Abraham J. *The Prophets.* New York: Harper & Row, 1962.

Hillers, Delbert R. "Amos 7:4 and Ancient Parallels." *Catholic Biblical Quarterly* 26 (1964): 221–25.

———. *Covenant: The History of a Biblical Idea.* Baltimore: Johns Hopkins University Press, 1969.

———. *Treaty-Curses and the Old Testament Prophets.* Rome: Pontifical Biblical Institute, 1964.

Hoffman, Yair. "The Day of the Lord as a Concept and a Term in the Prophetic Literature." *Zeitschrift für die alttestamentliche Wissenschaft* 93 (1981): 37–50.

———. "A North Israelite Typological Myth and a Judean Historical Tradition: The Exodus in Hosea and Amos." *Vetus Testamentum* 39 (1989): 169–82.

Holladay, John S., Jr. "Assyrian Statecraft and the Prophets of Israel." *Harvard Theological Review* 63 (1970): 29–51.

Holladay, William L. *The Root Šûbh in the Old Testament with Particular Reference to Its Usages in Covenantal Contexts.* Leiden: Brill, 1958.

Holwerda, David E. *Jesus and Israel: One Covenant or Two?* Grand Rapids: Eerdmans, 1995.

Hoppe, Leslie J. *There Shall Be No Poor among You: Poverty in the Bible.* Nashville: Abingdon, 2004.

Horst, Friedrich. "Die Visionsschilderungen der alttestamentlichen Propheten." *Evangelische Theologie* 20 (1960): 193–205.

Hubbard, David Allan. *Joel and Amos: An Introduction and Commentary.* Tyndale Old Testament Commentaries. Leicester: Inter-Varsity, 1989.

Huffmon, Herbert B. "The Treaty Background of Hebrew *Yāda*ʿ." *Bulletin of the American Schools of Oriental Research* 181 (1966): 31–37.

Hummel, Horace D. *Ezekiel 1–20.* Concordia Commentary. St. Louis: Concordia, 2005.

———. *Ezekiel 21–48.* Concordia Commentary. St. Louis: Concordia, 2007.

———. *The Word Becoming Flesh.* St. Louis: Concordia, 1979.

Hurtado, Larry W. "The Origin of the *Nomina Sacra*: A Proposal." *Journal of Biblical Literature* 117 (1998): 655–73.

Jacob, Edmond. *Theology of the Old Testament.* Translated by Arthur W. Heathcote and Philip J. Allcock. London: Hodder & Stoughton, 1958.

Janzen, Waldemar. *Mourning Cry and Woe Oracle.* Beihefte zur Zeitschrift für die alttestamentliche Wissenschaft 125. New York: De Gruyter, 1972.

Jaruzelska, Izabela. "Social Structure in the Kingdom of Israel in the Eighth Century B.C. as Reflected in the Book of Amos." *Folia Orientalia* 29 (1992–1993): 91–117.

Jemielity, Thomas. *Satire and the Hebrew Prophets.* Louisville: Westminster/John Knox, 1992.

Jeremias, Jörg. "Amos 3–6: From the Oral Word to the Text." Translated by Stuart A. Irvine. Pages 217–29 in *Canon, Theology, and Old Testament Interpretation: Essays in Honor of Brevard S. Childs.* Edited by Gene M. Tucker, David L. Petersen, and Robert R. Wilson. Philadelphia: Fortress, 1988.

———. *The Book of Amos: A Commentary.* Old Testament Library. Translated by D. W. Stott. Louisville: Westminster John Knox, 1998.

———. *Hosea und Amos: Studien zu den Anfängen des Dodekapropheton*. Tübingen: Mohr (Siebeck), 1996.

Johnson, Luke T. *Sharing Possessions: Mandate and Symbol of Faith*. Philadelphia: Fortress, 1981.

Johnston, Philip S. *Shades of Sheol: Death and Afterlife in the Old Testament*. Downers Grove, Ill.: InterVarsity, 2002.

Joyce Shelly, Patricia. "Amos and Irony: The Use of Irony in Amos's Prophetic Discourse." Ph.D. diss., Iliff School of Theology, 1992.

Kaiser, Walter C., Jr. "The Davidic Promise and the Inclusion of the Gentiles (Amos 9:9–15 and Acts 15:13–18): A Test Passage for Theological Systems." *Journal of the Evangelical Theological Society* 20 (1977): 97–111.

———. *Toward Old Testament Ethics*. Grand Rapids: Zondervan, 1983.

———. *The Uses of the Old Testament in the New*. Chicago: Moody, 1985.

Kapelrud, Arvid S. *Central Ideas in Amos*. Oslo: Oslo University Press, 1961.

Katzenstein, H. Jacob. *The History of Tyre: From the Beginning of the Second Millennium B.C.E. until the Fall of the Neo-Babylonian Empire in 539 B.C.E.* 2d ed. Jerusalem: Ben-Gurion University of the Negev Press, 1997.

Kennedy, George A. *The Art of Persuasion in Greece*. Princeton: Princeton University Press, 1963.

———. *Classical Rhetoric and Its Christian and Secular Tradition from Ancient to Modern Times*. 2d ed. Chapel Hill: University of North Carolina Press, 1999.

———. *New Testament Interpretation through Rhetorical Criticism*. Chapel Hill: University of North Carolina Press, 1984.

King, Philip J. *Amos, Hosea, Micah: An Archaeological Commentary*. Philadelphia: Westminster, 1988.

———. "The *Marzeaḥ* Amos Denounces—Using Archaeology to Interpret a Biblical Text." *Biblical Archaeology Review* 14/4 (July/August 1988): 34–44.

Kleinig, John W. *Leviticus*. Concordia Commentary. St. Louis: Concordia, 2003.

Kleven, Terence. "The Cows of Bashan: A Single Metaphor at Amos 4:1–3." *Catholic Biblical Quarterly* 58 (1996): 215–27.

Knierim, Rolf P. " 'I Will Not Cause It to Return' in Amos 1 and 2." Pages 163–75 in *Canon and Authority: Essays in Old Testament Religion and Theology*. Edited by George W. Coats and Burke O. Long. Philadelphia: Fortress, 1977.

———. *The Task of Old Testament Theology: Substance, Method, and Cases*. Grand Rapids: Eerdmans, 1995.

Koch, Klaus. *Amos: Untersuch mit den Methoden einer strukturalen Formgeschichte*. Part 1: *Programm und Analyse*. Part 2: *Synthese*. Part 3: *Schlüssel*. Alter Orient und Altes Testament 30. Kevelaer : Butzon & Bercker, 1976.

———. *The Prophets*. Vol. 1: *The Assyrian Period*. Translated by Margaret Kohl. Philadelphia: Fortress, 1983.

Kolb, Robert. *The Christian Faith: A Lutheran Exposition*. St. Louis: Concordia, 1993.

Kraeling, Carl H. "Music in the Bible." Pages 283–312 in *Ancient and Oriental Music*. Vol. 1 of *The New Oxford History of Music*. Edited by Egon Wellesz. London: Oxford University Press, 1957.

Kugel, James L. *The Idea of Biblical Poetry: Parallelism and Its History*. New Haven, Conn.: Yale University Press, 1981.

Kuhrt, Amélie. "Non-Royal Women in the Late Babylonian Period: A Survey." Pages 215–43 in *Women's Earliest Records: From Ancient Egypt and Western Asia*. Edited by Barbara S. Lesko. Atlanta: Scholars, 1989.

Laetsch, Theodore. *The Minor Prophets*. St. Louis: Concordia, 1956.

LaHaye, Tim, and Jerry B. Jenkins. *Are We Living in the End Times?* Wheaton: Tyndale, 1999.

Lambert, W. G. "A Neo-Babylonian Tammuz Lament." *Journal of the American Oriental Society* 103 (1983): 211–15.

Landsberger, Benno. "Tin and Lead: The Adventures of Two Vocables." *Journal of Near Eastern Studies* 24 (1965): 285–96.

Lang, Bernhard. "The Social Organization of Peasant Poverty in Biblical Israel." *Journal for the Study of the Old Testament* 24 (1982): 47–63.

LaRondelle, Hans K. *The Israel of God in Prophecy: Principles of Prophetic Interpretation*. Berrien Springs, Mich.: Andrews University Press, 1983.

Lawrence, Paul J. N. "Assyrian Nobles and the Book of Jonah." *Tyndale Bulletin* 37 (1986): 121–32.

Leeuwen, C. van. "The Prophecy of the *Yōm YHWH* in Amos v 18–20." Pages 113–34 in *Language and Meaning: Studies in Hebrew Language and Biblical Exegesis*. Edited by A. S. van der Woude. Oudtestamentische Studiën 19. Leiden: Brill, 1974.

LeFebvre, Michael. "Torah-Meditation and the Psalms: The Invitation of Psalm 1." Pages 213–25 in *Interpreting the Psalms: Issues and Approaches*. Edited by David Firth and Philip S. Johnston. Downers Grove, Ill.: InterVarsity, 2005.

Lemaire, André. *Inscriptions hébraïques*. Vol. 1: *Les ostraca*. Paris: Cerf, 1977.

———. "Tarshish-*Tarsisi*: Problème de Topographie Historique Biblique et Assyrienne." Pages 44–62 in *Studies in Historical Geography and Biblical Historiography: Presented to Zecharia Kallai*. Edited by Gershon Galil and Moshe Weinfeld. Supplements to Vetus Testamentum 81. Leiden: Brill, 2000.

Lemanski, Jay. "Jonah's Nineveh." *Concordia Journal* 18 (1992): 40–49.

Lemos, T. M. "Shame and Mutilation of Enemies in the Hebrew Bible." *Journal of Biblical Literature* 125 (2006): 225–41.

Lessing, R. Reed. *Interpreting Discontinuity: Isaiah's Tyre Oracle*. Winona Lake, Ind.: Eisenbrauns, 2004.

———. *Jonah*. Concordia Commentary. St. Louis: Concordia, 2007.

———. "Orality in the Prophets." *Concordia Journal* 29 (2003): 152–65.

———. "Satire in Isaiah's Tyre Oracle." *Journal for the Study of the Old Testament* 28 (2003): 89–112.

———. "Upsetting the Status Quo: Preaching Like Amos." *Concordia Journal* 33 (2007): 285–98.

Levenson, Jon D. *Creation and the Persistence of Evil: The Jewish Drama of Divine Omnipotence*. San Francisco: Harper & Row, 1988.

Levine, Baruch A. *In the Presence of the Lord: A Study of Cult and Some Cultic Terms in Ancient Israel.* Leiden: Brill, 1974.

Levy, Thomas E., and Mohammad Najjar. "Edom and Copper: The Emergence of Ancient Israel's Rival." *Biblical Archaeology Review* 32/4 (July/August 2006): 24–35, 70.

Lewis, C. S. *The Lion, the Witch, and the Wardrobe.* 1950. Repr., New York: Harper-Collins, 1978.

Lichtenstein, Murray H. "Biblical Poetry." Pages 105–27 in *Back to the Sources: Reading the Classic Jewish Texts*. Edited by Barry W. Holtz. New York: Summit, 1984.

Lichtheim, Miriam. *Ancient Egyptian Literature: A Book of Readings.* Vol. 1: *The Old and Middle Kingdoms*. Berkley: University of California Press, 1973.

Limburg, James. *Hosea–Micah*. Interpretation: A Bible Commentary for Teaching and Preaching. Atlanta: John Knox, 1988.

———. "Sevenfold Structures in the Book of Amos." *Journal of Biblical Literature* 106 (1987): 217–22.

Lindblom, J. *Prophecy in Ancient Israel*. Oxford: Blackwell, 1962.

Linville, James R. "What Does 'It' Mean? Interpretation at the Point of No Return in Amos 1–2." *Biblical Interpretation* 8 (2000): 400–24.

Lockwood, Gregory J. *1 Corinthians.* Concordia Commentary. St. Louis: Concordia, 2000.

Lohfink, Norbert. "Opfer und Säkularisierung im Deuteronomium." Pages 15–43 in *Studien zu Opfer und Kult im Alten Testament: Mit einer Bibliographie 1969–1991 zum Opfer in der Bibel*. Edited by Adrian Schenker. Tübingen: Mohr (Siebeck), 1992.

Long, Burke O. "Recent Field Studies in Oral Literature and Their Bearing on OT Criticism." *Vetus Testamentum* 26 (1976): 187–98.

———. "Reports of Visions among the Prophets." *Journal of Biblical Literature* 95 (1976): 353–65.

Longman, Tremper, and Daniel G. Reid. *God Is a Warrior*. Grand Rapids: Zondervan, 1995.

Lowry, Eugene L. *The Homiletical Plot: The Sermon as Narrative Art Form.* Rev. ed. Louisville: Westminster John Knox, 2001.

Luckenbill, Daniel David. *Ancient Records of Assyria and Babylonia*. 2 vols. Chicago: University of Chicago Press, 1926–1927.

Mandelkern, Solomon. *Veteris Testamenti Concordantiae Hebraicae atque Chaldaicae*. 4th ed. Tel Aviv: Schocken, 1962.

March, W. Eugene. "Prophecy." Pages 141–77 in *Old Testament Form Criticism*. Edited by John H. Hayes. San Antonio: Trinity University Press, 1974.

Margulis, Barry B. "Studies in the Oracles against the Nations." Ph.D. diss., Brandeis University, 1967.

Markoe, Glenn E. "The Emergence of Phoenician Art." *Bulletin of the American Schools of Oriental Research* 279 (1990): 13–26.

Martens, Elmer A. *God's Design: A Focus on Old Testament Theology*. 3d ed. North Richland Hills, Tex.: BIBAL, 1998.

Marti, Karl. *Das Dodekapropheton erklart*. Tübingen: Mohr, 1904.

———. *The Religion of the Old Testament: Its Place among the Religions of the Nearer East*. Translated by G. A. Bienemann. London: Williams & Norgate, 1907.

Marxsen, Willi. *Mark the Evangelist: Studies on the Redaction History of the Gospel*. Translated by James Boyce et al. Nashville: Abingdon, 1969.

Matthews, Victor H. *Old Testament Turning Points: The Narratives That Shaped a Nation*. Grand Rapids: Baker, 2005.

———. *Social World of the Hebrew Prophets*. Peabody, Mass.: Hendrickson, 2001.

Matthews, Victor H., and Don C. Benjamin. *Old Testament Parallels: Laws and Stories from the Ancient Near East*. 2d ed. New York: Paulist, 1997.

Matties, Gordon H. *Ezekiel 18 and the Rhetoric of Moral Discourse*. Atlanta: Scholars, 1990.

Mauchline, John. "Implicit Signs of a Persistent Belief in the Davidic Empire." *Vetus Testamentum* 20 (1970): 288–303.

Mays, James Luther. *Amos: A Commentary*. Philadelphia: Westminster, 1969.

———. "Justice: Perspectives from the Prophetic Tradition." *Interpretation* 37 (1983): 5–17.

———. "Words about the Words of Amos: Recent Study of the Book of Amos." *Interpretation* 13 (1959): 259–72.

Mays, James Luther, and Paul J. Achtemeier, eds. *Interpreting the Prophets*. Fortress: Philadelphia, 1987.

Mazar, Amihay. *Archaeology of the Land of the Bible*. 2 vols. New York: Doubleday, 1990.

McCarthy, Dennis J. *Old Testament Covenant: A Survey of Current Opinions*. Richmond: John Knox, 1972.

McCurley, Foster R. *Ancient Myths and Biblical Faith: Scriptural Transformations*. Fortress: Philadelphia, 1983.

McKane, W. "Prophecy and the Prophetic Literature." Pages 163–88 in *Tradition and Interpretation*. Edited by G. W. Anderson. Oxford: Clarendon, 1979.

McKay, Heather. "The Horse in Warfare in Ancient Israel: A Re-reading of the Biblical Texts." Paper presented at the annual meeting of the Society of Biblical Literature. Philadelphia, November 19–22, 2005.

McLaughlin, John L. *The* Marzēaḥ *in the Prophetic Literature: References and Allusions in Light of Extra-Biblical Evidence*. Supplements to Vetus Testamentum 86. Leiden: Brill, 2001.

Melugin, Roy F. "Amos in Recent Research." *Currents in Research* 6 (1998): 65–101.

———. "Prophetic Books and the Problem of Historical Reconstruction." Pages 63–78 in *Prophets and Paradigms: Essays in Honor of Gene M. Tucker*. Edited by Stephen Breck Reid. Journal for the Study of the Old Testament: Supplement Series 229. Sheffield: Sheffield Academic Press, 1996.

Mendenhall, George E. *Law and Covenant in Israel and the Ancient Near East*. Pittsburgh: Presbyterian Board of Colportage of Western Pennsylvania, 1955.

———. "The Relation of the Individual to Political Society in Ancient Israel." Pages 89–108 in *Biblical Studies in Memory of H. C. Alleman*. Edited by J. M. Myers, O. Reimherr, and H. N. Bream. Locus Valley, N.Y.: Augustin, 1960.

Meuser, Fred W. *Luther the Preacher*. Minneapolis: Augsburg, 1983.

Meyers, Carol. "The Family in Early Israel." Pages 1–47 in *Families in Ancient Israel*. By Leo G. Perdue, Joseph Blenkinsopp, John J. Collins, and Carol Meyers. Louisville: Westminster John Knox, 1997.

Meynet, Roland. *Rhetorical Analysis: An Introduction to Biblical Rhetoric*. Sheffield Academic Press: Sheffield, 1998.

Miller, J. Maxwell, and John H. Hayes. *A History of Ancient Israel and Judah*. London: SCM, 1986.

Miller, Patrick D. "The Human Sabbath: A Study in Deuteronomic Theology." *Princeton Seminary Bulletin* 6 (1985): 81–97.

———. "The Prophetic Critique of Kings." Pages 526–47 in *Israelite Religion and Biblical Theology*. Journal for the Study of the Old Testament: Supplement Series 267. Sheffield: Sheffield Academic Press, 2000.

———. *Sin and Judgment in the Prophets: A Stylistic and Theological Analysis*. Society of Biblical Literature Monograph Series 27. Chico, Calif.: Scholars, 1982.

Minor, Mark. *Literary-Critical Approaches to the Bible: An Annotated Bibliography*. West Cornwall, Conn.: Locust Hill, 1992.

Mitchell, Christopher W. *The Song of Songs*. Concordia Commentary. St. Louis: Concordia, 2003.

Möller, Karl. " 'Hear This Word against You': A Fresh Look at the Arrangement and the Rhetorical Strategy of the Book of Amos." *Vetus Testamentum* 50 (2000): 499–518.

Moscati, Sabatino. *The World of the Phoenicians*. Translated by Alastair Hamilton. London: Weidenfeld & Nicolson, 1968.

Mott, Stephen Charles. *Biblical Ethics and Social Change*. New York: Oxford University Press, 1982.

Motyer, J. A. *The Message of Amos: The Day of the Lion*. Downers Grove, Ill.: Inter-Varsity, 1998. Published in 1974 as *The Day of the Lion: The Message of Amos*.

Mowinckel, Sigmund. *He That Cometh*. Translated by G. W. Anderson. Oxford: Clarendon, 1956.

———. *Prophecy and Tradition: The Prophetic Books in the Light of the Study of the Growth and History of the Tradition*. Oslo: Dybwad, 1946.

———. *Psalmenstudien*. Vol. 2: *Das Thronbesteigungsfest Jähwas und der Usprung der Eschatologie*. Kristiania: Dybwad, 1922.

Muecke, Douglas C. "Irony Markers." *Poetics* 7 (1978): 363–75.

Muilenburg, James. "Form Criticism and Beyond." *Journal of Biblical Literature* 88 (1969): 1–18.

———. "The Linguistic and Rhetorical Usages of the Particle כי in the Old Testament." *Hebrew Union College Annual* 32 (1961): 135–60.

Munch, Peter A. *The Expression Bajjôm Hahuʾ: Is It an Eschatological Terminus Technicus?* Oslo: Dybward, 1936.

Murray, D. F. "The Rhetoric of Disputation: Re-examination of a Prophetic Genre." *Journal for the Study of the Old Testament* 38 (1987): 95–121.

Napier, B. D. "Community under Law: On Hebrew Law and Its Theological Presuppositions." *Interpretation* 7 (1953): 404–17.

Nembach, Ulrich. *Predigt des Evangeliums: Luther als Prediger, Pädagoge und Rhetor*. Neukirchen-Vluyn: Neukirchener, 1972.

Neusner, Jacob. *The Way of Torah: An Introduction to Judaism*. 6th ed. Belmont, Calif.: Wadsworth, 1997.

Niditch, Susan. "The Composition of Isaiah 1." *Biblica* 61 (1980): 509–29.

———. *Oral World and Written Word: Ancient Israelite Literature*. Louisville: Westminster John Knox, 1996.

Niebuhr, H. Richard. *Christ and Culture*. New York: Harper, 1956.

Niehaus, Jeff. "Amos." Pages 315–494 in *The Minor Prophets: An Exegetical and Expository Commentary*. Vol. 1: *Hosea, Joel, and Amos*. Edited by Thomas Edward McComiskey. Grand Rapids: Baker, 1992.

Noble, Paul R. "Amos' Absolute 'No.' " *Vetus Testamentum* 47 (1997): 329–40.

———. " 'I Will Not Bring "It" Back' (Amos 1:3): A Deliberately Ambiguous Oracle?" *Expository Times* 106 (1995): 105–9.

———. "The Literary Structure of Amos: A Thematic Analysis." *Journal of Biblical Literature* 114 (1995): 209–26.

Nogalski, James. "The Problematic Suffixes of Amos IX 11." *Vetus Testamentum* 43 (1993): 411–18.

Noth, Martin. *The Chronicler's History*. Translated by H. G. M. Williamson. Journal for the Study of the Old Testament: Supplement Series 50. Sheffield: JSOT Press, 1987. Translation of *Überlieferungsgeschichtliche Studien*, part 2.

———. *The Deuteronomistic History*. Journal for the Study of the Old Testament: Supplement Series 15. Sheffield: JSOT Press, 1981. Translation of *Überlieferungsgeschichtliche Studien*, pages 1–110 in the 2d ed. Schriften der Königsberger Gelehrten Gesellschaft: Geisteswissenschaftliche Klasse 18. Tübingen: Niemeyer, 1957.

Nouwen, Henri J. M. *Reaching Out: The Three Movements of the Spiritual Life*. Garden City, N.Y.: Doubleday, 1975.

Oded, Bustanay. *Mass Deportations and Deportees in the Neo-Assyrian Empire*. Wiesbaden: Reichert, 1979.

———. "The Phoenician Cities and the Assyrian Empire in the Time of Tiglathpileser III." *Zeitschrift des deutschen Palästina-Vereins* 90 (1974): 38–49.

———. "The Settlements of the Israelite and the Judean Exiles in Mesopotamia in the 8th–6th Centuries BCE." Pages 91–103 in *Studies in Historical Geography and Biblical Historiography: Presented to Zecharia Kallai*. Edited by Gershon Galil and Moshe Weinfeld. Supplements to Vetus Testamentum 81. Leiden: Brill, 2000.

Odell, Margaret S. *Ezekiel*. Smyth & Helwys Bible Commentary. Macon, Ga.: Smyth & Helwys, 2005.

Olmstead, A. T. *History of the Persian Empire: Achaemenid Period*. Chicago: University of Chicago Press, 1948.

Osborne, Grant R. *The Hermeneutical Spiral: A Comprehensive Introduction to Biblical Interpretation*. Downers Grove, Ill.: InterVarsity, 1991.

Otto, Eckart. *Theologische Ethik des Alten Testaments*. Stuttgart: Kohlhammer, 1994.

Otto, Rudolf. *The Idea of the Holy: An Inquiry into the Non-rational Factor in the Idea of the Divine and Its Relation to the Rational*. 9th ed. Translated by John W. Harvey. Oxford: Oxford University Press, 1928.

Ouellette, Jean. "Le mur d'étain dans Amos, VII, 7–9." *Revue biblique* 80 (1973): 321–31.

Paas, Stefan. *Creation and Judgement: Creation Texts in Some Eighth Century Prophets*. Leiden: Brill, 2003.

Patrick, Dale, and Allen Scult. *Rhetoric and Biblical Interpretation*. Sheffield: Almond, 1990.

Paul, Shalom M. "Amos III 15—Winter and Summer Mansions." *Vetus Testamentum* 28 (1978): 358–60.

———. *Amos: A Commentary on the Book of Amos*. Hermeneia. Minneapolis: Fortress, 1991.

———. "Fishing Imagery in Amos 4:2." *Journal of Biblical Literature* 97 (1978): 183–90.

———. "A Literary Reinvestigation of the Authenticity of the Oracles against the Nations of Amos." Pages 189–204 in *De la Tôrah au Messie: Études d'exégèse et d'herméneutique bibliques offertes à Henri Cazelles*. Edited by Maurice Carrez, Joseph Doré, and Pierre Grelot. Paris: Desclée, 1981.

———. *Studies in the Book of the Covenant in the Light of Cuneiform and Biblical Law*. Supplements to Vetus Testamentum 18. Leiden: Brill, 1970.

Perrin, Norman. *What Is Redaction Criticism?* Philadelphia: Fortress, 1969.

Perrin, Norman, and Dennis C. Duling. *The New Testament: An Introduction*. 2d ed. New York: Harcourt Brace Jovanovich, 1982.

Petersen, David L. *The Prophetic Literature: An Introduction*. Louisville: Westminster John Knox, 2002.

Pieper, Francis. *Christian Dogmatics*. 4 vols. St. Louis: Concordia, 1950–1957.

Polley, Max E. *Amos and the Davidic Empire: A Socio-Historical Approach*. New York: Oxford University Press, 1989.

Porter, Stanley E., and Thomas H. Olbricht, eds. *Rhetoric, Scripture and Theology: Essays from the 1994 Pretoria Conference*. Sheffield: Sheffield Academic Press, 1996.

Preus, J. A. O., III. "Liberation Theology: Basic Themes and Methodology." *Concordia Journal* 13 (1987): 6–26.

Procksch, Otto. *Geschichtsbetrachtung und geschichtliche Überlieferung bei den vorexilischen Propheten*. Leipzig: Hinrichs, 1902.

Raabe, Paul R. *Obadiah*. Anchor Bible 24D. New York: Doubleday, 1996.

———. "The Particularizing of Universal Judgment in Prophetic Discourse." *Catholic Biblical Quarterly* 64 (2002): 652–74.

———. "Why Prophetic Oracles against the Nations?" Pages 236–57 in *Fortunate the Eyes That See: Essays in Honor of David Noel Freedman in Celebration of His Seventieth Birthday*. Edited by Astrid B. Beck, Andrew H. Bartelt, Paul R. Raabe, Chris A. Franke. Grand Rapids: Eerdmans, 1995.

Rad, Gerhard von. *Das erste Buch Mose, Genesis: Übersetzt und erklärt*. Göttingen: Vandenhoeck & Ruprecht, 1956.

———. *Der heilige Krieg im alten Israel*. 3d ed. Göttingen: Vandenhoeck & Ruprecht, 1958.

———. *Old Testament Theology*. Translated by D. M. G. Stalker. 2 vols. San Francisco: Harper & Row, 1962–1965. Translation of *Theologie des Alten Testaments*. 2 vols. Munich: Kaiser, 1957–1960.

———. "The Origin of the Concept of the Day of Yahweh." *Journal of Semitic Studies* 4 (1959): 97–108.

———. *The Problem of the Hexateuch and Other Essays*. Translated by E. W. Trueman Dicken. London: Oliver & Boyd, 1966.

———. “The Theological Problem of the Old Testament Doctrine of Creation.” Pages 131–43 in *The Problem of the Hexateuch and Other Essays*. Translated by E. W. Trueman Dicken. London: Oliver & Boyd, 1966.

Rauschenbusch, Walter. *Christianizing the Social Order*. New York: Macmillan, 1913.

Redditt, Paul L., and Aaron Schart, eds. *Thematic Threads in the Book of the Twelve*. Beihefte zur Zeitschrift für die alttestamentliche Wissenschaft 325. Berlin: De Gruyter, 2003.

Reicke, Bo, and Leonhard Rost, eds. *Biblisch-Historisches Hantwörterbuch*. Göttingen: Vandenhoeck & Ruprecht, 1962–1979.

Rendtorff, Rolf. *Canon and Theology: Overtures to an Old Testament Theology*. Translated by Margaret Kohl. Minneapolis: Fortress, 1993.

Renz, Thomas. *The Rhetorical Function of the Book of Ezekiel*. Supplements to Vetus Testamentum 76. Leiden: Brill, 1999.

Reventlow, Henning Graf. *Das Amt des Propheten bei Amos*. Göttingen: Vandenhoeck & Ruprecht, 1962.

Richardson, H. Neil. “*SKT* (Amos 9:11): ‘Booth’ or ‘Succoth’?” *Journal of Biblical Literature* 92 (1973): 375–81.

Richter, Wolfgang. *Exegese als Literaturwissenschaft: Entwurf einer alttestamentlichen Literaturtheorie und Methodologie*. Göttingen: Vandenhoeck and Ruprecht, 1971.

Rimmon-Kenan, Shlomith. *Narrative Fiction: Contemporary Poetics*. New York: Methuen, 1983.

Ringgren, Helmer. *The Prophetical Conception of Holiness*. Uppsala: Lundequist, 1948.

Roberts, Colin H. “*Nomina Sacra*: Origins and Significance.” Pages 26–48 in *Manuscript, Society, and Belief in Early Christian Egypt*. London: Oxford University Press, 1979.

Rogerson, John W. *Old Testament Criticism in the Nineteenth Century: England and Germany*. London: SPCK, 1984.

Rosenbaum, Stanley N. *Amos of Israel: A New Interpretation*. Macon, Ga.: Mercer University Press, 1989.

Rosin, Robert. “The Reformation as Liberation—Reformers, Peasants, Marxists.” *Concordia Journal* 13 (1987): 47–65.

———. “The Reformation, Humanism, and Education: The Wittenberg Model for Reform.” *Concordia Journal* 16 (1990): 301–18.

Rossow Francis C. *Preaching the Creative Gospel Creatively*. St. Louis: Concordia, 1983.

Roth, Wolfgang M. W. “The Numerical Sequence x/x + 1 in the Old Testament.” *Vetus Testamentum* 12 (1962): 300–11.

Roux, Georges. *Ancient Iraq*. Cleveland: World, 1964.

Rowley, H. H. *Worship in Ancient Israel: Its Forms and Meaning.* London: SPCK, 1965.

Rudolph, Wilhelm. *Joel, Amos, Obadja, Jona.* Kommentar zum Alten Testament 13/2. Gütersloh: Mohn, 1971.

Saebo, Magne. "Yahweh as *Deus absconditus*: Some Remarks on a Dictum by Gerhard von Rad." Pages 43–56 in *Shall Not the Judge of All the Earth Do What Is Right? Studies on the Nature of God in Tribute to James L. Crenshaw.* Edited by David Penchansky and Paul L. Redditt. Winona Lake, Ind.: Eisenbrauns, 2000.

Schart, Aaron. "The Fifth Vision of Amos in Context." Pages 46–71 in *Thematic Threads in the Book of the Twelve.* Edited by Paul L. Redditt and Aaron Schart. Beihefte zur Zeitschrift für die alttestamentliche Wissenschaft 325. Berlin: De Gruyter, 2003.

Schmid, Hans Heinrich. "Creation, Righteousness, and Salvation: 'Creation Theology' as the Broad Horizon of Biblical Theology." Pages 102–17 in *Creation in the Old Testament.* Edited by Bernhard W. Anderson. Philadelphia: Fortress, 1984.

Schmidt, Daniel. "Another Word-Play in Amos?" *Grace Theological Journal* 8 (1987): 141–42.

Schrieber, Paul L. "Liberation Theology and the Old Testament: An Exegetical Critique." *Concordia Journal* 13 (1987): 27–46.

Sellin, Ernst. *Theologie des Alten Testaments.* Leipzig: Quelle & Meyer, 1933.

———. *Das Zwölfprophetenbuch: Übersetzt und erklärt.* Vol. 1: *Hosea–Micha.* 2d/3d ed. Kommentar zum Alten Testament 12/1. Leipzig: Deichert, 1929.

Silver, Morris. *Prophets and Markets: The Political Economy of Ancient Israel.* Boston: Kluwer-Nijhoff, 1983.

Simkins, Ronald A. *Creator and Creation: Nature in the Worldview of Ancient Israel.* Peabody, Mass.: Hendrickson, 1994.

Simundson, Daniel J. *Hosea, Joel, Amos, Obadiah, Jonah, Micah.* Abingdon Old Testament Commentaries. Nashville: Abingdon, 2005.

Smith, Gary V. "Amos 5:13: The Deadly Silence of the Prosperous." *Journal of Biblical Literature* 107 (1988): 289–91.

———. *Amos.* Rev. ed. Fearn, United Kingdom: Mentor, 1998.

———. *Hosea, Amos, Micah.* NIV Application Commentary. Grand Rapids: Zondervan, 2001.

———. *The Prophets as Preachers: An Introduction to the Hebrew Prophets.* Nashville: Broadman & Holman, 1994.

Smith, George Adam. *The Book of the Twelve Prophets: Commonly Called the Minor.* Vol. 1: *Amos, Hosea, and Micah.* Rev. ed. New York: Harper & Brothers, 1928.

Smith, Preserved, trans. *Luther's Correspondence and Other Contemporary Letters.* 2 vols. Philadelphia: Lutheran Publication Society, 1913–1918.

Soggin, J. Alberto. *The Prophet Amos: A Translation and Commentary.* Translated by John Bowden. London: SCM, 1988.

Steck, Odil Hannes. *The Prophetic Books and Their Theological Witness*. Translated by James D. Nogalski. St. Louis: Chalice, 2000.

Steiner, Richard C. *Stockmen from Tekoa, Sycomores from Sheba: A Study of Amos' Occupations*. Catholic Biblical Quarterly Monograph Series 36. Washington, D.C.: Catholic Biblical Association of America, 2003.

Steinmann, Andrew E. *Daniel*. Concordia Commentary. St. Louis: Concordia, 2008.

———. "The Order of Amos's Oracles against the Nations: 1:3–2:16." *Journal of Biblical Literature* 111 (1992): 683–89.

Stieglitz, Robert R. "Long-Distance Seafaring in the Ancient Near East." *Biblical Archaeologist* 47 (1984): 134–42.

Story, Cullen I. K. "Amos—Prophet of Praise." *Vetus Testamentum* 30 (1980): 67–80.

Strijdom, P. D. F. "What Tekoa Did to Amos." *Old Testament Essays* 9 (1996): 273–93.

Stuart, Douglas. *Hosea–Jonah*. Word Bible Commentary 31. Waco: Word, 1987.

Stulman, Louis. *Jeremiah*. Abingdon Old Testament Commentaries. Nashville: Abingdon, 2005.

Sweeney, Marvin A. "Form Criticism." Pages 58–89 in *To Each Its Own Meaning: An Introduction to Biblical Criticisms and Their Application*. Rev. ed. Edited by Steven L. McKenzie and Stephen R. Haynes. Louisville: Westminster John Knox, 1999.

———. *Isaiah 1–39: With an Introduction to Prophetic Literature*. Forms of the Old Testament Literature 16. Grand Rapids: Eerdmans, 1996.

———. *The Prophetic Literature*. Interpreting Biblical Texts. Nashville: Abingdon, 2005.

———. *The Twelve Prophets*. Vol. 1: *Hosea, Joel, Amos, Obadiah, Jonah*. Berit Olam. Collegeville, Minn.: Liturgical, 2000.

Terrien, Samuel. "Amos and Wisdom." Pages 108–15 in *Israel's Prophetic Heritage: Essays in Honor of James Muilenburg*. Edited by Bernhard W. Anderson and Walter Harrelson. New York: Harper, 1962.

Thiele, Edwin R. *The Mysterious Numbers of the Hebrew Kings*. 3d ed. Grand Rapids: Zondervan, 1983.

Thiselton, Anthony C. "The Supposed Power of Words in the Biblical Writings." *Journal of Theological Studies* 25 (1974): 283–99.

Thomas, D. Winton. "A Consideration of Some Unusual Ways of Expressing the Superlative in Hebrew." *Vetus Testamentum* 3 (1953): 209–24.

Trible, Phyllis. *Rhetorical Criticism: Context, Method, and the Book of Jonah*. Minneapolis: Fortress, 1994.

Tromp, N. J. "Amos V 1–17: Towards a Stylistic and Rhetorical Analysis." Pages 56–84 in *Prophets, Worship and Theodicy: Studies in Prophetism, Biblical Theology and Structural and Rhetorical Analysis and on the Place of Music in Worship*. Edited by A. S. van der Woude. Oudtestamentische Studiën 23. Leiden: Brill, 1984.

Tucker, Gene M. *Form Criticism of the Old Testament*. Philadelphia: Fortress, 1971.

Voelz, James W. "Biblical Charity: What Does It Entail and How Does It Relate to the Gospel—A New Testament Perspective." Pages 65–92 in *A Cup of Cold Water: A Look at Biblical Charity*. Edited by Robert Rosin and Charles P. Arand. St. Louis: Concordia Seminary Publications, 1996.

Vorster, Willem S. "Readings, Readers and the Succession Narrative: An Essay on Reception." *Zeitschrift für die alttestamentliche Wissenschaft* 98 (1986): 351–62.

Wal, Adri van der. *Amos: A Classified Bibliography.* 3d ed. Amsterdam: Free University Press, 1986.

Ward, James M. *Amos and Isaiah: Prophets of the Word of God.* Nashville: Abingdon, 1969.

Watson, Wilfred G. E. *Classical Hebrew Poetry: A Guide to Its Techniques*. Journal for the Study of the Old Testament: Supplement Series 26. Sheffield: JSOT Press, 1984.

Watts, John D. W. *Isaiah 1–33*. Word Biblical Commentary 24. Waco: Word, 1985.

———. *Vision and Prophecy in Amos*. Expanded anniversary ed. Macon, Ga.: Mercer University Press, 1997.

Weber, Max. *Ancient Judaism.* Translated by Hans H. Gerth and Don Martindale. Glencoe, Ill.: Free Press, 1952.

———. *The Sociology of Religion.* Translated by Ephraim Fischoff. Boston: Beacon, 1963.

Weiss, Meier. " 'And I Raised Up Prophets from amongst Your Sons': A Note about the History and Character of Israelite Prophecy." Pages 257–74 in vol. 1 of *Isac Leo Seeligmann Volume: Essays on the Bible and the Ancient World.* Edited by Alexander Rofé and Yair Zakovitch. 3 vols. Jerusalem: Rubinstein, 1983.

———. "Concerning Amos' Repudiation of the Cult." Pages 199–215 in *Pomegranates and Golden Bells: Studies in Biblical, Jewish, and Near Eastern Ritual, Law, and Literature in Honor of Jacob Milgrom.* Edited by David P. Wright, David Noel Freedman, and Avi Hurvitz. Winona Lake, Ind.: Eisenbrauns, 1995.

———. "The Origin of the 'Day of the Lord'—Reconsidered." *Hebrew Union College Annual* 37 (1966): 29–71.

———. "The Pattern of Numerical Sequence in Amos 1–2: A Re-examination." *Journal of Biblical Literature* 86 (1967): 416–23.

Wellhausen, Julius. *Die kleinen Propheten: Übersetzt und erklärt.* Berlin: Reimer, 1892.

———. *Prolegomena to the History of Ancient Israel*. New York: Meridian, 1957. Reprint of *Prolegomena to the History of Israel*. Translated by J. Sutherland Black and A. Enzies. Edinburgh: Black, 1885. Translation of *Prolegomena zur Geschichte Israels*. 2d ed. Berlin: Reimer, 1883. 1st ed. 1878.

Wendland, Ernst R. *The Discourse Analysis of Hebrew Prophetic Literature: Determining the Larger Textual Units of Hosea and Joel*. Lewiston, N.Y.: Mellen, 1995.

Wenham, Gordon J. *Genesis 1–15*. Word Biblical Commentary 1. Waco: Word, 1987.

———. *Story as Torah: Reading Old Testament Narrative Ethically*. Grand Rapids: Baker, 2000.

Westermann, Claus. *Praise and Lament in the Psalms*. Translated by Keith R. Crim and Richard H. Soulen. Atlanta: John Knox, 1981.

White, Lynn Jr. "The Historical Roots of Our Ecological Crisis." *Science* 155 (1967): 1203–7.

Wiesel, Elie. *Five Biblical Portraits*. South Bend, Ind.: University of Notre Dame Press, 1981.

Wilch, John R. *Ruth*. Concordia Commentary. St. Louis: Concordia, 2006.

Williams, James G. "The Alas-Oracles of the Eighth Century Prophets." *Hebrew Union College Annual* 38 (1967): 75–91.

Wilson, Robert R. *Prophecy and Society in Ancient Israel*. Philadelphia: Fortress, 1980.

Wiseman, Donald J. "Jonah's Nineveh." *Tyndale Bulletin* 30 (1979): 29–51.

———. "A New Stela of Aššur-naṣir-pal II. *Iraq* 14 (1952): 24–44.

Wittgenstein, Ludwig. *Philosophical Investigations*. Translated by G. E. M. Anscombe. New York: Macmillan, 1953.

Wolff, Hans Walther. *Amos the Prophet: The Man and His Background*. Translated by Foster R. McCurley. Philadelphia: Fortress, 1973.

———. *Confrontations with Prophets: Discovery the Old Testament's New and Contemporary Significance*. Philadelphia: Fortress, 1983.

———. *Joel and Amos*. Translated by Waldemar Janzen, S. Dean McBride, Jr., and Charles A. Muenchow. Hermeneia. Philadelphia: Fortress, 1977. Translation of *Dodekapropheton*. Vol. 2: *Joel und Amos*. Biblischer Kommentar Altes Testament 14/2. Neukirchen-Vluyn: Neukirchener, 1969.

Woolf, Bertram Lee, trans. *Reformation Writings of Martin Luther*. Vol. 1. London: Lutterworth, 1952.

Woude, A. S. van der. "Three Classical Prophets: Amos, Hosea and Micah." Pages 32–57 in *Israel's Prophetic Tradition: Essays in Honour of Peter R. Ackroyd*. Edited by Richard Coggins, Anthony Phillips, and Michael Knibb. Cambridge: Cambridge University Press, 1982.

Woudstra, Marten H. "Edom and Israel in Ezekiel." *Calvin Theological Journal* 3 (1968): 21–35.

Wright, Christopher J. H. *Deuteronomy*. New International Biblical Commentary, Old Testament 4. Peabody, MA: Hendrickson, 1996.

Wright, G. Ernest. "The Nations in Hebrew Prophecy." *Encounter* 26 (1965): 225–37.

Wuellner, Wilhelm. "Where Is Rhetorical Criticism Taking Us?" *Catholic Biblical Quarterly* 49 (1987): 448–63.

Wybrow, Cameron. *The Bible, Baconianism, and Mastery over Nature: The Old Testament and Its Modern Misreading*. New York: Peter Lang, 1991.

Yadin, Yigael. *The Art of Warfare in Biblical Lands in the Light of Archaeological Study*. Translated by M. Pearlman. 2 vols. London: Weidenfeld & Nicholson, 1963.

———. "Beer-Sheba: The High Place Destroyed by King Josiah." *Bulletin of the American Schools of Oriental Research* 222 (1976): 5–17.

Yadin, Yigael, et al. *Hazor II: An Account of the Second Season of Excavations, 1956*. Jerusalem: Magnes, 1960.

Young, Edward J. *My Servants the Prophets*. Grand Rapids: Eerdmans, 1952.

Younger, K. Lawson, Jr. "The Deportations of the Israelites." *Journal of Biblical Literature* 117 (1998): 201–27.

Zalcman, Lawrence. "Astronomical Illusions in Amos." *Journal of Biblical Literature* 100 (1981): 53–58.

Zimmerli, Walther. *Ezekiel*. Translated by Ronald E. Clements. Vol. 1. Hermeneia. Philadelphia: Fortress, 1979.

Introduction

In C. S. Lewis' *The Lion, the Witch, and the Wardrobe*, Mr. and Mrs. Beaver have this conversation with the children about the Christ figure, Aslan:

> "Is—is he a man?" asked Lucy.
>
> "Aslan a man!" said Mr. Beaver sternly. "… Aslan is a lion—*the* Lion, the great Lion."
>
> "Ooh!" said Susan. "… Is he—quite safe? I shall feel rather nervous about meeting a lion."
>
> "That you will, dearie, and no mistake," said Mrs. Beaver; "if there's anyone who can appear before Aslan without their knees knocking, they're either braver than most or else just silly."
>
> "Then he isn't safe?" said Lucy.
>
> "Safe?" said Mr. Beaver; "don't you hear what Mrs. Beaver tells you? Who said anything about safe? 'Course he isn't safe. But he's good."[1]

Yahweh certainly is not safe. He is terrifyingly dangerous for sinful people. Yet he is also good and gracious toward all who trust in him. There are biblical images that depict Yahweh as a caring Shepherd (Psalm 23) and a mighty Redeemer (Job 19:25), and some verses even compare him to a mother who nurses her infant children (Is 49:15; 66:9–13; Ps 131:2; cf. Num 11:12; 1 Thess 2:7; 1 Pet 2:2). But the church dare not let these images remove the claws and fangs of the Lion who roars from Zion (Amos 1:2; cf. 3:4, 8, 12; 5:19). Jesus, the crucified and risen Lord, is "the Lion of the tribe of Judah" (Rev 5:5). His words have teeth and his voice is like a roar.[2]

The Detroit Lions—a largely hapless football franchise—have as one of their cheers "Restore the roar!" The book of Amos has this as its singular goal: to restore the rightful roar of *the* Lion, the Lord Yahweh, the God of Israel, the triune God of the universe. The temptation is to put our hands over our ears to drown out his roar. The world, the devil, and the old Adam continue to urge the baptized to clip the claws on the Lion and clean up his bloody passion. The bride of Christ is called to holy reverence before the King of the nations. This Lion will never be safe, but he is very good.

---

1 Lewis, *The Lion, the Witch, and the Wardrobe*, 79–80.

2 In Rev 10:3 the mighty angel, who may be an angelomorphic appearance of the exalted Christ, "shouted in a great voice *as a lion roars* [ὥσπερ λέων μυκᾶται]. And when he shouted, the seven thunders spoke their voices." For the significance of this leonine voice, see Brighton, *Revelation*, 266, and for this angel as a possible Christophany, see Brighton, *Revelation*, 274–78. ESV translates the description of the exalted Christ's voice in Rev 1:15 (ἡ φωνὴ αὐτοῦ ὡς φωνὴ ὑδάτων πολλῶν) as "his voice was like the roar of many waters" (ESV). Similarly in Rev 14:1–2, where John sees the Lamb, ESV translates that the apostle heard "a voice from heaven like the roar of many waters and like the sound of loud thunder." Roaring and storm features like thunder and torrential waters signal theophany. See further the textual notes and commentary on Amos 1:2 and 3:8.

In Amos, the Lion Yahweh sends fires and earthquakes, locusts and drought, famine, disease, and an army bent on the complete annihilation of Israel. His wrath and anger are real. What unleashed such fury against a nation whom he calls "my people" (e.g., Amos 7:15; 8:2)? Is there any future after such devastation? How will God fulfill his promise to restore his people by resurrecting the tabernacle of David (9:11)? How does this messianic restoration apply now to his church as "the Israel of God" (Gal 6:16) consisting of believing Jews and Gentiles alike (Acts 15:16–17, quoting Amos 9:11–12)? And when will we dwell in the new creation with its Eden-like abundance (9:13–15)?

The book of Amos addresses these questions with a wide variety of rhetorical features that display a polished style, even as it is a straightforward, "in your face" message. Prophetic speech is inextricably tied to the Pentateuchal blessings and curses.[3] Amos' theology and thematic frame of reference come from the Mosaic covenant as it is articulated in Exodus, Leviticus, Numbers, and Deuteronomy. Amos was not a revolutionary trying to overturn the covenant and nation God had established, but a covenant preacher who harkened back to Israel's beginning as the people whom God elected to participate in his covenant of grace. In harmony with the eschatology of other prophetic books, he anticipated the eschatological fulfillment in the new covenant in Christ, in his church, and ultimately in the new heavens and earth (compare Amos 9:11–15 with Revelation 21–22).

Stuart identifies twenty-seven curses and ten restoration blessings in the Pentateuch.[4] He argues that in a Pentateuchal passage like Deut 4:21–31 the general contours of Amos' message are already laid out.[5] In these verses, Moses warns and invokes witnesses against Israel not to make idols (Deut 4:23) nor do anything that would provoke Yahweh to anger (Deut 4:25), for he is a consuming fire (Deut 4:24). But if the people choose to ignore these warnings, Yahweh will exile Israel and only a few will survive (Deut 4:27). If they seek Yahweh with all their heart and soul (4:29), he will not forget the covenant he established with the patriarchs (Deut 4:31). Building upon these types of Pentateuchal threats and promises, Amos interprets Israel's history through this dual lens of curse and blessing, disaster and restoration, Law and Gospel.

---

[3] Wellhausen's *Prolegomena to the History of Ancient Israel* (originally published in German in 1878) posits the opposite historical relationship: the Torah of Moses was written after the prophets. He supposes that the prophets—and especially Amos—were the originators of ethical monotheism, that they created Israel's religion largely from scratch (see the discussion of Wellhausen's work in "Form Criticism" in "Different Methods of Interpreting the Book of Amos" below, and Stuart, *Hosea–Jonah*, xxxi–xxxii). The position is summarized by Stuart: "As preachers prior to the composition of law, the OT prophets were in effect the inventors of biblical social ethics and to some extent personal ethics as well, and the creators of most of the covenantal ideas later systematized into what is now the bulk of the Pentateuch" (p. xxxi). Fortunately, this historically backward view, which was popular until the second half of the twentieth century, has now for the most part been given a quiet burial.

[4] Stuart, *Hosea–Jonah*, xxxii—xlii.

[5] Stuart, *Hosea–Jonah*, 288.

Amos not only calls for Israel to "hear" the roaring Word of Yahweh (e.g., Amos 3:1; 4:1; 5:1; 8:4), but he also mandates that the nation must care for the needs of other members of God's people who are impoverished and marginalized. The prophet witnesses to, speaks from, and hopes for an alternative world that most of his contemporaries cannot understand or accept. He wants them to feed the hungry, give water to the thirsty, provide shelter for the homeless, offer clothes to the naked, and look after the sick. Amos is not setting forth his own idea. He has been in Yahweh's council (Amos 3:7), so he knows that Yahweh earlier had rescued the barren woman (Gen 11:30; 21:1–7), redeemed his people from slavery and provided for their food, drink, clothing, and shelter (Exodus 14–17; cf. Deut 8:2–4), and then given them the command "do not take advantage of any widow or orphan" (Ex 22:21 [ET 22:22]). Yahweh's will in these ancient commands would be reiterated by Jesus as service rendered by Christians to himself (Mt 25:35–36).

Tragically the people of Israel did not respond in care and compassion. Toward them and all unbelievers Yahweh is a roaring Lion, ready to pounce upon his enemies and unleash upon them his ripping fangs and tearing claws. This Lion will bring about disaster after disaster, and not just against Israel. All the nations will be ushered before his throne of judgment because they too have ignored the needs of those whom Jesus would call "the least of these my brothers" (Mt 25:40).[6]

Amos declares that Israel's most sacred institutions and theological understandings—its divinely established temple, sacrificial and liturgical system of worship, priesthood, covenant, land entitlement, election, and kingship—will not avert disaster. Longstanding institutions associated with Yahweh's blessing, cherished belief systems, and a social structure that appears invincible will come to a cataclysmic end. He insists that the kings, priests, and leaders are engaging in an enormous deception. He calls it like he sees it: rotten, fake, treacherous—an unending process of evil. As such, Amos advocates a "religion against itself."[7]

The book of Amos probably constitutes the earliest collection of OT prophetic oracles that have been preserved as an independent literary work.[8] Amos contains not only the prophet's oracles and speeches but also a series of vision

---

[6] Those Jesus identifies as his "brothers," and whose treatment he equates with treatment of himself, are not just the poor and disadvantaged in general, but needy Christian believers, especially those whom he sends as his representatives and evangelists. One may see Gibbs, *Jerusalem and Parousia*, 217–20, and *Matthew 1:1–11:1*, 543–45. See also Voelz, "Biblical Charity: What Does It Entail and How Does It Relate to the Gospel—A New Testament Perspective," especially 79–80.

[7] Fretheim, *God and World in the Old Testament*, 160.

[8] The books of Samuel and Kings preserve oracles of earlier prophets that were incorporated into those historical books, not into a prophet's independent book. Amos dates to the early to mid-eighth century BC, and Hosea to the mid eighth century. The date of Joel is uncertain, but somewhere in the ninth–sixth centuries BC. See further "Amos' Place in the Minor Prophets" and "The Historical Setting of the Book of Amos" below in the introduction.

reports (7:1–9; 8:1–3; 9:1–4). Both his preaching and his visions reflect the life of a Judahite cattleman/farmer who was called to serve as a prophet in the Northern Kingdom. But the book is not just about "the life and times of Amos," nor about Israel's history in the mid-eighth century BC. Its major focus is *Yahweh*, who is the covenant God of Israel, the God who created and rules the universe—the triune God, the Father who would send his Son in the power of the Holy Spirit to save his people (Lk 1:35; 4:1, 14; Acts 10:38; Rom 1:1–4). In his book, Amos employs ten different titles to describe Yahweh, and they occur a total of eighty-six times.[9]

Standing with Amos is Israel's final Prophet, who also is called by different titles. Some believers confess him as "the Christ," the Greek equivalent of "the Messiah" (e.g., Mt 16:16),[10] others "Rabboni" (Jn 20:16), "the Son of God, … the King of Israel" (Jn 1:49), and even our "God and Savior" (Titus 2:13; 2 Pet 1:1). Like Amos, he also dares to turn his world of power politics upside down. He makes subversive proclamations such as "the last will be first" (Mt 20:16; cf. Mk 10:31; Lk 13:30). This Prophet has the zeal to make a whip and use it to cleanse his Father's house (Jn 2:15). He looks the religious leaders straight in the eye and says, "Woe to you, scribes and Pharisees, hypocrites! For you clean the outside of the cup and the dish, but inside they are full of greed and uncleanness" (Mt 23:25). And climactically he stands before his equivalent of the apostate priest Amaziah (Amos 7:10–17)—the high priest Caiaphas—and confesses, "From now on you will see the Son of Man sitting at the right hand of the Power and coming on the clouds of heaven" (Mt 26:64; cf. Dan 7:13; Mk 14:62). This prophet's name is "Jesus" because he saves his people from their sins (Mt 1:21). He alone is "the Lion of the tribe of Judah" (Rev 5:5; cf. Amos 1:2; 3:8). His resurrection marks the raising of the fallen tabernacle of David (cf. Amos 9:11–15; Lk 1:69; Jn 2:18–22), and through him God has raised up the new and living temple, his holy church (Acts 15:16–17; 1 Cor 3:16–17; 6:19–20; 2 Cor 6:16; Eph 2:19–21).

Jesus definitively revealed God's radical love *for all people*, but was executed for disrupting the religious and social order of the first-century Jewish and Greco-Roman establishments. He instituted a new and eternal kingdom of which he is the King (Jn 18:36; cf. Dan 2:44; 7:14). He associated with the poor and destitute, and was crucified because he welcomed sinners of all sorts into his kingdom simply through faith in him. "Though rich, he became poor for your sake, so that you by his poverty might become rich" (2 Cor 8:9).

To be sure, Jesus roars like a Lion, but he is also the Lamb of God who takes away the sin of the world (Jn 1:29, 36). His power is made perfect in weakness

---

[9] This analysis comes from Dempster, "The Lord Is His Name," 175. The figure is derived from the MT of Amos and may not be apparent in English translations. See further the commentary on 1:2.

[10] In the OT, the Hebrew מָשִׁיחַ, "Messiah," is a title for Christ in Ps 2:2; Dan 9:25–26; and perhaps in other passages such as 1 Sam 2:10, 35; Pss 18:51 (ET 18:50); 132:17.

(2 Cor 12:9). He allows soldiers to march him through the city streets on the Via Dolorosa, shouldering his crossbar, while blood drips from his butchered back. He permits these same executioners to strip him naked, shove him to the ground, and pin him to wood with their tools of torture. He accepts the spit and the insults without calling on his Father to dispatch twelve legions of angels (Mt 26:53).

The passion of our Lord is typified by the persecution of Amos. By cleansing the temple Jesus angered the priests, who, with the other Jewish leaders, betrayed him to the governor representing the king (Jn 19:14–15). By prophesying against the idolatrous temple at Bethel, Amos infuriated the priest Amaziah, who charged him with treason against the king (Amos 7:10–13). Amaziah and company did everything they could to cage the Lion and his prophet; if they could not cage him, they would kill him. Jesus, the Prophet (Lk 24:19; Acts 3:22–23), was killed on Good Friday, and his enemies and all the demons of hell thought they had vanquished the Lion. But coming forth from the tomb on Easter, the Lion's fierce love roars on! God's promise to restore both his people and his creation by raising up the falling tabernacle of David (Amos 9:11–15) stands fulfilled in the bodily resurrection of the Son of David, who has raised up his church and confers everlasting life on all baptized believers—those called by his name (cf. 9:12). Therefore Rev 5:5 boldly proclaims: "See, the Lion of the tribe of Judah … *has triumphed*!"

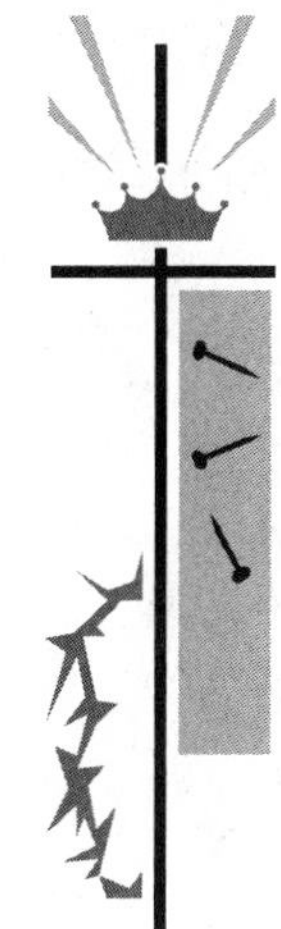

Amos Scholarship

Although Amos is comprised of only nine chapters with one hundred forty-six verses, it has been the subject of voluminous literature.[11] Almost every exegetical method and hermeneutical perspective has been used to investigate the book.[12] The result is that few prophetic books can claim an amount of secondary literature close to the volumes devoted to Amos. Van der Woude writes:

> In 1959 Mays … wrote that Amos "has had more than his proportionate share of scholarly attention and Amos-studies are already on the way to becoming a small library on their own." This statement holds true for the two following decades as well.[13]

---

[11] For example, van der Wal's compilation *Amos: A Classified Bibliography* lists approximately 1,600 titles written from AD 1800 through June 1986. In 1991 Hasel (*Understanding the Book of Amos*, 26) observed that more than eight hundred items had been written about Amos since the 1960s and that three hundred fifty of those did not appear in van der Wal's bibliography. Since Hasel's work was published, many more books and articles about Amos have appeared. At the present time, Carroll R. (*Amos—The Prophet and His Oracles*) provides the most up-to-date discussion and list of available resources for Amos scholarship.

[12] Auld, *Amos*, provides an overview of many interpretive issues in the study of the book of Amos.

[13] Van der Woude, "Three Classical Prophets: Amos, Hosea and Micah," 34, citing Mays, "Words about the Words of Amos," 259.

The enormous attention given to Amos is not difficult to explain. As the first of the inspired writing prophets, he stands at the head of a significant movement in Israel's history.[14] The oracles and narratives of earlier prophets are embedded in other books, for example, Elijah and Elisha in 1 and 2 Kings, but Amos begins the phenomenon of a prophetic book.

The issues in Amos research may be discussed in the categories of "behind the text," "within the text," and "in front of the text."[15]

"Behind the text" issues include archaeological findings as well as tools from the social sciences that seek to enable a better understanding of the prophet's historical and sociological milieu. For archaeology, the works of Shalom Paul and Philip King are noteworthy.[16] Max Weber's work is an example of anthropological and sociological strategies that attempt to get "behind the text" of Amos.[17] Such a social reconstruction of what was "behind the text" of Amos may be helpful, yet it has also been misused to advocate revolutionary power for, for example, Latin Americans, African-Americans, homosexuals, and feminists. It is a misreading of Scripture to attempt to use Amos to promote political revolt, nationalism, racism, or sexual perversion, which are contrary to the clear message of God's Word. Amos is a book about Yahweh and his people and a call to repentance and faith in him.

Other "behind the text" enterprises likewise compromise the truth that the Bible is the inspired and inerrant Word of God. These investigations seek to reveal the "real" Amos, and with it, they question the theological and literary integrity of the book. This line of inquiry begins with the belief that Amos predates the Mosaic covenant and the giving of the Torah. Amos is a champion of universal moral principles, or "ethical monotheism." In this view, Amos is a harbinger of the higher ethics of the Christian faith and a precursor to the social gospel. This position creates a chasm between prophetic theology and the sacrificial aspects of Israel's faith that are developed in Exodus 25–40, Leviticus, and much of Numbers and Deuteronomy, and which find their fulfillment in the sacrificial atonement of Christ.

In this way, these "behind the text" investigations—often called form, tradition, and redaction criticism—attempt to separate Amos from the Pentateuch. They also seek to separate the *ipsissima verba* of Amos (the "very words" he uttered) from later redactional editors, who get credit for the canonical form of the book. For example, in his commentary on Amos, first published in German in 1969, Wolff distinguished between what he thought were the original words

---

[14] Holladay says: "Like Melchizedek, Amos seems to have been born without benefit of ancestors" ("Assyrian Statecraft and the Prophets of Israel," 29).

[15] This section closely follows Carroll R., *Amos—The Prophet and His Oracles*, 31–51.

[16] See especially Paul, *Amos*, and the works by King cited in the bibliography, especially *Amos, Hosea, Micah*.

[17] See Weber, *Ancient Judaism*, especially 297–355. For an evaluation of Weber's work, see Carroll R., *Contexts for Amos*, 26–36.

of Amos and what was added by later editors: "Even a cursory examination of the book of Amos forces one to posit behind it a long history of literary growth."[18]

"Within the text" methods do not totally ignore the issues of archaeology, sociology, and literary history, but focus on what is actually written in the extant, finished text. In a move beyond the less-than-helpful "behind the text" methodologies, Jörg Jeremias in the 1980s began to argue that Amos needs to be read together with Hosea.[19] This direction of research led to a more holistic reading of Amos in light of the other minor prophets, with the belief that he must be interpreted as one among the twelve and not simply by himself. This movement resulted in renewed attention to the literary and rhetorical structures of Amos, with greater appreciation of its artistry and less focus on disjunction in the text. One advocate of this reading strategy is Roy Melugin, who singles out Wolff's redactional theory of the composition of Amos as an illustration of a "behind the text" theory that "stretch[es] meager evidence too far."[20] Melugin encourages more concern for synchronic literary readings of Scripture, since redactional strategies often rely on scholarly ingenuity divorced from historical controls. This is a move in the right direction.

"In front of the text" appropriations of Amos concentrate on applying its message to people today. Such approaches abound and often capitalize on the book's message of justice and righteousness. However, many reinterpret that message in contemporary political and nationalistic terms, rather than in theological terms that apply to the church and individual Christians in society. An example of such a reinterpretive "in front of the text" reading of Amos is the following paraphrase that substitutes modern peoples and political issues for the biblical ones:

> Thus says the Lord:
> For three transgressions of Iraq and for four,
> punishment will come;
> because they have destroyed the Kurdish people
> by denying them land, food, and dignity.
> So I will send a fire on the hills and valleys of Iraq. …
> Thus says the Lord:
> For three transgressions of the United States and for four
> and more, punishment will come;
> because you have been the great hypocrites of the earth:
> pointing your moralistic finger and expounding your pious rhetoric,
> while you commit the same atrocities as the other nations.[21]

---

[18] Wolff, *Joel and Amos*, 106. See further the discussion of Wolff's work in "Form Criticism" in "Different Methods of Interpreting the Book of Amos" below.

[19] See the collection of Jeremias' essays entitled *Hosea und Amos*.

[20] As noted by Carroll R., *Amos—The Prophet and His Oracles*, 43, who cites (on p. 197, n. 63), for example, Melugin, "Prophetic Books and the Problem of Historical Reconstruction."

[21] Ruth E. Frey, "Oracle against the Nations," in *Many Voices: Multicultural Responses to the Minor Prophets* (ed. Alice Ogden Bellis; Lanham, Md.: University Press of America, 1995),

This Commentary's Method

This commentary on Amos selectively employs aspects of all three of these reading strategies to interpret the book. "Behind the text" disciplines of archaeology and ancient Near Eastern history serve to enhance the understanding of several key passages.

The main focus, however, is on what is actually "within the text." God spoke to ancient Israel through his servants the prophets, and the writing prophets recorded their inspired messages in books incorporated into the sacred Scriptures. Through these inerrant, infallible Scriptures, God continues to speak authoritatively today. As we study each book, we follow the contours of its unique, distinctive features, and we also interpret its message in light of its larger context as one of the canonical Scriptures contained in the Old and New Testaments, which together comprise the Bible. The hallmark of faithful biblical exegesis from the early-church, medieval, and Reformation eras down to the present day is that it has sought to understand, proclaim, and apply the divine message that is actually "within the text." This method appreciates the unity and rhetorical power of Amos and results in an exegetically sound and theologically orthodox interpretation that benefits the church and her ministry.

This commentary's "in front of the text" applications of Amos rely on the definitive interpretation of the OT in the NT, focusing on the fulfillment in Christ. These applications also utilize the church fathers, and especially are guided by the theology of Luther and the Lutheran Confessions.

In these ways, this commentary seeks a balance between these three windows into the book of Amos. Detailed textual exegesis and Christian theological exposition go together. As Motyer writes:

> Exegesis without exposition is like a deep-freeze, full of good things but, as it stands, out of touch with reality and devoid of nourishment; exposition without exegesis is like a space-rocket, enjoying itself in its own orbit but oblivious now of the launching-pad from which it started.[22]

Amos' address to Israel is powerful and often abrasive, but in the end, he offers a hope that will never end (9:11–15). The Holy Spirit continues to speak through this word of Law and Gospel to the baptized, who are the new "Israel of God" (see Gal 6:16; Phil 3:3). Looking primarily in, but also behind and in front of the text, this commentary seeks to give the reader of Amos a new set of ears for listening to the Lion's roar (see Amos 1:2; 3:4, 8, 12; 5:19). This will lead to repentance and faith in the risen Son of David, and faithful preaching, joyful teaching, and humble serving in his name.[23]

12–13, quoted by Carroll R., *Amos—The Prophet and His Oracles*, 55 and 201, n. 6. Used by permission of University Press of America.

[22] Motyer, *The Message of Amos*, 10.

[23] For a discussion of the method of rhetorical analysis that this commentary employs, see "Rhetorical Analysis" and "Conclusions" in "Different Methods of Interpreting the Book of Amos."

The Structure and Outline of the Book of Amos

Scholars have made numerous attempts to outline the book of Amos using any number of different patterns and series. Gordis observes this outline: (1) the judgment oracles in chapters 1 and 2; (2) the oracles beginning with "hear this word" (3:1–15; 4:1–13; 5:1–6); (3) the accusations that begin with "woe" (5:7–17; 5:18–27; 6:1–14);[24] (4) the five visions in chapters 7–9; and (5) the oracle of hope (9:11–15).[25] Gese proposes a five-element pattern (two plus two plus one) in the oracles against the nations; in 4:6–13; and in the visions in chapters 7–9.[26] Limburg argues that Amos reflects a structural pattern of seven plus one,[27] while Hayes states: "The material in the book is best understood in terms of large rhetorical units."[28] Noble believes Amos consists of a superscription and three main parts: part 1 is Yahweh's word to the nations (1:2–3:8); part 2 is a palistrophic judgment oracle (3:9–6:14); and part 3 is the destruction and reconstitution of Israel (7:1–9:15).[29] Paul believes the present order of the book depicts independent collections arranged according to their genres, including the oracles against the nations (1:3–2:3); the woe oracles (5:18–27; 6:1–7); and the series of visions in chapters 7–9.[30] Gibson states: "We do not know on what principle his oracles were arranged."[31]

It is clear from the book that Amos did not arrange his oracles by genre type nor in a chronological sequence. It also is not valid to amend the text in order to achieve a numerical or logical consistency. Rather, the book of Amos is a literary presentation that has its own integrity. The prophet preached his sermons on various occasions, then deliberately arranged them, together with his visionary revelations, into the present form of the book. This has long been recognized by faithful interpreters, including E. W. Hengstenberg, a nineteenth-

---

24 Gordis advocates emending 5:7 to include הוֹי, "woe" ("The Composition and Structure of Amos," 225, n. 3).

25 Gordis, "The Composition and Structure of Amos," 217.

26 In order to produce his five-element pattern, Gese assumes that originally there were only five oracles against the nations: Damascus, Gaza, Ammon, Moab, and Israel. (He deems Tyre, Edom, and Judah to be secondary.) He groups the first four in two pairs (Damascus/Aram and Gaza/Philistia as the first pair; Ammon and Moab as the second pair) and sees the climax in the Israel oracle. He compares these five oracles to the fivefold refrain "but you did not return to me" in 4:6–13 and claims a developing pattern of increasing devastation in the punishments outlined in those verses ("Komposition bei Amos").

27 Limburg sees the pattern in the oracles against the nations; the seven questions followed by a climactic statement in 3:3–8; the seven verbs in the imperative or its equivalent followed by a climactic statement in 4:4–5; the seven verbs in the first person followed by a climactic statement in 4:6–12; the seven aspects of worship that Yahweh does not like followed by what he desires in 5:21–24; the seven behaviors followed by a climactic statement in 6:4–6; and in the seven punishing acts followed by a climactic general statement in 9:1–4 ("Sevenfold Structures in the Book of Amos"). See also his commentary *Hosea–Micah* on those passages.

28 Hayes, *Amos, the Eighth-Century Prophet*, 39.

29 Noble, "The Literary Structure of Amos: A Thematic Analysis."

30 Paul, *Amos*, 6–7.

31 Gibson, *Language and Imagery in the Old Testament*, 60.

century Lutheran, who simply divided the book into the sermons (chapters 1–6) and the visions (chapters 7–9):

> The very inscription [1:1] proves that we have before us a whole, composed at one time, and containing the substance of what the prophet had uttered previously, and in a detached form. …
>
> There is a plan in the arrangement of the book, which indicates that the book is not a collection of separate discourses, but that it bears an independent character. …
>
> But that … we have not before us pieces loosely connected with each other in a chronological arrangement, is evident from the fact, that the promises [9:11–15] stand just at the end of the whole collection. The prophet had rather to reprove and to threaten than to comfort; but yet he cannot refrain, at least at the close, from causing the sun to break through the clouds. Without this close [9:11–15] there would be wanting in Amos a main element [Gospel promises] of the prophetic discourse, which is wanting in no other prophet, and by which alone the other elements are placed in a proper light. …
>
> He foresees that, before salvation comes, all that is glorious, not only in Israel, but in Judah also, must be given over to destruction. Judah and Israel shall be overflowed by the heathen world, the Temple at Jerusalem destroyed, the Davidic dynasty dethroned, and the inhabitants of both kingdoms carried away into captivity. But afterwards, the restoration of David's tabernacle ([9:]11), and the extension of the kingdom of God far beyond the borders of the heathen world ([9:]12), take place. The most characteristic point is the emanation of salvation from the family of David, at the time of its deepest abasement.[32]

Andersen and Freedman offer the most compelling brief literary outline of Amos. Their analysis is as follows:

I. The Book of Doom: oracles against the nations and Israel (Amos 1–4)
   - A. Oracles against the nations (1:3–2:8)
   - B. The charge against Israel (2:9–4:13)

II. Woes and lamentations (chapters 5–6)

III. The Book of Visions (7:1–9:6)

IV. Epilogue (9:7–15)[33]

A fuller and slightly different outline of the book is as follows:

I. Superscription and introduction (1:1–2)

II. Judgments against the nations (1:3–2:16)
   - A. Aram (1:3–5)
   - B. Philistia (1:6–8)
   - C. Tyre (1:9–10)
   - D. Edom (1:11–12)
   - E. Ammon (1:13–15)
   - F. Moab (2:1–3)

---

32 Hengstenberg, *Christology of the Old Testament*, 1:356–57, 362.

33 Andersen and Freedman, *Amos*, 26.

G. Judah (2:4–5)
H. Israel (2:6–16)

III. Declarations concerning Israel (3:1–6:14)
   A. Accusations lodged against Israel (3:1–4:13)
      1. Yahweh's exclusive relationship with Israel (3:1–2)
      2. Prophecy verified (3:3–8)
      3. Proclamation concerning Israel's guilt and punishment (3:9–15)
      4. Prophetic satire against women and worshipers (4:1–5)
      5. Failure to respond to Yahweh's rebuke (4:6–13)
   B. Lamentation for Israel (5:1–3)
   C. Exhortation to seek Yahweh (5:4–17)
   D. Judgment on the Day of Yahweh (5:18–27)
      1. The Day of Yahweh (5:18–20)
      2. Detestable ritual practices (5:21–27)
   E. Warning to the secure and complacent (6:1–7)
   F. Certain destruction for the prideful house of Israel (6:8–14)

IV. Visions (7:1–9:15)
   A. Visions that do not come to pass (7:1–6)
      1. The vision of the locusts (7:1–3)
      2. The vision of the fire (7:4–6)
   B. Visions that do come to pass (7:7–9:10)
      1. The vision of the plaster (7:7–9)
      2. Historical interlude (7:10–17)
      3. The vision of the summer fruit (8:1–14)
      4. The vision of Yahweh beside the altar (9:1–10)
   C. Restoration through the resurrection of the tent of David (9:11–15)

These two outlines offer a *literary* analysis of the book. Andersen and Freedman also reconstruct a *chronological* development of Amos' ministry by means of the five visions described in chapters 7–9.[34] Of course, their hypothesis about the history of Amos' ministry is conjecture and cannot be verified.

---

[34] Andersen and Freedman, *Amos*, for example, 8, 73, 196–98. Polley also believes that to some extent the book reflects different phases in Amos' ministry (*Amos and the Davidic Empire*, 160). On the other hand, von Rad writes: "Little is gained by attempting to order and interrelate them, for each unit really stands on its own" (*Old Testament Theology*, 2:135). Stuart says: "The structuring of material in the first six chapters shows no special organizing principle" (*Hosea–Jonah*, 288). But Andersen and Freedman give the following rationale: "Amos is not alone in such arrangement of materials. The books of Jeremiah, Isaiah, and Ezekiel likewise combine biographical, autobiographical, historical, visionary, and oracular compositions" (*Amos*, 76). More specifically, they cite Jeremiah 25 as "a prophetic composition that in several particulars resembles the book of Amos as a whole. It documents similar phases in the development of the prophet's career and serves a similar apologetic purpose" (*Amos*, 82). In light of these other prophetic books, it is safe to assume that the book of Amos does not proceed along the lines of a strict chronological sequence.

Although Andersen and Freedman's reconstruction has not gone unchallenged, it appears to be a viable roadmap to make the journey through the phases of the prophetic ministry of Amos. This commentary engages their theory about the chronology, but of course it proceeds in the order of the canonical form of the text. Moreover, this commentary affirms that Amos was the author of the entire book, whereas Andersen and Freedman are unsure.[35]

When viewed from the perspective of Amos' five visions, a possible chain of events in his ministry, largely based on the analysis of Andersen and Freedman, is as follows:

Phase 1

1. Amos is called to be a prophet (3:8; 7:14–15).
2. He receives his first two visions and successfully intercedes for Jacob, who "is so small" (7:1–6). Amos' prayers do not cancel Yahweh's judgment, but postpone it, giving the prophet the opportunity to call Israel to repentance and faith.
3. Emboldened by these two visions, Amos summons Israel to repent, believe, and bear fruit that is fitting of repentance (chapters 5–6).
4. God's exhortations through Amos (e.g., "seek good and not evil so that you may live," 5:14) go unheeded by Israel.
5. Even the plagues cited in 4:6–11 do not turn Israel back to Yahweh.

Phase 2

1. Amos receives two more visions (7:7–9; 8:1–3) that indicate that Yahweh will not forgive the people any longer (7:8; 8:2) and that "the end is coming upon my people Israel" (8:2).
2. These visions result in Yahweh's eightfold "I will not revoke it [the planned punishment]" in 1:3–2:16.
3. Amos continues with his oracles in chapters 3–4, which end with the verdict "prepare to meet your God" (4:12).
4. These prophecies in chapters 1–4, perhaps spoken at Bethel, provoke Amaziah and lead to the priest's confrontation with Amos (7:10–17). In this way, Amos' third and fourth visions (7:7–9; 8:1–3) provide the necessary context for a proper understanding of this encounter between the prophet and the priest.

Phase 3

1. Amos delivers an apologia for phases 1 and 2 with a special focus upon punishment for Israel's leaders (8:4–14).
2. Vision 5 follows (9:1–4) with the ensuing destruction described in 9:5–10.

Phase 4

While hope for the near future is gone, God will fulfill his promise of restoration through raising David's falling tabernacle (9:11). There is a day (9:11)—indeed, "days are coming" (9:13)—when Yahweh will reverse the

---

[35] See, for example, Andersen and Freedman, *Amos*, 196–98.

curses pronounced in 1:2–9:10. A believing remnant of Israel (5:15; 9:14), along with a believing remnant from among the nations (9:12), will be restored in the new creation to dwell in it forever (9:15).

Phase 5

1. Amos' ministry ceases.
2. Two years later a massive earthquake validates Amos' preaching (1:1).
3. Shortly after the earthquake the finished book with its superscription (1:1) is circulated.

Whether or not these phases occurred in that historical order, it is apparent that the book of Amos does not unfold logically or chronologically.[36] Rather, it presents the climax of irrevocable judgment first (1:3–2:16) and then proceeds in retrograde fashion into the background and buildup of how Israel (like the other nations mentioned in 1:3–2:3) went so wrong, leading to the all-encompassing decision by Yahweh that he would not revoke. Then it concludes with God's promise of restoration through his raising of the tent of David—ultimately, the resurrection of the Davidic Messiah. God's people will be restored and comprise the new temple in Christ. This new Israel, including Gentile believers, will live forever in the new creation (9:11–15; Acts 15:16–18; Revelation 21–22, especially Rev 22:16).

Amos' Place in the Minor Prophets

Amos is the third book in the collection of the twelve books that comprise "the Minor Prophets," which follow "the Major Prophets," Isaiah, Jeremiah, and Ezekiel. "Minor" refers to their brevity, not to lesser importance. Recent scholarship has preferred to call the books from Hosea through Malachi "the Book of the Twelve."[37] The view that these twelve constitute a single "book" would make the collection comparable in size to their prophetic kinsman, Isaiah, Jeremiah, and Ezekiel. According to the Final Masorah (added at the end of each book by the Masoretes, the Hebrew scribes who copied the OT books in the sixth through tenth centuries AD, to ensure that the full text had been copied accurately), Isaiah consists of 1,291 verses. Jeremiah is slightly longer, with 1,364 verses, whereas Ezekiel has 1,273 verses. The Book of the Twelve has a

---

[36] Freedman, "Confrontations in the Book of Amos," 243, writes:

> Why the apparent order of events and oracles is reversed, or at least demonstrably not chronological is an intriguing question, which may never be answered satisfactorily, although examples abound in the literature of all nations in which the author or compiler preferred to organize available information according to another principle or system. In the case of Amos, one important effect is to position the Great Set Speech [chapters 1–2] against the eight small nations in the lands between Assyria to the north-east and Egypt to the south-west, at the very beginning of the book, thus focusing attention on the central and climactic message of the prophet.

[37] For example, that is the title of a chapter in Petersen, *The Prophetic Literature*, 169–214, that proceeds to discuss each of the minor prophets.

total of 1,050 verses. It is significant that the Masoretes referred to the Minor Prophets as שְׁנֵים עָשָׂר, the "Twelve."[38]

There is other ancient evidence that some considered these twelve prophets to constitute a collection. Sirach, written about 200 BC, includes this prayer: "May the bones of the Twelve Prophets send forth new life from where they lie" (Sirach 49:10 NRSV).[39] Jewish tradition generally considers these twelve prophets to be the fourth and last book (after Isaiah, Jeremiah, and Ezekiel) of the Latter Prophets in the Hebrew Scriptures.[40] The Talmud also stipulates that only three lines should separate the individual books of the Twelve Prophets from each other, whereas four lines normally separate biblical books.[41]

In recent centuries, neither Jewish nor Christian interpreters have typically interpreted the Twelve as one book. Until the beginning of the 1990s—apart from a few exceptions—the individual books of the Twelve were treated like other individual prophetic writings, without considering the possibility that each book perhaps should be read and understood in the context of the other eleven. However, at the end of the twentieth century, it became acceptable in scholarly circles to view these books as a literary unit.[42]

A foundational idea in recent scholarship is that the Twelve were arranged in the canon in such a way that the message of each builds on its predecessors, picking up concepts, words, and text types from them. The compilers of the Book of the Twelve wanted readers to look for, discover, and appreciate how the different thematic threads generate a colorful tapestry that reflects Yahweh's self disclosure in this corpus. This idea is in agreement with the overall historical order of the Twelve, which is generally chronological. Hosea, probably Joel, and Amos are the earliest ones, written in the eighth century BC, while Haggai, Zechariah, and Malachi are the latest, written in the late sixth and the fifth centuries BC.

"The Day of Yahweh" is a prominent theme in the Twelve. Joel and Amos probably are the oldest biblical books that contain this phrase, which occurs sixteen times in the OT, exclusively in the Prophets.[43] When "the Day of Yahweh" texts from the Twelve are placed together, the two themes of Law and Gospel emerge: it will be a day of destruction for the ungodly but also a day of salvation

---

[38] This title for them is used in the Final Masorah after the book of Malachi, which includes the total number of verses in the Twelve, and also the totals for Malachi and for the sum of the Prophets.

[39] As noted by Petersen, *The Prophetic Literature*, 169.

[40] Talmud, *Baba Bathra*, 14b, says: "The order of the Prophets is, Joshua, Judges, Samuel, Kings, Jeremiah, Ezekiel, Isaiah, and the Twelve Minor Prophets" (trans. Maurice Simon; London: Soncino, 1989). The rabbis go on to discuss why Isaiah is placed after Jeremiah and Ezekiel.

[41] Talmud, *Baba Bathra*, 13b (cf. Petersen, *The Prophetic Literature*, 169–70).

[42] For a discussion, see Redditt and Schart, Thematic Threads in the Book of the Twelve.

[43] See further the commentary on 5:18, 20, which are the only two Amos verses with the phrase. Related phrases about a "day" or "days" of judgment or salvation are in 1:14; 2:16; 3:14; 4:2; 5:8; 6:3; 8:3, 9, 10, 11, 13; 9:11, 13.

for the righteous. Usually it is described as a day of judgment, but it can also be the decisive time of grace.[44]

The prophets who spoke of this judgment day in the eighth century BC, including Amos, Isaiah (13:6, 9), and probably Joel, were initially referring to the defeat and exile of northern Israel in 722 BC and/or the Babylonian destruction of Jerusalem in 587 BC. Further fulfillments of their prophecies include Good Friday, the day when Yahweh executed his judgment against humanity's sin upon Jesus on the cross, and the final Judgment Day at the second advent of Christ. Yet the Last Day will also be the day of resurrection (cf. "that day" in 9:11) inaugurating eternal life for all believers in the new creation (cf. "the days are coming" in 9:13).

The prophets often use other phrases with "day" that are equivalent to "the Day of Yahweh." For example, Micah maintains that "those devising wickedness" (Micah 2:1) are singled out for wrath "on that day" (Micah 2:4). Obadiah 15 states that "the Day of Yahweh" is "against all the nations." Joel warns that "the Day of Yahweh" will bring destruction (Joel 1:15). Yet Joel also speaks of a time of blessing and the outpouring of the Holy Spirit (2:18–3:2 [ET 2:18–29]) as fulfilled on the day of Pentecost (cf. Acts 2; especially Acts 2:16–21). This era of grace precedes the "the Day of Yahweh" that is the Last Day, when the solar system and present universe will pass away (Joel 3:4 [ET 2:31]).

Other prophets among the Twelve add their specific nuances to "the Day of Yahweh" (e.g., Zeph 1:7, 14; Mal 3:23). It is the same event called a "day of trouble" in Nah 1:7 and Hab 3:16. Jonah is the only book in the Twelve that does not contain this theme. Since the motif is present but not common in Isaiah, Jeremiah, and Ezekiel,[45] its frequency in the Twelve is noteworthy. Isaiah's foci include David, Zion, and the Suffering Servant, while Jeremiah's burden is primarily on Judah's exile and return. Ezekiel's major motif is "the glory of Yahweh." Seen in this light, the Twelve's ongoing theme of "the Day of Yahweh" stands out all the more.

There are other connections between Amos and other books of the Twelve. Like Joel (chapters 1 and 2), Amos employs the curse of locusts to portray threats against the land (4:9; 7:1). Like Hosea (e.g., 6:1; 14:2–3), Amos is a preacher of repentance (4:6–11). Joel ends with Yahweh roaring from Zion (4:16 [ET 3:16]), while Amos begins with this roaring theophany (1:2). Like Hosea (3:5), Amos looks ahead to the new era and foresees God's restoration of his people under the Davidic Messiah (9:11). "The latter days" in Hos 3:5 and "on that day" in Amos 9:11 both are OT prophetic expressions that are shorthand for the end times, which begin with the first advent of Christ and culminate in his second coming, whereupon the promised restoration will be completed. Amos' eschatological vision of the new creation includes mountains dripping with sweet wine (9:13), as does Joel's (4:18 [ET 3:18]).

---

[44] See the commentary on "on that day" in 9:11 and "days are coming" in 9:13.

[45] For example, in Isaiah the theme appears primarily in Is 2:6–22, in his oracles against the nations (Is 13:6, 9; 22:5), and in a few later texts (e.g., Is 34:8).

Further comparisons between Amos and other books in the Twelve are as follows: Hosea, like Amos, depicts Yahweh as a lion (Hos 5:14; 13:7–8; Amos 1:2; 3:8; cf. Joel 1:6), who tears but who also heals (Hos 6:1). Hosea also contains a resurrection theme that transforms creation (Hos 6:1–3; 14:4–9) as does Amos 9:11–15. Both books end with salvation oracles. The second half of Joel has many salvation oracles. Joel 2:21–29 has similarities to Amos 9:11–15. Obadiah is an oracle against Edom, while Amos includes an oracle against Edom in 1:11–12. In like manner, Obadiah concludes with Yahweh's salvation taking place on Mount Zion (Obad 21), while Amos begins and ends with Zion/Davidic themes (1:2; 9:11). Micah's Gospel themes are also similar to those in the book of Amos. For example, Micah's picture of restoration as an abundance of vines and fig trees (Micah 4:4) is analogous to Amos 9:14–15. Both Nahum and Habakkuk announce that Yahweh is about to judge an oppressive empire (Assyria and Babylon, respectively). This will in turn usher in salvation for Israel. The book of Amos has this as a major theme: Yahweh will bring destruction on those who oppress vulnerable people (e.g., 1:3, 13; 2:6–8). This is good news for the oppressed! Zephaniah's promise of restored fortunes (Zeph 3:20) lies at the heart of Amos' salvation oracle (Amos 9:14), while Haggai, Zechariah, and Malachi are testimonies that the possibility of salvation for the remnant (Amos 5:15) was partially fulfilled in the postexilic Persian province of Yehud (Judea), then realized by the advent of Christ.

However, some have disagreed with the view that the Book of the Twelve exhibits an overall theme, plot, and direction greater than that of the sum of its twelve parts. For example, Ben Zvi expresses the following concerns.[46] First, the Book of the Twelve does not have a comprehensive heading or overall title. Second, the argument that catchwords form links between different prophetic books seems to be doubtful, since the mere fact that one more or less unspecific word occurs in two different literary units can be accidental in many cases. It is arbitrary to interpret such cases as deliberate links. Third, there is the danger that an interpretation of each book as part of the Twelve may conceal the original meaning of a book and may lead to misunderstanding it.

The best way to appropriate current scholarship on the Twelve is to utilize its canonical approach of interpreting the extant, final forms of each book in order to grasp certain elements of literary unity that divulge theological themes.[47] However, especially in light of concerns such as those expressed by Ben Zvi, it is important to treat each book individually before asking questions about how it fits into the larger group of the Twelve and into biblical canon as a whole.

Finally, we can note the position of the Twelve in the OT. The Hebrew OT is arranged into the Torah, the Prophets, and the Writings, so that the Twelve precede the Psalms and the rest of the Writings. The result is that the Hebrew OT concludes with 2 Chronicles. The last verse contains Cyrus' declaration that

---

[46] Ben Zvi, "Twelve Prophetic Books or 'The Twelve': A Few Preliminary Considerations."

[47] This methodology is similar to, though not identical with, that of Sweeney, *The Twelve Prophets*.

Yahweh had appointed him to rebuild the Jerusalem temple in Judah and Cyrus' decree permitting the Judeans to ascend to the temple (2 Chr 36:23). Therefore it focuses on the return back to the OT place of worship.

In the whole Bible, however, according to the ancient versions (LXX, Peshitta, Vulgate) and later translations, including English Bibles, the prophetic books are placed at the end of the OT. Therefore the OT concludes with the Twelve and its last book, Malachi. This results in a theological emphasis looking forward to the completion of God's plan of salvation in the advent of the Messiah, "the messenger of the covenant" (Mal 3:1) and "the sun of righteousness" (Mal 3:20 [ET 4:2]). The Savior will be attended by "Elijah the prophet," who repairs family relationships (a fruit of repentance) before the coming of the great and terrible Day of Yahweh (Mal 3:23 [ET Mal 4:5]). Thus the final word is the prophetic task of preaching Law and Gospel, repentance and the Christ who alone can save on Judgment Day.

The placement of the Twelve therefore affects how readers view Yahweh's plan for the future. Judaism thinks that God wants the nation back in the land with life centered and ordered in the earthly temple, as it was in the OT. Christianity embraces Yahweh's full plan of salvation, including the preparatory role of John the Baptist, who, as the Elijah promised in Malachi (Mt 11:12–14; 17:3–4, 10–12), is the forerunner of Jesus, Israel's greatest Prophet (e.g., Jn 6:14). He is God incarnate (Jn 1:14; Rom 9:5; Col 2:9; Titus 2:13), who saves his people from their sins (Mt 1:21–23) and rises as the new temple (Jn 2:18–22), the foundation of his church (Ps 118:22; Acts 4:11; Eph 2:19–21).

The Historical Setting of the Book of Amos

Amos dates to the first half of the eighth century BC. The first verse (1:1) states that the prophet ministered during the reigns of Uzziah of Judah (792–740 BC)[48] and Jeroboam ben Joash of Israel (793–753 BC)[49] and notes that Amos completed his ministry two years before a notable earthquake, likely the one that occurred around 760 BC (see the commentary on 1:1).

In the last thirty years of the ninth century BC, the Aramean kingdom repeatedly kept the Northern Kingdom of Israel in a defensive mode (e.g., 2 Ki 10:32–33; 13:7). However, Yahweh was merciful, and northern Israel was not destroyed (2 Ki 13:22–23). The Assyrian king Adad-nirari III (ca. 810–783 BC) started a westward expansion that included the conquest of the Aramean capital Damascus (796 BC). The result was a lull in the wars between Israel and Aram (or Syria) during the reigns of Uzziah (792–740 BC) and Jeroboam ben Joash (793–753 BC), the kings who were reigning when Amos prophesied (1:1).

---

48 The chronology of Israelite and Judean kings is complicated. These are the dates for Uzziah advocated by Thiele (*The Mysterious Numbers of the Hebrew Kings*, 118).

49 Thiele, *The Mysterious Numbers of the Hebrew Kings*, 116. The father's name is stated to differentiate this Jeroboam from the Northern Kingdom's founder, Jeroboam ben Nebat (cf. 1 Ki 11:26; 12:1–17). As a member of the royal house of Jehu, Jeroboam ben Joash was part of a dynasty that included Jehu, Jehoahaz, Jehoash, and Zechariah.

Assyria was dominant over Aram at this time but did not attempt any further expansion westward,[50] in part because Assyria was in an alliance with Israel at this time. This agreement dated from the reigns of Jeroboam ben Joash's great-grandfather Jehu (841–814 BC)[51] and his father Joash.[52] Living before the westward campaigns of Tiglath-pileser III, both Jeroboam ben Joash and Uzziah were able to take advantage of this political situation and expand their economic influence.[53] For example, Uzziah was able to field an army of 307,500 crack troops and achieve several military victories (2 Chr 26:1–15; cf. Is 2:6–7).

Andersen and Freedman write: "It was not until the accession of Tiglath-pileser III (745 B.C.E.) that this 'unnatural' state of affairs ended."[54] In fact, as Younger notes, during the reign of Tiglath-pileser III, northern Israel devolved from a prosperous nation to a vassal state and finally to a puppet state surrounded by Assyrian districts.[55] Everything fell apart *after* the death of King Jeroboam ben Joash, Amos' contemporary.

The exact duration of Amos' prophetic ministry cannot be dated with precision. In addition to the notice in 1:1 about a notable earthquake (likely the one that occurred ca. 760 BC), another factor that makes it likely that he completed his mission prior to 745 BC is that his oracles make no reference to the dramatic reversal in domestic political affairs after the death of Jeroboam ben Joash, nor does he give any direct indication that he knows of the westward territorial expansion of the Assyrian Empire under Tiglath-pileser III. Assyria is never mentioned in the book of Amos; the nation referred to several times (e.g., Amos 3:11; 6:14) as Yahweh's agent for punishing Israel remains anonymous. Whatever information may be gleaned from Amos' oracles against the nations (1:3–2:3) also alludes to events either contemporaneous to the initial stages of Jeroboam ben Joash's reign or, more likely, to the historical events prior to Amos' ministry. But by all accounts, those oracles reflect an era before the reign of Tiglath-pileser III. It is safe, therefore, to date the ministry of Amos to an earlier, rather than a later, time in Jeroboam ben Joash's reign.

Early in his rule, Jeroboam ben Joash changed the political map of northern Israel. Through military conquests he recovered and annexed the territories east of the Jordan (Amos 6:13), extended the northern border to Lebo-hamath, and enlarged the southern border all the way to the Dead Sea (2 Ki 14:25). The large extent of the Northern Kingdom coupled with the Southern Kingdom of

---

50 Assyrian history at this time is discussed by Grayson, "Assyria: Ashur-dan II to Ashur-nirari V (934–745 B.C.)," 271–76. See also the excursus "The Assyrian Empire."

51 Thiele, *The Mysterious Numbers of the Hebrew Kings*, 103.

52 The Jehu dynasty adhered to a pro-Assyrian policy. See the inscription on the Black Obelisk, where Jehu presents Shalmaneser with special tribute gifts (*ANET*, 281). Assyrian inscriptions do not mention any Israelite anti-Assyrian action until Pekah's revolt in around 734 BC.

53 Cf. Matthews, *Old Testament Turning Points*, 126.

54 Andersen and Freedman, *Amos*, 21.

55 Younger, "The Deportations of the Israelites," 201. For an overview of the reign of Tiglath-pileser III and its impact on Israel, see Younger, "The Deportations of the Israelites."

Judah when it was ruled by King Uzziah, Jeroboam ben Joash's vassal,[56] rivaled that of the united kingdom of David and Solomon in Israel's "golden age."

Judah's vassal status began after the Judean king Amaziah's failed revolt against more powerful northern Israel (2 Ki 14:8–14).[57] Judah remained a vassal of Israel during the ministry of Amos and was probably forced to pay a yearly tribute in order to maintain the empire's military and political infrastructure.[58] Judah had a subsistence-level agricultural economy so the imposition of taxes had serious implications, especially when natural catastrophes, such as drought, locusts, fires, and so forth, took their toll on the annual harvest. Living in this political situation, Amos repeatedly points out the poverty of his Judean kinsfolk and their hardships placed upon them by the north. Northern Israel, for its part, was forced to pay tribute to Assyria. The Northern Kingdom's rule over Judah, together with the relative passivity of Assyria, created for Jeroboam ben Joash a growing economy but a shrinking heart for those who were economically marginalized.

During this period, which some call the silver age of Israelite history,[59] northern Israel reached the summit of its material power, the height of its economic prosperity, and the pinnacle of its territorial expansion. The nation had all the signs that it believed were pointing to Yahweh's unlimited favor, and the future appeared to hold limitless possibilities (Amos 5:18a). Yahweh's protection was assumed to be unconditional, and thus the nation felt certain of its future.

Due in large part to the military victories of Jeroboam ben Joash (cf. Amos 6:13), it was perceived as the time in Israel to eat and drink and be merry (cf. Is 22:12–13; 1 Cor 15:32). Building activity was on the rise (Amos 3:15). Houses were more numerous, but only for those with the means to finance their purchase (Amos 3:15; 5:11; 6:8). Some homes were furnished elaborately with costly ivory (3:15; 6:4). The wealthiest could maintain separate residences for summer and winter (3:15). Political, legal, worship, and business leaders were enjoying affluence, eating meat—a tremendous luxury at this time—and drinking their

---

56 Judah was subordinate to Israel for most of the time between the reigns of Omri and Pekah (885–732 BC). The only exceptions were during the reigns of Jehoram (852–841), Jehu (841–814), and Jehoahaz (814–798), when northern Israel was itself a vassal to Damascus. For the dates of these kings, see Thiele, *The Mysterious Numbers of the Hebrew Kings*, 88, 99, 103, 105, 120.

57 After the conflict between Jeroboam ben Nebat and Rehoboam (1 Ki 12:1–17) that divided the Solomonic kingdom, Judah and Israel went back and forth between war (e.g., 1 Ki 14:30; 2 Ki 14:12; Isaiah 7) and peace (e.g., 1 Kings 22; 2 Kings 3).

58 As noted by Sweeney, *The Twelve Prophets*, 192–93. He writes: "In an agrarian economy, this means that the people of Judah would have to pay a share of their agricultural harvest and animal stock to both the Judean and the Israelite monarchies" (p. 193).

59 E.g., Paul, *Amos*, 1. These prosperous times in the eighth century are also depicted in Hos 12:9 (ET 12:8), where Ephraim (the Northern Kingdom) boasts, "I am very rich; I have become wealthy." This wealth was to a large extent concentrated in the hands of the few and was obtained through injustice (cf., e.g., Amos 2:6–8; 5:10–12; 8:4–6).

wine to the accompaniment of music (6:4–6). New music was being composed for celebratory occasions (6:5). Sacrificial offerings were skyrocketing (4:4–5), attendance at places of worship was rising (5:21–22), and these religious feasts were accompanied with festive music (5:23).[60] Women were putting demands on their husbands to keep their liquor cabinets well stocked (4:1). Business was booming, and dishonest trade meant even more profit for those who knew how to work the system (8:4–6).

The well-to-do felt secure in this robust economy, even if it meant others were suffering. The leaders even had the audacity to chant in effect, "We're number one" (6:1). If the present scene was silver, then the future looked golden. Popular thinking was that "the Day of Yahweh" would usher in a time of unprecedented prosperity (5:18a).

But the book of Amos reveals that what looked so good on the outside was completely rotten on the inside. Syncretistic worship of the Canaanite fertility god Baal, which is hinted at in 2:7c–d and 6:4–6 and clearly condemned in 8:14, meant that Israel's leaders had embraced a nonbiblical view toward the land, people, politics, worship, and business. This, in turn, created an upper class that unlovingly took advantage of Israel's lower classes. The economically disadvantaged were exploited (2:7a–b; 4:1; 8:4); their rights were violated through a well-organized partnership that included Israel's judicial, political, and religious power-brokers (e.g., 5:10, 12; 7:9–17).

Israel's charter in the Pentateuch dictated that every citizen had a right to own land (Lev 25:23–34; cf. 1 Kings 21). But these rights were being superseded due to the leaders lusting after Canaanite gods and goddesses. This syncretistic worship brought demonic "evil" (5:14) and a different way of ordering Israelite society. The Canaanite city-state had replaced the earlier tribal model that guaranteed justice and equity for all (e.g., Lev 19:15).

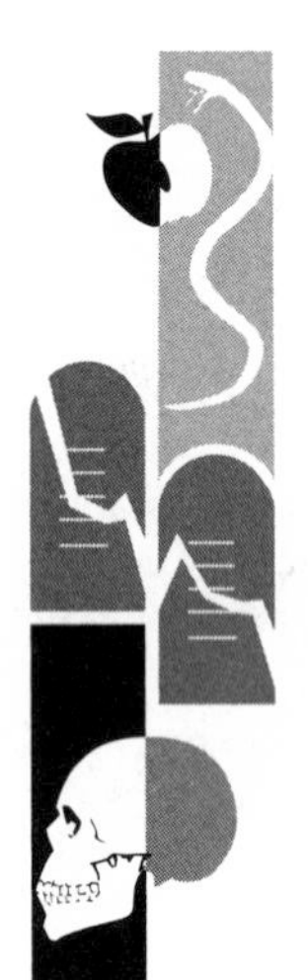

Living in this society of "haves" and "have nots," Amos announces that the lifestyles of the rich and famous were merely an allusion. The high-roller days of Jeroboam ben Joash were about to end. In a few short years, the good times would cease to roll. Storm clouds were gathering on the horizon, and soon a succession of great ancient Near Eastern empires would roll over Israel, and later Judah, and flatten them like pancakes. It was the task of Amos to announce that the judgment was about to strike, and to explain why.

Because apostate Israel presumed that Yahweh was a national deity who would always grant the nation military, political, and economic success, Amos' preaching amounted to treason (7:10–17). The idolatrous national sanctuary at Bethel, which Jeroboam ben Nebat had established and furnished with a golden calf supposedly representing the God who saved Israel through the exodus (1 Ki 12:28–33; cf. 2 Ki 10:29), was the ultimate symbol of this religious order. At this sanctuary, every word was uttered as a way to support the regime. Any

---

[60] For a detailed analysis on the different views of religion during the time of Amos, see Carroll R., " 'For So You Love to Do': Probing Popular Religion in the Book of Amos."

messenger at Bethel with a contrary "Word from Yahweh" could not be tolerated. Amos was just this kind of anti-Bethel, anti-Jeroboam[61] messenger from Yahweh. The result of his preaching was that he was not-so-politely asked to leave the premises and go back to where he belonged (7:12–13). But Amos did not leave without predicting Israel's defeat and exile (7:17).

The first of these conquerors would be the Assyrian monarch Tiglath-pileser III. Amos alludes to his reign of terror in 6:14. Before the reign of Tiglath-pileser III, periods of rapid Assyrian westward expansion culminated in equally abrupt collapses. Though prior Assyrian kings excelled in military prowess, they lacked the administrative skills necessary to sustain their conquests. However, with the ascension of Tiglath-pileser III, that deficiency was remedied. To the predatory viciousness of his forbears, he brought a new political cunning. Conquered areas were kept under control through a calculated policy of extortion, terror, and large-scale deportation. After Tiglath-pileser III, the subsequent Assyrian kings Shalmaneser V (726–722 BC) and Sargon II (722–705 BC) crushed Israel and leveled its capital city of Samaria, which fell in 722 BC. Massive numbers of people were exiled, fulfilling a major theme in the book of Amos (4:2–3; 5:5, 27; 6:7; 7:11, 17; 9:4).

Different Methods of Interpreting the Book of Amos

In the last century, scholars have employed several different strategies in their attempt to interpret Israelite prophecy. These are mirrored in Amos studies.[62] Of these, the three most prominent are form criticism, redaction criticism, and rhetorical analysis. What follows is a brief description of each methodology and how it has been employed by others to interpret the book of Amos. After these three summaries, this commentary will present its conclusions about the proper method of interpretation for Amos.

Form Criticism

Although there were forerunners to form criticism,[63] Hermann Gunkel is considered to be the founder of OT form-critical work.[64] Gunkel was greatly

---

[61] Amos preached against both Jeroboams of northern Israel: the incumbent apostate king, Jeroboam ben Joash, and the founder of the idolatrous sanctuaries, Jeroboam ben Nebat.

[62] Hayes reviews the history of Amos scholarship from the 1870s to the 1980s in *Amos, the Eighth-Century Prophet*, 28–39. Hasel calls a study of Amos "a type or paradigm—if not a microcosm—for the study of all of the prophetic writings of the Old Testament" (*Understanding the Book of Amos*, 11).

[63] The most notable forerunner is Bernhard Duhm. In *Die Theologie der Propheten als Grundlage für die innere Entwicklungsgeschichte der israelitischen Religion*, Duhm devoted himself to "the entire question of method and, therefore, performed much of the fundamental spadework needed in developing the procedures which were eventually adopted by the whole historical-critical approach" (Hayes and Prussner, *Old Testament Theology*, 130).

[64] March writes: "A discussion of form critical research must almost inevitably begin with the work of Hermann Gunkel, generally acknowledged pioneer of and inspiration for the discipline" ("Prophecy," 143). Barton and Sweeney agree. Barton writes: "OT form criticism is usually held to have begun with the work of Hermann Gunkel (1862–1932)" ("Form

impacted by the philosophical system of Hegelian idealism, whose central idea was the evolution from the simple to the more complex through thesis, antithesis, and synthesis. His goal was to apply the Hegelian framework to the study of Israel's literature.[65]

Gunkel believed that in ancient Israel an idea could be stated in only one way on any given occasion. In this way, OT genres appeared in a "pure manner." He believed that the oldest OT genres were "almost always completely pure."[66] Any mixture of genres was a sign of later scribal additions. Closely connected with his notion of an original purity of genres was Gunkel's belief that early oral productions were very brief. Buss writes: "One of the primary assumptions [of Gunkel and those who followed him] was that **early stages of literature contained short units**."[67]

Gunkel never produced a commentary on any prophetic book. However, an evaluation of his understanding of prophetic literature may be reached by looking at two of his works, *Die Propheten* and "Die israelitische Literatur,"[68] which are considered to be his most comprehensive treatments of this material. What follows is an analysis of how Gunkel understood prophetic pure forms, prophetic speech, and the difference in prophetic texts and prophetic speech.

First, Gunkel's pursuit of pure forms means that stylistic and syntactical changes, variations in meter, new literary genres, and the like, are indications of new prophetic oracles. Consequently, the original form, not the canonical form, was his focus of research.[69] Second, in keeping with his belief that authen-

---

Criticism," *ABD* 2:838). Sweeney writes: "The origins of modern form-critical research appear in the writings of Hermann Gunkel" ("Form Criticism," 60).

[65] Gunkel was also heavily influenced by the prior work of Wellhausen (*Prolegomena to the History of Ancient Israel*). Wellhausen's book first appeared in 1878; the English translation was published in 1885, using the second German edition (1883). In his commentary *Die kleinen Propheten*, Wellhausen provides the classic statement of nineteenth-century critical scholarship: the legal traditions of the Bible had developed late, so the eighth-century prophets had influenced that tradition, not simply reflected it. He believed that Amos was "the founder, and the purest type, of a new phase of prophecy" that emphasized "ethical monotheism" (*Prolegomena to the History of Ancient Israel*, 472–74).

[66] Gunkel, "Die israelitische Literatur," 54.

[67] Buss, *Biblical Form Criticism in Its Context*, 359.

[68] See Gunkel, "The Israelite Prophecy from the Time of Amos." Summaries of Gunkel's understanding of prophetic speech are in Hayes, "The History of the Form-Critical Study of Prophecy," 60–70; March, "Prophecy," 143–49; and Tucker, *Form Criticism of the Old Testament*, 55–57.

[69] Gunkel's approach is typified by his contemporary Karl Marti, who also speculated about prophetic texts (*The Religion of the Old Testament*, 4):

> We should even be fully justified in maintaining that in the course of time they have experienced all manner of alterations of a peculiar nature, just because they were intended to serve the interests of the religion of Israel. It is not only that careless transcribers have introduced unintentional alterations and that private owners of manuscripts have increased the length of their copies by the addition of new paragraphs at their own pleasure, but these old writings have been regularly edited.

tic prophetic speech was ecstatic, Gunkel believed that the primary prophetic communications were largely terse, ejaculatory, and often cryptic.

Gunkel imagined that prophets were incapable of writing long, well-reasoned compositions, which are characteristic of modern thinkers. Hence prophetic books are little more than a collection of beads on a string with literary context counting for little.[70] Because of his belief that prophets were ecstatic figures who delivered short and sporadic oracles, Gunkel divided up chapters and even verses and attributed the pieces to many prophets, disciples, editors, or redactors. He argued that since the basic forms of prophetic discourse were short and self-contained, the exegete's goal is to identify and isolate these short units in order to reconstruct the original message of the prophet.

The first form-critical work on Amos arose from Gunkel's students Walter Baumgartner and Emil Balla,[71] but the most influential of Gunkel's students in the study of prophetic literature was Sigmund Mowinckel. He distinguished four types of prophetic material: (1) various sayings, poems, and/or oracles in the first person, representing Yahweh's direct discourse through the prophet, which Mowinckel usually considered genuine; (2) narratives about prophets concerned with the occasions for speeches and prophecies, which he thought were influenced by legend; (3) speeches by the prophet in narrative form, which he believed were usually influenced by the postexilic community; and (4) hopeful prophecies, which he also considered postexilic and ungenuine.[72]

In following Gunkel, whose views he believed had "full and far-reaching justification,"[73] Mowinckel writes: "The original datum is the separate tradition, the separate narration, the separate local story, the separate stanza, etc., the binding together to larger units being a later stage in the history of tradition."[74] Therefore, the goal of the exegete is first to separate "from each other the single 'units' within the total complex of tradition."[75] Tradition "has arranged the

---

[70] Gunkel presumed that, "speaking generally, the Hebrew mind had not the type of genius required for lengthy productions, and so the shorter the pieces the more beautiful they are" (*What Remains of the Old Testament and Other Essays*, 29). He believed that because speaking was much more common than writing, "this explains the extreme brevity and small compass of the ancient compositions" (p. 62). Gunkel described the ancient listener as one "whose receptive power was very limited" (p. 62). Finally, he stated: "Just as we see the development of our children's minds in the gradually increasing amount that they can take in at a time, so we can trace one feature of the growth of civilization in the gradual increase of the literary units in Israel" (p. 63).

[71] Baumgartner, *Kennen Amos und Hosea eine Heils-Eschatologie*; Balla, *Die Droh- und Scheltworte des Amos*.

[72] Mowinckel, *Prophecy and Tradition*, 60–66.

[73] Mowinckel, *Prophecy and Tradition*, 23. He also writes: "The form criticism and tradition criticism of Gunkel and his 'school' have been of great importance for the study of the prophetic books" (p. 36).

[74] Mowinckel, *Prophecy and Tradition*, 11.

[75] Mowinckel, *Prophecy and Tradition*, 40. This is because "the relatively brief, in itself, complete and concluded, independent separate saying ('oracle') is the original and real form of prophet 'speech' " (p. 60).

sayings in groups; by association, sayings with the same 'catch-word' or with the same or cognate content, with the same address, ... etc."[76]

The Amos commentaries of William Rainey Harper and George Adam Smith reflect Gunkel's interest in pure forms as well as Mowinckel's methodology for separating original prophecy from scribal additions. For example, Harper lists the following passages in Amos as being secondary: the opening two verses (1:1–2), the oracles against Tyre, Edom, and Judah (1:9–10, 11–12; 2:4–5), the "doxologies" (4:13; 5:8–9; 9:5–6), the closing epilogue (9:8c–15), as well as other minor expansions.[77] Smith lists most of the above passages and notes additional contested passages.[78] For Harper and Smith, any type of discontinuity in the text of Amos indicates later additions.

The next generation of Amos scholars summarized and expanded these form-critical ideas. The most influential of them was Hans Walter Wolff, who followed Gunkel's major ideas in postulating that the book of Amos passed through a lengthy process of oral and literary transmission. Based on form-critical reading strategies, Wolff's commentary on Amos distinguishes three eighth-century literary strata, "all of which for the most part derive from Amos himself and his contemporary disciples," as well as three additional strata that are recognizable "by their distinctive language and different intentions."[79]

More specifically, Wolff believed the initial "words of Amos from Tekoa" (mainly chapters 3–6) were added to the visions and (most of) the opening oracles against the nations. He traced both of these layers of material to Amos. He attributed the third layer to a "circle of disciples" who added the biographical narrative in 7:10–17, while they also supplemented and reformulated earlier material. Wolff then postulated a fourth editorial layer, which supposedly emerged during the time of Josiah, when the king destroyed the sanctuary at Bethel (2 Ki 23:15). The fifth layer Wolff called the Deuteronomistic redaction, whose intent was to show that Judah stood under the same judgment as Israel. This layer includes 1:1; 1:9–12; 2:4–5; 3:1b; 3:7; 5:25–26; and 6:1aα. The last stratum was the postexilic eschatology of salvation in 9:11–15. Wolff's methodology assumed that each of these redactional levels arose as a reaction to specific historical events that necessitated an updating of the text.[80]

About the same time, James Luther Mays composed a commentary on Amos that was based in large part on the form-critical work of Gunkel.[81] Several years after Mays wrote his work, Klaus Koch published three volumes of his form-critical investigation of Amos.[82] Also representative of Amos scholarship at this

[76] Mowinckel, *Prophecy and Tradition*, 49.

[77] Harper, *Amos and Hosea*, cxxx–cxxxvi.

[78] Smith, *The Book of the Twelve Prophets*, 1:57, including n. 1.

[79] Wolff, *Joel and Amos*, 107.

[80] Wolff, *Joel and Amos*, 107–13.

[81] Mays, *Amos: A Commentary*.

[82] Koch, *Amos: Untersuch mit den Methoden einer strukturalen Formgeschichte*.

time is the work of Robert Coote, who believed that the book of Amos developed in three stages: (1) an eighth-century collection of oracles that addressed the ruling elite and predicted disaster; (2) a seventh-century collection that admonished and offered a choice to a more general audience in a new situation; and (3) a sixth-century, postexilic edition that reverses the seemingly irreversible word of judgment in the eighth-century collection.[83]

The primary goal of form-critical studies of Amos at this time was to probe behind the text to discover earlier oral sources presumed to be more ancient and revealing about the history, religion, sociology, and politics of early eighth-century Israel. The fundamental assumption was that the text was not the most fruitful object of extensive study. Rather, the primary value of the text lay in its being a depository for earlier oral materials that were more useful and interesting to these critical scholars. Thus the book was viewed as an aggregate of literary sources, often not pieced together very well and easily identified and separated out from later additions. There was little interest in studying extensive units of Amos as a literary piece or as a book that presents a coherent perspective of its own.

Those who supposedly finalized the text—often called redactors—were viewed as technicians, scissors-and-paste men, who added irrelevant comments to their material, frequently distorting its message and adding ideas that had little theological worth.[84] Amos scholarship continued to hold to Gunkel's belief that prophets originally delivered short rather than lengthy oracles.[85] Texts in Amos were divided and separated based on the idea that each original short text was "pure."

By the mid 1970s, a major shift was in the making as form critics began to place more emphasis on the work of hypothetical redactors.[86] This change is explained by Gene Tucker, writing in 1976:

> While the recognition and analysis of the preliterary materials must remain an important aspect of the form-critical endeavor, it is only a part of the task. There is a growing awareness that the form-critical questions, i.e., the search for what is typical in the linguistic expressions, can and should be applied to all stages of the literature, including material which did not have an oral prehistory.[87]

Amos scholarship was in a state of flux. While still distinguishing between the final text and earlier tradition,[88] the new critical goal was to place greater

---

[83] Coote, *Amos among the Prophets: Composition and Theology*.

[84] See, for example, Fohrer, *Introduction to the Old Testament*, 190–92; Eissfeldt, *The Old Testament*, 239–41.

[85] For further discussion of Gunkel's impact on prophetic scholarship, see Gordon, "A Story of Two Paradigm Shifts," 7–14.

[86] For an overview of this change in Amos scholarship, see Melugin, "Amos in Recent Research."

[87] G. M. Tucker, "Form Criticism, OT," *IDBSup*, 342.

[88] See Tucker, *IDBSup*, 343.

value on the additions. Classical form criticism was evolving into what scholarship now calls redaction criticism. The difference is in form criticism's archival text designed merely to preserve the prophet's words and redaction criticism's focus on an exhortational text that employs words of both the prophet and later editors as a means to motivate a community living decades, if not centuries after the prophet. Describing this evolution, Marvin Sweeney writes:

> The history of form-critical research demonstrates a shift from an early focus on the short, self-contained, "original" oral speech unit to an emphasis on the literary and linguistic structures and modes of expression of the much larger textual compositions in which smaller formal units function.[89]

Whereas Gunkel and those who followed him were determined to locate the original words of Amos, the work of redaction critics began to move the discussion in the direction of studying prophetic books as a whole.

Redaction Criticism

The term "redaction criticism" is "an attempt to represent in English the German word *Redaktionsgeschichte*, which Willi Marxsen[90] proposed as the designation for a discipline within the field of New Testament studies."[91] It was Gerhard von Rad who pioneered OT redaction criticism in a series of articles and books, especially *Das formgeschichtliche Problem des Hexateuchs*.[92] Following von Rad, Martin Noth contributed important works on the redaction of the so-called Deuteronomistic history (Joshua–2 Kings) and the work of the Chronicler (Chronicles; Ezra-Nehemiah).[93] Both of these scholars referred to their work as "tradition-historical." However, today that term is more commonly reserved for their thought about the history of Israel's religious and historical traditions, while the literary side of their interests is called redaction criticism.

Wolfgang Richter is a scholar who builds on the methods of von Rad and Noth. Richter engages texts on the basis of both their supposed *Sitz im Leben* and their *Sitz im Literatur*.[94] Sweeney notes: "Although Richter focuses largely on the synchronic level, a major goal of his research is to identify tensions within the text as a means to reconstruct its [hypothetical] diachronic or redac-

---

[89] Sweeney, "Form Criticism," 60.

[90] Marxsen, *Mark the Evangelist*.

[91] Perrin, *What Is Redaction Criticism?* 1. Perrin also notes that the method "could equally be called 'composition criticism' [*Kompositionsgeschichte*] because it is concerned with the composition of new material and the arrangements of redacted or freshly created material into new units and patterns, as well as with the redaction of existing material."

[92] Von Rad, *Das formgeschichtliche Problem des Hexateuchs* (Stuttgart: Kohlhammer, 1938); in English, *The Problem of the Hexateuch and Other Essays*. Barton writes of von Rad's work: "It is through his work above all that the redaction-critical approach has really established itself in Old Testament studies" (*Reading the Old Testament*, 47).

[93] Noth, *The Deuteronomistic History* and *The Chronicler's History*.

[94] Richter, *Exegese als Literaturwissenschaft: Entwurf einer alttestamentlichen Literaturtheorie und Methodologie*, 148.

tional history."[95] This way of reading texts is influenced by the belief that the prophetic word was capable of being adapted to new situations and of inspiring fresh oracles modeled on it.[96] Therefore, Richter views prophetic texts as testimonies to a living tradition that continually actualized old texts with new interpretations.[97]

Redaction critics frequently speak of this hypothesized literary growth of prophetic texts.[98] Michael Fishbane uses the concept of "explication."[99] Hermann Barth prefers the concept of "Adaption" as the tradents transferred older prophetic words into a new context.[100] Whatever term is used, there is a consensus among redaction critics that prophetic texts went through a process of continual realization and actualization beginning with the realm of oral tradition.[101]

Redaction critics imagine that so many interpretations have been placed on the original text that readers of Amos are not confronted with the "historical" prophet, but with the "presentation" of the prophet, to use a term coined by Peter Ackroyd.[102] The original quest for the authentic words of Amos, the program that formed the basis for form criticism, is now considered a futile enterprise. As these scholars assign more work to the redactional process, they

---

95 Sweeney, "Form Criticism," 67 (see also p. 86, n. 27), citing Richter, *Exegese als Literaturwissenschaft: Entwurf einer alttestamentlichen Literaturtheorie und Methodologie.* For example, Richter writes: *Eine Gattung kann nicht von vornherein auf einen "Sitz im Leben" eingeschränkt werden, sondern kann diesen ändern und sich dabei auch ändern* (*Exegese als Literaturwissenschaft*, 148). ("A genre cannot be a priori limited to one *Sitz im Leben* but can change this and also change itself by doing so.") Richter identifies changes by means of textual discontinuities, which he then interprets as evidence of composite authorship.

96 Fishbane calls redaction criticism "inner-biblical exegesis" (*Biblical Interpretation in Ancient Israel*, e.g., 542).

97 This tendency to have a higher view of redactors is summed up by the Jewish scholar Franz Rosenzweig. He holds that "R," the conventional symbol for "redactor," should be regarded as standing for *rabbenu*, "our rabbi/master," since it is from their hands that the Scriptures are received. This remark by Rosenzweig is cited in von Rad, *Das erste Buch Mose, Genesis* (see Barton, *Reading the Old Testament*, 47).

98 Steck, *The Prophetic Books and Their Theological Witness*, 236, n. 54.

99 Fishbane, *Biblical Interpretation in Ancient Israel*, 166–70. He speculates about the process by which redaction critics believe the Scriptures were passed down (pp. 542–43):

> The whole phenomenon of inner-biblical exegesis requires the latter-day historian to appreciate the fact that the texts and traditions, the received *traditum* of ancient Israel, were not simply copied, studied, transmitted, or recited. They were also, and by these means, subject to redaction, elucidation, reformulation, and outright transformation. Accordingly, our received traditions are complex blends of *traditum* and *traditio* in dynamic interaction, dynamic interpenetration, and dynamic interdependence.

100 Barth, *Die Jesaja-Worte in der Josiazeit*, 308.

101 Sweeney writes: "Redaction criticism is the study of the editorial formation of biblical literature. It is essentially a literary discipline" (*Isaiah 1–39*, 13). Steck writes: "The transmission no longer concretely elaborates the original historical circumstances and addressees in characteristic concentration. ... The texts of the prophetic books are thus largely stripped of the original communication between prophet and listener" (*The Prophetic Books and Their Theological Witness*, 55–56).

102 Ackroyd, "Isaiah I–XII: Presentation of a Prophet."

assign less to the author of Amos. This yields (according to the hypothesis) less reliable historical data about the prophet. Pushed to its extreme, redaction criticism concludes that any historical reconstruction of Amos is unrecoverable and that the book is likely an imaginative literary construct.

Redaction criticism does not reject the diachronic methods of form criticism, but it reorders priorities so that it examines biblical texts in their final context as literary wholes. Whereas form criticism understood texts in terms of their *beginning*, redaction criticism understands them in terms of their *end*. This feature distinguishes form criticism from redaction criticism in that the latter does not focus its attention on seeking the supposed *Urtext* uttered or written by the prophet. Rather, redaction critics seek to discover the successive stages in the hypothetical editorial process that supposedly led to the final text.[103] Redaction criticism is thus the study of the presumed editorial formation of biblical literature.[104] The focus has shifted from the pursuit of alleged original oral forms to the final literary form, that is, the real book.

Consequently, redaction critics jettison form criticism's swift access to the prophet and its marginal evaluation of the written book.[105] The view of the prophet as *speaker* that dominated in the era of form criticism no longer serves as the starting point for the question.[106] This shift away from form criticism at least begins to take prophetic books seriously as *books*. Redaction critics postulate that discontinuities occur in prophetic texts because later communities adapted the prophetic message to their current situations. An earlier text was changed to serve the purposes of the community.

The most in-depth redactional work on Amos is that of Jörg Jeremias. Jeremias attempts to ascribe most of the text of Amos to later redactors who were not interested in preserving the original words of the prophet, but rather sought to address audiences in contexts that were different from Amos.[107] His interpretive

---

[103] Thus the form-critical method of separating the prophetic core from the scribal husk does not change with redaction criticism. The only difference is that the latter places a higher value on the husk. This altered outlook is fittingly summed up by McKane: "Disciples are also prophets and so the tradition is indivisible, and a prophetic book is the record of the on-going life of a prophetic community" ("Prophecy and the Prophetic Literature," 186). Perrin and Duling write: "Once it was recognized that the final author was in fact an *author* and not merely a transmitter of tradition, it became natural and inevitable to inquire into his total literary activity as revealing his purpose and theology, not only into his redaction of previously existing tradition" (*The New Testament*, 236).

[104] Sweeney writes: "The setting of a text form therefore includes both its *Sitz im Leben* ('setting in life') and its *Sitz im Literatur* ('setting in literature')" (*Isaiah 1–39*, 12, citing Richter, *Exegese als Literaturwissenschaft*, 148). Barton writes that redaction criticism "takes the compilers of the various books seriously and tries to get inside their minds, to see what they were about when they combined source materials in ways that are superficially so puzzling" (*Reading the Old Testament*, 51).

[105] Steck writes: "One must exclude the fact that this flow is nothing more than an accident or a loose compilation" (*The Prophetic Books and Their Theological Witness*, 93).

[106] Steck writes: "We cannot directly reach the formerly oral work of the prophet" (*The Prophetic Books and Their Theological Witness*, 128).

[107] Jeremias, "Amos 3–6: From the Oral Word to the Text." In his commentary *The Book of Amos*, Jeremias sums up his redaction-historical proposal for the entire book (pp. 5–9).

assumption is that the prophet's message "can be recovered only through complicated, and in many instances only hypothetical, reconstruction."[108] Yet in the end, Jeremias despairs of locating Amos' exact words.[109]

Rhetorical Analysis

A more fruitful approach to understanding Amos is that of rhetorical analysis. This method pays attention to the literary features in the extant, canonical text that involve orality and the purpose of persuasion, and it also takes into account the historical setting. Martin Luther understood the value of rhetoric in biblical exegesis. He wrote:

> I am persuaded that without knowledge of literature pure theology cannot at all endure, just as heretofore, when letters [grammar and rhetoric] have declined and lain prostrate, theology, too, has wretchedly fallen and lain prostrate; nay, I see that there has never been a great revelation of the Word of God unless He has first prepared the way by the rise and prosperity of languages and letters, as though they were John the Baptists. ... Certainly it is my desire that there shall be as many poets and rhetoricians as possible, because I see that by these studies, as by no other means, people are wonderfully fitted for the grasping of sacred truth and for handling it skillfully and happily. ... Therefore I beg of you that at my request (if that has any weight) you will urge your young people to be diligent in the study of poetry and rhetoric.[110]

Soon after Luther outlined his theology in the 1518 *Heidelberg Theses*, he wrote to his teacher Jodocus Trutfetter:

> I simply believe that it is impossible to reform the Church unless the Canon Law, scholastic theology, philosophy and logic, as they are now taught, are thoroughly rooted out and other studies put in their stead. I am so fixed in this opinion that I daily ask the Lord, as far as now may be, that the pure study of the Bible and the Fathers may be restored.[111]

Summarizing and evaluating the modern study of rhetorical analysis is a daunting task.[112] Perhaps the most influential voice in rhetorical analysis has been that of James Muilenburg in his 1968 Society of Biblical Literature

---

108 Jeremias, *The Book of Amos*, 5.

109 Jeremias, *The Book of Amos*, 9.

110 Smith, *Luther's Correspondence*, 2:176–77 (cf. WA Br 3:50; AE 49:34).

111 Smith, *Luther's Correspondence*, 1:83–84 (cf. WA Br 1:170). The "other studies" that Luther advocated were those of Renaissance humanism. See Rosin, "The Reformation, Humanism, and Education: The Wittenberg Model for Reform," and Nembach, *Predigt des Evangeliums: Luther als Prediger, Pädagoge und Rhetor*.

112 The rediscovery of the importance of rhetoric has had a profound impact upon biblical studies, as seen in the growth in the number of articles, monographs, Festschriften, and conferences addressed to rhetorical analysis of biblical texts. See, for example *Rhetoric, Scripture and Theology: Essays from the 1994 Pretoria Conference* (ed. Porter and Olbricht). In the last twenty years more books and articles on rhetorical method and its application have appeared than in the previous century and a half. A look at Minor, *Literary-Critical Approaches to the Bible: An Annotated Bibliography*, confirms this impression. Of its 2,254 entries, the vast majority date after 1980 and very few were written before 1970.

presidential address, "Form Criticism and Beyond." In this ground-breaking paper, Muilenburg criticized form criticism because of its tendency to ignore the artistry and particularity of a text's literary features. He maintained that form criticism tends to "obscure the thought and intention of the writer or speaker," because it fixates on conventions, slights historical commentary, and separates form from content while isolating small units. It neglects the individual, personal, unique, particular, distinctive, precise, versatile, and fluid features of texts. Whereas form critics look for what is *typical*, Muilenburg argued for an investigation of the *particularities* of a given text. He advocated the study of large unified compositions and component genres that are built together into a rhetorical whole.[113]

Muilenburg's main interest was in the identification of formal devices such as parallelism, strophic structure, and repetition.[114] By employing such literary markers, he sought to overcome the arbitrary and atomistic methods of form criticism. In doing so, Muilenburg paved the way for a more holistic approach to biblical texts.

Many scholars have built on Muilenburg's work. Some have advocated taking the rhetorical method in different directions. One major example is Wilhelm Wuellner, who claimed that the rhetorical critics of the Muilenburg School were "victims of the fateful reduction of rhetorics to stylistics, and of stylistics in turn to the rhetorical tropes and figures."[115] In place of this "old" rhetorical method, Wuellner called for a "new rhetoric" that returns to the classical definition of rhetoric, *the art of persuasion*, and also includes social identification and transformation.[116] According to Terry Eagleton, this method of literary analysis examines "the way discourses are constructed in order to achieve certain effects." It sees "speaking and writing not merely as textual objects, to be aesthetically contemplated or endlessly deconstructed, but as forms of *activity* inseparable from the wider social relations between writers and readers, orators and audiences, and as largely unintelligible outside the social purposes and conditions in which they were embedded."[117]

Phyllis Trible divided the various methods that fall under the umbrella of rhetorical analysis into two branches.[118] First, some interpreters carry out Muilenburg's directive to devote attention to the structure of a passage.[119] Trible

---

[113] Muilenburg, "Form Criticism and Beyond," 4–7; the quote is on page 5.

[114] See Muilenburg, "Form Criticism and Beyond," 8–18.

[115] Wuellner, "Where Is Rhetorical Criticism Taking Us?" 451. Brueggemann also finds Muilenburg's type of rhetorical criticism "too enamored of style to notice speech as a means and source of power" ("At the Mercy of Babylon," 19).

[116] Wuellner, "Where Is Rhetorical Criticism Taking Us?" 461–63.

[117] Eagleton, *Literary Theory: An Introduction*, 205–6.

[118] Trible, *Rhetorical Criticism*, 25–52.

[119] See, for example, Meynet, *Rhetorical Analysis*, who seeks to establish specific organizational laws for biblical texts. Accordingly, his rhetorical analysis is concerned with the structure of the composition of texts, not their oral persuasive element.

calls this branch the study of "the art of composition."[120] Second, the branch represented by Yehoshua Gitay practices what Trible has named the study of "the art of persuasion."[121] Gitay outlines the structure of prophetic texts in classical rhetorical terms: thesis, argument for it and against alternatives, ethos, and pathos. In this move beyond Muilenburg, he highlights not only the stylistic features of prophetic texts, but their *persuasive* aspects as well.[122] For an interpreter not to consider a text's persuasive aspect is to present its structure as static. In actual presentation—written as well as oral—a text is dynamic and persuasive.

Dale Patrick and Allen Scult articulate this method that focuses on both stylistics and persuasion:

> We believe rhetorical criticism does indeed hold the key to realizing Muilenburg's vision, but not if it is unnecessarily confined to an analysis of stylistic devices.
>
> In order to lead to a deeper penetration into the particularity and concreteness of the text, the "rhetoric" in rhetorical criticism must be broadened to its fullest range in the classical tradition, namely, *as the means by which a text establishes and manages its relationship to its audience in order to achieve a particular effect.* This, of course, includes stylistic devices, but goes beyond style to encompass the whole range of linguistic instrumentalities by which a discourse constructs a particular relationship with an audience in order to communicate a message.[123]

Amos employs a number of rhetorical devices that are highlighted throughout this commentary. One of his favorites is that of repetition. Amos 1:3–2:16 contains five reoccurring expressions: (1) "thus says Yahweh"; (2) "because of three transgressions … and because of four …"; (3) "I will not revoke it"; (4) "I will send fire"; and (5) "and it will consume the/her fortresses." The imperative "hear!" appears as a structuring device in 3:1; 4:1; and 5:1. In 4:6–11, the prophet employs the fivefold statement "but you did not return to me." "Woe" appears in 5:18 and 6:1, while the five visions (7:1–9:4) are each introduced with a form of the verb רָאָה ("to see" in Qal; "to show" in Hiphil). Amos' first two visions repeat several phrases verbatim (see 7:1–6), and this same feature occurs in the second two visions (7:7–9; 8:1–3). Additional rhetorical devices

---

[120] Trible, *Rhetorical Criticism*, 40.

[121] Trible, *Rhetorical Criticism*, 41.

[122] See, for example, Gitay, "Reflections on the Study of the Prophetic Discourse," 215–21. See Black, "Keeping Up with Recent Studies XVI: Rhetorical Criticism and Biblical Interpretation." Black's contrast between the approach of Muilenburg and that of NT rhetorical critic George Kennedy is helpful: "For Muilenburg, 'rhetoric' is virtually synonymous with 'literary artistry'; for Kennedy, the term refers to the disciplined art of persuasion, as conceptualized and practised by Greeks and Romans of the classical and Hellenistic periods" (p. 254).

[123] Patrick and Scult, *Rhetoric and Biblical Interpretation*, 12. Barton opines: "[Prophets] did not enunciate theological systems or lay down general principles, but spoke rhetorically and with an awareness of the effect their words would be likely to have on their immediate audience" ("Ethics in Isaiah of Jerusalem," 94).

include a riddle in 3:3–8; sound plays in 5:5; 7:7–9; and 8:1–3; and rhetorical questions in 2:11; 5:18, 20, 25; 6:12; and 9:7. Amos is a master at Hebrew rhetoric as he attempts to move Israel's leaders to repentance and faith.

This approach to understanding Amos reveals that the book is rhetorically charged and is designed to persuade people. Amos, therefore, stands alongside his fellow prophets who were commissioned by Yahweh to be orators and authors of his living Word. From Elijah's jest that Baal did not answer his worshipers' prayers because he had "gone aside" to defecate (1 Ki 18:27) to Jeremiah's wry comparison of foreign idols to "scarecrows in a cucumber field" (Jer 10:5), the goal of prophetic preaching was to persuasively communicate that Yahweh is the only God, and his will and ways bring judgment to unbelievers but mercy and salvation to all who trust in him. Even a cursory examination of prophetic literature justifies the conclusion that oral communication was an essential feature of the prophets' ministries to their contemporaries. They committed Yahweh's words to writing for two reasons. First, their writings could serve as a kind of sermon text to facilitate their preaching to their listening audience. Second, their writings could communicate the divine message beyond their immediate hearers to a wider audience that would extend to future generations, including us (cf. 1 Cor 10:11; 1 Pet 1:10–12).

In addition to such reports or allusions in the prophetic texts themselves to their ministries of preaching and writing, it is clear from the form, style, and content of those texts that the prophets fundamentally were communicators.[124] Calls to "hear" using the imperative of שְׁמַע are common in prophetic literature.[a] The frequent use of שְׁמַע indicates that prophetic texts were meant to be read out loud.[125] Such communication continues in the church today through the oral reading of the prophetic and apostolic Scriptures.

(a) E.g., Is 1:2; 7:13; 48:1; Jer 10:1; Amos 3:1; 4:1; 5:1

However, the oral world described by Gunkel and other form critics was part of an evolutionary hypothesis whereby oral meant early and primitive, that is, pretextual.[126] He believed that oral compositions and their cultures predated the written OT texts. Recent scholars have argued against that reconstruction of the history of OT texts. For example, Susan Niditch suggests that the oral

---

[124] For studies on the speaking role of prophets, see, for example, Mays and Achtemeier, *Interpreting the Prophets*, and Smith, *The Prophets as Preachers*. Smith writes (pp. 6–7):

> The prophets functioned as spokesmen for God (Ex. 7:1–2; Jer. 1:4–10) so their main role was to communicate God's words to others. As God's messengers, they were not interested in just declaring the truth. …
>
> The prophets were preachers who communicated God's words in order to transform their audience's thinking and social behavior.

[125] See further Lessing, "Orality in the Prophets."

[126] Gunkel was influenced by Axel Olrik's 1908 study "Epic Laws of Folk Narrative," in *The Study of Folklore* (ed. Alan Dundes; Englewood Cliffs, N.J.: Prentice-Hall, 1965; Danish original, 1908; German translation, 1909), 129–41 (see Niditch, *Oral World and Written Word*, 2, 137).

world lives in the words of the written OT.[127] She critiques form and redaction criticism as follows:

> [Their] diachronic approach to orality and literacy is, however, misguided, devaluing the power of oral cultures and misconstruing the characteristics of orally composed and oral-style works. Such an approach ignores the possibility that written works in a traditional culture will often share the characteristics of orally composed works. It misrepresents ancient literacy as synonymous with literacy in the modern world of print, books, and computers and draws too artificial a line, chronological and cultural, between oral and written literatures.[128]

Instead of the presuppositions of form and redaction criticism, it is better to understand that "in any writing culture orality and literacy coexist and interact, as each influences the other. There is no 'great divide' between the oral and the written in the cultures of ancient Israel but a continuum."[129] Niditch maintains that the classical prophets could have written down their texts in order to perform them orally.[130]

Further evidence of this understanding is confirmed by the lack of separate vocabulary in the OT for reading. Instead, the same vocabulary is used for *both* the activities of preaching and reading. In both Hebrew and Aramaic, the most common verb so used is קרא, "to proclaim." Derived from the verb קָרָא is the noun מִקְרָא, which in the OT can refer to a "sacred assembly" of God's people called together (e.g., Ex 12:16; Is 1:13) or to the oral "reading" of the Scriptures before such an assembly (Neh 8:8).[131] Both terms are highly oral. In the OT era, reading was done aloud and usually in the presence of others. In 2 Kings 5, קָרָא, "read (aloud)," is interchangeable with אָמַר, "say, speak (aloud)." The king of Aram writes a letter for Naaman to take to Israel, asking that he be healed of leprosy (2 Ki 5:5). When Naaman appears in Israel's royal court, he immediately speaks (לֵאמֹר) the contents of the letter (2 Ki 5:6). Then Joram reads it aloud (כִּקְרֹא) for himself (2 Ki 5:7). A similar account is in 2 Ki 19:9–14 || Is 37:9–14.

At the heart of Israel's faith was the repeated public proclamation of the Torah, which Moses had written down in the books of Moses. "Then [Moses] took the book of the covenant and read (it) in the ears/hearing of the people [וַיִּקְרָא בְּאָזְנֵי הָעָם]. They said, 'All that Yahweh has spoken [דִּבֶּר] we will do, and we will listen/obey [וְנִשְׁמָע]'" (Ex 24:7). The public reading of the Torah was

[127] Niditch, *Oral World and Written Word.*

[128] Niditch, *Oral World and Written Word*, 3.

[129] Niditch, *Oral World and Written Word*, 78, citing Ruth Finnegan. Niditch doesn't gives a specific citation for Finnegan, but six works by Finnegan are listed in Niditch's bibliography (pp. 153–54), including Ruth Finnegan, *Literacy and Orality* (Oxford: Blackwell, 1988).

[130] Niditch, *Oral World and Written Word*, 117. She offers a detailed analysis of the orality of Isaiah 1 in "The Composition of Isaiah 1."

[131] In Rabbinic Hebrew, מִקְרָא continued to be used for a sacred convocation and for reading from the Scriptures, as well as for Bible study and teaching (see Jastrow, s.v. מִקְרָא).

to be repeated every seven years at the Feast of Booths (Deut 31:10–11). When Israel took possession of Canaan, Joshua saw to it that this reading was carried out (Josh 8:34–35). Another example of keeping thought and lips together was demonstrated by Hannah. "Now it came about, as she continued praying before Yahweh, that Eli was watching her mouth. As for Hannah, she was speaking in her heart; only her lips were moving, but her voice was not heard, so Eli thought she was drunk" (1 Sam 1:12–13). What would not get our attention today was attention-getting then: that a person would pray *silently*. Finally, note that in Acts 8:30, Philip "heard" (ἤκουσεν) the Ethiopian eunuch "reading" (ἀναγι νώσκοντος) the prophet Isaiah, specifically chapter 53, and overhearing his oral reading provided the opportunity for Philip to proclaim Jesus Christ as the fulfillment of the prophet's message. St. Paul also refers to the oral reading of his letters in assembled Christian congregations in Col 4:16 and 1 Thess 5:27.

This uniting of orality and literary features is foundational to George Kennedy's approach to rhetorical analysis. He writes: "To a greater extent than any modern text, the Bible retained an oral and linear quality for its audience."[132] In several prophetic sections of the OT, texts are represented as written first and then presented orally.[133] These texts were written on scrolls not simply as inspired literature, but also for the purpose of orality; that is, they were not composed simply for the silent perusal of the *eyes*, but to be read aloud for the *ears*.

The classic example is in Jeremiah 36. Baruch publicly read Jeremiah's scroll at the Jerusalem temple, where a fast had been declared. The royal officials summoned Baruch and took his scroll to the king in his winter palace, where it was read aloud to Jehoiakim. Jer 36:23 states: "When Jehudi would read three columns or four, [King Jehoiakim] would cut them off with the knife of the scribe and throw them into the fire that was in the brazier, until the entire scroll was finished." Yet "the Word of our God endures forever" (Is 40:8; cf. 1 Pet 1:25), and God was not to be outdone by the king. "Jeremiah took another scroll and gave it to Baruch the scribe, the son of Neriah, and he [Baruch] wrote on it from the mouth of Jeremiah all the words of the scroll that Jehoiakim king of Judah had burned in the fire. In addition, many other words like them were added" (Jer 36:32). The scroll that God had inspired the prophet to write was composed for *hearing*, and when it was destroyed, the inspired prophet directed his amanuensis to write down another text that Jeremiah dictated *orally*.

It is plausible, then, to hold that Amos under divine inspiration composed his book in writing in order to deliver it orally, either through reading it aloud

---

[132] Kennedy, *New Testament Interpretation through Rhetorical Criticism*, 5. He writes of ancient texts: "All literature was written to be heard, and even when reading to himself a Greek read aloud" (*The Art of Persuasion in Greece*, 4).

[133] That written texts were composed to be read aloud is also affirmed by, for example, Gitay, "Deutero-Isaiah: Oral or Written?" 190–94; *Prophecy and Persuasion*, 41; Vorster, "Readings, Readers and the Succession Narrative: An Essay on Reception," 353; and Conrad, "Heard But Not Seen: The Representation of 'Books' in the Old Testament."

or through memorizing it before speaking it.[134] For his original audience, his writing was a servant of his preaching. His written sermon served as an aide-mémoire. The prophet, well versed in an oral tradition, could have written his texts and then delivered them to his hearers. The book of Amos, therefore, is a sermon that is rhetorically constructed in order to gain a hearing and persuade people to "seek Yahweh and live" (5:6).

While the system of classical rhetoric can legitimately be used to analyze prophetic literature, there is a need for caution. The approach cannot simply be to determine how the discourses of the Hebrew prophets conform to the canons of classical Greek and Latin rhetoric. Thomas Renz writes:

> We do not know much about the training of scribes, priests, and prophets at that time, and in any case our own training in Hebrew language and in rhetorical analysis derives from sources different from theirs. Nevertheless, I attempt to show that we are able to grasp the nature of their arguments, as we are able to grasp the nature of their language to a sufficient degree to call it "understanding."[135]

Kennedy similarly connects classical rhetoric with that used in the Bible:

> Though rhetoric is colored by the traditions and conventions of the society in which it is applied, it is also a universal phenomenon which is conditioned by basic workings of the human mind and heart and by the nature of all human society. Aristotle's objective in writing his *Rhetoric* was not to describe Greek rhetoric, but to describe this universal facet of human communication.[136]

Kennedy also notes: "Rhetoric is a historical phenomenon and differs somewhat from culture to culture, more in matters of arrangement and style than in basic devices of invention."[137] Again, he writes:

> Though the Jews of the pre-Christian era seem never to have conceptualized rhetoric to any significant degree, the importance of speech among them is everywhere evident in the Old Testament, and undoubtedly they learned its techniques by imitation. In understanding how their rhetoric worked we have little choice but to employ the concepts and terms of the Greeks.[138]

---

[134] Of course, one exception where spoken dialogue must have preceded the writing of the text is the narrative account of Amos' confrontation with the priest Amaziah in 7:10–17.

[135] Renz, *The Rhetorical Function of the Book of Ezekiel*, 8. Crenshaw, "Education in Ancient Israel," surveys the OT and extrabiblical sources and concludes that they provide fragmentary information about the possible existence of schools that might have taught writing skills that could have been utilized by scribes, priests, and prophets (see also Crenshaw, *Education in Ancient Israel*, 85–113).

[136] Kennedy, *New Testament Interpretation through Rhetorical Criticism*, 10. Fox states this in his study of Ezekiel 37: "For in Israel we have a well-documented major rhetorical movement entirely independent of the classical tradition from which Western rhetoric and rhetorical criticism descend" ("The Rhetoric of Ezekiel's Vision of the Valley of the Bones," 5).

[137] Kennedy, *New Testament Interpretation through Rhetorical Criticism*, 8.

[138] Kennedy, *New Testament Interpretation through Rhetorical Criticism*, 11. OT rhetoric is discussed by Kennedy in *Classical Rhetoric and Its Christian and Secular Tradition from Ancient to Modern Times*, 137–43.

The Greeks became intellectually conscious of an impulse that is part of humanity's repertoire as communicators. They applied that impulse to the art of political discourse. Even though the Scriptures do not contain any theoretical elaboration about Israelite rhetoric, the art of rhetoric is evident in the divinely inspired Scriptures, including narrative, prophecy, and poetry, all of which announce God's redemptive work in history.

Not only does rhetorical analysis unite orality, literary form, and persuasion in its interpretive task, but it also adds the component of historical setting. It is important to capture the original "rhetorical situation" between the author and audience within the domain of the historical paradigm. Gitay writes: "The prophetic language is a reflection of both the rhetorical situation and the prophet's goal, and has to be studied accordingly."[139] Hayes and Irvine write: "A rhetorical situation involves an audience, a speaker, a topic or issue of mutual concern, a shared world of meaning, and an occasion for communication."[140] Fiorenza agrees: "Rhetorical criticism focuses on the persuasive power and literary strategies of a text that have a communicative function in a *concrete historical situation*."[141]

The interpretive method employed in this commentary is *rhetorical* to the extent that it assumes that the text is an inspired masterpiece of literary artistry composed for oral delivery in a specific historical situation and that God, speaking through his prophet Amos, has specific persuasive goals in mind. Therefore the present study interprets the book of Amos in a synchronic manner, seeing it as a unified whole. Roth's summary of steps for doing rhetorical analysis offers a helpful conclusion to the method being developed here: (1) determine the extent of the unit; (2) identify the rhetorical situation; (3) determine the rhetorical strategy, that is, what the speaker is attempting to accomplish; (4) identify the rhetorical technique; (5) analyze the unit as a whole, understanding that it is more than the sum of its individual parts.[142]

Gitay has been at the forefront of the approach that attends to rhetorical issues in the book of Amos.[143] Hayes structures his commentary in terms of "large rhetorical units rather than in terms of a multiplicity of small isolated texts."[144] Andersen and Freedman also eschew the scissors-and-paste reading strategies of form and to some extent redaction critics. Their position is that the messages in the different parts of the book, some of which might seem to be contradictory, are best explained as the result of Amos' different messages delivered over the course of his ministry, not as the signs of sloppy later redac-

---

[139] Gitay, "Reflections on the Study of the Prophetic Discourse," 221.

[140] Hayes and Irvine, *Isaiah, the Eighth-Century Prophet*, 61.

[141] Fiorenza, *Rhetoric and Ethic*, 108; emphasis added.

[142] W. M. W. Roth, "Rhetorical Criticism, Hebrew Bible," *DBI* 2:398. This is largely based on Kennedy, *New Testament Interpretation through Rhetorical Criticism*, 33–38.

[143] Gitay, "A Study of Amos's Art of Speech."

[144] Hayes, *Amos, the Eighth-Century Prophet*, 39.

tors.[145] Shalom Paul also postulates that much—if not all—of the book comes from the hand of Amos.[146]

Conclusions

Obviously there are many problems with form and redactional reading strategies. Chief among those problems is the amount of speculation involved by those who attempt to interpret Scripture using those methods. They supply subjective information that is outside of the biblical text and then interpret the text on the basis of their speculations. By linking exegesis to hypothetical historical reconstructions, these modes of interpretation compromise the integrity of the biblical text and destroy its theological message.[147] The reconstructed texts of form and redactional critics are hypothetical and unverifiable. What Ben Zvi writes about Hosea applies equally well to Amos:

> There is no indication that the intended readership of the book was asked to divide it into potential sources, read each of them separately and then reconstruct the possible redactional processes that led to the book in its present form.[148]

The rhetorical approach to the text of Amos challenges the assumptions and conclusions of form and redaction criticism.[149] The judgment that editors and intertextual scribes are responsible for the phenomena of discontinuity in Amos should be withheld. Rather, discontinuity can reflect the oral performance of the text. Niditch's words summarize the position taken in this commentary:

> We reject the romantic notion of an oral period in the history of Israel followed by the time of literacy in which Israelite literature becomes written and bookish. The oral and the literate interact throughout Israel's literary history, as is true also of the ancient Near Eastern cultures of Mesopotamia and Egypt. ...
>
> Given this assessment of Israelite aesthetics and the importance placed on the ongoing oral-literate continuum, source-critical theories become suspect, as do other theories about the composition of the Hebrew Bible that are grounded in modern-style notions about Israelites' use of reading and writing.[150]

---

145 Andersen and Freedman, *Amos*, 3–9.

146 Paul, *Amos*, 6.

147 After surveying the critical approaches to Amos, with a special focus upon the work of Wolff, Childs writes: "In my judgment, there is no greater indictment of the critical method than the theological bankruptcy of its homiletical model" (*Introduction to the Old Testament as Scripture*, 408–9).

148 Ben Zvi, *Hosea*, 5.

149 Paul, *Amos*, 6, states this opinion:

> Almost all of the arguments for later interpolations and redactions, including a Deuteronomistic one, are shown to be based on fragile foundations and inconclusive evidence. When each case is examined and analyzed on its own, without preconceived conjectures and unsupported hypotheses, the book in its entirety (with one or two minor exceptions) can be reclaimed for its rightful author, the prophet Amos.

Hasel likewise concludes that synchronic approaches like rhetorical analysis should have priority in Amos scholarship (*Understanding the Book of Amos*, 91–99).

150 Niditch, *Oral World and Written Word*, 134.

Greenstein also states:

> Source criticism has always rested on Western presuppositions and standards about logical sequence, the unacceptability of logical contradiction, the aesthetic blemish of duplication or repetition, and the ideal of consistency. Studies of orally performed literature in preliterate societies, however, demonstrate that "repetitions, doublets, false starts, digressions, rough transitions and the like so dear to the heart of biblical critics" tend to pervade oral literature. This means that the source critic's evidence of documentary difference may not represent difference at all. Without the discovery of independent documents attesting to the historical reality of sources, one simply is in no position to decide whether a discrepancy or duplication results from editorial splicing or a compositional sensibility that differs from the modern critic's. The source critic must in any event admit that the redactor found the end-result aesthetically acceptable. What was acceptable to an ancient redactor might also have been acceptable to an ancient author. For these and other reasons source critical conclusions must remain indecisive.[151]

Greenberg documents how Egyptologists, who once wrote off discontinuity in Egyptian texts, now view these texts more holistically.[152] In Egyptian literature, "there is a liking for the mixing of styles, a technique that culminates in the *Story of Sinuhe*, where the narration is interspersed with three poems."[153] Greenberg writes:

> We have no reason to suspect the plain evidence that the prophets composed from the first in various styles and forms, because they were learned in them and rhetorically skilled. ...
>
> We cannot gauge *a priori* what value an ancient author placed on consistency—especially if by being inconsistent he could best make his point.[154]

Greenberg maintains:

> A universal prejudice of modern biblical criticism is the assumption of original simplicity. A passage of complex structure, or one containing repetition, or skewing a previously used figure is, on these grounds, suspect of being inauthentic. Another widespread prejudice equates authenticity with topical or thematic uniformity. A temporal vista that progresses from present, to penultimate, to ultimate time is considered an artificial result of successive

---

[151] Greenstein, *Essays on Biblical Method and Translation*, 32–33 (including n. 14), quoting Long, "Recent Field Studies in Oral Literature and Their Bearing on OT Criticism," 195.

[152] Greenberg, "What Are the Valid Criteria for Determining Inauthentic Matter in Ezekiel?" 123. Greenberg goes on to note how the same set of affairs has marked the study of the legal taxonomy of Mesopotamian law collections. Here too scholarship that once eschewed discontinuity has come to recognize its brilliance (pp. 124–25). The methodology of form and redaction critics, uninformed by how ancient Near Eastern texts were composed, too quickly passes judgment on what was added and what was original (see Greenberg, "What Are the Valid Criteria for Determining Inauthentic Matter in Ezekiel?" 125–26, 135).

[153] Lichtheim, *Ancient Egyptian Literature*, 1:11, quoted by Greenberg, "What Are the Valid Criteria for Determining Inauthentic Matter in Ezekiel?" 123 (see also p. 124, n. 3).

[154] Greenberg, "What Are the Valid Criteria for Determining Inauthentic Matter in Ezekiel?" 132, 134.

> additions to a single-time original oracle. Doom oracles that end with a glimpse of a better future are declared composites on the ground of psychological improbability. Such prejudices are simply a prioris, an array of unproved (and unprovable) modern assumptions and conventions that confirm themselves through the results obtained by forcing them on the text and altering, reducing, and reordering it accordingly.[155]

Form and redaction criticisms' attempts to recover so-called original versions is an enterprise fraught with perils, obstacles, and difficulties; any results are partly if not largely guesswork. In the end, there is a significant difference between having a tangible text and trying to draw inferences or argue cases on the basis of a reconstructed hypothetical original text. What is reconstructed is finally of the critical scholar's own making. One must ask whether form and redaction critics have discovered a past reality or whether they have created one. They propose that discontinuities and alleged contradictions in the text were introduced by later authors or editors, based on the critics' own stylistic preconceptions derived from the modern Western world. Instead, those textual features are intentional elements of the original text that must be explained as the result of the inspired author's own peculiarities of style and particular theological purpose, since such features are evident throughout the OT prophetic literature.

Andersen's thesis is that in the OT some of the public behavior of prophets was abnormal[b] and that this abnormality carried over into their writings.[156] He writes: "To insist that biblical authors were always logical, and to use logic to interpret their writings, leads to grotesque results."[157] Paul Raabe notes: "It is precisely the nature of prophetic discourse to make sudden shifts on all levels of language, including style and imagery, and to juxtapose multiple, divergent, and even dissonant perspectives in much the same way as in the use of poetic parallelism."[158] It is therefore an anachronism to impose on the book of Amos modern criteria for writings to meet in order for them to be considered the unified work of a single author. Likewise, it is anachronistic to require a biblical book to conform to modern conventions for supposedly objective historical and scientific writings. It need not present discrete ideas in strict chronological or logical order in order for it to be authentic, didactic, and trustworthy theological proclamation. Every biblical text is God's own self-revelation through his chosen Spirit-filled author.

(b) See, e.g., 1 Ki 20:35–41; 2 Ki 1:7–8; Is 20:2–3; Ezek 4:1–5:4; 12:3–7; Hos 1:3–9; 3:1–2

A portrait combines *both* art and history. It is an artistic creation serving a referential end: the accurate portrayal of a real person at a certain time in history. On the one hand, in appreciating a portrait, one may admire its artistry: the consummate brushwork, the well-conceived composition, the judicious

---

[155] Greenberg, *Ezekiel*, 20.

[156] Andersen, "Linguistic Coherence in Prophetic Discourse."

[157] Andersen, "Linguistic Coherence in Prophetic Discourse," 146.

[158] Raabe, *Obadiah*, 17.

selection of detail. However, failure to recognize that all of this artistry is marshaled to serve a historical purpose—to capture a true and telling likeness of a historical person—will miss the main point. Approaching a portrait fully aware of its referential and historical intent but with little understanding of the artistic medium in which it is rendered also misses the point. The danger in such cases is that lack of awareness of *how* the medium communicates the message may lead to misunderstandings of just *what* the message is that the medium communicates.

Just as the best way to "read" a portrait and to grasp its significance is to *combine* competent appreciation of the artistic medium with historical knowledge of the person in his or her life setting, so the best way to read the book of Amos is to combine a competent appreciation of the rhetorical linguistic medium this prophet of Yahweh employed with historical knowledge of the peoples, places, and events to which he refers. The better the understanding is of the artistic workings of a portrait or biblical text, the better is the grasp of the historical subject depicted.

Amos is a portrait about Yahweh and his salvation for Israel and all nations. It portrays how the triune God acts in judgment and salvation, both of which climax in the crucifixion, atoning death, and bodily resurrection of the promised Son of David. This is how God has now resurrected "the falling tabernacle of David" (Amos 9:11): the risen Messiah is now gathering God's new Israel into himself to build the new temple, the Christian church, with the promise of everlasting salvation in the new creation. This is affirmed by the citation of Amos 9:11–12 in Acts 15:16–17 to support the acceptance of Gentiles into the apostolic church by Christ's grace alone, without the need to perform the works required by the Law of Moses (Acts 15:5; cf. Rom 3:20–28; Gal 2:16; 3:2–11). The apostles maintained that all baptized believers in Christ are members of God's kingdom of grace and co-heirs of all the blessings God had promised to Israel in the old covenant. Faith in this one true God, who has revealed himself definitively in the person and atoning work of his Son, is a necessary prerequisite for rightly interpreting Amos, and indeed all the Scriptures, since they all are portraits of him.

This commentary's rhetorical reading of Amos, like the proverbial bride, brings things old, new, and borrowed. Theological insights from faithful interpreters in the past are incorporated; beneficial ideas and methods initiated by earlier generations of scholars are expanded and refined. New information, such as that based on recently discovered texts or archaeological artifacts, is added to further the understanding of the book. Literary methods borrowed from rhetorical studies help illumine the distinctive features and message of the God-breathed text.

This approach to Amos respects the book's divine inspiration as well as its normative authority for Christian faith and life. Amos' sermons of Law and Gospel were designed to move ancient Israel to repent from its many sins and trust Yahweh's promise of the coming messianic salvation. The book continues to serve God's same dual purpose today. It calls us and all people to repent, lest we face the same fiery eschatological judgment.[159] At the same time, this portion of God's Word also grants and sustains faith in the salvation already accomplished for us by Jesus Christ, even as we await the consummation of all God's promises at Christ's return.[160]

[159] Judgment by fire is threatened for pagan nations in 1:4, 7, 10, 12, 14; 2:2; for unfaithful Judah in 2:5; and for apostate Israel in Amos 5:6. This corresponds to the NT warning of the everlasting fire of hell for all unbelievers (e.g., Mt 18:8; 25:41; Jude 7).

[160] The Gospel promise of Amos 9:11–15 has already been secured for all believers by the perfect life, atoning death, and glorious resurrection of Jesus Christ. However, only on the Last Day will God raise all believers bodily to abundant everlasting life in the new creation as portrayed in 9:11–15.

Amos 1:1–2

Superscription and Introduction

Amos 1:1–2

Superscription and Introduction

Translation

1 [1]The words of Amos, who was among the sheep breeders from Tekoa, which he perceived concerning Israel during the days of Uzziah the king of Judah and during the days of Jeroboam ben Joash the king of Israel, two years before the earthquake.

[2]He said:

"Yahweh from Zion roars,
and from Jerusalem he utters his voice.
The pastures of the shepherds mourn,
and the peak of Carmel withers."

Textual Notes

1:1 דִּבְרֵ֣י עָמ֔וֹס—The expression דִּבְרֵי, "the words of," in construct with a proper noun (here "Amos") appears elsewhere in the OT at the beginning of a book to indicate its author (Jer 1:1; Neh 1:1; cf. Eccl 1:1) or at the start of a chapter to indicate its author (Prov 30:1; 31:1). As such it serves as the book's title.[1] These first two Hebrew words represent the whole book as the product of a single individual author, Amos.

"Word" (דָּבָר) is not, as one might understand its translation, simply a verbal or grammatical unit. A divine דָּבָר is an objective entity, endowed by God with his own power to accomplish its stated goal, so it may be translated as either as a "word" from God, or the "event" God accomplishes through his words. *Yahweh's* words have power, not only to persuade or to reason, but also to bring about judgment and salvation (see, e.g., Is 55:10–11; Jer 23:29; Jn 17:17).

Amos' proper name עָמוֹס probably is derived from the verb עָמַס, which can mean "to load" something on a beast of burden or "to carry" a load. Ps 68:20 (ET 68:19) uses the verb to praise God, "our salvation," who daily "carries for us" our burdens. The noun form עָמוֹס could be patterned after the infinitive absolute and convey the verbal idea of "carrying" or mean "one who carries" a burden (see GKC, § 84[a] k). Alternatively, it might have a passive meaning: "carried [by Yahweh]." עָמוֹס appears in the OT only as the name of this prophet (1:1; 7:8, 10–12, 14; 8:2), but the verbal root עמס with a suffixed theophoric element also appears in the personal name עֲמַסְיָה, "Amasiah" (2 Chr 17:16), probably meaning "Yah(weh) carries."

---

[1] So Andersen and Freedman, *Amos*, 184. They believe the construct phrase means something like "the Story of Amos" or "Amos' Record" or "Amos' Report" (p. 185).

אֲשֶׁר־הָיָה בַנֹּקְדִים מִתְּקוֹעַ—Amos is described as one of the נֹקְדִים, "sheep breeders."[2] This noun occurs elsewhere in the OT only in 2 Ki 3:4. In form it is the Qal participle of the verb נקד, which, however, never occurs in the OT. 2 Ki 3:4 reports that King Mesha of Moab was a נֹקֵד who "used to pay as tribute to the king of Israel (the wool of) a hundred thousand lambs and the wool of a hundred thousand rams."[3] This implies that Amos belonged to a higher socioeconomic status than that of a menial shepherd, commonly denoted by רֹעֶה. More ambiguous is Amos' description in 7:15 of his divine call: literally, "Yahweh took me from behind the sheep," which could refer to the vocation of either a shepherd or a sheep breeder.

The town of Tekoa (תְּקוֹעַ, modern Khirbet Tequ'a) is about twelve miles south of Jerusalem and five miles south of Bethlehem.[4] To the west of Tekoa is cultivated land, and to the east is wilderness. In 1 Chr 11:5–6, Tekoa appears in a list of fortresses. It is called מִדְבַּר תְּקוֹעַ ("the wilderness of Tekoa") in 2 Chr 20:20. 2 Sam 14:2 may suggest that the village had a reputation for wisdom and sages since Joab sought from Tekoa a "wise woman" (אִשָּׁה חֲכָמָה) to help carry out his plan for reconciling David with his son Absalom.

אֲשֶׁר חָזָה עַל־יִשְׂרָאֵל—This relative clause, "which he perceived concerning Israel," modifies דִּבְרֵי עָמוֹס, "the words of Amos." Because prophets often see (Amos 7–9) *and* hear (3:7–8) from Yahweh, the best translation of the verb חָזָה in this context is "perceived." Usually חָזָה means "to see, look upon." It can have an ordinary object (e.g., a house in Job 8:17; a man in Prov 22:29) or have no object at all (Ps 11:4). The verb can also be used for seeing God himself (e.g., Ex 24:11; Num 24:4; Ps 17:15; Job 19:26). Although in prophetic literature חָזָה may appear in a non-technical sense (e.g., Is 33:17; Micah 4:11), the vast majority of attestations refer to seeing prophetic visions (e.g., Is 30:10; Lam 2:14). The noun חָזוֹן, "a vision," derived from the verb, is sometimes employed in the superscription referring to an entire prophetic book (Is 1:1; Obad 1; Nah 1:1). The use of חָזָה here indicates that the five visions revealed to Amos (7:1–3, 4–6, 7–9; 8:1–3; 9:1–4) are a significant part of his prophetic call. In fact, in 7:12 the priest Amaziah calls Amos a חֹזֶה, "seer, visionary."

The preposition עַל is used in the sense of "about, concerning." The proper noun יִשְׂרָאֵל, "Israel," may refer to the patriarch Jacob, the twelve-tribe group of his descendants who came out of Egypt, or the Northern Kingdom. After the fall of the Northern Kingdom in 722 BC, the term continued to be used for the northern survivors of the Assyrian destruction and exile; for Judah as the only recognizable continuation of the

---

2 The LXX translators apparently did not know the meaning of the term because they transliterated it in Amos 1:1 with νακκαριμ and in 2 Ki 3:4 with νωκηδ.

3 It would be unwise, however, to believe that Amos was in the same social and economic standing as King Mesha of Moab. Amos lived in a different country and at a different time, so the correspondence between the two may be slight (cf. Andersen and Freedman, *Amos*, 188). Based on Ugaritic cognates, Craigie believes that the word refers to one who manages shepherds. Understood in this way, Amos would have held a middle- to upper-class job ("Amos the *Nōqēd* in the Light of Ugaritic").

4 Cf. L. Axelsson, "Tekoa," *ABD* 6:343–44.

original nation; and in an eschatological sense for the restored and united people of God, the Christian church.

"Israel" appears thirty times in Amos. Andersen and Freedman present an argument for the following hypotheses:

1. When "Israel" by itself occurs in Amos, it probably designates the Northern Kingdom only.
2. When "Israel" is qualified in Amos with expressions like "house of," "sons of," or "my people," it probably refers to the twelve tribes, the united kingdom, or an ideal entity of the future.[5]

They summarize their proposals as follows:

> "Israel" when used alone refers to the northern kingdom only, just as Judah (which is always used alone in Amos) routinely refers to the southern kingdom. All other examples of Israel (with qualifiers) refer to an older or larger Israel, including the northern kingdom but not restricted to it. Of the other terms [used in Amos], Jacob refers to the larger entity, while Joseph and Isaac refer to the northern kingdom.[6]

בִּימֵ֣י ׀ עֻזִּיָּ֣ה מֶֽלֶךְ־יְהוּדָ֗ה—The reigning king of Judah is named first as the rightful king from the line of David, whence the Messiah will come (2 Samuel 7). In this context, בִּימֵ֣י, "in the days of," means "during the reign of." עֻזִּיָּ֣ה, "Uzziah," means "my strength is Yah(weh)," a combination of the noun עֹז and the theophoric element יָהּ.

וּבִימֵ֞י יָרָבְעָ֤ם בֶּן־יוֹאָשׁ֙ מֶ֣לֶךְ יִשְׂרָאֵ֔ל—The king of the apostate Northern Kingdom of Israel is stated second, since this group of Israelites cut themselves off from the gracious dwelling place of God in Jerusalem and from the royal line of David. יָרָבְעָם, "Jeroboam," may mean "may the people increase" if -יָרָבְ represents a form of the verb רָבַב or רָבָה. Another possibility is that the name could mean "the people contend [against God]" if -יָרָבְ is from the verb רִיב (see BDB, s.v. יָרָבְעָם, under the root רבב). The meaning of the name of his father, יוֹאָשׁ֙, "Joash," is uncertain but the theophoric element (-יוֹ) is a shortened form of "Yahweh." This Joash was the preceding king in Samaria (2 Ki 13:9–14, 25; 14:1, 8–17, 23, 27).

שְׁנָתַ֖יִם לִפְנֵ֥י הָרָֽעַשׁ׃—The dual form of שָׁנָה, "year," means "two years." The preposition לִפְנֵי may function locally (e.g., Gen 18:22), referentially (e.g., Gen 7:1), comparatively (e.g., 1 Sam 1:16), or, as here, temporally, meaning "before" (Waltke-O'Connor, § 11.3.1a).

The segholate noun רַעַשׁ (in pause, רָ֫עַשׁ), "earthquake," generally indicates some sort of shaking or quaking. The cognate verb רָעַשׁ, "to shake, quake," is associated with the presence of Yahweh: the earth trembles at his appearing or because he is angry (e.g., Judg 5:4; 2 Sam 22:8 [see also 2 Sam 22:9–16]; Is 13:13; Jer 10:10; Ps 68:9 [ET 68:8]).[7] Sometimes the shaking occurs because of Yahweh's judgment specifically on "the Day

---

5 Andersen and Freedman, *Amos*, 98–139. This is contrary to the opinion of Wolff that " 'house of Israel' refers to the state of the northern kingdom" (*Joel and Amos*, 164).

6 Andersen and Freedman, *Amos*, 126. This range of meaning for "Israel" is for the most part also operative in the books of Samuel and Kings (p. 136).

7 Cf. H. Schmoldt, "רָעַשׁ," *TDOT* 13:589–93.

of Yahweh": see the verb רָעַשׁ in Joel 2:10; 4:16 (ET 3:16) in connection with "the Day of Yahweh" in Joel 2:11; 4:14 (ET 3:14). What makes the earth quake in Joel 4:16 (ET 3:16) is that "Yahweh roars from Zion," the same phraseology in Amos 1:2. Cf. also the earthquake (רַעַשׁ, 1 Ki 19:11–12) that precedes the divine voice in 1 Ki 19:12–13.

In Amos 1:1, רַעַשׁ refers to a literal "earthquake" that is probably tied to an act of divine judgment that certified Amos' preaching. Since earth tremors and shocks are common in the region of Israel, this particular quake with the definite article, הָרָעַשׁ, "*the* earthquake," must have been historically significant and probably stronger than normal (see Waltke-O'Connor, § 13.5.1c, including example 2). The earthquake, therefore, is cited as a historical marker by which Amos' words can be dated. Since it came after Amos finished his book, it seems to have been Yahweh's ratification of the veracity of Amos' prophecies and a sign of their imminent fulfillment. Yet it also has Gospel implications (see the commentary).

Zech 14:5 also references an earthquake during the reign of Uzziah, which is likely this same earthquake. Archaeologists have tentatively located this cataclysm in the first half of the eighth century. Stratum VI at Hazor shows evidence of a great earthquake circa 760 BC.[8] This helps to date Amos' ministry. See further the commentary.

1:2 | וַיֹּאמַר—The subject of "he said" is Amos, who, however, speaks the "words" given him by God (1:1). The rest of 1:2 consists of four lines comprising two bicola. Each bicolon consists of two lines exhibiting synonymous parallelism.

יְהוָה מִצִּיּוֹן יִשְׁאָג—Literally, "Yahweh from Zion roars." An almost identical clause begins Joel 4:16 (ET 3:16). Normally such a sentence in Hebrew follows the sequence of verb, subject, and prepositional phrase. When this order is changed, it signals that the author is seeking to emphasize a certain word. In this case, the subject, יְהוָה, "Yahweh," appears before both the prepositional phrase מִצִּיּוֹן, "from Zion," and the verb יִשְׁאָג, "roars." The emphatic position of Yahweh's name accents that he is the one bringing about the mourning and withering judgment in 1:2 and the judgments throughout the rest of the book.

Amos also emphasizes "from Zion" syntactically by placing it before the verb "roars" but after "Yahweh." In the second half of this bicolon, וּמִירוּשָׁלַם, "and from Jerusalem," is fronted in like manner by its placement before the verb יִתֵּן, "gives." These syntactical positions of "Zion" and "Jerusalem" indicate that Yahweh's dwelling place is in Solomon's temple on Zion in Jerusalem and in the southern kingdom of Judah, as opposed to the idolatrous shrines at Bethel and Dan in the northern kingdom of Israel. In Is 8:18, the prophet states that Yahweh is "the one dwelling on Mount Zion" (הַשֹּׁכֵן בְּהַר צִיּוֹן). Amos' word order highlights this same fact.

The verb שָׁאַג refers to the roar of a lion, normally when it is about to attack.[9] This is distinct from the verb נָהַם, which denotes the "growl" of a lion *while* it is devouring its prey (BDB, s.v. נָהַם, 1). Roaring (שָׁאַג) is a strategic tactic of a lion because it paralyzes with fear or frightens away all who are within the large audible range (see, e.g.,

---

8 Yadin et al., *Hazor II*, 24–26, 36–37.

9 Cf. M. Graupner, "שָׁאַג," *TDOT* 14:232–35.

Judg 14:5; Is 5:29; Amos 3:4, 8; Ps 104:21).[10] The verb is used to describe Yahweh's roaring voice, which instills fear in sinners (Jer 25:30; Hos 11:10; Job 37:4). Zeph 3:3 uses the verb to liken the rapacious officials in Jerusalem who were oppressing the poor to roaring lions.

In every case, whether used of Yahweh or people, שָׁאַג evokes fear. Amos 1:2 attributes this roar to Yahweh, whose voice elicits the fear of judgment due to the overwhelming power of his word (cf. Amos 3:4, 8, 12; 5:19). In addition to passages where Yahweh roars, he is likened to a lion in Hos 5:14 and 13:7–8.

The metaphor is used in Rev 5:5 for Jesus, who is called "the Lion of the tribe of Judah, the Root of David" because he "has triumphed": by his death and resurrection he has defeated the devil, death itself, and humanity's sin by atoning for it. "The Root of David" refers to Jesus' descent from the chosen line of kings over Judah, the tribe from which God had promised to send the royal Messiah (Gen 49:10). That is part of the purview of "the tabernacle of David" in Amos 9:11.

The imperfect form of יִשְׁאָג in Amos 1:2 indicates a future action that is so imminent that it can be translated as present tense: "roars." The same is true of the imperfect יִתֵּן in the next colon: "gives/utters" (see the next textual note).

וּמִירוּשָׁלַם יִתֵּן קוֹלוֹ—The identical clause is in Joel 4:16 (ET 3:16). The implied subject of this second clause continues to be "Yahweh," whose name began the preceding parallel clause. It too consists of three words, but they are a prepositional phrase, verb, and direct object. As in the preceding line, a prepositional phrase denoting source or direction of origin, מִירוּשָׁלַם, "from Jerusalem," precedes the verb.

Jerusalem was the capital of Israel, and after the division of the nation it continued to be the capital of Judah.[11] It often stands for the country and its people, just as "Damascus" (e.g., Amos 1:3–5) and "Babylon" (e.g., Is 21:9) by metonymy mean the land and the people of the nations of which those cities were the capitals. The ark of the covenant was brought to Jerusalem by David (2 Samuel 6), who pitched a tent for it (1 Chr 15:1; 16:1; 2 Chr 1:4; cf. "the tabernacle of David" in Amos 9:11). After the temple was built by Solomon (1 Kings 6–8), the ark resided in it. The real presence of Yahweh enthroned on the cherubim atop the ark (e.g., 1 Sam 4:4) made Jerusalem Yahweh's holy city (Is 45:13; 60:14; Pss 46:5 [ET 46:4]; 48:2, 9 [ET 48:1, 8]).

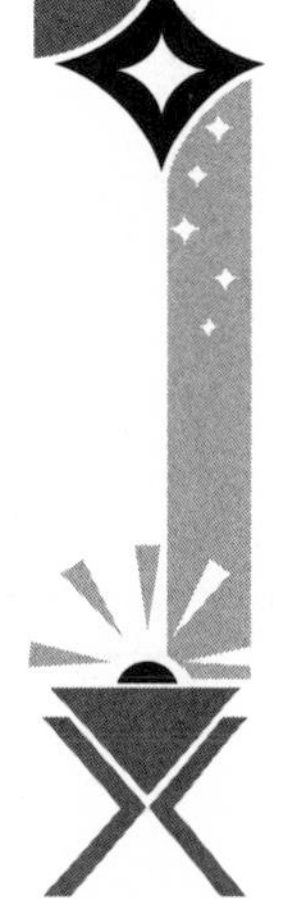

Solomon's temple was built with Phoenician assistance (e.g., 1 Kings 5), but Jerusalem was established by Yahweh (Is 14:32; Ps 87:1). He placed his name there (Deut 12:5, 11), and his glory dwelt there (1 Ki 8:11), a type of how his glory would dwell in the incarnate Christ ("tabernacled" in Jn 1:14; see also "glory" in Jn 2:11; 2 Cor 4:6). Through the person and work of Christ, Jerusalem will become even more glorious in the latter days—the church age, culminating in the return of Christ and the

[10] King writes: "No wild animal is so often mentioned in the Bible as the lion. This awesome beast, cited about 135 times in the Bible, often serves as a metaphor symbolizing destruction, power, or ferocity" (*Amos, Hosea, Micah*, 129). For example, in the Psalter, enemies are often portrayed as animals, particularly lions (see, e.g., Pss 7:3 [ET 7:2]; 10:9; 57:5 [ET 57:4]; 58:7 [ET 58:6]). In 1 Sam 17:37, David says that Yahweh delivered him "from the paw of the lion."

[11] Cf. H. Ringgren and M. Tsevat, "יְרוּשָׁלַםִ," *TDOT* 6:348–55.

eternal state (Is 2:1–5 || Micah 4:1–5; Ezek 40:2; Rev 21:2, 10). The NT understands the spiritual city of "Jerusalem" to be the home of Christians already now (Gal 4:26; Heb 12:22), where Jesus continues to dwell through his name, Word, and Sacraments (Mt 18:20; 28:19–20). In the eschaton, the church in glory will be the new Jerusalem (Revelation 21).

When the "voice" (קוֹל) of Yahweh is paired with the verb נָתַן (here the imperfect יִתֵּן, "gives/utters"), the combination often indicates some kind of "theophanic thunder."[12] The thunder in Amos 1:2 will have a reverse effect: instead of rain there will be drought (see the next two textual notes).

וְאָבְלוּ נְאוֹת הָרֹעִים—This line begins the second bicolon in the verse. The verb אָבַל usually means "to mourn." *HALOT* proposes the existence of a separate, homographic verb אבל II, "to dry up," but *DCH* includes drought as a possible reason for the mourning denoted by the single verb אבל I, which *DCH* defines as "**mourn, grieve**, because of calamity, drought, etc." That definition explains why וְאָבְלוּ is parallel with the verb in the following line, יָבֵשׁ, "to be dry, to dry up." Those two verbs are parallel also in Jer 12:4; 23:10; Joel 1:10.

The wider contexts in which אָבַל is used can be divided into two related groups: (1) mourning on account of death and (2) mourning on account of divine judgment.[13] Mourning on account of death is frequently accompanied by other rituals of lamentation, including the tearing of clothes (e.g., 2 Sam 13:30–31) and putting on sackcloth (Gen 37:34). Grief on account of judgment is accompanied by outward signs such as fasting, sackcloth, and prayer (e.g., Ps 35:13–14; Ezra 10:6; Neh 1:4). אָבַל may also describe creation's sorrow: the earth and the ground grieve (Hos 4:3; Joel 1:10). Likewise, in Amos 1:2, the subject of the mourning is "the pastures of the shepherds" because Yahweh's judgment is about to bring death to these places that normally provide life: vegetation for the sheep, which in turn provide wool, milk, and meat for the people. Amos 1:3–2:6 is a litany about Yahweh's "fire" (1:4, 7, 10, 12, 14; 2:2, 5) as the means he uses to enact judgment upon sinful peoples and their lands.

The construct phrase נְאוֹת הָרֹעִים, "the pastures of the shepherds," is unique in the OT, but the two plural words occur in close proximity in Zeph 2:6. נְאוֹת is the plural in construct of the noun נָוָה II, "pasture, meadow" (BDB). It is used in the more familiar phrase נְאוֹת (הַ)מִּדְבָּר, "(the) pastures of the wilderness" (e.g., Jer 9:9 [ET 9:10]; Joel 1:19–20; Ps 65:13 [ET 65:12]). Paul believes that Amos' phrase "mostly likely was selected here to describe the effect of the roar of God upon the shepherds themselves." The mourning of their pastures due to drought meant the end of their livelihood and also hardship and famine for the rest of the people. It is appropriate that Amos, a sheep breeder by profession (1:1; 7:15), draws on his own experience for this vivid imagery of the worst possible calamity.[14]

---

12 See Stuart, *Hosea–Jonah*, 301. See, for example, Pss 18:14 (ET 18:13); 46:7 (ET 46:6), where נָתַן קוֹל means "to thunder" (cf. Ps 29:3–5, 7–9). In the theophany at Sinai, קֹלֹת, "voices, sounds," signified Yahweh's thundering presence (Ex 19:16; 20:18).

13 Cf. A. Baumann, "אָבַל," *TDOT* 1:44–48.

14 Paul, *Amos*, 40.

The plainest meaning of the noun נָוֶה is that of a "pasture" or "meadow," a place where flocks gather to feed. נָוֶה usually is found in poetic contexts about Yahweh's judgment or salvation. Pastures can be the object of God's wrath (Jer 23:10) and judgment by fire (Joel 1:19–20). Similarly, Amos 1:2 makes pastures the first location of judgment and mourning in response to Yahweh's roar of judgment. Compare the lamentations over the pastures in Jer 9:9 (ET 9:10). Pastures can also be the location of God's promised blessings by his grace toward the faithful (Joel 2:22; Ps 65:13 [ET 65:12]). David in Ps 23:1–2 affirms that Yahweh, his gracious Shepherd, makes him lie down in "pastures of green grass."

וְיָבֵשׁ רֹאשׁ הַכַּרְמֶל׃—The Qal of יָבֵשׁ generally has the intransitive meaning "to be dry" or "to become dry." The Hiphil usually has the corresponding causative meaning, "to make dry, to dry up (water)," or to make plants "wither." The Qal and the Hiphil can be used in contexts of salvation, as when the flood waters dried up for Noah (Gen 8:7, 14) and when God parted the Red Sea for Israel's exodus (Josh 2:10; Ps 74:12–15) and held back the Jordan River for Israel to cross (Josh 4:23; 5:1).[15] But most often יָבֵשׁ is used in negative contexts of judgment, such as drought (1 Ki 17:7), a dying plant (Job 18:16), and death (Job 14:10–12). The withering of the herbage of the field is the result of God's judgment upon the wicked (Jer 12:4; 23:10; 50:38; 51:36). The city of Nineveh is consumed like dried stubble by the wrath of Yahweh (the related adjective יָבֵשׁ in Nah 1:10). The grass is dried out in Isaiah's oracle against Moab (Is 15:6). Similarly in Amos, יָבֵשׁ is used for Yahweh's judgment manifested in the desiccation of Mount Carmel (1:2) and in a drought that causes a field to wither (4:7).

The noun רֹאשׁ can designate the "top" or "summit" of a mountain (e.g., Gen 8:5; Ex 19:20; 24:17; Is 2:2; Ps 72:16). In this case, the mountain is הַכַּרְמֶל, part of a chain of hills and mountains that extend southeast from present-day Haifa.[16] The summit that is typically understood to be Mount Carmel is a headland that forms the northern part of the Bay of Acre. The proper noun כַּרְמֶל, "Carmel," derives from כֶּרֶם, "vineyard," and as such indicates that it is a place of abundant and lush vineyards (e.g., Is 33:9; 35:2; Jer 50:19; Nah 1:4; 2 Chr 26:10). Because of its close proximity to the Mediterranean Sea, it is well-watered and fertile. Its slopes and hill country are famous for their olives, grain, and vineyards. כַּרְמֶל as the common noun meaning "fruitful land" represents the opposite of מִדְבָּר, the "wilderness" (Is 32:15–16; Jer 4:26), and of יַעַר, "brush" (Is 29:17; 32:15). The withering of Mount Carmel signifies a major calamity (see also Is 33:9; Nah 1:4).

Here in Amos, Mount Carmel is important both as the epitome of fertility, which will cease, and for its northern location, which signifies Yahweh's word of judgment against the Northern Kingdom of Israel. Mount Carmel may have served as a northern boundary of the Northern Kingdom, separating it from Tyre. Together, "the pastures of the shepherds" and "the peak of Carmel" constitute a merism, implying the total devastation of all fertile places in Israel due to Yahweh's roar.

---

[15] Cf. H. D. Preuss, "יָבֵשׁ," *TDOT* 5:373–79.

[16] Cf. H. O. Thompson, "Carmel, Mount," *ABD* 1:874.

Commentary

Although "the words" are ascribed to "Amos," the prophetic formula "which he perceived" in 1:1 indicates that the content of the visionary book was revealed to him by Yahweh. The book is not of the prophet's own making, but was inspired by the Holy Spirit (see 2 Pet 1:19–21). Amos 1:1 locates Yahweh's vision concretely in history, tying it to the reigns of two eighth-century BC kings: Uzziah of Judah and Jeroboam ben Joash of Israel. Amos 1:1 also connects this prophecy to "the earthquake." The mention of this earthquake sets the primary theme for the book: Yahweh's earthquake-like judgment will shake Israel, Judah, and the nations, until everything comes crashing down. Only after that will Yahweh resurrect the tabernacle of David, inaugurating the kingdom of God brought by the Messiah, and ushering in the new creation with abundant life, when God's people will permanently dwell in the new land (9:11–15).

Amos 1:2 introduces the major motif of the undoing of creation. When Yahweh roars from Zion and utters his voice from Jerusalem, the whole creation is adversely affected. The interconnectedness between Yahweh, the ethics of people, and the cosmic order is an ongoing theme in the book.[17] Because of the absence of justice and righteousness (5:7, 15, 24; 6:12), the land experiences numerous ecological disasters (e.g., 4:6–13; 8:7–14). Yet because "mercy triumphs over judgment" (James 2:13), the book ends with Eden-like abundance (Amos 9:11–15). And so Amos begins and ends with creation and ethics, with Yahweh interacting with his human creatures as well as their natural environment. Creation laments and withers because of the sins of Israel, Judah, and the nations (1:2–2:16), while in 9:11–15 creation is restored because Yahweh promises a new Davidic king who will bring about justice and righteousness for all the people (cf. 2 Sam 8:15). This same theological dynamic is affirmed in the NT; see, for example, Rom 8:19–22, which describes the present era, in which creation is in bondage to decay, and Revelation 22, which describes the eternal dwelling of all the redeemed in Christ as a greater Eden.

Additionally, 1:1 provides key information about the prophet: where he is from, what he did for a living, and when the book was compiled.

Amos 1:1

Beginnings in the Bible are significant. Elie Wiesel stated: "As with every genuine work of art, [the] opening statement contains all that is to follow."[18] This is especially true for the book of Amos, as he offers the most complete superscription in all of the prophetic literature. It tells us about his vocation,

---

[17] Paradigmatic biblical narratives that explain this relationship include the curse on creation in Gen 3:14–19 and the judgment on Sodom and Gomorrah. Prior to their destruction, those cities were described in paradisiacal terms: כְּגַן־יְהוָה, "like the garden of Yahweh," that is, Eden (Gen 13:10). But because of the sin of homosexuality, Yahweh sent his judgment that left the area a permanent ecological disaster (Gen 19:24–28).

[18] Wiesel, *Five Biblical Portraits*, 101.

his place of residence, who the reigning kings of Judah and Israel were at the time of his ministry, and when he finished his book, two years before a well-known cataclysmic event.

"The Words of Amos"

The name "Amos" is derived from a Hebrew verb that can mean "to load" or "to carry a load." Luther associates the prophet's name with his message: "He can well be called Amos, that is 'a burden,' one who is hard to get along with and irritating."[19] In partial agreement, a modern scholar explains that "perhaps, the name is meant to be symbolic for the burden Amos must carry to be a messenger of doom or for the heavy load that he lays upon his hearers."[20] The weight he bears is that of proclaiming Yahweh's judgment that "the end is coming upon my people Israel" (8:2).

Following the phrase "the words of Amos" are two subordinate clauses, each one introduced with the relative pronoun אֲשֶׁר. The first אֲשֶׁר refers back to "Amos" and means "who," while the second אֲשֶׁר refers back to "the words" and means "which." The first clause introduces the prophet's vocation and hometown; the second indicates when he prophesied his words.

"Who Was among the Sheep Breeders from Tekoa"

As Amos later reaffirms, he was a layman, called to be a prophet while he was going about his ordinary vocation (7:14–15).[21] But what did he do before he was called to be a prophet? The first subordinate clause in 1:1 addresses this issue, which some believe is pivotal. Hasel writes: "It is believed that as his sociocultural background is grasped or reconstructed we have a key, if not *the* key, to his message."[22] Yet this task is not as easy as it might appear, for according to 1:1 and 7:14–15, Amos' vocation involved four types of work: he was בַּנֹּקְדִים, "among the sheep breeders"; a בּוֹקֵר, "livestock breeder"; a בּוֹלֵס שִׁקְמִים, "dresser of sycamore figs"; and he was called מֵאַחֲרֵי הַצֹּאן, literally, "from behind the sheep," which indicates that he was a shepherd.[23] As a shepherd like Moses and David, Amos is a type of Christ (e.g., Mt 25:31–32; Lk 15:3–7; Jn 10:1–18). Called to be a prophet, he also prefigures Christ, who is Israel's

---

[19] AE 35:320.

[20] Simundson, *Hosea, Joel, Amos, Obadiah, Jonah, Micah*, 163.

[21] Sweeney believes Amos may have been a Judean agriculturalist who appeared at Bethel to pay his part of Judah's tribute to Israel its suzerain (*The Twelve Prophets*, e.g., 231). He speculates that the motive of Amos was economic: he rejected Bethel because it was the place where the more affluent north collected its tribute from the poorer south. Amos wanted his home country of Judah to be free of this taxation and his Davidic state to be autonomous (cf. 9:11–15). However, Sweeney fails to account for the most important motive of Amos: he had heard Yahweh roar (1:2; 3:8), and he was divinely sent to be a herald of God's living Word.

[22] Hasel, *Understanding the Book of Amos*, 29.

[23] Steiner provides an in-depth study of these terms in *Stockmen from Tekoa, Sycomores from Sheba*.

greatest Prophet (Deut 18:15–20; Jn 7:40; Acts 3:22–26), the divine and prophetic Word made flesh (Jn 1:14; Rev 19:13; cf. 2 Pet 1:19).

The noun for "sheep breeder" appears only one other time in the OT, for Mesha, the king of Moab, who dealt in livestock by the hundreds of thousands (2 Ki 3:4). This suggests that Amos was not a lonely rustic, wandering from pasture to pasture with a few sheep under his care. A "sheep breeder" was a person of substance and influence. It is safe to assume, then, that the references in 7:14–15 to him as a "livestock breeder" and being called, literally, "from behind the sheep" are more general terms for the same vocation: one who works with livestock. Probably the term translated as "sheep breeder" could refer to dealing with both cattle and sheep. Amos was a major herdsman and a dealer in large and small kinds of livestock.

In light of the reference to "the Tekoites and their wealthy shepherds" in Neh 3:5, Driver suggests that this group of "sheep breeders" in Tekoa (Amos 1:1) probably consisted of "families following hereditary trades."[24] This may indicate that Amos was working in a family business of stock breeders who worked in distant pastures like the Shephelah (coastal plain), where sycamore trees grow.[25] This would then explain the prophet's words in 7:14, where he states that he was a "dresser of sycamore figs," because sycamore fig trees would not be found in or around Tekoa in the hill country.

Amos likely had only one principal vocation, not two or more separate ones. As a herdsman he would have reason to take care of sycamore trees. The sycamore tree provided both necessary food and shade for herds. The tree's dependence on large amounts of water would indicate that their location provided plenty of water for the animals to drink.[26]

The first subordinate clause in 1:1 continues with "*from* Tekoa," not "*in* Tekoa."[27] Tekoite herdsmen spent most of their time on the road because the town and its surrounding fields did not have enough pasturage. "All in all, the Tekoite herdsmen probably spent very little time at home."[28]

So what would it mean to be from Tekoa?[29] For one thing, Polley postulates that Amos' associations with Tekoa influenced his understanding of

---

[24] Driver, *Joel and Amos*, 128.

[25] Steiner, *Stockmen from Tekoa, Sycomores from Sheba*, 101, suggests this location.

[26] So Steiner, *Stockmen from Tekoa, Sycomores from Sheba*, 105–15. King also notes the possibility that "in exchange for grazing rights for their flocks, the shepherds dressed the sycamore fruit." He considers this "a plausible explanation" of "how Amos could be 'a herdsman, and a dresser of sycamore trees' at the same time" (*Amos, Hosea, Micah*, 117).

[27] Contrast Jer 1:1, which states that the prophet was among the priests "*in* Anathoth" (בַּעֲנָתוֹת).

[28] Steiner, *Stockmen from Tekoa, Sycomores from Sheba*, 89.

[29] Cf. Strijdom, "What Tekoa Did to Amos." Rosenbaum believes that Amos was a native of a northern town also named Tekoa and hence he was no stranger in northern Israel (*Amos of Israel*, 37–50). Koch also argues that Amos came from "a Galilean Tekoa, which is attested in post-biblical times" (*The Prophets*, 1:70). This position is based on a philological argument that the command in 7:12–13 is an order for Amos to flee from his own country and that

justice. The reforms of the Judahite king Jehoshaphat (872–848 BC)[30] noted in 2 Chronicles 19 indicate that the king appointed judges in each of the fortified cities of Judah and also appointed Levites, priests, and heads of families to render just judgments in Jerusalem. Since Tekoa was one of the fortified cities of Judah (2 Chr 11:5–12), Polley believes Amos was able to observe the proper administration of justice in his hometown.[31] This would have sharpened his discernment of the injustices perpetrated in Israel that Amos describes later in his book (e.g., 2:6–16).

It has been said, "You can take the man out of the country, but you can't take the country out of the man."[32] Tekoa was known for its military fortress and its role as an administrative center. It may also have been renowned for having some wise and faithful Israelite believers. For example, when Joab needed assistance in reconciling David and Absalom, he sought out "a wise woman" from Tekoa (2 Sam 14:2) who displayed Proverbs-like wisdom. It comes as no surprise, therefore, that in Amos there are several "home spun" wisdom sayings that could have been part of the genuine faith of the residents of the small town of Tekoa (e.g., Amos 3:3–6; 6:12).[33]

Amos was not "a son of a prophet" (7:14), meaning that he had not been among "the sons of the prophets" (e.g., 2 Ki 2:3–5). He had not been part of a group of disciples (such as Elijah had) gathered around another prophet of Yahweh. Prior to his call into the prophetic ministry, his training had come from field experience—*literally*. Based on the descriptions in his book, Amos probably had seen oak and cedar trees (2:9), what happens to field wagons that bear heavy loads (2:13), how the cattle of Bashan graze in the fields (4:1), and how wadis surge water through barren fields (5:24). During his time in the fields, Amos likely witnessed a lion devouring a lamb (3:12), drought and famine (4:6–8), blight and mildew (4:9), and the devastating effects of locusts (4:9; 7:1).

Although Amos was "from the sticks," his book demonstrates more than just a rural perspective. He was not only at home in the field of labor but also in the field of politics and international events. For example, Amos was familiar with large-scale moral atrocities committed by other countries (1:3–2:3). He was aware of the religious corruption in Israel in cities such as Bethel, Gilgal, and Beersheba (5:5). The prophet even went so far as to directly challenge northern Israel's king, Jeroboam ben Joash, and Amaziah, a leading priest at the idolatrous shrine at Bethel (7:10–17).

---

the charge of treason (7:10) makes no sense if Amos were not a northerner. Hasel considers these arguments but rejects them (*Understanding Amos*, 49–55), as does this commentary.

30 For these dates, see Thiele, *The Mysterious Numbers of the Hebrew Kings*, 96.

31 Polley, *Amos and the Davidic Empire*, 128–31.

32 As noted by Limburg, *Hosea–Micah*, 82.

33 Because of his connection to Tekoa, some suppose that Amos was heavily influenced by Israel's Wisdom tradition (cf. Wolff, *Amos the Prophet*; Limburg, *Hosea–Micah*, 82).

Amos also shows a fascination with houses. His preaching targets fortresses and royal houses (e.g., 1:4, 7, 10, 12, 14; 2:1), luxurious houses (3:15), great houses and little houses (6:11), and ultimately the abomination of the false shrine in northern Israel at Bethel (e.g., 3:14; 4:4; 5:5–6; 7:10, 13), the city whose name means "house of God" (Gen 28:17–19). Yahweh revealed to Amos what went on in these houses. In one vision, he saw Yahweh beside a wall built with a plumb line, illustrating a construction technique used for building these houses (7:7–8). He knew that some houses had furnishings made with ivory (3:15; 6:4) and that lavish feasting and drinking went on and on in some residences (4:1; 6:4–6). These houses—even the most fortified, decorated, luxuriant, and happy—will offer no shelter from Yahweh's judgment (5:19; 6:9).

From field to farm, from politics to parties, Amos' travels also brought him to places of worship. He saw that northern Israel had spurned the merciful God who had redeemed his people through the exodus and who had established his covenant of grace with them. In spite of their numerous songs and offerings (4:4–5; 5:23), they lacked faith in the one true and triune God, and had turned to idols. Much of Israel's religion had become a mechanism for reinforcing the society's status quo (5:21), which was marked with countless shenanigans of corruption, greed, self-indulgence, and violence. Amos includes hymns of praise to God (4:13; 5:7–9; 9:5–6) as evangelical pleas for the people to return to true worship, and also lamentations over the coming judgment for the impenitent (5:1–3, 16–17). Those who attended the places of false worship had their affections set not on Yahweh but on fleecing the poor in the marketplace (8:5–6). Amos knew this truth of history: a highly corrupt society is the result of people forsaking God. The Israelite leaders believed that they could dominate God's people by sheer force; they could have it all and be immune from divine judgment. Amos was compelled by Yahweh (cf. 3:8; 7:15) to preach boldly about this sorry state of affairs.

Somewhere, perhaps in Tekoa, Amos developed considerable skill as a rhetorician. He makes use of the following genres: (1) oracles against the nations (1:3–2:16); (2) graded numerical sayings (e.g., 1:3, 6, 9); (3) woe oracles (5:18; 6:1); (4) laments (5:1–3, 16–17); (5) hymns (4:13; 5:7–9; 9:5–6); (6) a curse formula (7:17); (7) wisdom argumentation from nature (3:3–8); (8) visions (7:1–9; 8:1–3; 9:1–4); (9) narrative (7:10–17); and (10) messianic eschatological promises (9:11–15).[34] Amos also makes effective use of rhetorical techniques and devices including similes (e.g., 2:9b; 5:24; 9:9), metaphors (e.g., 1:2; 2:9c; 6:12), merisms (e.g., 3:12, 15), repetition (4:6–11), and building to a climax (e.g., 1:3–2:16). One frequent technique is to accuse his listeners by quoting their own words (e.g., 2:12; 4:1; 5:14; 6:13; 7:16; 8:5–6, 14). His rhetoric and passion earned him a one-way ticket back to Tekoa (7:12–13). Such is the "reward" for a faithful preacher of God's Word (cf. Lk 4:22–30; 6:22–23)!

---

[34] Sweeney discusses genres of prophetic literature in *The Prophetic Literature*, 33–42. Watts also discusses and defines prophetic genres (*Vision and Prophesy in Amos*, 122–33).

Yet Amos was not a political activist advocating social revolt. Andersen and Freedman write: "In spite of his unremitting attacks on the power elite and bureaucratic establishment in every aspect—commercial, military, judicial, ecclesiastical—Amos never addresses the proletariat (whose just causes he has so much at heart), inciting them to secure for themselves the justice of which they have been deprived."[35] Although Amos does not state it in the following exact terms, his refusal to sanction some kind of "peasants' revolt" is due to the biblical principle that God is the ultimate administrator of justice. Vengeance belongs to Yahweh, and he will repay in his own good time and with exactitude (e.g., Deut 32:35, 41, 43; Is 34:8; 35:4; 63:4; Heb 10:30). God's people are never called to avenge prior wrongs; instead their proper response is to speak God's Word of Law and Gospel and show love and compassion for all (e.g., Ex 23:4–5; Lev 19:18; Rom 12:19–20; 1 Cor 13:5). In Mt 5:22–25, 43–48, Jesus commands God's people to love their brothers and their enemies alike. Heb 12:15 warns the believing baptized against harboring a "root of bitterness."

Amos' association with the small southern village of Tekoa indicates that he was an outsider to the northern Israelite establishment and its recognized leaders. Luther comments about Amos' humble background: "Moreover, God never made prophets out of the high priests or others of lofty station, but usually he raised up lowly and despised persons, even at last the shepherd, Amos."[36]

Luther also writes:

> So also today, to the wise men of the world those things appear to be strange (παράδοξα) which are said and written through the Gospel of Christ against so powerful a kingdom as that of the pope, extolled for so long by saintly men. After all, it is by the pope that kings and princes and all the learned, finally, the whole world, stand. This is what the prophet intends when he calls himself a shepherd of Tekoa. He indicates that both the place and the person are insignificant. This, however, is what the apostle Paul says in 1 Cor. 1:27, that God selected the foolish and weak things of the world to shame the wise and powerful people of the world.[37]

Moses (Ex 2:1–6), Elijah (1 Ki 17:1), and Jeremiah (Jer 1:1) were also prophets called by God from the fringes of society to challenge mainstream religious thinking and practices. Amos stands in this long line of men who were emboldened to preach the need for repentance to the powerful elite and the repressive leaders of their day, and who also proclaimed the eschatological Good News of the Gospel (Amos 9:11–15). This line of OT prophets culminates in the Prophet (Lk 24:19), Jesus of Nazareth (Mt 2:23; Jn 1:46), whom even the demons identify as none other than "the Holy One of God" (Mk 1:24; Lk 4:34), and whom believers acclaim as "our great God and Savior" (Titus 2:13). Jesus chose his apostles and established the office of the public ministry.

---

[35] Andersen and Freedman, *Amos*, 774.

[36] AE 32:9.

[37] "Lectures on Amos," AE 18:129–30.

Throughout the church age, he calls men into the pastoral ministry to continue his summons to repentance, to rebuke and correct, and to proclaim the forgiveness of sins and eternal life to all who believe (Eph 4:11–16; 1 Tim 2:7–3:7; 4:11–6:21; Titus 1:1–14).

Which He Perceived concerning Israel during the Days of Uzziah and Jeroboam

The second subordinate clause in Amos 1:1, introduced by the second relative pronoun אֲשֶׁר, referring back to Amos' "words," begins "which he saw/perceived." Amos' entire prophetic book could be called a divine "vision" in the broad sense (as in Is 1:1; Obad 1; Nah 1:1), making it appropriate for him to say that he "saw" the divine "words" revealed to him. In the narrower sense, however, the verb "saw" points to a central theological thrust of the book and the determinative factors that shaped Amos' ministry: his five visions (7:1–3; 7:4–6; 7:7–9; 8:1–3; 9:1–4).[38]

Dating "the days of Uzziah the king of Judah" and "the days of Jeroboam ben Joash the king of Israel" (1:2) is fraught with difficulty.[39] Thiele dates Uzziah's reign from 792 to 740 BC and Jeroboam ben Joash's from 793 to 753 BC.[40] Most scholars locate the prophetic career of Amos within the decade 765–755 BC.[41] One exception is Hayes, who dates the ministry of Amos to 750 BC.[42] It is safe, therefore, to place Amos' ministry in the first half of the eighth century BC.[43]

Amos places the Judahite king Uzziah first, before the northern king Jeroboam ben Joash, and in this way subtly states that Yahweh's Messiah will come from the tribe of Judah (Gen 49:8–12) and not from the seceded Northern Kingdom. 1 Sam 17:12 indicates that David was a Judahite. It was through the line of Judah and David and Uzziah, as well as many other southern kings (see

---

38 Watts is credited with the insight that Amos' visions in chapters 7–9 signal the different stages of the prophet's mission (*Vision and Prophecy in Amos*, 59–89).

39 Compare the general discussion of problems in establishing regnal chronology in Bright, *A History of Israel*, 229, n. 1. See also Thiele, *The Mysterious Numbers of the Hebrew Kings*.

40 Thiele, *The Mysterious Numbers of the Hebrew Kings*, 116, 118. Bright gives Uzziah's dates as 783–742 BC and Jeroboam ben Joash's dates as 786–746 BC (*A History of Israel*, 492).

41 Smith coordinates Yadin's dating of an earthquake in Israel in about 760 BC with the reference in 1:1 (*Amos*, 13, including n. 1, citing Yadin et al., *Hazor II*, 24–26, 36–37). Rosenbaum concludes that Amos prophesied circa 760 BC, plus or minus five years (*Amos of Israel*, 27). Andersen and Freedman, believing that Amos' ministry may have lasted more than a year, date it to the decade 765–755 BC (*Amos*, 19).

42 Hayes, *Amos, the Eighth-Century Prophet*, 38 (see also pp. 26–27, 45–47). Hayes pinpoints Amos' preaching at Bethel to a day or at the most a few days "just prior to the fall festival beginning the year 750–749" (p. 38).

43 Andersen and Freedman write: "These two kings enjoyed very long reigns, exceptional for those times: Uzziah ruled for fifty-two years and Jeroboam for forty-one, each setting a record for his kingdom up to that time" (*Amos*, 18–19). In spite of their lengthy reigns, the OT does not provide much detail on their lives. For Uzziah (Azariah), see 2 Ki 14:21–22; 15:1–7; 2 Chronicles 26. Regarding Jeroboam ben Joash, see 2 Ki 14:23–29.

Mt 1:6–16), that Jesus came into the world as Israel's final and perfect King (see, e.g., Is 9:1–6 [ET 9:2–7]; 11:1–9; Jer 23:5; Hos 3:5; Rom 1:3; Heb 7:14). He was born in the city of David, the "Bethlehem in the land of Judah" (Mt 2:6; see Micah 5:1 [ET 5:2]; Mt 2:1–16), and he brought the eternal kingdom of God/heaven (e.g., Mt 4:17; 5:3; 12:28), fulfilling the prophetic promise (e.g., Dan 2:44–45; 7:13–14, 22, 27).

Jeroboam ben Joash shares the name of the Northern Kingdom's apostate first king, Jeroboam ben Nebat. Because of Solomon's idolatry, God granted the ten northern tribes to Jeroboam ben Nebat while still affirming his messianic promise to the line of David and Jerusalem (1 Ki 11:29–39). However, Jeroboam ben Nebat did not remain faithful to Yahweh, but instead erected idolatrous temples at Dan and Bethel (1 Ki 12:25–33). By promoting these false alternatives to God's dwelling place in the temple on Mount Zion, Jeroboam ben Nebat became "a religious schismatic (against the Jerusalem Cult) and a theological heretic (against the truth of God)."[44] It comes as no surprise, then, that God, speaking through the Judean prophet Amos, is diametrically opposed to everything that proceeds out of the northern monarchy and the northern centers of idolatrous worship. Amos condemns Bethel often (3:14; 4:4; 5:5–6; and implicitly in 7:10, 13).

In other ancient Near Eastern countries, kings were the supreme and final authorities in the land, considered to be the personal representatives of their gods. But according to Deut 17:14–20, Israel's kings were subject to the highest authority, Yahweh, who expressed his will in the Torah, which the king was to read and obey throughout his life.[45] Although Uzziah (sometimes called Azariah in 2 Kings) committed one major transgression during his reign (2 Chr 26:16–21), he received the overall commendation that "he did what was right in the eyes of Yahweh" (2 Ki 15:3 || 2 Chr 26:4; see also 2 Ki 15:34 || 2 Chr 27:2). However, Jeroboam ben Joash received the opposite condemnation: "he did what was evil in the eyes of Yahweh. He did not turn away from all the sins of Jeroboam ben Nebat, who caused Israel to sin" (2 Ki 14:24).

"Two Years before the Earthquake"

The last part of Amos 1:1 mentions that Amos' ministry and writing ended "two years before the earthquake." This could mean "the earthquake predicted by Amos,"[46] which took place two years after he ceased receiving and recording visions from Yahweh. Amos 9:1–4, the fifth and last in the series of visions in chapters 7–9, begins with a prediction in which Yahweh commands the striking of the temple so that even the thresholds "shake, quake," using the verb that

---

44 Motyer, *The Message of Amos*, 86. "The sin(s) of Jeroboam (ben Nebat)" is an ongoing refrain in 1 and 2 Kings. 2 Ki 17:1–18 indicates that the Northern Kingdom fell to the Assyrian Empire (in 722 BC) in large part due to idolatry, including Jeroboam ben Nebat's decision to cast metal "images of two calves" (2 Ki 17:16).

45 Cf. Block, *The Gods of the Nations*, 21–33.

46 Andersen and Freedman, *Amos*, 194.

is cognate to the noun for "earthquake" in 1:1. This was the last of the prophet's visions chronologically, and he received it shortly before his ministry came to an end. The time between the conclusion of his preaching and this earthquake was relatively short: only two years. This earthquake vindicated Amos' ministry and demonstrated that he was indeed Yahweh's prophet, since it fulfilled the criterion for true prophecy given through Moses (Deut 18:21–22). While Amos might have added the superscription after the earthquake occurred, it is also possible that at the conclusion of his ministry, he added the superscription under divine inspiration to predict the earthquake that subsequently took place at that time.

Amos' reference to "the earthquake" contains geographical, historical, theological, and literary significance. Geographically, Israel is located along the Great Rift Valley that extends from northern Syria along the course of the Jordan River to the Dead Sea and into the Arabah (and beyond into Africa), making earthquakes common (e.g., 1 Sam 14:15; 1 Ki 19:11; cf. Mt 24:7; 27:51–53). Historically, most scholars believe this particular earthquake is the one attested in stratum VI of Hazor and dated to around 760 BC.[47] Earthquakes have occurred throughout Israel's history, so this one, "*the* earthquake," must have been extremely severe and noteworthy.

Theological significance was attributed to this earthquake three centuries later by the prophet Zechariah. Writing in the fifth century BC, he referred to it and the ensuing panic as a type of the fearful day of Yahweh's coming: "You shall flee as you fled from the earthquake in the days of Uzziah king of Judah. Then Yahweh my God will come and all holy ones with him" (Zech 14:5). This typological significance makes it likely that the earthquake "was interpreted as a fulfillment of some of his [Amos'] prophetic oracles" and "most probably authenticated his being accepted as a true prophet."[48] Amos met the biblical qualifications for being a true prophet (Deut 18:18–22; Jer 28:9; Ezek 12:21–28) because his prophetic vision of a temple-shattering quake in Amos 9:1 was followed by Yahweh's definitive action two years later. Then after about four more decades, his prophecies of judgment against northern Israel were fulfilled when God allowed the Assyrians to destroy the Northern Kingdom in 722 BC.[49]

---

[47] See Yadin et al., *Hazor II*, 24–26, 36–37. Yohanan Aharoni, an excavator of Beersheba, conjectures that the destruction of stratum III of that city may have been triggered by the same earthquake (as noted by King, *Amos, Hosea, Micah*, 21). See page 22 for an artist's rendering of the evidence of this earthquake at Hazor.

[48] Paul, *Amos*, 36.

[49] Isaiah, writing only decades after Amos, also incorporated the earthquake motif. Is 2:10–21 states that everything tall—trees, mountains, towers, ships, and the haughtiness of people—will be brought low. The theme continues in Is 13:13; 24:18–20; 29:6. Is 5:25 appears to be an indirect reference to Amos 1:1, while Is 6:4 may reflect Amos 9:1. After Amos and Isaiah, the earthquake motif became common in prophetic literature (e.g., Jer 4:23–26; Ezek 38:17–20; Nah 1:5; Hag 2:6–7). Freedman and Welch propose, "The convergence and coincidence of the earthquake's time, place, and magnitude with Amos's prediction combined to make an indelible impression on the prophetic community and its audience, and thus instigated the corpus

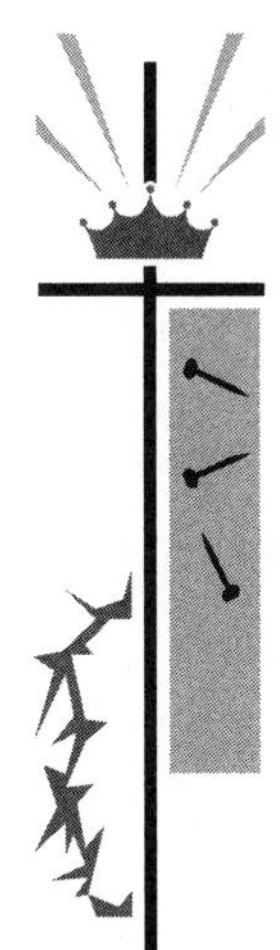

Theologically, the quake in 1:1 may also have had Gospel significance as a sign that God would fulfill his messianic promises in Amos, which center on the resurrection of David's tabernacle (9:11–15). Seismic shocks are often interpreted in the Bible as manifestations of Yahweh's presence (e.g., Ex 19:18; Hab 3:6; Ps 29:6). They will accompany Yahweh when he comes in the future, climactically in Jesus Christ.[a] In a vision, Ezekiel saw that the reassembly of dry bones and their resurrection were accompanied by the sound of an "earthquake" (רַעַשׁ, Ezek 37:7). This was fulfilled in a preliminary way by the resurrection of dead saints signaled by the earthquake upon the death of Christ (Mt 27:51–53; cf. Ezek 37:12; Jn 5:25; 11:43–44) and by the earthquake at Christ's own resurrection (Mt 28:2; cf. Acts 16:26). It will be fulfilled universally at the return of Christ, when all the dead shall be raised—believers to eternal life and unbelievers to everlasting judgment (Dan 12:2–3; Jn 5:28–29; compare Zech 14:5 to the descriptions of Christ's second advent in 1 Thess 4:16–17 and Rev 6:12–17).

(a) Is 29:6; Joel 4:16 (ET 3:16); Hag 2:20–22; Heb 12:26–27; Rev 6:12; 16:18

Literarily, this record of the earthquake provides a major theme throughout the book of Amos. The motif of the earthquake is most prominent in the fifth vision (9:1–4), where the verb רָעַשׁ, "quake, shake," appears (9:1). An earthquake is also implied in other Amos passages. Yahweh will punish (פָּקַד) the altars of Bethel and strike (Hiphil of נָכָה) the royal houses (3:13–15). Yahweh overturned (הָפַךְ) a part of Israel like he overturned Sodom and Gomorrah (4:11). Yahweh will strike (Hiphil of נָכָה) all of Israel's houses (6:11). The land will shake (רָגַז, 8:8). The earth will tremble (רָגַז) and rise and fall like the flooding and receding Nile (8:8; 9:5). While Yahweh brings fire on both Israel and the nations (chapters 1–2; 5:6; 7:4), in Amos he reserves earthquakes exclusively for Israel.

Summary of Amos 1:1

The divine message from Yahweh through Amos to Israel and the nations burst into space and time at a particular moment in history. Since the book is culturally and geographically specific (1:1), we must not universalize Amos' contents in a simplistic fashion, e.g., to justify liberation theology, which encourages the church to replace her ministry of Word and Sacrament with a social or political agenda.[50] Local contexts (Tekoa, Israel, Judah) and real-life situations (the days of Uzziah and Jeroboam ben Joash; the earthquake) are the particularities of this divine-human drama, as well as the proper context for its interpretation. This message of Law and Gospel will first condemn unbelief, infidelity, and idolatry, which were evident in Israel and perpetuated by Jeroboam. Yet Uzziah, a son of David, still reigned in Jerusalem, connecting 1:1 to the book's concluding promise that God will resurrect the tabernacle of David

---

of prophetic literature in the Hebrew Bible. It literally began with a Big Bang!" ("Amos's Earthquake and Israelite Prophecy," 197).

50 Stulman writes: "To extricate the message from its local context is to do violence to the essence of prophecy" (*Jeremiah*, 193).

(9:11–15). The earthquake attests the veracity of the book at the same time that it anticipates the future Day of Yahweh, when he shall come and reveal himself in the fullness of his majesty. Then all unbelievers shall be condemned and all believers in the Son of David will be raised to everlasting life.

Amos 1:2

This verse reflects "the motif of the manifestation of the Deity and the resultant catastrophic effects upon the cosmos and nature."[51] Texts with this motif have two parts: (1) a description of Yahweh and (2) a description of the accompanying upheavals in creation such as drought, fire, and/or earthquake.[52] Nah 1:3–5 vividly illustrates this motif. It includes two noteworthy verbs. "Dries it up" translates a different form of the verb translated as "withers" in Amos 1:2, and "quake" translates a verb cognate to the noun for "earthquake" in Amos 1:1:

> [Yahweh] travels in a whirlwind and storm. … He rebukes the sea and dries it up [וַיַּבְּשֵׁהוּ], and he makes all rivers fail; Bashan and Carmel languish, and the blossoms of Lebanon wither. The mountains quake [רָעֲשׁוּ] because of him, and the hills melt. The earth heaves before him, the world and all that dwell therein.[53]

Yahweh's roaring has effects that reach from Jerusalem to as far north as Mount Carmel. This is a fitting prelude to a message from Amos, whose mission is directed mostly against the Northern Kingdom, but who does not neglect the Southern Kingdom of Judah (2:4–5), and who includes surrounding pagan nations in 1:3–2:3.

In 1:2 the theophany depicts Yahweh as a roaring Lion, which is just the opposite of his "still small voice" spoken to Elijah (1 Ki 19:12).[54] The verse is often referred to as the theme of the book and a prelude to Amos' message, in much the same way as Jer 1:10 functions as the essence of the judgment and

---

[51] Paul, *Amos*, 38.

[52] Cf. Sweeney, *Isaiah 1–39*, 541.

[53] This translation is that of Paul (*Amos*, 38). See also, for example, Deut 33:2; Judg 5:4–5; 2 Sam 22:8; Is 24:18–20; Micah 1:3–4; Joel 2:1–3; 4:14–15 (ET 3:14–15); Hab 3:3–12; Ps 18:10–11 (ET 18:9–10); 68:34 (ET 68:33); 104:3. In Is 19:1, the prophet sees Yahweh riding on a swift cloud to Egypt; the vision expresses Yahweh's sovereign power over nature as well as over the Egyptian pantheon of gods.

[54] Heschel writes: "Most of us who care for the world bewail God's dreadful silence, while Amos appears smitten by God's mighty voice. He did not hear a whisper, 'a still small voice,' but a voice like a lion's roaring that drives shepherd and flock into panic" (*The Prophets*, 29). Egyptian iconography also employs lion imagery to demonstrate both royal and divine power. For example, one portrait of Ramses III depicts him with the head of a lion and describes him as "the lion, the lord of victory, concealed, going forward, and making a conquest—his heart is full of might" (Gardiner, *The Kadesh Inscriptions of Ramesses II*, no. R 2).

restoration proclaimed by Jeremiah. Thus Amos 1:2 introduces the prophet's message and sets the tone for the entire book.[55]

Whereas 1:1 titles the book "the words of Amos," the first words in 1:2, "Yahweh from Zion roars," assert the claim that Yahweh inspired and authorized the whole prophetic book. This combination of the divine author and his chosen human author indicates that Amos did not write by his own initiative; rather, he was led by the Spirit of Christ to record the very words of God that center in "the sufferings of Christ and, after these things, the glories" (1 Pet 1:11; cf. Amos 9:11–15; 2 Pet 1:19–21). Because "the words of Amos" (Amos 1:1) are Yahweh's words, the book is free from human error, and in its entirety it is the efficacious truth of God.[56] At the same time, Amos was not merely God's keyboard or animated computer drive, with no personal involvement in what he spoke or wrote. Amos was inspired to write within the fullness of his historical context, utilizing his language facilities, personality, and experiences.

The book of Amos is thus a collage of oracles, narratives, visions, and prayers, all covered by the transcendent claim of 1:2, that is, they all are inspired by the God of Israel, and all reach their goal in Jesus Christ. The source of Amos' speech is neither the Israelite establishment nor any other human agency. His book is no mere human artifact. Yahweh authorized Amos to present in word and action his will for Israel, Judah, the nations, and all peoples. Given the competing ideology that comes from the priest at Bethel, appealing to the king of northern Israel (7:10–17), this assertion regarding Amos' authority is critical. Thus 1:2 can be compared to the way St. Paul begins his epistles by asserting his authority as an apostle who was called by Christ himself and who is speaking on his behalf (e.g., Rom 1:1; 1 Cor 1:1).

As much as 1:1 tells us about the life and times of Amos, the first Hebrew word he utters in 1:2 is "Yahweh," the personal name of Israel's God. This indicates that *Yahweh*—not Amos nor anyone else—is the book's main focus.

Dempster has analyzed the use of "Yahweh" and divine titles in Amos. In the MT of Amos, ten different titles or combinations of a title with the Tetragrammaton are used to refer to Israel's God. The total number of occurrences of these is eighty-six. "Yahweh" appears eighty-one times in the book,

---

[55] Andersen and Freedman, *Amos*, 341, write of Amos 1:2:

> While the couplet of two bicola leads into the great oracle against the nations including Israel or against Israel among the nations, it also serves as an introduction to the whole work. It serves a dual purpose, being at once an introductory part of the prophecy that follows and a suitable exordium for the work as a whole.

Wolff likewise maintains: "It seems appropriately to have been placed at the head of the book as a motto summarizing the message of the prophet" (*Joel and Amos,* 119).

[56] Ferreiro writes:

> The beauty and fluidity of Amos's language is captivating. This alone caused Augustine to point out that Amos, whom he believed to be but a rustic shepherd without any formal training, could have expressed himself with sophisticated human language only under the inspiration of the Holy Spirit. (*The Twelve Prophets*, ACCS 14:83)

fifty-two times alone and twenty-nine times in conjunction with one of the titles. Only five times is God referred to by a title not in combination with the Tetragrammaton: three times as אֲדֹנָי, "Lord" (7:7–8; 9:1), and twice as אֱלֹהִים, "God" (4:11–12).[57] This is, therefore, a book about the God who established his gracious covenant with Israel, whose name is *Yahweh.* Each of the three doxological hymns (4:13; 5:8–9; 9:5–6) celebrates this fact with the words יְהוָה שְׁמוֹ, "Yahweh is his name" (4:13; 5:8; 9:6).

Just as the earthquake motif pervades the book of Amos (see "Two Years before the Earthquake" in the commentary on 1:1), so does lion imagery. Leonine references or allusions to Yahweh use the verb "roar" (שָׁאַג, 1:2; 3:4, 8) and nouns for "lion" (אַרְיֵה in 3:4, 8 and the synonym אֲרִי in 3:12; 5:19). As a herdsman, Amos heard the lion's roar when it caught its prey; he witnessed what a lion can do to its victim (3:4, 12). The automatic response upon hearing a lion's roar is sheer terror (3:8). When a lion comes near the only logical response is to flee to safety immediately (5:19). The imagery of Yahweh as a Lion in the book of Amos indicates that the curse of harm from wild animals, which was part of the covenant of Moses (Lev 26:22; Deut 32:24), will be carried out by Yahweh himself upon his unfaithful people who have broken the Mosaic covenant.

As such, *Yahweh's words have teeth in them.* He is an undomesticated Deity who is powerful enough to shatter all of Israel's conventional categories and systems of control (e.g., Amos 7:8–17). Yahweh intrudes into Israel's settled existence in unsettling ways. He comes to afflict the comfortable and hold them accountable because of their loveless actions toward the poor and needy. To become mesmerized with the evils of this present age and with its prince of darkness is to become blind to a much greater destructive entity: *Lion Yahweh.*

Several texts depict the lion as one of the most ferocious animals in Israel. 1 Kings 13 is a narrative about a prophet ripped apart by a lion as he was traveling on the road from Bethel to Judah. 1 Ki 20:35–36 is an account about another prophet killed by a lion. The presence of lions in eighth-century Samaria is also indicated by 2 Ki 17:25. The proverb writer calls the lion "the mightiest among the beasts" (Prov 30:30). Daniel, Peter, and John use the animal in their writings to denote terrifying power (Dan 7:1–4; 1 Pet 5:8; Rev 13:2).

However, in the new creation, lions will be tame (Is 11:6–7) or they and other vicious beasts will be completely absent (Is 35:9). And—in a different use of the motif—because a lion is the symbol for the tribe of Judah (Gen 49:8–12), Jesus the Savior is called "the Lion of the tribe of Judah" because he "has triumphed" over all enemies, both his and ours (Rev 5:5).

Joel 4:16a–b (ET 3:16a–b) is virtually identical to Amos 1:2b–c.[58] However, in many ways the two passages stand in contrast. In Joel, Yahweh roars toward

---

[57] Dempster, "The Lord Is His Name," 175.

[58] Since Amos 1:2b–c corresponds almost exactly with Joel 4:16a–b (ET 3:16a–b), the clauses could be part of broader prophetic language (cf. Jer 25:30b–c). This prophetic description

the end of the book. The setting seems to be the second coming of Christ (compare Joel 4:15 [ET 3:15] to Mt 24:29; Rev 6:12–13) to judge all unbelievers. The roaring of Yahweh occurs in "the Valley of Jehoshaphat [יְהוֹשָׁפָט, 'Yahweh judges']" (Joel 4:12 [ET 3:12]) when he will judge all the hostile, unbelieving nations. At the same time, he will save his people and transform creation to be miraculously abundant (Joel 4:16–18 [ET 3:16–18]; cf. Amos 9:11–15). In Amos, Yahweh roars at the beginning of the book. Creation withers. He roars not only against the nations, but especially against his own people, who have become like the idolatrous nations. Their judgment is imminent, as demonstrated by the earthquake only two years later (Amos 1:1). Northern Israel would fall only three or four decades after Amos preached.

In short, Yahweh's roar in Joel 4:16 (ET 3:16) is in a Gospel context of final deliverance to eternal life for God's faithful people, whereas in Amos 1:2, Yahweh's roar portends for God's unfaithful people the swift execution of judgment according to his Law (yet not without the Gospel promise at the conclusion of the book). Luther writes:

> It is metaphor then—or allegory, rather—when he says, "The Lord will roar." By this he signifies the great wrath and threat of God. It is as if he were saying: "The Lord, who is from Zion, who lives in Zion, or resides in Jerusalem—that Lord will roar. He is angry. He will stiffen His mane like an angry lion. Watch out! He is threatening you with destruction. For no matter how much you may hold Him in contempt, yet He is warning that He will devour you all. Moreover, for this devouring of you, He will use the teeth and throat of the Assyrians. This will happen to all of you unless you repent, etc."[59]

Yahweh's roaring comes from Mount Zion, which was in the southern tribe of Judah and in the city of Jerusalem—the temple mount.[60] This is the second subtle attack against the Northern Kingdom's claims that Yahweh was in their midst (1 Ki 12:28–30).[61] (The first was the placement of Uzziah before Jeroboam ben Joash in Amos 1:1.) In other theophanies, Yahweh speaks his

---

of Yahweh recalls the earlier image of him in the Torah of Moses as a warrior God (e.g., Ex 15:3).

59 "Lectures on Amos," AE 18:130–31.

60 Andersen and Freedman propose: "The identification of Zion//Jerusalem as the source of the prophecies that follow suggests further that this place is also where Amos received them" (*Amos*, 223). Understood this way, Amos may have had an experience similar to that of Isaiah (see Isaiah 6). Yahweh took up his dwelling in Zion after David brought the ark of the covenant to Jerusalem (2 Samuel 6–7) and Solomon built and dedicated the temple (1 Kings 8). Various Zion psalms affirm his dwelling place there (e.g., Psalms 46–48; 99). In the NT, God's promises are located in Jesus Christ (2 Cor 1:21). He is Immanuel, "God with us" (Mt 1:23), the new temple (Jn 2:19–22), and through him alone baptized believers have access to the Father and his throne of grace (Jn 14:6; Rom 5:2; Eph 2:18; Heb 10:19–20). Luke tells us that God initiated his plan of salvation in Christ at Jerusalem (Lk 1:8–17), and after Christ's death and resurrection there his Gospel would spread from Jerusalem to the entire world (Lk 24:46–53; Acts 1:8).

61 Sweeney, *The Twelve Prophets*, 200, writes:

"voice" (קוֹל) from above the ark of the covenant (Num 7:89), in the temple (Is 6:8), from atop Sinai (Deut 4:12, 33; 5:24; cf. 1 Ki 19:13), and from the heavens (2 Sam 22:14; see also Mt 3:17; Jn 12:28; Acts 11:9; 2 Pet 1:18; Rev 12:10; 14:13). In Jer 25:30, he "will roar" from on high and "utter his voice" from his holy habitation (his earthly or heavenly temple). Only in Amos 1:2 and Joel 4:16 (ET 3:16) does Yahweh roar from Zion and utter his "voice from Jerusalem."

The "voice" (קוֹל) of Yahweh, here issuing forth from the Jerusalem temple, is often associated with thunder (e.g., Ps 29:3–5, 7–9). But this thundering in Amos 1:2 ironically brings no rain; instead it inflicts drought and disaster, which are part of Yahweh's covenant curses upon Israel when they would break the divine covenant (Deut 28:15, 22–24; see also Is 5:6; 19:7; 42:15; Nah 1:3–5).[62] Yahweh, not the Canaanite god of fertility and rain—Hadad, also known as Baal, sometimes depicted with a bolt of lightning—controls the land (cf. Amos 8:14).[63] The earth belongs to Yahweh (Ps 24:1), and he controls its natural disasters. Yahweh also initiates a drought in Amos 4:6–8 and threatens one in 7:4–6. The result of Yahweh's theophany is that the pastures of the shepherds mourn because their flocks have died from the drought.[64] This drought is so extensive that it brings devastation to the pastures of the shepherds *and* to Mount Carmel, a sign of eschatological proportions. "It is the task of the book of Amos to proclaim such an end. … The end is always viewed as the consequence of the terrifying voice of Yahweh."[65]

Amos is not just using figurative language when he refers to the mourning of the land.[66] Rather, he is indicating that Yahweh has a relationship with the entire creation—the earth as well as the people inhabiting it (cf. Psalms

---

> Insofar as Amos calls for the destruction of the Beth El Temple, i.e., the royal temple of the northern kingdom of Israel (9:1–10), the death of Jeroboam ben Joash (7:10–17), and the restoration of the "fallen hut of David," he calls for the reunification of the entire nation Israel around YHWH's Jerusalem and the Davidic monarchy.

62 Yahweh's storm theophany is portrayed extensively in Ps 18:8–16 (ET 18:7–15).

63 Simkins, *Creator and Creation: Nature in the Worldview of Ancient Israel*, traces both the OT and the ancient Near Eastern ideas of how deities control nature.

64 Often in the OT, nature is anthropomorphized as rejoicing, lamenting, celebrating, and the like. For example Ps 98:7–8 states: "Let the sea thunder, and its fullness, the world, and those who live in it. Let the rivers clap their hands; let the mountains sing together for joy" (cf., e.g., Is 55:12). These texts are not poetic license, for just as the creation groans because of the curse of sin (Gen 3:17; Rom 8:19–22), it will rejoice when Christ comes again to make all things new (Ps 96:12–13; Rev 21:5).

65 Wolff, *Joel and Amos*, 125.

66 Andersen and Freedman, *Amos*, 229, write:

> This literary technique [poising statements between the actual and the figurative] is worth emphasizing at the beginning of our study, because it is characteristic of Amos' craftsmanship throughout the entire book. It is grounded in his visionary experiences, but it is always in contact with the phenomenal world. The prophet as visionary is not interested in a transcendental world, inaccessible to the rest of us.

24; 104; 147–150).[67] The theological order directly impacts the cosmic order. Just as Adam's sin brought decay and death on the entire creation (Genesis 3; Rom 8:18–22), so too the sin of Israel provokes the judgment of Yahweh that has negative effects on the land. The natural life-sustaining processes of creation are reversed so that chaos and death ensue. The land's beauty and order are threatened and become marred throughout the book of Amos (e.g., 4:6–11; 5:16–17; 7:1–6). Yet Yahweh also promises to raise the tabernacle of David (9:11) through the Savior, whose death and resurrection will reconcile heaven and earth. Only he is able to save people from everlasting destruction and bring about a new creation (9:13–15). Jesus, Son of David and Son of God, came and finished his mission to redeem humanity and secure a new created order (Jn 19:30). What believers have in Christ already now by promise will be brought to completion and fully realized on the Last Day (1 Cor 15:24–28; Phil 1:6; Revelation 21–22).

See also the excursus "The Land."

Summary of Amos 1:1–2

Just as the first verse identifies Amos and his context in space (Tekoa) and time (the days of Uzziah and Jeroboam ben Joash), the second verse identifies the impetus for the book and its ultimate Author. Amos heard the voice of Yahweh and compared his experience to hearing a lion roar, a roaring that causes pastures to mourn and forests to wither. Everything that follows in the book needs to be heard with this roaring in the background. Amos will personally encounter Yahweh as a Lion (3:4, 8), and this in turn will lead to Israel's encounter with Lion Yahweh (3:12; 5:19). Throughout the book, Yahweh appears as the roaring Lion looking to devour the pagan nations, Judah, and Israel. What set off this divine roaring? Amos 1:3–2:16 provides the answer to that question.

Even though this main theme is of God's terrifying and impending judgment, the Gospel is already latent in 1:1–2, and it will be developed more fully in 9:11–15. The earthquake (1:1) portends the ones at Christ's death and resurrection (Mt 27:51–54; 28:2) and at the end of the world (Rev 16:18). Amos places the Judean king Uzziah before the Israelite king Jeroboam ben Joash, and God's roar issues forth from Zion and Jerusalem, not from the apostate northern sanctuaries at Bethel and Dan. The preference for southern kings and the Jerusalem temple has messianic implications. Amos' hope is Yahweh's promise to resurrect the tabernacle of David (9:11), gather all people called by his name (9:12), and transform the withered creation (1:2) into a new Eden (9:13–15).

---

[67] Fretheim puts it this way: "The world could be imaged as a giant spiderweb. Every creature is in relationship with every other, such that any act reverberates out and affects the whole, shaking the entire web in varying degrees of intensity" (*God and World in the Old Testament*, 173). Compare, for example, Is 24:5; Jer 2:12; 14:4.

Excursus

Hebrew Poetry

The book of Amos, like most prophetic books, is composed mostly in poetry.[1] Amos was a man called by Yahweh and sent to speak Yahweh's words with poetic passion. His inspired book consists mostly of poetry, except for a few prose verses, including the superscription (1:1) and the narrative account of his confrontation with the apostate priest Amaziah (7:10–17; see also 6:10; 7:1–6). Paying attention to the poetic nature of Amos' oracles is not an exercise in aesthetics without interpretive value. Rather, a proper understanding of the prophet's poetry is at the heart of a proper exegetical process. Alter maintains: "We need to read this [Hebrew] poetry well because it is not merely a means of heightening or dramatizing the religious perceptions of the biblical writers."[2] Instead, since the Scriptures are the *ipsissima verba*, the "very words" of God, we must comprehend their poetic style in order to discern their true message of judgment and salvation as it applied to ancient Israel and as it applies to us today.

The most dominant feature of Hebrew poetry is parallelism, which is defined as "the presence of several poetic lines of a roughly comparable length that stand in a semantic relationship."[3] One typical set of two pairs of lines comes from Amos 1:2:

> Yahweh from Zion roars,
>   and from Jerusalem he utters his voice.
> The pastures of the shepherds mourn,
>   and the peak of Carmel withers.

Bishop Robert Lowth (1710–1787) called attention to what he termed *parallelismus membrorum*, that is, the correspondence of parallel lines and words in Hebrew poetry.[4] In 1981 Kugel broadened the understanding of parallelism. He expresses Hebrew poetic structures in a more helpful way by means of his formula "A, and what's more, B."[5] The second line intensifies and defines more

---

[1] For an overview of the history of the study of OT poetry, see Bartelt, *The Book around Immanuel*, 1–10, and Boadt, "Reflections on the Study of Hebrew Poetry Today." Boadt writes: "We might take a cue from ancient Biblical Hebrew itself, in which there is no one word that stands for 'poetry' as such over against 'prose.' There are words for many kinds of poems and songs, but these names do not always help identify the poetic vis-à-vis prose" ("Reflections on the Study of Hebrew Poetry Today," 157).

[2] Alter, "The Characteristics of Ancient Hebrew Poetry," 623.

[3] Petersen, *The Prophetic Literature*, 25.

[4] Lowth's standard work is *De sacra poesi Hebraeorum*, first published in Latin in 1753 (trans. G. Gregory, *Lectures on the Sacred Poetry of the Hebrews* [London: Tegg, 1835]).

[5] Kugel, *The Idea of Biblical Poetry*, 42 (see pp. 40–45). Alter writes: "Now, the greatest stumbling block in approaching biblical poetry has been the misconception that parallelism implies

specifically what is stated in the first; it does not merely repeat it. There is progression from line A to line B. The major focus of thought is not just line A, but the sum total of lines A and B together.

In the case of Amos 1:2, the words "roars" and "utters his voice" could be interpreted as standing in synonymous parallelism, as could "the pastures of the shepherds" and "the peak of Carmel." Yet the heart of the relationship between these lines involves more than redundant repetition. There is more going on. Employing Kugel's understanding of Hebrew poetry, the first pair of lines in Amos 1:2 not only equates Yahweh's roar with his uttered Word, but announces that Yahweh's roaring Word comes from Zion, the site of Solomon's temple in Jerusalem. That is where he dwells and speaks, not at any of the idolatrous shrines in northern Israel.

The idea of repetition with intensity also assists in the interpretation of the second pair of lines in Amos 1:2. Not only will the shepherds' pastures mourn, but one of the most fertile locales in all Israel, the peak of Mount Carmel, will dry up. This mountain catches rain from the Mediterranean Sea, making it an ideal place for lush vegetation (cf., e.g., Is 35:2; Amos 9:3). Yahweh's Word has the performative power to unleash a drought even upon Carmel!

Amos 1:2, then, announces two major themes of the book. Yahweh's roaring Word issues forth from Jerusalem, not the shrine at Bethel (which Amos denounces in 3:14; 4:4; 5:5–6; 7:10–17; 9:1–4), and this Word will bring about massive destruction to all of northern Israel's farmlands (cf. 4:6–11; 5:16–17; 7:1–6), even Carmel, the most fecund.

As he did for many of Israel's authors, Yahweh inspired Amos to employ poetry in order for his message to be more persuasive. But how is poetry different from prose? Lichtenstein claims that the power of biblical poetry lies in "its particular genius for effecting the direct, immediate involvement of its audience in a kind of emotional dialogue with both its form and content."[6] Poetry was the most frequent medium for the prophets due to its "powerful voice" in proclaiming Yahweh's message publicly; it "spoke more eloquently to the issue."[7] Freedman writes:

> The form and style, the selection and order of words, all play a vital role in conveying content, meaning, and feeling. In poetry, the medium and message are inseparably intertwined to produce multiple effects at different levels of discourse and evoke a whole range of responses: intellectual, emotional, and spiritual.[8]

---

synonymity, saying the same thing twice in different words" ("The Characteristics of Ancient Hebrew Poetry," 615). Like Kugel, in this article, Alter interprets Hebrew poetry along the lines of intensification, progression, and focusing.

6 Lichtenstein, "Biblical Poetry," 120.

7 Osborne, *The Hermeneutical Spiral*, 216.

8 Freedman, *Pottery, Poetry, and Prophecy*, 1–2.

Hence a major function of prophetic poetry is persuasion. Through it, the Holy Spirit works to influence and change people. Some of the same points about rhetoric made in this commentary's introduction[9] also pertain to the prophetic use of poetry. The miracle of divine inspiration, by which the prophet declares, "Thus says Yahweh" (e.g., 1:3), also engages the mind and creative faculties of the prophet, allowing him maximum use of his own rhetorical and literary talents as a preacher and poet. Thus the carefully articulated "words of Amos" (1:1) in memorable, compelling, persuasive poetic verse are, at the same time, "the words of Yahweh" (8:11).

The poetic mode of prophetic speech is not accidental to the prophetic office, but rather, as Brueggemann notes, "part of the strategy for letting the live word make a difference in historical reality."[10] Brueggemann continues:

> The shattering and forming of worlds is not done as a potter molds clay or as a factory makes products. It is done as a poet "redescribes" the world, reconfigures public perception, and causes people to reexperience their experience. To do that requires that speech must not be conventional, reasonable, predictable; it must shock sensitivity, call attention to what is not noticed, break the routine, cause people to redescribe things that have long since seem settled, bear surpluses of power before routine assessments.[11]

Another example of how Hebrew poetry works in Amos comes from 2:6d–8, where the prophet employs poetic parallelism to develop several powerful images:

> ... because they sell the righteous for silver
> and the needy for a pair of sandals.
> They trample the poorest of the poor into the dust of the earth,
> and they twist the way of the oppressed.
> And each man and his father go to the young woman,
> so that they defile my holy name.
> Upon seized garments they stretch themselves out
> beside every altar.
> They drink wine obtained through fines
> in the temple of their gods.

These pairs of parallel lines or sentences provide a catalog of sins. The basic order is social, economic, sexual, and finally liturgical sins. As lines of poetry, they communicate more than just a list. Rather, this catalog contains a "narrative movement" that climaxes at the end.[12] The implied locations of

---

[9] See "Rhetorical Analysis" and "Conclusions" in "Different Methods of Interpreting the Book of Amos" in the introduction.

[10] Brueggemann, "The Book of Jeremiah," 135.

[11] Brueggemann, "The Book of Jeremiah," 135, including n. 19, citing Paul Ricoeur, "Biblical Hermeneutics," *Semeia* 4 (1975): 27–148, especially page 31, for a discussion of "redescribing" the world.

[12] Alter writes: "The two most common structures, then, of biblical poetry are a movement of intensification of images, concepts, themes through a sequence of lines, and a narrative

the actions move from the marketplace, the courts at the city gate (where justice was twisted), and finally idolatrous temples, the likely site of what may be cultic prostitution with the "young woman" (2:7), and certainly shrines are the locations of the altars "in the temple of their gods" (2:8). That last Hebrew line indicates the climax of the previous places of action. All the actions are a violation of the divine covenant and an affront to Yahweh's gracious will for his chosen people, but the most heinous crimes are the drunken sexual sins in pagan temples. This is shocking! The Israelites loved the life of hedonism rather than a life with Yahweh (cf. 2 Tim 3:4). By saving the most explicit reference to idolatry for the last line, Amos' focus indicates that all of Israel's sins stem from religious apostasy. The worship of false gods rather than the one true God is Israel's fundamental problem—and the root problem of all fallen people. The prophet further highlights this in 5:25–26 and 8:14.

Repetition with intensity, one of the main hallmarks of Hebrew parallelism, provides a vivid way not only for Amos to bring charges against the abusive Israelites, but also to focus on the core of Israel's sin: idolatry, indulgence, and illicit sex. Working together, these iniquities are maximizing the pleasure of the elite, while at the same time destroying the marginalized in the land. This relationship between the breaking of the First Commandment (Deut 5:6–7) and the breaking of the Sixth and the Ninth Commandments (Deut 5:18, 21) gets at the heart of what was so wrong with Israel.

Just as Amos persuasively and memorably employs poetry to convey the Law, he is also adept at using his literary spiritual gift to announce the Gospel. Another good example of the poetic phenomenon of seconding, in which the first line is strengthened and elaborated by the second line, is the missional implication of two parallel lines in the messianic promise that God will raise up the falling tabernacle of David (Amos 9:11–15). Ultimately, this promise is fulfilled in the bodily resurrection of the crucified Messiah, Jesus Christ. His own body is the new temple (Jn 2:19–22), and the NT also affirms that all who are baptized into his body die and are raised (Rom 6:1–4) to be members of the church as the new temple (e.g., 1 Cor 3:16–17; Eph 2:21). The result of this resurrection is described in Amos 9:12:

> So that they will possess the remnant of Edom,
> that is, all the nations over whom my name is called.

The first line announces that Yahweh will enlarge his redeemed people. This expansion is depicted in OT language as enabling the restored Israel to take possession of the adjacent territory of the Edomites, who were a pagan people throughout the OT era, and few of whom would survive the divine judgment announced in 1:11–12. However, "the remnant of Edom" in the first line

---

movement—which most often pertains to the development of metaphorical acts but can also refer to literal events, as in much prophetic poetry" ("The Characteristics of Ancient Hebrew Poetry," 620).

is defined further in the second line as one of "all the nations over whom my name has been called." That is, in this messianic promise, the Edomites who are incorporated into the restored Israel are no longer pagans; instead, they bear the saving name of the one true God. In NT language, they have become disciples of Jesus Christ through Holy Baptism "in the name of the Father and of the Son and of the Holy Spirit" (Mt 28:19).

Therefore they are a "remnant" (Amos 9:12) not just in the sense of the few survivors, but also with the familiar OT meaning of the faithful remnant: those who are saved by grace alone, through faith alone. Therefore Yahweh's plan inaugurated by the Son of David is not only to redeem and restore ethnic Israelites, but rather for Israel's Messiah to redeem all the nations and gather a new people that includes believers from all peoples.[13] This promise in Amos is similar to the one spoken through Isaiah, where Yahweh says to his Servant:

> It is too small a thing for you, my Servant,
> to restore the tribes of Jacob
> and to return the preserved of Israel.
> I will also make you a light for the Gentiles,
> so that my salvation extends to the end of the earth. (Is 49:6)

Thus in the new (NT) era, not just faithful Israelites, but also Edomites and others from all nations will bear God's triune name and be incorporated into his new covenant people. This incorporation began in earnest in the book of Acts, where Jesus gave the promise "You will be my witnesses in Jerusalem and in all Judea and Samaria and to the ends of the earth" (Acts 1:8), and where we learn that three thousand people from many countries were baptized into Christ on Pentecost (Acts 2). This interpretation of Amos' poetry is further confirmed when it is quoted during the apostolic council in Acts 15 as biblical support for the unhindered inclusion of Gentiles into the infant church (Acts 15:16–17).[14]

---

[13] This is a theme throughout the OT. See the excursus "Mission in the Old Testament" in Lessing, *Jonah*, 151–69.

[14] See further the excursus "The Quotation from Amos 9 in Acts 15."

Excursus

The Land

A major theme in the book of Amos is God's creation of the universe and his ongoing relationship with the land of Israel. Amos begins with a reference to a memorable earthquake (1:1; cf. 9:1) and the notice that Yahweh is roaring in anger at his people's sin, causing the pasturelands to mourn and the usually fertile Mount Carmel to dry up (1:2). The land of Israel experiences drought (4:7–8), blight and mildew (4:9), locusts (4:9; cf. 7:1–3), and the threat of fire (5:6; 7:4–6). At the end of the book, Yahweh issues his eschatological and messianic promise to plant his redeemed people—the saved remnant of Israel and Gentiles—in the rejuvenated land overflowing with fertility that shall be their home for eternity (9:11–15).

Throughout Amos, the natural created world and the human world of religion, politics, war, and business are intimately intertwined. The human and nonhuman are so deeply interconnected that human sin has a devastating effect on the land. Luther offers this summary:

> Creation does not like to see a godless and damned person, but out of inexpressible mercy God has commanded her that she must be subjected to futility in this life (Rom 8[:20]) and serve such people, even against her will, so that she is troubled by it like a woman in childbirth. She would rather have nothing else than to be freed from such service to the damned and godless world, but she must have patience in the hope of redemption, for the sake of the children of God, who are yet to come to Christ and be brought to glory [Rom 8:22–23]. Otherwise the creation—sun, moon, stars, heaven, and earth—is also as much an enemy to sin as God himself is.[1]

Yahweh's will is to bring about *shalom* for the entire created order. God imputes his own righteousness to his redeemed people through faith, enabling them to show forth his holiness and faithfulness. Eschatologically, in the risen Son of David (Amos 9:11), God's righteousness will spill over into harmony and peace for the entire creation (Amos 9:13–15). The apostle Peter sums up the Christian hope in these terms: "According to his promise, we look forward to new heavens and a new earth in which righteousness dwells" (2 Pet 3:13).

The Link between People and Land

Amos is not the only prophet concerned with the land. Jeremiah typifies God's attentiveness to the land in his anguished cry "Oh land! Oh land! Oh land! Hear the Word of Yahweh" (Jer 22:29). Lengthy portions of Ezekiel are prophecies against the mountains and land of Israel (chapters 6–7) and against Mount

---

[1] Luther, *Von Jhesu Christo Warem Gott und Menschen und von seinem Ampt und Reich* (two sermons preached on Colossians 1), 1537 (WA 45.270; trans. Charles Schulz). Translation © Concordia Publishing House.

Seir (chapter 35), as well as Gospel promises of restoration for the mountains, land, and people of Israel (chapter 36). Indeed, from Genesis to Revelation, the land is a major theological motif.[2]

The bond between people and land is based on their common dependence on Yahweh, who created the world and everything in it as interdependent parts of a single, unified whole, which originally was very good (Gen 1:31). This relationship is stated classically in Gen 2:7:

> וַיִּיצֶר יְהוָה אֱלֹהִים אֶת־הָאָדָם עָפָר מִן־הָאֲדָמָה
> Then Yahweh God formed the man (out of) dust from the ground.

The Hebrew "Adam, mankind" (אָדָם) comes from the noun for "ground" (אֲדָמָה). The two are linked to each other in life, in death, and at the resurrection. After death the body decomposes into the dust of the earth until the bodily resurrection when "the earth will give birth to the dead" (Is 26:19; cf. Rev 20:13) and those "sleeping in the dusty ground" shall awake and be physically raised—believers to everlasting life and unbelievers to everlasting contempt (Dan 12:2–3).

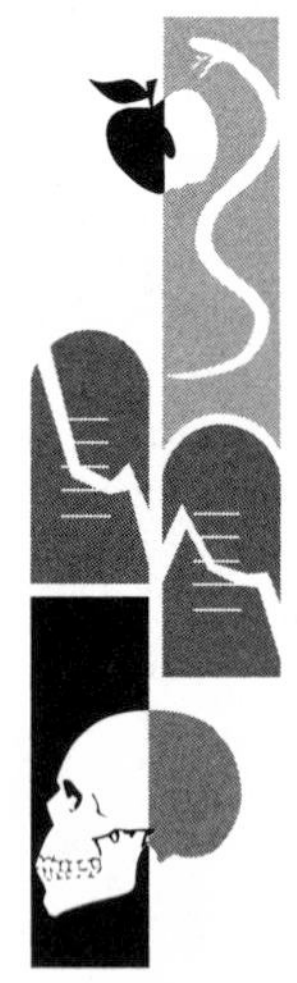

The tragic result of Adam and Eve's sin was that the ground brought forth thorns and thistles (Gen 3:17–18). Death came to our first parents and through them to all humanity. Death also came to animals and plants—all living creatures. As a result of rampant sin, the world was inundated by a flood (Genesis 6–8) that killed most of humanity and most of its animals. Sodom and Gomorrah became an ecological disaster because of human wickedness and the sexual perversion of homosexuality (Gen 13:10–13; 19:24–28). The plagues were disruptions in the created order that God caused in Egypt as part of his plan to save his people from slavery under Pharaoh and the gods of Egypt (Exodus 7–11) so that he could lead his redeemed people into the promised land. Prophets repeatedly link human sin with cosmic destruction (e.g., Jer 4:22–26; Hos 4:1–3) and also promise the new heavens and new earth that is the inheritance of all God's faithful servants (Isaiah 11; 65–66).

Throughout the OT, there exists a symbiosis between Yahweh, the people, the promised land, and the rest of creation.[3] Ben Zvi calls the holy land "the eco-theological place where a proper relation with YHWH is meant to be maintained."[4] Brueggemann writes: "It will no longer do to talk about

---

[2] Holwerda writes: "The biblical message is very earthy" (*Jesus and Israel*, 85). Martens notes that the word אֶרֶץ ("land") is the fourth most frequent noun in the OT, appearing 2,504 times (*God's Design*, 114).

[3] Cf. Habel, *The Land Is Mine*, 33–35, 75–96.

[4] Ben Zvi, *Hosea*, 73. Holwerda writes: "The gospel of salvation never becomes so spiritual that it loses its rootedness in creation, and its belief in the resurrection of the body remains absolutely foundational" (*Jesus and Israel*, 85).

Yahweh and his people but we must speak about Yahweh and his people *and his land*."[5]

The Old Testament Narrative of the Land

The primeval history in Genesis 1–11 and the patriarchal history in Genesis 12–50 set the parameters of land theology in the Bible.[6] In Genesis 1–11, people presumed upon the land and were expelled, first from Eden and later from Babel (Gen 3:23–24; 11:8; see also Gen 4:16; 6:7).

When Yahweh called Abram, he told him to "go ... to the land I will show you" (Gen 12:1). In Gen 12:7 Yahweh stated, "To your offspring I will give this land."[7] When Yahweh cut a covenant with Abram, it included this promise: "to your offspring I am giving this land" (Gen 15:18). So important was this promise that it was sealed by means of an ancient ceremony whereby animals were killed and cut in half (Gen 15:9–21). In, with, and under a blazing firepot and a torch, Yahweh passed through the slain animals, thus signifying this: "May the fate of the animals be the fate of the promise-maker if the promise is not kept."[8] When the patriarch was ninety-nine, Yahweh stated, "I will give to you and your offspring after you the land of your sojournings, all the land of Canaan, as an everlasting possession" (Gen 17:8). Yahweh renewed this promise, both to Isaac (Gen 26:3) and to Jacob (Gen 28:3–4, 13–15; 35:9–12). At the time of his death, Joseph reiterated the gift of the land (Gen 50:24).

In Genesis 12–50, the patriarchs trusted God's land promises but never received anything more permanent than a down payment (Genesis 23). They were sojourners or resident aliens who wandered in the land and lived there for a while (Deut 26:5; cf. 1 Pet 1:1; 2:11). They never received a lasting home in the earthly land but lived by faith in hopeful anticipation of receiving their permanent home in heaven (Heb 11:8–16).

Israel's first period of settlement in a land was when the sons of Jacob settled in Egypt under Joseph. They were given the best of the land (Gen 47:6) and made to dwell there in security and prosperity (Gen 47:27). Yet this was not *their* land. A pharaoh arose who did not remember Joseph, and so he enslaved Israel in this land (Ex 1:8–22). Then Yahweh came to Moses and reissued the patriarchal promise of the land (Ex 3:8, 17). While encamped at Mount Sinai (Exodus 19–Numbers 10), Yahweh's teaching on the land was dialectical. Israel's involvement was to always be with Yahweh and *his* land, never with the land only, as though the people would live in it apart from Yahweh. "The

---

5 Brueggemann, *The Land*, 5. Martens writes: "From the first, then, people and land belong together; both belong to Yahweh" (*God's Design*, 116).

6 Cf. Brueggemann, *The Land*, 15.

7 Martens states that the expression " 'to give' with reference to land is found about 150 times in the Bible" (*God's Design*, 306).

8 Martens, *God's Design*, 115.

gift cannot be received without its Giver."[9] Israel's relationship with God also was never purely spiritual, but was sacramental as Yahweh sustained his people and their faith through physical means attended by the gracious promises in his Word. Israel was to remain a faithful tenant in this land Yahweh was providing. The Israelites could never claim to be owners since they were merely caretakers of God's vineyard (Lev 25:23; cf. Is 5:1–7; Mt 21:33–46).[10]

After Yahweh gave his Torah at Mount Sinai, Israel stood on the brink of possessing the land. The spies sent out by Moses returned and reported that it was a good land but that the inhabitants were strong and their cities were fortified (Num 13:27–28). The assembly embraced "the bad report" (Num 13:32) that caused them to doubt Yahweh's earlier promises of the land. The result was a forty-year detour in the desert (Num 14:33–35).

Once those over twenty years of age had died and a new generation stood on the plains of Moab, Yahweh inspired Moses to deliver the book of Deuteronomy, which is full of theological reflections on the land. The book's message is—over and over again—that the land was a pure gift, flowing from Yahweh's grace (e.g., Deut 1:35; 6:10; 10:11; 12:10).[11] The land could not be earned, neither was it deserved. The Israelites were warned never to arrogate to themselves the land and its blessings by saying, "My power and the might of my own hand have produced this wealth for me" (Deut 8:17). The land was not given because of Israel's righteousness (Deut 9:6). Rather, God granted to Israel the righteousness that comes through faith (Gen 15:6; Romans 4; Galatians 4–5), and he provided the land as a pure gift, *sola gratia*.

The temptation would be that Israel's prosperity in the land would tempt the people to forget Yahweh, his goodness to them, and his gracious salvation through the exodus redemption (e.g., Deut 8:7–20). If the land was not to be lost, the Israelites must remember their experiences of Law and Gospel under God's hand: their barrenness and the gift of birth (Gen 11:30; 21:1–3), their slavery and God's deliverance into freedom (Exodus 1–14), their thirst and God's water from the rock (Ex 17:1–7; Num 20:1–12), and their hunger and God's provision of manna (Exodus 16). The frequent exhortation in Deuteronomy is "remember" (e.g., Deut 5:15; 7:18; 8:2; 15:15; 16:12); the people must never forget the gospel of the land (e.g., Deut 4:9; 6:12; 8:11).

Leviticus 26 and Deuteronomy 28 contain Sinaitic covenant blessings and curses (cf. also 1 Kings 8). Chief among the curses is exile from the land (e.g., Lev 26:33; Deut 28:63). While looking westward from the plain of Moab toward the land, Israel was to remember that just as Yahweh promised the land to his

---

[9] LaRondelle, *The Israel of God in Prophecy*, 136.

[10] Diepold writes: "Israel cannot claim an immediate relation to its land, cannot have it at its disposal in an autonomous way, cannot idolize the land into an absolute possession" (*Israels Land*, 109), translated and cited by LaRondelle, *The Israel of God in Prophecy*, 136 (see also p. 145, n. 5).

[11] Martens notes that in Deuteronomy "assertions about the land as gift occur thirty times" (*God's Design*, 120).

faithful believers, their idolatry would cause them to forfeit the land (Deut 8:19–20; 31:16–22; 32:1–43).

In a physical sense, Israel's history consisted of the patriarchal promise of land, the possession of land under Joshua and the kings, the loss of land during exile, and the return and reestablishment in the land. Both the historian of 2 Kings 24–25 and the author of Chronicles (2 Chronicles 36) made the loss of the promised land the tragic culmination of their narratives, while also offering the Gospel hope for the people of Israel beyond their land loss through the royal line of David (2 Ki 25:27–30), whence the Messiah would come, and a return to the land (2 Chr 36:22–23), in which the Messiah would be born.

As the centuries passed from Moses (fifteenth century BC) through the eras of Joshua, the judges, and into the united monarchy, it was only during the reign of Solomon (tenth century BC) that Israel finally received the full extent of the land promised to the patriarchs and Moses (1 Ki 5:1 [ET 4:21]). However, Solomon also implemented corps of forced laborers conscripted from all Israel, amassed great wealth through commerce and taxation, and expanded the government into a bulging bureaucracy (e.g., 1 Ki 5:27–30 [ET 5:13–16]; 9:15–23; 10:11–29). These diminished the Israelites' enjoyment of their God-given privileges in the land. Moreover, Solomon's marriage alliances included one with Pharaoh by way of marriage to Pharaoh's daughter (1 Ki 3:1; 7:8; 9:24). She was among the foreign wives who led Solomon into idolatry (1 Kings 11), the same transgression against the First Commandment that would eventually cause northern Israel and then southern Judah to be exiled and to forfeit the land. In a sense then, Solomon's reign was like a return to Egypt, for he lessened Israel's freedom and reduced the social order toward the pre-exodus situation of Israel's slavery in Egypt and oppression under foreign gods. Even though Yahweh in his grace had provided the land allotments to all Israelites as an identifying mark of his chosen people (Joshua 13–22), because of their sins, the Israelites began to lose the land that contained Yahweh's gift of life. Yahweh had predicted this (e.g., Deut 31:20).

One narrative that depicts the propensity of kings to unlawfully confiscate land is in 1 Kings 21. The relation of Naboth and his land was not that of an owner and his property (as Ahab and Jezebel believed), but rather an heir by faith and the divine gift that was his by Yahweh's grace. Ahab and Jezebel were led to this distorted view of the land due to their belief in Canaanite deities (e.g., 1 Kings 16:31–33). Elijah from Tishbe entered the scene after Naboth had been murdered and his land taken. The prophet's message reflected the truth that the land belonged to Yahweh. Elijah asserted that it was Yahweh's covenant with the patriarchs and the Torah given at Sinai and not royal prerogative that governed the land (1 Ki 21:17–29).

These same two conflicting theologies of the land also collide in Amos, especially in 7:10–17. The apostate priest Amaziah reflects a distorted theology of royal ownership of the land similar to that expressed in the royal abuses by Solomon, Ahab, and Jezebel. He takes offense at Amos' warning that Israel will be exiled because he wrongly assumes that Israel's king and subjects have an exclusive right to the land that not even Yahweh can take away. Amos follows in the way of Elijah and declares judgment on the northern king and kingdom because they have forsaken Yahweh and his righteousness and denied justice to the poor and oppressed Israelites.

Jeremiah was the prophet of the land par excellence. The story of Israel was from the land of Egypt to the land of inheritance, but by the time of Jeremiah's ministry, the people had so defiled the land by their unbelief, idolatry, and sins that it had become an abomination. No stronger antithetical word pair can be imagined than "inheritance" versus "abomination" (Jer 2:7).

Just as the apostasy of northern Israel (the major burden of Amos in the eighth century BC) resulted in its exile in 722 BC, so the infidelity of the Southern Kingdom of Judah prompted the destruction of the Jerusalem temple in 587 BC and exile to Babylon, which severed the Judeans from the land (Jer 24:8–10). A holy land (Ps 78:54) could not tolerate an unholy Israel (e.g., Lev 7:20–21). If unclean people inhabit the land for too long, the land must vomit out the occupants (Lev 18:24–28; cf. Hos 9:3).

Yet the Israelites and Judahites were not the only ones to leave the land. The temple had become so defiled by the people's sin that Yahweh himself vacated it to prepare for its destruction (Ezekiel 10–11). But Ezekiel, a prophet in exile, foresaw that Yahweh would resurrect, regather, and restore his landless people (Ezek 11:17; 34:13; 36:24; 37:1–14; chapters 40–48). In Ezek 43:1–9 Yahweh returned to a rebuilt temple in the center of the new promised land, and this temple was the centerpiece in the eschatological vision (Ezekiel 40–48) to be fulfilled in Revelation 21–22.

That final restoration of the new Israel in the new heavens and new earth was foreshadowed by Israel's return from Babylon, which also paved the way for the advent of Christ to the land (Is 40:3–5; Lk 3:4–6). Isaiah had promised that "Yahweh will return to Zion" (Is 52:8), and his return would enable that of the exiles (cf. Is 35:10; 51:11; 52:7) and the advent of the Suffering Servant (e.g., Is 42:1–9; 49:1–13; 50:4–11; 52:13–53:12). Those returning from exile once again received land as a gift of grace, as promised in Deut 30:1–5 and realized under the leadership of Zerubbabel, Ezra, and Nehemiah. The initial return to the land was made possible in 538 by Cyrus, a Persian king. So central was his mission in Yahweh's regiving of the land that Isaiah, writing some two centuries earlier, had called him "shepherd" (Is 44:28) and "messiah" (Is 45:1). Yahweh forgave and comforted his people (Is 40:2) and granted them a new beginning in the land. This divine act was almost as radical as the original promise to Abram in Gen 12:1–3 (cf. Isa 51:2). A central prophetic phrase in the OT that describes the new era of redemption is literally that God would "restore the restoration" of his people, as he promises in Amos 9:14 (see the commentary there). This restoration began with the return from exile, was inaugurated by the first advent of Jesus, and will be completed at the return of Christ, when all believers will be raised to everlasting life in the new heavens and new earth—the new promised land.

Throughout both Testaments and into the eschaton, the promised land is Yahweh's dwelling place with his redeemed, the physical place where the corporate people of God live before him and together worship him. During the NT era, the land theme finds its fulfillment in corporate worship centered around God's Word and the Sacraments of Baptism and Holy Communion. In the places where God's Word is faithfully proclaimed and his Sacraments are administered according to his biblical institution, God comes in his grace to save his people, forgive their sins, incorporate them into the body of Christ, and dwell among and within them. In church, those in Christ enjoy a Sabbath rest that anticipates the eternal worship celebration around the throne of God and the Lamb.

The neglect or ignorance of the biblical land texts can allow interpreters to construe salvation as an individual and personal relationship with God, a purely spiritual experience divorced from the incarnation of Christ, the church as his body, and his gracious bodily presence in the Sacrament of the Altar. The biblical teaching on the land, therefore, encompasses a full-bodied, fully engaged life that values creation and the "one holy catholic and apostolic church" (Nicene Creed), with the promise of bodily resurrection and eternal life when the bride of Christ becomes the wife of the Lamb, united with him forever in the new land (Revelation 21–22).

A recovery of a biblical theology of the land supports the connection between the First Article of the Creed and the Second and Third Articles. Under God the Father and Creator, Christians can join unbelievers in opposing evils that threaten ecological disasters that wreak havoc on large portions of humanity.[12] As scientists increasingly discover, God's creation is a marvelously (perhaps incomprehensibly) complex and sensitive network of interrelated parts. Yet Christians are uniquely gifted with the true understanding of the land and the natural world. They are not the products of a random, impersonal process of evolution, natural selection, and survival of the fittest. Instead, nature and the land are the handiwork of the same God who fashioned the world in six days and created Adam and Eve in his image to reign over his creation. Since the fall into sin, the creation has been subjected to futility (Rom 8:20) and unbelieving humanity is under the wrath of God. Surrounded by death and decay,

---

[12] A helpful essay that addresses the Christian stewardship of creation is Berry, "Christianity and the Environment: Escapist Mysticism or Responsible Stewardship." A negative connection between the Bible and ecology was articulated in the now (in)famous essay of Lynn White Jr. in which he proposed the thesis that the biblical notion of dominion over the earth, mandated by God in Genesis 1, is the reason why people have taken the liberty to exploit the earth ("The Historical Roots of Our Ecological Crisis"). However, God in Genesis 1 commands people to exercise his proper headship over the creation, not to abuse it. The issues raised by White are reviewed by Wybrow in *The Bible, Baconianism, and Mastery over Nature*.

mindful of the imminent end of the present world, the church's urgent mission is to proclaim the Gospel to the whole creation.[13]

Different Aspects of Land Theology in the New Testament

At first blush, the NT appears to have little to say about the land. It seems as though what is so important in the OT is almost entirely absent from the NT. But a closer look recognizes that land theology casts a long shadow over the books from Matthew to Revelation. In fact Brueggemann goes so far as to maintain: "It is sobering for New Testament exegesis to recognize that the single central symbol for the promise of the gospel is land."[14] Land theology in the NT is so multi-faceted that it requires discussion under several different categories.

1. *The land is a down payment.* In order to provide a proper burial place for Sarah, Abraham purchased the cave at Machpelah from Ephron the Hittite (Genesis 23). It was a "down payment" on a larger block of land.[15] The patriarchs never possessed the earthly land but lived by faith in hopeful anticipation of receiving their permanent home in heaven (Heb 11:8–16). The land was a foretaste of "a better country" with a heavenly city (Heb 11:10, 16). They were sojourners or resident aliens who had a place and lived there for a while, but they were always outsiders, never belonging, only possessing a burial plot in Machpelah. That is true for Christians as well. "Sojourners and exiles" is how 1 Pet 2:11 describes Christians during this earthly life (see also 1 Pet 1:1). "Enjoyment of the promise of the land has already begun, but only as a sign anticipating the future."[16]

Through Baptism into Christ (Acts 2:38–39) believers have already received the forgiveness of sins and the promised gift of the Holy Spirit, who is the "down payment" (ἀρραβών) of eternal salvation (2 Cor 1:22; 5:5; Eph 1:14). Similarly, the church celebrates the Lord's Supper as a foretaste of the feast to come, which is "the marriage supper of the Lamb" (Rev 19:9; see also Mt 26:29; 1 Cor 11:26), when "the bride" of Christ will become "the *wife* of the Lamb" (Rev 21:9). Thus Christians are those "who have been enlightened,[17]

---

[13] According to the textually disputed longer ending of Mark's Gospel, Jesus says, πορευθέντες εἰς τὸν κόσμον ἅπαντα κηρύξατε τὸ εὐαγγέλιον πάσῃ τῇ κτίσει, "go into all the world and preach the Gospel to the whole creation" (Mk 16:15).

[14] Brueggemann, *The Land*, 168.

[15] Martens, *God's Design*, 32.

[16] Holwerda, *Jesus and Israel*, 112.

[17] See also Heb 10:32. A connection between Baptism and enlightenment may also be supported by Eph 5:14; Col 1:12–14. In the early church, Justin Martyr maintained that in Holy Baptism, the Christian receives φωτισμός, "enlightenment" or "illumination" (*First Apology*, 61, cited in Greek in H. Conzelmann, "φῶς κτλ.," *TDNT* 9:357–58; ET: *ANF* 1:183). The Lutheran Confessions affirm that Christ offers his grace "in the Word and the holy sacraments. … But if such a person despises the instruments of the Holy Spirit and will not hear [the Word], no injustice is done him if the Holy Spirit does not illuminate him but lets him remain in the darkness of his unbelief" (FC SD II 57–58).

who have tasted the heavenly gift, … and who have tasted the good Word of God and the powers of the age to come" (Heb 6:4–5), but we will not receive the full meal with all its courses until Christ comes again and makes the new heaven and new earth (Rev 21:1).

2. *The land is an inheritance.* In Joshua 13–22, the tribes of Israel received portions of the land as their "inheritance" (נַחֲלָה). Lev 25:24–34 prescribes that if tracts of land were sold or traded to other clans, the inheritance was always to be returned in the Jubilee Year so that it would be a lasting possession of the original owner and his heirs. This idea carries into the NT in, for example, 1 Pet 1:4, where the apostle asserts that the Christian hope is an inheritance that, unlike the land, "is imperishable, unspoiled, and unfading." Paul likewise asserts, "And now I commend you to God and to the word of his grace, which can build you up and give you an inheritance among all those who are sanctified" (Acts 20:32).

3. *Living in the land is the abundant life.* Israel's land was "an exceedingly good land" (Num 14:7). It was a land that "drinks water by the rain of heaven, a land that Yahweh your God looks after" (Deut 11:11–12), "a land flowing with milk and honey" (e.g., Num 13:27; Deut 6:3; 11:9). As such "the land represented prosperity under God's watchful eye, fruitful fields and herds, an abundance of grain, wine, and oil, and numerous descendants."[18] Martens writes: "The land comes before long to symbolize the life with Yahweh in ideal conditions, a quality of life which might be characterized as the abundant life."[19] The land foreshadowed the abundant life that Jesus has come to give (Jn 10:10).

4. *The land is a foretaste of paradise restored.* In Deut 8:7–9 the land is extolled in Eden-like terms. Isaiah foresaw the restoration when God would make Zion's "wilderness like Eden, her wasteland like the garden of Yahweh" (Is 51:3). LaRondelle writes: "The full scope of Israel's prophets was not nationalistic, but universal, with an increasing cosmic dimension which took in heaven and earth (Isaiah 65:17; 24:21–23)."[20] Israel's land, then, was a foreshadowing of what Yahweh plans to re-create when Christ comes again. "The Church of Christ has no other hope, no other destiny, no other inheritance than the one that God gave to Abraham and Israel—a redeemed heaven and earth (Isaiah 65:17)."[21]

5. *The land is a place of rest.* In Deuteronomy, Yahweh promises the Israelites that when they enter the land, he will give them "rest from [their] enemies all around so that [they] live in safety" (Deut 12:10; see also Deut 25:19). Josh 1:13 recalls the words given to Moses: "Yahweh your God is pro-

---

[18] Holwerda, *Jesus and Israel*, 90.

[19] Martens, *God's Design*, 13. He also writes: "It is almost axiomatic that the prospect of dwelling in the land involved more than substituting a Palestinian address for an Egyptian address. At stake was the quality of life" (p. 218).

[20] LaRondelle, *The Israel of God in Prophecy*, 141.

[21] LaRondelle, *The Israel of God in Prophecy*, 144.

viding you a place of rest and will give you this land." This promise is partially and temporarily realized after Joshua's conquests (Josh 21:43). Similarly, the book of Hebrews indicates that Christians possess the land—described as the rest into which they have entered through Christ—in a way that even Joshua did not achieve for Israel (Heb 3:12–4:11). Jesus invites in Mt 11:28, "Come to me, all who are weary and burdened, and I will give you rest."

6. *Yahweh grants blessings to those in the land.* The land was where Yahweh poured out his blessings on Israel. Moses announces in Deut 28:11, "Yahweh will cause you to abound in prosperity, in the fruit of your womb and in the fruit of your livestock and in the fruit of your ground, upon the land that Yahweh swore to your fathers to give to you." In NT terms, God graciously imparts his gifts of forgiveness, life, and salvation "in Christ" (ἐν Χριστῷ, e.g., Rom 6:11, 23; 8:1, 39; 1 Cor 1:2, 4; Eph 1:12; 1 Thess 2:14). This is shorthand for incorporation into Christ through Baptism (e.g., Rom 6:1–4; Gal 3:26–29; Col 2:11–13) and by faith, and shorthand for participating in the body and blood of Christ through Holy Communion (e.g., 1 Cor 10:16–17). To be "in Christ" is equivalent to the location of OT believers "in the land," where they could come to the temple and participate in divine worship. The NT " 'Christifies' the old territorial holiness and thus transcends its limitations. This should not be regarded as the New Testament rejection of Israel's territorial promise, but rather as its fulfillment and confirmation in Christ."[22] Just as Yahweh blessed Israel with every blessing in the land, so God the Father grants every spiritual blessing to those in Christ (Eph 1:3).

7. *The land is a foreshadowing of the NT sacraments.* This has already been noted above a number of times in this excursus. Martens writes: "The land becomes a medium whereby Yahweh can make something clear about himself in a concrete way."[23] Yahweh used the land as a means to enrich and bless Israel. The cities that they did not build and the vineyards that they did not plant were Yahweh's instruments to graciously care for his people (e.g., Deut 6:10–12). God showed his love for his people as he provided water, bread, and wine in and through the land (Deut 7:13; 11:14). His people were to feast on bread and wine in his presence at the central sanctuary (Deut 14:23), where too the priests would enjoy bread and wine from the firstfruits of the people (Num 18:12). Just so, in the NT, God conveys the treasures of his Gospel through the waters of Holy Baptism (e.g., Mt 28:19; Jn 3:1–8; Titus 3:4–7; 1 Pet 3:18–22) and the Sacrament of Holy Communion (e.g., Mt 26:26–29; 1 Cor 11:23–27; cf. Jn 6:35–58).

8. *The land has a missional strategy.* Yahweh's gift of the land to Abraham and his descendants was strategic in its location. Two major trade routes, the Via Maris and the King's Highway, ran through the promised land and connected

---

[22] LaRondelle, *The Israel of God in Prophecy*, 142.

[23] Martens, *God's Design*, 311.

the two largest cradles of civilization, Egypt and Mesopotamia. The goal was for the nations to come into contact with Israel and through Israel to encounter Yahweh. God told Israel that her faithfulness to his covenant was to be "[her] wisdom and [her] understanding in the eyes of the peoples, who will hear all these statutes and will say, 'Surely this great nation is a wise and understanding people.' For what other nation is so great as to have gods near to it the way Yahweh our God [is near to us] whenever we call on him?" (Deut 4:6–7). In a similar manner, the church is empowered to be "a city on a hill [that] cannot be hidden" (Mt 5:14) so that through Christ, her light shines before the nations and they praise the Father in heaven (Mt 5:16).

9. *The occupants of the land.* God did not give the land to the strong and mighty (Ps 37:11). The promise to the patriarchs highlights this central paradox in the Bible's narrative about the land: it was first promised to elderly Abraham who had no heirs and was as good as dead. Then it was promised to his descendants as transients, temporary residents, and exiles (Deut 26:5–9). Deut 7:7 indicates that Israel was "the fewest of all peoples," yet it is to these weaklings that the land was gifted. Just as earlier in Israel's history the sojourners were promised the land and the Israelite slaves in Egypt were redeemed as Yahweh triumphed over Pharaoh in order to give them the land, so also in the NT, this same land theology continues. It is part of the theology of the cross (1 Cor 1:18–25). As the new chosen people of God, Christians remain "sojourners and exiles" in this life (1 Pet 2:11) with the eschatological promise that "the meek … will inherit the earth" (Mt 5:5), to be fulfilled in Revelation 21–22.

Jesus affirms that all the OT Scriptures testify to him (Jn 5:39), and that includes all of Israel's land promises. LaRondelle writes: "Israel's territorial promises are made sure in Christ and guaranteed through Him to all believers, whether Jew or Gentile."[24]

Dispensationalism, Eschatology, and the Land

One major misunderstanding of the Bible's teaching on the land comes from the relatively new system of theology termed "premillennial dispensationalism." At least two study Bibles advocate this way of interpreting the biblical promises of the land,[25] as do also some recent popular authors, including Hal Lindsey,[26] as well as Tim LaHaye and Jerry Jenkins, who co-wrote a series of novels called Left Behind.[27] Dispensationalists draw on texts including Amos 9:11–15, and its quotation in Acts 15, in order to support their belief that the

---

[24] LaRondelle, *The Israel of God in Prophecy*, 139–40.

[25] *The Scofield Reference Bible* (Oxford: Oxford University Press, 1909); *The Ryrie Study Bible* (Chicago: Moody, 1976).

[26] Hal Lindsey, *The Late Great Planet Earth* (Grand Rapids: Zondervan, 1970).

[27] Published by Tyndale, Carol Stream, Ill., 1995–2007. In *Are We Living in the End Times?* LaHaye and Jenkins demonstrate that the theology of their Left Behind series is premillennial dispensationalism.

OT land texts will be fulfilled literally by the regathering of Jewish people to reside in the historical territory of Israel in the present world. Some consider the establishment of the modern state of Israel in 1948 to be at least a partial fulfillment of the OT land promises, but most emphasize that the complete fulfillment will take place during a future millennium on this earth during which, they maintain, Christ will reign in Jerusalem, the temple will be rebuilt, and animal sacrifices will be resumed.[28]

Most Christians believe that all of God's promises are fulfilled in Christ (2 Cor 1:20), and so baptized believers in Christ, Jews and Gentiles alike, are the heirs—the only heirs—of God's promises (Gal 3:26–29). In contrast, dispensationalists believe that God has two different plans of salvation, one for Jews and another for Gentiles. They believe that God attached his land promises to ethnic Israel and that those OT promises continue to apply to the modern Jewish people, even though most of them do not believe in the Messiah. Dispensationalists (and many Israelis), citing passages such as Gen 17:7–8, believe that God granted the land to ethnic Israel forever.

However, that is the same error into which presumptuous Israel fell in the OT era. Arrogant Israelites believed that *they* were entitled to own the land permanently and so they could abuse their privileged position in it according to their whims, even allowing syncretism and idolatry in it. God punished this arrogance by allowing the Assyrians to exile northern Israel in 722 BC and the Babylonians to exile Judah in 587 BC. By separating the Israelites and Judeans from the land, God showed that their idolatry had caused them to forfeit their share in the inheritance he had promised to his people. In the covenant of Moses, the land and its blessings were promised to Israel conditionally, with the requirement that the people remain faithful and worship Yahweh alone; otherwise they would be cursed and exiled from the land (Deuteronomy 27–29).

The OT declares that the land of Canaan belongs to Yahweh (Lev 25:23; "my land" in Joel 1:6 and 2 Chr 7:20; cf. Ps 24:1). As the true owner, he is the one who promised it to Israel (e.g., Deut 6:10–11), and he is also the one who is able to take it away (Lev 26:33; Jer 16:18). Among the Israelites, Yahweh's land was not to be permanently bought or sold from one clan or tribe to another (cf. 1 Ki 21:1–16). It was not to be given away, let alone stolen or confiscated.

---

[28] For example, Archer rightly states that Amos 9:11–12 is about "the New Testament age," but then mistakenly claims that the description about the land in Amos 9:13–15 is a prophecy of "the millennial consummation" (*A Survey of Old Testament Introduction*, 317). *The Scofield Reference Bible*, 1343, states this about Acts 15:13–18, which includes James' quotation of Amos 9:11–12: "Dispensationally, this is the most important passage in the N.T. ... The verses which follow in Amos describe the final regathering of Israel, which the other prophets invariably connect with the fulfillment of the Davidic Covenant" (quoted by Kaiser, *The Uses of the Old Testament in the New*, 178). Kaiser partially agrees with that view in *The Scofield Reference Bible*, but offers important correctives (pp. 177–94). Yet Kaiser sides with many dispensationalists when he asserts that "the seminal reappearance of the state of Israel in 1948" was a historical confirmation that "God's offer to the Jews" (the OT land promise) has not been terminated" (p. 192).

The land in the OT was always a means toward a greater end: the coming of Jesus Christ to this land in the fullness of time to fulfill all the OT promises (Gen 17:1–7; Gal 3:13–14, 29; 4:4).

God's promises that he would restore and regather his people have already been fulfilled in the new covenant of grace in the Messiah: the new "Israel of God" (Gal 6:16), the Christian church, includes all baptized believers in Christ, both Jews and Gentiles (Gal 3:26–29; see also Rom 1:16; 10:8–13; Col 3:11). This inclusion of Gentiles alongside Jews in the people of God is the emphasis in Acts 15 when James cites from Amos 9.[29] The consummation of the land promises will take place after the return of Christ, when all believers will inherit the new heavens and the new earth as their home with God forever (Mt 19:29; 25:34; 2 Pet 3:10–13; Rev 21:1–5).

When Jesus speaks about the land (e.g., Lk 19:41–44), he makes no reference to it ever being restored to the Jewish people as an ethnic nation. In Lk 24:19–27, he does not sympathize with the Emmaus disciples and their hope for a redemption of Israel that meant the end of Roman occupation and freedom for Jews to govern their land (Lk 24:21). Instead, Jesus rebukes them for their dullness and slowness to understand the OT prophets, who wrote about him (Lk 24:25–27). He goes on to teach that everything in the OT (Lk 24:44) points to him and not to the nationalistic and territorial hope of an Israel as it was in the OT era. The redemption of Israel (and of all humanity) has been carried out through Jesus' perfect life, bloody death, and glorious resurrection. He teaches his disciples not to look backward nostalgically to OT Israel, but to look forward with eager expectation for the coming of Son of Man in his glory on the Last Day to usher in the new creation (Mt 24:30–31; Lk 21:25–28; cf. Dan 7:13–14; Isaiah 11; 65:17–25).

Jesus makes several explicit references to the land in the Gospels. The strongest is in the Beatitudes. In Mt 5:5 he quotes from Ps 37:11, where God promises that the meek will inherit the "earth" (אֶרֶץ). Note that in the psalm of David, the promise is not merely about the land of Israel, but the entire earth.[30] In light of the strong eschatological dimension of this section of Christ's Sermon on the Mount, this earth is the "new heavens and new earth in which righteousness dwells" (2 Pet 3:13).[31]

---

[29] See the excursus "The Quotation from Amos 9 in Acts 15."

[30] Some English translations rightly render אֶרֶץ in Ps 37:11 as "the earth" (e.g., KJV, NKJV), while others weaken the verse by translating the word as "the land" (e.g., RSV, NIV).

[31] Gibbs, *Matthew 1:1–11:1*, 244, writes:

> Jesus, the Son of God, promises to all such oppressed and spiritually powerless disciples the future eschatological inheritance of a new creation. ... The hope is both creational and eschatological. There will be a regeneration of all things (Mt 19:28) and a final Judgment Day ([Mt] 25:31–32). Those who have suffered oppression at the hands of wicked forces and wicked men will receive the blessings of God's great reversal on that day.

Until Pentecost, Christ's disciples may have shared the same nationalistic understanding of the land as other Jews of the first century. In Acts 1:6, they ask Jesus if he would now restore the kingdom to Israel. His response in Acts 1:7–8 indicates that his kingdom is in no way tied to a sovereign Jewish state, but will be spread by his disciples to other lands, reaching to the ends of the earth. The true "Israel of God" (Gal 6:16) had already been restored through his death and resurrection. After the coming of the Holy Spirit, the disciples began to use OT language concerning the land in new ways. In Rom 4:13, for example, Paul recalls God's promises in Genesis that Abraham and his seed would be heirs, but instead of saying that God pledged "land" (γῆ), he indicates that Abraham and his seed (all who believe) are heirs of the whole "cosmos" (κόσμος). By this he implies that already in the OT the promise of God looked forward to the new heaven and new earth (Rev 21:1). Peter likewise speaks of "an inheritance," language associated with the OT land promises (e.g., "inherit" or "inheritance" in Ex 32:13; Deut 1:38; often in Numbers 34–36; Joshua 11–21; see also Ps 78:52–55), but this first-century Jewish Christian contrasts it with the land of Palestine when he states that it "is imperishable, unspoiled, and unfading, kept in heaven for you" (1 Pet 1:4).[32] In light of how the OT promises are expanded in the NT and endowed with greater glory, the hope for possession of territory in earthly Israel seems "rather like lighting a candle when the sun is shining."[33]

The book of Hebrews is filled with texts that reinterpret the land in light of Christ's first and second advents. Christians have already entered the land through Christ in terms of the Sabbath rest in a way that even Joshua did not achieve for Israel (Heb 3:12–4:11). In Heb 11:13–16, the central Gospel motif is the land, where the pilgrimage of faith for all believers is pictured in three scenes: (1) setting out in faith from one's native land, as did Abraham; (2) the present context of wandering on this earth as a temporary sojourner here; and (3) the hoped-for homeland, which is far better: the heavenly city (Heb 11:16). Christians have already come to "the city of the living God, the heavenly Jerusalem" (Heb 12:22).

Premillennial dispensationalists suggest that the establishment of the modern state of Israel in 1948 is the start of the literal fulfillment of the land promises in the OT. Moreover, they contend that the fulfillment of the OT prophecies also requires that the temple be rebuilt in Jerusalem and animal sacrifices be reinstituted there. However, this is a misreading of the OT prophets. For example, the visionary prophecy of Ezekiel 40–48 is fulfilled in the sacrificial death and resurrection of Christ, who is the new temple and who builds up his church as

---

Davies writes: "Like everything else, the land also in the New Testament drives us to ponder the mystery of Jesus, the Christ, who by his cross and resurrection broke not only the bonds of death for early Christians but also the bonds of the land" (*The Gospel and the Land*, 375).

[32] See also 1 Pet 2:9–10, the apostle also takes terms that were exclusive to Israel in the OT and applies them to the corporate church, including all baptized believers in Christ.

[33] Chapman, *Whose Promised Land?* 167–68.

the new house of God. These prophetic chapters will be consummated in the eternal state (Revelation 21–22).[34]

It is clear from Scripture that the OT promises are to be read in the light of Jesus (Col 2:16–17). The OT revelations of God's acts in the history of Israel were types, shadows, images, and prefigurations of what God would accomplish in the Messiah. The NT announces the reality, substance, and fulfillment of those promises in the person and work of Jesus Christ (Lk 24:44; Jn 5:39). Therefore the question is not whether the land promises of the OT are to be understood literally or spiritually. Rather, the question is whether they should be understood as promises that God's people will return to the OT shadows that existed prior to the advent of Christ (as in dispensationalism) or as promises that now stand fulfilled in the NT realities of Christ and his church (as in traditional Christian eschatology). These NT realities, including the incarnation, death, and resurrection of Christ and his ongoing salvific ministry in his church through his Word and Sacraments, are both spiritual and physical. Christ's present ministry to God's chosen people will be completed in the bodily resurrection of all believers to everlasting life—spiritual and physical—in the tangible, palpable new creation.

When God's own self-revelation in the NT is allowed to guide the interpretation of his word in the OT, it becomes clear that God's people are the "one holy catholic and apostolic church" (Nicene Creed) consisting of all believers from the OT and NT eras. The modern state of Israel is not a prophetic realization of the promised messianic kingdom, which has now come in Jesus Christ. (Indeed, the majority of ethnically Jewish people in modern Israel are secular, not practicing religious Jews, much less believers in the King of the Jews.) His kingdom is not of this world (Jn 18:36). Furthermore, since the old covenant was merely preparatory for the new covenant in Christ, we should not expect the new wine to be poured back into old wineskins (cf. Mt 9:17). We should not require or expect Christ's kingdom to manifest the old Israelite distinctives, whether by its location in the land of Palestine, its capital in the earthly Jerusalem, its ethnic constituency, or its ceremonial institutions and practices at a temple. All those have been rendered obsolete forever by the once-for-all sacrifice of Christ (Heb 7:27; 9:12, 26; 10:10).

The land promises that God gave to Abraham and his seed were realized in Christ, Abraham's true Seed (Gal 3:16). All spiritual benefits are derived from Jesus, and apart from him there is no participation in the promises made to

---

[34] To be sure, Revelation 21–22 does not merely repeat Ezekiel 40–48. It transforms and in some ways completely transcends the OT prophecy, for example, by the absence of any temple except for God and the Lamb once slain (Rev 21:22). For the complex relationship between Ezekiel 40–48 and Revelation 21–22, one may see Hummel, *Ezekiel 40–48*, 1149–58, and Brighton, *Revelation*, 595–99, 611, 613–21.

Abraham.[35] Moreover, God's promises centered in "the Son of David" and "the Son of Abraham" (Mt 1:1) are not limited to any particular ethnic group; all are welcome at the King's table through faith in his Son. All believers, Jewish and Gentile alike, comprise the true Israel of God; all who have been baptized into Christ are the children of Abraham and heirs of the promises (Rom 2:28–29; Gal 3:26–29; Phil 3:3). Heirs now, Christians anticipate the full reception of their inheritance by grace when Christ comes again.

When premillennial dispensationalists point to the state of Israel established in 1948 as a concrete manifestation of God's presence, they overlook the visible and tangible signs that God *has* established as the means through which he comes to his people, forgives their sins, and strengthens their faith. 1 Jn 5:7–8 states: "For there are three that testify: the Spirit and the water and the blood, and the three are in agreement." God testifies to being present with his church right now by means of the Spirit-inspired and Christ-centered Old and New Testament Scriptures, the water of Holy Baptism into the triune name, as well as the true body and blood of Jesus in Holy Communion. The assurance that God is graciously working in the world is therefore not based on the return of Jewish people to their ancestral land, but rather on the sure Gospel promise of the forgiveness of sins, imparted in the means of grace, the Word and the Sacraments.

Jesus, Paul, and other NT writers interpreted the land promises as pointing ultimately to life after the resurrection in the new heavens and new earth. There is no teaching in the NT that ethnically Jewish people still have a divine right to the land or that the Jewish possession of the land would be an important—let alone central—aspect of God's plan for the world. The land was promised to Abraham, taken possession of under Joshua, lost in the Assyrian (722 BC) and Babylonian (587 BC) exiles, and regained by Judahite returnees after Cyrus' decree (538 BC). The destruction of Jerusalem and the temple in AD 70, following the rejection of Christ by the Jewish people as a whole, was predicted already in the OT (Dan 9:24–27) and by Jesus in the Gospels (e.g., Lk 21:5–6, 20).

The hope of the baptized, therefore, is not in current events in the land of Israel. Rather, they are called to fix their eyes on Jesus (Heb 12:1–3), even as they long and pray for his second advent. On that day, all the dead shall be raised, unbelievers shall be damned to hell, and all believers will be ushered into the eternal kingdom and promised land that is their true inheritance (Dan 12:2–3; Mt 25:31–46; Jn 5:28–29; Rev 20:11–15).

---

[35] Davies writes (*The Gospel and the Land*, 179, 182, 213, 217):

> In the Christological logic of Paul, the land, like the Law, particular and provisional, had become irrelevant. …
>
> The people of Israel living in the land had been replaced as the people of God by a universal community which had no special territorial attachment. …
>
> "The land" has been for him [Paul] "Christified." It is not the land promised as much as he had loved it that became his "inheritance," but the Living Lord, in whom was a new creation. …
>
> To be "in Christ" … has replaced "in the land" as the ideal life.

Amos 1:3–2:16

Judgments against the Nations

Introduction to Amos 1:3–2:16: Judgments against the Nations

Amos 1:3–2:16 is the longest unit in the book of Amos. In the first seven of its eight oracles, the prophet announces that Yahweh is about to send fire to destroy the sophisticated defense systems of Israel's neighbors. The speech comes to a shocking climax when Yahweh's most severe accusations are directed against Israel (2:6–16). The nation has been taking advantage of God's poor and the powerless in its midst, contrary to Moses' mandate in Deut 15:11.

Old Testament Prophets Who Speak to Other Nations

Although Jeremiah is the only prophet who is distinctly designated to be a prophet "over the nations" (Jer 1:10; cf. chapters 46–51), Isaiah (e.g., chaps. 13–23), Ezekiel (e.g., chaps. 25–32), and all of the Minor Prophets with the exception of Hosea address pagan nations. For example, later in the same (eighth) century BC Isaiah announces that Yahweh has a plan for all people, just as Amos had proclaimed:

> This is the plan that is planned concerning the whole earth
> [זֹאת הָעֵצָה הַיְּעוּצָה עַל־כָּל־הָאָרֶץ],
> and this is the hand that is stretched out over all the nations.
> (Is 14:26)[1]

Israel's prophets were heralds of this cosmic plan of God because Yahweh is the Judge of the entire universe (see, e.g., Ps 96:13).

As far back as the universal flood, Yahweh declared that he would not tolerate violence (Gen 6:11–13). He sent ten plagues against the Egyptians because of their violent oppression of the Israelites (Ex 3:7–9; 5:14–16). He sent Jonah to Nineveh because of the evil of the Ninevites (Jonah 1:2), which included violence (3:8). Yahweh is against any act that desecrates the status of people, since he created our original parents, Adam and Eve, in his own image and likeness (Gen 1:26). He has now redeemed all people through the sacrificial atonement of his Son in order to restore us to his image (Rom 8:29; 1 Cor 15:49; Col 1:15; 3:10; 2 Pet 1:4).

Amos is the first writing prophet to announce Yahweh's judgment on nations other than Judah and Israel. When Amos addresses Israel, he refers to God as אֱלֹהֶיךָ, "your God" (4:12; 9:15), but in 1:3–2:3 Yahweh speaks as the God who has jurisdiction over all the nations. Amos' hymns (4:13; 5:8–9; 9:5–6) in like manner proclaim Yahweh's lordship over the nations, as does

---

[1] Brueggemann writes: "The rhetoric of 'plan' is a device to speak of a *countergovernance* of the world that the would-be autonomous states do not acknowledge but cannot resist" (*Isaiah 1–39*, 113).

9:7, where God declares that he had brought out several other nations in their own "exoduses."

This international scope of Yahweh's dominion is a major theme in the Minor Prophets. For example, Joel records Yahweh's promise to repulse a northern army that had attacked his people Israel (2:20) and Yahweh's summons "among the nations" for warriors to assemble (4:9 [ET 3:9]) since he will judge "all the surrounding nations" (4:12 [ET 3:12]). Obadiah focuses exclusively on Edom. Yahweh twice calls Jonah to go and preach to Nineveh (Jonah 1:2; 3:1–2). Micah is shown a vision of the nations streaming to Zion (Micah 4:1–5), while Nahum is given "an oracle against Nineveh" (Nah 1:1). The vision Yahweh gives to Habakkuk is international as well: "Look at the nations and see. … I am raising up the Babylonians" (Hab 1:5–6). Zephaniah includes judgment oracles by Yahweh against foreign nations (Zeph 2:4–15). Haggai focuses on postexilic Israel's welfare, yet anticipates Yahweh's future cosmic action: "I am about to shake the heavens and the earth. I will overthrow the throne of kingdoms and destroy the strength of the kingdoms of the nations" (Hag 2:21–22). In Zechariah's first vision, Yahweh sends his messengers to travel "throughout the earth," and they report that they have done so (Zech 1:10–11). Through Malachi, Yahweh declares that his name will be "great among the nations" from east to west (Mal 1:11).

Yahweh responds to the heathen nations in judgment, but he also extends the promise of salvation to those who repent and believe in him. These OT prophecies and events foreshadow the inclusion of Gentiles into the Christian church on a large scale beginning on Pentecost.[2] For example, in the book of Jonah, the Assyrian Ninevites are moved by Jonah's preaching to repentance and faith (3:5–9); they "believed in God" (3:5), and Yahweh forgives them by his relenting and compassion (3:10; 4:11). Isaiah likewise envisions Yahweh's benevolence for the nations in, for example, Is 2:1–5; 19:19–25; 40:5; 56:6–7. In Is 19:20–22, the motif of the exodus is employed for the Egyptians whom Yahweh will rescue, while in Is 19:23, the scope of the healing and restoration extends from Egypt to the other major nation of the ancient Near East at that time, Assyria. In Is 19:24–25, the incorporation of these nations into the one people of God is evident by the application of "my people" to Egypt, just as it is applied to Israel elsewhere (e.g., Ex 3:7; Is 10:24; Hos 2:25 [ET 2:23]; Jer 2:11), and by the application of "the work of (my) hands" to Assyria, applied elsewhere to Israel (Is 60:21; 64:7 [ET 64:8]).

In Amos 9:7 Yahweh makes it clear that he has acted in unmerited kindness toward Israel, Philistia, and Aram. This suggests that God may have acted similarly toward all of the nations he condemns in Amos 1:3–2:3,[3] and indeed,

---

2 See Acts 2 and the excursus "The Quotation from Amos 9 in Acts 15."

3 Andersen and Freedman write: "We may assume that Amos would make the same claim and the same argument about the rest of the nations on the list: that Yahweh brought them to their present territory and has overseen their historical experience" (*Amos*, 352).

toward all nations on earth. Because God has displayed his goodness (e.g., Mt 5:45) and forbearance (Rom 3:25b) toward all peoples on earth, he expects them to respond according to the demands and requirements of his natural law, which is evident from nature and written on the human conscience (Rom 1:18–20; 2:14–15).[4] However, humanity's knowledge of natural law has been corrupted since the fall into sin, and no one is able to satisfy God's demands (Rom 3:1–20, citing various OT verses). Whether the nations know of Yahweh's providential guiding of their history or not, they still owe their life and existence to him, and he holds them responsible for their actions, for he is "the judge of all the earth" (Gen 18:25).

Amos' Oracles against Eight Nations (1:3–2:16)

Amos 1:3–2:3 constitutes the longest oracle against other nations in the Minor Prophets.[5] Whether delivered in times of warfare or public lamentation, in a royal court or a worship setting,[6] oracles against the nations either explicitly or implicitly normally boded well for Israel.[7] However, God speaking through Amos employs this genre in 1:3–2:3 and adapts it for his own purpose in order to make stinging accusations against his own unfaithful people, who had divided into two nations: Judah (2:4–5) and especially apostate northern Israel, which receives the longest and most severe condemnation (2:6–16). In the context of judgment oracles against other nations, Amos' Israelite audience would not have expected judgment oracles against Judah and Israel. Yahweh intends to include his divided unfaithful people among the heathen nations that are his enemies.[8]

---

[4] For natural law as the basis for the prophets' pronouncements of judgment on the pagan nations, see "The Transgressions of the Six Pagan Nations" below and also Lessing, *Jonah*, 88–90.

[5] For additional comments about the prophetic oracles against/about the nations, see Lessing, *Jonah*, 88–89, and 159–64 in the excursus "Mission in the Old Testament"; and Hummel, *Ezekiel 21–48*, 773–77. Some prophetic oracles have Gospel promises for Gentile nations and thus are better called "oracles *about* the nations." Such a promise regarding Edom, as a country representing the Gentiles, is found in Amos 9:12.

[6] It is impossible as well as unnecessary to choose one particular social setting for the oracles against the nations. Hayes wisely advises against evaluating all the oracles against the nations in the prophetic books based on one presumed setting ("The Usage of Oracles against Foreign Nations in Ancient Israel," 92). Clements maintains that there was no exclusive setting for the oracles against the nations (*Prophecy and Tradition*, 72). Mays believes that Amos has assimilated "forms and motifs from a variety of spheres and traditions to fashion a speech appropriate for his message" (*Amos*, 25). While Wolff believes that Amos has woven traditional elements and themes into "a particular kind of speech not previously heard in Israel," the uniqueness of Amos' oracle is due to its unique purpose and setting (*Joel and Amos*, 147–48).

[7] In the context of preparation for warfare, God's proclamation against the enemy could be matched with a specific promise of victory for the faithful nation (e.g., 1 Sam 15:1–7; 1 Ki 20:26–30).

[8] Isaiah employs the same rhetorical strategy when he includes Jerusalem (Is 22:1–14) in his oracles against the nations in chapters 13–23.

Thus Amos employs the genre of oracles against the nations not just to condemn unbelieving people, but also for the end purpose of announcing Law to unrepentant Israelites who thought they deserved nothing but Gospel.[9] In the same vein, St. Paul quotes from Israel's Scriptures (Pss 14:1, 3 || 53:2, 4 [ET 53:1, 3]) to convict Jewish people that they are just like Gentiles, since under the Law, "no one is righteous, not even one" (Rom 3:10; see Rom 3:9–20). Everyone is subject to Yahweh's judgment; both the chosen and the non-chosen must appear before his judgment seat (Rom 14:10b). The nations are condemned in Amos 1:3–2:3 because of their violation of Yahweh's general revelation or natural law (Rom 2:12a). Judah and Israel stand guilty of breaking Yahweh's Torah (Amos 2:4–16), so his written revelation condemns them (Rom 2:12b).

Amos' Oracles against the Six Pagan Nations (1:3–2:3)

The Transgressions of the Six Pagan Nations

Amos' first six oracles can be summarized as follows:

1. Damascus threshed Gilead with iron threshing sledges (1:3). This transgression was the use of harvest instruments as instruments for torturing subjugated Israelites.
2. Gaza captured the entire population of a city or region and sold the people to Edom as slaves (1:6). This transgression of taking captive an entire community was almost unprecedented in the ancient Near East.
3. Tyre delivered an entire captive population to Edom as slaves. This transgression violated a covenant Tyre had established with its "brothers" (1:9).
4. Edom pursued his brother (a people) with a sword and even slew his brother's pregnant women (1:11). This transgression killed both mothers and their unborn children.
5. Ammon ripped open the stomachs of pregnant women in Gilead (1:13). This transgression was barbaric murder of both mothers and their unborn children, the most vulnerable and innocent people in any society.
6. The Moabites burned the bones of the king of Edom to lime (2:1), probably to be used in plaster for a building. This transgression was a final act of desecration against the dead monarch.

The victims of these brutal actions were not nameless "collateral damage." They left behind a grieving father or mother, husband or wife, brother or sister, son or daughter. The main gist of Amos' oracles against the nations is that Damascus, Gaza, Tyre, Edom, Ammon, and Moab have violated Yahweh's moral Law, which they are obliged to keep and which they disregard at their own peril. Yahweh's natural order, inscribed on the hearts of all people, and

---

[9] Hummel writes: "Most commentators also agree that Amos here artfully uses the rhetorical device known as *captatio benevolentiae*. That is, first he gains his audience's attention and goodwill by condemning other people, saving his 'knockout blow' until he has them 'eating out of his hand' " (*The Word Becoming Flesh*, 312). This rhetorical device is evident also in 2 Sam 12:1–12; Is 5:1–7; Mt 21:33–46. This is the first of many texts in Amos where the prophet inverts a Gospel genre in order to proclaim Law (see also, e.g., 4:4–5; 5:18–20; 9:7).

even reflected by animals, is expressed in Is 1:3: "The ox knows his owner, and the ass the crib of his master; but Israel does not know, my people do not understand." While Isaiah (e.g., Is 29:22; 41:8; 51:2) affirms that Israel had a special relationship with Yahweh through the covenant he made with Abram in Gen 15:9–21, this opening passage in Isaiah emphasizes "the *unnaturalness* of Israel's rebellion, which is seen as standing in sharp contrast with the purely instinctive 'natural' reactions of animals"[10] (see also Jer 8:7).

The Western church has a long "natural law" tradition based on the recognition that the Scriptures affirm a natural knowledge of God, which is visible in creation and written on the human heart (e.g., Rom 1:18–20; 2:14–16). While this knowledge of God's existence, power, and goodness is not sufficient for salvation, it is the basis for natural law. Natural law is the reason why all societies feel they must have laws regarding justice in human conduct, based on moral and ethical standards of right and wrong. Yet the basis for Yahweh's judgments is not merely an internationally agreed upon code of ethics, what fallen people perceive to be the proper laws and standards. Rather, God judges people according to his own holy and righteous will, which is expressed in the Scriptures and is reflected in natural law. His divine will and Law is obligatory for all humankind, whether or not people recognize or accept it.[11]

The theological foundation of Amos' oracles against the nations is this understanding of God's immutable will, which is expressed in the Scriptures and reflected in natural law and (albeit imperfectly) in the natural knowledge of God. The prophet appeals to an innate order about human conduct that is—or should be—evident to all people as good and right. Amos declares that the perpetrators of evil will not "get away with murder." Reality is not shaped by realpolitik, nor will the ruthless and powerful finally have their way. In Yahweh's just universe, the wicked will receive their due punishment. While such a confession seems to run smack in the face of a world where plunder, death, injustice, and evil are rampant, it boldly confesses that exploitation is not the final word; God has the final word.[12] Amos testifies to Yahweh's righteous rule even in the midst of a world gone astray.

In Amos' oracles, the nations are not denounced for sins that they could not have been expected to recognize (e.g., disregarding the Torah or the Sabbath observance), but rather for their "crimes against humanity." Put another way, Amos preaches against the nations not simply because of their disobedience to Yahweh, but also for failing to follow the dictates of their own God-given moral sense. The theory of evolution, which does away with God the Creator,

---

[10] Barton, *Understanding Old Testament Ethics*, 37.

[11] Barton, *Understanding Old Testament Ethics*, 109–14, discusses four different kinds of explanations for the basis of God's judgments against the other nations in Amos 1–2. He calls one explanation an appeal to "universal law" (pp. 112–13), which he defines in a way similar to the description of natural law above. However, Barton rejects it as the basis for Amos 1–2.

[12] See "Yahweh's Long Memory and Last Word" below as one of the patterns in Amos' oracles against the nations.

and the monumental influence of Karl Barth, who made a radical distinction between natural revelation and biblical revelation and who viewed unfavorably texts like Acts 17:24–31; Rom 1:18–32; and Rom 2:12–16,[13] have caused many to neglect the doctrine of creation and the corollaries of natural revelation and natural law. But when these NT texts are read sympathetically and interpreted faithfully, it becomes clear that they express the same theology as prophetic oracles against the nations.

Paul's speech on the Areopagus in Acts 17 begins with the doctrine of creation. There is no mention of the people of Israel, of the patriarchs or the prophets, or of Moses or David. The apostle cites no OT passage. The only texts quoted explicitly are from two Gentile poets. The apostle's argument concludes with Jesus' resurrection (Acts 17:31), which he mentioned earlier in the conversation (Acts 17:18). Paul asserts that God "commands all people everywhere to repent" (Acts 17:30). Judgment and resurrection are themes of special revelation, but to prepare for his proclamation of them, Paul starts his argument with natural theology.

In a similar way, in Romans 1 and 2, Paul presents a series of arguments that contain natural theology. In Rom 1:18–32, Paul explains the wrath of God against human wickedness on the grounds that "what can be known of God is plain to them [all people], because God has shown it to them" (Rom 1:19). Ever since the creation of the world, God's invisible nature has been clearly perceived in the things that he has made. All people are therefore without excuse. Paul goes on to state that when God's creatures disregard their Creator's natural revelation, they degenerate into abominable sins (he cites homosexuality and lesbianism) and worship creatures in nature, eliciting judgment by God.

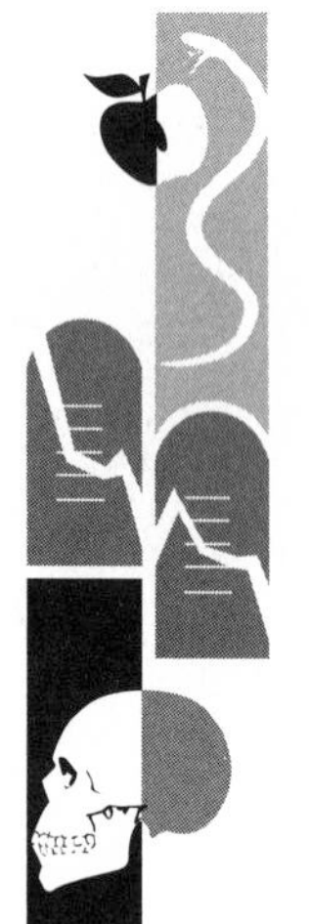

In Rom 2:12–16, Paul states that although Gentiles do not have the revealed Word of God that began with the Torah given to Moses, they nevertheless by nature (φύσις, Rom 2:14) behave in a way that reflects (positively or negatively) an awareness of God's Law. Gentiles "show the work of the Law written in their hearts, their conscience [συνείδησις] witnessing together with it, and their thoughts alternately accusing or even defending them" (Rom 2:15). Both of the words "nature" (φύσις) and "conscience" (συνείδησις) indicate that all human beings, as creatures of God, know something valid about God and his will. This innate knowledge has been confused and obscured by human sinfulness since the fall, but to the extent that it remains, it is consistent with the will of God expressed in the Second Table of the Ten Commandments—commandments that pertain to human relationships.

The Lutheran Confessions confirm this biblical witness about the Law: "Our first parents did not live without the law even before the fall. This law of God was written into the heart, for they were created in the image of God."[14]

---

[13] See, for example, Barth, *Church Dogmatics*, 2/1:85–254.

[14] FC Ep VI 2. See the discussion in Pieper, *Christian Dogmatics*, 1:531–33.

Although the nations Amos addresses are without special divine revelation, they are not exempt from moral responsibility. They do not have the Ten Commandments written in stone, but they do have standards from God about right and wrong written on their hearts. And because the nations have disregarded these ingrained laws, Yahweh will wage war against these inhumane war criminals.

God's Law Is Built into Creation

On this basis, Yahweh holds the six nations in Amos 1:3–2:3 accountable for their "crimes against humanity." Yahweh revealed his Torah to his chosen people, yet other nations have been and will be judged for "transgressions" (1:3, 6, 9, 11, 13; 2:1) against him and his will. Throughout the book of Amos, Yahweh is never *just* the God of Israel. In fact, in Amos, Yahweh is never given the title אֱלֹהֵי יִשְׂרָאֵל, "the God of Israel."[15] The God of Abraham, Isaac, and Jacob is first and foremost *the God of the universe*, and this remains true even when his own covenant people have rejected him as their God.

As Fretheim notes, the opening chapters of Genesis indicate that Yahweh was in a relationship with the world he created long before he ever created Israel. His relationship with Israel is a subset of his relationship with the entire cosmos. To be sure, Yahweh's action and revelation is especially focused on Israel, but this is only for the sake of the world. His election of Abram (Gen 12:1–3) is so that all the families of the earth in Genesis 10 will be blessed. "The election of the family of Abraham and Sarah is an initially exclusive move for the sake of a maximally inclusive end."[16]

The oracles against the six pagan nations presuppose that God fashioned the world so that its order reflects his own goodness. Consequently the divine Law is evident in the natural creation. This is already assumed in Gen 4:10–13, when God indicates to Cain that he should have known that murder is wrong.[17] Fretheim cites Yahweh's mandates in Gen 1:26–28 and 2:15–17 and then notes that Law is "a pre-sin reality, part and parcel of God's good creation."[18] Patriarchal narratives also testify to pre-Sinaitic divine Law. One example given by Fretheim is in Gen 26:5, where Yahweh says, "Abraham listened to my voice and kept my charge, my commandments, my statutes, and my laws [מִצְוֹתַי חֻקּוֹתַי וְתוֹרֹתָי]" (cf. Gen 18:19). The Law given by Yahweh to Israel at Sinai stands in continuity with the Law observed by Abraham.[19]

Israel's laws affirmed and elaborated the existing moral order that Yahweh had built into creation. That moral order could and should be discerned by all

---

[15] For example, the title is used thirteen times in Isaiah, forty-nine times in Jeremiah, and seven times in Ezekiel.

[16] Fretheim, *God and World in the Old Testament*, 18–19.

[17] Cf. Fretheim, *God and World in the Old Testament*, 135.

[18] Fretheim, *God and World in the Old Testament*, 135.

[19] Fretheim, *God and World in the Old Testament*, 136.

peoples and nations. Yahweh declared that the other nations would be able to see that Israel's laws were good (Deut 4:6) and that after Israel would be punished for violating the Torah, the other nations would perceive that Yahweh acted justly (Deut 29:23–27 [ET 29:24–28]; Jer 22:8–9). This shows that the nations who lacked the written Scriptures still had a basic moral standard of right and wrong that could detect human sin and affirm God's justice.[20]

When Amos speaks against foreign nations, his focus is not on what these nations have done to Israel and/or Judah, but what they have done to one another. Each nation is judged for cruel and inhumane treatment, for what we would call "crimes against humanity."[21] Amos declares that these crimes are even more serious than offenses against other people; the nations are guilty of crimes against *Yahweh*.[22] In every case, the punishment is focused on the political decisions of each nation, and each judgment consists of destructive fire, a sign of the "eternal fire" prepared for the devil and the final destination of all who die as unbelievers (Mt 18:8; 25:41; Jude 7).

The nations, even though they were not part of Israel, were subject to creational laws. "Nations are held accountable to creational law quite apart from their knowledge of the God who gave it."[23] The condemnations of the six nations in Amos 1:2–2:3 do not mention their idolatry or religious life.[24] Rather, they are condemned for cruel and inhumane treatment of fellow human beings. Yahweh's general revelation (e.g., Ps 19:2–7 [ET 19:1–6]) indicts the nations and makes it impossible for them to plead ignorance about how Yahweh desires people to care for one another.[25]

Patterns in Amos' Oracles against the Nations

In Amos 1:3–2:16, Yahweh's judgments follow a repeated pattern. Each of the oracles begins with the formula "because of three transgressions of [the

---

[20] Cf. Fretheim, *God and World in the Old Testament*, 137, who says this about the verdicts of such pagan nations: "That those who are not people of God can make such a determination successfully means that the laws are understood to conform to a standard other than 'God said so.' "

[21] Sumerian and Assyrian law codes and Hittite and Egyptian treaties, as well as ancient Near Eastern wisdom texts, all contain laws that guided behavior in the ancient Near East (cf., e.g., *ANET*, 159–206, 217–22, 412–30).

[22] In Rom 2:12–16, Paul asserts that no one has an excuse before God because his Law has been written on the hearts of all people.

[23] Fretheim, *God and World in the Old Testament*, 138. Psalm 19 links creation law with Torah; both are derived from Yahweh.

[24] Amos mentions false gods in 2:7–8; 5:26; and 8:14, but in all these cases he is addressing Israel as the perpetrator of idolatry.

[25] In addition to parallels between some Torah commandments and law codes of other ancient nations, we can also see similarity between Prov 22:17–24:22 and the Egyptian wisdom book The Instruction of Amenemope. Fretheim believes that the similarity shows that "God the Creator was actively engaged in the everyday experiences and reflections of other peoples who had thereby gained many valuable insights into the nature of life and the world" (*God and World in the Old Testament*, 202).

nation] and because of four, I will not revoke it [the punishment]." Then the accusation is stated, followed by the punishment. This basic form, an indictment followed by a statement of judgment, appears in many other prophetic books (e.g., Jer 5:10–17; Micah 1:5–7). However, the oracles in Amos 1–2, especially the first six, which are against the non-Israelite nations, exhibit at least eight distinctive patterns.

The Order of the Nations

The first of these patterns is the sequence of the nations. As each judgment unfolds, the order of the nations follows a geographical and social spiral that finally centers on Israel (2:6). The first three nations, Aram (represented by its capital, Damascus), Philistia (represented by Gaza), and Phoenicia (represented by Tyre), were the farthest away from Israel and had no direct ethnic connection with Yahweh's chosen people. The next three, Edom, Ammon, and Moab, were closer to Israel, sometimes geographically and always ethnically. Next, Judah is judged, and then the entire section culminates with the judgment of northern Israel.

The nations are presented in three different groups:[26]

1. The first three address city-states: Damascus, Gaza and her sister city-states, and Tyre.
2. The next three oracles are addressed to nations: Edom, Ammon, and Moab.
3. The last two address Judah and northern Israel, Yahweh's one covenant people who had divided after the reign of Solomon, when the northern tribes seceded from the messianic promise attached to the tribe of Judah (Gen 49:10) and royal line of David (2 Samuel 7).

Steinmann's study offers this analysis of Amos' order of the nations:

Amos' Oracles and Several Characteristics of the Nations

Text	*Nation*	*Presented as*	*Neighbor of*
1:3–5	Damascus	City-state	Israel
1:6–8	Gaza	City-state	Judah
1:9–10	Tyre	City-state	Israel
1:11–12	Edom	Nation	Judah
1:13–15	Ammon	Nation	Israel
2:1–3	Moab	Nation	Judah
2:4–5	Judah	Special (covenant) nation	Israel
2:6–16	Israel	Special (covenant) nation	Judah

The nations alternate between those bordering Israel and those bordering Judah, and the movement progressively gets closer to Israel and Judah's shared border. Damascus and Tyre (the first and third oracles) were on Israel's extreme north (northeast and northwest, respectively). Gaza and Edom (the second and

[26] See Steinmann, "The Order of Amos's Oracles against the Nations," 687.

fourth oracles) were to Judah's extreme south (southwest and southeast, respectively). Ammon (the fifth oracle) was east of Israel, while Moab (the sixth oracle) was east of Judah. Judah (the seventh oracle) shared the same border with Israel.[27] Viewed in this way, Amos moves geographically toward his rhetorical and theological goal: the oracle against Israel.

Sweeney offers another viable interpretation of Amos' ordering of the oracles. He believes that they are not arranged either historically or geographically, but in the order whereby an eastern empire such as Assyria would invade and defeat northern Israel. Beginning with Damascus/Aram, which was the first nation west of the Tigris and Euphrates Rivers, an advancing army would then pass through the Jezreel Valley. The march would continue south to Philistia in order to block any assistance for Israel from Egypt. The next target would be the Phoenician coast that would counter any Egyptian help from the sea. The strategy then leaves the Transjordan area (Edom, Ammon, Moab) sealed off for invasion. Finally, Judah and Israel, cut off from all possible help from their neighbors, are open to attack. Similar military maneuvers were followed by Hazael of Aram (2 Ki 12:18–19 [ET 12:17–18]) and Sennacherib (2 Ki 18:13, 17–37; 19:1–37 || Isaiah 36–37).[28]

Sweeney's proposal makes good tactical sense for the order of conquest, but it lacks clear reasoning to support the leap-frog order of conquest in the Transjordan, since Ammon is *north* of Moab. Steinmann's literary suggestion, therefore, makes more sense.

The Messenger Formula

A second pattern is that each of Amos' eight oracles is introduced by the well-known prophetic messenger/herald formula (*Botenformel*), כֹּה אָמַר יְהוָה, "thus says Yahweh" (see the first textual note on 1:3). The words that follow are not the musings of the prophet himself, nor of Israelites, but of the personal God who established his covenant with Israel and inspired the writing of the sacred Scriptures. God himself preaches through his called prophet, whose words therefore have divine authority certified by the invocation of God's name.

The Staircase Numerical Pattern

Third, the opening prophetic messenger formula is followed by a staircase numerical pattern, "because of three transgressions of [the nation] and because of four," with only the name of the nation varying in each case. (For "transgressions," see the second textual note on 1:3.) The same numerical staircase formula, "three … four," is in Prov 30:15, 18, 21, 29. The pattern of a graded

---

27 Steinmann, "The Order of Amos's Oracles against the Nations," 687. For further discussion on the logic behind Amos' order, see Paul, *Amos*, 11–15.

28 Sweeney, *The Twelve Prophets*, 203.

numerical sequence (a number and that number plus one) is a stylistic device used elsewhere in the OT[29] as well as in other ancient Near East documents.[30]

Weiss contends, however, that the numerical pattern in Amos is sui generis, unique both stylistically and structurally.[31] He notes that the number seven symbolizes completeness and contends that the phrase "because of three sins … and because of four" indicates that divine punishment will be forthcoming because the sins (totaling seven) have reached their completeness. He is aware that this suggestion is novel since in other contexts graded numerical sayings aren't used to indicate the totality of the two numbers.[32] Elsewhere in the OT, graduated numbers can signify an indefinite figure (e.g., 1 Sam 18:7; Ps 91:7), but in those cases no additional detailed illustrations follow. And when the literary device is employed to indicate a definite number, it is always immediately illustrated by specific examples whose sum is the total of the higher of the two numbers (Prov 6:16–19; 30:15–16, 18–19, 21–23, 29–31; cf. Job 5:19).[33] Weiss supports his suggestion by referring to the linguistic phenomenon of merism, by which two different components express a totality. He maintains that "the wholeness of a thing is demonstrated by two of its components and by two numbers, each of which and both together constitute a typological number for completeness."[34]

A slightly different understanding proposed by Soggin is that the phrase "because of three … and because of four" implies "innumerable crimes."[35] The nations are not judged based on isolated events but rather on their continued and repeated brutality. The refrain can be read in light of Amos 4:6–11, where sin after sin is met by God's call to repent, but then Yahweh's patience finally runs out. Creature must meet Creator; on this Yahweh will not change his will (cf. Amos 4:12).

Equally appealing is the argument put forth by Paul, who believes that Amos employs the literary scheme "three … four" in the same manner as he uses "seven … eight," the number of oracles against nations in 1:3–2:16 (six pagan nations, then Judah as the seventh and northern Israel as the eighth). "Both three and seven are typologically complete numbers, for which four and eight provide the complementary numerical parallelism and also add a climactic dimension." Paul notes that Amos' choice of three and four may have been influenced by the phrase "to the third and fourth generation" (Ex 20:5; 34:7;

---

29 For example, "one … two" is in Ps 62:12 (ET 62:11), and "six … seven" is in Prov 6:16 and Job 5:19. See GKC, § 134 s.

30 See, for example, Roth, "The Numerical Sequence x/x + 1 in the Old Testament."

31 Weiss, "The Pattern of Numerical Sequence in Amos 1–2."

32 Weiss, "The Pattern of Numerical Sequence in Amos 1–2," 420–21.

33 Cf. Weiss, "The Pattern of Numerical Sequence in Amos 1–2," 417.

34 Weiss, "The Pattern of Numerical Sequence in Amos 1–2," 421, citing Judg 12:14; Job 1:2–3.

35 Soggin, *The Prophet Amos*, 32.

Num 14:18; Deut 5:9), which "expresses the length and finality of God's retributive justice and punishment."[36]

The phrase "because of three … and because of four" indicates Yahweh's longsuffering; he has sought to postpone the judgment.[37] Yahweh is "slow to anger and abounding in steadfast love" (e.g., Joel 2:13; Jonah 4:2).[38] Jerome extrapolates:

> God will not punish us at once for our thoughts and resolves but will send retribution upon their offspring or upon the evil deeds and habits of sin, which arise out of the offspring. As he says by the mouth of Amos, "For three transgressions of such and such a city and for four I will not turn away the punishment thereof."[39]

God's antecedent will or first desire is to forgive sins and save people by his grace; that is why he puts off the Day of Judgment (2 Pet 3:8–10). However, although Yahweh is very patient, he does set a limit for each people, as he indicated already in Gen 15:16 for "the iniquity of the Amorites." "God is notably exasperated when his self-restraint is misinterpreted as indifference or acquiescence, when a stay in punishment, granted so that they may have every possible opportunity to repent, is used as an opportunity to commit more sins (Rom 2:1–11)."[40] When a nation's sins exceed the limit allowed by Yahweh in his patience, he changes from forbearance to wrath.

God's Judgment Is Irrevocable

Fourth, all of the oracles announce the absolute irrevocability of the divine decision as Yahweh declares, לֹא אֲשִׁיבֶנּוּ, "I will not revoke it." The referent of the third masculine singular object suffix, "it," is not clear. The nearest matching noun that would make sense as the antecedent is קוֹלוֹ, "his [Yahweh's] voice" in 1:2, and some scholars understand this to be the referent.[41] However, schol-

---

[36] Paul, *Amos*, 30.

[37] Motyer writes: "One way of expressing this truth about God is to say that He never punishes the sinner except after prolonged personal observation and ample opportunity for repentance" (*The Message of Amos*, 30, citing [in n. 6], e.g., Gen 18:20–21; Is 30:18; Acts 17:30–31; 2 Pet 3:8–9, 15). Three plus four equals a total of seven. Limburg discusses the role of the number seven in Amos and concludes that it is the most prominent number in the book ("Sevenfold Structures in the Book of Amos"). Amos uses literary units of heptads in 1:3–2:5; 2:6–8; 2:14–16; 3:3–6; 4:4–5; 4:6–11; 5:8–9; 5:21–23; 6:1–6; 9:1–4.

[38] For an exposition of this description of God that recurs in the OT, see Lessing, *Jonah*, 353–56, and "Jonah's Creedal Confession of Gracious Yahweh (4:2d–e)" on pages 367–70.

[39] Jerome, letter to Demetrias (letter 130; cited in Ferreiro, *The Twelve Prophets*, ACCS 14:86; cf. *NPNF*[2] 6:266).

[40] Andersen and Freedman, *Amos*, 231.

[41] This is noted by Andersen and Freedman, *Amos*, 235. Raabe understands the antecedent of "it" to be Yahweh's "voice" in 1:2 ("The Particularizing of Universal Judgment in Prophetic Discourse," 666). This line of interpretation sees continuity between Amos 1:2 and the oracles against the nations that follow.

ars have offered other interpretations.[42] Most English translations paraphrase: "I will not turn back [my wrath]" (NIV); "I will not revoke the punishment" (NRSV; similar is NASB); "I will grant them no reprieve" (NEB).

Andersen and Freedman believe that Amos' first two visions (7:1–6) inaugurated his ministry.[43] In those visions, Amos pleaded for "Jacob," and then Yahweh relented and did not carry out his prior decision to enact judgment. If that phase of Amos' ministry came first, then the Jerusalem Bible's translation of לֹא אֲשִׁיבֶנּוּ comes closest to the contextual meaning: "I have made my decree and will not relent."[44] This understanding also corresponds to the message of the third through fifth visions (7:7–9; 8:1–3; 9:1–4) and to Yahweh's assertion "I will never again forgive him" (7:8; 8:2), meaning "this time I will not change my course of action as I have done previously." Amos 4:6–11 indicates that Yahweh's plagues were meant to bring repentance, but the people did not repent; note the fivefold refrain throughout 4:6–11, וְלֹא־שַׁבְתֶּם עָדַי, "but you did not return to me" (e.g., 4:6), which uses a different form of the same verb translated as "revoke" in 1:3 and the later oracles against the nations. In chapters 1 and 2, which could have been revealed after the first two visions (7:1–6), Yahweh indicates that the time of forbearance is past and the opportunity for northern Israel to be spared is gone. Judgment will no longer be postponed.[45]

Just One Transgression Is Cited

A fifth pattern is shared by only the first six oracles, which are directed against the pagan nations. Even though Yahweh's accusation against each of the six is "because of three transgressions … and because of four," he goes on to describe just one specific transgression, although in all likelihood more than one transgression is implied. Simundson asks these pertinent questions: "Does

---

[42] For an overview of how various other scholars have understood the antecedent, see Wolff, *Joel and Amos*, 128, and Linville, "What Does 'It' Mean?" Knierim believes the antecedent is Yahweh's anger (" 'I Will Not Cause It to Return' in Amos 1 and 2," 170–75). Noble believes that the antecedent is deliberately ambiguous (e.g., Noble, " 'I Will Not Bring "It" Back' (Amos 1:3): A Deliberately Ambiguous Oracle?"). By "ambiguous," Noble means that Amos is saying that Yahweh won't revoke the threatened punishment but also that Yahweh won't revoke the promised restoration envisioned in 9:11–15 (pp. 108–9). That is a good argument for the unity of the book. Ceresko calls for translating the clause as "I will not let him return (to me)." He also argues for polysemy by changing the vocalization of the clause so that the text can also be read as "I will indeed fan/blow upon it [the fire of my fury]" ("Janus Parallelism in Amos's 'Oracles against the Nations' (Amos 1:3–2:16)," 487, following for the first translation Barré, "The Meaning of *lʾ ʾšybnw* in Amos 1:3–2:6," 622). Paul maintains that the antecedent of "it" is the punishment that is about to be spoken. He calls this an "anticipatory" sense (*Amos*, 46).

[43] Andersen and Freedman, *Amos*, 8. See "The Structure and Outline of the Book of Amos" in the introduction.

[44] Andersen and Freedman write: "The links between these oracles against the nations and the visions reported in chaps. 7 and 8 show that the events develop from an initial threat that was temporarily averted by Amos' successful intercession (7:1–6)" (*Amos*, 235).

[45] A comparable clause is in Num 23:20, where Balaam declares about his pronouncement of Yahweh's blessing upon Israel, וְלֹא אֲשִׁיבֶנָּה, "and I cannot take it back."

he skip the first three and go immediately to the most grievous example? Is the one transgression that is listed the one that finally wears out God's patience, the straw that breaks the camel's back? Or does the use of this formula imply repetition of wrongdoing that is endless, so many sins that one cannot really number them?"[46]

In contrast, God cites multiple transgressions by Judah (2:4–5) and especially by northern Israel (2:6–16), implying that their sins are more numerous or grievous.

The Citation of the Transgression

A sixth pattern is that all of the oracles use the preposition עַל, "because," followed by an infinitive construct with third masculine object suffix (usually plural, sometimes singular) to describe the transgression by each pagan nation, or the first cited transgression by Judah and Israel. These appear in 1:3, 6, 9, 11, 13; 2:1, 4, 6, for example, עַל־דּוּשָׁם, "because they threshed" (1:3), and עַל־הַגְלוֹתָם, "because they exiled" (1:6). The transgressions cited in the six oracles against the pagan nations are all corporate sins, perpetrated by the nation against another nation, its king, or its people. The transgressions of Judah are also corporate, but are against the special revelation of Yahweh and specifically the First Commandment: they rejected the Torah and fell into idolatry. Only the oracle against Israel cites transgressions by individuals against others within the nation.

Most of the transgressions by the six pagan nations cited in this way are war crimes committed during attacks (1:3, 11, 13) or subsequent inhumane treatment of those conquered (1:6, 9; 2:1). Helpless people were abused so that policies of the state could move forward. The setting is international; the issues are about warfare.

Yahweh's Long Memory and Last Word

The seventh pattern is held in common by the six oracles against the pagan nations. The war atrocities cited were probably committed as border wars from the late years of Solomon's reign (ca. 940 BC) down to, and perhaps including, the time of Amos (ca. 760 BC).[47] The citation of crimes committed over

---

[46] Simundson, *Hosea, Joel, Amos, Obadiah, Jonah, Micah*, 166.

[47] Sweeney, however, seeks to establish specific dates for these events in the ninth and eighth centuries (*The Twelve Prophets*, 204–12). Wright believes that the six nations were guilty of breaking their covenant relationships ("the system of vassal and parity treaties") with Israel that he presumes were established by the empire of David ("The Nations in Hebrew Prophecy," 236), yet there is not enough historical data from the Scriptures nor from extrabiblical sources about the existence and terms of such treaties nor about the events cited in Amos 1:3–2:3 to be that precise. Similar is the argument of Mauchline, "Implicit Signs of a Persistent Belief in the Davidic Empire," 288–92. The suggestions of Wright and Mauchline, however, seem unlikely because (1) none of the nations is explicitly condemned for rejection of a united Israel or treaties established during the empire of David, and (2) Tyre was never a part of that empire. It is more plausible and faithful to the text to conclude that these nations are being judged because they broke God's natural law.

some two centuries reveals that Yahweh does not forget the sins of the impenitent, but stores them up for the time of judgment. Yahweh takes the long view; sins, no matter when they were committed, constitute the reason for present punishments (cf., e.g., Ex 20:5; 1 Ki 14:14–16; 2 Ki 17:21–23). Raw human power that crushes fellow human beings cannot succeed in destroying God's kingdom and people (cf. Mt 10:28; Lk 12:4) and is not the final datum of history. Yahweh always has the last word.

Yahweh Punishes by Fire

The eighth pattern shared by the first seven oracles (but not by the oracle against Israel in 2:6–16)[48] is that they all end with the final verdict in which Yahweh, speaking in the first person, condemns each nation to punishment by fire: usually וְשִׁלַּחְתִּי אֵשׁ, "and/so I will send fire" (1:4, 7, 10, 12; 2:2; 2:5) and once its variant, וְהִצַּתִּי אֵשׁ, "and/so I will kindle fire" (1:14).[49] Death by fire was a means of capital punishment for heinous offenses (cf. Gen 38:24; Lev 20:14; Josh 7:24–25). Its purpose was the complete annihilation of evil. It also has eschatological significance. It recalls the conflagration of Sodom and Gomorrah, archetypes of abominable sinfulness (Genesis 19), and anticipates the everlasting fire of hell to which all unbelievers will be consigned on Judgment Day (Mt 3:12; 5:22; 13:40; Rev 20:9–10, 14–15).

---

[48] However, in Amos 5:6, Yahweh indicates that the fire of judgment can break out against Israel.

[49] Wolff calls this "divine pyrotechnics" (*Joel and Amos*, 158). A movement of fire that is similar, but one of grace, occurs in the narrative sequence in Exodus through Leviticus. Fire begins in the burning bush (Ex 3:2), descends on Sinai (Ex 19:18), and then takes up permanent residence on the altar in the tabernacle (Lev 6:6 [ET 6:13]).

Amos 1:3–5

Judgment against Aram

Translation

1 **[3]Thus says Yahweh:**
"Because of three transgressions of Damascus
and because of four, I will not revoke it,
because they threshed Gilead with threshing sledges of iron.
[4]So I will send fire against the dynasty of Hazael,
and it will consume the fortresses of Ben-hadad.
[5]And I will break the gate-bar of Damascus,
and I will cut off the ruler from the Valley of Aven,
and the scepter-bearer from Beth-eden.
And the people of Aram will go into exile toward Kir."
Yahweh has spoken.

Textual Notes

1:3 כֹּה אָמַר יְהוָה—The declaration "thus says Yahweh" introduces the book's first prophetic speech. It is repeated throughout the oracles against the nations (1:6, 9, 11, 13; 2:1, 4, 6), as well as elsewhere in the book (3:12; 5:4, 16; 7:17; see also 3:11 and 5:3, which have the variation "thus says the Lord Yahweh"). It is more assertive and emphatic than אָמַר יְהוָה, literally, "Yahweh said," which appears in 1:5, 15; 2:3; 5:17, 27; 7:3; 9:15 (see also 1:8; 7:6). The more solemn נְאֻם־יְהוָה, literally, "an oracle/utterance of Yahweh," or a similar variant occurs twenty-one times in Amos.[a] The highest degree of legal veracity is expressed by Yahweh's oath invoking himself as the supreme authority: נִשְׁבַּע אֲדֹנָי יְהוִה, "the Lord Yahweh swears" (4:2; 6:8; see also נִשְׁבַּע יְהוָה in 8:7). Of course, all of these expressions declare that the utterances are the very Word of God and so are absolutely true.

(a) Amos 2:11, 16; 3:10, 13, 15; 4:3, 5–6, 8–11; 6:8, 14; 8:3, 9, 11; 9:7–8, 12–13

In social use, the messenger formula "thus says …" probably had its genesis in the world of diplomacy. Sweeney explains:

> It is styled as a literal repetition of the words that were given to the messenger at the time that the messenger was commissioned by the sender (cf. Gen 32:1–5 [MT 32:2–6]). The messenger speech begins with the … messenger formula, and the message itself takes the form of a direct speech by the sender. Use of the form presupposes that the person who delivers the message speaks on behalf of the sender.[1]

For example, when King Sennacherib relates a message to King Hezekiah, Sennacherib's messenger begins, "Thus says the great king, the king of Assyria" (2 Ki 18:19; cf. 2 Ki 18:29). The authority behind the message lies not with the messen-

---

[1] Sweeney, *Isaiah 1–39*, 524.

ger but with the sender. Similarly, when Jacob communicates with his brother Esau, he sends messengers introducing his message with "thus says your servant Jacob" (Gen 32:5 [ET 32:4]). When Jephthah is involved in negotiations with the Ammonite king, his representatives begin with "thus says Jephthah" (Judg 11:15).

עַל־שְׁלֹשָׁה פִּשְׁעֵי דַמֶּשֶׂק וְעַל־אַרְבָּעָה—The same accusation formula is employed in all eight of the oracles against nations in chapters 1–2: the preposition עַל, "because of," followed by שְׁלֹשָׁה פִּשְׁעֵי, "three transgressions of," and the name of the offending city-state or nation, then וְעַל־אַרְבָּעָה, "and because of four [transgressions]" (1:3, 6, 9, 11, 13; 2:1, 4, 6). The repeated preposition עַל functions causally and is therefore translated as "because of" (see Joüon, § 170 h). עַל also functions this way later in each of the eight oracles; see the fourth textual note on 1:3.

The segholate noun פֶּשַׁע is a central term in the vocabulary of Amos. It appears ten times, always plural,[b] and the cognate verb פָּשַׁע is used twice in 4:4. The noun פֶּשַׁע is a legal term that usually means "transgression," "offense," or "crime." It can refer to sins committed by individuals or nations against other people (cf. BDB, 1 and 2), but usually it refers to transgressions against God (BDB, 3). It has this theological meaning especially in contexts where it appears alongside the synonyms עָוֺן, "iniquity," and חַטָּאָה or חַטָּאת, "sin" (see *HALOT*, 2 a–c). Words and phrases with those (and cognate) synonyms are in the same semantic field as פֶּשַׁע, and they appear in the following places in Amos: עֲוֺנֹתֵיכֶם, "your iniquities" (3:2); חַטֹּאתֵיכֶם, "your sins" (5:12); בַּמַּמְלָכָה הַחַטָּאָה, "upon the most sinful kingdom" (9:8); and כֹּל חַטָּאֵי עַמִּי, "all the sinners of my people" (9:10).

(b) Amos 1:3, 6, 9, 11, 13; 2:1, 4, 6; 3:14; 5:12

Whether the transgression is by an individual or a corporate nation, it remains within Yahweh's authority whether to punish or to forgive. The offenses in 1:3–2:16 prompt divine punishment, but in 9:11–15 Yahweh's final response is to proffer forgiveness and restoration through the line of David culminating in the Messiah.

The cognate verb פָּשַׁע usually has the theological meaning "*transgress* against God" (BDB, 2), but it can also have a more political meaning for a nation: "rebel, revolt" (BDB, 1) against an overlord.[2] For example, in 2 Ki 1:1 Moab rebels against its suzerain, the king of Israel. Since God has instituted all governmental authority to rule with justice on his behalf (Rom 13:1–6), rebellion against rightful authority is transgression against God. The verb can have both a theological and a political meaning in some contexts, as in Hos 8:1, where the verb פָּשַׁע is parallel with the idiom עָבַר בְּרִית, "to transgress [God's] covenant," and in Is 1:2, where Yahweh declares that his children, the Israelites, "have rebelled against me." If the noun in Amos has a political connotation, then it is that all eight nations in 1:3–2:16 have rebelled so often that their suzerain, Yahweh, must act with retribution.

---

2 Andersen and Freedman write: "The root *pšʿ* is used of rebellion against higher authority, and specifically of nations and their rulers revolting against their suzerains" (*Amos*, 26). Compare von Rad, *Old Testament Theology*, 1:263, who says that the term belongs to "the language of politics."

לֹא אֲשִׁיבֶנּוּ—The verb שׁוּב appears over one thousand times in the OT and has one of the broadest and most complex semantic ranges of any Hebrew verb.[3] Often the Qal of שׁוּב indicates that someone going in one direction turns back or returns to the place from which he started. This meaning is often quite literal and straightforward, indicating a simple, physical return (e.g., Gen 18:33; Is 38:8). The verb is frequently used together with the preposition מִן, "from," and in this construction, the emphasis can be on desisting and abandoning a current action (e.g., Jer 4:8, 28). In some texts, שׁוּב indicates a theological return, turning back to Yahweh in repentance and faith (e.g., Deut 4:30; Jer 3:7).

Many different suggestions have been offered for unraveling the unclear nuance of this verb repeated in Amos' oracles against the nations, אֲשִׁיבֶנּוּ, the Hiphil of שׁוּב with third masculine singular object suffix, "him/it." The Hiphil of שׁוּב can mean "to annul, revoke,"[4] and such a meaning is appropriate here.

The problem is with the object suffix. What is its antecedent? But this question looks in the wrong direction for the answer. The object suffix is proleptic, and its referent is found by looking *forward* in the book. Understood in this way, the mystery heightens the tension. What is it—exactly—that Yahweh will not revoke? What could it be? This rhetorical device allows anxiety to mount as the coming punishment is initially left ambiguous, only to be explained later. In the case of Israel (2:6–16), the coming punishment is explained by means of Amos' first four visions in 7:1–3, 4–6, 7–9; 8:1–3. The referent is Yahweh's decree that he makes in 7:8 and 8:2: he will no longer forgive Israel. See also the discussion of this clause under "God's Judgment Is Irrevocable" in the introduction to 1:3–2:16.

עַל־דּוּשָׁם בַּחֲרֻצוֹת הַבַּרְזֶל אֶת־הַגִּלְעָד׃—Again (see the second textual note on 1:3), the preposition עַל functions causally: "because of" (see Joüon, § 170 h). Here and in the corresponding clauses in each of the seven later oracles against the nations, עַל introduces an infinitive construct with a third masculine suffix, here דּוּשָׁם. See GKC, § 158 c, and "The Citation of the Transgression" in the introduction to 1:3–2:16.

The Qal of דּוּשׁ, "to thresh," usually refers to guided animals (usually cattle or oxen) trampling grain in order to separate the kernels from the husks (e.g., Jer 50:11; Hos 10:11).[5] Threshing could also be done with special sleds or implements (e.g., Is 28:28). The verb can also denote the trampling action of an animal, for example, one that crushes the eggs of an ostrich in the nest on the ground (Job 39:13–15). The verb דּוּשׁ may be used in a figure of speech for the destruction of mountains (Is 41:15), nations (e.g., Hab 3:12), or enemies (e.g., 2 Ki 13:7; Micah 4:13) in the same way that the stalks are destroyed when the grain is threshed. This is the verb's meaning in Amos 1:3, where the destruction of Gilead by Damascus is reported to have been by means of threshing.

---

[3] Cf. Holladay, *The Root Šûbh in the Old Testament*.

[4] See *HALOT*, s.v. שׁוּב, Hiphil, 6 (cf. 3); BDB, s.v. שׁוּב, Hiphil, 11; and Holladay, *The Root Šûbh in the Old Testament*, 101–2.

[5] Cf. H. F. Fuhs, "דּוּשׁ," *TDOT* 3:182–86.

Some lexicons list חָרוּץ as an adjective, for example, "*sharp*: of threshing instrument" (BDB, 1, citing Is 41:15), but it is used as a substantive noun here and in Is 28:27, where too it refers to a threshing sledge. The theological usage of חָרוּץ is exclusively tied to judgment and war. Twice in Isaiah the threshing sledge is used as a metaphor for Yahweh's punishment (Is 28:27; 41:15). This sledge was probably a wagon with low wheels and mounted teeth of iron (as indicated here by הַבַּרְזֶל) or flint on the underside. Niehaus believes that חָרוּץ in Amos 1:3 refers to "a type of threshing board with knives or sharp stones underneath. … This board was approximately seven feet by three feet and is used for threshing even today in Syria."[6] Wolff writes: "Grain was threshed by drawing over it a heavy sledge, the boards of which were curved upward at the front and the underside of which was studded with prongs; the use of iron knives, rather than flint stones, for these prongs in the iron age significantly increased the efficiency of the sledge."[7]

The Arameans used these boards attached to wagons against the citizens of Gilead. "Only prisoners of war were thus tortured; the custom was not uncommon of placing them on the ground like grain, and driving the machine over them."[8] Therefore the language of "thresh" and "threshing sledges" in Amos 1:3 may not be purely metaphorical, but also literal and exceedingly cruel.

"Gilead" is one proper place name that can take the definite article (הַגִּלְעָד). It is a compound of two words, גַּל, "hill" or "heap," and עֵד, "witness," coined by Jacob when he first marked his land with a heap of stones signifying the border between himself and Laban, an Aramean, and invoked God to be a witness to maintain this border (Gen 31:21–25, 44–53).[9] The region of Gilead was east of the Jordan River and extended from the Arnon River in the south to the Yarmuk River in the north. Machir, the firstborn of Manasseh, was named "the father of Gilead" (Num 26:29; Josh 17:1).

The word can be used for a territory (Gen 37:25) and can designate a "tribe" (Judg 5:17). It was the home of Jephthah (Judg 11:1–12:7). Moses conquered Gilead by defeating the Amorite kings Sihon and Og (Num 21:21–35; Deut 4:47–49; Josh 12:2–5). Reuben and Gad received their inheritance in the southern part of Gilead, and half of the tribe of Manasseh settled in the northern part of Gilead (Numbers 32; Joshua 13). Beginning with the time of the judges, Gilead was repeatedly overrun by the Ammonites (e.g., Judg 11:4–5; 1 Samuel 11).

Because Gilead bordered Aramean territory, it was often the first region to suffer from foreign military campaigns, which from the mid-ninth century on became extremely severe (e.g., 2 Ki 10:32–33). By the beginning of the eighth century, however, the Aramean attacks had stopped, and Israel was able to recuperate and restore its authority over the area, especially under Jeroboam ben Joash, who occupied Damascus and

---

6 Niehaus, "Amos," 341.

7 Wolff, *Joel and Amos*, 154.

8 Harper, *Amos and Hosea*, 18.

9 Cf. M. Ottosson, "Gilead (Place)," *ABD* 2:1020–21.

Hamath (2 Ki 14:25, 28). Later in the eighth century, Gilead was captured in 733–732 BC by Tiglath-pileser III who deported its inhabitants (2 Ki 15:29).

1:4 וְשִׁלַּ֫חְתִּי אֵ֫שׁ בְּבֵ֣ית חֲזָאֵ֑ל—The idiom וְשִׁלַּ֫חְתִּי אֵ֫שׁ בְּ-, "and I will send fire against … ," is repeated verbatim in 1:4, 7, 10, 12; 2:2, 5. See "Yahweh Punishes by Fire" in the introduction to 1:3–2:16. In all except 2:2, the accent on the verb remains on the penultimate syllable (-לַּ֫-) and is not shifted to the final syllable (as usual for a perfect with *waw* consecutive) because the following word is accented on its first (and only) syllable, אֵ֫שׁ. See GKC, § 49 m. The idiom also occurs in Ezek 39:6 and Hos 8:14, with Yahweh as the subject. He is also the subject of the third person idiom in Lam 1:13. A few other passages use second or third person forms of the Piel of שָׁלַח with אֵשׁ and the preposition בְּ when people are the agents of destructive fire (Judg 1:8; 20:48; 2 Ki 8:12; Ps 74:7). For בֵּ֣ית חֲזָאֵ֑ל, "the dynasty of [King] Hazael," see the commentary on 1:3–4.

וְאָכְלָ֖ה אַרְמְנ֥וֹת בֶּן־הֲדָֽד׃—The feminine noun אֵשׁ, "fire," is the subject of the feminine perfect with *waw* consecutive, וְאָכְלָה, "and it will consume." The direct object, the plural of אַרְמוֹן, refers to "fortresses," "palaces," or "citadels," spacious, strongly fortified houses that could be defended in time of war even if the city walls had fallen. The word may denote "not only the royal residence but also the buildings required by court officials."[10] Others consider the plural to refer to the dwellings of the rich, "rivaling in size and beauty and grandeur of construction the palaces of the kings."[11] The singular in 1 Ki 16:18 and 2 Ki 15:25 seems to refer to "an especially fortified section of the royal palace."[12]

All the oracles against the nations (except the one against Israel in 2:6–16) express the divine judgment with וְאָכְלָה אַרְמְנוֹת, "and it [the fire] will consume the fortresses" (1:4, 7, 10, 12, 14; 2:2, 5). One battle strategy in the ancient Near East was to set these buildings on fire by igniting their timbers. אַרְמְנוֹת is used mostly in contexts of conquest because these buildings would be special targets for attack and plunder. After the oracles against the nations, Amos also refers to these imposing structures in 3:9–11 and in 6:8; in 6:8 they are spoken of as objects of national pride.

For "Ben-hadad" (בֶּן־הֲדָד), which is parallel to "Hazael" in 1:4a, see the commentary on 1:4.

1:5 וְשָֽׁבַרְתִּי֙ בְּרִ֣יחַ דַּמֶּ֔שֶׂק—The noun בְּרִיחַ often denotes the large beams or bars that held shut the doors of the gates in a fortified city. King explains:

> The gate of an ancient city had wooden double doors, which were metal-plated to withstand fire. When the gates were closed, they were secured by a locking bar of bronze or iron which was positioned across the back of the double doors and held in place by sockets in the doorposts.[13]

---

[10] Grant and Rowley, *Dictionary of the Bible*, 717.

[11] Laetsch, *The Minor Prophets*, 12–13.

[12] King, *Amos, Hosea, Micah*, 67.

[13] King, *Amos, Hosea, Micah*, 75.

In Nah 3:13 the bars are made of wood, while they are bronze in 1 Ki 4:13. Normally the bar was anchored at each end in the gateposts; this made it impossible to forcibly open the gates either from the inside or outside. Only someone divinely empowered like Samson could lift up the gateposts, together with the doors, in order to overcome a city's bars (Judg 16:3). This same power of Yahweh will break the bar of Damascus.

Damascus (דַּמֶּשֶׂק) was conquered by David, who stationed troops there, and the Arameans then paid tribute to Israel (2 Sam 8:5–6 ‖ 1 Chr 18:5–6).[14] But in the tenth century BC, Damascus regained its independence and became the capital of a powerful Aramean kingdom that fought against Israel during Solomon's reign (1 Ki 11:23–25) and then various times in the ninth century (e.g., 1 Ki 15:16–22 ‖ 2 Chr 16:1–6; 1 Kings 20 and 22; 2 Ki 10:32–33; 2 Kings 13). At the beginning of the eighth century, Damascus was defeated by the Assyrians. The city-state became a vassal of Israel during the reign of Jeroboam ben Joash (2 Ki 14:25, 28). In 732 BC, it was incorporated into the Assyrian Empire. Damascus is located along the banks of the Barada River (the biblical Abana), which is the major source of water in the region.

וְהִכְרַתִּי יוֹשֵׁב מִבִּקְעַת־אָוֶן—The Hiphil of כָּרַת, "cut off," often refers to destruction during warfare, for example, the destruction of the Canaanite peoples in Josh 23:4; of Jabin of Hazor in Judg 4:24; of nations in Is 10:7; and of Judah in Jer 44:11. Its object here is the participle יוֹשֵׁב, which could be a collective singular, "the one dwelling," that is, "the inhabitants," as rendered by the LXX, κατοικοῦντας. However, the end of the verse refers to the inhabitants of the city as being exiled. So יוֹשֵׁב instead expresses Yahweh's vow to cut off the "one sitting" on the throne, the "ruler" of Damascus (cf. 2 Chr 16:2).[15] Compare, for example, Pss 2:4 and 22:4 (ET 22:3), where יוֹשֵׁב describes Yahweh as "enthroned." יוֹשֵׁב is one of several participles used by Amos as epithets to designate rulers. Later in this verse (Amos 1:5c), the parallel participial phrase וְתוֹמֵךְ שֵׁבֶט, literally, "and one who grasps/takes hold of a scepter," refers to Ben-hadad. In 1:8 the clause וְהִכְרַתִּי יוֹשֵׁב recurs, and the following parallel to יוֹשֵׁב is again וְתוֹמֵךְ שֵׁבֶט. Other analogous terms appear in 2:3: שׁוֹפֵט, "ruler, judge," and שָׂרִים, "princes, officers."

The construct phrase מִבִּקְעַת־אָוֶן is translated as a place name, "from the Valley of Aven," but its literal meaning is "from the valley of wickedness/idolatry." The pointing of אָוֶן (transliterated as "Aven") may be a cacophemism or malphemism for אוֹן, since LXX Amos 1:5 has ἐκ πεδίου Ων.[16] Its location may be Baalbek, whose name alludes to the worship of Baal, in the plain of Coele-Syria. In Greco-Roman times, Baalbek was given the Greek name Heliopolis ("city of the sun") when it was renamed after the Egyptian city by the same name, and the cult of sun worship was imported there from the Egyptian city. The Egyptian name for the Egyptian city of sun worship was Anûnû, which was rendered in Hebrew as אוֹן, "On" (Gen 41:45, 50; 46:20). In an oracle against Egypt, its city of On (אוֹן) is called אָוֶן, "wickedness/idolatry," as a cacophemism (Ezek

---

[14] Cf. W. T. Pitard, "Damascus," *ABD* 2:5–7.

[15] As noted by Andersen and Freedman, *Amos*, 253–54, whose analysis is followed in the rest of this textual note. They translate יוֹשֵׁב here and in 1:8 as "sovereign."

[16] Cf. Harper, *Amos and Hosea*, 19, and Niehaus, "Amos," 342–43.

30:17). A similar cacophemism is in Hos 4:15; 5:8; 10:5, where Bethel (בֵּית־אֵל, "house of God") is condemned by calling it בֵּית אָוֶן, "the house of wickedness/idolatry."

וְתוֹמֵךְ שֵׁבֶט מִבֵּית עֶדֶן—The participial phrase וְתוֹמֵךְ שֵׁבֶט is, literally, "and one who grasps/takes hold of a scepter." In this context, the noun שֵׁבֶט denotes an insignia of leadership and designates a ruler. Amos may have selected this phrase, "the exact semantic analogue" of which is documented in an ancient Aramaic inscription, because he was addressing his oracle against Damascus, the Aramean capital.[17] שֵׁבֶט refers to the scepter of a ruler, symbolizing authority and dominion, also in, for example, Judg 5:14 and Is 14:5. Several promises state that the Messiah himself will be God's royal "scepter" (Gen 49:10; Num 24:17; Ezek 21:15, 18 [ET 21:10, 13]) or will wield God's scepter (Is 11:4; Pss 2:9; 45:7 [ET 45:6]).

Elsewhere the noun שֵׁבֶט can denote a staff, stick, or rod, made of either wood or iron.[18] It could be used as a threshing rod, a gentler alternative to the threshing sledge, or as a shepherd's staff (Micah 7:14). Since a tribe was a political entity with rulers or leaders, שֵׁבֶט is often used by extension to denote the entire tribe, as prominently demonstrated in the many references to the "tribes" of Israel (e.g., Gen 49:28; Ex 24:4; Ezek 48:1).

Amos refers next to בֵּית עֶדֶן, Beth-eden, meaning "house of delight." This site also appears in the OT simply as עֶדֶן (2 Ki 19:12 || Is 37:12; Ezek 27:23). עֶדֶן probably is cognate to עֵדֶן, as in the garden of Eden (e.g., Gen 2:8, 10), and shares the same meaning, "delight, pleasure, exquisiteness." The Hebrew Beth-eden refers to the Aramean kingdom Bit-adini on the banks of the middle Euphrates River,[19] about two hundred miles north-northeast of Damascus.

וְגָלוּ עַם־אֲרָם קִירָה—The construct phrase עַם־אֲרָם, "the people of Aram," is singular but a collective consisting of many people, so it is the subject of the plural verb וְגָלוּ (GKC, § 145 b–c). "The people of Aram" were spread out across the area northeast of Israel. Quite often local groups of them were specified by phrases like "Aram of Damascus" (2 Sam 8:5–6) or "Aram of Zobah" (2 Sam 10:6, 8). Their numbers and influence were so great that their different dialects of Aramaic supplanted the Akkadian language and Aramaic became the diplomatic language of much of the ancient Near East (see 2 Ki 18:26 || Is 36:11).

Although the Qal of גָּלָה can express a wide variety of distinctions, its meanings fall primarily into two basic categories: "to uncover, reveal" (as in Amos 3:7) and "to emigrate, go away, go into exile."[20] The latter meaning has a negative connotation,

---

17 Paul, *Amos*, 52, including n. 90, who cites *KAI*, § 214.15, 20, 25, an inscription of Panammu I, who was the king of Samal during the first half of the eighth century BC.

The literary device of employing native vocabulary when referencing foreign nations also appears in Jonah 1:5, where מַלָּח, "sailor, seaman," is used, as also in an oracle against Tyre (on the Phoenician coast) in Ezek 27:9, 27, 29. Because מַלָּח is attested in Phoenician and appears in Ezekiel to reference Phoenicians, it is likely that מַלָּח is borrowed from Tyre and Sidon.

18 Cf. H.-J. Zobel, "שֵׁבֶט," *TDOT* 14:303–8.

19 King, *Amos, Hosea, Micah*, 50–51.

20 Cf. H.-J. Zobel, "גָּלָה," *TDOT* 2:476–88.

signifying defeat and deportation, as is evident here in Amos 1:5. Similarly, the Qal is used to describe the departure of Israel into exile in Amos 5:5; 6:7; 7:11, 17 (also, e.g., 2 Ki 17:23; Micah 1:16). Compare 1 Sam 4:21–22, where it refers to the departure of Yahweh's glory from Israel. The Hiphil stem of גָּלָה exclusively means "to take into exile," as Gaza is accused of doing in Amos 1:6. It also describes Yahweh as the one who causes Israel to go into exile in Amos 5:27 (see also Jer 29:4, 7, 14).

The noun קִיר usually means "wall" in Hebrew, while in Moabite it means "city."[21] In a few instances, קִיר is a proper name, as in Is 15:1, where it appears as a destroyed Moabite town, possibly the same place as Kir-hareseth (2 Ki 3:25; Is 16:7, 11; Jer 48:31, 36; cf. BDB, s.v. קִיר II). The location mentioned here in Amos 1:5, as well as in 2 Ki 16:9; Is 22:6; Amos 9:7, is apparently a different place (see BDB, s.v. קִיר III). In Is 22:6, קִיר is parallel to Elam, which was east of Babylon at the northern end of the Persian Gulf in the vicinity of Ur, the home of Abraham (Gen 11:27–32). In Amos 1:5, קִיר with the locative *he* (ָה-), "*toward* Kir," is the direction in which the Arameans are taken into exile by the Assyrians, and in 9:7, קִיר is named as having been the original home of the Arameans. However, its precise location is still largely debated. The suggestions have ranged from the area of Nineveh to southeastern Mesopotamia, perhaps as far as the territory adjacent to modern-day Iran.

אָמַר יְהוָה׃—"Yahweh has spoken" serves as Yahweh's signature, verifying that he himself spoke the preceding words. Like a bookend, it balances the opening "thus says Yahweh" (1:3). This same signatory formula, אָמַר יְהוָה, concluding the first oracle against the first nation also ends the oracles against Ammon (1:15) and Moab (2:3). Other signatory formulas conclude the second and last oracles against the nations (אָמַר אֲדֹנָי יְהוִה, 1:8; נְאֻם־יְהוָה, 2:16).

Commentary

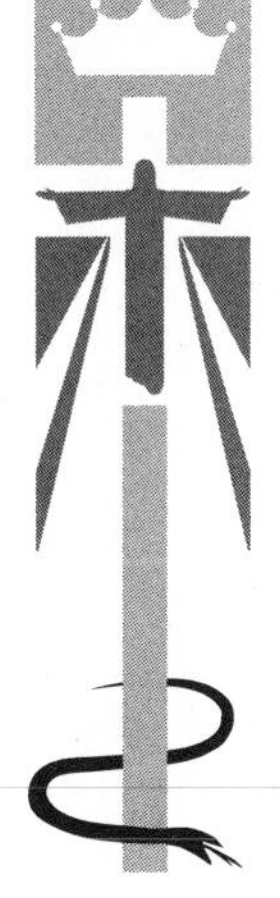

1:3 "Why do the nations conspire and the peoples plot in vain? The kings of the earth set themselves up, and the rulers take counsel together against Yahweh and against his Messiah: 'Let us burst their bonds asunder and cast their cords from us.' Enthroned in the heavens he laughs; the Lord mocks them" (Ps 2:1–4).

This royal, messianic psalm is an apt summary of Amos' oracles against the nations (1:3–2:16). Pagan nations, kings, and rulers of the ancient Near East revolted against their true Lord, Yahweh, and his anointed Davidic King, but Yahweh scoffs at such madness and promises to judge the rebels (1:3–2:3). Moreover, his own chosen people, Judah and Israel, had committed even worse transgressions than the pagans, and so they too will receive their just judgment (2:4–16). This is the major thrust of Amos 1–2.

Amos' initial oracle is not only spoken against Damascus. It becomes clear in 1:5 that the prophet also includes the Valley of Aven and Beth-eden. Therefore, 1:3–5 encompasses all "the people of Aram" (1:5), whose capital

[21] Cf. G. L. Mattingly and H. O. Thompson, "Kir," *ABD* 4:83.

city was Damascus.[22] It was an important Aramean city long before the reign of David, who captured it along with other Aramean states (2 Sam 8:3–8; 10:6–19). 1 Ki 11:23–25 indicates that Damascus became independent during Solomon's rule. Later, in the ninth century BC, Aram, headed by Damascus, became Israel's most pernicious enemy.

Yahweh's "I will not revoke it" declares that the issue is settled. While Amos' five visions in 7:1–9:4 come later in the book, chronologically they may have been revealed to the prophet earlier in his ministry, and they may furnish an organizing principle for the book.[23] Most readers read Amos linearly from 1:1 to 9:15, assuming that the book is laid out in a chronological fashion. However, many of the writing prophets were led by the Holy Spirit to arrange their blocks of material deliberately for theological purposes and not in strict chronological order.[24] Amos' ministry begins with Yahweh threatening judgment for Israel but then, after Amos pleads for his people, Yahweh relents twice, once at the end of each of the first two visions (7:1–3 and 7:4–6).

However, in the last three visions (7:7–9; 8:1–3; 9:1–4), Yahweh indicates that the time of grace has elapsed and that judgment must ensue. His statements in these visions "I will never again forgive him" (7:8; 8:2) as well as "and not for good" (9:4) replace the merciful retractions he granted earlier when Amos interceded for Jacob, who "is so small" (7:2, 5). The cycle of visions, therefore, is the background for the refrain "I will not revoke it" and indicates that the time of Yahweh's favor toward Israel has passed. If Israel can no longer escape judgment, then certainly the pagan nations cannot either. Therefore all the nations in 1:3–2:16 must appear before Yahweh's judgment seat (cf. Amos 4:12; Mt 25:31–32).

The word "transgressions"[25] describes the Arameans' military atrocities and accuses them of rebellion against Yahweh, who as the universal Creator and Monarch of all people is justly concerned about *every* nation and people.

---

[22] Is 17:1–3; Jer 49:23–27; and Zech 9:1–4 also include the city of Damascus in their oracles against foreign powers. In those passages too the capital city may represent the whole nation.

[23] See "The Structure and Outline of the Book of Amos" in the introduction.

[24] For example, Ezekiel supplies dates for most of his prophetic revelations, and they clearly are not all in chronological order, but are structured so that the book has the classical prophetic outline. For the stated dates of Ezekiel's oracles, see Hummel, *Ezekiel 21–48*, 740–41, and for the classical prophetic outline of the book, see Hummel, *Ezekiel 1–20*, 10–12. Daniel arranged his prophecies slightly out of chronological order to form interlocking Hebrew and Aramaic chiasms (see Steinmann, *Daniel*, 2, 22). Similarly, the four NT evangelists arranged their Gospel accounts in distinctive ways that are not always strictly chronological (but are historically true) in order to convey certain theological truths.

[25] The same Hebrew noun, פֶּשַׁע, appears in the accusations in all eight of the oracles (1:3, 6, 9, 11, 13; 2:1, 4, 6). The crimes of the nations entail military brutality, whereas Judah's crimes are rebellion against Yahweh's Torah (2:5), and Israel's crimes include disenfranchising the poor and needy among God's elect people (2:6–8). Because Judah and Israel are bound to Yahweh by a covenant relationship (3:1–2), they are specifically indicted for infractions against the revealed Torah.

"Offenses against him are punished directly, wherever they are committed and whoever the guilty party may be."[26] Yahweh's will is binding for all of humanity because he is the God of every nation under heaven. As a king musters his troops when his vassal rebels (2 Ki 3:5–6), so throughout Amos 1:3–2:5, Yahweh musters fire as his avenging force because his vassals have revolted against his will.[27]

Probably the Aramean threshing of Gilead took place during the last half of the ninth century when the Arameans under King Hazael invaded Gilead during the reigns of the northern Israelite kings Joram (2 Ki 8:28–29) and Jehu (2 Ki 10:32–33). The agricultural imagery of threshing is not used figuratively; rather, it describes the actual barbaric atrocity committed by the Arameans against Gilead. The Arameans used animals to drag weighted pieces of wood, studded on the underside with sharp iron or flint, back and forth across the prostrate bodies of the Gileadites. This war crime was comparable to the practice of skinning alive and impaling defeated foes.[28] This inhumane torture, treating people like stalks of grain and inflicting great pain, makes a mockery out of the sanctity of human life.

God originally fashioned man and woman in his image (Gen 1:26–27), and in Christ he has redeemed every person from every nation and of any age, from conception to the end of natural life. He desires to bring all people into his kingdom of grace through faith and sacramental incorporation. The abuse, dehumanization, or murder of any of his beloved creatures is a transgression against the triune God who is Creator, Redeemer, and Sanctifier.

1:4 Yahweh's judgment coming in the form of fire appears nine times in Amos (1:4, 7, 10, 12, 14; 2:2, 5; 5:6; 7:4). The pronouncement of punishment by fire is used in each of the oracles against the nations except the one against Israel (2:6–16), but Israel receives fiery judgment later in the book.[29] The motif is common among the prophets (e.g., Is 9:18 [ET 9:19]; Jer 11:16; Ezek 15:7), and Yahweh's fire often is indicative of his righteous anger, for example, "like the fire of my wrath" (Jer 4:4).[c]

(c) See also, e.g., Ezek 36:5; Nah 1:6; Lam 2:4; cf. Mt 3:12; 5:22; 13:40; Rev 20:9–10, 14–15

The motif of Yahweh's destructive fire engulfing pagan cities that commit abominations may be traced back to Genesis 19, where Sodom and Gomorrah, infamous for homosexuality, were consumed in a conflagration. The practice

---

26 Paul, *Amos*, 46. He also writes: "The innovation here is that Amos is sent not to chastise individuals, as his predecessors did, but entire nations" (p. 46, n. 12).

27 Cf. Paul, *Amos*, 46. Only the oracle against Israel in 2:6–16 does not refer to fire, but Yahweh's judgment to send fire against Israel occurs later, in 5:6 (see also 7:4).

28 A vassal treaty imposed by King Esarhaddon included the following consequence for disloyalty to himself as the covenant overlord: "Just as a honeycomb is pierced through and through with holes, so may holes be pierced through and through in your flesh, the flesh of your women, your brothers, your sons and daughters while you are alive" (*ANET*, 540).

29 Broadly speaking, the motif of the fire of judgment against Israel appears later in Amos (5:6; 7:4). Yahweh not only uses fire as a means for judgment against Israel, but also earthquakes (1:1; 3:15; 4:11; 8:8; 9:1, 5), an attacking army (6:14), the sword (7:9; 9:1), and he could use a lion, bear, or serpent (5:19; 9:3).

of Yahweh's earthly hosts, the army of Israel, burning enemy cities taken in divine warfare[30] goes back to Num 21:21–31, where Israel was victorious over the Amorite king Sihon. During Israel's conquest of idolatrous Canaan, the capture and destruction of pagan cities was often accompanied by burning (e.g., Josh 6:24; 8:8; 11:11; Judg 1:8).

The same practice was a military strategy throughout the ancient Near East, as confirmed by archaeological excavations. For example, an Assyrian relief depicting the capture of Thebes by Ashurbanipal shows the central gate of the city being torched by an Assyrian soldier.[31] Often in these ancient Near Eastern contexts, an engulfing fire meant an all-out frontal attack against a walled city. First flaming arrows were shot, followed by a battering ram that broke through the barred and fortified city gates, followed by wholesale slaughter, and ending with deportation.[32]

Each nation in Amos 1:3–2:5 is judged individually, but they all receive the same judgment: fire. This massive inferno may be similar to what Yahweh sent to kindle Sodom and Gomorrah (see Amos 4:11). Yahweh himself is described as a "devouring fire" (Deut 4:24; 9:3; Heb 12:29). His theophany that started the mustering of Israel as a nation was in the burning bush (Ex 3:2–10), and he redeemed his people by leading them as a pillar of fire by night (Ex 13:21–22). On Mount Sinai his presence brought with it fire (Ex 19:18), an event recalled by Moses in Deut 5:22–27. The glory of Yahweh is called a devouring fire in Ex 24:17. In his role as the Divine Warrior (Ex 15:3), Yahweh is *the* Arsonist par excellence. On Mount Carmel, Elijah was a witness to Yahweh's consuming fire as Yahweh defeated Baal and his prophets (1 Ki 18:24, 38). Elijah called down Yahweh's fire to destroy armed troops sent by the apostate king of northern Israel (2 Ki 1:10–14).

In Amos, the image of fire anticipates the Assyrian assaults that would come after his ministry, in the latter half of the eighth century BC (Amos 6:14). These events would be a dramatic portrayal of the revival of divine warfare, the theophanic manifestation of Yahweh. Strikingly, however, Yahweh will not fight *for* Israel as he did in the conquest of Canaan under Joshua. Instead, the divine warfare will be *against* Israel, and Yahweh's agent will be the army of another nation, which executes judgment on Israel since it had become apostate. Other

---

[30] For a theological study of OT Israel as Yahweh's earthly host carrying out his punitive will through warfare, one may see "Divine Warfare" in Harstad, *Joshua*, 256–69. An older critical standard work on holy war is by von Rad, *Der heilige Krieg im alten Israel.*

[31] Yadin, *The Art of Warfare in Biblical Lands in the Light of Archaeological Study*, 2:462. See also 2:420–21 for a relief depicting Sargon's assault on and igniting of the city of Kishesim.

[32] The Assyrian relief depicting the siege of Lachish by Sennacherib in 701 BC shows this process except that the arrows are not burning. This relief is shown and discussed in Yadin, *The Art of Warfare in Biblical Lands in the Light of Archaeological Study*, 2:428–37; it is also shown and briefly described in *ANEP*, §§ 372–73.

motifs connected to holy war include the following: mustering troops by a trumpet call (2:2; 3:6) and complete annihilation of the enemy (9:1–4, 10).

Yahweh's fiery war against Damascus in Amos 1:4 is directed toward "the dynasty of Hazael," the king who reigned in Damascus from 843 until about 796 BC.[33] Hazael brought about "evil" for Israel, even to the point of dashing little children to the ground and ripping open pregnant women (2 Ki 8:12). He seized from Jehu all of Israel's territory in the Transjordan (2 Ki 10:32–33) and continued his policy of terror throughout the reign of Jehoahaz (2 Ki 13:22). At one time, he had reduced Israel's army to a mere fifty horsemen, ten chariots, and ten thousand foot soldiers (2 Ki 13:7). Hazael also threatened to attack Jerusalem and was turned away only after Jehoash sent to him Jerusalem's treasures (2 Ki 12:18–19 [ET 12:17–18]).

Parallel to "the dynasty of Hazael" in Amos 1:4 is the phrase "the fortresses of Ben-hadad." Ben-hadad may have functioned as a throne name in much the same way as the term "pharaoh" functioned in Egypt. Apparently two Aramean kings called Ben-hadad preceded Hazael on the Aramean throne. Ben-hadad I, who was the son of Tabrimmon, ruled at the beginning of the ninth century BC. He was a treaty partner with Baasha, king of Israel, but later he allied himself with Asa, king of Judah (1 Ki 15:18–20). Ben-hadad II, who was either the son or grandson of Ben-hadad I, occupied the Aramean throne during the mid-ninth century. He was the major adversary of Ahab, king of Israel (1 Ki 20:1–34). However, he was assassinated by a usurper, the Hazael (2 Ki 8:7–15) named in Amos 1:4a. The third Ben-hadad was the son of Hazael (2 Ki 13:3, 24). He was a contemporary of the Judahite kings Amaziah (796–767 BC) and Uzziah (792–740) and the Israelite kings Joash (798–782) and Jeroboam ben Joash (793–753).[34] In Amos 1:4b, the prophet probably has in mind this last Ben-hadad, who ruled from about 796 until about 770 BC.[35]

Jer 49:27 quotes Amos 1:4 to indicate that Yahweh's promises to destroy Damascus were fulfilled in Jeremiah's day. The city's fortified "fortresses" or strongholds (Amos 1:4) were built to withstand the most intense attacks from the enemy for centuries, yet they were straw in the presence of Yahweh's fire (cf. 1 Cor 3:12–15).

1:5 To "break the gate-bar" of a city gate—in this case the city of Damascus—marks a decisive stage in the defeat of a city (cf. Judg 16:3). After the gate is broken open, the advancing army moves directly into the city (Jer 51:30; Lam 2:9). Yahweh, as the subject of the verbs "I will break" and "I will cut off" (Amos 1:5), indicates that he is the one who gives authority to the nation (Assyria) that will eventually enact this judgment.

---

33 Andersen and Freedman, *Amos*, 244, give these as "the most likely dates for this monarch."

34 Thiele, *The Mysterious Numbers of the Hebrew Kings*, 111, 113, 116, 118.

35 Andersen and Freedman, *Amos*, 246. They believe Ben-hadad was ruling when Amos delivered this oracle because his reign overlapped somewhat with those of Uzziah and Jeroboam ben Joash (cf. Amos 1:1). The year might have been about 775 BC (p. 249).

The parallel relationship between the Valley of Aven and Beth-eden forms a geographical merism, meaning that all Aramean territories from west to east—from Lebanon to Beth-eden on the Euphrates River—are destined for destruction.[36] In addition to the city of Damascus (1:5a), all of its allied territories will come under Yahweh's judgment.

The last part of the verse declares that "the people of Aram" would be exiled to Kir. 2 Ki 13:3 indicates that Aram had been Yahweh's tool of punishment against Israel. However, Yahweh would punish the Arameans by dethroning the nation's ruler and exiling the Aramean people.[37]

Yahweh's judgments were fulfilled about thirty years after Amos preached them. King Pekah of Israel and King Rezin of Aram/Damascus attacked Jerusalem (2 Ki 16:5; Isaiah 7), apparently trying to force King Ahaz of Judah into an anti-Assyrian coalition. Ahaz appealed to the Assyrian king Tiglath-pileser III for aid (2 Ki 16:7–8). In 732 BC, the Assyrians captured Damascus, killed Rezin, and "exiled [Damascus] to Kir" (2 Ki 16:9).

One of God's covenant curses for when Israel would prove unfaithful was for the people to be taken back to Egypt (Deut 28:68; see also Jer 43:5–7; Hos 8:13). By analogy, for Aram to return to Kir, its place of origin (Amos 9:7), implies the execution of Yahweh's curse. Just as Egypt meant slavery for Israel, Kir indicates Aram's return into oppression. Exile and deportation—in this case, Aram returning to Kir—is a dominant motif in Amos. The idea is expressed eleven times with the verb גָּלָה, "to (go into) exile" (1:5–6; 5:5 [twice], 27; 6:7 [twice]; 7:11 [twice], 17 [twice]), and with nouns for "exile" (גּוֹלָה in 1:15 and גָּלוּת in 1:6, 9).

Tiglath-pileser III was the Assyrian king who institutionalized exile as a part of his political strategy. He also began a new variation on the practice: he repopulated the vacated areas by relocating there exiles from other regions. This helped make exile permanent: not only were exiles sent to live in another land, other deportees were populated in the exiles' former land, making it much more difficult for exiles to return to their homeland since a new people was now firmly established in it. Assyrian exile, therefore, functioned as "a form of punishment, liquidation of rival powers, loyalty to empire, military conscription, source for craftsmen and unskilled laborers, and program of colonization, as well as population of urban centers and strategic sites."[38]

---

[36] For the locations of the Valley of Aven and Beth-eden, see the third and fourth textual notes on 1:5.

[37] For a similar account, see Is 10:5–19, where the Assyrians, who had been Yahweh's rod of anger (Is 10:5) against Israel, are subsequently placed under divine wrath. This means that Assyria is not an independent political force carrying out its own will; rather, it is Yahweh who "raises a signal for nations far away" (Is 5:26). Yet the unbelievers who are Yahweh's agents of judgment will themselves also be judged.

[38] Paul, *Amos*, 55, n. 112, citing Oded, *Mass Deportations and Deportees in the Neo-Assyrian Empire*.

This is one reason why the northern tribes of Israel, exiled by the Assyrians in 722 BC, never returned in any significant numbers, but were assimilated into their new locations. They essentially ceased to exist as distinct groups and became known as "the ten *lost* tribes."

In contrast, significant numbers of those exiled from Judah by the Babylonians around the time of the fall of Jerusalem (587 BC) later were able to return after the decree of Cyrus (538 BC). The tribe of Judah thus experienced a kind of resurrection, as Ezekiel foresaw (Ezek 37:1–14). The royal line of King David survived the Babylonian exile and lived on until the birth of the Son of David (Mt 1:1), through whom God fulfilled his promise of restoration (Amos 9:11–12; Acts 15:16–18).

Amos 1:6–8

Judgment against Philistia

Translation

1 **[6]Thus says Yahweh:**
"Because of three transgressions of Gaza
and because of four, I will not revoke it,
because they exiled an entire population into exile,
delivering them over to Edom.
[7]So I will send fire against the city wall of Gaza,
and it will consume her fortresses.
[8]And I will cut off the ruler from Ashdod,
and the scepter-bearer from Ashkelon.
And I will turn my hand against Ekron,
and the remnant of the Philistines will perish."
The Lord Yahweh has spoken.

Textual Notes

1:6 כֹּה אָמַר יְהוָה—For this messenger formula, see the first textual note on 1:3 and "The Messenger Formula" in the introduction to 1:3–2:16.

עַל־שְׁלֹשָׁה פִּשְׁעֵי עַזָּה וְעַל־אַרְבָּעָה—For this accusation formula, see the second textual note on 1:3 and "The Staircase Numerical Pattern" in the introduction to 1:3–2:16. Gaza (עַזָּה) was the southernmost of the Philistine pentapolis, which also included Ashkelon, Ashdod, Ekron, and Gath (see Josh 13:3; 1 Sam 6:17). Here in Amos 1:6, Gaza must function (by synecdoche of a part for the whole) for all of Philistia, since Yahweh's fire falls on the rest of Philistia too in Amos 1:7–8.

לֹא אֲשִׁיבֶנּוּ—See the third textual note on 1:3 and "God's Judgment Is Irrevocable" in the introduction to 1:3–2:16.

עַל־הַגְלוֹתָם גָּלוּת שְׁלֵמָה לְהַסְגִּיר לֶאֱדוֹם׃—This is the standard formulaic way in which the (first) transgression is cited in each of Amos' oracles. See the fourth textual note on 1:3 and "The Citation of the Transgression" in the introduction to 1:3–2:16. The six oracles against pagan nations cite only one transgression; see "Just One Transgression Is Cited" in the introduction to 1:3–2:16. However, the oracles against Judah and Israel cite multiple transgressions.

The clause הַגְלוֹתָם גָּלוּת שְׁלֵמָה is, literally, "they exiled a complete exile." The Hiphil infinitive construct of גָּלָה with subjective suffix, הַגְלוֹתָם, "their exiling," means "they exiled [others], took [others] into exile." For גָּלָה, see the fourth textual note on 1:5. The cognate accusative noun גָּלוּת, "exile, group of exiles," is derived from that same verb, as reflected in the translation: "they exiled … into exile." גָּלוּת שְׁלֵמָה, literally, "a complete exile," recurs in 1:9 and means the captivity of an entire population. Normally only a select group of people would be exiled, especially the political leaders and wealthy, influential citizens, since they would be the ones most likely to lead a revolt if they remained in their homeland (e.g., 2 Ki 24:14–16; Jer 52:28–30). Therefore Gaza committed a more heinous crime.

The Piel and the Hiphil stems of the verb סָגַר, "close, shut," mean "deliver over, hand over." Yahweh may deliver Israel over to its enemies to seal their downfall, as expressed by the Hiphil of סָגַר in Deut 32:30; Amos 6:8; and Lam 2:7. Amos rebukes Gaza for handing over their prisoners of war, presumably as slave labor,[1] לֶאֱדוֹם "to Edom." The equivalent of the Hiphil of סָגַר appears with this same technical meaning in extrabiblical Phoenician and Aramaic sources.[2]

1:7 וְשִׁלַּחְתִּי אֵשׁ בְּחוֹמַת עַזָּה—For this idiom for the punishment, וְשִׁלַּחְתִּי אֵשׁ בְּ, see the first textual note on 1:4 and "Yahweh Punishes by Fire" in the introduction to 1:3–2:16. חוֹמָה denotes the city wall that surrounded ancient walled cities, as in the parallel punishments in 1:10, 14.

וְאָכְלָה אַרְמְנֹתֶיהָ׃—See the second textual note on 1:4.

1:8 וְהִכְרַתִּי יוֹשֵׁב מֵאַשְׁדּוֹד—For וְהִכְרַתִּי יוֹשֵׁב מֵ-, see the second textual note on 1:5. "Ashdod" (אַשְׁדּוֹד) was one of the cities of the Philistine pentapolis, located on the Mediterranean coastal plain north-northeast of Ashkelon. Ashdod commanded the trade routes by land and sea to Egypt.[3] Josh 11:22 indicates that the Anakim, a race of giants, were exterminated from Israel but a population of them survived in Ashdod, Gaza, and in Gath. It is possible that the Philistine giant Goliath was a descendant of the Anakim.

In the conquest of Canaan, Judah was unable to conquer the inhabitants of the Mediterranean coastal plain, including the people of Ashdod, "because they had chariots of iron" (Judg 1:19). When the Philistines captured the ark of the covenant and it was taken to Ashdod (1 Sam 5:1–8), its inhabitants were punished by Yahweh with tumors (the Qere) or hemorrhoids (the Kethib in 1 Sam 5:6). In the eighth century, Uzziah captured Ashdod and Gath (2 Chr 26:3–6). Then Sargon took Ashdod in about 711 BC toward the end of his reign (Is 20:1).

וְתוֹמֵךְ שֵׁבֶט מֵאַשְׁקְלוֹן—For וְתוֹמֵךְ שֵׁבֶט, "scepter-bearer," see the third textual note on 1:5. "Ashkelon" (אַשְׁקְלוֹן) was the only Philistine seaport city and was one of the most important seaports in the eastern Mediterranean.[4] After Judah captured it (Judg 1:18), the city was later recaptured and inhabited by the Philistines. In the eighth century, the city became a vassal of the Assyrian king Tiglath-pileser III.[5]

וַהֲשִׁיבוֹתִי יָדִי עַל־עֶקְרוֹן—The OT has other common idioms for God (or his representative, e.g., Moses) extending (שָׁלַח or נָטָה) his hand (יָד) against (עַל) foes (e.g., Ps 138:7; Ex 7:5). However, this particular idiom with the Hiphil of שׁוּב, the object יָד, and the preposition עַל, "turn one's hand against," only occurs in a few OT verses and

---

1 Haran, "Observations on the Historical Background of Amos 1:2–2:6," 201–2.

2 Paul, *Amos*, 60.

3 See King, *Amos, Hosea, Micah*, 53, who notes that "in Iron Age II, Ashdod's gate and towers were similar in plan to those of Gezer, Megiddo, and Hazor."

4 King, *Amos, Hosea, Micah*, 53.

5 See *ANET*, 282–83.

usually refers to God striking people with a judgment. Wearied by Israel's idolatry and injustice, Yahweh declares to her, "I will turn my hand against you" (Is 1:25). God would turn his hand against Israel's enemies if Israel would again listen to him Ps 81:15 (ET 81:14). Zechariah 13 is a prophecy of the Davidic Messiah's atonement for the forgiveness of sins: God will strike the Shepherd on the cross, and the sheep (disciples) will be scattered (see Mt 26:31; Mk 14:27), and in that way God would turn his hand against the little sheep (Zech 13:7), but only temporarily—until Easter (cf. Amos 9:11). Ezek 38:12 is the only passage where God is not the subject of the idiom; in a vision of the eschatological battle, Gog plots to turn his hand against and pillage Israel, but Gog will be defeated.

"Ekron" (עֶקְרֹ֗ון), the northernmost city of the Philistine pentapolis, was about twenty-two miles west of Jerusalem. This prophecy by Amos in the mid-eighth century was fulfilled over the next century and a half.[6] Ekron was captured by Sargon II in 712 BC. In 701 BC, the king of Ekron remained loyal to the Assyrians and was imprisoned by Hezekiah. Sennacherib freed the king of Ekron and restored him as king.[7] Ekron was destroyed by Nebuchadnezzar in 603 BC.

וְאָבְדוּ֙ שְׁאֵרִ֣ית פְּלִשְׁתִּ֔ים—The construct phrase שְׁאֵרִ֣ית פְּלִשְׁתִּ֔ים, "the remnant of the Philistines," is governed by the feminine singular collective noun שְׁאֵרִ֣ית, which, however, refers to (plural, masculine and feminine) people, פְּלִשְׁתִּ֔ים, the "Philistines." That explains why the phrase is the subject of the plural verb וְאָבְדוּ֙. See GKC, § 145 e; Waltke-O'Connor, § 6.6b, example 1.

The noun שְׁאֵרִית, "remnant," often denotes those who are still alive after some form of disaster.[8] The word frequently appears in prophetic oracles against the nations (Is 14:30; 15:9; Jer 25:20; 47:4–5; 50:26; Ezek 25:16; Zeph 2:7, 9). Within the book of Amos, the Israelite tribe of Joseph is promised a remnant (5:15), as is Edom (9:12). In Edom's case, the remnant stands for what remains of the Gentile nations after their judgment by fire in 1:3–2:3, and the Gentile remnant will be called by God's name. This implies that God's eschatological Israel, reconstituted through the Davidic Messiah (9:11), will incorporate Gentiles.

The Philistines (פְּלִשְׁתִּ֔ים), whose place of origin is unknown, were among the Sea Peoples who migrated from the Aegean Sea to the Canaanite coast in the thirteen century BC.[9] In Amos 9:7, the prophet indicates that at one point in this migration they lived in Caphtor, the island of Crete. In about 1190 BC, the Egyptian pharaoh Rameses III defeated the Philistines and settled them in the Palestinian coastal towns of Gaza, Ashkelon, and Ashdod. Around 1150 BC, the Philistines overthrew their Egyptian overlords and formed the Philistine pentapolis, which included those three cities, plus Ekron and Gath. Each of these five cities was a city-state by a local ruler who also ruled the surrounding territory (Josh 13:3; 1 Sam 6:17–18; 27:2–5).

---

6 Cf. King, *Amos, Hosea, Micah*, 54.

7 See *ANET*, 287–88.

8 Cf. R. E. Clements, "שָׁאַר," *TDOT* 14:272–86.

9 Cf. H. J. Katzenstein, "Philistines (History)," *ABD* 5:326–28, and T. Dothan, "Philistines (Archaeology)," *ABD* 5:328–33.

Battles between the Philistines and Israelites are reflected in Judg 3:31; 14:1–16:30; 1 Sam 4:1–11; 7:5–14; 12:9; 13:1–14:52; 17:1–54; 18:27, 30; 19:8; 23:1–5, 27–28; 31:1–13; 2 Sam 5:17–25; 8:1; 21:15–22; 23:9–17; 2 Ki 18:8. During the eighth century, the Assyrian king Tiglath-pileser III began the policy of making these cities autonomous tribute-bearing states. Toward the end of the eighth century, Philistia's allegiance was torn between Assyria and Egypt. Hanno, the king of Gaza, joined a Syro-Israelite revolt against Sargon in about 722 BC. In 720 Sargon launched a campaign against Philistia and captured Hanno. Gaza became a loyal Assyrian vassal. Ashdod fell to Sargon in 712 (see Is 20:1). In 705 Sargon suddenly died, and this led several of Assyria's subject nations to rebel. When Sennacherib regained Assyrian control in 701, he deported the king of Ashkelon. Ashdod, Ekron, and Gaza were rewarded by the Assyrians for their loyalty. Additional military defeats of the Philistines, so that only a remnant was left, are reflected in Jer 25:17, 20; 47:4–5; and Ezek 25:16. But Amos, like Zeph 2:5, prophesies that even this remnant shall one day cease to exist.

אָמַר אֲדֹנָי יְהוִה׃—This is the only one of the oracles against the nations that ends with these exact words, "says the Lord Yahweh," but the same clause concludes Amos' second vision (7:6), and preceded by "thus" it begins prophetic oracles in 3:11 and 5:3. Here Yahweh in effect signs his name at the end to attest that the oracle consists of his own words. The fifth textual note on 1:5 points out that most of the oracles against the nations conclude with some signatory formula that balances the opening messenger formula, "thus says Yahweh" (as in 1:6).

The divine personal name יהוה, "Yahweh," most often stands alone in Amos. The second most common designation for God in Amos consists of this combination of the divine title and the divine personal name, אֲדֹנָי יְהוִה, "the Lord Yahweh," which appears twenty-one times in the book.[10] Normally the Masoretes point the Tetragrammaton with the vowels of אֲדֹנָי to make יְהוָה (e.g., Amos 1:2–3), directing the reader not to pronounce the divine name but instead to substitute "the Lord" for it. However, when the Tetragrammaton follows אֲדֹנָי, as here, they point the Tetragrammaton with the vowels of אֱלֹהִים to direct the reader to substitute "the Lord God" for "the Lord Yahweh." The earliest translators of אֲדֹנָי did not render the noun with the first person singular pronoun, "*my* Lord." The LXX almost always translates it with κύριος, not κύριός μου. In reference to Yahweh, אֲדֹנָי may mean "my Lord" (e.g., Gen 15:2), but in most cases it is better understood to mean "Lord par excellence, Lord of all" (see Waltke-O'Connor, § 7.4.3f).

Commentary

1:6–8 The first oracle (1:3–5) was against Damascus and all of "Aram," which will go into exile to "Kir" (1:5). Amos' second oracle invokes Yahweh's fire upon the Philistine city of Gaza. The coupling of Aram, Kir, and a Philistine city appears again toward the end of the book, in 9:7: "Did I not bring … the

[10] See Dempster, "The Lord Is His Name," 175. אֲדֹנָי יְהוִה occurs as a standalone title nineteen times (1:8; 3:7–8, 11; 4:2, 5; 5:3; 6:8; 7:1–2, 4 [twice], 5–6; 8:1, 3, 9, 11; 9:8) and as part of a longer title twice (3:13; 9:5).

Philistines from Caphtor and the Arameans from Kir?" Gaza, about three miles from the Mediterranean coast, was the southernmost of the Philistine pentapolis that consisted also of Ekron, Gath, Ashdod, and Ashkelon. In 1:6, Gaza represents, by metonymy, the entire Philistine realm, just as Damascus, the leading city of the Arameans, stands for the entire country in Amos 1:3–5.

1:6 The textual movement from Damascus (1:3–5) to Gaza is a move "from the battle-field to the board-room, from the camp to the counter."[11] The city-state of Gaza is not accused of exiling any particular nation but is ushered before Yahweh's judgment seat because of its practice of selling off an entire conquered people (not just the leading citizens), probably selling them as slaves. Self-serving power, concentrated in the hands of a few, resulted in writing off marginal people and making them hostages in another land. The Law of Moses allowed taking prisoners of war (Deut 20:10–11). However, Ex 21:16 indicates that the penalty for kidnapping and selling into slavery was death.

The major trading route from Gaza to Beersheba and then to Edom made Gaza's transportation of captive slaves quick and efficient. At the bargaining bench, Gaza, along with the other Philistine cities, delivered an entire population to Edom. Unlike the reference to Gilead in Amos 1:3, conspicuous by its absence here is any indication as to the exact people or region affected by this inhumane action. Furthermore, the exact number of people in this exile is not stated. It probably was the whole population of a city or a town, but it could have been of an entire region or country. Because the Edomites who purchased them from Gaza most likely employed the slaves in their copper and smelting operations, a continual supply of people power was a constant necessity because of the ongoing threat of injury and death involved in the dangerous work in their mines.

1:7–8 Because of this slave trade, Yahweh promises to send the same divine fire as in Amos 1:4 to bring about an inferno against Gaza (1:7). He will also cut off two of the Philistine rulers: "the ruler from Ashdod, and the scepter-bearer from Ashkelon" (1:8). Then he will turn his hand against Ekron (1:8), meaning that he will grasp it and exert his power to judge it. The implication probably is that each of the five Philistine cities will suffer all of these judgments: Yahweh's fire, the removal of their leader, and Yahweh's hand against them in judgment. In this way, the whole nation will be punished. Even "the remnant of the Philistines" that might survive some of these judgments eventually will perish (1:8).

A "remnant" (also 5:15; 9:12) refers to the survivors of a catastrophic devastation. Even a small remnant that subsists (cf. Is 1:9; 6:13; 11:1) gives hope for the future. But when the remnant is liquidated, no one is left and all hope perishes. In extreme circumstances, God's judgment may leave no chance for a remnant to survive (e.g., Josh 7:24–25). This is poetic justice for Philistia. In

---

[11] Motyer, *The Message of Amos*, 40.

the spirit of *lex talionis* (cf. Ex 21:24), Yahweh's verdict for those who exiled "an entire population" (Amos 1:6) is entire destruction.

Gath is the only city of the Philistine pentapolis not mentioned in this oracle. In fact no oracle against Philistia anywhere in the OT records all five names of these Philistine cities.[12] Perhaps Amos does not mention Gath because it was no longer independent.

Some thirty years after Amos' prophecy, Tiglath-pileser III, king of Assyria, captured Gaza in 734 BC in the course of his campaign against Israel. He wrote in his annals:

> As to Hanno of Gaza who had fled before my army and run away to Egypt, [I conquered] the town of Gaza, … his personal property, his images … [and I placed (?)] (the images of) my [… gods] and my royal image in his own palace … and declared (them) to be (thenceforward) the gods of their country. I imposed upon th[em tribute].[13]

Once Yahweh's inferno is kindled, it cannot be quenched (cf. Mk 9:43).

[12] In Jer 47:5–7, only Gaza and Ashkelon are mentioned. In Jer 25:20; Zeph 2:4–7; and Zech 9:5–7, Gath alone is conspicuous by its absence.

[13] *ANET*, 283 (the brackets, parenthesis, and ellipses are in *ANET*).

Amos 1:9–10

Judgment against Tyre

Translation

1 [9]**Thus says Yahweh:**
"Because of three transgressions of Tyre
and because of four, I will not revoke it,
because they delivered over an entire exiled population to Edom,
and they did not remember a covenant of brothers.
[10]**So I will send fire against the city wall of Tyre,**
and it will consume her fortresses."

Textual Notes

1:9 כֹּה אָמַר יְהוָה—For this messenger formula, see the first textual note on 1:3 and "The Messenger Formula" in the introduction to 1:3–2:16.

עַל־שְׁלֹשָׁה פִּשְׁעֵי־צֹר וְעַל־אַרְבָּעָה—For this accusation formula, see the second textual note on 1:3 and "The Staircase Numerical Pattern" in the introduction to 1:3–2:16. The city name צֹר, "Tyre," literally means "rock." The city was situated on a rocky island very close to the Phoenician coastline. Egyptian, Assyrian, biblical, and classical writings repeatedly refer to Tyre as the city in the midst of the sea.[1] Island Tyre was very much like modern Hong Kong or Manhattan: a financial center dependent on the mainland. Situated on the shore opposite the island city of Tyre was the mainland city of "Ancient Tyre" (Παλαίτυρος), which the Assyrians called Ú-*šu*-ú.[2]

Island Tyre is described in Is 23:7 as a city "whose origin is from ancient days." As a "bestower of crowns" (Is 23:8), Tyre colonized many lands. "Archaeological evidence testifies to the extent of Tyre's domination of international trade during the 8th and 7th centuries B.C.E."[3] Kings appointed by Tyre governed such colonies as Cyprus, Carthage, and Tarsus. Tarshish ships (destined for or coming from Tarsus) associated with coastal cities including Tyre (1 Ki 10:22; Is 23:1; Ezek 27:12, 25) point to the city's broad economic impact.[4] The most important ancient document detailing Tyre's economic influence is the lament over Tyre in Ezekiel 27. (See also Ezekiel 28, which depicts the fall of Tyre's king in terms of Satan's expulsion from Eden.) Although Ezekiel was a sixth-century BC prophet, his lament over Tyre is believed to reflect earlier Phoenician

---

1 Katzenstein, *The History of Tyre*, 9.

2 See Oded, "The Phoenician Cities and the Assyrian Empire in the Time of Tiglath-pileser III," 48, n. 57.

3 Bikai, "Phoenician Tyre," 49.

4 For Tarshish and ships associated with it, see Lessing, *Jonah*, 69–73, 75–76; Lemaire, "Tarshish-*Tarsisi*: Problème de Topographie Historique Biblique et Assyrienne," 47–49.

descriptions of the city and its trade.[5] So important was Tyre that the sinking of "Ship Tyre" creates repercussions to the ends of the earth (Ezek 27:33, 36). A perusal of the list of nations that traded with Tyre distinguishes three groups. Ezekiel 27 begins with Tarshish, Javan (Greece), Tubal, Meshech, and Beth-togarmah (27:12–14), then passes over to Dedan, greater Syria, Judah, Israel, and Damascus (27:15–20), and finally concludes with locations in Arabia and Mesopotamia (27:21–24). The city is spoken of in the following terms: "merchant of the peoples to many coastlands" (27:3), "your builders made your beauty perfect" (27:4), "your great wealth of every kind" (27:12), "Your wealth, your exports and your imports, your sailors and your pilots, your caulkers, and those who bring you imports" (27:27), and its king was "the signatory of perfection, full of wisdom and perfect in beauty" (28:12).

In this way, Ezekiel envisions Tyre as a "great metropolis, which resembled a 'glorious ship,' which all the nations of the ancient world vied with each other in ornamenting."[6] The city's wealth at the time of Tiglath-pileser III is attested by it giving Assyria the tribute of one hundred fifty talents of gold. "This is the largest amount of gold ever mentioned in any Assyrian tribute list."[7]

לֹא אֲשִׁיבֶנּוּ—For this declaration, see the third textual note on 1:3 and "God's Judgment Is Irrevocable" in the introduction to 1:3–2:16.

עַל־הַסְגִּירָם גָּלוּת שְׁלֵמָה לֶאֱדוֹם—Tyre's transgression is cited in the same form as the transgressions of other nations in Amos 1–2. See the fourth textual note on 1:3 and "The Citation of the Transgression" in the introduction to 1:3–2:16.

Much of this language is repeated from the citation of Gaza's transgression in 1:6. הַסְגִּירָם, the Hiphil infinitive construct of סָגַר, "deliver over, hand over," also occurs in 1:6 (לְהַסְגִּיר). The transgression of Gaza is described in 1:6 with the same phrases, גָּלוּת שְׁלֵמָה, literally, "a complete exile," translated here as "an entire exiled population," and לֶאֱדוֹם, "to Edom" (see the fourth textual note on 1:6). This means that Tyre, like Gaza, sold to Edom an entire population of captives as slaves. Normally only the higher classes of society would be deported, and only the useful workers would be sold as slaves. It was more inhumane to exile the entire population of a city or region and sell everyone into slavery.

וְלֹא זָכְרוּ בְּרִית אַחִים׃—After the infinitive הַסְגִּירָם in the preceding clause, the perfect verb זָכְרוּ continues to describe the sinful actions of Tyre (GKC, §§ 114 r; 158 c; Joüon, § 124 q). The verb זָכַר, "to remember," indicates the continuing presence in the mind and contemporary action consistent with that memory. The negated (לֹא) verb, "not to remember," is synonymous with forgetting (e.g., Gen 40:23; Is 17:10). זָכַר is not merely recalling benign facts or events, for it can be parallel with either of the verbs

---

5 For a detailed exposition, see Hummel, *Ezekiel 21–48*, 815–41. Cf. also van Dijk, *Ezekiel's Prophecy on Tyre*, and Katzenstein, *The History of Tyre*, 154. Elat hypothesizes about Ezekiel 27: "This prophecy originated from a Phoenician poem that glorified Tyre during her golden age from the beginning of the 10th until the second half of the 8th century B.C.E." ("Phoenician Overland Trade within the Mesopotamian Empires," 24).

6 Katzenstein, *The History of Tyre*, 161. See also Markoe, "The Emergence of Phoenician Art."

7 Elat, "Phoenician Overland Trade within the Mesopotamian Empires," 24.

שִׂים or עָלָה and עַל לֵב, "to place" or "to arise" and "on the heart" (e.g., Is 47:7; 57:11; 65:17), where the heart (לֵב) indicates not only the activity of the mind, but the action of the entire person. זָכַר often denotes a remembering that leads to action (e.g., Ex 6:5). In Amos 1:9, זָכַר denotes the observance of a covenant between two parties, as also in, for example, Gen 9:15–16; Ex 2:24; 32:13; Lev 26:42, 45; Ps 105:8.

The construct phrase בְּרִית אַחִים, "a covenant of brothers," is unique in the OT. In this context and again in 1:11, אָח does not mean a literal, familial "brother" but a treaty partner, who may be called a "brother" (e.g., Gen 26:28–31; 1 Ki 9:13; 20:32).[8] Both the particular covenant and Tyre's treaty partners are left unidentified. It is impossible to say whether this refers to earlier covenants between King David of Israel and Hiram, king of Tyre (2 Sam 5:11; 1 Ki 5:15b [ET 5:1b]; 1 Chr 14:1), or between Solomon and Hiram (1 Ki 5:15a, 26 [ET 5:1a, 12]; 2 Chr 2:2 [ET 2:3]; see the commentary on Amos 1:9–10). Perhaps it could refer to a renewal of a covenant between Tyre and Israel in Amos' time, during the reign of Jeroboam ben Joash, even though Scripture does not refer to such a covenant. Amos leaves the details "unidentified to place the emphasis upon the deplorable act itself rather than upon the specific party affected."[9]

1:10 וְשִׁלַּחְתִּי אֵשׁ בְּחוֹמַת צֹר—For the idiom וְשִׁלַּחְתִּי אֵשׁ בְּ, see the first textual note on 1:4 and "Yahweh Punishes by Fire" in the introduction to 1:3–2:16. חוֹמָה denotes a "city wall" as in 1:7, 14.

וְאָכְלָה אַרְמְנֹתֶיהָ׃—For the verb וְאָכְלָה and the object אַרְמְנוֹת, see the second textual note on 1:4.

Commentary

1:9–10 In these verses Tyre is accused of delivering an entire community of captives to Edom, even though it had a covenant relationship with the people taken captive. The charge echoes the previous oracle against Philistine cities (1:6–8), particularly Gaza, which was similarly accused of handing over an entire community to Edom (1:6). Like Gaza, Tyre is a powerful city on the Mediterranean coast that is guilty of the crime of trading slaves.[10] In Joel 4:4–8 (ET 3:4–8), both Philistia and Tyre are accused of the same crime of selling slaves, this time to the Greeks.[11]

Unlike the first two oracles, which were against the regions of Aram (1:3–5) and Philistia (1:6–8), this one specifically addresses one city, Tyre. Unlike the Philistia oracle (1:6–8), Amos' indictment against Tyre only accuses the city of selling a whole community, not first capturing it and then selling the people. Tyre apparently was not the conqueror, but served as the "middle man" that brokered people captured from surrounding nations and sold them to the highest bidder, which in this case was Edom.

---

[8] Fishbane, "The Treaty Background of Amos 1:11 and Related Matters," 314–15.

[9] Paul, *Amos*, 61.

[10] Cf. Paul, *Amos*, 57.

[11] Javan/Greece is named as a trading partner of Tyre also in Ezek 27:13. Haran, "Observations on the Historical Background of Amos 1:2–2:6," 201–7, discusses Tyre and Amos 1:9.

To "not remember a covenant of brothers" (1:9) means to not adhere to the conditions of the relationship established with a sworn oath. "Brothers" means that this was a parity covenant as opposed to a suzerain/vassal relationship, so it may be likened to an agreement between two brothers (e.g., Gen 31:43–54).[12] In 1 Ki 9:12–13 Hiram, king of Tyre, refers to Solomon as "my brother." In doing so, the Tyrian king is using a standard ancient Near Eastern term to denote a parity treaty.

Amos does not mention the names of Tyre's "brothers" (1:9), but they may have been Israelites. Israel and Tyre formed a political and commercial union under David and Hiram (2 Sam 5:11). This partnership continued between Hiram and Solomon (1 Ki 5:26 [ET 5:12]; 9:10–14), as well as with Ahab and Ethbaal (1 Ki 16:30–31). These relationships involving God's covenant people may have been the ones that Tyre betrayed.

Before the emergence of the Assyrian Empire with the reign of Tiglath-pileser III (745–727 BC), Tyre and the coastal areas extending farther south through Phoenicia stood at the extreme western end of Assyria's political horizon. But with the rise of the empire, Tyre and the other coastal cities became an important factor in Assyria's strategy in the west. In any struggle between a Mesopotamian power and Egypt for the control of Syria and Palestine, victory would go to the nation that acquired mastery of the Mediterranean ports. Control of Tyre and Phoenicia would guarantee the opportunity to exploit choice timber and highly skilled craftsmen, shipbuilders, and navigators.[13]

At least four Assyrian kings attacked the Phoenician coast, each with devastating results: Tiglath-pileser III (in 728–727 BC), Shalmaneser V (in 727 BC), Sennacherib (in 701 BC), and Esarhaddon (in 677 BC). The Babylonian king Nebuchadnezzar besieged Tyre for thirteen years before defeating it in 572 BC. But none of these attacks actually carried out Yahweh's threat in Amos 1:10 by destroying Tyre. The fulfillment did not come until the Greek conqueror Alexander the Great built a causeway to the island in 332 BC.[14] Yahweh's delays of judgment are not denials of his judgment. He will always fulfill his Word (cf. 2 Pet 3:2–9).

---

[12] As noted by Andersen and Freedman, *Amos*, 261.

[13] See Oded, "The Phoenician Cities and the Assyrian Empire in the Time of Tiglath-pileser III." On the economy and trade of the Phoenician cities, see Moscati, *The World of the Phoenicians*, 82–87.

[14] For the details, see Lessing, *Interpreting Discontinuity: Isaiah's Tyre Oracle*, 182–95.

Amos 1:11–12

Judgment against Edom

Translation

1 11 Thus says Yahweh:
"Because of three transgressions of Edom
and because of four, I will not revoke it,
because he pursued his brother with a sword,
and he destroyed his [brother's pregnant] women.
His anger seethed continuously,
and his fury raged incessantly.
12 So I will send fire against Teman,
and it will consume the fortresses of Bozrah."

Textual Notes

1:11 כֹּה אָמַר יְהוָה—For this messenger formula, see the first textual note on 1:3 and "The Messenger Formula" in the introduction to 1:3–2:16.

עַל־שְׁלֹשָׁה פִּשְׁעֵי אֱדוֹם וְעַל־אַרְבָּעָה—For this accusation formula, see the second textual note on 1:3 and "The Staircase Numerical Pattern" in the introduction to 1:3–2:16. "Edom" (אֱדוֹם) is located on both sides of the Wadi Arabah south of the Dead Sea. The name means "the red region" and is derived from the reddish sandstone located throughout the country.[1] Edom's major trade routes were the Desert Highway and the King's Highway. Both ran north from the Gulf of Aqaba through the country of Edom.[2] The country's economy was fueled from control over caravan routes from India and South Arabia to Egypt.[3] Edom dealt in slaves purchased from the Philistines and Tyre in the late ninth century and/or early eighth century (Amos 1:6, 9).

לֹא אֲשִׁיבֶנּוּ—For this declaration, see the third textual note on 1:3 and "God's Judgment Is Irrevocable" in the introduction to 1:3–2:16.

עַל־רָדְפוֹ בַחֶרֶב אָחִיו—The formula citing the transgression uses the preposition עַל, "because," followed by an infinitive construct with suffix (רָדְפוֹ). See the fourth textual note on 1:3 and "The Citation of the Transgression" in the introduction to 1:3–2:16. The clause is translated with a past tense finite verb: "because he pursued his brother with a sword." The context indicates that the suffix on the infinitive is subjective: רָדְפוֹ, "his [Edom's] pursuing," meaning that "he [Edom] pursued" (Waltke-O'Connor, § 36.1.1e, example 1). In the citations of (first) transgression by all the other nations except Moab (2:1), the infinitives have a plural suffix, but the suffix here and the following verbs

---

1 King, *Amos, Hosea, Micah*, 56.

2 See the map in B. MacDonald, "Archaeology of Edom," *ABD* 2:295.

3 King, *Amos, Hosea, Micah*, 56.

(וְשִׁחֵת ... וַיִּטְרֹף) are singular. The names of peoples can be used with either singular or plural verbs (Joüon, § 150 e).

The noun חֶרֶב, "sword," reappears in 4:10; 7:9, 11, 17; 9:1, 4, 10. In Amos it usually is employed by metonymy for warfare or violent death. Here the violence inflicted by Edom is condemned as contrary to God's will. However, in all of the other Amos passages, the "sword" is wielded by Yahweh himself (4:10; 7:9; 9:1) or by his agents who carry out his judgments (7:11, 17; 9:4, 10).

As in 1:9, אָח, "brother," refers to a nation or people that was a partner in a treaty or covenant with the offending nation, which violated the pact. The nation here is Israel. אָח also alludes to the fraternal kinship between Israel and Edom (see the commentary on 1:11).

וְשִׁחֵת רַחֲמָיו—The infinitive in the preceding clause (רָדְפוֹ) is followed here by a Piel perfect with *waw* consecutive, וְשִׁחֵת, which indicates recurring action: "*and* (on each occasion) *did cast off all pity*" (GKC, § 112 i; cf. § 114 r) or "*and* [repeatedly] *ruined* mercy" (Waltke-O'Connor, 32.2.5c, example 17).

In Amos the verb שָׁחַת occurs only here (the Piel perfect). Elsewhere in the OT, it occurs primarily in the Piel and Hiphil stems, both of which mean "to ruin, destroy, corrupt." The Piel typically refers to a completed action, while the Hiphil usually indicates a future, intended destruction.[4] When human beings are the subject, as here, the context usually refers to war (e.g., Josh 22:33; 1 Sam 23:10) or the perverse behavior of individuals (e.g., Prov 23:8) or groups of people (e.g., Zeph 3:7). The Piel can denote the killing of people (Num 32:15; 2 Sam 1:14) and the destruction of people along with other creatures (Gen 6:17; 9:15).[5]

The object of the verb is the noun (with suffix) רַחֲמָיו. The abstract plural noun רַחֲמִים can refer to human "compassion, mercy, pity" (e.g., Gen 43:30; 1 Ki 3:26; Dan 1:9; see BDB, 2). More commonly, רַחֲמִים denotes God's "grace" or "mercy" (see BDB, 1) and is often parallel with חֶסֶד, God's "loyal covenant faithfulness" (e.g., Ps 40:12 [ET 40:11]; Lam 3:22). Yahweh's רַחֲמִים can be manifest in various forms but is always of benefit to the recipient (e.g., Neh 9:19, 27–28, 31).

In Amos 1:11, רַחֲמָיו could refer to "his [Yahweh's] mercy" if Edom somehow corrupted or disregarded God's mercy by the way Edom dealt with God's chosen people Israel. Or it could mean that Edom "ruined its [own] compassion" in the sense that Edom was cruel and lacked any pity or compassion in its dealings with other peoples. That is the way Jerome's Vulgate (*violaverit misericordiam eius*)[6] and most English translations take the clause: Edom "cast off all pity" (KJV, RSV, ESV, NKJV) or "stifled his compassion" (NASB; cf. NIV). That understanding fits with the next two clauses of 1:11, which speak of Edom displaying anger and fury.

---

4 Cf. J. Conrad, "שָׁחַת," *TDOT* 14:584–93.

5 When Yahweh is the subject of שָׁחַת, his "destructive action is always a reaction to human sin" (Conrad, *TDOT* 14:590).

6 Jerome, *Commentariorum in Amos Prophetam* (CCSL 76:225), includes the Vulgate translation as well as a literal translation of the LXX into Latin as *violaverit vulvam super terram*, "he destroyed a womb upon the ground."

However, since the preceding parallel line, "because he pursued his brother with a sword," has a concrete human object ("his brother"), rather than an abstract object, רַחֲמָיו could have the corresponding concrete meaning "his [brother's pregnant] women," meaning that Edom did violence to the women—especially pregnant women and their children—belonging to the people that was its partner in a covenant treaty. The cognate noun רֶחֶם or רַחַם commonly means "womb" (e.g., Gen 29:31; 49:25; Ex 13:2), but it can refer to a woman taken captive or killed by attacking soldiers.[7] The LXX translated וְשִׁחֵת רַחֲמָיו here as καὶ ἐλυμήνατο μήτραν ἐπὶ γῆς, "and they destroyed a womb upon the ground." Understood in this way, רַחֲמָיו links this cited transgression by Edom to the crime of Ammon, who "ripped open the pregnant women of Gilead" (Amos 1:13).

Jerome's commentary connects the meanings "mercy" and "womb" by recalling how Jacob and Esau were twin brothers born from the single womb of Rebekah, so Esau's descendants (Edom) should have shown fraternal compassion for Israel:

> He [Edom] destroyed mercy, or his womb (or as Symmachus interpreted more plainly, his own bowels/compassion), forgetting the brotherhood, hardening the bowels/compassion of mercy, ignoring that he was a brother, and despising the womb of Rebekah, who in one act of birthing gave birth to twin infants.[8]

וַיִּטְרֹף לָעַד אַפּוֹ—Literally, "his anger [אַפּוֹ] tore [וַיִּטְרֹף] forever [לָעַד]," this is translated as "his anger seethed continuously" (cf. Waltke-O'Connor, § 33.3.1a, example 5). The verb טָרַף generally means to "tear apart" or "tear to pieces."[9] It can describe action by a wild beast of prey, as in Gen 37:33. Violent people, including the Messiah's enemies (Ps 22:14 [ET 22:13]; cf. Ps 22:22 [ET 22:21]); pagan nations, including Assyria (Nah 2:14 [ET 2:13]); and the abusive princes and false prophets of Israel (Ezek 19:3, 6; 22:25, 27) can be depicted as wild animals that tear apart (טָרַף) their prey. In Amos 1:11, the prophet's use of טָרַף compares savage human behavior with that of a rapacious beast (see also Gen 49:27; Deut 33:20). The cognate noun טְרֵפָה often refers to the carcass of an animal that has been "torn, killed" in the wild, rendering its meat unclean (e.g., Lev 17:15; 22:8). The cognate noun טֶרֶף often refers to the "prey" that a wild animal would tear with its teeth, as in Amos 3:4 (see also, e.g., Ezek 22:25, 27; Ps 124:6).

וְעֶבְרָתוֹ שְׁמָרָה נֶצַח׃—Literally, "and his fury [וְעֶבְרָתוֹ], he retained it [שְׁמָרָה] forever [נֶצַח]," this clause is translated as "and his fury raged incessantly." The feminine noun עֶבְרָה with suffix (וְעֶבְרָתוֹ) begins the clause as a *casus pendens* and is parallel to the immediately preceding word in the previous line, אַפּוֹ. The verb שְׁמָרָה is the third

---

7 In Judg 5:30, רַחַם רַחֲמָתַיִם, the singular and dual forms of the cognate noun רַחַם, "womb," is usually interpreted to be a vulgar expression more politely rendered as "a girl or two," denoting women taken by a conquering soldier. In the Moabite Mesha Inscription, line 17 has the feminine plural noun ורחמת (Gibson, *Hebrew and Moabite Inscriptions*, 75), which Gibson translates as "female slaves" (p. 76) or "concubines" (p. 81) and which *ANET* translates as "maid-servants" (p. 320). These women are among the seven thousand people killed by Mesha after he took Nebo, the town in which they lived.

8 Jerome, *Commentariorum in Amos Prophetam* (CCSL 76:226).

9 Cf. S. Wagner, "טָרַף," *TDOT* 5:350–57.

masculine singular perfect of שָׁמַר, meaning "*retain* wrath" (BDB, s.v. שָׁמַר I, 2 a, citing also Jer 3:5), with a third feminine singular suffix referring to וְעֶבְרָתוֹ. The expected form of the verb with suffix would be שְׁמָרָהּ but the *mappiq* is omitted in the suffix. For the form of the suffix, see Joüon, § 61 i, and GKC, § 58 g (which, however, also proposes a popular but unnecessary emendation). Moreover, the accent of the verb is retracted to the penultimate syllable (-מָ-) because the following word is accented on the first syllable (נֶצַח). This retraction is called נָסוֹג אָחוֹר or נְסִיגָה, which Joüon transliterates as *nsiga*. See Joüon, § 31 c.

Of the thirty-four instances of עֶבְרָה in the OT, in thirty-one it means "anger" or "wrath," including this sole instance in Amos, while in the remaining three it refers to human "arrogance."[10] Its common meaning can refer to the "anger" or "wrath" of either Yahweh or humans. The end result of עֶבְרָה is always destruction and punishment.

1:12 :וְשִׁלַּחְתִּי אֵשׁ בְּתֵימָן וְאָכְלָה אַרְמְנוֹת בָּצְרָה—For the phraseology, see the first and second textual notes on 1:4 and "Yahweh Punishes by Fire" in the introduction to 1:3–2:16. Here the two sites slated for destruction by fire are Teman (תֵּימָן) and Bozrah (בָּצְרָה).

Teman, originally the name of a grandson of Esau (Gen 36:11, 15), became known as a city or a district in Edom (Ezek 25:13). It is often used by metonymy for the entire country of Edom (Jer 49:7, 20; Obad 9) since it was a leading city. Eliphaz, one of Job's "friends," came from there (Job 2:11). "Edom … Teman" in Amos 1:11–12 is similar to the oracles against Moab and Judah, which first cite the country and then its leading city: "Moab … Kerioth" (2:1–3) and "Judah … Jerusalem" (2:4–5).

Bozrah may mean "fortified place."[11] It was located some twenty-five miles southeast of the Dead Sea and was the chief city in northern Edom (e.g., Is 34:6; 63:1).

Commentary

1:11 The next three oracles differ from those against Aram (1:3–5), Philistia (1:6–8), and Tyre (1:9–10) in that Edom (1:11–12), Ammon (1:13–15), and Moab (2:1–3) all were east of Israel. They were bound to Israel by geographical proximity, historical relationships, and consanguineous and ethnic ties. Edom, Ammon, and Moab are mentioned together also in, for example, Deut 23:4–8 (ET 23:3–7); Is 11:14; Jeremiah 48–49; Ezek 25:2–14; Dan 11:41.

Edom is referenced more than any other country in Amos' oracles against the nations (1:6, 9, 11; 2:1). This may be why "Edom" appears toward the end of the book in 9:12 as a synecdoche for all the nations who are destroyed by fire in 1:3–2:3. A "remnant of Edom," representing Gentiles from all nations, will be called by Yahweh's name (9:12) and will be saved by means of Yahweh's

---

[10] Cf. K.-D. Schunck, "עֶבְרָה," *TDOT* 10:426–30. The three passages where it denotes human arrogance are Is 16:6; Jer 48:30; Prov 21:24.

[11] King, *Amos, Hosea, Micah*, 56.

gracious rule through his resurrection of David's falling dynasty through the Messiah (9:11).[12]

Edom had already been implicated twice in the crime of trading slaves since it was the recipient of captive slaves from Gaza (1:6) and Tyre (1:9). Now the nation is charged with more transgressions. The first accusation is that "he pursued his brother with a sword" (1:11). In addition to a covenant or treaty between Edom and Israel, "brother" may also reflect Israel's kinship with Edom, since Jacob and Esau (the progenitor of Edom) were often referred to as brothers.[13] Edom's crime is then understood as a "violation of the customary ethos of kinship obligations."[14] This crime is more grievous because Edom's "brother" Israel was God's chosen people, making the crime a transgression against Yahweh himself (cf. Mt 25:41–46a; Acts 9:5). Amos 1:11 includes two allusions to the Jacob-Esau narrative. First, Isaac had declared in his "blessing" (curse?) of Esau, "You will live by your sword" (Gen 27:40), and here Edom "pursued his brother with a sword" (Amos 1:11). Second, Rebekah hoped that Esau's wrath would only be temporary (Gen 27:41–45; see חֵמָה, "wrath," in 27:44 and אַף, "anger," in 27:45), but years later Jacob still was afraid for his life (Gen 32:7–12 [ET 32:6–11]; 33:12–15). Here Amos says that Edom's "anger [אַף] seethed continuously, and his fury [עֶבְרָה] raged incessantly" (Amos 1:11).

At almost any point in OT history, a Hebrew writer could readily document Israel's grievances because of Edomite crimes.[15] Strained relations between the two nations are already reflected in the Jacob-Esau narratives. Gen 25:23 and 27:39–40 foretell that Edom will either be subject to his brother Israel or in revolt against him. At the time of Moses, Israel sought to pass peacefully through the nation of Edom on the King's Highway, but Edom opposed Israel "with the sword" (Num 20:18, 20). Edom was routed by Saul (1 Sam 14:47) and later brought under Israelite control by David (2 Sam 8:14). An exiled member of the Edomite royal family was an adversary of Solomon (1 Ki 11:14–22). Edom still lacked a king in the time of Jehoshaphat (1 Ki 22:48 [ET 22:47]), but it revolted against Jehoshaphat's son Jehoram (Joram) in the mid-ninth century (2 Ki 8:20–22; 2 Chr 21:8–10). Some believe that this revolt is the historical incident to which Amos 1:11 refers.[16]

The next clause in Amos 1:11 might level the abstract accusation that Edom showed no compassion or pity. However, רַחֲמָיו could literally mean "his wombs," referring to the wombs of Israel's women, and by metonymy

---

[12] See further the commentary on 9:11–12. For additional discussion of the Gentiles in Yahweh's plan to redeem all peoples in Christ, as revealed already in the OT, see "Mission in the Old Testament" in Lessing, *Jonah*, 151–69.

[13] See, for example, Gen 25:26; 27:40–41; Num 20:14; Obad 10, 12.

[14] Mays, *Amos*, 35. On the other hand, Fishbane believes this verse is referring to a political treaty ("The Treaty Background of Amos 1:11 and Related Matters").

[15] After Amos' lifetime, the Israelite-Edomite feud continued. See, for example, Is 34:5–15; Jer 49:7–22; Obadiah; Lam 4:21–22.

[16] See Paul, *Amos*, 63, including n. 201.

mean "his women," especially pregnant women. This commentary translates the clause concretely as "he destroyed his [brother's pregnant] women." If this understanding of the Hebrew is correct, Edom is not only guilty of turning the sword against "his brother," but also of using the sword to split open the wombs of pregnant Israelite women. Ammon is clearly accused of committing that atrocity in 1:13 (see the third textual note and the commentary on that verse). Thus both Edom and Ammon wielded the sword in order to kill females and their children in utero. This gruesome method of double murder could be compared to the widespread modern sin of abortion, which kills the child in the womb, and occasionally the mother too. Since "his [Edom's] brother" referred to Israel, this further act is all the more heinous because Esau (the father of Edom) and Jacob (Israel, the father of the twelve tribes of Israelites) were twins in the same womb (Gen 25:21–24).[17]

Amos creates a merism by accusing Edom of having persecuted men ("his brother") and pregnant women with their children ("his [brother's pregnant] women"). In this way the entire Israelite population was subjected to Edom's atrocities. These brutalities foreshadow the full manifestation of Edom's animosity toward Judah in 587 BC. At the time when the Babylonians sacked Jerusalem and destroyed the temple, the Edomites cried out, "Tear it [Jerusalem] down, tear it down to its foundations" (Ps 137:7). Yet Edom shall not escape its just judgment.

1:12 Because of these crimes, Yahweh promises to send fire against the chief Edomite cities of Teman and Bozrah. These fires of judgment were first kindled later in the eighth century when Edom was subjugated by Assyria, so that Edom was required to pay tribute to the Assyrian kings Tiglath-pileser III, Sennacherib, Esarhaddon, and Ashurbanipal (eighth–seventh centuries BC).[18] Eventually Edom was conquered in the sixth century by the Babylonian king Nebuchadnezzar (Jer 27:1–7).

---

[17] In Gen 25:22–24, Rebekah's womb is not denoted by the term רֶחֶם that is in Amos 1:11, but by three other Hebrew terms.

[18] *ANET*, 282, 287, 291, 294.

Amos 1:13–15

Judgment against Ammon

Translation

1 [13]Thus says Yahweh:
"Because of three transgressions of the Ammonites
and because of four, I will not revoke it,
because they ripped open the pregnant women of Gilead,
in order to enlarge their own territory.
[14]So I will kindle fire against the city wall of Rabbah,
and it will consume her fortresses
with a battle cry on a day of war,
in a storm on a day of tempest.
[15]And their king will go into exile,
he and his officers together."
Yahweh has spoken.

Textual Notes

1:13 כֹּה אָמַר יְהוָה—For this messenger formula, see the first textual note on 1:3 and "The Messenger Formula" in the introduction to 1:3–2:16.

עַל־שְׁלֹשָׁה פִּשְׁעֵי בְנֵי־עַמּוֹן וְעַל־אַרְבָּעָה—For this accusation formula, see the second textual note on 1:3 and "The Staircase Numerical Pattern" in the introduction to 1:3–2:16. "Ammon" (עַמּוֹן) was located in north-central Transjordan north of Moab. Ammon's financial base was derived from the trade routes it controlled.[1] Its capital city was "Rabbah" (רַבָּה, 1:14).

לֹא אֲשִׁיבֶנּוּ—For this declaration, see the third textual note on 1:3 and "God's Judgment Is Irrevocable" in the introduction to 1:3–2:16.

עַל־בִּקְעָם הָרוֹת הַגִּלְעָד—This cited transgression uses the same syntactical pattern as the other oracles; see the fourth textual note on 1:3 and "The Citation of the Transgression" in the introduction to 1:3–2:16. Amos employs the verb בָּקַע, "cleave or rip open" (see BDB, 1), only here. Its Qal infinitive construct has the nominal form of the third masculine plural suffix (בִּקְעָם) used subjectively: "their ripping open" means "they ripped open" (Joüon, §§ 65 a; 70 d). The Qal indicates that the Ammonites themselves ripped open the stomachs of pregnant women in order to destroy both the mothers and the children in their wombs. Waltke-O'Connor, 24.3.2d, including examples 4a and 4b, explains that the Qal of בָּקַע usually denotes action directly performed by the subject, as is true here, whereas the Piel can denote action performed indirectly, for example, commanded by a king but carried out by his soldiers (cf. the Piel in 2 Ki 8:12). בָּקַע can also designate the breaching of a city wall and hence by extension the conquering of a

---

1 King, *Amos, Hosea, Micah*, 57.

town (e.g., Ezek 26:10). In the Piel stem, בָּקַע can describe the activity of bears (2 Ki 2:24) and other animals (Hos 13:8) that maul and rip apart human beings.

The feminine adjective הָרָה, "pregnant," can be used as a substantive noun, as is its plural הָרוֹת here: "pregnant women, women with child" (BDB, s.v. הָרָה II). It is derived from the verb הָרָה, "conceive, become pregnant" (BDB, s.v. הָרָה I, 1), which often is followed by יָלַד, "to give birth" (e.g., Gen 4:1; Is 7:14).

לְמַעַן הַרְחִיב אֶת־גְּבוּלָם׃—This purpose clause introduced by לְמַעַן, "in order to," uses the Hiphil infinitive of רָחַב and the object גְּבוּל, a combination meaning "*enlarge* limit of territory" (BDB, s.v. רָחַב, Hiphil, 2). The verb occurs only here in Amos. The Hiphil stem of רָחַב, "to make broad, wide," comprises the majority of occurrences (twenty-one of twenty-five) of the verb in the OT.[2] It can apply to borders (Deut 12:20) and land (Gen 26:22). The enlarging of territory may be the result of God's blessing (Deut 33:20) or the result of brutal conquest, as in Amos 1:13.

The noun גְּבוּל denotes a border or boundary.[3] It recurs in 6:2, where again the concern is the size of the bounded territories. גְּבוּל is sometimes used to indicate an entire territory (2 Ki 10:32), the area surrounding a city (Josh 13:3), or as in Amos 1:13, the territory possessed by a nation (cf. Ezek 47:15). A גְּבוּל may be modified by a direction (e.g., "southern," Num 34:3), a topographical feature ("of [the wadi] Arnon," Num 22:36), or a country or people ("the border of Egypt," 1 Ki 4:21). In the ancient Near East, boundaries had theological implications because boundaries agreements were protected by the local god, "and a curse awaited anyone who violated the agreement."[4] To violate a nation's boundaries was to violate their god.

1:14 וְהִצַּתִּי אֵשׁ בְּחוֹמַת רַבָּה—The similar judgment וְשִׁלַּחְתִּי אֵשׁ בְּ, "and/so I will *send* fire against …" is in all but the last of the other oracles against the nations (1:4, 7, 10, 12; 2:2, 5). See the first textual note and the commentary on 1:4 and "Yahweh Punishes by Fire" in the introduction to 1:3–2:16. Like 1:14, both 1:7 and 1:10 also continue with בְּחוֹמַת, "against the city wall of …" But only this oracle uses the verb וְהִצַּתִּי, "and/so I will *kindle*." Both the Qal and the Hiphil of יָצַת, "kindle," often take the thing ignited as the direct object, and then בָּאֵשׁ ("with fire") follows as the instrument. Here, however, the fire itself (אֵשׁ) is the direct object of the verb, and the thing ignited (בְּחוֹמַת רַבָּה) is introduced with בְּ. This same construction occurs in other verses (e.g., Jer 17:27; 21:14; Ezek 21:3 [ET 20:47]; Lam 4:11). יָצַת is one of six Biblical Hebrew verbs that begin with -יָצ. In some forms of these verbs, the consonantal י is assimilated into the following צ and marked by a *daghesh* (-צּ-), as here. See GKC, § 71, and Joüon, § 77.

The city name "Rabbah" (רַבָּה) means "the great." Rabbah was the capital of Ammon (2 Sam 11:1 || 1 Chr 20:1; 2 Sam 12:27, 29). It was located on the upper course of the Jabbok River (cf. 2 Sam 12:27). Its fuller OT name was "Rabbah of the Ammonites" (e.g., 2 Sam 12:26) to distinguish it from other cities whose names sometimes included רַבָּה (e.g., "Sidon Rabbah" in Josh 11:8; 19:28; "Hamath Rabbah" in

---

2 Cf. R. Bartelmus, "רָחַב," *TDOT* 13:427–37.

3 Cf. M. Ottosson, "גְּבוּל," *TDOT* 2:361–66.

4 Ottosson, *TDOT* 2:366.

Amos 6:2). Rabbah was renamed Philadelphia after Ptolemy II Philadelphus (285–246 BC). It took on the name of Amman in the Middle Ages and is the capital of modern Jordan.[5]

וְאָכְלָה אַרְמְנוֹתֶיהָ—For this vocabulary, see the second textual note on 1:4.

בִּתְרוּעָה֙ בְּי֣וֹם מִלְחָמָ֔ה— The noun תְּרוּעָה recurs in 2:2 with the same meaning, "battle cry." "With a battle cry on a day of war" is similar to this clause in Josh 6:5, 20 describing when the Israelites conquered Jericho: יָרִ֥יעוּ כָל־הָעָ֖ם תְּרוּעָ֣ה גְדוֹלָ֑ה, "all the people cried a great battle cry." The next oracle in Amos, against Moab, uses similar language: בִּתְרוּעָ֖ה בְּק֥וֹל שׁוֹפָֽר, "in a battle cry with the blare of a shofar" (2:2). "A day of war" occurs also in 1 Sam 13:22; Hos 10:14; Prov 21:31. In this context in Amos, both it and "a day of tempest" (see the next textual note) are expressions that are equivalent to "the Day of Yahweh" (Amos 5:18–20) and to the "day(s)" of various calamities described in 2:16; 3:14; 4:2; 6:3; 8:3, 9–11, 13. The "day" in 1:14 is when Yahweh punishes his enemies using a foreign military power and/or theophanic elements in nature. In contrast is the Gospel "day" of resurrection in 9:11.

בְּסַ֖עַר בְּי֥וֹם סוּפָֽה׃—The nouns סַעַר, "storm, storm wind," and סוּפָה, "tempest, whirlwind," are synonyms that both possess the characteristics of onomatopoeia. Pronouncing the sibilant ס reproduces the sound of whistling wind as comes forth from the lips. The two nouns are parallel here and in Ps 83:16 (ET 83:15). (In Is 29:6 סוּפָה is parallel to סְעָרָה, and in Nah 1:3 סוּפָה and שְׂעָרָה are parallel.) Here the emphasis of these words is not on meteorological phenomena per se, but on their use as instruments of Yahweh's wrath (BDB, s.v. סַעַר).

The meaning of the noun סַעַר is closely related to its verbal cognate סָעַר, "to storm" (Qal), "to be troubled" (Niphal), and "to blow away" (Piel).[6] Moreover, סַעַר belongs to the semantic field of words that describe meteorological phenomena. Its feminine counterpart סְעָרָה is frequently paired with other meteorological words like "shower" and "hailstones" (Ezek 13:11) or "lightning" (Zech 9:14). In Jonah 1:4, Yahweh hurls a סַעַר upon the sea (see also Jonah 1:12).[7] In another OT text about a storm at sea, it is clear that סְעָרָה is always under the command of Yahweh (Ps 107:25, 29). Yahweh curbs and controls storms (described with various Hebrew terms in Pss 89:10 [ET 89:9]; 29:3; 77:17 [ET 77:16]; 97:2–5; 107:23–24; 148:7–8, as does Jesus in Mk 4:39.

The noun סוּפָה, "tempest," appears fifteen times in the OT. It infrequently refers to the meteorological event (as in Job 37:9), but is often used as a military metaphor (Is 5:26–28; 66:15; Jer 4:13) referring either to the army of a nation or to Yahweh himself as the military power that carries out destructive judgment.[8] That is its meaning in Amos 1:14.

---

5 Niehaus, "Amos," 354.

6 Cf. H.-J. Fabry, "סָעַר," *TDOT* 10:291–96.

7 See Lessing, *Jonah*, 100, 112, 117–19. Fabry notes: "Because meteorological phenomena are nowhere portrayed merely for the sake of scientific aims, even the completely realistic description of the mighty sea storm in Jonah 1 is already referring metaphorically to Yahweh's theophany" (*TDOT* 10:294).

8 Cf. K.-M. Beyse, "סוּפָה," *TDOT* 10:197–99.

Judgment is a common theme in storm theophanies (Jer 25:32; Job 9:17; cf. Job 38:1; 40:6), although the terrifying appearance of Yahweh may be to judge his enemies and deliver his faithful people (Is 29:5–6; Nah 1:2–3; Zech 9:13–14; Ps 83:14–16 [ET 83:13–15]). In Amos 1:14 in, with, and under the storm, Yahweh is depicted as manifesting his power to punish sin.

1:15 וְהָלַךְ מַלְכָּם בַּגּוֹלָה הוּא וְשָׂרָיו יַחְדָּו—The noun גּוֹלָה, "exile," occurs only here in Amos, but it is a synonym of the cognate noun גָּלוּת in 1:6, 9, and the cognate verb גָּלָה occurs twelve times (e.g., 1:5–6). For מַלְכָּם, "their king," some LXX manuscripts, especially in the Lucianic family, have μελχομ, apparently because they vocalized it as מִלְכֹּם, the Amorite god Milcom (1 Ki 11:5, 33; 2 Ki 23:13). Some commentators advocate emending מַלְכָּם to מִלְכֹּם here and in some other OT passages.[9] However, the context in Amos 1:3–2:3 indicates that Yahweh is prophesying against pagan nations and their leaders, not against their gods.[10] It is better, therefore, to retain the MT vocalization and translate the word as "their king," which is supported by the following וְשָׂרָיו, "and his officers." A suffixed plural of שַׂר recurs in 2:3. See further the commentary.

אָמַר יְהוָה׃—"Yahweh has spoken" is the formula that concludes this fifth oracle as well as the first and the sixth oracles (1:5; 2:3). In each of these oracles, it balances the opening messenger formula, "thus says Yahweh."

Commentary

1:13–15 The next two oracles are aimed at Ammon (1:13–15) and Moab (2:1–3). It is fitting for Amos to place these countries side by side since the progenitors of these two nations were conceived through Lot's drunken incestuous relationships with his two daughters (Gen 19:30–38).

1:13 Beginning with the period of the judges, the Ammonites were a thorn in Israel's side, often fighting to (re)capture from Israel part of Gilead (e.g., Judg 3:12–14; 11:4–33; 1 Sam 11:1–11; 2 Sam 8:11–12; 2 Chr 20:1–30). The multiple crimes of Ammon were easy for Amos to catalogue.[11] The final atrocity that kindled Yahweh's fiery wrath was that Ammon allowed their selfish ambition "to enlarge their own territory"[12] to lead them into butchering Gileadite women gestating children (Amos 1:13) because these helpless and "dispensable" people got in their way. Simundson writes: "One shudders to think of the viciousness of killing two lives with one slash for the sake of national expansion."[13]

This heinous act of ripping open the stomachs of pregnant women probably was referred to also in Amos' oracle against Edom (see the fifth textual note

---

9 See Wolff, *Joel and Amos*, 131–32, and BDB, s.v. מִלְכֹּם.

10 Later in the book, Amos does mention foreign deities (5:26; 8:14).

11 For other oracles against the Ammonites, see Jer 49:1–2; Ezek 21:33–37 (ET 21:28–32); 25:1–7; Zeph 2:8–11.

12 Ancient Near Eastern monarchs often boasted that they enlarged their borders. See Niehaus, "Amos," 354, for details. In Is 26:15, Yahweh is depicted as the one who enlarges the borders of Israel.

13 Simundson, *Hosea, Joel, Amos, Obadiah, Jonah, Micah*, 170.

and the commentary on 1:11). It is clearly described in 2 Ki 8:12; 15:16; and Hos 14:1 (ET 13:16), which use the same verb בָּקַע, "to rip open," as in Amos 1:13. Several biblical and extrabiblical texts refer to the same or similar horrific war crimes.[14] A Middle-Assyrian hymn records the appalling sins of Tiglath-pileser I (ca. 1114–1076 BC): "He slit the wombs of the pregnant woman, he gouged out the eyes of the infants, he cut the throats of their strong men."[15] A Neo-Babylonian lament includes this: "My eyes cannot look on my … the ripping of the mothers' wombs."[16] This gruesome practice was intended to keep the enemy from multiplying its population (cf. 2 Ki 8:12). Compare Pharaoh's command to kill Israel's male infants, whose purpose was to curtail Israel's population growth (Ex 1:8–22).

These ancient practices of murdering children in utero and of infanticide can be compared to the modern tragedy of abortion, which murders the child in the womb, and to the growing modern acceptance of selective infanticide. In stark contrast to these barbaric human sins, Yahweh promises that his reconstituted and renewed Israel, the Christian church, will nurture the weak and vulnerable people in the community: the blind, the lame, pregnant women, and women in labor (Jer 31:8). From the earliest days of the church, Christians have renounced abortion and infanticide. The *Didache* (second century AD) explains the Second Table of the Ten Commandments, including the Fifth Commandment, "You shall not murder," by including the prohibitions οὐ φονεύσεις τέκνον ἐν φθορᾷ, οὐδὲ γεννηθὲν ἀποκτενεῖς, literally, "you shall not murder a child by abortion; neither shall you kill a born [child]."[17] Instead Christians cherish all human life from the moment of conception to life's natural end, since God is the Creator and Redeemer of every person.

1:14 Ammon is held accountable for its barbaric behavior because it was a rejection of the Noahic covenant that places an invaluable price on every human being—so valuable that the only fair verdict for murder is capital punishment (Gen 9:6). As in all the other oracles against the nations except the one against Israel, Yahweh's response is fire. Yet in 1:14 Amos employs the verb "*kindle* fire" instead of "send fire" (1:4, 7, 10, 12; 2:2, 5). Both convey the same

---

14 See *ANET*, 288, 295, 302, and Cogan, " 'Ripping Open Pregnant Women' in Light of Assyrian Analogue." References to the dashing of children (against rocks) occur in Is 13:16; Nah 3:10; and Ps 137:9. In Hos 10:14, women and children are dashed against the ground together. More generally, the mutilation of enemy people was a common wartime strategy in the ancient Near East (Lemos, "Shame and Mutilation of Enemies in the Hebrew Bible"). Assyrian, Babylonian, and Egyptian art provides many examples of dismemberment. For pictures from Egyptian art, see *ANEP*, §§ 318, 319, 340, 348.

15 Paul, *Amos*, 68, including n. 242, citing Ebeling, "Ein Heldenlied auf Tiglatpileser I," 35, 37 (reverse, lines 3–4).

16 Lambert, "A Neo-Babylonian Tammuz Lament," 212 (reverse, line 19), cited by Paul, *Amos*, 68, including n. 243.

17 The Greek text is in *The Apostolic Fathers* (Loeb Classical Library; Cambridge, Mass.: Harvard University Press, 1977), 1:310, 312. The English translation by Kirsopp Lake in that volume is "thou shalt not procure abortion, nor commit infanticide" (pp. 311, 313).

idea. The synonym here is an example of what linguists term "internal variations within a schematic pattern."[18]

Unlike any of the other oracles, Yahweh adds to "fire" the judgments of "storm" and "tempest" (1:14). A great storm is sometimes associated with a theophany when Yahweh appears on his day to execute judgment (e.g., Is 29:6; Nah 1:3). "Storm" and "tempest" are messengers or attendants of Yahweh (Ps 83:16 [ET 83:15]; cf. Ps 104:3–4), who will destroy Rabbah, the capital of Ammon. Employing these natural phenomena, Yahweh will execute his judgment.

1:15 The day will come when the nation falls and the chief culprits, Ammon's king and its political leaders, will be exiled. Yahweh will humiliate the Ammonites when they are forced to watch their "king" and "his officers" march into captivity (1:15). The only other judgment in the oracles against the nations that results in exile is in the oracle against Damascus, where "the people of Aram will go into exile" (1:5). Because both the Arameans and the Ammonites perpetrated barbaric atrocities against Gilead, both will face deportation after their demise in battle. Yet while Yahweh in 1:5 declared that the entire population of Aram would be exiled, in 1:15 he warns that (only) the leadership of Ammon will face this judgment.

Some propose emending "their king" to "Milcom" (see the first textual note on 1:15). Elsewhere in his oracles against the nations, Amos only refers to one other "king" (מֶלֶךְ, 2:1). He usually refers to national leaders by means of other terms: יוֹשֵׁב, "one enthroned, a ruler" (1:5, 8), תּוֹמֵךְ שֵׁבֶט, "scepter-bearer" (1:5, 8), שׁוֹפֵט, "judge" (2:3), and שָׂרִים, royal "officers" (1:15; 2:3). However, emending the text of 1:15 destroys a play on words. The choice of the Hebrew word מַלְכָּם, *malcam*, "their king," helps Amos produce a subtle double entendre on the name of the Ammon's national deity, Milcom, spelled with the same Hebrew consonants (מִלְכֹּם, 1 Ki 11:5, 33; 2 Ki 23:13). The emendation also is contrary to a parallel text in Jeremiah, in another oracle that is against the Ammonites and their capital city Rabbah. Almost exactly the same wording as in Amos 1:15 (וְהָלַךְ מַלְכָּם בַּגּוֹלָה הוּא וְשָׂרָיו יַחְדָּו) is in Jer 49:3 (מַלְכָּם בַּגּוֹלָה יֵלֵךְ כֹּהֲנָיו וְשָׂרָיו יַחְדָּיו): Yahweh declares, "Their king will go in exile, his priests and his officials together [with him]."[19]

---

18 Paul, "A Literary Reinvestigation of the Authenticity of the Oracles against the Nations of Amos," 199, cited by Paul, *Amos*, 69, including n. 247.

19 Despite the evidence for retaining Hebrew text in both verses, some English translations emend one of the parallel passages. For example, ESV and NKJV have "their king" in Amos 1:15 but "Milcom" in Jer 49:3. NIV has "her king" (Amos 1:15) and "Molech" (Jer 49:3). NASB has "their king" (Amos 1:15) and "Malcam" (Jer 49:3).

Amos 2:1–3

Judgment against Moab

Translation

2 **[1]Thus says Yahweh:**
"Because of three transgressions of Moab
and because of four, I will not revoke it,
because they burned the bones of the king of Edom for lime.
[2]So I will send fire against Moab,
and it will consume the fortresses of Kerioth.
And Moab will die in tumult,
in a battle cry with the blare of a shofar.
[3]And I will cut off the judge from her midst,
and all her officers I will slay with him."
Yahweh has spoken.

Textual Notes

2:1 כֹּה אָמַר יְהוָה—For this messenger formula, see the first textual note on 1:3 and "The Messenger Formula" in the introduction to 1:3–2:16.

עַל־שְׁלֹשָׁה פִּשְׁעֵי מוֹאָב וְעַל־אַרְבָּעָה—For this accusation formula, see the second textual note on 1:3 and "The Staircase Numerical Pattern" in the introduction to 1:3–2:16. "Moab" (מוֹאָב) was located east of the Dead Sea south of Ammon and north of Edom. Its capital city was ʿAr, probably also called Kerioth; see the second textual note on 2:2. Moab was a brother nation of Ammon since both were the product of Lot's drunken incest with his daughters; his older daughter bore Moab and his younger daughter bore Ben-ammi, the father of the Ammonites (Gen 19:36–38). Therefore in Amos, the oracles against Ammon (1:13–15) and Moab (2:1–3) are adjacent to each other.

Moab and Israel had a long history of both friendship and discord. Kinship is expressed in Gen 19:36–37; Deut 2:9 and in the narrative of Ruth.[1] Their affinity is also evident in the similarity of their languages, as witnessed in the Mesha Stele, whose Moabite language is almost identical to Biblical Hebrew.[2]

---

[1] Ruth narrates the history of a Moabitess who was incorporated into Israel and the people of God saved through faith, and she was privileged to become an ancestress of the Savior, Jesus Christ (Mt 1:5). See Wilch, *Ruth*, 334, 337, 339, 361.

[2] The Mesha Stele, also known as the Moabite Stone, is an engraved stone that celebrates a victory of Mesha, a ninth-century BC king of Moab. It was written in the same Canaanite script used for ancient Hebrew inscriptions. The king relates his victory over Israel (cf. 2 Kings 3), which he dedicates to Chemosh, the national god of the Moabites. For the Moabite text of the Mesha Stele rendered in later Hebrew script, see Gibson, *Hebrew and Moabite Inscriptions*, 74–75. For a translation and discussion, see Gibson, pages 75–83, and also *ANET*, 320–21.

Animosity between Israel and Moab is displayed in the following narratives: In Num 25:1–9, Moabite women seduced Israel into apostasy at Baal Peor. The portly Moabite king Eglon was assassinated by the left-handed Benjaminite Ehud (Judg 3:12–30). And King Mesha of Moab rebelled after the death of Ahab, king of Israel, but then was defeated by Jehoram of Israel and Jehoshaphat of Judah (2 Ki 3:4–27). The biblical record stating the true history differs significantly from Mesha's boast in the Moabite Stone that "Israel perished utterly for ever!"[3] It was customary for pagan ancient Near Eastern kings to exaggerate their brags about their accomplishments. Ex 15:15; 1 Sam 14:47; and 2 Chr 20:1 are other texts that attest to strife between Israel and Moab.

לֹא אֲשִׁיבֶנּוּ—For this declaration, see the third textual note on 1:3 and "God's Judgment Is Irrevocable" in the introduction to 1:3–2:16.

עַל־שָׂרְפוֹ עַצְמוֹת מֶלֶךְ־אֱדוֹם לַשִּׂיד׃—For this standard way (עַל followed by an infinitive construct with suffix, here שָׂרְפוֹ) in which a national transgression is cited in each of the oracles against the nations, see the fourth textual note on 1:3 and "The Citation of the Transgression" in the introduction to 1:3–2:16. The Qal of שָׂרַף, "to burn," is transitive and usually is done for the purpose of destroying the object (so BDB, Qal, 2 a). Usually the object is a thing, but since the object here is עַצְמוֹת, "bones," this usage overlaps with the OT passages in which a person is burned (BDB, Qal, 2 b).

The noun שִׂיד usually denotes "lime" or "whitewash" as in "plaster" applied to a wall. Here with the preposition לְ the Vulgate renders it as *usque ad cinerem*, "entirely into ashes," while the LXX translates it as εἰς κονίαν, "into/for lime, plaster." If the phrase simply meant that the bones were reduced to fine ashes, probably a different Hebrew word would have been used, such as עָפָר or אֵפֶר or perhaps דֶּשֶׁן, which are common words for "ash."[4] The preposition לְ on לַשִּׂיד may mean "*into* lime," which would imply the total destruction of the corpse. But if the *lamed* is understood to denote purpose, "*for* lime, plaster," then, as outrageous as it appears, the Moabites burned the bones of an Edomite king in order to use his remains for the purpose of plastering and whitewashing stones or houses. The *lamed* could function to convey both truths: the Moabites may have disinterred the bones of a dead king and burned them *into* lime, then used the lime *for* the sealing of their building(s).

2:2 וְשִׁלַּחְתִּי־אֵשׁ בְּמוֹאָב—This is the standard idiom in Amos' oracles against the nations for Yahweh's judgment of sending fire. See the first textual note on 1:4 and "Yahweh Punishes by Fire" in the introduction to 1:3–2:16.

וְאָכְלָה אַרְמְנוֹת הַקְּרִיּוֹת—For the first two words, see the second textual note on 1:4. The noun with article הַקְּרִיּוֹת probably is the proper city name "Kerioth" (BDB, s.v. קְרִיּוֹת, 2), since there was a principal city in Moab by that name (Jer 48:24, 41), and its name has the article in Jer 48:41. There was another city by that name in Judah (Josh 15:25). Possibly הַקְּרִיּוֹת could be a unique plural of the common noun קִרְיָה, "city," as the LXX apparently understood it here, translating the word as τῶν πόλεων αὐτῆς, "of

---

[3] Moabite Stone, line 7 (Gibson, *Hebrew and Moabite Inscriptions*, 74, 76).

[4] See the discussion in Paul, *Amos*, 72.

its cities." But קרית appears on the Moabite Stone as the location of the main sanctuary of Chemosh, probably the proper name of the city. In lines 12–13, King Mesha of Moab boasts, "I brought back from there [Ataroth] the lion figure of David, and dragged it before Chemosh at Kerioth [בקרית]."[5] Kerioth's location is not certain. Andersen and Freedman believe that Kerioth is another name for ʿAr, the capital city of Moab, since both are dialectical variants of nouns meaning "city": Kerioth is related to קִרְיָה, "city," and ʿAr is related to עִיר, "city."[6] Kerioth probably was an alternate name for ʿAr of Moab (Num 21:28; Is 15:1). This is possible because ʿAr and Kerioth are never mentioned together in the OT. ʿAr was located in the Arnon Valley, near the border of Moab (Deut 2:18).

וּמֵ֣ת בְּשָׁא֔וֹן מוֹאָ֑ב—Normally countries are grammatically feminine; the feminine suffixes in 2:3 ("her midst … her officers") refer to Moab. However, here מוֹאָב must be the subject of the masculine Qal verb וּמֵת, which is a perfect with *waw* consecutive ("Moab *will* die") parallel to the perfects with *waw* consecutive that begin 2:2 (וְשִׁלַּחְתִּי) and 2:3 (וְהִכְרַתִּי). The noun שָׁאוֹן can refer to the "tumult" or chaotic din of war and battle (e.g., Is 13:4; 66:6; Jer 25:31; Hos 10:14).[7] In Ps 40:3 (ET 40:2), שָׁאוֹן has the unique meaning of "downfall" or "catastrophe." It may denote a jubilant and triumphant sound (Is 5:14; 24:8) or the powerful "roar" of waves (Jer 51:55; Ps 65:8 [ET 65:7]).

The force of שָׁאוֹן in Amos 2:2 is somewhat ambiguous because it could indicate either the din of Moab attacking a foreign foe or the sound of its defeat at home. However, the first two lines of 2:2 and the shofar in the next, parallel line (see the next textual note) imply that שָׁאוֹן refers to the sound of Moab being attacked on its home turf, defeated, and burned (2:2a). A similar description of the defeat and burning of Moab is given nearly two centuries later in Jer 48:45, where Moab is further described by the parallel phrase בְּנֵי שָׁאוֹן, "sons of tumult." That phrase probably refers to the tumult Moab inflicted on other peoples in its previous victories over them. שָׁאוֹן may have been a term associated with Moab's victories even before the time of Amos. However, Amos uses the term to signify Moab's defeat. Shalom Paul believes that "שָׁאוֹן thus is none other than an archaic appellation for Moab, and by employing the term here Amos creates a very effective double entendre to describe the attack of the Divine Warrior upon that nation—the שָׁאוֹן of arms shall 'disarm' the people of שָׁאוֹן."[8]

בִּתְרוּעָ֖ה בְּק֥וֹל שׁוֹפָֽר׃—The noun תְּרוּעָה means "battle cry" also in 1:14. The "battle cry" (תְּרוּעָה) and "shofar" (שׁוֹפָר) appear together in other verses too (e.g., Josh 6:5, 20; Jer 4:19; Zeph 1:16; Job 39:25). The שׁוֹפָר was a musical instrument made from a ram's horn that often functioned as a bugle in ancient warfare.[9] Its most prominent uses were by the attacking nation to assemble its army (Judg 3:27; 6:34; Jer 51:27), signal the beginning of a battle (Josh 6:5, 20), announce victory (1 Sam 13:3), or end the attack

---

5 Gibson, *Hebrew and Moabite Inscriptions*, 75–76.

6 Andersen and Freedman, *Amos*, 289.

7 Cf. K.-M. Beyse, "שָׁאוֹן," *TDOT* 14:237–38.

8 Paul, *Amos*, 74.

9 Cf. H. Ringgren, "שׁוֹפָר," *TDOT* 14:541–42.

(2 Sam 2:28), or, defensively, to warn the people of an approaching enemy (Amos 3:6; also Is 18:3; Neh 4:12, 14 [ET 4:18, 20]). Another prominent use of the שׁוֹפָר was in religio-political functions. The horn was sounded at Mount Sinai (Ex 19:16, 19; 20:18), at religious festivals (Lev 25:9; Ps 81:4 [ET 81:3]), and at the coronation of a new king (2 Sam 15:10; 1 Ki 1:34, 39, 41).

2:3 וְהִכְרַתִּי שׁוֹפֵט מִקִּרְבָּהּ—Yahweh is the implied subject of the Hiphil perfect with *waw* consecutive (marked by the shift of the accent to the final syllable), וְהִכְרַתִּי, "and I will cut off." The substantized participle שׁוֹפֵט, "judge, " must refer to the reigning king of Moab. שׁוֹפֵט functions in this verse in the same way that יוֹשֵׁב, "one enthroned/ruler," functions in 1:5, 8. For other terms for royalty in the oracles against the nations, see the commentary on 1:15. In the book of Judges (שֹׁפְטִים), the term שׁוֹפֵט refers to a Spirit-empowered warrior and theological leader raised up by Yahweh to save his people (see Judg 2:16–19). By the eighth century BC, however, it was used as a royal title (e.g., Is 33:22; 40:23). In Amos 2:3, it denotes "the king in his capacity as lawgiver and administrator of justice."[10]

The feminine singular suffixes on מִקִּרְבָּהּ, "from her midst," and שָׂרֶיהָ, "her officers" (see the next textual note), probably refer to מוֹאָב, "Moab" (thrice in 2:1–2), since countries normally are treated as grammatically feminine. It could also refer to the city of Kerioth in 2:2, since cities too are grammatically feminine, and if Kerioth is the capital city also called ʿAr, then the king would have reigned there with the nation's "officials."

וְכָל־שָׂרֶיהָ אֶהֱרוֹג עִמּוֹ—The suffixed plural of שַׂר refers to royal "officers" also in 1:15. The masculine suffix on עִמּוֹ, "with him," must refer back to the שׁוֹפֵט, "judge" (referring to the king) in the preceding line.

The verb הָרַג usually refers to one individual or collective group of people killing another individual or group of people.[11] It almost always appears when both the subject and object are people; only once does the killing involve an animal (Is 22:13). The human object of the killing can be an enemy in conflict (Gen 34:25; Josh 8:24; Judg 7:25) or a political opponent (1 Sam 16:2) or a personal rival (Gen 26:7). To be the subject of the verb הָרַג was considered in some contexts to be a crime (Ex 2:14; 21:14; 2 Sam 3:30).[12] Yahweh is the subject of הָרַג in Amos 2:3. In its other occurrences in Amos, it refers to Yahweh using the sword to kill people he had called to be his own, but who turned against him: unfaithful Israelites (4:10; 9:1, 4).

אָמַר יְהוָה׃—For this divine signature formula, see the last textual note on 1:5.

---

[10] Niehaus, "Amos," 359. The term is also used to describe King Jotham of Judah (2 Ki 15:5) as well as Yahweh as King and Judge of the whole earth (e.g., Gen 18:25; Judg 11:27; Is 33:22; Pss 7:12 [ET 7:11]; 94:32).

[11] Cf. H. F. Fuhs, "הָרַג," *TDOT* 3:449–57.

[12] However, the Fifth Commandment uses a different, more specific verb, רָצַח, "to murder" (Ex 20:13; Deut 5:17).

Commentary

2:1–3 Moab is the target of other prophecies inspired by Yahweh. Isaiah's oracles against the nations (chapters 13–23) include a lengthy oracle against Moab (chapters 15–16). Jeremiah (chapter 48), Ezekiel (25:8–11), and Zephaniah (2:8–11) also prophesy against Moab.

Through Amos, Yahweh accuses Moab of atrocities it committed against Edom, its southern neighbor. While the Edomites and Ammonites are judged because they destroyed the future, that is, children in their mother's wombs (1:11, 13), the Moabites fall under Yahweh's judgment because they destroyed the past by burning a dead Edomite king's bones. These three oracles are therefore woven together by means of a common theme: diabolically taking advantage of helpless people, a pregnant mother and the baby in her womb or a corpse in the grave.

In the ancient Near East, cemeteries and the remains of the dead were considered sacred. In the ancient world, horrific curses were invoked on those who dared to be grave robbers or desecraters.[13] "By removing and burning bones a person would have to believe that he was doing more harm to the dead than could be done to him [the burner] by the protective curse. Such a risky act must have been motivated by intense vindictiveness."[14] To burn someone's remains into lime "means to burn them to dust as the soil of Israel and Jordan is composed largely of eroded limestone."[15] This was the ultimate act of destruction, as witnessed by Josiah burning the bones of idolaters at Bethel to desecrate the pagan altar there (2 Ki 23:15–16) in fulfillment of an earlier prophecy (1 Ki 13:1–2).

It is fitting that in light of the biblical doctrine of *lex talionis* ("law of retribution"), Moab's burning will be met with Yahweh's burning. Moab's military fortress at Kerioth—the city where the Moabite god Chemosh had a temple[16]—will be engulfed in fire. Those who live by fire will die by fire. This kind of retribution is frequently displayed in prophetic judgment scenes: destroyers will be destroyed (Is 33:1); devourers will be devoured (Jer 30:16); reproachers will be reproached (Ezek 36:6–7); and plunderers will be plundered (Hab 2:8).[17]

Lex talionis reveals the juridical character of Yahweh's judgment. This law is evident throughout Amos. Because Israel had heaped up its ill-gotten gains in "fortresses" (אַרְמְנוֹת, 3:10), those "fortresses" will be destroyed (אַרְמְנוֹת, 3:11). Because they multiplied the din of their "songs" (שִׁרִים, 5:23), their "songs" will be turned into dirges (שִׁרִים, 8:10). Because they "are turning" justice to

---

13 See, for example, *ANET*, 661–62. Anderson and Freedman, *Amos*, 288, write: "This sacrilege was feared in antiquity, and graves were protected by curses (*KAI*, §§ 13–14)."

14 Anderson and Freedman, *Amos*, 288.

15 Sweeney, *The Twelve Prophets*, 212.

16 See the quotation of the Moabite Stone, lines 12–13, in the second textual note on 2:2.

17 These examples are noted by Raabe, *Obadiah*, 201, who cites Miller, *Sin and Judgment in the Prophets*.

wormwood (הָפַךְ, 5:7), Yahweh will "turn" their festivals into mourning (הָפַךְ, 8:10). Raabe writes:

> The correspondence pattern serves to depict the just nature of the punishment, not some strange fate coming "out of the blue" but a rational and appropriate punishment, one that fits the particular crime committed by the guilty party. According to Ezek 18:25–30 and 33:17–20, Yahweh's judgment is "fair" because he judges people "according to their ways."[18]

The personification of the country of Moab in Amos 2:2 indicates an important idea throughout the Bible—that of corporate solidarity. "Because of national sin, the nation will die, so completely that it will be like the death of an individual."[19] To be sure, any individuals who believe in the one true God and so are accounted righteous through faith will ultimately be saved, but they still may suffer the same fate in this life as their unbelieving countrymen.[20]

The expression "in a battle cry with the blare of a shofar" (2:2) indicates that the Assyrian invasions that would overwhelm the entire Levant later in the eighth century BC would not spare the Moabites. Brutality would be met by brutality. The leadership of the nation ("the judge … and all her officers") is singled out in 2:3, as it was in the oracles against Damascus (1:4–5), Gaza (1:8), and Ammon (1:15).

---

[18] Raabe, *Obadiah*, 201.

[19] Niehaus, "Amos," 358.

[20] See Ezekiel 18 and 33:1–20, which Ezekiel spoke to his fellow Israelites in exile. Israelite believers, including Ezekiel himself, and apostates alike had been taken captive to Babylon.

Amos 2:4–5

Judgment against Judah

Translation

2 [4]**Thus says Yahweh:**
"Because of three transgressions of Judah
and because of four, I will not revoke it,
because they rejected the Torah of Yahweh,
and his statutes they did not keep.
Their idols led them astray,
those that their fathers followed.
[5]**So I will send fire against Judah,**
and it will consume the fortresses of Jerusalem."

Textual Notes

2:4 כֹּה אָמַר יְהוָה—For this messenger formula, see the first textual note on 1:3 and "The Messenger Formula" in the introduction to 1:3–2:16.

עַל־שְׁלֹשָׁה פִּשְׁעֵי יְהוּדָה וְעַל־אַרְבָּעָה לֹא אֲשִׁיבֶנּוּ—For this accusation formula, see the second textual note on 1:3 and "The Staircase Numerical Pattern" in the introduction to 1:3–2:16. God accuses Judah with the identical phraseology that he used to accuse the pagan nations in 1:3–2:3. Judah (יְהוּדָה) was the fourth son of Jacob and the fourth son of Leah (Gen 29:31–35). The proper name is derived from the verb יָדָה, whose Hiphil means "to praise." The first part of the name (-יְהוּ) resembles the theophoric ending -יָהוּ, *yahu*, a form of Yahweh, which ends many Hebrew names (e.g., בְּנָיָהוּ, "Benaiah," 2 Sam 8:18; יִרְמְיָהוּ, "Jeremiah," Jer 1:1). Thus Judah means "praise Yahweh," as Leah explained in the context when she named him (Gen 29:35). Jacob's blessing of Judah also plays on the Hiphil of יָדָה (Gen 49:8).

The tribe consisting of Judah's descendents was the first tribe to occupy its land in southern Canaan (Judg 1:1–19). The core of Judah's territory was the mountain ridge between Bethlehem and Hebron.[1] During the second half of the ninth century BC, both northern Israel (2 Ki 10:32–33; 13:3, 22) and, apparently to an lesser extent, Judah (2 Ki 12:18–19 [ET 12:17–18]) were under the domination of King Hazael of Aram. Once the Aramean threat had passed (2 Ki 13:23–25), the Judean king Amaziah challenged Jehoash of Israel to war (2 Ki 14:8–14 || 2 Chr 25:17–24). At this point, Judah probably became Israel's vassal, for 2 Ki 14:12 states: "Judah was struck down before Israel, and every man fled to his tent." This relationship continued during the reigns of the next two Judean kings, Uzziah and Jotham. Amos' ministry was during the reign of Uzziah (Amos 1:1).

---

[1] For an overview of Judah's political history from about 1000 BC to 587 BC, see *Eerdmans Dictionary of the Bible*, 744–47.

לֹא אֲשִׁיבֶנּוּ—For this declaration, see the third textual note on 1:3 and "God's Judgment Is Irrevocable" in the introduction to 1:3–2:16. Again, God pronounces judgment on Judah in the identical way he pronounced judgment on the heathen nations in 1:3–2:3.

עַל־מָאֳסָם אֶת־תּוֹרַת יְהוָה—"Because they rejected the Torah of Yahweh" uses the standard formulaic way (עַל followed by an infinitive construct with suffix, here מָאֳסָם) in which a national transgression is cited in each of the oracles against the nations. See the fourth textual note on 1:3 and "The Citation of the Transgression" in the introduction to 1:3–2:16. In 2:4, however, a difference will emerge. The oracles against the pagan nations in 1:3–2:3 cited only one transgression (see "Just One Transgression Is Cited" in the introduction to 1:3–2:16). But this is the first of multiple transgressions cited in the condemnation of Judah in 2:4. The condemnation of Israel in 2:6–16 will cite even more transgressions.

The verb מָאַס generally means "to reject, refuse, despise" (see BDB). In Amos it recurs only in 5:21. It may refer to rejecting people, such as the Messiah as the necessary building stone (Ps 118:22) or a wife (Is 54:6).[2] It can also refer to rejecting abstract entities such as evil (Is 7:15–16). There is always some element of evaluation and choice involved in rejecting.

Many texts employ מָאַס to denote Yahweh rejecting people because they first rejected him. In Amos 5:21, Yahweh declares, "I hate, I reject" apostate Israel's religious festivals (see also 2 Ki 23:27; Jer 6:30; Ps 78:59, 67). Yahweh rejected Israel because they rejected his commandments (2 Ki 17:15; Is 5:24; Hos 4:6). Amos 2:4–5 makes a clear correlation between Judah's rejection of Yahweh's revealed Word and his consequent punishment of them.

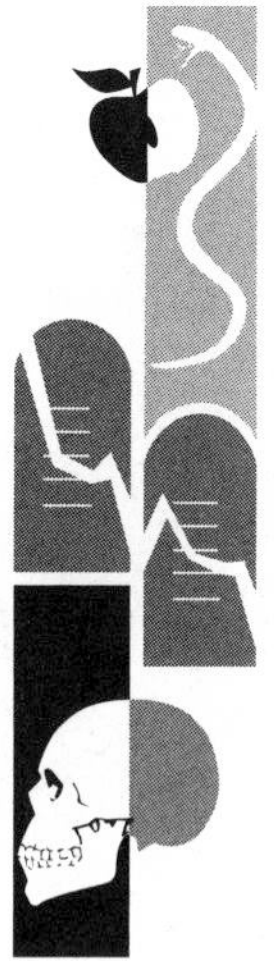

"Torah" (תּוֹרָה) occurs only here in Amos. It derives from the verb יָרָה, which in the Hiphil can mean "to instruct, direct, teach." "The Torah of Moses" refers to the divine revelation written in the Pentateuch (e.g., Josh 8:31–32; 1 Ki 2:3; Mal 3:22 [ET 4:4]). Already in Moses' day, "the Torah" could refer specifically to the Ten Commandments as the centerpiece of the Mosaic covenant (Ex 24:12). More generally, "the Torah" can refer to main parts of the Mosaic covenant (Ex 13:9); to the covenant as a whole, as often in Deuteronomy (e.g., Deut 1:5; 4:8, 44); and to the Pentateuch with emphasis on it as written (Deut 17:18–19). Here in Amos, its meaning likely centers on the Mosaic covenant, but in addition to the Pentateuch, it may well include later revelations of Yahweh and his will from the time of Moses (fifteenth century BC) down to the time of Amos (eighth century BC) as found in the other canonical books written during that period.

Looking toward the NT and Jesus Christ, Yahweh's תּוֹרָה, his provision of life through his incarnate Word, issues forth from Zion (Is 2:3 || Micah 4:2). The Suffering Servant of Yahweh brings a תּוֹרָה that even gives the hope of salvation through faith for the distant Gentile lands (Is 42:4). Thus the rejection of Yahweh's Torah in the OT era was tantamount to a rejection of the divine Word that would become flesh (Jn 1:14), Israel's Messiah.

---

[2] Cf. S. Wagner, "מָאַס," *TDOT* 8:47–59.

תּוֹרָה also appears as the synopsis or compendium of Yahweh's words for life. Particularly clear examples abound in the Psalms. Psalm 1 pronounces a beatitude upon the person whose "delight is in the תּוֹרָה of Yahweh, and on his תּוֹרָה he meditates day and night" (Ps 1:2; see also, e.g., Pss 40:9 [ET 40:8]; 78:5; 119:1, 29). God gave priests the role of preserving and teaching his תּוֹרָה (e.g., Deut 17:18; 31:9), but תּוֹרָה can also be taught by parents to their children. In Prov 1:8, "the Torah/teaching of your mother" stands in parallel to "the instruction of your father" (see also Prov 13:14). Similarly, Luther intended parents to use his Small Catechism to instruct their children as stated in the titles of most of the sections of the Small Catechism.

The LXX almost always translates תּוֹרָה with νόμος, "law," which emphasizes legislation, enforcement, reward, and punishment. However, since תּוֹרָה can be parallel to דְּבַר־יְהוָה, "the Word of Yahweh" (Is 1:10; 2:3 || Micah 4:2), "teaching," "instruction," or even "revelation" are better translations than "law" because they facilitate understanding the term primarily as one of Gospel: God's provision of life and salvation through his covenant and Word, now fulfilled in Christ and the new covenant in his blood. This sense is appropriate for תּוֹרָה in Amos 2:4. Tragically, Judah had rejected Yahweh's תּוֹרָה, and this in turn led to the people's worship of other gods that could not save or give eternal life, but only mislead them into everlasting death.

וְחֻקָּיו לֹא שָׁמָרוּ—The verb שָׁמַר, "keep, observe," and the noun חֹק, "statute," are commonly used for living by faith according to God's gracious covenant expressed in his Torah (e.g., Ex 12:24; 15:26; Deut 4:40), but sadly the verb is negated here (לֹא). The noun חֹק derives from the verb חָקַק, "to carve out, engrave" (e.g., Is 22:16; Prov 8:27). The noun usually denotes a divine "statute, command, order" (Jer 31:36; Micah 7:11) and is often paired with מִשְׁפָּט, "judgment, regulation for justice, ordinance" (e.g., Ex 15:25; Deut 5:1; 12:1), making the two words at times almost synonymous. God's "statutes" are part of his single Torah.

וַיַּתְעוּם כִּזְבֵיהֶם אֲשֶׁר־הָלְכוּ אֲבוֹתָם אַחֲרֵיהֶם׃—The Hiphil verb with direct object suffix, וַיַּתְעוּם, means "and they led them astray." The subject is כִּזְבֵיהֶם, "their lies/idols," modified by the relative clause with redundant pronoun אֲשֶׁר־הָלְכוּ אֲבוֹתָם אַחֲרֵיהֶם, literally, "which their fathers followed after them [after the lies/idols]." The relative clause is translated as a separate line to reflect the Hebrew order of clauses.

The line suggests that the theological lies fostered by idols (see below)—and by the demons behind such false gods (cf. Hos 4:12; 1 Cor 10:20–21)—are false shepherds who deceive and mislead God's sheep.[3] The Qal of תָּעָה, "go astray," can describe the aimless wandering of a lost animal (e.g., Ex 23:4; Job 38:41; cf. Ps 119:176) or person (e.g., Gen 37:15) or people who go astray spiritually (Is 29:24; Ezek 14:11). The Israelites went astray like sheep, each turning to his own way (Is 53:6). The Hiphil has the corresponding causative meaning: to lead or cause people to go astray, which is done by apostate rulers (2 Ki 21:9) and false prophets (Jer 23:13, 32).

In contrast, only God is able to regather and guide his people to salvation. After alluding to Isaiah 53 in 1 Pet 2:22–24, the apostle Peter declares: "For you were like

---

[3] Cf. Andersen and Freedman, *Amos*, 305.

sheep going astray, but you have returned now to the Shepherd and Overseer of your souls" (1 Pet 2:25). Yahweh is the Shepherd (Ps 23:1) who leads his people "in paths of righteousness" (Ps 23:3). Jesus is the Good Shepherd (John 10).

The noun כָּזָב usually means "a lie, falsehood, delusion." However, it is one of several abstract Hebrew words that can also be used to refer to idols—lying gods. Other words that can similarly refer to idols include הֶבֶל, "vanity" (Deut 32:21; 1 Ki 16:13, 26; Jer 2:5); שֶׁקֶר, "lie" (Jer 10:14–15); אֱלִיל, "nothingness" (Lev 19:4); אָוֶן, "wickedness" (Is 66:3); תּוֹעֵבָה, "abomination" (2 Chr 34:33); שִׁקּוּצִים, "detestable things" (Hos 9:10); גִּלּוּלִים, "excrement cylinders" (Ezek 22:3); and תֹּהוּ, "emptiness, worthlessness" (Is 44:9). These words appear in polemical texts as pejorative designations for false gods.

Andersen and Freedman disagree that in Amos 2:4 the plural of כָּזָב denotes "idols." They prefer to take the term as "lies," which are connected by synecdoche to false prophets.[4] For example, in Ezek 13:9 and 22:28, false prophets are condemned for disseminating pernicious כָּזָב, "falsehood" or, as a collective, "lies."

The commentary below allows for the possibility that the plural of כָּזָב may allude to false prophets and their lies. However, the relative clause in Amos 2:4 includes the idiom אַחֲרֵיהֶם ... הָלְכוּ, "they went/followed after them," which is common in Deuteronomy and Joshua–2 Kings in reference to following (believing in, worshiping) false gods.[5] For example, in Deut 4:3, Moses reminds Israel of "what Yahweh did with regard to the Baal of Peor—how Yahweh your God annihilated from among you everyone who walked after the Baal of Peor [הָלַךְ֙ אַחֲרֵ֣י בַֽעַל־פְּע֔וֹר]." See also, for example, Deut 8:19 and Jer 11:10. Therefore it seems most likely that כָּזָב in Amos 2:4 refers to pagan deities.

2:5 וְשִׁלַּחְתִּי אֵשׁ בִּיהוּדָה וְאָכְלָה אַרְמְנוֹת יְרוּשָׁלִָם׃—This double judgment by fire—which Yahweh sends against the nation and which consumes the fortresses of its capital city—is similar to the double judgments by fire in the oracles against the pagan nations. See the first and second textual notes on 1:4 and "Yahweh Punishes by Fire" in the introduction to 1:3–2:16.

Commentary

2:4–5 This brief oracle against Judah is the only address to this nation in Amos.[6]

2:4 The accusations citing the transgressions of Judah (2:4) and later those of northern Israel (2:6–16) reflect their status as the people called to be the one elect nation of God, but who divided themselves into two warring nations, and who have now spurned their Redeemer and rejected his revealed Word.

---

4 Andersen and Freedman, *Amos*, 302–5.

5 Niehaus writes: "In the ancient Near East the concept of walking after someone indicated a subordinate or, in some cases, a suzerain-vassal relationship" ("Amos," 361).

6 Besides 2:4–5, "Judah" is mentioned elsewhere in Amos only in passing in 1:1 and 7:12. "Jerusalem" (2:5) occurs elsewhere only in 1:2, where it is parallel to "Zion," which is condemned in the woe in 6:1, its only other occurrence in the book.

Nevertheless, Yahweh uses many of the same formulas and words to condemn Judah (2:4–5) and Israel (2:6–16) as he did in the previous six oracles against pagan nations (1:3–2:3).[7]

By rejecting God's special revelation of salvation, Judah and Israel have degraded themselves so that they have become no better than their heathen neighbors, who possessed only an obscured natural knowledge of God.[8] In the NT, St. Paul exhorts the elect people of God—all baptized believers in Christ—that we must not repeat the sin of OT Israel (e.g., 1 Corinthians 10). If we too abuse our divine calling, we will forfeit our status as God's saved people:

> So I say this and testify in the Lord that you must no longer walk as the Gentiles walk in the futility of their mind. They are darkened in their understanding and estranged from the life of God because of the ignorance that is in them due to the hardening of their hearts. Having lost all sensitivity, they have given themselves over to sensuality to indulge in every kind of impurity with a continual lust for more. *You, however, did not come to know Christ that way.* (Eph 4:17–20)

The people of Judah and Israel had come to know Yahweh when he redeemed them through the exodus, gave them his Torah, and led them victoriously in the conquest of the promised land. Yahweh's expectation, therefore, was that their lives in the world, empowered by this Gospel, would reflect his salvation, will, and ways. The reality, however, is that Yahweh through Amos grouped his divided people with the Gentiles, thereby indicating that they were no different, no less sinful. They had become in effect foreign nations who deserved judgment just like those heathen nations did.

Judah is not accused of mistreating fellow human beings, as were the six previous nations, but of spurning God's inspired Word:

> They rejected the Torah of Yahweh,
> and his statutes they did not keep. (2:4)

Yahweh's "Torah" means his Word, especially the Pentateuch, with its narrative of redemption, its plan of salvation, and its covenant that constituted Israel as God's holy people (see the fourth textual note on 2:4). Since the time of Moses, God had raised up prophets to call his people to remain faithful to, or to return to, his Torah. Since the prophets were Yahweh's means of speaking his Word, to reject one is to reject the other. Here Yahweh charges Judah with rejecting his Word, and the corresponding charge against northern Israel is that the people tried to silence the prophets (2:12).

The rejection (מָאַס, 2:4) began even before northern Israel separated from Judah. United Israel requested a king so that it could be like the other nations.[9]

---

[7] The textual notes on 2:4–5 point out these shared formulas and words.

[8] See the introduction to 1:3–2:16, especially "God's Law Is Built into Creation."

[9] It is not correct to state that Israel's request for a king was in and of itself a rejection of Yahweh. God promised kings in Gen 17:6, while in Deut 17:14–20, he provided a description for how the kings were to lead his people. The recurring problem with the monarchy was that as the

In 1 Sam 8:7, Yahweh tells Samuel, "You they did not reject [מָאָסוּ]; rather, I am the one they rejected [מָאֲסוּ] from reigning over them." Because the Israelites repeatedly rejected Yahweh, his gracious covenant, and his holy Word, eventually he in turn rejected them.[10] Later, in Amos 5:21, Yahweh will declare to Israel, "I reject [מָאַסְתִּי] your [religious] festivals."

The people of Judah rejected Yahweh when they disobeyed his Torah.[11] They also rejected Yahweh when they decided to follow false gods—idols, who embodied lies. This too was an ancestral and ongoing sin: "Their idols led them astray, those that their fathers followed" (Amos 2:4). The disregard for the Torah and the acceptance of other gods were often disseminated by means of lying false prophets. In Isaiah, those false prophets spoke "smooth things" (Is 30:10), while in Ezekiel Yahweh declared that he would put a stop to "vacuous vision or misleading divination" (Ezek 12:24).[12] In Jeremiah, these prophets proclaimed, "Peace, peace, when there is no peace" (Jer 6:14; 8:11). Based on Amos 5:18–20, it is safe to assume that the false prophets in Amos' time promised that the Day of Yahweh would be all sunshine and brightness. These prophetic lies said yes to Paul's question "shall we continue in sin so that grace may abound?" (Rom 6:1). They believed that Yahweh would never act in judgment toward *Israel*.[13]

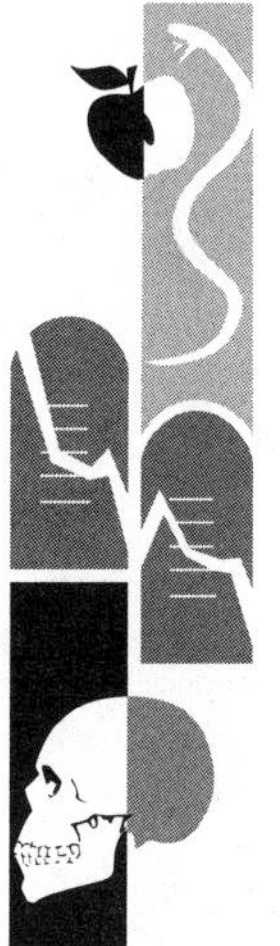

Lies ultimately come from Satan, the serpent who deceived Eve in the Garden of Eden with the words "you surely will not die" (Gen 3:4). This same enemy led the people of Judah not to believe the truth of God's Pentateuchal curses upon Israel when the people would go astray (Deut 28:15–68), in effect saying again, "You surely will not die." Since the sin of disbelieving the truth and believing the lie leads to death, Jesus declared that Satan "was a murderer from the beginning and has nothing to do with the truth. ... He is a liar and the father of lies" (Jn 8:44).

---

kings drifted away from the Torah and many lapsed into apostasy, they allowed and even pressured the people to conform to the pagan practices and beliefs of the neighboring nations (cf. 1 Sam 8:20).

[10] Cf. Andersen and Freedman, *Amos*, 296 (cf. also 2 Ki 17:20; 23:27). Andersen and Freedman, *Amos*, 300, write:

> Ezekiel often has "my judgments" and "my statutes" as objects of *mā'as* ["reject"] (5:6; 20:13, 16, 24); and one does not have to choose between a body of traditional regulations (priestly *torah*) or occasional oracular utterances (prophetic *torah*), for the prophets spoke as custodians and restorers of the requirements of the covenant (2 Kgs 17:23). Amos' indictment is accordingly quite broad.

[11] For a similar charge, see Is 5:24e–f.

[12] This is the translation of Hummel, *Ezekiel 1–20*, 328. See further the exposition of Ezekiel 13, "False Prophets and Prophetesses," in Hummel, *Ezekiel 1–20*, 365–77.

[13] A classic example of false prophecy is in 1 Kings 22. The false court prophets of Ahab, the king of Israel, promised that he would be victorious in battle, and Zedekiah even made horns of iron to emphasize the point. However, the true prophet Micaiah explained that Yahweh allowed a "lying spirit" (1 Ki 22:22) to speak through the false prophets to deceive the king into battle, where he would be killed, as indeed happened. Another classic example is in Jeremiah 28, where the false prophet Hananiah prophesied a quick end to Israel's Babylonian exile.

Amos' mention of "their fathers" (2:4) indicates that punishment comes upon the people of Judah because of their long history of sin. Beginning with the generation of Israelites redeemed in the exodus who grumbled and perished in the wilderness, a generation Yahweh loathed "for forty years" (Ps 95:10), Judah (as part of Israel) rejected his Torah, did not keep his statues, and was led astray after false gods.

2:5 At this point in the book of Amos, Yahweh proffers no mercy, no second chance even for Judah, the tribe from which the Ruler would come (Gen 49:10)—the Messiah, specifically from the line of King David (2 Samuel 7). Only at the end of the book, after God's scathing Law has done its work of convicting the people of their sins, will he extend the hope of the Gospel through the line of David (9:11) and "the Lion from the tribe of Judah, the Root of David" (Rev 5:5).

The imminent divine judgment for Judah is the same as that for the previous six nations: punishment by fire. 2 Ki 25:8–9 documents this judgment. In August of 587 BC, Nebuzaradan, acting on behalf of Nebuchadnezzar II, the king of Babylon, "burned the house of Yahweh, the house of the king, and all the houses of Jerusalem" (2 Ki 25:9). Jerusalem and the temple were destroyed. Waves of exiles from Judah were taken to Babylon periodically from 605 BC (see Dan 1:1–4) until 582/581 BC (see 2 Ki 24:12–14; 25:8–11; Jer 52:28–30).

Amos spent most of his ministry preaching not in Judah, but in northern Israel. His northern audience was in all likelihood filled with glee at the thought of Yahweh taking aim at Judah. Ever since the schism after the death of Solomon, their southern neighbors had accused the people of northern Israel of heterodox worship and practice (e.g., 1 Ki 13:1–6; 2 Chr 13:4–12; cf. 1 Ki 12:25–33). It was only fair that Judahites drink some of their own medicine!

Relations between Israel and Judah had been anything but peaceful in the decades preceding Amos' ministry. Joash (798–782 BC),[14] the father of the Jeroboam who was reigning in northern Israel when Amos prophesied, was provoked to war by Amaziah as detailed in 2 Ki 14:8–16 and 2 Chr 25:17–24. Joash responded by destroying the wall of Jerusalem, looting the temple and its royal treasuries, and taking hostages with him back to Samaria. The ninth century and the early eighth century had seen no love lost in this topsy-turvy familial relationship.

In fact, not only Judah, but Edom, Ammon, and Moab were historically related to Israel, and most of the time these people groups were engaged in "sibling rivalry." How satisfying it must have been to northern Israel to know that their wayward relatives were getting their just deserts! Yet Israel will be the target of divine wrath in the next oracle (2:6–16).

Moreover, this fiery judgment against Judah is not the last word in the book about the southern tribe. Instead, the book ends with a salvation oracle

---

[14] Thiele, *The Mysterious Numbers of the Hebrew Kings*, 111.

promising restoration for all repentant believers through the resurrection of David's tabernacle (9:11–15). Therefore Yahweh's Gospel promise continues to be attached to Judah (as in Gen 49:10), specifically in the Judahite line of David, and was fulfilled in David's greater Son and Lord (Psalm 110; Mk 12:35–37; Acts 2:34–36).

Amos 2:6–16

Judgment against Israel

Translation

2 [6]Thus says Yahweh:
"Because of three transgressions of Israel
and because of four, I will not revoke it,
because they sell the righteous for silver
and the needy for a pair of sandals.
[7]They trample the poorest of the poor into the dust of the earth,
and they twist the way of the oppressed.
And each man and his father go to the young woman,
so that they defile my holy name.
[8]Upon seized garments they stretch themselves out
beside every altar.
They drink wine obtained through fines
in the temple of their gods.
[9]Yet I myself annihilated the Amorite before them,
whose height was like the height of cedars, and he was strong like oaks.
I annihilated his fruit above and his roots below.
[10]And I myself brought you up from the land of Egypt,
and I led you in the wilderness for forty years,
to possess the land of the Amorite.
[11]And I raised up some of your sons to be prophets,
and some of your chosen men to be Nazirites.
Is this not so, O children of Israel?"
declares Yahweh.
[12]"But you made the Nazirites drink wine,
and you commanded the prophets, saying, 'You shall not prophesy at all!'
[13]Behold, I am creaking under you,
just as a wagon creaks when it is full of sheaves.
[14]Flight to a place of refuge will fail from the swift,
and the strong man will not exert his strength,
and the warrior will not save his life.
[15]And the archer will not stand,
and the one who is swift on his feet will not save himself,
and the one who rides the horse will not save his life.
[16]And the most courageous of heart among the warriors will flee naked on that day,"
declares Yahweh.

Textual Notes

2:6 כֹּה אָמַר יְהוָה—For this messenger formula, see the first textual note on 1:3 and "The Messenger Formula" in the introduction to 1:3–2:16.

עַל־שְׁלֹשָׁה פִּשְׁעֵי יִשְׂרָאֵל וְעַל־אַרְבָּעָה—This is the same accusation formula Yahweh used for the pagan nations in 1:3–2:3 and for Judah in 2:4. See the second textual note on 1:3 and "The Staircase Numerical Pattern" in the introduction to 1:3–2:16. Here יִשְׂרָאֵל, "Israel," refers to the northern nation of the divided kingdom, separate from the southern kingdom of Judah (2:4–5).

לֹא אֲשִׁיבֶנּוּ—This is the same declaration of judgment as used in the earlier seven oracles against the other nations. See the third textual note on 1:3 and "God's Judgment Is Irrevocable" in the introduction to 1:3–2:16.

עַל־מִכְרָם בַּכֶּסֶף צַדִּיק—Literally, "because of their selling for silver a righteous man," this transgression is expressed in the same formulaic way (עַל followed by an infinitive construct with suffix, here מִכְרָם) as the national transgression cited in each of the six oracles against the pagan nations and in the oracle against Judah. See the fourth textual note on 1:3 and "The Citation of the Transgression" in the introduction to 1:3–2:16. Against the six pagan nations in 1:3–2:3, Yahweh cited only one transgression; see "Just One Transgression Is Cited" in the introduction to 1:3–2:16. But for Judah Yahweh cited several transgressions (2:4). This transgression by northern Israel in 2:6 is just the first of seven charges cited against northern Israel in 2:6–8.

The Qal infinitive construct of מָכַר has a subjective suffix: מִכְרָם, "their selling," means "they sell." For the *hireq* in the first syllable, see GKC, § 61 b; Joüon, § 65 b. The participle and imperfect verbs in 2:7–8 imply that the cited sins of Israel were ongoing, and so this infinitive is translated as present tense ("they *sell*," not "sold") as are the verb forms in 2:7–8 (see the first textual note on 2:7). Usually the verb מָכַר involves a monetary transaction.[1] Elsewhere in the OT it can denote the sale of people as slaves (e.g., Gen 37:27–28, 36; Deut 21:14). This is the meaning of מָכַר in Amos 2:6, its only occurrence in this prophetic book. בַּכֶּסֶף, "for (the) silver," uses the preposition בְּ *pretii*, of price (BDB, s.v. בְּ, III 3 b) and the generic definite article (not translated) for the material of silver (Waltke-O'Connor, § 13.5.1g, including n. 12). The identical phrase בַּכֶּסֶף recurs in 8:6 with the same meaning.

Related is the use of the verb מָכַר for a person with debts larger than he can pay, who can sell himself to his creditor for six years (Deut 15:12; Jer 34:14). In a metaphorical sense, Yahweh can "sell, hand over" his people Israel to their enemies for various periods of time (Judg 3:8; 4:21; 10:7), but in that case neither money nor goods are given in exchange for them.

The adjective צַדִּיק, "righteous," is the most common word from the verbal root צדק.[2] It can describe the attribute of righteousness possessed by Yahweh and imputed to his people by grace. Yahweh demonstrates that he is צַדִּיק by his actions. He is righteous when he acts mercifully and saves sinners through faith (Is 45:21; Ps 116:5; cf. Zech

[1] Cf. E. Lipinski, "מכר," *TDOT* 8:291–96.

[2] Cf. B. Johnson, "צַדִּיק," *TDOT* 12:257–59.

9:9). He is also righteous when he punishes the wicked and establishes his righteous people (Jer 20:12; Zeph 3:5; Pss 7:10 [ET 7:9]; 11:7).

God's people are called "righteous," including Noah (Gen 6:9) and David (1 Sam 24:17–18 [ET 24:16–17]). This is a forensic term, since their actions demonstrated that they still remained sinful (Gen 9:20–22; 2 Samuel 11). Yet they repented from their sins and continued to believe in God as their Savior. Their righteousness was imputed to them through faith, as Gen 15:6 states about Abraham, the paradigmatic Israelite believer. Already the OT describes how the Messiah will "justify/declare righteous" (Hiphil of צָדַק) believers so that they are "righteous" (צַדִּיק); see Is 53:11. The NT has extensive arguments showing that the doctrine of forensic justification through faith in Christ was indeed the teaching of the OT and continues to be true for NT believers (e.g., Romans 4–5; Galatians 3). OT descriptions of the righteous are based on their faith relationship with Yahweh and his ways (Ps 1:6; Prov 2:20; Job 17:9). It is therefore abominable to treat the righteous wickedly (Ex 23:7; Is 5:13, 23; Prov 17:15, 26), since that is a transgression against righteous Yahweh himself (cf. Acts 9:4; 26:14).

In Amos 2:6, צַדִּיק could be a true singular and indefinite, "a righteous person," or a collective, substantive adjective, "righteous people." It is best understood as a collective adjective, "the righteous," because Israel's abuse of righteous people was a widespread practice.

The only other occurrence of צַדִּיק, "righteous," in Amos is in 5:12, where again it refers to the transgression of Israelites abusing righteous people in their midst. See also the discussion of "justice" (מִשְׁפָּט) in parallel with "righteousness" (צְדָקָה) in the second and third textual notes on 5:7.

וְאֶבְי֖וֹן בַּעֲב֥וּר נַעֲלָֽיִם׃—This second accusation in the transgression charged against Israel is repeated verbatim in 8:6. This is a second object clause for the infinitive in the previous clause, מִכְרָם, "they sell." The direct object is the noun אֶבְיוֹן, "the needy," a collective singular parallel to the direct object at the end of the preceding clause, צַדִּיק, "the righteous." (צַדִּיק is followed by the parallel אֶבְיוֹנִים in 5:12.) The Hebrew word order forms a poetic chiasm: "… for silver, the righteous and the needy, for two sandals."

The noun אֶבְיוֹן (2:6; 4:1; 5:12; 8:4, 6) is in the same semantic field as other terms for the destitute and powerless, including דַּל, "poor" (in 2:7 and 5:11 and parallel to אֶבְיוֹן in 4:1; 8:6) and עָנָו and עָנִי, "oppressed, afflicted, meek, humble" (the Qere and Kethib, respectively, parallel to אֶבְיוֹן in 8:4).[3] אֶבְיוֹן appears in a wide variety of contexts. For example, in the psalms, the אֶבְיוֹן receives help from Yahweh when he is threatened by his more powerful enemies (Pss 9:19 [ET 9:18]; 72:4, 12–13; 82:4). An אֶבְיוֹן is frequently identified as one who looks to and trusts in Yahweh (Pss 70:6 [ET 70:5]; 86:1). Yahweh hears the אֶבְיוֹן (Ps 35:10) and promises help by administering justice (Ps 140:13 [ET 140:12]), that is, by judging the oppressor and justifying the lowly believer. In the legal realm, the אֶבְיוֹן, the "needy" person, occurs in discussions about the Sabbath (Ex 23:11). The exploitation of the אֶבְיוֹן plays a particularly important role in Amos. In Amos 2:6 and 5:12, oppression of the אֶבְיוֹן goes hand-in-hand

[3] Cf. G. J. Botterweck, "אֶבְיוֹן," *TDOT* 1:29–41.

with the affliction of the צַדִּיק, "righteous." Injustice and oppression are intertwined, and both elicit Yahweh's wrath.

Used here as a preposition, בַּעֲבוּר, "for (the sake of)," functions in the same way as the preposition בְּ of price (see the previous textual note). In the OT, עֲבוּר always has the prefixed preposition בְּ. This combination recurs in Amos only in the identical phrase in 8:6.

The dual form (נַעֲלָיִם) of the noun נַעַל, "sandal," means "two sandals," that is, "a pair of sandals" (Joüon, § 91 c). The plural נְעָלִים, "sandals," occurs elsewhere in the OT but the dual occurs only in 2:6 and 8:6. "Objects that occur in pairs associated with paired body parts may be referred to with a dual, for example, נַעֲלַיִם '(a pair of) sandals' " (Waltke-O'Connor, § 7.3b).

2:7 הַשֹּׁאֲפִים עַל־עֲפַר־אֶרֶץ בְּרֹאשׁ דַּלִּים—Yahweh's third accusation against Israel begins with the attributive Qal participle of שָׁאַף II, "crush, trample upon" (BDB) with the article, הַשֹּׁאֲפִים, referring back to the same people denoted by the pronominal suffix on מִכְרָם, "they sell," in 2:6 (Joüon, § 138 e). The article on such a participle can function like a personal pronoun (GKC, § 126 b). Thus הַשֹּׁאֲפִים, "the trampling ones," means "they trample."

This charge in *participial* form indicates an *ongoing* sin. This is confirmed by the four following imperfect verbs (יַטּוּ ... יֵלְכוּ ... יַטּוּ ... יִשְׁתּוּ) in 2:7–8, which too are translated as present tense ("they twist," etc.). Therefore these accusations against Israel are unlike those enumerations of past sins in the oracles against the other nations (1:3–2:5).

Amos contains nineteen participles that describe the ongoing sins of Israel's leaders. While only two of them are preceded by הוֹי, "woe" (5:18; 6:1), Andersen and Freedman understand all of the participles in their contexts to imply woe to those people whom they describe.[4]

The verb שָׁאַף II, "trample," should not to be confused with the homonym שָׁאַף I, "gasp, pant" (BDB), although KJV, NKJV, and NASB render "pant after" and Sweeney argues that the possible meaning "pant after" may "convey the sense of effort made by those who chase their victims down in order to sell them for silver or sandals."[5] שָׁאַף II is a by-form of שׁוּף, "to crush, trample."[6] הַשֹּׁאֲפִים recurs in a similar context in 8:4, and other forms of שָׁאַף II are in Ezek 36:3; Pss 56:2–3 (ET 56:1–2); 57:4 (ET 57:3). In all these texts, it refers to people who destroy the power of others in order to defeat and humiliate them. The by-form שׁוּף, "crush," famously occurs in Gen 3:15, where God states that the Seed of Eve, Jesus Christ, will "crush" the head (all the power) of the serpent, while the serpent will "crush" his heel, that is, deliver a mortal wound that only lasts from Good Friday until Easter morning.

---

4 Andersen and Freedman, *Amos*, 462.

5 Sweeney, *The Twelve Prophets*, 215. That הַשֹּׁאֲפִים means "trample" is confirmed by the LXX, which translated it with τὰ πατοῦντα, from the verb πατέω, "to tread on, trample."

6 Compare GKC, § 72 p, for similar participial forms with middle א. There is no need to emend the text by deleting the *aleph* as is suggested by *BHS* and Stuart, *Hosea–Jonah*, 307.

The precise nuance of the prepositional phrase עַל־עֲפַר־אֶרֶץ, "on the dust of earth," has been interpreted in different ways. RSV, NRSV, and ESV translate, "trample the head of the poor into the dust of the earth," while NIV gives "trample on the heads of the poor as upon the dust of the ground."

The construct phrase בְּרֹאשׁ דַּלִּים, literally, "on the head of poor people," serves as the object of the verb "trample." It has been interpreted in different ways. Many take "head" as a reference to the body part. However, Bewer suggests that here ראשׁ means "greatest" or "chief" of the poor,[7] aptly translated as "the poorest of the poor." Certainly ראשׁ can have that meaning in other contexts. The noun דַּל is one of the common words in the semantic field describing the "poor," weak, destitute, and powerless, as also is אֶבְיוֹן (see the fifth textual note on 2:6). דַּל can refer to poor physical health (Gen 41:19), a distressed emotional state (2 Sam 13:4), or low standing in society (Judg 6:15).[8] Most often it describes a person's socio-economic status of poverty (Ex 30:15; Lev 14:21; Job 20:10). The poor are frequently contrasted with the rich (Lev 19:15; Ruth 3:10). Because of their poverty, they can be keenly aware of their need for an intercessor and the Savior (1 Sam 2:8; Is 25:4; Ps 72:13; in the NT, see Mt 5:3; Lk 4:18; 14:21).

דַּל appears four times in Amos (2:7; 4:1; 5:11; 8:6) and usually denotes the "poor." In some passages, it may be understood as "helpless," because the poor do not have money to pay taxes (5:11). The prophet speaks Yahweh's condemnation against the wealthy who oppress or enslave the poor. This abuse is abhorrent to Yahweh. דַּל is nearly synonymous with other Hebrew terms that denote poverty and need. It is parallel with עָנָו here (see the next textual note) and with אֶבְיוֹן in 4:1 and 8:6.

וְדֶרֶךְ עֲנָוִים יַטּוּ—The noun דֶּרֶךְ in construct with עֲנָוִים is the direct object of the verb יַטּוּ, literally, "they turn aside/pervert the way of oppressed people." This fourth charge against Israel employs the Hiphil of נָטָה. (The identical form יַטּוּ recurs in 2:8 but in a different sense.) In the Qal, נָטָה commonly means "to stretch out" or "extend."[9] In the Hiphil, it usually has the transitive meaning "to turn (something) aside, steer, direct," either in a physical sense or a spiritual sense. Thus Balaam turned his donkey (Num 22:23), while Joshua exhorted the Israelites to turn their hearts to Yahweh (Josh 24:23). In judicial contexts, the Hiphil of נָטָה often means "to twist/pervert" justice (see BDB, Hiphil, 3 g). God commands in Ex 23:6, "You shall not pervert [תַטֶּה] the justice of your needy one in his lawsuit." The Hiphil has a similar meaning in Amos 5:12 and also, for example, Deut 16:19; 24:17; Prov 17:23. With the preposition מִן, it can denote turning people away *from* the right way (Job 24:4). Job's complaint too is set in a legal context that expresses the action of the wealthy bullying the underprivileged, using courts to accomplish this treachery.

The Hiphil in Prov 17:23 has as its object a synonym of דֶּרֶךְ, namely, לְהַטּוֹת אָרְחוֹת מִשְׁפָּט, "to pervert the ways of justice." Similarly here Israel is turning—or

---

7 Bewer, "Critical Notes on Amos 2:7 and 8:4," 116. He asserts: "The very fact that the LXX knew just as little as modern scholars what to do with [this phrase] should put us on our guard. It speaks rather for than against the originality of the phrase" ("Note on Amos 2:7a," 201).

8 Cf. H.-J. Fabry, "דַּל," *TDOT* 3:217–30.

9 Cf. H. Ringgren, "נָטָה," *TDOT* 9:381–87.

better, twisting—the "*way* of the oppressed." NIV paraphrases: "deny justice to the oppressed," which could involve corruption in court at the city gate, as in Amos 5:12. In both 2:7 and 5:12, Yahweh probably is referring to the actions of the powerful who are abusing the legal system to control, manipulate, and deprive impoverished people of due justice. Andersen and Freedman, citing Job 24:1–4 and Mal 3:5, speculate that the expression may indicate fraud and the withholding of legal redress.[10]

The substantized adjective עָנָו, "oppressed, afflicted, humble," appears in Amos here and (the Kethib) in 8:4. It is derived from the verb עָנָה III, "be oppressed, afflicted, downcast" (see BDB, Qal). It connotes hardship, torment, pain, and despair, "the darkness of human experience, the shadow side of life."[11] The עֲנָוִים receive special protection by God's grace in Jesus Christ (Is 11:4 and 61:1, quoted by Jesus in Lk 4:18). Zech 7:9–10 indicates that God's people have the obligation to champion the weak and not to abuse power over them. The related noun עֳנִי, "affliction," usually leads to Yahweh's intervention, as when Yahweh sees the affliction of his people and takes redemptive action (Ex 3:7, 17; cf. Gen 29:32; 1 Sam 1:11; Ps 119:153).

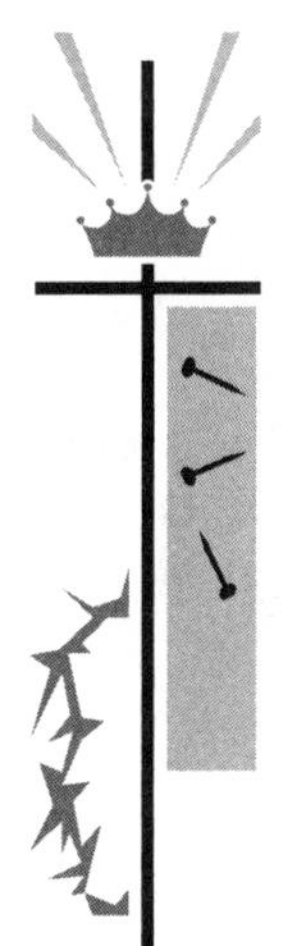

The LXX translates עֲנָוִים in Amos 2:7 with ταπεινοί, the "humble," while in 8:4 it employs πτωχοί, the "poor." In the NT, the πτωχοί are not simply poverty-stricken, but those who are invited to receive the riches of God's grace in his Son (Mt 5:3; 11:5; Lk 4:18). Paul describes the theology of the cross in terms of God choosing those who are weak, lowly, and despised to receive wisdom, righteousness, and redemption in Christ (1 Cor 1:26–30). He also proclaims that Christ, who was rich, became poor so that by his poverty we baptized believers might become rich in grace (2 Cor 8:9).

וְאִישׁ וְאָבִיו יֵלְכוּ אֶל־הַנַּעֲרָה—Literally, "a man and his father go to the young woman." There is a general consensus that this fifth accusation refers to a sexual sin.[12] However, its precise meaning is debated.

Both a father and his son are committing this transgression. Probably no marriage relationship exists between either of them and the young woman, so both father and son are committing adultery, and their sin is more heinous (akin to incest) because it is with the same woman. Even if the woman were the wife of the father or the son, so one of them would not be committing adultery, the other man would be committing adultery and incest. Leviticus clearly prohibits incestuous sexual relations, specifically between a man and his father's wife or between a father and his daughter-in-law (Lev 18:6–8, 15). For the former sin, the NT commands, "deliver such a man over to Satan for the destruction of his flesh" (1 Cor 5:1–5).

---

[10] Andersen and Freedman, *Amos*, 316.

[11] E. Gerstenberger, "עָנָה," *TDOT* 11:235; cf. further Gerstenberger, *TDOT* 11:234–52.

[12] Paul cites several similar statements that have sexual meanings in Akkadian and other Near Eastern texts (*Amos*, 82). Bronznick ("More on *HLK ʾL*") confirms Paul's work by relating the verb הָלַךְ here with the verb בּוֹא used elsewhere in the OT with אֶל to connote sexual intercourse. Bronznick cites the following verses as examples where בּוֹא אֶל has that meaning: Gen 16:2; 30:3; 38:8; 2 Sam 16:21. See also Wolff, *Joel and Amos*, 166–67; McLaughlin, *The* Marzēaḥ *in the Prophetic Literature*, 124.

The wording of the predicate, יֵלְכוּ אֶל־הַנַּעֲרָה, "go to the young woman," needs to be explained, since this phraseology (the verb הָלַךְ with the preposition אֶל and noun נַעֲרָה as its indirect object) does not occur elsewhere in the OT.

First, Amos may have chosen the verb הָלַךְ to connect this accusation verbally with the accusation against Judah in 2:4: הָלְכוּ אֲבוֹתָם אַחֲרֵיהֶם, literally, "their fathers followed after them [idols]."

Second, the idiom בּוֹא אֶל, "come (in)to," is common in the OT denoting sexual intercourse (see BDB, s.v. בּוֹא, Qal, 1 e). That common idiom explains the use of the same preposition here.

Third, the noun נַעֲרָה, "young woman, servant girl," is a common and general term. It can have a wide range of referents, including a single female (e.g., Gen 24:14), a married woman (e.g., Deut 22:15), a widow (e.g., Ruth 2:6), a concubine (e.g., Judg 19:3), or a female slave (e.g., 2 Ki 5:2–4). The word itself does not necessarily entail sexual activity or association with cultic activity, but the context here certainly describes sexual activity ("each man and his father go to the young woman," Amos 2:7) in a cultic context ("beside every altar … in the temple of their gods," 2:8). In the ancient Near East, ritual prostitution was part of pagan fertility worship, but different terms are used for a cultic prostitute such as זוֹנָה, "a prostitute" (e.g., Gen 38:15), or more specifically קְדֵשָׁה, literally, "a holy woman," meaning "sacral prostitute" (e.g., Deut 23:18 [ET 23:17]; Hos 4:14).

Even though נַעֲרָה is a general term for "young woman," that has not kept commentators from putting forth a multitude of arguments that in Amos 2:7 it refers to a "sacred" prostitute. The main reason is the cultic setting of the next verse. The fact that those who commit these sins are stretching out near altars in the temples of their gods (2:8) brings forth an image of cultic prostitution, which is adultery against Yahweh.[13]

The clause with the "young woman" in 2:7 and the following cultic scene in 2:8 imply that the men's action involved both sexual adultery (2:7) and theological whoredom (2:8). The Scriptures portray a link between sexual behavior and theological belief. Sexual and theological fidelity go together (Song of Songs; Eph 5:21–33), as do sexual sins and apostasy from God (1 Cor 6:9–10). Israel's infidelity toward God is portrayed as sexual promiscuity in Ezekiel 16 and 23, while the literal sexual promiscuity of Hosea's wife in Hos 1:2 signifies the apostasy of Israel. By breaking the Sixth and Tenth Commandments (Ex 20:14, 17; Deut 5:18, 21) the Israelites are breaking the First Commandment (Ex 20:3; Deut 5:7), and their violation of the First Commandment (worshiping other gods, as is clear in Amos 2:8) leads them into violating the Sixth and Tenth Commandments.

---

[13] Barstad, *The Religious Polemics of Amos*, 21–36, discusses the idea that the woman in 2:7c is a cult prostitute but rejects it in favor of her being a *marzēaḥ* hostess. He argues that no sexual activity is implied in 2:7c and that what 2:7c–8 condemns is attending a *marzēaḥ* feast. For the *marzēaḥ* feast, see the second textual note and the commentary on 6:7. However McLaughlin, *The* Marzēaḥ *in the Prophetic Literature*, 120–28, argues against Barstad, asserting that other *marzēaḥ* allusions in Amos (4:1; 6:4–7) do not support this interpretation and that the surrounding context supports the interpretation that 2:7 depicts a woman of a low class being mistreated or abused.

Since 2:7 does not use any specific term for a prostitute, this young woman probably belongs in the same category as the "poor" and "oppressed" in 2:7. The lack of a pejorative term like "prostitute" helps readers sympathize with her and see her purely as a victim. She represents one more example of the kinds of exploited people being denied justice in Israel.

לְמַעַן חַלֵּל אֶת־שֵׁם קָדְשִׁי׃—Usually לְמַעַן with an infinitive construct (here חַלֵּל) introduces a purpose clause. Andersen and Freedman believe that לְמַעַן implies willful intention to profane God's name.[14] However, the Israelites probably did not sin with the conscious purpose or goal of receiving God's wrath and punishment. Instead, profaning God's holy name is the result of sin. Hence לְמַעַן probably introduces a result clause.[15]

Characteristic language in Leviticus and Ezekiel, books with priestly and liturgical concerns, is the Piel of חָלַל, "to profane, desecrate," with the adjectival genitive שֵׁם קָדְשִׁי, "my [God's] holy name," as its direct object. This results from sins such as sacrificing children to the god Molech (Lev 20:3; cf. Lev 18:21) or worshiping fecal deities (Ezek 20:39; 36:18–23). Other abominations in the context of profaning God's name (Lev 18:21) include incest, adultery, homosexuality, and bestiality (Lev 18:6–23). When his name has been profaned, God acts in judgment and, later, salvation to resanctify his holy name (Ezek 20:9, 14, 22; 36:18–23; 39:7; cf. Lk 11:2; Jn 17:6, 17, 26).

By using this liturgical language for moral offenses, Amos, like Leviticus and Ezekiel, affirms that God's people are to reflect God's holiness in all aspects of daily life, not only during formal worship (Lev 19:2; 20:26; 1 Pet 1:15–16). Sexual sins, and not just worship infringements, profane Yahweh's holy name.

The noun קֹדֶשׁ recurs in 4:2 in reference to God's "holiness," and מִקְדָּשׁ, "sanctuary," is in 7:9, 13. For further comments about God's holiness, see the first textual note on 4:2 and the second textual note on 7:9.

2:8 וְעַל־בְּגָדִים חֲבֻלִים יַטּוּ אֵצֶל כָּל־מִזְבֵּחַ—Yahweh's sixth accusation begins with a reference to בְּגָדִים חֲבֻלִים, "garments taken in pledge" (BDB, s.v. חָבַל I, Qal, 2). The noun בֶּגֶד denotes a large square cloak used as a garment by day and a covering by night.[16] The verb חָבַל (here the Qal passive participle) means "*take* or *hold in pledge*" (BDB, s.v. חָבַל I, Qal, 2).[17]

The OT maintains a distinction between a pledge and a surety. Whereas a surety involves three parties, a pledge involves only two, usually with some exchange of goods.

---

[14] Andersen and Freedman, *Amos*, 319.

[15] See Joüon, § 169 g; Waltke-O'Connor, § 38.3b, including n. 25, citing Brongers, "Die Partikel לְמַעַן in der biblisch-hebräischen Sprache"; and Williams, § 198.

[16] Niehaus, "Amos," 367.

[17] Under the verb חָבַל I, BDB includes three different definitions (with supporting OT verses): "to bind," "to take or hold in pledge," and (in the Piel) "to writhe," that is, to be in birth labor. However, *HALOT* and other recent scholars (e.g., H. A. Hoffner, "חָבַל," *TDOT* 4:179–84; cf. C. P. Weber, "חָבַל," *TWOT*, § 592) believe that each of these definitions belongs to a separate homographic verb חבל. The one here means "to impound … to seize a pledge from a person" (*HALOT*, s.v. חבל II). Yet another homograph is listed separately in BDB (חָבַל II) and *HALOT* (חבל III): "to act corruptly." That provides a possible double entendre here in 2:8: the garments were pledged for repayment of the loan, and then they were taken by the corrupt actions of the wealthy.

A wealthy person could give a loan to a poor or needy person and take some of the poor person's belongings as a pledge or collateral, to make sure the debtor would eventually repay the loan. Some of the common belongings that could be taken in pledge were clothes (Deut 24:17; Amos 2:8), livestock (Job 24:3), and household utensils (Deut 24:6). However, God commanded that a widow's "garment" (בֶּגֶד) was never to be confiscated (Deut 24:17). Although a different word for "garment" appears in Deut 24:12–13, those verses admonish Israelites to return the garment "before the sun goes down."

Creditors were warned not to take necessities for life from their debtors. They were not allowed to take (part of) a mill for grinding grain (Deut 24:6), clothing from the very poor (Ex 22:25–26 [ET 22:26–27]; Job 22:6), or an ox or ass from the widow (Job 24:3). Livestock, clothing, and a mill were all necessary for sustaining life and making a living, so a creditor could not strip his debtor of these vital necessities.

The phrase here may refer to an injustice other than lawfully holding garments taken as collateral for a loan. It could refer to distrain, that is, forceful seizing of property. When a loan came due and a person defaulted on a debt, the lender might confiscate the debtor's property. There was no provision in the Torah or the OT allowing this treatment, so it was an injustice. This would explain why taking a garment in pledge (the verb חָבַל and the noun בֶּגֶד as its object) occurs in a context that speaks of perverting justice (Deut 24:17). Ezek 18:16 describes a righteous man as one who never takes in pledge (the verb חָבַל) and covers the naked with a garment (בֶּגֶד).

The identical verb יַטּוּ also occurred in 2:7 but with a different meaning. Here the Hiphil imperfect of נָטָה means "they recline" on the garments (BDB, Hiphil, 3 a). This clarifies the transgression. People were stretching themselves out (perhaps for sexual immorality, as described in 2:7) on illegally confiscated garments אֵצֶל כָּל־מִזְבֵּחַ, "beside every altar," that is, at various pagan places of worship.

וְיֵין עֲנוּשִׁים יִשְׁתּוּ בֵּית אֱלֹהֵיהֶם׃—Yahweh's seventh charge against Israel sarcastically indicts the nation for getting drunk on confiscated wine in heathen temples.

The uncommon verb עָנַשׁ means "to **impose a fine** on someone" (*HALOT*) and refers to monetary fines and indemnity (e.g., Ex 21:22; Deut 22:19). The hapax legomenon עֲנוּשִׁים may be the Qal passive participle, referring to people who have been "fined" (BDB; *HALOT*, s.v. עֲנוּשִׁים, 1), or it may be a related substantive, possibly meaning "fines" (*HALOT*, s.v. עֲנוּשִׁים, 2 a). Therefore וְיֵין עֲנוּשִׁים could mean "wine of/from fined people," that is, wine taken as payment for fines imposed on people. Or it could mean "wine of fines," that is, wine purchased with money exacted by imposing fines on people. The translation "wine obtained through fines" allows for either possibility. "It is impossible to know whether these fines were legal or not and whether the parties were actually guilty. Whatever the case, fines are not to be exacted in order to allow the wealthy to indulge their appetites."[18]

The interpretive decision for בֵּית אֱלֹהֵיהֶם is whether it refers to "the house/temple of their God" or "the house/temple of their gods." Because Amos may allude to

[18] Paul, *Amos*, 86–87.

sacred prostitution in 6:7 and he refers to multiple altars ("every altar") in 6:8, it is best to translate אֱלֹהֵיהֶם as "their [pagan] gods." Yahweh will name some of these gods in 5:26 and 8:14. The construct phrase בֵּית אֱלֹהֵיהֶם may well allude to בֵּית אֵל, Bethel, "house of God," the center of northern Israel's apostate worship named in 3:14; 4:4; 5:5–6; 7:10, 13. After the schism of northern Israel from Judah, Jeroboam established the false temples at Bethel and Dan and furnished them with golden calves, which he declared to be the saviors: "Behold your gods, Israel, who brought you up from the land of Egypt" (1 Ki 12:28).

Confirming the plural translation is the fact that this is the only place in the book where Amos uses the divine title אֱלֹהִים with a third masculine plural object suffix. In 4:12 and 9:15 Yahweh refers to himself as God with the second masculine singular pronominal suffix: אֱלֹהֶיךָ, "your God."

2:9 וְאָנֹכִי הִשְׁמַדְתִּי אֶת־הָאֱמֹרִי מִפְּנֵיהֶם—The dramatic reversal in this oracle is introduced by the pleonastic pronoun with adversative *waw*, וְאָנֹכִי, literally, "*but I* exterminated the Amorite before them." Such an unneeded pronoun preceding the inflected verb emphasizes the subject (GKC, § 135 a). This emphatic pronoun referring to Yahweh indicates that the roles are now reversed. Israel was the subject of the sinful actions in 2:6–8. Now Yahweh is the subject of the gracious actions in 2:9–11, and Israel is the object who benefited from those actions. What follows is a brief review of prior salvation history. For other references to the early history of Israel in Amos, see 3:1; 5:25; 9:7. Yahweh's salvific acts in 2:9–11 stand in stark antithesis to those of Israel's leaders, who were persistently taking advantage of the impoverished and abusing their status as God's redeemed people.

The verb שָׁמַד in the Hiphil stem means "to annihilate, exterminate."[19] It is employed to describe the complete annihilation of an enemy (e.g., Josh 7:12; 11:20; 1 Ki 13:34), as when Yahweh "destroyed them [the Rephaim] from before the Ammonites" and "destroyed the Horim" (Deut 2:21–22). For emphasis it is used twice in Amos 2:9. Elsewhere Amos employs it only in 9:8, where it occurs three times and Yahweh declares that he will exterminate the sinful kingdom (Israel), yet not completely exterminate the house of Jacob. Yahweh promises a remnant for Joseph (5:15) and even for the Gentile nations (9:12).

The preposition with the third masculine plural pronominal suffix, מִפְּנֵיהֶם, has a geographical meaning, "from before them," before the advancing Israelites, as in Ex 23:30; 34:11; Lev 18:24. It may also have the nuance "for them," that is, for the benefit of the Israelites, as מִפְּנֵיכֶם, "for you," is used in reference to the miracles God performed for them in Josh 2:10 and 4:23.[20] This conveys that salvation is accomplished by God alone, not in any part by his people, but his gracious actions are for their benefit.

The definite singular adjective used as a proper noun, הָאֱמֹרִי, "the Amorite," serves as a collective. Against those who believe that the Amorites were nomads from the Syro-Arabian desert, Mendenhall maintains that the Amorites had their homeland in

---

[19] Cf. N. Lohfink, "שׁמד," *TDOT* 15:177–98.

[20] Cf. Paul, *Amos*, 87.

northeast Syria and that the sedentary Amorite culture of northeast Syria continued from at least the Chalcolithic period (which began ca. 4200 BC) through the end of the Middle Bronze Age (which ended ca. 1550 BC). From northeast Syria, the Amorites emigrated to the east and to the west. Mendenhall notes: "By the end of the 3d millennium B.C. Amorites were already settled in fairly large numbers in the cities of Mesopotamia." During the Late Bronze Age (1550–1200 BC), it became impossible to define an Amorite ethnicity since the Amorites had assimilated into their surrounding cultures.[21] The OT identifies Amorites as one of the former occupants of the promised land (e.g., Gen 15:16, 21; Deut 1:7; 7:1).

In this context in Amos (2:9–10), Yahweh is recalling Moses' victories over Sihon and Og, who were Amorite kings (Deut 2:24–37; 3:1–11), as well as the conquest of the promised land under Joshua. Because the Amorites were idolaters, Yahweh warned Israel not to worship the Amorite gods (Judg 6:10; cf. Josh 24:15).

אֲשֶׁר כְּגֹבַהּ אֲרָזִים גָּבְהוֹ וְחָסֹן הוּא כָּאַלּוֹנִים—The relative pronoun אֲשֶׁר and the singular pronoun on גָּבְהוֹ and הוּא refer back to the singular הָאֱמֹרִי in 2:9a. The height of cedars and the strength of oaks are both proverbial (Is 2:13). The tall cedar is contrasted to its opposite in 1 Ki 5:13 (ET 4:33): Solomon "discoursed about trees, from the cedar [הָאֶרֶז], which is in Lebanon, to the hyssop, which comes out of the wall." Another merism in 2 Ki 14:9 compares a cedar tree to a thorn.

Because of its strength, wood from the oak tree (אַלּוֹן) was employed in making oars (Ezek 27:6). The only other occurrence of the adjective חָסֹן, "strong," in the OT is in Is 1:31, where the context likens the "strong" in Israel to an oak or terebinth that shall be burned (Is 1:29–31). The cognate adjective חֲסִין, "strong," occurs only in Ps 89:9 (ET 89:8) and describes Yah(weh).

The tree imagery involves two similes ("like …") here, but in the next line two metaphors.

וָאַשְׁמִיד פִּרְיוֹ מִמַּעַל וְשָׁרָשָׁיו מִתָּחַת׃—Now Yahweh speaks of the Amorite "tree" metaphorically: "I annihilated his fruit above and his roots below." וָאַשְׁמִיד is the Hiphil of שָׁמַד, as in 2:9a. Normally the first person singular of the imperfect is not shortened when it has *waw* consecutive (GKC, §§ 49 e; 53 n), hence the Hiphil form here is וָאַשְׁמִיד (not וָאַשְׁמֵד). However, for an exception, see the second textual note on 2:10.

2:10 וְאָנֹכִי הֶעֱלֵיתִי אֶתְכֶם מֵאֶרֶץ מִצְרָיִם—As at the start of 2:9, the pleonastic pronoun אָנֹכִי is emphatic: "and *I myself* brought you up from the land of Egypt." The OT commonly employs two different verbs, both in the Hiphil stem, to describe Yahweh's deliverance of Israel from Egypt: הֶעֱלָה, "to bring up" (e.g., Ex 3:8), and הוֹצִיא, "to bring out" (e.g., Jer 7:22). Amos uses הֶעֱלֵיתִי in 2:10 and again in 3:1 and 9:7. In this way, he indicates that the journey from Egypt to Canaan was a literal ascent from the lower delta region of the Nile River to the higher and mountainous promised land. The verb may also have the connotation of resurrection, since for Israel, Egypt was like a

---

[21] G. E. Mendenhall, "Amorites," *ABD* 1:199–202. The quote is on 1:200, where Mendenhall cites Giorgio Buccellati, *The Amorites of the Ur III Period*. Naples: Instituto Orientale di Napoli, 1966. For the dates of the archaeological periods, see King, *Amos, Hosea, Micah*, 9.

tomb of death and God by his grace brought his people up to the land with the promise of life (Deut 30:15–20).

In the Table of Nations, the progenitor named Egypt (מִצְרַיִם) appears as the son of Ham, along with the eponymic progenitors Cush (the father of Nubia), Put (the father of Libya), and Canaan (Gen 10:6). The OT primarily depicts Egypt as "the house of bondage" (e.g., Ex 20:2; Deut 6:12; Judg 6:8; Micah 6:4) or even an "iron-smelter" (Jer 11:4), an enemy whom Yahweh defeated to bring Israel out of slavery and into the promised land (Ex 6:6–8).

וָאוֹלֵךְ אֶתְכֶם בַּמִּדְבָּר אַרְבָּעִים שָׁנָה—"And I led you in the wilderness for forty years" refers to Israel's wilderness wandering. The Hiphil first singular imperfect of הָלַךְ with *waw* consecutive is an exception to the usual rule (GKC, §§ 49 e; 53 n) because it regularly has the shortened form וָאוֹלֵךְ (GKC, § 69 x). Paul notes that the Hiphil of הָלַךְ (only here in Amos) often connotes "leading and guiding with care" (e.g., Deut 8:2, 15; 29:4 [ET 29:5]; Josh 24:3; Is 42:16; Jer 2:6, 17; Pss 106:9; 136:16). "The point that is being made is that the Lord did not merely lead them through the wilderness but did so with provident care."[22] The LXX translates the verb in Amos 2:10 as περιήγαγον, "I led around," which implies God's continuous guidance during Israel's time in the wilderness.

The noun מִדְבָּר "refers to arid or semiarid regions whose scarcity of water makes them unsuitable for agriculture and farming settlements."[23] The word appears two hundred seventy times in the OT, forty-eight of them in the book of Numbers. Both occurrences in Amos (2:10; 5:25) are in the context of Israel's wilderness wanderings. A primary Law theme that runs through Exodus–Deuteronomy is Israel's rebellions against Yahweh and doubt of his gracious care (e.g., Ex 16:2; Numbers 14 and 16; Deut 9:7). But also during this time in Israel's history, as Amos underscores in 2:10, Yahweh continually provided for his people and repeatedly forgave their sins (Deut 2:7; Psalms 78; 105; and 106). For that reason Yahweh, the Husband of his bride, speaking through Hosea and Jeremiah, could refer to the wilderness period as newlywed Israel's honeymoon (Hos 2:16–21 [ET 2:14–19]) when the nation loved Yahweh with "bridal love" (Jer 2:2).

לָרֶשֶׁת אֶת־אֶרֶץ הָאֱמֹרִי׃—"To possess the land of the Amorite" accents that the land was purely a gift of grace that Israel did not earn or deserve. The infinitive construct of יָרַשׁ with *lamed* (לָרֶשֶׁת) forms a purpose clause (GKC, § 114 f): God's overarching purpose of the exodus and wilderness wanderings was for Israel to take possession of the promised land.

The ancient versions (LXX, Vulgate, and Syriac) generally translate יָרַשׁ by words referring to the inheritance of private property.[24] Of the one hundred sixty-one occurrences of the Qal of יָרַשׁ, all but eight have a direct object referring to what is inherited or possessed. In twenty-five cases, the verb means "take possession of, dispossess," and its object is an individual or a collective people. These people often were dispos-

---

22 Paul, *Amos*, 91.

23 S. Talmon, "מִדְבָּר," *TDOT* 8:91; cf. further Talmon, *TDOT* 8:91–118.

24 Cf. N. Lohfink, "יָרַשׁ," *TDOT* 6:368–96.

sessed through defeat in battle and war (e.g., Deut 31:3). In one hundred twenty-eight cases, the verb means "inherit" and its object is inanimate property of some sort. Often the verb conveys the idea of succession, the handing down of family property or leadership to the heir (e.g., Gen 21:10; Num 27:11; Deut 30:5; 2 Sam 14:7). Normally this happened by means of inheritance, as something, usually land, was passed down the family line.

2:11 וָאָקִים מִבְּנֵיכֶם֙ לִנְבִיאִים וּמִבַּחוּרֵיכֶם לִנְזִרִים—Yahweh employs the verb וָאָקִים, "and I raised up," to demonstrate that the OT prophets (נְבִיאִים) and Nazirites (נְזִרִים) were his gifts to Israel. Here God is saying that it was not the people themselves who chose certain individuals to fill these offices, nor were these offices established by Israel. Rather, just as the NT office of apostle and the office of pastor in the church have been established by Christ himself, so in the OT era, God chose and installed certain people to these ministerial offices for the good of his people.

With God as subject, the verb קוּם in the Hiphil stem refers to God raising up prophets (the Messiah as the Prophet in Deut 18:15, 18; other prophets in Jer 29:15), judges (e.g., Judg 2:16, 18), a priest (1 Sam 2:35), kings (the Messiah as King and Shepherd in Jer 23:5; 30:9; Ezek 34:23; other kings and shepherds in 1 Ki 14:14; Jer 23:4). God can also raise up disaster or enemies to punish his unfaithful people (2 Sam 12:11; 1 Ki 11:14, 23; Amos 6:14). The Hiphil of קוּם can be used for God establishing his covenant with individuals (e.g., Noah in Gen 6:18; Abraham in Gen 17:7), as well as with Israel (e.g., Lev 26:9; Deut 8:18).

The only other verses in Amos where God is the subject of the Hiphil of קוּם are in a Law and a Gospel passage, respectively. God warns that he will "raise up" a nation to oppress Israel because of her unfaithfulness (Amos 6:14). But God's final word in the book is his eschatological and evangelical promise to "raise up" both the falling tent of David and his ruins (9:11), which will allow a remnant of Gentiles to be ingrafted into his people and will rejuvenate the whole creation (9:11–15).

The repeated preposition מִן on מִבְּנֵיכֶם֙ … וּמִבַּחוּרֵיכֶם is partitive: "*some of* your sons … *some of* your young men."

The noun "prophet" (נָבִיא) may be derived from the Akkadian *nabu*, which means to "name" or "call." Amos employs the noun נָבִיא again in 2:12; 3:7; 7:14, and the cognate verb נָבָא, "to prophesy," in 2:12; 3:8; 7:12–13, 15–16. See also the fourth textual note on 7:12 and the second textual note on 7:14. A prophet was one called by God who "calls" or "proclaims" the divine Word. Yahweh places his words into his prophet's mouth (Num 22:38; Jer 1:9). The noun נָבִיא is a passive form (GKC, § 84[a] l) that implies that a prophet is one who has passively been "called" to discharge a divinely assigned task.

The verb נָבָא can be used for all forms of speech inspired by the one true God, such as the precise, poetic sayings of Amos (3:8). It can also be used for the self-induced (or demonic) utterances of false prophets, such as the shrieks of Baal's devotees (1 Ki 18:29). Thus the ravings of a lunatic could be characterized as "prophesying" (1 Sam 18:10). What is important for understanding the nuance of this verb is not simply the genre of the content of the speech, but the relationship between the speaker and God, or the speaker's relationship with other external supernatural powers.

The proper noun נָזִיר, basically transliterated as "Nazirite," occurs in Amos in 2:11–12. Amos 2:11 is the only place in the OT where Nazirites are described as people whom Yahweh raised up by his grace for the good of Israel. Num 6:2–21 prescribes how a man or woman can take a vow to be a Nazirite for a period of time, during which he or she is separated from others and consecrated to Yahweh. The only Nazirites known by name—Samson (Judg 13:5, 7; 16:17) and Samuel (1 Sam 1:11)—were consecrated as Nazirites from birth and for their entire life. Amos characterizes Nazirites by their abstinence from wine, in harmony with Num 6:3.

הַאַף אֵין־זֹאת בְּנֵי יִשְׂרָאֵל נְאֻם־יְהוָה׃—The use of the emphatic particle אַף with interrogative ה (as in, e.g., Gen 18:13, 23; Job 34:17; 40:8) here adds force to the following negative אֵין (see Waltke-O'Connor, § 16.3.5b): "Is this not so, O children of Israel?"

The concluding construct phrase נְאֻם־יְהוָה is, literally, "an utterance of Yahweh." It is similar to the signatory formulas in some of the oracles against the other nations; see the fifth textual note on 1:5. In the OT, the noun נְאֻם always is in construct with the following speaker. Most translations render the phrase with a verb, "declares Yahweh." נְאֻם־יְהוָה or a similar variant appears three hundred fifty-seven times in the OT, twenty-one times in the book of Amos. It concludes an oracle thirteen times: 2:11, 16; 3:15; 4:3, 5, 6, 8, 9, 10, 11; 9:7, 8, 12. Three times it is in the middle of a unit: 3:10; 6:14; 8:3. Five times it begins a unit along with other oracular introductions: 3:13; 6:8; 8:9, 11; 9:13.[25] Wolff explains that in comparison to the formula that concludes messenger speech, אָמַר יְהוָה, "Yahweh has spoken" (e.g., 1:5), נְאֻם־יְהוָה indicates "a more solemn affirmation of the certainty that it is Yahweh himself who confronts Israel through the prophetic oracle."[26]

2:12 וַתַּשְׁקוּ אֶת־הַנְּזִרִים יָיִן—The verb שָׁקָה almost always occurs in the Hiphil and with a double accusative, as here: "to give/cause someone [here הַנְּזִרִים] to drink something [here יָיִן]." Giving Nazirites wine to drink would tempt or force them into a direct violation of Yahweh's command in Num 6:3. The Qal of שָׁקָה is not used in the OT. Instead the Qal of שָׁתָה is used for the transitive with a single object: "to drink (something)."

וְעַל־הַנְּבִיאִים צִוִּיתֶם לֵאמֹר לֹא תִּנָּבְאוּ׃—The Piel verb צִוָּה with the preposition עַל means "lay charge upon" (BDB, s.v. צָוָה, Piel, 1 a), that is, "to command." לֵאמֹר, the Qal infinitive construct of אָמַר, "to speak, say," is "used to introduce direct discourse after verbs of saying and of mental activity (thinking, praying, etc.)" (Waltke-O'Connor, § 36.2.3e). In this case, לֵאמֹר introduces the direct quote לֹא תִּנָּבְאוּ, "you shall not prophesy at all!"[27] This prohibition couples the negative לֹא with an imperfect verb (תִּנָּבְאוּ) and thus indicates the most emphatic expectation of obedience (GKC, § 107 o). Ironically, this human command contradicts God's own call of these men into the prophetic office (2:11a; cf. 3:8). This same form of prohibition (לֹא followed by an imperfect) appears in the Decalogue (Ex 20:3–5, 7, 10, 13–17) indicating that—based upon Yahweh's salvific acts (Ex 20:2; Deut 5:6)—Israel must "not at all" participate in sins such as idolatry,

---

[25] Wolff, *Joel and Amos*, 143.

[26] Wolff, *Joel and Amos*, 144.

[27] For other direct quotations in Amos, see 4:1; 6:13; 8:5–6, 14; 9:10 (cf. 5:14).

adultery, stealing, and the others described in the commandments. The Niphal of נָבָא, "to prophesy," recurs in 3:8; 7:12–13, 15–16.

2:13 הִנֵּה אָנֹכִי מֵעִיק תַּחְתֵּיכֶם—This verse begins with the particle of immediacy, הִנֵּה, "behold" (its first occurrence in Amos) and the independent personal pronoun אָנֹכִי, "I." This last אָנֹכִי in the section (unlike the preceding two in 2:9–10) is followed by a participle, מֵעִיק. This syntactical construction (הִנֵּה אָנֹכִי followed by a participle) recurs only in 9:9. Here it probably indicates ongoing action, which is reflected in the translation "behold, *I am creaking* under you." The translation depends on the meaning of a rare verb that occurs in the OT only in this verse: the Hiphil participle מֵעִיק and in the next clause the Qal or Hiphil imperfect תָּעִיק. There are a number of possibilities.

First, the verb forms could be from עִיק, "to creak, groan" (see *DCH*, s.v. עיק). Yahweh creaks under the burden of the Israelites and their sins, just as a wagon creaks and groans under a heavy load. This commentary follows this first possible meaning. Andersen and Freedman say the root could be either עִיק or עוּק, "creak," the meaning that "can be hazarded simply because that is what an overloaded cart might do."[28]

A second, perhaps related explanation is that the Hebrew verb could mean "press" (*DCH*, s.v. עוק I). It could be cognate and equivalent in meaning to the Aramaic verb עוּק, whose Peal can mean "to be pressed, in distress" (see Jastrow, s.v. עוּק), and the Syriac verb ܥܘܩ, whose Peal can mean "be weary" and whose Aphel can mean "be weary, grieve, be in distress" (see Payne Smith, s.v. ܥܘܩ). Other possible cognates are two Hebrew nouns, each a hapax legomenon: עָקָה, "pressure" (Ps 55:4 [ET 55:3]) and מוּעָקָה, "compression, distress" (Ps 66:11). If so, Yahweh says he is pressed down, distressed, or weary under the load of (the sins of) the Israelites, just like a fully loaded wagon is under stress or pressure.

Third, the forms may be from עוּק, "be hindered," whose Hiphil could mean "to hinder" or "to sway" (see *DCH*, s.v. עוק II, and *HALOT*, s.v. עוק I, 1). A possible cognate is the Syriac Pael ܥܰܘܶܩ, "to hinder, impede" (Payne Smith, s.v. ܥܰܘܶܩ, b). In this case, Yahweh will hinder the way of the Israelites or make them sway like an overloaded wagon. Paul opts for this view and writes: "The movements of Israel shall be 'hampered, hindered' and thereby come haltingly to a stop. … They shall become totally transfixed."[29]

Fourth, the forms may be from עוּק, "to roar," with the Hiphil as causative, "to cause a roar" (see *DCH*, s.v. עוק III, and *HALOT*, s.v. עוק I, 2). This would connect the verse to Yahweh roaring in 1:2 and 3:8. However, loaded wagons generally do not roar.

Fifth, following possible Arabic and Ugaritic cognates, forms of עוק could mean "to split, divide," just as the wheels of a heavily laden wagon make furrows in the ground (see *HALOT*, s.v. עוק I, 3). Yahweh then could be predicting that he would split the earth under the Israelites with the earthquake recorded in 1:1.

כַּאֲשֶׁר תָּעִיק הָעֲגָלָה הַמְלֵאָה לָהּ עָמִיר׃—Literally, this is "just as the wagon that is full to itself (with) sheaf creaks." תָּעִיק is the feminine imperfect of the same verb used

---

[28] Andersen and Freedman, *Amos*, 333–34.

[29] Paul, *Amos*, 94.

in the preceding clause. Its subject is the feminine noun הָעֲגָלָה, which is modified by the adjectival clause הַמְלֵאָה לָהּ עָמִיר, implying that the wagon has been filled to its full capacity. The reflexive prepositional phrase לָהּ refers back to הָעֲגָלָה. The singular noun עָמִיר, a "sheaf" of grain, is an accusative of material, specifying what the cart is full of (see Waltke-O'Connor, § 10.2.3c), so it is translated as plural: "sheaves."

The noun עֲגָלָה describes a transport "wagon" that may be used in any number of circumstances,[30] in contrast to the chariot (רֶכֶב), which is an exclusively military vehicle. For example, Jacob used transport wagons in his move to Egypt (e.g., Gen 45:19; 46:5). Wagons were used in the transport of the tabernacle structure (Num 7:1–8; cf. Num 4:24–33) and to transport the ark of the covenant back from Philistia (1 Sam 6:1–14).

The transport wagon was also used for carrying the harvest and may have been used for threshing wheat (Is 28:23–29). These literal uses of the harvest wagon inform its metaphorical use. In Is 5:18, the wagon is likened to sin and guilt to which the people are tethered, just as oxen are tethered to the wagon. In Amos 2:13, Yahweh is like a harvest wagon that is heavily loaded with Israel's crimes. He is suffering under the weight of their ongoing transgressions.

2:14 וְאָבַד מָנוֹס מִקָּל—Literally, "refuge will perish from the swift," this means that even the swift person will not be able to escape judgment by fleeing to a place of safety. The noun מָנוֹס is based on the verb נוּס, "to flee." The two nouns from this verbal root differ slightly.[31] The noun מְנוּסָה indicates the *act* of fleeing (Lev 26:36; Is 52:12), whereas the noun here, מָנוֹס, typically indicates the *place* to which one flees, that is, a refuge or safe place. It can refer to Yahweh himself (2 Sam 22:3; Jer 16:19; Ps 59:17 [ET 59:16]). In three other verses (Jer 25:35; Ps 142:5 [ET 142:4]; Job 11:20), it appears in the same clause as in Amos 2:14: מָנוֹס as the subject of אָבַד with the preposition מִן attached to the person(s) who will not be able to find refuge. קָל is the pausal form of the adjective קַל, "light, swift, speedy," which recurs in 2:15.

Amos employs the verb נוּס, "to flee," in three verses, which express similar ideas. He who flees from judgment will not go unscathed (2:16; 5:19), and no one will escape (9:1).

וְחָזָק לֹא־יְאַמֵּץ כֹּחוֹ—Literally, "the strong will not strengthen/muster his strength." The adjective חָזָק is derived from the verb חָזַק, "to be/become strong."[32] The verb usually refers to individual people, as with Hezekiah's recovery from illness (e.g., Is 39:1) or the securing of one's position (e.g., Lev 25:35). Collectively, nations and peoples may become strong militarily (e.g., Josh 17:13), and this is often expressed figuratively (e.g., Ezek 30:21). The adjective in Amos 2:14 refers to an individual. The only other occurrence of a word from the root חזק in Amos is חֹזֶק, "strength," in 6:13, which refers to the collective strength of the people of Israel.

---

30 Cf. D. Kellermann, "עֲגָלָה," *TDOT* 10:451–55. See also *ANEP*, § 367, which pictures an Assyrian relief showing women and children being transported from a conquered town in wagons.

31 Cf. J. Reindl, "נוּס," *TDOT* 9:290–93.

32 Cf. F. Hesse, "חָזַק," *TDOT* 4:301–8.

The Piel of אָמֵץ usually means "to strengthen, give strength and courage" and is most frequently associated with strength or bravery in war and conflict.[33] In Ps 89:21–23 (ET 89:20–22), Yahweh promises to strengthen the Davidic king so that the king's enemies will not triumph over him. The Qal of אָמֵץ, "be strong, courageous" (along with the verb חָזַק, "be strong"), was an encouragement to Joshua and the Israelites as they drew near to conquer the promised land (Deut 31:6–7, 23; Josh 1:6–7, 9, 18; 10:25). In Amos 2:14, the inability to retain or muster one's strength means certain defeat. The cognate adjective in 2:16 is all the more shocking: "and the most courageous of heart [וְאַמִּיץ לִבּוֹ] among the warriors will flee naked on that day."

וְגִבּוֹר לֹא־יְמַלֵּט נַפְשׁוֹ׃—"And the warrior will not save his life." The noun גִּבּוֹר, which recurs in 2:16, "is an intensive form, and thus means a particularly strong or mighty person who carries out, can carry out, or has carried out great deeds, and surpasses others in doing so."[34] Although גִּבּוֹר can apply more generally to anyone who excels in a particular task or field (e.g., Gen 10:9; 1 Sam 9:1; Is 5:22), it is more commonly associated with military prowess (e.g., Jer 46:12; Hos 10:13). The term is used of the Nephilim (Gen 6:4), Nimrod (Gen 10:8–9), Goliath (1 Sam 17:51), and the Messiah, the "Mighty/Warrior God" (Is 9:5 [ET 9:6]). David had an elite enclave designated as his "mighty men" (גִּבֹּרִים, e.g., 2 Sam 10:7). Yahweh's angels who carry out his commands are also designated as גִּבֹּרִים (Ps 103:20), as are his angels who carry out his judgments (Joel 4:11 [ET 3:11]). In Amos 2:14, the term "properly refers to a soldier who by prowess and stature was unusually well suited to be a mighty warrior."[35]

The identical Piel imperfect of מָלַט used in 2:14 (יְמַלֵּט) recurs twice in 2:15. The Piel has a transitive meaning and often takes נֶפֶשׁ as its object. The negated clause יְמַלֵּט נַפְשׁוֹ in 2:14c, 15c means not to "deliver, save life" (BDB, s.v. מָלַט, Piel, 3, citing, e.g., 1 Sam 19:11; 2 Sam 19:6 (ET 19:5); Jer 48:6). In Amos 2:15b, the Piel is used absolutely with no object, לֹא יְמַלֵּט, so the translation supplies the object "will not save *himself*." Besides 2:14–15 the only other occurrence of מָלַט in Amos is in 9:1, where it appears in the Niphal stem and means "escape, be delivered" (cf., e.g., Gen 19:17; Judg 3:26; Job 20:20).

The noun נֶפֶשׁ is a cognate of the Akkadian *napištu*, "throat."[36] Since breath issues forth from the throat, the word took on the meaning "life" (see Gen 2:7). The KJV often translated נֶפֶשׁ as "soul," that is, the immaterial aspect of a human being, but the word usually denotes the entire person, body and soul together, as here. The meaning in Amos 2:14 is that the mighty warrior will not save his life. Dying under divine judgment also carries the implication of spiritual death, and after the bodily resurrection, the eternal perdition of the whole person in "the second death" (Rev 20:14–15).

2:15 וְתֹפֵשׂ הַקֶּשֶׁת לֹא יַעֲמֹד—The construct phrase וְתֹפֵשׂ הַקֶּשֶׁת, literally, "the one who holds the bow," is translated as "the archer." It designates a person who is skilled as an

---

[33] Cf. J. Schreiner, "אָמַץ," *TDOT* 1:323–27.

[34] H. Kosmala, "גִּבּוֹר," *TDOT* 2:373; cf. further Kosmala, *TDOT* 2:373–77.

[35] Niehaus, "Amos," 372.

[36] As noted by Niehaus, "Amos," 372. נֶפֶשׁ may occasionally have "throat" as its meaning (cf., e.g., Ps 69:2 [ET 69:1]; Jonah 2:6 [ET 2:5]).

archer and who could be the weapon-bearer in a two-man chariot. The verb תָּפַשׂ may connote "to be skilled or trained in" a respective field, for example, תֹּפֵשׂ כִּנּוֹר וְעוּגָב, "skilled in (playing) lyre and pipe" (Gen 4:21); תֹּפְשֵׂי הַמִּלְחָמָה, "skilled in the battle" (Num 31:27); and וְתֹפְשֵׂי הַתּוֹרָה, "skilled in the Torah" (Jer 2:8).[37] The phrase with the singular participle תֹּפֵשׂ הַקֶּשֶׁת appears only here in the OT, but similar phrases with the plural participle, תֹּפְשֵׂי מָגֵן, "shield holders," and תֹּפְשֵׂי דֹּרְכֵי קָשֶׁת, "holders (and) drawers of (the) bow," occur in Jer 46:9.

וְקַל בְּרַגְלָיו לֹא יְמַלֵּט—Since וְקַל בְּרַגְלָיו, literally, "the light one on his feet," is positioned between two military terms, it is likely that it refers to a foot soldier rather than a civilian. Specifically, he may be a runner who specializes in pursuing foes who are retreating. Ironically, instead of running forward, he will be running away in the face of battle. The only other time in the OT that קַל appears with רֶגֶל is in the identical expression קַל בְּרַגְלָיו in 2 Sam 2:18, when Asahel chases Abner (2 Sam 2:19) in the war between the houses of David and Saul.

For the predicate לֹא יְמַלֵּט and, at the end of the last clause in the verse, לֹא יְמַלֵּט נַפְשׁוֹ, see the third textual note on 2:14.

וְרֹכֵב הַסּוּס לֹא יְמַלֵּט נַפְשׁוֹ׃—The construct phrase וְרֹכֵב הַסּוּס is, literally, "he who rides the horse" (e.g., NASB). However, the phrase may instead refer to the driver of the horse-drawn chariot, that is, a charioteer. In the ancient Near East in the eighth century, the time of Amos, the primary military function of horses was to draw war chariots.[38] Mounted cavalry as a military strategy spread later with the dawning of the Persian Empire in 538 BC.[39]

2:16 וְאַמִּיץ לִבּוֹ בַּגִּבּוֹרִים עָרוֹם יָנוּס בַּיּוֹם־הַהוּא—The construct phrase וְאַמִּיץ לִבּוֹ, "courageous of/in his heart," uses the genitive לִבּוֹ to specify which part of the person is characterized as "courageous" (GKC, § 128 y). An indefinite adjective (אַמִּיץ) may function as a superlative when followed by a partitive genitive such as בַּגִּבּוֹרִים, "among the warriors" (GKC, § 133 g), so וְאַמִּיץ לִבּוֹ בַּגִּבּוֹרִים is translated as a superlative: "the *most* courageous of heart among the warriors." Compare לֵב in expressions for courage or cowardice in Gen 42:28; 1 Sam 17:32; 2 Sam 17:10; Ps 40:13 (40:12).

The adjective עָרוֹם is an accusative of state, which usually follows the verb, but here it precedes יָנוּס and so receives additional emphasis, literally, "*naked* shall he flee" (see GKC, § 118 n). Here עָרוֹם does not simply refer to a soldier's lack of armor. When applied to people, it always has the sense of nakedness in the strict sense of the word (e.g., Gen 2:25; Is 20:2; Job 1:21).

The verb יָנוּס, "he will flee," does not mean he will escape; Amos 2:14 implied no soldiers would survive. Normally in battle, flight implies a complete defeat (e.g., Ex 14:27; Is 13:14–15). A fleeing soldier could easily be cut down by pursuing troops.

The formula בַּיּוֹם הַהוּא, "on that day," designates a future time, often with eschatological significance. It occurs two hundred eight times in the OT, of which one hundred

---

37 Paul, *Amos*, 97.

38 Wolff, *Joel and Amos*, 172.

39 King, *Amos, Hosea, Micah*, 80.

nine are in the Latter Prophets. Only four prophetic books lack this formula: Jonah, Nahum, Habakkuk, and Malachi. Many instances in the OT simply refer to a future day and lack clear implications for eschatology.[40] Munch maintains that it can always be understood simply as a temporal adverb:[41] "on the same day," "then." In partial agreement, DeVries maintains that it can serve "as part of a transition to a following episode within the pericope."[42] But DeVries also refers to its frequent use in an epitome, "a summarizing characterization concerning a particular day in which Israel's God was in some way seen to be active in crucial confrontation with his people."[43]

While sometimes בַּיּוֹם הַהוּא simply is a temporal reference to a coming historical day, here in 2:16 and often elsewhere, it has eschatological overtones. It is equivalent to "a day of war" and "a day of tempest" (1:14), "the day when I punish the transgressions of Israel" (3:14), "the Day of Yahweh" (5:18 [twice], 20), "the evil day" in 6:3, and "a bitter day" in 8:10. The phrase בַּיּוֹם הַהוּא also occurs in 8:3, 9, 13. It is equivalent to הִנֵּה יָמִים בָּאִים, "behold, days are coming," in 4:2 and 8:11. Both בַּיּוֹם הַהוּא (9:11) and הִנֵּה יָמִים בָּאִים (9:13) appear in Amos' eschatological oracle of restoration in 9:11–15. In this light, the book of Amos has these sixteen specific references to a "day" or "days" that point to what Yahweh will do in the future. He will judge Israel and the nations because of their transgressions, then resurrect his people, which will include Gentiles, according to his sure and certain messianic promises to David (9:11).

נְאֻם־יְהוָה׃—See the second textual note on 2:11.

Commentary

Overview of the Oracle against Israel (2:6–16)

Genesis 1 exhibits a refrain at the end of each of the six days of creation (כִּי־טוֹב, "that it was good," Gen 1:4, 10, 12, 18, 21, 25) that climaxes with the Sabbath rest on the seventh day. Gen 2:1–3 breaks the pattern, and in doing so, the Sabbath stands out as chief among the days that Yahweh God created. In like manner, Amos' first seven oracles against nations (1:3–2:5) are ordered according to a set pattern, but this pattern is altered at the climax of his oracles against the nations: the oracle against northern Israel. This oracle is different in at least five ways:

1. It is longer than all the others.
2. It addresses sins in the marketplace, legal system, and religious life.
3. It contains no threat of Yahweh's judgment by fire.
4. Yahweh personally addresses northern Israel in the second person in 2:10–13, as opposed to his more impersonal addresses in the third person throughout 1:3–2:5.

---

[40] Cf. Gressmann, *Der Messias*, 83.

[41] Munch, *The Expression Bajjôm Hahu'*, especially p. 6, cited by DeVries, *Yesterday, Today and Tomorrow*, 57, including n. 2.

[42] DeVries, *Yesterday, Today and Tomorrow*, 61.

[43] DeVries, *Yesterday, Today and Tomorrow*, 136.

5. The oracle against Israel announces themes that are repeated and elaborated on throughout the rest of the book.

This oracle, therefore, is the culmination of Amos' oracles against the nations and the rhetorical goal of 1:3–2:5. The first seven oracles were small sparks of fire when compared to the mighty blaze that now falls upon northern Israel.[44] Wellhausen put it classically: *Das Gewitter schliesslich in Israel selber einschlägt*, "the thunderstorm finally smashes into Israel itself."[45]

This comes as a shocking surprise. Beginning with Aram (1:3–5) and ending with Judah (2:4–5), there have been seven oracles. Seven is a number commonly used in the Bible to denote completeness.[46] An eighth oracle is unexpected. Little did the audience (presumably Amos preached these oracles at Bethel) know that the prophet's analysis of the crimes of the nations was in reality a noose that was getting ready to tighten around their own throats.[47] Amos employs a rhetoric of entrapment that catches his hearers unawares (cf. 2 Sam 12:1–12; Is 5:1–7).

From 1:3 through 2:5, Amos' northern Israelite audience in all likelihood cheered and applauded after each neighboring nation was condemned. "Great preacher, this Amos!" was the mantra of the moment. The speech builds to a climax as four, five, then six pagan nations are placed under divine fire. With the next fiery judgment upon Judah the number reaches seven. The people could then safely assume that the Law part of the sermon had come to an end and only comforting Gospel would follow. Then the audience could conclude, "All is well that ends well!" It was probably time for the Aaronic Benediction (Num 6:22–27), a general dismissal, and then the normal post-service discussion of the events of the week, a bit more chit-chat, and then it would be time to go home. But Amos was not done preaching. The roaring Lion was not yet silent (1:2; 3:8; cf. 3:4, 12; 5:19). The ravaging fire had not yet reached its goal: *Israel*.

Amos' use of the seven-eight pattern was foreshadowed by the three-four pattern in the previous seven oracles ("because of three transgressions … and because of four"), which is also used in this eighth oracle as well.[48] Yet it is a surprise that there is an eighth oracle of judgment. The eighth also expresses the culmination and climactic finish for the entire unit (1:3–2:16). In the fol-

---

[44] This application of fire imagery to Israel is appropriate based on later passages in the book. Although judgment by fire is cited in the previous seven oracles but is not invoked in the oracle against Israel, later in 5:6 and 7:4, fire is Yahweh's means of judging the Northern Kingdom.

[45] Wellhausen, *Die kleinen Propheten*, 71 (trans. Paul, *Amos*, 21).

[46] See, for example, Gen 1:1–2:3; 4:15, 24; Lev 26:18, 21, 24; Dan 9:24–27; Mt 18:21–22; Lk 17:3–4; and often in the book of Revelation.

[47] Cf. Motyer, *The Message of Amos*, 50.

[48] See "The Staircase Numerical Pattern" in the introduction to 1:3–2:16.

lowing passages, the eighth represents the climax, but with a Gospel meaning, not condemnation:[49]

- Circumcision was to take place on the eighth day (Gen 17:12), the first day of the new week.[50] The first week signifies natural life, and the first day of the new week signifies the start of new life as a member of the covenant people of God.
- Jesus' resurrection was on "the first day of the week" (Mt 28:1–7), which set the pattern for Christian worship on that day (Acts 20:7). As the first week represented creation, the first day of the new week begins God's new era of re-creation, redemption, and renewal.
- The period of Aaron's ordination took place over seven days: "You shall not go outside the entrance of the tent of meeting for seven days ... for your ordination will require seven days" (Lev 8:33–35). Then immediately afterward, "on the eighth day Moses called Aaron. ... For today Yahweh will appear to you" (Lev 9:1–4).
- The eighth day of a domesticated animal's life was when it was consecrated to Yahweh: "You shall do the same with your cattle and your flocks; seven days it shall remain with its mother; on the eighth day you shall give it to me" (Ex 22:29 [ET 22:30]; cf. Lev 22:27).
- David was the eighth and the youngest son in his family. After the previous seven sons were examined and rejected, David was chosen to be king (1 Sam 16:10–12; 17:12).

Amos may have used the unusual literary pattern for two complementary reasons. First, it expresses finality and climactic culmination. Second, because the more usual scheme ended with seven, his northern audience, which was probably enjoying every bit of his diatribe, would psychologically be in a state of mind that would lead them to believe that he had reached the climax of his fulmination with his oracle against Judah (2:4–5). The moment he continued with his eighth—the last and unexpected oracle—they would have been completely surprised.[51] Catching them off-guard would allow the judgment oracle to penetrate their defenses more deeply and work repentance in their hearts.

The first seven oracles are short and to the point. In contrast, this oracle against Israel in 2:6–16 leads into the prophecies against Israel that continue throughout the rest of the book. It is—after all—to *Israel* that Amos was specifically sent (7:15). This oracle (2:6–16) contains the most detailed list of transgressions and accusations. The extensive and elaborate series of sins is spelled out so vividly precisely because Israel has benefited from being the elect nation of Yahweh (3:2).

Economic injustice, sexual sin, and idolatry head the list (2:6–8). Then follows recounting of Yahweh's past and gracious acts of salvation, for which Israel

---

49 See also Micah 5:4 (ET 5:5); Ps 90:10; 1 Ki 5:29 (ET 5:15) || 2 Chr 2:1, 17 (ET 2:2, 18). "This graduated sequential literary pattern is frequent in the literature of the ancient Near East" (Paul, *Amos*, 23–24, who cites examples).

50 Generally in the OT, days were counted inclusively. Thus a child born on what we call Sunday would be circumcised on the following Sunday.

51 Amos also makes use of a surprise ending in 3:1–2; 3:3–8; 4:4–5; 9:11–15.

shows no gratefulness (2:9–11). But the culmination of the sins is Israel's contempt for Yahweh's prophets and prophecy (2:12; see also 7:10–17; cf. 1 Thess 5:20). This initial section against Israel can be outlined in three parts:

1. Yahweh indicts Israel for oppression of the weak and incestuous idolatry (2:6–8). In this first section, Amos employs a heptad, a series of seven items, here seven accusations.[52]
2. Yahweh reminds Israel how he defeated her enemies and saved her when the nation was helpless and weak and gave her prophets and priests, whom she despised (2:9–12).
3. Yahweh assures Israel that he will defeat even the most courageous in her midst and render the nation weak (2:13–16).

The Israelites at Bethel might have responded to 2:6–16 as follows: "Hey, Amos. Your doctrine is flat out false! *We* are the elect of Yahweh! *We* are exempt from his judgment! And if *we* aren't, then what on earth does election mean if it doesn't mean that *we* have a favored status making us free to do whatever *we* want? Amos, you've got it all wrong!"

But no, Yahweh's prophet was right. Israel's sins were a greater abomination to Yahweh than were the sins of the pagan nations. The heathen peoples did not know Yahweh through his special revelation, and they mistreated foreigners. The Israelites knew better; they had heard Yahweh's Word and had been incorporated into his covenant people by grace, yet were guilty of oppressing fellow members of God's own brotherhood. Rebelling against Yahweh's clear Torah commands (e.g., Ex 21:2–11; Lev 25:35–43; Deut 15:7–18; 24:14–15), Israel's elite were oblivious to the needs of the poor and vulnerable. For them to oppress the poor members of Yahweh's people was an indication that they did not fear or believe in Yahweh himself (Lev 25:43; cf. 1 Jn 4:7–11).

Israel is not under condemnation because of military atrocities as were the pagan nations (1:3–2:3). Judah was explicitly condemned for rejecting the Torah and following idols (2:4), and the same grounds for condemnation are implicit in the accusations against Israel (2:6–8, 12). Israel's transgressions were committed against both tables of the Law: the First Table (the First through Third Commandments) regarding faith and worship of God and the Second Table (the Fourth through Tenth Commandments) regarding love for neighbor within the covenant people. They ignored the "more excellent way" of love (1 Cor 12:31–13:13) and shunned compassionate justice. Their guilt was evident in the realm of their daily behavior toward the marginalized people in the community of the faith. Israel's sins of injustice, oppression, sexual immorality, and idolatry stand in direct contradiction to what Yahweh had done for them (Amos 2:9–11). Yahweh describes their punishment not in terms of fire or destruction, but in terms of inescapable defeat: the picture is of an impotent army that is unable to fight and is therefore cut down completely (2:14–16).

---

[52] Cf. Paul, *Amos*, 76, including n. 330. Amos employs heptads in 1:3–2:5; 2:6–8; 2:14–16; 3:3–6; 4:4–5; 4:6–11; 5:8–9; 5:21–23; 6:1–6; 9:1–4.

Israel's Idolatrous Oppression of the Weak and Her Incestuous Idolatry (2:6–8)

2:6 The first charge against northern Israel relates to the illegal action of creditors selling debtors into slavery.[53] This dishonesty may refer to bribery in court, which was condemned in the Pentateuchal laws (e.g., Ex 23:6–8; Deut 16:18–20), as well as in other prophetic literature (e.g., Is 1:23; 5:22–23; Micah 3:9–12). It is also possible that the selling was of innocent people into slavery because of their exceedingly high debt (cf. 2 Ki 4:1).

In either case, Yahweh characterizes those who are being oppressed as צַדִּיק, "righteous," implying that they are believers justified through faith, making the crime against them more heinous. There are three possible implications. First, in this context "righteous" can connote a forensically "innocent party," a person who was judged innocent in a legal proceeding (cf. Ex 23:6–8; Deut 16:19). It would be illegal for such a person to be sold privately into slavery on the false charge (disproven in public court) of owing money ("for silver"). Second, "righteous" can imply righteous living (sanctification), so that "an honest man" is sold in order to repay creditors demanding compensation. "For silver" may denote what the "righteous" owed and could not pay.[54] A third suggestion is that the "righteous" was sold "for silver," that is, for a paltry sum so inadequate compared to the value of his life that it arouses Yahweh to anger.

Whatever the exact nature of the offense—and perhaps all three were occurring—the main point is that people were falling through the cracks in a society where there were no secular mechanisms to provide a safety net. Israelite society was supposed to be built on Yahweh's Torah and covenant, which made provisions to sustain all of God's people, from greatest to least. But when the nation rejected God's Word, social injustice became the norm.

Tertullian interprets "they sell the righteous (one) for silver" (2:6) in a Christological way. He writes about Jesus Christ:

> He might also have been betrayed by any stranger, did I not find that even here too he fulfilled a psalm: "He who did eat bread with me has lifted up his heel against me" [Ps 41:10 (ET 41:9)]. And without a price might he have been betrayed. For what need of a traitor was there in the case of one who offered himself to the people openly and might quite as easily have been captured by force as taken by treachery? This might, no doubt, have been well enough for another Christ but would not have been suitable in one who was accomplishing prophecies. For it was written, "The righteous one did they sell for silver" [Amos 2:6]. The very amount and the destination of the money, which on Judas's remorse was recalled "from its first purpose of a fee" and appropriated to the purchase of a potter's field, as narrated in the Gospel of Matthew

---

53 Amos 2:6–8 shares similar vocabulary with 8:4–6 and so the texts mutually interpret one another.

54 A person could choose to become a slave in order to pay off a debt, but the covenant limited the term of slavery to only six years. The slave had to be released in the seventh year unless he or she voluntarily decided to work permanently for the master (Ex 21:2–6; Deut 15:12–18).

> [Mt 27:3–10], were clearly foretold by Jeremiah: "And they took the thirty pieces of silver, the price of him who was valued, and gave them for the potter's field" [Mt 27:9; cf. Jer 19:1–13; 32:6–15; Zech 11:12–13].[55]

The "righteous" in Israel were not the only ones suffering; the defenseless and "needy" (אֶבְיוֹן, Amos 2:6) also had no means to protect themselves from being sold into slavery. Because the "righteous" and "needy" are parallel to one another, they are two descriptions of the same class of people. Sweeney writes: "The reference to the 'righteous' suggests that persons who were legally innocent were being sold into debt slavery, and the reference to the 'needy' indicates the reason for the sale."[56]

Throughout his book, Amos mentions members of the group of abused people by means of several different words. A listing is as follows:

1. "Righteous" (צַדִּיק) in 2:6; 5:12
2. "Needy" (אֶבְיוֹן) in 2:6; 4:1; 5:12; 8:4, 6
3. "Poor" (דַּל) in 2:7; 4:1; 5:11; 8:6
4. "Oppressed" (עָנָו or עָנִי) in 2:7; 8:4

People in this group were being abused economically (2:6, 8; 4:1; 5:11), judicially (2:7a–b; 5:10), and sexually (2:7c–d). All of these were not just social crimes, but religious offenses, sins by those called to be God's covenant people, perpetrated against those believers whom God deemed "righteous" (2:6). There was no justice or righteousness (5:7, 24; 6:12) for people on the edges of Israelite society because the nation was rotten at its core.

Israel's leadership was unable to embrace the severity of this social/religious situation because they were wrapped in a cocoon carefully spun out of economic prosperity and technical know-how. They demonstrated unshakeable confidence that their lifestyles would continue (5:18; 6:1, 3, 13; 9:10).

Yet it would be a misreading of Amos to believe that he idealized the poor or their poverty. The poor were not righteous *because* they had been denied their rights (cf. 5:11), but rather because Yahweh had reckoned righteousness to them through their faith (Gen 15:6; Hab 2:4; Rom 3:19–31). Responding to their gift of a righteous standing before Yahweh, we may assume that these poor people were faithful to their covenantal calling. However, their oppressors were not.

The purpose of Amos' advocacy for the poor is not to put them on a pedestal (cf. Mt 26:11), but to point out that the abusive Israelites will have to face judgment because of their treatment of these fellow members of God's people. Amos did not advocate class warfare or social revolt. The righteous poor will be vindicated by Yahweh and Yahweh alone.[57] The prophet's oracles call for

---

55 Tertullian, *Against Marcion*, 40, cited by Ferreiro, *The Twelve Prophets*, ACCS 14:88.

56 Sweeney, *The Twelve Prophets*, 215.

57 Gelin proposes that the Bible makes a transition from seeing poverty as a social problem to a religious metaphor (*The Poor of Yahweh*). Although Gelin demonstrates that this shift moved the focus away from material poverty to poverty in spirit, he also correctly points out that this transition does not mean that the Bible therefore minimizes or ignores the call for justice to

repentance and *conversion*, not *revolution*. Amos does not promote liberation theology, which confuses the church's mission of proclaiming the justifying Gospel with the political agenda of justice defined in socioeconomic terms.[58]

Although Amos takes up the cause of human need and destitution throughout his book, he never proposes concrete ways to eliminate poverty, nor does he restrict responsibility for social welfare to either of what we, in modern terms, would call the government or the private sector. However, throughout the book of Amos, Yahweh does make it clear that acting unjustly toward his poor is a *theological* issue. Material and economic poverty is the result of human sin, and taking advantage of the disadvantaged is not in accord with God's will. Yahweh hears the cries of his people who are enslaved in economic systems that create intense suffering (e.g., Ex 3:7).

Too often texts like Deut 15:11, "there will never cease to be some in need on the earth" (cf. also Mt 26:11; Mk 14:7; Jn 12:8), are read as expressions of fatalism, as though poverty is part of the natural order of the world and therefore there is nothing any of us can do about it. However, God created the world as a place of abundance and plenty (Genesis 1–2). It was only after the fall of Adam and Eve into sin that poverty entered the world and became part of all human societies. The forgiveness of sins in Jesus Christ brings the promise of eternal riches after the resurrection of all believers to everlasting life in the new creation. During the present era, failure to understand Yahweh's solidarity with his suffering people and his compassion toward all is a failure to understand his salvific will (cf. Mt 25:31–46). To ignore both material and spiritual poverty is to miss the Bible's call to marshal resources in order to minister to those in need, bring the Gospel to all, and proclaim the new creation in Christ as the ultimate end to this evil. Gelin writes: "Without pretending to extract from the Bible an economic treatise, we have no right to forget the social results of its religious principles."[59]

The sum of the divine Law is love for God and for one's neighbor. James 1:27 states: "Worship that is pure and undefiled to our God and Father is this: to care for orphans and widows in their distress and to keep oneself undefiled by the world." Andersen and Freedman write: "The issue of right behavior to one's neighbors is the ultimate test of true religion, if not its actual essence and substance. It is not a substitute for theology but its necessary adjunct."[60]

---

end oppression. For an overview of how poverty is addressed in the Bible, see Hoppe, *There Shall Be No Poor among You*.

58 A confessional Lutheran response to liberation theology is the theme of *Concordia Journal* 13/1 (1987). This volume contains articles by J. A. O. Preus III, "Liberation Theology: Basic Themes and Methodology"; Paul L. Schrieber, "Liberation Theology and the Old Testament: An Exegetical Critique"; and Robert Rosin, "The Reformation as Liberation—Reformers, Peasants, Marxists."

59 Gelin, *The Poor of Yahweh*, 112–13.

60 Andersen and Freedman, *Amos*, 92.

2:7 Amos refers to courts or other avenues that were to administer justice in 2:7–8 and 5:10, 12, 15, and he addresses the general state of national injustice in 3:10; 5:7–24; and 6:12. While none of the preceding seven oracles in 1:3–2:5 contains accusations in a participial form,[61] this verse begins with one: הַשֹּׁאֲפִים, literally, "those who are trampling." The participle indicates that this sin was an ongoing action.[62] Amos employs participles to describe Israel's obstinate behavior and in this way depicts the nation's sins as being continual.[63]

Paul comments on the ongoing nature of the "trampling": "They step upon the heads of the poor as though they were stepping upon the ground beneath them, that is, they treat the underprivileged with contempt and abuse."[64] After Amos, but also in the eighth century, Isaiah announces the same kind of crime: "What do you mean by crushing my people and grinding the faces of the poor?" (Is 3:15).

After the economic sins in Amos 2:6–7b the sexual sin in 2:7c is unexpected: "each man and his father go to the young woman." The distributive אִישׁ, "each man," indicates that large numbers of men were engaging in illicit sex. The definite article attached to the word הַנַּעֲרָה, literally, "the young woman" (Amos 2:7), may be a generic article, to be translated as "*a* girl," or the article may suggest a specific and fairly well-known female. Andersen and Freedman argue that in light of 2:8, with its description of "wine," "every altar," and a shrine of "their gods," this young woman is probably a sacred female prostitute.[65] Amos 8:14 too refers to Israel's syncretistic worship practices, which involved venerating pagan deities, including a goddess whom Amos calls "the Guilt of Samaria" and false gods in Dan and Beersheba, implying throughout Judah and Israel. It may be that the young woman in 2:7c was connected to pagan fertility worship, perhaps under the name of one of the fertility goddesses. If she was a cultic prostitute in the service of a goddess, then "each man and his father" were having sex with her in order to bring about fertility in their fields, flocks, and families.

This was not only a sexual sin, but also idolatry. It is the one true and triune God who grants and sustains all life. The worship of fertility gods and goddesses through cultic sex is an abomination against God and against the human bodies of the participants, whom he created and redeemed (cf. 1 Cor 6:9–20). Israel's true hope for life and fertility rested on Yahweh's good and gracious promises in his covenant with his people. He promised that if they remained faithful to

---

[61] Amos employs the infinitive construct to introduce the first sin in each of his eight oracles in 1:3–2:16. See "The Citation of the Transgression" in the introduction to 1:3–2:16.

[62] Compare Prov 6:16–19, a graduated numerical unit listing things that Yahweh hates. The actions there too are enumerated using participles, for example, וְיָדַיִם שֹׁפְכוֹת דָּם־נָקִי, "hands shedding innocent blood" (Prov 6:17b).

[63] Specific participles that indict Israel are in 2:7–8; 3:10; 4:1; 5:12, 18; 6:1, 3–6, 13; 8:4, 14; 9:10.

[64] Paul, *Amos*, 80.

[65] Andersen and Freedman, *Amos*, 318–19.

his covenant, he would bless them with fertility and abundant life (e.g., Deut 28:1–14). Their violation of the covenant made them forfeit that promise.

At the same time, given Yahweh's repeated concern for the oppressed, "the young woman" (Amos 2:7) may refer to an unwilling, abused woman. For example, she could be a female slave, who had no power to resist the sexual advances of her master and other members of the family.[66] If she was unmarried, then Deut 22:28–29 would apply: if a man rapes a girl he must marry her. According to Deut 22:25–27, if she was betrothed, then her attacker should be stoned (cf. also Deut 22:22–30). Therefore if she was an unmarried household slave who was first raped by one brother, he was to marry her, and subsequent attackers—the father as well as any other brothers—were to be stoned to death. In any event, the scenario with a son and father described in Amos 2:7 clearly violates the Sinai statutes against incestuous relations between a father and son and one woman (e.g., Lev 20:11–12).

This commentary allows for both of the possibilities outlined above: the young woman could be a sacred prostitute or an oppressed, violated woman. Both kinds of sexual perversion are condemned in the Torah. According to chapters 18 and 20 of Leviticus, the sexual perversions of the Canaanites who formerly inhabited Israel defiled the land and caused the land to vomit them out. The sexual sin here is part of the reason for the divine judgments executed upon the land in, for example, Amos 1:2; 4:7–11 (cf. 7:1–6).

Amos is not delineating an arcane set of sexual taboos, nor is he being excessively priggish. Rather, he is describing Israelite society in which religious sex, incest, and rape were tolerated and may even have become the norm. This defiled Yahweh's holy name and was an affront to his will. Men and women are to express their sexuality within the confines of an exclusive, heterosexual, and lifelong marriage (cf. Gen 2:24; Mt 19:4–6). Only such a marriage of believers can embody and proclaim the holy mutual love between Jesus Christ and his bride, the church (see the Song of Songs; Eph 5:21–33). God's holiness demands that "the marriage bed be kept undefiled" (Heb 13:4). Marriage is the only proper context for sexual intercourse. Yahweh declares that to ignore this command is to "defile [חַלֵּל] my holy name" (Amos 2:7). This recalls the same verb in the prohibition in the midst of Leviticus 18, a chapter that details Yahweh's will for sexual expression: וְלֹא תְחַלֵּל אֶת־שֵׁם אֱלֹהֶיךָ, "you will not defile the name of your God" (Lev 18:21). Sexual purity is an essential part of holiness for God's people.

Luther comments on this defilement of Yahweh's holy name recorded in Amos:

> The sum of all their wickedness reaches this point, and all things fall back to this point: they are blaspheming and profaning the holy name of God. The name of God has been invoked upon us, that is, by grace we have become the sons of God, coheirs with Christ. In short, we are called by the same names

---

[66] As noted by Simundson, *Hosea, Joel, Amos, Obadiah, Jonah, Micah*, 173.

> with which God is called. So long as we believe, we are called righteous, holy, wise—even gods! The name of God, however, is blasphemed and corrupted because of us and through us when we walk unworthily, when we live and behave otherwise than befits Christians, when we are given over to wickedness and uncleanness.[67]

The Israelites probably viewed the sins catalogued in 2:7 as small indiscretions. Some win, others lose; that's the way it is in the "real world." But Yahweh looked upon these sins with the utmost seriousness since they defiled his holy name. His people are called to be holy just as he is holy (Lev 11:44–45; 19:2; 20:7; 1 Pet 1:15–16; cf. Eph 1:4; 5:27).

2:8 The literary artistry of Amos is evident by the repetition of the verb יַטּוּ, which in 2:7 meant "twist" in the context of withholding justice from the righteous poor. Here the verb conveys another kind of perversion: heartless Israelites "stretch themselves out," reclining for a religious feast to pagan gods, as indicated by the references to "every altar," "drink wine," and "their gods." Amos 2:7–8 is the first of the Amos passages in which God condemns the syncretistic and idolatrous worship practices of northern Israel; see also 3:14; 4:4–5; 5:5–6, 14, 21–27; 7:9–17; 8:5, 10, 14; 9:1; and the excursus "The Sabbath." Stephen the protomartyr quotes Amos 5:25–27 in Acts 7:42–43 to confirm that the culmination of Israel's idolatry was their rejection of Jesus the Messiah.

The carousing Israelites were not lounging on their own garments, but on those they had illegally confiscated. Yahweh had commanded in the Torah, "If you lend money to one of my people among you who is poor, do not be like a moneylender to him; you shall not charge him interest. If you take your neighbor's cloak as a pledge, you shall return it to him by sunset" (Ex 22:24–25 [ET 22:25–26]; cf. also Deut 24:17). Amos addresses the Israelites in light of this Pentateuchal commandment. These revelers were going beyond the Pentateuchal "daylight possession" rule and using the garments to bed down at night in a pagan temple. What is worse, these actions were in idolatrous worship "beside every altar" and "in the temple of their gods" (Amos 2:8).

As is often the case, poor people fall from destitution into deep debt. The righteous poor person in Amos' day had only one item remaining in his possession, a בֶּגֶד, "garment," that served as a cloak by day and a blanket by night.[68] Amos is not the only prophet who indicts Israel for this behavior. Ezekiel uses the seizure or return of collateral as one of his criteria for distinguishing between a righteous man and a wicked one (Ezek 18:7, 12, 16; 33:15). However, Amos is singular in his denunciation of wealthy creditors who not only violate a law that is intended to protect the poor, but then use the confiscated garments to

---

[67] Luther, "Lectures on Amos" (AE 18:141). When he stated that believers are called "gods," he probably was thinking of Ps 82:6 and Jesus' citation of it in Jn 10:34–36.

[68] King notes that there is a fourteen-line Hebrew ostracon (an inscribed potsherd) found in the ancient fortress at Meṣad Ḥashavyahu that dates from about 625 BC that is a letter from a reaper who complained that his garment (בֶּגֶד) had been taken; he pleads for the military governor to intervene so that it might be returned (*Amos, Hosea, Micah*, 24–25).

"stretch themselves out beside every altar," indicating that they used the garments as bedding for illicit cultic sexual relations.

Moreover, these Israelites were drinking wine "in the temple of their gods" as part of an illegitimate pagan feast. The clause "they drink wine obtained through fines" is parallel with the first colon of the verse, "upon seized garments they stretch themselves out." Since the first offense is morally wrong, so is the later parallel. The poetic parallelism indicates that both actions were reprehensible to Yahweh.

Andersen and Freedman conclude that the perpetrators of these crimes were located in the marketplaces where people were sold (2:6), the city gate where loans were certified (2:8), the courts where fines were paid (2:8), and the shrines where their gods were worshiped (2:8).[69] If so, the main culprits were, under God, the magistrates who were to dispense justice and righteousness (cf. 5:7, 10, 24), the businessmen who were to deal fairly (8:4–6), the monarch and his royal officials who were to protect the vulnerable people in the land, and the priests and religious leaders, especially at Bethel, who should have structured worship in such a way that God's justice and righteousness would forever flow (cf. 5:24; 7:10–17).

Yahweh's compassion for the outcast and disenfranchised, coupled with his power and authority over all the nations, is demonstrated in Gen 11:30, where Sarai is described as being barren. It was through this socially ostracized old woman and her husband Abram that all the families of the earth would be blessed (Gen 12:3)—by the "Son of Abraham," the Savior, Jesus the Christ (Mt 1:1; cf. Mt 1:21). Yahweh remembered this covenant promise and came down to rescue his people when they were slaves in Egypt (Ex 3:6–8), while at the same time inflicting judgment upon the gods of Egypt (Ex 12:12). The theme of Yahweh's care for the powerless is also in legal portions of the Torah of Moses: in the portion often called the Book of the Covenant (e.g., Ex 22:21–26 [ET 22:22–27]; 23:2–3, 6–11), in the so-called Holiness Code (e.g., Lev 19:9–10, 15, 32; 25:35–38), and in Moses' recital of the covenant on the plains of Moab in Deuteronomy (e.g., Deut 14:28–29; 15:7–11; 26:12–15). The theme is frequent in the Psalter[a] and in Proverbs.[b]

(a) E.g., Pss 72:2–4, 12–14; 82:3–4; 107:41; 113:7; 132:15; 146:7

(b) E.g., Prov 14:21, 31; 19:17; 21:13; 22:9, 22–23; 23:10–11; 29:7, 14; 31:9, 20

Like Amos, other Israelite prophets join in having compassion for people on the margins. Is 10:1–4 directs a woe-saying against those who oppress widows, orphans, and the poor. The widow has no husband, the orphan no parent, the poor no money to provide the basic necessities of life. Jeremiah (e.g., 5:28; 7:6), Ezekiel (e.g., 16:49; 18:12), and Zechariah (e.g., 7:10) express Yahweh's concern for the poor. Yahweh takes up the cause of his helpless people.

God's compassion for the lowly is also expressed in the NT and is exemplified through his Son, Jesus Christ. After his conception, the Virgin Mary sings about it (Lk 1:46–55). Jesus preaches it (Lk 4:18–21). The disciples model it

[69] Andersen and Freedman, *Amos*, 321–22.

(Acts 4:32–37; 6:1–6). At the final judgment in Mt 25:31–46, Jesus blesses the faithful who reflected his own compassion toward fellow believers who were the strangers, the naked, the prisoners, and the hungry. Then he damns unbelievers for ignoring the needs of his people. Arand and Biermann sum up the relationship between righteousness before God and active righteousness (faith active through love [Gal 5:6]) expressed to one's neighbor in their article "Why the Two Kinds of Righteousness?" They define "passive righteousness": "Standing before God in heaven, human beings must leave all works behind on earth and seek nothing but the righteousness of Christ that is received by faith."[70] Active righteousness does not justify—only Christ can do that—but, propelled by the Holy Spirit, we Christians actively embrace "our God-entrusted tasks—tasks spelled out with sufficient specificity in the Law both revealed and written on human hearts—within our walks of life for the good of creation."[71]

The Holy Spirit works through the Word of God and the Sacraments of Holy Baptism and the Lord's Supper to justify the sinner before God and to enable his life of sanctification in relation to his neighbor. Thus these two kinds of righteousness accord with one another so that the Christian's righteousness before God yields the fruit of a godly life of active righteousness.

Amos 2:6–8 explains three of Israel's crimes: (1) wealth perverted justice; (2) illicit sex was rampant; and (3) participation at the altars of foreign gods was ongoing. These three charges set the stage for what Amos preaches against in the rest of his book. Although sexual sin is not a predominate concern in Amos, he employs the metaphor of the loss of virginity to depict Israel's apostasy and idolatry (5:1–17; cf. 8:14). Amos' primary rebuke falls against the financial exploitation of God's poor. He condemns bribery (5:12), luxury without concern for the poor (4:1; 6:4–6), and the unloving treatment of the needy (8:4).

Yahweh Had Saved Israel and Defeated Her Enemies (2:9–12)

2:9–12 This subunit of the Israel oracle (2:6–16) is marked off with Yahweh's "yet I" (2:9) and the words "but you" (2:12). These markers reinforce the Gospel/Law theme of this subunit, in which Yahweh ("I") contrasts his acts of salvation with the Israelites ("you"), who rejected him and his salvation, as exemplified by their abuse of the Nazirites and the prophets whom Yahweh raised up (2:12). The emphasis remains on what Yahweh has done to redeem his people. A first person singular verb ("I ...") occurs five times in this section, and twice it is reinforced with an independent personal pronoun (וְאָנֹכִי הִשְׁמַדְתִּי, "I myself annihilated," 2:9; and וְאָנֹכִי הֶעֱלֵיתִי, "I myself brought up," 2:10).

The oracles against the pagan nations (1:3–2:3) proclaimed Yahweh's judgment upon peoples who sinned on the international scale. The oracle against Judah (2:4–5) indicted the Southern Kingdom for specifically theological sins:

---

70 Arand and Biermann, "Why the Two Kinds of Righteousness?" 121.

71 Arand and Biermann, "Why the Two Kinds of Righteousness?" 119.

her rejection of the Torah, which was brought about in part by idolatry fueled by false prophets. In the earlier part of the oracle against Israel (2:6–8), Yahweh's wrath was kindled by theological sins that damaged society: contrary to the Torah, legal aid was denied the poor; the safety net designed to protect the dignity of the powerless among God's covenant people was quietly brought down; a father and son incestuously had relations with the same young woman; and sexual sins continued in drunken orgies in idolatrous temples. These mostly were "polite" sins that were acceptable within the apostate people. They took place within an outwardly orderly and civil society, but they were denounced in the same speech as the war crimes and atrocities committed by the heathen nations. Yet Israel's sins were even more reprehensible because Yahweh had poured out his covenant loving-kindness on the nation.

Yahweh's redeeming faithfulness described in 2:9–12 is placed in a context whose genre is that of a covenant lawsuit.[72] The affluence of Israel's elite had produced amnesia. Moses warned Israel never to forget Yahweh's acts of kindness (Deuteronomy 8), since those who remember nothing will feel free to do anything (cf. Jer 2:5–6). After forgetting their past redemption, the Israelites were bound to live unfaithfully in the present, which meant judgment in the future.[73] Yahweh therefore reminds them of his great acts of salvation on their behalf, how as a faithful suzerain he had taken care of his beloved vassal.[74] Devoted without reserve, Yahweh had delivered Israel from the land of Egypt, guided his people through the wilderness, and brought them to a land of bounty. By acting in such benevolent ways, the Overlord established his claim to the nation's loyalty.

Yet in spite of Yahweh's great acts of deliverance for Israel, the people responded with infidelity and ignored the will of their sovereign Savior to whom they owed absolute allegiance. For Israel's leaders, Yahweh's Gospel acts of redemption became dry and rote. Ironically, by means of this recapitulation of the Gospel and Israel's rejection of it, Amos establishes the reason for the *end* of Yahweh dealing with Israel on the basis of the Gospel.

---

[72] Bright states this of Amos and cites 2:9–12 as an example: "His attack was deeply rooted in theology. … On occasion he throws these crimes against the backdrop of the events of the exodus and the giving of the land" (*Covenant and Promise*, 84). Sweeney labels this genre "historical review" and lists the following texts, among others, as examples: Josh 24:2–13; 1 Sam 12:7–12; Neh 9:7–31; and 2 Chr 15:2–7 (*Isaiah 1–39*, 521). Other prophets often denote the covenant lawsuit genre by use of the term רִיב, *rib*, a legal "charge" or "accusation." Amos uses that term in 7:4 (see the textual notes and commentary there).

[73] Brueggemann, *Like Fire in the Bones*, 161, writes:

> The voiding of memory leads to a misreading of present reality. That misleading in turn leads to mis-action and mis-policy. Without the redefining voice of the old memory, the present historical process deteriorates into an enterprise of brute power and intimidation, a juggling of interests, an ideological manipulation of symbols.

[74] Compare, for example, Is 5:1–7; Ezek 16:1–63; and Micah 6:1–5 for similar prophetic recitals of Yahweh's benevolence for his beloved Israel even though she proved unfaithful.

The order of the great events of salvation in 2:9–10 is an inclusio that accents the events in the book of Joshua when Yahweh led Israel to take the land from the Amorites. The order is as follows:

1. Yahweh destroyed the Amorites (2:9).
2. Yahweh brought up Israel out of Egypt (2:10a).
3. Yahweh led Israel in the desert for 40 years (2:10b).
4. Yahweh destroyed the Amorites (2:10c).

While Hosea employs the patriarchal narratives in his citations of Yahweh's grace (e.g., Hos 9:10; 12:13 [ET 12:12]), Amos uses the exodus and conquest as his major motifs for attesting Yahweh's grace (see also 3:1; 9:7).

2:9 The collective phrase "the Amorite" (הָאֱמֹרִ֗י) can be used narrowly for the specific Amorite ethnic group[75] or in a broad sense as a term for all of the different kinds of inhabitants of Canaan prior to Joshua's conquest of the land (see Gen 48:22; Josh 24:15; Judg 6:10; 2 Sam 21:2). The Amorites were judged because they defiled Yahweh's land (Gen 15:16). Amos uses terms for trees—"cedars" and "oaks" (Amos 2:9)—to describe the Amorites because of their overwhelming size (cf., e.g., Num 13:28; Josh 14:12, 15; 15:14). In Deut 1:28 and 9:2, the Anakim (among the Amorites in the broad sense) are described as huge and insurmountable giants. Amos' Amorite tree imagery may also be a subtle reference to the worship of Asherah (cf. Deut 16:21–22). Asherah was a Canaanite fertility goddess often represented by a tree or pole planted in the ground beside an altar (e.g., Judg 6:25; 2 Ki 21:3).[76]

The imagery further suggests that Yahweh is against all that is proud and lofty. In Isaiah's "Day of Yahweh" poem (Is 2:6–22), Yahweh indicates that he is against "the cedars of Lebanon … and the oaks of Bashan" (Is 2:13), while twice the prophet indicates that "Yahweh alone will be exalted on that day" (Is 2:11, 17). John the Baptist employs similar judgment imagery when he warns, "Already the ax is lying at the root of the trees, and every tree therefore that does not bear good fruit is cut down and thrown into the fire" (Mt 3:10; cf. Jn 15:1–8).

Amos' tree metaphor continues with a description of the destruction "of his fruit above and his roots below" (Amos 2:9)—a merism depicting total extermination. These paired polar opposites, "fruit" (פְּרִי) and "root" (שֹׁרֶשׁ), are also used in 2 Ki 19:30; Is 14:29; 37:31; Jer 17:8; Ezek 17:9; and Hos 9:16. Amos reverses the conventional order by citing first the fruit at the top of the tree and then its roots. In this way, he emphasizes Yahweh's complete control over the Amorites; if they are high, he is higher (cf. Gen 11:5).

---

[75] The first textual note on 2:9 describes the specific ethnic group.

[76] In Ugaritic literature, El's consort was Athirat, a name that occurs as "Asherah" in the OT. A stylized tree symbolized both Athirat (the mother of the gods at Ugarit) and Asherah, yet intertestamental Jews forgot who Asherah was, and so the LXX and the Mishnah translate *Asherim* as "living trees." This led eventually to the KJV translation of "grove" (e.g., Ex 34:13; 2 Ki 17:10; Jer 17:2).

A statement that Yahweh had annihilated the fruit and roots employs metaphors that "would be quite familiar to a dresser of sycamore trees like Amos, who constantly had to deal with the threats posed by nature to the fruit trees which helped to provide him with a living."[77] The irony is that Israel, who by God's grace was able "to possess the land of the Amorite" (2:10), would soon be punished just as the Amorites had been punished: they would be expelled from the land (4:2–3; 5:5, 27; 6:7; 7:11, 17; 9:4).

Here, as well as in other places in Amos, Yahweh reverses commonly expected conclusions (e.g., 3:1–2; 4:4–5; 5:18–20). This verse employs the motif of salvation history, but not as a guarantee of Yahweh's acts of kindness in the future. Rather it is an indictment. Ironically, now salvation history is announced as reason for Yahweh's judgment.

2:10 This verse, like 2:9, begins with Yahweh's emphatic "I myself" (וְאָנֹכִי). While the same first person independent pronoun (וְאָנֹכִי) was employed in 2:9 to highlight what Yahweh did against the Amorites for the benefit of Israel, this second independent personal pronoun introduces his salvific actions with Israel herself.

Whereas the first seven oracles (1:3–2:5) referred to nations in the third person, here, for the first time, Yahweh addresses a nation—Israel—in the second person (אֶתְכֶם, "you" plural). This second person address continues through 2:13. In this way, the oracle takes direct aim at the covenant community whom Yahweh created by saving them from Egypt. Yahweh is now speaking directly to *his* chosen people. Heschel writes of this section in Amos: "The message of God is not an impersonal accusation, but the utterance of a Redeemer who is pained by the misdeeds, the thanklessness of those whom He has redeemed."[78]

The historical backdrop for Amos 2:10 begins in Exodus 14, which is the narrative of the exodus, while Exodus 15 is Moses' Song of the Sea, which celebrates Yahweh's salvation. After the exodus, Yahweh led Israel in the wilderness (Deut 8:15), fought for his people there (Deut 1:30–31), tested them (Deut 8:2), and provided for their needs (Deut 8:3–4). After forty years (Deut 8:1–5), Yahweh gave Israel a wonderful inheritance (Deut 8:6–10). The exodus, wilderness wanderings, and conquest accomplished at least four divine acts, two of judgment and two of salvation:

1. By the final plague, Yahweh judged the gods of Egypt (Ex 12:12).
2. Yahweh redeemed, guided, and disciplined a people to be faithful to himself (Ex 15:13; Deut 8:1–6).
3. By Israel's conquest of the land, Yahweh punished the iniquity of the Amorites after it was full (Gen 15:16).
4. By blessing Israel in the land, Yahweh demonstrated his faithfulness to his promise to Abraham (Gen 12:1–3; Deut 4:37–38).

---

[77] Sweeney, *The Twelve Prophets*, 217.

[78] Heschel, *The Prophets*, 32.

These acts of judgment and salvation for the sake of Israel are commemorated throughout the OT (e.g., Ex 20:1–2; Deuteronomy 5:6; 32; Joshua 24). Some early texts contain warnings not to forget Yahweh's grace (e.g., Deut 32:15–29; Josh 24:14–24), while later ones indicate that Israel forgot Yahweh and his acts of kindness. For example, through Hosea, probably a contemporary of Amos, Yahweh anguishes, "She [Israel] walked after her lovers, but me she has forgotten" (Hos 2:15 [ET 2:13]). In Jer 2:32, Yahweh states, "My people have forgotten me for days without number."

The exodus deliverance had become old news, and what is old is easily cast aside, dismissed, and forgotten instead of cherished in faith as the basis for future hope. In the same way, Christians can be tempted to forget the death and resurrection of Christ and their Baptism into him, or to neglect the Lord's Supper, even though these NT fulfillments of the OT Passover and exodus (e.g., 1 Cor 5:7; 10:1–4, 16–18) are the basis of our salvation and furnish our hope for eternal life.

2:11 The line of prophets that would culminate in the Prophet promised in Deut 18:15–20 created a chain of communication between Israel and Yahweh.[79] Yahweh's gift of the prophetic office was his ordained means by which his voice would continue to be heard in Israel and in the world between the time of Moses and the advent of Christ. Deut 18:15–18 indicates that each coming prophet would be like Moses in terms of being the authorized mediator of Yahweh's words. The promise entailed both a succession of prophets, who would serve to mediate Yahweh's Word, as well as the single individual who would be Yahweh's final Prophet, Jesus the Christ (Acts 3:12–26), the definitive Word of God (cf. Jn 1:1; Heb 1:1–2; Rev 19:13).

The office of the prophet, then, is important. Yahweh and his Torah do not change; people and their situations and circumstances do change. The prophets were to serve as interpreters of Torah in changing circumstances. In the Torah, God made no provision for a continuous line of prophets (whereas he established a permanent succession of priests), since each prophet was called only by Yahweh's initiative, and each was to speak only the words given to him. Prophets like Moses included Samuel (1 Sam 3:20), Elijah (1 Ki 18:36), and Elisha (1 Ki 19:16). These mediators held the ultimate power in Israel over against kings with their horses and chariots (cf. Ps 20:8 [ET 20:7]). In fact, Elijah and Elisha are both called "the chariotry of Israel and its horses" (רֶכֶב יִשְׂרָאֵל וּפָרָשָׁיו, 2 Ki 2:12; 13:14).[80] The prophetic Word endures forever (Is 40:8) and is efficacious and all-powerful (Is 55:10–11).

The spiritual leaders who are often paired in the OT with prophets—the priests (see, e.g., Jer 14:18; 23:11; Ezek 7:26)—are notable by their absence in

---

[79] Abraham was the first prophet (Gen 20:7). His primary role in this capacity was as a mediator between God and people (e.g., Gen 18:16–33; 20:7). Moses was also such a mediator (Ex 32:11–14; Deut 5:4–5; cf. Deut 34:10).

[80] Cf. Weiss, "And I Raised Up Prophets from amongst Your Sons."

Amos 2:11. This omission probably has something to do with prophet-priest conflict in Amos 7:10–17, where the northern priest Amaziah and his family come under Yahweh's judgment. Another likely reason for the absence of priests is that the priesthood of northern Israel was apostate from its inception since it was established by Jeroboam ben Nebat (1 Ki 12:31–32), not by God.

Mentioned together in Amos 2:11 with the prophets are Nazirites, who took vows that included abstaining from alcoholic drink, from cutting their hair, and from contact with the dead (Num 6:1–21). They "provided visible testimony of the humility of heart and purity of life that are appropriate before the Great King."[81] Instead of being a mouth-piece of Yahweh like a prophet, Nazirites were "regarded as models of an ascetic holy-man tradition who were ever before the Israelites as examples of dedication or commitment to Yahweh."[82] Samson was ordained to be a Nazirite for life from before his conception (Judg 13:2–7; 16:17). Hannah consecrated Samuel to Yahweh before his conception, and he too appears to have been a life-long Nazirite (1 Sam 1:9–11, 20–22). Other men and women could take a Nazirite vow for only a specific period of time (Num 6:2–4; cf. Acts 21:23–26).

Amos concludes this verse (2:11) with a rhetorical question,[83] demanding a response from his listeners and readers: "Is this not so, O children of Israel?" This powerfully sets forth the prophet's argument and challenges, "Can anyone deny these facts"? Chrysostom explained:

> The Lord accused the Israelites more severely and showed that they deserved greater punishment, because they sinned after receiving the honors that he had bestowed on them. He said, "You only have I known of all the families of the earth; therefore I will visit upon you your iniquities" [Amos 3:2], and again, "I took of your sons for prophets and of your young men for consecration" [LXX Amos 2:11].[84]

2:12 Amos employs chiastic parallelism with the preceding verse. He first refers to the people corrupting the Nazirites, who were mentioned last in 2:11, and second to the people muzzling the prophets, who were mentioned first in 2:11. By corrupting the Nazirites and silencing the prophets, the Israelites attempted to shut down every channel of divine communication.

The Nazirites were forced to drink wine and thereby break their vows of abstinence.[85] In light of the "party atmosphere" detailed by Amos in 2:7–8; 4:1; and 6:4–6, it comes as no surprise that Israelites were forcing Nazirites to

---

81 Niehaus, "Amos," 370.

82 Andersen and Freedman, *Amos*, 31.

83 For other rhetorical questions in Amos, see 3:3–8; 5:18, 20, 25; 6:2, 12; 8:8; 9:7.

84 Chrysostom, *On the Priesthood*, 6.10, quoted in Ferreiro, *The Twelve Prophets*, ACCS 14:89.

85 Breaking one part of the vow would violate the whole vow. Andersen and Freedman write: "The reference to their being made to drink wine contrary to the dedicatory vow seems to be exemplary and representative, rather then central. The point is that they are rendered unfit for their calling" (*Amos*, 31). Other eighth-century prophets connect the abuse of wine with false

drink. Perhaps the carousing Israelites were embarrassed by the fidelity of the Nazirites, or maybe they considered the vow of abstinence part of a by-gone era.

As an example of the silencing of the prophets, Yahweh could refer to Jezebel killing many prophets (1 Ki 18:4; cf. 1 Ki 19:2, 10), Ahab muzzling Micaiah ben Imlah (1 Ki 22:26–27), or Joram's attempt to kill Elisha (2 Ki 6:31). Yet the most immediate event is Amaziah's rebuke of Amos himself in Amos 7:12–13, where he commands the prophet, "At Bethel you shall never again prophesy." By silencing prophets, Israel attempted to silence Yahweh, who will confirm Israel in this sin when he promises a famine of hearing his word in 8:11.

On many other occasions, prophets met fierce opposition (cf., e.g., 1 Ki 13:4; 18:4; 19:2, 10; 22:26–27; Jer 2:30; 18:18). Is 30:10–11 is a classic rebuff of a prophet. 2 Ki 17:13 and 2 Chr 36:16 indicate that Israel's rejection of the prophets was one of the primary reasons why the north was exiled in 722 BC and the south in 587 BC. Stulman writes:

> Without the prophetic presence there is no poetry, imagination, generosity, or testimony to transcendence. Kings avert their eyes to human needs, economic inequities, and broken social systems. And there remain only "horses and chariots," unbridled greed, brutality, technology, and stinginess (see, e.g., Deut 17:14–20). ... Life flattens into settled categories, undisturbed and insensitive to what is truly going on.[86]

And so the prophets and Nazirites, the men God chose in Israel (Amos 2:11), were made to conform to their contemporary evil age (2:12; cf. Rom 12:1–2).

The leaders of Israel in Jesus' day did everything they could to silence him (e.g., Mk 3:6; Jn 11:53). In every age, God's spokesmen will meet opposition (Mt 5:11–12). This is certainly true about the men God calls into the pastoral ministry, as St. Paul warned Timothy already in the first century AD (2 Tim 4:1–4). But Jesus promises that he will continue to build his church on the rock of those who faithfully confess him, and neither hell nor anything else will ultimately defeat the advance of his kingdom (Mt 16:16–18; Jn 16:33).

Yahweh Will Defeat Even the Most Courageous in Israel (2:13–16)

2:13–16 Earlier in the oracle, Yahweh served as the accusing Judge (2:6–8) because Israel had abandoned her Redeemer (2:9–12). However, in 2:13 he is the one who suffers. His anguish will lead to the judgments described in 2:14–16.

---

prophets (e.g., Is 28:1–15; Micah 2:11; cf. Hos 4:18). Priests were forbidden from drinking alcoholic beverages when performing their duties (Lev 10:9).

[86] Stulman, *Jeremiah*, 222.

2:13 Yahweh continues to suffer because of Israel. Yahweh's heart is not one-dimensional anger. Even in wrath he is full of anguish, grief, pathos, and pain (cf. Jer 31:20). Yahweh cannot cease to care.

The wagon is overloaded with freshly cut sheaves. This is harvest imagery. In like manner, the fourth vision of Amos employs the imagery of harvested fruit (8:1–2), and the fifth vision features Yahweh cutting down all his people with a sword and by other means (9:1–4), perhaps recalling the harvesting of grain with a sickle. In the NT, the harvest is often connected with the final judgment at the end of the age (e.g., Mt 13:30, 39; Mk 4:29; Rev 14:14–19).

The overloaded wagon reflects Israel's abundance that was made possible through the nation's abuse of the poor.[87] The heaviness causes Yahweh to groan and suffer from the burden of carrying his people. By revealing Yahweh's sorrow over the situation, Amos 2:13 shows that Yahweh is not vengeful in his administration of justice, but grieves because he must punish. This continues the OT theme of God's suffering,[88] which culminates in the passion and vicarious atonement of God the Son, Jesus Christ.

Gregory the Great explains the suffering of God in 2:13 with these words:

> He [God] sometimes compares himself with deep condescension, on account of our infirmity, to objects without sense, as he says by the prophet, "Behold, I will shriek over you as a cart creaks when laden with hay" [Amos 2:13]. For since the life of the carnal is hay (as it is written, all flesh is hay [Is 40:6]), in that the Lord endures the life of the carnal he declares that he carries hay as a cart. And to creak under the weight of the hay is for him to bear with murmuring the burdens and iniquities of sinners. When therefore he applies to himself very unlike resemblances, we must carefully observe that some things of this kind are sometimes spoken of concerning God, on account of the effect of his doings, but sometimes to indicate the substance of his majesty.[89]

The first reference to Yahweh's suffering occurs in the prelude to the story of Noah in Genesis 6–9. The spread of sin introduced in Genesis 3 seems to reach a climax as Gen 6:5 states that every human thought and plan is continuously evil. Gen 6:6 states: "Yahweh regretted [וַיִּנָּחֶם] that he had made mankind on the earth, and he was deeply saddened in his heart [וַיִּתְעַצֵּב אֶל־לִבּוֹ]." This divine sorrow is emphatically expressed by the two Hebrew verbs used.[90] Further stress is added by "in his heart." The rampant evil that controls the hearts of all humanity according to Gen 6:5 is thus contrasted in Gen 6:6 with what Delitzsch

---

87 Amos makes this same point in 4:1 when he labels the women of Samaria "cows of Bashan."

88 Cf. Fretheim, *The Suffering of God: An Old Testament Perspective*.

89 Gregory the Great, *Morals on the Book of Job*, 6.32.7, cited in Ferreiro, *The Twelve Prophets*, ACCS 14:90.

90 This is the only time that both of these verbs occur together in the OT. Wenham points out that the verb עָצַב "is used to express the most intense form of human emotion, a mixture of rage and bitter anguish" (*Genesis 1–15*, 144).

calls Yahweh's "heart-piercing sorrow."[91] It is only with this sense of deep grief and disappointment that Yahweh decides to destroy all his earthly creatures, with the exception of Noah and his family and the animals on the ark, enabling a new start for creation (cf. 1 Pet 3:18–22).

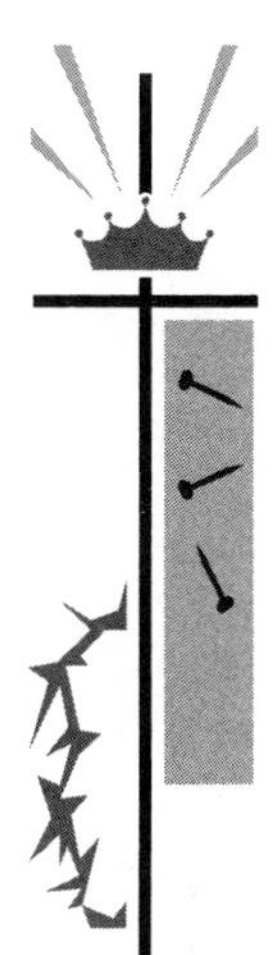

Yahweh's suffering for and with *Israel* begins in Ex 3:7: "Yahweh said, 'I have indeed seen the misery of my people in Egypt. I have heard them crying out because of their slave drivers, and I am intimately acquainted [יָדַעְתִּי] with their suffering.' " Is 1:13–14 and Hos 11:8–9 also depict Yahweh as suffering for his people. In Num 11:14–17, Moses, Yahweh's servant, complains about bearing the load of Israel (cf. Deut. 1:9–12).

In his Suffering Servant Jesus, God climactically bears the burden of Israel's sin (Is 52:13–53:12), and indeed the sin of the whole world (1 Jn 2:2). Jesus was laden with sin (Is 53:4–6) when he carried it in his body on the cross (2 Cor 5:21; 1 Pet 2:24). What Luther called "the joyous exchange" is that all our sins were imputed to Christ, and through faith in him alone, his righteousness is imputed to us (2 Cor 5:18–21).[92]

2:14–16 These last verses of the oracle depict the judgment against Israel that results from the people's sins recounted in the preceding part of the oracle. Each of the earlier oracles against other nations in 1:3–2:5 likewise concluded with declarations of judgment. In those declarations, the sole agent of destruction was divine fire that destroys fortified cities and causes the exile of kings, princes, and peoples. Amos 2:14–16 does not explicitly refer to fire nor even to Yahweh himself as the cause, but it implies that there will be an earthly agent who executes Yahweh's fiery judgment: an army. It is not until 6:14 that a nation (גּוֹי) is mentioned, but few specific details about it are given. Nevertheless, the nation that is Yahweh's agent of judgment can be identified as Assyria (see the excursus "The Assyrian Empire in the Eighth Century BC"). Andersen and Freedman write:

> Thanks to our knowledge of subsequent history and the insights provided by roughly contemporary and later prophets, we can identify this invader and conqueror as Assyria. Perhaps Amos did not wish or need to do so—Assyria had fought great battles in that area in the past [i.e., Shalmaneser III (858–824) who battled with Israel at Qarqar], and its illustrious all-conquering kings had washed their swords in the waters of the Great Western [Mediterranean] Sea.[93]

---

[91] Delitzsch, *A New Commentary on Genesis*, 1:233.

[92] The phrase *der fröhlich Wechsel* ("the joyous exchange") appears in Luther's German version of *The Freedom of a Christian* (WA 7.25), a work he originally wrote in Latin. The Latin version is translated in AE 31:327–77 (see especially 31:351–52), and the German version is translated in Woolf, *Reformation Writings of Martin Luther*, 1:349–79 (see especially 1:363–64). See also, for example, AE 26:172–79, 276–91 (the exchange is termed "this fortunate exchange" on 26:284); 30:225; 31:297–99; 48:12–13.

[93] Andersen and Freedman, *Amos*, 347.

The unit (2:14–16) employs seven examples to depict the helplessness of Israel: three in 2:14, three in 2:15, and a climactic one in 2:16. Some of the examples are repetitious, for example, "swift" in 2:14a and 2:15b, in order to achieve the total of seven. This heptad corresponds to the number of the seven nations in 1:3–2:5 that preceded the oracle against Israel, along with seven acts of rebellion by each of those nations ("for three sins of … and for four"). In 2:6–8, Israel too is cited for seven transgressions.[94] Amos 2:14–16 depicts the utter defeat of Israel's army, for fleeing in the midst of a battle (2:14a) means certain slaughter (e.g., Josh 7:5; Judg 4:16; 2 Chr 13:16–17). Every division and category of troops is threatened. In previous battles, Yahweh had thrown Israel's enemies into confusion (e.g., Judg 5:4; 1 Sam 14:15). Yahweh now plans to use this strategy *against* Israel. Complete pandemonium will overwhelm her army. This defeated army is the same military force in which Israel had so much pride (Amos 6:13).

The futility of trusting in military might is stated in other OT texts that use some of the same vocabulary as used in 2:14–16. For example, Ps 33:16–17 warns: "The king is not saved by a great army, and a *warrior* [גִּבּוֹר] is not delivered by great *strength* [כֹּחַ]. The *horse* [הַסּוּס] is a false hope for salvation; for all its great power, it *does not save* [לֹא יְמַלֵּט]." In Hos 1:7, God declares, "I will save them by Yahweh their God, but I will not save them by *bow* or by sword or by battle or by *horses* or by horsemen." See also Jer 46:5–6 and Eccl 9:11.

2:14 This verse contains the first triad of military positions that will fail. The first is the swift runner. One of the key characteristics of any military corps is its swiftness in battle (cf. 2 Sam 2:18; Jer 46:6; Lam 4:19; 1 Chr 12:9 [ET 12:8]). But in this verse, Amos maintains that there is no "flight to a place of refuge" for "the swift." The second and third positions are similar to each other: "the strong man" and "the warrior." The strong man who normally is brave will lose his courage, and the warrior will not be able to save his life by his prowess in battle. In Amos 5:19 and 9:1–4, the prophet reiterates this theme of no exit.

2:15 Amos' litany of seven punishments continues in this verse with the second group of three military positions that are doomed. The fourth is the bowman, who normally would shoot from a standing position, but he will not stand. The fifth is the "swift" runner, as in 2:14a, but his ability is expanded here by adding that he is "swift *on his feet*," that is, fleet of foot. But even he will not be able to save himself.

The sixth category mentioned probably is the chariot driver (see the third textual note on 2:15). The Israelite army of the eighth century may have had only a few of these soldiers, as suggested by the sarcastic jibe of the Assyrian Rabshakeh. He addressed Hezekiah's officials in 701 BC as follows: "Come now, make this wager with my master, the king of Assyria. I will give you two thousand horses if you can supply riders/drivers [רֹכְבִים] for them" (2 Ki 18:23

94 For other heptads in Amos, see 3:3–6; 4:4–5; 4:6–11; 5:8–9; 5:21–23; 6:1–6; 9:1–4.

|| Is 36:8). Of all the different kinds of soldiers, the horseman would have the best opportunity to "save his life" (Amos 2:15). Compare 1 Sam 30:17, where only those who mounted camels escaped David's onslaught. Yet Amos declares that even those with access to horses will not escape divine judgment on the coming Day of Yahweh.

2:16 The last category of soldier is the most courageous military man. Such elite warriors are the sort who would comprise the king's bodyguard and Israel's crack troops.[95] Even these warriors will run away in fear. An Assyrian text detailing the eighth campaign of Sennacherib describes the terrified flight of defeated enemies:

> They abandoned their tents and to save their lives they trampled the bodies of their (fallen) soldiers, they fled like young pigeons that are pursued. They were beside themselves (*lit.*, their hearts were torn)[;] they held back(?) their urine, but let their dung go into their chariots. In pursuit of them I dispatched my chariots and horses after them. Those among them who had escaped, who had fled for their lives, wherever they (my charioteers) met them, they cut them down with the sword.[96]

In the ancient Near East, war captives were often stripped naked. This had the practical effect of making covert escape difficult, but the chief end was public disgrace and humiliation. See 2 Sam 10:4–5 and Is 20:4.

The Israel oracle (2:6–16) shall be fulfilled "on that day" (בַּיּוֹם־הַהוּא). In OT narrative passages, the phrase may synchronize the events mentioned in contiguous passages. However, especially in prophetic texts, it often has an eschatological dimension. In the context of Amos, "on that day" in 2:16 is part of the "Day of Yahweh" theme that is fully developed by the prophet in 5:18–20. On that day, the entire Israelite army will be mown down. Israel's complete catastrophe occurred when her capital city Samaria fell to the Assyrian king Sargon II in 722 BC. Judgment on that day points to the final Judgment Day, the Last Day, when Christ "will come again with glory to judge both the living and the dead" (Nicene Creed).[97]

Amos had been in Yahweh's council (3:7). He knew that the different eras of Israel were all held in Yahweh's hand (cf. Ps 31:16 [ET 31:15]). The time of judgment pictured in 2:14–16 and throughout most of the book of Amos would one day give way to the time of grace. Amos was aware of that time as well (9:11–15). The raising of the tabernacle of David through the resurrection of Jesus Christ would inaugurate the church age, the time when all peoples are welcomed into the true Israel through faith in the King of the Jews (9:11–12).

---

[95] Andersen and Freedman, *Amos*, 340.

[96] Luckenbill, *Ancient Records of Assyria and Babylonia*, 2:128.

[97] For the "Day of Yahweh" theme, see the commentary on 5:18, 20, and also "Amos' Place in the Minor Prophets" in the introduction; the third textual note on 1:14; the first textual note on 2:16; and the second textual note and the commentary on 4:2.

His return will commence the resurrection of all the dead and the entrance of all believers into the eternal paradise (9:13–15).

The final phrase, literally, "oracle of Yahweh" (2:16), is a signatory formula. It functions as Yahweh's own signature, certifying the authenticity of the divine message.[98] It is Yahweh who speaks. He is fully aware of Israel's sins (2:6–8, 12). It is Yahweh who creaks and grieves (2:13). It is Yahweh who will execute judgment (2:14–16). Yet he is also the God who once saved Israel (2:9–11) and who will provide salvation for all (9:11–15).

Summary of Amos' Oracles against the Nations (1:3–2:16)

Amos' worldview started in the small rural town of Tekoa (1:1), which had a military fortification to protect Judah's southern flank (2 Chr 11:5–12). These surroundings provided Amos with the opportunity to learn about international events, especially as they related to warfare. Much of what Amos prophesies in 1:3–2:16 involves military concepts he probably learned from his interactions with the soldiers stationed in Tekoa.

Seven was the traditional number of enemies that suffered Yahweh's wrath when Israel defeated them to secure the land of Canaan in the fifteenth and fourteenth centuries BC (e.g., Deut 7:1; Josh 3:10, 24:11; Acts 13:19). While not an exact correspondence, the nations in the eighth century in Amos 1:3–2:16 are now the object of Yahweh's wrath. They, like their predecessors, will be driven out from their lands (1:5, 15) or annihilated (1:8; 2:3). This time, however, Judah (2:4–5) and Israel (2:6–16) are numbered with the transgressors. There is a total of seven nations if we count the six heathen powers in 1:3–2:3 plus the original Israel, now divided into the Southern Kingdom of Judah (2:4–5) and the Northern Kingdom of Israel (2:6–16). The divided and apostate people of God will likewise undergo judgment. Like the six pagan nations, Judah and Israel too will receive divine fire (2:5; 5:6; 7:4).[99] And Israel will be exiled (4:2–3; 5:5, 27; 6:7; 7:11, 17; 9:4).[100]

Yahweh had worked for the good of other nations (9:7) but 1:2–2:3 indicates he will also punish them for their crimes. Yahweh brought about salvation for Israel (2:9–11), but these tables will also turn because his people have rejected him. Yahweh will wage war against his own people, Israel. Although his means of judgment is not revealed, later in the eighth century Yahweh would raise up the Assyrians to enact the events described in 1:3–2:16. The Assyrians massacred entire cities, piled up corpses, impaled prisoners, and engaged in other atrocities.[101] In this way, Yahweh placed his torch to the tinder of all eight nations.

---

[98] See the second textual note on 2:11. For other signatory formulas in the oracles against the nations, see the last textual note on 1:5.

[99] See "Yahweh Punishes by Fire" in the introduction to 1:3–2:16.

[100] Judah too will be exiled some one hundred and fifty years after northern Israel's exile, but Judah's exile is not explicitly prophesied in Amos.

[101] See, for example, Bleibtreu, "Grisly Assyrian Record of Torture and Death."

This is how he responded to the helpless and afflicted people depicted as victims in 1:3–2:16. Yahweh is the "Father of the fatherless and the defending Judge of widows" (Ps 68:6 [ET 68:5]).

In Amos' oracles against the nations, Yahweh contends that the events about to happen will be no accident. They are not simply the consequence of geopolitical power plays, nor will they occur because of divine capriciousness. The dissolution of these nations and their well-established institutions will be the outcome of their rebellion against holy and righteous Yahweh. All must appear before the judgment seat of Christ (2 Cor 5:10; cf. Rev 20:11–15).

There are two different foundations for judgment in Amos 1:3–2:16. First, God's natural law written in creation and on the human conscience is common to all humanity, and it is the basis for his judgment against the pagan nations (1:3–2:3). The nations are indicted for behavior that most humans should find heinous: genocidal acts (1:6, 9), violence against noncombatants (1:13), and acts of ritual degradation (2:1). In 1948 the United Nations adopted the Universal Declaration of Human Rights, which reflects natural law, although imperfectly and inadequately. Article 1 states: "All human beings are born free and equal in dignity and rights. They are endowed with reason and conscience and should act towards one another in a spirit of brotherhood."[102]

Even though knowledge of the natural law has been corrupted by human sin, it remains written on the hearts of all people, so theoretically God could still inspire today a prophet to preach oracles similar to those of Amos against the heathen nations. Millions are killed by genocide, ethnic cleansing, and the slaughter of helpless infants still in the wombs of their mothers (see 1:11, 13). Millions more suffer or perish under economic enslavement, totalitarian political abuse, and the greedy consumption of goods by the wealthy at the expense of the poor. These sins still run rampant in the world today. Yahweh still hates these inhumane acts and considers them a rebellion against his plan for the world.

Second, God has made known his Law and Gospel through his special revelation in the Scriptures (2:4) and in the preaching of his prophets (2:11). The OT revelation was given only to Judah and Israel, and on this basis they will be judged (2:4–16). Judah and Israel are not only accused of breaking God's natural law, but especially of rejecting God's sacred Word. They not only abused impoverished people in their society, but also listened to false prophets and worshiped idols, disregarding Yahweh's acts of salvation.

Yahweh seeks justice and righteousness from his people (5:24). Righteousness is his gift to them through the forgiveness of their sins, and that passive righteousness that they receive leads, in turn, to their active righteousness in leading a life of faith that involves doing the right things, for example, giving aid to the widow and orphan.[103] Justice addresses the question of how

[102] As quoted by Drinan, *Cry of the Oppressed*, 23.

[103] See Luther, *Two Kinds of Righteousness* (AE 31:293–306).

God's people should respond to and display the righteousness he has imputed to them.

God's message of judgment against sin (of which Amos 1–2 is an example) is summarized by Stulman as Yahweh's "wrath of love," which he defines as "anger that grow[s] out of passionate affection for humanity and for Israel in particular."[104] Yahweh's judgments in Amos 1 and 2 are instrumental and proleptic, but not vindictive and universal. The judgments of fire are God's consequent will because of the sins of the peoples, but they are not his antecedent and ultimate will. Neither will he completely eradicate these nations, as shown by the survival of the remnants of Israel, Edom, and other nations in 9:11–12. God's intent is to destroy in order to recreate. Yahweh's judgment is penultimate; his ultimate goal is to show grace. This is realized in 9:11–15, where the fallen tabernacle of David is resurrected, Israel is reconstituted as the people of God incorporating the remnants of Edom and other nations who bear God's name, and the creation itself is rejuvenated.

[104] Stulman, *Jeremiah*, 21.

Amos 3:1–6:14

Declarations concerning Israel

3:1–8	Amos' Defense of His Ministry
3:9–15	Judgment against Samaria
4:1–5	Prophetic Satire
4:6–13	Plagues Produce No Repentance
Excursus	*Amos' Use of Earlier Biblical Texts*
5:1–3	Dirge over Fallen Israel
5:4–17	Seek Yahweh and Live!
Excursus	*The Church's Response to Ethical Issues*
5:18–20	The Day of Yahweh Is Darkness
5:21–27	Yahweh Hates Faithless Worship
Excursus	*The Prophets and Israel's Worship*
6:1–7	The First Will Be First into Exile
Excursus	*The Assyrian Empire*
6:8–14	Certain Destruction for the Prideful House of Israel

Amos 3:1–8

Amos' Defense of His Ministry

Translation

3 [1]Hear this word that Yahweh has spoken concerning you, O children of Israel, concerning the entire clan that I brought up from the land of Egypt, saying:

[2]"You alone have I chosen from all the clans of the earth.
Therefore I will visit upon you the punishment for all your iniquities."
[3]Do two walk together
if they have not met?
[4]Does a lion roar in the forest
if it does not have prey?
Does a young lion utter its voice from its lair
if it has not caught [prey]?
[5]Does a bird swoop down upon a trap on the ground
if it has no bait?
Does a trap spring up from the ground
if it has not surely caught [prey]?
[6]If the shofar is sounded in a city,
do the people not tremble?
If a disaster happens in a city,
did Yahweh not do [it]?
[7]Surely the Lord Yahweh does not do something
unless he reveals his counsel to his servants the prophets.
[8]A lion has roared;
who should not be terrified?
The Lord Yahweh has spoken;
who cannot prophesy?

Textual Notes

3:1 שִׁמְעוּ אֶת־הַדָּבָר הַזֶּה אֲשֶׁר דִּבֶּר יְהוָה עֲלֵיכֶם בְּנֵי יִשְׂרָאֵל—The plural imperative of שָׁמַע, "hear" (שִׁמְעוּ), that begins 3:1–8 recurs in 4:1 and 5:1 to begin chapters 4 and 5 (cf. 3:13; 8:4). The imperative serves as a macro syntactical marker that divides these chapters. It is also a literary marker that links them together. The verb שָׁמַע serves in a similar way in Micah 1:2; 3:1; 6:1.

The imperatival prophetic formula to "hear" word(s) spoken by Yahweh is rarer and more forcefully direct than the common messenger formula "thus says Yahweh" (see the first textual note on Amos 1:3). In Amos, only in 3:1, 8 is יהוה the subject of the verb דִּבֶּר.

The call to "hear" goes back to the creedal command of Moses, "hear, O Israel, Yahweh our God, Yahweh is one!" (שְׁמַע יִשְׂרָאֵל יְהוָה אֱלֹהֵינוּ יְהוָה ׀ אֶחָד, Deut 6:4; cf.

Deut 4:1; 5:1). The verb, therefore, connects Amos to Moses and the subsequent line of prophets like him (cf. Deut 18:15). As also in Is 1:2, 10; Jer 2:4; Hos 4:1, here too the imperative "hear" implies that Yahweh is entering into a covenant lawsuit with his people because they have renounced the creedal confession of Yahweh (Deut 6:4) by their idolatry.

"The children of Israel" (בְּנֵי יִשְׂרָאֵל) are called to listen to the prophetic message. According to Andersen and Freedman, in Amos when "Israel" is used with an adjacent term such as "my people," "the house of," or "the sons/children of" as here in 3:1, it probably refers to historic Israel, the twelve tribes, the united kingdom, the whole people (both north and south), or to the future ideal Israel.[1] In light of this and other such passages, for example, 1:2; 2:4–5; 6:1, it would be wrong to believe that Amos softened his critique of his native Southern Kingdom out of "patriotic prejudice." Both parts of the divided kingdom stand guilty before Yahweh.

עַל כָּל־הַמִּשְׁפָּחָה אֲשֶׁר הֶעֱלֵיתִי מֵאֶרֶץ מִצְרַיִם לֵאמֹר׃—This long prepositional phrase (excluding לֵאמֹר) is in apposition to the preceding prepositional phrase עֲלֵיכֶם בְּנֵי יִשְׂרָאֵל, "concerning you, O children of Israel," and it elaborates who the children of Israel are: the clan Yahweh redeemed from Egypt.

The closest English equivalent of מִשְׁפָּחָה is the originally Gaelic term "clan," meaning a group of individual families or households forming a major unit of the tribe and claiming common, unilinear descent from an ancestor. The noun מִשְׁפָּחָה is often used in quite unspecific ways for large social groups or nations (e.g., Gen 10:5, 32; 12:3) and even for species of animals (Gen 8:19). It can also be used for the Northern and Southern Kingdoms (Jer 33:24) and on one occasion for an individual tribe (Judg 13:2). In a more technical sense, a מִשְׁפָּחָה is the kinship unit between the tribe (שֵׁבֶט) and the ancestral household (בַּיִת or בֵּית אָב). However מִשְׁפָּחָה does not fit the general anthropological understanding of a clan, which does not usually involve residential commonality. The suggested translations "protective association of families"[2] and "subtribal unit"[3] are unwieldy although they convey the dimension of local cooperation involved in military protection.

This may be the only OT passage where the singular מִשְׁפָּחָה refers to "all Isr[ael]" (BDB, 1 f). Other passages use the plural to refer to "all the clans of the earth" (see BDB, 1 f, citing Gen 12:3; 28:14; Amos 3:2). The use of מִשְׁפָּחָה here for Israel demeans or demotes Israel from being a nation to merely being a clan within a nation. This is reinforced by 3:2, which refers to Yahweh electing Israel מִכֹּל מִשְׁפְּחוֹת הָאֲדָמָה, "from all the clans of the earth," which suggests that Israel was no different from other clans. The implication of these two verses is that all humanity is like a single nation comprised

---

1 Andersen and Freedman, *Amos*, 98–99, 102.

2 Gottwald, *The Tribes of Yahweh*, 257.

3 Andersen and Freedman write that the מִשְׁפָּחָה "is the largest subtribal unit, between tribe and family, and could be called a clan or phratry" (*Amos*, 380). See also Meyers, "The Family in Early Israel," 13. For an extensive study on מִשְׁפָּחָה, see Bendor, *The Social Structure of Ancient Israel*.

of the clans on earth (with Israel merely being one of those clans), and all are equally accountable to Yahweh (cf. 1:3–2:16; 9:7).

But how could Israel be *equal* to the other nations? One can almost hear the people's response to Amos: "You have made them equal to us!" (Mt 20:12). Yahweh affirms that he brought up Israel from Egypt, but later Yahweh will state that he brought up other peoples from other nations and caused their migrations (Amos 9:7).

3:2 רַק אֶתְכֶם יָדַעְתִּי מִכֹּל מִשְׁפְּחוֹת הָאֲדָמָה—Instead of the usual Hebrew syntax of verb, subject, and object, the object and adverb, רַק אֶתְכֶם, "only you," is placed first for emphasis, preceding the verb, יָדַעְתִּי, "I have chosen." *Israel's* election is the focus in the first part of this verse. Yahweh also chose (יָדַע) Jeremiah while still in his mother's womb (Jer 1:5) and appointed him as a prophet to the nations. Using similar words, St. Paul defends his apostolic vocation by asserting that God had "set [him] apart" before he was born and called him through grace (Gal 1:15).

The verb יָדַע can have a wide range of different nuances: "know, observe, realize, notice, find out, learn, recognize, perceive, care about, be acquainted with, have sex with, understand, have insight into, and even select or choose."[4] In Amos' context, יָדַע denotes a relationship between Yahweh and Israel (cf. BDB, 2; *HALOT*, 5 a) and means "to choose for a covenant partner."[5] It conveys the idea of a "covenantal commitment and not merely cognitive perception."[6]

"From all the clans of the earth" (מִכֹּל מִשְׁפְּחוֹת הָאֲדָמָה) is loosely connected to texts like Deut 10:15 but has its closest connection to Gen 12:3 and 28:14, where God issues the messianic promise to the patriarchs, וְנִבְרְכוּ בְךָ כֹּל מִשְׁפְּחֹת הָאֲדָמָה, "all the clans of the earth will be blessed through you"; Gen 28:14 adds וּבְזַרְעֶךָ, "and through your Seed." In Galatians 3 St. Paul interprets the patriarchal blessing promises as fulfilled in Christ, the Seed.

עַל־כֵּן אֶפְקֹד עֲלֵיכֶם אֵת כָּל־עֲוֺנֹתֵיכֶם׃—The phrase עַל־כֵּן, "therefore," is a compound preposition used adverbially (Waltke-O'Connor, § 11.3.2). It occurs only here in Amos. It is "reminiscent of the transition from evidence to verdict in covenant lawsuits."[7] The prophets commonly use לָכֵן, "therefore," to announce judgment, as does Amos in 3:11; 4:12; 5:11, 16; 6:7; 7:17.

---

4 Stuart, *Hosea–Jonah*, 322.

5 Cf. Huffmon, "The Treaty Background of Hebrew *Yādaʿ*." For other passages with similar meanings of יָדַע, see Gen 18:19; Ex 33:12, 17; Deut 9:24; 2 Sam 7:20; Jer 1:5; Dan 11:32. Paul understands the verb in Amos 3:2 to have a technical legal meaning: "to recognize as a legitimate suzerain or vassal and to recognize treaty stipulations as binding" (*Amos*, 102). Wolff also believes that in this context יָדַע designates election (*Joel and Amos*, 176).

6 Stuart, *Hosea–Jonah*, 321. Fretheim ("ידע," *NIDOTTE* 2:411–12) summarizes the meanings of יָדַע when used with Yahweh as its subject (one hundred twenty-three times out of the total of nine hundred forty-eight instances of יָדַע in the OT). They include (1) Yahweh's special relationship with people (e.g., Gen 18:19; Ex 33:12; Jer 1:5; Amos 3:2); (2) Yahweh's close familiarity with the lives of people (e.g., Jer 17:16; Pss 40:10 [ET 40:9]; 139:4); (3) Yahweh entering into Israel's experience (e.g., Ex 3:7; Deut 2:7) or the experience of individuals (Pss 31:8 [ET 31:7]; 142:4 [ET 142:3]); (4) Yahweh's knowledge that comes as a result of testing Israel (e.g., Deut 8:2; Judg 3:4) or individuals (e.g., Gen 22:12; Jer 12:3); (5) Yahweh's care and protection of his people (e.g., Ps 1:6; Hos 13:5).

7 Stuart, *Hosea–Jonah*, 321.

The varieties of translations for פָּקַד in the versions reflect that the verb, depending on its context, has an unusually broad semantic range that is difficult to pull together into one central definition.[8] The visitation of Yahweh may result in gracious promises and deliverance. When Yahweh visited (פָּקַד) Sarah, the result was the fulfillment of the promised son (Gen 21:1). He also visited the Israelites while they were captive in Egypt, and the result was their deliverance (Ex 4:31).

However, פָּקַד often refers to Yahweh punishing sinful actions by judging the offending people. Sometimes in such contexts, the verb has as its object a word for sin or iniquity, as here. God punishes the nation of Israel here in 3:2 and also in 3:14a, while he punishes apostate Israel's altars in Amos 3:14b. In the final analysis, what Yahweh's visitation or active presence delivers is dependent on whether he comes to bring grace or to punish sin. Amos 3 begins with פָּקַד in 3:2 and concludes with פָּקַד twice in 3:14, the only other Amos verse with the verb.

The LXX understood פָּקַד to denote punishment since here (and often elsewhere) it translates it with ἐκδικέω, "to judge, avenge, punish."

The noun עָוֹן occurs only here in Amos. It is related to terms for sin and guilt, as when parallel with חַטָּאת (Pss 32:5; 109:14).[9] עָוֹן can denote "iniquity" itself (BDB, 1) or, as here, the "consequence of, or punishment for, iniquity" (BDB, 3). Unabsolved guilt is punished by Yahweh (cf. Num 5:31). Often עָוֹן refers to iniquity as a concrete entity: it is present in the one who is guilty (1 Sam 20:8), it finds people (2 Ki 7:9), and it consumes them (Gen 19:15).[10]

The way Yahweh deals with עָוֹן can reflect either Law or Gospel. On the one hand, he is the one who serves as the catalyst for punishment (Ex 20:5), while on the other hand, he alone is capable of taking away iniquity and thus averting the punishment (2 Sam 24:10). Within worship contexts, עָוֹן occurs when a person defiles holy things, either intentionally or unintentionally (Lev 7:18; 17:16). Someone with עָוֹן may be put to death (Ex 28:43). The only solution for עָוֹן is atonement, which Yahweh delivers through sacrificial and priestly actions in the sanctuary (Ps 65:4 [ET 65:3]). He takes away עָוֹן by washing or wiping it away (Ps 51:4, 11 [ET 51:2, 9]). Simply being part of the ethnic people chosen by Yahweh does not guarantee a passport to forgiveness. According to Amos 3:2, when Yahweh visits Israel's עָוֹן he does so all the more severely *because* Israel is his chosen people.

3:3–6 The Hebrew questions in 3:3–6 are rhetorical and expect "no" for an answer. However, the last part of each question is phrased in the negative, with "not" or "no." For example, 3:6c–d asks:

---

8 Cf. G. André, "פָּקַד," *TDOT* 12:50–62. André proposes that the verb's basic meaning is "to determine the destiny" (*Determining the Destiny: PQD in the Old Testament*, 241). Watts writes: "It is the most meaningful word Hebrew possesses to define God's function in determining what will happen to a person or group in a given situation, whether they are under blessing or curse, or placed in battle or rescued from danger" (*Isaiah 1–33*, 326).

9 Cf. K. Koch, "עָוֹן," *TDOT* 10:546–62.

10 Wolff defines עָוֹן: "It focuses not so much on the attitude of deliberate malice as on the reality of the consequent act which issues in concrete results" (*Joel and Amos*, 177).

If a disaster happens in a city,
did Yahweh *not do* [it]?

The expected negative answer to each of the negatively phrased questions therefore functions rhetorically as an emphatic positive. For example, the implication of 3:6c–d is that if a disaster happens in a city, Yahweh *certainly did do* it.

The questions in 3:3–5 have the interrogative -הֲ at the beginning of the first clause. The interrogative -הֲ often is used for a rhetorical question expecting a negative answer (GKC, § 150 d). The second clause of each question in 3:3–5 has a negative particle (אֵין or לֹא) or the negative combination of particles בִּלְתִּי אִם־. (The constructions with בִּלְתִּי אִם־ in 3:3–4 and כִּי אִם־ in 3:7 can be called "exceptive clauses" [see GKC, § 163 c; Joüon, § 173 b; Waltke-O'Connor, § 38.6b; and the second textual note on 3:7].) These constructions in 3:3–5 mean that the first clause in each question does not happen unless the second clause has already happened. Therefore the second clause states a necessary condition for the first clause. The first clause states the resulting event, and the second clause gives the cause of the event.

The construction in each of the two questions in 3:6 is slightly different. The first clause of each question begins with אִם, which only rarely is used for direct questions, as here (Joüon, § 161 d), and the second clause includes the negative לֹא. The meaning of the construction in the second question of 3:6 is the same as that of the constructions in 3:3–5: the second clause is a necessary condition for the first clause. However, in the first question of 3:6, the first clause states a necessary and sufficient condition for the second clause: if the action described by the first clause happens, the action in the second clause is the inevitable result.

The purpose of all the questions in 3:3–6 is to bolster the assertions in 3:7–8.

3:3 הֲיֵלְכוּ שְׁנַיִם יַחְדָּו בִּלְתִּי אִם־נוֹעָדוּ׃—The verb נוֹעָדוּ is the Niphal of יָעַד, the most common stem of this verb. It can mean "meet at an appointed place and/or time." The plural verb is an example of a Niphal with a reciprocal meaning expressing mutual action (cf. Waltke-O'Connor, § 23.4e, including example 10). The "two" men (שְׁנַיִם) who "walk … together" (יֵלְכוּ … יַחְדָּו) must have met at some place and at some time before beginning their journey.

The LXX translated the second clause as ἐὰν μὴ γνωρίσωσιν ἑαυτούς, "unless they know each other," which implies that it read the Hebrew with a metathesis of נוֹעָדוּ as נוֹדְעוּ, the Niphal perfect of יָדַע.

3:4 הֲיִשְׁאַג אַרְיֵה בַּיַּעַר וְטֶרֶף אֵין לוֹ—The verbal expressions שָׁאַג, "to roar," and in 3:4c, נָתַן קוֹל, literally, "to give a voice," also appeared in parallel in 1:2; see the notes there. The verb שָׁאַג again with the noun אַרְיֵה as its subject will recur in 3:8. אַרְיֵה is the most common noun for "lion" in the OT. The roaring lion is commonly used figuratively for "a fearsome enemy which is eager for plunder."[11]

The noun יַעַר is a general word for "forest" and is not particularly limiting.[12] A forest may include thorns, thistles, underbrush, and thickets (Is 9:17 [ET 9:18]; 2 Sam

[11] G. J. Botterweck, "אֲרִי," *TDOT* 1:387, citing, for example, Is 5:29; Amos 3:4; Zeph 3:3.

[12] Cf. M. J. Mulder, "יַעַר," *TDOT* 6:208–17.

18:8–9). A יַעַר is usually a dangerous and sinister place, characterized by wild animals that live there (e.g., 2 Ki 2:24; Is 56:9; Ps 50:10).

הֲיִתֵּן כְּפִיר קוֹלוֹ מִמְּעֹנָתוֹ בִּלְתִּי אִם־לָכָד׃—The noun כְּפִיר is related to אַרְיֵה and denotes a "young lion" whose ravenous appetite for food motivates it to become skilled in catching prey (Ezek 19:3). מְעֹנָה can have either of two meanings: "hiding place" or "lair" (*HALOT*). Lions hunt from strategic hiding places; in Job 38:39–40 they crouch in their מְעוֹנוֹת, the plural of מְעֹנָה, and ambush their prey from a סֻכָּה. After making the kill, a lion may eat at the site or drag at least part of the prey back to its lair. Does this lion roar as it leaps from its hiding place and closes in on its prey (as in Judg 14:5), or does it roar after making the kill and while eating on the spot or after dragging the carcass back to its lair? Since the last part of the clause states that the lion has captured its prey, most likely מִמְּעֹנָתוֹ means "its lair."

The verb לָכַד (pausal: לָכָד) can have the literal meaning "to capture, catch" a wild animal as prey, as in Judg 15:4 and Amos 3:4–5.[13] Here and at end of 3:5, לָכַד is used absolutely, with no direct object, but English requires supplying an object: "caught [prey]." In other OT texts, לָכַד is used metaphorically, as when Yahweh captures nations or their warriors in judgment (e.g., Jer 48:44; 51:56). That usage may be relevant here since in Amos 3:8, the description of the lion will be applied metaphorically to Yahweh roaring through his prophet to judge the nation of Israel.

3:5 הֲתִפֹּל צִפּוֹר עַל־פַּח הָאָרֶץ וּמוֹקֵשׁ אֵין לָהּ—The noun צִפּוֹר, "bird," sometimes is construed as masculine, but here it is feminine since it is the subject of the feminine imperfect תִּפֹּל, "fall." The idiom נָפַל עַל, "fall upon," can mean to "attack" (BDB, s.v. נָפַל, Qal, 4 a). In this context, the bird "swoop[s] down upon" the trap's bait (מוֹקֵשׁ), intending to devour it.[14]

The phrase עַל־פַּח הָאָרֶץ, "upon a trap of the ground," can be rendered "a snare on the earth" (NRSV) or "a trap on the ground" (NIV). The parallel phrase in the second half of the verse is פַּח מִן־הָאֲדָמָה, where the "trap" springs up "from the ground." Therefore this פַּח must be a snare set on the ground, rather than a net suspended in the air or thrown. A פַּח is often used to trap birds (e.g., Ps 124:7; Prov 7:23). It can refer to a concealed noose, a net with cords (e.g., Ps 140:6 [ET 140:5]), or a pit for a person or an animal to fall into (e.g., Hos 9:8).

The noun מוֹקֵשׁ can refer to a "snare" (*HALOT*), a trap with a net or noose. Or it can refer more specifically to the "bait or lure in a fowler's net" (BDB), and that is its meaning here. A bird will not swoop down to a trap unless it has enticing bait.[15] מוֹקֵשׁ is sometimes parallel to פַּח (e.g., Pss 140:6 [ET 140:5]; 141:9). Often מוֹקֵשׁ has a figurative meaning. See further the commentary.

---

[13] Cf. H. Gross, "לָכַד," *TDOT* 8:1–4.

[14] Cf. Paul, *Amos*, 110.

[15] Paul, *Amos*, 111, cites 1 Sam 18:21: "Saul thought, 'I will give her [Michal] to him [David]; let her be the bait that lures him [לְמוֹקֵשׁ] to his death at the hands of the Philistines.' " Wolff, *Joel and Amos*, 180, 185, understands מוֹקֵשׁ to denote a "wooden missile" or some kind of throwing stick that causes the bird to fall to the ground, but that is not consistent with the first clause of 3:5.

הֲיַעֲלֶה־פַּח֙ מִן־הָ֣אֲדָמָ֔ה וְלָכ֖וֹד לֹ֥א יִלְכּֽוֹד׃—This is the counterpart to the preceding question: first the bird swoops down on the bait in the trap on the ground, and now the trap springs up from the ground to catch the bird. In form יַעֲלֶה could be either Qal or Hiphil, but in context it must be the intransitive Qal of עָלָה, "to arise, spring up." The bird triggers the snare, such as a stick bent under tension, and it now snaps up the noose or net hidden on the ground. The emphatic Qal infinitive absolute לָכוֹד preceding the negated imperfect of the same verb, לֹא יִלְכּוֹד, is reflected by saying that the trap "surely" has caught its prey. Such an infinitive absolute "is used to strengthen a question, and especially in impassioned or indignant questions" (GKC, § 113 q).

3:6 אִם־יִתָּקַ֤ע שׁוֹפָר֙ בְּעִ֔יר וְעָ֖ם לֹ֣א יֶחֱרָ֑דוּ—The שׁוֹפָר, "shofar," occurred in Amos in 2:2 as the offensive signal for attacking and defeating Moab. Here it is defensive, to warn the people of an approaching enemy, as also in Is 18:3 and Neh 4:12, 14 (ET 4:18, 20). It often is used with the active Qal (e.g., Hos 5:8) of תָּקַע, "to blow," or (as here) the passive Niphal of תָּקַע, to "be blown" (BDB, 1) or "is sounded."

The singular collective עָם, "people," is the subject of the plural Qal verb, יֶחֱרָדוּ "tremble, are terrified." This verb occurs only here in Amos. Elsewhere in the OT, it often describes the crippling fear that follows the arrival of terrifying news.[16] A common situation for such terror is war. Ezekiel describes the ensuing terror when Tyre will fall (Ezek 26:16–18). The appearance of an army strikes terror into the heart (e.g., 1 Sam 13:7; Is 10:29).

אִם־תִּהְיֶ֤ה רָעָה֙ בְּעִ֔יר וַיהוָ֖ה לֹ֥א עָשָֽׂה׃—The noun רָעָה occurs three hundred ten times in the OT. It frequently denotes theological, moral, or ethical "evil." However, here and often elsewhere it refers to calamity, disaster, or harm, which are perceived by sinful people as bad or evil even though they are allowed by God for his good purposes, especially to drive people to repentance. Therefore this verse can affirm that Yahweh is the subject of עָשָׂה, "do, perform," with רָעָה֙ as the implied object. As in the last clauses of 3:4 and 3:5 where לָכַד was used absolutely with no expressed object, here עָשָׂה is used absolutely, and the translation supplies the object "it," referring back to רָעָה֙ as its antecedent.

3:7 כִּ֣י לֹ֤א יַעֲשֶׂה֙ אֲדֹנָ֣י יְהוִ֔ה דָּבָ֑ר—Most translations take the conjunction כִּי as asseverative: "surely" (KJV, RSV, NIV, NASB; see BDB, 1 e). A few take it as causal, "for" (ESV), in which case it would be explicative (see BDB, 3 c), explaining the point of all the rhetorical questions in 3:3–6. The necessary conditions and cause-and-effect relationships described in 3:3–8 point to the cause-and-effect relationship between Yahweh roaring and the utterance of prophecy.

The noun דָּבָר can have a wide range of meanings. The verb עָשָׂה with דָּבָר as its object has the general meaning "do a thing," and דָּבָר has the broad meaning "something, anything" (BDB, s.v. דָּבָר, IV 6). The LXX rendered it πρᾶγμα, "event, affair, matter." Even though it refers to an action or event here, it may be linked to its common meaning, "word," by the verbal similarity between אֲדֹנָ֣י יְהוִ֔ה דָּבָ֑ר here and אֲדֹנָ֤י יְהוִה֙ דִּבֶּ֔ר in 3:8c. For אֲדֹנָי יְהוִה, see the fifth textual note and the commentary on 1:8.

[16] A. Baumann, "חָרַד," *TDOT* 5:167; cf. further Baumann, *TDOT* 5:166–70.

כִּי אִם־גָּלָה סוֹדוֹ אֶל־עֲבָדָיו הַנְּבִיאִים:—The combination כִּי אִם־, "unless," limits the preceding clause (BDB, s.v. כִּי אִם־, 2 a) by stating a necessary condition for it: Yahweh does not do something "unless he reveals his counsel to his servants the prophets." The grammarians describe this as an "exceptive clause" comparable to the exceptive clauses with בִּלְתִּי אִם־ in 3:3 and 3:4d (GKC, § 163 c; Joüon, § 173 b; Waltke-O'Connor, § 38.6b, including examples 1 and 3 and n. 31). The combination כִּי אִם־ often occurs after a negative statement such as לֹא יַעֲשֶׂה in 3:7a.

The Qal of גָּלָה can have the transitive meaning to "reveal" (BDB, 1), more commonly expressed by the Piel. Elsewhere in the OT, the combination גָּלָה (Qal) with the object סוֹד occurs only in Prov 20:19, and the Piel of גָּלָה is used with סוֹד only in Prov 11:13; 25:9. These Proverbs parallels attest to the connection between Amos 3:3–8 and Wisdom literature; see "Overview of Amos 3:3–8" below. Here גָּלָה takes the preposition אֶל (Joüon, § 133 b).

The object noun סוֹד appears only here in Amos but twenty-one times in the OT, always singular. It can denote either a "council" or the "counsel, plan" revealed in a council. The word suggests "a circle of trusted intimates who give their advice"[17] or a " 'circle' in which people consult with one another in a spirit of intimacy and trust."[18] סוֹד commonly appears in prophetic texts denoting Yahweh's council or counsel.[19] Yahweh's council includes angelic "holy ones" (Ps 89:8 [ET 89:7]). He graciously invites his prophets into his council to hear his Word so that they can preach it to the people, but false prophets do not have that privilege (Jer 23:18–22).

Yahweh's "servants" (the plural of עֶבֶד) include all who believe in and worship him (e.g., 2 Ki 10:23; Ps 134:1). All of Yahweh's people are "servants" (Lev 25:55), and Moses once wished that all of them would become prophets (Num 11:29). Here, after עֲבָדָיו the addition of הַנְּבִיאִים in apposition restricts the reference to faithful prophets. The description of Yahweh's prophets as his servants occurs elsewhere,[a] especially in Jeremiah.[20]

(a) E.g., 2 Ki 9:7; 17:23; 21:10; 24:2; Ezek 38:17; Zech 1:6

3:8 The construction in both 3:8a–b and 3:8c–d is the simple juxtaposition of a protasis and apodosis. The protasis expresses a condition that has been met (an event that has happened) and the apodosis expresses the consequence (GKC, § 159 b). The protasis has a perfect verb (שָׁאָג or דִּבֶּר), while the apodosis has the interrogative pronoun מִי as the subject of a negated imperfect (יִירָא or יִנָּבֵא). In both questions, the perfect expresses an action to be regarded as completed (GKC, § 159 h), hence the perfects are translated in English present perfect tense: "has roared … has spoken." The parallelism in 3:8 implies that the lion who has roared is Yahweh who has spoken, which results in Amos prophesying (3:8d). This is consistent with 1:2, where Yahweh roars, and the result is the content of the prophecy of Amos.

---

17 "סוֹד," *TWOT*, § 1471a, citing Pss 55:15 (ET 55:14); 83:4 (ET 83:3).

18 Wolff, *Joel and Amos*, 187.

19 Cf. H.-J. Fabry, "סוֹד," *TDOT* 10:171–76.

20 Jer 7:25; 25:4; 26:5; 29:19; 35:15; 44:4. See Young, *My Servants the Prophets.*

The imperfect יִירָא in 3:8a is translated modally in the (negated) English conditional mood, "who *should not* be terrified?" because the Israelites should have been struck with fear at Amos' preaching, but evidently most did not repent (see 4:6–11; 7:10–17). The imperfect יִנָּבֵא in 3:8b is translated with an English indicative, "who cannot prophesy?" because Amos did in fact respond to Yahweh's speaking by his prophetic ministry of preaching.

אַרְיֵה שָׁאָג מִי לֹא יִירָא—Amos repeats vocabulary from 3:4: a lion (the noun אַרְיֵה) roars (the verb שָׁאַג, here pausal: שָׁאָג). The verb שָׁאַג was also used for Yahweh roaring in 1:2.

The verb יָרֵא (here the Qal imperfect יִירָא), "be afraid," occurs only here in Amos and is a more common synonym of חָרַד in 3:6.

אֲדֹנָי יְהוִה דִּבֶּר מִי לֹא יִנָּבֵא׃—"The Lord Yahweh has spoken" recalls דִּבֶּר יְהוָה in 3:1, and the two clauses form an inclusio around 3:1–8 as a unit. These are the only two verses in Amos where God is the subject of the Piel verb דִּבֶּר.

For the Niphal of נָבָא, "to prophesy," see the second textual note and the commentary on 2:12.

Commentary

Amos' initial focus in his book envisions Yahweh as a lion who roars (1:2) and who is on the offensive against the pagan nations (1:3–2:3), against Judah (2:4–5), and climactically against Israel (2:6–16). In 3:1–6:14 the Lion continues to roar (see 3:4, 8, 12; cf. 5:19), pronouncing judgment upon Israel. Three collections of prophetic sayings begin with "hear this word" (3:1; 4:1; 5:1). First Yahweh reminds the Israelites of who they are (3:1–2); then he tells them who his prophet is (3:3–8). This is followed by judgment against northern Israel's capital city, Samaria (3:9–11), whose citizens revel in the perks of their "rich and famous" lifestyles (3:15; 6:1–6). The leaders busy themselves with religion (4:4–5; 5:21–23), "but they do not grieve over the ruin of Joseph" (6:6). Instead of repenting, they lead the nation further into apostasy and turn a blind eye toward the abuse of people on the fringes of their society. Samaria was a place of affluence and power but was indifferent toward the poor. This is why Yahweh has roared (1:2), and this is why he calls for justice and for righteousness (5:24).

The outline of chapter 3 is as follows:[21]

- 3:1–2: A summary of the Israel oracle of 2:6–16
- 3:3–8: Justification for Amos' prophetic ministry
- 3:9–11: Condemnation of Samaria, the political capital of the Northern Kingdom
- 3:12: Interlude about the future of the Northern Kingdom
- 3:13–15: The destiny of Bethel, the ecclesiastical counterpart of Samaria

---

[21] Cf. Andersen and Freedman, *Amos*, 369.

The oracles against the nations cover seven peoples in 1:3–2:3 and end with the announcement of an earth-shaking punishment upon northern Israel (2:6–16).[22] At least two questions arise from the first two chapters in the book. The first is "isn't Israel the nation elected by Yahweh?" The second is "who is this Amos anyway?" Amos 3:1–2 answers the first question, while 3:3–8 deals with the second.

Amos 3:1–2

3:1–2 These two verses are "a paradigm of his [Amos'] prophetic faith" and "a terse summary of the theological basis of his message."[23] They also function as a "minirecapitulation" of chapters 1 and 2.[24]

The biblical doctrine of election must not be abused by libertine antinomianism, the fallacy that the elect can sin with impunity and never fall from grace. The Lutheran Confessions state that the fault of such failure "does not lie in God or his election, but in their [the unbelievers'] own wickedness."[25]

Whereas Yahweh knows all of the nations (1:3–2:3; 9:7), he elected Israel and redeemed only this people from Egypt. They were the only people he chose to be in a covenant relationship with him (Deut 7:6). Amos 3:1–2 announces that Yahweh is the God who brought Israel up from Egypt (cf. Ex 20:2) and established an exclusive relationship with the nation. It is, however, on the grounds of this relationship that will he punish Israel. Privilege has its perils. The elect nation had Yahweh's covenant and promise, but this means that the Israelites are held to a higher standard than the pagan nations, and their transgressions against their redeeming God are all the more serious.

The relationship between Yahweh and Israel is expressed by strong I/you language: "concerning *you* ... *I* brought up ... *You* alone have *I* chosen ... *I* will visit upon *you*." These verses remind both Israel and Judah that they were placed into an interpersonal relationship. "The entire clan" (3:1) of both northern and southern Israel has been chosen and known by God; now both will be judged.

---

22 It would be a mistake, however, to think that the seven oracles leading up to the one against northern Israel were employed simply as a rhetorical device intended to put Israel off guard before delivering the final knockout punch. Yahweh's target is Israel, but he is also concerned with all peoples on earth. Yahweh "comes to judge the world. He will judge the inhabited world in righteousness and the peoples in his faithfulness" (Ps 96:13).

23 Mays, *Amos*, 56.

24 Paul, *Amos*, 100–1. He goes on to write: "Just as Israel climaxes the catalogue of oracles against the nations, here, too, they are singled out within the context of all the other 'families of the earth' " (p. 101). Andersen and Freedman, *Amos*, 32, write:

> This emphatic assertion, a condensation and crystallization of the essential elements concerning Israel (and Judah) in the Great Set Speech of chaps. 1–2, also serves as the heading and summary of what follows in the next two chapters and is thus a pivotal expression or bridge between the two sections, lying at the center of Part I—a nuclear expression of the whole message and its meaning and tenor.

25 FC Ep XI 12. For a thorough exposition of the biblical doctrine of election, see FC Ep and SD XI, "God's Eternal Foreknowledge and Election."

Amos' audience might have concluded at the end of 3:1 that the exodus was a sign of Yahweh's ongoing and eternal favor (cf., e.g., Num 24:8; Judg 6:13; 1 Ki 8:50–51), that the exodus forever guaranteed Israel's favored standing before Yahweh. In the next verse, however, Amos flatly contradicts this expectation.[26] The unusual use of "clan" as a title for all Israel indicates that Israel has been demoted. Israel is not called a "people" (עַם) or a "nation" (גּוֹי), but merely a "clan" (מִשְׁפָּחָה, 3:1), like "all the (other) clans of the earth" (3:2).

3:2 In light of the oracles against the nations in 1:3–2:16, the first half of this verse might seem odd. In the opening oracles of the book, Yahweh indicates that he knows what has been transpiring among all the nations. How then can Yahweh say, literally, "I have known" *only* Israel? In this context, the verb denotes his choice and election of Israel to stand in a unique, redemptive covenant relationship with himself.[27] Here to "know" involves more than God's omniscience. In doctrinal terms, the verb means "to foreknow" and "to elect to salvation." The same theology is expressed in Rom 8:29–30:

> For those whom God foreknew he also predestined to be conformed to the image of his Son. ... Those whom he predestined he also called, and those whom he called he also justified, and those whom he justified he also glorified.[28]

Israel's election was completely undeserved and came from Yahweh's grace alone (Deut 7:6–8; 9:4). The Israelites were attractive to God only because of his love for them; they were not loved because they were attractive.[29] Chosen and loved by Yahweh, Israel was called to be his missionary to the nations (Gen 12:1–3; Ex 19:5), as embodied by the Suffering Servant in Is 42:6; 49:6; 52:13–53:12.

Election to grace always originates and depends entirely on God himself and is rooted in his mercy and love (Deut 7:7–8; Jn 15:16). Those who are elected and called to faith by the power of the Holy Spirit are empowered to respond with faithfulness. Abraham was declared righteous (Gen 15:6), and through the Seed of this obedient believer, God's blessing would come to "all

---

[26] In Amos 3:1–2 the prophet begins with the exodus motif as salvation and ends in judgment. In like manner in 9:7–15, Amos begins with the theme of the exodus, only to turn it into an act of judgment which then ends in salvation.

[27] Amos' use of יָדַע in 3:2 is similar to the language of Hos 13:4–5: "Yet I have been Yahweh your God ever since the land of Egypt; you know [תֵּדָע] no God but me, and besides me there is no savior. It was I who knew [יְדַעְתִּיךָ] you in the wilderness." There are several points of comparison between Amos 3:1–2 and these verses in Hosea. First, the language of knowing is used to describe the relationship of Yahweh to Israel in both contexts, though in Hosea the act of knowing is reciprocal, not one-sided as in Amos. Divine first-person language is used in both texts. Explicit reference is made to the exodus tradition in Amos 3:1 as well as in Hos 13:4. In Hosea the language of knowing elaborates the intimate and saving relationship that Yahweh has with those addressed; in Amos this same vocabulary becomes the prelude to punishment.

[28] See further the doctrinal discussion of Amos 3:2 as well as Ps 1:6; Rom 11:2; Gal 4:9 and other passages in Pieper, *Christian Dogmatics*, 1:450 and 3:488.

[29] Cf. Luther, *Heidelberg Disputation*, § 28 (AE 31:41, 57–58).

the clans of the earth" (Gen 12:3; 22:18). Israel witnessed Yahweh's acts of salvation (Ex 19:4) and was called to be "a kingdom of priests" (Ex 19:6; cf. 1 Pet 2:6–9). The Messiah's disciples are grafted into the Vine (Jn 15:5) so they can bear fruit (Jn 15:16). And it is because the baptized have been called out of darkness that they declare God's wonderful praises (1 Pet 2:9).[b] Amos is but one voice in this grand chorus that proclaims Yahweh's electing grace that also empowers the elect to live for him. Like other biblical writers, Amos does not deny Israel's covenantal status, but suggests that the status carries with it added responsibility.

(b) Cf. Jn 15:15–16; 1 Thess 1:4–5; 2 Tim 2:10; Titus 1:1; 2:14; James 2:5; 2 Jn 1

Amos blends election ("chosen," 3:2) with the patriarchal blessing (כֹּל מִשְׁפְּחוֹת הָאֲדָמָה, "all the clans of the earth," occurs in the OT only in Gen 12:3; 28:14; and Amos 3:2). However, he uses these words ironically.[30] He does not state that it is because of Israel's sins that the nation is judged; it is rather because of Israel's *covenant status*. The irony consists of making election to blessing the basis for judgment.[31] Just as he does in 2:9–11, the prophet takes a Gospel tradition and places it within the context of a judgment oracle.

John the Baptist too cites God's election and patriarchal blessing promise, then denies that ethnic descent without faith avails: "And do not suppose that you can say to yourselves, 'We have Abraham as our father.' I tell you that out of these stones God can raise up children for Abraham" (Mt 3:9; see also Lk 3:8). The theological principle behind the words of Amos and John is articulated by Jesus: "From everyone to whom much has been given, much will be required; and from the one to whom they entrusted much, much more will be asked" (Lk 12:48). Peter indicates that judgment must "begin with the household of God" (1 Pet 4:17), while James writes that God has entrusted teachers in the church with special responsibility, and so they will be judged all the more strictly (James 3:1). Wolff summarizes it well: "He first calls to account those whom he has first called as his own."[32]

Amos employs a prominent biblical theme of the Sinaitic covenant: relationship, reminder, and response. It is first articulated with Abraham, where Yahweh initiates the relationship (Gen 12:1–3) and reminds the patriarch of his promises (e.g., Gen 15:7; 22:17–18). These gifts received in faith and imputed righteousness (Gen 15:6) in turn empower a response from Abraham, for example, his near-sacrifice of Isaac (Gen 22:1–14). The theme is echoed with variations in Ex 20:1–17. The prologue to the Ten Commandments is a declaration that Yahweh has created a saving relationship: "I am Yahweh your God, who brought you out of the land of Egypt, out of the house of slavery" (Ex 20:2). As Yahweh's

---

30 Andersen and Freedman claim the verse displays Amos' "characteristic vigor and irony" (*Amos*, 381).

31 Wolff writes: "Contrary to the normal procedure, therefore, it is not an infraction of the law which is the reason for punishment, but rather it is Yahweh's own saving act which establishes the ground for punishment" (*Joel and Amos*, 175).

32 Wolff, *Joel and Amos*, 172.

new creation from Egypt (Ex 19:5–6), the people now are in a position to begin, albeit imperfectly, to follow his will expressed in the Decalogue.

Following this same progression, Amos reiterates the Sinaitic covenant by calling Israel to affirm the relationship, remember Yahweh's grace, and respond with justice and righteousness. But now Israel has denied this threefold plan of Yahweh. The people boasted that because of election they were "the foremost of the nations" (Amos 6:1). Because of their "most favored nation" status, they believed that "the evil will not overtake nor confront us" (9:10).[33] The leaders were at ease in Zion and confident in Samaria (6:1) for they were sure that Yahweh was with them (5:14). Enjoying their economic success (4:1; 6:4–5; 8:5–6) and celebrating their victories on the battlefield (6:13), they were sure that "the Day of Yahweh" would be for them a day of light and not darkness (refuted by Amos in 5:18–20). They presumed that God would always be on their side.[34] The shocking surprise in 3:2 is this: *because* of their relationship with Yahweh, they will be punished all the more.[35]

This, however, was not a "bolt out of the blue." The Israelites never inherited God's grace simply because of their ethnic descent. Those who fell into unbelief and infidelity always forfeited God's blessings. For example, during the period of the judges the nation was caught in a cycle of sin, discipline, repentance, salvation, and then back to sin (e.g., Judg 2:10–23). Yahweh sent foreign raiders in order to punish his people and move them to repentance. Amos' audience must have excised the book of Judges from their collective memory; how else could they have embraced a theology that guaranteed blessing regardless of their behavior?[36]

One might conclude that northern Israel's imminent historical collapse in 722 BC occurred because of poor foreign policy, weak military preparation,

---

[33] Motyer writes: "The people to whom Amos spoke had devalued the doctrine of election into a non-moral doctrine of divine favouritism: Israel was God's 'pet,' surrounded by a divine imperial preference, protected, subsidized, the recipient of many unique allowances and special pleadings" (*The Message of Amos*, 50). He goes on to say: "Special privileges, special obligations; special grace, special holiness; special revelation, special scrutiny; special love, special responsiveness ... the church of God cannot ever escape the perils of its uniqueness" (p. 68; the ellipsis is his).

[34] Andersen and Freedman, *Amos*, 30, note:

> People would naturally react by saying that the idea [expressed in 3:1–2] was unthinkable and impossible because they were Yahweh's people and he was their God—while they were bound to him, he was also bound to them. ... They were tied together indissolubly in a mutual assistance pact. In drawing his conclusion Amos could not be more wrong; hence he could not be a prophet at all, and certainly not a true one.

[35] A surprise ending is employed by Amos also in 2:6–16; 3:3–8; 4:4–5; 9:11–15.

[36] This same self-delusion was rampant during the days of Jeremiah (e.g., Jer 2:35). Judahites were living in denial, believing that Yahweh would never punish the nation (e.g., Jer 6:13–15; 14:13–14). Jeremiah saw the people's misplaced trust in the temple as the chief basis for this delusion (Jer 7:4), because some thought it automatically protected the nation from destruction (Jer 7:1–14). James warns that to claim to believe in Christ while not producing any works is hypocrisy; that kind of faith is dead and possessed even by demons (James 2:14–19).

foolish government, or aggressive imperialism. Amos cuts through conventional perceptions and underneath the commonsense explanations to the real issues, which are covenantal and theological. Israel's elite ignored Yahweh's counsel (2:12), treated him as though he was second-rate (5:26), believed themselves above the Law (4:4; 7:10–11), and ignored their election status and responsibilities (2:6–11; 3:1–2).

Overview of Amos 3:3–8

In 3:1–2 Yahweh answered the first question that was posed by Israelites who objected to the oracle against Israel in 2:6–16: "Doesn't Israel have a favored-nation status that exempts it from judgment?" Now Yahweh proceeds to respond to the second objection raised by those who heard the oracle in 2:6–16: "Who is *Amos* to preach such a sermon? By whose authority does he say these things?" Amos 3:3–8 is the answer. Yahweh's prophet issues a series of rhetorical questions that use analogies from common experience in Israel's life. Amos was challenged by his contemporaries who were urging him not to prophesy (2:12; 7:10–17) so it was necessary to present the theological reason for his oracles.

Essentially the same challenge was put to Jesus, Israel's greatest Prophet, by his contemporaries who questioned his authority (e.g., Mt 21:23–27; Mk 6:1–3). Yet as the Son of Man, he has the authority to execute judgment (Jn 5:27). All authority in heaven and on earth has been entrusted to him, and his divine authority is the basis for those who baptize, teach, and minister in his stead (Mt 28:19–20; cf. Mk 6:7; Lk 9:1; 10:19; Rev 11:3). St. Paul found himself a situation similar to that of Amos and defended his apostolic authority for the purpose of strengthening faith in the Gospel he preached (2 Cor 11:16–12:13). Down to the present day, pastors have faced hostile challenges to their ministries, and the best response is to invoke the authority of the Lord who has called them into the office of the ministry. This is what Amos does in 3:3–8.

The genre of these verses has been called a "wisdom saying"[37] or a "didactic disputation."[38] Biblical Wisdom literature often uses the theology of creation, including animals and natural phenomena (the First Article of the Creed), to support the revealed theology of God's judgment and salvation (the Second Article of the Creed) and the implications for the people of God (the Third Article of the Creed). The series of sayings progresses toward the conclusion that Israel

---

[37] See Sweeney, *Isaiah 1–39*, 543, who defines the genre as "a short didactic saying, based on experience or tradition, that inculcates some value or lesson." It occurs most widely in sapiential writings (e.g., Job 6:5–6; 8:8–13, 38–39). The questions often move from insignificant observations to those that are much more ominous. Cf. also Terrien, "Amos and Wisdom." In *Amos the Prophet*, Wolff maintains that there is an extensive Wisdom influence in Amos. Both Terrien and Wolff catalogue similarities between Amos' rhetoric and the terminology and style of Wisdom literature, but this has been critiqued by Crenshaw, "The Influence of the Wise upon Amos."

[38] Wolff, *Joel and Amos*, 183.

is punished (3:9–15; cf. 2:14–16) because its people were chosen for salvation (3:1–2; cf. 2:9–11) but were unfaithful (3:9–15; cf. 2:6–8, 12–13).

The rhetorical questions in 3:3–6 find their answer in the assertions in 3:7–8. Each of Amos' questions involves a cause-and-effect relationship or a necessary precondition for the consequent action.[39] However, in 3:3–5, 6c–d, the effect or result is stated in the first clause, and the cause or necessary condition is given in the second clause. The heart of the passage is the assertions in 3:7–8, which provide the real answer to the rhetorical questions: Israel's unfaithfulness is the cause that has provoked Yahweh's consequent judgment, and Lion Yahweh's roaring judgment is the cause that necessitates Amos' preaching. The lion imagery from 3:4 and 1:2 is resumed in 3:8, which affirms that Yahweh's speaking is the cause and also the essence of Amos' prophesying. Yahweh's Word is the prophet's words, and the former compels the latter.[40]

Amos employs the genre of oracles against the nations in 1:3–2:5 to surprise his hearers in 2:6–16. Here he uses a Wisdom genre to shock an unsuspecting audience. Another literary similarity between chapters 1–2 and 3:3–8 is that in both sections, Amos uses the pattern of the graduated ascending number scheme of seven and then a climactic eighth. In chapters 1–2 there were seven oracles (against pagan nations and Judah) before the surprising final one against northern Israel, the main target. There are seven rhetorical questions in 3:3–6, and then the climactic ones come in 3:8. The eighth and ninth questions catch Amos' audience off guard because Amos often expresses himself in heptads.[41]

Amos' first question (3:3) is self-evident and pictures a harmonious relationship that is designed to gain a hearing with the audience.[42] The next six questions, in three related pairs, are about harm and danger. The lion seizes his prey in the first pair. The trapper is the one who seizes the prey (a bird) in the second pair. This trapper could represent Yahweh.[43] In the sixth question, the trouble (an attacking army) may have been allowed or sent by Yahweh, and in the seventh question, the trouble (disaster) unmistakably comes from Yahweh

---

[39] Paul, *Amos*, 104, says this about the rhetorical questions: "This didactic device, which is commonly assumed to be drawn from folk wisdom, is anchored in the premise that every event has its immediate cause, and every cause, in turn, leads to its own concomitant result."

[40] Other prophets express the same divine compulsion to preach using other imagery (e.g., Jer 20:9). The apostles too were compelled to preach (e.g., Acts 10:42; 19:21; Rom 1:15; 15:20; 1 Cor 9:16).

[41] Seven acts of rebellion ("because of three transgressions of ... and because of four") are cited for each of the seven nations in 1:3–2:5. Israel too is cited for seven transgressions (2:6–8). Amos 2:14–16 employs seven examples to depict the utter defeat of Israel. For other heptads in Amos, see 4:4–5; 4:6–11; 5:8–9; 5:21–23; 6:1–6; 9:1–4. Cf. Gordis, "The Heptad as an Element of Biblical and Rabbinic Style."

[42] Isaiah follows a similar rhetorical strategy in his Song of the Vineyard in Is 5:1–7. In Is 5:1 he begins with a love song, but by the end (Is 5:7), he surprises his listeners by indicating that *they* are the fruitless vineyard.

[43] So Andersen and Freedman, *Amos*, 33.

himself. Each question includes a negative and expects a negative answer, so the result is an emphatic positive: "Yes, that is obviously so!"

Except for 3:6a–b, the order in the questions is to present the effect first and the cause second. However, at the end of the sequence, the order is reversed in the two questions in 3:8 since they first name the cause and then the resulting effect second. "A lion has roared; who should not be terrified?" (3:8a–b). The normal response to a roaring lion is a racing heart, a stomach knotted with terror, and feet that are ready to run on adrenaline. One thought consumes a person's mind: "I am about to die!" Amos heard Lion Yahweh roar, and through Amos, he roared to Israel (1:2; 3:8; cf. 3:4, 12; 5:19). Yahweh spoke his Word, so Amos *had to* prophesy. He was compelled to speak because Yahweh first spoke to him. He could not do otherwise. Those who attempt to silence the prophet (2:12; 7:10–17) seek to silence Yahweh, but to no avail; he will be heard!

Amos 3:3–8

3:3 The first question asks whether two people would walk together if they had never met. The answer is "of course not"; people only walk together when they have met and agreed to do so. For example, when Abraham and his son Isaac climb up Mount Moriah, they walk together as planned. "The two of them walked together" (וַיֵּלְכוּ שְׁנֵיהֶם יַחְדָּו) in Gen 22:6, 8 is remarkably similar to "Do two walk together?" (הֲיֵלְכוּ שְׁנַיִם יַחְדָּו) in Amos 3:3.

3:4 A lion may roar right before, during, and/or after the kill.[44] The two questions in this verse point to two different growls in a lion's hunt.[45] The first is the lion's roar "in the forest" (בַּיַּעַר) after it has seen and stalked its prey and is closing in for the kill. This is the same kind of roar described in Is 5:29, where lions first roar and then seize their prey. The second is the cry of victory that the lion emits "from its lair" (מִמְּעֹנָתוֹ) after it has made the kill and dragged the prey back to its den. Compare Ps 22:14 (ET 22:13), where the lion roars as it tears its prey.

3:5 The two opposite verbal expressions with נָפַל עַל, "swoop down upon … the ground," and עָלָה מִן, "spring up from the ground," indicate the two stages in the capture of a bird. First it is lured down to the snare, and then the noose or net is released and snaps up the bird. The cause of the bird's capture is the מוֹקֵשׁ, the "bait" or "lure."

The snaring of the bird probably alludes to the apostasy of Israel. Proverbs can refer to a net or trap set for a bird as a metaphor for enticements that lure a person into sin and death (Prov 1:17–18; 7:21–23; 29:5). Some texts use מוֹקֵשׁ, "snare, bait, lure," to refer to the influence of pagans, including false worship and idolatry, which can ensnare God's people to their eternal destruction (e.g., Ex 23:33; Deut 7:16; Judg 2:3; 8:27; Ps 106:36). These OT texts can be compared to the NT use of σκάνδαλον, a "scandal, stumbling block" or cause of

---

[44] Andersen and Freedman, *Amos*, 395.

[45] Cf. Paul, *Amos*, 110.

spiritual downfall. It can be a sinful person, an enticement to sin, or false doctrine (e.g., Mt 13:41; 16:23; 18:7; Rom 16:17; Rev 2:14). Even though he is the Savior, Christ crucified is himself called a "stumbling block" since many take offense at him and refuse to believe in him, leading to their destruction, as happened to most of ethnic Israel (Rom 9:30–33; 11:9–11). See also 1 Cor 1:23; 1 Pet 2:8; and "the scandal [σκάνδαλον] of the cross" in Gal 5:11.

3:6 The questions in 3:3–5 involve a journey and events in the wild. In 3:6 the prophet changes his focus to events "in a city" (בְּעִיר twice). In 3:6a–b Amos also reverses the sequence in 3:3–5 by placing the cause before the effect. The sounding of the shofar causes the people to tremble. (These changes coincide with the introduction of interrogatory particle אִם twice in 3:6 versus -הֲ, used consistently in 3:3–5.)

When blown in the field, the shofar could be employed in any number of military maneuvers: attacking, defending, or retreating (e.g., Josh 6:5, 20; 1 Sam 13:3; 2 Sam 18:16). However, when the shofar is sounded in a city (e.g., Jer 6:1, 17; Hos 5:8), the blast warns the city residents of an advancing enemy; they must prepare to be attacked (Ezek 33:2–6). This is why the result is that the citizens are terrified (Amos 3:6). Here the attacker is Yahweh himself, and the city represents Israel. The unfaithful Israelites should prepare to receive divine judgment.

The NT uses the "trumpet" (σάλπιγξ) similarly as the signal to prepare for battle; it must be clear and distinct to get people's attention (1 Cor 14:8). In Revelation 8–9, the first six trumpets announce divine judgments that afflict the inhabitants of earth, especially unbelievers, whom God seeks to move to repentance, rather than kill (Rev 9:4–6). On the Last Day, the trumpet blast signals the end of the period of clemency toward unbelievers and their final, eternal judgment, but it also announces the day of resurrection to everlasting life for all in Christ (Mt 24:31; 1 Cor 15:52; 1 Thess 4:16; Rev 11:15–19).

Amos 3:6c–d reverts to the usual pattern: "if a disaster happens in a city" (the effect or result), "did Yahweh not do [it]?" (the cause). The answer to this question is not as self-evident as the answers to the other questions. Whenever disaster strikes, are all people to conclude that God has caused the calamity and that it is divine judgment for the sins of those who suffer?

Other Scripture passages address this issue from a different perspective. God allowed Satan to afflict righteous Job, and he gained a stronger and more profound faith (Job 42). Jesus interprets martyrdom and a deadly "accident" not as evidence that the victims were punished by God for being worse sinners, but as warning signs that should prompt all of us to repent of our own sins, lest we too perish (Lk 13:1–5). Ultimately the issue of suffering is resolved in the passion and vicarious atonement of Christ, whose bitter sufferings and death have procured for us the plenary forgiveness of sins and the promise of resurrection to life beyond all tears and pain (Rev 21:4). Furthermore, it is God the Son, the God-man, who carries out the judgment on behalf of God the Father, since the Son's own sufferings, death, and vindicating resurrection have earned him the right to judge the living and the dead (Jn 5:22–30; Acts 10:42; 17:31; 2 Tim 4:1). His verdict will be damnation for all unbelievers, but justification and acquittal of all believers.

Amos is addressing impenitent Israelites who have taken the position that no evil will ever befall *their* city. They think that their membership in ethnic Israel makes them immune from divine judgment. This smug and self-righteous attitude is evident in 6:1 and 9:10 and is implied in 5:14, 18. "Amos here, as elsewhere, demolishes these popular sentiments and time-honored beliefs and reaches completely opposite conclusions."[46] Amos is subtly suggesting that the unidentified city in 3:6 is the capital of northern Israel, Samaria. The oracles against the nations mentioned the cities of Damascus (1:3); Beth-eden (1:5); Gaza (1:6); Ashdod, Ashkelon, and Ekron (1:8); Tyre (1:9); Teman and Bozrah (1:12); Rabbah of the Ammonites (1:14); Kerioth (2:2); and Jerusalem (2:5). Here the prophet makes it clear that Yahweh is responsible for the punitive judgments that will befall *these* cities as well.

A related theological issue is the meaning of רָעָה, "evil, disaster" (3:6). The context of this verse indicates that it refers to divine judgment upon Israel in the form of a city-wide calamity, which could be inflicted by a conquering army (cf. 3:11–15) or an earthquake (cf. 1:1). The Lutheran dogmatician Gerhard affirms:

> God wills the *evil of punishment*, that is, the punishment for sin, in the order of justice. However, that is properly and of itself not evil, because it is the work of divine justice punishing sins, and thus it is opposed to evil.[47]

Gerhard then cites Amos 3:6 and clarifies that "God does not will the *evil of fault* [an evil committed by a person who thereby becomes culpable] … because that is opposed to His righteousness and goodness. Ps. 5 [5:5 (ET 5:4)]: 'You are not a God who wills iniquity.' "[48] God himself is holy, and his will is always righteous. He expresses his will in his Word and is always faithful to his Word (cf. 2 Tim 2:13). It was Satan who brought evil into the world by seducing Adam and Eve to rebel against God and his will expressed in his Word (Gen 3:1). Yet God continues to reign over the creation even though it has fallen into sin. He exercises his power over the world by means of his Word (cf. Ps 147:15–20; 2 Pet 3:5–7), which includes his accusing Law and his justifying Gospel.

Divine disaster is an expression of Yahweh's judging Law. The condemnation of sin is his *opus alienum*, his "alien work" that drives sinners to repent, while justifying sinners for Christ's sake is his *opus proprium*, his "proper work" performed in the person of Christ and by the Gospel of forgiving grace. Lutheran theology often connects God's alien work with his hiddenness and

---

46 Paul, *Amos*, 112.

47 Gerhard, "On the Nature of God," § 281 (*On the Nature of God and on the Most Holy Mystery of the Trinity*, 247).

48 Gerhard, "On the Nature of God," § 281 (*On the Nature of God and on the Most Holy Mystery of the Trinity*, 247).

emphasizes that God carries out his proper work through his revealed Gospel in his Word and Sacraments.[49]

God himself describes these two kinds of works through Isaiah:

> I am Yahweh, and there is no other.
> I form light and create darkness;
> I make peace [שָׁלוֹם] and create disaster [רָע].
> I, Yahweh, do all these things. (Is 45:6–7; cf. Is 28:21)

In reflecting upon Amos 3:6, John of Damascus understands that "evil" can refer to what is intrinsically evil, but it can also have a second, phenomenological meaning—what people perceive as injurious or harmful—and that God can use such "evil" for his salvific purposes:

> It is, then, customary for sacred Scripture to speak of his [God's] permission as an action and deed, but even when it goes so far as to say that God "creates evil" and that "there is not evil in a city which the Lord has not done," it still does not show God to be the author of evil. On the contrary, since the word *evil* is ambiguous it has two meanings, for it sometimes means what is by nature evil, being the opposite of virtue and against God's will, while at other times it means what is evil and painful in relation to our sensibility, which is to say, tribulation and distress. Now while these last seem to be evil, because they cause pain, actually they are good because to such as understand them they are a source of conversion and salvation. It is these last that Scripture says are permitted by God. Moreover, one must know that we too cause them because involuntary evils spring from voluntary ones."[50]

Kolb addresses evil from the standpoint of God's lordship:

> God's control over evil is so complete that he could even claim it for his own purposes. He claimed responsibility for light and darkness, for "weal" and "woe" or "prosperity" and "disaster" (Is. 45:7). He could say, "Against this family I am devising evil, from which you cannot remove your necks" (Micah 2:3 RSV). He causes blindness and deafness even as he gives sight and hearing (Ex. 4:11). Amos could console his hearers by explaining, "Does evil befall a city unless the Lord has done it?" (Amos 3:6). None of these passages offers an explanation for the origin of evil. None of these passages can be easily dismissed by saying that what we view as evil—for instance, blindness—may not really be evil from God's point of view. The message of these passages points to a deeper truth. God is lord over evil. God has the whole world in his hands. God masters and moves all human history. Without

---

[49] Luther discusses the differences between *Deus absconditus* and *Deus revelatus* in *The Bondage of the Will* (AE 33:138–40, 145–46). In *God Hidden and Revealed*, Dillenberger offers a thorough and valuable summary of various interpretations of Luther's *Deus absconditus*. Elert, *The Structure of Lutheranism*, 117–26, also discusses the *Deus absconditus* and its place in the doctrine of God. The phrase *Deus absconditus* comes from the Vulgate translation of Is 45:15. For discussions of the theme in the OT, see Balentine, *The Hidden God: The Hiding of the Face of God in the Old Testament*, and Saebo, "Yahweh as *Deus absconditus*: Some Remarks on a Dictum by Gerhard von Rad."

[50] John of Damascus, *Orthodox Faith*, 4.20, cited by Ferreiro, *The Twelve Prophets*, ACCS 14:92.

piercing the mystery of evil these passages affirm God's lordship over everything, even evil.[51]

Questions 6 and 7 in Amos 3:6 indicate that the prophet is moving in on his rhetorical goal. At the end of this verse "Yahweh" appears for the first time in 3:3–8. Amos has progressively zoomed in toward the target of this section: the city of Samaria. The seventh question in 3:3–6 gives a sense of finality to the series. It is startling, then, that Amos continues into 3:7–8.[52]

3:7 In 3:6 Amos declared that a city does not suffer judgment unless Yahweh has decreed it. Now in this verse, he indicates that Yahweh decrees it through a prophet. The prophet preaches to the city in order to confirm to its citizens that it was *Yahweh* who brought the calamity.

The reference to "his servants, the prophets" (3:7) links this statement to 2:11–12. Beginning with Moses, Yahweh had sent a number of prophets who were his mouthpieces (cf. Ex 4:14–16; 7:1; Deut 18:15–20). Amos stands in this long line of prophets. Yahweh reveals his counsel to him. God also enables him to correctly interpret current events (4:6–11), and he intercedes for Israel with God (7:1–6).

Like 3:6, this verse too must be interpreted in light of its immediate context. Yahweh is speaking about his judgment of northern Israel and its capital city, Samaria; it is this divine counsel that he has revealed to Amos. The verse should not be interpreted more broadly to mean that Yahweh always reveals to his prophets everything that he will do in the future. "It is not that Yahweh does nothing at all without telling the prophets; rather, he does nothing by way of covenant-lawsuit judgment without telling them."[53] Other OT passages confirm this. For example, Yahweh revealed to Noah his plan to destroy most of humanity (Gen 6:13–21) and to Abraham his plan to destroy Sodom and Gomorrah (Gen 18:17–21). The judgments of northern Israel and the southern kingdom of Judah were predicted through many prophets, and Yahweh even warned of judgment for various foreign nations (e.g., Amos 1:3–2:3; Isaiah 13–23; Ezekiel 25–32; Jonah 1:2; Obadiah; Nahum).

The prophets were Yahweh's closest confidants, his right-hand men. Amos was taken by Yahweh (7:15) into his council, and it was probably there that the prophet received his visions of chapters 7–9.[54] Amaziah labels him a "seer" (חֹזֶה, 7:12), presumably of visions he had seen in Yahweh's council. Having been in this council, Amos carries with him a transcendent authority that the apostate priestly and royal authorities could not nullify, try as they might (7:10–17). His message was not his word (contra 7:11), but Yahweh's Word. Furthermore, prophets could even be God's consultants. Yahweh consults with Amos in vary-

---

51 Kolb, *The Christian Faith: A Lutheran Exposition*, 75.

52 A surprise ending is employed by Amos also in 2:6–16; 3:1–2; 4:4–5; 9:11–15.

53 Niehaus, "Amos," 380.

54 So Andersen and Freedman, *Amos*, 399.

ing degrees throughout the five visions in chapters 7–9. Yahweh not only speaks his Word to Amos, he also listens and responds to the prophet's intercessions (7:2–3, 5–6).

By having access to Yahweh's council, the prophets could see (cf. "perceived, saw" in 1:1) what others could not. For example, when Israel's army in Dothan was surrounded by a Syrian army, Elisha saw that "those who are with us are more than those who are with them" (2 Ki 6:16). Elisha prayed that Yahweh would open the eyes of his apprentice, and the man saw that the surrounding mountains were filled with angelic chariots (2 Ki 6:17). In contrast, false prophets are excluded and rebuked: "If they had stood in my council [בְּסוֹדִי], they would have made my people hear my words, and they would have turned them from their evil way" (Jer 23:22).

Christ is the final Prophet who has provided the definitive revelation of the divine counsel, the redemptive plan of God that involves both judgment and salvation. Because of his atonement and reconciling work, we who have been baptized in the triune name (Mt 28:19) have gained access to the Father through the power of the Holy Spirit (Rom 5:2; Eph 2:18). Through the Word and in the Sacrament of Christ's body and blood, we are in communion with the triune God. In Christ, the divine mystery, long hidden from the human race, has been revealed to us (Rom 16:25; Eph 1:9; Col 2:2; 1 Tim 3:16), and we have confidence that when we draw near to God, we will receive from him mercy and grace (Heb 4:16; 10:19–22).

"To obtain such faith God instituted the office of the ministry" for the preaching of the Gospel and administration of the Sacraments (AC V). Pastors are called into the apostolic office to be "stewards of the mysteries of God" (1 Cor 4:1; see also Eph 3:1–10). Imitating Paul, they are not to shirk from proclaiming "the whole counsel of God" (Acts 20:27). The divine counsel is revealed in God's Word, which pastors are ordained to preach to God's people and to all. They announce that "the mystery of God, which he evangelized to his servants the prophets," will be fulfilled at the seventh trumpet, upon the return of Christ (Rev 10:7).

3:8 Throughout 3:3–7, Amos followed a well-designed and carefully structured argument.[55] An introductory question (3:3) led to the example from the animal world about a lion and its prey (3:4). Then 3:5 connected the animal world (a bird) with the human world (the fowler). Human enmity was the subject of 3:6a–b, then 3:6c–d connected human disaster with Yahweh. "The examples all depict the parties involved as being in situations in which they are ensnared or overpowered by some stronger force, be it animal, human, or divine."[56] In this way the textual unit moves to the certainty of no escape for the audience.

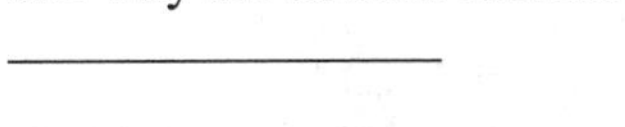

[55] Cf. Paul, *Amos*, 106.

[56] Paul, *Amos*, 106. Amos also employs this theme of entrapment in 5:18–20 and 9:1–4.

With this pattern of cause and effect established, 3:8 connects the last link: the causal relationship between Yahweh and his prophet. The cause-and-effect relationships in the earlier verses now vindicate Amos' vocation. Yahweh's roar has compelled Amos to prophesy; he cannot remain silent (cf. Is 62:1). Amos did not choose Yahweh; Yahweh chose him (cf. Jn 15:16). This means that the human attempts to silence him (Amos 2:12; 7:12–13) are in vain; in fact, they are a frontal attack against Yahweh himself (cf. Lk 10:16).

In a far greater way, Jesus was also compelled to carry out his ministry. In Luke's Gospel, his first declaration about his divine mandate comes in Lk 2:49: "Did you not know that I must [δεῖ] be in the things of my Father?" Nine more times in Luke the impersonal verb δεῖ marks the Savior's determination to fulfill his mission. For example, in Lk 9:22 Jesus says, "It is necessary [δεῖ] for the Son of Man to suffer many things and be rejected by the elders, chief priests, and scribes, and be killed, and on the third day be raised." In Lk 22:37 he states, "I tell you that this which stands written must [δεῖ] be fulfilled in me: 'And he was numbered with transgressors' [Is 53:12]."

Following the pattern of his Lord, St. Paul tells the church in Corinth, "Yet when I preach the Gospel, it is no boast for me for a necessity is laid on me. Woe to me if I do not preach the Gospel!" (1 Cor 9:16). A true prophet has no option but to speak, regardless of the consequences for himself or for anyone else.

Summary

The redemptive covenant relationship Yahweh established with Israel through the exodus is the presupposition of Amos' indictment in 3:1–2. Yahweh does not exhort Israel to act justly on the basis of any inherent goodness nor by human effort. Rather, righteous actions are to flow from faith in the Gospel promise Yahweh made in Eden (Gen 3:15) and elaborated to the patriarchs. The Israelites received a down payment toward the fulfillment of that promise when they inherited the promised land.

The principle at work in Amos' rhetorical questions in 3:3–8, namely, that events occur for a reason, connects Yahweh's election of Israel (3:1–2) with what will befall Israel (3:9–15). Such a connection is part of Yahweh's counsel and is embedded in his orders of creation and redemption. Yahweh is not capricious, and his actions are not random or whimsical.

In his judgment and wrath, Yahweh is an attacking lion. As in 1:2, Yahweh's roar compels Amos to preach (3:8).[57] When the prophet appears before the hostile priest Amaziah in 7:10–17, it is because he has been summoned by God (7:14–15). In this he is similar to the prophet Jeremiah, who could not contain Yahweh's fiery wrath and was compelled to preach it (Jer 6:11; 20:9). If God's

---

[57] Compare Acts 4, where the authorities prohibited the apostles from preaching, but they were compelled to speak (Acts 4:20). After a sermon that interpreted Psalm 2 as fulfilled in Christ, the Christians were filled with the Holy Spirit and spoke the Word of God with boldness (μετὰ παρρησίας, Acts 4:31).

judgment demands proclamation, how much more does his Gospel of salvation compel his ministers to preach! Paul states in Acts 20:24: "I do not account my life as of any value to myself if only I may finish my race and the ministry I received from the Lord Jesus: to testify to the Gospel of God's grace." Finishing the race while testifying to the Gospel is every the goal of every faithful pastor, and indeed of every Christian.

Amos 3:9–15

Judgment against Samaria

Translation

3 [9]Make known to the fortresses in Ashdod
and to the fortresses in the land of Egypt,
and say, "Gather yourselves upon the mountains of Samaria,
and see the great tumult in her
and the oppression in her midst."
[10]"They do not know how to do what is right," declares Yahweh,
"they who are treasuring up violence and destruction in their fortresses."
[11]Therefore, thus says the Lord Yahweh:
"An enemy—and surrounding the land.
He will strip from you your strength,
and your fortresses will be plundered."
[12]Thus says Yahweh:
"Just as a shepherd rescues from the mouth of a lion
two legs or a tip of an ear,
thus the children of Israel who are living in Samaria will be rescued
with only a corner of a bed or a foot of a couch."
[13]"Listen and testify against the house of Jacob,"
declares the Lord Yahweh, the God of armies.
[14]"Indeed, on the day when I punish the transgressions of Israel,
I will punish the altars of Bethel,
and the horns of the altar will be cut off,
and they will fall to the ground.
[15]And I will strike the winter house
along with the summer house.
The houses of ivory will perish,
and the great houses will come to an end,"
declares Yahweh.

Textual Notes

3:9 הַשְׁמִ֙יעוּ֙ עַל־אַרְמְנ֣וֹת בְּאַשְׁדּ֔וֹד וְעַֽל־אַרְמְנ֖וֹת בְּאֶ֣רֶץ מִצְרָ֑יִם—The Hiphil imperative of שָׁמַע, "to cause to hear, make known," governs both prepositional phrases with עַל. Here עַל probably means "make known *to*" since it can be used for that meaning, which is more often expressed with אֶל. It is also possible that עַל means "upon" with the idea that heralds will stand on top of the fortresses to proclaim the message to gather.

אַרְמוֹן recurs in 3:10–11 and refers to majestic homes like those inhabited by royalty. It is the same term for "fortress" used often in the oracles against the nations in 1:3–2:5. See the second textual note on 1:4.

Since Yahweh uses the plural imperative, he may be calling other prophets in addition to Amos to preach. Or the plural may be a literary device that addresses "hypothetical persons and is used for literary effect."[1] Compare the plural imperatives spoken by Yahweh in Is 40:1 (נַחֲמוּ נַחֲמוּ); 62:11; Hos 5:8.

The LXX translates בְּאַשְׁדּוֹד, "in Ashdod," as ἐν Ἀσσυρίοις, "in Assyria," apparently reading the Hebrew as בְּאַשּׁוּר. On the other hand, the Vulgate translates בְּאַשְׁדּוֹד as *Azoti*, "Ashdod." Perhaps the reason for the LXX translation is that Assyria and Egypt (the second, parallel country here) regularly occur in tandem (e.g., Is 7:18; 19:23–25; Hos 11:5, 11).

Ashdod is mentioned earlier in Amos 1:8, and so it is not surprising that the Philistine city is mentioned again here, its only other occurrence in the book. Paul argues that Assyria is nowhere mentioned in the book of Amos because most, if not all, of Amos' prophecies were completed before the Assyrian expansion to the west under the leadership of Tiglath-pileser III.[2] Andersen and Freedman argue for the LXX reading, "Assyria," since "Ashdod … is never used in parallel with Egypt elsewhere in the Bible."[3] They also maintain: "It is not sensible to threaten a nation with destruction [Ashdod in 1:8] and then invite it to be a witness or observer. If 'Egypt' is correct [in 3:9], and it must be, then Ashdod [in 3:9] is wrong, and something else is needed. The only reasonable possibility is Assyria."[4] However, Niehaus persuasively argues: "Since Assyria was not at this time a perennial enemy of Israel, Ashdod, which represents the Philistines, is thus an appropriate nation to address in this regard."[5] Moreover, "Ashdod" (אַשְׁדּוֹד) creates paronomasia with "destruction" (שֹׁד) in 3:10.

Normally a word in construct (אַרְמְנוֹת) is followed directly by the noun it governs, but twice here the preposition בְּ is attached to the following noun (בְּאַשְׁדּוֹד … בְּאֶרֶץ). This is uncommon (GKC, § 130 a), but it occurs occasionally elsewhere, for example, הָרֵי בַגִּלְבֹּעַ, "the mountains of/in Gilboa" (2 Sam 1:21) and כְּשִׂמְחַת בַּקָּצִיר, "like rejoicing of/in the harvest" (Is 9:2 [ET 9:3]).

וְאִמְרוּ הֵאָסְפוּ עַל־הָרֵי שֹׁמְרוֹן וּרְאוּ מְהוּמֹת רַבּוֹת בְּתוֹכָהּ—Samaria (שֹׁמְרוֹן) became the capital city of the Northern Kingdom during the reign of Omri (885–874 BC;[6] see 1 Ki 16:23–24).[7] It was the third capital of the Northern Kingdom, after Shechem (1 Ki 12:1, 25) and Tirzah (e.g., 1 Ki 15:33; 16:6, 8, 23–24). Omri bought the land and built a city, which was about forty-two miles north of Jerusalem. Samaria was located on a

---

1 Niehaus, "Amos," 383.

2 Paul, *Amos*, 116.

3 Andersen and Freedman, *Amos*, 374.

4 Andersen and Freedman, *Amos*, 406.

5 Niehaus, "Amos," 383.

6 Thiele, *The Mysterious Numbers of the Hebrew Kings*, 88.

7 Cf. King, *Amos, Hosea, Micah*, 36; see also N. Avigad, "Samaria (City)," *NEAEHL* 4:1300–10; J. D. Purvis, "Samaria (City)," *ABD* 5:914–21.

hill about three hundred feet above a valley and "was readily defensible, well located along major trade routes, and within a fertile region cultivated with olive orchards and vineyards."[8]

The noun מְהוּמָה is used in the plural (מְהוּמֹת) only twice in the OT, in Amos 3:9 and 2 Chr 15:5. In both instances, it is modified by the plural adjective רַבּוֹת ("many"). The plural is intensive (GKC, § 124 e), hence "great tumult," indicating confusion, panic, tumult, and chaos when Yahweh enacts his judgment in the context of holy war. The phrase indicates that Yahweh is already carrying out his holy war in Samaria due to the city's perversion of justice and righteousness (Amos 5:7, 24; 6:12). Related texts with the singular מְהוּמָה are, for example, Deut 7:23; 1 Sam 5:9; 14:20; Zech 14:13. Amos passages that use other vocabulary for Yahweh's holy war include 2:14–16; 5:18–20; 9:1–4.

וַעֲשׁוּקִים בְּקִרְבָּהּ׃—The noun עֲשׁוּקִים is an abstract plural meaning "oppression, exploitation," that occurs elsewhere only in Job 35:9 and Eccl 4:1. It is derived from the verb עָשַׁק, "oppress," which occurs in Amos 4:1. Lev 19:13 prohibits Israelites from oppressing (עָשַׁק) or robbing their neighbor.

3:10 וְלֹא־יָדְעוּ עֲשׂוֹת־נְכֹחָה נְאֻם־יְהוָה—The implied subject of the negated plural verb וְלֹא־יָדְעוּ is the residents of Samaria, rather than the Philistines or Egyptians, although 3:9 simply referred to the feminine singular city "Samaria," שֹׁמְרוֹן. As an adjective, נָכֹחַ means "straight, right." נְכֹחָה is an example of the feminine form of an adjective used as an abstract noun (Joüon, § 134 n). The context in Amos 3:10 concerns "what is right" morally, ethically, and theologically. For נְאֻם־יְהוָה, see the second textual note on 2:11.

הָאוֹצְרִים חָמָס וָשֹׁד בְּאַרְמְנוֹתֵיהֶם׃—The implied antecedent of the Qal plural participle with article הָאוֹצְרִים is the residents of "Samaria" (3:9). Normally אָצַר means "to store up, treasure up" valuable food or precious commodities, so it is being used ironically here with the direct objects חָמָס וָשֹׁד.

The noun חָמָס, "violence," recurs in Amos only in 6:3. It encompasses a broad range of violent and abusive activities. Just like blood (Is 1:15), "violence" can stain someone's hands (Job 16:17). חָמָס "connotes violence done to people, including even the violence of false witness (Exod. 23:1; Deut. 19:16), as well as attempted physical harm (2 Sam. 22:3, 49) and bloodshed (Judg. 9:24 …)."[9] In his holiness and righteousness, Yahweh cannot ignore the חָמָס of Israel; he must punish the perpetrators (Ezek 12:19; Zeph 1:12).

The second direct object noun, שֹׁד, often refers to the "destruction" of personal property. Examples of parallel words include שֶׁבֶר, "breaking, breach, crash" (e.g., Is 59:7; Jer 48:3), and כָּזָב, "lie, falsehood" (Hos 12:2 [ET 12:1]). In Amos 5:9, שֹׁד refers to the destruction of a country through war. When חָמָס and שֹׁד are paired (Jer 6:7; 20:8;

---

8 King, *Amos, Hosea, Micah*, 36.

9 Niehaus "Amos," 384.

Ezek 45:9; Hab 1:3), they represent "the lawlessness and corruption of the society"[10] and could simply be rendered as "murder and robbery."[11]

3:11 לָכֵ֗ן כֹּ֤ה אָמַר֙ אֲדֹנָ֣י יְהֹוִ֔ה—Prophetic judgment oracles commonly enumerate sins and then use the conjunction לָכֵן, "therefore," to introduce the sentence of judgment for those sins. Amos uses לָכֵן again in 4:12; 5:11, 13, 16; 6:7; 7:17.

צַ֖ר וּסְבִ֣יב הָאָ֑רֶץ—The noun צַר has been interpreted in different ways. BDB lists four homographs: צַר I, "narrow," and צַר II, "distress" (from צרר I); צַר III, "adversary, foe" (from צרר II); and צַר IV, "hard pebble, flint" (from צרר III). It is probably best to understand it here as the third word, meaning "foe, enemy," as in, for example, Gen 14:20; Num 10:9; Josh 5:13; Is 9:10 (ET 9:11).

The syntax is, literally, "an enemy, and around the land." Some follow the Vulgate's *circumietur*, "be encompassed," and emend וּסְבִיב to יְסוֹבֵב, the Poel imperfect of סָבַב, meaning "[the enemy] will surround." Then the gist of 3:9–10 would be this: "Just as the witnesses 'gathered' around to bear testimony, so shall the enemy—but this time in order to attack!"[12] Howevere, there is no need to emend the text. The *waw* is best understood as explanatory (GKC, § 154 a, n. 1 b): the word describes the enemy as "surrounding the land."

וְהוֹרִ֤ד מִמֵּךְ֙ עֻזֵּ֔ךְ וְנָבֹ֖זּוּ אַרְמְנוֹתָֽיִךְ׃—The Hiphil of יָרַד usually means "bring down," but it can mean "to take/strip off" jewelry (Ex 33:5). The noun עֹז means "strength" or "might." Metaphorically it can refer to God as the believer's "strength" (Pss 28:7–8; 46:2 [ET 46:1]).

The verb בָּזַז is a close synonym of שָׁלַל; the words are parallel in Is 10:6; Ezek 26:12; 29:19; 38:12–13; 39:10. Both mean "to plunder, take spoils of war."[13] וְנָבֹזּוּ is the Niphal perfect with *waw* consecutive (GKC, § 67 t; Joüon, § 82 m). בָּזַז appears almost exclusively in the context of war and conquest, and typically it is a city that gets plundered. All sorts of items may be taken as plunder, especially animals like cattle and sheep (e.g., Num 31:32–34; Deut 2:35), but also food made from grain (2 Ki 7:16) as well as people (Gen 34:29; Num 31:9). As a mode of divine judgment, the plundering of a city or nation is prominent in prophetic texts. Yahweh judges by using Assyria (Is 10:5–6) and Babylon (Jer 20:5) to plunder the national treasures and the population of Israel and Judah. But what goes around comes around: the nations who plunder Israel will also be plundered (Ezek 39:10).

3:12 כֹּה֮ אָמַ֣ר יְהוָה֒—This is the same prophetic messenger formula first used in 1:3; see the first textual note on 1:3.

כַּאֲשֶׁר֩ יַצִּ֨יל הָרֹעֶ֜ה מִפִּ֣י הָאֲרִ֗י ... כֵּ֤ן יִנָּצְלוּ֙—The verse is a comparison between two acts of salvaging. The comparison uses the conjunction כַּאֲשֶׁר, "just as," and the adverb כֵּן, "thus, so also." Both actions are expressed by the verb נָצַל, first the Hiphil (יַצִּיל) and

[10] Paul, *Amos*, 117.

[11] Wolff, *Joel and Amos*, 194.

[12] Paul, *Amos*, 118.

[13] Cf. H. Ringgren, "בזז," *TDOT* 2:66–68.

then the Niphal (יִנָּצְלוּ). Most often נָצַל appears in the Hiphil stem, usually with Yahweh as its subject, meaning "to save, rescue" someone from something.[14] A person may be saved from death (Ps 56:14 [ET 56:13]), danger (Ex 2:19), slavery (Ex 6:6), enemies (1 Sam 30:8), or from every fear (Ps 34:5 [ET 34:4]). However, the act of saving described in Amos 3:12 is ironic. Although the lamb is rescued, it is only delivered in parts, not whole and alive, so this is a death sentence and not a blessing of salvation. The shepherd "rescues" only a few worthless pieces from a carcass that has been devoured and destroyed. Similar is the implication of 4:11c, which is the only other Amos passage with נָצַל, "save, snatch."

The Hebrew definite article can be used with a noun referring to an indefinite, undefined person or thing (BDB, s.v. הַ, 1 d; GKC, § 126 q–r), and so הָרֹעֶה means "*a* shepherd, *any* shepherd." The same kind of article occurs on הָאֲרִי, "a lion," both here and in 5:19. The same employment of the article in an indefinite way occurs also on other words in 5:19; see the first textual note on 5:19.

שְׁתֵּי כְרָעַיִם אוֹ בְדַל־אֹזֶן—The noun כֶּרַע always refers to the "leg" of an animal (e.g., Ex 12:9; 29:17; Lev 1:9, 13; 4:11) and always occurs in the dual (here: כְרָעַיִם) since animal legs occur in pairs. The numeral שְׁתֵּי emphasizes that only "two of" the animal's four legs are rescued (GKC, § 88 f). The other remnant Amos mentions is part of an "ear" (אֹזֶן). The word in construct with it (בְדַל־) appears only here in the OT. Probably בָּדָל means "severed piece" (BDB), and so the construct phrase can be rendered as "tip of the ear."[15] These body parts are opposite extremities,[16] but none of the vital organs in between will be saved.

כֵּן יִנָּצְלוּ בְּנֵי יִשְׂרָאֵל הַיֹּשְׁבִים בְּשֹׁמְרוֹן—The article on the participle הַיֹּשְׁבִים functions as a relative pronoun. The modifying clause הַיֹּשְׁבִים בְּשֹׁמְרוֹן narrows down the focus to those Israelites "who are living in Samaria."

בִּפְאַת מִטָּה וּבִדְמֶשֶׁק עָרֶשׂ׃—The Israelites who will be rescued will not be able to keep their possessions. Instead, they will emerge from the destruction only "with" (בְּ) parts of two items, denoted by two construct phrases: פְּאַת מִטָּה and דְּמֶשֶׁק עָרֶשׂ. The governed noun in each phrase, מִטָּה and עֶרֶשׂ, are synonyms for a "bed" or "couch." Both recur in Amos only in 6:4. The governing nouns, פֵּאָה and דְּמֶשֶׁק in construct, denote specific parts of the bed. פֵּאָה generally refers to the corner or side of something, such as the corner of a table (Ex 25:26), a field (Lev 19:9), a face (Lev 13:41), or, as here, a bed.[17]

Much more difficult to understand is the noun דְּמֶשֶׁק.[18] Some emend it to דַּמֶּשֶׂק, "Damascus,"[19] which is in 1:3, 5; 5:27, but that does not fit the context here. Because its derivation is unknown, the best solution is to understand it as having a meaning

---

[14] Cf. F. L. Hossfeld and B. Kalthoff, "נצל," *TDOT* 9:533–40.

[15] Paul, *Amos*, 119.

[16] Cf. Paul, *Amos*, 119.

[17] An Assyrian bas relief depicts the Assyrian king Ashurbanipal reclining on his bed (*ANEP*, § 451).

[18] For a discussion, see Paul, *Amos*, 121–22.

[19] E.g., NIV and Hayes, *Amos, the Eighth-Century Prophet*, 134–35. The emendation requires three changes in pointing: adding a *patach* and *daghesh forte* and changing *shin* to *sin*.

similar to its preceding parallel word, פֵּאָה, "corner." It must refer to another extremity of a bed. Paul writes:

> In the light of the first half of the verse, in which the prophet uses the imagery from bottom (legs) to top (ear) to create an anatomical merism, it stands to reason that here, too, he names chiastically the two opposite sides of the bed, from top to bottom: פֵּאָה ("front/head") and דְמֶשֶׁק, which in the present context would then represent the "rear/foot" of the bed. Only the meager polar opposites will be saved; all the rest will be destroyed.[20]

3:13 שִׁמְעוּ וְהָעִידוּ בְּבֵית יַעֲקֹב—The final section of verses (3:13–15) begins with the Qal imperative שִׁמְעוּ, "hear," which inaugurates new sections also in 3:1; 4:1; and 5:1. Its Hiphil imperative, הַשְׁמִיעוּ, begins a section in 3:9. The second imperative, וְהָעִידוּ, is the Hiphil of the verb עוּד, which occurs only here in Amos. The Hiphil of עוּד can express two related meanings.[21] First and more specifically, in a juridical context it describes the activity of testifying for the sake of identifying and condemning a guilty party (1 Ki 21:10, 13). It may also include the calling of witnesses in order to testify (Is 8:2). The witnesses summoned, however, need not be people, since Yahweh may call heaven and earth as witnesses (Deut 4:26; 30:19; 31:28; cf. Is 1:2). In Amos 3:13, עוּד has a juridical sense accenting the prophet's use of a covenant lawsuit (cf., e.g., Deut 8:19; Mal 2:14; Ps 50:7), which Amos alludes to in 7:4 with the verb רִיב. Second and more generally, the Hiphil of עוּד can denote making an authoritative statement: "warn" (1 Sam 8:9), "forbid" (Ex 19:21), "admonish" (Neh 9:29), "threaten" (Deut 8:19), or "reproach" (Neh 13:15).

Here the Hiphil of עוּד takes the preposition בְּ on בְּבֵית to introduce the party whom the witness is to testify "against." The same idiom is in, for example, Deut 4:26, where Moses calls the heavens and the earth to testify against Israel:

> הַעִידֹתִי בָכֶם הַיּוֹם אֶת־הַשָּׁמַיִם וְאֶת־הָאָרֶץ
>
> I call as witnesses against you today the heavens and the earth.

The construct phrase בֵּית יַעֲקֹב recurs in Amos 9:8. It goes back to Gen 46:27, where it refers to the living patriarch and his extended family. Yahweh uses it for all Israel in Ex 19:3. It is often used in prophetic literature (e.g., Is 2:5; Jer 2:4; Micah 2:7).

נְאֻם־אֲדֹנָי יְהוִה אֱלֹהֵי הַצְּבָאוֹת׃—For נְאֻם, see the second textual note on 2:11. Divine titles that include יהוה אֱלֹהֵי (הַ)צְּבָאוֹת, "Yahweh, the God of (the) armies/hosts," recur in 4:13; 5:14–16, 27; 6:8, 14. But in the OT, those titles are less common than the shorter יְהוָה צְבָאוֹת, "Yahweh of armies," which is contained in the divine title in 9:5. The shorter form may involve an ellipsis so that יְהוָה צְבָאוֹת means "Yahweh, (the God) of armies" (see GKC, § 125 h). The titles refer to Yahweh's command over his armies. Those armies include the hosts of angels in heaven, who war against both spiritual and

[20] Paul, *Amos*, 122.

[21] Cf. H. Simian-Yofre and H. Ringgren, "עוּד," *TDOT* 10:495–516.

earthly powers of evil (e.g., Josh 5:14; 2 Ki 6:17), and also the earthly armies of God's saints, the church militant (Is 13:4).[22] Andersen and Freedman write:

> The name "Yahweh of hosts" has associations with earlier warfare in the period of conquest and consolidation that culminated in David's triumph. It involved the participation of heavenly troops, and its revival suits the theme of cosmic warfare in the prophets.[23]

3:14 כִּי בְּיוֹם פָּקְדִי פִשְׁעֵי־יִשְׂרָאֵל עָלָיו—Literally, the syntax is "indeed, on the day when I punish the transgressions of Israel upon it [Israel]." With the disjunctive accent, כִּי is not the causal conjunction but is asseverative: "indeed." בְּיוֹם with the infinitive construct פָּקְדִי forms a temporal clause: "on the day *when* I punish." For the "day" of Yahweh's punishment, see further the commentary. For פָּקַד, "visit (sins) upon [עַל], punish," see the second textual note on 3:2. The construction פָּקַד עַל recurs in the next line of 3:14. פֶּשַׁע is the same noun for "transgression" used in the oracles against the nations in 1:3–2:16. See the second textual note on 1:3.

וּפָקַדְתִּי עַל־מִזְבְּחוֹת בֵּית־אֵל וְנִגְדְּעוּ קַרְנוֹת הַמִּזְבֵּחַ וְנָפְלוּ לָאָרֶץ׃—The construction פָּקַד עַל, "visit (sins) upon, punish," was used with guilty people in 3:2, 14a, but here the inanimate "altars of Bethel" (מִזְבְּחוֹת בֵּית־אֵל) are punished. Here the noun מִזְבֵּחַ first appears in the plural (construct: מִזְבְּחוֹת) and then in the singular. The plural suggests that the false cult at Bethel had multiple altars, while the singular suggests that there was one chief altar that was horned. Probably the chief altar was used for animal sacrifice, while some of the lesser altars could have been for incense. In 2:8 Yahweh referred to multiple altars in Israel ("every altar") that were sites of immorality as part of pagan worship. Amos employs the definite singular הַמִּזְבֵּחַ again in 9:1, where most likely it again refers to the main altar at Bethel in apostate northern Israel. When this prophecy was finally fulfilled by Josiah, he destroyed the main altar and the Asherah as well as other shrines (2 Ki 23:15–19).

The noun מִזְבֵּחַ is derived from the verb זָבַח, "to sacrifice," and it denotes a "sacrificial site."[24] Altars for worshiping other gods are often critiqued by prophets (e.g., Jer 11:13; Hos 8:11; 10:1). In Ezek 6:4–6, 13, Yahweh predicts the destruction of altars as part of the end of idol worship.

The noun קֶרֶן may refer to animal horns, either literally or symbolically.[25] Horns may symbolize power (Deut 33:17) or peril (Ps 22:22 [ET 22:21]). Animal horns could be used as instruments (Josh 6:5) or flasks for anointing oil (1 Sam 16:1, 13). In religious usage, ancient altars commonly had horns on each of their four corners, as did Yahweh's sacrificial altar (Ex 27:2) and presumably also his incense altar, although the number of its horns and their location is not specified (Ex 30:2). The blood of sacrificed animals was smeared on the horns of Yahweh's incense altar (Ex 30:10; Lev 4:7, 18) and the horns of his sacrificial altar (e.g., Lev 4:25, 30, 34). A wanted man might

---

22 For the roles of Christ and holy angels in the spiritual warfare that affects God's saints on earth, see Steinmann, *Daniel*, 481, 502–6, 559–60.

23 Andersen and Freedman, *Micah*, 409–10.

24 Cf. C. Dohmen, "מִזְבֵּחַ," *TDOT* 8:209–25.

25 Cf. B. Kedar-Kopfstein, "קֶרֶן," *TDOT* 13:167–74.

seek sanctuary by grasping the horns of the sacrificial altar (1 Ki 1:50–51; 2:28). When the horns of an altar were cut off, it was desecrated and useless.

3:15 וְהִכֵּיתִי בֵית־הַחֹרֶף עַל־בֵּית הַקָּיִץ—The verb נָכָה, "to strike (down)," denotes the killing or injuring of people and appears primarily in the Hiphil stem.[26] Its basic meaning is "the use of physical force against others, resulting in infringement on their personal existence."[27] It is used in connection with Yahweh's judgments (e.g., Ex 3:20; Num 32:4; Ezek 32:15; Pss 135:8, 10; 136:10, 17). In prophetic texts, God may strike by means of military attacks (Is 10:24), angelic messengers (Ezek 9:5–8), or pestilence in various forms (Jer 21:6; cf. "sword, famine, wild beasts, and pestilence" in Ezek 14:21 with the Hiphil of כָּרַת). Amos employs the Hiphil of נָכָה again in 4:9; 6:11; and 9:1.

Literally, "the house of winter" (בֵּית־הַחֹרֶף) refers to a winter residence, while "the house of summer" (בֵּית הַקָּיִץ) refers to a summer residence that would be in a relatively cooler location. The preposition עַל is used in the sense of "in addition to, along with."

וְאָבְדוּ בָּתֵּי הַשֵּׁן—The noun שֵׁן usually means "tooth," but it can also refer to a tusk and ivory. In the ancient Near East, the principal sources of commercial ivory were African and Asian elephants.[28] The description of the houses in Samaria as "the houses of ivory" (בָּתֵּי הַשֵּׁן) does not mean that the buildings themselves were constructed out of ivory. Rather, the phrase is an example of synecdoche with a part standing for the whole (*pars pro toto*). King explains that it refers to "domiciles adorned with sumptuous ivory paneling and to furniture decorated with elaborate ivory inlays." King also notes as another example of synecdoche "the house of the forest of Lebanon," a part of Solomon's palace so named because of its extensive use of cedar imported from Lebanon (1 Ki 7:2–5).[29] King goes on to say that the most ivory uncovered by archaeologists was in Megiddo and in Samaria. In Samaria over five hundred ivory fragments were found dating to the ninth or, more likely, the eighth century BC. Thus some scholars call the reign of Jeroboam ben Joash "the ivory age."[30] 1 Ki 22:39 refers to a house built by King Ahab (874–853 BC)[31] as "the house of ivory" (בֵּית הַשֵּׁן).

וְסָפוּ בָּתִּים רַבִּים—The Qal perfect verb סָפוּ may be from the hollow verb סוּף, "to come to an end, cease," whose Qal occurs three other times in the OT (Is 66:17; Ps 73:19; Esth 9:28). Or it could be from the third-*he* verb סָפָה, whose Qal usually has a transitive meaning, "to sweep away, destroy." However, its Qal may have an intransitive meaning, "be swept away," in Jer 12:4 unless the form there is from סוּף. As a parallel to the intransitive verb וְאָבְדוּ in the preceding line, either סוּף or סָפָה with an intransitive meaning makes sense in this context, but סוּף is a closer semantic parallel.

---

26 Cf. J. Conrad, "נכה," *TDOT* 9:415–23.

27 Conrad, *TDOT* 9:417.

28 King, "The *Marzeaḥ* Amos Denounces," 37. The disappearance of elephants in the ancient Near East occurred in part because of the killing of elephants for ivory (p. 39).

29 King, *Amos, Hosea, Micah*, 139.

30 King, *Amos, Hosea, Micah*, 142–43.

31 Thiele, *The Mysterious Numbers of the Hebrew Kings*, 94.

The adjectival phrase בָּתִּים רַבִּים is best understood as "great houses" rather than "many houses." It refers to the mansions of Samaria's upper class. The same idea is conveyed by means of the parallelism in Is 5:9: "Great houses [בָּתִּים רַבִּים] shall become a desolation; large and good ones [גְּדֹלִים וְטוֹבִים] will have no inhabitant."

נְאֻם־יְהוָה:—See the second textual note on 2:11. The most important significance of "declares Yahweh" is that it establishes that the prophet's words are Yahweh's words, so the prophet's faithful ministry has more authority than any other authority, including the king or a priest (cf. 7:10–17).

Commentary

Amos 3:9–11 states themes that 3:12–4:13 addresses in more detail. A few examples will suffice. In 3:9 the nation is described as having "oppression [וַעֲשׁוּקִים] in her midst," while in 4:1 the prophet lambastes women who are "oppressing" (הָעֹשְׁקוֹת) the poor. Israel's excess is typified by her majestic residences called "fortresses" (3:10–11), and 3:15 mentions winter and summer homes along with homes of ivory. Israel's lack of repentance detailed throughout 4:6–11 demonstrates that "they do not know how to do what is right" (3:10). The entirety of 3:9–4:5 is directed against the royal ruling class of citizens living in Samaria.

Wolff labels the genre of 3:9–15 an "instruction to heralds," a "genre whose life-setting was the occasion when emissaries were commissioned."[32] Ashdod and Egypt are called as witnesses against Israel in this judicial image. The summons is a rhetorical device since the chapter never reports what these peoples do or say, or even if they heard the summons.[33]

For the elite of Israel, who call themselves the first among the nations (6:1), to be judged by the likes of the pagan Philistines in Ashdod and the Egyptians strikes at the heart of indignity. Ashdod has already been singled out as one of the chief sinners (1:6–8). Likewise Egypt, the country that had enslaved Israel before the exodus, represented the dregs of society.[34] The implication is that Israel, whom Yahweh redeemed from Egypt and claimed as his own (3:1–2), is a greater sinner than those two nations. That same implication is also the message of 1:3–2:16. Earlier Yahweh had reminded Israel of her election to grace (2:9–11; 3:1–2), but Israel's sins in response, as well as Yahweh's consequent judgment, form the basis for this section.

3:9 This verse begins a new oracle with the Hiphil imperative of שָׁמַע, "to make known." The plural verbs here, "make known … and say" (הַשְׁמִיעוּ … וְאִמְרוּ), may indicate that Yahweh commanded not only Amos to

---

32 Wolff, *Joel and Amos*, 191. Is 40:1–11 is structured in a similar way as the imperative verbs are addresses to heralds to announce comfort and the advent of God.

33 Smith, *Amos*, 163.

34 Motyer writes: "Those who had no special revelation and who had never experienced special redemption can rise up and judge the social misdemeanors of those who were uniquely privileged towards God but seemed to think nothing of despising, abusing and oppressing their fellow members of the family of grace" (*The Message of Amos*, 83).

summon witnesses to see Israel's sins, but also that other (unknown) prophets were to join in the proclamation to call the witnesses. In 2:11 Yahweh had declared, "And I raised up *prophets* [לִנְבִיאִים] from among your sons."[35] The plurality of heralds, and the two regions they summon as witnesses (Ashdod and Egypt), may indicate an observance of Israel's Torah, which stipulated that at least two witnesses must be summoned to bear testimony to acts of injustice (Deut 17:6; 19:15; cf. 1 Ki 21:10). These prophets are—in a rhetorical manner—to make Samaria's sin known to Ashdod and Egypt. The tables have turned. The pagan nations in 1:3–2:3 were judged for their crimes. Now two of Israel's archrivals—heathen Ashdod and Egypt—are called on to testify against Israel!

Although geographically Samaria sat on top of a single hill (1 Ki 16:24), and although the singular הַר, "mountain," appears in Amos 4:1 and 6:1, so many witnesses from Ashdod and Egypt are summoned in 3:9 that they will need several of the surrounding mountains to accommodate the crowd. The mountains around Samaria are higher than the hill upon which the city stood, so they provide the best vantage point from which the witnesses could peer down into Samaria.[36] As they look on, they witness massive turmoil as well as ongoing social and economic oppression.

3:10 The Israelites "do not know how to do what is right," a veiled expression indicating that their theology was perverse, as were also their ethics. They had acquired their goods by means of extortion. This is affirmed by the next line: "they who are storing/treasuring up violence and destruction in their fortresses."[37]

Storehouses have been unearthed in Megiddo in northern Israel and Beersheba in southern Judah.[38] Agricultural products were placed in them and later sold in the marketplace (cf. 8:4–6). Amos may have agricultural storehouses in mind, as well as repositories for gold, silver, and other valuable commodities. The people who were treasuring up goods by means of violence were ignoring the prayer of Prov 30:8–9: "Remove vanity and false word(s)

---

[35] Andersen and Freedman understand the first two of the four plural imperatives in this verse to be addressing heavenly messengers (*Amos*, 374–75).

[36] Paul, *Amos*, 116. Wolff lists the elevations of the surrounding mountains, but thinks too literalistically when he claims that since they are four or more kilometers (close to three miles) from Samaria, "they are too distant to provide a vantage point from which to observe the oppression of people in the city" (*Joel and Amos*, 190).

[37] According to Andersen and Freedman, *Amos*, 404, the participles הָאוֹצְרִים, "who are treasuring up" (3:10), and הַיֹּשְׁבִים, "who are living" (3:12), may imply that Yahweh declares "woe" to these people. Andersen and Freedman (*Amos*, 462) maintain that the "woe" followed by a participle in 5:18 signals that all of the other participles directed against Israel imply a "woe" before them, beginning with the first participle in the book, which was in 2:7 (see the first textual note on 2:7), and continuing through 9:10. There are nineteen such participles that describe the ongoing actions of Israel's oppressive upper class. These "participial people" (my phrase) are described in the most oppressive and arrogant of terms.

[38] Silver, *Prophets and Markets*, 37.

far from me. Give me neither poverty nor riches, but feed me the food I need. Otherwise, I may be full and deny (you) and say, 'Who is Yahweh?' " See also Jesus' words about treasure in Mt 6:21; 12:35; 19:21; the condemnation in James 5:3; and St. Paul's counsel in 1 Tim 6:6–19.

The rapacious activity Amos denounces reflects how Canaanite culture had corrupted Israel. The Canaanites were involved in merchant trade, and "Canaanite" can mean "people who practice sharp, exploitive economics and politics."[39] The trade of Phoenician artisans is evidenced, for example, in the well-known ivories (cf. "the houses of ivory" in 3:15) from palaces at Samaria and Nimrud, where ivory decorative panels of Phoenician style have been found in profusion.[40] Hos 12:9 (ET 12:8) condemns Ephraim (northern Israel) for having been brought down by the Canaanite spirit of whoredom and mercantilism. The Canaanite religious, economic, and religious impact on northern Israel was tremendous during the reign of Jeroboam ben Joash, when Amos ministered (see 1:1). They wanted to have Yahweh as their God but also the economic program fostered by Baal. But "no one can serve two masters" (Mt 6:24), let alone the true God as well as a false god.

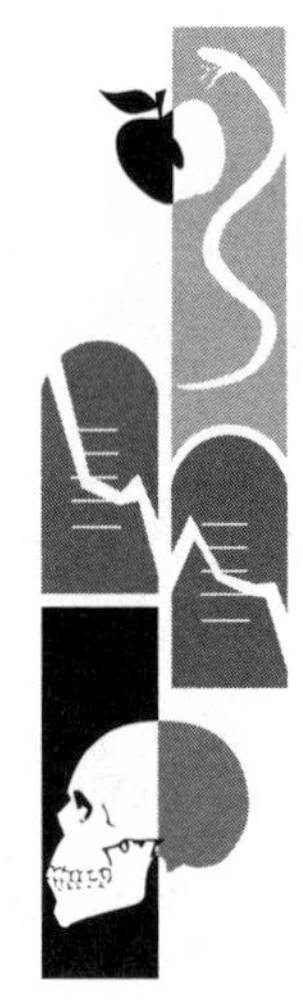

Amos' oracles only address the spiritual side of Canaanite fertility worship in passing (e.g., 2:7; 6:7; 8:14), but it was the religious apostasy of Israel's leaders that fueled the harsh treatment of the poor. The two are different sides of the same coin. Whoring after other gods brought with it brutal socioeconomic policies. The big banks in Samaria were buying up land, displacing people, and creating a poverty class. By storing up violence and robbery, the elite conformed themselves to a Canaanite worldview of getting and grabbing—a worldview prevalent in societies today. This "treasuring up" (Amos 3:10) was in contrast to what Jesus says, "Do not store up for yourselves treasures on earth" (see Mt 6:19–21).

The wealthy officials in Samaria were placing their treasures (and thus their hearts) in their high-end homes and storehouses, which together are called "fortresses" (אַרְמְנוֹת, 3:10–11). The "fortresses" of pagan cities and nations come under attack in each of Amos' oracles against the heathen nations in 1:3–2:3 (see 1:4, 7, 10, 12, 14; 2:2). Throughout the book, "fortresses" are residences of royalty, government officials, and the wealthy. By using the same term for the "fortresses" in Israel as those in the pagan nations, Yahweh implies that those in his own land built from ill-gotten wealth (and that were also used to protect such wealth) were no better than those built by the ungodly.

Archaeological excavations indicate that the palace of Ahab, who reigned in Israel after the death of his father, Omri (874–853 BC), was part of a larger

---

39 Brueggemann, *Like Fire in the Bones*, 202. See, for example, Is 23:8.

40 See Mazar, *Archaeology of the Land of the Bible*, 503–5. For discussions of ancient Near Eastern trade, see Stieglitz, "Long-Distance Seafaring in the Ancient Near East," and Bikai, "The Phoenicians: Rich and Glorious Traders of the Levant." On the ivories, see further the commentary on 3:15.

complex of buildings.[41] The majority of the ivories unearthed in Samaria have been identified with "the house of ivory" erected by Ahab (1 Ki 22:39).[42] Most of the ivories were ornamental furniture decorations.[43] Amos condemns the lavishness of ivory furnishings in 3:15 and 6:4.

Jaruzelska surmises:

> Since the palaces mentioned in the Book of Amos were decorated with ivory, and since similar embellishments have been uncovered in the Samaria acropolis, we are allowed to think that those condemned by Amos in the discussed passage [3:9–11] may have dwelt close to the king's court, thus being indeed royal functionaries.[44]

Also among the archaeological finds of Samaria are sixty-three ostraca. Jaruzelska cites the suggestion of Lémaire that the names of the addressees on some of these ostraca refer to royal officials who had been granted fiefs by the king of northern Israel (cf. 1 Sam 8:14). She also notes the opinion of Aharoni that these royal officials of Samaria owned not only fiefs but private, inherited land as well. On the basis of those opinions, she concludes that those who dwelt in the "fortresses" mentioned in Amos 3:10–11 "could be identified with great landowners. Furthermore, the gains dishonestly acquired by them would derive from an accumulation of land involving the dispossession of small tenants"[45] (cf. Is 5:8).

In addition to the Israelite royal officials implicitly condemned throughout 3:9–15, Yahweh through Amos will also condemn northern Israel's judges (5:10–17), its monarchy (7:9, 11), a leading representative of its false clergy (7:10–17), and its merchants (8:4–14). These five groups constitute the leaders who do not grieve over "the ruin of Joseph" (6:6), the wretched state of Israel's poor, oppressed, and theologically misled people. These groups are also prime examples of "all the sinners of my people" (9:10) for whom there is no hope or future apart from repentance and faith in the promised Son of David (9:11).

3:11 Amos arrives at the first of his seven uses of "therefore" (לָכֵן) to introduce judgment.[46] The murderers will not get away with murder! Amos does not specify who the "enemy" (צַר) is, while in 6:14 he only mentions a "nation." By refusing to be more specific, the prophet points to the fact that ultimately Yahweh is the executioner of judgment (cf. 9:4). Yahweh has at his disposal fire (1:4–2:5; 5:6; 7:4); lions, bears, and snakes (5:19–20; 9:3 [cf. 1:2; 3:4, 8,

---

41 Jaruzelska, "Social Structure in the Kingdom of Israel in the Eighth Century B.C. as Reflected in the Book of Amos," 98, citing Mazar, *Archaeology of the Land of the Bible*, 503.

42 Mazar, *Archaeology of the Land of the Bible*, 503.

43 Mazar, *Archaeology of the Land of the Bible*, 505.

44 Jaruzelska, "Social Structure in the Kingdom of Israel in the Eighth Century B.C. as Reflected in the Book of Amos," 98.

45 Jaruzelska, "Social Structure in the Kingdom of Israel in the Eighth Century B.C. as Reflected in the Book of Amos," 99–100 (see also p. 116, nn. 54–55), citing Lemaire, *Inscriptions hébraïques*, 1:76, and Aharoni, *The Samaria Ostraca* (in Hebrew), 281.

46 See the first textual note on 3:11.

12]); the sword (7:9); and earthquakes (1:1; 3:15; 4:11; 8:8; 9:1, 5). By using these impersonal terms, the historical agent of destruction remains anonymous throughout the book of Amos. Since Amos preached his oracles before Assyria rose to be the dominant world power, he does not indicate which nation would be "the rod of [Yahweh's] anger" (Is 10:5). Isaiah, who preached later in the eighth century and into the seventh, did name Assyria (e.g., Is 7:17–20).

"He will strip from you your strength" (Amos 3:11) echoes the covenantal curse in Deut 28:52. "Your fortresses will be plundered" expresses Samaria's punishment as poetic justice. The "fortresses" where Samaria's officials stored their plunder and loot (Amos 3:10) will be the site of their judgment ("fortresses" in 3:11; cf. Rev 2:22, where a bed is the place of punishment for an adulteress). The other punishments articulated in Amos 3:11 are also fulfillments of Torah curses pronounced on Israel in advance for when she would break the covenant: enemy occupation of the land (see Deut 28:47–57) and loss of possessions (see Deut 28:31).[47]

3:12 Although this verse begins with the common prophetic messenger formula "thus says Yahweh," the formula does not signal a break in the unit. The focus is still on "the children of Israel who are living in Samaria" (3:12). Yahweh invokes the image of an attacking lion, which is implicit also in 1:2; 3:4, 8; 5:19, and which Amos may well have witnessed during his own pastoral experience (cf. 1:1; 7:14–15). The message has legal overtones.[48] Ex 22:12 (ET 22:13) states that a man who is caring for another man's animal is acquitted of responsibility for the loss of the animal (and does not have to repay the owner) if he brings the torn remains to its owner as evidence that a wild animal is to blame. (Jacob in Gen 31:39 says that as a shepherd he did not make use of this right.) Just like the witnesses in Amos 3:9, this legal testimony is also based on visual evidence.[49]

Amos the shepherd-prophet will be innocent of the blood of the unrepentant Israelites because he preached Yahweh's Word to them. He warned them about the coming wrath of Lion Yahweh (1:2; 3:8; cf. 3:4, 12; 5:19), but most ignored his sermons. Therefore Amos carried out his prophetic and pastoral office faithfully and is absolved of responsibility for the guilt of those he called to repentance. See also Ezek 3:17–21; 33:1–20; Mt 10:14–15.

Yahweh sometimes enabled his saints to perform a miraculous rescue. David rescued sheep from both lions and bears (1 Sam 17:34–37). On a snowy day, Benaiah went down into a pit and killed a lion (2 Sam 23:20), which was a menace to sheep. However, most sheep did not experience such a miracle.

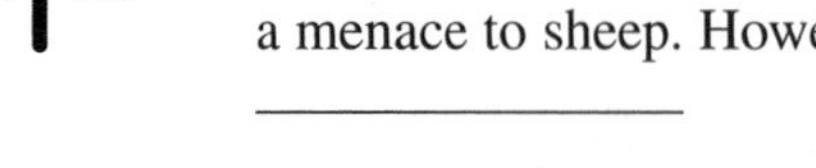

[47] Cf. Stuart, *Hosea–Jonah*, 331.

[48] As noted by Paul, *Amos*, 119.

[49] Andersen and Freedman write: "The purpose of rescuing a bit or two of the animal is for identification and to provide proof to the owner that the shepherd was not negligent, and that the animal from the flock was actually eaten and not merely a stray (or indeed taken by the shepherd for his own purposes)" (*Amos*, 373).

That will include the impenitent sheep of Israel, whose "rescue" is described as really no rescue at all. Severed body parts, "two legs" and "a tip of an ear" (Amos 3:12), will be all that is left of them when they are "rescued" from Lion Yahweh (1:2; 3:8; cf. 3:4, 12). This is one of the most commonly recognized examples of irony in Amos.[50] Death is death, no matter what leftover body parts remain. The leftovers are nothing other than the proof of a total loss. Yahweh is not employing a pastoral image innocently, but is ironically evoking a "rescue" that spells doom for Israel.

When the term "Israel" in Amos is modified by, for example, "the house of," "the sons/children of," or "my people," it probably indicates the entire twelve-tribe nation (e.g., 3:1). However, in 3:12 "the children of Israel" is restricted by the following relative clause "who are living in Samaria." Here, therefore, the reference is especially to the Northern Kingdom, particularly to the residents of its capital city and especially the royal officials.[51]

Beds in the ancient Near East were luxury furniture. They were typically associated with the well-to-do. Amos 6:4 describes wealthy people as reclining comfortably on beds of ivory. Yahweh's reference to the parts of a bed should be understood in light of the previous description of a slain lamb's remnants. Only a few small pieces of the bed will be saved. Destruction is destruction, no matter what leftover parts remain. "The scraps of furniture somehow resemble the bits of the animal, suggesting that all that will be salvaged will be a few miserable and useless pieces."[52] This action will fulfill Yahweh's covenant curse of death and destruction on unbelieving Israel (e.g., Lev 26:21–22; Deut 4:26; 28:20).

Other prophets often speak of the salvation of a faithful remnant of Israel (e.g., Is 10:20–22; 11:11; Jer 23:3) and even of a saved remnant from Gentile nations (e.g., Is 17:3; 19:18–25; Ezek 16:53). However, Amos 3:12 does not promise a living remnant. In 5:3, 15 and 9:11, God promises that a remnant of Israel will be saved, and he issues a corresponding promise for the Gentile nations in 9:12.

If the only remaining parts of their earthly existence are pieces of beds and couches, what kind of people are they? Do they have any of the Holy Scriptures? Why are there no pieces of the Torah, which the priests were to keep and read to the people each year of release (Deut 31:9–13), and which the king was to read daily (Deut 17:18–20)? Are any scrolls of the Psalter left? It was to be the Israelites' hymnal.

What *is* left over indicates the priorities of Israelites: beds and couches. These symbolize bodily care, personal pampering, luxury, and idleness (cf. 4:1; 6:4–6). While the poor were left without a garment to cover them at night (2:8), Israel's opulent were sleeping on comfortable couches and beds. "But woe to

---

[50] Cf., e.g., Good, *Irony in the Old Testament*, 144; Mays, *Amos*, 67; Paul, *Amos*, 120; Wolff, *Joel and Amos*, 197; Smith, *Amos*, 167.

[51] Andersen and Freedman, *Amos*, 102–3 (see also pp. 98–99).

[52] Andersen and Freedman, *Amos*, 409.

you who are rich, for you have already received your comfort. Woe to you who have been filled now, for you will hunger. Woe to you who are laughing now, for you will mourn and weep" (Lk 6:24–25).

3:13 The last section (3:13–15) begins with the commands to "listen and testify against the house of Jacob."[53] "Listen" (שִׁמְעוּ) is a different form of the same verb translated in 3:9 as "make known" (הַשְׁמִיעוּ). In 3:9 God summoned Ashdod and Egypt to gather around Samaria as witnesses, and they are the ones now commanded to "listen and testify." This call for witnesses with its impending judgment resembles Is 1:2, where Yahweh calls the heavens to "listen" and the earth to "give ear" to his charge that his children have rebelled against him. It also reflects the Israelite law that required a minimum of two witnesses in order to convict someone charged with a crime (Deut 19:15). Israel's royal leaders are on trial, Ashdod and Egypt are the witnesses, and Yahweh is the Judge who will remove two of their chief sources of security: their idolatrous altars and their mansions (Amos 3:11, 14–15).

"The house of Jacob" (בֵּית יַעֲקֹב, 3:13) here refers especially to the Northern Kingdom of Israel. The conniving patriarch Jacob/Israel ever casts his shadow over the nation. "Jacob" brings to mind lies, half-truths, and a deceptive character. The apple hasn't fallen far from the tree. "The house of Jacob" also introduces one of the main themes of 3:13–15: *houses*. Bethel (בֵּית־אֵל, literally, "the *house* of God") is Yahweh's target in 3:14, while in 3:15, he also takes aim at "the winter house" (בֵּית־הַחֹרֶף), "the summer house" (בֵּית הַקָּיִץ), "the houses of ivory" (בָּתֵּי הַשֵּׁן), and "the great houses" (בָּתִּים רַבִּים).

3:14 Yahweh promises that he will punish Israel for her transgressions on a certain "day." This is related to the "Day of Yahweh" theme.[54] "On the day when I punish the transgressions of Israel" (כִּי בְּיוֹם פָּקְדִי פִשְׁעֵי־יִשְׂרָאֵל עָלָיו) has much of the same vocabulary as Ex 32:34: "On the day when I punish, I will punish them for their sin" (וּבְיוֹם פָּקְדִי וּפָקַדְתִּי עֲלֵיהֶם חַטָּאתָם). "In Exodus the punishment refers to the golden calf incident, and in Amos the threat is leveled against the central altar of Bethel, where Jeroboam I had also set up a golden calf. The sins of the past, which abide in the present, will once more be extirpated."[55]

The temporal clause "*when* I punish" leaves no last chances for escape; judgment is unavoidable. In Amos' fourth vision, Yahweh says, "The end is coming upon my people Israel" (8:2). To those sinners who repent, Yahweh extends the promise of forgiveness and restoration (7:1–6; 9:11–15), but here to the impenitent idolaters and their city he only promises judgment.

---

[53] Andersen and Freedman understand the plural imperatives "listen and testify" to be addressed to heavenly heralds, the same heralds whom they understand to be addressed by the plural imperatives "make known" and "say" in 3:9 (*Amos*, 376).

[54] For "the Day of Yahweh," see the commentary on 5:18, 20. See also "Amos' Place in the Minor Prophets" in the introduction; the third textual note on 1:14; the first textual note and the commentary on 2:16; and the second textual note and the commentary on 4:2.

[55] Paul, *Amos*, 124–25.

Yahweh does not always execute his justice immediately. He may delay it to a later generation. The complete judgment for the sin of all humanity was executed some eight centuries after the time of Amos. God "made him who knew no sin to be sin on our behalf, so that we might become the righteousness of God in him" (2 Cor 5:21). Good Friday was *the* day when God punished his own Son for our transgressions so that we might receive forgiveness and pardon that will avail on the final Judgment Day.

"Generational sin" is articulated in the Ten Commandments, where Yahweh promises to punish the sins of the fathers up to the third and fourth generations of those who hate him (Ex 20:5).[a] The prophet Ahijah announces that the punishment for the sins of Jeroboam ben Nebat will fall upon his descendants (1 Ki 14:1–18). Jehu ben Hanani declares that Baasha's descendants will pay for Baasha's sins (1 Ki 16:1–4). Yahweh's punishment may be fast or slow in coming (cf. "yet forty days" in Jonah 3:4) because he is "slow to anger" (e.g., Joel 2:13; Jonah 4:2). Nevertheless, it will arrive, regardless of what his people think (cf. Amos 9:10).

(a) Cf. Ex 34:6–7; Lev 26:39–44; 2 Samuel 13–19; 1 Ki 17:18; 2 Ki 22:19–20

Much has been written about a supposed turn in the OT from the generational accountability for sin articulated in the Pentateuch to a doctrine of individualistic accountability as stated in Jeremiah and Ezekiel.[56] Some believe that during the exile the doctrine of individual responsibility began to undermine the understanding of corporate and generational sin (e.g., Jer 31:29–30; Ezekiel 18).[57] However, a convincing case cannot be made to substantiate a gradually emerging individualism that replaced the previous emphasis on the corporate group. Kaiser writes of Ezekiel 18:

> This chapter, however, sets forth no new doctrine, but combats a fatalistic view of life engendered by self-pity and a one-sided emphasis of moral collectivism or corporate solidarity.[58]

The crimes of Israel noted in Amos 3:14 are so acute that Yahweh promises to punish the two centers of the nation. The sanctuary in Bethel (3:14) was the center of Israel's errant religious life. The winter and summer houses in 3:15 were the epitome of the elite lifestyles of Israel's wealthy leaders.

The first reference in Amos to "Bethel" is in 3:14. During the time of Amos in the eighth century BC, this city, located about twelve miles north of Jerusalem, was the primary religious center of northern Israel. This is why Bethel is named so frequently in Amos (3:14; 4:4; 5:5–6; 7:10, 13) and why these references to it occur within the forceful condemnations of northern Israel's syncretistic,

---

[56] Cf., e.g., Mendenhall, "The Relation of the Individual to Political Society in Ancient Israel." Halpern mistakenly argues that individual responsibility emerged in Israel as a result of the monarchy's undermining of the solidarity of the traditional kinship groups of households, clans, and tribes ("Jerusalem and the Lineages in the Seventh Century BCE: Kinship and the Rise of Individual Moral Liability").

[57] The debate is summarized in Matties, *Ezekiel 18 and the Rhetoric of Moral Discourse*, 115–25. For a theological exposition of Ezekiel 18, see Hummel, *Ezekiel 1–20*, 532–47.

[58] Kaiser, *Toward Old Testament Ethics*, 70.

(b) Amos 2:7–8; 3:14; 4:4–5; 5:5–6, 14, 21–27; 7:9–17; 8:5, 10, 14; 9:1

idolatrous worship.[b] The city also functioned as the royal sanctuary (7:13). The apostate church and the corrupt state were intertwined, but instead of the king serving God, the king used the gods at Bethel to strengthen his grip on the nation isolated from the true sanctuary in Jerusalem.

Both Abraham and Jacob offered true worship at Bethel (Gen 12:8; 35:7). At Bethel Jacob had a vision of a ladder reaching from heaven to earth on which angels were ascending and descending (Gen 28:10–18). But by Amos' time, Bethel had long since lost its identity as a contact point between heaven and earth. Jeroboam ben Nebat had made it one of his two chief shrines for idolatrous worship (1 Ki 12:25–33; 13:1–2). Hosea, a contemporary of Amos, mentions and condemns the Bethel sanctuary often (Hos 4:15; 5:8; 10:5, 15). The plural "*altars* of Bethel" (Amos 3:14) indicates that polytheistic worship was the norm in northern Israel (cf. 2:8; 6:4–7; 8:14). Bethel's main altar was destroyed during the reformation of Josiah in about 623 BC (2 Ki 23:15).

Yahweh's sacrificial altar at the temple in Jerusalem was the place where the blood of sacrifices was sprinkled or poured and on which the sacrifices were burned so that atonement could be attained (e.g., Lev 1:4–5; 4:1–21; 5:1–10). Since it was a place of atonement, a guilty person might grasp the horns of the altar to seek asylum (cf. Ex 21:12–14; 1 Ki 1:50; 2:28). The altars of northern Israel were sites of false worship, so God provided no forgiveness through them. Their destruction and the loss of their horns would show Israel that they were not a means of receiving forgiveness nor were they a safe haven (cf. Amos 8:12). The destruction of a sanctuary (probably at Bethel) with its altar also appears in Amos' last vision (9:1–4). "In a paradoxical fashion and contrary to all popular expectations, the end of Israel's cultic existence would be brought about by their very own God."[59]

3:15 Not only does Amos declare that the religious center at Bethel (literally, "the house of God") is under Yahweh's judgment, in this verse he turns his attention toward Israel's royal officials and their houses.[60] Those "who enjoy the present life of pomp, pleasure, and prosperity (see 6:4–6)"[61] are about to see their party and oppressive lifestyle come to an end.

The word "house" (בַּ֫יִת) appears four times in this verse. Yahweh will "strike" (וְהִכֵּיתִ֫י) the winter and summer houses, and those with ivory will "perish" (וְאָבְד֫וּ). Both of these verbs are also used in covenantal curse texts. "Strike" (the Hiphil of נָכָה) appears in, for example, Lev 26:24; Deut 28:22, 27–28, 35, while "perish" (אָבַד) is used in, for example, Lev 26:38; Deut 4:26; 28:20, 22.

---

59 Paul, *Amos*, 124.

60 Barkay's study on the eighth-century Judean royal place in Ramat Raḥel (between Jerusalem and Bethlehem) illustrates how houses depict the extravagant lifestyles that were possible at that time ("Royal Palace, Royal Portrait?").

61 Paul, *Amos*, 125.

"The winter house" and "the summer house" do not refer to two different parts of the same house (cf. Judg 3:20), but rather to two separate homes.[62] Palestine's climate can be severe, with cold winters and scorching summers. The epitome of luxury would be to own a home for each season.[63] King Ahab of the Northern Kingdom was once part of this elite group. His winter house was in the warmer Jezreel Valley (1 Ki 21:1), while his summer house was at a higher, cooler elevation in the capital city Samaria (1 Ki 21:18).[64] Israel's royal houses had inlays of ivory (Ps 45:9 [ET 45:8]), yet Solomon in all his glory only owned a "great throne of ivory" (כִּסֵּא־שֵׁן גָּדוֹל, 1 Ki 10:18 ǁ 2 Chr 9:17).

In Amos 3:14–15, Yahweh states, "On the day when I punish ... I will punish ... And I will strike down ..." Although Yahweh will employ another unnamed nation (Assyria) to do this (cf. 6:14), *he* is the one who will stand behind the imminent devastation when northern Israel will lose both of her places of refuge, the sacred (3:14) and the secular (3:15). The prophecy of the destruction and fall of Samaria was fulfilled during the three-year siege ending with the final conquest of Samaria by Assyria in 722 BC (2 Ki 17:1–6). The destruction of the altar of Samaria was accomplished during Josiah's reformation (2 Ki 23:15–19).

Summary of Amos 3:1–15

Chapter 3 of Amos is composed of three parts: (1) judgment (3:1–2), (2) disputation (3:3–8), and (3) oracles of judgment (3:9–15). Although these appear to be separate sections, they combine to form a unit. The theme of the chapter as a whole is that Lion Yahweh has roared, impelling the prophet into ministry (3:8). The Lion will roar again when he comes in judgment for Israel's royal officials (3:12). Other scholars too argue that the chapter is a unity with a central theme. For example, Gitay identifies the chapter's theme as "the recognition that God reveals himself not only in matters of success but also in terms of sins

---

62 Cf. Paul, "Amos III 15," and Wolff, *Joel and Amos*, 201. King uses archaeological evidence from Samal (in modern Turkey) and from Ugarit to conclude: "The prophet [Amos] is referring to two geographically distinct buildings" (*Amos, Hosea, Micah*, 64–65). He also ventures to suggest that "the largest house" and "the smallest house" of 6:11 might refer to the winter and summer houses, respectively.

63 The extravagance of living in two houses is attested by the fact that even some foreign kings were not able to enjoy such luxury. King Barrakab of Samal (ca. 730 BC) writes in an inscription: "My fathers, the kings of Sam'al, had no good house. They had the house of Kilamu, which was their winter house and also their summer house" (*ANET*, 655). However, according to Xenophon, *Cyropaedia*, 8.6.22, the Persian king Cyrus had capitals and palaces in Susa, Ecbatana, and Babylon and took advantage of temperate seasons in each location. See also Olmstead, *History of the Persian Empire*, 162–84, who discusses these capitals during the time of Darius I, who built yet another capital in Persepolis.

64 Archaeological excavations at Samaria unearthed some of the ivories that adorned these buildings, testifying to their grandeur. For pictures and descriptions of some of these ivories, see Crowfoot and Crowfoot, *Early Ivories from Samaria*; N. Avigad, "Samaria (City)," *NEAEHL* 4:1304–6; King, "The *Marzeaḥ* Amos Denounces."

and punishment."[65] Jeremias, in like manner, demonstrates that the different elements of the chapter are connected by the theme of "Yahweh's *pqd*," or visitation.[66] The verb פָּקַד, "to visit, punish," occurs in 3:2, 14 (twice) and nowhere else in the book.

Samaria—a city of pride and excess—will see its houses ruined, its furniture burned, its wealth confiscated, its comforts taken, its leaders captured, killed, and exiled. Its way of life will be forever "gone with the wind." "Every kind of sickness and every kind of smiting" (Deut 28:61) is about to visit this dark city on a hill. On that "day" (3:14; cf. 2:14–16; 5:18–20) everything will vaporize. Every royal mansion will fall, but Yahweh's ultimate destruction will be upon the house of worship at Bethel (cf. 9:1). The end of the earthly lives of these unfaithful Israelites is a sign of their eternal destruction in hell.

Deut 8:18 indicates that it is Yahweh who gives strength to his faithful people, and this may result in them gaining wealth that includes homes, wells, vineyards, and fields (Deut 8:6–9). In Scripture, God also provides warnings that wealth may erode faith (e.g., 1 Tim 6:9, 17; James 5:3–6) and bring about ungodly pride (cf. Rev 3:17). It is incumbent, therefore, not to make all-encompassing statements about wealth that only consider one or two biblical texts. The Bible teaches a variety of viewpoints, and each sends a distinct message within its context. Perhaps Johnson gets at the heart of what the Scriptures teach in this realm: "The way we use, own, acquire, and disperse material things symbolizes and expresses our attitudes and responses to ourselves, the world around us, other people, and, most of all, God."[67]

---

[65] Gitay, "A Study of Amos's Art of Speech," 296.

[66] Jeremias, "Amos 3–6," 222–24.

[67] Johnson, *Sharing Possessions*, 40. Smith writes: "The broader principles of Scripture condemn anyone (rich and poor) who centers attention on gaining possessions, finds ultimate value and self-esteem in wealth, is preoccupied and motivated only by expanding material security, and places hope and satisfaction in money" (*Hosea, Amos, Micah*, 293).

Amos 4:1–5

Prophetic Satire

Translation

4 **[1]Hear this word, O cows of Bashan,**
who are on the mountain of Samaria,
who are oppressing the poor,
crushing the needy,
saying to their husbands, "Bring that we may drink!"
[2]The Lord Yahweh swears by his holiness:
"Surely days are coming against you,
and he will take you away by means of hooks,
and the last group of you by means of fishhooks.
[3]Through breaches you will go forth, each woman straight ahead,
and you will be thrown to Hermon,"
declares Yahweh.
[4]"Go to Bethel and transgress,
to Gilgal and transgress even more.
Bring your sacrifices for every morning,
for every third day your tithes.
[5]Burn from unleavened bread a thank offering,
and proclaim freewill offerings—make it heard!
For you love to do this, O children of Israel,"
says the Lord Yahweh.

Textual Notes

4:1 שִׁמְעוּ הַדָּבָר הַזֶּה—The plural imperative שִׁמְעוּ, "hear," also begins sections in 3:1, 13; 5:1. It is masculine even though it is addressed to the female "cows" (see the next textual note). In Hebrew, masculine forms often replace feminine ones (GKC, § 144 a; Joüon, § 150 a). See also the sixth textual note on 4:1, which discusses the masculine suffix on לַאֲדֹנֵיהֶם.

פָּרוֹת הַבָּשָׁן אֲשֶׁר בְּהַר שֹׁמְרוֹן—The masculine noun פַּר denotes a "steer," but פָּרוֹת is the plural of the feminine noun פָּרָה, "heifer, cow" (BDB, s.v. פָּרָה I, under the root פרר III). בָּשָׁן is one of the Hebrew proper place names that regularly takes the definite article. Bashan is a fertile plain located on both sides of the Yarmuk River in the Transjordan. It was famous for the flocks and cattle that fattened themselves on its rich pastures (e.g., Deut 32:14; Ps 22:13 [ET 22:12]). Ezek 39:18 refers to "cattle" that are "the fatlings of Bashan" (פָּרִים מְרִיאֵי בָשָׁן). For שֹׁמְרוֹן, see the second textual note on 3:9.

הָעֹשְׁקוֹת ... הָרֹצְצוֹת ... הָאֹמְרֹת—The article is used on these three attributive Qal feminine plural participles to refer back to the definite construct phrase פָּרוֹת הַבָּשָׁן, "*the* cows of Bashan" (Joüon, § 138 e). In the translation, the article is omitted because of the use of "O" in the vocative phrase.

הָעֹשְׁקוֹת דַּלִּים—The verb עָשַׁק, "to oppress," occurs only here in Amos, but it is the root of the abstract plural noun עֲשׁוּקִים that is used in 3:9. For דַּל, see the last textual note on 2:6 and the first textual note and the commentary on 2:7.

הָרֹצְצוֹת אֶבְיוֹנִים—The verb רָצַץ may have the literal meaning "to crush." Egypt is described as a crushed (broken) reed (2 Ki 18:21 ‖ Is 36:6). The verb often has an ethical dimension to it as well.[1] In Amos 4:1, as well as passages in other biblical books, רָצַץ occurs with the verb עָשַׁק, "to oppress, wrong" (Deut 28:33; 1 Sam 12:3–4; Hos 5:11).

For אֶבְיוֹן, see the last textual note and the commentary on 2:6. The words "poor" (דַּלִּים) and "needy" (אֶבְיוֹנִים) are in the same semantic field. They are often parallel with one another, as again in 8:6 (also, e.g., in 1 Sam 2:8; Ps 72:13). "These words are not absolute synonyms because certain contexts invest דַּל with a sense of weakness and poverty, while אֶבְיוֹן generally connotes the sense of need."[2]

הָאֹמְרֹת לַאֲדֹנֵיהֶם הָבִיאָה וְנִשְׁתֶּה׃—The noun אָדוֹן, "lord," is used occasionally to denote a "husband" (Gen 18:12; Judg 19:26–27; Ps 45:12 [ET 45:11]; cf. 1 Pet 3:6, which refers to Gen 18:12). The NT compares the relationship between husband and wife to that between the Lord and his church (Eph 5:21–33). The Hebrew words used more often for a husband are בַּעַל and אִישׁ. Paul writes: "The reason this specific term was selected may very well be due to the intention of the prophet to relate אֲדֹנֵיהֶם ('their lords') with the following verse, where in contrast the true 'Lord' (אֲדֹנָי) appears."[3] The masculine pronominal suffix יהֶם- is used even though it refers to the wives: "*their* husbands" (GKC, § 135 o). The irony is that these nagging wives who demand that their lords bring them drinks will meet their Lord and God (Amos 4:12b), who will come not to add to their joy but to bring judgment and misery (cf. 8:10).

הָבִיאָה is the emphatic form of the Hiphil singular imperative of בּוֹא (see Joüon, § 48 d).

4:2 נִשְׁבַּע אֲדֹנָי יְהוִה בְּקָדְשׁוֹ כִּי ...—The verb שָׁבַע often means "to swear, take an oath." It is so used in reference to Yahweh's oath to the patriarchs promising land to them (e.g., Deut 1:8, 35).[4] The idiom נִשְׁבַּע ... כִּי, literally, "to swear ... that," expresses an oath that is a positive affirmation that something will happen. See Joüon, § 165 b, and Waltke-O'Connor, § 40.2.2b, including example 1. When שָׁבַע appears in the Niphal stem, followed by the preposition בְּ (here on בְּקָדְשׁוֹ), the בְּ introduces the power invoked that secures the oath. As the subject of שָׁבַע twice elsewhere in Amos, Yahweh swears by his life, or נֶפֶשׁ (6:8), and by "the pride of Jacob" (8:7), a circumlocution for himself. The exact oath here appears again in the OT only in Ps 89:36 (ET 89:35): נִשְׁבַּעְתִּי בְקָדְשִׁי, "I have sworn by my holiness," where Yahweh emphasizes his everlasting commitment to the house of David—salvation for Christ's sake. *TWOT* notes:

---

1 Cf. H. Ringgren, "רָצַץ," *TDOT* 13:641–43.

2 Niehaus, "Amos," 392.

3 Paul, *Amos*, 129.

4 Cf. I. Kottsieper, "שָׁבַע," *TDOT* 14:311–36.

> To swear in the Old Testament was to give one's sacred unbreakable word in testimony that the one swearing would faithfully perform some promised deed, or that he would faithfully refrain from some evil act.[5]

In Amos, Yahweh only swears in condemnation against certain groups of people, like the exploitative upper class (4:2; 8:7), or Samaria (6:8). In other OT books, Yahweh may swear (שָׁבַע) when describing his irrevocable favor for his people (e.g., Is 45:14–25; 54:9; Jer 51:12–14).

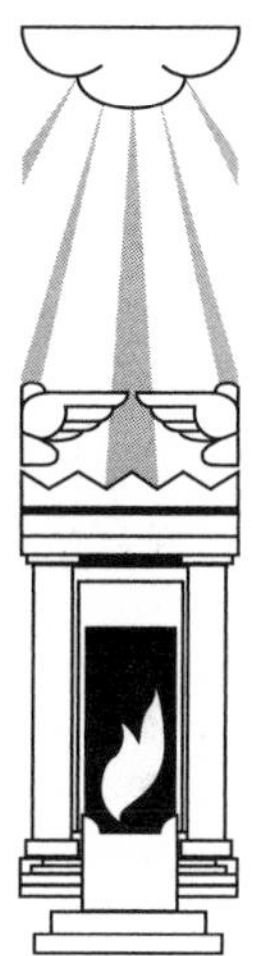

The noun קֹדֶשׁ refers to Yahweh's "holiness."[6] The only other occurrence of קֹדֶשׁ in Amos is in reference to Yahweh's "holy name" in 2:7. Micah 1:2 uses קֹדֶשׁ in connection with judgment when Yahweh comes out of his "holy" temple. Likewise, in Zeph 3:11, קָדְשִׁי ("on my *holy* mountain") appears in connection with judgment when Yahweh puts an end to arrogance. It is cognate to the adjective קָדוֹשׁ, which can describe the central divine attribute of the "holy" God in contradistinction to human sinfulness (e.g., Is 1:4), and which is the term in the Trisagion (Is 6:3) of Isaiah 6, the theophany that causes Isaiah to confess his uncleanness and inadequacy (Is 6:5). The divine epithet with the adjective קָדוֹשׁ, "the Holy One of Israel," is especially frequent in Isaiah, often in contexts of judgment (e.g., Is 5:24; 31:1; 37:23). Yet the epithet may also refer to Yahweh as the gracious God, the Creator to whom people can look (Is 17:7), the one on whom the remnant will lean (Is 10:20), and the one in whom the poor will exult (Is 29:19).

כִּי הִנֵּה יָמִים בָּאִים עֲלֵיכֶם—Here כִּי introduces the contents of the oath (GKC, § 157 b). See also the previous textual note. For similar uses of כִּי in the context of an oath, see, for example, Gen 22:16; 1 Ki 1:13, 17, 30; Jer 22:5. This commentary takes it as asseverative: "surely" (so also Waltke-O'Connor, § 40.2.2b, example 1).

The deictic particle הִנֵּה ("behold") is often employed with participles and designates future time (GKC, § 116 p).

The phrase יָמִים בָּאִים, "days are coming," recurs in Amos 8:11 and 9:13. It "is an expression often used in eschatological descriptions" and indicates a new period of time.[7] It is equivalent to other eschatological references to "the Day of Yahweh" (5:18–20) or Yahweh's "day(s)" of judgment in 1:14; 2:16; 3:14; 6:3; 8:3, 9–11, 13. The aspect of judgment is emphasized by the preposition עֲלֵיכֶם used in the sense of disadvantage, "against you," which has the masculine form of the suffix even though the reference is to the women/cows. See the last textual note on 4:1.

וְנִשָּׂא אֶתְכֶם בְּצִנּוֹת—The pointing of נִשָּׂא, the Piel perfect of נָשָׂא, follows that of a third-*he* verb (GKC, § 75 oo). The perfect with *waw* consecutive (וְנִשָּׂא) is used here to

---

5 "שָׁבַע," *TWOT*, § 2319.

6 Cf. W. Kornfeld and H. Ringgren, "קדשׁ," *TDOT* 12:521–45. Sellin writes: "God is holy. Herein we touch on that which constitutes the deepest and innermost nature of the God of the Old Testament" (*Theologie des Alten Testaments*, 18–19). The expression of Yahweh's holiness occurs in songs of salvation (Ex 15:11; 1 Sam 2:2). It pervades Leviticus (a book about priests and worship) and Ezekiel (a book by a priest) as well as Isaiah. The classic study is Otto, *The Idea of the Holy*. The prophetic inheritance of the priestly and liturgical concern for holiness is affirmed by Ringgren, who writes: "The prophets obviously accepted the cultic notion of holiness, as it is preserved to us in the ritual laws of the Pentateuch" (*The Prophetical Conception of Holiness*, 18).

7 Paul, *Amos*, 130.

announce future events (GKC, § 112 x). The form itself could also be the Niphal perfect, but "*he* will be taken away" does not fit in this context with the following direct object אֶתְכֶם ("you").

The rest of this verse is full of lexical difficulties.[8] The noun צִנָּה is fairly common with the meaning "large shield" (BDB, s.v. צִנָּה III). Most likely the word here is a homograph meaning a "hook" or "barb" (BDB, s.v. צִנָּה I). A masculine cognate צֵן appears only in Job 5:5 and Prov 22:5 and apparently means "thorn" or "barb" (BDB). Almost all English translations render צִנּוֹת as "hooks" and the corresponding construct phrase סִירוֹת דּוּגָה in the next line as "fishhooks."

Paul translates צִנּוֹת as "baskets," while suggesting "pots" for סִירוֹת.[9] He believes that neither term refers to "fishhooks," and that the image Amos is creating is that of catching, packing, and transporting fish in these kinds of containers.[10]

Some interpreters object to the traditional understanding of the words as a reference to fishing gear because the metaphor of cows that Amos begins in 4:1 and continues in 4:3 would be interrupted by the fish imagery. Some interpret the words as referring to parts of a bridle that could be put on a cow to lead it. The LXX renders בְּצִנּוֹת with ἐν ὅπλοις, "with weapons, tools." Kleven comments: "Although the LXX never uses ὅπλον for a rope, the Greek may well be naming a bridle which includes both a hook and reins."[11] Wolff argues that סִירוֹת means "harpoons" that were used as cattle prods.[12] See also the next textual note.

וְאַחֲרִיתְכֶן בְּסִירוֹת דּוּגָה׃—The noun אַחֲרִית, "latter part, end," can have a temporal meaning or a spatial meaning. Here it might have a spatial meaning that refers to the "hind part" of the cows (*HALOT*, 1). However, since the cows are being led away into exile, the spatial meaning more likely refers to the "last group" or "end" of the traveling group or line of women. Andersen and Freedman translate it as "rear guard" or "stragglers."[13]

One noun סִיר refers to a "pot" often used for cooking (BDB, s.v. סִיר I). However, the word here probably is a rare homograph that means "thorn" and elsewhere always occurs in the masculine plural form סִירִים (Is 34:13; Hos 2:8 [ET 2:6]; Nah 1:10; Eccl 7:6) but here occurs in a feminine plural form meaning "hooks" (BDB, s.v. סִיר II). It is possible for a noun to have both masculine and feminine forms (GKC, § 124 e). סִירוֹת is in construct with the abstract feminine noun דּוּגָה, which refers to the activity of "fishing." It occurs only here in the OT, but it is related to other words for "fish" and "fishermen" from the root דגה (and/or דוג or דיג).

---

8 Cf. Paul, *Amos*, 130–35, or Paul, "Fishing Imagery in Amos 4:2."

9 Paul, *Amos*, 134. He goes on to write: "The former [צִנּוֹת] is well attested by its cognates, … and the latter [סִירוֹת] is well documented in the Bible itself."

10 Paul, *Amos*, 134, who cites a prophetic text from Mari where captives are placed in a fisherman's basket: "Then I, Dagan, will make the Benjaminite sheiks wriggle/writhe in a fisherman's basket and deliver them in front of you."

11 Kleven, "The Cows of Bashan," 223.

12 Wolff, *Joel and Amos*, 207. He says that such a harpoon "may have been considered a cattle prod peculiar enough to be suited to this unusual and violent deportation."

13 Andersen and Freedman, *Amos*, 424.

4:3 וּפְרָצִים תֵּצֶאנָה אִשָּׁה נֶגְדָּהּ—The noun פֶּרֶץ, "breach," comes from the root פרץ, which "describes a breakthrough, a break-in, or an outbreak."[14] פֶּרֶץ is used for breaches through the walls of a city.[15] In 1 Ki 11:27 Solomon patches up the breach in the wall around the city of David. Job employs the word in a simile (Job 30:14): his contemporaries despised and attacked him like invaders pouring into a city through a wide breach in the city wall. A breach in a wall always signifies a loss of security and safety.

Walls were normally broken (cf., e.g., Neh 1:3; 2:13) by an attacking army using a battering ram.[16] Then the invaders could lead the captive inhabitants of the city out through the same breaches. The implication here is that the city wall of Samaria will be breached in many places, signifying that the destruction is so massive that it is unnecessary to exit through the city gate.

The idiom אִשָּׁה נֶגְדָּהּ is, literally, "each woman straight ahead of herself." For the function of אִישׁ and אִשָּׁה as distributive pronouns, see GKC, § 139 b; Joüon, § 147 d. The masculine equivalent appears in Josh 6:5, 20, describing how Israelite soldiers marched into the city of Jericho after its wall had completely fallen: אִישׁ נֶגְדּוֹ, "each man straight ahead," since no part of the wall remained.

The imagery here may also suggest that the women like "cows" will go out of Samaria like animals escaping from a pen whose fence has broken down.[17] If so, this adds further irony and insult to the women.

וְהִשְׁלַכְתֶּנָה הַהַרְמוֹנָה נְאֻם־יְהוָה׃—The verb is pointed as a Hiphil second person feminine perfect with the unusual longer ending תֶּנָה- instead of תֶּן- (GKC, § 44 k). The verb שָׁלַךְ ("to throw") appears only in the Hiphil and Hophal stems.[18] The Hiphil would mean "and you [the women/cows] will throw toward Hermon." However, the women are being taken captive, so the active Hiphil does not make sense in this context. The translation "and you will be thrown" follows the LXX rendition with ἀπορριφήσεσθε, the future passive of ἀπορρίπτω, "to throw away," whose passive means "to be cast (forth), to be cast out" (LEH). This meaning is also supported by the Vulgate. The LXX probably read the unpointed Hebrew text as a Hophal, vocalizing it as הָ- instead of הִ-. The Hiphil of שָׁלַךְ recurs in 8:3. It is used in Deut 29:27 (ET 29:28) to warn that Yahweh will "throw" Israel into exile, and the Hophal is used in Jer 22:28 to say that King Jehoiachin of Judah and his family are "thrown" into exile.

הַהַרְמוֹנָה baffles commentators. It appears to be a place name הַרְמוֹן with the definite article and locative ending (הָ-), "to the Harmon." It is a geographical location to which the "cows of Bashan" will be deported. הַרְמוֹן occurs only here in the OT and its identity is unknown; see BDB and *HALOT*. Most English versions follow the MT and translate with something like "to Harmon." Andersen and Freedman tentatively iden-

---

14 Andersen and Freedman, *Amos*, 424.

15 Cf. J. Conrad, "פֶּרֶץ," *TDOT* 12:109.

16 See King, *Amos, Hosea, Micah*, 70–87, for a discussion on the art of warfare in the ancient Near East.

17 Andersen and Freedman, *Amos*, 424.

18 Cf. W. Thiel, "שׁלך," *TDOT* 15:88–96.

tify Harmon with the region beyond Damascus in Aram.[19] The LXX translates it as εἰς τὸ ὄρος τὸ Ρεμμαν, "to the mountain of Remman," apparently dividing הַהַרְמוֹנָה into two words, הַר רִמּוֹנָה. Sweeney says that the reference is to Mount Hermon, the snow-capped peak on the border between Israel and Aram, near the region of Bashan.[20] That would entail emending -הַהַ to -הַחֶ yielding הַחֶרְמוֹנָה, "to (Mount) Hermon." This suggestion appears to be the best. Mount Hermon is close to Bashan, which is referenced in 4:1. Understood this way, the "cows of Bashan" (4:1) will be led back to their pasture. At any rate, the text, however interpreted, leads to one conclusion: the Israelites will be sent into exile.

For the signatory formula נְאֻם־יְהוָה, see the second textual note on 2:11. It recurs at the end of 4:5 with the expanded divine title אֲדֹנָי יְהוִה.

4:4–5 These two verses have seven commands. In form six are imperatives (בֹּאוּ, וּפִשְׁעוּ, הַרְבּוּ, וְהָבִיאוּ, וְקַרְאוּ, הַשְׁמִיעוּ) and one is an infinitive absolute (וְקַטֵּר) that functions as an imperative. In this context, they function as sarcastic imperatives. Waltke-O'Connor, § 34.4b, also notes that imperatives can be used sarcastically, and it cites וּפִשְׁעוּ in 4:4 as an instance (example 17). There is often a gloating quality in passages using sarcastic imperatives. By employing expressions such as "flee, turn back" (Jer 49:8; cf. Jer 49:30); "hide in the dust" (Is 2:10); "awake … and weep" (Joel 1:5); and "sit in the dust" (Is 47:1), prophets could mock their enemies.[21] Other groups of seven that Amos employs are in 1:3–2:5; 2:6–8; 2:14–16; 3:3–6; 4:6–11; 5:8–9; 5:21–23; 6:1–6; 9:1–4.

4:4 בֹּאוּ בֵית־אֵל וּפִשְׁעוּ הַגִּלְגָּל הַרְבּוּ לִפְשֹׁעַ—The Qal imperative בֹּאוּ does double duty: "go [to] Bethel … [and go to] Gilgal …"[22] Both Bethel and Gilgal are accusatives of places that are destinations of travel so they are translated with the English preposition "to" (see GKC, § 118 d).

Bethel (בֵּית־אֵל) appears seven times in Amos (3:14; 4:4; 5:5 [twice]; 5:6; 7:10, 13). It has its roots in earlier periods of Israel's history when it was a site of genuine worship (e.g., Gen 28:11–22; cf. Judg 20:18). However, it was transformed by Jeroboam ben Nebat (1 Ki 12:28–33) to be one of the two chief sanctuaries of the Northern Kingdom (the other was at Dan; see Amos 8:14) that were false substitutes for the Jerusalem temple. In the book of Amos, Bethel signifies everything that is wrong with northern Israel. It is no surprise that the pivotal confrontation between Amos and Amaziah takes place at Bethel (7:10–17).

---

[19] Andersen and Freedman, *Amos*, 425. They also note 5:27, where Yahweh vows to exile Israel to the region "beyond Damascus" (מֵהָלְאָה לְדַמָּשֶׂק). See also 1:5 in light of 9:7.

[20] Sweeney, *The Twelve Prophets*, 226.

[21] See also, for example, Jer 46:3–4, 9a–b, 11, 19; Nah 2:2 (ET 2:1); 3:14–15. Examples similar to Amos 4:4–5 include these: "Keep listening, but do not comprehend; keep looking, but do not understand" (Is 6:9). "Stupefy and be in a stupor; blind yourselves and be blind! Be drunk, but not from wine; stagger, but not from strong drink!" (Is 29:9).

[22] The LXX misses the irony that is employed by the imperatives when it translates them as aorists: εἰσήλθατε εἰς Βαιθηλ καὶ ἠνομήσατε καὶ εἰς Γαλγαλα ἐπληθύνατε τοῦ ἀσεβῆσαι, "you entered Bethel and acted lawlessly, and you multiplied acting in ungodliness at Gilgal."

The verb פָּשַׁע appears two times in this verse (the imperative וּפִשְׁעוּ and the infinitive construct לִפְשֹׁעַ) and nowhere else in Amos. However, the plural of the cognate noun פֶּשַׁע describes crimes against humanity as "transgressions" in the oracles against the nations (1:3–2:16). Even though Yahweh issues the imperative command וּפִשְׁעוּ, it is not his will for the people to "transgress." Rather, he is engaging in satire. How ironic: Israel's worship is an act of sinning and rebelling against Yahweh!

Gilgal (with the article: הַגִּלְגָּל) occurs in 4:4; 5:5. It is mentioned together with Bethel also in 1 Sam 7:16; Hos 4:15 (Beth-aven); Amos 5:5. The etymology of its name conveys the meaning of "circle" or "wheel" (Is 28:28). As a location, it was Israel's first encampment in Canaan west of the Jordan River and may have been so designated due to its circle of stones (Josh 4:8, 20). Josh 5:9 records the etymology: when Israel crossed the Jordan into the promised land at Gilgal, Yahweh thereby "rolled away" (the verb גָּלַל) from Israel "the reproach of [being slaves in] Egypt." Gilgal was a sacred site from the time of the conquest until the time of Amos (e.g., Josh 4:19–20; 5:2–10; 1 Sam 7:16; 10:8; 11:14–15), but like Amos, another eighth-century prophet, Hosea, condemned the evil that was being done there (Hos 4:15; 9:15; 12:12 [ET 12:11]). Gilgal's exact location continues to confound scholars, but it is clear that in the time of Amos the city was part of the Northern Kingdom.

While הַרְבּוּ is a Hiphil imperative, "multiply, magnify," it is coordinated with the infinitive לִפְשֹׁעַ. It is best to translate הַרְבּוּ adverbially, "greatly, repeatedly, all the more, even more," and to render the infinitive לִפְשֹׁעַ, "transgress," as the main verb in the clause.[23] When the Hiphil of רָבָה is used with such an infinitive it can have a variety of adverbial forces, including "do much, abundantly, greatly, often" (BDB, s.v. רָבָה, Hiphil, 1 d (1), which translates the phrase here as "transgress greatly"). Most versions render the phrase as "multiply transgression" (KJV, RSV, ESV, NASB).

וְהָבִיאוּ לַבֹּקֶר זִבְחֵיכֶם לִשְׁלֹשֶׁת יָמִים מַעְשְׂרֹתֵיכֶם׃—The repeated preposition לְ on לַבֹּקֶר and לִשְׁלֹשֶׁת has distributive force: "*every* morning … *every* three days" (see BDB, s.v. לְ, 5 i (a)). The offering of voluntary sacrifice every morning and of a tithe every three days is far in excess of what is required by Israel's worship regulations.[24] In the OT, tithes were never offered with such frequency, making this a sarcastic taunt. Deut 14:22–23 commands the Israelites to bring their tithes to the central sanctuary every year, while every third year the Israelites were to gather and distribute their tithes in their own towns (Deut 14:28; 26:12).

---

[23] GKC, § 114 n, note 2, explains this about such coordinated infinitives: "In almost all these examples the principal idea is properly contained in the infinitive, whilst the governing verb strictly speaking contains only a subordinate adverbial statement, and is therefore best rendered in English by an adverb."

[24] Paul (*Amos*, 140) cites other scholars who do not take the לְ as distributive and so interpret the sacrifices as one-time events offered by a worshiper. These other scholars "have suggested that what is being referred to here reflects an otherwise unattested custom of offering a sacrifice on the morning after the arrival of the worshiper at the sanctuary." Cf. Wolff, *Joel and Amos*, 219; Hayes, *Amos, the Eighth-Century Prophet*, 143–44. However, in light of the satirical nature of the passage in general, the distributive sense seems most likely.

(a) E.g., Ex 12:27; 18:12; 23:18; 34:25; Lev 17:5–9; 22:29; 23:37; Num 15:3, 5, 8; Deut 12:6, 11, 27; 18:3

The noun זֶבַח, "sacrifice," could refer to a variety of sacrifices[a] and is used, often with שְׁלָמִים, especially for the peace offering (Leviticus 3; 7:11–36; 23:19).[25] It connotes the slaughtering of animals by means of the shedding of blood. However, the Torah stipulated that such sacrifice was to be performed at the central sanctuary, which during the monarchy was the Jerusalem temple. There were no commands to offer sacrifice anywhere else, such as at Bethel or Gilgal. The prescription (first given in Ex 29:38–42) for the twice-daily sacrifices to be offered at the central sanctuary does not use the noun זֶבַח, but it is possible that the "sacrifices" to be offered "every morning" in Amos 4:4 are a parody of the divinely ordained daily sacrifice offered at the Jerusalem temple.

The "tithe" (מַעֲשֵׂר), or offering of one-tenth, was commanded by God to support the Levites and the disadvantaged (Num 18:21–29; Deut 14:22–29; 26:12). In Gen 14:20 Abraham gave Melchizedek a "tithe" from his entire wealth as a spontaneous gift of thanks. In Gen 28:22 Jacob pledged to give God a tenth of everything he had. In 1 Sam 8:15 Samuel warned the Israelites that a king would take a tenth from their fields and vineyards in order to distribute it among his officials. In Amos 4:4, מַעֲשֵׂר is used specifically as a religious offering.

4:5 וְקַטֵּר מֵחָמֵץ תּוֹדָה—The Piel infinitive absolute וְקַטֵּר in this context functions as a Piel imperative (GKC, § 113 z; Joüon, § 123 x).[26] The verb קָטַר does not occur in the Qal stem, but appears around forty times in Piel and seventy times in Hiphil. Its Piel means "*make sacrifices smoke*, offer them by burning" (BDB). The offering to be burned might be part of an animal (e.g., Lev 9:10, 13–14; 1 Sam 2:15–16) or a handful of grain (Lev 9:17; Num 5:26).

The infinitive is a morphological break from the six surrounding plural imperatives in Amos 4:4–5. Amos also breaks a series of seven when he has six instances of וְשִׁלַּחְתִּי אֵשׁ, "so I will send fire," in 1:3–2:5, but uses another verb, וְהִצַּתִּי אֵשׁ, "so I will kindle fire," in 1:14.

The noun חָמֵץ, "leavened bread," here denotes a grain offering that apparently accompanied the animal sacrifices in 4:4. The preposition מִן on מֵחָמֵץ is best understood as partitive: "some of, from." Leavened bread was normally forbidden on the altar with blood sacrifices (e.g., Ex 23:18; Lev 2:11), and it was to be banished from households for seven days during the Passover and the Feast of Unleavened Bread (Ex 12:15). However, there is one provision for its proper use with a peace offering. Lev 7:13 states: "Along with the sacrifice of his peace offering of thanksgiving [תּוֹדַת שְׁלָמָיו], he shall present his offering with cakes of bread made with yeast [לֶחֶם חָמֵץ]." However, since the context here in Amos refers to sacrifices not prescribed in the Torah, the Israelites may have been using leavened bread in ways contrary to the Torah of Moses.

The תּוֹדָה, "thank offering," was a subcategory of the peace offering (Lev 7:11–15). It was voluntary, not required. A worshiper would offer it to express thanks for Yahweh

[25] See Kleinig, *Leviticus*, 33–39.

[26] Two examples of an imperatival infinitive absolute occur in the Decalogue: זָכוֹר, "remember" the Sabbath day (Ex 20:8), and שָׁמוֹר, "keep, observe" the Sabbath day (Deut 5:12).

answering a prayer. It was offered by means of bread or cakes that accompanied a meat sacrifice.[27]

וְקִרְאוּ נְדָבוֹת הַשְׁמִיעוּ—The נְדָבָה, "freewill offering," like the thank offering, was a subcategory of the peace offering (Lev 7:16) and was voluntary. Freewill offerings were brought for the construction of the tabernacle (Ex 35:29; 36:3). They were offered "in gratitude to the Lord for the blessings received from him ([Lev] 7:16; Deut 16:10)."[28]

כִּי כֵן אֲהַבְתֶּם בְּנֵי יִשְׂרָאֵל נְאֻם אֲדֹנָי יְהוִה׃—The implication of "*you* love" (אֲהַבְתֶּם) is that the Israelites were engaged in worship practices that pleased themselves, not in the divinely ordained worship that is pleasing to God through faith. Here בְּנֵי יִשְׂרָאֵל is a vocative phrase.

For the signatory formula נְאֻם אֲדֹנָי יְהוִה, see the second textual note on 2:11.

Commentary

Satire in Amos

Amos 4:1–5 is ripe with satire. Women are fattened cows ready for the slaughter. Bethel and Gilgal are apostate religious centers that are the centers of sin. Scholars often note Amos' sophisticated appropriation of forms and traditions and his carefully crafted language.[29] For example, Crenshaw argues that Amos uses worship words and ideas (as in 4:4–5) throughout his book to make contact with his audience, only to turn the themes against Israel. He writes: "Amos employs cultic materials as a point of contact and reverses their import, indicating that he viewed the salvation offered by the cult as a damnable delusion."[30] Amos' reversal of traditional symbols and images is what literary critics call satire.[31] He stands in the prophetic tradition of employing satire to announce Yahweh's judgment. (See also 6:12–13.)

Amos needed to use this unfamiliar language because the familiar had become settled, closed, fixed, certain, and oppressive. He could not have been effective if he was tied to stereotyped language, because stereotyped language is a language of cliché. The immediate danger of cliché is the audience's passive

---

[27] See Kleinig, *Leviticus*, 168–74.

[28] See Kleinig, *Leviticus*, 93 (see also pp. 170–71).

[29] Among commentators there appears to be near unanimous agreement on Amos' literary art. Wolff marvels that in the two dozen short oracles one finds a "wealth of rhetorical forms" (*Joel and Amos*, 91). Mays hails Amos as one who displays "remarkable skill at using all the devices of oral literature available in Israel's culture" (*Amos*, 6). Andersen and Freedman note that Amos is one of the most "versatile verbal craftsmen" among the prophets (*Amos*, 144). They are particularly fascinated by the structural and thematic dimensions that unify the whole book literarily (*Amos*, 17–18). Paul speaks of Amos' "distinctive literary style" (*Amos*, 7), as well as the way he uses literary traditions and conventions with "creative sophistication" (*Amos*, 4).

[30] Crenshaw, "Amos and the Theophanic Tradition," 214.

[31] Mays says that Amos "does seem to take up the themes of the theological tradition from his audience and use them in a way that was completely 'unorthodox' and unexpected" (*Amos*, 57). For an overview of OT satire, especially as it relates to the prophets, see Lessing, "Satire in Isaiah's Tyre Oracle," 91–95.

response. That is what Homer meant when he spoke about the poet's creativity: "For men praise that song the most which comes the newest to their ears."[32] Amos employed satire in order to gain a hearing from people who were not interested in what he had to say (see 2:12; 7:10–17).

Overview of Amos 4:1–5

Amos addresses a nation whose economy was up and whose deficit was down. Israel's religious institutions were thriving, and its military enabled its people to feel secure. Although on the outside everything looked great, Yahweh and Amos saw that the inside was rotten to the core (cf. Mt 23:27). And the prophet could smell it from as far away as Tekoa.

The relationship between 3:9–15 and 4:1–5 is one of general sins to specific sins. Whereas the latter part of chapter 3 calls Ashdod and Egypt to serve as witnesses on the hills of Samaria (3:9), 4:1–5 takes aim at specific targets: Israel's women who are on the same hills and the nation's worship, which was all fluff and no substance. The point of both sections is the same: Israelite society was self-indulgent, selfish, and utterly corrupt. The Israelites seem to have organized their lives around three deadly independent personal pronouns: "me," "myself," and "I." Such self-centeredness is the hallmark of privileged and complacent unbelievers today as well.

Violent Exile of the "Cows of Bashan" (4:1–3)

The prophecy of 4:1–3 falls into the pattern of the accusation (4:1), followed by the announcement of the punishment (4:2–3). Amos complains that the opulent women of Samaria are "oppressing the poor" and "crushing the needy" (4:1).[33] Just as a bowl is crushed and broken (Eccl 12:6), so the needy are being destroyed. These two charges are analogous to those made against men of northern Israel in Amos 2:6–7. The women's punishment (4:2–3) will correspond to their crimes. These two verses are the first explicit expression of Israel's exile in Amos. Others are in 5:5, 27; 6:7; 7:11, 17; 9:4.

The prophet's third judgment is more subtle. He quotes the women's words to their husbands: "Bring that we may drink!" (4:1) and accuses them of being obsessed with parties filled with alcoholic beverages. They insisted that their husbands bring home enough money to make their luxurious lifestyles possible. These actions were not directly cheating the poor in the marketplace (8:5–6) or denying them justice in the courts (5:11–12). However, their demands on their husbands encouraged the men to carry out the cheating and perversion of justice in order to pay for the excesses of the "cows" (4:1). Therefore the women too were responsible for "the ruin of Joseph" (6:6c).

---

[32] Homer, *Odyssey*, 1.351–52, quoted by Gitay, "Reflections on the Study of the Prophetic Discourse," 213.

[33] For examples of how Wisdom literature addresses this same theme, see, for example, Prov 14:31; 22:16; Eccl 4:1–3.

This becomes clear when 4:1–3 is compared with 8:4–8. Both texts begin with "hear" (שִׁמְעוּ) and consist of an accusation and an announcement of punishment. In both passages, the accusation concerns mistreatment of the poor, and in both Amos quotes the Israelites' own words against them. Each section also introduces the announcement of punishment with an oath formula: "the Lord Yahweh swears" (4:2; similar is 8:7). Amos 2:6–7; 4:1–3; and 8:4–8 are parallel in theme and structure. Amos 4:1–3 addresses women, while 8:4–8 addresses men. All are guilty (cf. Rom 3:23).

The greedy leaders portrayed throughout the book of Amos may be compared to Zacchaeus in the NT. As an Israelite ("a son of Abraham," Lk 19:9) who had become a wealthy chief tax collector on behalf of the Roman Empire (Lk 19:2), he was enmeshed in an oppressive economic system and financially benefited from it. When called by Jesus, Zacchaeus pledged to give half of his wealth to the poor and to reimburse fourfold anyone whom he had defrauded (Lk 19:8). In the person of Jesus, salvation came to the house of this man who had been lost but was saved (Lk 19:9–10). Unfortunately, however, most of those who heard Amos' preaching did not respond with repentance and faith (4:6–11; 9:10). Nevertheless, God still would fulfill his Gospel promises at the advent of Christ and extend the invitation to all, Israelites and Gentiles alike, to live in paradise for eternity (9:11–15).

4:1 The imperative "hear" begins a new unit (see the first textual note on 4:1). Nevertheless, chapter 4 is connected to chapter 3 by "the mountain of Samaria" (3:9; 4:1; cf. 3:12) as well as Amos' concern for the poor and oppressed ("oppression" in 3:9 and "oppressing" in 4:1). In this way, chapter 4 elaborates on the punishments listed against Israel in 3:9–15, which in turn clarify the initial oracle against Israel in 2:6–16.[34] The words "poor" and "needy" also connect 4:1 to 2:6–7, which employs the same terms. The picture of life in Israel painted in 2:6–3:15 becomes more specific in chapter 4.

Rather than confining himself to whole categories in 4:1, Amos vividly depicts and dramatizes one specific instance of Israel's sin: the gluttony of Israel's leading women.[35] In doing so, he employs some of the most provocative and colorful language in the book. In order to describe their greed and self-indulgence, Amos invokes the imagery of well-fed cows to refer to the upper-class women of Samaria. The husbands of these women were the royal elites who were "treasuring up violence and destruction" (3:10), the wealthy magistrates of large estates (5:11–12), the priestly cast (7:10–17), and/or the miserly mer-

[34] Cf. Andersen and Freedman, *Amos*, 412.

[35] For a similar attack against uppity women, see Is 3:16–26. The placement of that passage in Isaiah, like Amos 4:1–5, appears after Isaiah's general rebuke in Is 3:1–15. The loss will be so severe that seven women will compete for one man (Is 4:1). Yahweh repeatedly declares that he will judge Israel and Judah because of idolatry as well as their mistreatment of the poor (e.g., Jer 7:1–15). The horizontal and vertical issues of faith are interrelated.

chants (2:6–7; 8:4–6). The sinful ambitions of these men were fueled, in part, by their demanding wives.

These women probably had no direct contact with the impoverished peasants in Israel. They may have never grasped the fact that their lavish lifestyles were made possible by the sweat and toil of the poor. But these "cows of Bashan" (4:1), on account of their insatiable greed, were just as guilty as their husbands in the repression and impoverishment of the lower classes in Samaria, for if someone is a member of a privileged class that profits from structural evil and if that person does nothing to try to help others, he or she is guilty before God (e.g., Lk 16:19–31).[36] Structural evil is just as damaging to people as is personal evil.[37]

This is the only instance in the Bible where women are compared to cows, and obese ones at that (see the second textual note on 4:1).[38] Whereas many modern societies prefer women to be thin, in the ancient Near East, where many lived from hand to mouth, the rich prided themselves on having enough food to make themselves fat. Being overweight was a sign of wealth and social status (e.g., Judg 3:17).

Some commentators argue that the feminine gender is a figure of speech and that Amos is calling men female cattle.[39] It is true that this section of Amos is full of satire, but that interpretation is hard to reconcile with the statement that the "cows" were "saying to their *husbands*" (Amos 4:1). It is best not to reverse the genders but to understand that God's target is the snooty women of Samaria who were living like animals. Bodily pleasures occupied their lives, and they had no time for those things that promote a devout spiritual life toward Yahweh (cf. Col 3:1–7).

Amos in the course of his many travels[40] probably witnessed the beautiful cattle in the pasturelands of Bashan, where fertility was a perpetual guarantee of abundance. "In both instances, their every need was supplied—to the pampered women by 'their lords,' and to the beautiful cattle by nature and by their herdsmen."[41]

---

[36] Jesus does not suggest that Lazarus' poverty was the result of oppression by the rich man (who traditionally is named "Dives," meaning "rich"). The rich man is guilty of the sin of *omission*. This indifferent unbeliever neglected to help, and his sin sent him to eternal torment in the fires of hell (Lk 16:19–31).

[37] For a treatment of structural or systemic evil that includes a discussion of St. Paul's teaching on principalities and powers, see Mott, *Biblical Ethics and Social Change*, chapter 1.

[38] However, Ephraim is called a calf in Jer 31:18, and Israel is called a cow in Hos 4:16. Symmachus translated פָּרוֹת הַבָּשָׁן, "the cows of Bashan" in Amos 4:1 as αἱ βόες εὔτροφοι, "the well-fed cattle." In other places in the OT as well as in other ancient Near Eastern texts, the comparison of women to animals is meant to be a positive praise of their beauty. See, for example, Song 4:1–7; 8:14, and Mitchell, *The Song of Songs*, 789–820.

[39] As noted by Andersen and Freedman, *Amos*, 416.

[40] See the commentary on 1:1 regarding the facts that Amos was from Tekoa and was a nomadic herdsman and a tender of sycamore trees.

[41] Kleven, "The Cows of Bashan," 215.

The Hebrew participles in Amos 4:1 indicate the unchanging picture of this sinful situation: "oppressing" (הָעֹשְׁקוֹת), "crushing" (הָרֹצְצוֹת), and "saying" (הָאֹמְרֹת) demonstrate this perpetual state of affairs. These women, "by their incessant demand upon their husbands to provide for their gluttonous needs to carouse and feast, are responsible for goading them on to impoverish even further the poor."[42] They are consumers, users, and non-producers, so self-absorbed that they can think of no one but themselves. Amos summons these party-hardy pretties to "act decently, as in the daytime, not in orgies and drunkenness" (Rom 13:13), because the Day of Yahweh was near (Amos 5:18–20).

These complacent women are perhaps some of the same revelers depicted in 6:1–6. In 9:10 the upper classes are quoted as saying, "The evil will not overtake nor confront us." Those who denied that Yahweh will ever come in judgment are quoted by Isaiah with these words: "Come, let me take wine; let us fill ourselves with strong drink; and tomorrow will be just like this day, great beyond excess" (Is 56:12).

In the apostolic era—and today—the same kinds of sentiments are expressed by scoffers who assume that the Lord Jesus Christ will never return. They do not realize that the time before Judgment Day is given so that we may repent and believe and thus inherit the eternal promised land (2 Pet 3:1–13).

Amos 4:1 concludes with a direct quote in which the women say in essence, "It's party time any time when our husbands serve up the drinks."[43] Micah also addresses this preoccupation with alcohol: "If a man following wind and falsehood tells lies, 'I will prophesy for you regarding wine and strong drink,' he would be the prophet for this people" (Micah 2:11).[44] Excessive consumption is a manifestation of one's economic *position*, and in the case of Samaria's rich and well-to-do, their ability to keep indulging in alcohol was the result of economic *oppression*.

Paul states positively in 1 Tim 3:11, "Likewise, their [the deacons'] wives are to be reverent, not slanderers but sober [νηφαλίους] and trustworthy in everything." Amos' "cows of Bashan" (4:1) are just the opposite. They revel in their drinks (as do the men in 2:8), and in doing so, they ignore the divine wisdom given to Israel, not to "eat the bread of wickedness" nor "drink the wine of violence" (Prov 4:17; cf. Prov 31:4–5).

While Amos does not employ the word *marzēaḥ* here to denote the feasting, he does use the term in 6:7. Some scholars argue that the three essential elements of the *marzēaḥ* feast—upper class participants, a pagan religious connection, and the drinking of alcohol—are in 4:1.[45] However, if the prophet is

---

[42] Paul, *Amos*, 128.

[43] For other direct quotations in Amos, see 2:12; 6:13; 8:5–6, 14; 9:10 (cf. 5:14).

[44] Proverbs condemns dissolute living. See, for example, Prov 20:1; 21:17; 23:29–35; 31:4–7. Isaiah too points out this sin. See, for example, Is 28:1, 3, 7–8; 29:1.

[45] These are the three elements according to McLaughlin, *The* Marzēaḥ *in the Prophetic Literature*, 66, 214, who also argues that Amos 4:1 does refer to a *marzēaḥ* feast (pp. 109–19).

alluding to the *marzēaḥ* feast, he does not call it that as such because the feast itself is not his primary concern here. Rather, Amos focuses on the injustice brought about by this feasting. In a similar fashion in 6:1–7, the prophet does not condemn drinking and parties per se. His main concern is that people were doing so while neglecting "the ruin of Joseph" (6:6c).

4:2 Yahweh uses an oath formula three times in the book of Amos: 4:2; 6:8; 8:7. Each time he invokes himself or one of his attributes—here "his holiness." Yahweh's oaths are frequently part of Gospel themes, including his promise of the land (Gen 24:7; 50:24; Ex 13:5; 33:1; Num 11:12; Deut 6:10, 18) and his messianic promises (Pss 89:4; 36, 50 [ET 89:3; 35, 49]; 110:4). Yahweh also uses oaths in judgment contexts, as for the punishment of prolonged wilderness wandering (Num 32:10–11; Deut 1:34–35; 2:14; Josh 5:6; Ps 95:11). In other prophetic texts, Yahweh swears concerning the judgment of Judah (Jer 22:5; 44:26) as well as the destruction of foreign nations (Is 14:24–25; Jer 49:13; 51:14).

Yahweh's oath in Amos 4:2 confirms his judgment on the women in Samaria. On oath in 6:8 he abhors Jacob's pride, while in 8:4–7 the oath is made against those who crush the poor. In each of these cases, the oath is given in a conventional pattern that appears elsewhere in the OT. Yahweh "swears by" something (שָׁבַע plus בְּ attached to a noun). God always fulfills his Word, but when he swears an oath, he gives his Word even greater solemnity and gravity. Human oaths were often validated by an appeal to a deity (e.g., 1 Ki 1:30; Amos 8:14), but when Yahweh takes an oath there is a double warranty. He is both the God who makes the vow and the one who guarantees it by an appeal to his very self or to some aspect of his character, for example, his holiness or his great name.

The NT recalls how God confirmed with an oath the certainty of his promises to Abraham in Genesis (Heb 6:13–20) and his promise of the eternal priestly office of Jesus Christ in Psalm 110 (Heb 7:20–22). A common way in which Jesus adds solemnity to his words and ratifies the certainty that they will come true is by ἀμήν, "amen, truly" (e.g., Mt 24:34), or sometimes a double ἀμήν: "amen, amen" (e.g., Jn 3:5; 5:24).

In Psalm 89, after Yahweh elaborates his messianic promise to establish the Davidic kingship universally and forever, he declares, "I swore by my holiness" (נִשְׁבַּעְתִּי בְקָדְשִׁי, Ps 89:36 [ET 89:35]). The context also includes his declaration that he will punish those who abandon his Torah and violate his commands (Ps 89:31–33 [ET 89:30–32]). Similarly in Amos, "Yahweh swears by his holiness" (4:2) that he will enact the covenant curses on unfaithful Israel.

Yahweh swears that "days are coming," referring to days of judgment with eschatological significance. The use of the phrase in 4:2 is similar to other eschatological phrases involving "day(s)" in Amos: "a day of war" and "a day

Barstad suggests that the *marzēaḥ* feast in 6:4–7 is the background for 4:1 (*Religious Polemics*, 42). See also the second textual note and the commentary on 6:7.

of tempest" (1:14); "on that day" (2:16; 8:3, 9, 13); "the day when I punish the transgressions of Israel" (3:14); "the Day of Yahweh" (5:18, 20); "the evil day" (6:3); and "a bitter day" (8:10). "On that day" (9:11) and "days are coming" (9:13) also appear in 9:11–13, but in the context of resurrection and eschatological blessings in the new creation. See further the commentary on 5:18–20.

Yahweh has a day when Samaria's leading women will be taken away with fish hooks. The negative imagery of fishermen or fish hooks catching people occurs in other OT texts (e.g., Ezek 29:4–5; Hab 1:14–17). In Jer 16:16 Yahweh dispatches of a group of fishermen and hunters on a seize-and-capture mission against unfaithful Israelites in Judah: "Behold, I am sending for many fishermen ... and they shall catch them. And afterward I will send for many hunters, and they shall hunt them from every mountain and every hill and out of the clefts of the rocks." The imagery is used positively by Jesus, who promises that his disciples will be "fishermen of men" (ἁλιεῖς ἀνθρώπων, Mt 4:19; Mk 1:17).

Amos has in mind something similar to what is pictured on reliefs that show Assyrian kings holding their enemies by ropes tied to rings or hooks in their faces.[46] The punishment fits the crime. Those Israelites who treat others like animals will themselves be treated like animals. Soldiers will drive hooks into their bodies and carry them off like a butcher drags away a side of beef.

Israel was exiled in 722 BC after the three-year siege and eventual Assyrian victory over Samaria (2 Ki 17:3–6). The battle may have been prolonged by the death of the Assyrian monarch Shalmaneser V in 722 BC, as well as the ensuing revolts throughout the empire as Sargon II sought to consolidate his rule. Sargon II describes the fall of Samaria with these words:

> The ruler of Samaria [King Hoshea], in conspiracy with another king, defaulted on his taxes and declared Samaria's independence from Assyria [cf. 2 Ki 17:4–6]. With the strength given me by the divine assembly, I conquered Samaria and its covenant partner, and took ... prisoners of war [cf. 2 Ki 17:23; 18:11]. ... I conscripted enough prisoners to outfit fifty teams of chariots. I rebuilt Samaria, bigger and better than before. I repopulated it with people from other states which I had conquered, and I appointed one of my officials over them, and made them Assyrian citizens.[47]

4:3 The "cows of Bashan" (4:1) will be led into exile through the breaches (וּפְרָצִים, 4:3) in the broken-down city wall of Samaria. (Eschatologically, God will restore the metaphorical "breaches" by the resurrection of the tabernacle of David in 9:11.) The women will proceed in single file, "each woman straight ahead" (אִשָּׁה נֶגְדָּהּ, 4:3), just like animals. Then they will be "thrown" all the way "to Hermon." Amos is referring to the deportation of northern Israel, which is an ongoing theme in the rest of the book (5:5, 27; 6:7; 7:11, 17; 9:4). The poetic

---

[46] *ANEP*, §§ 440, 447. *ANEP*, § 440, shows an Assyrian king holding ropes tied to rings in the noses of four captives. In § 447, a stele from Zinjirli depicts Esarhaddon holding two captives by a rope attached to a ring or hook in each man's face (*ANEP*, pp. 300–1).

[47] Annals of Sargon II, quoted in Matthews and Benjamin, *Old Testament Parallels*, 175.

justice is this: the "cows of Bashan" (4:1) in Samaria will return to their pasture. They will be led away northward, toward Mount Hermon, which is near the region of Bashan. This judgment is guaranteed twice. In 4:2 "Yahweh swears by his holiness," and the section of 4:1–3 ends with God's signatory formula "declares Yahweh" (4:3).

Parody of Israel's False Worship (4:4–5)

4:4–5 After his attacks on the upper class women in 4:1–3, in 4:4–5 the prophet broadens his scope to include all the northern Israelites by means of a parody on their worship, using terminology drawn from the divinely ordained worship in the Torah, but stating that the result of Israel's heterodox worship is sin after sin.

4:4 The prophet imitates the liturgical call to worship that Israel's orthodox priests would issue ("go … bring …"), but sarcastically describes the unfaithful Israelites as responding with offering excessive sacrifices at alternative shrines ("Bethel … Gilgal") that were false substitutes for the Jerusalem temple, where God's people were to offer genuine worship in faith (e.g., Deut 12:5–7). For Bethel, see the second textual note and the commentary on 3:14, the first textual note on 4:4, and the commentary on 7:13. Even though the outward rites might appear to be the same as the God-pleasing worship specified in the Torah, the Israelites were performing them in the wrong places and offering their sacrifices to the wrong gods. Bethel was characterized by syncretistic worship: the two golden calves made by Jeroboam ben Nebat, one of which was in Bethel, supposedly were the gods who had redeemed Israel from Egypt (1 Ki 12:28–29) when in fact it was Yahweh alone who had saved his people. (The same issue was in Amos 2:8–9: the Israelites were sinning beside altars not consecrated to the God who had delivered them.) Gilgal probably was one of the other sites where Jeroboam ben Nebat had constructed temples (1 Ki 12:31). Israel's corrupt and idolatrous worship not only violated the spirit and letter of the Torah, it also caused justice and righteousness to be thrown down and poisoned (cf. Amos 5:7, 24; 6:12).

Ps 95:6–7 is a familiar liturgical piece in the Office of Matins: "O come, let us worship and bow down; let us kneel before Yahweh/the LORD, our Maker. For he is our God, and we are the people of his pasture and the sheep of his hand." These verses display a two-part structure: (1) the invitation, using imperative verbs; (2) the reasons for offering worship, expressed by clauses introduced with כִּי: "*for* he is our God …" That God has redeemed people to be his own is the reason why they respond in faith. Ps 81:2–8 (ET 81:1–7) functions in a similar manner.[48] It begins with multiple worship invitations (morphologically imperatives) to praise God, including injunctions for worship behavior: "blow the shofar at the new moon, at the full moon on our feast day" (Ps 81:4 [ET 81:3]). These imperatives are followed by the reasons for worship introduced with כִּי:

[48] Cf. Ward, *Amos and Isaiah*, 129–32.

"*for* it is a statute for Israel, an ordinance of the God of Jacob ..." (Ps 81:5–8 [ET 81:4–7]).[49] A pilgrim coming to the Jerusalem temple would anticipate these kinds of invitations in Psalms 81 and 95. Perhaps the false clergy ordained by Jeroboam ben Nebat (1 Ki 12:31) would issue the same kinds of invitations at the shrines in Bethel and Gilgal.

Amos offers an invitation as well, but turns the established pattern on its head. Imitating the call to worship, Amos 4:4 begins with the imperative of בּוֹא, "go/come," the same imperative that functions as a call for pilgrims to worship in Pss 95:6; 96:8; 100:2, 4. This is the first of seven imperatives in Amos 4:4–5.[50] "Go to Bethel," Amos cries out. Then the other shoe drops. Instead of continuing with the theme of worship, kneeling or bowing down to Yahweh, the one true God, he commands, "and transgress" (וּפִשְׁעוּ). Amos' paradoxical invitation, which begins with "go ... and transgress" (בֹּאוּ ... וּפִשְׁעוּ), is another case where the prophet uses the element of surprise.[51] "Transgress" is cognate to the noun "transgression" used throughout 1:3–2:3 to describe the transgressions of the heathen nations. There it refers to crimes against humanity, moral and ethical horrors that even unbelievers know are wrong. The shock in 4:4 is that the same idea is used to describe Israel's worship life!

Imagine this sign on a marquee outside of a Christian sanctuary: *Come to this church and sin!*

The frequent and generous offerings Israel was bringing according to 4:4–5 sound more like a list that a church would draw up to describe an ideal member of the year, rather than an indictment for excommunication! After all, the people were attending "church" and going beyond the call of duty with their daily offerings and tithes (ten percent of their income) every three days. Israel had the outward form of godliness but denied its power (2 Tim 3:5). Pseudo-worship of gods substituting for Yahweh is transgression against Yahweh (1 Ki 12:28–30). Worship had been transformed into a fraudulent form of escape for the elite who practiced social oppression and then flocked into the pews at every opportunity. The worship sites had become barriers to true faith; they had to be destroyed (Amos 9:1–4).

In 2:8 Amos describes the oppression as occurring "beside every altar" (אֵצֶל כָּל־מִזְבֵּחַ). Two places with such altars are now named: Bethel and Gilgal. They had been important sites in God's salvation of his people during the patriarchal age and the conquest, respectively. But by the time of Amos in the eighth century, they were centers of idolatry in northern Israel (Hos 4:15; cf. Micah 6:5). In Amos 5:4–5, Beer-sheba in the southern kingdom of Judah is added to the list, indicating that although the prophet's main target was the Northern Kingdom, he never excused the Southern Kingdom.

---

49 For this use of כִּי in priestly Torah, see, for example, Lev 7:22–25; 19:5–8; Deut 14:4–8, 21.

50 See the textual note on 4:4–5.

51 For other surprising endings, see 2:6–16; 3:1–2; 3:3–8; 9:11–15.

Jerusalem was to be the only legitimate place to worship Yahweh (e.g., Deut 12:5–6). Moreover, it antedated these other places as the site of true worship. Gen 14:18–20 expresses how Melchizedek was king of Jerusalem and priest of God Most High. He brought victorious Abraham bread and wine, prefiguring the Lord's Supper. He then blessed Abraham and received a tithe from him. This priest and his office prefigured Jesus Christ in his eternal office as High Priest (Ps 110:4; Heb 5:5–10; 6:19–20; 7:1–17).

The second colon in Amos 4:4 intensifies the first: as the Israelites increased their visits and offerings at their shrines they—"*even more*"—increased their transgressing. In the third and fourth lines of 4:4, the second masculine plural pronominal suffixes—"*your* sacrifices" (זִבְחֵיכֶם) and "*your* tithes" (מַעְשְׂרֹתֵיכֶם)—strike at the heart of the problem. Unfaithful Israel's worship does not involve *Yahweh*; if it did, Amos would have called them "*his* sacrifices" and "*his* tithes." Paul writes: "The cult has become an anthropocentric staff of life, but theocentrically it is void of all substance."[52]

Israelite men were to appear before the Lord at the central sanctuary (at least) three times a year (Ex 23:14–17; 34:23; Leviticus 23; Deut 16:1–17), but there was no requirement for them to offer sacrifice daily. They were to bring their tithes from the produce of the land not every third day, but every year and every three years (Deut 14:22, 28; 26:12; see the second textual note on Amos 4:4). When Yahweh commands them to bring "sacrifices for every morning" and "tithes" for "every third day," he "cynically urges them to continue their multitude of useless acts that will not appease God."[53]

4:5 The first part of 4:5 indicates that externally Israel's worship followed the correct forms (see the first and second textual notes on 4:5). But internally the hearts of the people were far from Yahweh (cf. Is 29:13; Mt 15:8). This worship consisted of offerings of unleavened bread, thank offerings, and freewill offerings. The faithless Israelites "love to do" (Amos 4:5) these acts, but the love of God does not come to them through these rites because they lack faith. Israel's love was focused not on Yahweh and neighbor (Deut 6:5; Lev 19:18), but only on the religious rituals at idolatrous shrines.[54]

Worship was fulfilling Israel's felt needs ("for *you* love to do this, O children of Israel"), but it was not fulfilling Yahweh's desire for *mercy* and sacrifice (cf. 1 Sam 15:22; Hos 6:6; Mt 9:13; 12:7). The loyalty of the Israelites was to their own actions, not to their Lord, for "they loved the sacrificial system" that they had devised, and that was contrary to the Torah, "more than they loved their poor and oppressed neighbors."[55] This is a far cry from the apostolic admonition to "present your bodies as a living sacrifice" (Rom 12:1), with the ensuing exhortation to "associate with the lowly" (Rom 12:16). What the Israelites were

---

[52] Paul, *Amos*, 140.

[53] Smith, *Hosea, Amos, Micah*, 298.

[54] Cf. Stuart, *Hosea–Jonah*, 338.

[55] Niehaus, "Amos," 397.

doing at their idolatrous shrines can be compared to what the Judahites later did at the Jerusalem temple, when they made Yahweh's "house of prayer into a den of thieves" (Jer 7:11; Lk 19:46).

It was the role of Israel's priesthood to teach the people about Yahweh's salvation and the liturgical worship through which they received his grace and expressed their faith in him (e.g., Leviticus 1–4; 2 Chr 15:3). But the northern Israelites lacked true knowledge of Yahweh due to an incompetent and illegitimate priesthood (1 Ki 12:31–32) as both Amos (7:10–17) and his approximate contemporary Hosea (4:4–10) declared. Therefore the Israelites' sacrifices were useless and their sanctuaries godless. The people along with their priests and king would soon receive divine judgment (Hos 5:1). The worship sites, along with the false priesthood, are the chief targets in Amos' oracles of judgment.[b]

(b) Amos 2:7–8; 3:14; 4:4–5; 5:5–6, 14, 21–27; 7:9–17; 8:5, 10, 14; 9:1

The sacrifices and liturgical worship Yahweh prescribed in the Torah were his gracious gifts. But in the context of Israel's blatant unrighteousness and impenitence, even those sacrifices and offerings, which they presented at idolatrous shrines, became a mockery and a sin.

Summary

In Gen 12:7–8 Abraham worshiped Yahweh in response to the "precious and great promises" (2 Pet 1:4) given to him in Gen 12:2–3. All the peoples of the earth would be blessed through him and his Seed (see Galatians 3). On seeing a vision of God, Jacob made an oath of devotion to Yahweh (Gen 28:12–22). Moses reverently hid his face from the presence of Yahweh when he heard him speaking in the burning bush (Ex 3:1–6). When the tabernacle (Exodus 40) and Solomonic temple (1 Kings 8) were erected according to God's instructions, Israel worshiped Yahweh in faith. In these instances, worship was a humble response to Yahweh's redemption and saving presence.

Not so with the Israelites in Amos' day. Women are able to go from party to party because their husbands are dishonest in the marketplace (8:4–6). The worship rituals were worthless anthropocentric inventions contrary to those God himself had instituted in his Word. Instead of the divine service given in the Torah, the people were sacrificing to idols, which means they were serving demons (see 1 Cor 10:20–21). In light of this dire situation, Amos attempts to shock the Israelites into repentance. He inverts the priestly call to divine worship, and in doing so he employs biting satire. Mays writes: "Amos usurps the role of the priest and exhorts the congregation in a shocking parody of ecclesiastical language that must have sounded like irreverent blasphemy."[56] The inspired prophet's rhetorical strategies apparently failed to drive the Israelites to repentance. The next passage (4:6–13) lists Yahweh's plagues, and five times Yahweh reminds Israel that "you did not return to me" (4:6, 8, 9, 10, 11).

---

[56] Mays, *Amos*, 74.

Amos 4:6–13

Plagues Produce No Repentance

Translation

4 [6]"I myself even gave to you clean teeth in all of your cities,
and lack of food in all your places,
but you did not return to me,"
declares Yahweh.
[7]"I myself even withheld from you the rain
while there were still three months before the harvest.
I would send rain on one city,
and on another city I would not send rain.
One plot would receive rain,
but another plot on which it would not rain would dry up.
[8]Two or three cities staggered to another city to drink water,
and they were not satisfied,
but you did not return to me,"
declares Yahweh.
[9]"I struck you with blight and mildew;
the multitude of your gardens, your vineyards, your fig trees, and your olive trees the locust devoured,
but you did not return to me,"
declares Yahweh.
[10]"I sent against you pestilence in the manner of Egypt.
I killed with the sword your best soldiers,
together with your captured horses.
I made the stench of your camp ascend even into your noses,
but you did not return to me,"
declares Yahweh.
[11]"I overturned you
just as God overturned Sodom and Gomorrah,
and you became like a burning stick snatched from the fire,
but you did not return to me,"
declares Yahweh.
[12]"Therefore, thus will I do to you, O Israel,
because this is what I will do to you:
prepare to meet your God, O Israel!"
[13]Indeed, behold, he who forms mountains and who creates wind,
and who declares to mankind his thoughts,
who makes dawn [into] darkness,
and who treads on the high places of the earth,
Yahweh, the God of armies, is his name.

Textual Notes

4:6 וְגַם־אֲנִי נָתַתִּי לָכֶם—The unneeded personal pronoun אֲנִי, "I," preceding the inflected verb נָתַתִּי, "I gave," emphasizes the subject (GKC, § 135 a) and the combination is rendered as "I *myself* gave." The first clause of 4:7 similarly has the equivalent emphatic pronoun אָנֹכִי, as also at the beginning of 2:9 and 2:10.

נִקְיוֹן שִׁנַּיִם בְּכָל־עָרֵיכֶם—The abstract noun נִקָּיוֹן is derived from the verb נָקָה, "to be empty, clean, innocent."[1] The noun usually means "innocence," but here it means "cleanness," and in the construct phrase "cleanness of teeth" it is translated adjectivally: "clean teeth." This indicates a lack of food, as confirmed by the following parallel line. The LXX did not understand the idiom and translated it with γομφιασμὸν ὀδόντων, "toothaches."

וְחֹסֶר לֶחֶם בְּכֹל מְקוֹמֹתֵיכֶם—The abstract noun חֹסֶר, "a lack, absence, need," occurs elsewhere only in the covenant curses in Deut 28:48, 57. It is derived from the verb חָסֵר, "to lack, need, want," often used in connection with the basic necessities of life. The verb is negated in Ps 23:1: "I shall not want." Yahweh brings about the lack of basic necessities in order to discipline his people (see also Deut 2:7; 8:2; Ezek 4:17; cf. the first temptation of Christ in Mt 4:1–4; Lk 4:1–4).

וְלֹא־שַׁבְתֶּם עָדַי נְאֻם־יְהוָה׃—This refrain is repeated at the end of 4:6, 8–11. For the signatory formula נְאֻם־יְהוָה, see the second textual note on 2:11.

The *waw* on וְלֹא־ is adversative: "*but* you did not return to me." In many OT passages, שׁוּב indicates a theological return, a turning back to Yahweh, the Creator and Redeemer. Thus it involves repentance and saving faith. In Amos שׁוּב has this meaning only in this refrain.[2] Similar is Is 9:12 (ET 9:13): וְהָעָם לֹא־שָׁב עַד־הַמַּכֵּהוּ, "but the people did not return to the one [God] who struck them." See also שׁוּב עַד־ in Deut 4:30; 30:2; Is 19:22; Joel 2:12; Job 22:23; Lam 3:40.

4:7 וְגַם אָנֹכִי מָנַעְתִּי מִכֶּם אֶת־הַגֶּשֶׁם—The personal pronoun אָנֹכִי is emphatic; see the first textual note on 4:6. The verb מָנַע and noun גֶּשֶׁם occur in Amos only here. In prophetic contexts, the verb מָנַע, "to withhold," is used with an aspect of creation as its object (here הַגֶּשֶׁם, "the rain") within a proclamation of judgment.[3] In Jer 3:3 and Amos 4:7, Yahweh withholds rain in order to punish. Job 38:15 states that Yahweh withholds the light of day from the wicked. The Niphal stem of מָנַע in Joel 1:13 indicates that grain and drink offerings were withheld from the temple (probably by means of drought killing crops) in order to bring the people to repentance. גֶּשֶׁם is a general word for "rain." In Israel most of the rain falls during the winter, from November through February. Here גֶּשֶׁם refers to these winter rains, which were essential for the crops to experience initial growth. See the next textual note.

בְּעוֹד שְׁלֹשָׁה חֳדָשִׁים לַקָּצִיר—Literally, "yet three months to the harvest" confirms that גֶּשֶׁם in the preceding clause refers to the winter rains. The barley harvest normally

---

1 Cf. G. Warmuth, "נִקָּיוֹן," *TDOT* 9:561–63.

2 The Qal of שׁוּב has a transitive meaning in 9:14, and the Hiphil has different transitive meanings in 1:3, 6, 8, 9, 11, 13; 2:1, 4, 6. See the third textual note on 1:3.

3 Cf. H.-J. Fabry, "מָנַע," *TDOT* 8:421–27.

took place in April or early May. The Feast of Firstfruits was celebrated at the beginning of the barley harvest. The wheat harvest normally occurred in May–June. The Feast of Weeks, or Pentecost, was normally celebrated during the wheat harvest.

וְהִמְטַרְתִּי עַל־עִיר אֶחָת וְעַל־עִיר אַחַת לֹא אַמְטִיר—The verb מָטַר occurs a total of four times in 4:7. Its Hiphil (once in each of these two clauses) means "to send/cause rain or hail," and God is normally the subject. In the OT, the verb always occurs in the Hiphil except for the one instance of the Niphal, to "be rained upon" (BDB) or "to receive rain," in the next clause.

The ultimate accent on וְהִמְטַרְתִּי indicates that it is the perfect with *waw* consecutive, and it is followed by the imperfect אַמְטִיר and then the imperfects תִּמָּטֵר and תַמְטִיר later in the verse. These verbs are epexegetical in that they further explain the preceding statement phrased with a perfect: "I … withheld [מָנַעְתִּי] from you the rain." These verbs have frequentative or durative force referring to past time, and so they are translated with "would," for example, "I would send rain." This force is conveyed in most English translations, for example, RSV, ESV, NASB, but not NIV. See GKC, § 112 h, note 3, and Waltke-O'Connor, § 32.2.3e, example 27.

The repeated noun אַחַת (pausal: אֶחָת) has the idiomatic meaning "one … another" (BDB, s.v. אֶחָד, 6).

חֶלְקָה אַחַת תִּמָּטֵר—The noun חֶלְקָה, "plot (of land),"[4] is a synonym of שָׂדֶה, "field," and can be used in construct with it (e.g., Gen 33:19; Ruth 2:3; 4:3). חֶלְקָה often refers to a plot of land that was part of a larger agricultural field.

וְחֶלְקָה אֲשֶׁר־לֹא־תַמְטִיר עָלֶיהָ תִּיבָשׁ׃—The imperfect תַמְטִיר is an example of a third feminine verb used impersonally for a natural phenomenon: "*it* would rain." See GKC, § 144 c, and Joüon, § 152 e (both of which wrongly doubt the text). The subject of the feminine imperfect תִּיבָשׁ, "dry up," is the feminine noun חֶלְקָה at the start of the clause. For יָבֵשׁ, see the fifth textual note on 1:2, its only other occurrence in Amos.

4:8 וְנָעוּ שְׁתַּיִם שָׁלֹשׁ עָרִים אֶל־עִיר אַחַת לִשְׁתּוֹת מַיִם וְלֹא יִשְׂבָּעוּ—The verb נוּעַ, "to reel, stagger, shake," also appears in 8:12 and twice in 9:9. It is used in some contexts with שִׁכּוֹר, "drunkard" (Is 24:20; Ps 107:27), so it may evoke the image of an inebriated man tottering to and fro.[5] In Gen 4:12, 14, נוּעַ describes the nomadic wandering that Cain must endure, while in Lam 4:14–15 it depicts confused wandering. In Ps 109:10 the psalmist curses his enemy, wishing that his foe's children would wander about. Paul writes that here the Israelites "are portrayed as taking a zigzag course not because of drunkenness but due to dehydration, unable to find adequate water sources to slake their thirst."[6]

The juxtaposition of the numerals "two, three cities" forms a staircase numerical pattern like that in 1:3–2:16,[7] but here it simply indicates a small and indefinite total number (GKC, § 134 s), that is, several cities.

---

4 Cf. K.-D. Schunck, "חָלַק," *TDOT* 4:444–47.

5 Cf. H. Ringgren, "נוּעַ," *TDOT* 9:293–95.

6 Paul, *Amos*, 145.

7 See "The Staircase Numerical Pattern" in the introduction to 1:3–2:16.

Elsewhere in Amos, the verb שָׁתָה, "to drink," usually has "wine" as its object (2:8; 5:11; 6:6; 9:14; cf. 4:1), but here the object of the infinitive לִשְׁתּוֹת is מַיִם, "water."

וְלֹא־שַׁבְתֶּם עָדַי נְאֻם־יְהוָה׃—See the fourth textual note on 4:6.

4:9 הִכֵּיתִי אֶתְכֶם בַּשִּׁדָּפוֹן וּבַיֵּרָקוֹן—For the Hiphil of נָכָה, "strike," see the first textual note on 3:15. The definite article is used (with the preposition בְּ) on both nouns, literally, "with the blight and with the mildew," but the article is generic and need not be translated (see GKC, § 126 n (c); Waltke-O'Connor, § 13.5.1g, example 43). When referring to plagues, שִׁדָּפוֹן and יֵרָקוֹן always appear together (Deut 28:22; 1 Ki 8:37 ‖ 2 Chr 6:28; Amos 4:9; Hag 2:17).

The first of these, שִׁדָּפוֹן, denotes "blasting, blight," which could be caused by a scorching sirocco wind. The LXX translates שִׁדָּפוֹן in Deut 28:22 and 2 Chr 6:28 as ἀνεμοφθορία, "wind damage." The noun שִׁדָּפוֹן is cognate to the verb שָׁדַף in, for example, Gen 41:6: "seven ears of grain, thin and *scorched* [וּשְׁדוּפֹת] by the east wind." This wind is well known in the Near East as the *khamsin* or *sharav*. When it blows today in the Near East, it is not unusual for the temperatures to reach 110 degrees Fahrenheit and the humidity gets as low as two percent. This wind is capable of blocking out the sun with the dust that it raises. As it blows harder, it becomes more destructive.

The noun יֵרָקוֹן "refers to the brownish yellow withering color of the grain."[8] The withering could be caused by the sirocco or by parasites or other plant diseases. שִׁדָּפוֹן and יֵרָקוֹן appear together in Deut 28:22 in the context of a covenant curse pronounced on Israel when it would become unfaithful. 1 Ki 8:37 (‖ 2 Chr 6:28) lists שִׁדָּפוֹן and יֵרָקוֹן alongside other disasters such as famine, locusts, and plague.

הַרְבּוֹת גַּנּוֹתֵיכֶם וְכַרְמֵיכֶם וּתְאֵנֵיכֶם וְזֵיתֵיכֶם—This is the long direct object of the verb יֹאכַל (see the next textual note). The Hiphil infinitive construct הַרְבּוֹת apparently functions as a noun here, as the infinitive absolute does rarely elsewhere (BDB, s.v. רָבָה, Hiphil, 1 e (5)). Hence it is translated as "the *multitude* of your gardens, your vineyards, your fig trees, and your olive trees." ESV renders it as an adjective: "your *many* gardens." Compare Prov 25:27, where הַרְבּוֹת has an adjectival meaning: "to eat much [הַרְבּוֹת] honey is not good."

יֹאכַל הַגָּזָם—The collective noun גָּזָם refers to "locusts" that were "devouring, devastating" (BDB).[9] Its etymology probably pertains to the grasshopper's cutting or biting activity.[10] There are eight more Hebrew words for the locust or grasshopper in the OT. Four of the terms appear in both Joel 1:4 and 2:25. The different words do not refer to difference species but rather to successive stages in the growth and life cycle of the locust.

וְלֹא־שַׁבְתֶּם עָדַי נְאֻם־יְהוָה׃—See the fourth textual note on 4:6.

---

[8] Paul, *Amos*, 146. Wolff includes this definition for יֵרָקוֹן: the "turning pale of the tips of the green grain due to the build-up of [parasitic] worms" (*Joel and Amos*, 221). Both Paul and Wolff cite Gustaf Dalman, *Arbeit und Sitte in Palästina* (Gütersloh: Bertelsmann, 1928), 1/2.326.

[9] See Crenshaw, *Joel*, 88–94, for a discussion on locusts in the OT and in ancient Near Eastern literature.

[10] Crenshaw, *Joel*, 88.

4:10 שִׁלַּחְתִּי בָכֶם דֶּבֶר בְּדֶרֶךְ מִצְרַיִם—The noun דֶּבֶר, which occurs only here in Amos, is a general term for any kind of potentially fatal disease or pestilence.[11] Because of the terminal nature, some speculation exists that the root is derived from the Ugaritic *dbr*, "death." More commonly, its derivation is sought in the Akkadian *dibiru*, "calamity." דֶּבֶר always refers to a divinely sent punishment, so it represents Yahweh's judgment. He can send it against another nation (e.g., Ex 9:3), but more frequently the target is apostate Israel (e.g., Jer 14:12; 21:6–7, 9; Ezek 28:23). The same general term for "pestilence" refers to the fifth plague against Egypt (דֶּבֶר in Ex 9:3), and here "in the manner of Egypt" (בְּדֶרֶךְ מִצְרַיִם) further clarifies that Yahweh will punish Israel with the same kind of judgment he sent as the fifth plague against Egypt. Disobedient Israel is no better than that pagan nation.

הָרַגְתִּי בַחֶרֶב בַּחוּרֵיכֶם—For the verb הָרַג, see the second textual note on 2:3. There it refers to Yahweh killing Moabites, who were enemies of his people. However, in its other occurrences in Amos, it refers to God using the "sword" (חֶרֶב, here with בְּ of means) to kill people he had called to be his own, but who had turned against him: the unfaithful Israelites (4:10; 9:1, 4). In the Amos passages with "sword" (except for 1:11), it is wielded by Yahweh himself (4:10; 7:9; 9:1) or by his agents who carry out his judgments (7:11, 17; 9:4, 10). Yahweh is the ultimate sword bearer in the book (cf. Josh 5:13–14). According to Odell, metaphors that describe the effects of Yahweh's sword belong to two different semantic fields. The first is that of fire, as suggested by the flashing brilliance of the polished blade (e.g., Is 66:16; Ezek 21:20, 33 [ET 21:15, 28]; Nah 2:14 [ET 2:13]; 3:15). The sword is also pictured as a consuming animal because it eats human flesh (e.g., Is 1:20; Jer 12:12) and gets drunk on human blood (e.g., Is 34:5; Jer 46:10). Odell writes: "Again, this is a commonplace in the ancient Near East; there is widespread archaeological evidence of sword hilts crafted to resemble the gaping mouth of a wild animal, usually a lion."[12]

Here the victims are denoted by the plural of בָּחוּר, a "*young man* (choice, in the prime of manhood)" (BDB), which was in 2:11 and recurs in 8:13. While it can refer to young men living as civilians, such men would be enlisted in the army in times of war, and they would be the most vigorous of Israel's troops. Therefore בַּחוּרֵיכֶם is translated as "your best soldiers." The following line refers to horses that would be used in the military, so it supports the military interpretation of בַּחוּרֵיכֶם.

עִם שְׁבִי סוּסֵיכֶם—Literally, "with the capture of your horses," this could imply that along with killing the young men (4:10b), Yahweh will also kill Israel's horses (so NIV, NASB), which Israel had captured from its enemies or which were captured from Israel. Or it could mean that in the battle that killed the young men, Yahweh also caused Israel's horses to be captured by the enemy (so KJV, RSV, ESV). Normally the noun שְׁבִי refers to the "captivity" (BDB, 1) of people sent into exile or, more concretely, to "captives" (BDB, 3) taken in war—usually people but sometimes also animals (Num 31:26; cf.

---

11 Cf. G. Mayer, "דֶּבֶר," *TDOT* 3:125–27.

12 Odell, *Ezekiel*, 268.

Num 31:12, 19).[13] The cognate verb (the Niphal of שָׁבָה) is used in Ex 22:9 (ET 22:10) to refer to an animal that is "captured [נִשְׁבָּה]." Here שְׁבִי may refer to the "act of *capture*" (BDB, 2). In one of the covenant curses, שְׁבִי refers to the Israelites' children being taken from them into "captivity" (Deut 28:41), and the word has a similar meaning in Jer 15:2; 43:11, where the contexts (like Amos 4:10) refer to other people killed by the "sword" (חֶרֶב). Here some emend שְׁבִי to צְבִי, "beauty, pomp,"[14] but that is inferior, and the ancient versions (LXX, Vulgate, Syriac, and Targum) support the MT.

וָאַעֲלֶה בְּאֹשׁ מַחֲנֵיכֶם וּבְאַפְּכֶם—Israel's defeated camp is filled with rotting corpses that emit the sickening smell of death. Yahweh causes the stench to ascend into the nostrils of the few surviving Israelites. In form, the verb וָאַעֲלֶה could be either the intransitive Qal or the Hiphil of עָלָה, but since it has a direct object (the construct phrase בְּאֹשׁ מַחֲנֵיכֶם), it must be the transitive Hiphil: "*I made* the stench … *ascend*." The noun בְּאֹשׁ refers to the "stench" (BDB) of the rotting corpses, which Yahweh sends up the nostrils of those Israelites still living. Similar is the warning in Is 34:3 expressed with בְּאשׁ and the intransitive Qal of עָלָה: "as for their corpses, their stench will arise [יַעֲלֶה בָאְשָׁם]." Cognate to the noun בְּאשׁ is the verb בָּאַשׁ, "to stink," which can refer to decaying carcasses of frogs (Ex 8:10 [ET 8:14]), fish (Is 50:2), and flies (Eccl 10:1).

The noun מַחֲנֶה can refer to the "camp" of all Israelites, including civilians, women, and children (e.g., Deut 29:10 [ET 29:11]), and it is frequently used with that meaning in Leviticus, Numbers, and Deuteronomy. It can also refer more specifically to an army camp of soldiers, as in, for example, Deut 23:10 (ET 23:9); Josh 8:13; Judg 4:15. Either meaning could fit here, but it is probably best to take it in the widest sense referring to all kinds of Israelites, especially since the cataclysmic destruction in the following verse, 4:11, would take the lives of all inhabitants. מַחֲנֵיכֶם is one of the "apparent plurals" of a noun ending in ה with a suffix, but it really is the singular noun (see Joüon, § 96C e). The *waw* on וּבְאַפְּכֶם is emphatic: "I made the stench of your camp ascend *even* into your noses" (see Waltke-O'Connor, § 39.2.1b, including example 7; GKC, § 154 a, note 1 (b)).

וְלֹא־שַׁבְתֶּם עָדַי נְאֻם־יְהוָה׃—See the fourth textual note on 4:6.

4:11 הָפַכְתִּי בָכֶם—The verb הָפַךְ often simply means "to turn," but it is used with the specific meaning to "overturn, overthrow" in reference to God's destruction of Sodom and Gomorrah (Gen 19:21, 25, 29; Deut 29:22 [ET 29:23]; Jer 20:16; Lam 4:6) and also for him destroying other things (e.g., Job 9:5). See BDB, s.v. הָפַךְ, Qal, 1 b. The preposition בְּ with pronominal suffix (בָכֶם) could be partitive,[15] "I overturned *some of you*" (similar are KJV, RSV, NIV, ESV), in which case this plague, like other ones in this passage, is selective. Or the preposition בְּ could introduce a predicate as an accusative (cf. BDB, s.v. בְּ, I 7 b; Joüon, §§ 125 m; 133 c), "I overthrew *you*" (NASB), in which case this final plague is comprehensive, affecting all the Israelites. The destruc-

[13] Cf. B. Otzen, "שָׁבָה," *TDOT* 14:286–94.

[14] Cf. Paul, *Amos*, 148.

[15] Andersen and Freedman, *Amos*, 444, maintain that the partitive use of בְּ "is unusual, but it seems to be the only plausible explanation here." Usually Hebrew expresses a partitive idea with the preposition מִן.

tion of Sodom and Gomorrah affected all of the residents of those cities save Lot and his daughters.

כְּמַהְפֵּכַת אֱלֹהִים אֶת־סְדֹם וְאֶת־עֲמֹרָה—The verbal noun מַהְפֵּכָה, "an overturning, overthrow," is indissolubly linked in the OT with the destruction of Sodom and Gomorrah, to which it refers in every OT occurrence (Deut 29:22 [ET 29:23]; Is 13:19; Jer 49:18; 50:40; Amos 4:11) except possibly Is 1:7, which, however, may allude to it. The destruction of Sodom and Gomorrah is the most-often-cited narrative from Genesis in the rest of the Bible, mentioned around twenty times. The construct form מַהְפֵּכַת of the noun מַהְפֵּכָה is unusual because the *tsere* is retained (-פֵּ-) instead of reduced to *shewa* (מַהְפְּכַת־). See Joüon, §§ 97C b; 97E b. מַהְפֵּכָה is a verbal noun formed by the nominal prefix מ and the verb הָפַךְ, "to overturn" (see the preceding textual note). Such verbal nouns can take direct objects (GKC, § 115 d) as indicated here by the direct object marker אֶת־ repeated before "Sodom" (סְדֹם) and "Gomorrah" (עֲמֹרָה).

The clause כְּמַהְפֵּכַת אֱלֹהִים אֶת־סְדֹם וְאֶת־עֲמֹרָה, "as God overturned Sodom and Gomorrah," occurs verbatim in Is 13:19 and Jer 50:40; in both verses the coming destruction of Babylon is compared to their destruction. Almost the same clause occurs in Jer 49:18 as a comparison for the destruction of Edom and in the covenant curse in Deut 29:22 (ET 29:23) for Israel when it would break the Sinaitic covenant.

Some interpreters find it strange that Yahweh, speaking in the first person, should then refer to himself in the third person as "God" (אֱלֹהִים). However, note the redundant repetition of "Yahweh" in Gen 19:24 in the original account of the destruction: "Yahweh rained down on Sodom and on Gomorrah fire and sulfur *from Yahweh* from heaven." The repetition emphasizes that the destruction was not some accident of nature, but a specific judgment of Yahweh that he himself executed. Similarly, the inclusion of "God" in Amos 4:11 (and similar passages) emphasizes that it was God who carried out the judgment of the cities notorious for their sin of homosexuality and that God himself will execute a similar judgment against his people who have forsaken him and broken his covenant.

Some commentators propose that "God" is not only the source of the action, but also a kind of superlative that emphasizes the tremendous size of the destruction. Thomas argues that in some verses אֱלֹהִים or אֵל can be used to express the superlative insofar as it brings something into comparison with God, but that argument may downplay the significance of the references to God.[16]

וַתִּהְיוּ כְּאוּד מֻצָּל מִשְּׂרֵפָה—The noun אוּד denotes a "burning stick, firebrand," and occurs in the OT only in Is 7:4; Amos 4:11; and Zech 3:2, which has a very similar phrase (אוּד מֻצָּל מֵאֵשׁ). The Hophal participle מֻצָּל (from נָצַל) does not mean that the whole stick is "saved, rescued," but merely that after much of the stick has already been incinerated, the remainder will be "snatched, pulled out" of the "burning (fire)" (שְׂרֵפָה). This is slightly more hopeful than the similar theological point made in 3:12, the only

---

16 Thomas, "A Consideration of Some Unusual Ways of Expressing the Superlative in Hebrew," especially p. 210–15. He believes that אֱלֹהִים or אֵל have a superlative force in Gen 23:6; 30:8; Ex 9:28; 1 Sam 14:15; Jonah 3:3; Pss 36:7 (ET 36:6); 80:11 (ET 80:10); Job 1:16. For an analysis of the proposal by Thomas and others and for an exposition of Jonah 3:3 that affirms the full theological significance of "God" there, see Lessing, *Jonah*, 278–81.

other Amos verse with נָצַל, where only pieces of a dead and dismembered sheep were "rescued" from Lion Yahweh. See the second textual note on 3:12.

וְלֹא־שַׁבְתֶּם עָדַי נְאֻם־יְהוָה׃—See the fourth textual note on 4:6.

4:12 לָכֵן כֹּה אֶעֱשֶׂה־לְּךָ יִשְׂרָאֵל עֵקֶב כִּי־זֹאת אֶעֱשֶׂה־לָּךְ—In prophetic texts לָכֵן, "therefore," often introduces a climactic judgment. See the first textual note on 3:11.

Both of these repetitious clauses use the imperfect of עָשָׂה, "to do," suggesting an imminent ongoing activity of continually disciplining Israel in the future so that the nation might repent. Both times אֶעֱשֶׂה is followed by לְּךָ (pausal: לָּךְ) with conjunctive *daghesh forte* in the first consonant of the monosyllabic לְּךָ (see GKC, § 20 c (a) (1)). The preposition לְ ("*to* you") may have the nuance of disadvantage: "*against* you" (see BDB, s.v. לְ, 5 g (b) (γ)).

Paul notes that the repeated idiom עָשָׂה לְ, "do to," echoes earlier curse formulas.[17] In Lev 26:16, the introduction to the long list of covenant curses in Lev 26:16–39 begins with Yahweh declaring, אַף־אֲנִי אֶעֱשֶׂה־זֹּאת לָכֶם, "surely I myself will do this to you." An individual swearing an oath can also declare, כֹּה יַעֲשֶׂה־לִּי אֱלֹהִים, "so may God do to me [if I do not fulfill this oath]" (1 Ki 2:23; cf. Josh 10:25).

הִכּוֹן לִקְרַאת־אֱלֹהֶיךָ יִשְׂרָאֵל׃—The Niphal of כּוּן (imperative: הִכּוֹן) can have passive meanings ("be established") or, as here, the middle meaning "prepare oneself, get ready" (see BDB, 3). Moses uses it to tell the Israelites to prepare themselves for Yahweh's theophany on Mount Sinai: Israel was to prepare to meet God through a three-day purification (Ex 19:11, 15). In 2 Chr 35:4 Josiah commands Israel to "prepare" (Qere: וְהָכִינוּ; Kethib: וְהִכּוֹנוּ) to celebrate Yahweh's Passover. Brueggemann comments on Amos 4:12c: "It is apparent that we are not dealing simply with a stern threat or warning nor with a call to repentance, but with *a liturgic formula of preparation for covenant-making or renewal* which includes both threat and call to repentance. … The phrase is a call to return to covenant, but it is filled with the potential threat that failure to repent will transform the confrontation into combat."[18]

Besides Amos 4:12 and the Kethib וְהִכּוֹנוּ in 2 Chr 35:4, the Niphal imperative of כּוּן appears elsewhere in the OT only in Ezek 38:7, where Yahweh warns the eschatological enemy Gog, "prepare [הִכֹּן] and ready yourself [וְהָכֵן לְךָ]" for the final battle when God will defeat him and all his troops. This is the same final battle described in Rev 20:7–10, where Satan and his hordes launch a final assault against God's saints but are defeated at the return of Christ. The Hiphil and Hophal stems of כּוּן appear in other warfare contexts, for example, Jer 51:12; Prov 21:31.

Therefore הִכּוֹן in Amos 4:12 involves a double entendre. The prophet is summoning Israel to repent and adhere to the Sinai covenant, established when Yahweh appeared to and met the Israelites. But knowing that they will refuse to repent, Yahweh is also calling the nation to prepare for the military onslaught of Assyria, which will conquer northern Israel in 722 BC, about four decades after the ministry of Amos. The parallels to Ezek 38:7 and Rev 20:7–10 also suggest ironically that instead of Israel being the faithful

---

[17] Paul, *Amos*, 150.

[18] Brueggemann, "Amos IV 4–13 and Israel's Covenant Worship," 2, 6.

people whom God will deliver from Satan's onslaught on the Last Day, the idolatrous Israelites are actually among the troops of Satan who war against his faithful saints!

The infinitive construct לִקְרַאת is from the verb קָרָא, "to meet, encounter." Because of his election and redemption of Israel (2:9–10; 3:1–2), Yahweh still calls himself אֱלֹהֶיךָ, "*your* God," even though he now comes in judgment. יִשְׂרָאֵל is vocative.

4:13 This hymn-like verse includes five participles used as titles for God: "he who forms [יוֹצֵר] ... and who creates [וּבֹרֵא] ... and who declares [וּמַגִּיד] ... who makes [עֹשֵׂה] ... and who treads [וְדֹרֵךְ]." Waltke-O'Connor maintain that "the use of participial titles for God is especially important in the old poetry of the Pentateuch (e.g., Deut 32:39) and Former Prophets (e.g., 1 Sam 2:6–8) and in some of the prophets (e.g., Amos 4:13; 5:8–9; 9:5–6; Isa 43:1; 44:2, 24; 45:7, 9, 11, 18) and in Job (e.g., 5:9; 9:9–10; 25:2)" (§ 37.3d, note 28).[19]

כִּי הִנֵּה יוֹצֵר הָרִים וּבֹרֵא רוּחַ—The verb יָצַר, "to form, shape, fashion," appears primarily in the Qal stem, of which seventeen participial forms refer to a "potter" (e.g., Is 29:16; Jer 18:4). With Yahweh as subject, יָצַר describes him as molding and shaping clay. The verb first appears in the OT in Gen 2:7–8, where Yahweh "formed" (וַיִּיצֶר) Adam from dust of the ground. This action of Yahweh, with his hands in the dirt, is stunning. It indicates the degree to which he is willing to enter into his creation to create and sustain life.[20]

In Amos 4:13 Yahweh, the divine potter, forms the mountains (הָרִים), which are mentioned as part of his creative activities in, for example, Is 40:12; Ps 65:7 (ET 65:6); Prov 8:25. The mountains serve as a synecdoche for the remainder of the created order, as confirmed by the second participle in the prophet's doxology, וּבֹרֵא. Yahweh formed the mountains in the visible realm, and he also created the wind in the invisible realm (cf. Ps 104:4; Jn 3:3–8).

Besides Amos 4:13, יָצַר is coupled with בָּרָא only in Isaiah (Is 43:1, 7; 45:7, 18), also in descriptions of Yahweh as in Amos 4:13. Participles of both verbs are used as divine titles in Is 43:1; 45:7, 18. These texts portray Yahweh as the one who creates the universe (Is 45:7, 18) and who also creates and redeems his people (Is 43:1, 7). While he created everything for his good purposes (Is 45:18), he also creates judgment (Is 45:7) against those who rebel against him by their sin and unbelief.

In the OT the Qal of בָּרָא is the most common verb for "to create." It always has Yahweh as its subject and never has an object of material or means that he uses in

---

[19] Deut 32:39 lacks any participial titles for Yahweh. However, Waltke-O'Connor may have intended to cite other verses with participial titles in the ancient poetry of Deuteronomy, such as Deut 32:18; 33:3, 12, 16, 20, 26.

[20] In Amos, the only other occurrence of יָצַר is in 7:1, where again the Qal participle depicts Yahweh as יוֹצֵר, "forming, creating," something. There the context begins as one of judgment, since Yahweh is creating "a locust swarm" that would have devastated Israel's crops. However, after Amos' intercession for Yahweh to forgive, Yahweh relents by his grace and does not send the locusts (7:2–3). In no other OT passage does בָּרָא, "create," take רוּחַ, "wind; spirit; Spirit," as its object noun, but there is one OT passage where the verb יָצַר, "form, create," takes the object noun רוּחַ. Zech 12:1, like Amos 4:13, acclaims Yahweh the Creator with participial titles: he alone is "the one who spreads out the heavens [נֹטֶה שָׁמַיִם] and who lays the foundation of earth [וְיֹסֵד אָרֶץ] and who forms the spirit of man inside him [וְיֹצֵר רוּחַ־אָדָם בְּקִרְבּוֹ]."

creating. The verb always indicates *creatio ex nihilo*, either when referring to the original creation or when referring to redemption when described as a new creation. The Scriptures connect Yahweh as the sole, unaided Creator with his work as the Redeemer who is entirely responsible for salvation. See, for example, Is 43:1–25, with בָּרָא in Is 43:1, 7, 15, and Ps 51:9–16 (ET 51:7–14) with בָּרָא in Ps 51:12 (ET 51:10). People cannot contribute to, prompt, cooperate, or assist in their redemption through any merit or works. Instead, salvation is the result of divine monergism. Yahweh alone can create in us a new heart and spirit (Ps 51:12 [ET 51:10]; Ezek 11:19; 36:26). The NT affirms this too: God alone can grant us a new birth by water and the Spirit (Jn 3:5; Titus 3:5–6). "If anyone is in Christ, he is a *new creation*" (2 Cor 5:17; cf. Gal 6:15).

וּמַגִּיד לְאָדָם מַה־שֵּׂחוֹ—The Hiphil of נָגַד frequently means "to declare, make known." Often the subject is Yahweh or his agent(s), in which case the verb refers to divine revelation (see BDB, Hiphil, 2).

The noun שֵׂחַ is a hapax legomenon, but probably it is related to the verb שִׂיחַ, which in Prov 6:22 refers to "instructing, teaching" (*HALOT*, s.v. שׂיח II, 1 d), and to the noun שִׂיחַ, which in Sirach can mean "wisdom, discourse" (*HALOT*, שִׂיחַ II, 4 b). The LXX renders the clause here in Amos 4:13 as ἀπαγγέλλων εἰς ἀνθρώπους τὸν χριστὸν αὐτοῦ, "declaring to men his Christ/Anointed One." Recensions of the LXX translate שֵׂחוֹ with some term for a divine announcement or expression of thought: ἡ ὁμιλία αὐτοῦ (Aquila), τὸ φώνημα αὐτοῦ (Symmachus), τὸν λόγον αὐτοῦ (Theodotion). The Vulgate has *eloquium suum*.[21] The third masculine singular suffix on שֵׂחוֹ is ambiguous; does it refer to Yahweh making known "his" own thoughts, or does Yahweh make known to mankind "his" (man's) thoughts or plans (cf. Pss 94:11; 139:2; Lk 5:22; 6:8; Heb 4:12)? In light of Amos 3:7 (also 2:11; 7:15), which refers to Yahweh's self-revelation through his prophets, the pronominal suffix probably refers to Yahweh, who reveals his thoughts through his prophetic Word (cf. Is 55:8–11; Ps 40:6 [ET 40:5])).

עֹשֵׂה שַׁחַר עֵיפָה—Most interpreters and translations understand the participle עֹשֶׂה, "maker," to be in construct (עֹשֵׂה) with its direct object, שַׁחַר, "dawn," which is then followed by the accusative of the product into which the dawn is made, עֵיפָה, "darkness" (GKC, § 116 g, note 1). "Who makes dawn [into] darkness" signals a reversal of creation, when there was darkness and Yahweh made light shine (Gen 1:2–3). This interpretation fits the larger context of this oracle of judgment, including Yahweh overturning Sodom and Gomorrah (Amos 4:11). It also fits with the description of "the Day of Yahweh" in 5:18 as a "day" (יוֹם) unlike a normal day because it is "darkness and not light" (חֹשֶׁךְ וְלֹא־אוֹר). See also 5:20 and 8:9. Similar are the constructions in 5:8a, where the same participle is in construct with its direct objects (עֹשֵׂה כִימָה וּכְסִיל), and in 5:8c, where the first noun is the object and the second (without a preposition) is the product, followed by a finite verb: וְיוֹם לַיְלָה הֶחְשִׁיךְ, literally, "day [into] night he darkens," that is, "he darkens day into night."

---

[21] Cf. *HALOT*, s.v. שֵׂחַ. Some point to the obvious acoustic value of the root and discern an audible expression of positive or negative emotion. Still others insist that the core meaning lies in the internal mental and emotional activity that in some cases gives rise to an audible outcry. See J. Hausmann, "שׂיח," *TDOT* 14:85–89.

However, since neither of the nouns, שַׁחַר עֵיפָה, has a preposition, it might be remotely possible that the second noun could be the object ("darkness") and the first one could be the product ("[into] dawn"). In 5:8b the second noun is the object: וְהֹפֵךְ לַבֹּקֶר צַלְמָוֶת, literally, "turning into morning the shadow of death," that is, "turning the shadow of death into morning," but the preposition לְ on the first noun (לַבֹּקֶר) clearly shows that it is the product. If the construction in 4:13 meant "making darkness into dawn," it would have a more hopeful meaning. That meaning is advocated by Paul, who, however, arrives at it by a different and circuitous route. He defines the nouns with the opposite of the customary meanings: שַׁחַר means "blackness" and עֵיפָה means "[into] daybreak." Paul then points out that the noun עֵיפָה is from the root עיף, which could be metathesized to form the root יפע, whose verb means "to shine forth." Although the normal meaning of שַׁחַר is "dawn" (e.g., Gen 19:15; Song 6:10), the word here could be derived from a different homographic root and refer to the color black.[22]

וְדֹרֵךְ עַל־בָּמֳתֵי אָרֶץ—"And who treads on the high places of the earth" evokes the idea of Yahweh's power as a mighty warrior. By beginning this hymn with "mountains" and ending it with the plural of בָּמָה, "high place, height," Amos creates an inclusion that highlights Yahweh's strength. (בָּמָה recurs in 7:9, where it refers to idolatrous worship on "high places"; see the first textual note on 7:9.)

Almost identical to the participial description of Yahweh here is Job 9:8, where Job refers to Yahweh as the sole Creator of the heavens and then accords him the title וְדוֹרֵךְ עַל־בָּמֳתֵי יָם, "he who treads on the high places of the sea." This title also highlights Yahweh's power over all creation, including his ability to control unruly forces (the sea) that are far too powerful for mere humans to master. Jesus fulfills that description of Yahweh when he walks on the water (Mt 14:23–33; cf. Mk 4:37–41).

The phrase בָּמֳתֵי אָרֶץ occurs three other times in the OT. In a similar description of Yahweh in Micah 1:3, Yahweh "descends and treads on the high places of the earth" (וְיָרַד וְדָרַךְ עַל־בָּמוֹתֵי [בָּמֳתֵי] אָרֶץ). In both Amos 4:13 and Micah 1:3, the phraseology indicates Yahweh's epiphany to judge Israel. In contrast, in Deut 32:13 and Is 58:14, Yahweh causes his faithful people to participate in his own victory over evil as he enables them to ride on "the high places of the earth." Compare Mt 14:29, where Jesus enables Peter to walk on the water.

יְהוָה אֱלֹהֵי־צְבָאוֹת שְׁמוֹ׃—For the divine title "Yahweh, God of armies," see the second textual note on 3:13.

Commentary

Amos 4:6–13 within the Book

Amos 4:6–13 has 2:6–16 as its counterpart.[23] Whereas 2:6–16 describes Israel's wickedness in contrast to Yahweh's grace, 4:6–13 describes Israel's

---

[22] Paul, *Amos*, 155, including n. 156, who cites Joel 2:2 for this meaning of שַׁחַר: "A day of darkness and gloom, a day of densest cloud, spread like soot [כְּשַׁחַר] over the hills." He maintains that this שַׁחַר would be related to the adjective שָׁחֹר ("black," e.g., Lev 13:31; Zech 6:2).

[23] Rudolph notes that 2:6–16 and 4:4–13 have similar structures. They each have three parts: first, the exposure of Israel's sin; second, the recital of Yahweh's acts that, so far, have not

unwillingness to repent in spite of the repeated warning signals that Yahweh provided for the Israelites. Whereas 2:9–11 cites Yahweh's redemptive historical actions for his people Israel, 4:6–11 cites Yahweh's historical judgments. This litany (4:6–13) is an example of "a prophetic judgment speech that draws upon the liturgical hymns of praise [see 4:13] and the historical reviews."[24] The result of these spurned opportunities will be something yet unspecified, as 4:12 only indicates that Israel will meet Yahweh.

Most of the book of Amos is poetic, with the major exceptions being the introduction (1:1) and the narrative account of the prophet's confrontation with the priest Amaziah in 7:10–17. While 4:13 certainly is poetry, 4:6–12 is more prose-like; it is halfway between narrative and poetry.[25] Perhaps Amos employs elevated prose in these verses in order to provide variation from his earlier oracles. His goal was to convince Israel to repent and believe in Yahweh, who was behind the plagues, which Israel had failed to interpret rightly. Amos had been in the heavenly council (3:7), so he was able to interpret them as Yahweh's judgment on Israel.

The Torah of Moses contains blessings for faithful Israel as well as curses for when the people would rebel against their Savior God and turn to other gods (e.g., Leviticus 26; Deuteronomy 27–28). Several times in the covenant curses in Leviticus 26, Yahweh warns that the people will be punished by a multiple of "seven" (שֶׁבַע) times for their unfaithfulness toward the God who had redeemed them (Lev 26:18, 21, 24, 28). It is not surprising, then, that Amos 4:6–11 includes *seven* curses, just as he frequently employs heptads elsewhere in his book.[26] Yahweh speaks the following first person singular verb forms. The first two are strengthened by an emphatic first person pronoun (translated "myself"). The three verbs in 4:7 refer to the same curse (the second one), since they all describe drought imposed on selected areas.

---

succeeded (in moving Israel to repentance); and third, the announcement of punishment. The middle sections (2:9–12; 4:6–11) differ in that 2:9–12 recounts Yahweh's acts of grace while 4:6–11 recounts his acts of judgment, yet both end (2:12; 4:11) with statements that Yahweh's goal for Israel was not achieved (*Joel, Amos, Obadja, Jona*, 172).

[24] Sweeney, *The Twelve Prophets*, 228. Elsewhere he describes this genre as a "historical review" of Israel's past history (e.g., Josh 24:2–13; 1 Sam 12:7–12; see also Psalm 136) and writes this about it: "It frequently aids in persuading people to follow a specific course of action or to adapt a specific viewpoint. It can therefore appear in prophetic literature as a means to justify an announcement of judgment" (Sweeney, *Isaiah 1–39*, 521).

[25] Berlin believes that prophetic prose may be understood as a conscious literary and rhetorical strategy ("The Prophetic Literature of the Hebrew Bible"). This contrasts with the view that it is a chronological devolution. Kugel believes that biblical poetry is vastly complex with combinations that vary widely even within a single genre. Failing to recognize what he calls "middle ground" blunts the rhetorical thrust of many passages (*The Idea of Biblical Poetry*, 86, 94).

[26] Amos employs heptads also in 1:3–2:5; 2:6–8; 2:14–16; 3:3–6; 4:4–5; 5:8–9; 5:21–23; 6:1–6; 9:1–4.

1. "*I myself* even *gave* to you clean teeth" (אֲנִי נָתַתִּי, 4:6).
2. "*I myself* even *withheld* from you the rain" (אָנֹכִי מָנַעְתִּי, 4:7).
   "*I would send rain* on one city" (וְהִמְטַרְתִּי, 4:7),
   and on another city *I would not send rain*" (לֹא אַמְטִיר, 4:7).
3. "*I struck* you with blight and mildew" (הִכֵּיתִי, 4:9).
4. "*I sent* against you pestilence" (שִׁלַּחְתִּי, 4:10a).
5. "*I killed* with the sword your best soldiers" (הָרַגְתִּי, 4:10b).
6. "*I made* the stench of your camp *ascend*" (וָאַעֲלֶה, 4:10d).
7. "*I overturned* some of you" (הָפַכְתִּי, 4:11).

With these first person verbs Yahweh declares that he ("I") was the one who was directly intervening in Israel's history. This heptad of curses is followed by a climactic eighth word from Yahweh, which is not another statement about a fulfilled curse, but an announcement of imminent encounter: "prepare to meet your God, O Israel!" (4:12).[27]

Interspersed among the seven curses is the fivefold recurring refrain " 'but you did not return to me,' declares Yahweh" (4:6, 8, 9, 10, 11).[28] This same movement of progressive plagues met by the people's refusal to repent was characteristic of the ten plagues Yahweh sent against the pagan nation of Egypt leading up to the exodus. Thus Israel is no more responsive to God than was idolatrous Egypt! Similarly, the refrain in Amos 1:3–2:6, "because of three transgressions of … and because of four …" was applied equally to six pagan nations, then to Judah, and finally to northern Israel, implying that they were all equally sinful. Jer 5:3 echoes the anguish of Yahweh in Amos 4:6–11: "You struck them, but they did not become sick; you exterminated them, but they refused to receive discipline. They made their faces harder than stone; they refused to repent." The refusal of sinful people to respond to God when he pours out his wrath is an integral part of Paul's argument in Rom 1:18–32, and also the cycles of plagues in Revelation (Rev 9:20–21; 16:9, 11). Rom 2:4–5 provides an apt summary of the theology of Amos 4:6–13:

> Do you despise the wealth of his [God's] kindness and forbearance and patience, not knowing that God's kindness leads you toward repentance? But because of your stubbornness and your unrepentant heart, you are storing up for yourself wrath on the day of wrath and revelation of God's righteous judgment.

The coming day of wrath is described in Amos 2:14–16; 5:18–20; and 9:1–4. (See the commentary on 5:18–20.)

---

[27] Other examples of this numerical pattern where a heptad is followed by a climatic eighth statement are in 1:3–2:16 and 5:21–24.

[28] Other pentads appears in 7:17 and 9:2–4, and the five visions make up a pentad: 7:1–3; 7:4–6; 7:7–9; 8:1–3; 9:1–4.

God's Blessing and His Curses in Amos 4:6–13

Israel's worship life as described in 4:4–5 appears disconnected with the harsh realities of hunger, thirst, crop failure, and military defeat as these are described in 4:6–11. Yahweh in his grace promised to bless those participating in the legitimate worship rites specified in the Torah and performed in faith at the Jerusalem temple, his dwelling place on earth (see, e.g., Deuteronomy 16). In Joel, for example, Yahweh calls the people to repentance as he issues the worship commands to "assemble" at the Jerusalem temple (Joel 1:14), "blow a shofar in Zion" (Joel 2:1), and "rend your heart and not only your clothes" (Joel 2:13). Then he extends the hope that he "may turn and change his previous decision [to execute judgment] and leave behind him a blessing, a grain offering and a drink offering for Yahweh your God" (Joel 2:14).

Amos describes how the apostates in northern Israel were performing excessive worship observances but not in faith, and instead of at the Jerusalem temple, at idolatrous shrines of their own invention (4:4–5). Therefore instead of the covenant blessings promised in the Torah, Israel received its covenant curses (4:6–11). This section (4:6–13) begins with a first person singular verb plus pronoun for emphasis: "I myself even gave …" (וְגַם־אֲנִי נָתַתִּי, 4:6). This is similar to the refrain in Lev 26:16, 24, 28, 41, where Yahweh's words "surely I …" (אַף־אֲנִי) indicate that he is the initiator of covenant curses against Israel. As the Israelites were busying themselves with empty religious exercises (Amos 4:4–5), Yahweh was busying himself with trying to get them to awaken from their fantasies and fictions and turn back to him. They were living in the murk of half-truths and flat lies; oh that "the eyes of their hearts would be enlightened" (Eph 1:18) to see their true spiritual state!

The same kind of divine blessing and curse pertain to worship today. When Christians gather in faith around God's Word and Sacraments, God promises to bless them with his abundant grace in Jesus Christ, forgiving their sins and granting them everlasting life. Jesus Christ suffered God's curse for us in order to redeem us from the curses of the Law, so that we might receive God's blessing through faith alone (Gal 3:10–14). However, when worship is not centered on Christ as he comes to us through God's Word and Sacraments—when the participants lack faith in Christ, engage in manmade rites, and direct their worship toward false gods, as in Islam, Hinduism, Buddhism, animism, humanism, and earth-centered New Age religions—such worship is idolatry. They cannot receive God's blessings of salvation, and instead they remain under God's curse of judgment (e.g., Jn 3:18; 1 Jn 5:20–21).

The Israelites' refusal to see the curses in Amos 4:6–11, which are patterned after the covenant maledictions in the Torah, as coming from the hand of Yahweh indicates how far their worship had deviated from the divine service given in the Pentateuch. The seven plagues and corresponding covenant curses from the Torah are as follows:[29]

1. Famine ("clean teeth," Amos 4:6): Lev 26:26, 29; Deut 32:24.
2. Drought ("withheld ... the rain," Amos 4:7): Lev 26:19; Deut 28:22–24.
3. Agricultural "blight and mildew" (Amos 4:9): Deut 28:22.[30]
4. "Pestilence" (Amos 4:10a), that is, human disease: Lev 26:16, 25; Deut 28:21–22, 61; 32:24. Specifically, "pestilence in the manner of Egypt" (Amos 4:10a) fulfills the curses that refer to imposition of the diseases "of Egypt": Deut 28:27, 60; see also Deut 7:15.
5. Defeat by "the sword" (Amos 4:10b–c): Lev 26:25, 33, 36–37; Deut 28:22; Deut 32:25.
6. "The stench of your camp" (Amos 4:10d–e) refers to reeking corpses. The dead Israelites could have been killed by the fulfillment of any of a wide variety of covenant curses. The surviving Israelites would be forced to inhale the stench especially if they resorted to cannibalism, as in the covenant curse in Deut 28:53–57.
7. Being "overturned" like Sodom and Gomorrah (Amos 4:11): Deut 29:21–23 (ET 29:22–24).[31]

Whereas the covenant curses in Leviticus 26 and Deuteronomy 28 and 32 speak of what would happen to Israel in the future, Amos employs the curse genre in a new way by relating the curses to what had already happened. "The manifold disasters that have overtaken the people are none other than the very implementation and actualization of these curses."[32] These disasters describe a succession of setbacks that a farmer or cattleman like Amos (cf. 1:1; 7:14–15) might experience in the worst of all possible years. Amos does not assign these plagues to any specific times or places. Plagues tend to have a snowball effect, and they might have happened in a relatively short period of time. There is also no need to believe that 4:6–11 proceeds in strict chronological order.[33]

---

[29] Wolff lists the relationships between Amos 4:6–11 and the covenant blessings and curses in Leviticus 26; Deuteronomy 28; and 1 Kings 8 (*Joel and Amos*, 213). See also Reventlow, *Das Amt des Propheten bei Amos*, 75–90.

[30] Amos 4:9 goes on to refer to the devouring locust, which recalls the covenant curses with locusts and other pests in Deut 28:38–39, 42.

[31] See also "Sodom" and "Gomorrah" in Deut 32:32 and cataclysmic destruction by fire sent by Yahweh in the covenant curse of Deut 32:22.

[32] Paul, *Amos*, 143.

[33] Andersen and Freedman, *Amos*, 417, believe that the plagues are connected, but not necessarily sequential:

> Plagues tend to multiply, and one disaster often leads to another. The first four often accompany one another, because famine frequently follows drought, and the weakening effect on flora and fauna is not difficult [to understand]. ... What is portrayed here is a list or series of calamities that are compatible with one another and reinforce one another's effects.

4:6 The first of the plagues is famine.[34] When there is no food, people's teeth remain clean. The extent of this famine covered all of Israel, for Amos says, "in all of your cities" and "in all your places."[35] As opposed to the countryside, Amos frequently targets cities and those who live in them for Yahweh's judgment (e.g., chapters 1–2; 3:6, 9; 4:1; 6:1). The prophet's concept of city is that of a city-state, or in modern terms, a country or nation.[36]

It is not known precisely when this famine occurred. In all likelihood it is one that Amos' living audience had experienced, not the earlier ninth-century famine during the days of Elijah (1 Ki 17:1). As the book of Amos progresses, a far worse famine is threatened: a famine of the hearing of Yahweh's Word (Amos 8:11).

In spite of the famine described in 4:6, Israel stubbornly refused to return to Yahweh, an obdurate lack of response that Amos records five times in this section (4:6, 8, 9, 10, 11). Yahweh's voice is that of a jilted lover who attempted to get his beloved's attention, but all in vain.

4:7 A hardened and obstinate Israel received another plague. The second curse is a drought due to the winter rains being withheld (see the first and second textual notes on 4:7). In Israel the harvest season—of first barley and then wheat—takes place in the months of April, May, and June. This harvest would amount to nothing without nourishment from the winter rains.

" 'Selective' raining"[37] on one town and not another or on one field and not another is unusual for God, who "sends rain on the righteous and the unrighteous" (Mt 5:45). However, he had used this same selective strategy prior to the exodus when he aimed some plagues only at the Egyptians (e.g., Ex 8:18 [ET 8:22]; 9:26; 10:22–23; 12:22–23). Because such selective rain occurred rarely, Amos implies that Israel should have realized that the nation was under *divine* discipline.

4:8 The drought not only affected the farmer (4:6–7) but also those living in Israel's towns and cities. Thirsty people staggered like drunks, desperately seeking water.

Because the "city(-state)" (עִיר) is analogous to "nation" (גּוֹי), the migrations were on a more international scale.[38] Yahweh's decision to execute such a massive judgment when Israel fell from faith was promised in the similar Pentateuchal curses of Lev 26:26 and Deut 28:30–31, 38–40. These maledictions belong in the genre of "futility curses," for the parched people looked

---

[34] In one of the earliest studies on covenant curses in ancient Near Eastern texts, Hillers notes that the appearance of famine in these curses was "so general and obvious in nature" that it did not need comment (*Treaty-Curses and the Old Testament Prophets*, 62).

[35] Famine is "throughout the land" in, for example, Gen 12:10; 26:1; 2 Ki 4:38; Ruth 1:1 (cf. 2 Sam 21:1; 1 Ki 17:1).

[36] Andersen and Freedman, *Amos*, 440. See, for example, 1:3, where Damascus includes Syria, and 1:6, where Gaza includes Philistia.

[37] Paul, *Amos*, 144.

[38] Similar journeys due to famine are recorded in, for example, Gen 26:1 and 2 Ki 8:1–6.

and looked, but found no relief.[39] Stiff-necked, the people still did not return to Yahweh.

4:9 Even if some crops survived drought (4:7–8), they could be destroyed by the plagues of blight, mildew, and locusts. The farmers had little defense against the scorching sirocco and the devastating blight it inflicts on crops. In the ancient world, of course, there were no pesticides or fungicides to combat agricultural threats of plant diseases and locusts.[40] A farmer like Amos would be familiar with these kinds of agricultural problems.[41] People were at the mercy of Yahweh, who as Creator controls both history and the elements of nature.

The judgment of locusts in 4:9 is analogous to the eighth plague that Yahweh inflicted upon Egypt (Ex 10:1–20). Using similar terms (e.g., vines, fig trees, locusts), Ps 105:33–34 describes punishments against the Egyptians. The terminology comes from the covenantal curses listed in Deut 28:38–42. The next verse (Amos 4:10) builds on the exodus connection.

Amos 4:9 illustrates the temporal nature of wealth and riches. Jesus says: "Do not store up for yourselves treasures on earth, where moth and rust destroy" (Mt 6:19). Israel's agricultural treasures had been decimated, but its people still refused to humble themselves before Yahweh (cf. James 4:6, 10).

4:10 Whereas 4:9 was about the death of crops, this verse describes three death sentences carried out against the Israelites themselves. Just as Yahweh promised to "send" (the Piel of שָׁלַח) fire against five of the six pagan nations and Judah in 1:3–2:5, so here he sends "pestilence" (דֶּבֶר). This term is employed in Torah curse texts (Lev 26:25; Deut 28:21). "In the manner of Egypt" alludes to the manifold disasters Yahweh had inflicted on Egypt to prepare for the exodus. Amos 4:10 is ironic in that Israel was treated like heathen Egypt when it refused to let God's people go. The tables had turned, and *now Yahweh's very own people were his chief enemy!*

Yahweh's ten plagues against the Egyptians were as follows:[42] blood; frogs; gnats; flies; pestilence striking the livestock; boils hitting people and livestock; hail striking people, livestock, and agriculture; locusts; darkness;[43] and the killing of the firstborn of people and livestock.[44] Amos 4:9 referred to locusts, which

---

39 Cf. Hillers, *Treaty-Curses and the Old Testament Prophets*, 28–29. Other futility curses include Gen 3:17–19; Hos 4:10; 5:6; Amos 5:11.

40 Cf. Crenshaw, *Joel*, 91–94. A locust plague is the basis for Amos' first vision in 7:1–3.

41 See "Who Was among the Sheep Breeders from Tekoa" in the commentary on 1:1.

42 See also the lists in Pss 78:42–51 and 105:26–36.

43 The ninth plague was especially devastating to Egyptian religion because the sun god Ra (or Re) was one of its chief gods.

44 The plagues were not natural events; they demonstrated *divine* intervention. Some were an *intensification* of phenomena that could occur naturally, but others were supernatural. Yahweh initiated all of them (e.g., Ex 7:19–20; 10:21–23; 12:29) and announced in advance exactly when some of them would occur (e.g., Ex 9:5–6, 18–25; 12:12–13). In response to Moses' intercession, Yahweh stopped some of them (e.g., Ex 8:4–9, 25–27 [ET 8:8–13, 29–31]). Yahweh sent some of them only on the Egyptians, while sparing the Israelites (e.g.,

were the eighth plague, and 4:10 refers to pestilence, which was the fifth plague. The ten plagues were arranged in the form of three series of calamities, with three afflictions in each series. The tenth is climactic and lies outside the series in that it is Yahweh's most devastating curse.

The plagues were Yahweh's judgments against "all the gods of Egypt" (Ex 12:12). The Egyptian magicians duplicated the first sign—the turning of rods into serpents (Ex 7:11–12)—and also duplicated the first two plagues: turning water into blood (Ex 7:22) and conjuring up frogs (Ex 8:3 [ET 8:7]). However, when it came to the third plague, the gnats, the magicians were unable to copy this miracle (Ex 8:14 [ET 8:18]). This led to their confession that the events occurring were the product of "the finger of God" (Ex 8:15 [ET 8:19]; cf. Ex 31:18; Deut 9:10; Lk 11:20).

Here in Amos the natural plagues of blight, mildew, and locusts (4:9) were followed by the sword (חֶרֶב, 4:10), that is, warfare. Israel's "best soldiers," its elite combat troops, were cut down in battle. They also lost their war horses. Amos may be alluding to the time when Hazael reduced the horsemen in Israel to just a few (2 Ki 13:7), or he may be thinking of a military setback closer to his own day. Since an enemy army would try to capture the horses for their own use, rather than kill them, the horses that died may have perished because of injury or disease.

The stench of bodies in the Israelites' camp would result from death by all manner of causes. That the surviving Israelites are forced to inhale the stench through their noses may imply close contact with the dead, perhaps through cannibalism (Deut 28:53–57). It may also imply that the dead were not buried, but were left strewn on the ground (cf. Ezek 37:1–14).

Despite this catastrophe, Israel refused "to draw near to God" (James 4:8). The pharaoh at the time of the exodus reacted to Yahweh's plagues in a similar manner. Because he kept hardening his own heart (Ex 8:11, 28 [ET 8:15, 32]; 9:7, 34), Yahweh hardened Pharaoh's heart (Ex 10:1).

4:11 The plague recorded in this verse is the most drastic and destructive since it is compared to the upheaval and annihilation of Sodom and Gomorrah.[45]

Sodom appears thirty-nine times in the OT, and Gomorrah appears nineteen times, always in association with Sodom. Attempts to identify the locations of Sodom and Gomorrah have focused near the southern end of the Dead Sea. The narratives involving the cities appear in Genesis 13–14, 18–19, and they consist of Lot's relocation to Sodom and a war of liberation fought under the leader-

---

Ex 8:18 [ET 8:22]; 9:26; 10:22–23; 12:22–23). The plagues were orderly, moving from the least intense to the most.

[45] Hillers calls this image a "parade example for sudden destruction" (*Treaty-Curses and the Old Testament Prophets*, 75). Yahweh often cites his prior judgment of Sodom and Gomorrah in contexts where he is warning Israel against the violation of his covenant (e.g., Deut 29:21–22 [ET 29:22–23]; Is 1:9–10; Jer 23:14).

ship of Abraham, followed by the history of the cities' destruction. Yahweh, in his righteous judgment, had determined that he would destroy Sodom and Gomorrah because of their people's sexual perversion—in particular, their practice of homosexuality. Their pride and inhospitable treatment of the two angelic visitors only confirmed the outcry that had risen to heaven against them. When Abraham learned of the coming judgment, he pleaded for the safety of the righteous and secured only the escape of Lot and his family from Sodom (Gen 19:29).

Outside the book of Genesis, the destruction of Sodom and Gomorrah becomes a paradigm for the prophetic judgment Yahweh executes against all sinners, including the most rebellious and degenerate people. The formulaic expression in Amos 4:11 recurs in other OT passages (see the second textual note on 4:11). Amos does not indicate that the abomination of homosexuality was practiced in Israel in his day, but he does mention other sexual sins (e.g., 2:7). However, his main focus is on the unbelief and pride of Israel (e.g., 6:8). The confidence of the Israelites in wealth and position, maintained by their abuse of the lowly, is especially what incurs Yahweh's judgment.

The prophet's comparison of Israel's judgment to the destruction of these cities is rooted in the covenant curse of Deut 29:22 (ET 29:23), which uses some of the same Hebrew terminology: when Israel rebels against her God, her judgment will be

> like the overturning of Sodom and Gomorrah, … which God overturned in his anger and wrath.
>
> כְּמַהְפֵּכַ֞ת סְדֹ֤ם וַעֲמֹרָה֙ ... אֲשֶׁר֙ הָפַ֣ךְ יְהוָ֔ה בְּאַפּ֖וֹ וּבַחֲמָתֽוֹ

The destruction of Sodom and Gomorrah by fire from heaven (Gen 19:24) is the most extreme form of Yahweh's judgment and the ultimate act of destruction in the OT. Other prophets too compare apostate Israel to one or both of these degenerate cities (e.g., Is 1:9–10; Ezek 16:46–56).

The NT too cites the destruction of Sodom and Gomorrah as a prefiguration of the eternal condemnation of all unbelievers on Judgment Day at the second advent of Christ (Mt 10:15; 2 Pet 2:6–11; Jude 7; see also, e.g., Lk 17:28–30; Rom 9:29; Rev 11:8). All the dead shall be raised bodily, and all those who lack faith in Christ will be condemned to bodily torment and everlasting perdition in the fires of hell (e.g., Is 66:24; Dan 12:2; Lk 16:23–28).

Homosexuality is an "abomination" in God's sight (תּוֹעֵבָה, Lev 18:22; 20:13). Same-sex activity is a perversion of God's created order, eliciting God's wrath (Rom 1:18, 26–28). It is incompatible with Christian faith, a vile sin against one's own body, and those who do such things will not inherit the kingdom of God (1 Cor 6:9–11, 18–20; Rev 22:15).[46]

[46] See the excursus "Homosexuality" in Lockwood, *1 Corinthians*, 204–9. "Dogs" in Rev 22:15 is a reference to homosexuals. Deut 23:19 (ET 23:18) uses the Hebrew term כֶּלֶב, "dog," for a male prostitute.

The earthquake motif of Amos 1:1 and 9:1 that brackets the entire book of Amos might appear here too if the overturning of Sodom and Gomorrah involved quaking and shaking. In any case, it involved fire (Gen 19:24), and the fire motif is present here as Amos likens the Israelite survivors of the covenant curses to a "burning stick" (אוּד) rescued from the fire. Destruction by fire is another covenant curse, for in Deut 32:22, Yahweh states, "For fire has been kindled by my anger [כִּי־אֵשׁ קָדְחָה בְאַפִּי], one that burns to Sheol below. It will consume the land and its produce and set ablaze the foundations of the mountains."

The rescue in Amos 4:11 of the unconsumed part of the burning stick offers a bit more hope than the mock rescue in 3:12, and certainly more than in 6:9. It can be compared to the remnant promise in 5:3. It implies that Yahweh will save at least some (the part of the stick not yet incinerated) from the catastrophe described in 4:11. This, in turn, relates to the expressions of hope for a saved remnant of Israel in 5:15 and a saved remnant of the Gentile nations in 9:12.

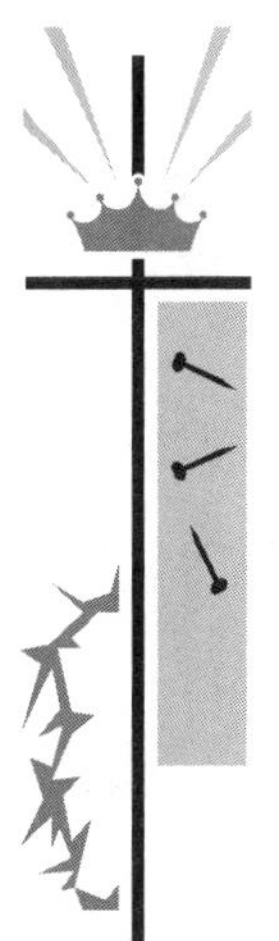

Luther likewise believes that 4:11 promises a remnant and supports basic Christian theology of Law and Gospel. He writes, first paraphrasing 4:11:

> "Just as one single brand, kindled and taken from the fire, must not be compared with the burning of the entire house; so also that remnant of you is not compared with the entire people." In this way, too, as the Lord is about to justify us, He deals with us, terrifies and so shames our consciences that we believe that it is all over with us, as if He intended to condemn us eternally. Yet, He always leaves us some hope, lest we utterly lose hope. He snatches us away like a brand from the fire. This passage and similar ones, then, have been written both to terrify and to comfort. They terrify those who have a stiff neck and persevere obstinately in their own righteousness. They comfort the humble and afflicted who recognize their sin. Blessed is the man who understands this.[47]

Tragically, however, 4:11 concludes with the fifth and final instance of the refrain " 'but you did not return to me,' declares Yahweh." Even though he spared a remnant, hardened Israel as a whole did not repent. John Cassian (or Cassianus) reflects on this:

> They [who refuse to repent] do not deserve to be saved by the Lord's visitation or to be healed by temporal afflictions. They are like those 'who in despair have handed themselves over to lasciviousness in the working of every error, unto uncleanness' [Eph 4:19]. In their hardness of heart and with their frequent habit of sinning, they are beyond the purgation of this very brief age and the punishment of the present life.[48]

Amos 4:6–11 describes the fulfillment of seven covenant curses, not ten, the number of completeness, and the full number of the plagues against Egypt. This

---

[47] Luther, "Lectures on Amos" (AE 18:154).

[48] John Cassian (or Cassianus), *Conferences*, 6.11.6, cited by Ferreiro, *The Twelve Prophets*, ACCS 14:95.

implies that there is still time for some Israelites to repent and return to Yahweh. The full number has not yet been reached (cf. Gen 15:16 and the "because of three transgressions of … and because of four …" in 1:3–2:16).

According to Andersen and Freedman's reconstruction of the chronology of the book of Amos, chapter 4 was written before Yahweh had yet uttered the refrain in chapters 1 and 2: "I will not revoke it [my judgment]."[49] Even if there is not a one-to-one correspondence, the list of plagues in 4:6–11 roughly correlates with the threatened judgments in the prophet's visions in chapters 7–9.[50] During the first two visions, which include catastrophes of locusts and fire, Amos' intercessory prayers moved Yahweh to spare Jacob because "he is so small" (7:2, 5). Yahweh's reprieve gave Amos the opportunity to warn Israel, and he did so by means of his oracles in chapters 5–6. But his message fell on deaf ears. Because Israel failed to return to Yahweh, there would be no more divine reprieve (7:8; 8:2). The end had come (8:2). The final nail in the coffin was the northern priest Amaziah's rejection of Amos (7:10–17; cf. 2:12). Northern Israel's sins had piled up ("three … four," 2:6). The only option was for the Northern Kingdom to "prepare to meet your God" (4:12).

Amos 4:6–11 is therefore pivotal in the book. Israel ignored both Amos' preaching in chapters 5–6 as well as Yahweh's plagues in 4:6–11. Yahweh's patience had run its course; he would not revoke his decision to come in judgment (2:6).

4:12 During these plagues, northern Israel had been at the proverbial "eleventh hour." But with 4:12 the clock struck midnight. It was time for judgment. Israel had not known "the time of [her] visitation" (Lk 19:44). Yahweh had become weary with sending warning shots across the bow. His patience had worn thin. Now Israel would not meet a prophet like Amos or even experience more plagues. The nation would no longer experience agents of judgment; instead they would meet the Judge. This is much more frightening than plagues. Yahweh says in effect, "You haven't seen anything yet."[51]

This is also terrifying because Yahweh does not spell out what he intends. Twice he introduces it in an indefinite and unspecified way: "*thus* [כֹּה] will I do to you, … because *this* [זֹאת] is what I will do to you."[52] Not knowing what it is makes the threat all the more ominous.[53] The decision not to define the punishment increases anxiety.

---

[49] E.g., Andersen and Freedman, *Amos*, 8. See the discussion of Andersen and Freedman's theory in "The Structure and Outline of the Book of Amos" in the introduction.

[50] Andersen and Freedman, *Amos*, 445.

[51] Stuart, *Hosea–Jonah*, 339.

[52] Amos uses זֹאת seven times (2:11; 4:12; 7:3, 6; 8:4, 8; 9:12). Andersen and Freedman write: "It [זֹאת, 'this'] has a specific theological sense: it always refers to something or, more specifically, to the thing that Yahweh has done, is doing, or will do, or has said, or has revealed in a vision. The *z't* [זֹאת, 'this'] in every case is a result of divine decision" (*Amos*, 452).

[53] Yahweh also leaves his listeners and readers in suspense in chapters 1–2 with his repeated use of לֹא אֲשִׁיבֶנּוּ, "I will not revoke it," without explaining what "it" is (1:3, 6, 9, 11, 13; 2:1, 4, 6).

Amos changes from addressing the Israelites in the plural as in the preceding verses (e.g., the refrain "but you [second masculine *plural* verb, שַׁבְתֶּם] did not return to me") to addressing them in the singular in the repeated expression אֶעֱשֶׂה־לְּךָ, "I will do to *you*."[54] This change indicates that imminent judgment is now addressed to *each individual* in Israel. The singular continues in the use of the same masculine *singular* suffix in the judgment "prepare to meet *your* God [אֱלֹהֶיךָ]."

"Prepare to meet your God" appears to be a strange form of punishment. Such language has its context in the Sinai revelation when Moses counseled Israel to prepare for Yahweh's theophany. In Ex 19:15 Moses uses another Niphal form of the same verb when he commands the Israelites to be "prepared" for Yahweh's advent on the third day. The words in Amos 4:12 "to meet your God" (לִקְרַאת־אֱלֹהֶיךָ) reflect Ex 19:17, where Moses brought the Israelites out of their camp "to meet God" (לִקְרַאת הָאֱלֹהִים). Through Amos, Yahweh extends an invitation to Israel using words that sound like his prior encouragement through Moses for them to come into his presence and receive the revelation of the gracious covenant from him, their Redeemer God (cf. Ex 20:1–2). However, this call for covenant renewal is actually an announcement of judgment.[55]

The only other time in Amos that Yahweh describes himself as אֱלֹהֶיךָ, "your God,"[56] is in 9:15, which is the decidedly comforting conclusion of the eschatological and messianic promise of 9:11–15. Seen in light of 9:15, 4:12 may offer a glimmer of hope of final salvation for a faithful remnant after the impending judgment of the people who as a whole had forsaken their God. "Your God" also harkens back to the covenant formula of Ex 6:7, where Yahweh declares himself to be "your God" and calls Israel "my people."

This hopeful note would be strengthened if Yahweh is described in 4:13 as he "who makes darkness into dawn" instead of "dawn into darkness" (see the fourth textual note on 4:13). In any event, in the book as a whole, the darkness of judgment in 4:12 will give way to the brightness of the coming "days" of resurrection and restoration in 9:11–15. Yahweh's anger may last for a moment, but his favor lasts a lifetime, into eternal life. "Weeping endures for a night, but joy comes in the morning" (Ps 30:6 [ET 30:5]). Yahweh's judgment will give way to his mercy for all believers, for he is bound to be Israel's God through his unconditional Gospel promises to Adam and Eve (Gen 3:15) and to the patriarchs (e.g., Gen 12:2–3; 17:7), fulfilled and sealed in Jesus the Christ (Mt 1:1; Gal 3:29).

---

54 The Hebrew expression is repeated, although English requires different word order in translation: "thus *will I do to you* ... because this is what *I will do to you.*" In the second occurrence, לְּךָ appears with the equivalent pausal pointing לָּךְ.

55 In other places in Amos, Yahweh turns Gospel traditions upside down in order to announce Law. See also 2:9–11; 3:1–2; 4:4–5, 13; 5:8–9, 18–20; 7:8; 8:2; 9:1, 4, 5–6, 7, 10.

56 אֱלֹהֶיךָ also appears in 8:14, but "your god" in that passage refers to the false god Israel worshiped at Dan.

4:13 Throughout chapters 1–4, Amos depicts the gruesome and all-too-frequent atrocities of people. The catalog includes inhumane warfare, social injustice, greed, drunkenness, fornication, and apostasy. Paul's list of sins in Rom 1:18–32 and Gal 5:19–21 are apt summaries of these chapters. But in the midst of this deep darkness, there is a ray of light. The hymn celebrating the goodness and justice of Yahweh in Amos 4:13 stands in stark contrast with evil of humanity. Humanity destroys. Yahweh creates and re-creates. He reveals his redemptive plan, judges those who reject it, but saves all who repent and believe.

This is the first of three doxologies or hymns in the book; the others are in 5:8–9 and 9:5–6.[57] They all describe God using participles. These doxologies are often labeled "creation hymns" because some of their participles describe God's acts of creation, for example, יוֹצֵר, "who forms" (4:13), וּבֹרֵא, "and who creates" (4:13), עֹשֵׂה, "who makes" (4:13; 5:8), הַקּוֹרֵא, literally, "the one who calls" (5:8; 9:6), and הַבּוֹנֶה, "the one who builds" (9:6). These participles—functioning as epithets or titles—describe the activity of Yahweh. Similar participial hymns appear in Isaiah 40–66; Jeremiah; and Job, and Isaiah and Jeremiah sometimes include the name formula "Yahweh of armies/hosts is his name."[58]

Of the five participles that are divine titles in 4:13, the first two focus on God the Creator, as summarized in the First Article of the Apostles' Creed: "I believe in God, the Father Almighty, Maker of heaven and earth." In addition to God's general revelation of himself in his creation, the hymn also refers to his special revelation through his prophets and other writers of the sacred Scriptures: he "declares to mankind his thoughts." His revealed will in the Scriptures centers on him as Savior and Redeemer, as summarized in the Second Article of the Apostles' Creed: "and [I believe] in Jesus Christ, his only Son, our Lord ..." The later hymns in Amos and especially 9:11–15 will have much more to say about Yahweh as Redeemer.

---

[57] Sweeney defines the genre of such hymns as "a pithy, highly lyrical acclamation of divine glory and righteousness (e.g., 2 Sam 7:29; 1 Chr 17:27) that often functions in relation to hymns of praise (e.g., Psalm 135) and communal thanksgiving songs (e.g., Psalms 118; 136)" (*Isaiah 1–39*, 519). Amos' hymns have been subjected to multiple investigations. This commentary believes that these three hymns were composed by Amos himself under divine inspiration and that they each serve an important purpose in their particular location within the book. However, critical scholars have expressed other views. Form-critical investigation has been done by Crenshaw, *Hymnic Affirmation of Divine Justice*; "The Influence of the Wise upon Amos"; and "Amos and the Theophanic Tradition." Cf. also Story, "Amos—Prophet of Praise." For a survey, see Paul, *Amos*, 152–53. Niehaus argues that the three hymns are not separate parts of one hymn, but that each of the three is a hymn in its own right, and he cites other ancient parallels: "These are no more fragments of a hymn than were their Assyrian counterparts, which, like them, are nevertheless written in a hymnic style that was very ancient, appearing in the prologue of Hammurabi's law code (*ANET*, pp. 164–65), with antecedents in Sumerian inscriptions of even earlier date" ("Amos," 483).

[58] Other examples of hymns and poetic speeches with participial divine titles include Is 43:1; 44:2, 24; 45:7, 9, 11, 18; 54:5; Job 5:8–16; 9:4–10. In the context of participial praise, the name formula "Yahweh of armies/hosts is his name" appears three times in Isaiah (47:4; 51:15; 54:5) and five times in Jeremiah (10:12–16; 31:35; 32:18; 50:34; 51:19; see also Jer 33:2).

However, this hymn also accents his role as Judge and Destroyer. Yahweh reverses creation (Gen 1:2–3) as he "makes dawn [into] darkness" (Amos 4:13; see also 5:8, 18; 8:9). The one who formed order out of chaos can mete out judgment by allowing his creation to revert into chaos (cf. Jer 4:23). We must remember this, lest we adopt the smug attitude that says, "The evil will not overtake nor confront us" (Amos 9:10). Judgment is also the theme of the acclamation that Yahweh "treads on the high places of the earth" (4:13). The highest, most arrogant aspirations of men and the most powerful of his enemies are beneath his feet.

In the ancient Near East, each nation and tribal group worshiped its own deity. Against this worldview, Yahweh asserted that he was not just one among many gods (polytheism), nor was he the primary god to be worshiped among several others (monolatry). Rather Yahweh was—and is—the one and only God; there is no other. Andersen and Freedman write:

> He was the maker and ruler of the universe who alone was worthy of the title, who brooked no rivals, had no consort or progeny, was dependent on no one and nothing, and exercised a full monopoly of power and authority.[59]

Amos' hymns of praise call Israel to acknowledge this claim. Yahweh is not—like many of the other deities in the ancient Near East—some local, parochial, domestic deity. As he says through Jeremiah, "I am the one who fills heaven and earth" (Jer 23:24). Creation is a sign and measure of Yahweh's capacity to act in ways beyond what Israel thought possible. This theme in Amos is of tremendous theological importance as it gives depth and meaning to Yahweh's acts of judgment and salvation, both of which involve creation.[60]

The praise of God is entirely consistent with his execution of just judgments, by which he displays his holiness and righteousness. For example, Revelation often intersperses hymnic praises of God (e.g., Rev 11:17–18; 15:3–4; 16:5–7; 19:1–8) among extended passages that portray God finally executing his wrath on the sinful, unbelieving world and the forces of evil. By these judgments against evil, God eventually vindicates the persecuted believers who have hoped

---

[59] Anderson and Freedman, *Amos*, 43. Knierim, *The Task of Old Testament Theology*, 14, says:

> Yahweh may be Israel's God in oneness and exclusivity, but if he is not Israel's God because he is first of all God of all reality and of all humanity, he is a nationalistic deity or an individualistic idol, one among others, actually a no-god. Without the critical notion of universality, the affirmation of Yahweh's oneness and exclusivity does not substantiate the affirmation of his true deity.

[60] For an exposition of the biblical theme of creation as it relates to OT prophecy, see the excursus "Yahweh, the Creator God" in Lessing, *Jonah*, 143–50. In contrast, older critical OT scholarship tended to neglect the doctrine of creation, as shown by these misguided words of von Rad, "The Theological Problem of the Old Testament Doctrine of Creation," 142:

> Our main thesis was that in genuinely Yahwistic belief the doctrine of creation never attained to the stature of a relevant, independent doctrine. ... Because of the exclusive commitment of Israel's faith to historical salvation, the doctrine of creation was never able to attain to independent existence in its own right.

in him, even as he vindicated his Christ (cf. Ps 22:2–6, 9 [ET 22:1–5, 8]; Mt 27:22–24) by defeating his foes and raising him from the dead (Ps 16:8–11, quoted in Acts 2:22–36). It is in that same spirit that we should view the hymns in Amos.

The first doxology (4:13) follows the recital of the plagues in the judgment oracle in 4:6–12. The second, if one accepts de Waard's chiastic analysis, is imbedded in an oracle of judgment.[61] The third doxology comes at the end of the five visions of impending judgment in 7:1–9:4. In this way the doxologies are drawn into the rhetoric of judgment.[62] The praise evokes in suffering believers a trusting confidence that Yahweh in his righteousness eventually will deliver them from all evil, but for unbelievers the doxologies ironically reinforce that his judgment is unavoidable and inescapable. For them such hymnic language serves to evoke fear rather than joy.

Amos may have sung his hymns to his original audience. Moses, Israel's paradigmatic prophet (cf. Deut 18:15–18), composed poetic songs (e.g., Ex 15:1–18; Deut 31:30–32:43), as did Isaiah (5:1–7) and Ezekiel (33:32). Other prophetic texts too are poetic and liturgical (e.g., Isaiah 12; Joel 1–2; Habakkuk 3).

In Amos 4:13 the first two participles, "he who forms (יוֹצֵר) … and who creates (וּבֹרֵא)," refer to Yahweh's acts in creation. In addition to the original creation (Genesis 1–2), these participles also refer to his ongoing work of sustaining and caring for the universe, his *creatio continua*. The use of "mountains" and "wind" pairs the most stable element of creation with the most moveable. This creates a merism whereby Amos asserts that Yahweh has created everything. Merism also appears in Gen 1:1, where "the heavens and the earth" are the two contrasting realms created by God and whose entire contents are his handiwork. While creation reveals God's eternal power and divine nature (Rom 1:19–20), the next participial phrase, "who declares to mankind his thoughts" (Amos 4:13), refers to God's special revelation of judgment and salvation through his inspired prophets and Scripture writers. "Who makes dawn [into] darkness" refers to his activity in judgment (cf. Ex 10:21–22), especially toward the end of the world (Mk 13:24; Acts 2:20; Rev 6:12; 8:12). "Who … treads on the high places of the earth" expresses Yahweh's dominion over the entire world and also points to his final conquest over all evil and all who rebel against him. Ultimately God conquers sin, death, and the devil through Christ's victory on the cross and by his bodily resurrection from the empty tomb. God the Father has subjected all of Christ's enemies to be merely a footstool under his feet (see Pss 8:7 [ET 8:6]; 110:1). Christ crushes Satan underfoot (Gen 3:15; 1 Cor 15:25–27; Eph 1:22; Heb 2:8), and all in Christ have the promise that on the Last Day Satan shall be crushed under their feet as well (Rom 16:20).

[61] De Waard, "The Chiastic Structure of Amos V 1–17."

[62] Crenshaw claims: "Amos has changed the meaning of the material to a dreadful threat" ("Amos and the Theophanic Tradition," 212).

The hymn ends with the full doxological title "Yahweh, the God of armies, is his name." This full title recurs at the end of 5:27, while the shorter title "Yahweh is his name" is in 5:8; 9:6. This holy-war title explains what kind of God unfaithful Israel must "prepare to meet" (4:12). "The use of the name at this climactic point is a reminder of the terror of the God of Sinai who came again and again into the history of Israel."[63] Yet God's angelic troops also fight *for* his penitent believers on earth, and so this same divine title offers the comfort of deliverance and eschatological victory for them (cf., e.g., Mk 13:27; Lk 2:9–14).[64]

Summary

Throughout Amos 4:6–11, the prophet rehearses Yahweh's attempts to get Israel to return to him. His chastisements displayed his fatherly concern and love for his wayward child (cf. Heb 12:6), but instead Israel ignored Yahweh, and the nation's last state became worse than its first (cf. 2 Pet 2:20).[65] The curses may have prompted the Israelites to increase their idolatrous worship (2:7–8; 4:4–5; 5:5), yet Yahweh was seeking repentance, faith, justice, and righteousness and that the Israelites would abandon their aberrant worship, which he hates (5:21–27). He was looking for a response similar to the one described in Ps 78:34:

> When he slew them, then they sought him,
> and they returned [וְשָׁבוּ] and earnestly sought God.

Amos in 4:4–5 reworks the genre of priestly, Levitical portions of the Torah. In 4:6–12 he reworks the biblical genres of God's holy war and theophany. And in 4:13 he reworks the genre of liturgical praise. As a creative craftsman of genres the inspired prophet's new word to Israel announces the shocking realization of Yahweh's imminent punishment of the apostate shrines at places such as Bethel and Gilgal (4:4) and the destruction of those who worship there.

Is 9:12 (ET 9:13) provides a fitting commentary on Amos 4:6–13:

> The people did not return [לֹא־שָׁב] to him [Yahweh] who struck them,
> nor did they seek Yahweh of hosts.

Yahweh works through historical events, both natural disasters and international affairs.[66] He strikes his people in order to bring them back to himself. He executes judgments on sinners now with the goal that they will repent, believe, and be raised to eternal life on the Last Day, lest they die in unbe-

---

[63] Brueggemann, "Amos IV 4–13 and Israel's Covenant Worship," 13.

[64] For the roles of Christ and the holy angels in the spiritual warfare that affects God's saints on earth, see Steinmann, *Daniel*, 481, 502–6, 559–60.

[65] For similar prophetic descriptions of how obdurate Israel failed to repent when Yahweh fulfilled his covenant curses, see, for example, Is 1:2–9; Jer 2:30; 5:3; Ezekiel 16; 20.

[66] As Amos had asked rhetorically in 3:6, "If a disaster happens in a city, did Yahweh not do [it]?" Other examples of Yahweh attempting to teach people using the events of history or natural disasters, but to no avail, are in Is 42:18–25; Jer 2:30; 5:3; Rev 9:13–21; 16:8–11.

lief, perish eternally, and be raised to everlasting contempt on Judgment Day (Is 66:12–24; Dan 12:2–3). He poured out his judgment on his own Son, who suffered and died for all humanity, and then rose again victoriously, fulfilling the participial hymn:

> Yahweh kills and he makes alive;
> he makes descend to Sheol and he raises up. (1 Sam 2:6; cf. Ps 16:9–11)

The disasters in Amos 4:6–11 were sent to chastise Israel and bring the nation back to their Creator and Redeemer (cf. Deut 4:29–31; 8:5; 30:1–10). If the people would not return, then they would meet their God as the Judge who would condemn them for eternity (Dan 12:2; Rev 20:11–15).

The first hymn in Amos (4:13) indicates that Yahweh is not a mere local deity who is competing with the gods of the nations to be supreme. No! Yahweh is the God of all creation, and all other so-called gods are "the work of the hands of men" (Ps 115:4). "Faith in God the Creator was perceived and experienced as the all-embracing framework, as the fundamental, all-underlying premise for any talk about God, the world, Israel, and the individual,"[67] and it remains so today. Creation is the beginning of Yahweh's work in the world. His revealed Word and his acts of judgment and salvation serve to condemn sin and move people to repentance and faith. His self-revelation culminates in the Word made flesh, Jesus Christ, the sinless one who suffered the entire divine judgment for humanity's sin, then rose victoriously from the dead to guarantee the bodily resurrection to eternal salvation for all who trust in him. This work of redemption will be completed on the day when God ushers in his new creation, already begun now in Christ (Is 65:17–25; 2 Cor 5:17; Gal 6:15; Rev 21:5). Amos' placement of three hymns in the book (4:13; 5:8–9; 9:5–6) highlights Yahweh as the Creator and eschatological Re-creator.

[67] Rendtorff, *Canon and Theology*, 107–8.

Excursus

Amos' Use of Earlier Biblical Texts

As Yahweh speaks through Amos, he moves the prophet to draw on earlier biblical texts in order to sharpen his accusations against the sins of the Israelites and to drive them to repentance, so that they might rightly receive and believe the Gospel promise that concludes the book (9:11–15). The prophet reuses older OT texts so that the older ideas move in new ways to confront Israel. It is important, therefore, for the reader to be alert to the earlier citations and allusions in the book of Amos, as he often employs them in shocking and surprising ways.[1]

Amos shows a keen knowledge of the Pentateuch. In his three hymns of praise (4:13; 5:8–9; 9:5–6), he displays his awareness of the creation narrative in Genesis 1–2. Amos is familiar with Yahweh's destruction of Sodom and Gomorrah because of their sexual abomination (4:11; cf. Genesis 18–19) and alludes to the messianic promises given to the patriarchs in Gen 12:3 and 28:14 (Amos 3:2). The prophet is aware of the regulations of the Sinai covenant (Amos 2:4), such as returning a garment taken in pledge (Amos 2:8; see Ex 22:25–26 [ET 22:26–27]; Deut 24:12–13). Amos speaks against the rich crushing the poor (Amos 2:7) who do not share their abundance (see Ex 22:20–23 [ET 22:21–24]; Deut 16:11, 14) and employs exodus themes and theology, as well as the conquest of the promised land (Amos 2:9–11; 4:10; 9:7; see Exodus 14–15; Numbers 13–14; Deuteronomy 1; 29). The prophet is also acquainted with the Nazirite vow (Amos 2:11; see Numbers 6) and cites terminology from the worship regulations in Leviticus in his satire of unfaithful Israel's deviant worship (Amos 4:4–5; see the textual notes and commentary on those verses).

Yet the parts of the Pentateuch that Amos employs most frequently are the covenant blessings and curses (Leviticus 26; Deuteronomy 27–30). The blessings promise Yahweh's gifts as long as the people remain faithful to his Sinaitic covenant of grace, but the curses warn of the horrors that shall be fulfilled when Israel forsakes her God. The covenant blessings and curses are so prominent in Amos that Bramer labels the genre of Amos as "a covenant enforcement document."[2]

---

[1] Scholars differ as to what part of Israel's literary past is most evident in Amos. Rosenbaum (*Amos of Israel*, 85) lists these biblical themes and the scholars who claim that each was the most influential for Amos: wisdom (Wolff), theophany (Crenshaw), covenant (Brueggemann), pre-Israelite prophecy (Gottwald), and the book of Psalms (Kapelrud). Rosenbaum cites, for example, Wolff, *Amos the Prophet*; Crenshaw, "Amos and the Theophanic Tradition"; Brueggemann, "Amos IV 4–13 and Israel's Covenant Worship"; Gottwald, *The Tribes of Yahweh*; Kapelrud, *Central Ideas in Amos*.

[2] Bramer, "The Literary Genre of the Book of Amos," 45. On pages 46–48, Bramer charts passages from Amos and links them with similar passages from the Pentateuch. Though

Amos also demonstrates an awareness of OT texts and themes later than the Torah of Moses. He issues a liturgical call to worship (Amos 4:4–5) that resembles calls in the Psalms (81:2–6 [ET 81:1–5]; 95:6–7; 100:4). He is adept at graded numerical sayings (e.g., 1:3, 6, 9) and riddles (3:3–8; 6:12), both of which are associated with Wisdom literature; funeral dirges (5:1, 17; 8:10); hymns (4:13; 5:8–9; 9:5–6) reminiscent of those in the Psalms; and vivid similes and metaphors (e.g., 3:12; 5:24; 9:9). Amos' woe oracles (5:18; 6:1) and visions (7:1–9; 8:1–3; 9:1–4) represent genres found in abundance in other OT prophetic books.

The prophets build on the older divine revelations as they apply them to their contemporaries and prepare the people for the coming of Christ. Jesus and the NT affirm this Christological and eschatological perspective of the OT prophets (e.g., Lk 24:25–27; Acts 3:18–24; Rom 1:2; 1 Pet 1:10–12). From the time of the early church on, interpreters have recognized that the prophets drew on earlier biblical texts and applied them to their contemporaries. Luther pointed to their reliance on the Torah: "For prophecy was nothing else than the burnishing, activating—if I may speak thus—and application of the [L]aw."[3]

More recently, Gerhard von Rad has pointed out that OT prophets like Amos reappropriate earlier texts in the OT. Von Rad employed the term *Vergegenwärtigung*, which could be translated as "a fresh presentation," "updating," or "reactualization."[4] With this term he maintained that prophets reactualized older biblical traditions in light of their new contexts. von Rad quotes Is 43:18–19 to introduce the second volume of his *Old Testament Theology*: "Remember not the former things nor consider the things of old. For behold, I purpose to do a new thing."[5] For von Rad the term "former things" refers to earlier texts. The phrase "a new thing" refers to the prophetic recasting and reshaping of those earlier writings. The new message is consistent with older texts, while at the same time being innovative. Older texts are adapted for new situations. They sparkle with new meanings, not contradictions.

In this move, von Rad proceeds against older critical ideas—especially those of Wellhausen—that assumed that prophets, and especially Amos, were innovators.[6] Von Rad treats the prophets as creative communicators who *reshaped* older texts for new situations. He writes: "For the prophets were never as orig-

---

not exhaustive, Niehaus also includes a chart in his commentary documenting connections between Amos and the Pentateuch ("Amos," 322).

3 Luther, *Against Latomus*, AE 32:225. Luther's Latin (WA 8.105) is quoted in von Rad, *Old Testament Theology*, 2:3, n. 2.

4 See von Rad's use of the term in *Theologie des Alten Testaments*, 2:6; 118, n. 10; 122; 329 (ET: *Old Testament Theology*, 2:vi; 105, n. 11; 108–9; 319; see also 2:177 [on Amos 9:7]; 2:394–95).

5 Von Rad, *Old Testament Theology*, 2:1.

6 See Wellhausen, *Prolegomena to the History of Ancient Israel*, 472–74.

inal, or as individualistic, or in such direct communion with God and no one else, as they were then [by older critical scholars] believed to be."[7]

By employing earlier themes and texts Amos narrates how, in terrible grandeur, Yahweh himself appeared to him and recruited him to deliver Yahweh's words (1:1–2; 3:7–8) to a people that already had the scrolls with God's older words. The oldest of Yahweh's revelations were recorded in Genesis, with the creation and patriarchal narratives, followed by his mercy in rescuing Israel from Egypt through the exodus. The covenant at Sinai followed, and then Israel received Yahweh's gift of the promised land. For almost seven hundred years before the time of Amos (eighth century BC), Israel had known the biblical language used for recording these events in the fifteenth (Moses) and fourteenth (Joshua) centuries BC.

The words of Yahweh through Amos are in the same theological tradition as his words through Moses and the other prophets and writers. They are a revelation of judgment and salvation from the same unchanging triune God to the same people he had created and redeemed to be his own, but who now are further down the road of history. This new book of Holy Scripture also shares cultural assumptions, structures of meaning, language, and literary features with the preceding Scriptures. To communicate through Amos, Yahweh used the language of his audience and connected his new revelation to his previous ones, which had become part of Israel's cherished religious traditions.[8]

Jesus and NT writers employ the same interpretive method of drawing on earlier sacred texts as did Amos. For example in Matthew 12, Jesus says, "One greater than the temple is here" (Mt 12:6); "One greater than Jonah is here" (Mt 12:41); and "One greater than Solomon is here" (Mt 12:42). What is Jesus doing when he compares himself to the Jerusalem temple, Israel's wisest and most powerful king, and a prophet who was swallowed by a big fish, then was resurrected in order to bring Gentiles to saving faith? Just like Amos, Jesus reappropriates earlier texts for his current situation. But Jesus goes farther than Amos. Christ announces that he is Yahweh's final and definitive "new thing" (see Is 43:19). He has come to demonstrate how all of Israel's earlier texts testified to the salvation he accomplished for all people through his sinless life, atoning death, and glorious resurrection (e.g., Lk 24:25–27; Col 2:16–17).

Following in the hermeneutical footsteps of Jesus, Paul takes Is 52:7, which praises the messenger who preaches the Good News of salvation through God's reign, and applies it to the evangelist who preaches the Good News of the resurrection of Christ (Rom 10:15). Paul makes some important modifications to the LXX. First, he omits the phrase ἐπὶ τῶν ὀρέων ("upon the mountains"), which refers to the mountains around Jerusalem, in order to emphasize that the quote applies to Christian preachers throughout the whole world. Second, instead of

7 Von Rad, *Old Testament Theology*, 2:3–4.

8 See further the excursus "Preaching Like Amos."

the more general LXX phrase ἀκοὴν εἰρήνης, literally, "hearing [the message] of peace," the apostle identifies the message more specifically as the Word that gives faith: "faith comes through hearing, and hearing through the Word of Christ" (ἄρα ἡ πίστις ἐξ ἀκοῆς, ἡ δὲ ἀκοὴ διὰ ῥήματος Χριστοῦ, Rom 10:17). Third, the apostle transforms the singular herald in the MT and the LXX (πόδες εὐαγγελιζομένου) into the plural to represent multiple evangelists (οἱ πόδες τῶν εὐαγγελιζομένων) who can then travel throughout the whole world. In this way, Paul identifies all faithful Christian pastors who "preach" (κηρύσσω appears in Rom 10:8, 14–15) with the herald of salvation in Is 52:7.

Amos 5:1–3

Dirge over Fallen Israel

Translation

5 [1]Hear this word that I am lifting up against you as a funeral dirge, O house of Israel:

[2] "Virgin Israel has fallen, and she will not rise again.
She is abandoned on her ground with no one raising her up."
[3]For thus says the Lord Yahweh:
"A city that marches forth with a thousand
will have a hundred left,
and [a city] that marches forth with a hundred
will have ten left of the house of Israel."

Textual Notes

5:1 שִׁמְעוּ אֶת־הַדָּבָר הַזֶּה—This same announcement formula, "hear this word," began chapters 3 and 4. See the first textual note on 3:1.

אֲשֶׁר אָנֹכִי נֹשֵׂא עֲלֵיכֶם קִינָה—The verb נָשָׂא can mean to "lift up" the voice (BDB, Qal, 1 b (5)), more specifically with a term for a solemn and formal utterance, such as קִינָה (BDB, Qal, 1 b (6)). The noun קִינָה, which recurs in 8:10, refers to a funeral dirge or lament for the dead.[1] In its two uses in the historical books of the OT (2 Sam 1:17; 2 Chr 35:25), a dirge is uttered over deceased individuals.[2] For example, in 2 Sam 1:17, "David lamented this lamentation" (וַיְקֹנֵן דָּוִד אֶת־הַקִּינָה הַזֹּאת) over the deaths of Saul and Jonathan. A formal קִינָה often has a poetic rhythm of three accented words followed by two accented words, a "limping" meter that is demonstrated in Amos 5:2a (see the first textual note on 5:2). A professional singers guild might perform a dirge (cf. 5:16). The OT prophets employ the קִינָה genre for nations or whole peoples. This is evident in Amos 5:1, where the prophet calls for a dirge to be lifted up for Virgin Israel because her demise is imminent. This premature dirge, before her actual "death" and exile, has the force of an imperative call for repentance. If Amos' preaching brings about Israel's repentance, Yahweh may cancel his plan to destroy the people (see Jer 18:7–10). Jonah's preaching caused Nineveh's repentance, and Yahweh then reversed his threatened judgment, and the Ninevites were saved through faith (Jonah 3:4–10).[3]

---

1 See Hummel, *Ezekiel 1–20*, 557–59. Budde ("Das hebräische Klagelied") was the first modern exegete to identify and define the *qinah* meter. His work has only been modified slightly by Garr, "The Qinah." Eissfeldt writes that the prophetic dirge is a lament "over something still in the future, but represented as the downfall, already in the past, of the people or of some other community. … We find it first in Amos" (*The Old Testament*, 95–96).

2 Cf. G. Fleischer, "קִינָה," *TDOT* 13:17–23.

3 See Lessing, *Jonah*, 296–341.

The idiom "to lift up a dirge" (נָשָׂא קִינָה) in Amos 5:1 is its oldest occurrence in the OT. The later prophets Jeremiah (7:29; 9:9 [ET 9:10]) and Ezekiel (19:1; 26:17; 27:2, 32; 28:12; 32:2) will employ it too. Amos summons his Israelite audience to listen to their own funeral, ironically while they are still alive! Block points out that in the OT a prophetic dirge (קִינָה) normally (1) opens with an exclamation of mourning, (2) is addressed directly to those who are dead, and (3) compares the present loss with the past greatness of the deceased.[4]

בֵּית יִשְׂרָאֵל׃—"House of Israel" is a vocative.

5:2 נָֽפְלָה֙ לֹֽא־תוֹסִ֣יף ק֔וּם בְּתוּלַ֖ת יִשְׂרָאֵ֑ל—This line displays the characteristic meter of the קִינָה, with three beats or accents (on נָֽפְלָה֙, the construct phrase לֹֽא־תוֹסִ֣יף, and ק֔וּם) followed by two accented words (בְּתוּלַ֖ת and יִשְׂרָאֵ֑ל). To produce this rhythm לֹֽא־ has *maqqeph* and no full accent, only *metheg* (-לֹֽ), so that the construct phrase לֹֽא־תוֹסִ֣יף has only a single full accent, *munach* (-סִ֣-). In contrast, and also to produce this rhythm, another word in construct, בְּתוּלַ֖ת, lacks *maqqeph* and receives the full accent *tiphcha* (-לַ֖-), so that the construct phrase בְּתוּלַ֖ת יִשְׂרָאֵ֑ל has two accented words.

The feminine noun בְּתוּלָה in the construct phrase בְּתוּלַ֖ת יִשְׂרָאֵ֑ל, literally, "the virgin of Israel," is the subject of the feminine verbs נָֽפְלָה֙ and תוֹסִ֣יף. The construct phrase means that Israel *is* a virgin—theologically and metaphorically, in the same sense that the church is the virgin bride of Christ. Hence the phrase can be translated as "Virgin Israel" (GKC, § 128 k; Waltke-O'Connor, § 9.5.3h, including example 53).

Ugaritic, Aramaic, Akkadian, and Arabic cognates of בְּתוּלָה imply that it denotes a young girl at the age of puberty or just afterwards, who probably would be a virgin.[5] In biblical usage, בְּתוּלָה usually refers to a "virgin" (BDB), as is clear in, for example, Deut 22:19; Ezek 44:22. בְּתוּלָה recurs in Amos 8:13 in the plural in the phrase "the beautiful maidens," parallel to "the young men," and the emphasis there is not on virginity, but on prime health (ruined by drought). The cognate abstract plural noun בְּתוּלִים means "virginity" or "tokens [proof] of virginity" (BDB), as is clear in Deut 22:14–15, 17, 20. With fifty OT occurrences, בְּתוּלָה is much more common than עַלְמָה, the technical term for *virgo intacto* in Is 7:14, which occurs only seven times in the OT (aside from the plural in musical notation in psalm superscriptions).[6] בְּתוּלָה frequently serves as a personification of a people, a nation, a city, or a land. Amos may be using the term to reflect Israel's status as Yahweh's bride.[7] Other prophets develop that theme at length (e.g., Jeremiah 2–3; Ezekiel 16 and 23; Hosea 1–3), just as the NT portrays the church as the virgin bride of Christ (e.g., 2 Cor 11:2; Eph 5:21–33; Revelation 21–22).

The verb נָפַל, "to fall," can denote the demise of a nation (e.g., Is 21:9: נָֽפְלָה֙ נָֽפְלָ֔ה בָּבֶ֔ל, "fallen, fallen is Babylon"; Jer 51:8; cf. Rev 18:2) or of individuals (e.g., 2 Sam 1:19, 25, 27; 3:34; Is 3:25), usually in battle.

---

4 Block, *Ezekiel*, 1:592–93.

5 Cf. J. Bergman, H. Ringgren, and M. Tsevat, "בְּתוּלָה," *TDOT* 2:338–43.

6 For עַלְמָה in Is 7:14, one may see Mitchell, *The Song of Songs*, 568–69, 588–91 (on Song 1:3), and Gibbs, *Matthew 1:1–11:1*, 99–101 (on Mt 1:23).

7 Andersen and Freedman, *Amos*, 474.

In לֹא־תוֹסִיף קוּם, the infinitive קוּם expresses the main verbal idea and the Hiphil of יָסַף (תוֹסִיף) functions adverbially: "she will not rise again."

Almost the same entire clause, וְנָפְלָה וְלֹא־תֹסִיף קוּם, occurs in Is 24:20. Similar is וְנָפְלוּ וְלֹא־יָקוּמוּ עוֹד in Amos 8:14.

נִטְּשָׁה עַל־אַדְמָתָהּ אֵין מְקִימָהּ׃—The image continues of Virgin Israel lying dead on the ground. "The corpse lies there unattended and ignored, 'abandoned' by God."[8] The Qal of נָטַשׁ usually means "to abandon, forsake" and in poetry often appears parallel to עָזַב, "leave behind."[9] The Niphal perfect here has the corresponding passive meaning, "abandoned," as Yahweh's judgment for her sins, as the active Qal means in Is 2:6. Whatever is abandoned by God is considered lost and spiritually dead.

The particle אֵין signifies the nonexistence of the Hiphil participle with objective suffix, מְקִימָהּ, "(some)one raising her." In Amos, only Yahweh is able to "raise up" someone or something, as stated with the Hiphil of קוּם in 2:11; 6:14; 9:11 (twice). No human help is available for those whom God has abandoned. Yet there is also no need for mere human help when God restores his people by raising up the tabernacle of David (9:11) since God's action is all sufficient.

5:3 כִּי כֹה אָמַר אֲדֹנָי יְהוִה—This is an expanded version of the prophetic messenger formula, used, for example, in 1:3; see the first textual note on 1:3. For the divine title אֲדֹנָי יְהוִה, see the fifth textual note on 1:8.

הָעִיר הַיֹּצֵאת אֶלֶף תַּשְׁאִיר מֵאָה—This and the following clause both describe examples of the literal decimation of Israel's forces. Cities in Israel will muster their soldiers, but for every ten that set out, only one will return alive. The loss of ninety percent of the military would mean that the cities' very existence is precarious.

The first example is about a city that is able to muster one thousand soldiers. The article is used with הָעִיר because "the city" is one present in the mind of the prophet, but it does not refer to any specific city, so in English it should be translated as indefinite: "a/any city that ..." (see GKC, § 126 q). The noun עִיר is feminine, hence the feminine participle הַיֹּצֵאת and the imperfect verb תַּשְׁאִיר, both of which are repeated in the next clause.

The verb יָצָא can mean to "march forth" into battle (e.g., Deut 20:1; 2 Sam 18:2–4; see BDB, Qal, 2 c). While the participle with article הַיֹּצֵאת serves as a relative clause modifying הָעִיר, the whole city would not march out; only its soldiers would go forth into war. The noun אֶלֶף, "a thousand," can be explained as an asyndetic subject complement that indicates the number from the city who march. A different grammatical explanation is that here יָצָא has acquired a transitive meaning and that אֶלֶף is its object, but the meaning of the clause would be the same, "to go forth with" a thousand soldiers (GKC, § 117 z).

The Qal of שָׁאַר has the intransitive meaning "be left over, remain."[10] The Niphal is used for the vestiges of the Canaanite nations that remained after the holy war when

---

8 Wolff, *Joel and Amos*, 236.

9 Cf. J. Lundbom and H.-J. Fabry, "נָטַשׁ," *TDOT* 9:407–12.

10 Cf. R. E. Clements, "שָׁאַר," *TDOT* 14:272–86.

Israel conquered the land (Josh 23:4, 7, 12). Remnants of such peoples served to bear witness to the destruction of the majority. Their witness was not one of joy but of dread, as they would have to endure defeat, oppression, and other sufferings caused by losing the war. Such connotations are relevant for Amos 5:3. The Hiphil of שָׁאַר often has the transitive meaning "to spare, leave (survivors), leave (a remnant) alive," with the conquerors as the subject and the surviving members of the defeated foes as its object (see BDB, 1). Only here in the OT does the subject of the Hiphil include the people who are also the direct object of the verb. The subject is הָעִיר, "the city," and the direct object, מֵאָה, refers to the "hundred" from the city that return alive from the war. Here the Hiphil means that the city will "preserve, keep alive, have (some survivors) left" (see BDB, 3; *HALOT*, 2).

Amos uses the verb שָׁאַר only here in 5:3 (twice). He uses the cognate noun שְׁאֵרִית three times, once negatively for heathen Philistia (1:8), once hopefully for Israel (5:15), and once in a Gospel promise for Edom representing converted Gentiles (9:12).

וְהַיּוֹצֵאת מֵאָה תַּשְׁאִיר עֲשָׂרָה—This repeats the two verbs from the preceding clause. Both numbers in the preceding clause are reduced by a factor of ten: instead of a thousand, there are just "a hundred" (מֵאָה) departing soldiers; and instead of a hundred, there are only "ten" (עֲשָׂרָה) survivors.

לְבֵית יִשְׂרָאֵל׃—The preposition לְ is used as a circumlocution for the genitive (GKC, § 129 g), hence "ten left *of the house of Israel.*"

Commentary

Introduction to Amos 5:1–17

Amos in chapter 5 warns Israel and calls the people to repentance. His announcements of irrevocable judgment in chapters 1–4 (e.g., "I will not revoke it," 2:6) are reflected in the funeral dirge that depicts Israel as already fallen (5:1–2). Historically, this downfall happened some forty years after the ministry of Amos when Assyria conquered northern Israel in 722 BC. Yet a small remnant will survive (5:3). For all who hear Amos preaching before the disaster, and for those who survive it, there is still time to "produce fruit in keeping with repentance" (Lk 3:8). The prophet's preaching includes this Gospel hope (e.g., 5:6a, 14–15). The sirens are sounding and national disaster is imminent, but there is still an opportunity for Israel to turn back to Yahweh.

This same message was heralded by Jesus in Mt 4:17: "Repent, for the reign of God is near." It is our impending death and the future judgment on the Last Day that give the present message such urgency. Every day we Christians recall our Baptism into Christ, die to sin, and rise to new life in him by the power of the Spirit, confident that if we have been buried with him we shall also be united with him in our resurrection on the Last Day (Rom 6:1–13). NT ethics frequently have this eschatological frame of reference (e.g., Rom 13:11–14; 2 Pet 3:11–12; 1 Jn 3:2–3), which is the same framework for the ethical exhortations in Amos.

The dirge of Amos 5:1–3 literarily follows logically after the theophanic confrontation in 4:12. The impending encounter of the unrepentant Israelites with their God can mean only one thing: death. Israel is called to lament its own death, which will come about through a terrible military downfall that will leave only ten percent of its soldiers alive (5:3).

While "thus says Yahweh" in 5:4 begins a new section of prophecy (5:4–17), the funeral dirge in 5:1–3 relates to it. De Waard believes all of 5:1–17 is deliberately structured as a chiasm with the doxology (5:8–9) at its center.[11] This explains why the doxology separates the accusations in 5:7 from the accusations in 5:10–13, which otherwise would go together. The following is based on his analysis:

A Lament over the death of the nation (5:1–3)
  B Call to seek Yahweh and live (5:4–6)
    C Accusations of no justice (5:7)
      D Hymn to Yahweh (5:8a–e)
        E "Yahweh is his name" (5:8f)
      D' Hymn to Yahweh (5:9)
    C' Accusations of no justice (5:10–13)
  B' Call to seek Yahweh and live (5:14–15)
A' Lament over the death of the nation (5:16–17)

The whole of 5:1–17 is similar to an ancient elegy in the OT, David's lament over the deaths of Saul and Jonathan in 2 Sam 1:19–27.[12] Amos 5:1–17 shares the following elements with David's funerary dirge:[13]

1. A description of the death (Amos 5:2–3; 2 Sam 1:19, 23, 25, 27)
2. The call for the survivors to respond (Amos 5:3–6, 14–15; 2 Sam 1:20)
3. A direct address to the deceased (Amos 5:7–13; 2 Sam 1:26)
4. A call to lament (Amos 5:1, 16–17; 2 Sam 1:21, where the mountains are called to mourn)

These similarities suggest that Amos is employing an ancient genre and changing it to suit his rhetorical purposes.[14] In this case, he is lamenting the death of a nation that—during his ministry—is still very much physically alive, but spiritually dead (see Eph 2:1; Rev 3:1).

---

[11] De Waard, "The Chiastic Structure of Amos V 1–17." Tromp identifies the structure somewhat differently, but he also argues that 5:1–17 is crafted as a unity ("Amos V 1–17").

[12] Israelites also lamented imminent death due to sickness, oppression, or injustice (e.g., Psalms 6 and 13; Jer 11:18–20). And the prophets record laments for the impending destruction of surrounding nations (e.g., Is 15:1–9; 23:1–14; Jer 48:36–44; Ezek 27:1–36). Cf. Westermann, *Praise and Lament in the Psalms*, 261–62.

[13] What follows is based on Stuart, *Hosea–Jonah*, 344.

[14] Amos inverts the following genres/doctrines in order to accuse Israel: oracles against the nations (1:3–2:16), the exodus and conquest (2:9–16; 9:7), election (3:2), the priestly call to worship (4:4–5), and the Day of Yahweh (5:18–20).

Amos 5:1

The chapter is addressed to the "house of Israel" in the vocative (5:1). Thus the chapter begins much like chapter 3 ("O children of Israel," 3:1) in that "Israel" is qualified with a term ("children of," 3:1; "house of," 5:1). In both texts, the qualification probably indicates that all Israel, both north and south, is being addressed.[15] This interpretation of chapter 5 is confirmed by the expressions "Virgin Israel" in 5:2 and "the house of Israel" in 5:3–4.

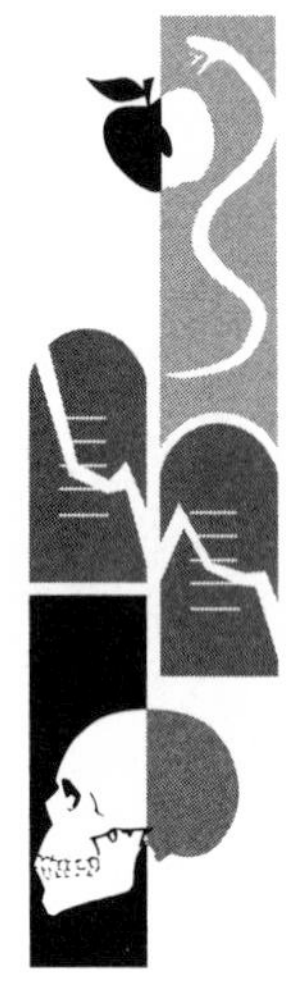

Yahweh announces that he is lifting up a קִינָה, a "dirge" or mournful funeral poem. This genre is not a eulogy in praise of the deceased, but a lament over their disgraceful demise. Similar to this lament over Israel prior to the fall of the Northern Kingdom is the dirge (קִינָה, Ezek 19:1, 14) over Israel prior to the fall of the Southern Kingdom in Ezekiel 19. But perhaps the most appalling OT dirge (קִינָה, Ezek 32:2, 16) is the lament in Ezekiel 32 over Pharaoh and Egypt as they are sent down into the "pit" and "Sheol" (Ezek 32:18–21), that is, to eternal perdition in hell. Similar in the NT are Jesus' woes over the inhabitants of unrepentant cities who will be damned on Judgment Day (Mt 11:21–24). The closest NT parallel is the lament over the antitype of OT Babylon: spiritual Babylon the harlot (Rev 17:1–7), whose dirge begins, "Fallen, fallen is Babylon!" (ἔπεσεν ἔπεσεν Βαβυλών, Rev 18:2), just like Israel is "fallen" (נָפְלָה) in Amos 5:2.

While those who die in unbelief lie "fallen" in hell for eternity, Yahweh extends a Gospel promise of resurrection that applies to all who repent and believe: "I will raise up the falling [הַנֹּפֶלֶת] tabernacle of David" (9:11; see further the commentary there).

Typical elements of prophetic dirges include the following: (1) the genre label "dirge" (קִינָה); (2) the idiomatic verb נָשָׂא, "to lift up"; (3) mourning and lamentation (as in 5:16–17); (4) satire of the former glory compared to the present disgrace of the deceased;[16] and (5) the dirge as a predictive prophecy of a *future* fall depicted as a past event; the "death" is a fait accompli. It is not surprising that Amos employs this genre, since 5:16 indicates that he was aware of lament singers. The irony is that, at least physically, the prophet's Israelite audience is still very much alive, although "dead" in their "trespasses and sins" (Eph 2:1; cf. Rev 3:1).

Amos' dirge is similar to somber funeral music in a minor key. Those who heard Amos 5:1 would naturally ask, "Who died?" The answer in 5:2 is this: "You have, but you are not yet aware of it!" The dirge communicates Israel's folly; death negates all of her claims of invincibility (e.g., 6:13; 9:10).

When people lamented in the ancient Near East, they often groaned and wept aloud, shaved their heads, tore their clothing, wore sackcloth and ashes,

---

[15] Andersen and Freedman, *Amos*, 106–7 (see also pp. 98–99).

[16] Jemielity writes: "A sizeable chunk of the text of Ezekiel, chapters twenty-five through thirty-two, for instance, prominently features mock lamentations on the demise of some of Israel's pagan neighbors and traditional enemies" (*Satire and the Hebrew Prophets*, 94).

and sometimes hired professional mourners (cf. Mt 9:23–24). As Amos delivered this oracle, he could have employed at least some of these mourning practices. Yahweh commanded the prophet Ezekiel to shave his head (Ezek 5:1) and groan in public as prophetic signs (Ezek 21:11–12 [ET 21:6–7]). The rhetorical strategy of both prophets was to convince Israel that the nation was as good as dead. At the same time, Yahweh promises through Amos that those who are dead may, through repentance and faith, be raised to new and everlasting life (Amos 5:4, 14–15; 9:11–15; cf. Lk 15:24, 32).

Jesus wept for a time when Lazarus died (Jn 11:35). He also wept when Jerusalem rejected his repeated attempts to gather the city to himself (Mt 23:37). Paul likewise was in anguish over his countrymen who, for the most part, rejected the Gospel of their long-promised Messiah, "the Christ, who is God over all, blessed forever" (Rom 9:1–5).

Amos 5:2

"Fallen" (נָפְלָה) in this context (cf. 5:3) denotes a major military defeat. David lamented Abner with similar words: "As one falls [כִּנְפוֹל] before wicked sons you have fallen [נָפָלְתָּ]" (2 Sam 3:34). The verb is employed similarly in 2 Sam 1:19, 25, 27 and Lam 2:21 as a euphemism for death.

The title בְּתוּלַת יִשְׂרָאֵל ("Virgin Israel") in Amos 5:2 is the oldest occurrence in the OT of this title for the people.[17] During Amos' ministry in the eighth century BC Israel was still in her youth; she was enjoying a successful political, military, and economic season. And yet the shock of it all is that this nation—still with the best years of her life ahead—has experienced a premature death.[18] "Its early demise before achieving adult maturity makes its situation ever so more tragic."[19] Put another way: "The pathos is that the relations possible in the covenant between Yahweh and [virgin] Israel were never fully realized."[20] Compare Ezekiel 16, written a century and a half later, where Jerusalem is pictured as an infant girl raised by Yahweh, who then marries her when she has grown up, but she commits adultery against him.

Yahweh declares that "Virgin Israel ... will not rise [קוּם] again" (5:2). The nation's wounds are fatal, too deep and severe for her to recover on her own.

---

[17] בְּתוּלַת יִשְׂרָאֵל appears in Deut 22:19, but there it refers to an individual woman: a "virgin of Israel" was any virgin bride who became married and then was wrongfully accused by her husband of not having been a virgin. Hayes claims that in Amos 5:2 "Virgin Israel" refers to the city of Samaria because feminine imagery is commonly employed in the OT for cities but not for Israel as a people (*Amos, the Eighth-Century Prophet*, 155). But it is better to understand the title "Virgin Israel" to mean that Amos is mourning over all of Israel, both the Northern and Southern Kingdoms.

[18] Jephthah's daughter also laments her early death. In Judg 11:37 she goes out with her friends for two months in order to weep because as a young woman she is about to die (וְאֶבְכֶּה עַל־בְּתוּלַי). "Daughter Zion" in Isaiah is also cut down in her prime (e.g., Is 1:8; 10:32).

[19] Paul, *Amos*, 160.

[20] Andersen and Freedman, *Amos*, 474.

Can the dead rise? Only Yahweh is able to raise the dead. The causative Hiphil of the same verb, קוּם, "to rise," is used in Hos 6:2:

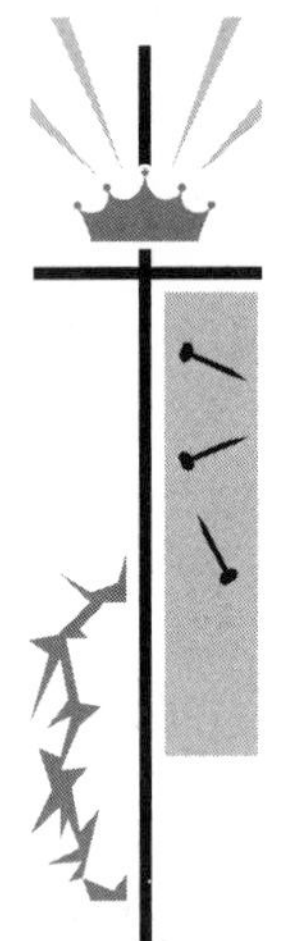

> He [Yahweh] will make us alive after two days;
> on the third day he will raise us up [יְקִמֵנוּ] so that we may live before him.

In Amos, Yahweh uses the causative Hiphil of קוּם, "to rise," twice in a similar sense in the messianic promise in 9:11:

> On that day I will raise up [אָקִים] the falling tabernacle of David.
> I will repair their breaches,
> and his ruins I will raise up [אָקִים].

Israel will not be able to lift herself up by her own power. Yahweh will do it climactically in David's greatest Son, Jesus, whose resurrection empowers those who are dead to come to life, by grace through faith (cf. Eph 2:1–10).[a]

(a) See also Is 25:8; 26:19; Job 14:7–14; 19:25–27; Dan 12:2–3

Amos 5:3

This verse employs standard Israelite military terminology for troops. Soldiers were organized by tens, fifties, hundreds, and thousands (e.g., Ex 18:21; Num 31:14; 1 Sam 10:19; 18:13; 2 Sam 18:1). However, only a tenth of all the troops sent by a city will survive. Throughout judgment oracles in Amos, God targets cities, for example, Damascus (1:3), Gaza (1:6), Tyre (1:9), and Samaria (3:12). Only when the breaches and ruins surrounding David's tabernacle will be repaired (9:11) will the devastated cities be rebuilt and once again inhabited—not only by the remnant of Israel, but also by the saved remnant of Gentiles (9:12, 14). The eschatological hope for the baptized is in the Jerusalem above (Gal 4:26; Heb 12:22). At the second coming of Christ, this completely restored city will come down "out of heaven from God, prepared as a bride beautifully dressed for her husband" (Rev 21:2).

But before this happens, the cities among the nations addressed in the oracles in 1:3–2:3, as well as the cities in Judah and Israel (2:4–16) must experience crushing military defeats. Amos describes the defeats of northern Israel in 2:14–16; 4:10; 6:8–10; 7:9.

Amos 5:3 activates the covenant curse in Deut 32:30 for the Israelites when they betray their God and Redeemer, who then forsakes them: "How could one [enemy] chase a thousand [Israelites] or two cause ten thousand to flee unless their Rock had sold them and Yahweh had delivered them up?" Israel's ranks are decimated from a thousand to a hundred to ten and to finally to zero, and only Yahweh could have permitted it. "You are left few in number whereas you were as numerous as the stars of the sky" (Deut 28:62). The words of Amos 5:3 are to be read in light of 3:6:

> If a disaster happens in a city,
> did Yahweh not do [it]?

Summary

In 5:1–3 the prophet intones a funeral lament for a nation physically alive but spiritually dead. The people called upon to hear are the deceased in the lament. This incongruity is evident in the opening call itself, as if God says, "Listen to your own obituary!" The Israelites are addressed as unburied corpses. The perfect verbs "has fallen" and "is abandoned" (5:2) suggest that death has already come upon the nation Israel, here personified as a young virgin. Her potential as a wife and mother remains unfulfilled. The repetition in 5:2 of the verb קוּם, first in the Qal, "she will not *rise* again," and then in the Hiphil, "no one *raising* her *up*," sharpens the image of national disaster and helplessness. Her apostasy from her Creator and Redeemer has left her barren, abandoned, dead, and without hope even for burial. The nation who is engaged in death-dealing lifestyles (e.g., 2:6–8; 4:1; 8:4–6) is itself *dead*. The only possible hope for resurrection to new life is through repentance and faith in the triune God.

Amos 5:4–17

Seek Yahweh and Live!

Translation

5 [4]For thus says Yahweh to the house of Israel:
"Seek me and live!
[5]But do not seek [at] Bethel,
and do not go to Gilgal,
and do not travel to Beersheba.
For Gilgal surely will go into exile,
and Bethel will become nothing."
[6]Seek Yahweh and live,
lest he rush like fire upon the house of Joseph,
and it will consume with no one extinguishing it for Bethel,
[7][O you] who are turning justice into wormwood,
and righteousness they throw to the ground.
[8]The Maker of the Pleiades and Orion,
who turns the shadow of death into the morning,
and who darkens day into night,
who summons the waters of the seas
and who pours them out upon the face of the earth—
Yahweh is his name—
[9]who causes destruction to flash upon a stronghold,
so destruction comes upon a fortification.
[10]They hate an arbiter in the gate,
and one speaking honestly they abhor.
[11]Therefore because you trample on the poor
and you take from them a tax of grain,
houses of hewn stones you have built,
but you will not live in them.
Choice vineyards you have planted,
but you will not drink their wine.
[12]For I know that many are your transgressions
and mighty are your sins,
[you] who are enemies of a righteous man,
[you] who are taking a bribe,
and needy people they thrust away in the gate.
[13]Therefore the prudent man in that time will be silent,
for it is an evil time.

14Seek good and not evil so that you may live,
and then it would be so: Yahweh, the God of armies, [would be] with you,
as you claim.
15Hate evil and love good,
and establish justice in the gate.
Perhaps Yahweh, the God of armies, will be gracious to the remnant of Joseph.
16Therefore thus says Yahweh, the God of armies, the Lord:
"In the city plazas there will be lamentation,
and in the streets they will say, 'Woe, woe!'
And they will summon the farmer to mourning
and [to] lamentation the ones skilled in wailing.
17In all the vineyards will be lamentation,
because I will pass through your midst," says Yahweh.

Textual Notes

5:4 כִּי כֹה אָמַר יְהוָה לְבֵית יִשְׂרָאֵל—For the messenger formula כֹּה אָמַר יְהוָה, see the first textual note on 1:3. In this chapter, modified forms of the formula occur also in 5:3 and 5:16. "House of Israel" probably refers to both the Northern Kingdom and the Southern Kingdom; see the commentary on 5:1.

דִּרְשׁוּנִי וִחְיוּ׃—The same two imperatives are repeated in the first line of 5:6 (cf. 5:14). The relationship between the two Qal plural imperatives is that of an action and its consequence or result. "The first imperative contains … a condition, while the second declares the consequence which the fulfillment of the condition will involve. … The consequence is, as a matter of fact, intended or desired by the speaker" (GKC, § 110 f). Yahweh declares that if the people "seek me" in penitent faith, then they will "live" as a result of his grace. His gracious desire is that they will seek him and so live. Joüon, § 116 f C 3, explains the construction as a direct volitive (the first imperative, by which the speaker directly states his will for the audience: "seek me") followed by an indirect volitive (the second imperative, by which Yahweh indirectly expresses his will that Israel should then "live"). Joüon, § 168 a, note 2, points out that the force of the second imperative, וִחְיוּ, "and live," is the same as that of a final or purpose clause, which is normally expressed with a telic particle, as in 5:14, where Yahweh declares, "Seek good … *so that you may live* [לְמַעַן תִּחְיוּ]."

The verb דָּרַשׁ, "to seek," occurs in 5:4, 5, 6, 14, but occurs nowhere else in the book. It can be a technical term for seeking Yahweh in repentance and faith, connoting total dedication and renunciation of all other gods (5:4, 6). Such faith leads to seeking good (5:14). Conversely, it can also refer to seeking other gods with faith in them, expressed by visiting their sanctuaries (5:5). Seeking Yahweh can involve worshiping at his holy sanctuary (e.g., Deut 12:5–6; 2 Chr 1:5). Believers can also seek Yahweh's will through oracles delivered by a faithful prophet (e.g., 2 Ki 22:13). Yahweh prohibits his people from seeking him through a medium, divination, attempting to contact the dead, or other occult methods (Deut 18:10–11). Sometimes those who seek a word from Yahweh may be deceived if they resort to false prophets (1 Ki 22:5–6).

5:5 וְאַל־תִּדְרְשׁוּ בֵּית־אֵל—The prohibition is expressed by the jussive or imperfect תִּדְרְשׁוּ negated with אַל (see GKC, § 107 p). Most English translations take בֵּית־אֵל as the direct object: "Do not seek Bethel," as if Bethel itself were a deity. However, if it were the direct object it probably would be preceded by אֶת, as in דִּרְשׁוּ אֶת־יְהוָה in 5:6. Instead, בֵּית־אֵל in 5:5 may be an accusative of location, with an implied direct object: "Do not seek [God or any false gods] at Bethel." This is confirmed by the following two parallel prohibitions, both of which speak of traveling to a location of an idolatrous shrine, rather than to Yahweh's temple in Jerusalem. For Bethel, which recurs again in this verse and in 5:6, see the second textual note and the commentary on 3:14, the first textual note on 4:4, and the commentary on 7:13.

וְהַגִּלְגָּל לֹא תָבֹאוּ וּבְאֵר שֶׁבַע לֹא תַעֲבֹרוּ—These two prohibitions use the strongest negative, לֹא, with imperfect verbs (תָבֹאוּ … תַעֲבֹרוּ), the same construction used for the prohibitions in the Ten Commandments. For Gilgal, see the first textual note on 4:4.

Beersheba was a major city in the Negev. Its name means "well of seven" or "well of oath" (Gen 21:25–31; see also Gen 26:26–33). It is often used to indicate the southern extremity of the promised land (e.g., Judg 20:1; 2 Sam 24:2). In the tribal allotment of land, Beersheba was given to Simeon (Josh 19:1–2), but this territory was soon assimilated by Judah. Beersheba recurs in Amos 8:14. In both verses Amos implies that this city in southern Judah also was the location of an idolatrous shrine.[1] Northern Israel had no monopoly on syncretistic apostasy.

כִּי הַגִּלְגָּל גָּלֹה יִגְלֶה—The infinitive absolute גָּלֹה functions adverbially to strengthen the affirmation (Joüon, § 123 e; GKC, § 113 n), and it modifies the imperfect of the same verb, יִגְלֶה: "Gilgal *surely* will go into exile." Gilgal's judgment is filled with assonance (cf. Joüon, § 123 u, note 1) and wordplay that can be transliterated as *hagilgal galoh yigleh*. Paul lists attempts to replicate Amos' literary pun, including "Gilgal shall weep gall," "Gilgal shall compensate commensurately," "the Rolling City shall rock and roll," "Gilgal shall go into galling exile," and "Gilgal shall taste the gall of exile."[2]

Normally the Hebrew names of cities and towns are feminine, but both Gilgal and Bethel are the subjects of masculine verbs: here הַגִּלְגָּל … יִגְלֶה and, in the next clause, וּבֵית־אֵל יִהְיֶה. Apparently the names of these towns originally were masculine appellatives (GKC, § 122 h). City names beginning with בֵּית־ are masculine (Joüon, § 134 g; Waltke-O'Connor, § 6.4.1d).

וּבֵית־אֵל יִהְיֶה לְאָוֶן׃—Yahweh warns that Bethel (בֵּית־אֵל) will become אָוֶן, "nothing." This likely involves a pun because another eighth-century prophet, Hosea, three times malphemistically calls Bethel "Beth-aven" (בֵּית־אָוֶן), that is, "house of nothing" (Hos 4:15; 5:8; 10:5). Since "Bethel" means "house of God," "Beth-aven" implies that the "god" whose shrine was there is really "nothing."

---

1 For a description of a horned altar found at Beersheba, see King, *Amos, Hosea, Micah*, 102–4.

2 Paul, *Amos*, 163, n. 41, who has translated some of these puns into English from German. Wellhausen rendered it in German as *Gilgal wird zum Galgen gehn*, "Gilgal will go to the gallows" (*Die kleinen Propheten*, 5; trans. Paul, *Amos*, 163, n. 41). Paul, *Amos*, 163, n. 42, gives these other examples of paronomastic puns on names of cities: 2 Sam 1:20; Is 10:29–30; Jer 6:1; Hos 12:12 (ET 12:11); Micah 1:10–15; Zeph 2:4.

While אָוֶן can have other meanings, including "disaster" (*HALOT*, 1 and 2), "idolatry" or, concretely, "idols" (BDB, 2), and "wickedness" (BDB, 3), and such meanings could be appropriate for Hos 4:15; 5:8; 10:5 (e.g., "Beth-aven" means "house of idolatry/wickedness"), "nothingness" is more appropriate for it here (*HALOT*, 4). Paul argues for "nothing," based on אָוֶן in Is 41:29, where it appears beside אֶפֶס, "non-existence," רוּחַ, "wind," and תֹהוּ, "emptiness."[3] The LXX translates לְאָוֶן in Amos 5:5 as ὡς οὐχ ὑπάρχουσα, "like that which is not."

5:6 דִּרְשׁוּ אֶת־יְהוָה וִחְיוּ—The same two imperatives from 5:4 are repeated; see the second textual note on 5:4. Here דִּרְשׁוּ takes the direct object אֶת־יְהוָה instead of the pronominal suffix (נִי-) that was in 5:4.

פֶּן־יִצְלַח כָּאֵשׁ בֵּית יוֹסֵף—The Qal of צָלַח displays a wide range of meanings, perhaps because of two different homographic roots (so BDB, but not *HALOT*).[4] For a discussion of its possible meanings here, see *HALOT*, s.v. צָלַח, Qal, 1 c 1. צָלַח often has the intransitive meaning "to succeed, prosper" (see BDB s.v. צָלַח II), but that is not appropriate for this context with Yahweh, named in the preceding clause, as the implied subject ("lest Yahweh succeed like fire"). צָלַח meaning "to rush" takes an accusative of place in 2 Sam 19:18 (ET 19:17): וְצָלְחוּ הַיַּרְדֵּן, "they rushed (into) the Jordan." Most likely the construction here is similar, with בֵּית יוֹסֵף as the accusative object, although English requires a preposition: "lest he rush like fire (upon) the house of Joseph" (see BDB, s.v. צָלַח I). God the Holy Spirit is the subject of צָלַח with a similar meaning in passages where the Spirit "comes, rushes" upon (עַל) a person: Samson (Judg 14:6, 19; 15:14), Saul (1 Sam 10:6, 10; 11:6; cf. 1 Sam 18:10), or David (1 Sam 16:13).

Grammatically it is possible that בֵּית יוֹסֵף is a vocative: "lest he rush like fire [upon you], O house of Joseph." The message of the clause would be the same. The next verse (5:7) likely begins with a vocative. However, within 5:6 the construct phrase בֵּית יוֹסֵף is parallel to the construct phrase with preposition at the end of the next clause, לְבֵית־אֵל, which is an indirect object (not a vocative). Most English translations take "the house of Joseph" as the indirect object (not as a vocative). The LXX translates the clause as ὅπως μὴ ἀναλάμψῃ ὡς πῦρ ὁ οἶκος Ιωσηφ, "so that the house of Joseph will not flame up like fire."[5]

In any case, this clause identifies "fire" as the means of Yahweh's judgment upon the house of Joseph.

The name "Joseph" (יוֹסֵף) appears in Amos in 5:6, 15; 6:6, where it refers to all of northern Israel. The name appears over two hundred times in the OT, and it most commonly denotes the first son of Jacob and Rachel. Rachel's name for him is explained by her prayer, "May Yahweh add [יֹסֵף] to me another son" (Gen 30:24), in which she uses the Hiphil jussive of יָסַף, "to add, increase." While "Joseph" means "may he [God] add," it also forms a pun on the verb אָסַף, "to remove," in the preceding verse, for in

---

3 Paul, *Amos*, 164.

4 Cf. J. Hausmann, "צָלַח," *TDOT* 12:382–85.

5 Paul, *Amos*, 165, argues that several verbs of motion in Hebrew and Akkadian may also refer to the act of burning.

Gen 30:23 Rachel states that by enabling her to conceive Joseph "God has removed [אָסַף] my reproach."

Later in the OT, "Joseph" can denote the tribes of Ephraim and Manasseh, the two sons of Joseph (e.g., Deut 27:12). Ephraim, the younger son, received the predominant blessing by Jacob, as if he were the firstborn (Gen 48:11–20), and in fulfillment of that blessing, Ephraim became the strongest of the northern tribes. Thus "Ephraim" was often used by the prophets as shorthand for all of northern Israel.[6] Similarly, but less frequently, "Joseph" was used as a shorthand name for the entire Northern Kingdom, as also in Obad 18 and Zech 10:6 (cf. Ezek 37:16, 19).

In Amos 5:6 "the house of Joseph" refers to the Northern Kingdom prior to the coming judgment. "The ruin of Joseph" in 6:6 implies that the judgment is imminent. "The remnant of Joseph" in 5:15 envisions the future time after the decimating judgment has already happened and Yahweh has graciously spared a few survivors.

וְאָכְלָה וְאֵין־מְכַבֶּה לְבֵית־אֵל׃—The subject of the feminine verb וְאָכְלָה is the (usually) feminine noun אֵשׁ, "fire," in the preceding clause. The fire is then the implied object of וְאֵין־מְכַבֶּה, literally, "and there is no one quenching." In the OT, the Piel participle of כָּבָה occurs only in this clause that describes Yahweh's unquenchable fiery judgment (Is 1:31; Jer 4:4; 21:12; Amos 5:6). לְבֵית־אֵל uses the preposition לְ in the sense of advantage (see BDB s.v. לְ 5 g (*b*)): "… no one quenching [the fire] for the sake/benefit of Bethel."

5:7 The syntactical relationship between this verse and the preceding one is difficult. So too is the syntactical relationship between the two clauses of this verse. Most translations understand the participle with article, הַהֹפְכִים, as a vocative: "[O you] who are turning …" (see GKC, § 126 e). Some translations take הַהֹפְכִים as a third person description continuing the reference לְבֵית־אֵל at the end of 5:6, "for Bethel, for those who turn justice …" (NASB).

In the second clause of 5:7, Yahweh continues to refer to Israel, but instead of another participle he uses a third person perfect verb, הִנִּיחוּ, "*they* throw." The same switch occurs in the second half of 5:12, where two vocative participles are followed by a third person verb, and all refer to the Israelites: "[you] who are enemies of [צֹרְרֵי] … [you] who are taking [לֹקְחֵי] … they thrust away [הִטּוּ]." Some English versions smooth the syntax by translating as if both lines of 5:7 were second person vocatives (RSV, ESV, NIV) or by making both lines third person (NASB).

Andersen and Freedman interpret the participles in this section as referring to the same people denoted by participles who receive the "woe" oracles in 5:18 and 6:1. They write:

> There is no reason to claim that the people who desired the Day of Yahweh (5:18) were different from those in 5:7, 10–12; or 6:1–7, 13. They came from different walks of life—merchants, magistrates, soldiers—but their general

---

[6] E.g., Is 7:2, 5, 8–9; Jer 31:9, 18, 20; Ezek 37:16, 19; Zech 9:10. Cf. S. Herrmann, "Ephraim (Person)," *ABD* 2:551, who notes that "Ephraim actually encompassed the real territorial center of this geopolitical region [that of the entire Northern Kingdom]."

outlook was the same, and they amounted to one consolidated class, which doubtless embraced all branches of public leadership, including clergy.[7]

הַהֹפְכִים לְלַעֲנָה מִשְׁפָּט—In Amos 5 the pair of synonyms "justice" (מִשְׁפָּט) and "righteousness" (צְדָקָה in the next clause) appears twice, here in an accusation against Israel and in 5:24 in a description of how Yahweh expects his people to treat others. Righteousness and justice are major themes in chapters 5 and 6. מִשְׁפָּט and/or צְדָקָה occurs in 5:7, 15, 24; 6:12. Outside of chapters 5–6, the only other verses with a word cognate to either of the nouns are 2:3, where Yahweh declares that he will cut off the "judge" (שׁוֹפֵט) from Moab, and 2:6, where Yahweh condemns Israelites who were selling the "righteous" (צַדִּיק) for silver. צַדִּיק also occurs in 5:12.

Several interpreters speculate that the definite article on the Qal participle הַהֹפְכִים is a remnant of an original הוֹי, "woe," to which the text should be emended.[8] If so, this would be the first of the three woe oracles in Amos; the other two occurrence of הוֹי are in 5:18 and 6:1. But this emendation is unwarranted. The construction of the verb הָפַךְ with the preposition לְ (here on לְלַעֲנָה) means "to turn [something in]to the opposite."[9] This is the construction and meaning in all the Amos verses with the verb הָפַךְ (5:7–8; 6:12; 8:10) except for 4:11, where the verb means "to overturn, destroy."

Both here and in 6:12 the direct object of הָפַךְ is מִשְׁפָּט, "justice." This noun is prominent in Amos and appears in 5:7, 15, 24 and 6:12. In three of these four verses, it precedes and is parallel to צְדָקָה, "righteousness" (5:7, 24; 6:12). It is derived from the verb שָׁפַט, which has a broad range of meanings and is usually translated as "to judge," but which can refer to saving God's people as well as carrying out judgment on his foes, as in the book of Judges, where individual judges (שֹׁפְטִים) are also called "savior" (מוֹשִׁיעַ) since Yahweh uses them to "save" (Hiphil of יָשַׁע) Israelites (see, e.g., Judg 2:16–18; 3:9; 6:36). The noun מִשְׁפָּט has several different meanings, including "justice," "judgment," and "verdict."[10] It can refer to Yahweh's attribute of "justice, right, rectitude" (BDB, 2 a), and to his expressions of his own righteousness through his "ordinances, just decrees, standards of justice" in his revealed Word (cf. BDB, 3). Often it can involve forensic justification. Understood in this way, there is considerable overlap between Yahweh's justice (מִשְׁפָּט) and righteousness (צְדָקָה). For example, Micah 7:9 states:

> וְעָשָׂה מִשְׁפָּטִי יוֹצִיאֵנִי לָאוֹר אֶרְאֶה בְּצִדְקָתוֹ׃
>
> He [Yahweh] will carry out justice for me; he will bring me forth into the light, and I will see his righteousness.

The Torah was the foundation for Israel's legal system because in it Yahweh revealed his own standards of justice and righteousness. Amos uses מִשְׁפָּט to encompass the theological justice that Yahweh intended for the justification of his people and for their moral and ethical well-being. It is rooted in Yahweh's own justness and righteousness. For this reason, מִשְׁפָּט in Amos 5:7a is parallel to צְדָקָה, "righteousness," in

---

7 Andersen and Freedman, *Amos*, 465.

8 Cf. Andersen and Freedman, *Amos*, 483–85.

9 Paul, *Amos*, 166, n. 77.

10 Cf. B. Johnson, "מִשְׁפָּט," *TDOT* 9:86–98.

5:7b. מִשְׁפָּט can often mean "what is right and proper, righteousness … the God-given norm to ensure a well-ordered society."[11]

Tragically, the Israelites were perverting Yahweh's justice into לַעֲנָה, "wormwood," a plant with a bitter and repulsive taste. The noun occurs a total of eight times in the OT. Wolff writes:

> This little bush-like plant, which can reach a height of 1.2 meters and has finely pinnate leaves, thrives in the area stretching from Spain across north Africa and as far as Iran. In early winter it blossoms and bears fruit. In Palestine it grows primarily in the Negeb, in the Wilderness of Judah, and in the Transjordan region.[12]

לַעֲנָה is parallel with רֹאשׁ (or מֵי־רֹאשׁ) in Amos 6:12 as well as in Deut 29:17 (ET 29:18); Jer 9:14 (ET 9:15); 23:15; and Lam 3:19, and in these contexts רֹאשׁ denotes "poison." לַעֲנָה may be used metaphorically to describe the damnation of unbelievers (Deut 29:17 [ET 29:18]), the misery of exiles (Jer 9:14–15 [ET 9:15–16]), or intense suffering (Lam 3:15, 19). In Prov 5:4 the sweet words of the temptress are in reality as dangerous as wormwood (לַעֲנָה) or a two-edged sword.

Wormwood is a plant that lies close to the ground, which is relevant for the next clause, where Yahweh speaks of the Israelites throwing righteousness down upon the ground.

וּצְדָקָה לָאָרֶץ הִנִּיחוּ׃—The noun צְדָקָה, "righteousness," recurs in 5:24 and 6:12. It is cognate to the adjective צַדִּיק, "righteous," in 2:6 and 5:12; see the fourth textual note on 2:6. Some studies of the root צדק have stressed its connection with deliverance and salvation.[13] When ascribed to a person, צְדָקָה, "righteousness," signifies that the person is justified through faith and stands in a right relationship with Yahweh because of his grace, as evident, for example, in Gen 15:6 and Jer 23:6. Odell writes:

> Modern readers tend to overlook [the] relational quality [of צְדָקָה] and assume that righteousness is a term for moral uprightness. … It would be mistaken to overlook the demand for moral uprightness, but it is equally problematic to ignore that these moral requirements are rooted in relationships with God and one another.[14]

The psalmist speaks of Yahweh's צֶדֶק, "righteousness," and אֱמוּנָה, "faithfulness," as twin attributes that serve as standards for his judgment (Ps 96:13). Jeremiah closely links צְדָקָה, "righteousness," with מִשְׁפָּט, "justice," and חֶסֶד, "loyal covenant faithfulness," as attributes of Yahweh that form a wise person's knowledge of him (Jer 9:23 [ET 9:24]). Isaiah declares that "the result of righteousness will be peace, and the work of righteousness will be tranquility and trust forever" (Is 32:17).

The most frequent word parallel to צְדָקָה is מִשְׁפָּט, and these two words are paired together almost fifty times in the OT. For מִשְׁפָּט, see the preceding textual note. Yahweh's

---

[11] Johnson, *TDOT* 9:92, including n. 31, citing P. Uys, *Nederduitse gereformeerde teologiese Tydskrif*, 9 (1968): 185.

[12] Wolff, *Joel and Amos*, 245–46.

[13] Cf. H. Ringgren and B. Johnson, "צָדַק," *TDOT* 12:239–64.

[14] Odell, *Ezekiel*, 166.

righteousness (צְדָקָה) is the underlying basis for justice. Put another way, justice denotes the honoring of relationships defined according to the norm of Yahweh's righteousness. Studies on justice and righteousness have generally gone in one of two directions, either focusing on the horizontal realm, where they apply to (or fail to characterize) human relationships, or on the vertical realm, where they apply to God's relationship with people. It is best to understand God's justification of his people through faith as the basis for justice as an expression of that relationship. Jeremiah declares that Yahweh's gift of imputed righteousness comes through the Davidic King who will be called יְהוָה ׀ צִדְקֵנוּ, "Yahweh is our righteousness" (Jer 23:6; cf. Mt 3:15; 5:6). God declares all believers in Christ righteous through faith apart from works (e.g., Rom 1:17; 3:21–28). God's gracious work in the believer is the reason for the justice and righteousness that is (and is to be) evident in the lives of his people.

The Hiphil of נוּחַ (here הִנִּיחוּ) has two different sets of meanings.[15] The first is "to bring rest," and it often occurs in Gospel contexts, as when Yahweh gives his people rest (e.g., Josh 1:13, 15). The second includes "to force down, throw or thrust down," which often appears in judgment contexts. Amos 5:7 refers to violently throwing down righteousness upon the ground. This may recall 2:7: "They trample the poorest of the poor into the dust of the earth." The Hiphil of נוּחַ occurs with לָאָרֶץ elsewhere only in Is 28:2, where Yahweh hurls hail and rainwater to earth and casts down to the ground with his hand.

5:8–9 The description of the Israelites' sins breaks off at the end of 5:7 and then resumes in 5:10. The two intervening verses (5:8–9) are a hymnic description of Yahweh that is the climax of a chiasm. See "Introduction to Amos 5:1–17" in the commentary on 5:1–3. The paean of Yahweh in 5:8–9 abounds in participial divine titles, as do the other two hymns in Amos, in 4:13 and 9:5–6. See the textual notes and commentary on 4:13.

5:8 עֹשֵׂה כִימָה וּכְסִיל—As in 4:13, the Qal participle of עָשָׂה is used as a divine title for God as the "Maker" of creation (although it was translated in 4:13 in the present tense, "who makes," since that verse refers to God's ongoing work; see the first and fourth textual notes on 4:13). As in 4:13, the participle is in construct (hence -שֵׂ- instead of -שֶׂ-) with the direct object(s) that Yahweh made. Here there are two direct objects, כִּימָה וּכְסִיל, and so this is one of the rare cases in the OT where a single word (עֹשֵׂה) is in construct with two words (כִּימָה וּכְסִיל). Similar is the construction in Gen 14:19, where a participle is in construct with two direct objects: Yahweh is קֹנֵה שָׁמַיִם וָאָרֶץ, "Creator of heaven and earth." See GKC, § 128 a, including note 3.

The proper noun כִּימָה refers to the Pleiades. Etymologically כִּימָה means "herd," "group," or "heap" (see *HALOT*), and in its three OT occurrences, it is always coupled with כְּסִיל, "Orion" (Amos 5:8; Job 9:9; 38:31). The Pleiades are a herd of stars, "an open galactic star cluster in the constellation Taurus; it has seven prominent stars

[15] Cf. H. D. Preuss, "נוּחַ," *TDOT* 9:277–86.

and is visible to the naked eye."[16] The proper noun כְּסִיל refers to Orion, also known as "the Hunter."

וְהֹפֵךְ לַבֹּ֫קֶר֙ צַלְמָ֔וֶת—Literally, "turning into the morning (the) shadow of death," the accusative צַלְמָ֔וֶת is the direct object of the participle וְהֹפֵךְ, and the prepositional phrase לַבֹּ֫קֶר֙ is the product into which the direct object is made or changed. Thus the meaning is "turning the shadow of death into the morning." The same idea can be expressed by a double accusative construction, as in the following clause. See the next textual note and Joüon, § 125 w, including note 2; Waltke-O'Connor, § 10.2.3c, including note 22.

Hebrew compound nouns are rare, but צַלְמָוֶת is the combination of צֵל, "shadow," and מָוֶת, "death." Besides its eighteen OT occurrences, the compound noun is also attested in Rabbinic Hebrew (see Jastrow). The LXX translates it with σκιὰ θανάτου, as in, for example, Is 9:1 (ET 9:2); Ps 23:4 (LXX Ps 22:4). The NT translates צַלְמָוֶת in Is 9:1 (ET 9:2) with σκιὰ θανάτου in Mt 4:16. σκιὰ θανάτου also appears in Lk 1:79, which may draw on Is 9:1 (ET 9:2); 42:7. Despite this longstanding history of understanding the word as a compound noun, many modern scholars[17] protest based on the paucity of other compound nouns and advocate repointing it here and throughout the OT to צַלְמוּת, which would be an abstract feminine singular noun meaning "deep darkness," although that noun is unattested in the OT or rabbinic literature.

וְי֖וֹם לַ֣יְלָה הֶחְשִׁ֑יךְ—Hebrew verbs that refer to making something into something else frequently take two accusatives, and the first is the direct object while the second (which can be called a predicative or object complement; see Joüon, § 125 w) is the product or thing into which the direct object is made (GKC, § 117 ii). Here the Hiphil perfect הֶחְשִׁ֑יךְ, "he makes [something] dark," is preceded by the two accusatives. The first is the direct object וְי֖וֹם, "day," and the second accusative, לַ֣יְלָה, "night," is the product into which he darkens the day. The idea is more commonly expressed by the construction with a single accusative for the direct object and a prepositional phrase for the product; see the preceding textual note.

It is unusual to find a perfect verb used for frequentative present-tense action, especially since the perfect הֶחְשִׁ֑יךְ is preceded and followed by participles (e.g., וְהֹפֵךְ ... הַקּוֹרֵ֣א) that are parallel to it in meaning and that similarly describe God's frequent and ongoing actions. See Joüon, § 112 l.

הַקּוֹרֵ֣א לְמֵי־הַיָּ֔ם וַיִּשְׁפְּכֵ֖ם עַל־פְּנֵ֣י הָאָ֑רֶץ—The identical wording recurs in 9:6. The idiom קָרָא לְ, "call to," often means "summon" (BDB, s.v. קָרָא, 5 a). The Qal participle הַקּוֹרֵ֣א is followed by an imperfect with *waw* consecutive, וַיִּשְׁפְּכֵ֖ם, whose temporal significance is to be understood in the same way as that of the participle (GKC, § 111 u; Joüon, § 118 r). Both refer to present-tense and continuing or repeated actions: Yahweh "summons" the waters of the seas "and pours them" on the face of the earth.

יְהוָ֥ה שְׁמֽוֹ׃—This affirmation recurs in 9:6. It is a shorter version of the affirmation "Yahweh, the God of armies, is his name" in 4:13 and 5:27.

---

16 Niehaus, "Amos," 418.

17 E.g., Andersen and Freedman, *Amos*, 491.

5:9 Desperate scholars have suggested emendations for six of the eight Hebrew words in this verse, but none are needed.

הַמַּבְלִיג שֹׁד עַל־עָז—The rare verb בָּלַג always occurs in the Hiphil but appears elsewhere only in Ps 39:14 (ET 39:13); Job 9:27; 10:20, where it means, "smile, look cheerful" (see BDB, 1). Here with Yahweh as its subject and שֹׁד, "destruction," as its object, it probably means "cause to flash" (*HALOT*, 1; similar is BDB, 2), which is supported by an Arabic cognate verb. The LXX rendered the participle as ὁ διαιρῶν, which may mean "who dispenses" (LEH, s.v. διαιρέω).

The preposition עַל could mean either "upon" or "against." The adjective עַז, "strong, mighty," could refer to an individual or to a people or nation, as in, for example, Num 13:28; Deut 28:50. Here it is used as a substantive. Since its parallel in the next clause is מִבְצָר, a city "fortification," עַז may refer to a "stronghold." While עַז is from the verb עָזַז, such a meaning is supported by the noun מָעוֹז, "refuge, protection," from the related verb עוּז.

וְשֹׁד עַל־מִבְצָר יָבוֹא׃—This is a telic clause: Yahweh performs the action described in the preceding clause with the purpose or result "so destruction comes upon a fortification." The noun שֹׁד, "destruction," was the object in the preceding clause but is the subject of the Qal verb יָבוֹא, "comes," in this clause. The ancient versions apparently understood the verb as a causative Hiphil form of בּוֹא, which would mean "he brings."[18] That change would harmonize this second clause with the first clause, which had a causative Hiphil participle (הַמַּבְלִיג) describing Yahweh as the cause of judgment. But no emendation is necessary.

5:10 The description of Israel's sins that was abruptly suspended at the end of 5:7 resumes in 5:10.

שָׂנְאוּ בַשַּׁעַר מוֹכִיחַ—The verb שָׂנֵא, "to hate," appears in Amos only in 5:10, 15, 21; 6:8. It often entails consequent actions based on hatred, as when it appears as a technical term in the laws of divorce (Deut 24:3).[19] Hatred originates in the heart (e.g., Lev 19:17) and "self" (נֶפֶשׁ, e.g., 2 Sam 5:8). The verb appears in Wisdom texts describing the foolish dislike of truthful speech: for example, "the one who hates reproof [וְשֹׂנֵא תוֹכַחַת] is senseless" (Prov 12:1; cf. Prov 15:10); "bloodthirsty people hate the one who is blameless [יִשְׂנְאוּ־תָם]" (Prov 29:10; cf. Prov 26:28). In contrast, Yahweh calls for his people to "hate evil" (Amos 5:15). Yahweh himself hates northern Israel's syncretistic worship (5:21) and its fortresses (6:8), just as he hates idolatrous Asherah pillars (Deut 16:22) and robbery and iniquity (Is 61:8).

Amos refers to a city "gate" (שַׁעַר) only in 5:10, 12, 15. This was normally "a complex of rooms along a corridor built into a city wall. It could house guards, but also afforded a place for the discussion and settlement of disputes."[20] The area in and around the gate was where people met, judicial cases were heard, decisions were made, and judgments were passed (e.g., Deut 21:18–21; 22:13–21; Is 29:21; Job 5:4; Ruth 4:1–12).

---

[18] For the discussion, see Paul, *Amos*, 170, including n. 110. For example, the LXX translates יָבוֹא with ἐπάγων, "one who brings."

[19] Cf. E. Lipinski, "שָׂנֵא," *TDOT* 14:164–74.

[20] Niehaus, "Amos," 419–20.

Prov 22:22 prohibits injustice there: "do not crush the needy in the gate." King writes: "The benches along the walls of the rooms, contiguous to the gate, were for the city council elders who passed judgments and settled disputes."[21]

Therefore the city "gate" was synonymous with the civil court. Amos uses the term in this sense (Amos 5:10, 12, 15): where a believer could stand in the assembly of Yahweh's covenant people, speak the truth of Yahweh, and rebuke those who were in the wrong. Unfortunately, the picture in Amos 5:10, 12, 15 is that unfaithful evildoers prevailed there.

מוֹכִ֑יחַ is the Hiphil participle of יָכַח, which in the Hiphil means "to set right, to show what is right."[22] It can have a forensic or pedagogic sense. The pedagogical sense appears most frequently in Wisdom literature to describe the activity of a father (e.g., Prov 3:12), a teacher (e.g., Ps 94:10), or a sage (e.g., Prov 15:12). In this connection it sometimes appears in parallel with the verb יָסַר, "to discipline, chasten, admonish" (e.g., Ps 6:2 [ET 6:1]). In the judicial process of hearing legal cases, the Hiphil of יָכַח can be used for those who adjudicate and render a right decision (e.g., Gen 31:37). The substantive participle is so used here, to identify the "arbiter" who calls for truth and seeks to ensure that justice is done, but he is hated for doing so. The next clause confirms that his role is primarily verbal.

וְדֹבֵ֥ר תָּמִ֖ים יְתָעֵֽבוּ׃—Literally, "one speaking (what is) honest they abhor," this clause further describes the corrupt situation in the city gates—the legal courts—where the leaders and elders sought to obstruct justice. Qal participles of דָּבַר occur almost forty times in the OT, but Piel forms of דָּבַר are far more common. The singular adjective תָּמִים can refer to what is "sound, honest, true, innocent, blameless." The phrase וְדֹבֵר תָּמִים can be rendered adverbially: "the one speaking honestly, blamelessly, with integrity." It is similar to the expression הוֹלֵךְ תָּמִים, "the one walking blamelessly, with integrity," (Ps 15:2; Prov 28:18), who "shall be saved" (Prov 28:18). The forensic righteousness and holiness of the believer results in words and living characterized by these same divine gifts and qualities. Yahweh commands his people to be "perfect, blameless" (תָּמִים) before him (Deut 18:13), even as Yahweh himself is righteous and his work is תָּמִים, "perfect" (Deut 32:4). He is "perfect" (תָּמִים) in knowledge (Job 37:16).[23]

The Piel of תָּעַב means "to abhor, treat as an abomination." Deut 7:26 illustrates the severity of the verb as it combines the infinitive absolute with the imperfect: Yahweh commands his people, "You shall utterly abhor [וְתַעֵ֥ב ׀ תְּתַעֲבֶ֖נּוּ]" what is an abomination to Yahweh and what has been consigned by him to destruction. The psalmist uses the same two verbs, "to hate" and "to abhor," that are parallel in Amos 5:10: "I hate and abhor falsehood, but your Torah I love" (Ps 119:163).

5:11 לָ֠כֵן יַ֣עַן בּוֹשַׁסְכֶ֞ם עַל־דָּ֗ל—For לָכֵן, "therefore," see the first textual note on 3:11. Usually it introduces the punishment pronounced by Yahweh, as in 5:13, 16. However, here the next word is יַעַן, "because," which usually introduces the sins that

[21] King, *Amos, Hosea, Micah*, 75.

[22] Cf. G. Mayer and H.-J. Fabry, "יכח," *TDOT* 6:64–71.

[23] Cf. B. Kedar-Kopfstein, "תָּמַם," *TDOT* 15:699–711.

have prompted Yahweh's punishment. The combination לָכֵן יַעַן, "therefore because …" occurs only here in the OT. In 5:11 Yahweh describes two offenses (trampling the poor and taking a grain tax from them) before he pronounces the first punishment (those who do those things will not live in their houses of hewn stones).

The verb בּוֹשַׁסְכֶם appears to be the Poel infinitive construct of בָּשַׁס, "to trample" (cf. GKC, § 61 e). While בָּשַׁס is a hapax legomenon, it probably is a by-form of בּוּס, "to trample." Since Polel forms of בּוּס occur in other OT passages, it is possible that בּוֹשַׁסְכֶם is the Polel of בּוּס but instead of the expected form, בּוֹסַסְכֶם, the first ס has been replaced with שׂ. Other Hebrew words in the OT attest the interchange of ס and שׂ. Israel's trampling of the poor was a transgression against Yahweh described previously in 2:7.

וּמַשְׂאַת־בַּר תִּקְחוּ מִמֶּנּוּ—The construct phrase מַשְׂאַת־בַּר probably denotes "a tax of grain." The noun מַשְׂאֵת refers to a tax in 2 Chr 24:6, 9, and here it could be an "exacted or enforced *gift*" (BDB, 4 c). In Gen 43:34, מַשְׂאֵת refers to an "allotment" or "portion" of food. The noun בַּר, "grain," recurs in Amos 8:5–6.

בָּתֵּי גָזִית בְּנִיתֶם וְלֹא־תֵשְׁבוּ בָם—The Israelite leaders were so wealthy they could afford to build (בְּנִיתֶם, Qal of בָּנָה) houses made of hewn stone. The construct phrase בָּתֵּי גָזִית is, literally, "houses of hewing," and the noun גָּזִית, "cutting, hewing," almost always refers to stones cut to size for construction. These were extravagant homes, as witnessed by the fact that King Solomon used hewn stone for his dwelling (1 Ki 7:9, 11–12). The temple was also built with hewn stones (1 Ki 5:31 [ET 5:17]; 6:36; 1 Chr 22:2). The cut stones would fit together smoothly without gaps, so these structures were solid, as opposed to drafty mud-brick houses (cf. Is 9:9 [ET 9:10]). King writes: "The finest examples of this building technique are at Samaria, where Omri and Ahab built the royal city in the ninth century B.C.E. … This type of construction contrasts sharply with the usual walls, consisting of stone foundations topped with bricks which were generally plastered."[24] Similarly, Yahweh had condemned northern Israel's officials in 3:15, who possessed both winter and summer houses as well as large houses (cf. 6:11) with ivory inlays.

Yahweh pronounces the first punishment in 5:11 as he tells the Israelites who had constructed opulent houses for themselves, "You shall not dwell in them" (וְלֹא־תֵשְׁבוּ בָם).

כַּרְמֵי־חֶמֶד נְטַעְתֶּם וְלֹא תִשְׁתּוּ אֶת־יֵינָם׃—The construct phrase כַּרְמֵי־חֶמֶד, literally, "vineyards of desire," is an attributive genitive, hence "choice vineyards." The noun חֶמֶד always appears in such a construct chain to describe desirable vineyards (Is 27:2; Amos 5:11), fields (Is 32:12), or young men (Ezek 23:6, 12, 23).

The verb נָטַע, "to plant," appears in Amos only in 5:11 and 9:14–15. When people are its subject, its object usually is a tract of cultivated plants such as vineyards (e.g., Amos 5:11; 9:14; Ps 107:37), olive trees (Deut 6:11), or gardens or parks with all types of trees (Eccl 2:5).[25] When Yahweh is the subject of נָטַע, quite often he "plants" a nation or a people in their land (e.g., Ps 80:9 [ET 80:8]; 1 Chr 17:9). This is its mean-

---

[24] King, *Amos, Hosea, Micah*, 65–67.

[25] Cf. J. Reindl, "נָטַע," *TDOT* 9:387–94.

ing in Amos 9:15 in the eschatological promise that Yahweh will plant his redeemed people in the new creation.

The corresponding curse for the unfaithful Israelites is "you will not drink their wine" (וְלֹא תִשְׁתּוּ אֶת־יֵינָם).

5:12 כִּי יָדַעְתִּי רַבִּים פִּשְׁעֵיכֶם וַעֲצֻמִים חַטֹּאתֵיכֶם—The two parallel adjectival phrases (רַבִּים פִּשְׁעֵיכֶם and וַעֲצֻמִים חַטֹּאתֵיכֶם) are substantival clauses that serve as direct objects of the verb יָדַעְתִּי, "I know" (Joüon, § 157 b). The parallelism reinforces the severity: "many [רַבִּים] are your transgressions and mighty [וַעֲצֻמִים] are your sins." For פֶּשַׁע, "transgression," see the second textual note on 1:3. חַטָּאת, "a sin," occurs in Amos only here.

צֹרְרֵי צַדִּיק לֹקְחֵי כֹפֶר וְאֶבְיוֹנִים בַּשַּׁעַר הִטּוּ׃—The syntax is difficult. In the preceding half of the verse, Yahweh addressed the Israelites in the second person plural (e.g., חַטֹּאתֵיכֶם, "*your* sins"). Therefore the best solution is to interpret this second half of the verse in the same way as 5:7, where the first clause continued a second-person address to the Israelites and then in the second clause Yahweh switched to a third-person description of them. Hence the translation renders the two participles (צֹרְרֵי ... לֹקְחֵי) as second person plural addresses, "[*you*] who are enemies of [צֹרְרֵי] ... [*you*] who are taking [לֹקְחֵי]," and then the final clause with the third person verb is translated literally, "*they* thrust away [הִטּוּ]."

Twice a Qal plural participle is in construct with its direct object. The first construct phrase is צֹרְרֵי צַדִּיק, literally, "enemies of a righteous man." The OT contains several homographic verbs צָרַר. While this could be צָרַר I, to "bind, tie up" (BDB), more likely it is צָרַר II, to "shew hostility toward ... vex, harass," which often occurs as a participle, "vexer, harasser" (BDB) or "adversary, enemy."[26] The participle is commonly rendered as "enemies" (e.g., Ps 23:5). The participle is in the covenant promise that if the Israelites listen to and obey Yahweh's words, their enemies will be the enemies of Yahweh himself (Ex 23:22). In Amos, the usage is reversed: the Israelite leaders have become the enemies of the righteous, and so they are enemies of Yahweh himself. Therefore Amos 5:12 is a covenant curse.

In Amos the only other occurrence of צַדִּיק, "righteous," is in 2:6, where too Yahweh condemns the transgression of the Israelites who are abusing righteous people in their midst. See the fourth textual note on 2:6. See also the second and third textual notes on 5:7, which has the nouns מִשְׁפָּט ("justice") and צְדָקָה ("righteousness"), which recurs in 5:24; 6:12.

The second participial construct phrase is לֹקְחֵי כֹפֶר, "[you] who are taking a bribe." לָקַח with כֹּפֶר as its object is used for taking a bribe also in 1 Sam 12:3. The verb לָקַח with שֹׁחַד, "bribe," as its object is used in, for example, Ex 23:8; 1 Sam 8:3; Ps 15:5. Isaiah has similar accusations that use the noun שֹׁחַד without the verb לָקַח (Is 1:23; 5:23). Amos employs כֹּפֶר, which usually refers to a material gift that establishes an amicable relationship between parties (e.g., Ex 21:30).[27] It can denote compensation

---

[26] Cf. H. Ringgren, "צָר II," *TDOT* 12:464–68.

[27] Cf. B. Lang, "כִּפֶּר," *TDOT* 7:288–303. See also Levine, *In the Presence of the Lord*, 61–62.

or reparation to the offended party or a ransom for the offender. Amos, however, uses the noun to speak of a perversion of this system. Instead of the guilty party giving reparations to the party he has injured, he gives a bribe to the corrupt judge, who then excuses the unlawful oppression. Justice and righteousness have been subverted. Therefore in this context, כֹּפֶר means something like "hush money."

The final clause of the verse switches to a third person perfect verb with an iterative or durative sense: וְאֶבְיוֹנִים בַּשַּׁעַר הִטּוּ, "and needy people they (repeatedly, continually) thrust away in the gate." Amos earlier used the Hiphil of נָטָה to mean "to twist, pervert" the way of the oppressed (see the second textual note on 2:7). Here it has the related meaning to "thrust away" people so as to deny them justice (see BDB, Hiphil, 3 g). For אֶבְיוֹן and other words in its semantic field, see the fifth textual note on 2:6. It frequently appears in the formulaic expression עָנִי וְאֶבְיוֹן, "(the) oppressed and needy" (e.g., Deut 24:14; Jer 22:16).[28] These terms are parallel in Amos 8:4. And in 4:1 and 8:6, אֶבְיוֹן is parallel to דַּל, "poor." Here in Amos 5:12, אֶבְיוֹן is parallel to צַדִּיק, "a righteous man," as it was in 2:6. Those who should champion the cause of the righteous and needy have become corrupt.

5:13 לָכֵן הַמַּשְׂכִּיל בָּעֵת הַהִיא יִדֹּם—For לָכֵן, "therefore," see the first textual note on 3:11. Here, as usual, it introduces a divine judgment. The rare Qal of שָׂכַל means to "be prudent" (BDB), and the common Hiphil often means to "act … prudently" (BDB, 5). The verb almost always refers to believers who act based on faith and knowledge of Yahweh and his grace. Thus Dan 12:3 has the eschatological promise:

> Those who are prudent/wise [וְהַמַּשְׂכִּלִים] will shine
> like the brightness of the sky,
> and those who bring many to righteousness
> like the stars forever and ever.

Most English translations take the participle הַמַּשְׂכִּיל here as referring to a faithful person who is spiritually "prudent" (KJV, RSV, ESV, NIV, NASB). The Hiphil verb can also mean to "prosper, have success" (BDB, 6). Some argue that the participle means "the prosperous person" and refers to the corrupt but prosperous magistrates being judged in 5:11–12.[29] If so, הַמַּשְׂכִּיל would be an antonym of צַדִּיק in 5:12. However, that argument overlooks the fact that the Hiphil verb is used for faithful believers, and so הַמַּשְׂכִּיל most likely is a synonym of צַדִּיק in 5:12.

The temporal expression בָּעֵת הַהִיא, "in that time," points toward "the Day of Yahweh" motif in 5:18–20.

Most lexicons, translations, and commentaries take the verb יִדֹּם as the Qal imperfect of דָּמַם, to "be silent," which can refer to maintaining silence "in grief," as in Lam 2:18; 3:28 (so BDB, s.v. דָּמַם I, 1; similar is *HALOT*, s.v. דָּמַם I, 2). This is also how the LXX understood the verb, since it translated with σιωπήσεται. Morphologically יִדֹּם could also be from the homographic verb דָּמַם II, to "wail" (BDB, *HALOT*), or from

---

[28] Cf. J. G. Botterweck, "אֶבְיוֹן," *TDOT* 1:27–41.

[29] E.g., Smith, *Hosea, Amos, Micah*, 315; cf. also Smith, "Amos 5:13: The Deadly Silence of the Prosperous."

a proposed homograph דָּמַם III, "to perish" (*HALOT*), although BDB and *HALOT* list Amos 5:13 under דָּמַם I. Paul understands יִדֹּם to be from דָּמַם II, to "moan, groan, sigh," which he sees in Is 23:2, where דֹּמּוּ is parallel to the preceding הֵילִילוּ, "wail," in Is 23:1.[30] If this is correct, then the sighing here would correspond with the weeping and wailing in Amos 5:16–17.[31]

Instead of choosing between silence or mourning, the verb could be a double entendre implying both. The discerning believer will mourn in stunned silence because of Yahweh's judgment of the extreme wickedness of that time. Nearly two centuries after the time of Amos, Yahweh predicts to Ezekiel that his beloved wife would die when the temple in Jerusalem (God's beloved city) would be destroyed by the Babylonians (Ezek 24:16–27). Yahweh uses the Qal imperative of דָּמַם I, "be silent," adverbially in the double command for his prophet to "groan silently" (הֵאָנֵק ׀ דֹּם, Ezek 24:17) and not to perform any of the customary mourning rites to anticipate the utter grief of the stricken Israelites when the city would fall.

כִּי עֵת רָעָה הִיא׃—This second reference in the verse to a future "time" (עֵת) also alludes to "the Day of Yahweh" theme in 5:18–20. עֵת is a feminine noun, hence the feminine form of the adjective רַע, "evil," which recurs in reference to a "day" in 6:3. רַע also appears in 5:14–15, where it refers to the aspirations and deeds of the Israelites that were "evil," as illustrated in Ezek 6:11, where Yahweh commands his prophet to cry, " 'Alas,' because of all the evil abominations [כָּל־תּוֹעֲבוֹת רָעוֹת] of the house of Israel."[32] It may also refer to disaster as a divine judgment; see the second textual note and the commentary on 3:6, which uses the noun רָעָה. Here עֵת רָעָה refers to a time of both human evil and also divine judgment, as also in Ps 37:19.

5:14 דִּרְשׁוּ־טוֹב וְאַל־רָע לְמַעַן תִּחְיוּ—The Qal imperative דִּרְשׁוּ, "seek," is repeated from 5:4, 6, where its object was Yahweh, and where it was followed by the imperative וִחְיוּ, "and live," expressing the consequence or result of seeking Yahweh. The same thought is expressed here but with an imperfect, לְמַעַן תִּחְיוּ, "so that you may live." The particle לְמַעַן can introduce either a purpose or a result clause, and both nuances may be intended here (cf. Joüon, §§ 168 a, note 2; 169 g). Yahweh's will is that the people live. See Ezek 18:23, 32; 33:11.

The prohibition וְאַל־רָע involves an ellipsis, with the reader to supply in thought a form of the preceding verb "to seek." Since וְאַל־רָע has the negative that normally is used with a jussive (אַל is not normally used with an imperative), the reader is most likely to supply a jussive form corresponding to the preceding imperative דִּרְשׁוּ, as if the text were וְאַל תִּדְרְשׁוּ רָע (GKC, § 152 g; cf. Amos 5:5).

---

30 Paul, *Amos*, 175–76.

31 Paul, *Amos*, 175, writes:

> The symmetrical chiastic structure of the composite pericope of vv 1–17 has been noted previously. The second and fourth sections begin on the similar note "to seek" the Lord and/or good (vv 4, 14). The fourth section then terminates with a public lamentation (vv 16–17). Thus it is also possible that the second section, followed by the third, which delineates the punishments, could also conclude on a similar mournful tone.

32 Cf. C. Dohmen and D. Rick, "רעע," *TDOT* 13:560–88.

In Amos, טוֹב, the adjective "good," appears in 5:14–15 and in a comparative sense in 6:2. The related noun טוֹבָה occurs in 9:4. In both 5:14 and 5:15, טוֹב is used as a substantive, "(what is) good," and it is contrasted with its antonym, the adjective רַע used as a substantive, "(what is) evil" (cf. רָעָה in the preceding textual note). The same contrast is expressed many times with these antonyms elsewhere in the OT (e.g., Gen 2:9, 17; 3:5, 22; Deut 1:39; Is 5:20; Micah 3:2).[33] טוֹב can refer to an attribute of Yahweh, as in the frequent call for praise of Yahweh "because he is good" (e.g., Pss 106:1; 107:1; 136:1; 1 Chr 16:34).

וִיהִי־כֵ֞ן יְהוָ֧ה אֱלֹהֵי־צְבָא֛וֹת אִתְּכֶ֖ם כַּאֲשֶׁ֥ר אֲמַרְתֶּֽם׃—This second half of the verse is a second purpose/result clause that follows the command "seek good." Yahweh uses the jussive יְהִי (from הָיָה) with conjunctive *waw* and כֵּ֞ן to express another purpose/result clause that is his will: literally, "may it be so: [that] Yahweh, the God of armies, [would be] with you, as you [now falsely] claim [that he is]."[34] Compare יְהִי expressing Yahweh's will in, for example, Gen 1:3, 6. Similar jussive expressions are used by people who pray that Yahweh would be with someone.[a]

(a) E.g., 1 Sam 20:13; 2 Sam 14:17; 1 Ki 1:37; 8:57; 1 Chr 22:11, 16; 2 Chr 19:11

For יְהוָה אֱלֹהֵי־צְבָאוֹת, see the second textual note and the commentary on 3:13. This divine title recurs in 5:15–16.

5:15 שִׂנְאוּ־רָע֙ וְאֶ֣הֱבוּ ט֔וֹב—These imperatival commands elaborate the themes from 5:4, 6, 14. "Hate evil" (שִׂנְאוּ־רָע) echoes the command in 5:14 not to seek "evil." "Love good" (וְאֶהֱבוּ טוֹב) echoes the commands to "seek" Yahweh (5:4, 6) and "(what is) good" in 5:14.

וְהַצִּ֥יגוּ בַשַּׁ֖עַר מִשְׁפָּ֑ט—The Hiphil of יָצַג means to "place, set up" an object (see BDB).[35] The Hebrew OT has several other common verbs meaning to "set" or "place," but יָצַג is relatively uncommon (sixteen occurrences in the OT), which suggests that יָצַג may be reserved for situations of special emphasis. BDB calls it "a vivid and forcible syn[onym]" of the frequently used verb שִׂים. In contrast to 5:7, where Yahweh said of the Israelites, "righteousness they throw to the ground," here Yahweh calls for Israel to "establish" justice in the gate. For מִשְׁפָּט, "justice," see the second textual note on 5:7.

אוּלַ֗י יֶחֱנַ֛ן יְהוָ֥ה אֱלֹהֵי־צְבָא֖וֹת שְׁאֵרִ֥ית יוֹסֵֽף׃—The adverb אוּלַי, "perhaps," expresses a hope (BDB, 1) rather than a certain promise. The Qal of חָנַן, "to be gracious," almost always takes an accusative of the person to whom Yahweh is gracious (see BDB, s.v. חָנַן, Qal, 2 a and b). Here שְׁאֵרִית יוֹסֵף is its object. The LXX, the Vulgate, and virtually all English translations understand the construction to mean that "perhaps Yahweh … will be gracious *to* the remnant of Joseph." Elsewhere in the OT, Qal imperfect forms of חָנַן without a suffix always have a single נ, for example, יָחֹן in Deut 28:50, so the form here, יֶחֱנַן, is unique (cf. GKC, § 67 cc; Joüon, § 82 k).

The verb חָנַן is used in the OT to express justification by grace alone, as in, for example, the Aaronic Benediction (Num 6:25). It implies "the bestowal of pardon and

---

33 Cf. I. Höver-Johag, "טוֹב," *TDOT* 5:296–317.

34 GKC, § 109 k, argues that the jussive here has no voluntative or volitional meaning and is equivalent to an imperfect. However, that seems to disregard the strong volitional meanings of the verbs in the first half of the verse.

35 Cf. B. Johnson, "יצג," *TDOT* 6:250–53.

favor by one in a superior position upon one who is dependent upon him."[36] The cognate adjective חַנּוּן, "gracious," only modifies Yahweh. Its meaning is illustrated in Ex 22:25–26 (ET 22:26–27), which describes an abuse similar to the one in Amos 2:8:

> If you take as a pledge the garment of your neighbor, return it to him before the sun sets, because it is his only covering; it is his garment for his body. In what else will he sleep? When he cries out to me, I will hear, for I am compassionate [כִּי־חַנּוּן אָנִי].

Yahweh hears the cry of the needy believer, especially one who is being abused by others, and he responds purely out of his gracious compassion. Compare Acts 9:4–5.

For "Joseph," see the second textual note on Amos 5:6. שְׁאֵרִית, "remnant," occurred in 1:8 in a context of judgment against the heathen, and it recurs in 9:12 in a Gospel context of salvation for believing Gentiles. Here the term implies judgment, since only a remnant of Israel is left, but also the hope of salvation when Yahweh is gracious toward those who are spared.

5:16 לָכֵן כֹּה־אָמַר יְהוָה אֱלֹהֵי צְבָאוֹת אֲדֹנָי—For לָכֵן, "therefore," see the first textual note on 3:11. For the messenger formula כֹּה־אָמַר יְהוָה, "thus says Yahweh," see the first textual note on 1:3. For the divine title יְהוָה אֱלֹהֵי (הַ)צְּבָאוֹת, see the second textual note and the commentary on 3:13. Only here in the OT is that divine title expanded by the addition of אֲדֹנָי.

בְּכָל־רְחֹבוֹת מִסְפֵּד וּבְכָל־חוּצוֹת יֹאמְרוּ הוֹ־הוֹ—"Open places, plazas" (plural of רְחוֹב) were spacious areas in a city, often near the gate, where groups of people could gather, talk, listen—or mourn, as also in Is 15:3 and Jer 48:38. The "streets" (plural of חוּץ; see BDB, 2 a) were the paths between city homes and are locations of mourning also in Is 15:3 and 24:11.

The noun מִסְפֵּד, "lamentation," is used in this verse twice and again in 5:17. It may have a narrower meaning than אֵבֶל, "mourning,"[37] which is parallel to it in the second half of 5:16. At Jacob's death (Gen 50:10), מִסְפֵּד refers to an initial lamentation or funeral ritual (perhaps accomplished on the first day), while אֵבֶל refers to a longer period of mourning that lasted seven days.

The cries of the people are expressed with the twofold הוֹ־הוֹ, a double "woe." הוֹ appears only here in the OT, but it is similar to הוֹי, which occurs in 5:18 and 6:1. See the first textual note on 5:18. Other similar cries include אוֹי (e.g., Is 6:5; Jer 4:31), אוֹיָה (Ps 120:5), הֶאָח (e.g., Ezek 25:3; Ps 40:16 [ET 40:15]), and הָהּ (Ezek 30:2).[38]

וְקָרְאוּ אִכָּר אֶל־אֵבֶל—The noun אִכָּר is a collective that means "farmhands," as opposed to farm owners.[39] Yahweh may have selected them as mourners here "because

---

[36] Paul, *Amos*, 177–78.

[37] Cf. J. Scharbert, "סָפַד," *TDOT* 10:299–303.

[38] For a list of other interjections in the OT, see GKC, § 105 a–b. See also Janzen, *Mourning Cry and Woe Oracle*, 19–27.

[39] The word appears six other times in the OT: Is 61:5; Jer 14:4; 31:24; 51:23; Joel 1:11; 2 Chr 26:10.

they were the ones accustomed to raise their voices in joy"[40] at a bountiful harvest (cf. 9:13–15). The call of farm workers to mourning echoes the opening theme of the withering of the fields in 1:2. See also the mourning in the vineyards in the next verse, 5:17.

וּמִסְפֵּד אֶל־יוֹדְעֵי נֶהִי׃—Some speculate that the word order of וּמִסְפֵּד אֶל־ should be reversed to וְאֶל־מִסְפֵּד, which would be parallel to אֶל־אֵבֶל in the preceding clause. However, וּמִסְפֵּד can be understood as an accusative of location and the destination to which the wailers are summoned. The preposition with אֶל־יוֹדְעֵי נֶהִי can be understood to follow the verb וְקָרְאוּ in the previous clause: "they will call *to*, summon." The Qal active participle of יָדַע, "to know," can refer to people who possess certain skills. For example, in Gen 25:27, Esau is יֹדֵעַ צַיִד, "skilled in hunting." 1 Sam 16:16 refers to a musician יֹדֵעַ מְנַגֵּן בַּכִּנּוֹר, "skilled in playing the lyre," and 1 Ki 9:27 refers to יֹדְעֵי הַיָּם, "those skilled in [sailing] the sea." The participial construct phrase יוֹדְעֵי נֶהִי, "the ones skilled in wailing," probably denotes a type of guild that was professionally trained.[41] Jeremiah describes a group of professional mourning women using the adjective הַחֲכָמוֹת, "wise, skilled" (Jer 9:16 [ET 9:17]).[42]

The noun נְהִי, "wailing," may specifically mean a "mourning song" (BDB gives both possible meanings). It appears six other times in the OT: Jer 9:9, 17–19 (ET 9:10, 18–20); 31:15; Micah 2:4.

5:17 וּבְכָל־כְּרָמִים מִסְפֵּד—Israel's "vineyards" (כְּרָמִים) would be places of abundance under Yahweh's grace, as in the eschatological messianic promise of 9:14. However, in every other instance in Amos, the "vineyards" of unfaithful Israel suffer pronouncements of divine judgment (4:9; 5:11, 17).

כִּי־אֶעֱבֹר בְּקִרְבְּךָ אָמַר יְהוָה׃—The advent of Yahweh, "I will pass through your midst," is a warning of judgment for unbelievers but also a promise of redemption and life (5:4, 6, 14) for those who repent and believe. The same dual implication of judgment and salvation is in the announcement "prepare to meet your God" in 4:12.

Commentary

This section follows the funeral lament over Israel in 5:1–3, and the language of mourning and lamentation concludes this section (5:16–17). Apostate Israel was spiritually dead, and many would perish some forty years after the ministry of Amos, when the Northern Kingdom would fall to Assyria in 722 BC. Yet this section is a new oracle marked by Yahweh's repeated invitation for his audience to seek him and live (5:4, 6, 14). Yahweh is coming soon ("I will pass through your midst," 5:17; cf. 4:12), but there is still time to repent and be saved at his advent, for he will be gracious to the faithful remnant (5:15). This

---

40 Paul, *Amos*, 179, n. 205. In Joel 1:11 farm laborers are summoned to be ashamed (cf. Jer 14:4).

41 Wolff, *Joel and Amos*, 249.

42 Wolff opines: "They must … have been knowledgeable concerning the comprehensive ceremonial requirements of fasting: rending of clothes, wearing of 'sackcloth,' shearing the hair, sprinkling dust on the head, and much else besides (cf. 8:10)" (*Joel and Amos*, 249).

is essentially the same message proclaimed by the church as she awaits the second advent of Jesus Christ, who is both Judge and Savior.

Amos earnestly hopes that the dead nation (5:1–3) will come to life. Yahweh is the Creator, Destroyer, and Re-creator (5:8–9). He may graciously grant resurrection life, as he promises to do through raising the tabernacle of David in 9:11–15. This life, however, will not be dispensed in Gilgal, Beersheba, or Bethel (5:5). These were idolatrous sanctuaries set up as alternatives to the temple in Jerusalem, contrary to Yahweh's command (cf. 1 Ki 12:24–33; see also the textual notes and commentary on Amos 4:4). Two of the cities (Gilgal and Bethel) were in schismatic northern Israel, and Beersheba may also have been controlled by northern Israel during Amos' time. Failing to seek Yahweh will result in the destruction of Bethel (and by extension, Beersheba and Gilgal), as well as those who worship there (5:16–17).

Exhortation to Seek Yahweh and Live (5:4–7)

5:4 Amos 5:4–7 exhibits the genre of a prophetic admonition.[43] Following the annihilation of ninety percent of the cities' troops in 5:3, these next verses offer a glimmer of hope. Yahweh has decimated the nation, but he has left survivors who may yet live by his grace.

Yahweh's plea uses the pair of verbs "seek" (דָּרַשׁ) and "live" (חָיָה) three times in this section (5:4, 6, 14). He does not desire the death of anyone, but desires all to repent, be saved, and live. This biblical theme of Yahweh's will regarding unbelief resulting in death and the gift of eternal life through faith is articulated in, for example, Deut 30:15–16, 19–20; Ezek 18:23, 32; 33:11; Rom 6:23; 1 Tim 2:3–4. Seeking Yahweh leads to life instead of the death announced in Amos 5:1–2 and portrayed in 5:3. If people repent, Yahweh may change his action from his announced judgment to grace (5:15c; cf. 7:3, 6), so that the death sentence will be commuted.[44]

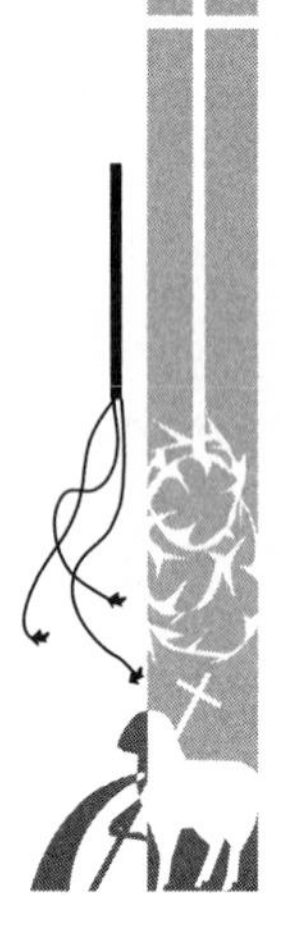

Ultimately, this change is rooted in the atonement of Christ, who suffered the entirety of divine judgment against humanity's sin, so that all believers may pass from death to life (cf. Jn 5:24; Rom 6:13). This is anticipated in Amos, since to seek (דָּרַשׁ) Yahweh means to reject the idolatrous northern worship establishment (5:4–6; 9:1–4), as well as to anticipate Yahweh's fuller manifestation from Zion and Jerusalem (the site of the temple [1:2]) by means of the resurrection of the Davidic tabernacle and rebuilding of the city of God (9:11–12). God will raise up a new temple in Christ (cf. Jn 2:19–22; 4:20–26; 1 Cor 3:16–17; 6:19) that will be the locus of divine worship not only for the faithful "remnant of Joseph" (Amos 5:15) but indeed for Gentile believers as well, "all the nations

---

[43] As noted by Sweeney, *Isaiah 1–39*, 513. Sweeney believes that Is 1:16–17 and Jer 25:3–7 are also in this genre.

[44] See the excursus "When Yahweh Changes A Prior Verdict," in Lessing, *Jonah*, 324–41. Jer 18:1–12 offers the most sustained OT theological reflection on this.

over whom my name is called" (9:12). In this way—and in this way only—will justice and righteousness continually flow (5:24; cf. 2 Sam 8:15).

Amos 5:4 is a part of a literary inclusio with 5:6 and forms a chiastic pattern. In 5:4 Yahweh implores the Israelites to "seek me and live," while in 5:5 they are commanded *not* to seek Yahweh in Bethel, Gilgal, or Beersheba.[45] Then in 5:6 the people are again exhorted to "seek Yahweh and live." In this way, Amos mandates that the people must not seek Yahweh at the false worship centers in Israel and Judah because these were stimulants to sin (cf. 4:4) as well as places of death (cf. 9:1–4). Israel must seek *Yahweh* to live, and he dwells in Zion (1:2)—ultimately in Christ (Is 7:14; Mt 1:23). Seeking God in any other place, or seeking any other god, will only bring death.

The nation's leaders, its military (Amos 5:3), and its worship places may all be dead—but Israel's God is not! In Deut 30:20, Moses makes the promise that "he [Yahweh] is your life." Because Yahweh is alive, Israel may live as well. The offer is stated this way in Deut 30:6: "Yahweh your God will circumcise your heart and the heart of your offspring so that you can love Yahweh your God with all your heart and with all your being, *in order that you may have life* [לְמַ֫עַן חַיֶּֽיךָ]." Life is what Yahweh wants for all of his creation. The free gift of everlasting life is given to all believers in Jesus Christ (Jn 5:24; 10:10; 17:3). Believers possess this life already now through faith, and will enter into all its fullness on the Last Day (Is 25:6–9; Dan 12:2–3; Revelation 21–22).

5:5 Bethel, the first sanctuary mentioned in this verse and then again in 5:6, was northern Israel's chief worship center. The city is also mentioned in 3:14 and 4:4, as well as twice in Amos' confrontation with Amaziah (7:10, 13). The primary target of the verse—if not the entire book—is *Bethel*.[46]

Bethel was historically connected with Jacob. Genesis records two encounters he had with Yahweh in this place. The first time was when he was fleeing from Esau (Gen 28:10–22). At night he saw a vision and concluded, "Yahweh is in this place" (Gen 28:16). He arrived with a mischievous past but left with a future hope. Jacob's second visit to Bethel was on his return from Paddan-aram (Gen 35:1–15). He left with Yahweh's confirmation of his new name, Israel (Gen 35:10; cf. Gen 32:28–29 [ET 32:27–28]). Jacob's two experiences with Yahweh at Bethel were renewing and recreating. This makes Amos' words in 5:4–5 all the more shocking. The false god that Jeroboam ben Nebat had erected there—a golden calf—had displaced Yahweh and caused Israel to sin (2 Ki 10:29). Consequently the only thing dispensed at Bethel was *death*.[47]

---

[45] This is part of Yahweh's ongoing diatribe against Israel's perversions of divine worship. See also 2:7–8; 3:14; 4:4–5; 5:14, 21–27; 7:9–17; 8:5, 10, 14; and 9:1–4.

[46] Andersen and Freedman, *Amos*, 479, citing the chiastic arrangement that lists Bethel first and last. Hosea also takes direct aim at this worship center. Several times he calls it בֵּית אָוֶן, "the house of iniquity/nothing" (Hos 5:8; 10:5).

[47] For the history of Bethel, see further the commentary on 3:14.

On the heels of the admonition not to seek Yahweh in Bethel comes the command not to go to Gilgal either. The location is mentioned in passing in Deut 11:30, but enters the OT narrative in a prominent way in Josh 4:19, when Israel camps there prior to her invasion of Jericho. At Gilgal, Israel was reconstituted as Yahweh's people by means of circumcision and the Passover celebration (Josh 5:2–12). Gilgal was where the gift of manna ceased and Israel first tasted "the produce of Canaan" (Josh 5:12). The site later became the base of Joshua's military operations (e.g., Josh 9:6; 10:6; 14:6). Later still, Gilgal was where Saul's monarchy was confirmed (1 Sam 11:14–15). The irony in Amos 5:5 is that Gilgal—the ancient location of inheritance, possession, and monarchy—would go into exile. Like Bethel and Beersheba, Gilgal was connected with ancient promises, but in the current state of affairs, it offered nothing but doom.

The threat of exile is a recurring theme in Amos (4:2–3; 5:5, 27; 6:7; 7:11, 17; 9:4). Throughout Israel's history, the nation was aware that Yahweh could employ foreign nations to exercise his judgment upon her (e.g., Lev 26:33; Deut 28:64–68; Judg 2:14–15). Amos, however, never mentions Assyria, the nation that would be Yahweh's agent to carry out the judgment prophesied in Amos.[48] This comes as no surprise, for during Amos' prophetic ministry (ca. 760 BC), Assyria was dormant, beset by internal strife. But a few decades later through Isaiah, Yahweh would name "Assyria" as "the rod of my anger" (Is 10:5).

The Judean town of Beersheba is sandwiched between the first and second appearances of Gilgal in Amos 5:5. Yahweh condemns this southern city again in 8:14. It had associations with Abraham, Isaac, and Jacob (e.g., Gen 21:14, 31–33; 22:19; 26:23–25; 46:1). For example, it was at Beersheba that Abimelech and Phicol said to Abraham, "God is with you in all that you do" (Gen 21:22). Later Yahweh made this promise to Isaac while he was in Beersheba: "Fear not, for I am with you" (Gen 26:23–24). As an old man Jacob arrived in Beersheba on his trip to Egypt, and there God said, "Do not be afraid to go down to Egypt, for I will make you into a great nation there" (Gen 46:3). The town was a place where the three patriarchs were comforted with the assurance of Yahweh's presence and blessing in their lives.

What horror, therefore, it must have been to hear Amos warn, "Do not travel to Beersheba" (5:5). The ancient site could no longer furnish an encounter with the living God. As its just judgment the idolatrous high place at Beersheba was destroyed by Josiah about 623 BC, about a century and a half after the ministry of Amos (2 Ki 23:8).[49]

The reference to Beersheba indicates that, while the primary target in Amos remained Bethel, Yahweh was also concerned about worship and social abuses in the south; see also 1:1–2; 2:4–5; 6:1.[50] The construction of the temple in

---

48 See the excursus "The Assyrian Empire."

49 Cf. Yadin, "Beer-Sheba: The High Place Destroyed by King Josiah."

50 Sweeney believes Beersheba was under northern authority in the eighth century because of inscriptions and drawings found at Kuntillet Ajrud, or Horvat Teiman, which include the

Jerusalem by Solomon in the tenth century BC (1 Kings 6–8) had made it the central site for Israel's worship, as mandated by the Torah (e.g., Deuteronomy 12; see also 1 Ki 9:3; 2 Chr 13:9–11). Although Amos is silent about worship practice in Jerusalem, later in the eighth century, Isaiah has much to say about the kind of worship going on there. Isaiah's sermon in 1:10–20 sounds much like Amos' oracle in 5:21–27.

The strong rejection of northern Israel's worship in 5:5 is because of the supremacy Yahweh places on justice and righteousness (cf. 5:7, 24; 6:12). It is not that the commandments and proper liturgical, sacrificial worship are at odds with one another. Rather, the Israelites neglect the former while practicing only a perverted form of the latter.[51] In Mt 23:23, Jesus admonishes the religious leaders of his day:

> Woe to you, scribes and Pharisees—hypocrites! For you tithe the mint, dill, and cumin, but you have forsaken the weightier matters of the Torah: justice, mercy, and faith. It is necessary to practice these without neglecting those.

5:6 The chiasm in 5:4–6 ends with the same two imperatives with which it began: "*seek* Yahweh and *live*" (דִּרְשׁוּ ... וִחְיוּ). Israel is not summoned to the heterodox worship centers, which only increase rebellion (4:5). Rather, Yahweh's people are to seek him alone, and "always" (Ps 105:4). The God of Israel has now come in the person of his Son "to seek and to save the lost" (Lk 19:10). The response of faith is to seek the risen and living Savior (Mt 28:5–7; Lk 11:9; Col 3:1).

If the Israelites will not pursue Yahweh, they will be consumed in fire.[52] If they do not repent, "everything will go up in flames, down in ashes, and away in exile."[53] The fire will be unleashed upon "the house of Joseph" (5:6), that is, the Northern Kingdom. No one and nothing will be able to quench this fire (cf. Is 1:31; Jer 4:4; 21:12). Jesus, citing Isaiah, warns that hell is a place "where their worm does not die and the fire is not quenched" (Mk 9:47–48, quoting Is 66:24).

Cyprian interprets Amos 5:6 in the following way:

> Therefore, while there is time, look to the true and eternal salvation, and, since the end of the world is now at hand, out of fear of God turn your minds to God. Let not your powerless and vain dominion in the world over the just and the meek delight you. Remember that in the fields the tares and the darnel have dominion over the cultivated and fruitful corn, and you should not say that evils happen because your gods are not worshiped by us. But you should realize that this is God's anger, this is God's censure, so that he who

---

statement "I bless you by YHWH of Samaria and his asherah" (*The Twelve Prophets*, 234, including n. 64, citing King, *Amos, Hosea, Micah*, 104–6).

[51] Andersen and Freedman write: "The point is that if there is injustice in the gate [5:10, 15] and oppression and mistreatment of the poor and helpless [2:6–8], then the worship of the perpetrators … is false and worthless" (*Amos*, 481–82).

[52] Judgment by fire is also pronounced in 1:4, 7, 10, 12, 14; 2:2, 5; 7:4.

[53] Andersen and Freedman, *Amos*, 47.

is not recognized for his blessings may at least be recognized for his judgments. "Seek God, and your soul shall live." Acknowledge God even though it is late. For Christ advises and teaches this, saying, "Now this is everlasting life, that they may know you the only true God and him whom you have sent, Jesus Christ" [Jn 17:3]. Believe him who by no means deceives. Believe him who has foretold that all these things would come to pass. Believe him who will give the reward of eternal life to those who believe. Believe him who by the fires of Gehenna will inflict eternal punishments on the disbelieving.[54]

5:7 Israel has turned "justice" (מִשְׁפָּט) into wormwood and thrown down "righteousness" (וּצְדָקָה) in spite of the fact that Yahweh calls his people to "establish justice in the gate" (וְהַצִּיגוּ בַשַּׁעַר מִשְׁפָּט, 5:15) so that justice and righteousness will flow "like an ever-flowing wadi" (כְּנַחַל אֵיתָן, 5:24).

Schmid maintains that justice is connected to righteousness, which, in turn is centered upon the idea of order.[55] The right ordering of the world brings about justice and well-being for the entire created order. Schmid believes that righteousness (צְדָקָה) refers to a harmonious world order built by Yahweh into the very infrastructure of creation. Wherever righteousness is practiced by human beings in the sociopolitical sphere, that action is in tune with creation, and it fosters the proper integration of social and cosmic orders. When people do not practice righteousness, the creation is impacted in negative ways. Justice, righteousness, politics, faith, and creation are therefore interrelated as "aspects of one comprehensive order of creation."[56]

"Justice" (מִשְׁפָּט) in the full biblical sense is not possible for sinful human beings without justification. Justice begins with Yahweh crediting righteousness to all who believe (Gen 15:6; Rom 3:21–31). The passive gift of righteousness that comes through faith alone in Jesus Christ empowers active righteousness, "faith working through love" (Gal 5:6), that builds up the church at the same time that it proclaims the justifying Gospel of Jesus Christ to the world and seeks a more just and humane society. In Amos 5:24, the prophet pictures justice and righteousness as a surging, churning, and cleansing stream. These sanctifying waters flow from God's grace in Christ, bestowed in Holy Baptism, the Word, and the Sacrament of the Altar. They lead all in Christ to fulfill the two great commandments (Mk 12:30–31). Justice and righteousness are "self-giving and neighbor-regarding."[57]

"Justice" (מִשְׁפָּט) and "righteousness" (צְדָקָה) do not occur together in the legislation of the Torah. However, Yahweh describes justified Abraham as someone who will instruct his children and his household after him to do "righteousness and justice" (צְדָקָה וּמִשְׁפָּט, Gen 18:19). The words appear together in Wisdom texts, for example, Prov 16:8 and 21:3. Wisdom, hypostasized in the

[54] Cyprian, *To Demetrian*, 23, quoted in Ferreiro, *The Twelve Prophets*, ACCS 14:98–99.

[55] Schmid, "Creation, Righteousness, and Salvation."

[56] Schmid, "Creation, Righteousness, and Salvation," 105.

[57] Benne, *Reasonable Ethics*, 62.

preincarnate Christ (Prov 8:22–31), declares, "I walk in the path of righteousness [צְדָקָה], in the ways of justice [מִשְׁפָּט]" (Prov 8:20). Another set of texts, closely related to the Wisdom proverbs of Solomon (Prov 1:1; 10:1; 25:1) are those that describe King David and his son King Solomon. 2 Sam 8:15 states:

וַיְהִי דָוִד עֹשֶׂה מִשְׁפָּט וּצְדָקָה לְכָל־עַמּוֹ׃

David was enacting justice and righteousness for all his people.

The Queen of Sheba looked at Solomon in all his glory and said:

Praise be to Yahweh your God, who has delighted in you and placed you on the throne of Israel. Because of Yahweh's love for Israel, he has made you king to maintain justice and righteousness. (לַעֲשׂוֹת מִשְׁפָּט וּצְדָקָה, 1 Ki 10:9 ‖ 2 Chr 9:8; cf. Ps 72:1)

Both the royal and Wisdom themes of justice and righteousness are fulfilled in Christ, the Son of David and King of Israel, and the wisdom of God (1 Cor 1:18–25). However, what characterized the lives of faithful believers like Abraham and the reigns of David and Solomon was the very antithesis of what characterized northern Israel in the middle of the eighth century BC. The nation was perverting justice into wormwood, a plant that leaves a bitter taste of poison in the mouth. Bitterness marked the give-and-take of personal interaction between Israel's leaders and Yahweh's impoverished people.[58] Later in the eighth century, Isaiah too accused Israel of perverting justice and righteousness (e.g., Is 1:21; 5:7; 28:17). Jeremiah indicated that in the seventh century, King Josiah had cultivated justice and righteousness for the poor and the oppressed saints in Judah (Jer 22:15–16), but King Zedekiah, whose name means "Yahweh is righteous," was one of the leaders who scattered and destroyed Yahweh's flock (Jer 23:1).

(b) Is 9:5–6 (ET 9:6–7);16:5; 55:3–5; Jer 23:5; 30:9; 33:15; Ezek 34:23–24; 37:24–25; Hos 3:5; Zech 12:7–12; 13:1

Yet Yahweh promised "a righteous Branch" (צֶמַח צַדִּיק, Jer 23:5–6). The word "branch" (צֶמַח) is used as a messianic title also in Zech 3:8 and 6:12. And the image appears in Is 11:1, though expressed with different Hebrew words: חֹטֶר, "twig," and נֵצֶר, "shoot/sprout." (נֵצֶר, *netser*, might be the basis of Matthew's citation of OT prophecy in Mt 2:23 that the Messiah would be a Nazarene.) Isaiah 11 begins with the image of the shoot from the stump of Jesse, alluding to the stump image earlier in Is 6:13. The use of "Jesse" rather than "David" in Is 11:1 and again in Is 11:10 indicates that this new king is not only of the lineage of David, but indeed a new David. The affirmation that the Messiah comes from the house of David is also affirmed elsewhere.[b] Matthew's genealogy (Mt 1:6, 17), Luke's birth narrative (Lk 2:4), and Paul's sermon in Acts 13:22–23 confirm that this promise of a Messiah is fulfilled in Jesus. According to Is 52:13–53:12, the way in which the Shoot will bring forth his righteous rule, peace, and restoration (Is 9:1–6 [ET 9:2–7]; 11:1–16)

[58] Cf. Motyer, *The Message of Amos*, 132. He goes on to write, citing Jer 7:11 as a commentary on this passage in Amos, that the people were "praying on their knees in the temple and preying on their neighbours everywhere else!"

is through his humble suffering, vicarious death for the sin of the people, and victorious resurrection.

The Davidic King "will enact justice and righteousness in the land" (וְעָשָׂה מִשְׁפָּט וּצְדָקָה בָּאָרֶץ, Jer 23:5). He will be called "Yahweh is our righteousness" (יְהוָה ׀ צִדְקֵנוּ, Jer 23:6). Jesus is the ultimate righteous King of David's line. Through his faithful ministry, atoning death, and glorious resurrection (cf. Amos 9:11), God has provided justification and righteousness for all in him (e.g., Rom 5:12–21; 2 Cor 5:21). He invites all the poor and needy to receive abundance in the kingdom of God (e.g., Lk 1:51–53; 4:17–21).

The primary indictment in the book of Amos is Israel's corruption of Yahweh's justice and righteousness (מִשְׁפָּט וּצְדָקָה, 5:7, 24; see also 6:12). These divine attributes, which Yahweh bestows on his faithful people through his covenant of grace, were to differentiate Israel from the pagan nations. In Deut 4:8, Yahweh says:

וּמִי גּוֹי גָּדוֹל אֲשֶׁר־לוֹ חֻקִּים וּמִשְׁפָּטִים צַדִּיקִם כְּכֹל הַתּוֹרָה הַזֹּאת

And what other nation is so great as to have such righteous decrees and laws as all this Torah?

The charter of Israel's existence called the people to be holy like their God (e.g., Lev 11:44–45; 20:26). Yahweh's people were to display fair and just ethical actions in the religious, commercial, political, and interpersonal realms. Yahweh, unlike other gods, is the King who "loves justice" (מִשְׁפָּט אָהֵב, Ps 99:4), who accomplishes "justice and righteousness" in Jacob (מִשְׁפָּט וּצְדָקָה, Ps 99:4). He is intolerant of injustice, critical of the greedy and powerful, and rescues the weak who trust only in his power. He is mightily at work in history to bring about his unique form of justice for all (Rom 5:6–11), and he blesses and satisfies those "who hunger and thirst for righteousness" (Mt 5:6).

(c) Amos 2:7–8; 3:14; 4:4–5; 5:5–6, 14, 21–27; 7:9–17; 8:5, 10, 14; 9:1

But in following other gods,[c] the Israelites adopted systems of belief and behavior that were opposed to Yahweh's command to "love your neighbor as yourself" (Lev 19:18). They worshiped fertility gods and goddesses whose veneration involved violence, oppression, injustice, and sexual license (2:6–8). Their actions reflected the myths about these gods rather than the historically true narrative of Yahweh, who redeemed them from Egypt and granted them the inheritance of the promised land. 2 Ki 17:15 and Jer 2:5 indicate that the object of worship becomes the pattern for life:

וַיֵּלְכוּ אַחֲרֵי הַהֶבֶל וַיֶּהְבָּלוּ

And they walked after what was worthless, and so they became worthless.

How will justice and righteousness enter the world in a definitive manner? In Amos 9:11–15 the prophet is shown the coming days when Yahweh will resurrect "the falling tabernacle of David" (סֻכַּת דָּוִיד הַנֹּפֶלֶת). The Son of David would show divine mercy to Jew and Gentile alike (e.g., Mt 15:22–28; 20:29–34), fulfilling Amos 9:11–12. The restoration of divine worship in righteousness through the risen Son will cause justice and righteousness to abound, re-create God's people for eternity, and usher in the new creation. This central concern of Amos for justice and righteousness (5:7, 24; 6:12) will only be fulfilled in Jesus the Christ.

What was true about worship in Amos' day remains true today. Those who worship the one true and triune God, who became incarnate in his Son, are called to be imitators of Christ (e.g., 1 Cor 11:1; Phil 2:5–11; see the excursus "The Church's Response to Ethical Issues"). In contrast, the capricious god worshiped by Muslims breeds terrorism and violence; Hinduism perpetrates the oppressive caste system that dehumanizes the lowly; and other religions as well not only fail to deliver but actually deprive their adherents of Yahweh's justice and righteousness.

The Second Hymn in Amos (5:8–9)

5:8 Amos 5:8–9 contain the second of three hymns in the book; the other two are in 4:13 and 9:5–6. These are commonly called creation hymns, yet they also depict Yahweh's judgment and salvation. They proclaim that Yahweh is not only the God of Israel (3:2) but indeed "the Creator of the heavens and the earth" (Gen 14:19, 22).[59] The inclusion of this second hymn (5:8–9) in the oracles of judgment that extends throughout 5:1–17 functions to drive home the threat of punishment. Israel will not escape Yahweh's judgment. As the Creator of all that exists, Yahweh is able to marshal all the forces of the cosmos to pursue and destroy the unbelieving people.

That Yahweh "summons the waters of the seas" and "pours them out upon the face of the earth" (5:8) can describe the continuing process by which Yahweh creates rainfall. Yet this description, repeated verbatim in 9:6, may refer especially to the universal flood in the days of Noah that wiped out all unbelieving humanity.[60] This would strengthen the point that Israel will not be able to avoid punishment. Wenham notes:

> The flood is presented as a great act of decreation, destroying human and animal life, covering the plants and mountains, so that the earth returns to the watery chaos that existed before the second day of creation. Noah, the survivor of this chaos, becomes as it were another Adam, the forefather of the human race after the flood.[61]

When the flood inundated the entire earth, every person perished save for the "eight souls" in the ark, prefiguring salvation through Christian Baptism by

---

[59] Andersen and Freedman, *Amos*, 51–52, write:

> It is essential to the book's premises and conclusions that the God of Israel, the one so deeply involved in the history and affairs of his people, also be identified as the supreme ruler of the universe and the director of the destiny of all the nations. … So these hymns simply spell out the necessary truth behind and underlying everything else in the book.

[60] So Waltke-O'Connor, § 33.3.5b, example 4, n. 21.

[61] Wenham, *Story as Torah*, 34. If Amos 5:8 recalls the forty days and forty nights of heavy downpour that created the Noahic flood, then, although Yahweh promised never again to destroy *the whole earth* with a flood (Gen 9:11), the prospect remains that he may decide to inundate *specific areas*.

the power of Christ's resurrection (1 Pet 3:18–22). The original creation was completed within seven days, so "eight" marks the start of a new creation, even as Christ was raised on the first day of a new week.

In the context of Amos' indictment against those "turning" (הַהֹפְכִים) justice into wormwood (5:7), the hymn praises Yahweh's power as the one "who turns [וְהֹפֵךְ] the shadow of death into the morning" (5:8). The catch-phrase "turn into" (הָפַךְ לְ-) appears in both 5:7 and 5:8. Paul writes:

> Israel was accused of having turned justice into (הַהֹפְכִים לְ-) wormwood. Now it will have to face the Lord, the Creator and ruler, who among his many formidable feats turns pitch-darkness into (הפך לְ-) dawn. ... Those who are guilty of social inversion shall now witness and suffer cosmic inversion.[62]

The unfaithful Israelites changed what was just into what was bitter, and this created *death*. On the other hand, Yahweh changes "the shadow of death" into morning in order to bring *life*. The use of הָפַךְ with Israel is anti-creational; the same verb with Yahweh indicates the sustaining of creation. Over against those who subvert creation, Yahweh is faithful; he not only sustains what he has made but he also brings the new creation in Christ (2 Cor 5:17; Rev 21:1–5).

By using the verb הָפַךְ in adjacent verses but opposite contexts, Amos highlights the vast differences between Yahweh and Israel. Yahweh's ways are not Israel's ways (cf. Is 55:8). Sinful human actions bring social and spiritual darkness, and people themselves are unable to change their condition. On the other hand, Yahweh's action ushers in light. Just as on the first day of creation he called forth light to shine out of the darkness (Gen 1:2–5), so also he has caused the light of Christ to shine into the darkness of this fallen world to give the hope of resurrection to eternal glory (Jn 1:4–5; 2 Cor 4:4–6, 14).

Yet just like Amos 4:13, the hymn in 5:8–9 is a doxology of judgment for those who reject the God being praised. Yahweh "darkens day into night" (5:8), signaling that his clemency has its limits, and the time of judgment will come for the impenitent. Jesus uses a similar image in Jn 9:4. Amos again has inverted a well-known motif in order to shock his audience into repentance and an awareness of the impending disaster.[63] The hopeful action here of turning darkness to light foreshadows Amos 5:18–20, where Yahweh reverses the idea: on the day of his judgment those who have squandered the chance to repent will receive no light, only *darkness*.

Amos demonstrates his delight in heptads[64] as he employs seven verbs in the hymn.[65] The constellations "Orion" (כְּסִיל) and "Pleiades" (כִּימָה) are also

---

[62] Paul, *Amos*, 167–68.

[63] The prophet also does this in, for example, 2:6–16; 3:1–2; 4:4–5; 5:18–20; 9:7.

[64] Amos employs heptads also in 1:3–2:5; 2:6–8; 2:14–16; 3:3–6; 4:4–5; 4:6–11; 5:21–23; 6:1–6; 9:1–4.

[65] The seven Hebrew verbs in 5:8–9 are translated as follows: "Maker ... who turns ... and who darkens ... who summons ... and who pours ... who causes (destruction) to flash ... comes."

paired in Job 9:9 and 38:31. Job 9:9 lauds Yahweh with the same epithet used here, the substantized participle עֹשֵׂה meaning "the Maker, Creator."

"Yahweh is his name" appears in all three hymns (5:8; 9:6; and expanded in 4:13). The repetition of the sacred and saving covenant name "Yahweh" (see Ex 3:13–17) is characteristic of Israel's hymns.[d]

(d) E.g., Pss 46:8–9, 12 (ET 46:7–8, 11); 80:5, 20 (ET 80:4, 19); 107:1–2, 6, 8, 13, 15, 19, 21, 24, 28, 31, 43

5:9 While 5:8 portrays Yahweh as all-powerful in creation, 5:9 shows him as all-powerful in the realm of human events. The Creator is also the Lord over the nations.[66] Israel's leaders were placing their confidence in their fortresses and luxurious homes (e.g., 3:10–11, 15), but Yahweh is able to take aim and destroy these habitations (5:9, 11; 6:11).

Seek Good, Not Evil, So That You May Live (5:10–17)

5:10–11 The hymn of 5:8–9 extols Yahweh as the Maker of the stars, the one who changes night into day and day into night, the one who commands the waters of the seas, and the one who also turns strongholds into rubble. This is bracketed by Amos' description of people who resist change and who refuse to repent (cf. 4:6–11). They go to Bethel, Beersheba, and Gilgal (5:5) for syncretistic worship that destroys justice and righteousness (5:7). The judges, elders, leaders, and witnesses pervert justice in the gate (5:10). The description of the unfaithful Israelites broke off in 5:7 and was interrupted by the hymn in 5:8–9, but now it resumes in 5:10. Motyer writes: "It is a supreme argument for the verse order as it is that it enables us to follow the worshiper through what was (if this hymn is a sample) a superb spiritual experience and see him emerge on the other side exactly the same person."[67] Outwardly the Israelites might appear to have the form of godliness, but inwardly they deny its power (cf. 2 Tim 3:5).

Amos begins 5:10 with a third person plural verb: "they hate" (שָׂנְאוּ). Perhaps, for a brief moment, the Israelite audience is tempted to think, "Very well, Amos is finally addressing *those* people. It's about time!" But in 5:11 he changes to second person plural verbs: "you ..." Amos becomes an arbiter speaking honestly, like those in the gate whom the Israelites hate. Is 29:21 elaborates on Amos 5:10 by further describing how the unfaithful Israelites opposed such a person: "for the arbiter in the gate they lay a snare" (וְלַמּוֹכִיחַ בַּשַּׁעַר יְקֹשׁוּן).[68] Likewise, Jesus was opposed by unbelieving Jewish people who set traps for him (e.g., Mk 12:13; Lk 11:53–54; 20:20, 26).

An OT passage illustrating the role of an "arbiter, adjudicator" (מוֹכִיחַ) is Job 9. Job laments that he has no such person to mediate his dispute with Yahweh

---

[66] This is the understanding of Zalcman, "Astronomical Illusions in Amos," 57–58. He writes: "The contrast of Divine Omnipotence (as expressed in the cosmic order) with the vain and important posturings of mortal man (especially of rulers and of 'the Wise') becomes a recurrent theme in OT thought" (p. 58). Other OT texts (e.g., Is 40:22–23; 45:12–13; Ps 33:6–10; cf. Ps 146:3–6) also juxtapose Yahweh as Lord over creation with his lordship over history.

[67] Motyer, *The Message of Amos*, 112.

[68] See Is 1:23 and Micah 3:1–3, 9–11; 7:1–3 for other examples of prophetic complaints about Israel's corrupt legal system.

(Job 9:33). Such an arbiter or mediator would place his hands on Job and God like a referee separating the pugilists in a boxing match, take away Job's fear of God, and enable Job to speak with God amicably (Job 9:33–35). Job envisions the ultimate purpose of the mediator as reconciliation. Ultimately, this role is carried out by Jesus Christ, the mediator between God and humanity who has accomplished our reconciliation (Rom 5:10–11; 2 Cor 5:18–19; 1 Tim 2:5).

An arbiter could assist the disenfranchised. The first judges in Israel were the idea of Jethro, as a means to alleviate the burden placed upon Moses (Ex 18:14–26). Candidates were chosen who displayed fear of God and exemplary faithfulness (Ex 18:21). The book of Numbers relates that judges were selected based upon proven leadership (Num 11:16–17), while Deuteronomy recounts that they were chosen by means of their intellectual qualities (Deut 1:9–18). In Deut 16:18, Moses commands the people to appoint judges and officers. The command uses a second person singular verb, which is usually understood in Deuteronomy as addressing the whole people. Not just the king, but *all of the people of God are responsible to ensure that justice is done.* The judges are "to judge the people with righteous judgment" (וְשָׁפְטוּ אֶת־הָעָם מִשְׁפַּט־צֶדֶק, Deut 16:18). This is part of the divine arrangement that will permit the people to "live and possess the land" that Yahweh will give them (Deut 16:20).

The Judean king Jehoshaphat brought about judicial reforms by appointing judges in the cities of the land (2 Chr 19:4–11). He counseled them (2 Chr 19:6–7):

> Consider carefully what you do, because you are not judging for man but for Yahweh. He is with you in the matter of justice. Now let the fear of Yahweh be upon you. Be careful what you do, for with Yahweh our God there is no injustice or partiality or taking a bribe.

The condemnation in Amos 5:10–12, 15 is particularly relevant for the corrupt judges. They are another class of Israelite leaders to come under Yahweh's judgment, besides the royal officials in 3:9–15, who lived in fortresses (3:10) and had winter and summer homes (3:15). The judges likely were among those who lived in homes of hewn stone and owned vineyards (5:11). In contrast to the vineyards mentioned in 4:9 (cf. 9:14), the qualifying term "choice" is added in 5:11. These vineyards were planted in fertile soil, and their owners were making a rich profit from the vineyard's wine. One result of Yahweh's judgment upon these corrupt leaders is that all of their vineyards—and by extension, their owners—will lament (5:17).[69]

These corrupt judges sought to provide legal protection to those who illegally abused weaker members of society. They presided over kangaroo courts

---

[69] Yahweh metaphorically describes Israel itself as a vineyard in Is 5:1–2. It is planted "on a very fertile hill," בְּקֶרֶן בֶּן־שָׁמֶן, literally, "on a horn, a son of oil." This highly figurative phrase is used only here in the OT to describe a geological formation that is superabundant in fertility. However, the vineyard of Israel proves unfruitful, and so Yahweh will destroy it (Is 5:4–7).

of the highest order.[70] The judicial actions in 5:7 and 5:10 are contrasted with Yahweh's actions in 5:8–9.[71] The human courts turn justice into wormwood and throw righteousness to the ground, creating social chaos.

The land belongs to Yahweh, as well as the fruits thereof (Ps 24:1). Yahweh is the legal landowner. Lev 23:22 states: "And when you reap the harvest of your land, do not completely reap the very edges of your field, and do not gather the gleanings of your harvest. Leave them for the poor and the alien. I am Yahweh your God" (cf. Lev 19:9). Lev 19:10 furthermore forbids farmers to pass through their fields a second time to gather what was missed the first time (cf. Deut 24:19–22). In this way, the destitute were to be cared for in Israel, as illustrated by the narrative of Ruth (e.g., Ruth 2:2–3). Because it is Yahweh's nature to be generous (cf. Ps 23:5; 1 Jn 3:1), he calls his people to demonstrate generosity.

But Israel's leadership would have none of it. According to Amos 5:11 the greedy leaders were taking "a tax of grain" from the poor. This may imply that they were taxing and obstructing gleaners, in violation of the Torah. The gist of the passage therefore is this: "You impose a burden on the poor, and you take from him even the measure of grain to which he is entitled."[72] By having to pay taxes on what they harvested, the poor and needy were forced to finance the lifestyles of the judges with their expensive homes and valuable vineyards. Israel's "well-to-dos" were getting richer, while at the same time the nation's "have nots" were becoming poorer. Jesus prohibited such arrogance among his followers, whom he calls to be servants (Mt 20:25–27).

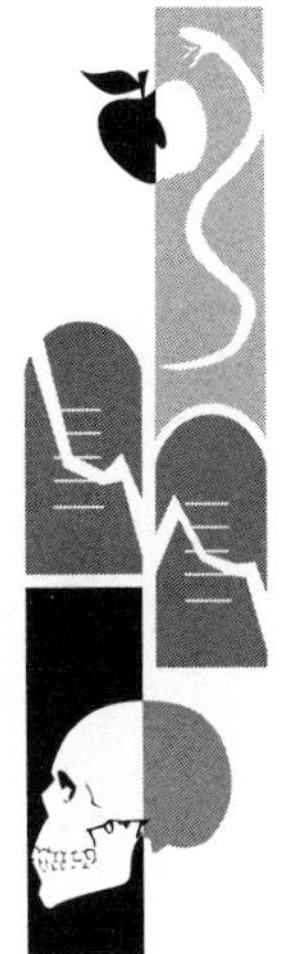

In 5:11 Amos announces a futility curse upon the leaders.[73] This curse reverses their expectations and makes the punishment fit their crime.[74] Those who illegally confiscated poor people's food will lack drink. They enhanced their property by their abuse, so they will have their property taken from them. These experts in "legalese" will not live in their houses made of hewn stone, nor will they enjoy wine from their choicest vineyards.[75] This reverses the gracious gifts received by the Israelite ancestors who entered the promised land and lived in houses they did not build, enjoyed wells of water that they did not

[70] Mays writes of such courts: "The rights of the widow, the fatherless, and the weak to protection against the economic process were widely ignored. The result was a growing differentiation between rich and poor" ("Justice: Perspectives from the Prophetic Tradition," 9). Similarly, Ezek 7:23 (cf. Ezek 9:9) condemns what Greenberg calls "judicial murder" (*Ezekiel*, 1:154).

[71] Amos' first hymn (4:13) also contrasts Yahweh's work with that of people.

[72] Andersen and Freedman, *Amos*, 501.

[73] Compare the similar curse in 4:8. On the curse of futility or uselessness, see Hillers, *Treaty-Curses and the Old Testament Prophets*, 28–29.

[74] The positive expectation is behind the question posed by St. Paul when discussing Christian ministry: "Who plants a vineyard but does not eat of its fruit?" (1 Cor 9:7). Of course the man who plants the vineyard should be sustained by its fruit! Congregations are obligated to support the livelihood of their faithful pastors and their pastors' families (1 Cor 9:4–14).

[75] For similar divine judgments upon homes and produce, see, for example, Deut 28:30, 38–40; Micah 6:14–15; Zeph 1:13.

dig, and ate and drank from vineyards and olive trees that they did not plant (Deut 6:10–11; Josh 24:13). Yahweh therefore will execute the covenant curses upon the unfaithful Israelites in Amos' day by taking away their houses and crops. Amos 5:11 fulfills the curses in Deut 28:30, 33, 39, 51 that foresaw how the Israelites would break the gracious covenant God established with them through Moses and be punished for it. Israel would lose the promised land it had received under Joshua. These curses can be compared to the expulsion from God's vineyard of the Jewish people who rejected their Messiah (Lk 20:9–19).

Yet Yahweh's final word in Amos, and in the Bible as a whole, is not curse but eschatological blessing. A remnant of Israel and the Gentiles will be saved by grace alone (9:11–12), and this faithful remnant will inherit a miraculously fruitful new creation (9:13–15). Both 5:11 and 9:14 include the same sequence of the four verbs "build" (בָּנָה), "live, inhabit" (יָשַׁב), "plant" (נָטַע), and "drink" (שָׁתָה). The totality of the curse in 5:11 will be completely reversed in the age to come. This is the same messianic promise expressed in Is 65:21–22, and it will be fulfilled after the return of Christ, the resurrection, and the establishment of the new heavens and new earth, as depicted in Revelation 21–22.

5:12 Yahweh, as the Creator, Redeemer, and Judge of all (5:8–9), knows and sees *all.* He is intimately aware of how Israel's leaders and judicial thieves were making a killing. The adjectives "many" (רַבִּים) and "mighty" (עֲצֻמִים) describe their transgressions and sins. Ironically these words once described the greatness of God's people. By his grace he enabled them to grow in Egypt to be "great, *mighty* [עָצוּם], and *many* [רָב]" (Deut 26:5). The pharaoh who "did not know Joseph" (Ex 1:8) acknowledges this about Israel using a comparative construction with the same words: "look, the people of the children of Israel are *more and mightier* than we are" (הִנֵּה עַם בְּנֵי יִשְׂרָאֵל רַב וְעָצוּם מִמֶּנּוּ, Ex 1:9). The irony expressed in Amos is that Israel now has "many" transgressions and "mighty" sins!

The "righteous man" and the "needy" (Amos 5:12) were victims in the very place where they should have expected to be treated with equity. Justice was thrust aside.[76] "And needy people they thrust away in the gate" (וְאֶבְיוֹנִים בַּשַּׁעַר הִטּוּ, 5:12) is the exact opposite of Yahweh's mandate in Ex 23:6: "you shall not thrust away the justice of your needy person" (לֹא תַטֶּה מִשְׁפַּט אֶבְיֹנְךָ). See also Deut 16:20; 24:17.

5:13 Yahweh will be the final Judge. He will vindicate the righteous, whom he himself has justified, and silence their accusers (Rom 8:31–39). The spiritually prudent or insightful person need say nothing, only let Yahweh speak and act. The "evil time" (Amos 5:13) of silence that will be followed by lamentation (5:16–17) is the same day of Yahweh's judgment described in 1:14;

[76] For similar charges, see, for example, Is 10:2; Mal 3:5; Prov 17:23; 18:5.

2:14–16; 3:14; 4:2; 5:18–20; 6:3; 8:3, 9–11, 13. See further the commentary on 5:18–20.

5:14–15 Amos 5:14–15 is at the center of the book, almost to the word.[77] These verses are bracketed by the preceding and following verses, each of which begins with "therefore" (לָכֵן, 5:13 and 5:16). They are also joined together as a chiasm with the key terms "good" (טוֹב) and "evil" (רָע):

Seek *good*
    and not *evil* …
    Hate *evil*
and love *good* …

There are 1,009 words in the MT of 1:1–5:13 and 1,006 words in 5:16–9:15.[78] Speaking of Hebrew rhetoric, Meynet writes:

> Instead of developing its argumentation in a linear way, in the Graeco-Roman fashion, to a conclusion which is the point of resolution of the discourse, it is organized most of the time in an involutive manner around a center which is the focal point, the keystone, through which the rest finds cohesion. The center of a concentric construction most of the time presents certain specific characteristics: it is often of a different shape and genre than the rest of the text, it is very often a question, or at least something which is problematic, which in all cases is enigmatic.[79]

These two verses summarize the entire message of the book, which may be stated as follows: "Seek Yahweh and forsake corrupt worship shrines, for in him alone you will live. Then Yahweh, the God who commands his armies in heaven and on earth, will be with you and not against you. He will be gracious to his faithful people, no matter how few or oppressed a remnant they may be."

Yahweh is concerned with proper worship and also with his people displaying righteousness in life (cf. Micah 6:8). Zeph 2:3 develops the same theme of seeking Yahweh and its resulting way of life:

בַּקְּשׁוּ אֶת־יְהוָה ... בַּקְּשׁוּ־צֶדֶק בַּקְּשׁוּ עֲנָוָה

Seek Yahweh; … seek righteousness; seek humility.

---

77 As noted by Andersen and Freedman, *Amos*, 53.

78 Andersen and Freedman, *Amos*, 465.

79 Meynet, *Rhetorical Analysis*, 175. The OT contains other examples of rhetorical emphasis achieved by placing equal numbers of words before and after a key passage. In Jonah 1:4–15, there are ninety-four Hebrew words from the scene's beginning in 1:4 to the beginning of the speech in 1:9 and ninety-four words in 1:10–15. Both the chiastic structure and the exact balance of words serve to place the focus of the scene on 1:9, which is Jonah's confession of faith. Similarly, Bartelt argues in *The Book around Immanuel* that Is 7:14, Isaiah's prophecy that Immanuel will be born to the virgin, is at the midpoint of Isaiah 2–12. In Moses' Song by the Sea (Ex 15:1–18), the rhetorical questions in Ex 15:11 are at the center. In Psalm 23 the words "for you are with me" (כִּי־אַתָּה עִמָּדִי, Ps 23:4) are in the numerical middle of the psalm, since there are twenty-six Hebrew words before and twenty-six after that clause.

True, saving faith and good works must be *distinguished* (Eph 2:8–9), but they must never be *divorced* (Eph 2:10). Faith manifests itself in works of love toward God and neighbor.

5:14 Similar language in 5:4, 6 exhorted Israel to seek *Yahweh* and live. The exhortation in 5:14 is to seek "good" and not "evil" in order that the people may live.[80] Amos 5:14–15 is expressing the same message about good and evil intertwined with life and death as Deut 30:15–20 (see also Deut 4:1) and as St. Paul expresses in Rom 12:9, 21; 16:19. "Good" (טוֹב) can be used as an attribute of God (see the first textual note on 5:14). God the Son declared, "Only one is good," God alone (Mt 19:17). God is the source of all that is good, and whoever seeks and finds God finds everything good (cf. Mt 7:11; Philemon 6; James 1:17). "Do not imitate evil, but good. He who does good is from God, but he who does evil has not seen God" (3 Jn 11).

Apart from the one true and triune God there is no good and no life, only evil and death. The antonymous phrase, "and not evil" (Amos 5:14), relates to the commands to avoid false gods and idolatry, into which Israel had fallen (5:5–6; 8:14; and especially 5:26–27). At its core idolatry involves the worship of demons (Lev 17:7; Deut 32:17; Ps 106:37; 1 Cor 10:20–21), and behind the demons is the devil, Satan (Rev 12:9; 20:2), who is called "the evil one" in, for example, Mt 5:37; 6:13; Jn 17:15; Eph 6:16. The traditional Christian liturgy for Holy Baptism asks this question: "Do you renounce the devil and all his works and all his ways?"[81] The baptized Christian is called and empowered to die to sin and evil daily, and to be raised to new life in Christ, abounding in every good work (Rom 6:1–11; Eph 2:8–10; Col 1:10).

Ambrose comments on Amos 5:14:

> Let us hurry to him in whom is that highest good, since he is goodness itself. He is the patience of Israel calling you to repentance, so you will not come to judgment but may receive the remission of sins. "Repent," he says [Mt 4:17]. He is the one of whom the prophet Amos cries, "Seek you good." He is the highest good, for he needs nothing and abounds in all things. Well may he abound, for in him dwells bodily the fullness of divinity [Col 2:9]. Well may he abound, of whose fullness we have all received, and in whom we have been filled, as the Evangelists says [Jn 1:16].[82]

As in 5:4, 6, the verb "to live" (חָיָה) reappears in 5:14. Yahweh created Adam and Eve to live and warned them not to disobey and die. He yearns for all people to repent, believe, and so live. His desire for life is climactically offered and bestowed in Jesus Christ. Jn 1:4 states this about Jesus: "In him was life, and the life was the light of men." In Jn 6:35 Jesus says, "I am the bread of life."

---

[80] The antonymous pair "good" (טוֹב) and "evil" (רַע) appear in, for example, Gen 2:17; 31:24; Lev 27:10; Is 5:20; Pss 34:15 (ET 34:14); 52:5 (ET 52:3). Compare the cognate verbs in Is 1:16–17: "cease to do evil, learn to do good" (חִדְלוּ הָרֵעַ׃ לִמְדוּ הֵיטֵב).

[81] E.g., *LW*, p. 201.

[82] Ambrose, Letter 79, quoted in Ferreiro, *The Twelve Prophets*, ACCS 14:100.

In Jn 6:68 Peter confesses to him, "You have the words of eternal life." In Jn 10:10 he asserts, "I have come that they may have life and have it abundantly." To a weeping Mary and Martha at the death of their brother Lazarus, Jesus says in Jn 11:25, "I am the resurrection and the life." In Jn 14:6 he announces, "I am the way and the truth and the life." Those who have been baptized into the death and resurrection of Jesus are empowered to walk in new life, a life that will never end (Rom 6:1–11). Jude exhorts the baptized, "Keep yourselves in God's love as you wait for the mercy of our Lord Jesus Christ to bring you to eternal life" (Jude 21).

Tragically, Israel was deluded. The people thought they had Yahweh and life. Yahweh cites their own words or thoughts in order to correct them.[83] They claimed that the God of hosts was "with" them, terminology that refers to God's gracious, saving presence (e.g., Is 7:14; 8:8; Mt 1:23; 18:20; 28:20). But Israel thought this grace was proven by "the good fortune, prosperity, and military and economic success of the northern kingdom."[84] The leaders believed that Yahweh's will was to prosper them and never to harm them, no matter how great or mighty their sins (5:12). God, however, always calls for repentance and faith. He confirms that what they are saying would be true, if—and this is a big *if*—they seek Yahweh and not Canaanite fertility deities. Grace is not a commodity that can be presumed upon and taken for granted. God's people must daily die to sin and rise to new life by the power of the Holy Spirit in order to reach the resurrection to eternal life (Rom 6:1–11; Phil 3:8–12).

5:15 The members of Israel's judicial corps believed that they possessed "the good life" with their stone-hewn houses and lush vineyards (5:11), but their path led to death (cf. Ps 1:6). The only route to life was to hate evil—to renounce their false gods and syncretistic worship that only served the evil one—and to love good, especially Yahweh, who alone is the source of all that is good. Israel's leaders were to "hate evil" with the same kind of passion by which they "hate an arbiter in the gate" (שָׂנְאוּ בַשַּׁעַר מוֹכִיחַ, 5:10). Instead of overturning and throwing down justice and righteousness (5:7), they were called to rectify the dismal situation: "establish justice in the gate" (5:15), which was where public business was transacted.

The accounts in, for example, Genesis 23 and 34 and Ruth 4 illustrate transactions in the city gate. Supervision was carried out by elders or other leaders. Witnesses could testify to the truth before a decision was made, or after a decision was rendered they could attest the validity of the legal record. Andersen and Freedman write:

> Everyone had a right to be there, and all citizens had a right to speak. Everything was given publicity, and even without written titles and affidavits, the community as a whole would be able to keep track of the property of its members. Promises were confirmed and protected by oaths, which is

[83] He does this also in 2:12; 4:1; 5:18; 6:13; 8:5; 9:10.

[84] Paul, *Amos*, 177; cf. also Wolff, *Joel and Amos*, 250.

where God came into it. Things were done "in front of God," which might require the presence of principals and witnesses at the shrine.[85]

Yahweh issues no guarantee that if the people repent and reestablish justice he will automatically void his sentence of judgment against them. The third colon of 5:15 begins with אוּלַי, "*perhaps*," analogous to the phrase מִי־יוֹדֵעַ, "who knows?" in 2 Sam 12:22; Joel 2:14; and Jonah 3:9.[86] Both ideas express humility and faith. Yahweh will act as he pleases, which may or may not conform to human patterns and expectations (cf. Ps 115:3). The Israelites' repentance will not automatically force Yahweh's hand. His decision to respond with grace is his alone; it cannot be manipulated or preprogrammed. The legal leaders' hope is not in their repentance or ethical renewal; it is solely in Yahweh's hands.

God may allow his repentant believers to suffer disaster and even temporal death, yet he alone remains their sure hope for resurrection to eternal life (cf. "live" in Amos 5:4, 6, 14), as expressed by Job: "Even if he kills me, in him will I hope" (Job 13:15; see also Job 19:25–27). In this way, grace remains *grace*. Salvation is not grounded in human repentance, but rather in Yahweh's compassion: "*perhaps* Yahweh, the God of armies, will be gracious" (Amos 5:15). In Article V, "Concerning the Office of Preaching," the Augsburg Confession states this same truth:

> Through these [the Gospel in the Word and Sacraments], as through means, he [God] gives the Holy Spirit, who works faith, *when and where he pleases*, in those who hear the Gospel.[87]

Seeking Yahweh will not *force* him to call off catastrophe. There is no mechanical relationship between human acts of piety or worship and Yahweh's saving action. In fact, the relationship is the reverse: God draws people to himself, and then empowered by the Holy Spirit, they respond in faith (Song 1:4; Jn 6:44; 12:32). The conditional sentence ("perhaps …") in Amos prevents any simple *quid pro quo* understanding of the relationship between human action and divine action. The prophet knows that Yahweh is not obligated to turn away from his judgment, even though he does relent twice when Amos intercedes (7:3, 6).

"The remnant of Joseph" (שְׁאֵרִית יוֹסֵף, 5:15) is a clear expression in Amos of the Gospel hope of a remnant saved by grace. Hasel believes there is a threefold usage of the remnant theme in Amos.[88] The first set of passages (3:12; 4:1–3; 5:3; 6:9–10; 9:1–4) speaks of survivors but offers no hope of a gracious future for them. The second and third are genuine promises of eschatological salvation and restoration, for a remnant from Israel (5:15) and for a remnant

---

[85] Andersen and Freedman, *Amos*, 309.

[86] For "who knows?" see Lessing, *Jonah*, 315–16. Ex 32:30; Zeph 2:3; and Lam 3:29 use אוּלַי, "perhaps," in the same sense as מִי־יוֹדֵעַ, "who knows?" in 2 Sam 12:22; Joel 2:14; and Jonah 3:9.

[87] Emphasis added.

[88] Hasel, *The Remnant*, 392–94.

from Edom and other nations (9:11–12). Therefore Hasel maintains that in Amos 5:15 "the remnant motif is used for the first time in an eschatological sense."[89] Andersen and Freedman concur that "as long as there is a remnant of Joseph (a tenth, a hundredth, a thousandth [5:3, 6:9]), perhaps Yahweh will be gracious."[90] This commentary agrees with Hasel that 5:14–15 and 9:11–12 extend Gospel hope, but it believes that 4:11 is the first among the Gospel remnant passages in Amos and that 5:3 also leaves room for hope.

"Joseph" (5:15) suggests the kind of people who will endure as God's OT church after the Assyrian conquest of northern Israel in 722 BC. The oppressed, marginalized believers will be a testimony to Yahweh's preserving grace even though everyone and everything appeared to be stacked against them. Joseph was sold by his brothers into slavery, but "Yahweh was with Joseph" (Gen 39:2; cf. "Yahweh … [would be] *with* you," Amos 5:14). Joseph spurned adultery with Potiphar's wife and was imprisoned for his virtue, but again "Yahweh was with Joseph" (Gen 39:21). While in prison, still "Yahweh was with him" (Gen 39:23). Finally, after Pharaoh had two dreams that no one could interpret except Joseph, Jacob's favorite son was exalted in Egypt in the blink of an eye when Pharaoh asked, "Can anyone like this be found, a man in whom is the Spirit of God?" (Gen 41:38).

Just as Joseph was rejected by his brothers and suffered exile, ridicule, imprisonment, and finally vindication (Genesis 37–50), the faithful Israelites who were abused (cf. Amos 6:6c) likewise would eventually be rescued and vindicated for eternity (9:11–15). These are the ones who have "an end-time future and a hope" (אַחֲרִ֖ית וְתִקְוָֽה, Jer 29:11). Throughout the book of Amos, and indeed throughout the Scriptures, the Gospel promises are for the meek and lowly (Mt 5:3–12). On the other hand, the arrogant political, legal, priestly, and business leaders are only promised judgment. It is this latter group that consists of "all the sinners of my people" who will die by the sword (Amos 9:10).

An overview of the biblical theme of remnant begins with Adam and Eve since God did not immediately carry out the sentence of death (Gen 2:17), but preserved them so they could perpetuate the human race, particularly the line of the promised Seed (Gen 3:15) who would destroy the works of the devil (1 Jn 3:8). Eve expresses faith in that promise with her explanation of the name of her first son (Gen 4:1).[91] The remnant theme continues with the flood narrative (Genesis 6–9) when Yahweh preserved Noah and his family.[92] The salvation of

---

89 Hasel, *The Remnant*, 393.

90 Andersen and Freedman, *Amos*, 511.

91 Eve's explanation is, literally, "I have begotten a man, Yahweh." She apparently believed that her first son was Yahweh incarnate, the Seed who would crush the serpent's head, fulfilling Gen 3:15. Since the Seed would not be born for several thousand more years, her faith was premature, but nevertheless she expresses faith, and so the faithful remnant theme in Scripture began.

92 Hasel, *The Remnant*, 146, 389, thinks the remnant theme in Scripture does not begin until the flood narrative.

eight lives in the ark continued the human race and prefigured the salvation of all who are baptized into the risen Christ (1 Pet 3:18–22). In the Abraham narrative, Yahweh condescends to save Lot and his two daughters even after his angels could not find a meager ten righteous people in Sodom and Gomorrah (Gen 18:32). The Jacob narrative connects Yahweh's covenantal promise of universal blessing through the Seed to the survival of a remnant stemming from Jacob himself, and God reiterates to Jacob his earlier covenantal promises to Abraham and Isaac (Gen 28:13–14; 32:10, 13 [ET 32:9, 12]). The Joseph cycle follows, where Joseph forgives his brothers for selling him into slavery by recognizing, "God sent me before you to preserve for you a *remnant* [שְׁאֵרִית] on earth and to keep alive for you a great group of escapees [פְּלֵיטָה]" (Gen 45:7). The prophet Elijah thought that he alone was the remnant in his time, but Yahweh promised, "Yet I will leave seven thousand in Israel, all the knees that have not bowed to Baal" (1 Ki 19:18).

These promises of a remnant are based on Yahweh's everlasting covenant of grace, first promised to Adam and Eve (Gen 3:15) and confirmed with Abraham and his descendants (Gen 12:1–3; 17:7; Gal 3:26–29). Yahweh will never nullify this promise (Mt 16:18). Judgment may come and remove those who claim to be members but are not (cf. Jn 15:2, 6), while it also purifies those who are true believers (cf. Heb 12:7–11).

Along with Amos, fellow eighth-century prophets Micah (e.g., Micah 2:12) and Isaiah (e.g., Is 1:8–9; 7:3; 10:20–22) likewise promise a remnant. They too foresaw that Yahweh would spare a remnant from Shalmaneser V and Sargon II, who defeated northern Israel (722 BC), as well as from Sennacherib, who surrounded Jerusalem (701 BC), and from Nebuchadnezzar, who conquered Judah and destroyed the Jerusalem temple (587 BC).[93]

Through the later prophets who ministered during the exile in the sixth century BC, Jeremiah (e.g., Jer 23:3) and Ezekiel (e.g., Ezek 11:13–17), Yahweh narrowed down the theme as he spoke of the faithful remnant coming not from the few who had avoided deportation from Judah, but from the Judeans suffering in exile in Babylon. The restoration prophets, Haggai (late sixth century BC) and Zechariah (late sixth century and fifth century BC), promised a remnant made up of those repatriated in the postexilic Persian province of Yehud (e.g., Hag 1:12–15; Zech 8:6–12).

The common denominator in each era is that the remnant does not consist of those who manage to avoid suffering. Rather, the remnant consists of those whom Yahweh enables by his grace to continue to believe in him and be faithful to him despite their experiences of tragedy, loss, and grief in this sinful world that stands under God's righteous judgment. Ultimately, the remnant theme culminates in the sinless one who is fully righteous, but who nevertheless

---

[93] Hasel, *The Remnant*, 402, asserts that Isaiah carried on the tradition of Amos' remnant theme while also solidifying its eschatological usage. Isaiah proclaimed an eschatological remnant that would be purified by a divine purging (e.g., Is 1:25–26; 10:20–22).

suffered the entirety of God's righteous judgment on sin (Is 52:13–53:12).[94] He embodies the true Israel (Mt 2:15).[95] Through baptismal incorporation into him, all believers become the heirs of Abraham and comprise the true "Israel of God" (Gal 3:26–29; 6:16). Thus the OT remnant theme finds its fulfillment in the Christian church, a faithful remnant of which will continue until Christ returns (Mt 24:22–24).

5:16 "Therefore" (לָכֵן) forms an inclusio with the same word beginning 5:13, where too it began a new section in this judgment oracle. This rhetorical technique of bracketing 5:14–15 by the repetition of "therefore" in 5:13, 16 highlights the remnant promise in 5:14–15 as a major emphasis of Amos' preaching.

The dirge that began in 5:1–3, lamenting Virgin Israel's untimely death, reappears again in 5:16–17. In 5:1–3 a single speaker, "I" (either Yahweh or Amos speaking for him), uttered the lament. Now professional singers, "the ones skilled in wailing," and recruited mourners, even "the farmer" (5:16), will join in the lament in the squares and streets of the city. It seems that Israel's professional mourners included women (e.g., Jer 9:19 [ET 9:20]; Ezek 32:16), but men could also chant laments (e.g., 2 Sam 1:11; 3:33; 2 Chr 35:25). Customs connected with mourning included tearing the robes, wearing sackcloth, sitting in ashes, throwing ashes on the head, cutting/shaving the hair and beard, and beating the chest with cries of lament.[e] In the case of Amos 5:16, because the calamity will be so devastating, there will not be enough professional mourners, so even farmhands will be invited to join in the requiem for the dead.

(e) E.g., 2 Sam 3:31; 13:19; Is 32:12; Jer 7:29; 48:37–38; Amos 8:10; Lk 10:13; 18:13

The prophetic use of "woe" can include a call for vengeance as well as mourning.[96] Lamentation over the dead leads to a cry for vengeance against those who are deemed responsible for the calamity. This lamentation-vengeance pattern fits the movement of Amos 5–6, where the "woe" oracles (5:18; 6:1; cf. 5:16) are embedded in descriptions of lamentation and death. Chapters 5 and 6 address the same Israelite audience, "first as the murdered victim and then as those guilty of murder."[97] The reason for Yahweh's judgment and the ensuing mourning is the Israelites' behavior that consistently denied justice and thwarted righteousness (5:7, 10–12).

---

[94] The declaration that the Suffering Servant "will see [his] seed" (Is 53:10), that is, that he will have spiritual offspring, continues the Genesis remnant theme sketched above from Gen 3:15 through the patriarchal promises, and connects to baptized Christians as "the seed of Abraham" (Gal 3:29).

[95] For Matthew's portrayal of Jesus, God's Son, as the nation, God's son, see Gibbs, *Matthew 1:1–11:1*, 139–45.

[96] Janzen, *Mourning Cry and Woe Oracle*, 27–34. Janzen's study notes the biblical connections between lamentation and the cry for revenge: David's lament over Saul and Jonathan (2 Sam 1:19–26) includes a curse of the mountains of Gilboa (2 Sam 1:21); his lament over Abner (2 Sam 3:33–34) is followed by a call for vengeance (2 Sam 3:39). Note also Psalm 137, where exilic situations of mourning are followed by cries for vengeance against the Edomites and Babylonians.

[97] Joyce Shelly, "Amos and Irony," 89.

The repetition of "lamentation" (מִסְפֵּד) twice in 5:16 and once in 5:17 emphasizes that the dirge of 5:1 is going to extend throughout the land ("in the city plazas … in the streets … in all the vineyards," 5:16–17). The immensity of the disaster is likewise conveyed by Amos' threefold use of "all" (כֹּל), twice in 5:16 and once in 5:17. The entire people will suffer because of the theological failure of the leaders.

"Yahweh, the God of armies" (יְהוָה אֱלֹהֵי (הַ)צְבָאוֹת) appears twenty-two times in the OT, and in Amos in 3:13; 4:13; 5:14–16, 27; 6:8, 14, sometimes in combination with other divine titles. Yahweh is the commander in chief of the heavenly and earthly armies, and he is about to launch a frontal attack on his own people! The nature of the onslaught is defined in the next verse.

5:17 This verse continues the theme of 5:16. It also concludes the dirge begun in 5:1–3. The funeral lamentation (מִסְפֵּד) appears in the most unlikely locale: a *vineyard*. Normally vineyards were the centers of exuberant joy (e.g., Judg 9:27; Jer 48:33). A similar description appears in Is 16:10: "Rejoicing and gladness are gone from the fertile field; and in the vineyards [וּבַכְּרָמִים] there is no singing for joy or shouting." The "choice vineyards" (Amos 5:11) of the leaders are going to experience funeral dirges.

Together 5:16 and 5:17 state that there will be wailing *everywhere* ("city plazas," "streets," and "vineyards"), as well as wailing by *everyone*: the unskilled "farmer" and "the ones skilled in wailing." Amos employs the genre of a funeral lament in a proleptic manner: the future has exploded into the present and is now turning the unbelievers' joy into sorrow, their glee into mourning, and their life into death. In 722 BC the Northern Kingdom experienced defeat and destruction brought on by the Assyrians (2 Ki 17:5, 18, 20, 23). In 587 BC the south underwent a similar judgment (2 Ki 25:1–21).

The final warning is an eerie sequel to the final plague against Egypt. "I will pass through your midst" (אֶעֱבֹר בְּקִרְבְּךָ, Amos 5:17) is very similar to Ex 12:12, "I will pass through the land of Egypt" (וְעָבַרְתִּי בְאֶרֶץ־מִצְרַיִם), as well as Ex 12:23, "Yahweh will pass through to strike Egypt" (וְעָבַר יְהוָה לִנְגֹּף אֶת־מִצְרַיִם). As Yahweh passed through Egypt and killed the firstborn of every human and animal, this time he will launch his attack against apostate Israel's citizenry. When Yahweh passes through, it will not be to destroy Israel's enemies, but rather to destroy unfaithful *Israel*![98]

Summary

Amos begins this section with a thorough rejection of Israel's syncretistic worship centers in Bethel, Gilgal, and Beersheba. These places, once the location of Yahweh's blessings and promises, were sites of false worship (cf. Mt

[98] Amos 4:9–10 also alludes to the plagues against Egypt while predicting judgment against Israel. Andersen and Freedman write: "In view of the account of the series of plagues in Amos 4:6–11, the correspondence between the treatment to be accorded Israel for its defiance of God and that which was meted out to Egypt at the time of the Exodus seems both plausible and probable" (*Amos*, 516).

21:13; Mk 11:17; Lk 19:46). The chief culprits in Amos 5:4–17 are the leaders, judges, elders, and witnesses who neglected justice and righteousness. Little did they know that Yahweh—who is the Creator, Redeemer, and Judge (5:8–9)—would turn against them to become Israel's Destroyer (5:17). The magistrates' fancy homes and sprawling vineyards receive Yahweh's special interest. These will be taken away and the perverters of righteousness will lament.

But Yahweh extends an offer of hope. It is not too late to seek Yahweh and live, to seek good and hate evil. In doing so, the leaders might join the remnant of Joseph, made up of the repentant believers in the land (5:15). If they do not repent, the lament begun by one speaker in 5:1 will be picked up in every place by everyone. Even professional mourners will be needed because Yahweh promises to pass through Israel in the same way he had passed through all of the homes in Egypt to strike down the firstborn. Moses' words in an earlier era appropriately summarize 5:4–17: "They are a nation perishing [without divine] counsel; they have no discernment. If only they would be wise and understand this and discern what their end will be" (Deut 32:28–29; cf. Jer 49:7–8; Obad 8).

The NT issues the same call as in Amos 5:4, 6, 14: seek God and live! Everlasting life is found in Jesus Christ and in him alone (Jn 1:4; 17:3). This life comes only by grace and through faith, and it overflows in doing good to others (Eph 2:8–10). When Christ's forerunner, John, came, he preached repentance and administered a baptism for the forgiveness of sins (Lk 3:3). He cried, "Repent, for the reign of heaven is near" (Mt 3:2). He called for the people to express their repentance and faith by giving to the needy: "Anyone who has two shirts should share with the one who has none, and whoever has food should do likewise" (Lk 3:11). In the early church, the Christians shared with one another so that the needs of all believers were met (e.g., Acts 2:41–47; 4:34–37).

The Israelites in Amos' day were religious (e.g., Amos 4:4–5; 5:21–23), but they rejected Yahweh's grace, and so they themselves failed to be gracious toward each other. Therefore Yahweh's visitation will cause them to mourn (5:16–17). The day of his visitation is the subject of 5:18–20.

Excursus

The Church's Response to Ethical Issues

Today there were global tragedies of horrific proportions. Worst of all, such disasters will happen again tomorrow and will be repeated on each subsequent day. In our world in 2008, the daily death toll includes thirty-five thousand children who perish from malnutrition and starvation.[1] Thousands of babies in utero are killed each day through abortion. Genocide is taking place, and Muslims are killing Christians daily. In fact, more Christians have been martyred in the past century than in all the previous centuries combined. Does the message of the book of Amos apply to this? And how should the church respond, based on the Scriptures, to corrupt governments, the lack of education and health services in the two-thirds world, the AIDS crisis, unjust laws, slavery, human trafficking, the forced prostitution of women and children, and countless other evils that are not only ethical issues but also harsh realities in countries around the globe?

Throughout Amos, Yahweh decries the moral and ethical sins of Israel, as well as those of other nations. The list of transgressions is as varied as it is long. In the oracles against Gentile nations (1:3–2:3), Yahweh's chief contention is that the nations should have known better than to enact horrific "crimes against humanity."[2] Damascus, the capital of the Aramean Empire, was guilty of butchering Gileadites with threshing sledges (1:3). Gaza (1:6) and Tyre (1:9) are called to account because of their inhumane slave trade. Edom demonstrated a lack of compassion toward a nation with which it had a covenant (probably Israel), actually pursuing it with a sword (1:11). The Ammonites were culpable for slicing open the wombs of pregnant women (1:13), while the Moabites had desecrated an Edomite king's remains (2:1).

However, Judah (2:4–5) and Israel (2:6–16), the divided people of God, are held to the higher standard: "the Torah of Yahweh" (2:4), the written Scriptures.[3] Their chief sin was that they had broken the covenant, including violations of the Ten Commandments. Israel's breaches of the Sinaitic covenant included abandoning Yahweh and pursuing false gods (2:8; 4:4; 5:5–6, 14, 25–27; 7:9; 8:14; 9:1); abusing the righteous and the poor (2:6–8; 4:1; 5:12; 8:4–6); sexual sins (2:7c); the excessive use of alcohol (4:1; 6:6); and perverting righteousness and justice in the civil legal system (5:7, 10–12, 15).

---

1 As noted in Clark and Rakestraw, *Readings in Christian Ethics*, 2:339.

2 See further "Amos' Oracles against the Six Pagan Nations (1:3–2:3)" in "Introduction to Amos 1:3–2:16: Judgments against the Nations."

3 See the commentary on 2:4 and "Overview of the Oracle against Israel (2:6–16)" in the commentary on 2:6–16. See also "Introduction to Amos 1:3–2:16: Judgments against the Nations."

Just as God expected Israel at the time of Amos to remain faithful to the Torah of Moses and warned of imminent judgment for the impenitent, so too God expects the church to remain faithful to the testimony of the Scriptures, and on that basis the church is to address the rampant sins in the world today, especially when they are found among the people of God. However, the church is not called primarily to be a political actor, a social transformer, or an aggressive interest group. If it acts *primarily* as any one of these, it loses its own integrity and reason for being. The church is the body of Christ, the communion of believers in the triune God. Yet Jesus has left his disciples in the world in order to witness to the world (Mt 5:13–16; Jn 17:11–17). This is the tension the church continually finds itself in. It is called upon to preach the Gospel and administer the Sacraments, while also engaging the moral and ethical issues of the day.

Jesus gave his apostles the mandate to make disciples from among all the nations by baptizing in the triune name and teaching the observance of all that he had commanded (Mt 28:18–20). The Great Commission does not mean the church can remain passive or silent regarding the ethical issues facing people, since Jesus himself often preached and taught about moral, ethical, and social topics during his ministry. Jesus not only offers the free gift of life *after* death, but he also empowers the baptized for life *before* death. And Christians in this life are called, as they have opportunity in their vocations, to intercede for the helpless, assist needy orphans and widows, heal the diseased, uplift the lowly, empower the disenfranchised, and reach out to all the vulnerable and lowly people, even as our Lord showed concern for such people during his earthly ministry. See, for example, Mt 15:22–28 (the healing of the Canaanite woman's sick daughter); Mk 10:46–52 (the healing of blind Bartimaeus); Lk 8:41–56 (the raising of Jairuis' dead daughter and the healing of the woman with the flow of blood).

Unfortunately a type of dualism can infect the church so that it divorces spiritual issues from physical care and from social and political issues. Many Christians believe that being "spiritual" means focusing exclusively on otherworldly piety. They have been taught that a "spiritual" person is one whose eyes are cast heavenward in prayer and contemplation, thinking only of the joys of the life to come, with eyes closed to the surrounding world. They think that living "spiritually" requires passive detachment from this world, transcending to a higher, more sublime realm. Christians may think that to be "spiritual" means disregarding the bodily needs of earthly life (contrary to, e.g., Eph 5:29) and ignoring the needs of others in the body of Christ and in the world. They may seek to escape by focusing only upon the invisible realities and eternal mysteries of God's holiness. A "spiritual" person may be consumed with the agenda "to win souls for Jesus." However, God the Creator fashioned people with bodies as well as souls. Salvation in the biblical sense is fellowship with the Creator through his flesh-and-blood Son, in communion with the church as a living witness to the world.

The OT in general, and Amos in particular, challenges the church to renounce the type of dualism where spiritual issues are divorced from moral, ethical, physical, and social concerns, as if the latter were of no spiritual significance, and as if God has no solution for them to offer the world. The incarnation, death, and resurrection of Christ has secured the promise of resurrection into the new creation for all believers—for all who are called by the triune God's saving name (Amos 9:11–15; Acts 4:12; Revelation 21–22). Moreover, God's gracious presence in his church now through his Word and Sacraments enables the body of Christ to be a living agent of change in society, working to help restore humanity to God's design. "The vertical dimension of faith—our confidence in the justifying grace of God in Christ—is accompanied by horizontal effects."[4]

Benne posits a diagram that assists the church in faithfully interacting with moral and political issues of the day.[5] The diagram consists of three concentric circles. The core circle in Benne's model has Jesus Christ at its center, surrounded by the biblical witness to his life, death, and resurrection, together with essential biblical doctrines such as the Trinity, eschatology, and mission. This core circle includes the central moral vision consisting of the Ten Commandments; the calling of Christians to faith active in love; the priceless value of all human life, since it has been created by God and redeemed by Christ; and the sanctity of marriage as the lifelong union of one man and one woman. These positions are firm and cannot be compromised. The next concentric circle represents the church's attempts at applying its religious and moral view to the dynamic world around it. "Theological reflection on society, the arts, science, and so on, and social teaching on economics, politics, and society are examples of this extension of Christian meaning."[6] The third circle consists of the church's position on specific public policy issues.

In addressing current issues, the church must begin at the center with foundational beliefs and then move to the second and third circles. However, two qualifications are helpful. First, each step beyond the core circle means there is a higher likelihood that Christians may disagree. Second, it is of paramount importance for the church to distinguish between the three realms and not to conflate the circles or collapse the outside circles into the middle. For example, assisting the poor, working toward fairer wages, lobbying for a more humane way to address immigration, and similar efforts are actions that lie in the second circle, and specific policy decisions, such as establishing the minimum wage or the numbers of immigrants to allow in, lie in the third circle.

The efforts that lie in the second and third circles may be good for society, but they do not bestow the forgiveness of sins for Christ's sake. They do

---

[4] Benne, *Reasonable Ethics*, 106.

[5] Benne, *Reasonable Ethics*, 70–72.

[6] Benne, *Reasonable Ethics*, 71.

not save people or bring the kingdom of God. That only happens by means of the Gospel of Jesus Christ, which is in the core circle. Salvation will never be accomplished by political reforms or social achievements. Christians are resident aliens in this world (Phil 3:20; 1 Pet 1:1, 2:11). Success at solving political and social problems can only bring provisional order and temporal peace. The church must be involved in public life, but this involvement is penultimate. Freely offering the gifts of the Gospel in God's Word and Sacraments is the *central* and *ultimate* way in which the church acts in this world. The church faces the danger that it may place too much emphasis on current issues and not enough on the eternal issue.

One example of how to keep the three circles distinct is in an exchange between the Protestant minister William Sloane Coffin and Henry Kissinger during the Vietnam War. Kissinger said to Coffin something like this: "If you're so smart, why don't you tell us what to do in Vietnam." To which Coffin replied, "Mr. Secretary, my job is to say to you, 'Let justice roll down like mighty waters' [Amos 5:24]. Your job is to get the plumbing in place."[7]

Niebuhr analyzes these models for the church to address social ills:[8]

1. Christ against culture (e.g., the Amish, who attempt to withdraw from the culture)
2. Christ above culture (e.g., the Roman Catholic Church, which seeks to create a synthesis led by the church)
3. Christ transforming culture (e.g., the Reformed tradition, which works to convert the culture to the will of God)
4. Christ of culture (e.g., liberalism's program of absorbing Christ into the culture)
5. Christ and culture in paradox (e.g., the Lutheran tradition)

Benne expounds on the fifth alternative, Christ and culture in paradox.[9] This alternative is built upon the doctrine of God's two kingdoms: the state, which governs by God's authority (Jn 19:11; Rom 13:1–6), and the church, which rests on the authority of Christ himself (Mt 16:15–19; 28:19–20). The distinction between these two kingdoms[10] is taught by Jesus in, for example, Mt 22:21. Whereas the other four approaches described by Niebuhr all seek to resolve the tension between the church and the state, the Lutheran teaching of the two kingdoms under God is content to live with this tension unresolved—

---

[7] As noted by Brueggemann, *Like Fire in the Bones*, 200.

[8] Niebuhr, *Christ and Culture*; cf. Benne, *Reasonable Ethics*, 75.

[9] Benne, *Reasonable Ethics*, 75. Benne writes (p. 102):

> The paradoxical vision leads to a different way of construing the public role of religion than does the Reformed or the Catholic. Its themes serve as guardians of the radicality and universality of the Gospel, of a proper understanding of the church's task, and of the two ways that God reigns. Churches ignore these themes at their great peril.

[10] The phrase "doctrine of the two kingdoms" was not coined until the 1930s, as noted by Childs ("Ethics and the Promise of God," 98). However, the doctrine of God's two modes of governance has been a part of the Lutheran theological heritage ever since Luther's publication in 1523 of "Temporal Authority: To What Extent It Should Be Obeyed" (AE 45:75–129).

until Christ returns. In both realms, the goal should be to overcome sin and bring the fallen creation back into harmony with God. But the means are different. In the left-hand kingdom, the instrument is the law, and governments and rulers use physical force and military power to accomplish their ends. In the right-hand kingdom, the instrument is the Gospel, and the church exercises spiritual power as it calls for repentance and invites people to believe, live by faith, and act in love.

The church engages the kingdom of the left first by equipping and empowering the baptized to be faithful in their vocations. One goal is to reeducate people who underestimate the importance of what they may merely call their "jobs" or "occupations," and lead them to see their work through the lens of *vocation.* A vocation is a call (Latin: *vocatio*) by God to serve him in a particular capacity for his glory (1 Pet 2:12) and for the good of others. Each Christian may have a number of vocations at the same time as part of different relationships, for example, as an employee or homemaker, husband or wife, father or mother, neighbor, citizen, and church member. A biblical understanding of vocation enables Christians to see their work in society as a way for them to express their love for God and for their neighbors, rather than envisioning the marketplace only as a place where wealth is accumulated.

The church has the divine mandate to proclaim the Gospel of Jesus Christ throughout the world and make disciples by baptizing in the triune name and by teaching all that Christ has commanded (Mt 28:19–20; Mk 16:16–20; Lk 24:45–48; Acts 1:1–8). As the church carries out this mission, it teaches and empowers those in Christ so that they can faithfully speak to current issues in the four vocational orders where God has placed them: marriage and family, work, public life, and the church.[11] As the members of Christ's body are nurtured and grow and mature, they make an impact on society through their public and private lives. Churches are called upon to educate and equip their laity to engage the world ethically in their respective vocations.[12] Benne calls this the "ethics of character."[13]

As the church heeds Amos' prophetic call for the people of God to channel his justice and righteousness into the world, there are at least three dangers. First, the church may expect to change the fallen world more than it can and may offer the world a false hope of utopia. Second, the church may neglect or abandon her true mission, which is the proclamation of the Gospel and administration of the Sacraments. Third, the church or Christians may simplistically take verses out of context and apply them to complex issues. This third danger

---

[11] Fredrickson, "Pauline Ethics," encourages Christian congregations to imitate St. Paul by shaping their members toward more ethical and just ways of living. For example, in Rom 13:8–14 the apostle instructs how the baptized are called upon to live in the public sphere.

[12] Benne writes: "Affecting people by catechetically and sacramentally affirming their identity in Christ is arguably the most fundamental and potentially the most effective way the church affects economic life" (*Reasonable Ethics*, 195).

[13] Benne, *Reasonable Ethics*, 197.

is especially important to bear in mind when citing passages about OT Israel, since it was both God's church and his state, whereas in the NT era, the kingdom of God cannot be equated with any government or nation (Lk 17:21; Rom 14:17).

By offering the hope and love and eternal life in Christ that already now belong to baptized believers, "the Lutheran vision leads to a nonutopian view of history that is not cynical."[14] The church works for relative victories while it prays for the consummation of the kingdom of God at the parousia, when it shall come to pass that "the kingdom of the world has become [the kingdom of] our Lord and of his Christ" (Rev 11:15). At the second coming of Christ, God will establish the new heavens and new earth and reign there among all his redeemed and risen people forever (Amos 9:13–15; also Is 65:17–25; Dan 12:2–3; Revelation 22). By anticipating that glorious future kingdom that God alone can and will establish, the church through its preaching, liturgy, and catechesis undercuts the morally ambiguous kingdom of this world and its pretentious estimation of itself. The church best confronts injustice in the world by being like her Lord: different than, but active in—not separate from—the world.

---

[14] Benne, *Reasonable Ethics*, 79.

Amos 5:18–20

The Day of Yahweh Is Darkness

Translation

5 [18]**Woe to those longing for the Day of Yahweh!**
What good is the Day of Yahweh for you?
It will be darkness and not light.
[19]**[It will be] just as if a man flees in fear from a lion,**
and a bear meets him,
or he enters the house and rests his hand upon the wall,
then a snake bites him.
[20]**Is not the Day of Yahweh darkness and not light,**
gloom without brightness?

Textual Notes

5:18 הוֹי הַמִּתְאַוִּים אֶת־יוֹם יְהוָה—The common interjection הוֹי, often signifying "woe," occurs in Amos in 5:18 and 6:1. It is a synonym of the rare הוֹ in 5:16. הוֹי is a characteristic feature of the genre of a "woe oracle," which is attested in the communal life of Israel.[1] Andersen and Freedman write: "The Woe is more than a warning or even [a] threat: it is an assurance, a promise, even an oath. They [the Israelites] are targeted, their days are numbered, and their execution is nigh."[2] In the context of Amos it might even mean that Israel was already spiritually dead, especially since 5:1–3 was a funeral lament as if the nation had already perished. הוֹי can be used to lament a death that has already taken place, as in, for example, הוֹי אָחִי (1 Ki 13:30; proleptic but similar is Jer 22:18).[3]

The woe interjection הוֹי is typically followed by a participle or noun that describes the malady of the person(s) being addressed. Here it is the Hithpael participle הַמִּתְאַוִּים of אָוָה I, whose Hithpael means "desire, long for" (BDB). It denotes a deep-rooted aspiration.[4] In the Piel, אָוָה I usually has as its subject the person's נֶפֶשׁ, "life, soul, being." This construction is used to say, for example, that the wicked desire evil (Prov 21:10),

---

[1] For the genre of the woe oracles, see Gerstenberger, "The Woe-Oracles of the Prophets." הוֹי appears almost exclusively in the Latter Prophets, with 1 Ki 13:30 as the only exception. Out of fifty-one occurrences in the OT, Isaiah uses it twenty-one times (e.g., Is 5:8, 11, 18, 20–22). However, it does not always signify "woe" or a warning. For example, in Is 55:1 הוֹי begins a Gospel invitation.

[2] Andersen and Freedman, *Amos*, 48.

[3] Clifford categorizes three uses of הוֹי in the OT: (1) to describe funeral laments; (2) to get attention; and (3) to introduce announcements of doom ("The Use of *Hôy* in the Prophets," 458). He places Amos 5:18 in the first category.

[4] Cf. G. Mayer, "אָוָה," *TDOT* 1:134–37.

while the believer desires Yahweh (Is 26:9). For the meaning of the verb see further the commentary.

The Hithpael sometimes takes the preposition לְ, but it can often take an accusative object; here it takes the direct object אֶת־י֣וֹם יְהוָ֑ה. The construct phrase י֣וֹם יְהוָ֑ה occurs in Amos only in 5:18 (twice) and 5:20 and elsewhere in the OT only in Is 13:6, 9; Ezek 13:5; Joel 1:15; 2:1, 11; 3:4 (ET 2:31); 4:14 (ET 3:14); Obad 15; Zeph 1:7, 14 (twice); and Mal 3:23 (ET 4:5). It is a possessive genitive, "Yahweh's Day," referring to the day on which Yahweh manifests himself by acting decisively in human history. See further the commentary.

לָ֥מָּה־זֶּ֛ה לָכֶ֖ם י֣וֹם יְהוָ֑ה—This idiomatic question (see BDB, s.v. מָה, 4 d) has the interrogative לָ֫מָּה; the demonstrative pronoun זֶה (with conjunctive *daghesh*, זֶּ֛ה־), which strengthens the question (BDB, s.v. זֶה, 4 e); and the preposition לְ in the sense of a dative of advantage (BDB, s.v. לְ, 5 g (*b*)): literally, "what is this for you (for your benefit), the Day of Yahweh?" It means "what good is the Day of Yahweh for you?" (see NKJV). A similar question is posed by Rebekah in Gen 27:46: she loathes her life because of her Hittite daughters-in-law and asks, לָ֥מָּה לִּ֖י חַיִּֽים, "what good for me is life?" Many English translations assume that the question in Amos 5:18 asks about the reason for the desire in the preceding clause, for example, "why do you long for the day of the Lord?" (NIV; similar is NRSV).

הוּא־חֹ֖שֶׁךְ וְלֹא־אֽוֹר׃—The personal pronoun הוּא refers back to יוֹם in י֣וֹם יְהוָ֑ה in the preceding two clauses. "It [the day] (will be) darkness and not light." Gen 1:2–5 uses the same nouns, יוֹם, חֹשֶׁךְ, and אוֹר, but there God caused the "light" to shine out from the "darkness," separated them, called the light "good," and thus created the first "day." Here the "day" reverses creation, and instead of bringing "light," it brings "darkness." See the same vocabulary in 5:20. לֹא is used here to negate the substantival predicate אוֹר (GKC, § 152 d).

5:19 כַּאֲשֶׁ֨ר יָנ֥וּס אִישׁ֙ מִפְּנֵ֣י הָאֲרִ֔י—The Qal of נוּס is also in 2:16 and 9:1; in both verses it refers to fleeing from mortal danger in battle at the time of divine judgment. Here the mortal danger is posed by אֲרִי, a "lion," the same noun used also in 3:12. As with the synonym אַרְיֵה in 3:4, 8, and with אֲרִי in 3:12, here too the comparison to a "lion" points to Yahweh as the real danger menacing his unfaithful people. Besides the nouns for "lion" in 3:4, 8, 12; 5:19, the verb שָׁאַג, "roar" (1:2; 3:4, 8) is a leonine depiction of or allusion to Yahweh.

The article on הָאֲרִ֔י is used with the noun to refer to an indefinite, undefined person or thing (BDB, s.v. הַ, 1 d; GKC, § 126 q–r), hence "*a* lion." The same kind of article is on הַדֹּ֑ב, "*a* bear," and הַנָּחָשׁ, "*a* snake," in subsequent clauses of 5:19.

The combination מִפְּנֵי (the preposition מִן and the plural of פָּנֶה) often has a causal meaning, "because of, for fear of" (BDB, s.v. פָּנֶה, II 6 a), which justifies the translation "flees *in fear from* a lion."

וּפְגָע֖וֹ הַדֹּ֑ב—The Qal of פָּגַע is the first in a series of four perfect verbs with *waw* consecutive (וּפְגָעוֹ ... וּבָא ... וְסָמַךְ ... וּנְשָׁכוֹ ...) that follow the imperfect יָנוּס in the preceding clause. The perfect *waw* consecutive verbs all denote actions subsequent to the imperfect: the man *first* flees (יָנוּס) from the lion, *then* a bear confronts him (וּפְגָעוֹ); or if after fleeing the lion, he *then* enters a house and *next* rests his hand on the wall

(וְסָמַךְ ... וּבָא), *finally* the snake bites him (וּנְשָׁכוֹ). See GKC, § 112 m (α), and Joüon, § 119 q.

The Qal of פָּגַע indicates movement and can mean to "*meet*" (BDB, 1) or "*encounter* with hostility" (BDB, 3).[5] The pronominal suffix (וֹ-) refers back to אִישׁ, the fleeing "man." The OT refers to bears (דֹּב) that inhabited Israel and sometimes attacked people (2 Ki 2:24; cf. 2 Sam 17:8; Prov 17:12). As a shepherd, David fended off both lions and bears (1 Sam 17:34–37). Like a "lion" (Amos 3:4, 8, 12; 5:19), a "bear" (דֹּב) too can be used as a metaphor (Lam 3:10) or in a simile (Hos 13:8) for Yahweh attacking in judgment. The encounter with the bear here is no accident of nature; rather, it is the deliberate execution of divine judgment, as also in 2 Ki 2:24.

In the eschatological new creation, the "bear" will be harmless after the Shoot from the stump of Jesse has established enduring peace between God and redeemed humanity (Is 11:1–7).

וּבָא הַבַּיִת וְסָמַךְ יָדוֹ עַל־הַקִּיר—The fleeing man now enters (perfect of בּוֹא) a house (the article on הַבַּיִת may indicate "*his* house") and "rests" (וְסָמַךְ) his hand on the house's "wall" (קִיר, not a city wall, חוֹמָה).

וּנְשָׁכוֹ הַנָּחָשׁ׃—The Qal of נָשַׁךְ often means "to bite"[6] as also in 9:3, where again its subject is נָחָשׁ, a "snake, serpent." Other OT passages refer to the bite of a serpent (e.g., Gen 49:17; Num 21:6–9; Jer 8:17). Only in Micah 3:5 do people "bite" (נָשַׁךְ): the deceitful prophets who falsely announce "peace" are "biting [God's faithful people] with their teeth."

The noun נָחָשׁ, "snake, serpent," first appears in the OT referring to the devil in the fall narrative in Genesis 3, where it was the craftiest creature (Gen 3:1).[7] The serpent is a master at hiding in camouflage and striking suddenly (Gen 49:17). The bite of venomous snakes can be fatal, as was the devil's deception of Eve. In some contexts, נָחָשׁ is synonymous with other serpentine terms for Satan, including לִוְיָתָן, "Leviathan" (Is 27:1). Rev 12:9 and 20:2 identify "the serpent" (ὁ ὄφις) as "the dragon," "the devil," and "Satan." In Revelation 12 he seeks to destroy the woman who first represents OT Israel; then the Virgin Mary; then the NT church, the bride of Christ. God can preserve victims of snakebite from death (Num 21:7–9; Deut 8:14–15; Mk 16:17–18; Jn 3:14–15; Acts 28:3–6). The promise of Rom 16:20 is that God will soon crush Satan under the feet of Christ's disciples.

Here, as in Num 21:6 and Amos 9:3, the serpent is Yahweh's agent of righteous judgment. Compare 1 Cor 5:5 and 1 Tim 1:20, where St. Paul refers to delivering impenitent sinners over to Satan—probably via excommunication—to attempt to move them to repentance, lest they perish eternally.

In Amos' sequence of divine judgment in 5:19, the serpent is the last enemy, and even if the fleeing man is able to escape the preceding dangers, he will not be able to avoid the serpent's fatal bite. In 9:2–4 the "serpent" is the danger in the fourth (9:3) of

---

5 Cf. P. Maiberger, "פָּגַע," *TDOT* 11:470–76.

6 Cf. A. S. Kapelrud, "נָשַׁךְ," *TDOT* 10:61–65.

7 Cf. H.-J. Fabry, "נָחָשׁ," *TDOT* 9:356–69.

five possible scenarios, and the point of the whole passage (9:2–4) is the same as that of 5:19: a person might be able to avoid one kind or agent of punishment, but in the end, Yahweh will still bring him into judgment. Compare Is 14:29, an oracle against Philistia, where the oppressor meets a sequence of a serpent (נָחָשׁ), an adder, and a flying fiery serpent.

5:20 הֲלֹא־חֹשֶׁךְ יוֹם יְהוָה וְלֹא־אוֹר—The compound of the interrogative -הֲ and the negative לֹא introduces a question that expects an answer in the affirmative (BDB, s.v. לֹא, 4 b). The noun חֹשֶׁךְ, the construct phrase יוֹם יְהוָה, and the negated predicate וְלֹא־אוֹר are all repeated from 5:18.

וְאָפֵל וְלֹא־נֹגַהּ לוֹ׃—The adjective אָפֵל, "gloomy" (BDB), is used as a substantive, "gloom." It occurs only here in the OT but is attested in Rabbinic Hebrew meaning "dark" (Jastrow). The OT attests cognates including אֹפֶל and אֲפֵלָה, which appears in the covenant curse of Deut 28:29: the covenant-breaker will grope around at noon like a blind man groping in "gloom." The LXX translates אָפֵל as γνόφος, "thick darkness," used for the Sinai theophany in Heb 12:18. Compare ζόφος in Heb 12:18; 2 Pet 2:4, 17; Jude 6, 13. The phrase וְלֹא־נֹגַהּ לוֹ, uses לְ for possession (see BDB, s.v. לְ, 5 b (*a*)): literally, "and no brightness belonging to it."

Commentary

A Day That Is Night (5:18–20)

Yahweh again announces the complete reversal of what is expected.[8] "The Day of Yahweh" will not be a bright "day" at all, but rather a night of judgment. It will be darkness at noonday. Even if a person manages to escape one form of judgment, another will come, ending in the serpent's fatal bite. All of this will fall upon the Israelites because they had turned eschatology into escapism. They thought the Day of Yahweh was no reason to repent and seek Yahweh (as he pleaded for them to do in 5:4, 6, 14). For them it had become a mirage, an illusion, a day in which Yahweh would come, vindicate the nation's false religious hopes, prosper its endeavors, and make all its delusions come true. Yahweh announces the harsh reality: it will be a day of darkness and not light.

God employs a woe oracle, a rhetorical question, and a gripping simile to shock his audience out of their lukewarm indifference (cf. Rev 3:16). Who was his audience? The book as a whole is aimed especially at the apostate Northern Kingdom of Israel (e.g., 2:6–16), although it also encompasses unfaithful Judah (2:4–5) and representatives from the Gentile nations that comprise the rest of humanity (1:3–2:3). Instead of seeking Yahweh in faith at his temple in Jerusalem, people were worshiping in syncretistic shrines at other locations (e.g., 4:4–5; 5:5). Elsewhere Amos targets Israel's government officials who were making a killing—literally—to store up ill-gotten gain (3:11); legal experts who turned justice into wormwood and threw righteousness to the ground (5:7); tradesmen who trampled the poor and needy (2:7; 8:4); and

---

[8] A dramatic reversal is also present in 2:9; 3:1–2; 4:4–5; 5:21–27; 6:1–7; 8:9–10; 9:11–15.

the priest Amaziah, representing the clergy who served the false royal theology and enforced the status quo rather than serving the true God (7:10–17). In short, these Israelites abused other members of the covenant people, "small" Jacob (7:2, 5), and deluded themselves into thinking that "the evil will not overtake nor confront us" (9:10).

The day of judgment that would come on northern Israel in 722 BC anticipates the similar judgment on Judah in 587 BC. It also anticipates the destruction of Jerusalem and the permanent end of the temple in AD 70, and finally Judgment Day, when Christ will come again. The warning for ancient Israel is reiterated for all humanity throughout the Scriptures by their depiction of the eschatological "day." Judgment Day will come, and none shall escape. "The *day* of the Lord will come like a thief in the *night*" (1 Thess 5:2), and "the sun shall be turned into darkness" (Acts 2:20, quoting Joel 3:4 [ET 2:31]). It will be a day of lamentation and death for all unbelievers (cf. Amos 5:16–17).

Yet there is hope. The darkness on the day of judgment in 5:18–20 points toward Good Friday, when the sum total of divine judgment for humanity's sin was suffered by Jesus Christ on the cross. The day turned into night for three hours as darkness reclaimed the earth and creation came undone (Mk 15:33; cf. Gen 1:2). But when it was finished (Jn 19:30), pardon on Judgment Day had been secured for all believers, with the promise of unending day (Rev 21:23–25).

The Gospel "day(s)" in Amos 9:11, 13 are the flip side of the dark day of judgment. Easter is the day of resurrection, fulfilling the promise in Amos 9:11. Christ's atonement has opened paradise to all believers (Lk 23:43; Rev 2:7). "Days are coming" (Amos 9:13) when they shall enjoy the miraculous bounty of the new creation, the paradise in the new heavens and new earth that will be the dwelling place of the redeemed forever after they are raised to everlasting life. Therefore each "Lord's day" (Rev 1:10), and indeed every day when God's Word is heard or read, is a day calling for repentance and faith in anticipation of the final day (Heb 3:7–4:7).[9]

In his influential book *He That Cometh*, Sigmund Mowinckel argues that for the OT books, the term "eschatology" should only be applied to Daniel and other apocalyptic works, though the beginnings of it can be traced back to Isaiah 40–66. He, therefore, understands texts like Amos 5:18 merely to promise a theophanic intervention of Yahweh.[10] Yet Amos contains the following elements that support a fully eschatological interpretation of "the Day of Yahweh": (1) the threat of imminent judgment (e.g., 1:14; 2:6–8); (2) the promise of life and restoration by God's grace (e.g., 5:4, 6, 14–15; 9:11–15); and (3) the reign of the Davidic King, the Messiah (9:11), who is the source of restor-

---

[9] Longman and Reid, *God Is a Warrior*, 91–192, trace the OT theme of "the Day of Yahweh" into the NT. The key texts they cite include Mt 12:28; 24:29–31; Mk 13:24–27; Lk 10:18; 21:25–28; 1 Cor 15:24–27; Col 2:14–15; and Rev 19:11–21.

[10] Mowinckel, *He That Cometh*, 125–54.

ing grace and life. Related phrases about a "day" or "days" that declare similar or related eschatological theology in Amos are 1:14; 2:16; 3:14; 4:2; 6:3; 8:3, 9, 10, 11, 13; 9:11, 13. All except those in 9:11, 13 are in contexts that speak of a day of judgment, when Yahweh will manifest his wrath because of the people's sin in violation of his Law. The noteworthy Gospel exceptions are in the salvation oracle in 9:11–15.

It is now a consensus among most scholars that "the Day of Yahweh" encapsulates OT eschatology.[11] The day is eschatological "in the sense of an end of the present world order which can either be within the flow of history or, in an absolute and final sense, at the end of all history."[12]

The Day of Yahweh (5:18)

Apostate Israel was trying to keep God the Judge at a safe distance. The people's mantra was "the Lion must remain caged!" as they tried to silence his prophets (cf. 2:12; 7:10–17), but the Lion roars anyway (1:2; 3:4, 8, 12; cf. 5:19). Recall that in 4:4–5, Yahweh ridiculed the Israelites' worship practices, which were not according to the Torah; he called the gifts they offered at idolatrous shrines "*your* sacrifices" and "*your* tithes," which "*you* love to do" instead of loving God or neighbor. It appears as though the last thing Israel wanted or expected in worship was to encounter their God on *his* terms, but now they will meet him (4:12)! It will be a day of darkness and not light.

The unfaithful Israelites yearning for Yahweh to intervene probably included leaders who wanted to entrench themselves even further in power to stifle all opposition, and also those less fortunate who were being abused and wanted their chance to be on top and take their revenge against their oppressors. Yet all of those motivated by the quest for power, prestige, and vengeance were wrong. Their expectations about this day are completely the opposite of what they will experience on it.

The woe cry of the mourning people predicted in 5:16–17 is the result of God's declaration of "woe" (5:18), which is a frequent genre marker in prophetic literature.[13] Central to the sighs of mourning was the Hebrew cry הוֹי, usually translated "woe," "ah," or "alas." Much like church bells tolling to announce a funeral, when someone cried out, "Woe" (הוֹי), in Israel, one would immediately ask, "Who has died?" For the Israelites listening to Amos, the answer is "*You*!" When Amos announced a "woe," the effect was comparable to the audi-

---

[11] E.g., Hoffman, "The Day of the Lord as a Concept and a Term in the Prophetic Literature."

[12] Hasel, "The Alleged 'No' of Amos and Amos' Eschatology," 3.

[13] Sweeney, *Isaiah 1–39*, 543, reviews the debates regarding the genre's origin and cites the most important secondary literature. Woe oracles may appear as individual units, as are the only two in Amos (5:18; 6:1), or in clusters, for example, Is 5:8–24; Isaiah 28–33; Hab 2:6–20. Amos is the earliest prophet to use הוֹי in a woe oracle (as recognized by, e.g., Williams, "The Alas-Oracles of the Eighth Century Prophets," 88, and Janzen, *Mourning Cry and Woe Oracle*, 84), although later in the eighth century, Isaiah uses it often.

ence hearing its death announced on a news broadcast or reading their names in the obituary column of the newspaper.

Amos is refuting a view widely held among the unfaithful Israelites that "the Day of Yahweh" would usher in more of Yahweh's blessings. His prophetic discourse, once again, takes a positive popular opinion and turns it upside down.[14] Contrary to Israel's deceptive theology of success and prosperity, Yahweh's arrival will not be a day of national victory and celebration but a night of horrific disaster and defeat. Amos opposes "popular eschatology" by presenting "Yahwistic eschatology, in which the divine demands count and the divine-human relationships are at the center, transforming and shaping all inter-human relationships."[15] The eschatological "day" will bring judgment upon all those who were abusing fellow members of God's people (as detailed throughout Amos) and who were visiting the syncretistic shrines in the vain hope of thereby securing God's favor.[16]

Blinded by their boundless optimism, the Israelites were oblivious to the clouds of wrath that were swiftly gathering all around them (6:14; 9:10). God's prophet, however, is not bedazzled or beguiled by the apparent success of the nation's economic, political, and religious state of affairs. He is well aware of the toxic waste that lays buried directly underneath Israel's faltering foundation and that this waste will soon destroy the land.

Amos announces "woe to those longing for [הַמִּתְאַוִּים] the Day of Yahweh" (5:18). While the verb (the Hithpael of אָוָה) can express holy desire (Ps 45:12 [ET 45:11]) or understandable longing (e.g., 2 Sam 23:15), most often it refers to sinful coveting or craving (e.g., Deut 5:21; Prov 13:4; 21:26; 23:3, 6). Num 11:4–34 documents how the Israelites "longed for" the food they had enjoyed in Egypt and desired to return there rather than continue in the salvation God had accomplished for them through the exodus (cf. also Ex 16:2–3). Amos 5:18 uses the same verb (the Hithpael of אָוָה) that appears in Num 11:4, 34 (also Ps 106:14) describing the longing or craving of the people, who were punished by death. In fact, Num 11:34 uses the identical participle used in Amos 5:18 as well as a cognate noun:

> He called the name of that place Kibroth-hatta'avah ["the graves of *longing*"] because there they buried the people *who were longing* [הַמִּתְאַוִּים].

Just as Israel yearned to return to Egypt, so the Israelites at the time of Amos longed for the Day of Yahweh because of what they thought it would

---

[14] In addition to 5:18–20, Amos has dramatic reversals in 2:9; 3:1–2; 4:4–5; 5:21–27; 6:1–7; 8:9–10; 9:11–15. Stuart, *Hosea–Jonah*, 354, writes:

> Like the student who receives an "F" for a paper he thought was brilliant, or the employee fired after doing what he thought was excellent work, or the person whose spouse suddenly announces that he or she wants a divorce when the marriage seemed to be going so well, the Israelites were undoubtedly stunned by such a reversal of their expectations.

[15] Hasel, "The Alleged 'No' of Amos and Amos' Eschatology," 18.

[16] For condemnations of Israel's false worship, see the commentary on 2:7–8; 3:14; 4:4–5; 5:5–6, 14, 21–27; 7:9–17; 8:5, 10, 14; 9:1.

bring them. In both cases the desires were sinful, and in both cases the nation was judged. The Day of Yahweh came upon northern Israel about four decades after the time of Amos, when it was conquered by Assyria in 722 BC. Then the southern kingdom of Judah fell to Babylon in 587 BC. Shortly later, almost two centuries after the time of Amos, a band of Judeans who had abducted Jeremiah returned to Egypt (Jer 41:16–43:13) only to face sword, famine, and plague (Jer 42:17, 22). Israel ceased to exist as a nation, at least for a time, as darkness hung over the promised land.

The ninth of the ten plagues on Egypt was darkness (Ex 10:21–29), which was visible evidence of divine judgment (e.g., Is 13:10; Joel 2:10; Mt 27:45). Then the climactic tenth plague, the death of the firstborn, took place under cover of darkness (Ex 11:4–5; 12:12, 29–31, 42). The exodus narrative (Ex 14:19–21) and covenant at Sinai (Ex 20:21; Deut 5:22–23) both include the motif of theophany in darkness. The first theophany in darkness was terrifying for the Egyptians (Ex 14:19–21) and the second one terrified Israel (Ex 20:21; Deut 5:22–23). The Law of Moses also included the covenant curse of groping at noon as if in complete darkness (Deut 28:29). Darkness could mean only one thing for the apostate Israelites: they were under God's curse for breaking his covenant. What is more, they were as accursed as the Egyptians (see also Amos 4:10; 5:17).

"Darkness" (חֹשֶׁךְ) is common feature in "the Day of Yahweh" texts.[17] By repeating the phraseology of "darkness and not light" in 5:18, 20, Amos creates an inclusio that emphasizes darkness as part of Yahweh's judgment (see also 8:9). "The truth is that the Day of the Lord will be the Night of the Lord."[18] The Day of Yahweh will bring a return to the chaos described in Gen 1:2:

> And the earth was formless and void, and *darkness* was upon the face of the deep.
>
> וְהָאָרֶץ הָיְתָה תֹהוּ וָבֹהוּ וְחֹשֶׁךְ עַל־פְּנֵי תְהוֹם

Jeremiah has this same idea in mind in his "chaos vision" in Jer 4:23–26. In Jer 4:23 he writes: "I looked at the earth, and behold, it was formless and void; [I looked] to the heavens, and their light did not exist" (וְאֵין אוֹרָם). Jeremiah searches for light only to find darkness (see also Jer 13:16).

Origen comments on Amos 5:18:

> Perhaps we will understand what has been written if we deal with a Gospel text spoken by the Savior, which expresses it in this way: "Work while it is day. The night comes when no one can work" [Jn 9:4]. … He has called this age the day, but the darkness and the night the consummation because of punishments. For "why do you desire the Day of the Lord? And it is darkness and

[17] See, for example, Is 13:9–10 (which uses the cognate verb חָשַׁךְ, "to be dark"); Joel 2:1–2; Zeph 1:15. In, for example, Is 9:1 (ET 9:2) and Job 18:6, darkness "symbolizes danger, hidden things that one cannot see, an absence of safety, and no divine protection" (Smith, *Hosea, Amos, Micah*, 324). Contrast Ps 27:1.

[18] Andersen and Freedman, *Amos*, 57.

not light," says the prophet Amos [5:18]. If you can envision after the consummation of the world what the gloom is, a gloom that pursues nearly all of the race of humans who are punished for sins. The atmosphere will become dark at that time, and no longer can anyone ever give glory to God, since the Word has given orders to the righteous, saying, "Go, my people, enter into your rooms, shut the door, hide yourself for a little season, until the force of my anger has passed away" [Is 26:20].[19]

Amos and Joel probably are the oldest OT books that include the phrase "the Day of Yahweh."[20] Amos uses "the Day of Yahweh" three times within the three verses of 5:18–20. Other prophets also use closely related expressions, including "the day of vengeance (for Yahweh/our God)" (יוֹם נָקָם, Is 34:8; 61:2; 63:4); "the day of Yahweh's anger" (יוֹם אַף־יְהוָה, Zeph 2:2–3; Lam 2:22); "the day of the burning of his anger" (יוֹם חֲרוֹן אַפּוֹ, Is 13:13; Lam 1:12); and "the day belonging to Yahweh" (יוֹם לַיהוָה, Is 2:12; Ezek 30:3; 46:13).[21]

Scholars have debated the possible settings and origin of the prophetic "Day of Yahweh" genre, but such investigations have ironically yielded about as much darkness as light.[22] Von Rad, who has been particularly influential, cites as the foundational text Isaiah 13.[23] The oracle against Babylon heads Isaiah's oracles against the nations (Isaiah 13–23), and chapter 13 describes judgment in general, universalistic terms, as also does the oracle against Tyre, which ends the section (Isaiah 23). The "Day of Yahweh" (Is 13:6, 9) is a day of darkness (Is 13:10; cf. Amos 5:18, 20). On this day, Yahweh will come in person to fight, and his enemies will lose heart, and their courage will fail (Is 13:7–8; cf. Ex 15:14–16; Josh 2:9, 24). This day also exhibits cosmic changes: the stars will darken (Is 13:10), and the earth will shake (Is 13:13). The slaughter will be terrible (Is 13:14–22).

Von Rad states that "the Day of Yahweh encompasses … the rise of Yahweh against his enemies, his battle and his victory."[24] This day is much like "the day of Jezreel" (יוֹם יִזְרְעֶאל, Hos 2:2 [ET 1:11]), "the day of Midian" (יוֹם מִדְיָן, Is 9:3 [ET 9:4]), "the day of Egypt" (יוֹם מִצְרַיִם, Ezek 30:9), and "the day of Jerusalem" (יוֹם יְרוּשָׁלָםִ, Ps 137:7). Each of these refers to a time when Yahweh will execute a decisive defeat of the named enemy. Hence "the Day of Yahweh" is like saying "the *battle* of Yahweh" (cf. "the battles of Yahweh" in Num 21:14;

---

[19] Origen, *Homilies on Jeremiah*, 12, quoted in Ferreiro, *The Twelve Prophets*, ACCS 14:102.

[20] "The Day of Yahweh" appears in Amos in 5:18 (twice), 20. The other OT texts that include it are Is 13:6, 9; Ezek 13:5; Joel 1:15; 2:1, 11; 3:4 (ET 2:31); 4:14 (ET 3:14); Obad 15; Zeph 1:7, 14 (twice); and Mal 3:23 (ET 4:5).

[21] Cf. Weiss, "The Origin of the 'Day of the Lord'—Reconsidered," especially his charts following page 60.

[22] For a survey of various views, see van Leeuwen, "The Prophecy of the *Yōm YHWH* in Amos v 18–20." See also von Rad, "The Origin of the Concept of the Day of Yahweh"; Weiss, "The Origin of the 'Day of the Lord'—Reconsidered"; Barstad, *The Religious Polemics of Amos*, 89–110; Wolff, *Joel and Amos*, 255; Mays *Amos*, 103–5; and Paul, *Amos*, 182–84.

[23] Von Rad, "The Origin of the Concept of the Day of Yahweh," 99–100.

[24] Von Rad, "The Origin of the Concept of the Day of Yahweh," 103.

1 Sam 18:17; 25:28). From narratives such as Exodus 14; Joshua 6–8; Judges 5–7; and 1 Samuel 15, the Israelites to whom Amos preached would have known what had happen on days of Yahweh in the past. Israel's longing for the Day of Yahweh was a desire for Yahweh to appear in order to defeat the nation's enemies. The irony is that apostate Israel herself had become God's enemy!

No Escape (5:19)

This night will be a time of no escape (cf. Jer 48:44). There will be nowhere to run and nowhere to hide. Amos expresses one of his common themes: the inescapability of Yahweh's judgment.[25] He does this by means of a simile that portrays one catastrophe after another. Any appearance of escape is really the assurance of disaster (cf. 9:3). The sequence of events is "out of the frying pan and into the fire." And although the text portrays a single person on the run, the individual figure stands for all of unfaithful Israel (cf. 3:12; 5:1).

In the OT, attacks from lions and bears usually were fatal.[26] The snake's bite was not only dangerous, but throughout the OT, encounters with snakes were almost always deadly.[27] Harm from wild beasts was a fulfillment of a covenant curse (Lev 26:22; Deut 32:24). This is reflected in Yahweh's words in Ezek 14:21: "For thus says the Lord Yahweh: 'How much worse will it be when I send against Jerusalem my four terrible judgments: sword and famine and evil beasts [וְחַיָּ֣ה רָעָ֔ה] and plague.' "

The point in Amos 5:19 is that the unbelieving people's safety was an illusion, and it was temporary. The man thought he had escaped once and surely would be delivered the next time. On the contrary, he will be bitten precisely in the moment he feels the most secure. Even if Israel felt safe now, disaster was waiting in the wings. The nation was going to fall and never rise again (Amos 5:2). Ultimately, it would be the people's rejection of their Messiah that would lead to the destruction of the temple in AD 70 and the permanent end of the earthly nation (Matthew 23).

St. Paul states it this way in his admonition "let he who thinks he stands watch out lest he fall" (1 Cor 10:12). In 1 Cor 9:24–27 the apostle indicates that he does everything he can to fight such illusionary contentment. He uses the colorful word ὑπωπιάζω, literally, "to hit under the eye," to describe what he does to control his body (as if, in a mixed metaphor, he gives his whole body a black eye) and bring it into bondage (δουλαγωγῶ), so that he would not be disqualified (ἀδόκιμος) from salvation by losing faith in the very Gospel he preached (1 Cor 9:27). Such apostasy was part of Israel's history, as Amos knew, and as Paul outlines in 1 Cor 10:1–13. The sacramental language in 1 Cor 10:1–5 connects the exodus redemption with Holy Baptism and the Lord's Supper; Israel had received the same salvation in Christ that we receive through God's Word

---

[25] See also, for example, 2:14–16; 9:1–4.

[26] See, for example, 2 Ki 2:24; Hos 13:7–8 (cf. 1 Sam 17:34–37).

[27] See, for example, Gen 3:1–19; Num 21:6–9; Jer 8:17; Amos 9:3.

and Sacraments.[28] The apostle's sober admonition in 1 Cor 10:12 is based on the recognition that the baptized and communicant Christian can fall into disbelief and judgment in the same way that Israel had.

Luther comments:

> *As if a man fled from the face of a lion* [Amos 5:19]. Now He [the Lord] is threatening a terrible death to those despisers. It is as if He were saying: "Go ahead! Completely despise the Word of the Lord! You are secure. You think that it will not come to pass that you will fall into the coming evil. But that is why it will be impossible for you not to be destroyed, as it is impossible for a man to escape who flees from a lion and meets a bear. Therefore you will be unable to escape. When you become confident that you are going to get away, you run into the midst of evil. I will remove all of your protection."[29]

Again, the Day of Yahweh Will Be Darkness (5:20)

Darkness and gloom are creation undone. A person groping around in the darkness reenacts the ninth plague against Egypt (Ex 10:21–29) and indicates fulfillment of a Pentateuchal covenant curse upon the apostate people. Deut 28:29 warns: "at noonday you will grope about like a blind man [יְמַשֵּׁשׁ הָעִוֵּר]." Smith writes:

> Amos is against any slanted view of God that deceptively reimagines God as a loving power who will pour out his blessings on his people regardless of their behavior. God is a warrior who will wipe out all evil—both the abhorrent idolatry of pagans and the rebellious sinfulness of his own people.[30]

Summary

"The Day of Yahweh" is a recurring theme in the prophets (e.g., Is 2:6–22; Joel 2:1–11). Yahweh will punish apostate Israel and also judge the nations. But all who have repented and called upon Yahweh's name in faith will be saved, for there shall be a saved remnant of believers from Israel (Amos 5:15; 9:11) and from the Gentile nations (Amos 9:12; see also Joel 3:5 [ET 2:32]; Acts 2, especially Acts 2:21). The books of Ezekiel and Zephaniah unfold in this three-part action: judgment upon Israel (Ezekiel 1–24; Zephaniah 1); judgment upon the nations (Ezekiel 25–32; Zephaniah 2); and restoration for the faithful remnant saved by grace alone (Ezekiel 33–48; Zephaniah 3).

Amos indicates that Israel's theology and practices had become unjust and unrighteous. This was why the Day of Yahweh would be "darkness and not light" (5:18, 20). The covenant of salvation Israel had received in the past was no guarantee of future security since the nation had broken the Sinai covenant. Amos proclaims, "You had better think again before longing for Yahweh to

---

[28] See Lockwood, *1 Corinthians*, 321–27.

[29] Luther, "Lectures on Amos" (AE 18:164).

[30] Smith, *Hosea, Amos, Micah*, 330.

appear and settle matters of right and wrong. In order to eliminate evil he will eliminate *you*, because *you* are evil!"

Imagery of light and darkness is often prominent in theophanic texts. Some of these passages (e.g., Deut 33:2–3, 26–29; Hab 3:3–15; Ps 68:8–9, 33–36 [ET 68:7–8, 32–35]) feature Yahweh as the military defender of his faithful people and the bringer of rain and fertility. But Amos warns that Yahweh's theophany from his temple on Zion will be to act as Israel's enemy and the harbinger of drought (Amos 1:2).

Paul notes that Amos' rhetoric in 5:18–20 repeats the syllable *lo*, usually in the negative לֹא ("no, not, without") and once in a prepositional phrase (לוֹ, "[belonging] to it").[31] The last two, וְלֹא־נֹגַהּ לוֹ, literally, "and no brightness (belonging) to it," are combined in the translation "without brightness." The uses of *lo* are, in order:

- "And *not* light" (וְלֹא־אוֹר, 5:18)
- "Is *not*" (הֲלֹא, 5:20)
- "And *not* light" (וְלֹא־אוֹר, 5:20)
- "And *no* brightness" (וְלֹא־נֹגַהּ, 5:20)
- "*To it*" (לוֹ, 5:20)

By means of this fivefold *lo*, Amos, in staccato-like fashion, creates a cumulative auditory effort that announces Yahweh's "no" upon Israel. The coming day will be like the plagues of 4:6–11, and for the impenitent apostates there will be no escape (see also 2:14–16; 9:1–4).

The only hope for Israel and for that matter for all people is Yahweh's final word to mankind: his incarnate Word, Jesus (Jn 1:14; Rev 19:13). God's gracious yes in the Gospel of Jesus Christ (cf. 2 Cor 1:20–21) justifies all believers and removes from them the no of the Law's condemnation (Rom 8:1). It is with an OT prophetic depiction of this Gospel that Amos concludes his book (9:11–15), and it is with a vision of the consummation of that prophetic promise that God concludes the entire Scriptures (Revelation 21–22).

---

[31] Paul, *Amos*, 186–87.

Amos 5:21–27

Yahweh Hates Faithless Worship

Translation

5 21“I hate, I reject your festivals.
I do not delight in the sacrificial smell of your sacred assemblies.
22For if you offer up to me your whole burnt offerings and your grain offerings,
I will not accept [them].
And the peace offering of your fatted calves
I will not gaze upon.
23Remove from me the din of your songs,
and the music of your lutes I will not hear.
24“But let justice roll like the waters,
and righteousness like an ever-flowing wadi.
25“Sacrifices and grain offering did you bring near to me in the wilderness for forty years,
O house of Israel?
26You took up Sikkuth, your king,
and Kiyyun, your images,
your star gods,
which you made for yourselves.
27So I will exile you beyond Damascus,”
says Yahweh, whose name is the God of armies.

Textual Notes

5:21 שָׂנֵאתִי מָאַסְתִּי חַגֵּיכֶם—The two Qal perfect verbs have a “quasi-stative meaning” that expresses a state of mind (Joüon, § 112 a) and are best translated in the present tense: “I hate” and “I reject” (GKC, § 106 g). Their syntactic relationship is asyndeton, with no conjunction (*waw*) connecting them. These two verbs are not juxtaposed in this way anywhere else in the OT. The staccato asyndetic syntax increases the emotion of the “impassioned description” (GKC, § 154 a, note 1, (a)). שָׂנֵאתִי could be translated adverbially, modifying מָאַסְתִּי as the main verb: “I reject with utter hatred.”[1]

In legal contexts שָׂנֵא indicates that the relationship has ended. For example, Yahweh in Mal 1:3 recalls how he chose Jacob for the line of the messianic promise but וְאֶת־עֵשָׂו שָׂנֵאתִי, “Esau I hated” (cf. Jer 12:8). In marriage contexts, שָׂנֵא, “to hate,” implies a cessation or rejection of the conjugal relationship (e.g., Deut 22:13–16; 24:3; cf. 2 Sam 13:15; Ezek 16:37). By means of this verb in Amos 5:21, Yahweh indicates that his gracious relationship with Israel is ending (“the end is coming,” Amos

[1] Niehaus, “Amos,” 431.

8:2), although he will promise messianic restoration in the coming "day" and "days" (9:11–15).

The verb מָאַס, "to reject," also implies the termination of a relationship.[2] Either Yahweh or people may serve as the subject. Because Israel rejected Yahweh (2 Ki 17:15), he rejected them (2 Ki 17:20). This verb conveys Yahweh's exasperation and revulsion over Israel's worship practices. Its antonym is בָּחַר, "to choose" by grace. Yahweh chose Israel purely out of his love (Deut 7:7). Now because of the people's infidelity, he is severing this relationship so they no longer will be beneficiaries of his Mosaic covenant promises.

The noun חַג, "festival, feast,"[3] can refer to any of Israel's three pilgrimage festivals provided in the Torah: (1) Passover and Unleavened Bread, celebrating Israel's deliverance from Egypt and held at the beginning of the barley harvest; (2) Weeks or Pentecost, held seven weeks later during the wheat harvest; and (3) Booths or Tabernacles, the celebration of Yahweh's gracious provisions during Israel's forty-year wilderness wanderings and held at the time of the grape and olive harvests (see, e.g., Ex 23:14–16; 34:18, 22, 25). חַג may also denote the "festal sacrifice" itself (e.g., Ex 23:18; Mal 2:3; Ps 118:27).

The description and terminology in Amos 5:21–23 indicate that the northern Israelites were imitating the worship practices Yahweh had instituted in the Torah, but they had adulterated their worship with idolatry. This is also the picture in 4:4–5. The plural of חַג here refers to "*religious* feasts" (NIV; emphasis added), but ones not celebrated in faith according to the Torah.

וְלֹא אָרִיחַ בְּעַצְּרֹתֵיכֶם׃—The Hiphil of רִיחַ means "to smell, perceive an odor," and the preposition בְּ is sometimes attached to what is smelled (Ex 30:38; Lev 26:31). The LXX (οὐ μὴ ὀσφρανθῶ) and the KJV translate the clause here in Amos 5:21 literally, "I will not smell," but that misses the connotation of delight and favor, which is reflected in the translation above: "I do not delight in the sacrificial smell of ..." When Yahweh is the subject in the context of sacrificial worship, the verb indicates his gracious and delighted acceptance of the sacrifice (Gen 8:21; 1 Sam 26:19) and connotes his grace toward the person offering it. Related to the verb is the noun רֵיחַ, which is common in Leviticus in the phrase רֵיחַ נִיחוֹחַ, describing the "pleasing aroma" of sacrifices prescribed by Yahweh and acceptable to him when offered faithfully (e.g., Lev 1:9, 13).[4] However, the verb is negated in the covenant curse in Lev 26:31: Yahweh will *not* smell (accept) the sacrifices of apostate Israel, but will destroy their sanctuaries. Amos 5:21 fulfills that covenant curse.

The noun עֲצָרָה (sometimes spelled עֲצֶרֶת) usually denotes a "sacred *assembly*" (BDB, 1).[5] The *daghesh* (-צְּ-) in the suffixed plural בְּעַצְּרֹתֵיכֶם, literally, "in your assemblies," sharpens the pronunciation of the sibilant צ and makes its *shewa* more audible (GKC, § 20 h). In the Torah of Moses, the singular of this noun refers to either of two

2 Cf. S. Wagner, "מָאַס," *TDOT* 8:47–59.

3 Cf. B. Kedar-Kopfstein and G. J. Botterweck, "חַג," *TDOT* 4:201–13.

4 See Kleinig, *Leviticus*, 57–58, 65–66, and for the fulfillment in Christ, pages 66–68.

5 Cf. D. P. Wright and J. Milgrom, "עֲצָרָה/עֲצֶרֶת," *TDOT* 11:314–15.

assemblies for worship mandated by Yahweh. One was on the seventh and last day of the Feast of Unleavened Bread (Deut 16:8). The other was on the day after the Feast of Booths (Lev 23:36; Num 29:35; obeyed in Neh 8:18). The noun can also refer to an ad hoc observance (Joel 1:14; 2:15). It is used in 2 Ki 10:20 for an assembly in northern Israel for Baal worship. In Amos 5:21, Yahweh rejects the sacred assemblies of apostate northern Israel because they were replete with idolatry (see also Is 1:13). Amos' use of the suffixed plural בְּעַצְּרֹתֵיכֶם, literally, "in *your* assembl*ies*," parallel to the preceding suffixed plural חַגֵּיכֶם, "*your* festival*s*," implies that Yahweh rejects *all* of northern Israel's worship assemblies because they were not *his* (the ones he mandated for divine service), but were humanly devised in the service of other gods (that is, demons [1 Cor 10:20–21]).

5:22 כִּי אִם־תַּעֲלוּ־לִי עֹלוֹת וּמִנְחֹתֵיכֶם—This is the protasis of a conditional sentence: literally, "for if you offer to me whole burnt offerings and your grain offerings …" The apodosis is the short next clause (see the next textual note). Usually the two particles כִּי אִם are closely joined (BDB, s.v. כִּי אִם־, 2). However the context indicates that Amos 5:22 is one of the passages where כִּי and אִם each retain their separate force: "for if" (BDB, s.v. כִּי אִם־, 1 b).[6]

In form תַּעֲלוּ could be Qal, but since it has the direct objects עֹלוֹת וּמִנְחֹתֵיכֶם, it must be the Hiphil of עָלָה, "cause to ascend (in flame), offer sacrifice" (see BDB, 8). The Hiphil frequently takes the cognate accusative noun עֹלָה, "whole burnt offering." This was distinctive among the sacrifices of Israel because this offering was enjoyed by Yahweh alone; none of it fed the priests or the people (Lev 1:3–17).[7] The daily offering sacrificed at the central sanctuary consisted of a whole burnt offering in the morning and one in the evening, each consisting of a year-old male lamb, together with a grain offering and a drink offering, and their smoke arose to Yahweh as a "pleasing aroma" (Ex 29:38–46; Lev 6:1–11 [ET 6:8–18]).[8] In prophetic texts, עֹלָה is usually mentioned in conjunction with other sacrifices, but here and often elsewhere it has the pride of first place, acknowledging it as the most important of the sacrifices (e.g., Is 43:23; 56:7; Jer 6:20; 14:12).

The second masculine plural pronominal suffix on וּמִנְחֹתֵיכֶם is backward gapped and therefore does double duty,[9] applying also to עֹלוֹת, as reflected in the translation ("*your* whole burnt offerings and *your* grain offerings").

The noun מִנְחָה can have a more general meaning of an "*offering* made to God, of any kind, whether grain or animals" (BDB, 3).[10] However, coupled with עֹלָה, as in Amos 5:22, מִנְחָה may have the more specific meaning of a "grain offering" (BDB, 4).

---

6 Weiss, "Concerning Amos' Repudiation of the Cult," 204, argues that here כִּי is asseverative or deictic, intended to strengthen the negational אִם, hence "even if."

7 See Kleinig, *Leviticus*, 37–66, and for the fulfillment in Christ, pages 66–68. Cf. D. Kellermann, "עֹלָה," *TDOT* 11:96–113.

8 For a theological explanation with the fulfillment in the self-offering of Christ and his benefits provided to us in the Lord's Supper, see Kleinig, *Leviticus*, 141–53.

9 As noted by Paul, *Amos*, 190.

10 Cf. H.-J. Fabry and M. Weinfeld, "מִנְחָה," *TDOT* 8:407–21.

A grain offering was to accompany the daily public morning and evening sacrifice (Ex 29:40–41), and the Torah also provided for a private grain offering (Lev 2:1–16; cf. Lev 6:7–11 [ET 6:14–18]).[11] Grain offerings were a mixture of oil (and sometimes frankincense) and flour or meal, and they were to be offered at the central sanctuary. The burning of the מִנְחָה was the part of the ritual that created the "pleasing aroma" (Lev 6:8 [ET 6:15]). The nouns עֹלָה and מִנְחָה occur also in Is 43:23 in a polemical attack against unfaithful Israel's worship. The use of the different terms together suggests that the prophets have the entire corrupted worship service in view.

The people of northern Israel may have offered the kind of sacrifices specified in the Torah, but they did not offer them at the central sanctuary, which since the time of Solomon was the Jerusalem temple. This was a major sin in Yahweh's eyes (Amos 5:5).

לֹא אֶרְצֶה—The Qal of רָצָה often has God as subject and means he is "pleased with, favorable to" people (BDB, 1 a).[12] In worship contexts, as here, רָצָה is usually understood to mean that God "accepts" worshipers or their sacrifices (see BDB, 2). Here the negated verb is used absolutely (i.e., with no direct object), and it is best to take it as meaning that God accepts neither the unfaithful Israelites nor their offerings. As the divine-human relationship finds its most intimate expression in worship, רָצָה becomes a technical term that denotes either the favorable or unfavorable acceptance of an animal sacrifice and/or the worshiper who offers it.[a]

(a) E.g., Lev 1:4; 19:7; Jer 14:12; Hos 8:13; Ps 51:18 (ET 51:16)

The verb רָצָה is one of the key grace terms in the OT when it refers to God showing his favor. The Israelites did not conquer the land by their own power, but instead by Yahweh's right hand, by his arm, and by the light of his face "because you [Yahweh] showed favor to them" (כִּי רְצִיתָם, Ps 44:4 [ET 44:3]). The verb is used to express justification through faith alone: "Yahweh shows favor" (רוֹצֶה יְהוָה) to those who fear him and trust in his grace (Ps 147:11). In Moses' blessing of the tribes, רָצָה is parallel to בָּרַךְ as God "blesses" (Deut 33:11), and his people are "blessed" (Deut 33:24). See also Deut 33:23, where the cognate nouns רָצוֹן and בְּרָכָה are parallel. In Is 42:1 Yahweh uses רָצָה to declare that his Servant is "my chosen one, in whom my soul delights/is pleased" (בְּחִירִי רָצְתָה נַפְשִׁי), and this is part of the OT background for the words of the Father over God the Son, ἐν ᾧ εὐδόκησα, "in whom I am well pleased," spoken at his Baptism (Mt 3:17) and again at his transfiguration (Mt 17:5). Matthew the evangelist also quotes almost the entirety of Is 42:1–4 in Mt 12:18–21 to explain the dynamics of Jesus' earthly ministry, including his rejection by the Jewish leaders—a parallel to the rejection of Amos (see especially Amos 7:10–17).

[11] For a theological explanation with the fulfillment in Christ and the bread in the Lord's Supper, see Kleinig, *Leviticus*, 69–82.

[12] Cf. H. M. Barstad, "רָצָה," *TDOT* 13:618–30.

וְשֶׁ֥לֶם מְרִיאֵיכֶ֖ם לֹ֥א אַבִּֽיט׃—The noun שֶׁלֶם denotes a "peace offering."[13] It is common in the plural, but the singular is attested in the OT only here.[14] In all likelihood Amos is referring to what is usually called זֶבַח (הַ)שְּׁלָמִים, literally, "(the) sacrifice of peace offerings" (e.g., Lev 3:1, 3; 4:10, 26; 7:20; Num 6:17–18; 1 Sam 10:8; 1 Ki 8:63), or sometimes just שְׁלָמִים, "peace offerings" (e.g., Lev 6:5 [ET 6:12]; 7:14, 33; Num 6:14). The rubrics for this voluntary offering are given in Lev 3:1–17, with some additional instructions about the role of the priests in Lev 7:28–36. It is a sacrificial meal of communion shared by the one bringing the sacrifice, the officiating priest, and God. Probably שֶׁלֶם is etymologically related to שָׁלוֹם, "peace."

The noun מְרִיא denotes a "fattened animal" or "fatling."[15] It does not occur in the Torah but in later texts that describe it as a class of animals from either herds or flocks that were offered in sacrifice (2 Sam 6:13; 1 Ki 1:9, 19, 25; Is 1:11). Ezekiel uses the term figuratively to portray the slain troops of Gog as the sacrifice of fatlings (Ezek 39:18). In the sole exception to sacrificial usage, the Shoot of Jesse endowed with the Spirit (the Messiah [Is 11:1–5]) will bring a new creation in which the "fatling" will lie down in harmony with the calf and the lion (Is 11:6).

The LXX translates the clause in Amos 5:22 as καὶ σωτηρίου ἐπιφανείας ὑμῶν οὐκ ἐπιβλέψομαι, literally, "and the appearances of your peace offering(s) I will not look upon (favorably)." Apparently the LXX took מְרִיאֵיכֶם as a form of the noun מַרְאֶה with a suffix. The LXX usually translates זֶבַח (הַ)שְּׁלָמִים as θυσία (τοῦ) σωτηρίου (e.g., Lev 3:1, 3).

The Hiphil of נָבַט, "to look at," can have the nuances "to look graciously at" (*HALOT*, 2 c) or "to accept favourably" (*HALOT*, 4, citing Amos 5:22).[16] The verb may denote Yahweh's attention toward one who prays to him (e.g., Pss 13:4 [ET 13:3]; 84:10 [ET 84:9]; Lam 5:1). In the OT, it is only in this verse that נָבַט refers to Yahweh's reaction to sacrifices, and the verb is negated.

5:23 הָסֵ֥ר מֵעָלַ֖י הֲמ֣וֹן שִׁרֶ֑יךָ—The previous two verses referred to the Israelites with second person plural forms, but this verse shifts to second person singular forms, including הָסֵר, the singular Hiphil imperative of סוּר, and the singular suffix on שִׁרֶיךָ. Then 5:25–27 shifts back to second person plural forms referring to Israel. *BHS* notes that scholars have suggested emending the singular forms in 5:23 to plural, but that is unwarranted. Such shifts in form appear in other OT texts and in ancient Near Eastern literature.[17]

---

[13] For a theological explanation with the fulfillment in Christ and the Sacrament of Holy Communion, traditionally preceded by the *Pax Domini*, "the *peace* of the Lord be with you always," see Kleinig, *Leviticus*, 83–96.

[14] Cf. T. Seidl, "שְׁלָמִים," *TDOT* 15:105–16.

[15] Cf. R. J. Way, "מְרִיא," *NIDOTTE* 2:1105–6.

[16] Cf. H. Ringgren, "נבט," *TDOT* 9:126–28.

[17] Such shifts are common in Deuteronomy, for example. In Deut 5:1 Moses begins his discourse to Israel with a singular imperative, then employs second person plural suffixes and verbs later in the same verse and in 5:4–5. Second person singular verbs and suffixes are used in 5:6–21, then second person plural forms reappear in 5:22–24. Niehaus, "Amos," 432, cites similar shifts in extrabiblical texts. Andersen and Freedman, *Amos*, 528, mention that the

The Hiphil of סוּר, "to remove," often is used with the combination of prepositions מֵעַל, "from [מִן] upon [עַל]," when the thing removed is something like clothing or a figurative burden (BDB, s.v. סוּר, Hiphil, 1). Yahweh's use here of מֵעָלַי, literally, "from upon me," may figuratively portray unfaithful Israel's worship songs as a heavy and unwanted burden.

That connotation is strengthened by הֲמוֹן שִׁרֶיךָ, "the din of your songs." The noun שִׁיר can refer to a liturgical worship "song" and is so used often in superscriptions of psalms (e.g., Psalms 45–46; 120–134) as well as the superlative "Song of Songs" (Song 1:1). Amos likely refers to songs that the apostate Israelites believed would count as worship pleasing to God. However, Yahweh probably implies otherwise by the noun הָמוֹן in construct with the songs. הָמוֹן has a broad semantic range. It can refer to a throng of pilgrims in liturgical celebration (Ps 42:5 [ET 42:4]), but more often it refers to a loud jumble of noises or disorganized, violent movement, for example, of an army (1 Ki 20:13; Joel 4:14 [ET 3:14]).[18] In Ezek 26:13 the identical construct phrase (but with a feminine suffix) refers to the songs of Tyre, which Yahweh will terminate when he judges the pagan city, the most prosperous center of commerce on the coast of Palestine. In the context of Amos 5:23 הָמוֹן refers to the irritating tumult of Israel's songs as well as their sheer number. They are too loud and annoying for Yahweh!

וְזִמְרַת נְבָלֶיךָ לֹא אֶשְׁמָע׃—The noun זִמְרָה can refer to both vocal and instrumental "music."[19] Like שִׁיר, it can be part of God-pleasing worship (e.g., Ex 15:2; Is 51:3; Ps 98:5). The construct phrase וְזִמְרַת נְבָלֶיךָ is "a reference to music that expresses praise and thanksgiving."[20] The noun נֵבֶל refers to a stringed instrument, and it has been rendered as "harp," "lute," or "lyre," although it should not be anachronistically equated with later instruments by those names. The Vulgate translates it here with *lyra*, "lyre." It was a common stringed instrument in ancient Israel (see, e.g., Pss 33:2; 144:9).[21]

Yahweh's denunciation implies that Israel's instrumental music is not accompanied by any theological substance and is not an expression of faith in him. Therefore he refuses to listen to it.

5:24 וְיִגַּל כַּמַּיִם מִשְׁפָּט וּצְדָקָה כְּנַחַל אֵיתָן׃—For the parallel nouns מִשְׁפָּט, "justice," and צְדָקָה, "righteousness," see the second and third textual notes on 5:7. The noun צְדָקָה,

---

singular forms in 5:23 may indicate that Amos has shifted his address to an individual such as Amaziah the priest (whom Amos confronts in 7:10–17) or Jeroboam ben Joash, the contemporary king of northern Israel.

18 Cf. A. Baumann, "הָמָה," *TDOT* 3:414–18.

19 Cf. C. Barth, "זמר," *TDOT* 4:91–98.

20 Weiss, "Concerning Amos' Repudiation of the Cult," 208.

21 According to M. Görg, "כִּנּוֹר," *TDOT* 7:201–3, the נֵבֶל and the כִּנּוֹר represent two different kinds of lyres, and the נֵבֶל is the larger of the two. His discussion includes the religious role of lyres, their depiction in artistry, and their players. Kraeling, "Music in the Bible," 296, says that the נֵבֶל was "probably a harp with as many as ten strings." See *ANEP*, § 199, for a picture showing two lyres, one with twelve strings and one with six. King opines: "The fact that *nebel* may also signify 'leather bottle' or 'jar' may account for the bulky shape of the musical instrument. … The *nebel* has twelve strings" (*Amos, Hosea, Micah*, 154).

"righteousness," also occurs in 5:7 and 6:12. The adjective צַדִּיק is used as a substantive, "a righteous man," in 2:6 and 5:12. See the fourth textual note on 2:6.

The *waw* on the jussive Niphal וְיִגַּל (Joüon, § 82 m) is adversative, "*but* let roll" (GKC, § 163 a). Amos creates a sharp contrast between Israel's worship described in 5:21–23 and the ethical life of faith desired and enabled by Yahweh in 5:24. In the Qal, גָּלַל has the transitive meaning "to roll (something), roll (something) away," and the usual object is a stone (Gen 29:3, 8, 10; Josh 10:18; 1 Sam 14:33; Prov 26:27).[22] The verb is the root of the place name Gilgal (Amos 4:4; 5:5; see the first textual note on 4:4). The Niphal occurs elsewhere in the OT only in Is 34:4, and it has an intransitive meaning, here "to roll along, flow," referring to the unstoppable rolling of a torrential wadi. Wolff translates it as "let cascade."[23]

The noun נַחַל refers to a "wadi," which normally would become only a trickle of water or be completely dry during Palestine's arid seasons, although the lower reaches of some wadis, such as the Kishon (Judg 5:21) and the Jabbok (Deut 2:37), have water in them year round. But here נַחַל is modified by the adjective אֵיתָן, "ever-flowing" (BDB, 1 [under the root ינן]). The same phrase, נַחַל אֵיתָן, is used in Deut 21:4 for "a wadi with a perennial stream." Ps 74:15 refers to "ever-flowing rivers" (נַהֲרוֹת אֵיתָן). In Ex 14:27 אֵיתָן is even used for the normal depth and currents of the sea.

Since a wadi in northern Israel normally would dry up in the dry season every summer, Yahweh may be pointing toward the miraculous new creation in 9:13, where planting and harvesting are no longer seasonal, but continue all the time.

5:25 הַזְּבָחִים וּמִנְחָה הִגַּשְׁתֶּם־לִי בַמִּדְבָּר אַרְבָּעִים שָׁנָה—While the noun הַזְּבָחִים could have the article ("the sacrifices"), it probably has the interrogative -הֲ, reflected in the translation: "sacrifices and grain offering did you bring near to me?" When the first consonant of a noun has a *shewa* (זְבָחִים), the interrogative usually has *patach* and is followed by *daghesh forte*, hence -הַזְּ (see GKC, § 100 l). If an ignorant speaker is asking for information, such a question could receive either a positive or negative answer, but if the question is merely rhetorical, it usually has a negative force (GKC, § 150 d). Here the omniscient God asks a question whose answer he knows: Israel as a whole did *not* offer him faithful worship during the wilderness wanderings. The LXX and the NT (Acts 7:42) accurately translate it as a question that expects a negative answer by beginning it with μή. The entire clause is a question, and it may have an exclamatory or incredulous tone (cf. Waltke-O'Connor, § 40.3b, example 3; Joüon, § 161 b).

For מִנְחָה, see the first textual note on 5:22. For the noun זֶבַח, "sacrifice," see the second textual note on 4:4.

The usual and frequent liturgical verb for bringing an offering (or bringing people, e.g., priests) before God is the Hiphil of קָרַב, "to bring near," used one hundred forty-seven times in Exodus, Leviticus, and Numbers.[24] הִגַּשְׁתֶּם is the Hiphil of נָגַשׁ, which has the same meaning, "to bring near" (BDB), but it is much less common as a liturgi-

---

22 Cf. G. Münderlein, "גלל," *TDOT* 3:20–23.

23 Wolff, *Joel and Amos*, 264.

24 For the theological significance, see Kleinig, *Leviticus*, 44–45, commenting on Lev 1:2, where the Hiphil of קָרַב occurs twice.

cal term for offering sacrifice. It is, however, so used in, for example, Ex 32:6; Lev 2:8; 8:14. The Hiphil of נָגַשׁ recurs in Amos 6:3 and 9:10, but not in worship settings.

The accusative phrase אַרְבָּעִים שָׁנָה denotes an extent of time: "*for* forty years."

בֵּית יִשְׂרָאֵל׃—As in 5:1 and 6:14, the context indicates that this phrase is a vocative.

5:26 וּנְשָׂאתֶם אֵת סִכּוּת מַלְכְּכֶם וְאֵת כִּיּוּן צַלְמֵיכֶם—Probably the perfect Qal verb וּנְשָׂאתֶם has conjunctive *waw* and continues the description in 5:25 of Israel's past idolatry during the wilderness wanderings, when they "took up" or "carried along" idols as their false gods. The last clause of 5:26 clearly refers to past action (עֲשִׂיתֶם, "you made"). The LXX and the NT (Acts 7:43) translate וּנְשָׂאתֶם as past tense with a second aorist, καὶ ἀνελάβετε, "and you lifted up." In the LXX and the NT ἀναλαμβάνω can have the nuance of taking up something to adopt it as one's own or of taking up something to carry it along or away (see LEH and BDAG). KJV and NASB translate וּנְשָׂאתֶם as past tense.

Morphologically it is possible that וּנְשָׂאתֶם has *waw* consecutive and then it would refer, from the perspective of Amos, to the future, as in ESV: "you [Israel] shall take up" the idols to carry them into exile. This would refer to the exile of northern Israel in 722 BC about four decades after the ministry of Amos, and it would apply to Judah's exile in 587 BC. Among commentators, Paul translates it as "and you shall carry off" and connects this clause with the impending exile Yahweh predicts in 5:27.[25] However, it is best to follow the LXX and the NT and see 5:26 as a description of past events, as in 5:25. Yahweh then announces the future exile in the next verse, 5:27.

The proper names of the two false gods, סִכּוּת, "Sikkuth," and כִּיּוּן, "Kiyyun," are pointed according to the same *qittul* pattern as the nouns גִּלּוּל, "excrement god, dung deity, fecal idol" (alluding to cylindrical shape), and שִׁקּוּץ, "detested thing."[26] The noun גִּלּוּל is most frequent in the OT in Ezekiel (e.g., Ezek 6:4–6), and he also uses שִׁקּוּץ, which is usually rendered "abomination" in Dan 9:27; 11:31; 12:11. These vocalizations satirize the Assyrian astral deities. They are not gods at all but excrement and abominations. The linguistic device of vocalizing a word so as to produce a negative connotation is called cacophony or dysphemism.

The usual pronunciation of the first astral deity was Sakkuth (instead of the MT's סִכּוּת, "Sikkuth"). 2 Ki 17:24–30 records how after the Assyrians conquered the Northern Kingdom in 722 BC, they forced Babylonians to settle in Samaria, and these Babylonians erected in northern Israel their deities, including "Sukkoth-benoth" (סֻכּוֹת בְּנוֹת), which probably is the same as Sakkuth. Sakkuth was another name for Adar, the Assyrian god of war and the chase.[27] In some Mesopotamian and Ugaritic texts, Sakkuth is identified with Ninurta, and secondarily with Saturn, as one of the leading

---

[25] Paul, *Amos*, 188, 194.

[26] For the scatological meaning of גִּלּוּל as "fecal deity," see Hummel, *Ezekiel 1–20*, 192–93, commenting on Ezek 6:4. Hummel, like others, believes the form of גִּלּוּל is patterned after that of שִׁקּוּץ.

[27] Niehaus, "Amos," 433.

gods in the pantheon.[28] Ninurta (or Ninib) was also associated with water, along with rivers, oceans, rain, and so forth. The supreme rank of this deity becomes clear in the epithet that follows in Amos 5:26, מַלְכְּכֶם, "your king." For the form of the suffixed noun, see Joüon, § 88C a* 4.

The name of the god כִּיּוּן is another deliberate dysphemism, this time of the Akkadian Kaiwan, an appellation of the star god Saturn.[29] "Most likely, then, preserved here in the Book of Amos is a rare glimpse of a Mesopotamian astral cult."[30] In the MT, this god, כִּיּוּן, is further described by צַלְמֵיכֶם, "your images." The plural might suggest that this god was represented by several images.

The translation above reflects the MT, whose accents indicate that each of the two object clauses have the identical syntax: the direct object marker, the name of a god, and a descriptive noun in apposition to that name. Yahweh states that the Israelites took up two objects:

אֵת סִכּוּת מַלְכְּכֶם	Sikkuth, your king
וְאֵת כִּיּוּן צַלְמֵיכֶם	and Kiyyun, your images

Then the final clause of the verse (see the next textual note) describes both deities as "your star gods, which you made for yourselves." However, many English translations rearrange the syntax to be smoother, for example, "Sikkuth your king and Kiyyun, your images" (NASB), so that the plural "images" refers to both Sikkuth and Kiyyun. After "Sikkuth your king," ESV has "Kiyyun your star-god" (as if the Hebrew had כּוֹכַב אֱלֹהֵיכֶם צַלְמֵיכֶם instead of צַלְמֵיכֶם כּוֹכַב אֱלֹהֵיכֶם), and then it describes both gods as "your images that you made." That departs even farther from the MT, but it results in a translation that is closer to Acts 7:43, which calls only the second deity "the star of your god Rephan" (καὶ τὸ ἄστρον τοῦ θεοῦ [ὑμῶν] Ῥαιφάν), and which then calls both deities "the images you made" (τοὺς τύπους οὓς ἐποιήσατε).

Additional differences between the MT of 5:26–27, the LXX, and Acts 7:43 (which follows the LXX closely, but not exactly) are as follows:

MT	*LXX*	*Acts 7:43*
סִכּוּת, Sikkuth	τὴν σκηνήν, the tabernacle	τὴν σκηνήν, the tabernacle
מַלְכְּכֶם, your king	τοῦ Μολοχ, of Molech	τοῦ Μόλοχ, of Molech
כִּיּוּן, Kiyyun	Ραιφαν, Rephan	Ῥαιφάν, Rephan
דַּמָּשֶׂק, Damascus	Δαμασκοῦ, Damascus	Βαβυλῶνος, Babylon

The MT vocalization of "Sikkuth" is a deliberately distorted form of the name of the Assyrian god Sakkuth, that is, Ninurta or Ninib. The LXX translators, working with an unvocalized Hebrew text, vocalized the consonants as the same word that appears in Amos 9:11, סֻכַּת, the singular construct of סֻכָּה (see the second textual note on 9:11). The LXX translators probably understood this "tabernacle" to be the shrine

28 Paul, *Amos*, 195.

29 Paul, *Amos*, 196.

30 Paul, *Amos*, 197.

of the god Sikkuth. The NT follows the LXX, and the Vulgate's *tabernaculum* reflects the same reading.

In place of the suffixed מַלְכְּכֶם, the LXX seems to have read only the consonants מלכ, and instead of vocalizing them as מֶלֶךְ ("king"), it vocalized them as מֹלֶךְ, "Molech," a deity to whom the Canaanites offered child sacrifice in the time of Moses (Lev 18:21; 20:2–5) and which was venerated by the Ammonites in the era of the monarchy (1 Ki 11:7; cf. 2 Ki 23:10; Jer 32:35). Probably the proper name of this deity was to be pronounced as *melech*, "king," but in the OT, it is deliberately vocalized with the vowels for בֹּשֶׁת, "shame."

In place of כִּיּוּן, the name of the second Akkadian astral deity, Kaiwan (Kiyyun), a scribal confusion between *kaph* and *resh* accounts for Ραιφαν, Rephan, in the LXX, followed by the NT.

The LXX accurately reflects "Damascus" in the MT, but the NT's "Babylon" appears to combine or subsume the exile of northern Israel in 722 BC under the exile of Judah in 587 BC to Babylon. Since the Jewish people in Judea in the NT era traced their heritage to the Judeans who returned from exile in Babylon, the use of "Babylon" in Acts 7:43 was a more direct (and more offensive) accusation by St. Stephen the protomartyr that his fellow Jews who rejected Jesus were idolaters. This helps explain why they became enraged and stoned him (Acts 7:54–60).

כּוֹכַב֙ אֱלֹהֵיכֶ֔ם אֲשֶׁ֥ר עֲשִׂיתֶ֖ם לָכֶֽם׃—The construct phrase, literally, "the star of your gods," has an epexegetical genitive, meaning that "your gods [Sikkuth and Kiyyun] are [each merely] a star." It is translated as "your star gods." Their impotence is emphasized by the idiom of the verb עָשָׂה plus לְ, "which you made for yourselves." This idiom is often used for people making idols (e.g., Ex 20:4; 1 Ki 14:9; Hos 8:4).

5:27 וְהִגְלֵיתִ֥י אֶתְכֶ֖ם מֵהָ֣לְאָה לְדַמָּ֑שֶׂק—The Qal of גָּלָה, "go into exile," describes Israel's exile in 5:5; 6:7; 7:11, 17. The causative Hiphil, "to exile, cause (people) to go into exile," was used for Gaza's transgression in 1:6, but only here in Amos does it refer to Yahweh exiling Israel. The adverb הָלְאָה, "beyond," may be temporal (e.g., Lev 22:27; Ezek 39:22) or spatial (e.g., Gen 19:9; Num 32:19), as here. It both has the attached preposition מִן with a comparative force ("farther *than*") and takes the preposition לְ, as also in Gen 35:21 and Jer 22:19.

For the dramatic substitution of "Babylon" in Acts 7:43 in place of "Damascus" in MT and LXX Amos 5:27, see the first textual note on 5:26.

אָמַ֛ר יְהוָ֥ה אֱלֹהֵֽי־צְבָא֖וֹת שְׁמֽוֹ׃—For the divine title יְהוָה אֱלֹהֵי (הַ)צְּבָאוֹת, see the second textual note and the commentary on 3:13. The same title is followed by שְׁמוֹ at the end of 4:13, where שְׁמוֹ serves as a predicate ("Yahweh, God of armies, *is* his name"). Here the syntax is, literally, "says Yahweh, the God of armies—his name." Almost all English translations smooth the syntax by using a relative clause: for example, "says Yahweh, *whose* name is the God of armies."

Commentary

The Message of Amos 5:21–27

Normally in the prophets Yahweh spells out the sins of his audience and then announces the impending punishment. However in Amos 5:18–27 this order is partially reversed. The prophet cited the punishment for unfaithful northern Israel by means of the coming Day of Yahweh in 5:18–20. Now he announces Yahweh's rejection of Israel's worship in 5:21–23. After a call for justice and righteousness in 5:24, he details the reason for Yahweh's judgment and rejection in 5:25–26, culminating in a restatement of the punishment in 5:27.

After turning the popular belief about the Day of Yahweh on its head (5:18–20), Yahweh attacks apostate Israel's worship as a case in point as to why the day will "be darkness and not light" (5:18, 20). The juxtaposition of 5:21–27 and 5:18–20 indicates that Israel's syncretistic worship, which lacks any ensuing justice and righteousness (5:24), is a prime reason why the Day of Yahweh will be a day of no escape (5:19). The message of 5:21–27 continues what Yahweh said earlier in 4:4–5 and 5:4–6.

When put together, these texts make it clear that worshiping Yahweh in faith leads to living the way Yahweh wants people to live—and that corrupt worship leads to corrupt living. The Israelites were trying to patronize Yahweh through their worship so that they could then set him aside and get on with "real business" (cf. 8:4–6). But Yahweh is no cardboard cutout. He is the living God with real anger and real love. He is deeply affected by Israel's "rite without right."

God is intensely concerned with public worship.[31] In the OT era, just as in the NT era, if worship is conducted according to God's institution in his Word, then through it he bestows his grace, forgiveness, and salvation upon all who receive his blessings in faith. But if it is not, then worship becomes a manmade ritual devoid of any salvific divine activity. God rejects and even hates such worship (5:21). The participants will reap judgment.

The Northern Kingdom of Israel had forsaken God's temple in Jerusalem and the divine worship conducted there. That was the central sanctuary where Israel was to participate in the worship Yahweh had instituted in the Torah of Moses. But instead northern Israel frequented the idolatrous shrines that Jeroboam ben Nebat had erected at Bethel and Dan (1 Ki 12:26–33). Amos frequently refers to the one at Bethel,[32] and he also mentions false worship sites at Dan (8:14), Gilgal (4:4; 5:5), and Beersheba (5:5; 8:14). These sites were syncretistic, meaning that they combined the veneration of pagan deities with the (ostensible) worship of the one true God.[33] This admixture made the worship even more reprehensible to God.

It is fitting, then, that in Acts 7:42–43 Stephen the protomartyr quotes Amos 5:25–27 as a key proof text to confirm that throughout the long history of Israel, the incorrigible people had been characterized by idolatry. Stephen's point is

---

[31] See further the excursus "The Prophets and Israel's Worship."

[32] For Bethel, see the second textual note and the commentary on 3:14, the first textual note on 4:4, and the commentary on 7:13. The temple whose destruction God commands in 9:1 must be the one in Bethel (see 3:14).

[33] Amos passages in which God condemns the syncretistic and idolatrous worship practices of northern Israel are 2:7–8; 3:14; 4:4–5; 5:5–6, 14, 21–27; 7:9–17; 8:5, 10, 14; 9:1. See also the excursus "The Sabbath."

that the culmination of Israel's apostasy is its rejection of Jesus the Messiah. However, the infant church was based on the foundation of the Jewish-Christian apostles, and it quickly expanded with the large-scale influx of Gentile converts beginning on Pentecost. Therefore it fulfilled the eschatological vision in Amos 9:11–15 of the new people of God consisting of a believing remnant of Israel plus a believing remnant of Gentiles, as James affirms when he quotes Amos in Acts 15.[34]

Yahweh Rejects Faithless Israel's Sacrifices and Songs (5:21–23)

5:21 The remaining verses in chapter 5 are part of Amos' ongoing critique of Israel's worship life. This preaching will inevitably lead to his confrontation with the apostate northern priest Amaziah in 7:10–17, which results in the priest's attempted gag order against the prophet (7:16; cf. 2:12).

Amos continues his rhetoric of dramatic reversal.[35] Whereas one would expect Yahweh to take delight in Israel's worship—after all, he had instituted the divine worship prescribed in the Torah—Yahweh is repulsed by the worship life of the faithless people. They are breaking the First Table of the Decalogue, especially the First Commandment (Ex 20:1–11), by their worship of other deities (Amos 5:26), and they are also neglecting the Second Table of the Ten Commandments (Ex 20:12–17).[36]

Earlier in the chapter, Yahweh described Israel's magistrates as those who "*hate* an arbiter in the gate" (שָׂנְאוּ בַשַּׁעַר מוֹכִיחַ, 5:10), and he called for them to "*hate* (the) evil (one) and love (the) good (One)" (שִׂנְאוּ־רָע וְאֶהֱבוּ טוֹב, 5:15). Now in 5:21, it is Yahweh who declares, "I *hate*, I reject" (שָׂנֵאתִי מָאַסְתִּי) Israel's worship. Because those responsible for justice and righteousness in the community hate the one who attempts to correct them (5:10) and fail to love the One who alone is truly good (5:15), Yahweh in turn hates their worship because justice and righteousness are not flowing from their liturgical life (5:24). "I, Yahweh, love justice" (Is 61:8); he is the one who justifies and sanctifies his people. But when they reject him, their lives are characterized by injustice.

Yahweh's declarations of his attitude and disposition, "I hate, I reject … ," show that he is immersed in his relationship with Israel. Yahweh's personal involvement is displayed by the six first-person singular verbs in 5:21–23 that have him as their subject. In 2:13 Yahweh had compared himself to a creaking, overly burdened wagon. The heaviness causes Yahweh to groan and suffer from the burden of carrying Israel. Ultimately, this suffering of God is fulfilled in the vicarious atonement of the Suffering Servant, Jesus Christ, who carries to the cross the burden of humanity's sin and makes satisfaction for it (Is 53:4–5).

---

34 See the excursus "The Quotation from Amos 9 in Acts 15."

35 In addition to 5:21–27, a dramatic reversal is present in 2:9; 3:1–2; 4:4–5; 5:18–20; 6:1–7; 8:9–10; 9:11–15.

36 For a similar text, see Is 1:11–15, which shares similar ideological motifs and vocabulary with Amos 5:21–24.

Yahweh's abhorrence should not be absolutized into a complete rejection of Israel's worship life. After all, it was Yahweh who gave the Israelites these gifts of sacrifice and song in the first place. But they had adopted a positive answer to Paul's question in Rom 6:1: "Shall we go on sinning so that grace may abound?" Instead of the apostle's fervent μὴ γένοιτο, in essence, "God forbid!" (Rom 6:2), the Israelites responded, "Yes, yes, a thousand times yes! We love to sin and Yahweh likes to forgive. Let both parties do what they love the most!" Their conscience had become seared (cf. 1 Tim 4:2). They believed that Yahweh had unconditionally promised to be with them (Amos 5:14) so that no evil could ever befall them (9:10).

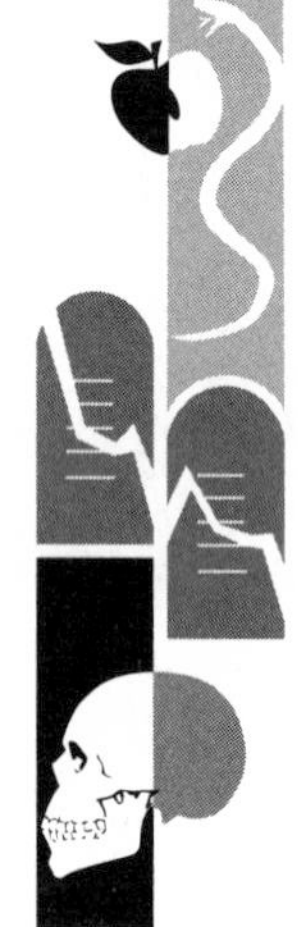

Yahweh in 5:21 reminds Israel of Lev 26:31, which is a curse rejecting Israel's worship, a curse to be fulfilled when Israel broke the covenant of Moses, as it had in Amos' day. There Yahweh declares, "I will not smell with delight [וְלֹ֥א אָרִ֖יחַ] the pleasing aroma of your offerings." The identical Hebrew phrase וְלֹ֥א אָרִ֖יחַ appears in Amos 5:21. The Levitical malediction indicates that the nation is now under Yahweh's curse. He rejects Israel's festivals because the people have rejected him and his covenant of grace. This is similar to 1 Sam 15:23, where Samuel tells Saul, מָאַ֙סְתָּ֙ אֶת־דְּבַ֣ר יְהוָ֔ה וַיִּמְאָסְךָ֖ מִמֶּֽלֶךְ, "you rejected the Word of Yahweh; therefore he has rejected you from (being) king" (cf. Hos 4:6).

The antidote to the Levitical curse is seen in the NT, which cites the liturgical language of the aroma of sacrifice pleasing to God. Christ gave himself up as the all-sufficient atoning sacrifice that rendered to God "a fragrant aroma" (ὀσμὴν εὐωδίας, Eph 5:2). Baptized believers are "the fragrant aroma of Christ" (Χριστοῦ εὐωδία) to others (2 Cor 2:15; see 2 Cor 2:14–16), and through faith in Christ, our offerings are "a fragrant aroma, an acceptable sacrifice, pleasing to God" (ὀσμὴν εὐωδίας, θυσίαν δεκτήν, εὐάρεστον τῷ θεῷ, Phil 4:18).

5:22–23 These verses qualify the abstract language of hatred and rejection in 5:21 by citing more specific rejections of faithless Israel's worship practices. In moving from 5:21 to 5:22–23, Yahweh goes from mentioning the festivals and assemblies as a whole to describing his hatred of their specific parts. Yahweh expresses a heptad[37] of verbs in 5:21–23 to completely denounce Israel's unfaithful worship: "I hate," "I reject," "I do not delight," "I will not accept," "I will not gaze upon," "remove," and "I will not hear." Yahweh's attitude toward the nation's worship is as follows: "I don't want to smell it, I don't want to see it, and I don't even want to hear it." This "heptad of negation"[38] represents a complete and comprehensive repudiation. Just as the seven judgments against the nations in 1:3–2:5 were followed by the climactic judgment against Israel in

---

[37] Amos employs heptads also in 1:3–2:5; 2:6–8; 2:14–16; 3:3–6; 4:4–5; 4:6–11; 5:8–9; 6:1–6; 9:1–4.

[38] Paul, *Amos*, 192.

2:6–16, here too the heptad is followed by a climactic eighth item, which is in 5:24.[39]

Amos 5:21–23 also rejects northern Israel's worship by using seven different liturgical terms: (1) "festivals"; (2) "sacred assemblies"; (3) "whole burnt offerings"; (4) "grain offerings"; (5) "peace offering"; (6) "songs"; and (7) "music." This list of seven indicates that Yahweh completely rejects Israel's faithless worship.

In 5:23 Yahweh turns his attention away from the animal sacrifices (5:21–22) and toward Israel's songs and music. God-pleasing worship included the singing of psalms and instrumental music as liturgical expressions of faith (e.g., 2 Sam 6:12–19; 1 Chronicles 15–16; Psalms 149–150). But Yahweh's ears could no longer bear the cacophony of choruses coming from the unfaithful people who lacked justice and righteousness (Amos 5:24).

Some of the identical terminology in this rejection is repeated some two centuries later when Yahweh pronounces this judgment upon the island city of Tyre, a pagan Canaanite stronghold (Ezek 26:13):

> I will put an end to *the din of your songs*, and the sound of your harps will not be heard again.
>
> וְהִשְׁבַּתִּ֖י הֲמ֣וֹן שִׁירָ֑יִךְ וְק֣וֹל כִּנּוֹרַ֔יִךְ לֹ֥א יִשָּׁמַ֖ע עֽוֹד

Similar is the judgment in Rev 18:22, which describes the day the music will die in Babylon (the great harlot who is the antitype of the church, the virgin bride of Christ) when she is destroyed at the return of Christ (Revelation 17–19).

What is true of pagan worship and partying is now also true of apostate Israel. The indictment that Yahweh's chosen people have become just like the unbelieving nations was also expressed by including the oracles against Judah (2:4–5) and Israel (2:6–16) with the oracles against the pagan nations (1:3–2:3). Israel will be likened to the other nations in a different way in 9:7, where Yahweh describes how he has acted upon other peoples in terms of exodus and deliverance.

Yahweh began 5:21–27 by addressing Israel in the second person *plural* (5:21–22), but in 5:23 he uses the second person *singular,* perhaps to confront each of the worshipers individually. The singular imperative "remove" (הָסֵר, 5:23) could apply to the priest overseeing worship, such as Amaziah at Bethel (7:10–17). In 5:25–27 the plural suffixes reappear.

The musical terms "songs" and "lutes" (שִׁיר and נֵבֶל) in 5:23 appear again in 6:5, where Yahweh rejects Israel's music. Coupling these texts together indicates that Yahweh views all the music in northern Israel as repugnant. A "song" (שִׁיר) is the opposite of a "funeral dirge" or "lament" (קִינָה, 5:1; 8:10). Yahweh

---

[39] Weiss maintains that 5:21–24 contains eight clauses that follow a seven-plus-one pattern similar to the oracles in chapters 1 and 2, with the eighth section driving home the point of the prophecy ("Concerning Amos' Repudiation of the Cult," 200–2).

had called Israel to repent and mourn by uttering a dirge over them (5:1–3) and warning that they would lament (5:16–17), but the people refused and continued their festal songs. Therefore he will turn their "festivals" into "mourning" and their "songs" into a "funeral dirge" (8:10).

The lack of lamentation fits with two conspicuous absences in the list of offerings in Amos 5:21–23. It does not include the "sin offering" (חַטָּאת, e.g., Lev 4:8, 14; 16:3, 5–6; Num 19:9, 17; 2 Chr 29:21, 23–24) or the "guilt offering" (אָשָׁם, e.g., Lev 14:12–14, 17, 21; 19:21–22), which were essential in the divine worship instituted in the Torah.[40] Because the Israelites had a high view of themselves (cf. 6:1; 9:10), they apparently felt their sin and guilt was not serious enough to require sacrificial atonement.

In 5:21 Yahweh shuts his nostrils. In 5:22 he closes his eyes. By the end of 5:23 he has plugged his ears.

Let Justice and Righteousness Flow (5:24)

5:24 This verse is the climactic eighth statement in 5:21–24. The problem is both Israel's worship and also Israel's conduct outside of worship. If justice and righteousness[41] are not present, "religious life, with all its ritual accoutrements, becomes a sham."[42] Unless people seek Yahweh (5:4, 6, 14), they are dehydrated, dry, and dead.[43]

At the heart of 5:24 is a water metaphor:[44]

> But let justice roll like the waters,
> and righteousness like an ever-flowing wadi.

When David was in the wilderness, "a dry and weary land where there is no water," he thirsted for Yahweh and looked for him at his sanctuary (Ps 63:1–3 [ET superscription and 63:1–2]). In the annual cycle of Israel's worship, the time of the festival of Sukkoth or Booths coincided with the beginning of the rainy season. ("Tabernacle, booth" in 9:11 is related to that festival; see the commentary on 9:11.) The OT often refers to the gushing forth of springs and rivers as a description of God's gracious gifts of life and salvation (e.g., Is 12:3;

---

[40] For an overview of their theological importance among the offerings, see Kleinig, *Leviticus*, 33–43. Instead of "guilt offering," Kleinig calls the אָשָׁם the "reparation offering."

[41] Amos couples these two words also in 5:7 and 6:12. See the second and third textual notes and the commentary on 5:7.

[42] Paul, *Amos*, 192. Paul also writes: "In the surrounding cultures, the two [justice and righteousness] are the concern of the king, who sponsored social reforms in order to implement social justice. The innovation in Amos is that he demands such action on the part of the entire population" (*Amos*, 192, n. 46).

[43] Wolff writes: "That which Israel has perverted into wormwood and poison (5:7; 6:12) was meant to effect blessing and prosperity among the people, just as the streams and rivers of a land bring the gift of fertility and life" (*Joel and Amos*, 264).

[44] Amos draws on imagery of the country also in, for example, 2:13; 3:3–5, 12; 6:12; 9:9. For a discussion of how Amos' background may have influenced his book, see the commentary on 1:1.

35:6–7; Pss 104:10–17; 107:35–38). Speaking through Isaiah, Yahweh refers to the need for cleansing water that removes sin, and he promises that his people will be redeemed by "justice" and "righteousness" (Is 1:16–27).

Amos connects Israel's longing for rain and fertility with God's yearning for his people to have justice and righteousness. People will enjoy God's blessings for eternity only if they have a right relationship with him through faith. Then his gifts of justification and righteousness by grace will overflow in their actions of justice and righteousness in their life and behavior toward one another. The apostle John affirms the same thing in 1 Jn 4:19–21.

"Waters" and "ever-flowing wadi" (Amos 5:24) are parallel, and they complement each other in that the meaning of "waters" is made clearer by the following reference to a wadi that is "ever-flowing, never-failing, perennial, permanent" (אֵיתָן). "An ever-flowing wadi" flows steadily throughout the year because its source is not just the rain that falls from the sky, but it is also supported by a wellspring or underground reservoir.[45]

What is this additional source? Since Yahweh is Israel's only source of life (5:4, 6, 14), he too is the sole spring of life-giving waters. This water could be obtained through the divine service established by God for the central sanctuary—in Amos' era, the Jerusalem temple. The liturgical worship there with God's Word and the ordained sacrifices furnished the forgiveness of sins and the wellspring that enabled God's people to live a life characterized by righteousness and justice. A wadi with a year-round torrential flow emphasizes divine power for life, permanence, and dependability, even in the arid season.

Tragically, northern Israel was not seeking Yahweh in the proper worship at Jerusalem, but was visiting idolatrous shrines elsewhere (e.g., 5:5; 8:14). Consequently the religious, ethical, and moral conduct of the people was like a wadi that had dried up. Later Amos will confront the apostate priest Amaziah at the false shrine in Bethel sponsored by the king of northern Israel (7:10–17). Amaziah can be likened to the religious leaders described by Jude who offer water only to disappoint their adherents. False teachers are "waterless clouds driven by the wind" (νεφέλαι ἄνυδροι ὑπὸ ἀνέμων παραφερόμεναι, Jude 12). They claim to offer life-giving water but instead entrap people in sin; for them eternal gloom[46] has been reserved (2 Pet 2:17–19).

The water imagery of Amos 5:24 anticipates the Sacrament of Christian Baptism, the new birth "through water and the Spirit" (Jn 3:5). Jesus alone offers the free gift of "living water" that wells up to become a spring within the baptized believer (Jn 4:7–15; 7:38–39), and Amos 5:24 may well be part of the OT background of "the Scripture" (Jn 7:38) Jesus cites for this promise.[47] Baptismal

---

[45] Weiss, "Amos' Repudiation of the Cult," 210.

[46] See the commentary on 5:18, 20, which speak of "darkness" and "gloom."

[47] Jesus' promise of "living water" flowing within the believer seems to draw most directly on Song 4:15. One may see Mitchell, *The Song of Songs*, 844–46, 868–73, and also the more general discussion "The Song and the Sacraments" on pages 311–54.

water delivers his love and then overflows through the baptized into lives and deeds of justice and righteousness in world. Baptismal cleansing and new life are made possible because of Christ's sacrificial death upon the cross and his glorious resurrection (Titus 3:4–7; 1 Pet 3:18–22). Blood and water flowed from his riven side (Jn 19:34). Only the Christian life begun in Baptism enables justice and righteousness to cascade as a river of life and mercy.

Israel's Idolatry and Exile (5:25–27)

5:25 Andersen and Freedman assess the difficulties of 5:25–27 and how those verses interrelate with the rest of the book; they conclude that the verses "are among the most puzzling and problematical in Amos studies."[48] What is clear, however, is that in order to advance the argument from 5:21–24 to 5:25, Yahweh presents evidence of idolatry from Israel's forty-year wilderness wanderings. During this time Israel was led by Yahweh (cf. Amos 2:10), and even though the Israelites were given the gift of the Levitical worship rites in the Pentateuch, they also engaged in the golden calf apostasy (Exodus 32), the cowardly rejection of the land promise (Numbers 13–14), Korah's rebellion (Numbers 16), and the orgiastic worship of Canaanite fertility deities at Baal Peor (Numbers 25).

The point of this history in the context of Amos is that sacrifice and ritual alone are not enough. Yahweh gave these gifts to furnish his people with his justice (justification) and righteousness, which are received *through faith*, and which empower his redeemed people for faithful living. But the writer of Hebrews comments on this period of Israel's history: "We have received the Gospel just as they did, but the word of the message did not benefit them, because they were *not* united *by faith* with those who listened" (Heb 4:2).

The negative answer to Yahweh's rhetorical question,[49] "sacrifices and grain offering did you bring near to me in the wilderness for forty years?" does not conflict with the Torah passages where God commanded Israel to set up the tabernacle (Exodus 25–31) and begin a life of sacrificial worship (e.g., Ex 17:15; 24:4–8; Leviticus and Numbers). It does, however, mean that Israel as a whole did not carry out this worship faithfully during the wilderness years. Yahweh called the people he had redeemed to worship him exclusively, renouncing all other gods (Ex 20:2–6). A few Israelites (Joshua and Caleb) remained steadfast, but such worship was not the hallmark of Israel. Instead, the people were characterized by doubts, grumblings, rebellions, and outbreaks of gross idolatry.

5:26 The initial verb is most naturally taken as referring to past action: during the wilderness wandering, Israel "took up" false gods by worshiping them. Yet the verb could be translated as future tense: Israel "will take up" its

---

[48] Andersen and Freedman, *Amos*, 530. For another discussion of the issues, see Brown, "Amos 5:26: A Challenge to Reading and Interpretation."

[49] This strategy of asking rhetorical questions is also in 2:11; 3:3–8; 5:18, 20; 6:2, 12; 8:8; 9:7.

false gods to carry them into exile so the people can continue their idolatry in foreign lands. If so, this would be a proleptic reference to the exile Yahweh will describe in the next verse (5:27). The verb may be an ironic double entendre: the punishment for Israel taking up false gods is that the people will be forced to go into exile, and there they will worship the false gods of their captors!

Sikkuth and Kiyyun were Assyrio-Babylonian astral deities and objects of Israel's syncretistic worship in the eighth century BC. Breaking the First Commandment is one of the chief reasons Amos critiques Israel's worship life so severely (4:4–5; 5:21–23; 8:14). Yahweh's covenant people had adopted foreign deities and made images of them to worship.[50]

In the ancient Near East, worshipers would carry the statutes of their gods in processionals.[51] Amos indicates that the Israelites will carry their false gods into exile. This contrasts with the worship Yahweh ordained in the wilderness: Israel carrying the ark of the covenant (e.g., Num 10:35–36). In turning this divine ritual on its head, Amos indicates in the next verse that Israel will process—right into exile![52] This kind of reversal is one of the prophet's most frequent rhetorical maneuvers.[53]

Yahweh satirizes the astral deities both by the distorted forms of their names (see the first textual note on 5:26) and by their description as "star gods" that were manmade ("you made for yourselves"). Yahweh alone is the God who created the constellations (5:8) and all the stars (כּוֹכָבִים, Gen 1:16; Jer 31:35; Ps 8:4 [ET 8:3]). Moreover, "Star" is a title for the Messiah (Num 24:17; cf. 2 Pet 1:19; Rev 22:16), attested by the nativity star (Mt 2:1–12). God's gracious promise is to multiply Abraham's descendants to be like the stars in the sky (e.g., Gen 15:5; 22:17), which is being fulfilled in all baptized believers in Christ, who are the sons of Abraham and heirs of the promise (Gal 3:26–29). Eschatologically all believers shall be raised to shine like the stars (Dan 12:3; cf. Rev 2:28).

---

[50] Idols are lifeless and cannot interact with or save those who worship them (Jer 10:3–5; Ps 115:4–7). Pagan gods cannot be moved or affected (see 1 Ki 18:27–29). The prohibition of images in Ex 20:4–5 protects Yahweh's uniqueness as the only God who can interact with his people. He alone is able to respond to prayer and show mercy, as he does, in, e.g., Amos 7:1–6.

[51] "Their idols are on beasts and livestock" (Is 46:1) depicts a common sight at Babylon's annual New Year's Festival. Images of Marduk and Nebo were carried throughout the town in festal procession. Is 46:7 also describes such a parade. The people who follow such idols are sent into exile (Jer 48:7; 49:3; Hos 10:5, 8). Wolff makes these comments about images of deities placed on standards: "Such standards are known from Mesopotamia. Besides the bull-standard from Mari, we would direct attention here especially to a brick orthostat from late eighth-century Assyria, upon which a multi-colored enamel mosaic depicts a supplicant with a standard, standing before a god" (*Joel and Amos*, 265). See *ANEP*, §§ 305, 535.

[52] Andersen and Freedman write: "Here it is the Israelites who have adopted Assyrian gods and made images of them for worship, who will take those gods with them into exile—ironically, back to the place of their (the gods') origin" (*Amos*, 544).

[53] In addition to 5:21–27, a dramatic reversal is present in 2:9; 3:1–2; 4:4–5; 5:18–20; 6:1–7; 8:9–10; 9:11–15.

Idolatrous people made God's creations into gods. But the one true and triune God is made by no one: "the Father uncreated, the Son uncreated, the Holy Spirit uncreated" (Athanasian Creed, 8).[54]

5:27 Yahweh of hosts is the one who is commanding Israel's exile. He bluntly states in the initial words in this verse, "I will exile you." As commander in chief, he is the one responsible for decreeing and executing Israel's exile. Yahweh explicitly predicted the deportation and exile of northern Israel for the first time in 4:2–3. It is an ongoing theme in the rest of the book (5:5, 27; 6:7; 7:11, 17; 9:4).

There is a possible play on words between the verb "to roll" (the Niphal of גָּלַל) in 5:24 and "to exile" (the Hiphil of גָּלָה) in 5:27. This could be paraphrased by saying that because justice and righteousness do not roll down through the unfaithful people (5:24), Yahweh will roll them away into exile.

"Beyond Damascus" (מֵהָלְאָה לְדַמָּשֶׂק, 5:27) is ironic in light of 2 Ki 14:28. Within Amos' lifetime, King Jeroboam ben Joash extended northern Israel's boundaries (2 Ki 14:25) so that the Israelites could safely go as far as Damascus. This time, however, the prophet promises that Israel will go even farther: beyond Damascus and into *exile*. This reflects the Pentateuchal covenant curse that unfaithful Israel will be banished to a distant land (Deut 28:36, 64–68; 29:27 [ET 29:28]; cf. Deut 30:4). Yahweh can do this because he is the commander of all the armies in heaven and on earth, including Assyria (cf. Amos 6:14), the country that would conquer northern Israel in 722 BC.

Summary

Amos delivered a devastating diatribe against Israel's distorted concept of worship. The nation was called to be a channel by which all the families of the world would be blessed through Abraham and his Seed (Gen 12:3; 18:18; 22:18; 26:4; 28:14; Romans 4; Galatians 3), so that God's justice (justification) and righteousness would come to one and all. But the wadi was bone dry because Israel's worship had become a syncretistic mixture of idolatry and self-aggrandizement, rather than the means for Yahweh's gracious will to shape his people and impact the whole world.[55] Beneath the veneer of worship, the people were not seeking Yahweh (as he invited in 5:4, 6, 14). Instead, they were seeking to control Yahweh, setting limits on Yahweh, and ultimately rejecting Yahweh. Worship was not consumed *with* Yahweh so it will be consumed *by* Yahweh.

Yahweh is not a "safe" or "nice" God.[56] He is not a therapeutic God or a warm and fuzzy God. He is a jealous God (Ex 20:5) who is offended by Israel's fickle faith and spiritual adultery. His rejection of Israel's worship involves several different senses: smell (5:21), sight (5:22), and hearing (5:23). His disgust is

---

[54] *LSB*, p. 319.

[55] See further the excursus "The Prophets and Israel's Worship."

[56] See further the beginning of the introduction.

completely "sensible."[57] He rejects Israel's worship in toto because the Israelites had rejected the heart of his Torah in toto: exclusive love for him (Deut 6:4–5; 11:1, 13; 30:6; Mt 22:37) and love for their neighbor (Lev 19:18; Mt 22:39).

Justice and righteousness (Amos 5:24) are God's gifts in worship, gifts that bear their proper fruits in the daily lives of faithful worshipers. But the apostate people were turning these divine gifts into bitterness and casting them to the ground (5:7; cf. 6:12).[58] The nation's liturgy had masqueraded itself as true piety, and in the process Israel became callous to the cause of justice and righteousness. Yahweh's response promises an ironic twist of fate. Israel will be thrust out of the land and led into exile. The people's gods—imported from foreign lands—will go back to their home. Israel trusted these gods, and they failed her; Yahweh, whom they failed to trust, will abandon the nation.

In the late seventh or early sixth century, Jeremiah's temple sermon (Jer 7:1–15) would echo Amos' same motifs. Liturgy and ethics are inseparable. Worship divorced from compassionate conduct is, according to Jeremiah, "deception" (הַשָּׁקֶר, Jer 7:4). Those who use worship to cheat and defraud will not find Yahweh. True worship, Jeremiah contends, is demonstrated in the practice of justice towards the sojourner, the orphan, and the widow (Jer 7:5–7). In this sermon, Jeremiah shatters the national myth of Zion's invincibility (cf. Micah 3:12). If the people and their worship become corrupt, Yahweh will no longer inhabit Israel's sanctuary or protect the people who worship there. Jeremiah reminds his audience of the tabernacle at Shiloh, which the Philistines had plundered in the days of Samuel (Jer 7:12–15; see 1 Samuel 4–6). When the sacred temple seethes with injustice, when worshipers become inhumane, the place and the people will be destroyed.

2 Ki 17:23–24 and chapters 24–25 verify that Amos' prophecy was divinely inspired. Yahweh sent the Northern Kingdom into Assyrian exile in 722 BC. Then Judah was exiled to Babylon in 587 BC.

The same prophetic concern expressed through Amos would be enacted by the Messiah when he would cleanse the corrupted Jerusalem temple and call the people to righteousness. The failure of the Jewish people as a whole to respond in faith would lead to the destruction of the temple in AD 70 and the diaspora. Yet God would fulfill his promise to resurrect the tabernacle of David (Amos 9:11; Jn 2:18–22) and gather a faithful remnant of both Israelites and Gentiles (Amos 9:12) to be his new and living temple, to be kept free of idolatry (1 Cor 6:19–20; 2 Cor 6:16; 1 Pet 2:5; 1 Jn 5:21).

---

[57] Paul, *Amos*, 189, n. 10.

[58] Amos gives details about their perversions of worship in 2:7–8; 3:14; 4:4–5; 5:5–6, 14, 21–27; 7:9–17; 8:5, 10, 14; 9:1.

Excursus

The Prophets and Israel's Worship

Introduction

It seems as though the attitude of Israel's leaders during the ministry of Amos was like this: anything goes as long as the rituals and sacrifices are done in good order. They might have been thinking, "The Day of Yahweh [5:18–20] will bring us eternal glory in God's kingdom, so until then we will coast through our earthly life." They imagined that they were "Sabbath saints" and that their abundant worship rites (5:21–23) gave them license to be sinners throughout the rest of the week. But Yahweh's call for ever-flowing justice and righteousness (5:24) indicates that faith and ethics cannot stop and start like a wilderness wadi that floods with water in the rainy season and then dries up. God's gift and expectation is for abiding faith that continually overflows in righteousness, like a perennial stream that never fails.[1]

Yahweh uses satire in 4:4–5 to critique unfaithful Israel's worship as a vacuous imitation of the divine service established in the Torah. In 5:4–6 and 5:21–27, he condemns Israel's worship as utterly repugnant. In 7:10–17 Yahweh sends his prophet Amos to confront and oppose the priest Amaziah at Bethel.[2] Both 4:4–5 and 5:21–23 use some vocabulary that is also found in the worship rituals instituted in Exodus and Leviticus, but in these prophetic passages, Yahweh condemns the Israelites' rites.

Scholarly Responses

Some critical scholars have speculated that Amos and other prophets[3] were opposed to the sacrificial and liturgical worship prescribed in the Torah. According to these scholars, the prophets believed that Yahweh did not institute Israel's worship life nor take any pleasure in it. Rather, God only cared about the nation's ethical life.[4]

In the past two hundred years, the relationship between Israel's prophets and the nation's worship life has gone through several different stages of interpretation. The oldest critical response promoted the idea that there was an

---

1 These words of Barth are descriptive of Amos 5:21–27: "Everything is in order, but everything is also in the greatest disorder. The mill is turning, but it is empty as it turns. All the sails are hoisted, but no wind fills them to drive the ship. The fountain adorned with many spouts is there, but no water comes" (*Evangelical Theology*, 135).

2 A full list of the Amos passages that condemn northern Israel's worship must include 2:7–8; 3:14; 4:4–5; 5:5–6, 14, 21–27; 7:9–17; 8:5, 10, 14; 9:1 (the Bethel altar). See also the excursus "The Sabbath."

3 See, for example, Is 1:10–20; Micah 6:6–8.

4 See Rogerson, *Old Testament Criticism in the Nineteenth Century*, 28–78, 257–89.

irreconcilable difference between the two. The argument went something like this. Prophets—especially Amos—were the founders of "ethical monotheism."[5] Their goal was to "de-ritualize" Israel's religion, and they sought to accomplish this through a complete denunciation of the nation's sacramental worship life. The vocation of the prophet was to be anti-liturgical worship, anti-sacrifice, and anti-priest. This critical view went hand-in-hand with the old source-critical method of interpreting the OT. (Not coincidentally, many of these critics disliked sacramental Christian worship as practiced in the Roman Catholic and Lutheran traditions.) This method denied that the Torah of Moses preceded the prophets. Instead, proponents of this method held that Amos and other prophets were militating against the liturgical movements and traditions that eventually would be codified in the priestly ("P") portions of the Torah. These portions supposedly were written last of all, in the postexilic era, centuries after the ministries of many prophets, including Amos.

Over the last two centuries, source criticism gave way to form criticism and redaction criticism, and then these destructive critical methods have largely been replaced by newer, more constructive literary methods such as rhetorical analysis.[6] As this has happened the old critical view of a strict dichotomy between the Word-based prophet and the worship-based priest has softened. Scholars increasingly have recognized that some prophets were supporters of sacrificial worship (e.g., Joel and Habakkuk), and several prophetic oracles were interpreted to be liturgically based and an integral part of Israel's worship life. For example, Isaiah's call came when he was in the Jerusalem temple (Isaiah 6), and he envisions the rebuilding of the temple in the era of Cyrus (Is 44:28) and the restoration of God-pleasing sacrificial worship (Is 66:20–23). Jeremiah (Jer 33:11, 18) and especially the prophetic priest Ezekiel (Ezek 20:40–42; chapters 40–48) likewise foresee the restoration of holy sacramental worship.[7] The postexilic prophets Haggai and Zechariah also advocate the rebuilding of the temple, along with the reestablishment of its worship life.

Dialectical Negation

Furthering this healthy understanding of the biblical connection between prophets and Israel's worship is Bartelt's study entitled "Dialectical Negation:

---

5 See Hummel, *The Word Becoming Flesh*, 156–58.

6 For a survey of these methods, see "Different Methods of Interpreting the Book of Amos" in the introduction. This commentary renounces historical-critical methods and instead uses rhetorical analysis and historical-grammatical interpretation, affirming the plenary inspiration and authority of Scripture. See "This Commentary's Method" in the introduction.

7 Ezekiel 40–48 envisions an eschatological temple as the center of the richly liturgical worship life of God's redeemed people. It finds its proleptic fulfillment now in the sacramental worship of the Christian church and will be fully realized in the eternal state. For an overview, see Hummel, *Ezekiel 21–48*, 1149–58.

An Exegetical Both/And."[8] He begins by calling attention to Amos 5:21–24 and other prophetic texts (e.g., Jer 7:22; Hos 6:6; Joel 2:13) that appear to completely reject Israel's worship life. In order to promote the view that God's ministry in the OT era encompassed *both* the prophet (a minister of the Word) *and* the priest (a minister of the sacrificial and sacramental worship) he promotes the term "dialectical negation," which embraces the idea that some texts that appear to be "either/or" propositions are best understood as examples of "both/and" thinking.

Dialectical negation also appears in the NT. For example, Peter states this about the OT prophets:

> Concerning this salvation, the prophets who prophesied concerning the grace for you searched carefully and inquired, seeking what person or time the Spirit of Christ within them was indicating as he predicted the sufferings of Christ and after these the glories. It was revealed to them that *they were not serving themselves, but you*, in these things which now have been announced to you through those who preached the Gospel to you by the Holy Spirit sent from heaven—things angels yearn to look into. (1 Pet 1:10–12)

These verses seem to give the impression that prophets were *not* preaching to their contemporaries nor for later generations of the OT people of God, but instead were *only* preaching for the benefit of NT believers. Bartelt writes: "However, if one translates what Peter says in verse 12 as dialectical negation, the integrity of the prophets as preachers to their own time is preserved: 'It was revealed to them that they were not (just) serving themselves, but [*also*] you.' "[9]

Dialectical negation proposes that in some texts the ideas that appear contradictory are in fact complementary. The prophets do not contradict what the Torah says about God's desire for worship. Instead, when the prophets condemn Israel's abuses and perversions of worship—practices that deviated from the Torah and were performed without faith—these divine spokesmen are actually complementing and upholding the Torah, which calls for the worship rites to be performed in faith, in gratitude for God's redemption. This is certainly true of Amos, since his denunciations are of northern Israel's syncretistic worship, which was accompanied by immorality, laced with idolatry, and performed at false alternative shrines instead of the Jerusalem temple, the dwelling place of Yahweh, God the Redeemer.[10] Similarly, employing dialectical negation assists in the interpretation of Jer 7:21–23, which appears to be a wholesale rejection

---

[8] Weiss also employs the term "dialectical negation." After his analysis of Amos 5:21–24 he writes: "It may even be worthwhile to consider the possibility that the absolute negation of the cultic acts witnessed by the prophet is in fact merely a 'dialectical negation,' a rhetorical technique employed in order to emphasize with greater force his historically conditioned demand for 'justice and righteousness' " ("Concerning Amos' Repudiation of the Cult," 214).

[9] Bartelt, "Dialectical Negation," 63.

[10] See Amos 2:7–8; 3:14; 4:4–5; 5:5–6, 14, 21–27; 7:9–17; 8:5, 10, 14; 9:1 (the Bethel altar).

of Israel's worship life.[11] In that passage, Yahweh appears to say that he did *not* give the prescriptions in Leviticus for whole burnt offerings and other sacrifices; instead, he *only* asked his people to listen to (believe and obey) his spoken Word. However, using this "both/and" reading strategy, we may augment the translation of Jer 7:21–23 with "only" and "also":

> This is what Yahweh of armies, the God of Israel, says: "Add your whole burnt offerings to your other sacrifices, and eat the meat! For I did not speak to your fathers, and I did not command them *only*[12] about whole burnt offering and sacrifice in the day I brought them out from the land of Egypt. Rather, I *also* commanded them this word, saying, "Listen to my voice, and I will be your God and you will be my people. You will walk in the whole way I command you, so that it may go well with you."

Yahweh employs hyperbole to illustrate the primacy of faith, love, and faithfulness toward him. This primacy does not contradict the Torah; in fact, it affirms the Torah (see, e.g., Deut 6:1–6, 20–25; 7:6–9). Dialectical negation sharpens Yahweh's rhetoric. The sarcastic imperative "eat the meat!" appears to contradict the Torah prescriptions by inviting the lay people to eat from the whole burnt offering and other sacrifices.[13] But this sarcasm is no different than that in Amos 4:4, where Yahweh tries to shock the people into repentance by exhorting them to sin all the more at their idolatrous shrines:

> Go to Bethel and transgress,
> to Gilgal and transgress even more.
> Bring your sacrifices for every morning,
> for every third day your tithes.[14]

Torah and Worship

Torah teaching was to be a standard feature of faithful worship. This close connection between Torah and worship is presupposed in Yahweh's indictment

---

[11] An example of an interpreter who interprets the text as a rejection of the absolute good of sacrificial worship is Barstad. He summarizes his view, which is similar to, but tamer than, that of Wellhausen (*The Religious Polemics of Amos*, 116–18):

> One of the conclusions which we *have* to draw from these passages of the prophets [like Jer 7:21–23], if we pay attention to the texts, is that the sacrificial cult is *unnecessary*. Even if the prophets do not in fact forbid the cultic sacrifices (which would indeed have been impossible), they make the value of the cultic sacrifices *relative*.

See the discussion of Wellhausen in "Form Criticism" in "Different Methods of Interpreting the Book of Amos" in the introduction.

[12] The NIV adds the word "just" in "I did not just give them commands about burnt offerings and sacrifices" (Jer 7:22) in order to accent that the relationship between Israel carrying out the worship rites and the people's faithful response to the Word is not "either/or" but "both/and."

[13] The whole burnt offering was to be consumed in its entirety on the altar. The only sacrifice that God permitted lay people to eat was from the peace offerings (Lev 7:11–36). For a listing of the offerings and the parts that could be eaten by the priests or lay people, see figure 4 in Kleinig, *Leviticus*, 38.

[14] See further the commentary on Amos 4:4.

in Amos 5:21–27.[15] The OT prophetic promise is that the eschatological revelation of Yahweh's Torah would take place from Jerusalem (Is 2:2–4; Micah 4:1–5). That promise now stands fulfilled in Christ's ministry and journey to Jerusalem, the site of his death, resurrection, and ascension, and the place from which he sent out his apostolic missionaries into all the world (Acts 1:4–8). Yet it also awaits its consummation in the new Jerusalem after his return (Revelation 21; cf. Acts 1:11). Grounded in God's messianic promise, the sacrificial and sacramental worship God gave Israel in the Torah was to empower and inspire a response of love. This is how Isaiah (Is 1:10–20) and Jeremiah (Jer 7:1–20) also interpret worship.

The Psalter was Israel's hymnal, and it bears abundant marks of its use in liturgical worship. It contains ethical admonitions for righteous living by faith so that the faithful can worship rightly; see, for example, Psalms 15; 24; and 51. LeFebvre notes that Psalm 1 intends that all the psalms are to be read through the prism of Torah faithfulness ("Torah" occurs twice in Ps 1:2).[16] The Torah-formed life is bounded by faithfulness (Psalm 1) and praise (Psalm 150). It is not surprising, therefore, that Jesus rejected the tithe of the Pharisees because they disregarded the important responses that are to flow out of worship: justice, mercy, and faithfulness (Mt 23:23). And just like Isaiah (Is 29:13), Jesus describes the people of his day with these words: "This people honors me with their lips, but their heart is far from me" (Mt 15:8–9).

Faith leads the believer to walk in the way of good works (Eph 2:8–10). Just as faith cannot be divorced from works, neither can adoration be severed from ethics. Yahweh hates fake worship. This is why Amos alerts the Israelites to the futility of their worship. They will fail in their attempts to circumvent the way of justice and righteousness (see Amos 5:7, 12, 15, 24; 6:12) with extravagant but idolatrous liturgical rites. They cannot use false worship as a masquerade for saving faith and true faithfulness to God's Word. Samuel asked disobedient Saul:

> Does Yahweh have as much delight in burnt offerings and sacrifices as he does in listening to the voice of Yahweh? Behold, to listen is better than sacrifice, and to hearken is better than the fat of rams. (1 Sam 15:22)

In the same Spirit, Amos declares that religious observances cannot substitute for God-given righteousness with moral integrity. Worship apart from love toward God and neighbor only creates an illusion of security. When worship anesthetizes people to the pain of the world it becomes skewed and can only lead to irrevocable disaster, exile, and eternal death (5:1–3, 16–20, 27). Yahweh alone is the source of all that is good, and he yearns for his people to seek him and find everlasting life (5:4, 6, 14).

---

[15] See further "The Message of Amos 5:21–27" in the commentary on 5:21–27.

[16] LeFebvre, "Torah-Meditation and the Psalms: The Invitation of Psalm 1."

The liturgical and sacrificial worship God instituted in the OT was for the purpose of strengthening the people's faith in him, furnishing communion with him and with each other, and granting them everlasting salvation through the forgiveness of their sins. It was a means to this end, not an end in itself. That is why Yahweh declares that he delights in loyal covenantal love more than sacrifices, and in people knowing him more than whole burnt offerings (Hos 6:6; Ps 40:7 [ET 40:6]). Jesus affirms this when he cites Hos 6:6 in the NT (Mt 9:13, 12:7). Ultimately, the OT sacrificial system is fulfilled by the sacrificial atonement of Jesus Christ on the cross, and as the risen Lord distributes the saving benefits of his atonement to his people through the divine service of Word and Sacrament in the Christian church.[17]

Loving worship of God and love toward one's neighbor is rooted in the covenant of grace God established in the OT. This gracious covenant was the basis for the preaching of the prophets, who looked for its fulfillment in Christ (1 Pet 1:10–12). This same grace is now poured out (cf. Amos 5:24) through the new covenant in the shed blood of Christ. When Christ was asked to name *the* greatest commandment, he responded by citing from the Torah, specifically from Deuteronomy (6:4–5; 11:1, 13; 30:6) and Leviticus (19:18):

> "You shall love the Lord your God with all your heart and with all your soul and with all your mind." This is the first and greatest commandment. The second is like it: "You shall love your neighbor as yourself." On these two commandments the whole Torah and the Prophets hang. (Mt 22:37–40)

The lawyer asked Jesus for one commandment, but he gave him two. The love of God we receive and give in worship is intimately connected to loving people in the world. Like faith itself, the ability to love one's neighbor comes only from God as his Holy Spirit works in us through his Word and Sacraments. "We love because he first loved us" (1 Jn 4:19).

The Lutheran Confessions and Worship

The Lutheran Confessions affirm this relationship between God-given faith, love for God, and love for one's neighbor. Article XIII of the Augsburg Confession briefly summarizes the Christian view of sacramental worship:

> It is taught among us that the sacraments were instituted not only to be signs by which people might be identified outwardly as Christians, but that they are signs and testimonies of God's will toward us for the purpose of awakening and strengthening our faith. For this reason they require faith, and they are rightly used when they are received in faith and for the purpose of strengthening faith.

Worship, the reading of God's Word, and the Sacraments do not grant a right standing before God *ex opere operato*, merely by doing them apart from faith in Christ. AC XXIV 28–30 states:

[17] See Kleinig, *Leviticus*, 1–13.

> St. Paul taught that we obtain grace before God through faith and not through works. Manifestly contrary to this teaching is the misuse of the Mass by those who think that grace is obtained through the performance of this work, for it is well known that the Mass is used to remove sin and obtain grace and all sorts of benefits from God, not only for the priest himself but also for the whole world and for others, both living and dead. …
>
> The holy sacrament was not instituted to make provision for a sacrifice for sin—for the sacrifice [of Christ on the cross] has already taken place—but to awaken our faith and comfort our consciences when we perceive that through the sacrament grace and forgiveness of sin are promised us by Christ. Accordingly the sacrament requires faith, and without faith it is used in vain.

Thus through his Word and Sacraments God grants and strengthens saving faith in Christ. This Christian faith leads to good works. AC VI 1–2 affirms:

> Faith should produce good fruits and good works and that we must do all such good works as God has commanded, but we should do them for God's sake and not place our trust in them as if thereby to merit favor before God. For we receive forgiveness of sin and righteousness through faith in Christ, as Christ himself says, "So you also, when you have done all that is commanded you, say, 'We are unworthy servants' " (Luke 17:10).

Conclusion

Yahweh calls for the people to abandon their idolatrous shrines and instead to seek him, live (Amos 5:4–6, 14), and let righteousness and justice flow (5:24). This call shows that the worship sacrifices and ceremonies he gave Israel in the Torah were his means of granting the people faith, everlasting life with him, and a righteous life. God desires both devotion and devotions.

Yahweh's critiques in Amos against Israel's worship life appear to contradict his commands through Moses only if these prophetic criticisms are isolated from their larger context in the book of Amos. He was against sacrifices that were combined with injustice, immorality, and idolatry (2:4, 7–8; 8:5–6), vain offerings of their own invention at false shrines without the inward sacrifice of a broken and contrite heart (4:4–5; 8:14; Ps 51:19 [ET 51:17]). For the same reason he despised their faithless songs and the music they improvised at their idolatrous banquets (5:23; 6:5–7; 8:10).[18] When the sacrificial system and ceremonial laws became a *substitute* for faithful living, then the prophets inveighed heavily against them (e.g., Is 58:6–7).[19] As 1 Jn 3:18 states using dialectical negation: "Little children, let us *not love* [only] in word nor [only] in speech but [also] in deed and truth." And so it was not the worship that Yahweh had given

---

18 Isaiah too preached against the sacrificial aspects of Israel's corrupt worship and included faithless prayer in the same category (Is 1:13–15).

19 Paul, *Amos*, 139, says: "When the cult became a substitute for moral behavior, it was condemned." A similar view is held by Rowley, *Worship in Ancient Israel*, 144–75.

Israel that was the problem. The people were not worshiping faithfully; it was the people in the worship services who were the real problem![20]

And the solution? Just as an ever-flowing wadi must be supplied by a well-spring or reservoir (see the commentary Amos 5:24), so a life of doing what is right and just can only be supplied by God. Amos sees that this life from God comes through the resurrection of the tabernacle and line of David, which culminates in Christ (see the commentary on 9:11).

[20] Wolff writes: "Amos does not turn against the cultus but against the participants in it" (*Joel and Amos*, 220).

Amos 6:1–7

The First Will Be First into Exile

Translation

6 **[1]Woe to you who are complacent on Mount Zion**
and who feel secure on Mount Samaria,
the most distinguished ones of the foremost of the nations,
to whom the house of Israel comes.
[2]Travel to Calneh and look,
and go from there to Hamath Rabbah,
and descend to Gath of the Philistines.
Are you better than those kingdoms?
Are their territories greater than your territory?
[3]You who are thrusting off the evil day,
you bring near the seat of violence!
[4]Those lying on beds of ivory,
sprawling upon their couches,
eating lambs from the flock
and calves from the midst of the stall,
[5]improvising tunes with the lyre,
like David they compose [music] for themselves [using] musical instruments,
[6]drinking wine from sacred bowls,
with the choicest of olive oils they anoint themselves,
but they do not grieve over the ruin of Joseph.
[7]Therefore now they will go into exile as the first of the exiles,
and the *marzēaḥ* feast of the sprawlers will depart.

Textual Notes

6:1 הוֹי הַשַּׁאֲנַנִּים בְּצִיּוֹן—For הוֹי, see the first textual note on 5:18.

The plural adjective with article הַשַּׁאֲנַנִּים, literally, "the carefree/complacent ones," serves as a vocative address to the Israelites, and so it is translated as "*you* who are complacent." Similarly, the plural participle with article הַמְנַדִּים at the beginning of 6:3 is translated as a vocative. Each of the next three verses also begins with a plural participle with article (הַשֹּׁכְבִים in 6:4; הַפֹּרְטִים in 6:5; and הַשֹּׁתִים in 6:6), but they are translated as third-person descriptions because of the third-person forms elsewhere in those verses.

The adjective שַׁאֲנָן is derived from the verb שָׁאַן which appears only five times in the OT, always in the Palel conjugation (see GKC, § 55 d), meaning "be at rest, peaceful, carefree, self-confident."[1] The contexts with the verb all carry positive connotations

---

1 Cf. W. Thiel, "שַׁאֲנָן," *TDOT* 14:265–67.

suggesting restful, peaceful conditions with God's grace and protection (e.g., Jer 30:10). The adjective too can be used with a salvific sense when it describes the hope of Israel (Is 32:18; 33:20). However, more frequently the adjective carries negative connotations of illusory security, perhaps going as far as proud arrogance and hubris (e.g., Is 32:9, 11). Amos employs the adjective in that sense as a substantive, "a carefree, arrogant, complacent person."

The noun הַר, "mountain," in the next clause is backward-gapped, so בְּצִיּוֹן is translated as "on *Mount* Zion." הַר does double duty since Zion is a mountain and the city of Samaria is on a mountain. Zion (the temple mount with the old city of David) in the first clause is parallel to "Mount Samaria" in the second clause. Both royal properties were separately obtained and governed outside of standard tribal administrations (cf. 2 Sam 5:6–9; 1 Ki 16:23–24), and so both were in a privileged position from their inception. This view is contrary to the LXX, which translated הַשַּׁאֲנַנִּים בְּצִיּוֹן as τοῖς ἐξουθενοῦσιν Σιων, "those who despise Zion," suggesting that it understood both clauses as addressed to the northern Israelites. But Amos addresses the southern kingdom elsewhere in his book (see the commentary), so it is fitting that the "woe" here applies first to those in "Zion."

וְהַבֹּטְחִים בְּהַר שֹׁמְרוֹן—For שֹׁמְרוֹן, "Samaria," see the second textual note on 3:9.

The verb בָּטַח with the preposition בְּ can mean "to trust in" and refer either to saving faith in God (BDB, s.v. בָּטַח, Qal, 3 a and d) or to false trust in persons or things (BDB, s.v. בָּטַח, Qal, 3 b and c, which cites Amos 6:1), so this clause could address woe to "those trusting *in* Mount Samaria." However, the parallel use of בְּ on בְּצִיּוֹן in the preceding clause has the spatial meaning "*on* Zion," so בְּהַר שֹׁמְרוֹן probably means "*on* Mount Samaria." בָּטַח can have the more general meaning "to feel secure, be unconcerned, careless."[2] As a parallel counterpart in this bicolon to הַשַּׁאֲנַנִּים, the prophet is employing בָּטַח to denote a facile optimism and false confidence. It has the same meaning in Prov 14:16: "the wise person fears [Yahweh] and turns away from evil, but a fool is hotheaded and *overconfident/reckless* [וּבוֹטֵחַ]." See also בָּטַח in Deut 28:52 and Prov 11:28. That Israelites were denying the reality of coming judgment is noted later in Amos 6:3 and 9:10. The only certain support for life rests in Yahweh; only in him is trust rightly grounded (Ps 37:5). The prophetic statements about trust in Amos 6:1 and Jer 17:7 have a strong connection to those in Wisdom literature; see, for example, the verb בָּטַח in Pss 32:10; 84:13 (ET 84:12) and the cognate noun מִבְטָח in Prov 22:19.

נְקֻבֵי רֵאשִׁית הַגּוֹיִם—The Qal passive participle in construct, נְקֻבֵי, "the distinguished ones of," is from the verb נָקַב, which can mean "to pierce" (e.g., 2 Ki 12:10 [ET 12:9]; Job 40:24; 40:26 [ET 41:2]).[3] Boring a hole in the ear could identify a person and establish ownership (the verb רָצַע in Ex 21:6). This may explain how נָקַב can also mean "to designate, distinguish" in Gen 30:28 and Is 62:2, and then the Qal passive participle means "distinguished" (see BDB, s.v. נָקַב, Qal, 2). The Niphal is similarly used for people who are appointed or designated for a high office (e.g., Num 1:17; Ezra 8:20).

---

2 Cf. BDB, s.v. בָּטַח, Qal, II, and A. Jepsen, "בָּטַח," *TDOT* 2:88–94.

3 Cf. J. Scharbert, "נָקַב," *TDOT* 9:551–53.

A construct phrase can be used for a superlative, and the construct chain here is, literally, "the distinguished of the first of the nations," that is, the most distinguished or highest aristocrats of what they believed was "the *foremost* nation" (Waltke-O'Connor, § 14.5e, including example 53). In this context רֵאשִׁית, "first," does not denote temporal primacy (as in, e.g., Gen 1:1), but pride of rank, place, or position (Waltke-O'Connor, § 14.5e). "Thus the carefree attitude of the elite class of Samaria is rooted in the sense of belonging to the patently superior people."[4] Balaam warned, "First among the nations [רֵאשִׁית גּוֹיִם] is Amalek, but its end is to perish forever" (Num 24:20). The leaders of Amos' day ignored this destiny of those who position themselves as "king of the hill."

Amos will reuse רֵאשִׁית, "first," in 6:6, where the context requires translating as "the *choicest* of olive oils." Then he will create irony by using the related noun רֹאשׁ for "the *first* of the exiles" in 6:7. While English obscures this threefold use of Hebrew terms for "first" in 6:1, 6–7, the title of this pericope, "The *First* Will Be *First* into Exile," reflects the usage.

וּבָאוּ לָהֶם בֵּית יִשְׂרָאֵל׃—Literally, "the house of Israel comes to them" means that people from all over Israel come to the aristocracies in Zion and Samaria because of these leaders' influential position (see the commentary). The preceding two clauses had participles (וְהַבֹּטְחִים ... נְקֻבֵי), but the description here continues with a perfect with *waw* consecutive, וּבָאוּ (Joüon, § 119 r; cf. GKC, § 112 n).

6:2 עִבְרוּ כַלְנֵה וּרְאוּ—The second of the two Qal imperatives could be rendered with a purpose clause: "cross over [עִבְרוּ] to Calneh *in order* to see [וּרְאוּ]." עָבַר often refers in a general sense to traveling or changing location with purposeful or goal-oriented motion.[5] The city name כַלְנֵה is spelled כַּלְנוֹ in Is 10:9. The exact location of the city is unknown. It was one of four cities that were centers for the kingdom of Nimrod (Gen 10:10).[6] Little is known about the city, which was the capital of the greater kingdom of Pattin (also known as Unqi), a kingdom in the lower valley of the Orontes River. The city appears as *Kullani(a)* in Akkadian sources. It was defeated by the Assyrian king Tiglath-pileser III in 738 BC, when it was assimilated into the Assyrian kingdom.[7]

וּלְכוּ מִשָּׁם חֲמַת רַבָּה—After arriving in Calneh the travelers are directed to "go from there" (וּלְכוּ מִשָּׁם) to an accusative of destination (see GKC, § 118 f), חֲמַת רַבָּה, transliterated as Hamath Rabbah, meaning "Hamath the great." The feminine adjective רַבָּה, "great" or perhaps "capital," differentiates this Hamath from Hamath-zobah in 2 Chr 8:3. It was common practice in the ancient Near East to differentiate cities in this way, for example, Great Sidon and Little Sidon.[8] Elsewhere the place name is always vocalized חֲמָת and the reduction of the *qamets* to *patach* here (-מַ-) indicates that it is in construct with the adjective (Joüon, § 131 n; GKC, § 125 h; cf. Joüon, § 96D d; GKC,

---

4 Wolff, *Joel and Amos*, 274.

5 Cf. H. F. Fuhs, "עָבַר," *TDOT* 10:413–24.

6 Cf. S. A. Meier, "Calneh," *ABD* 1:823–24; Paul, *Amos*, 201–2.

7 Cf. *ANET*, 282–83.

8 *ANET*, 287.

§ 126 y). Hamath Rabbah was located on the Orontes River in upper Syria, about a hundred and fifty miles north of Dan. Paul writes: "Like Kullani [Calneh], the name Hamath Rabbah may have originally designated the capital city and was subsequently extended to represent the entire kingdom or was itself the name of the great state of Hamath."[9] The city-state may have been under the control of Jeroboam ben Joash (see 2 Ki 14:25), Amos' contemporary (Amos 1:1), but it was conquered by the Assyrian king Tiglath-pileser III during his campaign in 738 BC.[10]

וּרְד֣וּ גַת־פְּלִשְׁתִּ֔ים—Next, the travelers are to "go down, descend" (imperative of יָרַד) to "Gath of the Philistines." This differentiates this Gath from several other cities in the OT named Gath (e.g., Gath-hepher in 2 Ki 14:25; Gath-rimmon in Josh 19:45). The location of Gath of the Philistines is still disputed by scholars.[11] Gath was subjugated by King Uzziah of Judah (2 Chr 26:6), a contemporary of Amos (1:1), but later lost to the Aramean king Hazael (see the commentary). The Philistine cities were threatened or conquered by the Assyrians several times in the latter part of the eighth century, beginning with the campaign of the Assyrian king Tiglath-pileser III in 734 BC.[12] Gath was taken by the Assyrian king Sargon II in 711 BC in his campaign against the king of Ashdod.[13] Assyrian dominance over Gath continued through Sennacherib's invasion in 701 BC.[14]

הֲטוֹבִים֙ מִן־הַמַּמְלָכ֣וֹת הָאֵ֔לֶּה אִם־רַ֥ב גְּבוּלָ֖ם מִגְּבֻלְכֶֽם׃—As in 6:12, the first rhetorical question begins with the interrogative -הֲ, and the second question begins with אִם. The second person suffix on the final word, מִגְּבֻלְכֶֽם, "than your territory," implies that the initial adjective with interrogative, הֲטוֹבִים֙, should be translated with a second person pronoun: "are *you* better … ?" The adjective טוֹב, "good," with the preposition מִן forms a comparative clause, "better than." The adjective רַב, "large, great," with the preposition מִן on מִגְּבֻלְכֶֽם forms another comparative clause, "greater than." The noun גְּבוּל can refer to the "boundary" of a country or, as here, its enclosed "territory." Its singular can be a collective, and גְּבוּלָ֖ם is translated with a plural, "their territories," because of the preceding references to a number of different city-states, each with its own territory.

6:3 הַֽמְנַדִּ֖ים לְי֣וֹם רָ֑ע וַתַּגִּישׁ֖וּן שֶׁ֥בֶת חָמָֽס׃—The syntax is difficult. A first view, reflected by this commentary's translation, is that the masculine plural participle הַֽמְנַדִּ֖ים has the definite article and is a vocative address to the Israelites addressed in the second person in 6:2d–e: "… your territory, *O you who put far away* the day of disaster" (ESV; emphasis added). This view is supported by the next verse, 6:4, which begins with a participle with article (הַשֹּׁכְבִים֙) that describes the Israelites. The second clause of the verse has a verb (וַתַּגִּישׁ֖וּן, "you bring near") that clearly speaks to the Israelites in the second person. The participles beginning the relative clauses at the start of 6:3 (הַֽמְנַדִּ֖ים); 6:4 (הַשֹּׁכְבִים֙); 6:5 (הַפֹּרְטִ֖ים); and 6:6 (הַשֹּׁתִ֤ים) have the article, but the participles in the two

[9] Paul, *Amos*, 202–3.

[10] See 2 Ki 18:34 and *ANET*, 282–83.

[11] Cf. J. D. Seger, "Gath," *ABD* 2:908–9.

[12] Cf. Sweeney, *The Twelve Prophets*, 244; Paul, *Amos*, 204.

[13] *ANET*, 286 (cf. Is 20:1).

[14] Sweeney, *The Twelve Prophets*, 244.

relative clauses later in 6:4 (וּסְרֻחִים ... וְאֹכְלִים) lack the article (Joüon, § 138 e; Waltke-O'Connor, § 37.5b, including example 17). Such variation is common in poetry.

A second view is that 6:3 begins a new sentence and the *he* on הַמְנַדִּים is the interrogative: "*do you put off* the day of calamity?" (NASB; emphasis added). Supporting this view is the fact that the preceding half verse, 6:2d–e, consists of two questions, the first of which begins with the *he* interrogative (הֲטוֹבִים). Compare the first textual note on 5:25, where הַזְּבָחִים probably has the interrogative -הֲ (rather than the definite article).

The verb נָדָה occurs only twice in the OT, both in the Piel meaning "to exclude, thrust away."[15] In both passages, arrogant people are rejecting God in some way. In the other occurrence, Yahweh speaks through Isaiah to encourage those who tremble at his Word because their enemies will be ashamed: "your brothers who hate you, who exclude you [מְנַדֵּיכֶם] because of my name, … will be put to shame" (Is 66:5). Here in Amos 6:3, Israel's elite are "thrusting off the evil day" by refusing to think about Yahweh's coming judgment, but it shall overtake them anyway.

The object of the participle is לְיוֹם רָע, introduced with the preposition לְ (GKC, § 117 n; Joüon, § 125 k). The adjectival phrase יוֹם רַע, "evil day," appears only here in the OT, but the construct phrase יוֹם רָעָה, "day of evil," appears in, for example, Jer 17:17–18; Ps 27:5; Prov 16:4, and the plural construct phrase יְמֵי רָע, "days of evil," occurs in Ps 49:6 (ET 49:5); 94:13. The "evil day" is theologically equivalent to other phrases with "day" in Amos: "a day of war" and "a day of tempest" (1:14); "that day" (2:16; 8:3, 9, 13); "the day when I punish the transgressions of Israel" (3:14); "the Day of Yahweh" (5:18, 20); and "a bitter day" (8:10). These expressions for judgment refer initially to the onslaught of the Assyrian army against Samaria, which resulted in Samaria's fall in 722 BC. See the commentary on 5:18, 20. Yet Amos also predicts a Gospel "day" and "days" (9:11, 13).

The verb וַתַּגִּישׁוּן is a Hiphil of נָגַשׁ. This is one of the rare cases where an imperfect with *waw* consecutive also has paragogic *nun* (Joüon, § 44 e). Waltke-O'Connor (§§ 31.1.1a, note 2, and 31.7.1a, note 48) argues based on Ugaritic and the Amarna texts that in form וַתַּגִּישׁוּן could be a third-person masculine plural, which would fit the third-person references to Israel in 6:4–7. However, the existence of such a third-person imperfect with -ת in Hebrew is questionable, and the participle (הַמְנַדִּים) can be understood as a vocative address to Israel in the second person ("*you* who are thrusting off"), which fits the second-person verb וַתַּגִּישׁוּן. The *waw* consecutive with imperfect often refers to past tense, and that could be the meaning here: by sinning Israel had already "brought near" violence. However, the first half of the verse refers to future (but imminent) violent judgment from God (on "the evil day"), and it makes more sense to take this clause as referring to the coming judgment Israel has provoked. The present-tense translation above, "you bring near," reflects that וַתַּגִּישׁוּן is parallel with the participle הַמְנַדִּים in the first colon of the bicolon.

The LXX translates the second half of the verse with two present participles: οἱ ἐγγίζοντες καὶ ἐφαπτόμενοι σαββάτων ψευδῶν, "those who are bringing near and

---

15 See BDB and P. J. J. S. Els, "נדה," *NIDOTTE* 3:33–34.

taking hold of false Sabbaths." The LXX apparently vocalized שֶׁבֶת as the plural of שַׁבָּת. The Peshitta also translated with a participle and apparently vocalized שֶׁבֶת as שַׁבָּת: ܘܡܩܪܒܝܢ ܫܒܬܐ ܕܚܛܘܦܝܐ, "and those bringing near a Sabbath that is seized by violence." The Vulgate renders with a second-person present active indicative: *et adpropinquatis solio iniquitatis*, "and you approach the seat of iniquity."

Amos referred to Israel's sins of חָמָס, "violence," earlier in 3:10. The interpretation of שֶׁבֶת חָמָס hinges on the meaning of שֶׁבֶת, which could be either of two rare nouns. The שֶׁבֶת derived from יָשַׁב, "to sit, dwell," refers to the seat of Solomon's throne in 1 Ki 10:19 || 2 Chr 9:18 and to a dwelling place in Num 21:15; Obad 3. BDB (s.v. שֶׁבֶת I, under the root ישׁב) defines the phrase here as "*a seat* (*throne*, or *enthronement*) *of violence*," and most English translations reflect this understanding. This would refer to Assyria's violent conquest of northern Israel in 722 BC, the Assyrian "reign of terror" (NIV). The second noun שֶׁבֶת, "cessation," occurs in Ex 21:19; Is 30:7; Prov 20:3 and is derived from the verb שָׁבַת, "to cease." If Israel brings near "a cessation of violence," this would refer to God terminating Israel's violent sins (the meaning of חָמָס in Amos 3:10) by destroying the nation itself. Paul writes: "Whatever the exact meaning of this enigmatic expression is, the intention of the prophet is clear: The leaders of the north are directly responsible for precipitating and accelerating the very misfortune that they claim will never overtake them."[16]

6:4 הַשֹּׁכְבִים֙ עַל־מִטּ֣וֹת שֵׁ֔ן—The attributive participle הַשֹּׁכְבִים֙, "those lying (down)," refers to people reclining to feast during a gala event, as made clear by the rest of the verse, although it might also refer to sleeping off the effects of an alcoholic party (cf. 2:8; 4:1; 6:6). Amos used the singular מִטָּה, "couch, bed," in 3:12 and referred to שֵׁן, "ivory (inlays)" of houses, in 3:15. The construct phrase מִטּ֣וֹת שֵׁ֔ן, "beds/couches of ivory," means that these lavish couches were decorated with ivory inlays.[17] Such couches are mentioned only here in the OT but are documented in Akkadian sources,[18] and Hezekiah gave some as tribute to Sennacherib.[19]

וּסְרֻחִ֖ים עַל־עַרְשׂוֹתָ֑ם—The Qal passive participle סְרֻחִים recurs in plene form (סְרוּחִים) at the end of 6:7 with the same substantive meaning, "people who are sprawling,"[20] like a blanket draped over a bed. In Ex 26:12–13 the verb סָרַח and cognate noun סֶרַח describe the curtains that "hang over" the back of the tabernacle. This is how Amos pictures those who sprawl about in indolence, draping themselves over their expensive beds in a drunken stupor. The noun עֶרֶשׂ, "bed, couch," occurred earlier in 3:12 and is a synonym of מִטָּה.

וְאֹכְלִ֤ים כָּרִים֙ מִצֹּ֔אן וַעֲגָלִ֖ים מִתּ֥וֹךְ מַרְבֵּֽק׃—The Israelites were dining on delicacies. The prepositional phrase כָּרִים֙ מִצֹּ֔אן, "lambs from the flock," connotes "the pick of the

---

[16] Paul, *Amos*, 205.

[17] King, *Amos, Hosea, Micah*, 148.

[18] For the details, see Paul, *Amos*, 205, including n. 51; cf. King, *Amos, Hosea, Micah*, 148–49.

[19] *ANET*, 288.

[20] See BDB, s.v. סָרַח, Qal 1, and R. S. Hess, "סרח," *NIDOTTE* 3:287–88.

flock"[21] because the lamb (כַּר) was the best animal in the herd (cf. Deut 32:14; Is 16:1). Similarly, it was more luxurious to eat a tender "calf" (עֵגֶל) than a grown bovine. The noun מַרְבֵּק by etymology means a "tying place" but refers to a "feeding stall" where animals were confined and fattened.[22] The calves in Amos 6:4 were well fed, fattened to perfection, and then butchered for the affluent. The witch at Endor had a fattened "calf of a feeding stall" (עֵגֶל־מַרְבֵּק) in her house, and she prepared it for Saul (1 Sam 28:24). The phrase כְּעֶגְלֵי מַרְבֵּק, "like calves of a feeding stall," appears in Mal 3:20 (ET 4:2) as a simile for the prosperity of God's redeemed people because of the advent of the Messiah, "the Sun of righteousness." It also describes well-fed mercenary soldiers in Jer 46:21.

6:5 הַפֹּרְטִים עַל־פִּי הַנָּבֶל—The exact meaning of the hapax legomenon verb פָּרַט is open to debate. Its Qal participle הַפֹּרְטִים is variously understood as meaning "those who pluck [stringed instruments]," "those who improvise [music]," "those who sing songs," or "those who howl."[23] The LXX renders the phrase οἱ ἐπικροτοῦντες πρὸς τὴν φωνὴν τῶν ὀργάνων, "those who are clapping/applauding to the sound of instruments," while the Vulgate has *qui canitis ad vocem psalterii*, "you who sing to the sound of a stringed instrument." The translation above reflects general idea of making songs by improvising tunes.

The prepositional phrase עַל־פִּי, literally, "according to the mouth of," means "according to the sound of" an instrument (see BDB, s.v. פֶּה, 2 e; cf. 6 d (1)). The stringed instrument נֵבֶל, "lyre," is sometimes incorrectly translated "harp" (e.g., RSV). A harp does not employ a neck, whereas a lyre does. The Psalms and Chronicles often refer to playing the נֵבֶל for religious festivals and services, as in Amos 5:23. The context of 6:5–7 indicates that Amos is describing a *marzēaḥ* feast that had religious implications; see the second textual note and the commentary on 6:7.

כְּדָוִיד חָשְׁבוּ לָהֶם כְּלֵי־שִׁיר׃—The simile כְּדָוִיד, "like David," indicates that the musical innovators compared themselves to Israel's greatest psalmist. The grammar of this clause can be understood in three different ways. First, in this context, the verb חָשַׁב may mean "to invent" (BDB, 5) and take the direct object כְּלֵי־שִׁיר, literally, "instruments of song/music." חָשַׁב conveys artistic talent to "invent, devise" artwork in, for example, Ex 31:4; 35:32; 2 Chr 2:13 (ET 2:14). For accounts of David's connections with musical instruments see, for example, Neh 12:36; 1 Chr 23:5; 2 Chr 29:26–27. A second possibility is to understand חָשַׁב in its more common sense of "to think, consider," and translate the clause as "they *think* regarding themselves that [their] musical instruments are like David's." However, David probably did not invent new musical instruments.[24] Instead, he composed new music on kinds of instruments that already

---

[21] Niehaus, "Amos," 439.

[22] See BDB. Wolff writes: "רבק means 'to bind tightly' (Arabic *rabaqa*); the מרבק is the enclosure where animals are restrained from moving about freely so that they can be fattened, hence 'fattening-pen' " (*Joel and Amos*, 276). King discusses the high probability that these stables were located within, not separate from, places of residence (*Amos, Hosea, Micah*, 149–53).

[23] For discussions, see *HALOT* and Paul, *Amos*, 206.

[24] So Freedman, "But Did King David Invent Musical Instruments?"

existed in Israel. Therefore the third possibility is most likely: חָשַׁב means "to compose (music)" and כְּלֵי־שִׁיר is an accusative of means: "like David they compose [music] for themselves [using] musical instruments." This is the direction taken by NIV ("improvise on musical instruments") and NASB ("have composed songs for themselves"). As with נֵבֶל "lyre," in the preceding clause, שִׁיר, "song, music," in this clause frequently is associated with worship and liturgy, as in the superscriptions to Psalms 120–134, each of which is called a "song [שִׁיר] of ascents" for pilgrims traveling up to the Jerusalem temple. The Israelites described in Amos 6:5 (wrongly) imagine that they too are composing God-pleasing worship music.

6:6 הַשֹּׁתִים בְּמִזְרְקֵי יַיִן—The verb שָׁתָה, "to drink," takes the preposition בְּ in an instrumental sense, "drink *with* sacred bowls," but English idiom requires "drink *from* sacred bowls" (cf. GKC, § 119 m, note 1).

Both the noun מִזְרָק, "sacred bowl," and the verb from which it is derived, זָרַק, "to pour out, sprinkle," are closely associated with liturgical worship.[25] The noun appears thirty-two times in the OT and elsewhere always refers to sacred bowls (e.g., Ex 27:3; 38:3; Num 4:14; 1 Ki 7:50). The Vulgate (*bibentes in fialis vinum*) reflects the MT, but the sacrilegious context of Amos 6:6 may be the reason why the LXX and Peshitta omit any reference to bowls and translate בְּמִזְרְקֵי יַיִן as meaning that the Israelites were drinking "filtered wine" (LXX: διυλισμένον οἶνον; Peshitta: ܚܡܪܐ ܡܨܠܠܐ, with the Pael passive participle of ܨܠܠ). A מִזְרָק was large in size, so normally people would not drink from one, but instead would drink from a כּוֹס, "cup." An inordinate consumption of wine is an element of a *marzēaḥ* feast (מַרְזֵחַ, 6:7). Amos' use of מִזְרָק indicates both gross excess and also blasphemous profanation of sacred vessels.[26] Similar sacrilege occurs in Dan 5:2–23, where the Babylonian King Belshazzar holds a banquet at which the guests drink wine from the gold vessels seized from the Jerusalem temple and praise their gods made of metal, wood, and stone.[27]

וְרֵאשִׁית שְׁמָנִים יִמְשָׁחוּ—This clearly means "with the finest of oils they anoint themselves." מָשַׁח is one of the Qal verbs that can have either a transitive meaning ("to anoint" someone or something) or a reflexive, middle meaning, as here: "they anoint themselves" (see Joüon, § 41 a). The construct phrase וְרֵאשִׁית שְׁמָנִים, literally, "the first of (olive) oils," serves as a superlative, as did the phrase with רֵאשִׁית in 6:1 (see the third textual note on 6:1). The instrumental בְּ in the preceding clause could do double duty and serve for וְרֵאשִׁית שְׁמָנִים.[28] Or וְרֵאשִׁית שְׁמָנִים may be an accusative of means or a com-

---

[25] Cf. G. André, "זָרַק," *TDOT* 4:162–65.

[26] Wolff writes: "No doubt one normally drank from a 'goblet' (כּוֹס) rather than from such a bowl. If the society accused by Amos nevertheless used bowls for drinking, its intemperance is thereby exposed" (*Joel and Amos*, 276). King writes: "Amos may have mentioned the use of sacred vessels at the *marzeaḥ* to underscore its sacrilegious nature. Also, he may have mentioned the use of vessels of large capacity to emphasize that inordinate drinking was an integral part of the *marzeaḥ*" (*Amos, Hosea, Micah*, 158). Paul, *Amos*, 208, states that the wording refers "to the quantity and abundance of wine imbibed and the manner in which they [members of the wealthy class] conducted their excessive drinking exercises."

[27] See Steinmann, *Daniel*, 271–73, 282–85.

[28] So Andersen and Freedman, *Amos*, 557.

plement accusative (cf. Waltke-O'Connor, § 10.2.1h). שֶׁמֶן, "olive oil," appears around two hundred times in the OT.[29] Like "wine" in the preceding clause, olive oil was a major agricultural product in Israel and a chief export.[30] In passages such as 6:6, שֶׁמֶן refers to oil applied to the body to moisten skin. Niehaus writes: "Usually plain olive oil was used (Deut. 28:40; Mic. 6:15), but the wealthy might have added spices and perfumes to it (Mark 14:3–5)."[31]

וְלֹא נֶחְלוּ עַל־שֵׁבֶר יוֹסֵף׃—The verb חָלָה encompasses a broad range of meanings, summarized as "to have a state of bodily weakness."[32] Contextually חָלָה may denote physical sickness, disease, injury, or mental illness. In some contexts, the verb can take on the meaning "to be sick about, grieved over, worried and concerned about."[33] The Qal has this meaning in 1 Sam 22:8, where Saul complains to his officials, "No one is concerned [וְאֵין־חֹלֶה] about me." The Niphal perfect here in Amos 6:6 has essentially the same ingressive-stative meaning as the Qal: "they *do* not *become sick* (*Niphal*) over the ruin of Joseph" (Waltke-O'Connor, § 23.6.1b, example 1b). For the Qal and Niphal of first guttural verbs, the preformative often takes *seghol* (נֶחְלוּ) in place of *patach* (-נַח). See GKC, § 63 e.

The noun שֵׁבֶר is the construct form of שֶׁבֶר (GKC, § 93 k), which derives from the verb שָׁבַר, "to break."[34] The noun often refers to the "breaking, fracture" of the people of Israel personified as an individual (BDB, 1, citing, e.g., Jer 8:21; 14:17; Lam 2:11). "In prophetic writing it has the meaning 'crushed' and is applied to the ruin of the nation in war."[35]

For "Joseph," see the second textual note on 5:6. The construct phrase שֵׁבֶר יוֹסֵף, "the ruin of Joseph," occurs only here in the OT. It is analogous to שֶׁבֶר עַמּוֹ, "the ruin of his people" (Is 30:26; cf., e.g., Jer 6:14; 8:11, 21; Lam 2:11).

6:7 לָכֵן עַתָּה יִגְלוּ בְּרֹאשׁ גֹּלִים—For לָכֵן, "therefore," see the first textual note on 3:11. In addition to its usual temporal meaning "now," the particle עַתָּה can also have a logical or emphatic force (Waltke-O'Connor, § 39.3.4f).

Amos explicitly mentions the exile of northern Israel for the first time in 4:2–3. It is an ongoing theme in the rest of the book (5:5, 27; 6:7; 7:11, 17; 9:4). It is made explicit here by the two uses of the Qal of גָּלָה, "to go into exile," first the imperfect יִגְלוּ and then the substantive participle גֹּלִים. In Amos this verb refers to the exile of Israel also in 5:5, 27; 7:11, 17. בְּרֹאשׁ, literally, "at the head," adverbially modifies יִגְלוּ, mean-

---

29 The main enemy of olive trees was the locust (cf. Amos 4:9).

30 Cf. King, *Amos, Hosea, Micah*, 159–61, who notes: "Touching on so many aspects of life, olive oil had multiple uses in biblical times: in food preparation, as an unguent for softening the skin, in offering sacrifice, as fuel for lamps, for medicinal purposes, for the preparation of cosmetics, and as a lubricant" (p. 159).

31 Niehaus, "Amos," 440.

32 Cf. K. Seybold, "חָלָה," *TDOT* 4:399–409.

33 Paul, *Amos*, 209.

34 Cf. B. Knipping, "שָׁבַר," *TDOT* 14:367–81.

35 Andersen and Freedman, *Amos*, 565.

ing that the aristocrats will go into exile "first" in the long line of deportees forcibly marched away.

וְסָר מִרְזַח סְרוּחִים׃—The subject of the singular verb וְסָר, "depart," is the singular noun מַרְזֵחַ in the construct phrase מִרְזַח סְרוּחִים. For the passive participle סְרוּחִים, "sprawling," see the second textual note on 6:4.

In the context of Amos 6:1–7, מַרְזֵחַ is best transliterated as the technical term "*marzēaḥ* (feast)."[36] The term and cognates are attested in a variety of Semitic languages from different periods, including Eblaite, Ugaritic, Phoenician, and the later Aramaic dialects of Nabatean, Palmyrene, and Rabbinic Aramaic.[37] Because these extrabiblical texts come from different cultures, and some predate (those from Ebla and Ugarit) or postdate (those written in the Aramaic dialects) Amos and Jeremiah by many centuries, one must be cautious in using them to reconstruct precisely what these two Israelite prophets were addressing by the term.

In extrabiblical texts, מַרְזֵחַ denotes a pagan ritual. According to McLaughlin, the three main elements of the *marzēaḥ* feast are upper-class participants, a (pagan) religious connection, and excessive drinking of alcohol.[38] Several texts also indicate a possible connection with a funeral banquet, but that element is absent from most of the extrabiblical texts. In general, the banquet seems to be a time for joyful eating and drinking.[39] Social standing and money are necessary to join in the revelry.

Amos 6:4–7 contains the three main elements associated with a *marzēaḥ* feast in extrabiblical texts: (1) wealthy participants, who can afford to recline "on beds of ivory" (6:4), eat choice meat ("lambs … calves," 6:4), and anoint themselves "with the choicest of olive oils" (6:6); (2) a pagan religious connection (the possible eating of sacrificial meat in 6:4; the composing of liturgical songs "like David" in 6:5; "drinking wine from sacred bowls" and anointing themselves with oil as if for a divine office or sacred meal in 6:6); and (3) excessive drinking (see the first textual note on 6:6).[40] Although the occasion for the feasting does not appear to be a death, there is an allusion to death in the context: "the ruin of Joseph," the impending death of the nation, over which Israel should but does not "grieve" (6:6).

It is possible, but far from certain, that 2:7–8 and 4:1 refer or allude to a *marzēaḥ* feast without including the term; see the commentary on those verses.

---

36 So, for example, King, *Amos, Hosea, Micah*, 137.

37 McLaughlin, *The* Marzēaḥ *in the Prophetic Literature*, 9–79, discusses the pertinent ancient Near Eastern *marzēaḥ* texts beginning with two texts from Ebla that date to the second half of the third millennium through the sixth century AD Madeba map, which describes Baalpeor (cf. Num 25:1–9) as "a *marzēaḥ* house." See also Barstad, *The Religious Polemics of Amos*, 130–42; King, "The *Marzeaḥ* Amos Denounces—Using Archaeology to Interpret a Biblical Text"; and *HALOT*, which gives "**cultic celebration** with revelry" for Amos 6:7 and "funerary meal" for Jer 16:5, the word's only other OT occurrence. An ancient Near Eastern banquet with drinkers and a musician is represented pictorially in *ANEP*, § 637.

38 McLaughlin, *The* Marzēaḥ *in the Prophetic Literature*, 66, 214.

39 See McLaughlin, *The* Marzēaḥ *in the Prophetic Literature*, 66–79, 214, and Barstad, *The Religious Polemics of Amos*, 139–40.

40 See McLaughlin, *The* Marzēaḥ *in the Prophetic Literature*, 80–128, and Barstad, *The Religious Polemics of Amos*, 138–42.

About a century and a half after the time of Amos, מַרְזֵחַ appears once more in the OT. In Jer 16:5 it is used in the context of a funeral feast. LXX Jer 16:5 translates מַרְזֵחַ with θίασος, "orgy, mourning feast" (LEH).[41] Yahweh tells Jeremiah, "Do not enter a house of mourning [בֵּית מַרְזֵחַ], and do not go to lament or console them" (Jer 16:5). The "house of mourning" is also called a "house of feasting" (בֵּית־מִשְׁתֶּה, Jer 16:8), where people eat and drink as part of the funeral rites.

Although the term מַרְזֵחַ does not appear in Num 25:1–9, such a feast may be what seduced Israelite men at Baal-peor to commit adultery with Moabite women in their worship of Baal.

Commentary

Amos' preaching in chapters 5 and 6 calls Israel to repent. If the people would abandon their sins and seek Yahweh, as he implores them to do (5:4, 6, 14), he might still relent from judgment, as he does in Amos' first two visions (7:1–3 and 7:4–6). But Israel refuses to repent (4:6–11) and does not heed the warnings in chapters 5 and 6. Yahweh has sent Amos to his people (7:15), but they do not listen. Therefore the nation would experience "ruin" (6:6) and the leading citizens would lead the way into exile (6:7). This would happen some four decades after the ministry of Amos, when northern Israel would fall to Assyria in 722 BC. "That judgment did not materialize without warning, but only after a long, agonizing effort to warn and exhort and encourage the people to repentance. Only when all efforts had failed and further attempts were effectively prevented did the gears shift and the period of grace end."[42]

"Woe" (6:1) marks a new warning and is another funeral lament over Israel.[43] This "woe" corresponds to the "woe" in 5:18. These are the only two Amos verses with הוֹי, "woe." In both verses, הוֹי, "woe," immediately precedes a participle, and the larger units containing each verse both conclude with a declaration of exile (5:27; 6:7). Both 5:18–27 and 6:1–7 employ "lyre" (נֶבֶל) and "song" (שִׁיר, 5:23; 6:5). Both convey the same theme: the coming "day" of judgment, "the Day of Yahweh" (יוֹם יְהוָה, 5:18, 20), which will be "the evil day" (יוֹם רָע, 6:3).

This juxtaposition prompts Paul to write: "Both religious and secular celebrations are abominable if morality is absent."[44] However, the celebrations that Yahweh rejects in both 5:21–27 and 6:1–7 are religious.[45] The Israelites imag-

---

[41] In Amos 6:7, the LXX translates וְסָר מִרְזַח סְרוּחִים as καὶ ἐξαρθήσεται χρεμετισμὸς ἵππων ἐξ Εφραιμ, "and the neighing of horses will be removed from Ephraim."

[42] Andersen and Freedman, *Amos*, 61.

[43] A previous funeral lament over Israel was in 5:1–3 (cf. also 5:16–17).

[44] Paul, *Amos*, 199.

[45] Cf. Andersen and Freedman, *Amos*, 550. See also Carroll R., "For So You Love to Do," 175–76. For 5:21–27, see the commentary on those verses. Andersen and Freedman propose: "Amos 6:1–6 is directed against a group of national leaders from the capital cities of both countries, who have gathered at the great shrine at Bethel in order to celebrate a festive occasion" (*Amos*, 552).

ine that their musical compositions are like the liturgical songs of the psalmist David (6:5), and they are guzzling wine from "sacred bowls" (6:6). They are anointing themselves (6:6), perhaps likening themselves to prophets, priests, or kings (cf. "like David" in 6:5). Mention of a *marzēaḥ* feast in 6:7 confirms the interpretation that the activities in 6:4–7 are religious and are polluted by pagan influence (see the second textual note on 6:7). Israel's religious activities mix sacred practices with idolatry and are performed at alternative worship sites; they are perversions of the divine service God instituted to be performed at his holy temple.[46]

Amos 6:4–6 calls this upper class to task for their pampered prosperity and boisterous banquets, for greed and arrogant security, for self-indulgence and a life of *carpe diem*. Luther describes these people as follows:

> Furthermore, he is prophesying against the princes and aristocrats of the people, who abounded in luxury and all riches. But he does not accuse them of wickedness in this, that they are wealthy, but that they acquired that wealth by deceitfully plundering and oppressing the poor, as we have seen earlier. Otherwise the possession of wealth is not bad. Acquiring wealth unjustly and misusing it—this is bad.[47]

Lying on beds and couches, eating meat from lambs and fattened calves, and composing songs are activities of people who indulge themselves in luxury and leisure. The self-gratifying upper class had no concern for the perilous state of Israel ("the ruin of Joseph," 6:6). Is 22:13 captures the thrust of this laissez-faire attitude:

> Behold, joy and revelry, killing cattle and slaughtering sheep, eating meat and drinking wine! [You say, "Let us] eat and drink, for tomorrow we die!"

The apostle Paul quotes from Is 22:13 to illustrate how futile life would be apart from the crucified and risen Christ, and without hope in our own resurrection from the dead to life eternal by his grace:

> If the dead are not raised, let us eat and drink, for tomorrow we die. (1 Cor 15:32)

Christ has been raised from the dead, and his atonement and resurrection endow our present life with a far greater purpose than gluttony and drunkenness. However, those without faith are still in their sins, and unless they repent, they will perish eternally (cf. 1 Cor 15:17–18).

Unbeknownst to the faithless Israelite revelers condemned by Amos, their idolatrous feasting is preparing them for the everlasting grave. Because of the self-indulgence and self-confidence that are rampant among the Israelites, Yahweh announces that the ones who deemed themselves "first" in prestige

---

[46] Condemnations of northern Israel's syncretistic worship, which perverted the divine worship ordained in the Torah and was performed at other locations besides the Jerusalem temple, are in 2:7–8; 3:14; 4:4–5; 5:5–6, 14, 21–27; 7:9–17; 8:5, 10, 14; 9:1. For Judah's apostasy from the Torah, see the commentary on 2:4–5.

[47] Luther, "Lectures on Amos" (AE 18:168).

and luxury (רֵאשִׁית, 6:1, 6) will be the "first" to go into exile (רֹאשׁ, 6:7). This is a dramatic reversal of the meaning of "first" and of the place occupied by the apostates. English translations obscure the connection, but the repeated Hebrew term רֵאשִׁית, which is translated as "foremost" in 6:1 and "choicest" in 6:6, is closely related to the Hebrew term רֹאשׁ translated as "first" in 6:7. Amos 6:1–7 reaches its climax with the prophetic "therefore" (לָכֵן) introducing the sentence of judgment in the bicolon of 6:7, which marks the end of the unit.

6:1 In chapter 6 Amos continues his preaching against the crème de la crème (cf. 3:15; 4:1), Israel's complacent aristocrats. The opening verse indicates that Amos 6:1–7 is an oracle against those who dwell in both northern Israel and the southern kingdom of Judah. "Mount Zion" and "Mount Samaria" are the capitals of the two kingdoms, Zion in the south and Samaria to the north.[48]

Amos was directed chiefly to preach against the north (7:15). Most of the place names in the book are in the north, and among the oracles against the nations (1:3–2:16), the one against northern Israel is the longest (2:6–16). Yet the reference to the southern kingdom by way of "Mount Zion" (the temple mount in Jerusalem, with the old city of David) is in keeping with Amos' mission. At the start of the book Yahweh roars from Zion (1:2), and 2:4–5 is an oracle against Judah. The book concludes with the promise of the resurrection of the tabernacle of David (9:11–15). It was in the southern kingdom that David's dynasty continued during the divided monarchy and then after the exile, until the arrival of the "Son of David" (Mt 1:1) to fulfill the prophets (e.g., Mt 26:56; Lk 1:70; 18:31), including the prophecy of resurrection (e.g., Lk 24:25–27).

"The house of Israel" in Amos 6:1 probably includes both the north and the south.[49] Judah became a vassal state of Israel beginning with the rule of Amaziah of Judah (796–767 BC) and Jehoash of Israel (798–782 BC),[50] and this relationship continued during the time of Amos (ca. 760 BC). Dignitaries from "Mount Zion" may have visited those on "Mount Samaria" (6:1) to enjoy a feast together. Both groups of leaders, those from the north and those from the south, are the chosen of the chosen, but they will be chosen to lead the way into exile (6:7). The Assyrians and later the Babylonians (2 Ki 24:11–16; 25:10–12, 18–21; Jer 52:24–30) deported mostly the royalty, nobility, and leading citizens. This strategy destabilized the conquered country and made it easier to exert control over it. The loss of the local leaders also inhibited the possibility of organized revolt.

---

[48] For another prophetic example of Zion as the capital of Judah, see, for example, Is 1:8. For another example of Samaria as the capital of Israel, see, for example, Is 36:19.

[49] Andersen and Freedman, *Amos*, 110–11, argue that in Amos when the term "Israel" is qualified by another term, such as "the house of" in 6:1, then it probably refers to the divided kingdom including both the north and the south (see also pp. 98–99).

[50] For the details, see 2 Ki 14:8–14. For the dates of those kings, see Thiele, *The Mysterious Numbers of the Hebrew Kings*, 111, 113.

Those "who are complacent on Mount Zion" and those "who feel secure on Mount Samaria" (Amos 6:1) were indulging in unbridled "pleasure without conscience,"[51] completely self-absorbed in their "have no cares" community. They might have said something like this to the meddlesome Amos: "Leave us alone to enjoy our days. Life is too short to be tormented with guilt about people whose problems are too big and too complex for us to fix anyway!" In 7:10–17 the apostate priest Amaziah will rebuke Amos for prophesying against the northern kingdom and its idolatrous worship cultus.

The leaders should have been like King Josiah, who initiated Judah's theological reformation in about 623 BC, and whom Yahweh describes with these words:

> He adjudicated the cause of the poor and needy, and so it was good. Is not this the knowledge of me?" declares Yahweh. (Jer 22:16; cf. James 1:26–27)

Knowing Yahweh, who has pity on the weak and needy (Pss 12:6 [ET 12:5]; 72:13; Ezek 34:16), is demonstrated in the vigilant observance of justice and righteousness for all, including the weakest brother in Christ (Rom 15:1; 1 Corinthians 8). But Amos laments Israel's oppression of the weak and lack of concern for "the ruin of Joseph" (6:6; cf. 5:10–12, 16–20) and the people's perversion of justice and righteousness (5:7; 6:12; cf. 5:15, 24).

The third colon in 6:1, "the most distinguished ones of the foremost of the nations," applies to both groups of aristocrats in 6:1a–b, those from Judah ("Mount Zion") and those from northern Israel ("Mount Samaria"). "First, foremost" (רֵאשִׁית) is ironic in that these leaders will also be the *first* to go into exile (יִגְלוּ בְּרֹאשׁ גֹּלִים, 6:7). If these leaders are first in anything, it is that they are first in pride, arrogance, and self-absorption, traits that epitomize human sin. Yahweh had chosen to love the people of Israel even though they were "the fewest of all the peoples" (Deut 7:7), but now these prima donnas were number one in self-esteem. Scripture offers only one source of confidence: "Yahweh of armies, blessed is the man who trusts in you" (Ps 84:13 [ET 84:12]).[52]

The last colon of Amos 6:1, "to whom the house of Israel comes," is vague about the reason for the journeys. It may imply that "the Israelites (or delegations from other cities) 'come to' these preeminent notables [at Zion and Samaria] either for advice or in order to petition them against injustice."[53] The populace could come in order to render honor and service, bring tribute or taxes, learn from, and/or seek legal redress from the leaders. The colon may imply a kind of idolatry: all Israelite men were to make three annual pilgrimages to the central sanctuary (in Amos' day, the Jerusalem temple) to worship Israel's God

---

[51] Gandhi, as quoted by Stulman, *Jeremiah*, 212.

[52] "Who trusts" in Ps 84:13 (ET 84:12) translates the singular of the same participle that is in Amos 6:1, where וְהַבֹּטְחִים is translated as "and who feel secure" (see the second textual note on 6:1). The theological meaning of "trusts" is well illustrated in Jer 17:7 with the Qal imperfect of בָּטַח, the same verb whose participles are in Amos 6:1 and Ps 84:13 (ET 84:12).

[53] Paul, *Amos*, 201.

there (Ex 23:14–17; 34:23–24; Deut 16:16), but the people were instead making pilgrimages to human leaders.

6:2 Yahweh continues to speak to the complacent and smug "distinguished ones" (Amos 6:1). He orders them to travel to three locations. About two decades after the ministry of Amos the first two city-states, Calneh and Hamath Rabbah, fell to Assyria in 738 BC during a western military campaign of Tiglath-pileser III (745–727 BC), who had earlier (ca. 743 BC)[54] exacted tribute from the Israelite king Menahem (2 Ki 15:19–20) and who, between 738 and 732, conquered most of the nations surrounding northern Israel and took much of Israel's territory (2 Ki 15:29; 1 Chr 5:26; see also 2 Ki 16:5–9), leaving only Samaria and a small region around it under Israelite control.[55] Shalmaneser V (726–722 BC), the successor of Tiglath-pileser III, would initiate the campaign against Samaria that would lead to its fall in 722 BC (2 Ki 17:1–6) under his successor, Sargon II (722–705 BC). The third kingdom in Amos 6:2, "Gath of the Philistines," together with the four other cities that formed the Philistine Pentapolis,[56] experienced military defeat at the hands of the Assyrians several times, including the conquest of Gath and Ashdod by Sargon II in 711 BC.[57]

Many critical commentators assume that Amos 6:2 was a later addition to the book of Amos, written after the fall of the three city-states it names.[58] But that critical assumption is not correct for at least two reasons. First, there is no textual evidence that 6:2 comes from a hand other than Amos' or from a time later than the rest of the book. Second, the verse would make no sense as a warning for Israel to repent and avoid the destiny of these other kingdoms if Israel was already experiencing the fury of the Assyrian war machine.[59] Paul aptly states that Amos must have compared Israel to the other kingdoms "while Israel was luxuriating in good fortune, prosperity, and security, … still enjoying the dolce vita described in the following verses," so that "the poignancy of the prophet's words would constitute an ominous threat against their presumed confidence in immunity from all foreign incursions. It stands to reason, therefore, that the verse must precede the western campaigns of the Assyrian king [Tiglath-pileser III]."[60]

God directs Israel to consider Calneh, Hamath Rabbah, and Gath of the Philistines. He raises two questions. First, is the theological condition of Israel

---

[54] See Thiele, *The Mysterious Numbers of the Hebrew Kings*, 124–28.

[55] See Younger, "The Deportations of the Israelites," 202–4.

[56] Amos 1:6–8 names the four other cities of the Philistine Pentapolis, but not Gath. The presence of Gath here completes the list, so that the book of Amos names all five Philistine cities.

[57] See the third textual note on 6:2.

[58] Cf. Paul, *Amos*, 201. Isaiah, writing in the second half of the eighth century BC, refers to Calneh as Calno and Hamath Rabbah as simply Hamath in Is 10:5–11, and his context indicates that these city-states had already been conquered by Assyria.

[59] For the chronology and relationship between Assyria and northern Israel, see the excursus "The Assyrian Empire."

[60] Paul, *Amos*, 203.

any "better than" these pagan city-states? Second, Israel should also ask whether the territories (and, by implication, the military strength) of these city-states were "greater" than Israel's. The obvious answer to both questions is a resounding no!

In answer to the first question, Israel was thoroughly infected with the same kinds of idolatry that permeated its pagan neighbors. As for the second question, these city-states were smaller and militarily weaker than northern Israel at the time of Amos, so they would not be able to afford any significant military help for Israel when Israel would be attacked by Assyria.[61] The southern kingdom of Judah was, in Amos's day, a vassal to northern Israel, so neither would Judah be able to rescue Israel from Assyria. Nor would any nation be able to fend off an attack sponsored by Yahweh! The leaderships of Judah and Israel must have "ears to hear" (cf. Mt 11:15) that the threat of an Assyrian invasion from the north would be as great for them as it would be for Calneh, Hamath, and Gath.[62]

So why does Amos single out these three city-states? Perhaps it was because the geographical line of an Assyrian conquest from the north would run through Calneh, continue to Hamath, and conclude with Gath.[63] The route from Calneh to Hamath had been followed by the army of the Assyrian king Shalmaneser III in the mid-ninth century. And in the late ninth century, the Aramean king Hazael conquered Gath and then threatened Jerusalem but was placated by gifts (2 Ki 12:18–19 [ET 12:17–18]). Hazael had earlier taken northern Israel's territory east of the Jordan and had most likely made Israel an Aramean vassal (2 Ki 10:32–33).[64] The three cities were not under Assyrian control during the lifetime of Amos, but the past conquests of them by Assyria and Aram provided a clue as to what a major Mesopotamian empire might do in the future.[65] If one of these empires invaded again and followed previous military strategies, would Israel and Judah be able to muster an army to stop its advance? Yahweh's questions indicate that they would not.

The pragmatic thrust of Amos 6:2 is this: Israel's aristocrats needed to repent and trust in their God rather than in their military might under Jeroboam ben Joash. This boasting was an illusion (cf. Amos 6:13). Calneh, Hamath Rabbah, and Gath of the Philistines were vulnerable against a Mesopotamian

---

[61] See the excursus "The Assyrian Empire."

[62] This is the view taken by Sweeney, *The Twelve Prophets*, 243–44. Smith concludes that Amos "is just contrasting the lack of complacency and illegitimate optimism in these cities with the excessive complacency in Samaria. These cities understand that they are vulnerable to attack and must be prepared to defend themselves at all times. They are not the biggest or the best, so there is no illusion about their security" (*Hosea, Amos, Micah*, 339).

[63] Cf. Sweeney, *The Twelve Prophets*, 244.

[64] Cf. W. T. Pitard, "Hazael," *ABD* 3:83.

[65] Amos does not name the "nation" that will be Yahweh's tool of judgment (6:14). Later in the eighth century, Isaiah identifies this nation as Assyria (e.g., Is 7:17; 10:5). See the excursus "The Assyrian Empire."

empire, and so were Israel and Judah. Amos wanted his hearers to respond with the words of Ps 20:8 (ET 20:7): "Some [trust] in chariotry, others [trust] in horses, but we will invoke the name of Yahweh our God." In this way they would follow Solomon's exhortation to "trust in Yahweh with all your heart" (Prov 3:5) as opposed to trusting in their apostate leaders (Amos 6:1) and the military and political might of their empires.

6:3 "The evil day" is the same "Day of Yahweh" described more fully in 5:18–20 and mentioned elsewhere in Amos (see the commentary on 5:18–20 and the textual note on 6:3). Yahweh's appointed day to bring northern Israel to an "end" (8:2) would come in 722 BC. The eschatological "day" of judgment also points to the outpouring of the Father's wrath at humanity's sin upon his sinless Son, Jesus, on Good Friday; the baptismal judgment and killing of the old Adam (Rom 6:1–6; Eph 4:22; Col 2:11–13; 3:9); the Christian's confession of sins and the absolution granted by the pastor; as well as the Last Day, when all the dead shall be raised bodily, those who have lived apart from Christ will be cast into outer darkness forever, and all believers shall be glorified in the fullness of eternal life (Dan 12:2–3). All of these are an "evil day" (Amos 6:3) for unbelievers (and for the sinful nature that persists in each believer during this life [Romans 7]), while in terms of the Gospel, they are days of new life and grand celebration for all believers.

But Israel's leaders will have none of this kind of preaching. Living in denial, the only music the nation wants to face is its own (6:5). Denial is the mechanism of the elite in Amos 9:10, where Yahweh quotes "all the sinners of my people" as saying, "The evil will not overtake nor confront us." Paradoxically, the more they deny reality, the more they hasten (וַתַּגִּישׁוּן, "you bring near," 6:3) the day of their disaster.

6:4 The drunken party labeled in 6:7 as a *marzēaḥ* feast includes the actions described in 6:4–7 (except for the forced exile in 6:7a). Is 22:12–14; 28:7–8; and Hos 7:3–7 are other eighth-century descriptions of similar feasts of debauchery, but Jer 16:5 is the only other OT passage that specifically mentions a *marzēaḥ* feast (see the second textual note on 6:7). Amos probably had heard of these feasts and perhaps even observed them. If he is again inverting an ancient theme of grace from the Pentateuch,[66] then perhaps Amos is standing on its head the theme of a sacred banquet with Yahweh, as in, for example, the Passover in Exodus 12; the meal on Sinai in Ex 24:9–11 (cf. Is 25:6–9); and the communion sacrifices in Leviticus 3 and 7:11–21. In this case, in place of a feast celebrating Yahweh's gracious presence and redeeming victory, the Israelites are indulging in a sacrilegious banquet in which Yahweh's name is not even mentioned.

---

[66] Amos, writing in the eighth century BC, sometimes cites a theme of God's grace from the fifteenth century BC Torah of Moses, but in Amos God reverses the theme into condemnation because Israel has broken the covenant of Moses. See, for example, the commentary on 3:2; 5:17; 9:7.

The items that head the description are "beds" with inlays of "ivory" (see the first textual note on 6:4). Fragments of ivory inlays from these status symbols have been uncovered in an excavation of the city of Samaria.[67] The Israelites are said to be "sprawling" (6:4), that is, reclining on their luxurious furniture to eat and get drunk (see also 6:7, where they are described as "sprawlers"). Next, the prophet rebukes the people for eating the choicest cuts of meat from lambs and calves. Meat was rarely eaten in everyday meals. It was consumed by some Israelites on sacred occasions, such as at the three annual major festivals attended by adult men (Ex 23:14–17; 34:23–24; Deut 16:16), the offering of communion sacrifices (Lev 7:15–18),[68] and the sacrifice of the firstborn of the herd or flock (Deut 12:17–18). In contrast to those holy and infrequent occasions, the habitual and sumptuous consumption of meat by the Israelites in Amos 6:4 indicates their wealth and gluttony. Paul writes: "These epicurean gourmets dine on nothing less than chateaubriand, on the most tender, tastiest, and choicest of meats."[69] But so much feasting made these leaders fat, obdurate, and too dense to understand Yahweh's ways (cf. Deut 32:13–15).

6:5 The privileged classes in Zion and Samaria were living the high life, just like kings. In fact, in this verse these people were comparing themselves to the king who was the father of Israel's psalmody: David. These party-goers considered themselves to be as pious and godly—and as good poets and composers—as King David. What a farce! David composed many psalms and songs (2 Sam 23:1; cf. 1 Sam 16:16, 23), but these glorified Yahweh by confessing human sin, extolling God's gift of forgiveness and righteousness by grace alone (e.g., Psalm 32 [cf. Rom 4:7] and Psalm 51), and prophesying about the crucified, risen, and exalted Christ (Psalms 16; 22; 110). David's faith was evident in the righteousness and justice he administered for all the people (2 Sam 8:15). Judah and Israel's leaders were living a lie; they were as far away from David's faith and piety as possible.

6:6 Amos moves from lounging, eating, and musical merrymaking to excessive drinking from large sacred bowls.[70] A modern analogy might put it this way: these partiers had taken wine that had been reserved for Holy Communion

---

[67] See N. Avigad, "Samaria (City)," *NEAEHL* 4:1304–6; Crowfoot and Crowfoot, *Early Ivories from Samaria*, especially pp. 31–32 and plates 14–15.

[68] See Kleinig, *Leviticus*, 168–74.

[69] Paul, *Amos*, 205.

[70] See the first textual note on 6:6. Is 24:7–9 is another judgment oracle that condemns the eating, singing, and drinking of unbelievers:

> The new wine mourns,
>   the vine withers;
> all the merrymakers groan.
>   The gaiety of the tambourines is stilled,
> the din of the revelers has stopped,
>   the joyful harp is silent.
> No longer do they drink wine with a song;
>   strong drink is bitter to its imbibers.

and were drinking it, not even from glasses, but straight from the bottle. "Their god is their belly" (Phil 3:19). They do not serve Yahweh; they serve their own appetites (Rom 16:18). By their selfish gluttony and abuse of holy vessels they are eating and drinking to their own judgment (cf. 1 Cor 10:20–22; 11:29).

Those who were part of the "first/foremost" of the nations (רֵאשִׁית הַגּוֹיִם, Amos 6:1) were anointing themselves with the "first/choicest of olive oils" (רֵאשִׁית שְׁמָנִים, 6:6). A special holy oil mixed with spices according to a divine recipe was to be used exclusively for anointing the priests and the sacred appointments of the tabernacle; misuse of it was cause for excommunication from God's people (Ex 30:22–33). Oil was also used to anoint prophets and kings (e.g., 1 Ki 19:16; 2 Ki 9:3). Anointing with oil might indicate preparation for participation in a divine feast (Ps 23:5) or priestly service (Psalm 133). While Amos 6:6 provides no specifics about the kind of oil or the motivation of the revelers, perhaps they thought of themselves in priestly and royal terms, even as they likened themselves to King David in 6:5.

Several OT texts combine wine, oil, and divine love to indicate that the combination furnishes the finest pleasures an Israelite believer could experience (Song 1:2–3; 4:10; cf. Ps 104:15; Eccl 9:7–8).[71] On the other hand, abstinence from wine and oil is indicative of repentance and mourning. For example, Daniel says: "In those days I, Daniel, was mourning for three weeks. I ate no choice food; no meat or wine entered my mouth; and I did not anoint myself at all until the fulfillment of the three weeks" (Dan 10:2–3; cf. Micah 6:15). Daniel uses the ordinary Hebrew verb for "anoint," סוּךְ, while the Hebrew verb for "anoint" used in contexts of worship or holy anointing to a divine office (prophet, priest, king) is מָשַׁח, which is what Amos employs in 6:6. The use of this verb in the context of other terms often employed in sacred contexts, including the "lyre" (6:5) and "sacred bowls" (6:6), as well as the pagan religious term "*marzēaḥ* feast" in 6:7, indicates that Amos is describing syncretistic religious revelry.[72]

At the end of the verse Amos—in characteristic style—drops another verbal missile in his attempt to arouse the inebriated Israelites from their spiritual stupor.[73] The first five verses consist mostly of bicola (pairs of parallel lines). However, 6:6 is a tricolon, with the third and last colon (line) being the most shocking: "but they do not grieve over the ruin of Joseph." In the midst of their "party hearty" atmosphere, the leaders remained oblivious to the ruin of their nation.[74] "The ruin of Joseph" (שֵׁבֶר יוֹסֵף) refers to the brokenness of the people because of their sins against each other and even more to the divine judgments

---

[71] For a Christological and sacramental exposition of wine and oil in the context of divine love in Song 1:2–3 and 4:10 in light of the rest of Scripture, one may see Mitchell, *The Song of Songs*, 299–354, 582–88, 860–61.

[72] This is the view of most commentators. See, for example, Paul, *Amos*, 210–12.

[73] Amos has a knack for surprise endings; see 2:6–16; 3:1–2; 3:3–8; 4:4–5; 5:18–20; 9:7–8.

[74] Isaiah presents a similar view in chapter 1 of his book. In Is 1:4–8 he describes Israel as the "sinful nation" and "people weighed down with iniquity" (Is 1:4) and their ensuing wounds "from the sole of the foot to the head" (Is 1:6).

inflicted on the apostate nation, as described by the series of devastating plagues in 4:6–11, as well as the military defeats described in 5:3 and 6:9–10. These must have wreaked havoc on the impoverished people.

Yet those most responsible—the apostate aristocrats—were apathetic. They acted as though nothing had happened. Their worldview was an illusion; it denied the true state of the nation's spiritual peril. They were conducting business and religion as usual. They refused to repent (4:6–11).

It is fitting that Amos speaks of "the ruin of Joseph" (6:6) because it was Joseph who cried out in distress when his brothers threw him in the pit (Gen 42:21). While he wept, the brothers sat down and ate a meal (Gen 37:25). Joseph and his brothers were members of the same family, sharing the same flesh and blood. One would expect love and compassion to be the hallmark of their relationship. In like manner, Israel's leaders were too busy lounging on couches and strumming away on their musical instruments to care about "the ruin of Joseph." They ate, drank, and were merry, much like Joseph's brothers when they cast him into the pit. Judas' betrayal of Jesus after the Last Supper is the epitome of brotherly hatred and betrayal (Mk 14:17–21).

"Joseph," the brother abused by his older siblings, is a cipher here in Amos 6:6 for the poor and oppressed people throughout the book of Amos (e.g., 2:6–7; 4:1; 5:11; 8:4) who were, together with the elite, in the same family of brothers called "the sons of Israel" (e.g., Ex 1:7). Yahweh redeemed the nation to be a community of "brothers" who "dwell together in unity" (Ps 133:1). Deuteronomy 12–26 is replete with this theme (e.g., Deut 15:2–3, 7–8). Many of the laws, such as those dealing with indebtedness, slavery, and the poor, demand specific treatment for members of the community based on the fact that Israel was a community *bound by ties of brotherhood*. The king was to be a brother Israelite (Deut 17:15), and the Prophet like Moses whom God would raise up as his definitive spokesman was to be "from among your brothers" (Deut 18:15; cf. Rom 9:5). Deuteronomy and the rest of the Torah provide regulations that protect and preserve marginal groups—slaves, widows, orphans, and strangers—in the brotherhood of Israel, since all the OT believers equally are members of the *una sancta*, "one holy catholic and apostolic church" (Nicene Creed).

Although Yahweh warns that he will "rush like fire upon the house of Joseph" (5:6), those who repent can trust that "Yahweh, the God of armies, will be gracious to the remnant of Joseph" (5:15), and they shall be among the believers gathered from the remnants of Israel and the Gentiles in the messianic restoration (9:11–15).

6:7 Yahweh uses the noun רֹאשׁ, "first, head," related to a noun in 6:1, 6, where the faithless Israelites considered themselves "the *foremost* of the nations" (רֵאשִׁית הַגּוֹיִם) and pampered themselves with the "*choicest* of olive oils" (רֵאשִׁית שְׁמָנִים). Now in a dramatic reversal,[75] he promises these leaders that

[75] In addition to 6:1–7, a dramatic reversal is present in 2:9; 3:1–2; 4:4–5; 5:18–20; 5:21–27; 8:9–10; 9:11–15.

they will continue in their preference for the finest and the best—for they will be first at the head of the parade of exiles (בְּרֹאשׁ גֹּלִים)! The unfaithful Israelite aristocrats will maintain their elite status all right: Yahweh has reserved for them first place. They will be "honored" as the first to leave their homeland![76] The noise of the party's music and revelry will give way to a sober silence when the merrymakers are marched into exile.[77] This will be the day their music dies (cf. Psalm 137)!

The "sprawlers" (סְרוּחִים, Amos 6:7; see also 6:4) were lying around, eating, drinking, and making merry. The exile of northern Israel by Assyria—hinted at in 6:14—took place after a three-year siege of Samaria that ended in 722 BC (2 Ki 17:5–6). Sargon II, the Assyrian king who finished the siege of Samaria that was started by Shalmaneser V, writes in an inscription that he exiled 27,290 Samarian inhabitants and formed them into a contingent of fifty chariots.[78]

Summary

The leaders of Judah and Israel were enjoying the best lifestyle that money could buy. They were "lovers of pleasure rather than lovers of God" (2 Tim 3:4) as they sought to please their senses by eye, ear, touch, taste, and smell. These elites preferred the cushion instead of the cross. The syncretistic activities in 6:4–7 are in the context of a religious setting, "the *marzēaḥ* feast" (6:7). This was an event associated with pagan deities (see the second textual note on 6:7).[79] Amos rebukes those who attend this ongoing party because of its pernicious theology and immoral excess,[80] which are causing "the ruin of Joseph" (6:6), the breakdown of covenantal life, injuring the vulnerable in Israel's society and precipitating divine judgment. Apostasy from Yahweh is the root cause of the nation's problems, and restoration requires repentance and faith that is active in love.

After Amos' sequence of seven verbs in 6:4–6 ("lying … sprawling … eating … improvising … they compose … drinking … they anoint themselves") comes the climactic eighth verb, which is negated: "but they do not grieve over

---

[76] Amos 6:1 warns both the complacent on Mount Zion, representing the southern kingdom of Judah, and those on Mount Samaria, representing the northern kingdom of Israel. After Assyria conquered northern Israel in 722 BC, the exiles were dispersed and never returned in any significant numbers. This contrasts with the southern kingdom of Judah. The Babylonians took waves of exiles from Judah beginning in 605 BC (Dan 1:1–4); in 597 BC; in 587 BC, when Jerusalem fell; and again in 582/581 BC (Jer 52:28–30). Large numbers of Judeans returned from exile after permission was granted by the edict of Cyrus in 538 BC.

[77] Here, as he does elsewhere (5:27; 6:14; 7:17), Amos ends a judgment oracle with the promise of exile.

[78] As quoted in Miller and Hayes, *A History of Ancient Israel and Judah*, 338 (cf. Luckenbill, *Ancient Records of Assyria and Babylonia*, vol. 2, § 55; *ANET*, 284–85).

[79] See also, for example, Barstad, *The Religious Polemics of Amos*, 127–42. Barstad believes that in light of 5:26 and 8:14, "polemics against foreign deities play a major role in the preaching of Amos" (p. 141, n. 96).

[80] Freedman, "But Did King David Invent Musical Instruments?" 51, suggests that the songs condemned by Amos were "scurrilous, obscene or blasphemous, and possibly all three."

the ruin of Joseph." The partygoers' faith is noticeably absent, as is Yahweh himself. The leaders of Judah and Israel (6:1) might have gained the whole world, but in the process they forfeited their own souls (cf. Mt 16:26; Lk 9:25).

Jesus tells a parable about an affluent man, one of the notables of his own day, who wore only the best clothing and consumed only the finest food (Lk 16:19–31). Outside the door of his home lay a man named Lazarus, who was hungry and poor. The faithless rich man did not persecute Lazarus, nor did he drive him away. *He was simply indifferent to him.*

The leaders of Amos' day exhibited a similar attitude. They ignored Yahweh's call for justice and righteousness and did nothing to heal, feed, and clothe members of God's people who were impoverished. In Lk 6:24–25 Jesus offers a fitting commentary on such merrymakers:

> Woe [οὐαί, equivalent to הוֹי in Amos 6:1] to you who are rich,
> for you have already received your consolation.
> Woe [οὐαί] to you who are full now,
> for you will go hungry.
> Woe [οὐαί] to you who laugh now,
> for you will mourn and weep.

Basil the Great comments on Amos 6:6:

> Just as it is not proper to provide ourselves with worldly trappings like a silver vessel, or a curtain edged with purple, or a downy couch, or transparent draperies, so we act unfittingly in contriving menus that deviate in any important way from our usual diet. That we should run about searching for anything not demanded by real necessity but calculated to provide a wretched delight and ruinous vainglory is not only shameful and out of keeping with our avowed purpose; it also causes harm of no mean gravity when they who spend their lives in sensual gratification and measure happiness in terms of pleasure for the appetite see us also taken up with the same preoccupations that keep them enthralled. If, indeed, sensual pleasure is evil and to be avoided, we should on no occasion indulge in it, for nothing that is condemned can at any time be beneficial. They who live riotously and are anointed with the best ointments and drink filtered wine come under the denunciation of Scripture. Because she lives in pleasure, the widow is dead while she is living [1 Tim 5:6]. The rich man is debarred from paradise because he lived in luxury upon earth [Lk 16:25]. What then have we to do with costly appointments?[81]

[81] Basil the Great, *The Long Rules*, question 20, quoted in Ferreiro, *The Twelve Prophets*, ACCS 14:106.

Excursus

The Assyrian Empire

The nation of Assyria is never named in Amos,[1] but it looms large in the background as the military power that would defeat the Northern Kingdom of Israel in 722 BC, some four decades after Amos, who ministered in the 760s BC, warned of Israel's coming destruction.[2] This impending threat is confirmed by other eighth-century prophets, including Hosea (e.g., Hos 1:5; 9:3) and Isaiah (e.g., Is 7:17–20; 8:4, 7; 10:5), who do name Assyria. Archaeology and cuneiform evidence indicates that Assyria as a nation endured for thousands of years. Its geographic center was triangular in shape, formed by the Kurdish mountains to the north, the Tigris River to the west, and the Upper Zab River to the east. Assyria's major civilization centers of Ashur, Nineveh, Arbela, and Calah fell within this triangle or were in its proximity.[3] The following kings of Assyria were contemporaries of Amos and of the king of northern Israel he names in Amos 1:1, Jeroboam ben Joash (793–753 BC[4]):

1. Adad-nirari III (810–783 BC)
2. Shalmaneser IV (782–773 BC)
3. Ashur-dan III (772–755 BC)
4. Ashur-nirari V (754–745 BC)[5]

More specifically, the years 782–745 BC, during the reigns of Shalmaneser IV, Ashur-dan III, and Ashur-nirari V, were a time of great political instability in the realm of Assyria, which was marked by local autonomy.[6] For example, an important Assyrian official named Shamshi-ilu seems to have enjoyed a long and successful career (ca. 792–752 BC), for during the reign of Shalmaneser IV (782–773 BC), this Shamshi-ilu records on two stone lions at the Syrian city of Til Barship his victory over Argishtish, king of Urartu, without making any mention of the Assyrian king. According to Roux, this silence about the reigning king is "unprecedented in Assyrian records."[7] Nor is Shamshi-ilu an exception. It is possible to identify a number of other important officials who, although

---

1 Yahweh does point in the direction of Assyria by warning that Israel will go into exile "beyond Damascus" in Amos 5:27. Also, in 5:26 he satirizes the names of Assyrian astral deities. The threat of exile is a recurring theme in Amos (4:2–3; 5:5, 27; 6:7; 7:11, 17; 9:4).

2 See "The Historical Setting of the Book of Amos" in the introduction.

3 A. K. Grayson, "Mesopotamia, History of (Assyria)," *ABD* 4:732.

4 Thiele, *The Mysterious Numbers of the Hebrew Kings*, 116.

5 These dates are based on relative dating. See Lemanski, "Jonah's Nineveh," 42.

6 See Lemanski, "Jonah's Nineveh," 44–46, and Grayson, *ABD* 4:743–44, who calls this period the "Interval" due to the fact that this was the lowest point in the history of Neo-Assyria.

7 Roux, *Ancient Iraq*, 251.

paying nominal allegiance to the Assyrian king, appear to have exercised considerable independence during the first half of the eighth century BC.[8]

This helps to explain why northern Israel prospered so greatly during the reign of its king Jeroboam ben Joash (named in Amos 1:1; 7:9–11). There was no central government in Assyria to organize effective military campaigns against Israel. The book of Amos describes northern Israel's wealth and military strength during this period, but warns that they would not last.

This state of affairs was short lived. Tiglath-pileser III (745–727 BC) consolidated Assyrian power and began a series of westward marches. The Northern Kingdom began to feel the squeeze as Assyria began to flex its muscles. In about 743 BC,[9] Tiglath-pileser III exacted tribute from the Israelite king Menahem (2 Ki 15:19–20) and, between 738 and 732, he conquered most of the nations surrounding northern Israel and took much of Israel's territory (2 Ki 15:29; 1 Chr 5:26; see also 2 Ki 16:5–9), leaving only Samaria and the hill country of Ephraim under Israelite control.[10] Inside northern Israel, assassinations and political instability began to destroy the country after the death of Jeroboam ben Joash in 753 BC. 2 Ki 15:8–31 narrates the reigns of those who followed him: Zechariah, Shallum, Menahem, Pekahiah, and Pekah. The last northern king was Hoshea, who dared to withhold tribute from Shalmaneser V (726–722 BC). This Assyrian king and his successor, Sargon II (722–705 BC), responded with vengeance, imprisoning Hoshea and besieging Samaria. In 722 BC, Samaria was destroyed, and thousands of Israelites were exiled (2 Ki 17:1–6). Northern Israel forever ceased to be a nation. This destruction fulfilled Amos' many prophecies of divine judgment upon the apostate Northern Kingdom.

It was during the subsequent reign of the Assyrian king Sennacherib (704–681 BC) that Nineveh became the capital of the Assyrian Empire.[11] Sennacherib enlarged the city's circumference from 9,300 cubits (approximately three miles) to 21,815 cubits (approximately seven miles).[12] The entire prophecy of Nahum, delivered sometime before Nineveh's downfall in 612 BC, gives a picture of the Assyrian capital, "the city of bloodshed" (Nah 3:1). Nineveh was full of lies, booty, and dead bodies without end (Nah 3:1–3). It was a city that Nahum likened to a shapely harlot out to seduce all nations (Nah 3:4). Picturing Nineveh's

---

[8] Lawrence, "Assyrian Nobles and the Book of Jonah," 125–26.

[9] See Thiele, *The Mysterious Numbers of the Hebrew Kings*, 124–28.

[10] See Younger, "The Deportations of the Israelites," 202–4.

[11] Thus Nineveh was not the capital of Assyria during the reign of Jeroboam ben Joash (793–753 BC), Amos' contemporary. Although Calah remained the nominal capital, during the "Interval" (782–745 BC), "the Assyrian empire was … totally fragmented into a number of virtually independent states ruled by former Assyrian governors" (Grayson, *ABD* 4:743). See also A. K. Grayson, "Calah," *ABD* 1:808, and "Nineveh," *ABD* 4:1119.

[12] In comparison, Babylon, the largest Mesopotamian city, covered two thousand five hundred acres. Jerusalem grew from about ten acres at the time David made it the capital to forty acres by the eighth century. After the fall of Samaria in 722 BC, Jerusalem almost quadrupled in size to about one hundred fifty acres (as noted in Broshi, "The Expansion of Jerusalem in the Reigns of Hezekiah and Manasseh," 23–24).

downfall, Nahum asks, "What has become of the den of lions?" (Nah 2:12 [ET 2:11]). He shouts, "Woe to the city of bloodshed! All of her is full of lies and plunder. [Her] prey never departs" (Nah 3:1). The book ends with these ominous words: "All who hear the news of you clap their hands over you. For upon whom has your evil not come continuously?" (Nah 3:19; cf. Zeph 2:13–15). Nahum celebrates with glee the downfall of Assyria because the empire's reign of terror had spread throughout the ancient Near East. The pagan nation that Yahweh had used to chastise his unfaithful people would not escape divine judgment for its own crimes (e.g., Is 10:5, 12, 24–24).

The Assyrians became infamous for deporting entire populations to distant lands (2 Ki 15:29; 17:6; cf. 2 Ki 18:31–32 || Is 36:16–17), the same crime that had been committed by Gaza (Amos 1:6) and Tyre (1:9). In order to squash future revolts, Assyria removed populations of rebel kingdoms and mixed them with other exilic groups and with the indigenous population of the place to which they were moved.[13] The fact that Israelite exiles were taken to areas in Mesopotamia is attested by a list of West Semitic names found on an Assyrian ostracon.[14] "In fact, Israelite names continue to appear in Assyrian economic and military documents throughout the seventh century."[15] Exiles from the Northern Kingdom apparently lived on for some time, as noted in the deuterocanonical book of Tobit (1:1–3).

Besides its practice of deporting and relocating populations of conquered enemies, Assyria also gained infamy for its cruel and inhumane warfare. A prime illustration is provided by this boastful battle rhetoric of Ashur-nasirpal II (883–859 BC):

> I built a pillar over against his city gate, and I flayed all the chief men who had revolted, and I covered the pillar with their skins; some I walled up within the pillar, some I impaled upon the pillar on stakes, and others I bound to stakes round about the pillar. …
>
> I stormed the mountain peaks and took them. In the midst of the mighty mountain I slaughtered them; with their blood I dyed the mountain red like wool. With the rest of them I darkened the gullies and precipices of the mountains. I carried off their spoil and their possessions. The heads of their warriors I cut off, and I formed them into a pillar over against their city; their young men and their maidens I burned in the fire.[16]

Bleibtreu observes: "Assyrian national history, as it has been preserved for us in inscriptions and pictures, consists almost solely of military campaigns and

---

13 See Becking, *The Fall of Samaria*, 61–62, 82.

14 Becking, *The Fall of Samaria*, 80–83.

15 Matthews, *Old Testament Turning Points*, 129. See also Oded, "The Settlements of the Israelite and the Judean Exiles in Mesopotamia in the 8th–6th Centuries BCE," 92–99.

16 Luckenbill, *Ancient Records of Assyria and Babylonia*, vol. 1, §§ 443, 447. For Assyrian reliefs showing impaled victims, see *ANEP*, §§ 362, 368, 373.

battles. It is as gory and bloodcurdling a history as we know."[17] Ashur-nasirpal II again boasts:

> In strife and conflict I besieged (and) conquered the city. I felled 3,000 of their fighting men with the sword. I carried off prisoners, possessions, oxen (and) cattle from them. I burnt many captives from them. I captured many troops alive: I cut off of some their arms (and) hands; I cut off of others their noses, ears, (and) extremities. I gouged out the eyes of many troops. I made one pile of the living (and) one of heads. I hung their heads on trees around the city.[18]

Ashur-nasirpal II also relates this defeat and post-battle punishment of a rebellious vassal:

> I felled with the sword 800 of their combat troops, I burnt 3,000 captives from them. I did not leave one of them alive as a hostage. I captured alive Hulaya their city ruler. I made a pile of their corpses. I burnt their adolescent boys (and) girls. I flayed Hulaya their city ruler (and) draped his skin over the wall of the city.[19]

The OT describes Assyria as idolatrous and full of pride (e.g., Is 10:5–19). Despite its hubris, Yahweh used this people as his instrument to execute his wrath upon Israel for breaking his covenant of grace. Within Isaiah, Assyria or its king is featured as (among other things) a killer bee for which Yahweh whistles (Is 7:18); the razor that he uses to shave the head, genitalia, and beard of the nations and expose them in shame to the world (Is 7:20); and the rod of Yahweh's anger and the staff of his fury (Is 10:5). Assyria is probably the unnamed force that devours the countryside surrounding Jerusalem, leaving the city tottering like a pathetic hut (Is 1:7–8). The representative of Sennacherib taunted Hezekiah by saying, "I will give you two thousand horses if you are able to set riders on them" (2 Ki 18:23 || Is 36:8), and he proclaimed to the inhabitants of Jerusalem—in the Hebrew language no less—that they were destined to "eat their own dung and drink their own urine" (2 Ki 18:26–27 || Is 36:11–12).

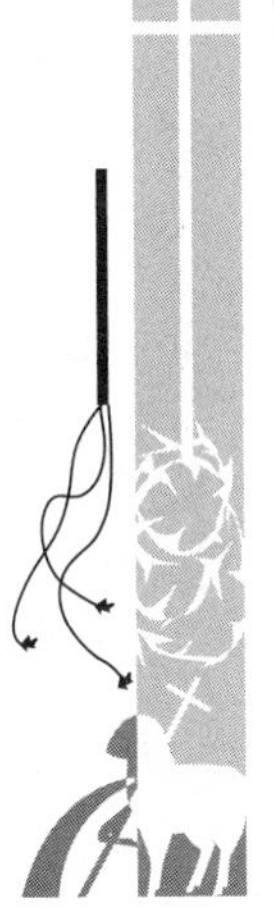

Among Israel's enemies in the eighth century BC, Assyria was truly the chief of sinners (cf. 1 Tim 1:15). Yet in the fullness of time (cf. Gal 4:4), the same kind of horrifying and humiliating violence that God allowed Assyria to inflict on Israel as his judgment would be inflicted on God's own Son. The Assyrian practice (described above) of impaling defeated victims was a precursor of the Roman practice of crucifixion.[20] The sinless Christ was scourged and hung upon the shameful cross, where he suffered the divine judgment for the transgressions of all humanity. By voluntarily becoming the victim and then triumphantly rising, Christ disarmed and defeated sin, death, the devil, and all

17 Bleibtreu, "Grisly Assyrian Record of Torture and Death," 52; cf. Bleibtreu, "Five Ways to Conquer a City."

18 Grayson, *Assyrian Royal Inscriptions*, 2:126.

19 Grayson, *Assyrian Royal Inscriptions*, 2:126.

20 See Hengel, *Crucifixion*, 22–23, including n. 4.

the forces of evil (cf. 2 Cor 2:14; Col 2:13–15). Through the resurrection of the tabernacle of David, God has raised up a remnant of people who constitute his new Israel, gathered from both the stock of Israel and the Gentiles, all marked by his saving name (Amos 9:11–12).

Amos 6:8–14

Certain Destruction for the Prideful House of Israel

Translation

6 [8]The Lord Yahweh swears by himself,
declares Yahweh, the God of armies:
"I am loathing the pride of Jacob,
and his fortresses I hate.
I will deliver over the city and its contents."
[9]If it happens that ten men survive in one house, they will die.
[10]And when a relative who is an embalmer will carry one away to take bones out from the house, he will say to whoever is in the recesses of the house, "Is anyone still with you?" And he will say, "No one." And he will say, "Silence! For you should not invoke the name of Yahweh!"
[11]Look, Yahweh is indeed commanding, and he will strike the largest house into fragments as well as the smallest house into splinters.
[12]Do horses run on a cliff?
Does someone plow [the sea] with oxen?
Yet you turn justice into poison
and the fruit of righteousness into wormwood.
[13]You are rejoicing about Lo-debar,
saying, "Was it not by our strength that we took for ourselves Karnaim?"
[14]"Indeed I am about to raise up against you, O house of Israel,
declares Yahweh, the God of armies,
a nation.
They will oppress you from Lebo-hamath to the Wadi of the Arabah."

Textual Notes

6:8 נִשְׁבַּע אֲדֹנָי יְהוִה בְּנַפְשׁוֹ—The same basic oath formula is used in all three of Yahweh's oaths in Amos (4:2; 6:8; 8:7). See the discussion of the oath formula in the first textual note and the commentary on 4:2, which advocate the view that in all three oaths, Yahweh swears by himself. In the normal phraseology of God taking an oath, the preposition בְּ is attached to the power or attribute of God that is invoked as the guarantor of the oath. In 4:2 God swears בְּקָדְשׁוֹ, "by his holiness," and here he swears בְּנַפְשׁוֹ, "by himself." In the OT, the specific oath formula נִשְׁבַּע … בְּנַפְשׁוֹ, "I swear … by myself," appears again only in Jer 51:14. The clause is a variant of בִּי נִשְׁבַּעְתִּי, "by myself I swear," in, for example, Gen 22:16 and Is 45:23. Yahweh's invocation of himself—the eternal, omnipotent, and immutable God—"expresses and stresses the implacable and irreversible nature of the impending punishment."[1]

[1] Paul, *Amos*, 213.

נְאֻם־יְהוָה אֱלֹהֵי צְבָאוֹת—This entire phrase (with the addition of the article on צְבָאוֹת) recurs in 6:14. For the signatory formula נְאֻם יְהוָה, see the second textual note on 2:11. For יְהוָה אֱלֹהֵי (הַ)צְבָאוֹת, see the second textual note and the commentary on 3:13.

מְתָאֵב אָנֹכִי אֶת־גְּאוֹן יַעֲקֹב—The construction with a participle (מְתָאֵב) and a pronoun (אָנֹכִי) often has an ongoing, durative force, hence "I am loathing, I continue to loathe." In all likelihood, the Piel participle מְתָאֵב is a by-form of the verb תָּעַב, "to loathe, abhor," which is common in the Piel, and which in 5:11 is parallel to the verb in the next clause of 6:8, שָׂנֵא, "to hate." The two verbs are also parallel in Ps 119:163. A homographic verb תָּאַב, "to long for, desire," occurs in Ps 119:40, 174, but the OT has no other instance (besides Amos 6:8) of תָּאַב meaning "to loathe." Yahweh is the subject of the Piel of תָּעַב, "to loathe," in, for example, Pss 5:7 (ET 5:6); 106:40. In the Torah, the cognate noun תּוֹעֵבָה often refers to actions or persons that God regards as an "abomination" (e.g., Lev 18:22, 26–27, 29–30; 20:13), including in the construct phrase "abomination of Yahweh" (תּוֹעֲבַת יְהוָה), a subjective genitive (e.g., Deut 7:25; 12:31; 17:1; 18:12). The verb here implies that Israel has violated the Torah, as other Amos verses make explicit (e.g., 2:4 regarding Judah).

The construct phrase גְּאוֹן יַעֲקֹב, "the pride/majesty of Jacob," recurs in 8:7. It has been interpreted in a variety of ways. The abstract noun גָּאוֹן can signify the "exaltation, majesty" of God (BDB, 1 b), of nations (BDB, 1 a), or of the creation (BDB, 1 c). It can also have the negative meaning "pride" (BDB, 2). In the OT, the occurrences of גָּאוֹן are almost equally divided between references to Yahweh's majesty, including that which he reveals by redeeming his people (e.g., Ex 15:7) or in judging human sin (e.g., Is 2:10, 19, 21), and humanity's foolish pretension to majesty.[2] גָּאוֹן is employed in a negative sense in, for example, Ezek 7:20 (Israel wrongly turned God's "ornament," the temple, into their source of presumptive "pride"); Is 13:19 (the arrogance of Babylon); Is 13:11 (Yahweh will punish the "pride" of insolent people throughout the world); and Is 14:11 (down to "Sheol" and hell goes the "pride, pomp" of the king of Babylon, who, in the context, stands as a type of fallen Lucifer and a warning that the eternal grave awaits all unbelievers). Prov 8:13 states that Yahweh hates "pride, arrogance" (גָּאוֹן), while Prov 16:18 states that "pride precedes destruction" (לִפְנֵי־שֶׁבֶר גָּאוֹן; cf. שֶׁבֶר in Amos 6:6).

Most interpreters believe the phrase here refers to faithless Israel's arrogant pride based on the nation's military power, wealth, and affluence. This fits the context, since Yahweh loathes it. The ancient versions understood it this way: the LXX renders it by ὕβρις, "hubris," and the Vulgate translates with *superbia*, "pride, haughtiness."

וְאַרְמְנֹתָיו שָׂנֵאתִי—This short clause is parallel to the preceding one. Yahweh used the same powerful verb שָׂנֵאתִי, "I hate," in reference to Israel in 5:21. For אַרְמוֹן, "fortress" or majestic, royal home, see the second textual note on 1:4 and the commentary on 3:9. By using the identical term, the plural of אַרְמוֹן, "fortresses," that recurs in all of

---

[2] Cf. D. Kellermann, "גָּאוֹן," *TDOT* 2:348–50. Gowan, *When Man Becomes God*, 20–23, notes other roots commonly used to indicate pride. He writes: "The greatest concentration of concern about the dangers of *hybris* in the Old Testament [is] in passages which are concerned with the great nations of the earth" (p. 29).

the judgment oracles against pagan nations (1:4, 7, 10, 12, 14; 2:2), Yahweh implicitly equates Israel with the heathen nations. The "fortresses" of Judah (2:5) and of northern Israel (3:10–11; 6:8) are no different than those inhabited by other unbelievers.

וְהִסְגַּרְתִּ֖י עִ֥יר וּמְלֹאָֽהּ׃—In the Qal, סָגַר means "to shut, close." The Hiphil, as here, often implies blocking off all possibility of escape so as to "deliver up" (BDB, 1) or hand someone over to a victor. Its compound object is the feminine noun עִיר, "city," and וּמְלֹאָהּ, "and her/its fullness." מְלֹא can mean the "entire contents" (BDB, 3), which would include all the people, animals, wealth, and possessions. "Her/its fullness" suggests the magnitude of the city's affluence.

6:9 וְהָיָ֗ה אִם־יִוָּ֨תְר֜וּ עֲשָׂרָ֧ה אֲנָשִׁ֛ים בְּבַ֥יִת אֶחָ֖ד וָמֵֽתוּ׃—This conditional sentence (אִם, "if …") at first envisions the possibility of survivors, then negates that possibility. The lack of any survivors will be reinforced in 6:10. The Niphal of יָתַר, "be left over, remain," can refer to those "surviving in" (בְּ) a "house" (בַּיִת here and in, e.g., Jer 27:21) or some other location (see BDB, s.v. יָתַר, Niphal). In Classical Hebrew fashion, the Niphal imperfect יִוָּתְרוּ is followed by perfect verbs with *waw* consecutive, each of which continues the sequence in the description of the hypothetical chain of future events. If "ten men survive," then וָמֵתוּ, "they will die." The sequence continues in 6:10: after the deaths, וּנְשָׂאוֹ, literally, "he [a relative] will carry him [one of the ten corpses] away" for burial (see the next textual note). Then a sequence of interactive dialogue follows, with each utterance introduced by the perfect with *waw* consecutive וְאָמַר, which occurs three times in 6:10.

6:10 וּנְשָׂא֞וֹ דּוֹד֣וֹ וּמְסָרְפ֗וֹ—The verb וּנְשָׂאוֹ has the compound subject דּוֹדוֹ וּמְסָרְפוֹ. The third masculine singular pronominal suffix repeated on the verb, noun, and participle, literally, "*his* relative and *his* embalmer will carry *him* away," may refer to one of the ten men who died at the end of 6:9. Or the singular might refer distributively to all ten of the dead (GKC, § 145 m). Since the context attaches no importance to which of the ten dead is involved, the pronouns are translated indefinitely: "*a* relative who is *an* embalmer will carry *one* [of the dead] away." The verb נָשָׂא, "to pick up, carry away," can refer to carrying a dead body to a grave for burial, as for Jacob (Gen 47:30; 50:13) or Saul and his sons (1 Chr 10:12).

The noun דּוֹד can refer specifically to an "uncle," or more generally, as here, to a "relative, kinsman." מְסָרְפוֹ is the only instance in the OT of the Piel stem of שָׂרַף, "to burn," and the only time it is spelled סָרַף. The Qal of שָׂרַף can refer to burning bones (Amos 2:1) and bodies, but in at least some OT passages, it may refer to burning spices for embalming or anointing the body as part of a funeral rite. For this meaning BDB, s.v. שָׂרַף, Qal, 2 a, cites Jer 34:5 and 2 Chr 16:14. Perhaps related is the Mishnaic Hebrew verb שָׂרַף that occurs in the Piel, is sometimes spelled סָרַף, and means "to cover with resin" (Jastrow, s.vv. סָרַף and שָׂרַף III; cf. also the noun שְׂרָף, "resin, gum"). Some commentators and translations take this line of interpretation, for example, "the one who anoints him for burial" (ESV). According to Paul, this custom is well attested in the Mishnaic period.[3] He cites Mishnah, *Shabbath* 23:5: "They may make ready [on

---

[3] Paul, *Amos*, 215–16.

the Sabbath] all that is needful for the dead and anoint (סָכִין) and wash it." The Jewish custom of anointing and embalming with spices is also attested in the NT in the preparation of the body of Jesus (Mt 26:6–12; Mk 16:1; Jn 19:39–40).

Paul believes that דּוֹדוֹ וּמְסָרְפוֹ refers to two different people: "The passage here is thus describing how the dead man's kinsman (דודו) and the one who is responsible for the proper last burial rites of anointing the body (מְסָרְפוֹ) are carrying the corpse out of the house."[4] However, the *waw* on וּמְסָרְפוֹ could be epexegetical, so that the two terms both refer to the same person,[5] as reflected in the translation adopted above, "a relative *who is* an embalmer." This is supported by the two occurrences later in the verse of the singular verb וְאָמַר, "and he will say," with this person as the speaker.

Another possibility is that מְסָרְפוֹ denotes someone who lights "an honorary funeral fire."[6] Yet another is that he "burns the structure [the house] to purify the site from the effects of corpses who have been left to rot for some period of time and then removes the bones for proper interment."[7]

לְהוֹצִיא עֲצָמִים מִן־הַבַּיִת—The Hiphil infinitive לְהוֹצִיא forms a purpose clause: the relative "will carry away" (וּנְשָׂאוֹ) the corpse, literally, "in order to take out bones from the house." עֲצָמִים, "bones," might mean that the flesh had already rotted off of the bones, but in this context, it is more likely that by synecdoche it refers to the whole corpse or "remains" (BDB, s.v. עֶצֶם, 1 f) of the man who has recently died. "The house" (הַבַּיִת) from which the bones are removed must be the "house" in which the ten men died in 6:9.

וְאָמַר לַאֲשֶׁר בְּיַרְכְּתֵי הַבַּיִת—The kinsman-embalmer speaks to (לְ) a person described by a vague relative clause, "who(ever) is in the recesses of the house." The dual (or plural) construct of יַרְכָה or יְרֵכָה, "*recesses* or *innermost part*" (BDB, 2), here refers to the room or chamber of a house that is farthest from the door, least accessible, and most hidden. Elsewhere יַרְכְּתֵי can refer to the "recesses, cargo hold" of a ship, to which Jonah withdraws to avoid Yahweh (Jonah 1:5);[8] to "the depths of the pit," which is Sheol, to which the king of Babylon, as a type of Satan, is banished (Is 14:15); or to "the farthest parts" of the earth (מִיַּרְכְּתֵי־אָרֶץ), from which comes the tempest of Yahweh's judgment in the face of international evil (Jer 25:32).

הַעוֹד עִמָּךְ—The relative asks this question, literally, "is [anyone] still with you?" It is a circumlocution for "is anyone still alive?"[9]

וְאָמַר אָפֶס—The terse reply is אָפֶס, "no one," a term "expressing non-existence … nought" (BDB, 2 and 2 b; cf. GKC, § 152 s). In Modern Hebrew, אֶפֶס is used for "zero."

---

4 Paul, *Amos*, 216.

5 As suggested by Andersen and Freedman, *Amos*, 572.

6 A possibility suggested by Niehaus, "Amos," 444, citing 2 Chr 16:14.

7 Sweeney, *The Twelve Prophets*, 246. The problem with this understanding is that normally only the bodies of criminals were burned (e.g., Lev 20:14; 21:9; Josh 7:15, 25).

8 See Lessing, *Jonah*, 103–4.

9 Smith, *Hosea, Amos, Micah*, 341.

וְאָמַר הָס כִּי לֹא לְהַזְכִּיר בְּשֵׁם יְהוָה׃—The relative speaks again to the person in the recesses of the house. הַס is an interjection, "hush! keep silence!" (*HALOT;* cf. Waltke-O'Connor, § 40.2.5c). It recurs in 8:3. In some passages, it is associated with the fear and dread that arise from a theophany or in a sanctuary where Yahweh's presence is immanent (e.g., Hab 2:20; Zeph 1:7; Zech 2:17 [ET 2:13]).[10] Here the word suggests fear that further speaking may provoke Yahweh to return to the house, and that can only mean one thing: more death!

The causal clause with כִּי explains the call for silence. When זָכַר, "to remember," is used in the Hiphil with שֵׁם, "a name," and/or a proper name (here יְהוָה), it means "to call upon, invoke" the name.[11] The Hiphil verb in this sense can take the preposition בְּ attached to the name invoked. The Hiphil of זָכַר is used for invoking "the name of Yahweh" (בְּשֵׁם יְהוָה) also in Ps 20:8 (ET 20:7), and similar wording is in, for example, Is 26:13. The force of the Hiphil infinitive construct here, לְהַזְכִּיר, may be rendered as "you/no one should invoke the name of Yahweh!" See GKC, § 114 l (cf. Waltke-O'Connor, § 36.2.3f, including example 45). Since wrathful Yahweh has been executing judgments, invoking him could bring judgment on the few who remain alive.

6:11 כִּי־הִנֵּה יְהוָה מְצַוֶּה—The causal כִּי introduces the reason for the preceding command not to invoke Yahweh by name. יְהוָה is modified by the attributive participle מְצַוֶּה. The divine name is also the implied subject of the perfect verb with *waw* consecutive that starts the next clause, וְהִכָּה (see the next textual note), literally, "Yahweh is commanding, and he will strike," which could be rendered as "Yahweh is giving the command to strike." Scripture can state that God himself performs an action even if the action is carried out by an intermediary. Yahweh was the subject of the Hiphil perfect of נָכָה with *waw* consecutive also in 3:15; see the first textual note on 3:15. In 9:1 Yahweh will speak the Hiphil imperative הַךְ, giving the command for another person to "strike" the idolatrous temple at Bethel. Yahweh will carry out the destruction of Israel predicted in Amos through Assyria as his intermediary.[12]

וְהִכָּה הַבַּיִת הַגָּדוֹל רְסִיסִים וְהַבַּיִת הַקָּטָן בְּקִעִים׃—The Hiphil of נָכָה takes two parallel direct object clauses, each consisting of three words. In both phrases, הַבַּיִת, "the house" and its following adjective (הַקָּטָן ... הַגָּדוֹל, "the large ... the small") have the definite article, forming superlatives: "the larg*est* house ... the small*est* house." See GKC, § 133 g. This merism expresses that *every* house will be included in the judgment. These houses would include the "winter" and "summer" homes mentioned in 3:15.[13]

Each adjectival phrase about a house is followed by a plural noun in the accusative (without a preposition) that describes the product "into" which the house is turned as it is destroyed. This noun רָסִיס means "a fragment." It occurs only here in the OT, but postbiblical Hebrew and other Semitic languages attest related verbs meaning "to chop" and nouns for things "chopped up" (see BDB and *HALOT*, s.v. רָסִיס II). A homograph

---

[10] Cf. Paul, *Amos*, 216.

[11] See Niehaus, "Amos," 444–45, and BDB, s.v. זָכַר, Hiphil, 3 a. Cf. *HALOT*, s.v. זָכַר, Hiphil, 4. For the same usage of זָכַר in the Hiphil, see Is 48:1.

[12] See the excursus "The Assyrian Empire."

[13] Cf. King, *Amos, Hosea, Micah*, 65.

meaning "drop of dew" occurs in Song 5:2. The noun בָּקִיעַ occurs elsewhere in the OT only in Is 22:9, where its plural refers to "breaches" in a city wall, and here its plural can be rendered "rubble" (*HALOT*) or "splinters." It is derived from the common verb בָּקַע, "to split, break open or through."

6:12 הַיְרֻצוּן בַּסֶּלַע סוּסִים—This is the first of two rhetorical questions beginning the verse.[14] As in 6:2, the first begins with the interrogative -הֲ, and the second begins with אִם. The Qal imperfect of רוּץ, "to run," has the interrogative -הֲ and a paragogic *nun*. No other OT verse has סוּס, "a horse," as the subject of רוּץ, but compare Joel 2:4; Esther 8:10. The noun סֶלַע usually refers to a "cliff, crag" (BDB, 1) or "precipice." The preposition בְּ here means "on (the side of)." Horses cannot negotiate a cliff even when walking slowly, let alone while running or galloping. In contrast, mountain goats easily traverse, ascend, or descend a cliff. Many English translations have "(up)on rocks," but the question could then be misunderstood as allowing for a positive answer, since horses are able to negotiate some rocks and moderately rocky ground.

אִם־יַחֲרוֹשׁ בַּבְּקָרִים—As it stands, the question here with the impersonal (GKC, § 144 d) habitual imperfect יַחֲרוֹשׁ reads, "does someone plow with oxen?" The noun בָּקָר is a generic term for large herd animals, including cattle and oxen. It rarely occurs in the plural as here. Usually it is a collective, as in Job 1:14, where the singular הַבָּקָר is the subject of the verb חָרַשׁ, "to plow."

This question in the MT would elicit the answer "yes, of course!" However, this obvious truth would undermine what Amos is trying to communicate at this point, namely, that Israel's behavior is absurd. Amos' rhetorical strategy in this passage requires that this be a question that expects a negative answer.

One way to arrive at an absurd question that expects a negative response is to take בַּסֶּלַע in the preceding clause as doing double duty: "Does someone plow with oxen *on a cliff*?" This construal is implied by translations that include the adverb "there," that is, "does one plow *there* with oxen?" (ESV; see also KJV, NIV, NASB). A second solution, preferred by many interpreters and some translations, is to redivide the consonants of בַּבְּקָרִים and repoint them to read בַּבָּקָר יָם, "does one plow the sea with oxen?" (RSV).[15] The question is nonsensical and demands the answer "no, impossible!"

The ancient versions vary. The Peshitta has ܐܘ ܕܒܢܝܢ ܒܗܘܢ ܦܕܢܐ, "or do they plow with them [with the horses in the preceding question]?" The Vulgate has *aut arari potest in bubalis*, "or is it possible to plow with gazelles/wild oxen?" The LXX has εἰ παρασιωπήσονται ἐν θηλείαις, probably meaning "Will they [horses] keep silent among females/mares?" (see LEH, s.v. θῆλυς). The LXX assumes that the verb is from the homograph חָרַשׁ II, "be silent, speechless," and apparently reads בַּבְּקָרִים as בַּנְּקֵבִים, the plural of נְקֵבָה.

---

[14] "A rhetorical question is basically the posing of a question which requires no answer since either the speaker or the listener (or even both of them) already knows the answer" (Watson, *Classical Hebrew Poetry*, 338). See also Joüon, § 161. For other rhetorical questions in Amos, see 2:11; 3:3–8; 5:18, 20, 25; 6:2; 8:8; 9:7.

[15] This solution is advocated by, for example, GKC, § 123 a, note 1; Paul, *Amos*, 218; Andersen and Freedman, *Amos*, 577–78.

כִּי־הֲפַכְתֶּם לְרֹאשׁ מִשְׁפָּט וּפְרִי צְדָקָה לְלַעֲנָה׃—The Qal verb הֲפַכְתֶּם, "you have turned, you turn," has two parallel object clauses. Each clause has a direct object (מִשְׁפָּט ... וּפְרִי צְדָקָה) and a prepositional phrase (לְרֹאשׁ ... לְלַעֲנָה) that states what the Israelites are turning the direct object into. Normally the noun רֹאשׁ means "head, first," as it does elsewhere in Amos (e.g., 6:7; 8:10). But a homograph רֹאשׁ II refers to a "poisonous plant" (e.g., Hos 10:4) or a serpent's "venom" (e.g., Deut 32:33). It can be used to qualify a substance such as poisoned water (e.g., Jer 8:14) and serve as a motif of Yahweh's judgment in the water of bitterness (cf. Num 5:11–28). Here in Amos 6:12, רֹאשׁ is translated generally as "poison," although its botanical meaning is supported by the following references to לַעֲנָה, "wormwood" (see the second textual note on 5:7) and "fruit" (פְּרִי), a term that can be used metaphorically in either a positive (e.g., Is 3:10; Prov 11:30) or negative (e.g., Hos 10:13; Micah 7:13) sense.

For מִשְׁפָּט, "justice" (also in 5:7, 15, 24) and its parallel noun צְדָקָה, "righteousness" (also in 5:7, 24), see the second and third textual notes on 5:7.

6:13 הַשְּׂמֵחִים לְלֹא דָבָר—The Qal of שָׂמַח, "to rejoice at, in, about," can take a variety of prepositions, including לְ, as here. In light of the second person plural verb referring to Israel in 6:12c, the Qal participle with the definite article, הַשְּׂמֵחִים, is translated with a second person pronoun, "*you* are rejoicing." The same was done in 6:1, 3; see the first textual note on 6:1.

The first of two cities in this verse is Lo-debar, a transliteration of its spelling לוֹ דְבָר in 2 Sam 9:4–5. The location of Lo-debar is generally identified as modern-day Tel el-Ḥammeh, north of the Jabbok River in northern Gilead.[16] Here and in 2 Sam 17:27, the city is spelled לֹא דָבָר, which means "no word/reason" or "a nothing" (GKC, § 152 a, note 1). This spelling is "an intentional paronomastic parody."[17] The LXX translates the phrase literally as οἱ εὐφραινόμενοι ἐπ' οὐδενὶ λόγῳ, "those rejoicing for no word/reason," while the Vulgate has *qui laetamini in nihili*, "you who rejoice in nothing." Even though 2 Sam 17:27–29 indicates that at one time the city was significant, Israel's rejoicing in the eighth century over Lo-debar is equivalent to rejoicing over *nothing*. As far as Yahweh is concerned, it does not exist.

הָאֹמְרִים הֲלוֹא בְחָזְקֵנוּ לָקַחְנוּ לָנוּ קַרְנָיִם׃—The translation of the quotation follows the Hebrew word order to convey its emphasis: "was it not *by our strength* that we took for ourselves Karnaim?" The phrase with the noun חֹזֶק, "strength," implicitly condemns Israel for hubris and lack of faith in Yahweh. It was he who redeemed Israel from Egypt by the חֹזֶק, "strength," of his hand (Ex 13:3, 14, 16) and enabled the Israelites to take possession of the promised land. See also the adjective חָזָק, "strong," in reference to Yahweh in, for example, Deut 3:24; 4:34; 5:15; Is 40:10; Ps 136:12.

The name of the second city, קַרְנַיִם, "Karnaim," may be a shortened form of Ashteroth-karnaim (Gen 14:5), meaning "Astarte of two horns." Astarte was a fertility goddess. More likely, Karnaim and Ashteroth (Josh 12:4) were sister cities, located in

---

16 Paul, *Amos*, 219.

17 Paul, *Amos*, 219. For another example of prophetic paronomasia against geographical sites, see Micah 1:10–15.

close proximity to each other. Karnaim is identified with modern day Sheikh es-Saʿad in central Bashan and is located on a northern tributary of the middle Yarmuk River.[18] קַרְנַיִם is a dual form of קֶרֶן, "horn." Since a horn of a bull symbolizes power and might (e.g., Zech 2:4 [ET 1:21]), the city's name, which means "double horn," denotes a very strong city. An Israelite might grasp the horns of an altar for protection (1 Ki 2:28).[19] Although the Israelites have defeated Karnaim, and thereby in a sense taken hold of the "two horns," they are anything but safe from the roaring Lion (see 1:2; 3:4, 8, 12; 5:19). The next verse warns that Yahweh will raise up a nation against Israel. When this happens there will be no safe haven. For the apostates death will be certain.

6:14 כִּי הִנְנִי מֵקִים עֲלֵיכֶם בֵּית יִשְׂרָאֵל נְאֻם־יְהוָה אֱלֹהֵי הַצְּבָאוֹת גּוֹי—The construction with הִנֵּה and pronominal suffix (הִנְנִי) plus participle (מֵקִים) denotes imminent action, "I am (soon) raising up, about to raise up" (see GKC, § 116 p). The Hiphil of קוּם often refers to God raising up a person to accomplish his divine purpose, either for salvation (e.g., וַיָּקֶם יְהוָה מוֹשִׁיעַ, "Yahweh raised up a savior," Judg 3:9) or for judgment (e.g., 1 Ki 11:14; 14:14). בֵּית יִשְׂרָאֵל is a vocative. For נְאֻם יְהוָה, see the second textual note on 2:11. Here the divine title is expanded by the addition of אֱלֹהֵי הַצְּבָאוֹת, for which, see the second textual note on 3:13. The direct object of the participle מֵקִים is the last word in the clause, the noun גּוֹי, "nation." It normally denotes a political entity, while עַם normally refers to an ethnic group. The lack of an article on גּוֹי may be for the sake of amplification (GKC, § 125 c).

וְלָחֲצוּ אֶתְכֶם מִלְּבוֹא חֲמָת עַד־נַחַל הָעֲרָבָה׃—The imminent future action represented by the participle in the preceding clause is continued here by the Qal perfect with *waw* consecutive, וְלָחֲצוּ (Joüon, § 119 n). The implied subject of the plural verb is the troops of the "nation" (גּוֹי) at the end of the preceding sentence. לָחַץ means "to squeeze, press, oppress" (see BDB). The verb can be used literally with an individual as the object (e.g., Num 22:25).[20] Figuratively, לָחַץ can mean "to oppress" someone who is vulnerable or of inferior standing (e.g., Ex 23:9). More commonly it refers to the subjugation of one nation or people by another or its king (e.g., Judg 4:3; 2 Ki 13:4; Ps 106:42). It is in this sense that Amos employs the verb, but ultimately it is Yahweh who will subjugate apostate Israel.

Lebo-hamath (לְבוֹא חֲמָת) is a city whose name literally means "the entrance of Hamath." Its exact location is still disputed.[21] This city is frequently named as the limit of the northern extent of Israel (Num 13:21; Judg 3:3; 1 Ki 8:65; 1 Chr 13:5).

"The Wadi of the Arabah" (נַחַל הָעֲרָבָה) appears only here in the OT. It probably refers to a wadi that empties into the Dead Sea itself or nearby into the Jordan Valley. Some OT verses (e.g., Deut 3:17; Josh 3:16; 2 Ki 14:25) refer to the Dead Sea as יָם הָעֲרָבָה, "the Sea of the Arabah." 2 Ki 14:25 states that the north-to-south extent of the northern kingdom of Israel during the height of the reign of Jeroboam ben Joash

---

[18] Paul, *Amos*, 219. Karnaim is mentioned in 1 Macc 5:26, 43–44.

[19] Cf. Sweeney, *The Twelve Prophets*, 248.

[20] Cf. J. Reindl, "לָחַץ," *TDOT* 7:529–33.

[21] See T. F. Wei, "Hamath, Entrance of," *ABD* 3:36–37.

(the reigning king during the ministry of Amos [1:1]) was "from Lebo-hamath to the Sea of the Arabah," which probably is the same as "from Lebo-hamath to the Wadi of the Arabah" in Amos 6:14. These two places create a merism from north to south that denotes the entire Northern Kingdom.

Commentary

A new section begins in 6:8, marked by Yahweh's oath against Israel's corrupt leadership. The next new section starts in 7:1, which inaugurates the series of five visions. When compared to the tight organization evident in the oracles against the nations (1:3–2:16) and the list of plagues (4:6–11), 6:8–14 is less cohesive and more miscellaneous. It does, however, connect with 6:1–7 in that it outlines the consequences of decadent leadership.

6:8 Yahweh is the Creator of the universe and the Lord over it (4:13; 5:8–9; 9:5–6). As the supreme authority he "swears by himself" (6:8); no higher guarantor of the oath can be invoked (Heb 6:13–14). The omniscient triune God has no trouble discerning Israel's arrogant actions and inner pride. "The pride of Jacob" refers to the hubris of the double kingdom, both northern Israel and Judah in the south.[22] It is an apt description of the attitude of the leaders from both the south ("Mount Zion," 6:1) and north ("Mount Samaria," 6:1) who are condemned in 6:1–7.

This arrogance of the aristocrats is demonstrated throughout the book. They imagine that since Yahweh has called and redeemed Israel to be his elect people (2:9–11; 3:1–2), no evil can overtake them (9:10), no matter how many and how grievous their sins are. Fueling their self-confidence are their ill-gotten riches (2:6–7; 3:9–10; 5:11–12), military might (2:14–16; 5:3), and frequent lavish religious rites, although saturated with idolatry (2:4, 8; 4:4–5; 5:21–26; 6:4–7).

Yahweh's charge against the loathsome "pride of Jacob" is summed up in this dictum of Luther:

Omne peccatum est superbia, "every sin is pride."[23]

This recapitulates mankind's original sin inherited from Adam and Eve, whom the serpent seduced with the false promise of becoming like God (Gen 3:5). This original sin is the root cause of all the actual sins of omission and commission, resulting in the reign of death over all humanity apart from Christ and saving faith in him (Rom 5:12–21).

God defines saving faith as including a renunciation of pride: "the fear of Yahweh is to hate evil, pride, and arrogance" (יִרְאַת יְהוָה שְׂנֹאת רָע גֵּאָה וְגָאוֹן, Prov 8:13). St. Paul calls the baptized not to think too highly of themselves, but to have a sober judgment according to the measure of faith given to each (Rom 12:3). He also calls all in Christ to have the same humility as Jesus himself,

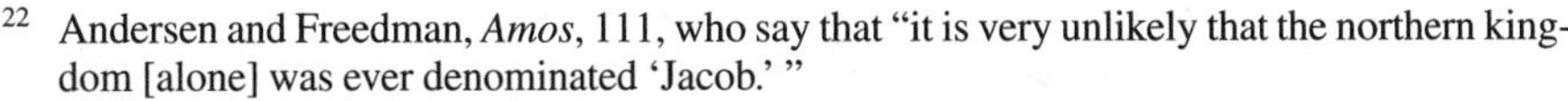

[22] Andersen and Freedman, *Amos*, 111, who say that "it is very unlikely that the northern kingdom [alone] was ever denominated 'Jacob.' "

[23] WA 3.568.20; AE 11:49.

who, though being God the Son, emptied himself, took on the form of a slave, and was obedient to death, then was exalted as Lord (Phil 2:5–11).

About a century and a half after Amos, Jeremiah would admonish the Israelites in Judah not to boast in wisdom, might, or wealth, but in the knowledge of Yahweh (Jer 9:22–23 [ET 9:23–24]). The admonitions to Israel against pride apply a fortiori to Gentiles. Although Yahweh would use Assyria as the "nation" (Amos 6:14) that would chastise prideful northern Israel by conquering it in 722 BC, he would also judge Assyria for its arrogance (Is 10:5–16). Then he would use Babylon to punish the proud southern kingdom of Judah by conquering it and destroying the temple in 587 BC, but eventually he would humiliate Babylon for its own "pride" (גָּאוֹן, Is 13:11) and send the Babylonian king down to Sheol (Is 14:4–21) because of his "pride" (גָּאוֹן, Is 14:11, as in Amos 6:8). Moab (Is 16:6–14) and Edom (Obad 1–16) also would be condemned for their hubris.[24]

In Amos' day, the arrogance of Israel and Judah's leaders had been fostered by the victories of Jeroboam ben Joash (793–753 BC),[25] the reigning king of northern Israel (Amos 1:1). Yahweh had used this king to bring about good for the sake of his people (2 Ki 14:26–28; cf. Gen 45:8–11; 50:20; Rom 8:28). He changed Israel's map when he extended the country's northern border to Lebo-hamath (the entrance of Hamath, probably south of Kadesh) and the southern border to the Dead Sea (2 Ki 14:25; Amos 6:14). Uzziah (792–740 BC),[26] the reigning king in Judah (Amos 1:1) and Jeroboam ben Joash's vassal, also achieved impressive military victories (2 Chr 26:1–15; cf. Is 2:6–7). The large extent of the Northern Kingdom under Jeroboam ben Joash coupled with the Southern Kingdom of Judah when it was ruled by King Uzziah rivaled that of the golden age of united Israel under David and Solomon. Yet even with its expanded borders, Israel allowed no room for Yahweh. Jeroboam ben Joash was economically successful but spiritually bankrupt, and northern Israel, especially its leaders, followed his lead. "Complacency, affluence, strong cities, huge military fortresses, and military victories in the past have created a spirit of invincibility and false security that God hates."[27]

God abhors not only the elite's inordinate pride, but also the Israelites' houses (see the commentary on 6:11), some so lavish they can be called "fortresses" (3:10–11; 6:8). The "fortresses" of pagan Gentiles were repeatedly the target of Yahweh's fire in the oracles against the nations (see the fourth textual

---

[24] Several OT passages depict arrogant pagan kings who aspired to be like gods, but who then were deposed and sent down to Sheol, to destruction in hell. Their hubris and fall typify that of Satan, who tried to usurp God but was thrown down from heaven. Compare the king of Babylon in Is 14:12–15; the king of Tyre in Ezek 28:11–19; and Pharaoh in Ezek 31:8–18 to the fall and judgment of Satan in Lk 10:18 and Rev 12:7–9; 20:2–3, 7–10.

[25] Thiele, *The Mysterious Numbers of the Hebrew Kings*, 116.

[26] Thiele, *The Mysterious Numbers of the Hebrew Kings*, 118.

[27] Smith, *Hosea, Amos, Micah*, 337.

note on 6:8), and Yahweh hates with equal fervor the "fortresses" of northern Israel (3:10–11; 6:8) and of Judah (2:5).

The Hebrew verb שָׂנֵא, "to hate, " first occurred in Amos describing Israel's hatred of judicial correction and the speaking of truth (5:10). Then the verb recurred when Yahweh called Israel instead to "hate evil and love good" (5:15). But Israel refused to do so, provoking Yahweh to declare, "I hate, I reject your festivals." His rejection of the nation's syncretistic worship (5:21–27), finds its culmination in 6:8–10, where he imposes the penalty of death. Those who "will die" are "all the sinners of my people" (9:10).

The judgment is that Yahweh "will deliver over the city and its contents" (6:8). In all likelihood this refers to the capital of northern Israel: the city of Samaria.

To whom will Yahweh hand the city over? The closest he gets to answering this question in the book of Amos is in 6:14, when he ominously, yet simply, states that it will be "a nation" (גּוֹי). Later in the eighth century, other prophets will identify this nation as Assyria (e.g., Is 8:4; Hos 11:5).

6:9 After a broad description in 6:8 of the coming disaster, Lion Yahweh moves in for the kill (cf. 1:2; 3:4, 8, 12; 5:19). The word "house" (בַּיִת) in 6:9–11, 14 functions as a catchword within this section.[28] There are several possible interpretations of its significance. Amos may be announcing an ironic twist to the feasting in 6:4–7: those gathered in a house for revelry, perhaps to commemorate the dead, will themselves die![29] Or the "house" (בַּיִת) may allude to Bethel, whose name means "house of God" (בֵּית־אֵל), but which northern Israel had turned into a site of idolatry with a temple that Yahweh will destroy (9:1–4).[30] Another possible interpretation is that Amos is literarily reaching back to the ten survivors from each city in 5:3. After the military defeat of each group of one hundred, each band of ten survivors may have crowded into a single house. Yet even in the presumed safety of their own home they will find no refuge (see also 5:19).[31] This small remnant of "ten" (5:3; cf. Gen 18:32), one-tenth (cf. Is 6:13) of the original hundred, will face death. The exact nature of the catastrophe is left undefined, as also in, for example, Amos 4:12; 6:14. Vintage Amos!

Earlier Yahweh lamented that the nation was dead (5:1–3). Throughout chapters 5 and 6 he repeatedly posts "drop dead" signs (cf. 5:2, 5, 18–20, 27; 6:1, 7). Here 6:9 portrays the performative power of his earlier words.

---

[28] As noted by Stuart, *Hosea–Jonah*, 363.

[29] This is the view of Paul, *Amos*, 214, n. 15. Sometimes a "*marzēaḥ* feast" (6:7) was associated with a funeral; see the second textual note on 6:7.

[30] For Bethel, see the second textual note and the commentary on 3:14, the first textual note on 4:4, and the commentary on 7:13.

[31] On the theme in Amos of the impossibility of escape from Yahweh, see 2:13–16; 5:18–20; 9:1–4.

6:10 This verse is a close-up picture of what the death announced in 6:9 will look like. As the camera zooms in, Amos depicts a relative removing from within a house the remains of the dead for burial.

A corpse is unclean, and contact with a dead body would render a person unclean (Num 9:6–10; 19:11–13). Priests were forbidden from having contact with a corpse except for that of a close relative (Lev 21:1–4), and the high priest was forbidden from all such contact, even with his dead father or mother (Lev 21:10–11). Such contact would profane Yahweh's name (Lev 21:6) and his sanctuary (Lev 21:12). But a lay relative may remove the corpse from the house. It would be a curse for the dead person not to be buried.[32] "Bones" (Amos 6:10) might suggest that the devastation has literally "sliced and diced" people into severed body parts.[33] The well-fed people of 6:4–7 have become skeletons, a shadow of their former selves. Their remains must be picked up, anointed, and buried.

The embalmer asks whether anyone else is alive, and the answer is "no one" (אָפֶס). This fulfills the covenant curse upon Israel for violating the Sinai covenant: there remains "no one [אָפֶס], either slave or free" (Deut 32:36).

"The name of Yahweh is a strong tower; to it the righteous man can run and be protected" (Prov 18:10). However, during this time of Yahweh's wrath upon his apostate people, if they call upon his name in the house of the dead, this invocation would only cause *more* bones of dead people to require collection and burial. The name of Yahweh brings death to those who are under his curse (2 Ki 2:24). He is a roaring, attacking Lion who prompts immediate flight (1:2; 3:4, 8, 12; 5:19).

6:11 Once again the precise agent of Yahweh's judgment is not named.[34] However, his command to destroy the houses could be fulfilled by the earthquake that occurred two years after the conclusion of Amos' ministry,[35] which may also have been the event that climactically shattered the altar and temple at Bethel (3:13–15; 9:1).

---

[32] Ancient Near Eastern treaty curses often speak about leaving the slain in the open to be eaten by scavengers or to rot. This treatment of covenant breakers appears regularly in the annals of the Assyrian kings Sennacherib, Esarhaddon, and Ashurbanipal. See, for example, the following: "The corpses of their warriors I [forbade] to be buried" (Esarhaddon, quoted in Luckenbill, *Ancient Records of Assyria and Babylonia*, vol. 2, § 521). "Their corpses they hung on stakes, they stripped off their skins and covered the city wall(s) with them" (Ashurbanipal, quoted in Luckenbill, *Ancient Records of Assyria and Babylonia*, vol. 2, § 773). In the OT the most shocking vision of this curse is in Ezek 37:1–14, where the dry, unburied bones are those of the Israelites who have suffered under Yahweh's curse for breaking his covenant, but for the penitent Yahweh promises resurrection and restoration. See Hummel, *Ezekiel 21–48*, 1074–85.

[33] 2 Ki 6:24–33 is a vivid description of this kind of havoc. The siege of Ben-hadad, king of Aram, against Samaria lasted so long that within the starving city a donkey's head sold for eighty shekels of silver, and people resorted to cannibalism.

[34] This is also the case in, for example, 3:11; 4:2–3; 5:2–3; 6:7–8, 14; 7:17; 8:8.

[35] See "Two Years before the Earthquake" in the commentary on 1:1.

The Israelites' multiple and lavish homes came under judgment in 3:15 and 5:11, including those opulent enough to be called "fortresses" (3:10; 6:8). Continuing his tirade against houses, Yahweh specifies "the largest house" (הַבַּיִת הַגָּדוֹל) and "the smallest house" (הַבַּיִת הַקָּטֹן) for destruction. By creating this merism, Yahweh indicates that all of Israel's houses will be demolished. The nation's field of dreams will be turned into a life of nightmares, surrounded by ruins.

6:12 This and the following verse are loaded with satire.[36] It begins with a pair of rhetorical questions[37] that are based upon the principle of *reductio ad absurdum.*

"Do horses run on a cliff?" The obvious answer is "no." The next question is even more absurd, whether "Does someone plow with oxen?" envisions plowing "on the side of a precipice" or "the sea."[38] Luther comments on this verse in light of Amos' personal background as a herdsman from Tekoa (1:1):

> Again we have a rustic metaphor of the Tekoan rustic. This shepherd is always consistent. He remembers the farm animals, the horses and the cows. Perhaps the prophet wants this to mean cows that will be kept for threshing rather than for plowing; or that pregnant or calving cows are not suitable for plowing. Otherwise we are certain that they plowed with oxen or cows. The sense of the metaphor is as if he were saying: "Those people are useless. They are not at all fit for that for which the Lord uses them. They are absolutely useless for every ministry of God. God has no use for them. Since He is so weary of them, He despises and rejects them. They no longer please Him."[39]

God can cite the obedience of the animals within the order of creation in order to shame his disobedient and rebellious people (Is 1:3; Jer 8:7; cf. Jer 13:23). The rhetorical questions about what would be insane behavior in the animal world point to the habitually insane way of life in apostate Israel. Just as it would be contrary in the natural world for horses to run on the side of a cliff or for oxen to plow a precipice or the sea, so it is unnatural for Israel to corrupt justice and righteousness (Amos 5:7; 6:12). Horses that tried to gallop on a rocky cliff would immediately fall to their deaths. Oxen likewise would perish if they were harnessed to plow the side of a crag or the sea (in which both the plower and the animals would drown).

Just so, all of Israel's actions fall into the same category: complete folly! The most nonsensical behavior is Israel's death by apostasy and idolatry, which is spiritual suicide. The perversion of divine justice and righteousness is poison and wormwood. This mixture will soon kill the nation.[40]

---

[36] See "Satire in Amos" in the commentary on 4:1–5.

[37] For other rhetorical questions in Amos, see 2:11; 3:3–8; 5:18, 20, 25; 6:2, 12; 8:8; 9:7.

[38] For these two possibilities, see the second textual note on 6:12.

[39] Luther, "Lectures on Amos" (AE 18:172).

[40] For condemnations of Israel's syncretistic worship, which perverted the divine justice, righteousness, and worship given in the Torah, see the commentary on 2:7–8; 3:14; 4:4–5; 5:5–6, 14, 21–27; 7:9–17; 8:5, 10, 14; 9:1. See also the excursus "The Prophets and Israel's Worship"

6:13 The historical background of these next two verses is given in 2 Ki 14:23–29, where the historian describes the victories of Jeroboam ben Joash. Those verses are consistent with Amos 6:14. The expansion of Israel's borders evoked memories of Israel's golden age under the leadership of David and Solomon. Popular opinion was that the Day of Yahweh was almost at hand (cf. 5:18–20)! The divine plan was in motion, and Israel imagined that it was about to rule "from sea to sea, and from the Euphrates River to the ends of the earth" (Ps 72:8). But for the unfaithful people, the Day of Yahweh will only be a day of darkness (5:18–20), an "evil day" (6:3), and most bitter (8:10).

Yahweh's response to Israel's gloating over its recent military victories is to respell the name of the city "Lo-debar" (לֹו דְבָר, 2 Sam 9:4–5) to "Lo'-dabar" (לֹ֣א דָבָ֑ר, Amos 6:13), meaning "nothing"! This is similar to other prophetic rebukes that use לֹא, "no, not," in, for example, Is 31:8 and Hos 1:9. The other city named here, Karnaim, is located in the region of Bashan. Israel's victories over both are as fleeting as dust in the wind.

Yahweh continues with another quotation of his Israelite adversaries.[41] In this quote are three Hebrew first-person forms: "Was it not by *our* strength that *we* took for *ourselves* Karnaim?" (6:13). Israel continues its "pride" over its achievements (6:8). The words of Ps 115:1, "*not to us*, O Yahweh, *not to us*, but to *your* name give glory," are as far away from these boasters as the east is from the west. It is not by human might or by power that Israel has defeated its enemies, but by Yahweh's Spirit (cf. Deut 9:4–6; Zech 4:6). "The horse is prepared for the day of battle, but to Yahweh belongs victory" (Prov 21:31).

6:14 Following on the heels of Israel's boastful rejoicing in 6:13, this verse comes as a shock. How could such a well-oiled military machine ever lose a battle?[42] How could the oppressors become the oppressed? The answer is that Yahweh is "*the* God of armies"(אֱלֹהֵ֥י הַצְּבָאוֹת, 6:14), the military commander par excellence. He plans to bring a nation that will oppress the oppressing Israelite aristocracy. "A nation" (גּוֹי), a short noun that is "undefined, unspecified, and unidentified,"[43] will be Yahweh's means of judgment against "the house

---

in the commentary on chapter 5 and the excursus "The Sabbath" in the commentary on chapter 8. Stephen the protomartyr quotes Amos 5:25–27 in Acts 7:42–43 to confirm that the culmination of Israel's idolatry was the people's rejection of Jesus the Messiah.

God rejects idolatry as demon worship (Lev 17:7; Deut 32:17; Ps 106:37; 1 Cor 10:20–21), and behind the demons is the devil, Satan (Rev 12:9; 20:2). See the commentary on Amos 5:14.

[41] Other quotes of the Israelites are in 2:12; 4:1; 6:13; 8:5–6, 14; 9:10 (cf. 5:14).

[42] Amos delights in countering Israel's expectations. For dramatic reversals of what is expected, see 2:9; 3:1–2; 4:4–5; 5:18–20; 5:21–27; 6:1–7; 8:9–10; 9:11–15.

[43] Paul, *Amos*, 220. See the excursus "The Assyrian Empire."

Yahweh employs this same rhetorical strategy in Jeremiah when he threatens that "a nation" will subjugate the house of Israel, at that time, Judah (Jer 5:15–17), and he withholds the nation's identity (Babylon) until later, beginning in Jer 20:4.

of Israel" (6:14), which in the context of the book of Amos probably includes Judah in the south as well as Israel in the north.[44]

The triune God customarily chooses to work through appointed means. In this case he will judge unfaithful Israel by means of the Assyrian Empire.[45] Yahweh judged Egypt by the ten plagues and accomplished Israel's deliverance through the Red Sea by means of the wind and waves (Exodus 7–15). God caused the birds and animals to serve Nebuchadnezzar in his work of judgment against Judah (Jer 27:6). But the most common means of divine destruction in the OT was Yahweh's use of foreign empires. In Jer 50:25 Yahweh calls the nations "the vessels of his wrath" (cf. Is 10:5; 13:5). He used Nebuchadnezzar and called him "my servant" (Jer 25:9; 27:6; 43:10).

Yet he would also appoint Cyrus the Persian to facilitate the return of the repentant exiles to Judah (Is 44:28; 45:1–7, fulfilled in Ezra 1:1–11). Ultimately, it is by means of the crucifixion of his own sinless Son that God executes his judgment against the iniquity of all humanity, and by means of the resurrection of that same appointed Man comes the promise of salvation on the day when he judges the world in righteousness (Acts 17:31). Until that day, God continues to work through his appointed means—his Word and Sacraments—to convict sinners of their need for the Savior, to work repentance and faith, and to justify all believers, sealing them with the Spirit for the day of salvation.

At the time Amos was prophesying (ca. 760 BC), Assyria was not yet a world power. "The enemy [is] yet unnamed and popularly unexpected."[46] Amos' ministry was about a decade and a half before the rise of the Assyrian king Tiglath-pileser III (745–727 BC). Tiglath-pileser III exacted tribute from the Israelite king Menahem (2 Ki 15:19–20). He took much of northern Israel's territory (2 Ki 15:29; 1 Chr 5:26; see also 2 Ki 16:5–9), leaving only Samaria and a small region around it under Israelite control.[47] And he conquered most of the nations surrounding northern Israel, including Damascus (2 Ki 16:9), which had in the past been a buffer state between Israel and Assyria. During the reign of Tiglath-pileser III, Judah became a vassal of Assyria (2 Ki 16:7–8).

Shalmaneser V (726–722 BC) adopted his father's policy of westward expansion and made King Hoshea of Israel his vassal (2 Ki 17:3). Hoshea, much like his predecessors (e.g., Is 30:1–2; 31:1–3), looked to Egypt for military aid

---

[44] Andersen and Freedman, *Amos*, 113 (see also pp. 98–99). They believe the military victories in 6:13 indicate that Uzziah in the south and Jeroboam ben Joash in the north

> may have assisted each other while each pursued his own objectives. … It is hard to imagine either operating so freely across national borders without an alliance or at least a cooperative understanding between them securing the internal border and allowing them to draw troops and equipment from that border in order to attack elsewhere. (*Amos*, 113)

[45] God frequently accomplishes his divine work through human beings. Here Yahweh's judgment is put into action through human troops: the Assyrians. Cf. Koch, *The Prophets*, 1:154–55.

[46] Stuart, *Hosea–Jonah*, 366.

[47] See Younger, "The Deportations of the Israelites," 202–4.

(2 Ki 17:4), but help never arrived. In a punitive action, Shalmaneser attacked Samaria. After a three year siege, the city fell in 722 BC, bringing the end of the northern kingdom of Israel (2 Ki 17:5–6). The subsequent king of Assyria, Sargon II (722–705 BC), was primarily responsible for the exile of the citizens and the repopulation of the city with foreigners who had been exiled from other nations.[48] All of these events fulfilled the prophecy of Amos.

Israel's hubris in 6:13 would be short lived. The people, especially their leaders, were enjoying the pleasures of sin, but only for a short time (cf. Heb 11:25). The Assyrians were about to flex their muscles.[49] What Israel had gained (2 Ki 14:25–27; Amos 6:13) would soon be lost.

The principle of *lex talionis* applies here, but instead of "an eye for an eye," it is "a land for a land." Yahweh in his grace enabled Israel to conquer Canaan and its diverse pagan inhabitants. But because of Israel's infidelity, the land would again be controlled by the power of a pagan empire, Assyria. Ironically, the judgment corresponds to Joshua's conquest of the land: in both cases a single overwhelming invasion brings Canaan under the control of one central power.

Summary

This unit begins and ends with the same four Hebrew words (נְאֻם־יְהוָה אֱלֹהֵי צְבָאוֹת, 6:8, 14), literally, "an utterance of Yahweh, the God of armies." The section is also tied together by Yahweh's repeated threats involving fortresses and houses, quite possibly with the royal residence functioning as ground zero (cf. 7:9).

Andersen and Freedman write:

> It is fairly easy to read the book of Amos in the light of the cataclysmic events of the late eighth century and to observe how correct he was. But the oracles must be considered in their own time and context and in the light of the circumstances of the man who launched the divine thunderbolts when the land was at peace and enjoying unusual prosperity—when, as almost a direct response and consequence of his words, [Israel's] victories increased, [its] borders were expanded, and the words of rival [false] prophets were being amply fulfilled.[50]

Large scale deportations of other peoples had already happened in the ancient Near East (see 1:6, 9).[51] The threats announced in 5:5, 27; 6:7, 14; 7:11, 17; and 9:4 should not have come as a total shock. God would fulfill the ancient warning he had given Israel already in the time of Moses (fifteenth century BC, some seven centuries before Amos) for when his people would forsake

---

48 See Younger, "The Deportations of the Israelites."

49 The first textual note on 6:14 explains the significance of the construction with הִנֵּה plus the participle מֵקִים, "I am about to raise up."

50 Andersen and Freedman, *Amos*, 601.

51 Wolff notes that the Urartean practice of exile during this era would sometimes include as many as fifty thousand people displaced at one time (*Joel and Amos*, 89 and 151, including n. 102).

him (Deut 28:63–65; 29:27 [ET 29:28]; 31:27–29; 32:15–35). Yet his purpose was not to utterly destroy them, but to drive them to repentance that they might return to him and receive his salvation through faith (Deut 32:36–43). This is his work of Law and Gospel according to his ancient covenant, now fulfilled in the death and resurrection of Christ:

> I kill and I make alive.
> I wound and I heal. (Deut 32:39)

Amos 7:1–9:10

The Visions

Introduction to Amos' Five Visions

7:1–6 Visions That Do Not Come to Pass

Introduction to Amos 7:1–6: Two Visions That Do Not Come to Pass

7:1–3 The First Vision: The Locusts

7:4–6 The Second Vision: The Fire

7:7–9:10 Visions That Do Come to Pass and the Reasons Why

Introduction to Amos 7:7–9; 8:1–3; and 9:1–4: Three Visions That Do Come to Pass

7:7–9 The Third Vision: The Plumb Line

7:10–17 Amos and Amaziah

8:1–3 The Fourth Vision: The Basket of Summer Fruit

8:4–6 Hucksters and Hypocrites on Holy Days

Excursus *The Sabbath*

8:7–14 A Famine of Yahweh's Word

9:1–4 The Fifth Vision: Yahweh Topples the Temple

9:5–6 Yahweh Shakes the Earth

9:7–10 The Final Judgment

Introduction to Amos' Five Visions

Prophets were sometimes called "seers" (1 Sam 9:9). Therefore it is not surprising that references to their visions are prominent in their oracles.[1] The book of Amos begins with a reference to the visionary character of the prophecy: "The words of Amos ... which *he saw/perceived* [חָזָה]" (see further the commentary on 1:1). This verb and its cognate noun חָזוֹן are attested in the introductions to some other prophetic books, such as "the vision of Isaiah" (חֲזוֹן יְשַׁעְיָהוּ, Is 1:1; see also Obad 1; Micah 1:1; Nah 1:1; Hab 1:1). Prophetic visions often occur in a series. For example, Ezekiel's inaugural call comes in the form of a vision of Yahweh's Glory (chapters 1–3); he then sees the Glory depart from the Jerusalem temple (chapters 8–11) and concludes the book with a vision of the return of the Glory to an eschatological temple (chapters 40–48). Jeremiah has two sequential visions (Jer 1:11–19), and Zechariah 1–6 contains eight visions.[2] Revelatory visions from Yahweh are central to the overall ministry and message of Israel's prophets.

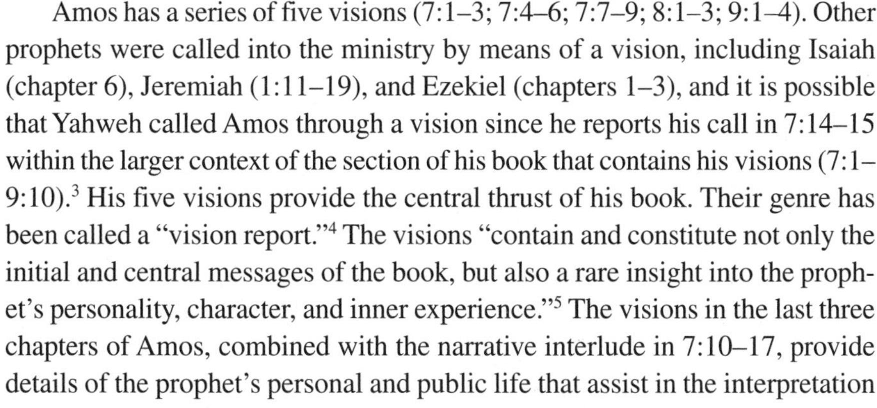

Amos has a series of five visions (7:1–3; 7:4–6; 7:7–9; 8:1–3; 9:1–4). Other prophets were called into the ministry by means of a vision, including Isaiah (chapter 6), Jeremiah (1:11–19), and Ezekiel (chapters 1–3), and it is possible that Yahweh called Amos through a vision since he reports his call in 7:14–15 within the larger context of the section of his book that contains his visions (7:1–9:10).[3] His five visions provide the central thrust of his book. Their genre has been called a "vision report."[4] The visions "contain and constitute not only the initial and central messages of the book, but also a rare insight into the prophet's personality, character, and inner experience."[5] The visions in the last three chapters of Amos, combined with the narrative interlude in 7:10–17, provide details of the prophet's personal and public life that assist in the interpretation

---

[1] Scholars have attempted to classify the different kinds of prophetic visions in the OT. For example, Lindblom divides visions into two groups: pictorial, where attention is directed to something seen, and dramatic, where action is the essential component (*Prophecy in Ancient Israel*, 122–37). Long offers three categories: oracle visions, for example, Amos 7:7–9; 8:1–3; word visions, for example, Amos 7:1–6; and revelatory mystery visions, for example, Zechariah 1–6 ("Reports of Visions among the Prophets").

[2] In contrast to Amos, whose five visions depict the destruction of Israel, Zechariah's eight visions in chapters 1–6 form a counterpart: they envision Israel's restoration and glorious future. This is discussed by Schart, "The Fifth Vision of Amos in Context," 59.

[3] Von Rad opines: "The peasant Amos's call is almost certainly to be connected with the reception of the five visions" (*Old Testament Theology*, 2:131).

[4] Sweeney (*Isaiah 1–39*, 542). He writes about them: "In their literary contexts, they authenticate and convey the prophetic message."

[5] Andersen and Freedman, *Amos*, 613, writing about Amos' first four visions. They also write: "The Book of Visions is the heart of the book of Amos because it tells us how Amos became a prophet, what he saw and heard in the presence of his God, and the nature of the message he brought back with him from those experiences" (pp. 725–26).

of chapters 1–6 as well as the messianic promise that concludes the book in 9:11–15.

Amos' visions involve both the Northern and Southern Kingdoms. Throughout the book, and indeed throughout the OT, "Jacob," "my people Israel," "the children of Israel," and "the house of Israel" regularly refer to the entire people called to be God's own nation: Israel as a whole. In the five visions, "Jacob" appears in 7:2, 5, while the title "my people Israel" is in 7:8 and 8:2. This means the visions apply to the entire people of God.[6] Yet the last verse of the third vision targets the northern kingdom: "Israel" and "the house of Jeroboam" (7:9; for Jeroboam, the king of northern Israel, see 1:1). When "Israel" appears without modification in 7:9 and elsewhere in Amos, it denotes only the Northern Kingdom.[7] In the fifth vision (9:1–4), Yahweh orders the demolition of a temple, which must be the idolatrous one at Bethel in northern Israel. The main focus of all five of the visions is the impending destruction of northern Israel. Like the rest of the book, the emphasis is that northern Israel was ripe for its destruction in 722 BC, some four decades after the ministry of Amos, which would fulfill his prophecies.

In the first two visions, Yahweh threatens to destroy Israel, but Amos intercedes and the judgment is postponed. These extensions of God's mercy probably reflect the earlier part of the prophet's ministry after his call. The second two visions announce the end of the time of Yahweh's clemency toward the Northern Kingdom. In the fifth vision, Yahweh gives the command to execute the judgment he had announced in the third and fourth visions. It is the climactic vision because it is separated from the preceding four visions (8:4–14 intervene between the fourth and fifth visions) and because it is fifth.[8] The only verbal connection between the first four visions and the fifth is the verb רָאָה, "to see." Each of the first four visions begins with the verb in the Hiphil, meaning "to show, reveal": כֹּה הִרְאַנִי אֲדֹנָי יְהוִה וְהִנֵּה, literally, "thus the Lord Yahweh showed me, and behold …" (7:1, 4; 8:1; the same wording but without the divine title is in 7:7). The participle of that verb, רֹאֶה, occurs in Yahweh's repeated question to Amos in the third and fourth visions, "what are you seeing?" (7:8; 8:2). The fifth and final vision begins with the Qal of the verb: "I saw" (רָאִיתִי, 9:1).

Yet the fifth vision strikes a different chord than the others. Paul writes of 9:1–4:

> There is no similar opening or concluding formula; the prophet is only a witness to a scene in which the sole "object" seen is the Lord himself; there is no dialogue, and thus no interpretation is necessary. The dénouement, described

---

6 So Andersen and Freedman, *Amos*, 631.

7 Andersen and Freedman, *Amos*, 631.

8 The five visions form a complete pentad, so they comprise a unity. Amos employs pentads elsewhere in the book. Amos 4:6–11 has the fivefold refrain " 'but you did not return to me,' declares Yahweh" (4:6, 8, 9, 10, 11). Another pentad consists of the five curses or threats in 7:17. There are five conditional sentences in 9:2–4 that express a fivefold concept of the impossibility of escaping from divine judgment.

by five successive threats, has arrived. This vision is the finale. The disaster is definitive and decisive.[9]

There is a logical progression involved in the sequence of the five visions. They exhibit repetition with intensification, which is a classical Hebraic literary feature.[10] "The repetition underlies their importance as well as authenticates their veracity."[11]

Amos' visions comprise a unity that can be subdivided "into three separate literary units—the first pair, the second pair, and the fifth."[12] Each of the first four visions is structured similarly,[13] but the fifth has a different structure. The first two visions are of disaster averted.[14] The next three are of judgment that is implemented.[15] The following exhibits how each vision recapitulates the former and adds greater urgency and severity. In each of the two pairs, the second vision confirms the first and makes it clear so that there will be no mistake as to what Yahweh plans to do. Then in the fifth vision Yahweh carries out his plan: the judgment from which he relented in the first two visions and that he then announced in the third and fourth visions.

The First Pair

- Vision 1: Yahweh threatens punishment against the agricultural land by means of locusts. Amos intercedes and Yahweh relents.
- Vision 2: Yahweh threatens to judge the land and the underground water sources by fire. Amos intercedes and Yahweh relents.

The Second Pair

- Vision 3: The plumb line or plaster[16] indicates that Yahweh will no longer relent as he did in the first two visions.
- Vision 4: The entire nation is visited with devastation. The ripe fruit spells "the end" (8:2).

---

[9] Paul, *Amos*, 225.

[10] See further the excursus "Hebrew Poetry" in the commentary on Amos 1. Besides the visions of Amos, repetition is evident in the two dreams of Joseph (the sheaves, and the sun, moon, and eleven stars [Gen 37:5–10]) and the two dreams of Pharaoh (the seven cows and the seven ears of grain [Gen 41:1–7]). Joseph explained that both of Pharaoh's dreams conveyed the same divine message (Gen 41:25–32).

[11] Paul, *Amos*, 224, speaking of Amos' first four visions.

[12] Paul, *Amos*, 223.

[13] See Niehaus, "Amos," 450, who also notes that Jeremiah's visions in Jer 1:11–12; 1:13–19; 24:1–10 follow the general structure of Amos' first four visions.

[14] See further "Introduction to Amos 7:1–6: Two Visions That Do Not Come to Pass."

[15] See further "Introduction to Amos 7:7–8:3: Two Visions That Do Come to Pass."

[16] See the textual note on אֲנָךְ in 7:7 for a discussion of the word's meaning.

The Last Vision

- Vision 5: The apostate Bethel temple is destroyed, and none of the unfaithful Israelites escapes Yahweh's judgment.

The intercessory role of Amos decreases as the judgments become more and more severe. In the first two visions, he successfully pleads for Israel, and Yahweh reverses his prior verdict. In the next two visions, Amos only answers Yahweh's questions with a word or two. In the climactic fifth vision, Yahweh alone speaks and Amos is completely silent. In visions 1 and 2, Israel is at the eleventh hour; in the last three visions the clock has struck midnight. In this way the visions exhibit a logical and sequential progression.

God the Father strengthened his own beloved Son for his ministry with a revelatory vision of the descending Spirit (Mt 3:16–17). After Isaiah saw Yahweh enthroned in his temple (Is 6:1–7), he was able to declare, "Here am I. Send me" (Is 6:8). Moses (Exodus 3) and Paul (Acts 9) received visions that called them into ministry and fortified them to be faithful despite the opposition they would face. Amos too was empowered for his ministry by seeing his five divine visions. After beholding Yahweh himself, it would be unlikely for the prophet to be intimidated by King Jeroboam ben Joash (1:1; 7:10–11), the priest Amaziah (7:10–17), or any other human authority.[17] Just like Paul, Amos was "not disobedient to the heavenly vision" (Acts 26:19), but went about preaching with boldness because he had been in Yahweh's presence (cf. Amos 3:7–8). While the immediate message of these visions is judgment, the final words Yahweh will speak through his prophet will be a vision of resurrection, restoration, and eschatological blessing for God's redeemed—gathered from both Israel and the Gentiles into the tabernacle of David (9:11–15).

---

[17] Andersen and Freedman write: "After facing Yahweh in vision and voice, in dialogue and decision, the prophet is fully equipped to perform his earthly mission" (*Amos*, 625).

Introduction to Amos 7:1–6: Two Visions That Do Not Come to Pass

Amos' first two visions (7:1–3 and 7:4–6) go together. In both, Amos repeats his plea "How can Jacob stand? For he is so small!" (מִי יָקוּם יַעֲקֹב כִּי קָטֹן הוּא, 7:2, 5). In both visions, Yahweh reverses his prior verdict of judgment and says that the threatened destruction will not occur (7:3, 6). The visions are further connected by the verb אָכַל, "to eat, consume, devour," in 7:2 and 7:4. In the first vision, Amos prays, "O Lord Yahweh, please forgive!" (סְלַח־נָא, 7:2), and Yahweh relents. In the second vision, he petitions, "O Lord Yahweh, please cease!" (חֲדַל־נָא, 7:5), and Yahweh stops the destruction. In both visions, Yahweh's mercy triumphs over his judgment (James 2:13). Yahweh's change of a previous decision, however, does not completely cancel his judgment. He grants Amos time to proclaim his Word, hoping Israel will repent. However, Israel refuses to repent, and this is critical for understanding the manner in which God's warnings progress into the actual execution of judgment. Evidence of this progression is seen when one compares the first two visions to each other, including the two petitions of Amos (7:2, 5).[1]

Amos' two intercessions in these visions indicate that a prophet's role was not only to see visions and preach but also to pray for the people so that they might be forgiven. Moses is Israel's paradigmatic prophet (cf. Deut 18:15), and one of his roles was to intercede for Israel (e.g., Ex 32:11–14; Deut 5:5). Amos follows in this tradition.[2]

There is a close connection between the first two visions and the prior plagues God sent against Israel as described in Amos 4:6–11.[3] In both cases, Yahweh sent agents of judgment for the purpose of moving Israel to repentance so that the nation as a whole might escape complete destruction. Ironically, in the visions Yahweh is the one who relents and changes his course of action. As

---

1 Wolff perceives this difference: "The first petition aims at Israel's guilt, pleading that it be washed away and that all reasons for the punishing intervention thus be removed. The second petition has in view only Yahweh's punishment. … There is no forgiveness of guilt; there is only delay of punishment. Amos wins forbearance, not pardon" (*Joel and Amos*, 303).

2 In contrast, a century and a half later, the guilt of Judah had grown so great that Yahweh prohibits Jeremiah from pleading for him not to execute his judgment on the southern kingdom. Several times Yahweh forbids the prophet from interceding (Jer 7:16; 11:14; 14:11–12). In Jer 15:1–4 Yahweh's rejection of prophetic intercession is even more emphatic. Even if two great intercessors, Moses and Samuel, would pray for Judah, they would fail to persuade Yahweh to be graciously disposed toward "this people" (Jer 15:1). The message is clear: if these heroes of yesteryear could not avert disaster, surely Jeremiah's own prayers will fail. In a similar vein, Yahweh declares through Ezekiel that even if Noah, Daniel, and Job were living in Judah, it would not escape his judgment, although these three righteous men would be saved (Ezek 14:14, 20).

3 This is the position of Andersen and Freedman, *Amos*, 66.

recorded in chapter 4, the unfaithful Israelites did not repent or return to their God (4:6, 8–11). Because the plagues listed in chapter 4 did not "produce fruit in keeping with repentance" (Lk 3:8), Amos proclaims, "Prepare to meet your God" (Amos 4:12). Visions 3, 4, and 5 depict what will happen when Israel meets Yahweh in his wrath. It will be a catastrophic end. Yet the end of the book envisions a remnant from Israel and the Gentiles that will repent and be saved (9:11–15).

Amos 7:1–3

The First Vision: The Locusts

Translation

7 [1]This is what the Lord Yahweh showed me: behold, he was creating a locust swarm at the time when the late-sown crop was beginning to sprout, and behold, it was the late-sown crop after the reaping of the king!

[2]When it finished consuming the vegetation of the land, I said, "O Lord Yahweh, please forgive! How can Jacob stand? For he is so small!"

[3]Yahweh changed his verdict about this. "It will not happen," said Yahweh.

Textual Notes

7:1 כֹּה הִרְאַנִי אֲדֹנָי יְהוִה—This formula begins the first, second, and fourth visions (7:1, 4; 8:1) and כֹּה הִרְאַנִי also begins the third vision (7:7). The beginning of the fifth vision includes the Qal of רָאָה (9:1). הִרְאַנִי is the Hiphil perfect of רָאָה, "to see," with a direct object suffix referring to Amos as the recipient of the vision. The Hiphil of רָאָה usually has the causative meaning "to show, reveal" something to someone. Its semantic range can include auditory as well as visionary experiences. In each of the five visions, Amos explains what he *saw* as well as Yahweh's *words and conversations*, so the visions include both seeing and hearing.[1] Similar uses of רָאָה in the Hiphil that refer to God imparting revelatory prophetic visions are in, for example, 2 Ki 8:13; Jer 38:21; Zech 2:3 (ET 1:20); 3:1.

For the divine title אֲדֹנָי יְהוִה, "(the) Lord Yahweh," which recurs in 7:2, see the fifth textual note on 1:8.

וְהִנֵּה יוֹצֵר גֹּבַי בִּתְחִלַּת עֲלוֹת הַלָּקֶשׁ—The demonstrative particle with conjunction וְהִנֵּה introduces what Amos sees in each of the first four visions (7:1, 4, 7; 8:1). It also recurs again later in this verse. The implied subject of the participle יוֹצֵר is Yahweh, the author of the vision, who is "creating" the plague. The verb יָצַר can refer to God's activity as Creator (BDB, 2 a, citing, e.g., Gen 2:7–8, 19; Is 45:18; Amos 4:13; Pss 95:5) or to God planning a course of action (BDB, 2 b, citing, e.g., Is 22:11; 46:11). The LXX diverges from the MT in several parts of the verse and renders יוֹצֵר גֹּבַי as ἐπιγονὴ ἀκρίδων, "offspring of locusts." The singular collective noun גֹּבַי refers to a "swarm of locusts" and occurs elsewhere in the OT only in Nah 3:17. It may refer to the larva stage of locusts, just after they have hatched.[2] For the unusual nominal form of גֹּבַי, see

---

1 Cf. Wolff, *Joel and Amos*, 296. Stuart notes that רָאָה in the Hiphil can mean "reveal" and "inform" as well as "make visible" (*Hosea–Jonah*, 371).

2 So Paul, *Amos*, 227.

GKC, § 86 i. Amos used another term for locusts, הַגָּזָם, in 4:9. Locusts destroy all types of vegetation (see Joel 1:4).[3]

The temporal clause בִּתְחִלַּת עֲלוֹת הַלָּקֶשׁ is, literally, "in the beginning of the coming up of the late crop." The term לֶקֶשׁ, "late crop, sown in the late spring," occurs in the OT only in this verse, but is attested in the Gezer Calendar,[4] "where it comes after the first season of sowing. Because that calendar is an almanac of farming tasks, *lqš* there probably means 'late sowing' rather than 'spring growth.' "[5] It refers to the crops sown after the "late spring rains," which are denoted by the cognate noun מַלְקוֹשׁ (e.g., Deut 11:14), and which fall during the months of March and April. These crops are not grains, but crops "such as vegetables and onions."[6] A locust attack in late spring would destroy both the earlier planting of grain as well as the later planting of vegetables. This would be a particularly acute tragedy for an agriculturally based population.

וְהִנֵּה־לֶקֶשׁ אַחַר גִּזֵּי הַמֶּלֶךְ׃—This additional temporal clause further clarifies the disastrous timing of the locust plague. הִנֵּה with a substantive (לֶקֶשׁ) can require supplying a pronoun and the copula, as here: "behold, *it was* the late-sown crop after the reaping of the king" (see GKC, § 147 b). The noun גֵּז is related to the verb גָּזַז, "to shear." גֵּז can refer to the shorn "wool, fleece" of sheep (Deut 18:4; Job 31:20). But in the agricultural context here, it probably refers to the "**reaping** of crops" (*DCH*). It likely has the related meaning "mown field of crops" (*DCH*) in a messianic prayer for the king as God's son to bless the nation: יֵרֵד כְּמָטָר עַל־גֵּז, "may he descend like rain upon a harvested field" (Ps 72:6). Here in Amos 7:1, גֵּז likely refers to "some royal prerogative of reaping (for example, fodder for horses) that took place toward the end of the late-rain season."[7]

7:2 וְהָיָה אִם־כִּלָּה לֶאֱכוֹל אֶת־עֵשֶׂב הָאָרֶץ—As in 7:4, immediately after Amos sees the judgment (7:1), it has already wreaked destruction within the vision (7:2a). Here it has "finished consuming the vegetation of the land."

The combination וְהָיָה אִם־ forms a temporal clause and is simply translated "when" (BDB, s.v. אִם, 1 b (4) (*a*)). Instead of the perfect with conjunctive *waw* (וְהָיָה), classical Biblical Hebrew usage would be an imperfect with *waw* consecutive (וַיְהִי); see Joüon, § 119 z (cf. GKC, § 112 *uu*).

---

[3] Dillard, "Joel," 256, writes:

> It was only in 1921 that the mystery of the locust was solved. Prior to this date researchers wondered what became of the locust during the years in which there were no outbreaks. In 1921 B. P. Uvarov demonstrated that the swarming locust was none other than an ordinary species of grasshopper. However, when moisture and temperature conditions favored a large hatch, the crowding, unceasing contact, and jostling of the nymphs begin to stimulate changes in coloration, physiology, metabolism, and behavior, so that the grasshopper nymphs make the transition from solitary behavior to the swarming gregarious and migratory phases of the dreaded plague.

[4] See Gibson, *Hebrew and Moabite Inscriptions*, 2.

[5] Andersen and Freedman, *Amos*, 741.

[6] Paul, *Amos*, 227.

[7] Paul, *Amos*, 227.

The implied subject of the singular verb כִּלָּה is the collective singular גֹּבַי, the "locust swarm" in 7:1. The Piel of כָּלָה often means "to complete, finish" an action,[8] and with this meaning it often takes an infinitive construct introduced by לְ (see BDB, s.v. כָּלָה I, Piel, 1 c), as here: לֶאֱכוֹל, "to eat, consume." Relevant here is another common meaning of the Piel of כָּלָה, to "destroy, exterminate" (see BDB, 2 c). Israel's crops would have been completely consumed if Yahweh had not responded graciously to Amos and relented from his plan.

The construct phrase עֵשֶׂב הָאָרֶץ, "the herbage of the land," is a comprehensive phrase for all "plant growth necessary for man and animal."[9] This same phrase describes what the locusts devoured in the eighth plague against Egypt (Ex 10:12, 15). Yahweh is treating apostate Israel just like he treated pagan Egypt (cf. 4:10).

וָאֹמַר אֲדֹנָי יְהוִה סְלַח־נָא—The Qal of סָלַח, "to forgive," refers to "an absolute and total pardon of sin."[10] נָא, the particle of entreaty rendered as "please," often is attached to a preceding imperative (BDB, 1), and it reinforces that the suppliant is appealing to God's mercy, rather than any legal right or obligation for God to fulfill his prayer. In the OT סָלַח is used only with God as its expressed or implied subject (e.g., Ex 34:9; Num 14:19–20; Jer 33:8; and negated in 2 Ki 24:4). This helps explain why those who did not believe in the divine nature in Jesus accused him of blasphemy because he forgave sins (Mk 2:1–12). The Niphal of סָלַח in the context of sacrificial worship expresses Yahweh's promise that sins will be forgiven (Lev 4:20–5:18; also Lev 5:26 [ET 6:7]; 19:22; Num 15:25–28).

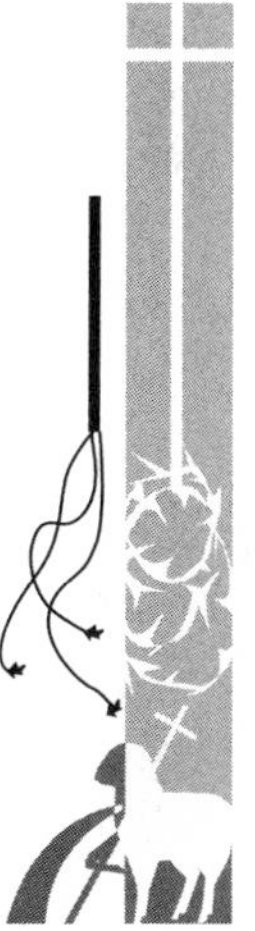

Here the Qal is used in a supplication for Yahweh to forgive, as also in, for example, Ex 34:9; Num 14:19 (the only other OT occurrence of סְלַח־נָא); 1 Ki 8:30, 34; Dan 9:19. The contexts of these supplications show that forgiveness is rooted in God's gracious covenant and that he promises this forgiveness through the new covenant (Jer 31:31–34) in the blood of Christ, shed for the forgiveness of sins (Mt 26:28). Amos' plea in 7:2 does not deny the justice of the plague on sinful Israel, but begs for forgiveness for the people Yahweh had redeemed and called to be his own.

מִי יָקוּם יַעֲקֹב—This question, has an apparently unique usage of the interrogative pronoun מִי, which normally means "who." Most translations and interpreters consider it to mean "*how* can Jacob stand?" (so *HALOT*, 7, citing also Ruth 3:16). Closer to the usual usage of מִי would be the understanding "who is Jacob that he can stand?" (Waltke-O'Connor, § 18.2d, note 10).[11] The Qal of קוּם can mean "to stand, endure" (see BDB, 7 a, c). This question is repeated in 7:5, and "Jacob" refers to all Israel also in Amos 3:13; 6:8; 8:7; 9:8.

כִּי קָטֹן הוּא׃—In this context, the adjective קָטֹן has a comparative sense, "*too* small," or absolute superlative sense, "*so* small." Here קָטֹן does not refer to "small" size but to a lack of standing. It describes a person who has no legal credentials to make a claim

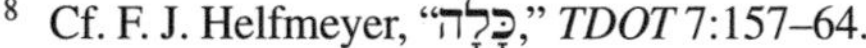

[8] Cf. F. J. Helfmeyer, "כָּלָה," *TDOT* 7:157–64.

[9] Paul, *Amos*, 228.

[10] Paul, *Amos*, 228. Cf. J. Hausmann, "סָלַח," *TDOT* 10:258–65.

[11] Niehaus, "Amos," 452, argues that in this context מִי means "in what condition or capacity?" and he cites Is 51:19 and Ruth 3:16.

for himself. He is completely dependent on the compassion of another person, namely, God.[12] In a legal setting, קָטֹן refers to those who are vulnerable to abuse because they lack power or influence (e.g., Deut 1:17). When referring to a person, קָטֹן can refer to a "young" brother, who lacks the privilege of the firstborn (e.g., Judg 1:13). Jacob himself was described with the closely related adjective הַקָּטָן, "the smaller/younger" son of Rebekah, in contrast to Esau, who was הַגָּדוֹל, "the larger/older" son, the firstborn (Gen 27:15, 42). Jacob himself also prayed with the cognate verb קָטֹן in Gen 32:11 (ET 32:10), where he confessed that he did not deserve any of the blessings of grace God had given him: "I am too small/unworthy [קָטֹנְתִּי] for all the mercies and all the faithfulness that you have shown to your servant." Yahweh affirms a similar truth about the whole nation when he declares that he did *not* choose Israel because it was greater than other peoples (לֹא מֵרֻבְּכֶם מִכָּל־הָעַמִּים); instead, Israel was the "fewest" of all the peoples (כִּי־אַתֶּם הַמְעַט מִכָּל־הָעַמִּים). But he chose the nation anyway purely out of his love and fidelity to his covenant promise (Deut 7:7–8).

By calling Israel "small," Amos admits that the people have no intrinsic worthiness or merit before God and are completely unable to earn his love or favor. The only hope for them—and for any person—is God's own grace and unmerited favor, which he has now demonstrated in Christ (Rom 3:19–31).

7:3 נִחַם יְהוָה עַל־זֹאת—This clause is repeated in 7:6, and these are the only two Amos verses with the Niphal of נָחַם. With God as subject, it means "to change a verdict, reverse a decision," usually with the connotation that God is "moved to pity" and has "compassion" (see BDB, s.v. נָחַם, Niphal, 1). Some older translations say that God "repented" (KJV, RSV), but that is inappropriate in modern English because God and his judgments are righteous, and Israel well deserves the punishments threatened in 7:1–3 and 7:4–6. Saying that God would "regret" or "become remorseful" (*HALOT*, 1 and 1 a) about his plans could also be misunderstood as implying some fault or evil on God's part. Other translations give "relented" (ESV, NKJV) or "changed His mind" (NASB). See further the commentary.

The feminine of the demonstrative adjective, זֹאת, "this," is typically used for an abstract concept or idea (GKC, § 122 q). Here it refers to the action of punishing Israel with the locust plague.

לֹא תִהְיֶה אָמַר יְהוָה׃—Just as the feminine זֹאת was in the preceding clause, the feminine verb תִהְיֶה is used with the abstract idea of the punishment as its implied subject. Quite similar is וְלֹא תִהְיֶה with an implied abstract subject in Is 7:7. The verbal clause here in Amos 7:3 will be repeated in 7:6 with the feminine pronoun הִיא as its subject. Joüon, § 152 b (see also § 152 c), cites Amos 7:6 and says "the feminine is used when the meaning is vague." But "abstract" is more accurate.

Commentary

Amos sees his first vision sometime during late spring. The "late-sown crop" (7:1) consists of vegetables and other non-grain crops. A plague at this

[12] Brueggemann, "Amos' Intercessory Formula," 387.

time, after the last sowing and before the first harvesting, would destroy all the crops for the entire year. The entire growing season would be ruined since the last time to plant any crop had transpired. In the face of this utter disaster, Amos does not base his plea upon Israel's repentance or worthiness, but solely upon Yahweh's grace. And his intercession is met by God's favor. Yahweh relents from letting the locusts completely devour the vegetation.

7:1 A locust plague indicated that Israel was under a curse for violating the covenant of Moses. Yahweh confirmed his promises to the patriarchs and established Israel as his nation by redeeming them from Egypt in the fifteenth century BC. At that time he warned that when the people would violate his Word and break his covenant, "You shall take much seed out to the field but gather little because the locust [הָאַרְבֶּה] will consume it. … Locusts [הַצְּלָצַל] will take over all your trees and the fruit of your land" (Deut 28:38, 42).

The timing of this plague is critical; this is why Amos 7:1 has two temporal clauses as chronological markers. If a locust plague attacked in the late spring, the results were catastrophic. They destroyed both the late-spring vegetable crops (לֶקֶשׁ) as well as the more developed but as-yet unharvested grain crops sown earlier. If the locusts arrived earlier, the late-spring crops would not have sprouted, and so they would be spared. If the locusts came later, the grain would already have been harvested safely. The timing in 7:1 means that the locusts would arrive when they could maximize their destruction. Adding insult to injury, it was also after the king had taken part of the harvest (cf. 1 Sam 8:14–15; 1 Ki 4:7–5:8 [ET 4:7–28]).

Amos sees the locust plague while Yahweh is in the process of "creating" it (7:1). The prophet perceives that the worst possible agricultural enemy is coming at the worst possible time. If not halted immediately, the people would have to face the worse possible hardship: an entire year of total famine.

7:2 This vision recalls the earlier locust plague described in 4:9. Obdurate Israel had behaved like pagan Egypt did during the time of Moses. When Yahweh sent the plagues recounted in 4:6–11 against his own people, the Israelites refused to repent and return to their God. Similarly now, 7:2 gives no indication that this locust swarm would succeed in driving Israel to repentance. The only hope was for Amos to intercede. He does not try to excuse unfaithful Israel's apostasy, plead extenuating circumstances, invoke the frailty of human nature, or cite the force of temptations. Amos begs for forgiveness, not because Israel's sins were small, but because Jacob itself was "so small," that is, utterly lacking any merit or worthiness before God (see the fourth textual note on 7:2). Amos casts himself and his people solely upon the mercy of God (cf. James 5:16), as he will do again in Amos 7:5.[13]

---

[13] In other OT passages, Yahweh responds to intercessory prayer purely out of his mercy, despite the sinfulness of the people he spares. See, for example, Gen 18:22–33; 20:1–7; Ex 32:11–14; Num 11:1–2; 14:11–25.

Amos is praying for "Jacob" (7:2), whose ruin should have caused the people to lament and repent (6:6). Since so much of Amos' book consists of judgment and condemnation, it would be easy to misinterpret him as a "fire and brimstone" preacher who delights in telling people that they are going to be obliterated by God. A quick reading of the book might convince someone that Amos is a "turn or burn" zealot who travels north from Tekoa and dumps Yahweh's wrath at Bethel in a heartless manner. But nothing could be farther from the truth. The heart of the prophet is depicted in his twofold plea, "How can Jacob stand? For he is so small" (7:2, 5). To know this about Amos is to understand that throughout the rest of the book his disturbing oracles against Israel, Judah, and the pagan nations are not spoken with sadistic glee.

Amos' prophetic intercession appeals to Yahweh to act on the basis of his gracious covenant promise, first issued to Abraham (Genesis 12–17), then reaffirmed for Isaac and Jacob.[14] Already the patriarch Jacob himself had petitioned Yahweh to be merciful toward him, not because he in any way deserved mercy, but because of Yahweh's gracious promises to Abraham and Isaac (Gen 32:10–13 [ET 32:9–12]).

"Jacob" in Amos 7:2, 5 refers to the double kingdom of both north and south.[15] Because the vision entails the threat against the entire people of Yahweh, it takes on greater seriousness. The prophet's prayer avails. The Israelites are given a reprieve—for a time.[16] The compassion Yahweh shows here echoes a number of earlier texts. For example, seven centuries earlier, in the time of Moses, Yahweh heard the cry of his oppressed people and delivered them from spiritual, economic, and political bondage in Egypt (Ex 3:7–9). In the covenant of Moses, he promised to respond to the cries of Israel's widows and orphans (Ex 22:21–23 [ET 22:22–24]). Now in the eighth century BC, Yahweh has raised up Amos to intercede on behalf of the Israelites, who should have been praying for their own forgiveness.

Chrysostom understands Amos' intercession in his first and second visions as typical of prophetic intercession:

> It is, after all, the practice of the prophets and the just to grieve not only for themselves but also for the rest of humankind. If you're inclined to check that, you will find them all giving evidence of this compassion—for example, you can listen to Jeremiah, "Who will pour water on my head, and provide a fountain of tears for my eyes?" [LXX Jer 8:23] or Ezekiel, "Alas, Lord, you will destroy what remains of Israel?" [Ezek 9:8] or Daniel lamenting in these

---

14 Cf. Brueggemann, "Amos' Intercessory Formula."

15 Andersen and Freedman, *Amos*, 114–15. They note that in the OT, "Jacob" never refers exclusively to the Northern Kingdom (p. 99).

16 Amos ministered in the 760s BC. Some forty years later, in 722 BC, God would execute his wrath against the Northern Kingdom of Israel by allowing Assyria to conquer it and exile its leading citizens. See the excursus "The Assyrian Empire."

words, "You have made us few in number by comparison with the Gentiles," or Amos, "Think better of this, Lord."[17]

"O that all of Yahweh's people were prophets" (Num 11:29) with an interceding heart like that of Amos! Amos emulated the Messiah to come, Jesus, who looked at the multitudes, who were harassed and helpless, like sheep without a shepherd, and he had compassion on them (Mt 9:36; Mk 6:34). Israel's greatest Prophet, the sinless Son of God, supplicated and interceded for all humanity by offering himself as the atoning sacrifice that avails for all sin and rebellion.

> Christ Jesus is the one who died, and even more is the one who was raised, who also is at the right hand of God, who indeed is interceding for us. (Rom 8:34)

The Holy Spirit, who dwells within baptized believers in Christ, also has an intercessory role as he "intercedes for the saints according to the will of God" (Rom 8:27) with "groanings too deep for words" (Rom 8:26).

7:3 Yahweh "changed his verdict" (נִחַם, as also in 7:6).[18] This indicates that instead of carrying out the fully justified Sinai covenant curse upon apostate Israel, he freely chooses to act in pure grace by forgiving the people's sin. In no respect do they deserve his forbearance or merit the blessings promised in the Torah of Moses. "They rejected the Torah of Yahweh," broke its statutes, and worshiped idols, as Amos 2:4 states about Judah, and so they deserve nothing but Yahweh's judgment "fire" (2:5; 5:6; 7:4). Nevertheless, the triune God delights in showing mercy to the undeserving. He is the God "who justifies the ungodly" (Rom 4:5; cf. Rom 5:6) solely by his grace in Jesus Christ. His response fulfills Amos' intercessory petition "please forgive!" (סְלַח־נָא, 7:2).

Yahweh's change of verdict from Law to Gospel—from judgment to forgiveness—in 7:3, 6 is one of the key Gospel motifs in the book, along with its concluding messianic promise of resurrection and eschatological blessing in 9:11–15. Ultimately these OT Gospel motifs are based on the sacrificial atonement of Jesus Christ, which is the reason why God can cancel his righteous verdict of judgment and instead show mercy and compassion. Yahweh pours out his wrath as his "alien work" (*opus alienum*, a phrase Luther cited from the Vulgate of Is 28:21).[19] He does this because he is righteous, and he seeks to drive impenitent people to contrition and faith. His conferral of grace and mercy is his proper work (*opus proprium*), in which he delights. The sum total of his judgment against humanity's iniquity was inflicted on Christ as he hung on the cross, and the Lamb of God thereby took away the sin of the world (Is 53:5–7; Jn 1:29, 36). His free grace in Christ is received solely through faith,

---

[17] Chrysostom, *Homilies on Genesis*, 29.7, quoted in Ferreiro, *The Twelve Prophets*, ACCS 14:108.

[18] See the excursus "When Yahweh Changes a Prior Verdict" in Lessing, *Jonah*, 324–41.

[19] See, for example, AE 2:134, including n. 3, and AE 14:335.

by both OT and NT believers alike (Romans 4–5; Galatians 3). For believers "there is now no condemnation" (Rom 8:1).

Here Yahweh reverses his earlier decision to send the locusts and devour the land. Tragically, however, the Israelites would quickly demonstrate that they lack repentance and faith. There is a close parallel to Israel's faithless behavior in the wilderness. After Israel believed the bad report of the ten faithless spies, Moses prayed, "Please forgive the iniquity of this people" (סְלַח־נָא לַעֲוֹן הָעָם הַזֶּה, Num 14:19), even as Amos prayed the first two identical Hebrew words, "Please forgive!" (סְלַח־נָא, Amos 7:2). Yahweh responded to Moses by affirming, "I have forgiven according to your word" (סָלַחְתִּי כִּדְבָרֶךָ, Num 14:20); the people were spared, although that faithless generation of Israelites perished during the forty years in the wilderness without reaching the promised land. Yahweh affirms to Amos that the judgment "will not happen" (Amos 7:3), at least not to that generation of Israel. Some forty years would go by from the time of Amos (ca. 760 BC) until the judgment would strike the next generation when Assyria conquered northern Israel in 722 BC. For apostate Israel the judgment is delayed, not denied.

For the knowledge of God, his people are dependent upon his self-revelation in the Scriptures. The unfolding of changing events in subsequent earthly history can show how God has indeed been faithful to his Word of both Law and Gospel. God himself, however, is immutable and omniscient. He knows beforehand all things—what he will do and how people will (or will not) respond. When God changes his verdict toward people or redirects events in earthly history, this does not in any way conflict with his immutability and omniscience, which must be confessed as essential doctrines of God. Jerome (ca. AD 347–420) says this of God's foreknowledge: "In stripping Him of foreknowledge you also take away His divinity."[20] Augustine (AD 354–430) maintains: "To confess that God exists, and at the same time to deny that He has foreknowledge of future things, is the most manifest folly."[21] Luther argues that God has an exhaustive understanding of the future:

> How religious, devout, and necessary a thing it is to know [of God's foreknowledge]. For if these things are not known, there can be neither faith nor any worship of God. For that would indeed be ignorance of God, and where there is such ignorance there cannot be salvation, as we know.[22]

The biblical teaching affirms God's ability to change his verdict as well has his absolute knowledge of the entire future. In a profound way, Yahweh's change from Law to Gospel (Amos 7:3, 6) and from Gospel to Law (Amos 1–2)

---

[20] Jerome, *Dialogue against the Pelagians*, 3.6 (*NPNF*² 6:475).

[21] Augustine, *The City of God*, 5.9 (*NPNF*¹ 2:90).

[22] Luther, *The Bondage of the Will* (AE 33:42).

shows that Yahweh is "perfect in knowledge" (Job 37:16) and that "his understanding has no limit" (Ps 147:5).[23]

Summary

1 Sam 3:1 states that during the time of Eli the high priest, the revelation of the Word of Yahweh was rare, and a vision seldom burst forth (אֵין חָזוֹן נִפְרָץ). This was due in part to the corrupt priesthood of Eli's sons, Hophni and Phinehas, and Eli's refusal to do anything about them (e.g., 1 Sam 2:12–17, 22–25). Israel faced a similar situation in the early part of the eighth century BC. The priesthood was apostate (as exemplified by Amaziah in Amos 7:10–17), and Israel tried to silence the prophets (2:12), so the Word of Yahweh was rare. In the days of Eli, Hophni, and Phinehas, Yahweh raised up Samuel (1 Samuel 3) to bring about a reformation in Israel. So also in the days of Jeroboam ben Joash (Amos 1:1; 7:9–13) and Amaziah, Yahweh burst forth upon Amos, called him to be a prophet (7:14–15) and charged him to confront Israel's idolatrous status quo.

In Amos' first two visions, the prophet's response to Yahweh is more active than deferential, more alarmed and reactive than submissive. He approaches Yahweh much like Jacob did in his all-night wrestling match with the divine Man, Yahweh (Gen 32:23–33 [ET 32:22–32]). Prophets have a long history of pleading for God to show mercy. In Gen 20:7, the second of the narratives in which Abraham purports that Sarah is his sister, God tells Abimelech, "Now return the man's wife; for he is a prophet, and he will pray for you, and you shall live." Here Abraham—as a prophet—functions as an intercessor, and God promises to answer his prayer by bestowing life. Earlier in Genesis, Abraham interceded on behalf of Sodom, and the result was that Lot and his daughters were saved (Gen 18:22–33). Moses in Num 21:7 prayed on behalf of Israel, and in response, Yahweh told Moses to make a bronze serpent and put it on a pole so that those who had been bitten by the serpents could look at it and live.

And just as Moses lifted up that bronze serpent in the wilderness, Jesus, God the Son, was lifted up on the tree of the cross so that everyone who believes in him may have eternal life (Jn 3:14–15). He is the greatest prophetic intercessor in the Bible, who continually intercedes with the Father on behalf of sinners (Is 53:12; Rom 8:34). The great High Priest offered the one perfect sacrifice that is fully efficacious to blot out all transgressions, and he continues to make intercession for his people (Heb 7:23–27). Lk 23:34 records Jesus' intercession for those who were crucifying him: "Father, forgive them, for they do not know what they are doing" (πάτερ, ἄφες αὐτοῖς, οὐ γὰρ οἴδασιν τί ποιοῦσιν). Climactically, Jesus not only prays for his enemies, but the sinless one assumes their sin (2 Cor 5:21) and rises again for their justification (Rom 4:25; see Amos 9:11).

---

[23] For further discussion of how God's immutability and foreknowledge relate to passages in which God changes his verdict or relents, see the excursus "When Yahweh Changes a Prior Verdict" in Lessing, *Jonah*, 324–41.

The Spirit dwelling in all baptized believers in Christ also intercedes for them when they do not know how or what to pray (Rom 8:26–27). Paul, after the manner of Jesus, repeatedly interceded for the unsaved Jews of his day (Rom 9:1–5; 10:1) and constantly offered prayers for the preservation of the saints in faith and in good works (e.g., 1 Thess 1:2; 2:13; 2 Tim 1:3).

Amos 7:4–6

The Second Vision: The Fire

Translation

7 [4]This is what the Lord Yahweh showed me: behold, the Lord Yahweh was calling for a covenant lawsuit by fire, and it devoured the great deep and started to consume the land.

[5]I said, "O Lord Yahweh, please cease! How can Jacob stand? For he is so small!"

[6]Yahweh changed his verdict about this. "It too will not happen," said the Lord Yahweh.

Textual Notes

7:4 כֹּה הִרְאַנִי אֲדֹנָי יְהוִה—See the first textual note on 7:1.

וְהִנֵּה קֹרֵא לָרִב בָּאֵשׁ אֲדֹנָי יְהוִה—The idiom קָרָא לְ can mean to "summon" (BDB, s.v. קָרָא, 5 d, citing this verse) or "call for." Since Yahweh is the subject here, it might be rendered "to demand, initiate, set in motion." The noun רִיב can denote a "dispute" and more specifically a "legal case" (cf. BDB, 3), that is, a "covenant lawsuit," an accusation against Israel for violating the divine covenant of Moses that was the constitution of the nation.

The following prepositional phrase בָּאֵשׁ, "by fire," assumes that Israel has already been found guilty and its legal judgment is executed by this means of punishment. "Fire" (אֵשׁ) was the means of judgment previously in 1:4, 7, 10, 12, 14; 2:2, 5; 5:6. This is the last occurrence of אֵשׁ in the book. In all these verses, the feminine noun אֵשׁ is the implied subject of feminine forms of the verb אָכַל, "consume," which occurs in the next two clauses of 7:4. The verb אָכַל, "consume, eat," was also in 7:2, where the locusts were the implied subject, and so אָכַל is a catch-word joining the first (7:1–3) and second (7:4–6) visions of Amos.

Some scholars have proposed emending לָרִב בָּאֵשׁ, but the text makes good sense as it stands.[1] The verse shares similarities with Joel 1:19–20.

וַתֹּאכַל אֶת־תְּהוֹם רַבָּה—As in 7:1–2, immediately after Amos sees the judgment, it has already caused catastrophic destruction. The imperfect with *waw* consecutive, וַתֹּאכַל, denotes completed action: "it devoured the great deep." For אָכַל, see the preceding textual note.

The feminine noun תְּהוֹם appears thirty-six times in the OT with a variety of nuances. Often it has a more strongly theological connotation than the other words for water, an ocean, a river, or a flood. It always lacks the definite article but here is preceded

---

1 See Paul, *Amos*, 230–31, for a discussion. Wolff, *Joel and Amos*, 292–93, 298, following Hillers, "Amos 7:4 and Ancient Parallels," 221–23, proposes emending the phrase to לִרְבִב אֵשׁ, "for a rain of fire."

by ‑אֶת, suggesting that the word is intrinsically definite, almost personified as a proper name, "the Deep." Normally the LXX translates תְּהוֹם with ἡ ἄβυσσος, "the abyss," as in Amos 7:4. The singular תְּהוֹם may refer to the primeval ocean deep, which God created already on the first day (Gen 1:2; cf. Ps 104:6; Prov 8:27–28). After the creation was completed in six days, תְּהוֹם subsequently may refer to the depth of the seas or oceans, including subterranean waters and the sources from which God summoned the universal deluge in the time of Noah (Gen 7:11). The plural is used for oceans and bodies of water (e.g., Ps 135:6), including the waters of the Red Sea, which covered the drowned Egyptians during the exodus (Ex 15:5; cf. the metaphorical singular in Ezek 31:15).

In Amos 7:4 תְּהוֹם denotes all the water that sustains terrestrial life, including the source of all the springs and rivers as well as the oceans that feed clouds and rainfall. After the fire consumed this source of all water, all life on land would quickly wither and die.

Older critical scholars, especially those who followed Hermann Gunkel and the history of religions school, supposed that תְּהוֹם derived from the Akkadian *Ti'âmat*, the name of the primordial goddess in Mesopotamian mythology, whose carcass was divided to create the world.[2] However this derivation is unlikely. If תְּהוֹם were derived from *Ti'âmat* it probably would have a middle consonant *aleph* (א) as well as a feminine ending (‑מָה). The consensus now is that the Hebrew does not come directly from the Akkadian, but that both words derive independently from a common proto-Semitic root *tiham*.[3] Nevertheless, OT writers may include an implicit polemic against pagan Babylonian mythology, which describes Marduk's primordial and mythic victory over Tiamat. In the OT it is Yahweh alone who is Lord over "the deep" and uses it for his own purposes. Yahweh alone controls history and accomplishes judgment and salvation. See further the commentary.

וְאָכְלָה אֶת־הַחֵלֶק׃—In contrast to וַתֹּאכַל, the imperfect with *waw* consecutive beginning the preceding clause, the perfect וְאָכְלָה with conjunctive *waw* may have an ingressive meaning: the fire "*began/started* to consume the land."[4] חֵלֶק often refers to a "portion, tract" of land and here seems to refer to the whole "land" of Israel (BDB, 2 and 2 e) in contrast to the watery "deep" (תְּהוֹם).

7:5 וָאֹמַר אֲדֹנָי יְהוִה חֲדַל־נָא—This is parallel to Amos' earlier prayer. See the second textual note on 7:2. Here the imperative חֲדַל replaces the earlier imperative סְלַח. Most commonly חָדַל means "to cease, come to an end."[5] Coupled with the infinitive of another verb, it can be used to indicate the cessation of activity such as the building of Babel (Gen 11:8) or praying (1 Sam 12:23). In a number of passages, including here, חָדַל is used without a complement and means "cease, forbear, refrain" (see BDB, 2,

---

2 Gunkel, *Creation and Chaos in the Primeval Era and the Eschaton*, 75–79 (cf. pp. 14–20, 253–69).

3 Johnston, *Shades of Sheol*, 119–20.

4 GKC, § 112 tt, wrongly states that the perfect here is an error or incorrect mode of expression. Waltke-O'Connor, 31.1.1d, including note 4, mentions the possibility that both verbs, וַתֹּאכַל ... וְאָכְלָה, are preterites.

5 Cf. D. N. Freedman and J. Lundbom, "חָדַל," *TDOT* 4:216–21.

and *HALOT*, 3). The exact phrase חֲדַל־נָא does not appear elsewhere in the OT, but the imperative without נָא occurs a number of times, including Job 7:16 and 10:20, where Job pleads for God to leave him alone.

מִי יָקוּם יַעֲקֹב—See the third textual note on 7:2, which has the identical clause.

כִּי קָטֹן הוּא׃—See the fourth textual note on 7:2, which has the identical clause.

7:6 נִחַם יְהוָה עַל־זֹאת—See the first textual note on 7:3, which has the identical clause.

גַּם־הִיא לֹא תִהְיֶה אָמַר אֲדֹנָי יְהוִה׃—For emphasis, this adds the adverb גַּם and the feminine pronoun הִיא as the subject of the identical verbal clause that was in 7:3: "*it too* will not happen." See the second textual note on 7:3. The adverb גַּם can immediately precede a pronoun that it emphasizes. See Waltke-O'Connor, § 39.3.4c–d, including examples 10 and 11. Whereas 7:3 concluded with אָמַר יְהוָה, "said Yahweh," 7:6 has an expanded divine title: אָמַר אֲדֹנָי יְהוִה, "said the Lord Yahweh."

Commentary

Amos' second vision, the vision of fire, closely parallels his first vision (7:1–3). The first vision was of a locust plague that would devastate the crops. This second vision is more comprehensive because the fire consumes both the water sources and the entire land. "The great deep" (תְּהוֹם, 7:4) implies that the divine fire is cosmic in its implications. It points toward the universal judgment and the fiery conflagration of the whole earth, and indeed the entire universe (2 Pet 3:7–12), at the second coming of Christ, who will "judge both the living and the dead" (Nicene Creed). However, just as Amos interceded in 7:2, he does so again in 7:5. Amos pleads with Yahweh and is met with the same gracious relenting (7:6). Israel will continue—for a time. Even so, the present world will continue, but it too shall come to its appointed end. Yet the intercession of Christ will spare all believers from everlasting judgment by fire.

7:4 The term for a "covenant lawsuit" (רִיב) reinforces what is evident elsewhere throughout much of the book of Amos: Yahweh is judging his people Israel because they have broken his covenant. Judah's rejection of the Torah of Moses was explicit in 2:4. The condemnations of Israel's idolatry fault the people for violating the Decalogue and perverting the divine worship ordained in the Torah.[6] Amos 7:4 is similar to Micah 6:1–8, which uses the same term: "For Yahweh has a *covenant lawsuit* with his people" (כִּי רִיב לַיהוָה עִם־עַמּוֹ, Micah 6:2).[7] Yahweh is the Judge, his prophet is the prosecuting attorney, and Israel is the defendant who is guilty of breaking the covenant of Moses. The verdict is that Yahweh must implement the covenant curses (e.g., Lev 26:14–39; Deut 28:15–68). These curses are reflected most prolifically in Amos 4:6–11,

---

6 For condemnations of northern Israel's syncretistic worship, see the commentary on 2:7–8; 3:14; 4:4–5; 5:5–6, 14, 21–27; 7:9–17; 8:5, 10, 14; 9:1 (the Bethel temple).

7 For a discussion of how extrabiblical covenant lawsuits may relate to Amos, see Niehaus, who cites parallels between Hittite treaties, Deuteronomy, and prophetic books ("Amos," 318–23).

where Yahweh expounds the plagues suffered by Israel as fulfillments of the Sinai covenant curses punishing Israel for its sins.[8]

Here the punishment is by means of fire. Amos refers to Yahweh's destructive fire throughout his oracles against the pagan nations and Judah in 1:3–2:5, as well as in the judgment against the house of Joseph in 5:6. This implies that Israel is no less sinful than its heathen neighbors, who will be judged with fire. Andersen and Freedman write:

> The similarity of this Fire to the one that destroys all of the major cities in the region in chaps. 1–2 and the unidentified cities in the last plague of 4:11 is important. Indeed we believe it is the same Fire throughout. The visions, the creation hymn[s], and the judgment oracles all have the same cosmic outlook, in which Yahweh is perceived as the Maker and Destroyer of the whole universe.[9]

Amos, an agriculturalist (see 1:1 and 7:14–15), was acutely aware that a fire in a field during the dry season would destroy vast expanses of crops. Amos may have seen this vision during the dry season, just as he may have received the vision of summer fruit (8:1–3) at the time of the fruit harvest in late summer.[10] But this vision encompasses more than just crops. Amos couples the earthly reality of fire with the cosmic imagery of "the great deep" (תְּהוֹם, 7:4). If the underground waters and springs are consumed by flames, then all life will soon perish. This is no ordinary field fire. Only Yahweh could be behind such a cosmic catastrophe (cf. Is 45:7). Yahweh's fire is consuming the tillable soil as well as the underground sources of water. By means of this merism the prophet is witnessing a total destruction. The result of this second plague is a cataclysm.

Other biblical authors too employ cosmic ideas in order to speak about God's actions in history. This language reinforces the theological dimension of historical events. A classic example is Moses' hymn in Ex 15:1–18, which applies creation motifs to Yahweh's judgment of the Egyptians and his salvation of Israel through the Red Sea. Twice the hymn refers to the "depths" (Ex 15:5, 8), the plural of the term in Gen 1:2 and Amos 7:4. In the first reference, the "depths" covered the Egyptians who drowned (Ex 15:5). In the second reference, Yahweh caused the "depths" to congeal so that Israel could safely cross through the sea to salvation and new life (Ex 15:8). This was a kind of baptism for Israel (1 Cor 10:1–4). The death and resurrection motifs associated with the sea and its "depths" relate to death and resurrection with Christ in the Sacrament of Christian Baptism (Rom 6:1–6; Col 2:11–13).

---

8 Cf. McCarthy, *Old Testament Covenant*, and Paul, *Studies in the Book of the Covenant in the Light of Cuneiform and Biblical Law*.

9 Andersen and Freedman, *Amos*, 746.

10 Andersen and Freedman, *Amos*, 741, suggest: "It is therefore possible that Amos' visions all took place in a single year, with the second one—cosmic fire—having as its real-world counterpart an excessively hot summer."

The connections between creation and redemption imply that God's actions in salvation history are implementing his plan from before the foundation of the world (Is 48:12–17; Mt 25:34; Eph 1:4; 1 Pet 1:20; Rev 13:8). Moreover, these actions anticipate the final judgment and the new creation, the new heaven and new earth (Isaiah 11; 65:17–25; Revelation 21–22). As he acts in history, God is judging sin and establishing his new creation in Christ (cf. 2 Cor 5:17; Gal 6:15).

Other texts likewise interpret the exodus redemption in both historical and cosmic terms. The cosmic language helps prevent people from thinking that events were "natural" or actions by "Mother Nature." For example, Is 51:9–10 asks the arm of Yahweh:

> Are you not the one who hacked up Rahab,
> pierced the sea monster [תַּנִּין]?
> Are you not the one who dried up the sea,
> the waters of *the great deep* [תְּהוֹם רַבָּה, as in Amos 7:4]?

Yahweh's salvation of Israel through the Red Sea exodus was a defeat of Satan, the devil. The parting of the sea split and hacked up the sea monster (cf. the "serpent" at "the bottom of the sea" in Amos 9:3). This strengthens the baptismal connection to the victorious death and resurrection of Christ, by which he defeated Satan and death forever.[11] In the larger context of Isaiah, the fifteenth century BC deliverance of Israel from slavery in Egypt is a type of the coming deliverance of exiled Israel from bondage in Babylon through Cyrus (Is 44:28; 45:1), and especially a type of the redemption to be accomplished by the Servant, who will suffer and atone for the sins of the people, die, and rise again to make intercession for all transgressors (Is 52:13–53:12).

Tragically, however, in Amos 7:4 unfaithful Israel has forsaken the covenant of salvation initiated by the Red Sea deliverance and to be fulfilled in Christ. The apostate people have excluded themselves from God's grace and so find themselves under judgment.

7:5 Amos' intercession is similar to his plea in the first vision (see the commentary on 7:2), yet it is distinguished by the change from the stronger prayer for God to "forgive" (סָלַח, 7:2) to the petition for him merely to "cease" (חָדַל, 7:5) inflicting the plague. In this appeal, Amos only attempts to stop the fire from destroying everything and everyone. Perhaps here Amos already realizes that since the people will not repent they are unable to receive forgiveness through faith. In his final three visions (7:7–9; 8:1–3; 9:1–4), their impenitence

[11] A parallel text to Is 51:9–10 is Ps 74:12–14, where Asaph recalls how Yahweh had accomplished "salvation" by splitting the sea and crushing the heads of the sea monster Leviathan. This recalls the first Gospel promise in Scripture, that the Seed of Eve would crush the head of the serpent who deceived Adam and Eve into sin (Gen 3:15). It also anticipates the promise to all in Christ that "the God of peace will crush Satan under your feet soon. The grace of our Lord Jesus Christ be with you" (Rom 16:20). The final crushing defeat of Satan will take place at the return of Christ (Rev 20:10; cf. Rev 12:9). Then all the dead in Christ shall be raised to everlasting life; this is the final victory (Dan 12:2–3; 1 Corinthians 15).

makes the situation so dire that Amos will not attempt to intercede for Israel. In the next vision, Yahweh will declare that he will no longer forgive the people or overlook their sins (7:8), and in the final vision Yahweh commands the execution of his inescapable judgment on them (9:1–4).

7:6 But the time of mercy has not yet expired. As in the first vision (7:1–3), Yahweh reverses the specific judgment he had threatened. The verse repeats the identical wording from 7:3 with three additional Hebrew words (see the second textual note on 7:6). God overlooks the transgressions of Israel—for a time. See the commentary on 7:3.

Summary

Amos' first two visions not only reveal Yahweh's grace, but they also bring Amos the prophet into a sharper focus. He intercedes not once, but twice for those called to be the people of God. He is not a "fire and brimstone" preacher who delights in placing sinners into "the hands of an angry God."[12] Amos seeks neither revenge nor retribution, but mercy and grace for the undeserving. Yahweh's cancellation of the two judgments gives Amos time to continue his preaching, even though, as Yahweh laments about the people in the ongoing refrain in 4:6–11, "But you [plural] did not return to me" (וְלֹא־שַׁבְתֶּם עָדַי).

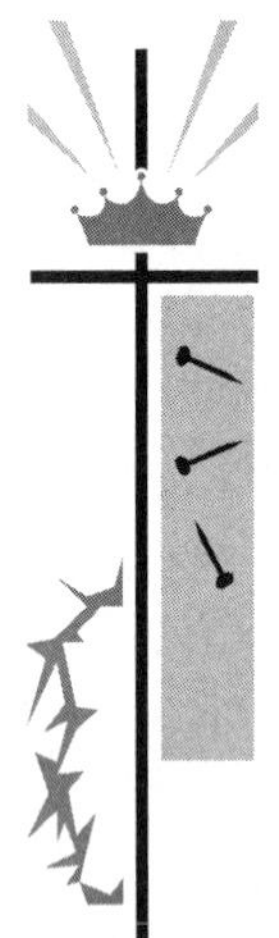

A God who is willing to change his course of action from judgment to clemency—from Law to Gospel—and a prophet who is willing to intercede for the people means that Israel has a hope and a future (cf. Jer 29:11). Yet the next three visions (Amos 7:7–9; 8:1–3; 9:1–4) will show that the apostate nation will experience the most severe judgment, a punishment that will destroy the idolatrous temple in Bethel (9:1). "The end" (8:2) will come when northern Israel falls to Assyria in 722 BC, some forty years after the ministry of Amos. But the eschatological vision at end of his book reveals a future era of grace. Yahweh, who reverses judgments in Amos' first two visions (7:3, 6), will do so again. In the greatest reversal in the book, Yahweh's final words promise forgiveness, restoration, and resurrection to new life (9:11–15). God's immutable will enables his primary attributes to remain at the forefront. His proper work is to show steadfast love and mercy, as he will demonstrate definitively in the person of Jesus Christ.

---

[12] "Sinners in the Hands of an Angry God" is the title of sermon preached by Jonathan Edwards in AD 1741.

Introduction to Amos 7:7–9; 8:1–3; and 9:1–4: Three Visions That Do Come to Pass

Amos' ministry of gloom and doom almost ended before it began. In the first two visions, his efforts at intercession were successful: Yahweh relented from judgment (7:3, 6). The prophet might have thought that this success with Yahweh would be a springboard to his success with Israel. Amos might have even started making plans to return home to Tekoa (1:1). Soon it would be back to life as normal, on the farm with the figs. Yet just as the plagues listed in 4:6–11 had failed to move Israel's aristocrats to repent, so too Amos' preaching fell on deaf ears (see chapters 5 and 6). The third (7:7–9) and fourth (8:1–3) visions confirm that since Israel refused to heed the divine warnings, the nation would not escape judgment (see also, e.g., 4:12; 5:18–20; 6:7–14). The fifth vision (9:1–4) announces the destruction of the temple at Bethel, the epicenter of everything so wrong in Israel.

In Is 49:8 Yahweh states, "In the time of favor I have answered you, and on the day of salvation I have helped you" (cf. 2 Cor 6:2). But for apostate Northern Israel the time of favor and the day of salvation had ended. This end of grace is marked by the differences between the first two visions (7:1–6) and the last three (7:7–9; 8:1–3; 9:1–4). Whereas Yahweh relented in the visions of the locusts and the fire, the visions of the plumb line, the basket of summer fruit, and Yahweh standing beside the altar show that judgment will come upon Israel.[1] Yahweh is weary of relenting (נִלְאֵיתִי הִנָּחֵם, Jer 15:6).

In his first two visions, Amos understood what he saw. But in the third and fourth visions he needs an explanation.[2] Just as the first two visions have a common stylistic structure, so the next two are related to one another by the question "what are you seeing, Amos?" (מָֽה־אַתָּ֤ה רֹאֶה֙ עָמ֔וֹס, 7:8; 8:2).[3] In both instances, Amos responds tersely by naming the item Yahweh shows to him. Also in contrast to the first two visions with their global scope, these next two are more mundane. Amos sees a plumb line used for constructing a wall and a basket of summer fruit. Yahweh then interprets each item. The third and fourth visions are related to the first and second by means of Yahweh's statement "I will never again forgive him" (לֹֽא־אוֹסִ֥יף ע֖וֹד עֲב֥וֹר לֽוֹ, 7:8; 8:2). That is to say, he had overlooked the sins of the Northern Kingdom for the better part of two centuries,[4]

---

[1] About four decades after the preaching of Amos, this judgment came in the form of the Assyrian conquest and deportation of northern Israel in 722 BC.

[2] In this way, Amos is like Daniel (e.g., Dan 7:15–28; 8:15–27; 12:5–13) and Peter (Acts 10:9–35).

[3] Horst calls both texts *Wortspielvisionen*, "wordplay visions" ("Die Visionsschilderungen der alttestamentlichen Propheten," 201).

[4] Jeroboam ben Nebat and the Northern Kingdom seceded from King Rehoboam and Judah in about 930 BC. Jeroboam promptly erected the idolatrous shrines at Bethel and Dan (1 Ki 12:26–33), and worship at those sites continued through the time of Amos (ca. 760 BC).

and in the first two visions (7:3, 6), he had forgiven or delayed judgment. But now the time of mercy has expired. The phrase "never *again*" creates a direct connection to the first two visions in which—based upon Yahweh's mercy in response to Amos' intercessory prayer—the people *had been* spared.

In contrast to the third and fourth visions, where Amos needed an explanation, he knows at the outset of the fifth that Yahweh is about to execute judgment, and he listens to Yahweh's order to destroy the temple at Bethel (9:1–4). In this vision, Amos makes no intercession, there is no relenting by Yahweh, and the prophet is not engaged by Yahweh in any conversation. In contrast to the use of רָאָה in the Hiphil in the first four visions, "The Lord Yahweh/he *showed* me" (7:1, 4, 7; 8:1), Amos employs רָאָה in the Qal in 9:1, "I *saw* the Lord," signaling that the last vision is decidedly different. The fifth vision lacks any wordplay, metaphor, or analogy; it is a literal, straightforward depiction of imminent historical action.

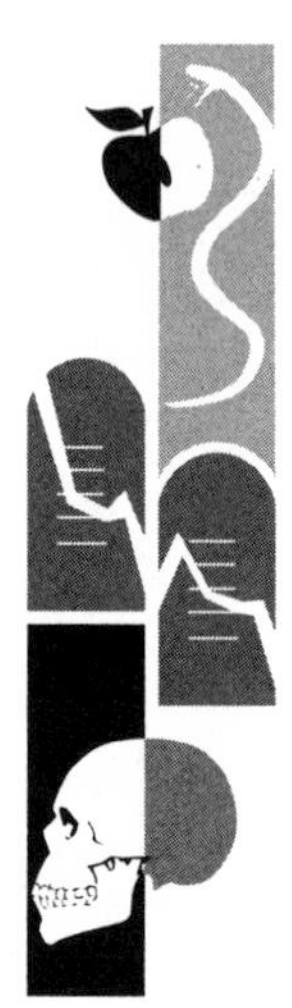

Both the third and fourth visions end with interpretive statements. Amos 7:9 describes the destruction of Isaac's high places and the house of Jeroboam ben Joash, while 8:3 portrays lamentation at the temple over the many dead bodies. And both 7:7–9 and 8:1–3 are followed by explanatory sections: the third vision is followed by 7:10–17, Amos' confrontation with Amaziah, while the fourth vision is followed by 8:4–14, a prophetic judgment speech, which also precedes the fifth and final vision, 9:1–4.

Unlike the previous two visions, in the last three Yahweh's mind is set. The faithless Israelites and their elite will be punished. The eightfold לֹא אֲשִׁיבֶנּוּ, "I will not revoke it" from chapters 1 and 2,[5] is behind Yahweh's refusal to allow Amos any active role in these three visions.[6] The prophet's silence is a preview of the terrible silence—the silence of death—with which the visions conclude. See "silence!" in 8:3 (also 6:10) and the inescapable deadly judgment in 9:1–4.

In forming an envelope around the decisive showdown between Amos and Amaziah in 7:10–17, the third and fourth visions define the main message of the book. Amaziah's rejection of Yahweh's Word epitomizes the apostasy of the entire Northern Kingdom. It signals that the eleventh hour has passed and the clock of divine retribution is about to strike midnight.

The third vision (7:7–9; the first vision in the second pair of visions) is the most obscure because of debate about the meaning of the key word אֲנָךְ (7:7–8, traditionally "plumb line") and the lack of a divine explanation of its exact significance.[7] But this much is clear: the religious establishment (the idolatrous "high places … and the sanctuaries") will be destroyed, and the ruling dynasty of Jeroboam over northern Israel will be dethroned (7:9). This dual message is confirmed in 8:1–3 and 9:1–4.

---

5 See "God's Judgment Is Irrevocable" in the introduction to 1:3–2:16.

6 "It is as though Yahweh, now finally determined on a course of action, wished to prevent the prophet from intervening in any way, and to compel the prophet to carry out his appointed mission" (Andersen and Freedman, *Amos*, 621).

7 See the second textual note on 7:7. For an overview of the history of interpretation, see Cooper, "The Meaning of Amos's Third Vision (Amos 7:7–9)."

Amos 7:7–9

The Third Vision: The Plumb Line

Translation

7 [7]This is what he showed me: behold, the Lord was standing by a wall [constructed with] a plumb line, and in his hand was a plumb line.

[8]And Yahweh said to me, "What are you seeing, Amos?"

And I said, "A plumb line."

And the Lord said, "Behold, I am about to place a plumb line in the midst of my people Israel. I will never again forgive him.

[9]"The high places of Isaac will be desolated,

and the sanctuaries of Israel will be ruined.

And I will arise against the house of Jeroboam with the sword."

Textual Notes

7:7 כֹּה הִרְאַנִי—See the first textual note on 7:1. This third vision uses the same introductory formula as the first, second, and fourth visions (7:1, 4; 8:1) but without the divine title אֲדֹנָי יְהוִה intervening between כֹּה הִרְאַנִי and וְהִנֵּה.

וְהִנֵּה אֲדֹנָי נִצָּב עַל־חוֹמַת אֲנָךְ וּבְיָדוֹ אֲנָךְ׃—The Niphal participle נִצָּב, "standing," together with the Qal participle רֹאֶה, "seeing," in 7:8 (cf. also שָׂם, "placing, about to place," in 7:8), helps readers picture the vision in progress and view it from the prophet's perspective. The Niphal of נָצַב often means "*station oneself, take one's stand*, for a definite purpose" (BDB, 1 a). It "expresses anxious expectation of something about to happen."[1] The preposition עַל often means "beside, by."[2] נִצָּב עַל־ recurs in 9:1, where Amos sees Yahweh "standing by" the altar.

The noun clause at the end of the verse appended with *waw*, וּבְיָדוֹ אֲנָךְ, functions as a circumstantial clause (GKC, § 156 b) that could be translated as "the Lord was standing … *with/while he had* a plumb line in his hand."

The noun אֲנָךְ appears twice in this verse, twice in 7:8, and nowhere else in the OT. It presents one of the most perplexing interpretive problems in the book of Amos. The traditional meaning "plumb line" (or a synonym such as "plummet") has been given in standard Biblical Hebrew lexicons over the last century (Gesenius [which has *Blei* and synonyms], BDB, *HALOT*, *DCH*) and is standard in English translations. This was a cord with a weight on its end. It could measure whether or not a structure was vertical or leaning at an angle, and whether the structure was vertically straight, with all of its stones or components aligned in a straight line. A plumb line could be suspended so that it hung down along the line that was to be the corner or side of a wall that was being built. Builders could place each layer of stones or bricks directly on top of one

---

[1] J. Reindl, "יצב/נצב," *TDOT* 9:522.

[2] See Laetsch, *The Minor Prophets*, 183, and Andersen and Freedman, *Amos*, 834–35.

another, with the corner or edge of each stone touching the plumb line. This method of construction ensured that the stones or bricks were aligned and that the wall was thus even and perpendicular to level ground. The prophet Zechariah refers to "the plumb line [הָאֶבֶן הַבְּדִיל, literally, 'the tin stone'] in the hand of Zerubbabel" in a context that speaks about building the second temple (Zech 4:9–10).[3]

Various Semitic and non-Semitic cognates (see *HALOT*) suggest that אֲנָךְ refers to either tin or lead, both of which are heavy metals that are malleable. אֲנָךְ is cognate to the Akkadian *annaku*, "tin."[4] Either tin or lead or an alloy of both would be suitable as the weight for a plumb line. Tin weighs about the same as silver and is twice as heavy as iron.[5] Lead is twice as heavy as tin. The OT refers to lead (עֹפֶרֶת) used as a weight (Zech 5:7–8) and as sinking rapidly in water (a metaphor for the Egyptians in Ex 15:10). In the OT era, lead (עֹפֶרֶת) and tin (בְּדִיל) were among the metals that were mined, smelted, refined, and traded (Num 31:22; Ezek 22:18, 20; 27:12; cf. עֹפֶרֶת in Job 19:24). אֲנָךְ occurs at least twice in Rabbinic Hebrew in passages that are dependent on Amos 7:7–8, and in at least one, it probably means "plumb-line" (Jastrow, s.v. אֲנָךְ II, citing *Midrash Rabbah Leviticus*, 33; see also *Midrash Rabbah Lamentations*, 25).

The construct phrase חוֹמַת אֲנָךְ in Amos 7:7 then refers to "a wall [constructed with] a plumb line," that is, "a vertical wall" (NASB), "a wall that had been built true to plumb" (NIV). Such a wall would be vertically straight, with all the stones or bricks in line. It would also be stronger and more stable than a wall constructed without a plumb line, which could be uneven and lean. The three later occurrences of אֲנָךְ (7:7–8) also refer to a plumb line, and in the last one it clearly is a metaphor. Both the plumb line itself and the wall constructed with it represent a strict, absolute standard by which Yahweh now judges Israel. Just as a plumb line is used to construct a straight wall without irregularities or curvature—without deviating from the norm—so Yahweh will judge Israel using his unbending requirement for justice and righteousness. He will punish the Israelites because they have strayed from his standard and are crooked. The result of Yahweh placing אֲנָךְ in the midst of his people (7:8) is the demolition and ruin of Israel's idolatrous shrines (7:9a) and the slaughter of the dynasty of Jeroboam (7:9b).

This interpretation is consistent with the ongoing theme of Amos expressed in other passages where Yahweh desires that his people display justice and righteousness (e.g., 5:7, 15, 24; 6:12) and threatens to judge the people for deviating from his Torah and commandments (e.g., 2:4) and for rejecting his prophets and their words (e.g., 2:12; 7:10–17). It is also consistent with other passages that describe God as evaluating and judging his people by means of a (metaphorical) "measuring line" (קָו, 2 Ki 21:13; Is 34:11) and "plumb line" (מִשְׁקֹלֶת, 2 Ki 21:13; plural of אֶבֶן in Is 34:11). In Lam 2:8 God uses a "line" (קָו) to evaluate the city "wall" (חוֹמָה) of Jerusalem, which

---

3 For an Egyptian illustration from the thirteenth century BC showing a plumb line, see Galling, *Biblisches Reallexikon*, illustration 3 under *Holzbearbeitung*, or Reicke and Rost, *Biblisch-Historisches Hantwörterbuch*, illustration 8 under *Holz*.

4 Landsberger, "Tin and Lead: The Adventures of Two Vocables." Landsberger argues that אֲנָךְ must refer to "tin" and not to "lead." However, *HALOT* includes "lead" as a possibility based on cognates to the Hebrew.

5 Tin (the element Sn) has the atomic number 50 and an atomic weight of 118.71.

he then causes to be destroyed. Because Yahweh is judging Israel with this exact and precise standard instead of a lenient or flexible standard, he will not forgive his people any more (Amos 7:8).

Many other suggestions for the meaning of אֲנָךְ have been offered in the history of interpretation. The LXX understands אֲנָךְ to refer to a hard metal or diamond. It translates the last part of 7:7 as ἐπὶ τείχους ἀδαμαντίνου καὶ ἐν τῇ χειρὶ αὐτοῦ ἀδάμας, "upon a wall of adamantine, and in his hand was adamant." The Peshitta agrees with the LXX and translates all four occurrences of אֲנָךְ with ܐܕܡܘܣ, "adamant." The Vulgate has this translation: *super murum litum et in manu eius trulla cementarii*, "beside a plastered wall, and in his hand was a trowel of a mason."

In the last century, some scholars have argued for other views. Paul suggests that חוֹמַת אֲנָךְ could mean "a wall (made out) of tin."[6] No other OT passages or ancient Near Eastern texts refer to a literal tin wall, but there are passages that refer to metaphorical or symbolical metal walls. For example, Yahweh promises Jeremiah, "Behold, today I myself am making you into a fortified city, into a pillar of iron, and into walls of bronze [וּלְחֹמוֹת נְחֹשֶׁת]" (Jer 1:18). These symbolize strength in the face of opposition and attacks. Tin, however, is softer than bronze. The message in Amos' vision could be that Israel is a weak tin wall that is about to come crashing down.[7]

Andersen and Freedman present a complicated argument for taking חוֹמַת אֲנָךְ as a "plastered wall," but they say that the next two occurrences of אֲנָךְ refer to "a lump of tin" and that the final occurrence of אֲנָךְ means "grief, wrong, oppression."[8]

Sweeney cites the Rabbinic Hebrew verb אָנַךְ, "to rub, polish ... to glaze vessels" (Jastrow), and cognate noun אֲנָךְ, "onyx; a glaze" (Jastrow), and argues that the first three occurrences of the noun refer to plaster: Amos sees "a plastered wall, and YHWH would be standing with plaster in the divine hand to represent the repair work."[9] However, this pictures Yahweh's activity as constructive, which does not fit in the context of this vision, which is an oracle of judgment and destruction. Sweeney recognizes that "plaster" is nonsensical in the fourth occurrence of אֲנָךְ, when Yahweh says, "I am about to place אֲנָךְ in the midst of my people Israel" (7:8c). He compares 7:7–9 to 8:1–3, which has a similar structure and contains a pun with קַיִץ, "summer (fruit)," and קֵץ, "end." He then argues that another pun involving אֲנָךְ may be present in 7:7–9, and proposes that here אֲנָךְ may form a pun by assonance with אֲנָחָה, "groaning, sighing"

---

6 Paul, *Amos*, 235.

7 The view of Paul essentially agrees with the conclusion of Landsberger, "Tin and Lead: The Adventures of Two Vocables." Landsberger argues that אֲנָךְ must mean "tin" and that חוֹמַת אֲנָךְ must refer to a wall made of tin, "this metal being a symbol of (a) softness, (b) uselessness, unless alloyed to another metal, [and] (c) perishability" (p. 287).

8 Andersen and Freedman, *Amos*, 754, 756–59. For the last meaning, they cite the Babylonian Talmud, *Baba Metzi'a*, 59a, as does Jastrow, s.v. אֲנָךְ I. However, the meaning of אֲנָךְ in that passage of the Talmud is at least partially dependent on its meaning in Amos 7:7–8, as noted by Jastrow.

9 Sweeney, *The Twelve Prophets*, 254. Sweeney first argues that "tin does not provide a suitable weight for use in a plumbline," but later in the same paragraph he notes that in Zech 4:10, הָאֶבֶן הַבְּדִיל, " 'the tin stone,' is used to describe a plummet," and so that verse "demonstrates that tin could be employed for a plumbline."

in grief (e.g., Is 21:2; 35:10; Ps 31:11 [ET 31:10]; Job 3:24; Lam 1:22). Yahweh will place groaning in the midst of Israel by carrying out his judgment.[10] The nouns אֲנָךְ and אֲנָחָה sound similar even though they are from different roots.

Stuart follows a similar approach but says that the fourth occurrence of אֲנָךְ is a pun on the verb אָנַק, "to moan, groan" after a disaster, as in Jer 51:52 and Ezek 26:15.[11]

Cooper, following an older view, proposes that in 7:8c אֲנָךְ should be emended to אָנֹךְ, an alleged short form of the pronoun אָנֹכִי, so that Yahweh would say, "I am putting I/myself in the midst of my people Israel."[12] Cooper states: "Having threatened Israel with destruction by natural agents (locusts, 7:1–3, and fire, 7:4–6), God now moves against the people Himself."[13] Yahweh's presence as the direct agent of judgment is a recurring theme in Amos (4:12; 5:1, 17; 6:8). However, this view requires a torturous construal of the grammar.[14]

7:8 וַיֹּאמֶר יְהוָה אֵלַי מָה־אַתָּה רֹאֶה עָמוֹס—"And Yahweh said to me, 'What are you seeing, Amos?'" will be repeated in 8:2 but without יְהוָה אֵלַי.

וָאֹמַר אֲנָךְ—The terse, one-word reply of Amos refers only to the central feature of the scene in 7:7: the "plumb line."

וַיֹּאמֶר אֲדֹנָי הִנְנִי שָׂם אֲנָךְ בְּקֶרֶב עַמִּי יִשְׂרָאֵל—The demonstrative הִנֵּה (here with pronominal suffix, הִנְנִי) and the participle (שָׂם) form a *futurum instans* (GKC, § 116 p): "I am soon placing, about to place." This construction is often used in prophetic announcements of impending divine judgment, as also in 2:13; 6:11, 14; 9:9. The significance of Yahweh placing a "plumb line" (אֲנָךְ) in the midst of Israel, whom he still calls "my people" (עַמִּי), is clarified by the following clause about strict judgment.

לֹא־אוֹסִיף עוֹד עֲבוֹר לוֹ׃—Literally, "I will not continue again to pass over for him," this divine declaration is repeated in 8:2. The Hiphil of יָסַף, to "*do again* or *more*" (BDB, 2 a), often is followed by an infinitive (here עֲבוֹר). In this construction, the form of יָסַף is best rendered adverbially, and the infinitive serves as the main verb. The addition of the adverb עוֹד, "ever, again," makes the negative (לֹא) declaration even more emphatic: "I will *never again* forgive (for) him." The Qal of עָבַר, "to cross, pass by," can have the nuance of "overlook, forgive" (BDB, 1 j, citing Micah 7:18 and Prov

---

[10] Sweeney, *The Twelve Prophets*, 255. Another interpreter who relies on a comparison of 7:7–9 to 8:1–3 is Cooper, "The Meaning of Amos's Third Vision (Amos 7:7–9)," 17–18.

[11] Stuart, *Hosea–Jonah*, 373. Others who offer some kind of theory that אֲנָךְ is a play on a word like אָנַק, "moan," include Horst, "Die Visionsschilderung der alttestamentlichen Propheten," and Ouellette, "Le Mur d'Etain dans Amos 7:7–9."

[12] Cooper, "The Meaning of Amos's Third Vision (Amos 7:7–9)," 18–20. He follows the view proposed by Prätorius in 1915 (Franz Prätorius, "Bemerkungen zu Amos," *Zeitschrift für die alttestamentliche Wissenschaft* 35 [1915]: 12–25, especially pp. 22–23).

[13] Cooper, "The Meaning of Amos's Third Vision," 19.

[14] This view proposes emending the text to produce the construction הִנְנִי שָׂם אָנֹךְ, with אָנֹךְ being a shortened form of אָנֹכִי, literally, "behold, I am placing, I," which would mean, "behold, I myself am placing." The pronoun אָנֹךְ/אָנֹכִי would be an emphatic repetition of the *subject* of the participle, *not* the direct object of the participle. To say "behold, I am placing myself," Classical Hebrew could use an intransitive (reflexive, middle) verb or another construction, such as the direct object marker אֵת with a pronoun, that is, הִנְנִי שָׂם אֹתִי (which would lack any pun on אֲנָךְ).

19:11 as well as Amos 7:8; 8:2). The person "to" whom God does (or here, does not) grant forgiveness is introduced by לְ in Micah 7:18 as well as Amos 7:8; 8:2. The singular pronoun on לוֹ refers back to עַמִּי יִשְׂרָאֵל, "my people Israel" and also is consistent with יִשְׂחָק, "Isaac," representing the whole people in the next verse (7:9).

The meaning of the condemnation in 7:8 and 8:2 is clarified by the fuller idiom in Micah 7:18, which is, in contrast, a Gospel affirmation of God's grace toward the faithful "remnant" of his people: "Who is a God like you, who forgives sin [נֹשֵׂא עָוֹן] and who passes over transgression for the remnant of his inheritance [וְעֹבֵר עַל־פֶּשַׁע לִשְׁאֵרִית נַחֲלָתוֹ]?"

7:9 וְנָשַׁמּוּ בָּמוֹת יִשְׂחָק—The Niphal of שָׁמֵם is best translated as a passive, "be desolated, destroyed." The Niphal can include both the psychological state of punished people who are "appalled" (e.g., Jer 4:9; Ezek 4:17; Lam 4:5) and geographic and physical conditions.[15] In addition to the subject here, "the high places of Isaac," other subjects that can be "desolated" include "cities" (Amos 9:14, the only other occurrence of the Niphal of שָׁמֵם in the book; also Is 54:3) and "your [Judah's idolatrous] altars" (Ezek 6:4). It is used in the Sinai covenant curse that unfaithful Israel's "ways" will be desolated (Lev 26:22; other forms of שָׁמֵם are in the curses in Lev 26:31–32, 34–35, 43). The Niphal forms are almost uniformly passive; the subjects have experienced the force of a destruction that overwhelmed them. Most frequently it is Yahweh who produces such desolation either directly (e.g., 1 Sam 5:6) or through agents (e.g., Ezek 30:12).

The noun בָּמָה can refer generally to a lofty ridge or a high piece of ground (e.g., Deut 32:13; Amos 4:13). Its most prominent OT usage is to identify a "high place" for Canaanite worship activities (e.g., of Moab in Jer 48:35).[16] These could be a hill or natural height that was further built up by people for their worship. After Israel conquered the land of Canaan under Joshua, many of the Canaanite high places were simply adopted for the proper worship of Yahweh (e.g., 1 Sam 9:12–24). Yahweh's epiphany to Solomon at the high place at Gibeon showed that this worship was salutary (1 Ki 3:2–5). After Solomon built and consecrated the temple (1 Kings 6–8), it was to be the one central sanctuary God had prescribed in the Torah. In Exodus, God commanded the construction of the tabernacle, and in Deuteronomy he predicted and ordained that Israel would have one central site for worship.[a] However, after Solomon constructed the temple, some worship at the high places continued, and the syncretistic nature of these sites eventually led to their condemnation by the prophets (e.g., Hos 10:8). בָּמוֹת here in Amos 7:9 denotes such syncretistic sites that likely combine some elements of the worship of Yahweh with the worship of indigenous pagan deities of fertility and nature. The destruction of such "high places" fulfills the covenant curse in Lev 26:30.

(a) See, e.g., Deut 12:5, 11, 14, 18, 21, 26; 14:23–25; 15:20; 16:2, 6–7, 11, 15–16

The proper name יִשְׂחָק, "Isaac," reappears in 7:16. For this spelling, see also Jer 33:26 and Ps 105:9. It is a softened form of יִצְחָק (e.g., Gen 17:19, 21).[17] Spelled either way, the name is derived from the verb צָחַק, "to laugh, play, jest" (Gen 17:17; 18:12–13,

---

[15] Cf. I. Meyer, "שָׁמֵם," *TDOT* 15:238–48.

[16] Cf. K.-D. Schunck, "בָּמָה," *TDOT* 2:139–45.

[17] Cf. R. Bartelmus, "צָחַק/שָׂחַק," *TDOT* 14:58–72.

15; 21:6). Genesis offers three possibilities for its origin: the incredulous laughter of the parents at the birth announcement (Gen 17:17; 18:12–15), Sarah's laughter after giving birth (Gen 21:6a), and/or the laughter of those hearing of the miraculous birth (Gen 21:6b).

וּמִקְדְּשֵׁי יִשְׂרָאֵל יֶחֱרָבוּ—The noun מִקְדָּשׁ, "sanctuary," is formed by affixing a preformative *mem* to the verbal root קָדַשׁ, "to be holy." A qualitative difference sets Yahweh and items dedicated to him apart from everything and everyone else, so that they are holy. Subjects of the verb קָדַשׁ include, for example, the priests and the priestly vestments (Ex 29:21) and the altar and anyone touching it (Ex 29:37). The singular noun מִקְדָּשׁ can designate Yahweh's one central "sanctuary" (e.g., Lev 16:33; 19:30; Ezek 5:11). The plural, which appears in Amos 7:9, necessarily refers to false alternative sites since God had declared in the Torah that there was to be one central sanctuary (see the preceding textual note). The singular מִקְדָּשׁ occurs in 7:13, where it refers to the idolatrous "sanctuary" at Bethel as the king's "sanctuary."

The Qal of חָרֵב displays two distinct semantic fields: "to be dry" or, as here, "to be ruined, in ruins; laid waste, destroyed."[18] These may represent two separate homographic verbs (BDB) or different meanings of the same verb (*HALOT*). Yahweh used similar language in the covenant curse in Lev 26:31: he warned that he would reduce the cities of unfaithful Israel to "ruin" (the cognate noun חָרְבָּה) and cause its "sanctuaries" (the plural of מִקְדָּשׁ, as in this clause) to be desolated (Hiphil of שָׁמֵם, whose Niphal was used in the preceding clause of Amos 7:9). Other prophetic judgment oracles use the Qal of חָרֵב meaning "to be in ruins" to refer to apostate Israel (e.g., Jer 26:9; Ezek 6:6; 12:20). But Yahweh also issues the eschatological messianic promise that Jerusalem (his church) will be rebuilt (Is 60:10–11), and those who do not serve her will be the ones who are "ruined" (Is 60:12; see also the Hiphil of חָרֵב in Is 49:17).

וְקַמְתִּי עַל־בֵּית יָרָבְעָם בֶּחָרֶב׃—Often the Qal of קוּם means "to arise" for hostile action and takes the preposition עַל, "against" (BDB, s.v. קוּם, Qal, 2). Similarly, Yahweh used the causative Hiphil of קוּם in 6:14 with עַל, "I am about to raise up against you … a nation."

For the proper name יָרָבְעָם, "Jeroboam," see the fifth textual note and the commentary on 1:1. He is named again in 7:10–11.

In Amos, except in 1:11, חֶרֶב, the "sword," is always wielded by Yahweh himself (4:10; 7:9; 9:1) or by his agents who carry out his judgments (7:11, 17; 9:4, 10).

Commentary

7:7 This third vision has the same structure as the fourth (see the commentary on 8:1–3). Yahweh has in his hand a plumb line, which was used to construct a straight, solid wall. What does this signify? Throughout the earlier phase of Amos' ministry, Yahweh tried to repair and rebuild the fallen nation, and twice he relented from executing judgment (7:1–6). However, these attempts failed; see his fivefold refrain, "but you did not return to me" (4:6, 8, 9, 10,

[18] Cf. O. Kaiser, "חָרַב," *TDOT* 5:150–54.

11). Israel's broken walls and cracked foundations will be repaired only when Yahweh resurrects the falling tabernacle of David (9:11).

The NT proclaims that this Davidic restoration arrives in Jesus Christ. Matthew declares that Jesus comes from the line and house of David (Mt 1:1, 6; see also Lk 2:4). Jesus is called "the Son of David" by two blind men (Mt 9:27), while James references Amos 9:11–12 in speaking of the inclusion of Gentiles together with Jews in the church of Jesus Christ (Acts 15:15–17).[19] Jesus is "the *root* and the descendant of David" (Rev 22:16; cf. Rev 5:5). This implies that he is not only the "branch" from Jesse (Is 11:1; cf. Is 4:2; Jer 23:5; 33:15), the one to come as the new David (Ezek 34:23–24; 37:24–25), but that he is greater than David himself; indeed, he is David's Lord (Psalm 110; Mt 22:42–46; Mk 12:35–37; Lk 20:42–44). He is the preexistent Ruler from eternity (Micah 5:1 [ET 5:2]), who shall reign on David's throne forever (Is 9:6 [ET 9:7]; cf. Dan 2:44; 7:18; Lk 1:33). Through the new and greater David, not only will Israel be restored to Yahweh but so will the entire creation (Jn 3:16; Rom 8:19–23). This will not be done with a plumb line or with stone walls and plaster, "but with his [Christ's] holy and precious blood and with his innocent sufferings and death."[20] Upon this Christ the kingdom of God is built (Is 28:16; Mt 16:16–18; 1 Cor 3:10–14; Eph 2:20–21).

7:8 Yahweh asks Amos, "What are you seeing?"[21] Amos responds with אֲנָךְ, the word from 7:7 that probably means "plumb line." Yahweh then tells Amos that he is placing it in the midst of "my people Israel" and that he will no longer forgive them. This means that strict judgment is coming.[22] There may also be a pun on the word אֲנָךְ implying that the judgment will bring "groaning" in lamentation (see the second textual note on 7:7).

Yet Yahweh still applies to the nation the term עַמִּי, "my people," evoking the endearing covenant bond (e.g., Ex 3:7, 10; 5:1). "My people Israel" (Amos 7:8) probably refers to both the northern and southern kingdoms.[23] In Isaiah, Yahweh refers to Israel at the time of judgment as "this people" (הָעָם הַזֶּה, e.g., Is 6:9; 29:13), but in a time of salvation, he lovingly refers to "my people" (עַמִּי, e.g., Is 40:1; 43:20; 65:19) and even includes converted Gentiles with the gracious label (Is 19:25). Hosea uses the term עַמִּי in both Law and Gospel contexts (e.g., Hos 1:9; and 2:1, 3, 25 [ET 1:10; 2:1, 23]). Yahweh declares through Amos that it is precisely *because* they are "my people" (also 8:2; 9:10) that their apostasy is so shocking and the judgment will be so devastating (see Amos 3:1–2; 1 Pet 4:17).

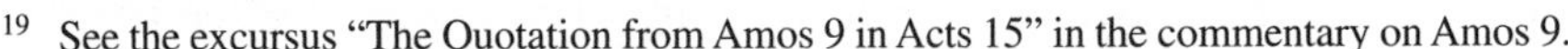

[19] See the excursus "The Quotation from Amos 9 in Acts 15" in the commentary on Amos 9.

[20] Based on 1 Pet 1:18–19, Luther wrote this in his Small Catechism (SC II 4).

[21] He will pose the same question to Amos again in 8:2 and, in later centuries, to Jeremiah (1:11; 24:3) and Zechariah (5:2).

[22] He will execute this judgment on northern Israel some forty years after Amos' ministry in 722 BC through Assyria, the unnamed "nation" in 6:14. See the excursus "The Assyrian Empire."

[23] Andersen and Freedman, *Amos*, 115 (see also pp. 98–99).

Yahweh again is employing a Gospel term (עַמִּי) ironically: because the people have spurned his grace, they have merited the coming condemnation.[24]

Unlike the first two visions (7:1–3 and 7:4–6), this time Amos does not attempt to intercede. His silence indicates that the die is cast and there will be no last minute reprieve as there was in 7:3, 6. Yahweh will not "pass by, forgive" (עֲבוֹר, 7:8) the nation for its sin. Instead, Yahweh will "pass through" Israel's midst in judgment (5:17, using the same verb, עָבַר), just as he passed through Egypt and struck down the firstborn of both people and animals (עָבַר in Ex 12:12, 23). And just as there was weeping and wailing in Egypt (Ex 12:30), so there will be groaning and grief in Israel.

7:9 The two foundations of the Northern Kingdom's life are targeted for annihilation: the spiritual center, resting on the idolatrous "high places" and "sanctuaries," and the political center, the king's house or dynasty. The false shrines at Bethel and elsewhere have already been in Amos' line of fire (e.g., 2:8; 3:14; 4:4; 5:5; see also 8:14; 9:1). But here, for the first time in the book, Yahweh names "Jeroboam" in a judgment oracle, and the judgment will be that Yahweh will pursue the king's house "with the sword" (7:9). Two verses later, the priest Amaziah will interpret this oracle as meaning that "by the sword Jeroboam will die" (7:11). Violent judgment for the royal household by means of "the sword" is given only in these two Amos verses.

Amos first attacks the apostate nation's places of worship. He refers to the people as "Isaac," parallel to "Israel," and both patriarchal names call to mind Yahweh's enduring grace and fidelity toward the patriarchs themselves and toward all their descendants down to this period of history (the eighth century BC, prior to the judgment against northern Israel in 722 BC).

Yahweh had commanded Israel to destroy the Canaanite "high places" (בָּמוֹת, Num 33:52) and idolatrous shrines (Deut 7:5). "High places" were pagan worship sites that persisted and were targeted during the reformations of the godly kings Hezekiah and Josiah (2 Ki 18:1–6; chapters 22–23). They are also condemned in, for example, Jer 17:1–4 and Ezek 6:2–6. "High places" were illegitimate centers of worship because Deut 12:1–7 indicates that the only sanctioned place of worship was to be the one place where Yahweh would cause his name to dwell. During David's reign, he moved the tabernacle to Jerusalem (2 Samuel 6), which then became the site of Solomon's temple (1 Kings 6–8).

Prophets like Amos confront unfaithful kings like Jeroboam ben Joash throughout much of the OT. Prophets arose and intensified as the monarchy strayed farther from the Torah covenant. Yahweh commissioned the prophet Samuel to instruct Israel's first king Saul, so from the inception of the monarchy, prophets were to monitor the authority of the king. These spokesmen were reminders "that power has its limits, that kings are not gods, and that politi-

---

[24] Besides 3:1–2 Yahweh inverts Gospel language into judgment also in, for example, 2:9–11; 3:1–2; 4:4–5, 12, 13; 5:8–9, 18–20; 8:2; 9:1, 4, 5–6, 7, 10.

cal arrangements are provisional."[25] Prophets often found themselves speaking against the state, yet sometimes they saw eye to eye with rulers.[26]

In the rest of the ancient Near East, the role of the king was central, and it went unchallenged. In essence kings were given a blank check to rule on behalf of a nation's patron deities. The Law Code of Hammurabi, for example, is clearly directed from the king to his people and seeks to regulate *their* conduct, *not his*.[27] This was not to be so in Israel. Deut 17:14–20 indicates that the king was to be a servant of Yahweh's Torah, given through Moses. The king was not to consider himself better than the rest of the people, who were "his brothers" (Deut 17:20). The prophets and psalmists affirm the subservient role of the king under God and according to his Torah: he is to display "truth and meekness and righteousness" (Ps 45:5 [ET 45:4]).

By circumscribing the power of the king, Deut 17:14–20 highlights the supremacy of Yahweh, *Israel's true King* (see also, e.g., Ex 15:18; Is 33:22; Pss 10:16; 29:10; 93:1). Israel's success would not be achieved through any of the means used by the surrounding nations, such as military might and political alliances, but only through faith and trust in Yahweh. Jeroboam ben Joash failed to heed these words of Moses in Deuteronomy. He lived as though he was in charge, as though he could have it his way on his terms. But in doing so, Amos says, the king has set himself and his nation on a one-way road toward judgment and death (cf. Amos 4:10; 9:1, 4).

"The house of Jeroboam" (בֵּית יָרָבְעָם, 7:9) may mean the king's family; the Jehu dynasty, of which Jeroboam ben Joash was a member; and/or the entire Northern Kingdom, which was under his rule. Andersen and Freedman write:

> Most of the oracles in the first set against the nations [1:3–2:3] include a threat against the ruler, his capital, or both, as well as exile for the nation (1:5) or for the king and his court (1:15). The oracle against Israel (2:6–8) does not include any punishment. Amos 7:9 supplies this lack.[28]

The agent of judgment against the house of Jeroboam ben Joash is the "sword" (חֶרֶב), used here as a synecdoche of a part for the whole, indicating judgment by warfare.[29] Whereas Yahweh had said in 6:14 that he was "about to raise up … a nation," here in 7:9 there is no specific mention of an enemy agent. Yahweh himself will "arise against" the king's house and execute judgment. This prophecy was fulfilled when Zechariah, the son of Jeroboam ben Joash (2 Ki 15:8), was assassinated. 2 Ki 15:10 states: "Shallum ben Jabesh conspired against him [Zechariah]. He smote him in front of the people, put him to death, and became king in his place." This was also in fulfillment of what

25 Stulman, *Jeremiah*, 206.

26 King Hezekiah enjoyed a good relationship with Isaiah during the Assyrian crisis of 701 BC (2 Kings 19 || Isaiah 37).

27 See *ANET*, 163–80.

28 Andersen and Freedman, *Amos*, 761.

29 For the "sword" as shorthand for judgment, see, for example, Ex 5:3; Deut 32:25; Is 1:20.

Yahweh had said earlier to Jehu: "Four generations of your descendants will occupy the throne of Israel" (2 Ki 15:12).

Amos 7:9 is strikingly similar to covenant curses in Lev 26:30–33, which reads:[30] "I will destroy your high places [וְהִשְׁמַדְתִּ֞י אֶת־בָּמֹֽתֵיכֶ֗ם]. … And I will desolate your sanctuaries [וַהֲשִׁמּוֹתִ֖י אֶת־מִקְדְּשֵׁיכֶ֑ם]. … And I will unsheathe the sword [חָ֑רֶב] against you." The similarities between the two texts can only indicate one thing: Yahweh's covenant curses in the Torah of Moses are about to be enacted against the house of Jeroboam ben Joash and the people's idolatrous worship shrines.

Summary

After his visions, Amos is prepared to go face to face with Amaziah (7:10–17).[31] The prophet's courage at the idolatrous shrine at Bethel in the presence of the apostate priest, who accuses him of treason against the king, comes from his visions, where Amos saw Yahweh himself. The narrative of 7:10–17 is strategically placed between the prophet's third (7:7–9) and fourth (8:1–3) visions to underline the fact that Amos does not back down in the presence of the priest who represents the king, for he has been in Yahweh's council (3:7).

Yahweh had given Jeroboam ben Nebat the Northern Kingdom conditionally in the tenth century BC (1 Ki 11:31–38). Since both he and his namesake successor in the eighth century, Jeroboam ben Joash, ignored the divine will and maintained shrines to other gods, there was only one option: exile. Amos' third and fourth visions are consistent with his sermons of doom for Israel (e.g., 5:1–3, 18–27). No wonder Amaziah tried to rid Bethel of Amos (7:10–17). The book will end with a Gospel promise (9:11–15) not unlike Isaiah's prophetic call to comfort the afflicted (Is 40:1). But for now Amos has a call to afflict the comfortable.

---

30 This is noted by Paul, *Amos*, 237. See also Stuart, *Hosea–Jonah*, 373.

31 Freedman, "Confrontations in the Book of Amos," 241, writes:

> In brief, we hold that there are two accounts of confrontations, one between prophet and priest and the other between prophet and God, and that they are deliberately juxtaposed, not because they proceed simultaneously (which would be a possibility at least) but because one set of circumstances influences the other, and the somewhat unusual behavior of the prophet in the confrontation at Bethel can be understood and is explained by the former and much more decisive confrontation already experienced by the prophet.

Amos 7:10–17

Amos and Amaziah

Translation

7 10Then Amaziah, the priest of Bethel, sent [a message] to Jeroboam, king of Israel: "Amos has conspired against you in the midst of the house of Israel. The land is not able to endure all of his words.

11"For thus says Amos: 'By the sword Jeroboam will die, and Israel will certainly go into exile from its land.' "

**12Then Amaziah said to Amos, "O seer, flee quickly to the land of Judah, and
eat food there, and there you may prophesy. 13But at Bethel you shall never again
prophesy, for it is the sanctuary of the king; it is the house of the kingdom."**

**14Then Amos answered and said to Amaziah, "I [was] not a prophet, nor [was]
I a son of a prophet. Rather, I [was] a livestock breeder and a dresser of sycamore
figs. 15But Yahweh took me from [tending] sheep, and Yahweh said to me, 'Go,
prophesy to my people Israel.' "**

16"But now, hear the Word of Yahweh, you who are saying, 'Do not prophesy against Israel' and 'Do not preach against the house of Isaac.'

17"Therefore thus says Yahweh: 'Your wife will be a prostitute in the city, and your sons and your daughters will fall by the sword. Your land will be parceled out with a measuring line, and as for you, in an unclean land you will die. And Israel will certainly go into exile from its land.' "

Textual Notes

7:10 וַיִּשְׁלַח אֲמַצְיָה כֹּהֵן בֵּית־אֵל אֶל־יָרָבְעָם מֶלֶךְ־יִשְׂרָאֵל לֵאמֹר—The expression וַיִּשְׁלַח אֶל, "and he sent to," connotes the sending of a message (as in 2 Sam 11:6), which is then quoted following לֵאמֹר. This wording occurs also in, for example, Gen 38:25 and 1 Ki 21:14.

"Amaziah" (אֲמַצְיָה) means "Yahweh is mighty." Sadly, as is often the case with OT theophoric names, this name does not indicate the character of its bearer.

The title כֹּהֵן בֵּית־אֵל, "the priest of Bethel," is unique. This priest is identified with his location, rather than with the one true God or a false deity. This is similar to the way in which pagan priests are named according to their location: "Potiphera, the priest of On" (Gen 41:45, 50; 46:20), and Jethro, "the priest of Midian" (Ex 2:16; 3:1; 18:1). Faithful priests are never designated by their location; the OT never refers to, for example, "priest of Jerusalem/Zion." Eli is the only priest named in a construct phrase as "the priest of Yahweh" (כֹּהֵן ׀ יְהוָה, 1 Sam 14:3). A prepositional phrase describes Melchizedek as "priest to God Most High" (כֹהֵן לְאֵל עֶלְיוֹן, Gen 14:18).

For the proper name יָרָבְעָם, "Jeroboam," see the fifth textual note and the commentary on 1:1.

קָשַׁר עָלֶיךָ עָמוֹס בְּקֶרֶב בֵּית יִשְׂרָאֵל—The basic sense of the verb קָשַׁר is "to bind."[1] It can have a positive connotation, as in the command to bind Yahweh's commandments to the hands (Deut 6:8). The more common meaning, however, is "to conspire." In this sense, קָשַׁר refers primarily to persons bound in a conspiracy with the goal of deposing and slaying the reigning king, for example, Baasha conspired and murdered Nadab in 1 Ki 15:27; Zimri conspired and murdered Elah in 1 Ki 16:9–10; Shallum conspired and murdered Zechariah ben Jeroboam (2 Ki 15:10); and Hoshea conspired and murdered Pekah in 2 Ki 15:30. This is how the word should be understood in Amos 7:10.

לֹא־תוּכַל הָאָרֶץ לְהָכִיל אֶת־כָּל־דְּבָרָיו׃—Amaziah portrays Amos' oracles as being so abundant that "the land is not able to contain/endure all of his words." Compare Jn 21:25, where the evangelist states that if all the deeds of Jesus were recorded, "the world itself could not contain the written books." The feminine noun (with article) הָאָרֶץ is the subject of תוּכַל, the feminine Qal imperfect of יָכֹל, to "be able," which usually takes an infinitive construct of another verb with לְ, as here, לְהָכִיל. In the Hiphil, כּוּל can mean "to contain, hold," as a cistern contains water (see BDB, 1, and *HALOT*, 1).[2] Jeremiah uses it to declare that he is weary of holding in Yahweh's wrath, and he is ordered to pour it out (Jer 6:11; cf. Jer 20:9, where he says about Yahweh's Word, "I am weary of containing it [כַּלְכֵל, Pilpel infinitive construct of כּוּל], and I am not able [וְלֹא אוּכָל]"). The Hiphil of כּוּל can also express that people cannot "endure" Yahweh's wrath, day, or words spoken through his prophet (see BDB, 2, and *HALOT*, 2, which both cite Jer 10:10; Joel 2:11; Amos 7:10).

7:11 כִּי־כֹה אָמַר עָמוֹס—Amaziah claims to be quoting Amos. Both statements in the quote correspond in some measure to what Amos says elsewhere. See the next two textual notes.

בַּחֶרֶב יָמוּת יָרָבְעָם—The "sword" (חֶרֶב) is frequently employed as a metonymy for a violent death or death by war (e.g., Jer 14:15). Just two verses earlier, in Amos 7:9, Yahweh declared that he would arise against the house of Jeroboam "with the sword" (בֶּחָרֶב). Yahweh wielded the "sword" against Israel's soldiers in 4:10, and threatens to use it against Israelites in 7:17; 9:1, 4, 10. The historical narrative in 2 Ki 14:29 does not state how Jeroboam ben Joash died. However, his son Zechariah was slain in a coup (2 Ki 15:10), thus fulfilling Amos' prophecy in 7:9.

וְיִשְׂרָאֵל גָּלֹה יִגְלֶה מֵעַל אַדְמָתוֹ׃—Amos will repeat this exact wording of Amaziah in his response at the end of 7:17. The same verbal construction, the Qal infinitive absolute of גָּלָה preceding its imperfect, גָּלֹה יִגְלֶה, was in the earlier judgment כִּי הַגִּלְגָּל גָּלֹה יִגְלֶה, "for Gilgal surely will go into exile" (see the third textual note on in 5:5). The infinitive absolute functions adverbially ("surely, certainly") to strengthen the affirmation (Joüon, § 123 e). Amos also prophesied exile for Israel using גָּלָה in 5:27; 6:7. In Amaziah's communication to Jeroboam, he is accurately summarizing the message of Amos. For the noun אֲדָמָה, see the fourth textual note on 7:17.

7:12 וַיֹּאמֶר אֲמַצְיָה אֶל־עָמוֹס—Amaziah now begins his rebuke of Amos.

---

[1] Cf. J. Conrad, "קָשַׁר," *TDOT* 13:196–201.

[2] Cf. A. Baumann, "כּוּל," *TDOT* 7:85–89.

חֹזֶה לֵךְ בְּרַח־לְךָ אֶל־אֶרֶץ יְהוּדָה—The noun חֹזֶה, literally, "seer," is in form the participle of חָזָה, "to see, perceive." The verb often refers to prophets who receive divine revelation, including Amos; see the third textual note on 1:1. The noun is a standard term for a faithful prophet of Yahweh, who may perceive revelation both by hearing and by seeing.[3] The noun refers to such true prophets as Gad (e.g., 2 Sam 24:11) and Iddo (e.g., 2 Chr 9:29). It can be parallel to נָבִיא, "prophet" (e.g., 2 Sam 24:11; 2 Ki 17:13; Is 29:10). See also the second textual note on 7:14, which discusses the synonyms רֹאֶה, "seer," and נָבִיא, "prophet." Only in Micah 3:7 does the noun חֹזֶה (in the plural) refer to "seers" who were false prophets and occult practitioners, as does the plural participle חֹזִים, "those seeing," in Is 47:13; Ezek 13:9, 16; 22:28.

The expression לֵךְ בְּרַח־לְךָ, literally, "go, flee for yourself," is rendered as "flee quickly." The two Qal imperatives (of הָלַךְ and בָּרַח) with the prepositional phrase in a reflexive sense (see BDB, s.v. לְ, 5 h; Joüon, § 133 d) mean that Amos was to flee immediately.

וֶאֱכָל־שָׁם לֶחֶם—Literally, "and eat there [your] bread," this probably was an idiom for "earn a living" (cf. Gen 3:19). True prophets were sometimes sustained by gifts of food (e.g., 1 Sam 9:7–8; 2 Ki 4:8; cf. the apostle's mandate for the support of Gospel ministers in 1 Cor 9:11, 14). False prophets could demand food and practice simony (Micah 3:5, 11).

וְשָׁם תִּנָּבֵא׃—The adverb שָׁם, "there," is placed first for emphasis, as is "Bethel" in the next clause at the start of 7:13. Amaziah uses an imperfect of permission, תִּנָּבֵא, "there you *may* prophesy," as if Amos requires the priest's human approval to speak God's Word!

Amos employs the Niphal of נָבָא, "to prophesy, speak on behalf of God" in 2:12; 3:8; 7:12–13, 15–16. Passages that clearly portray the role of a true "prophet" (the cognate noun נָבִיא) include Ex 7:1–2; Deut 18:18; Jer 1:5–6, 17, as well as Amos 7:10–17, the passage in the book in which the vocabulary for prophetic activity is most prominent. For נָבִיא, "prophet," see also the first second note on 7:14. Scholars have not reached a consensus about the root meaning of the verb, but in all likelihood it signifies that God calls someone to a specific task of preaching a particular divine message.[4] It is no accident, therefore, that extended *call* narratives appear in several prophetic books (e.g., Isaiah 6; Jeremiah 1; Ezekiel 1–3). These call narratives, like Amos 7:10–17, show that a prophet was called and empowered to preach Yahweh's Word of judgment and salvation faithfully in the face of fierce and even violent opposition from the very people of God to whom he was to minister.

7:13 וּבֵית־אֵל לֹא־תוֹסִיף עוֹד לְהִנָּבֵא—The place name וּבֵית־אֵל is first for emphasis, as reflected in the translation. The Hiphil of יָסַף plus an infinitive construct (here לְהִנָּבֵא, the Niphal of נבא with לְ) means "to do [something] again, more." The negative particle לֹא and the adverb עוֹד plus the imperfect expresses an emphatic negative

[3] Sweeney, *The Twelve Prophets*, 259. For example, Isaiah uses the verb חָזָה for perceiving a "vision" (חָזוֹן, Is 1:1), a "word" (הַדָּבָר, Is 2:1), and a "pronouncement" (מַשָּׂא, Is 13:1). Cf. A. Jepsen, "חָזָה," *TDOT* 4:280–90.

[4] Cf. Petersen, *The Prophetic Literature*, 6.

command: "you shall not at all, at any time, ever prophesy again at Bethel." The same construction is in 7:8 and 8:2, where Yahweh declares, "I will never again forgive" (see the fourth textual note on 7:8). Amaziah intends this prohibition to be permanent and irreversible. With it, Amaziah places himself among those cited in 2:12 who command Yahweh's prophets not to prophesy.

כִּי מִקְדַּשׁ־מֶלֶךְ הוּא—The construct phrase מִקְדַּשׁ־מֶלֶךְ occurs only here in the OT. Literally, "a sanctuary of a king" can be rendered with an adjectival genitive: "a royal sanctuary."

וּבֵית מַמְלָכָה הוּא׃—This next construct phrase בֵּית מַמְלָכָה, "a house of (the) kingdom," means "a temple of the kingdom," that is, the Northern Kingdom's state temple in Bethel. בַּיִת may mean "temple" (e.g., 1 Ki 6:1–3; 7:50; 2 Chr 1:18; 29:3). The phrase does not refer to the northern palace or royal residences, since they were in Samaria (see the first and second textual notes on Amos 3:9 and the commentary on 3:10, 15).

7:14 וַיַּעַן עָמוֹס וַיֹּאמֶר אֶל־אֲמַצְיָה—Amos responds to Amaziah's presumptuous orders.

לֹא־נָבִיא אָנֹכִי—In the first of two famous declarations, Amos first denies that he is a נָבִיא, "prophet." For the implication, see the commentary. Both this and the next declaration use לֹא, which creates a more forceful negation of the nominal clauses than would be the case with the usual nominal negative אֵין (Joüon, § 160 c).

In Amos, the noun נָבִיא always refers to true prophets of Yahweh (2:11–12; 3:7; 7:14). Occasionally נָבִיא is used as far back as the patriarchal era (Gen 20:7) and the time of Moses (e.g., Ex 7:1; Deut 13:2, 4, 6 [ET 13:1, 3, 5]; 18:15–22).[5] However, apparently "seer" (the participle רֹאֶה) was more common early in the history of the established nation, but the preferred term became נָבִיא. 1 Sam 9:9 reflects the change: previously, a person seeking God would say, "Let us go to the seer [רֹאֶה], for the person now called a prophet [נָבִיא] formerly was called a seer." The participle רֹאֶה is used verbally for Amos in 7:8 and 8:2 in Yahweh's question "what are you seeing?" A synonym of the nominal רֹאֶה, "seer," is חֹזֶה (see the second textual note on 7:12).

Prophets could represent the people before Yahweh and intercede for them, as Amos does in 7:2, 5[6] (cf. the "sacrificial" role of the pastor before God). Or they could represent Yahweh to the people, and even speak for him in the first person, as Amos does throughout the book (e.g., 5:4; cf. the "sacramental" role of the pastor). Yahweh's power could enable them to perform miracles in the everyday world (e.g., 2 Ki 4:38–41), envision the cosmic world (e.g., Amos 7:4; Zech 1: 7–17), or participate in the divine council (1 Ki 22:2–28; Isaiah 6; Amos 3:7). "Prophets were truly boundary figures, standing between the world of the sacred and secular."[7]

וְלֹא בֶן־נָבִיא אָנֹכִי—Next Amos denies that he is "a son of a prophet" (בֶן־נָבִיא). This singular phrase occurs only here in the OT. The plural בְּנֵי־הַנְּבִיאִים occurs in 1 Ki 20:35; 2 Ki 2:3, 5, 7, 15; 4:1, 38; 5:22; 6:1; 9:1, always referring to disciples of true prophets.

---

5 Cf. H.-P. Müller, "נָבִיא," *TDOT* 9:129–50.

6 Cf. Petersen, *The Prophetic Literature*, 7.

7 Petersen, *The Prophetic Literature*, 7.

Amos 7:14 is the only instance of either phrase in the books of the writing prophets. The phrases indicate vocational status rather than biological descent (although the biological sons of Isaiah had prophetic names and significance [Is 7:3–9; 8:1–4, 18] as did the children of Hosea [Hos 1:2–2:3 (ET 1:2–2:1)]). They refer to the disciples, associates, and supporters of prophets, "persons *belonging to the guild of prophets*" (GKC, § 128 v). Unlike the prophets themselves, their "sons" did not ordinarily receive oracles directly from Yahweh. Rather, they were beholden to their master, heard the divine Word through him, and helped him carry out his commission (e.g., 2 Ki 9:1–3).

כִּֽי־בוֹקֵ֥ר אָנֹ֖כִי וּבוֹלֵ֥ס שִׁקְמִֽים׃—After the preceding two negative declarations by Amos, כִּי has the restrictive sense "rather, instead" (cf. Joüon, § 172 b; Waltke-O'Connor, § 39.3.5d, including example 16 and note 100). Both of the masculine singular Qal active participles, בוֹקֵר and וּבוֹלֵס, are used as substantive nouns that denote professions. Both occur in the OT only here. בּוֹקֵר, "livestock breeder," is related to בָּקָר, "large bovines, cattle, oxen." This does not contradict Amos 1:1, where Amos is described as בַּנֹּקְדִים, "among the sheep breeders." Paul notes that the "all-embracing term" in 1:1 "may refer to either a breeder of cattle or herdsman of sheep and goats."[8] Similarly, a בּוֹקֵר, "livestock breeder," may also have tended sheep and goats. This aligns with Amos' statement in the next verse that, literally, "Yahweh took me from behind the sheep [הַצֹּאן]" (7:15).

The construct phrase וּבוֹלֵס שִׁקְמִים refers to one whose occupation was to "handle/dress the sycamore fig."[9] No other word from the root בלס is attested in the OT, but בּוֹלֵס is related to Arabic, Ethiopian, and Egyptian words for a "date" or "sycamore fig" (see *HALOT*). This meaning is confirmed by the following plural of שִׁקְמָה, "sycamore fig," *ficus sycomorus*, a tall tree with small fruit. Sycamore fig trees flourished in lower-elevation lands, for example, Egypt (Ps 78:47) and in the Shephelah (1 Ki 10:27; 1 Chr 27:28). It is unlikely that they grew anywhere close to Amos' hometown of Tekoa, so he likely traveled to carry out this occupation (see the commentary on 1:1). Since the fruit on these trees gets infested with a type of insect, the top of the fruit needs to be punctured so that the insects can come out. This makes the fruit edible.[10] The "dressing" process may also refer to the practice of slitting the sycamore fig before it ripens, a process that ensures it will turn sweet.[11] This task is reflected by the LXX translation of the occupation as κνίζων συκάμινα, "one who pricks/nips/scratches mulberry trees." The verb κνίζω is a technical term connected with sycamore horticulture.[12]

---

[8] Paul, *Amos*, 248.

[9] Wolff correctly cautions: "We do not know whether the compound expression בולס שקמים ('one who slits mulberry figs') designates only someone who actually performed the work or might also refer to someone who supervised such labor" (*Joel and Amos*, 314).

[10] Driver writes: "The fruit is infested with an insect (the *Sycophaga crassipes*), and till the 'eye' or top has been punctured, so that the insects may escape, it is not eatable" (*Joel and Amos*, 212).

[11] Wolff, *Joel and Amos*, 314. King discusses the procedure and provides illustrations of knives used for cutting sycamore figs (*Amos, Hosea, Micah*, 116–17).

[12] See Steiner, *Stockmen from Tekoa, Sycomores from Sheba*, 8–17.

7:15 וַיִּקָּחֵנִי יְהוָה מֵאַחֲרֵי הַצֹּאן—The *waw* is disjunctive, "but," contrasting Amos' preceding vocations to Yahweh calling him into the ministry. When Yahweh is the subject of the verb לָקַח and he "takes" a person, it can mean "select, choose" (cf. BDB, Qal, 4 d) and refer to calling the person into a high office, for example, placing Adam in Eden to keep it (Gen 2:15), calling Abraham and promising him the land (Gen 24:7), redeeming Israel to be his people (Deut 4:20; cf. Deut 4:34), or choosing Jeroboam ben Nebat to be king over the northern tribes (1 Ki 11:37). The compound מֵאַחֲרֵי (the prepositions מִן plus אַחֲרֵי), literally, "Yahweh took me *from behind* the sheep" (see GKC, § 119 b; Waltke-O'Connor, § 11.3.3a), precisely describes the location "from" which Yahweh called him, since a shepherd often follows "behind, after" (אַחַר or אַחֲרֵי) his flock while tending them (cf. 2 Sam 7:8 ‖ 1 Chr 17:7; Ps 78:70–71).

This clause recalls the pastoral vocation of Moses when he was called by Yahweh (Ex 3:1). Like Amos (7:4), Moses had a vision of fire (Ex 3:2). Both prophets were on missions that were accompanied by divine plagues aimed at bringing a nation to repentance (Ex 7:14–12:42; Amos 4:6–11). Both were intercessors for Israel (Ex 32:11–14; Amos 7:1–6). Both also oversaw the death of one era and the dawn of another.

This clause is remarkably similar to the words of Yahweh that Nathan spoke to David: "I myself took you from the pasture, from after [tending] the sheep" (אֲנִי לְקַחְתִּיךָ מִן־הַנָּוֶה מֵאַחַר הַצֹּאן, 2 Sam 7:8 ‖ 1 Chr 17:7; cf. Ps 78:70–71). Thus Amos is connected to not only Moses but also to David. Moses and David became leaders by divine election. Yahweh had promised that he would choose his people's king (Deut 17:15) and also raise up a Prophet like Moses (Deut 18:15). Amos has, in like manner, been chosen by Yahweh for his divine task.

וַיֹּאמֶר אֵלַי יְהוָה לֵךְ הִנָּבֵא אֶל־עַמִּי יִשְׂרָאֵל׃—Amos quotes Yahweh as ordaining him with the command לֵךְ, "go," the same Qal imperative of הָלַךְ Amaziah had used in 7:12 to try to persuade the prophet to abandon his ministry. Amos, however, obeys God rather than men, as also did the apostles (Acts 5:29). For the Niphal of נָבָא (imperative הִנָּבֵא), see the fourth textual note on 7:12. The covenant label עַמִּי, "my people," does not preclude preaching judgment to them, since the surrounding visions use it in judgment contexts (7:8, 8:2; see also 9:10).

7:16 וְעַתָּה שְׁמַע דְּבַר־יְהוָה—The word וְעַתָּה, "but now," has another adversative *waw* as Amos has finished his description of his call and now prophesies against Amaziah and Israel. וְעַתָּה is a standard introduction to prophetic oracles (e.g., Is 43:1; 44:1; Jer 18:11). It begins the main part of Amos' response, thus distinguishing his preliminary discourse (7:14–15) from the chief oracle (7:16–17), which is דְּבַר־יְהוָה, "the Word of Yahweh."

אַתָּה אֹמֵר לֹא תִנָּבֵא עַל־יִשְׂרָאֵל—The clause אַתָּה אֹמֵר, "you (who) are saying," may express a challenge in a dialogue (e.g., Ex 2:14; 33:12; 1 Ki 18:11, 14). Amos' quotation is milder than the words Amaziah used in 7:13. Here Amos uses the normal wording for a permanent prohibition, לֹא with an imperfect (תִנָּבֵא, the Niphal of נָבָא, "to prophesy"; see the fourth textual note on 7:12). The priest had used the strongest possible construction with the adverb עוֹד and an additional imperfect (תוֹסִיף) that was adverbial. See the first textual note on 7:13.

וְלֹא תַטִּיף עַל־בֵּית יִשְׂחָק׃—This clause is synonymously parallel to the preceding clause. The Hiphil of נָטַף, "to preach/prophesy," is parallel to the Niphal of נָבָא, "to prophesy," also in Ezek 21:2, 7 (ET 20:46; 21:2). The Qal of נָטַף has the basic sense "to drip" (e.g., Judg 5:4; Joel 4:18 [ET 3:18]; Prov 5:3).[13] Its Hiphil denotes "to preach/prophesy" and occurs in four other passages pertaining to preaching and prophesying. The two in Ezekiel (21:2, 7 [ET 20:46; 21:2]) are imperatives from Yahweh himself for the priestly prophet to "preach." The other two are in Micah. Micah 2:6 quotes false prophets who are ironically described as attempting to muzzle orthodox preaching by their own preaching. They were saying, אַל־תַּטִּפוּ יַטִּיפוּן לֹא־יַטִּפוּ לָאֵלֶּה, literally, " 'You shall not preach,' they preach. 'They should not preach these things.' " Micah 2:11 uses נָטַף to discredit false prophets who were only looking for more alcohol: "If a man should follow a spirit and deceive with falsehood, [saying,] 'I will preach for you [אַטִּף לְךָ] about wine and strong drink,' he would be the preacher for this people [וְהָיָה מַטִּיף הָעָם הַזֶּה]".[14]

"Against the house of Isaac" is parallel to "against Israel" in the preceding clause of 7:16. "Isaac" refers to the Northern Kingdom, as does its parallel "Israel." Amaziah would not have prohibited Amos from preaching in the Southern Kingdom of Judah. In fact, prophesying in Judah is exactly what Amaziah encouraged Amos to do (7:12).

7:17 לָכֵן כֹּה־אָמַר יְהוָה—For לָכֵן, "therefore," see the first textual note on 3:11. For the prophetic messenger formula, כֹּה אָמַר יְהוָה, "thus says Yahweh," see the first textual note on 1:3.

אִשְׁתְּךָ בָּעִיר תִּזְנֶה—Literally, "your wife in the city will be a prostitute." בָּעִיר, "in the city," is in an emphatic position preceding the verb and means "in public."[15] Amos proclaims that Amaziah's wife is going to become a public prostitute. A prostitute was as low as a woman could go vocationally, morally, and religiously. זָנָה often has the literal meaning "*be* or *act as a harlot*" (BDB, 1), and it also frequently refers to "*intercourse with other deities*, considered as harlotry, sts. [sometimes] involving actual prostitution" (BDB, 3).

In the OT, the language of harlotry is intertwined with that of idolatry; both are involved in many verses with זָנָה, for example, Ex 34:15–16; Lev 17:7; Deut 31:16; Jer 3:1; Hos 1:2; 2:7 (ET 2:5); and especially Ezekiel 16 and 23.[16] Cognate nouns are used similarly. For example, in 2 Ki 9:22 Jehu stated that Israel would have no peace as

---

13 Cf. H. Madl, "נָטַף," *TDOT* 9:395–402.

14 There is no biblical support for connecting the Hiphil of נָטַף meaning "to preach" with the physical dripping denoted by its Qal (and by its Hiphil in Amos 9:13). This is contra Wolff, who believes that the Hiphil of נָטַף is related to the "dripping" or "driveling" of saliva. He writes: "The word describes the delivery of an impassioned discourse, with drops spraying from the mouth of the speaker or his saliva freely flowing. The verb need not always have a pejorative sense; it can also be used to depict the vehement speaking of the prophet in the context of a commission from Yahweh" (*Joel and Amos*, 315, citing, for the last point, Ezek 21:2, 7 [ET 20:46; 21:2]).

15 Paul, *Amos*, 250. A similar curse of Tyre, pictured as a woman, is in Is 23:17. Deut 22:23–25 contrasts rape or fornication "in the city," בָּעִיר, with "in the field," בַּשָּׂדֶה.

16 Cf. S. Erlandsson, "זָנָה," *TDOT* 4:99–104.

long as the many "prostitutions of Jezebel" (זְנוּנֵי אִיזֶבֶל), Joram's pagan Tyrian mother, and "her sorceries" (וּכְשָׁפֶיהָ) continued. Wisdom literature warns against a "prostitute" (זוֹנָה) as a wicked and deceitful woman (Prov 6:26; 7:10; 23:27; 29:3). In the parallelism of Prov 23:27, a "prostitute" (זוֹנָה) is called a "foreign woman" (נָכְרִיָּה), meaning that she is outside both the marriage bond and the covenant community of believers in the one true God. Israel's commercial contacts brought the nation into contact with the worship of foreign gods, and so the profit idolatrous Samaria gained from commercial trade is called the fee charged by a prostitute (Micah 1:7). Nah 3:4, an oracle of judgment against Nineveh, the capital of Assyria at that time, likens the city to a prostitute who seduces other nations with idol worship and occult arts.

וּבָנֶיךָ וּבְנֹתֶיךָ בַּחֶרֶב יִפֹּלוּ—Yahweh pronounces upon the sons and daughters of Amaziah the same punishment of death "by the sword" (בַּחֶרֶב) that was forthcoming for the house of Jeroboam (בֶּחָרֶב, 7:9; see also בַּחֶרֶב in 7:11). See the commentary on 7:9 and the second textual note on 7:11. The Qal of נָפַל (here יִפֹּלוּ), "to fall," often refers to a "violent death" (BDB, 2 a).

וְאַדְמָתְךָ בַּחֶבֶל תְּחֻלָּק—The noun אֲדָמָה, "land," recurs in this and the next two clauses, in which it has different shades of meaning. It may refer to the entire world (e.g., Gen 12:3; Amos 3:2), dirt and soil (e.g., Gen 2:7; Amos 3:5), the boundaries of a country (e.g., Is 14:1), or land as a personal possession (e.g., Gen 47:23). This first time in Amos 7:17 it refers to the land that was the personal possession of Amaziah. The second and third instances both denote a country. This use of אֲדָמָה in more than one sense in one verse finds a parallel in Gen 47:26, where Joseph decreed about "the land of Egypt [אַדְמַת מִצְרַיִם]" that Pharaoh owned one fifth of it, but none of "the land of the priests [אַדְמַת הַכֹּהֲנִים]." In an agrarian society, control over the land was crucial to survival. Yet in Israel, the ultimate owner of the land was Yahweh (e.g., Lev 25:23). Whoever received a portion of the land received a portion of Yahweh's inheritance (Josh 22:24–27).

Most commonly, the verb חָלַק, "to apportion, divide, distribute," refers to giving that portion due by law or custom.[17] The Qal of חָלַק can mean "to distribute" the inheritance within a family (e.g., Prov. 17:2). The Piel is sometimes used when Joshua assigns portions of the conquered promised land to the tribes of Israel (e.g., Josh 13:7; 19:51). Elsewhere the Piel can be used when victors divide up the spoils of war (e.g., Gen 49:27; Ex 15:9; Is 9:2 [ET 9:3]; cf. Is 53:12). The Pual here, with "land" as its subject, probably includes the passive of both nuances: Amaziah's inherited land in Israel will be conquered (by the enemy "nation" in 6:14), then divided up and allotted to others from that victorious people. Compared to the transitive Qal of חָלַק, its Pual has the corresponding resultative sense: "be apportioned" (Waltke-O'Connor, § 25.3a, including example 1).

The preposition בְּ in an instrumental sense ("by means of") is prefixed to חֶבֶל, a "measuring-cord, line" (BDB, 2) or "survey line" (NKJV).

---

[17] Cf. M. Tsevat, "חָלַק II," *TDOT* 4:447–51.

וְאַתָּה עַל־אֲדָמָה טְמֵאָה תָּמוּת—While the exact adjectival phrase אֲדָמָה טְמֵאָה, "unclean land," occurs only here, similar concepts of land defilement occur in the Torah and other prophets, including Micah 2:10 and Zech 13:2 (cf. Hos 9:3). The homographic adjective and verb טָמֵא, "(to be) unclean," are most commonly employed in the context of Israel's liturgical worship life in Leviticus. It was the duty of a priest to distinguish between what was unclean and clean (Lev 10:10).[18] That which was טָמֵא had to be kept out of the presence of Yahweh. Israelites who became "unclean" needed to be purified before they could resume full life within the community of Israel in communion with Yahweh. The people had to keep the land of Israel clean because it was the place where Yahweh dwelt (Num 35:34). If the people defiled themselves by idolatry, sexual immorality, and other violations of God's laws, they would cause the land itself to become unclean so that it would vomit them out, just as it had expelled the pagan Canaanites (Lev 18:24–30; 20:22–26).

Amos prophesies that Amaziah will perish in an "unclean land," a land of pagan foreigners who do not worship the one true God of Israel and who therefore are utterly cut off from any hope of salvation. Josh 22:19 best defines the idea: "If the land [אֶרֶץ] of your possession is unclean [טְמֵאָה], cross over into the land of Yahweh's possession, where the tabernacle of Yahweh dwells [שָׁכַן־שָׁם מִשְׁכַּן יְהוָה]."[19] Yahweh's sanctifying presence is what makes the land and the people there holy (Lev 20:8; 21:15, 23; 22:9, 16, 32; see also Ezek 37:28). A land devoid of Yahweh's presence therefore must be unclean. Banishment to such a land (cf. 1 Sam 26:19; Ps 137:4) should have been especially scandalous to Amaziah, a priest, since maintaining ritual cleanness was a central part of the priestly duties mandated in the Torah (e.g., Lev 10:10–11; cf. Ezek 44:23).

וְיִשְׂרָאֵל גָּלֹה יִגְלֶה מֵעַל אַדְמָתוֹ׃—Amos repeats verbatim the second prophecy Amaziah attributed to him. See the third textual note on 7:11.

Commentary

In reading a book, special attention needs to be devoted to its opening. Rimmon-Kenan says: "Information and attitudes presented at an early stage of the text tend to encourage the reader to interpret everything in their light."[20] The book of Amos begins with a reference to an earthquake in 1:1 (שְׁנָתַיִם לִפְנֵי הָרָעַשׁ, "two years before the earthquake"), and Amos' oracles repeatedly refer to shaking and quakes caused by God (3:15; 4:11; 8:8; 9:1, 5; and in a Gospel context, the last clause of 9:13). The climactic fifth vision (9:1–4) begins with a depiction of the Lord standing beside the idolatrous Bethel altar, saying, "Strike the capital [of the pillar] so that the thresholds shake [וְיִרְעֲשׁוּ הַסִּפִּים]." The chief agent of the divine shaking of northern Israel would be Assyria (the unnamed "nation" in

---

[18] Cf. G. André and H. Ringgren, "טָמֵא," *TDOT* 5:330–42.

[19] The Cisjordan tribes said this when they discovered that the Transjordan tribes had constructed an altar apart from the tabernacle, which was then at Shiloh (Josh 22:10–12). Even though this altar was on the west side of the Jordan, the Cisjordan tribes initially considered such an altar to be a breach of the divine covenant and grounds for war. See Harstad, *Joshua*, 690–93.

[20] Rimmon-Kenan, *Narrative Fiction*, 121.

6:14), which would conquer it in 722 BC, some four decades after the ministry of Amos, fulfilling his prophecies (e.g., 5:27). About a century later (ca. 623 BC), King Josiah of Judah would destroy the main altar at Bethel (fulfilling Amos 9:1–4) as well as other idolatrous shrines (2 Ki 23:15–19). But these earth-shaking catastrophes were triggered by Yahweh's Word (3:7–8). The toppling of every false pretense in Israel continues here in 7:10–17, another passage that reverses the religious sensibilities and expectations of the people.[21]

The narrative of 7:10–17 is tied to the prophet's third vision (7:7–9) by the syntax of the first word in 7:10, וַיִּשְׁלַח, literally, "and he sent." The imperfect verb with *waw* consecutive joins the narrative to the preceding vision. A second link between the third vision and the Amos-Amaziah confrontation is in 7:11. There Amaziah accuses Amos of saying that Jeroboam will die by "the sword," thus rephrasing Yahweh's warning at the end of the vision report in 7:9 that he "will arise against the house of Jeroboam with the sword."[22] Strategically sandwiched between the third and fourth visions (7:7–9; 8:1–3) that announce "the end" (8:2) of Israel, this prose section serves as the interpretive guide for the visions, as well as for the entire book. It accentuates the prophet's themes and clarifies his overall message.

Amaziah envisions Amos to be—as Ahab viewed Elijah—a "troubler of Israel."[23] Amaziah is like the priests Eli (1 Sam 3:1–13) and Caiaphas (Jn 11:49–50), who also ironically appear to be the last people on earth to know the mind of God. As a representative of the Northern Kingdom, Amaziah cannot tolerate Amos' anti-Israel rhetoric. He seeks to ban Amos from Bethel,[24] the official but idolatrous place of worship for northern Israel, and send him back home to Tekoa. The prophet's refusal to knuckle under evokes bitter opposition and earns him the label of communal pariah.

The apostate priest Amaziah was a vigilant defender of the royal self-deception. Backed by the full weight of the unfaithful nation's state-church and

---

[21] For other dramatic reversals, see 2:9; 3:1–2; 4:4–5; 5:18–20; 5:21–27; 6:1–7; 8:9–10; and especially the Gospel reversal in 9:11–15.

[22] Stuart rightly considers 7:10–17 as properly placed in the present form of the book, and he points out how it is linked to its context in a number of ways (*Hosea–Jonah*, 369–70). See also Hubbard, *Joel and Amos*, 211. In contrast, Hayes (*Amos, the Eighth-Century Prophet*, 230–31) supposes that an early editor placed 7:10–17 in its present location in the book. He therefore discusses 7:10–17 at the end of his commentary and isolates it from the setting in which it is presently placed. Similarly, Soggin, *The Prophet Amos*, 125–33, incorrectly places his discussion of this section near the end of his commentary.

[23] The phrase עֹכֵר יִשְׂרָאֵל, "troubler of Israel," occurs twice in the OT. The phrase is applied appropriately to Achan (1 Chr 2:7; see other forms of the verb עָכַר in Josh 6:18; 7:25) because his disobedience caused the Israelites to be defeated the first time they attacked Ai (Joshua 7). The second occurrence of the phrase is in 1 Ki 18:17, where Ahab wrongly applied it to the faithful prophet Elijah because he opposed the king and his state-sponsored idolatry.

[24] For Bethel, see the second textual note and the commentary on 3:14 and the first textual note on 4:4 as well as the commentary on 7:13.

king, he strove to preserve the status quo that ignored Yahweh's will. Amos, on the other hand, was a spokesman of Yahweh, the zealous advocate of divine justice and righteousness. Committed to the discharge of his divinely assigned task, Amos stood outside the central power structures of the nation and delivered a message that condemned and announced the destruction of all of Israel. No wonder Amaziah opposed him! Israel's greatest Prophet, Jesus, recalls how Israel had rejected the prophets God had sent them in the OT era (Mt 21:33–46; 22:1–6; Lk 13:34), and these are apt depictions of Amaziah's treatment of Amos.

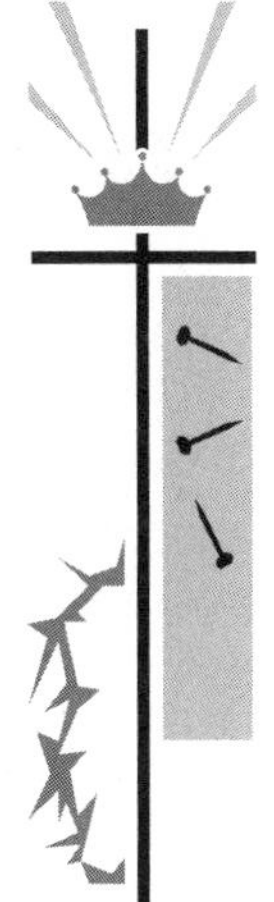

The uncredentialed and unconnected Amos confronts Bethel's power brokers and shatters their entrenched assumptions. He refuses to allow the public square to remain naked.[25] The Lion roars here as well.[26] Amos not only denounces the faithless empire, he also models a different way to live: deep compassion for the small (cf. 7:2, 5), undeserving people of Israel, who had been led astray. Amos says, in effect, "If you are tired of what the empire has to offer, I invite you into a different way of life where everything is backward and upside down. The last are first and the first are last, the poor ones are blessed and the mighty are cast from their thrones."[27] Jesus Christ came to announce the coming of this radical kingdom (Mk 1:15; Lk 1:52–53), and through his own ministry, death, and resurrection, he fulfilled the mission of all the OT prophets, including that of Amos.[28]

The narrative in Amos 7:10–17 is couched in the third person, even though it was written by Amos. This is common style in the Torah and OT Prophets,[29] as

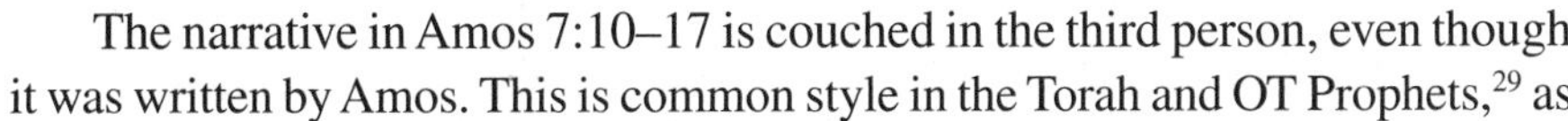

[25] See Richard John Neuhaus, *The Naked Public Square: Religion and Democracy in America* (Grand Rapids: Eerdmans, 1984). By "naked public square," Neuhaus means public discourse that has no Judeo-Christian voice.

[26] For Yahweh as the Lion who roars through his prophet, see the beginning of the introduction and 1:1; 3:4, 8, 12; 5:19.

[27] These reversals characterize the theology of the cross. Compare the condemning reversal in 6:1–7, where the "first," the arrogant and powerful people, will be "first" into exile, and the Gospel reversal in 9:11–15, where God promises to raise up the fallen tabernacle of David and restore a believing remnant from the nations.

[28] The persecution of Amos by the apostate religious establishment of Israel in his day, represented by the priest Amaziah, typifies the Jewish leaders' rejection of Jesus as well as his passion. Yet the vindication of Amos' prophetic ministry by the ensuing "earthquake" (1:1) prefigures the victorious death and resurrection of Christ, which were accompanied by earthquakes (Mt 27:50–53; 28:2; cf. Acts 16:26). See the explanation of the parallels between Amos and Christ in the beginning of the introduction. For the earthquake, see the sixth textual note and the commentary on 1:1. See also the commentary on 9:11–15, which prophesies the resurrection of the tabernacle of David, the restoration of a believing remnant from Israel and the Gentiles, and the eschatological new creation.

[29] For example, Moses speaks of himself in the third person throughout Exodus–Numbers. Isaiah and Jeremiah are among the OT prophets who begin their books with third-person references to themselves. See the discussion and the ancient Near Eastern references to this literary technique in Niehaus, "Amos," 460.

well as in other ancient Near Eastern literature. The narrative is a prophetic confrontation story[30] that takes place at Bethel[31] and is presented in four parts:

1. Amaziah the priest reports to Jeroboam ben Joash, accusing Amos of conspiracy (7:10–11).
2. Amaziah orders Amos to cease his prophetic activity at Bethel (7:12–13).
3. Amos responds with his *apologia*: he is Yahweh's called messenger (7:14–15).
4. Amos concludes with an oracle of judgment against Amaziah, his family, and Israel (7:16–17).

Miller presents this narrative as a conflict between the different perspectives of Amos and Amaziah:[32]

Amaziah's Perspective	*Amos' Perspective*
Jeroboam ben Joash is king.	Yahweh is King.
"Thus says Amos" (7:11).	"Thus says Yahweh" (7:17).
"By the sword Jeroboam will die" (7:11).	Yahweh "will arise against the house of Jeroboam with the sword" (7:9).
"Amos has conspired ..." (7:10).	"Yahweh took me, ... and Yahweh said to me, 'Go, prophesy' " (7:15).
Amos should prophesy in *Judah* (7:12).	"Yahweh said to me, 'Go, prophesy to *my people Israel*' " (7:15).
Amaziah says to Amos, "Flee quickly" (7:12).	"Yahweh said to me, '*Go*, prophesy to my people Israel' " (7:15).

Which perspective will Israel and its leadership choose? Do they see themselves as part of a typical ancient Near Eastern city-state in which the king and priesthood are supreme or as the covenant people of Yahweh, who reigns supreme? Should the aristocrats seek to preserve their own safety, or should they be concerned with the will and ways of Yahweh? Are they going to remain comfortable fleecing the poor (e.g., 2:6–7; 4:1; 5:11; 8:4, 6)? Will they opt for the "status-quo loving" Amaziah or the "boat-rocker" Amos and his roaring God?

The confrontation has several connections with the ripples caused by the healing of the crippled beggar in Acts 3. After Peter and John were charged no longer to speak in the name of Jesus (Acts 4:17–18), they responded, "For we

---

[30] Sweeney, *Isaiah 1–39*, 518. Sweeney writes of this genre: "Constituent elements include: (1) the deliverance of the message by the prophet; (2) the confrontation by the opposition, who denies the validity of the message or the authority of the prophet; and (3) the punishment of the opponent that vindicates the prophet." The genre appears also in, for example, Jeremiah 26–28; 36.

[31] Other confrontations occur in the OT between a prophet and a king (or his representative) at a worship site. See, for example, 1 Ki 18:17–40 and Jeremiah 26 and 36.

[32] Miller, "The Prophetic Critique of Kings," 531.

cannot but speak of the things we have seen and heard" (Acts 4:20). Following meditation upon Psalm 2 (Acts 4:23–30), the entire church was filled with the Holy Spirit and "spoke the Word of God with boldness [μετὰ παρρησίας]" (Acts 4:31).[33] More healings brought more arrests (Acts 5:15–18). An angel released the apostles from prison, and because Peter and the other apostles spoke about Jesus, they were brought before the Sanhedrin (Acts 5:19–28). When asked to explain why they had not heeded the earlier command not to teach about Jesus, they replied, "We must obey God rather than men" (Acts 5:29). The chapter ends with Acts 5:42: "and every day, in the temple and from house to house, they did not stop teaching and proclaiming the Good News that Jesus is the Christ." The courage of the early church is the same boldness reflected by Amos. Both were compelled to stand up for the truth of God's Word.

It is as though Amos, in trying to be a Good Samaritan (cf. Lk 10:25–37), realized that the Jericho road itself had to be transformed so that people wouldn't continue to get beaten and robbed. The prophet believed that the path from Jericho to Jerusalem had to be destroyed and rebuilt (cf. Is 40:3–4; Lk 3:4–5) so that the people could come to God—and he to them. The system producing broken people had to be changed. This is the burden of Amos' book, and this is the reason he confronted the priest Amaziah at the apostate shrine in Bethel.

Amaziah Accuses Amos of Conspiracy against Jeroboam (7:10–11)

7:10 Amaziah is called "the priest of Bethel"[34] (כֹּהֵן בֵּית־אֵל), presumably meaning that he was the head of the local priestly hierarchy.[35] OT priests were to be guardians of Israel's sacred times, places, and traditions. They were to view life as "organized along structural lines emanating from the Temple."[36] It was their responsibility to offer proper sacrifices to Yahweh, to teach and apply the Torah in matters of ritual holiness, and to make juridical decisions at the central sanctuary (Deut 17:8–13). The Torah assumes that while the priests carried out these tasks of ministry, they would also support the state institution, which was to govern righteously on behalf of God. But in northern Israel, both the priesthood and the state had defected from Yahweh's Word.

Having heard the alarming pronouncements from Amos, Amaziah the priest sends a message to the king that warns of a conspiracy. "Israel" when it is connected in Amos with a qualifying word or phrase, as here in "the house of Israel,"

---

[33] The noun παρρησία appears five times in Acts (2:29; 4:13, 29, 31; 28:31) while the verb (παρρησιάζομαι) appears seven times (9:27–28; 13:46; 14:3; 18:26; 19:8; 26:26).

[34] Bethel is an ancient Yahwistic site linked both to Abraham (Gen 12:8; 13:3) and Jacob (e.g., Gen 28:19; 31:13; 35:1). See the second textual note and the commentary on Amos 3:14, the first textual note on 4:4, and the commentary on 7:13.

[35] He may be compared and contrasted with named priests who presumably were the high priest of the tabernacle or Jerusalem temple, including Eli at Shiloh (1 Samuel 1–4) and Abiathar and Zadok at Jerusalem (2 Sam 8:17; 1 Ki 2:26–28, 35).

[36] Neusner, *The Way of Torah*, 42.

probably refers to both the north and the south.[37] Although Amaziah's major concern was the north, the south was a vassal of the north at this time,[38] so he recognizes that Amos' words are having a negative impact all over the promised land. Nothing in Amos' previous oracles in the book suggests that he is involved in an organized revolt. Nonetheless, Amaziah has ample cause for suspicion. Prophets had instigated rebellion against two previous Israelite dynasties, resulting in their deposition (1 Ki 11:29–12:24; 19:15–18; 2 Ki 9:1–37).

Not only has this outsider Amos predicted a violent end to the reigning dynasty (Amos 7:9), he has also challenged the efficacy of Israel's syncretistic worship life (4:4–5; 5:5, 21–23), thereby undercutting the two mainstays of national existence. Were that not enough, Amos has also announced that Israel's armies would be defeated (5:3), its cities looted (6:8), its idolatrous high places and sanctuaries destroyed (7:9), and its people sent into exile (e.g., 6:7). Amaziah has had enough! "The land is not able to contain/endure all of his words" (7:10). The priest implicitly compares Israel to a giant vat, filled to the point of bursting with the relentless flow of Amos' threats.[39] The prophet is like Jesus, whose new wine bursts the old wineskins of Israel (Mt 9:17).

As this prophet versus priest narrative unfolds, it needs to be kept in mind that according to the Torah, true prophets and faithful priests were to have complementary roles as both built up the faith of Israel. Some prophets were also priests by lineage.[40] For example, Jeremiah was born into a priestly family that resided in Anathoth, a small town not far from Jerusalem (Jer 1:1). This priestly house traced its roots to Abiathar, who was exiled to the ancestral dwelling of Anathoth for having supported Adonijah rather than Solomon (1 Ki 2:26–27). Ezekiel was a priest as well (Ezek 1:3), again as a result of his birth. Zechariah was another prophet born into a priestly family. His genealogy, "Zechariah son of Berechiah son of Iddo" (Zech 1:1), is also attested in Nehemiah's list of priestly families (Neh 12:16).

The connection between prophets and priests often is stronger than simply a matter of lineage. In the book of Joel, the prophet functions as an intercessor like a priest. When locusts attack (Joel 1:4), the prophet summons the people to engage in ritual lamentation at the temple (Joel 1:13–14). Joel then speaks words

---

[37] Andersen and Freedman, *Amos*, 117 (see also pp. 98–99). They write: "With some amazement we ascribe the usage here to the double kingdom as an appropriate arena for this supposed conspiracy instead of the northern kingdom alone" (p. 117).

[38] With only a few short exceptions, Judah was Israel's vassal for most of the time between the reigns of Omri and Pekah (885–732 BC). See "The Historical Setting of the Book of Amos" in the introduction.

[39] Andersen and Freedman write (*Amos*, 793):

> The words [of Amos] cannot be neutralized or contained; they burst the bonds and restraints, and work in the city and the state, bringing about the reality of which they speak. They are self-fulfilling because they have the power to produce results in conformity with their contents. Once said they have a life of their own, and the outcome is already inherent in their contents.

[40] Cf. Petersen, *The Prophetic Literature*, 7.

that the priest would have spoken to Yahweh (Joel 1:19). In response to the people's calls for help, Yahweh speaks through Joel, affirming that the prayers of the people have been heard (Joel 2:18–27). In all of this, Joel functions very much like a priest. Moreover, Habakkuk proclaims that "Yahweh is in his holy temple" (Hab 2:20) and then proceeds to pray a psalm (Hab 3:1–19). Haggai is concerned about rebuilding Yahweh's temple. Malachi envisions genuine worship: " 'In every place incense will be brought to my name, and a pure offering, because my name will be great among the nations,' says Yahweh of armies" (Mal 1:11). Prophets and priests were to oppose one another only when one party had defected from his divine calling. In the case of Amos and Amaziah, it was the priest who had deviated from his office by serving at the idolatrous alternative altar at Bethel and by opposing the Word of Yahweh spoken by Amos.

7:11 Amaziah's words "for thus says *Amos*" (כִּי־כֹה֙ אָמַ֣ר עָמ֔וֹס) ignore or even deny that *Yahweh* is speaking through the prophet. The normal prophetic utterance begins "thus says Yahweh" (כֹּה אָמַר יהוה, e.g., 1:3, 6, 9). The priest makes it appear that Amos is speaking on his own accord rather than as a spokesman for Yahweh. He wants to construe Amos as a political threat and not an authoritative theological voice that the king might be willing to tolerate or even believe. Amaziah "de-theologizes" Amos' message, inferring that the prophet is speaking only for himself. This explains, in part, why Amos provides his *apologia* in 7:14–15 as well as in 3:3–8. He has been in Yahweh's counsel (3:7). He has heard the Lion roar (1:2; 3:8; cf. 3:4, 12; 5:19).

Amaziah not only belittles Amos by denying that his message is from Yahweh, his quote of Amos is not a word-for-word citation of the prophet's oracle in 7:9. Yahweh himself had stated, "I will arise against the house of Jeroboam with the sword" (7:9). The priest changes the wording to this: "for thus says Amos: 'By the sword Jeroboam will die' " (7:11). Amaziah narrows down the judgment specifically to the person of the king. The term "sword" frequently functions as a metonymy for a violent death or death in war (e.g., Is 1:20; Jer 14:15).

As a symbol for the status quo, Amaziah also "conveniently" forgets to mention the reason for Yahweh's judgment: Israel's economic, sexual, ethical, spiritual, and legal crimes. Amaziah also omits Amos' words about the destruction of Israel's sanctuaries in 7:9, as well as the prophet's threat of imminent exile (e.g., 5:27), which is a covenant curse (Deut 28:64–68).[41] Amaziah feels he must place a gag order upon Amos as soon as possible (cf. Amos 2:12). Jesus warns his disciples that people will speak "all kinds of evil against you falsely on my account" (Mt 5:11). Amaziah's twisting of Amos' words is an OT example of that kind of persecution, the kind to which Jesus referred when he said, "For in this way they persecuted the prophets who were before you" (Mt 5:12).

---

[41] Amos warns of exile also in 4:2–3; 5:5, 27; 6:7; 9:4.

The only report concerning the death of Jeroboam ben Joash is in 2 Ki 14:29, which states: "Jeroboam rested with his fathers, with the kings of Israel. And Zechariah his son reigned in his place." Nevertheless, the house—or dynasty—of Jeroboam did die by the sword (2 Ki 15:8–12), fulfilling the Word of Yahweh uttered through Amos.

Amos 7:11 presents Amaziah "as an expert in diplomacy and conflict management; no doubt such skills had helped him to attain his position as the number one person at the number one religious establishment in the country."[42] Everything about him reeks of a veneered, cosmetic faith. He is enmeshed in public relations, image building, and salesmanship. In reporting the contents of Amos' preaching, he conveniently avoids the sticky issues of idolatry, unrighteousness, oppression, poverty, and social injustice, while portraying Amos as a religious fanatic. The priest is the consummate religious leader who has reduced Yahweh's call to ensuring his own job efficiency and job security. He does not recognize that he has been visited by a prophet (cf. Lk 19:41–44). Amaziah speaks what people want to hear; Amos speaks the truth that Yahweh wants them to hear. Jeremiah's rebuke of the priests in his day is a fitting description of Amaziah: "The priests do not say, 'Where is Yahweh?' Those who handle the Torah do not know me. The shepherds have rebelled against me" (Jer 2:8). Amaziah is self-serving, self-legitimating, and in the end, self-destroying (Amos 7:17).

Amaziah Orders Amos to Cease Prophesying at Bethel (7:12–13)

7:12 "Sent" in 7:10 assumes that Amaziah has sent a letter to the king. A messenger from Bethel carrying the note would need to travel about twenty-five miles to reach Jeroboam ben Joash, who would presumably be living in Samaria, the nation's capital. The king's response would take days to receive. It may be best to assume that Amaziah does not wait for a reply but takes matters into his own hands and immediately commands Amos to cross the border and return to Tekoa in Judah.[43]

The fact that Amaziah has banned Amos from Bethel is indication enough that his presence is deemed a mortal threat to the empire. In a similar way, Jeremiah is evicted from the Jerusalem temple for speaking the Word of Yahweh

---

[42] Limburg, *Hosea–Micah*, 118.

[43] Regarding Jeroboam's silence in the text, Paul asks these pertinent questions (*Amos*, 240):

> Did he find no reason to trouble himself about such an incident and therefore refrained from sending a reply? Did Amaziah act on his own authority even before he received an answer? Or was he carrying out a royal order on the authority of the king, whose response was omitted from the text? Because there is no way of decisively deciding the issue, it must remain an enigma.

As other situations where a king did not confront a prophet face to face, Stuart cites 1 Ki 22:8, where Ahab does not desire a meeting with Micaiah ben Imlah, and Jer 36:23–24, where Jehoiakim ignores Jeremiah by burning a scroll of the prophet's words. Stuart writes: "A king could not risk appearing petty and insecure by responding officially to prophetic threats" (*Hosea–Jonah*, 376).

(Jer 36:5). But removing Yahweh's prophets will not silence Yahweh. His Word endures forever (Is 40:8; 1 Pet 1:25).

The phrase בְּרַח־לְךָ (Amos 7:12) appears also in Num 24:10–11, where Balak says to Balaam, "I summoned you to curse my enemies, and instead you have blessed them these three times. Now flee [בְּרַח־לְךָ֣] to your own place." Balaam and Amos are similar in that both prophets deliver oracles from Yahweh that are unpopular, speaking in places not their homeland. The expression בְּרַח־לְךָ appears to be "the correct manner and proper protocol for the deportation of a VIP (very important prophet)."[44]

The command "eat food there" may mean "to earn a living," and Amaziah may be implying that Amos is a professional prophet, a person who makes his living by issuing prophetic oracles. Amos should go and get paid in Judah! True prophets were sometimes remunerated (e.g., 1 Sam 9:7–8; 2 Ki 4:42). Within the timeframe of the writing prophets, false prophets and prophetesses accepted payment for their oracles (Ezek 13:17–19; Micah 3:5, 11), yet there is no indication that Amaziah believes Amos is a false prophet. The priest simply does not want Amos to deliver his oracles in Bethel. Two times in Amos 7:12, Amaziah indicates that Amos may continue his prophesying "there" (שָׁם), in Judah. Bethel and northern Israel are off limits.

Amaziah's response is similar to that of Pashhur upon hearing Jeremiah speak almost two centuries later. Jeremiah delivers his message in the Jerusalem temple, and Pashhur, its chief administrative officer, notices the prophet's seditious oracles. Actually he listens to them (Jer 20:1) without truly hearing (Jer 19:15). Pashhur does not tolerate Jeremiah's threat that Yahweh is against Jerusalem and that it will suffer irrevocable consequences for its unfaithfulness (Jer 19:14–15). Pashhur then strikes Jeremiah and puts him in stocks at the upper Benjamin Gate of the temple (Jer 20:2). As the guardian of the state and its sacred precincts, Pashhur lashes out against this unofficial "outsider." Once released from prison, Jeremiah—reminiscent of Amos against Amaziah—delivers a scathing rebuke. He renames Pashhur "terror all around" and then explains the symbolic action: Yahweh will make Pashhur a "terror" to himself and others. The king of Babylon will plunder and pillage Judah and Pashhur. He and his fellow priests will be exiled to Babylon, where he will eventually die (Jer 20:3–6).

Israel's military victories (Amos 6:13) prompted the unfaithful nation to say, "Yahweh is with us" (see 5:14) and "Evil will not overtake, nor will it confront us" (9:10). Business was good, even if it was a bit underhanded (8:4–6). Free time was spent at parties (6:1–6), drinking (4:1), or simply kicking back in luxurious homes (3:15). They thought that even better days were ahead, for the Day of Yahweh was drawing nigh (5:18, 20). In such a context, they thought that a call to repent was not needed. In fact, such preaching seemed unpatriotic.

---

[44] Paul, *Amos*, 242.

No wonder Amos was reported to the authorities and Amaziah attempted to run him out of town. Quite possibly he could have been imprisoned or killed.[45]

7:13 Amaziah's injunction "at Bethel *you shall never again* prophesy" (לֹא־תוֹסִיף עוֹד) needs to be interpreted in light of Yahweh's twofold declaration, "*I will never again* forgive him" (לֹא־אוֹסִיף עוֹד, 7:8; 8:2) in the two visions that frame this encounter. Amaziah wants "never again" to listen to Amos, which expresses the unbelief of the obdurate nation, which in turn is the reason Yahweh says that he will "never again" forgive the people. When Amaziah breaks off his relationship with Amos, he is at the same time ending his relationship with Yahweh. Jesus says, "He who listens to you listens to me, and he who rejects you rejects me, and he who rejects me rejects him who sent me" (Lk 10:16; cf. Mt 10:40; Mk 9:37).

Luther comments:

> This account is well worth noting. In it one can see what … ungodliness is and what it thinks of the Word of God, how it despises everything that is of God in order to keep its own things safe. Here the wicked priest Amaziah mocks and despises the pious prophet Amos, a contemptible, lowly shepherd. So he urges the king not to believe the prophecy of Amos. He says that it is a lie since Amos indeed speaks against the king and against the kingdom which they were very sure God had instituted. This is how the wicked blind and mislead each other with their wickedness, as the apostle says in 2 Tim. 3:13: "Evil men and impostors will go on from bad to worse, deceivers and deceived." He now adds the wicked doctrine of the wicked priest.[46]

Amaziah refers to Bethel as "the sanctuary of the king" (מִקְדַּשׁ־מֶלֶךְ הוּא) and "the house of the kingdom" (וּבֵית מַמְלָכָה הוּא, Amos 7:13). The shrine was, in effect, the religious arm of the state, an extension of the monarchy and a powerful instrument of its policies. It was the engine that drove Israel's dominant ideology.[47] The phrases come close to meaning something like "Israel's state shrine." At this place the only words tolerated are those that support the status quo.

By claiming that the shrine at Bethel is akin to "the national cathedral," Amaziah connects the state with Israel's worship life. Bethel amounts to the king's personal chapel, and its priests are his employees who serve his will. This status was conferred a century and a half before the time of Amos, in about

---

[45] Andersen and Freedman write (*Amos*, 734):

> The encounter was not simply a violent argument between two headstrong men who differed on matters of local propriety and protocol. It was the irreconcilable conflict between opposing spokesmen for the one God: the primate of the leading sanctuary in the north and the undocumented visionary from the south. In fact, the one speaks for himself and the interests of those who share power and prestige ostensibly in the name of and for the sake of Yahweh, but not in actuality, while the other speaks for the same deity but out of a genuine experience in vision and dialogue.

[46] Luther, "Lectures on Amos" (AE 18:176).

[47] Monarchial control of the state religion in the north had been the policy since its inception; see 1 Ki 12:26–33; 16:26, 30–33; 18:4, 19.

920 BC, by Jeroboam ben Nebat, following the breakup of the Davidic empire (1 Ki 12:26–33). Although Yahweh had promised Jeroboam that he would make Jeroboam's dynasty as enduring as David's if Jeroboam would walk in his ways (1 Ki 11:38), Jeroboam thought that he needed to secure his subjects' allegiance and presumed that this would not occur as long as northerners continued to go south to worship at the true temple in Jerusalem. He felt that the glory of Zion had to be neutralized.

Toward that end, he appropriated the ancient holy site at Bethel and established another worship center at the other end of his kingdom in Dan. In those places he built new temples, erected golden calves, reorganized the religious calendar, and replaced the hereditary Levitical priesthood with a different priestly order loyal to himself. Northern Israel's first king created a false but effective alternative to the established worship in Jerusalem. In place of the Solomonic temple, the incarnational dwelling place of Yahweh, with its appointed festivals and pilgrimages, the Northern Kingdom had a separate religious structure of its own, closely identified with the new dynasty. Because of its own religious staff, liturgy, and history, the apostate north felt that southern outsiders like Amos were neither needed nor heeded.

Amos prophesied against Bethel in about 760 BC. Nearly a century and a half later, in about 623 BC, Yahweh used Josiah as his agent of judgment to demolish the altar and high place at Bethel (2 Ki 23:15–16).

Amos' *Apologia*: Yahweh Called Him to Prophesy (7:14–15)

7:14 A "hireling" (Jn 10:13) flees and abandons the flock to the wolf because he does not care for the sheep. But a true shepherd will remain and faithfully speak on behalf of the sheep that are harassed and helpless. Amos is this kind of shepherd; he preaches for the sake of those few who may repent and believe. He speaks up for the poor, the crushed, and the needy in Israel. He will not leave; here he stands! Amos' response to Amaziah in 7:14–15 is the prophet's claim that his message is genuine despite his lack of prior status as a prophet or a prophetic associate. Because of his divine call, he is not about to go away or back down. Amos will not be muzzled, even by the priest giving orders with the royal authority of the king.

Amos is not concerned about public opinion or the estimation of the incumbent priest and king. His sole concern is the commission he has received from Yahweh. In defending his office, he uses words that constitute the best-known *crux interpretum* of the book. The prophet's description of himself in 7:14–15, which lies at the heart of this narrative, is "one of the most crucial and obscure passages in all the prophetic literature."[48] Wolff states the issue as follows:

> The question [is] whether the nominal clauses in 7:14 refer only to the prophet's past, or whether they intend to say something about his present status as well. This is a heated discussion because it includes the question of the

[48] Blenkinsopp, *A History of Prophecy in Israel*, 33.

self-understanding of Amos, and thereby also the problem of distinguishing between independent and officially sanctioned prophetism.[49]

Part of the reason why Amos eschews the traditional title of a prophet is because such an institutional association could be a sellout to the corrupt state in the same way that the institutional northern priesthood was. He would not want to be associated with the false prophets who gratuitously supported the kings of northern Israel, such as those court prophets who are contrasted with the true prophet Micaiah in 1 Kings 22. See also Micah 3:5–7, 11. For later Judean false prophets and prophetesses, see Jeremiah 28 and Ezekiel 13.[50] When Amaziah confronts him, Amos takes the opportunity to distance himself from any prior association with a prophet or his disciples. Moreover, he asserts that he makes his living through agriculture, so when he speaks on Yahweh's behalf it is not for material gain.[51]

The prophet's Hebrew words in Amos 7:14 consist only of nouns, participles, particles, conjunctions, and the threefold repetition of the independent personal pronoun "I" (אָנֹכִי). There is no verb nor explicit indication of whether Amos is talking about the past or the present.[52] English must supply verbal forms with a tense that indicates what period of his life Amos is describing, either his past vocation or his present calling. If the first clause were translated "I *am* not a prophet," referring to Amos' current status, it would contradict statements that Amos *is* a prophet (e.g., 1:1; 3:7–8), as well as his prophetic speech throughout the book. Moreover, it would conflict with what he says in the next verse, namely that Yahweh commanded him to "go, prophesy" (לֵךְ הִנָּבֵא, 7:15). Amos affirms that "the Lord Yahweh does not do something unless he reveals his counsel to his servants the prophets" (3:7), and he engages in various prophetic roles throughout the book. Amos receives visions, proclaims messages of doom and also sermons of salvation (notably 9:11–15), intercedes for people (7:2, 5), faces this challenge to his prophetic calling (7:10–17), reports what he is told by Yahweh, and calls people to repentance and faith.

Therefore the best way to translate the clause is this: "I *was* not a prophet, nor *was* I a son [disciple] of a prophet." This agrees with the LXX's twofold use of the imperfect verb ἤμην, "I was," in 7:14, and it also comports well with the context, where Amos recalls his occupation before be became a prophet.

Amos "did not go to prophet school, take seminars on how to be a prophet, or join the guild of practicing prophets."[53] Amos essentially is saying to Amaziah,

---

[49] Wolff, *Joel and Amos*, 312.

[50] For an exposition of false prophets and prophetesses in Ezekiel, see Hummel, *Ezekiel 1–20*, 364–77.

[51] Compare Zech 13:4–5: "On that day the prophets will be ashamed, each because of his vision when he prophesies. They will not put on a [prophet's] garment of hair in order to deceive. He will say, 'I am not a prophet. I am a man who works the ground.' "

[52] GKC, § 141 f, states this about Hebrew noun clauses: "To what period of time the statement applies must be inferred from the context."

[53] Simundson, *Hosea, Joel, Amos, Obadiah, Jonah, Micah*, 219.

"I'm not prophesying for profit, nor did any other prophet teach me to prophesy. Your comment about earning a living back in Judah is not pertinent and will not succeed in getting rid of me." Andersen and Freedman suggest: "By distancing himself from professional prophets and prophetic guilds Amos reveals himself as a lone figure, one who is unclassifiable, but with a unitary focus and guided by a personal vision."[54] Paul writes:

> He [Amos] is also asserting that his present prophetic activity is due entirely to his being selected by the Lord, who commanded him to address northern Israel. Thus, although he formerly had no connections with any prophets or prophetic guilds, he now is a prophet of Yahweh, and Yahweh's authority supersedes Amaziah's.[55]

Limburg notes that "by the time of Jeremiah, 'prophet' seems to have become a tainted word, since those who bore that office were often ungodly and immoral (Jer. 23:9–[40]), lackeys, hangers-on, and yes-men who spoke only soothing words of comfort (Jer. 23:17)."[56] Probably with such false prophets in mind, Amos makes the statement "I was not a prophet." Amos is not on the payroll of the king or his royal temple; he has no financial reason to engage in prophecy. Amos also identifies himself as a farmer and worker, the kind of person often pictured in the book as oppressed (2:6–7; 5:11–12; 8:4–6), not as an aristocrat, the kind of person often portrayed as an oppressor.[57] Amos' call was somewhat like that of Elisha, who abandoned his career in agriculture to assist Elijah (1 Ki 19:19–21).

Gregory the Great includes Amos 7:14–15 in his reflections on the work of the Holy Spirit:

> How good it is to raise up eyes of faith to the power of this worker, the Holy Spirit, and to look here and there at our ancestors in the Old and New Testaments. With the eyes of my faith open, I gaze on David, on Amos, on Daniel, on Peter, on Paul, on Matthew—and I am filled with a desire to behold the nature of this worker, the Holy Spirit. But I fall short. The Spirit filled a boy who played upon the harp, and made him a psalmist; on a shepherd and herdsman who pruned sycamore trees, and made him a prophet; on a child given to abstinence, and made him a judge of his elders; on a fisherman, and made him a preacher; on one who persecuted the church, and made him the teacher of the Gentiles; on a tax collector, and made him an Evangelist. What a skilled worker this Spirit is! There is no question of delay in learning what the Spirit teaches us. No sooner does the Spirit touch our minds in regard to anything than we are taught; the Spirit's very touch is teaching. The Spirit

---

54 Andersen and Freedman, *Amos*, 790.

55 Paul, *Amos*, 247.

56 Limburg, *Hosea–Micah*, 117.

57 The oppressors in Amos include royal officials (3:9–15), judges (5:10–12), rich women (4:1), military leaders (6:13), and merchants (2:6–8; 8:4–6). For Amos' profession, see the commentary on "who was among the sheep breeders from Tekoa" in 1:1. Cf. Giles, "A Note on the Vocation of Amos in 7:14," and Dearman, *Property Rights in the Eighth-Century Prophets*, 18–33.

changes the human heart in a moment, filling it with light. Suddenly we are no longer what we were; suddenly we are something we never used to be.[58]

Amaziah does not perceive Amos' divine calling. By rejecting Amos, he loses what Jesus later offers: "Whoever receives a prophet in the name of a prophet will receive a prophet's reward" (Mt 10:41). Those who receive Amos and his message find reprieve (Amos 7:3, 6; 9:11–15); those on the side of Amaziah find no mercy.

7:15 In 7:15 Amos continues his defense of his office. Just as the apostle Paul defended his apostolic office (e.g., Acts 22:1–23:11; Gal 1:11–2:14) for the sake of the Gospel he preached (e.g., Gal 1:6–10), Amos is not concerned about himself, but about his audience's credence in the divine message he speaks. Since he speaks Yahweh's Word, his hearers should believe his preaching, repent, believe, and be saved.

Amos' call suggests that he stands in the same line as the great leaders of Israel, David and Moses. When Amos says, literally, "Yahweh took me from behind the sheep" (וַיִּקָּחֵנִי יְהוָה מֵאַחֲרֵי הַצֹּאן), his claim connects him to Moses (Ex 3:1) and David (2 Sam 7:8).[59] A prophet's connection to Moses demonstrates that his ministry is legitimate (see Deut 18:15–20). These allusions to Moses and David suggest that Amos, with no thought of personal advancement or motivation, also responded to a spontaneous call by Yahweh to serve in an authoritative capacity. In this way, Amos 7:14–15 employs a genre that could be titled "the commission of a prophet."[60]

Just as God sent leaders to Israel in Moses, David, and now Amos—all former shepherds—so the new Israel is led by the greatest Shepherd—the Good Shepherd, Jesus the Christ, God the Son (Jn 10:11, 14). Jesus is the definitive paradigm for all the true prophets who preceded him and all the faithful ministers of the Gospel who follow him. The Christ eschewed the apostate religious societies of Israel in his day and denounced them for their hypocrisy, lack of compassion, and greed (e.g., Matthew 23). He gave his life as the sacrificial offering that enables the sheep of both Israel and Gentiles to be incorporated by grace into God's flock (Jn 10:11, 15–18, fulfilling Amos 9:11–12).

---

58 Gregory the Great, *Forty Gospel Homilies*, 30, quoted in Ferreiro, *The Twelve Prophets*, ACCS 14:109–10.

59 Stuart writes (*Hosea–Jonah*, 377):

> Since the offices of king and prophet were legitimately only by divine election (Deut 17:15; 18:15) and since David and Amos were both involved in sheep raising, it is quite possible that Amos consciously intended for Amaziah to see the similarity. Israelites had once accepted a Judean as their king, recognizing his divine appointment (2 Sam 5:1–3).

See also Ps 78:70–71, where the same verb used in Amos 7:15, לָקַח, "to take," denotes Yahweh's choice of David.

60 Sweeney, *Isaiah 1–39*, 516, defines the genre that he terms "commission" as "an authoritative charge given by a superior to a subordinate." Other OT examples of a call into the holy ministry or to continue that work include Ex 3:1–10; 1 Ki 12:22–24; 19:15–16; 21:17–19; Isaiah 6; Jeremiah 1; and Ezekiel 1–3.

It was *Yahweh*—whom Amos mentions twice in this verse—who seized the prophet and charged him to go and prophesy to "my people Israel." Yahweh still calls them by that covenant phrase, yet it does not exempt them from judgment; see his use of the same phrase in 7:8 and 8:2, where he declares he will never again forgive them. In Amos when "Israel" is qualified by a term such as "my people" (or "the house of" or "the sons/children of" or "virgin"), the phrase probably refers to all twelve tribes. Thus Amos' call is to both the Northern and Southern Kingdoms.[61] In this aspect Amos is no different from his contemporaries. Other eighth-century prophets, including Hosea, Micah, and Isaiah, likewise received oracles for both the north and the south.[62] They considered the destinies of both nations to be bound up with each other, as together they comprised the people Yahweh had redeemed from Egypt and established as his covenant people in the land. Yahweh's continuing history with his people involved both. Moreover, even the Gentile nations fall within the scope of Yahweh's judgment (1:3–2:3) and also his messianic plan of salvation (9:12).

2 Chr 16:9 states: "As for Yahweh, his eyes range throughout the whole earth to strengthen them whose hearts are fully his." Yahweh's search within the ranks of the false northern court prophets was in vain, so he chose a herdsman/farmer from Tekoa named Amos. Amos might have asked something like, "Who is adequate for these things?" (2 Cor 2:16). But as this confrontation with Amaziah demonstrates, Amos could also affirm with Paul, "We are not like the many who are peddling the Word of God, but [we preach] from sincerity, from God" (2 Cor 2:17).

Amos' Oracle of Judgment against Amaziah (7:16–17)

7:16 Amos does not flinch. The neutral preposition "prophesy *to* [אֶל] my people Israel" in 7:15 is replaced here by the repeated adversarial preposition: Amaziah tries to prohibit Amos from carrying out his call to "prophesy *against* [עַל] Israel … preach *against* [עַל] the house of Isaac." Amos' first two visions (7:1–3 and 7:4–6) indicate a period in his ministry when Amos preached "to" Israel and interceded for the people, and Yahweh relented from executing judgment against them. But with the nation's lack of repentance, the message became more confrontational. In the third (7:7–9) and fourth (8:1–3) visions and in this confrontation with Amaziah (7:10–17), the divine message is harsh

---

61 Andersen and Freedman, *Amos*, 118–20 (see also pp. 98–99).

Amos' call to the Southern Kingdom is supported by the following: the *Judean* king Uzziah (1:1); "Yahweh from *Zion* roars, and from *Jerusalem* he utters his voice" (1:2); the oracle against *Judah* (2:4–5); "woe to you who are complacent on *Mount Zion*" (6:1); the vision of the resurrected tabernacle of *David* (9:11–15). Although much of Amos' ministry was directed toward the north, and toward Bethel in particular, Amos was commissioned to preach to both Judah and Israel.

62 For example, most of Hosea's oracles are directed against the Northern Kingdom, but oracles that include the south are in, for example, Hos 1:7; 3:5; 12:12–14 (ET 12:11–13). Micah and Isaiah, on the other hand, speak predominately to the Southern Kingdom, but their books also contain oracles against the north, for example, Micah 1:3–7; Is 7:1–25; 17:3; 28:1.

judgment. Yet Yahweh's final words will be a consoling Gospel promise and invitation for Israelites and Gentiles alike to be included in the new people of God and the new creation through faith in the Son of David (9:11–15).

7:17 Having made the claim for divine authority in 7:14–15, Amos will affirm Amaziah's charge that Amos was preaching "against" Israel (7:16) by now proclaiming a fourfold oracle against Amaziah and a prophecy against Israel in 7:17. The five maledictions in 7:17 relate to other pentads in the book.[63]

The fourfold oracle against Amaziah is the only one in the book directed at a specific individual.[64] The initial judgments on the priest focus upon his family. Often in Scripture whole families suffer under the divine judgment meted out for the sins of the head of the household (e.g., Joshua 7; 2 Sam 12:7–18; cf. Mt 18:25). For prophetic judgments of death for other disobedient priests and their children, see 1 Sam 2:34 (Eli's sons) and Jer 20:1–6 (Pashhur and his sons).

These passages expresses collective retribution.[65] Also involved is the principle of headship. The most obvious biblical examples of the head affecting the entire body are the imputation of the sin of Adam (the father of the human race) to the entire human race, and the imputation of the righteousness of Christ (the head of the church) to all believers (Rom 5:12–21; Eph 4:1–16; 5:22–33).[66] The wife and sons of Amaziah suffer punishment at least in part for his opposition to Yahweh, his Word, and his prophet. Yet these close relatives may well have shared Amaziah's unbelief and hostility toward the true God and his prophetic Word. It is likely that they supported his occupation as a priest at the idolatrous shrine in Bethel, which was diametrically opposed to the divine worship provided in the Torah and centered at the Jerusalem temple. Therefore passages such as Amos 7:17 need not conflict with the biblical doctrine of individual accountability to God, with individual justification or condemnation (e.g., Ezek 14:12–20; chapter 18; 33:10–20; Hab 2:4; Psalm 1).

This type of "prophetic announcement of punishment against an individual"[67] normally begins with the characteristic לָכֵ֗ן, "therefore."[68] A subgenre of this announcement of punishment is evident in narratives about prophets who confront antagonists. For example, when King Ahab ignores the prophet Micaiah

---

[63] Amos 4:6–11 has the fivefold refrain " 'but you did not return to me,' declares Yahweh" (4:6, 8, 9, 10, 11). There are five conditional sentences in 9:2–4 that express a fivefold concept of the impossibility of escaping from divine judgment. The five visions make up a pentad: 7:1–3; 7:4–6; 7:7–9; 8:1–3; 9:1–4.

[64] However, Yahweh also targeted "the house of Jeroboam" (7:9), a prophecy to which Amaziah refers in 7:11.

[65] Collective guilt and retribution are evident in many biblical texts even though they are generally foreign to the Western legal tradition of regarding each individual as liable only for his or her own actions.

[66] Pieper, *Christian Dogmatics*, 1:540, n. 26, quotes Meisner, *Anthropologie*: "In any body … that which the head does, as far as it is the head, is rightly imputed to the whole body. … The acts of the *pater familias* [are imputed] to the whole family."

[67] Sweeney, *Isaiah 1–39*, 530. Other examples include Is 22:15–19 and Jer 20:1–6.

[68] For לָכֵ֗ן, "therefore," see the first textual note on 3:11.

ben Imlah (1 Ki 22:2–28), the monarch dies in a battle at Ramoth Gilead (1 Ki 22:29–40). When the Assyrian king Sennacherib through his field commander defies Yahweh, the king is later assassinated by his sons Adrammelech and Sharezer (Is 36:1–37:38). Similar maladies are inflicted upon Jeroboam ben Nebat when he tries to seize the prophet who prophesies against the Bethel altar (1 Ki 13:1–4), as well as others who fail to give proper respect to Elijah and Elisha (e.g., 2 Ki 1:9–16; 2:23–24; 5:19b–27). Hananiah mocks Jeremiah and as a result dies two months later (Jeremiah 28). In a similar way, Amaziah will also die for trying to censor the words of Yahweh through Amos.

Amos continues to turn from his defensive *apologia* (7:14–15) to an offensive assault against Amaziah. Whereas in 7:11 Amaziah derogatorily said, "Thus says *Amos*" (כֹּה אָמַר עָמוֹס), now Amos counters with "thus says *Yahweh*" (כֹּה־אָמַר יְהוָה). The order of the condemnations is surprising. One would expect the first target to be Amaziah himself. However, the prophet begins with the priest's wife, then addresses the fate of his children and his land, and concludes with Amaziah. And yet the emphatic pronoun "and as for you" (וְאַתָּה, 7:17) places the cause of all the maledictions on the priest's doorstep.[69]

Amos states that Amaziah's wife will become a public prostitute. This does not suggest a choice on her part. The harsh reality of a woman's experience in a time of war and conquest by a foreign enemy is that she could be raped by enemy soldiers.[70] She also could be forced to become a prostitute.

In the ancient Near East, to be a prostitute was considered a most abysmal destiny. For example, in the Gilgamesh Epic, Enkidu describes the life of a prostitute: she is "one debarred from any family-life, subject to physical abuse from drunkards, living alone in the recesses of the city-walls, poorly clothed, barefoot and a prey to all insults."[71] The link between poverty and prostitution is apparent in a Sumerian text, the Cursing of Agade, where the prostitute and the male pauper appear in adjacent curses: "May your poor hurl his precious children into the water, may the prostitute stretch herself out in the gate of her brother."[72] Likewise, certain treaty curses suggest the prostitute's low social status. The treaty between Ashur-nirari V of Assyria and Matiʾilu of Arpad has this imprecation:

> If Matiʾilu sins against this treaty with Ashurnirari, king of Assyria, may Matiʾilu become a prostitute, his soldiers women, may they receive [*a gift*] in the square of their cities (i.e. publicly) like any prostitute.[73]

---

69 Note the same pronoun in the similar rhetorical move by Nathan when he confronts David: "*you* are the man" (אַתָּה הָאִישׁ, 2 Sam 12:7).

70 Luther explains "will be a prostitute" as meaning "that is, she will be raped" ("Lectures on Amos," AE 18:178).

71 Summarized by Kuhrt, "Non-Royal Women in the Late Babylonian Period," 236.

72 *ANET*, 650.

73 *ANET*, 532–33.

Amos next proclaims that Amaziah's sons and daughters "will fall by the sword" (7:17). The "sword" occurs in Amos' visions (7:9; 9:1, 4; also 9:10), and it frames this narrative (7:11, 17). Ironically, the high priest ordered Amos to end his preaching at Bethel (7:13). When his sons and daughters fall by the sword, Amaziah's line will come to an *end*. Children were too young to be of any use to a conqueror and were considered as extra mouths to feed; therefore they were often eliminated. Several Pentateuchal curses address the loss of wife and children (e.g., Deut 28:30, 41; 32:25), and the phrase "your sons and your daughters" occurs in covenant curses in Deut 28:32, 53.

The next curse is the confiscation and apportionment of Amaziah's land. The parceling out of "your land" (with the singular Hebrew pronominal suffix on וְאַדְמָתְךָ, translated as "your") may refer to the nation of northern Israel (clearly the meaning of "land" in the last sentence of 7:17), the city of Bethel, the priest's private property,[74] or all of these locales together. The land will be measured and given as spoil to the conquering army.[75]

Amos continues next with the curse that Amaziah will die in "an unclean land," that is, a foreign country that worships idols and has immoral practices. This presupposes that he will be exiled there as a result of Israel's imminent military defeat (6:14). A foreign land would, of course, lack the presence of an Israelite sanctuary and be considered unclean. For Amaziah, a priest whose life was devoted to what was thought to be holy, to die in an unclean land meant he would become unclean himself. In the same spirit as "an eye for an eye, a tooth for a tooth" (Ex 21:24), because Amaziah tried to stop Amos from fulfilling his holy vocation, in the future he will not be able to fulfill his own vocation.

These four judgments pertaining to Amaziah's wife, children, land, and place of death presuppose the fifth judgment: Israel's exile, which is an ongoing theme in Amos.[76] Exile fulfills the Mosaic covenant curses upon Israel in Lev 26:38–39. Amos repeats verbatim in 7:17 what Amaziah in 7:11 had accused him of preaching, namely, that "Israel will certainly go into exile from its land." The word "land" (אֲדָמָה) appears three times in this verse. From the OT perspective, to be separated from the land with the dwelling place of Yahweh meant that his people would not be able to dwell with him; thus they would have no hope or future.[77]

---

[74] When referring to the priest Abiathar and the priestly family of Jeremiah, both 1 Ki 2:26–27 and Jer 32:6–15 use שָׂדֶה, "field," rather than אֲדָמָה, "land." Nevertheless, these texts may indicate that some priests owned land.

[75] For a similar thought, see Jer 6:12.

[76] The deportation of northern Israel is a judgment in Amos 4:2–3; 5:5, 27; 6:7; 7:11, 17; 9:4.

[77] This central importance of the temple in the land is expressed in, for example, Solomon's prayer in 1 Kings 8. In the NT perspective, geographic location is not an essential part of the relationship between God and his people (e.g., Jn 4:20–26). Rather, God comes to dwell with his people in the person of Christ and through his Word and Sacraments, which are efficacious throughout the entire world (e.g., Mt 28:19–20).

In the Hebrew word order of the five curses in 7:17, the person or object cursed is emphatically positioned first. The first word at the beginning of each of the curses is as follows:

1. אִשְׁתְּךָ, "*your* wife"
2. וּבָנֶיךָ וּבְנֹתֶיךָ, "and *your* sons and *your* daughters"
3. וְאַדְמָתְךָ, "and *your* land"
4. וְאַתָּה, "and as for *you*"
5. וְיִשְׂרָאֵל, "and Israel"

The rhetorical affect is akin to "you, you, you, you, and all of you!"

The narrative began abruptly, "then Amaziah … sent" (7:10), without any reference to the time or place, with which Hebrew narratives normally begin. It ends just as suddenly. The narrative appears to end at its climax, when the tension is at its height.

Did Amaziah repent? What happened to Amos? When Jeremiah was accused of treason he was arrested and thrown in jail (Jer 37:11–38:13). Micaiah ben Imlah was held in custody to await a final verdict from the king, who never returned (1 Ki 22:26–28). Was Amos henceforth allowed to wander around the Northern Kingdom freely so he could continue to preach against it? Probably not. He may have been placed under house arrest or even martyred.[78] Perhaps he was expelled to Tekoa and a guard was stationed at the border of northern Israel to prohibit his reentrance. The future of Amos is left unresolved.

In this way the narrative places its readers into the story and employs the rhetoric of entrapment.[79] Amos used this same literary strategy when he initially focused on the sins and punishments of other nations (Amos 1:3–2:5) in order to trap Israel under judgment (2:6–16). Israel's response to Yahweh's Word through Amos up to 2:5 was to assume that the nation's prosperity was a sign of divine blessing and that its considerable religiosity[a] was sufficient to guarantee its future well-being. As the people sat comfortably in their sins—not grieving over the ruin of Joseph (6:6)—Amos had them in the palm of his hand. In 2:6–16 he hit the unsuspecting Israelites with Yahweh's judgment against *them*.

(a) Cf. Amos 2:7–8; 3:14; 4:4–5; 5:5–6, 14, 21–27; 7:9–17; 8:5, 10, 14; 9:1

After 7:17 readers find themselves asking questions about what happened to Amaziah and Amos, but these are the wrong questions. The narrative engages

[78] The same questions surround Paul's trial before Caesar in Rome (Acts 28:17–31) as Luke leaves his narrative open. Compare the unresolved ending in Jonah 4:10–11.

[79] Nathan employs the rhetoric of entrapment when he confronts David after the king's adultery with Bathsheba. The prophet crafts a parable for David that is about a rich man with many flocks who steals a poor man's pet lamb. David immediately recognizes that injustice has been done by the rich man and promptly pronounces judgment. At this point Nathan says to David, "You are the man" (2 Sam 12:7). It is the king who is guilty of gross injustice. David recognizes Yahweh's Word in Nathan's parable and immediately repents. Other examples of the rhetoric of entrapment include the woman from Tekoa in 2 Samuel 14 and Isaiah's Song of the Vineyard in Is 5:1–7. The short ending of Mark (16:1–8) functions in like manner, ending abruptly. It is as if Mark, after describing the reaction of the women to the risen Jesus, hands the reader a pen and says, "Here, now that Jesus has appeared alive, write how this will shape *your* life."

all readers and asks them this question: "What will *your* future be like? How will *you* respond to the divine Word? Will you live after the pattern of Amaziah or of Amos?"

Summary

Behind Amos stands Yahweh; behind Amaziah stands Jeroboam ben Joash. The prophet is called and ordained by the God of Israel. The priest is ordained by the highest human authority in the idolatrous land. Amos and Amaziah represent two perspectives, two commitments, and two ways of living. To say that the priest and the prophet crossed paths is to understate the force of the narrative. According to a fundamental law of physics, the force of impact depends upon the momentum (mass times the velocity vector) of both colliding objects. Amos and Amaziah were both moving quickly, but from totally opposite directions. One was bent on promotion, the other on devotion. One was a tyrant, the other a servant. One was consumed with self-interest, the other consumed with loving small people. One manipulated, slandered, and coerced; the other preached, prayed, and interceded. One was backed by the weightiest human authority; the other carried the weight of divine authority.

In this way Amaziah functions in the book as the archetype of all opponents of God and his spokesmen. Schmidt goes so far as to suggest that in Amaziah's name, אֲמַצְיָה, "mighty is Yah(weh)," the verbal element (-אמצ, from אָמַץ, "to be mighty") forms a wordplay on the same verb (אָמַץ) in 2:14, "the strong man will not *exert his strength*," and on the cognate adjective אַמִּיץ in 2:16, "the most *courageous* of heart among the warriors will flee naked on that day." These words from אמץ describe people "who are powerful by human standards but whose power is futile in the face of the harsh judgment of 2:14–16."[80] Amaziah then is a cipher for all of the mighty and influential people in the book who stand defiant against Yahweh and his prophet Amos.

Amaziah's reaction to Amos is expected; the darkness is never able to stand in the light (cf. Jn 3:19–20). His rejection of Yahweh's Word explains why Yahweh says in the third and fourth visions, "I will never again forgive" Israel (7:8; 8:2). Amaziah's rejection of Amos is Israel's rejection of Yahweh. The ostracism of the prophet betrays the people's renunciation of their God. In this way Amos is a suffering servant of Yahweh in the same line as Moses (e.g., Num 11:11) and climactically Jesus (e.g., Is 52:13–53:12; Mk 10:45). The rejected prophet is a symbol of hope and courage for disciples of Jesus, who are similarly oppressed (Mt 5:11–12; Lk 6:20–26).

Amos' courage in the face of Amaziah is part of a long tradition in which prophets dare to challenge the sinful establishment. Moses confronts Pharaoh with Yahweh's thunderous "let my people go" (e.g., Ex 5:1). Nathan courageously puts his prophetic career on the line when he thunders to David, אַתָּה הָאִישׁ, "you are the man" (2 Sam 12:7). Elijah takes the heat from Ahab,

---

80 Schmidt, "Another Word-Play in Amos?" 141.

who calls him the "troubler of Israel" (1 Ki 18:17). Jeremiah daringly writes Yahweh's Word again after the king had sliced and burned it (Jer 36:20–32). And Daniel's interpretation of Nebuchadnezzar's dream of the night subverts Nebuchadnezzar's illusion of the day (Dan 3:31–4:34 [ET 4:1–37]).

Standing in the tradition of Moses, Nathan, Elijah, Jeremiah, Daniel, and Amos, and fulfilling their ministries, is Israel's mightiest Prophet ("a prophet mighty in deed and word," Lk 24:19). Moses and all the prophets testify to this Prophet, who took the greatest stand. Climactically, he stood before the first-century equivalent of Amaziah—the high priest Caiaphas—and confessed, "In the future you will see the Son of Man seated at the right hand of the Power and coming on the clouds of heaven" (Mt 26:64; cf. Mk 14:62). Jesus was crucified not only for being a faithful Prophet and for living out a love that disrupted the Jewish Greco-Roman social order,[81] but as the Suffering Servant he also bore the transgressions of humanity, died in the place of all sinners, and made atonement for all (Is 52:13–53:12). He rose again victoriously and justifies all believers so that they are righteous (Is 53:11–12). He instituted the new kingdom of God, of which he himself is the King (Jn 18:36).[82]

[81] Benne writes: "It is instructive to remember that the one person who did live fully out of *agapé* love ended up on a cross, crucified by the best and brightest of the time" (*Reasonable Ethics*, 98).

[82] For further discussion of parallels between Amos 7:10–17 and the ministry of Christ, see the beginning of the introduction.

Amos 8:1–3

The Fourth Vision: The Basket of Summer Fruit

Translation

8 [1]This is what the Lord Yahweh showed me: behold, it was a basket of summer fruit. [2]Then he asked, "What are you seeing, Amos?"

And I said, "A basket of summer fruit."

Then Yahweh said to me, "The end is coming upon my people Israel. I will never again forgive him.

[3]"The singing women of the palace will wail on that day," declares the Lord Yahweh. "Many corpses, thrown in every place. Silence!"

Textual Notes

8:1 כֹּה הִרְאַנִי אֲדֹנָי יְהוִה—See the first textual note on the identical wording in 7:1.

וְהִנֵּה כְּלוּב קָיִץ׃—The noun כְּלוּב probably comes from a verb meaning "to weave" (*HALOT*). In Amos 8:1–2 כְּלוּב denotes a "basket" (BDB, *HALOT*), and in its only other OT occurrence, it refers to a "bird cage" (Jer 5:27).

The noun קַיִץ can denote either the season of "summer" or "fruit," which could be picked in summer.[1] It is related to the verb קִיץ, "spend the summer," which occurs only in Is 18:6. The noun means "summer" in, for example, Gen 8:22; Amos 3:15; and Ps 74:17. קַיִץ denotes fruit that is harvested at the end of the summer, especially figs, in, for example, 2 Sam 16:1–2; Is 16:9; Micah 7:1. When קַיִץ appears by itself in a harvest context, as it does here, it always refers to fruit. The eighth and last month of the agricultural year on the seventh line of the Gezer Calendar is called ירח קץ,[2] "a month of summer fruit." This corresponds to the fruit harvest in late summer and early fall. This may have been the time of year when Amos saw this vision, just as it is possible that he received the vision of judgment by fire (7:4–6) during an excessively hot summer.

As pointed in the MT, the pronunciation of קַיִץ, *qayits*, is close to that of the word in 8:2b on which it is a pun, קֵץ, *qeyts*. However, the phonological correspondence may have been even closer in the eighth-century BC Hebrew spoken by Amos' northern Israelite audience. The older or northern dialectical pronunciation of קַיִץ could have been as a monosyllable קַיְץ, *qayts*, before the addition of the anaptyctic *hireq* to produce the two-syllable word קַיִץ. Therefore קַיִץ and קֵץ would have sounded almost identical.[3]

---

1 Cf. J. Hausmann, "קַיִץ," *TDOT* 13:24–26.

2 Gibson, *Hebrew and Moabite Inscriptions*, 2.

3 GKC, § 93 v, and Joüon, §§ 88C a*, a, and f, explain that the original form of nouns of the pattern בַּיִת, זַיִת, and so on was *qatl* with consonantal *yod*. In the case of קַיִץ, this means the original form was קַיְץ. See also Andersen and Freedman, *Amos*, 757.

8:2 וַיֹּאמֶר מָֽה־אַתָּה רֹאֶה עָמוֹס—This is a shortened form of the same narration of Yahweh's question in 7:8. See the first textual note on 7:8.

וָאֹמַר כְּלוּב קָיִץ—As in 7:8, Amos gives a terse reply that focuses on the one central item in the preceding vision: here, כְּלוּב קָיִץ, the "basket of summer fruit," repeated from 8:1.

וַיֹּאמֶר יְהוָה אֵלַי בָּא הַקֵּץ אֶל־עַמִּי יִשְׂרָאֵל—In form בָּא could be either a prophetic perfect, "has come," signaling that God has already fixed the judgment that will arrive soon, or the participle, "is coming." The participle, reflected in the translation, is supported by the participle Yahweh used in the clause הִנְנִי שָׂם, "behold, I am placing/about to place" (7:8) in the parallel interpretation in the third vision, which shares the same structure as this fourth vision.

Yahweh creates another wordplay, this time between קַיִץ ("summer") and קֵץ ("end"), which originally sounded almost identical (see the second textual note on 8:1). In 5:5 Amos punned with the alliterative הַגִּלְגָּל גָּלֹה יִגְלֶה ("Gilgal surely will go into exile"). He performed a similar literary maneuver in 5:26 with סִכּוּת ("Sikkuth") and כִּיּוּן ("Kiyyun") for their vowels are taken from the words גִּלּוּל ("idol") and/or שִׁקּוּץ ("detested thing"). The name אֲמַצְיָה ("Amaziah," 7:10–12, 14) may be a play on the verb אָמֵץ ("be mighty, exert strength," 2:14) and the adjective אַמִּיץ ("mighty one," 2:16). The third vision (7:7–9) may involve a wordplay between אֲנָךְ ("plumb line") and אֲנָחָה ("groaning"; see the second textual note on 7:7).

In the prophets, the noun קֵץ usually refers to the "end" of a period of time, marked by God carrying out a judgment and/or intervening in history with salvation, just as does "the Day of Yahweh" (see the commentary on 5:18–20). קֵץ is especially frequent in Daniel.[4] It is often the subject of the verb בּוֹא, "to come," as here (also, e.g., Gen 6:13; Jer 51:13).[5] Ezekiel refers to the imminent fall of Jerusalem to Babylon when he employs קֵץ five times in Ezek 7:2–6, and three of those times it is the subject of the same verb form here, בָּא. The noun קֵץ probably is derived from the verb קָצַץ and is related to the verb קָצָה, both of which mean "to cut off."

Amos' usage of the noun is eschatological and should be equated with the eschatological statements of judgment throughout the book.[a] קֵץ has a similar meaning in Dan 12:13, where it refers to the end of the world and the resurrection of Daniel together with all believers (see Dan 12:2–3) after the return of Christ. NT passages such as Mt 24:6, 13–14: Phil 3:19; 1 Pet 4:7 likewise employ τέλος, "end," to denote the final hour of judgment for unbelievers and redemption for believers at the parousia of the Lord. Christ himself is "the beginning and the end" (Rev 22:13; cf. Rev 21:6).

(a) E.g., Amos 1:14; 2:14–16; 4:2; 5:18–20; 6:3; 8:9–11, 13

As in Amos 7:8, 15, Yahweh uses the covenant label עַמִּי יִשְׂרָאֵל even though he is decreeing judgment, which is so severe precisely because he had called this people to be his own and they rebelled. See especially 3:1–2.

לֹא־אוֹסִיף עוֹד עֲבוֹר לוֹ׃—This is repeated verbatim from the third vision. See the fourth textual note on 7:8.

---

4 It is in Dan 8:17, 19; 9:26; 11:6, 13, 27, 35, 40, 45; 12:4, 6, 9, 13. See Steinmann, *Daniel*, 409, and his commentary on other verses with the word.

5 Cf. S. Talmon, "קֵץ," *TDOT* 13:78–86.

(b) Is 14:31; 65:14; Jer 25:34; 47:2; 48:20, 31; 49:3; Ezek 21:17 (ET 21:12); Hos 7:14

8:3 וְהֵילִילוּ שִׁירוֹת הֵיכָל בַּיּוֹם הַהוּא—The Hiphil of יָלַל, "to howl," is onomatopoeic, imitating the sound of its action.[6] It suggests "the ultimate degree of lamentation, an extraordinary wail of agony."[7] It is often associated with זָעַק or צָעַק, "to cry out,"[b] or סָפַד, "to lament" (Jer 4:8; 49:3; Joel 1:13; Micah 1:8).

The feminine plural שִׁירוֹת occurs only here in the OT, but it is obviously related to the noun שִׁיר, "song," and verb שִׁיר, "to sing." The feminine plural participle of the verb, שָׁרוֹת, "singing women" or "songstresses" (BDB), is in 2 Sam 19:36 (ET 19:35); Eccl 2:8; and 2 Chr 35:25. In all these passages, these women are associated with the royal court. Some suggest emending שִׁירוֹת in Amos 8:3 to שָׁרוֹת, but this is unnecessary because at least once in the OT שִׁיר refers to a "singer."[8] In Ezek 33:32 Yahweh tells the prophet, "You are like a singer to them" (וְהִנְּךָ לָהֶם כְּשִׁיר). שִׁירוֹת most likely is that same noun in the feminine plural.

שִׁירוֹת is in construct with the noun הֵיכָל, which occurs only here in Amos. It may denote a royal "palace" (e.g., Dan 1:4; Ps 144:12; Prov 30:28), a "temple," or more specifically, the Holy Place in Solomon's temple.[9] Because the "singing women" are associated with the royal court, here הֵיכָל probably refers to Jeroboam ben Joash's royal residence, his "palace" in Samaria. When the apostate priest Amaziah referred to the Bethel temple in 7:13, he used different Hebrew terminology when he called it "the sanctuary of the king" (מִקְדַּשׁ־מֶלֶךְ) and "the house of the kingdom" (בֵּית מַמְלָכָה).

נְאֻם אֲדֹנָי יְהוִה—For נְאֻם, see the second textual note on 2:11.

רַב הַפֶּגֶר בְּכָל־מָקוֹם הִשְׁלִיךְ הָס׃—With one exception (Gen 15:11), the noun פֶּגֶר refers to human corpses, and it implies death by violence.[10] The Hiphil of שָׁלַךְ, "to throw," appears in Amos 4:3.[11] Here the singular is impersonal, literally, "[someone] will throw." The implied subject is a (lone?) survivor of the judgment, and the implied object is the collective singular הַפֶּגֶר, "the corpse(s)." For the sake of English and to avoid a plural subject of an active verb, which could imply many survivors, the verb is translated with a passive, "thrown." For an abundance of corpses after Yahweh's judgment, leading to the call for הַס, "silence!" see also 6:9–10. For הַס, see the sixth textual note on 6:10.

The corpses are "thrown" and so are left unburied "in every place" (בְּכָל־מָקוֹם). Compare Nah 3:3, where there are so many unburied corpses that people stumble over them. Without burial they would emit a foul smell (Is 34:3). A corpse might be thrown into a cistern (Jer 41:9) or left for birds and wild animals to consume (1 Sam 17:46; Ezek 39:17–20). The angel of Yahweh struck down a hundred and eighty-five thousand Assyrians so that the enemy became corpses (the plural of פֶּגֶר in 2 Ki 19:35 || Is 37:36). In the eschaton, the rotting, burning corpses of raised unbelievers will be eternally abhorrent (Is 66:24).

---

6 Cf. A. Bauman, "ילל," *TDOT* 6:82–87.

7 Bauman, *TDOT* 6:84.

8 This follows Paul, *Amos*, 254–55.

9 Cf. M. Ottosson, "הֵיכָל," *TDOT* 3:382–88.

10 Cf. P. Maiberger, "פֶּגֶר," *TDOT* 11:479–82.

11 Perhaps a Hophal was intended there; see the second textual note on 4:3.

Commentary

Whereas the third vision (7:7–9) ends with the desolation of the high places and the death of Israel's ruling dynasty (7:9), this fourth vision ends with the death of the people (8:3). The cry "silence!" (הָס) at the end of 8:3 is connected to 6:10, where הַס is also uttered in sheer terror. The fear expressed in 6:10 was that invoking the name of Yahweh could provoke his further wrath upon the survivors. Here the silence follows the recognition of the huge number of corpses of those who perished under Yahweh's wrath.

Just as the first (7:1–3) and second (7:4–6) visions have the same structure, so the third vision (7:7–9) and this fourth vision exhibit the same pattern.

1. Yahweh shows Amos a vision (8:1; cf. 7:7).
2. Yahweh asks Amos what he is seeing (8:2a, repeating 7:8a).
3. Amos answers by repeating the catchword (8:2b; cf. 7:8b) from the initial vision (8:1; cf. 7:7).
4. Yahweh interprets the vision with a pun based upon the catchword (8:2c; cf. 7:8c) as a judgment upon "my people Israel" (8:2c, repeating 7:8c).
5. Yahweh states, "I will never again forgive him [Israel]" (8:2d, repeating 7:8d).
6. Yahweh describes the destruction and death that will result from the termination of his forbearance (8:3; cf. 7:9).

In the fourth vision, Yahweh utters one of the most climactic statements in the book: "the end is coming upon my people Israel" (8:2).[12] This means that the time of forbearance (cf. Lk 13:8) had run its course. The harvest was at hand because opportunities to repent went unheeded (Amos 4:6–11). It was now time for weeping and gnashing of teeth (cf. Mt 8:12) until a silence even more horrific than the wailing enfolds everyone. In many ways, this vision is the epitome of Amos' preaching. In it he announces the end of Israel's world, the world presided over by kings and priests and magistrates and officials and businessmen who imagine themselves secure and stable and safe. Yahweh had constituted the nation of Israel according to his gracious covenant through Moses. But now the people had reorganized themselves in rebellion against Yahweh's covenant faithfulness (e.g., the "transgressions" in 2:4, 6; 3:14; 5:12), and so he will impose the covenant curses,[13] and their world must and certainly will end.

For northern Israel, the end would come about forty years after the ministry of Amos (ca. 760 BC), when it would fall to Assyria in 722 BC.[14] The Southern Kingdom of Judah would cease with its fall to Babylon in 587 BC. Yet these cataclysmic events would not terminate God's kingdom. The final prophetic oracle in Amos is the promise of the resurrection of David's tabernacle and a regath-

---

[12] It is likely that throughout Amos "my people Israel" encompasses both northern Israel and the Southern Kingdom of Judah (Andersen and Freedman, *Amos*, 98–99, 121).

[13] For the execution of curses in the covenant of Moses, see especially the commentary on 4:6–11 and on רִיב, "covenant lawsuit," in 7:4.

[14] See the excursus "The Assyrian Empire."

ering of a believing remnant from among both Israel and the Gentile nations (9:11–12), and it is this people of God who will inherit everlasting life in the new creation (9:13–15).

8:1–2 In the first two visions, the judgments pictured were obvious: a locust plague (7:1–3) and a devastating fire (7:4–6). In contrast, in the second two visions the pictured judgments (7:7–8; 8:1–2) are much more enigmatic. This fourth vision is aptly labeled a "wordplay vision,"[15] and the third vision too may involve a wordplay.[16] Yahweh is the one who gives all the visions, but in the third and fourth, he alone is able to interpret the meaning (cf. Mt 13:10–23).

A "basket of summer fruit" must have been familiar to Amos who, along with working with livestock (1:1; 7:14), earned part of his living in agriculture (7:14). קַיִץ, "fruit," could refer to fresh figs that were harvested in the summer during the months of August and September. Rhyming in 8:2 with קַיִץ, *qayits* or *qayts*,[17] "fruit," is קֵץ, *qets*, "end," which in this context refers to the Day of Yahweh (5:18–20). Agrarian minds understand the connection between "fruit" and the "end." The time of harvest invokes the ideas of ripeness, decay, and finality.

The two nouns resemble each other in spelling and pronunciation.[18] Together they indicate that the fruit is ripe, the harvest is here, and the end is coming for Israel.[19] The earlier prophecies of Ahijah of Shiloh against the house of Jeroboam ben Nebat (1 Ki 14:1–13), Jehu ben Hanani against the house of Baasha (1 Ki 16:1–4), and Elijah against the house of Ahab (1 Ki 21:17–24) were directed against specific dynasties. So too was Yahweh's judgment against the house of Jeroboam ben Joash in Amos 7:9b (cited in 7:11). But here in Amos, Yahweh announces the end of the *nation*. Israel's death and destruction (cf. also 5:1–3; 6:8–10; 7:9a) is predicted in the Pentateuchal covenant curses for when Israel would forsake their redeeming God (see, e.g., Deut 4:26; 28:20–22; 30:17–19; 31:16–17).

8:3 What normally would be a time of rejoicing over the harvest ironically becomes mayhem. The word "end" means the end of Israel, and that end will occur "on that day," which is a reference to the Day of Yahweh.[20] The "day"

---

15 Cf. the discussion in Paul, *Amos*, 253.

16 See the second textual note on 7:7.

17 See the second textual note on 8:1.

18 A similar pun on words is in Jer 1:11–12, where Yahweh shows Jeremiah a branch from an almond tree (שָׁקֵד, *shaqed*), and then promises that he will be watching over (שֹׁקֵד, *shoqed*) his Word of judgment in order to fulfill it.

19 The NEB translates the two words similarly to bring out the idea of the right time for divine judgment: " 'A basket of ripe summer fruit.' … 'The time is ripe for my people Israel.' " The Jerusalem Bible focuses upon the theological state of the people: " 'A basket of ripe fruit.' … 'My people Israel is ripe for destruction.' "

20 For the Day of Yahweh, see especially the commentary on 5:18, 20. See also "Amos' Place in the Minor Prophets" in the introduction; the third textual note on 1:14; the first textual note and the commentary on 2:16; and the second textual note and the commentary on 4:2. Related phrases about an eschatological "day" or "days" are in 1:14; 2:16; 3:14; 4:2; 6:3; 8:3, 9, 10,

of destruction for the Northern Kingdom will arrive in the year of 722 BC with the Assyrian conquest of Samaria. The Southern Kingdom's "day" will commence with the Babylonian assaults culminating in the destruction of Jerusalem and the temple in 587 BC. These judgments, as well as the demolition of the Herodian Jerusalem temple in AD 70, portend the verdict of everlasting judgment on all unbelievers on the final day when Christ comes again. Yet God's judgment against humanity's sin was executed upon the sinless Son of God, whose death razed the temple of his body, and whose bodily resurrection is the guarantee that all believers shall rise to everlasting life on the Last Day (Amos 9:11–15; Jn 2:18–22).

Ground zero will include the royal palace in Samaria, where the songstresses performed for the king. The sight of wholesale death at the king's palace will prompt the female singers to lament in short, staccato outbursts: "Many corpses, thrown in every place. Silence!"[21] Unburied corpses are a sign that people are under Yahweh's curse (Lev 26:30; cf. Deut 21:23, quoted in Gal 3:13; Ezek 37:1–2), and those corpses will defile the land (Ezek 39:12). Without a place of burial, corpses may be consumed by birds and wild beasts (Ezek 39:4–5) or dogs (2 Ki 9:36) or left to rot like dung in the fields (Jer 16:4; Nah 3:3). Under such horrific circumstances, it is best not to utter even one word (cf. Amos 6:10).

Summary

Solomon's kingdom fell apart due to idolatry and corruption that fostered unbiblical worldviews (1 Ki 11:1–8). The king allied himself with Egypt by marrying a daughter of Pharaoh (1 Ki 3:1; 7:8; 9:24; 11:1). In a sense then, Solomon's reign took Israel back to a condition of bondage as in Egypt. The people were enslaved to other gods. Moreover, Solomon's bloated administration burdened the people with taxation and forced labor (1 Ki 4:7; 5:27 [ET 5:13]). The reign of Jeroboam ben Joash over northern Israel, with his acquisition of land and economic prosperity, was not only a return to Solomonic splendor, but also Solomonic vice. It too would come to an end since Yahweh terminated his forgiveness of the apostate people (Amos 8:2). The cause of Israel's death (cf. 5:1–3, 16–20; 6:1), so graphic in 8:3, was not murder, but suicide, since Israel's false worship[22] and abusive policies toward the impoverished killed the nation.

11, 13; 9:11, 13. The final two passages, 9:11 and 9:13, are in the concluding Gospel promise of the messianic era of salvation. See the commentary on 9:11–15.

[21] Smith writes: "All one can do is gasp in horror at the enormity of the slaughter, turn one's eyes away from the mutilated carnage and bloated bodies, and flee from the unbearable stench of death and rotting flesh" (*Hosea, Amos, Micah*, 382).

[22] See 2:7–8; 3:14; 4:4–5; 5:5–6, 14, 21–27; 7:9–17; 8:5, 10, 14; 9:1. See also the excursuses "The Prophets and Israel's Worship" and "The Sabbath." Stephen quotes Amos 5:25–27 in Acts 7:42–43 to confirm that the culmination of Israel's idolatry was the people's rejection of Jesus the Messiah.

But is this end for Israel *absolute*? Does Amos insist that God's OT people will come to an end that is total and comprehensive? Koch writes: "Amos certainly proclaims unconditional disaster, but he does not proclaim it wholesale."[23] This is similar to several texts in the book of Jeremiah. In the context of several judgment oracles that appear to announce the absolute end of Judah, Jeremiah also states that the end is not going to be complete (Jer 4:27; 5:10, 18; 30:11; 46:28). While the end of Judah's military and political institutions is envisioned in much of Jeremiah, "I will not make a full end" (e.g., Jer 4:27) indicates Yahweh's dogged faithfulness to his promises made to Abraham, Isaac, and Jacob. This same commitment is what finally prevails in the book of Amos. Yahweh is no quitter. After judgment he will bring about salvation. In the future there will be a remnant, and it will include not only believing Israelites, but also Gentiles who will be called by God's saving name (see Amos 5:15; 9:11–15).

---

[23] Koch, *The Prophets*, 1:70.

Amos 8:4–6

Hucksters and Hypocrites on Holy Days

Translation

8 [4]Hear this, you who trample upon the needy
so as to eliminate the oppressed of the land,
[5]saying, "When will the New Moon be over so we may sell corn,
and the Sabbath so we may open grain [bins],
to make the ephah smaller and to make the shekel heavier,
to distort with dishonest scales,
[6]to buy the poor for silver,
and the needy for a pair of sandals—
so we may sell the chaff of grain."

Textual Notes

8:4 שִׁמְעוּ־זֹאת הַשֹּׁאֲפִים אֶבְיוֹן—Regarding the Qal participle הַשֹּׁאֲפִים, "who trample," see the first textual note on 2:7, which has the identical participle. For אֶבְיוֹן, which recurs in 8:6, and other words in its semantic field, see the fifth textual note on 2:6. The parallel word in the next clause, עֲנִיֵּי or עֲנָוֵי, is one of those words in its semantic field.

וְלַשְׁבִּית עֲנִוֵּי־אָרֶץ׃—The Hiphil infinitive construct (with the preposition לְ) לַשְׁבִּית is a contracted form of לְהַשְׁבִּית, which occurs in Ps 8:3 (ET 8:2). Here the preformative ה is elided (Joüon, § 54 b; cf. GKC, § 53 q). The meaning of the Qal of שָׁבַת is "to cease, end, finish, rest."[1] In the Qal, שָׁבַת is used to refer to the first Sabbath, when God rested after having finished his work of creating (Gen 2:2–3), and to his people observing the Sabbath (Ex 16:30). It may also denote the ceasing of Yahweh's provision of manna (Josh 5:12) or the ending of a celebration (Is 24:8). In the Hiphil, the verb means "to cause to cease, eliminate, put an end to" (e.g., Is 13:11; 2 Chr 16:5). This is its meaning in Amos 8:4 as the prophet accuses the oppressors of eliminating needy people by means of their dishonest practices in the marketplace.

Joüon, § 124 p, argues that the infinitive with וְ and לְ here and sometimes elsewhere may have the same value as the preceding verb (in 8:4, הַשֹּׁאֲפִים), in which case לַשְׁבִּית could be translated "and who eliminate." However, an infinitive with לְ can also form a purpose or result clause (Waltke-O'Connor, § 36.2.3d), as reflected in the translation "*so as to* eliminate."

The form עֲנִוֵּי־ represents the Qere עֲנִיֵּי־ and the Kethib עֲנָוֵי. The Qere is the masculine plural construct form of עָנִי, "an oppressed person," which occurs only here in Amos, while the Kethib is the same form but from עָנָו, also meaning "an oppressed person." Its plural was in 2:7; see the second textual note on 2:7. Both words are from the

---

[1] Cf. E. Haag, "שָׁבַת," *TDOT* 14:381–86.

verb עָנָה II, "to oppress." Either word produces a similar meaning in this context. עָנִי may be a biform of עָנָו.

8:5 לֵאמֹר מָתַי יַעֲבֹר הַחֹדֶשׁ וְנַשְׁבִּירָה שֶּׁבֶר—The temporal interrogative מָתַי asks "when?" and the Qal imperfect of עָבַר refers to time and means "be past, over" (BDB, Qal, 4 d). The verb's subject, חֹדֶשׁ, refers to the New Moon celebration or first day of the month. References to the New Moon celebration indicate that it was a standard religious observance in Israel.[2] It was not, however, on the same level as the divinely instituted Sabbath and the three major festivals of Passover and the Feast of Unleavened Bread, Weeks (Pentecost), and Booths (Sukkoth). Celebration of the New Moon feast included offerings of two bulls, a ram, seven male lambs, grain and flour mixed with oil, wine, and a male goat (Num 28:11–15). Because the New Moon is listed with other festivals (e.g., Num 10:10; Is 1:14) and with the Sabbath (e.g., 2 Ki 4:23; Is 1:13; Col 2:16), by custom (but apparently not by the Law), it was a time for people to refrain from buying and selling. Paul states: "Although cessation from work on that day may be inferred from such passages as 1 Sam 20:5; 2 Kgs 4:23; Ezek 46:1, 3, it is clearly cited only here."[3]

The Hiphil cohortative וְנַשְׁבִּירָה and the Qal cohortative וְנִפְתְּחָה in the next clause are each in a dependent clause that expresses purpose: "so we may sell … so we may open." See Waltke-O'Connor, § 34.5.2b, including example 6, and Joüon, § 116 c.

The noun שֶׁבֶר I or שֵׁבֶר (Amos 6:6) means "a breaking, fracture, breach." The homograph שֶׁבֶר II refers to "corn" or "grain" also in, for example, Gen 42:1–2 and 43:2. For the cognate verb, see the third textual note on Amos 8:6. The noun שֶׁבֶר and the noun in the next clause, בַּר, "grain," are synonyms (e.g., Gen 42:1–3, 19, 25–26). The word "corn" was chosen for the translation of שֶׁבֶר to distinguish the two synonyms here, however, it refers to "corn" in the general sense of "grain," not to New World maize. The major grain crops in ancient Israel were wheat and barley.

וְהַשַּׁבָּת וְנִפְתְּחָה־בָּר—The Sabbath (שַׁבָּת) was the seventh day of the week. It was a celebration of both God's creation (Gen 2:1–3; Ex 20:11), as well as his redemption or new creation of Israel through his defeat of the Egyptian army (Exodus 14; Deut 5:15).[4] On it work was prohibited (Ex 20:8–11; 34:21; Lev 23:3) and a special offering was required at the temple (Num 28:9–10). Isaiah (e.g., Is 56:2; 58:13–14), Jeremiah (e.g., Jer 17:21–22), and Ezekiel (e.g., Ezek 20:12–13; 23:38) emphasize that keeping the Sabbath was a sign of Israel's faith in Yahweh. The "New Moon" and the "Sabbath" are paired together in Amos 8:5 as they are in, for example, Is 1:13–14 and Hos 2:13 (ET 2:11). This probably indicates that the New Moon was like the Sabbath in that all work was prohibited on it.

Here וְהַשַּׁבָּת is the subject of the verb יַעֲבֹר, "be over," which was in the previous clause and which does double duty. It need not be repeated in English translation.

---

2 See Num 10:10; 28:11–15; 29:6; 1 Sam 20:5, 18, 24, 27, 34; 2 Ki 4:23; Ps 81:4 (ET 81:3); Neh 10:34.

3 Paul, *Amos*, 257–58.

4 Cf. E. Haag, "שַׁבָּת," *TDOT* 14:387–97.

The Qal cohortative וְנִפְתְּחָה expresses purpose (see Waltke-O'Connor, § 34.5.2b; Joüon, § 116 c): "so we may open." The object, בַּר, "grain," implies "grain bins, containers."

לְהַקְטִין אֵיפָה וּלְהַגְדִּיל שֶׁקֶל—The verbs now become infinitive constructs with לְ in 8:5c–6, except for the last verb in 8:6, which is an imperfect (נַשְׁבִּיר). The two infinitive constructs here signal what the dishonest sellers intend to do (לְהַקְטִין, "to make smaller"; וּלְהַגְדִּיל, "and to enlarge, make heavier") once the holidays are over. The verbs קָטֹן, "be small," and גָּדַל, "be large," are antonyms. The Hiphil forms here have the corresponding causative meanings, which are translated as comparatives, "make smaller" and "make heavier," because they will be smaller and heavier, respectively, than the standard norms. The Hiphil of קָטֹן occurs only here in the OT.

The noun אֵיפָה, "ephah," is an Egyptian loanword (*HALOT*). It was a unit of dry measure probably equivalent in preexilic times to between ten and twenty liters[5] (between about nine and eighteen quarts).

The noun שֶׁקֶל, "shekel," is related to the verb שָׁקַל, "to weigh." It may have been equivalent to around 11.4 grams[6] (about 0.4 ounces). It was a standard measure of weight used for gold, silver, and other commodities.

וּלְעַוֵּת מֹאזְנֵי מִרְמָה׃—The intent to tamper with the scales is indicated by the Piel infinitive of עָוַת, "to make crooked, pervert." Wolff writes: "In our context perhaps [it] connotes not merely 'falsifying' in general (e.g., by over-weighting the norm-bowl), but quite specifically 'bending' out of shape the cross-beam of the balances."[7]

The noun מֹאזְנַיִם, "scales, balances," always occurs in the dual, here in construct. The verbal root of the noun מִרְמָה, "deceit, treachery," is רָמָה, "to beguile, act treacherously."[8] Solomon's wisdom in Proverbs condemned the use of cheating balances: מֹאזְנֵי מִרְמָה תּוֹעֲבַת יְהוָה, "dishonest scales are an abomination to Yahweh" (Prov 11:1; cf. Prov 16:11; 20:10, 23). In Micah 6:11, Yahweh asks rhetorically: "Shall I acquit [a man] with wicked scales [בְּמֹאזְנֵי רֶשַׁע], with a bag of dishonest weights [אַבְנֵי מִרְמָה]?"

8:6 לִקְנוֹת בַּכֶּסֶף דַּלִּים—The verb קָנָה can be a commercial term, "to acquire, purchase." Amos employs the verb only here, where it is an antonym of מָכַר, "to sell" (Amos 2:6).

בַּכֶּסֶף, "for silver," uses the preposition בְּ *pretii*, of price (BDB, s.v. בְּ, III 3 b). The identical phrase בַּכֶּסֶף also occurs in 2:6 with the same meaning. See the fourth textual note on 2:6.

---

5 M. A. Powell, "Weights and Measures," *ABD* 6:903. Although not used in Amos, the homer (חֹמֶר, e.g., Lev 27:16; Is 5:10; Hos 3:2) was equal to ten ephahs. The related word חֲמוֹר means a "donkey" (e.g., Gen 49:14; Ex 13:13). The חֹמֶר, "homer," was "equivalent to the load that this beast of burden could carry" (King, *Amos, Hosea, Micah*, 23).

6 Powell, *ABD* 6:906.

7 Wolff, *Joel and Amos*, 327.

8 Cf. M. Kartveit, "רמה," *TDOT* 13:500–503.

Amos employs the noun דַּל, "poor," also in 2:7; 4:1; 5:11, and he uses the noun in the next clause, אֶבְיוֹן, "needy," also in 2:6; 4:1; 5:12; 8:4. See the fifth textual note on 2:6 and the first textual note on 2:7.

וְאֶבְיוֹן בַּעֲבוּר נַעֲלָיִם—For the identical phrase, see the fifth textual note on 2:6.

וּמַפַּל בַּר נַשְׁבִּיר׃—The noun מַפָּל occurs only here and in Job 41:15 (ET 41:23).[9] It comes from the verb נָפַל, "to fall." Here it means something like "chaff," "refuse," "sweepings," or "leftovers." It is in construct with בַּר, the same noun for "grain" used in 5:11 and 8:5. נַשְׁבִּיר is not the common verb שָׁבַר, "to break," but a homograph that probably is a denominative from שֶׁבֶר, "grain, corn," the noun used in 8:5. In the Qal, the verb means "to buy grain," and in the Hiphil, "to sell grain," as here and also in, for example, Gen 42:6; Deut 2:28; and Prov 11:26.

Commentary

Yahweh's destruction of "the high places of Isaac" and "the sanctuaries of Israel" foreseen in Amos' third vision (7:7–9) and his demolition of the royal palace and its attendants in the fourth vision (8:1–3) provide the background for the rest of chapter 8. Amos 8:4–6 states why Bethel and Samaria will experience Yahweh's wrath, while 8:7–14 defines the nature of this wrath. Just as the showdown between Amos and Amaziah (7:10–17) is placed between the first three visions (7:1–3; 7:4–6; 7:7–9) and the fourth vision (8:1–3), so 8:4–14 is inserted between the fourth vision (8:1–3) and the fifth (9:1–4). Both sections (7:10–17 and 8:4–14) interrupt the visions (7:1–3; 7:4–6; 7:7–9; 8:1–3; 9:1–4).

Since Amos was a businessman before he became a prophet (1:1; 7:14–15), he had some knowledge of Israel's economic system, which had become a perverse abomination to Yahweh. The movers and shakers in Israel's marketplaces were consumed with money, loan debts, interest, capital gains, and wealth. They had little time for the "weightier matters" (Mt 23:23) of justice, righteousness, and the love of Yahweh. Their mantra was "there will never be enough to go around so we must continue to get *more*!" This consumerism drove the businessmen to accumulate more and more stuff and propelled them to not only "seize the day," but also to illegally seize their neighbor's goods.

These tradesmen are one of four distinct groups of leaders in the book of Amos that come under Yahweh's critical eye. They first appear in 2:6–8. In order of appearance, the others are (1) the royal officials (3:9–15), including Jeroboam ben Joash (1:1; 7:9–11); (2) the judges (5:10–12); and (3) the priests, with Amaziah being the paradigmatic leader of this group (7:10–17).

8:4 This verse introduces the rest of chapter 8, which belongs to the time of Amos' ministry after the following events, which can be arranged in topical order from graceful to judgmental:

---

9 In Job 41:15 (ET 41:23), it refers to Leviathan's layers of flesh. The OT contains related nouns from נָפַל, including מַפֶּלֶת, "fall," which appears eight times in the OT, with six in Ezekiel's prophecies against Tyre (Ezek 26:15, 18; 27:27) and Egypt (Ezek 31:13, 16; 32:10).

1. His first two visions, in which Yahweh relented from judgment (7:1–3; 7:4–6)
2. His preaching for Israel to repent, seek Yahweh, and live (chapters 5–6)
3. Israel's refusal to repent (4:6–11)
4. His next two visions, in which Yahweh does not relent from judgment (7:7–9; 8:1–3)
5. His confrontation with Amaziah and harsh personal judgment against him (7:10–17)

After these revelations and experiences there was nothing left but to reinforce and sharpen the theme of Israel's imminent destruction.

Amos 8:4 is a close parallel to 2:7 in both content and thrust: literally, "those who trample upon the needy" (הַשֹּׁאֲפִים אֶבְיוֹן, 8:4) and "those who trample upon the dust of the earth on the head of the poor ones" (הַשֹּׁאֲפִים עַל־עֲפַר־אֶרֶץ בְּרֹאשׁ דַּלִּים, 2:7). Amos 8:4 also displays the characteristic imperative organizational marker "hear" (שִׁמְעוּ) that Amos employs in 3:1, 13; 4:1; and 5:1. The masculine plural participles הַשֹּׁאֲפִים, "those who trample," in 8:4 and הַנִּשְׁבָּעִים, "those who swear," in 8:14 provide an inclusio around 8:4–14. They also link "those who trample" with "those who swear" and indicate that dishonest business practices are rooted in syncretistic worship.[10] Proper attitude and behavior in the Second Table of the Ten Commandments flows out of correct priorities in the First Table. Conversely, if one's relationship with God is skewed, one's behavior toward others will be misdirected too.

Yahweh has compassion upon the poor and needy (e.g., Ex 23:10–11; Deut 15:7–11). It is for this reason that Jesus announces that he comes "to bring Good News to the poor" (Lk 4:18; cf. James 2:5). Service rendered to those in Christ, no matter how lowly they may be, is service rendered to the Lord himself (Mt 25:40). The apostles agreed that "we should remember the poor" (Gal 2:10), and St. Paul gathered an offering for needy Christian believers in Jerusalem (1 Cor 16:1–3). But Israel's aristocrats were too busy turning a profit to hear the cries of the needy.

8:5 Amos frequently quotes words of the accused (2:12; 4:1; 6:13; 8:14; 9:10; cf. 5:14). This quote, running through 8:6, is similar in vocabulary and tone to 2:6–7. In 2:6–7 the prophet condemns those who sell people; here he accuses those who buy people. Together the picture is of the members of Israel's entrepreneurial class who cannot wait until the non-working and non-profit-making days are over so that they may continue to treat people heartlessly like merchandise.

Amos' indictment is against those who follow the letter of the Law in terms of keeping the Sabbath and the New Moon festivals, but fail to keep the spirit when they cheat their fellow citizens on non-festival days with their wheeling

---

[10] Andersen and Freedman write: "The two groups described in [8:]4 and [8:]14 overlap heavily, if they are not entirely congruent" (*Amos*, 832).

and dealing.[11] This propensity to fulfill outward religious obligations while neglecting justice and righteousness is also condemned by Amos in 4:4–5 and 5:21–27. "Though their shops were closed on such days [New Moons and Sabbaths], their minds were open to the concerns of their businesses, which would be operating at full tilt the minute the holy day came to an end."[12]

Limburg observes that Israel's businessmen divided their lives into watertight compartments, one marked "religion" and the other labeled "marketplace." "Religion, after all, is religion and as for the rest—well, business is business!"[13] Behind this façade of religious activity, their attitude revealed that they honored Yahweh with their lips, but their hearts were far from him (cf. Is 29:13; Mt 15:8).

The businessmen were making a killing by selling skimpy amounts of grain using oversize weights.[14] They ignored the mandate that honest balances, measures, scales, and weights were commanded by Yahweh (e.g., Lev 19:35–36; Deut 25:13–15). These wheelers and dealers had two sets of weights and two sets of measuring containers. To those who came selling their grain they offered an oversized bushel basket; they would then outfox those buying grain by using a smaller bushel. In this way the ephah was made small by using a smaller than proper container and the shekel was enlarged by making its standard weight (ca. 11.4 grams or .04 ounces) heavier. Sellers thought they were selling more, while buyers thought they were getting more.

By employing two sets of weights, middlemen could gain the upper hand on both buyer and seller. And to add more money in their coffers, these "prudent" businessmen would add chaff or other useless material to a sack of grain they were selling so that what was thought to be "grade A" was less than the best. Yahweh was aware of these tricks of the trade, and his will "has to do with the whole of life, holy day and holy place, but also every day and every place."[15] It was to their own peril that these merchants ignored Yahweh's words through Amos because the day would surely come when they would be forced to hang

---

[11] Matthews and Benjamin cite a Middle Kingdom (2134–1786 BC) text from Egypt that also speaks about the responsibility of the wealthy to provide fair treatment to the poor but also about common negligence of that responsibility:

> You are the chief steward, [y]ou are my lord. You are my last hope, [y]ou are my only judge. When you sail the Lake of Justice, [f]airness fills your sails. You father the orphan, [y]ou husband the widow. … [But t]hose who distribute the grain put more in their own ration. Those authorized to give full measures short their people. Lawmakers approve of robbery. (A Farmer and the Courts in Egypt, quoted in Matthews and Benjamin, *Old Testament Parallels*, 217, 219)

[12] Limburg, *Hosea–Micah*, 120.

[13] Limburg, *Hosea–Micah*, 122.

[14] The Israelite system of weights and measures was probably developed from the Babylonians (King, *Amos, Hosea, Micah*, 23). In excavations at Tirzah (the second capital of the Northern Kingdom), shops from the eighth century were unearthed that used two sets of weights: one for buying and one for selling (Mays, *Amos*, 144).

[15] Limburg, *Hosea–Micah*, 122.

this sign outside their shops: *Out of Business.* Note the eschatological markers "on that day" (8:9, 13), "a bitter day" (8:10), and "days are coming" (8:11).

It is possible that the merchants were in partnership with the religious leaders, perhaps urging them to shorten the sacred times for the sake of monetary gain (even as modern parishioners may request, "Shorten the church service, Pastor").[16] Such a partnership would be at least one reason why Amaziah was so quick to escort Amos out of town. In 5:10–12 the merchants and the magistrates appear as collaborators in fraud and cover-up, so it wouldn't be impossible to propose that all of the aristocrats—royal officials, judges, priests, and merchants—were in cahoots. Their theme was "no nickel is too small!"

A proper relationship with Yahweh was centered upon the Sabbath[17] and the Jerusalem temple but also included the shops and the shekel. Northern Israel was worshiping at false shrines (not at Jerusalem)[a] and following fake business practices. Near the beginning (2:6–8), the middle (4:1–3), and the end (8:4–6) of his book, Amos has the same message: apostate Israel is trampling, oppressing, and crushing the most marginalized members of its society. This kind of dishonesty in buying and selling was a common problem in the eighth century. Both Hosea (12:8 [ET 12:7]) and Micah (6:9–11) address this evil. Honesty in business is also a concern in the book of Proverbs (e.g., Prov 11:1; 16:11; 20:10, 23).

(a) See Amos 2:7–8; 3:14; 4:4–5; 5:5–6, 14, 21–27; 7:9–17; 8:5, 10, 14; 9:1

"The love of money," Paul warns, "is a root of all kinds of evil" (1 Tim 6:10). It was this misplaced love that once kept a young rich ruler out of the kingdom of God (Mt 19:16–22). Jesus warns of the addictive power of "mammon" (μαμωνᾶς), a word appearing four times in the NT (Mt 6:24; Lk 16:9, 11, 13). "Mammon" is the transliteration of the Aramaic word for money or wealth (BDAG). Jesus employs the word to indicate that money has an egocentric force, a power that enslaves hearts and minds. Mammon is money *deified.*

8:6 The cheating businessmen did not confine their trade to grain; they also dealt in purchasing people. The more they were able to drive people into debt, the more likely it would be that the paupers would be forced to sell themselves as slaves to remain financially viable. Amos 8:6 reveals the plan: "the more we cheat, the more slaves we will be able to buy and sell." The first part of 8:6 coincides with 2:6d–e, except that 2:6d uses the verb מָכַר, "to sell," whereas 8:6 uses קָנָה, "to buy." The marketers are making a profit from both selling (2:6d–e) and buying (8:6) human beings.

If an Israelite could not get enough money together to pay off a debt, he could be sold into slavery (Ex 21:1–6; Deut 15:12–18). A man could serve only for a maximum of six years, but a woman might serve for the rest of her life if she became designated for marriage by her owner. When Amos states that the poor were bought and sold for silver, he points out a practice that was tolerated

[16] Nehemiah's problem was also created by commercial greed in that the people in Jerusalem in his day were conducting their business *on the Sabbath* (Neh 13:15–22).

[17] See the excursus "The Sabbath."

in the Torah. What is *intolerable*, however, is that people were being forced into slavery for a relatively small debt: a pair of sandals (2:6; 8:6).

The marketplace had become the center for deceiving and defrauding the defenseless. The merchants' greed was insatiable; their self-indulgence knew no limits. They exploited the "nameless" people located at the bottom of the social hierarchy in order to improve their own stations in life. No one was able to rectify these "business moves"—no one, that is, except Yahweh, who "executes justice [מִשְׁפַּט] for the orphan and the widow and loves the sojourner" (Deut 10:18), who is the "Father of orphans and protector of widows" (Ps 68:6 [ET 68:5]).

While other nations practiced power politics and economics rooted in greed and self-interest,[18] the people of Israel were called to be different: they were to be holy, even as Yahweh is holy (Lev 19:2). Yahweh's people were summoned to embrace and embody the Torah, and the quintessential qualities of the Torah include righteousness and justice. These divine qualities, proffered also through Amos (5:15, 24; cf. 5:7; 6:12), preclude every form of greed and exploitation. Or stated positively, righteousness and justice involve the movement "from hostility to hospitality,"[19] especially in relation to people on the fringes of society. God's will for his OT covenant people continues into the new covenant in Christ. As the apostle exhorts, "So then, as we have opportunity, let us do good to all, most especially to those who are of the household of the faith" (Gal 6:10; cf. Mt 25:31–46; 1 Tim 5:8).

Summary

Psalm 92 is entitled "A Psalm; A Song for the Day of the Sabbath."[20] The poem begins:

> It is good to give thanks to Yahweh,
> and to sing praise to your name, O Most High. (Ps 92:2 [ET 92:1])

The tradesmen described by Amos in 8:4–6 had no such affection for Yahweh's gift of the Sabbath.[21] The holy day was a reluctant duty, not a delight—a day of begrudged obligation, not a time of holy celebration. The psalmist calls anyone with this attitude "a stupid man [who] does not know" and "a fool" (Ps 92:7 [ET 92:6]). In Israel the phrase "business ethics" appeared to be an oxymoron as dubious as "government efficiency."

Israel's inception included the mandate that there be equal access to land (Num 26:53–56; 33:53–54; 36:1–12). Yahweh had given everyone in Israel an

---

[18] Compare, for example, the Tyrian queen Jezebel's manipulation, deception, and murder (1 Kings 21).

[19] Nouwen, *Reaching Out*, 45.

[20] The only other psalm whose superscription dedicates it for the Sabbath is LXX Ps 37:1. After translating the Hebrew superscription in MT Ps 38:1, it adds περὶ σαββάτου so that it reads "for the memorial/remembrance of the Sabbath" (εἰς ἀνάμνησιν περὶ σαββάτου).

[21] See further the excursus "The Sabbath."

ancestral allotment of land (Joshua 13–21). Yet in the ninth and eighth centuries, the nation was transformed into more of a Canaanite state where the wealthy increased their possession of land by means of economic leverage and social power. Some other prophetic texts use words related to "Canaanite" for a "trader" (כְּנַעָן, Is 23:8; כְּנַעַן, Ezek 16:29; Zeph 1:11; כְּנַעֲנִי, Zech 14:21), probably with negative connotations. Corrupt businessmen supported economic activity that created upper and lower classes. Israel's elite confiscated more and more land through dishonest practices (cf. Is 5:8; Amos 2:6–8; 5:12). They sold less food than was honest for more currency than was honest (8:5–6). The influence of Canaanite religion upon Israel brought with it Canaanite business practices.[22]

The protection and care for the poor and needy was part of Yahweh's summons to Israel. The Jubilee was Yahweh's way of restructuring Israel's assets to remind the nation that all property and land belonged to him. Israel was an exodus people who must never return to a system of slavery (Lev 25:42). The Jubilee was to take place every fiftieth year, preceded by a "Sabbath's Sabbath," or the forty-ninth year (Lev 25:8–12). The Jubilee aimed to dismantle social and economic inequality by releasing each member from debt (Lev 25:35–42), returning forfeited land to its original owners (Lev 25:25–28), and freeing slaves (Lev 25:47–55). The monarchy and priesthood were charged with the enforcement of the Jubilee and fair standards of trade (e.g., Deut 17:8–13, 18–20). Jeroboam ben Joash and Amaziah the priest of Bethel (Amos 1:1; 7:10–17) were guilty because they were proponents of "business as usual." They conveniently forgot the mandate in Lev 25:17: "do not oppress each other, but fear your God, for I am Yahweh your God."

Yahweh hears the cry of his oppressed people (Ex 2:23) and feels their pain (Ex 3:7; cf. Acts 9:1–2, 5). Everyone who has been restored to a right relationship with God through his forgiveness is granted the same ears and heart to be merciful to others (cf. Mt 18:21–35). But deep down, within every son and daughter of Adam and Eve, there exists an insatiable desire to look at their neighbor's spouse, manservant, maidservant, ox, donkey, indeed, anything that belongs to their neighbor and long for them all to be "mine!" People disregard the Ninth and Tenth Commandments, which state, "You shall not covet" (Ex 20:17).

The verb "covet" (חָמַד) in Ex 20:17 covers the entire sequence from seeing to desiring to possessing. For example, Achan confesses in Josh 7:21: "I *saw* among the spoil a beautiful mantle from Shinar and two hundred shekels of silver and a bar of gold weighing fifty shekels, and I *coveted* them [וָאֶחְמְדֵם], and I *took* them." This sequence leads to Yahweh's judgment. James 1:15 states:

---

22 For condemnations of northern Israel's syncretistic and idolatrous worship, which incorporated some aspects of Canaanite religion, see the commentary on 2:7–8; 3:14; 4:4–5; 5:5–6, 14, 21–27; 7:9–17; 8:5, 10, 14; 9:1 (the Bethel temple). See also the excursuses "The Prophets and Israel's Worship" and "The Sabbath."

"After desire has conceived, it gives birth to sin, and sin, when it is finished, brings forth death." By treating their fellow Israelites as commodities, the merchants of Amos' day denied their core identity as Yahweh's people. *Those once oppressed in Egypt became the oppressors of their own countrymen.*

There is a sickness and madness in Western society called consumerism—the notion that life consists in having and getting and spending and controlling and using and eating. This system places stress on accumulation and believes that meaning and security come by "more." How shall those baptized into Christ live in a world with its titanic desire to acquire? How are the words of Paul in Phil 4:11 able to make sense: "I have learned in whatever circumstances I am to be content"? And just how do people live in a society that screams at them daily to buy things they don't need with money they don't have to impress people they may not even like?

By the washing of water with the Word (Eph 5:26; cf. Mt 28:19), Yahweh placed his mark of ownership upon the baptized. He made this promise, "I have redeemed you; I have called you by name. You are mine" (Is 43:1). In those belonging to God the Father through the redeeming work of Jesus, the Holy Spirit empowers a life that combats greed, dishonesty, and vice. Asaph's contentment with Yahweh is the gift and goal of the people of God:

> Who [but you] have I in heaven?
> Besides you, I desire nothing on earth. (Ps 73:25)

Excursus

The Sabbath

The Israelite merchants' observance of the Sabbath in name only (Amos 8:5) was a serious violation of the Sinaitic covenant. For them the day was merely a lost opportunity for profit. They failed to keep the Sabbath day holy (Ex 20:8; Deut 5:12). This was an omission that endangered the Israelite community as the people of God and therefore carried the threat of grave consequences (Ex 31:14–15). Later prophets would cite the violation of the Sabbath as the reason for Judah's demise. Jeremiah, speaking for Yahweh, blames the destruction of Jerusalem and its temple on the nation's failure to keep this day holy (Jer 17:19–27). So does the priestly prophet Ezekiel (Ezek 20:12–24). Israel's greatest Prophet, the Lord Jesus, also reprimanded the improper appropriation of the day: "The Sabbath was made for man, not man for the Sabbath" (Mk 2:27).

The Sabbath is rich in spiritual and social significance. Its origin is as old as creation (Gen 2:1–3). The Hebrew verb "to be holy" (קָדַשׁ) first appears in the establishment of the Sabbath to mark it as distinct from the previous six days. Gen 2:3 states: "God blessed the seventh day and hallowed it" (וַיְקַדֵּשׁ אֹתוֹ). The contrast in Gen 2:3 is between the sacred, the realm of God, and his good creation. The focus in the first six days of creation is on the human world, the realm of God's creatures. But on the seventh day no act of creation takes place. The focus is instead on Yahweh alone, who is described as resting. This prompts the sacred activity of worship in the human world. The holiness of the seventh day is a sign of Yahweh's own holiness, which distinguishes him from his entire creation.

Holiness is intrinsic to Yahweh (Is 5:24; 6:3; Ps 89:19 [ET 89:18]) and a characteristic of the region of heaven (Deut 26:15; Ps 20:7 [ET 20:6]). Genesis 1 illustrates the distinction between the sacred and the ordinary. The first two humans were good and blessed, and they even bore the image of God, but they were not called holy (Gen 1:26–30). The same is true for the rest of creation in Genesis 1. It is good, even "very good" (Gen 1:31), but it is not described as holy. Holiness is only introduced on the seventh day, as a moment in time, not as an object within creation.

The fall into sin (Genesis 3) produced an enormous gulf between the holy God and his now-dying creation. Yet holiness broke into creation when Yahweh appeared to Moses and called him to lead the redemption of his people; the theophany created "holy ground" (Ex 3:5). The Passover and the first day of the Feast of Unleavened Bread were to be the occasion of a "holy assembly" (Ex 12:16), and when Yahweh delivered his people, he was acclaimed as "majestic in holiness" (Ex 15:11; cf. Ex 15:13). Moreover, at Sinai Yahweh declared his intention that all Israel be "a kingdom of priests and a holy nation" (Ex 19:6).

All members of God's people, regardless of their social status, were to receive the benefits of Yahweh's holy Sabbath. The day was a celebration of both the original creation (Ex 20:11) and the new creation through salvation (Deut 5:15). It served as a sign of the divine covenant (Ex 31:12–13; Ezek 20:12, 20), a marker for holy days (Lev 23:15–16), and a reminder of Yahweh's powerful deliverance from servitude in Egypt (Deut 5:15). Israel was free from slavery to oppressors and false gods and liberated to serve the living God. Miller maintains: "If Exodus was God's redemptive activity to give sabbath to slaves, then sabbath now is human non-activity to remember the Exodus redemption."[1] The benefit of Sabbath rest extended to aliens and sojourners in Israel and even domesticated animals (Ex 23:12; Deut 5:14).

The Sabbath was a gift not only for people but also for serving animals because, as Fretheim notes, the Sabbath commandments in Ex 20:11 and Ex 31:17 are linked to the creation account. The laws undergirding the Jubilee Year demonstrate that the land also must have its Sabbaths (Lev 25:1–24). Neglect of these mandates would have a negative effect upon the land (Lev 26:27–45). "If Sabbath is not kept, that neglect can have adverse effects upon the entire creation."[2] This is one reason why the book of Amos describes so much undoing of creation, for example, the earthquakes and shaking caused by Yahweh in 1:1; 3:15; 4:11; 8:8; 9:1, 5 (the quaking is compared to the rise and fall of the Nile River in 8:8 and 9:5); the lack of rain in 4:7; the locust attacks in 4:9 (see also 7:1); and the darkening of the sun in 8:9 (cf. 5:8, 18–20). The link is clear: desecration of the Sabbath meant destruction of *people, land, and animals.*

The Sabbath was kept by OT believers as they followed Yahweh's ordinances (Ezek 20:12–20) and offered prescribed sacrifices (Num 28:9–10) and as the priests and Levites performed the specific duties of their offices (Lev 24:8; 2 Chr 23:4, 8). Undergirding this was the cessation of all economic activity (e.g., Ex 20:10; Deut 5:14; Neh 13:15–22) because Yahweh "rested on the seventh day" (Ex 20:11). The work stoppage emphasized that Israel was not the owner but the beneficiary and manager of Yahweh's gracious resources (Deut 8:10–18). The Sabbath was a constant reminder of the answer to Jesus' question, "Is not life is more than food, and the body more than clothing?" (Mt 6:25).

Consumption and achievement were to cease one day in seven, and God still enabled life to go on. Work was to cease so that God's redeemed could remember that the reason for living was not merely to desire and then acquire. Israel was created for more than "life, liberty, and the purchase of happiness."

Honest work is part of Yahweh's good creation (Gen 2:15) and not to be disparaged (2 Thess 3:11–13). Yet the human enterprise becomes sinful abuse

---

1 Miller, "The Human Sabbath," 88.

2 Fretheim, *God and World in the Old Testament*, 62–63. Odell notes that in the rest of the ancient Near East "human beings were made to work and serve the gods, while only the gods rested." She asserts that "human participation in the sabbath signifies a daring claim that human beings share in the divine image" (*Ezekiel*, 251).

when it treats people like commodities that may be used and thrown away. All human beings have value, apart from their economic and geopolitical utility. From the moment of conception, every person is a creation of God, and through incorporation into the covenant of grace (in the NT era, through Holy Baptism [Col 2:11–13]), each person receives the benefits of God's redemption and becomes an heir of all the divine promises. The Sabbath celebrated this reality. Those who honored the spirit and the letter of this day of rest were following Yahweh's temporal framework for creation and redemption.

"The pattern for those created in the image of God is work/rest, not just rest."[3] And in Amos' day, he had to preach that it was rest/work, *not just work.* The Sabbath, therefore, says yes to the value of people while at the same time it says no to the insidious need for more and the frantic frenzy for upward mobility. But the businessmen of Amos' day would have none of this. They were begrudging the New Moon and the Sabbath (Amos 8:5). Their motto was "time is money!"

Yahweh's gift of the Sabbath finds its ultimate expression in Jesus (Col 2:16–17). After suffering for the sins of the world on Good Friday, he observed the Sabbath by his rest in the tomb on Holy Saturday before rising on the first day of the new week (cf. Lk 23:56). He offers the free gift of salvation so that all human work that seeks justification before God may be placed aside (Mt 11:28–29). The writer of Hebrews confirms the promise of Jesus. He also transforms the Sabbath rest. "There remains, then, a Sabbath rest for the people of God, for whoever enters his [God's] rest also rests from his works, just as God did from his own [works]" (Heb 4:9–10). At the time of death, Jesus gives rest to all believers as they await their bodily resurrection into the everlasting new creation with its eternal Sabbath rest. John puts it this way: "Then I heard a voice from heaven saying, 'Write: Blessed are the dead who die in the Lord from now on.' 'Yes,' says the Spirit, 'that they may rest from their labors, for their works will follow them' " (Rev 14:13).

[3] Fretheim, *God and World in the Old Testament*, 319.

Amos 8:7–14

A Famine of Yahweh's Word

Translation

8 [7]Yahweh swears by the pride of Jacob, "I will never forget any of their deeds.

[8]On account of this shall not the land shake
and each one living in it mourn?
And all of it will ascend like the Nile
and be tossed and sink like the Nile of Egypt.
[9]"And it will happen on that day," declares the Lord Yahweh,
"that I will bring in the sun at midday
and I will cause darkness for the earth in a day of light.
[10]And I will turn your festivals into mourning
and all of your songs into a funeral dirge.
And I will put on all loins sackcloth
and upon every head baldness.
And I will make it like mourning for an only son
and its end like a bitter day.
[11]"Behold, days are coming," declares the Lord Yahweh,
"when I will send a famine in the land—
not famine for bread,
and not thirst for water,
but rather to hear the words of Yahweh.
[12]And they will wander from sea to sea
and from north to east.
They will go back and forth to seek the Word of Yahweh,
but they will not find [it].
[13]"On that day the beautiful maidens will faint,
and the young men from thirst.
[14]Those who swear, 'By the Guilt of Samaria,'
and who say, 'As your god lives, Dan,'
and, 'As lives the Way of Beersheba'—
they will fall, and they will never rise again."

Textual Notes

8:7 נִשְׁבַּע יְהוָה בִּגְאוֹן יַעֲקֹב—The oath formula with the Niphal of שָׁבַע, "to swear," with the preposition בְּ is also used in 4:2 and 6:8. See the first textual note on 4:2 and the first textual note on 6:8. In those passages, God swears "by himself" (בְּנַפְשׁוֹ, 6:8) or by one of his attributes, "by his holiness" (בְּקָדְשׁוֹ, 4:2). The phrase גְּאוֹן יַעֲקֹב, "the pride of Jacob," also appears in 6:8. See the third textual note on 6:8. Besides Amos 6:8 and

8:7, there are two other occurrences of the construct phrase "the pride of Jacob" in the OT. Nah 2:3 (ET 2:2) describes Yahweh as restoring "the pride/majesty [גְּאוֹן] of Jacob as the pride/majesty [גְּאוֹן] of Israel," and both construct phrases must refer to the splendor of the restored people of God. In Ps 47:5 (ET 47:4), "the pride/majesty of Jacob" is parallel with "heritage," and seems to refer to the land of Israel.

There are at least three different possibilities for the meaning of the phrase in 8:7:[1]

1. Yahweh himself is "the pride/majesty of Jacob." According to this view, "Yahweh swears by the pride of Jacob" in 8:7 is equivalent to "Yahweh swears by himself" in 6:8. Marti interprets the phrase as a straightforward name for Yahweh and paraphrases the clause in 8:7 as "as truly as I am the pride of Jacob."[2] In a number of passages, גְּאוֹן is an attribute of God (BDB, s.v. גָּאוֹן, 1 b, under the root גאה). See, for example, גְּאוֹן in Micah 5:3 (ET 5:4).
2. It refers to Israel's inheritance, that is, the promised land, as apparently in Ps 47:5 (ET 47:4). גָּאוֹן appears in a positive sense in Is 4:2, where the fruit of the land is the pride of Israel's survivors, and in Ps 47:5 (ET 47:4), where Yahweh chooses the pride of Jacob, whom he loves.
3. Israel's attitude of pride brought about by the nation's military power, wealth, and affluence. Wolff understands it in 8:7 to refer to Israel's arrogance as it did in 6:8.[3] Andersen and Freedman understand גְּאוֹן יַעֲקֹב in 8:7 to include "everybody in both kingdoms or perhaps primarily the leadership, but especially [the] grasping, greedy, and oppressive merchants who are front and center."[4] These elite aristocrats display an attitude that is the opposite of life envisioned by Paul in Phil 2:3–4: do "nothing from strife or conceit, but in humility consider others better than yourselves, each of you not looking out only for your own interests, but also for the interests of others."

It appears most likely that in 8:7 "the pride of Jacob" refers to Yahweh himself. There is a close parallel between the first clause of 6:8, where Yahweh swears "by himself," and this clause in 8:7, where Yahweh swears "by the pride/majesty of Jacob." Hos 5:5 and 7:10 speak of "the pride/majesty of Israel" as an appellation for Yahweh.

אִם־אֶשְׁכַּח לָנֶצַח כָּל־מַעֲשֵׂיהֶם׃—After an oath formula, the hypothetical particle אִם "becomes an emph[atic] negative" (BDB, s.v. אִם, 1 b (2)). The verb שָׁכַח usually means "to forget" and may connote "to abandon, leave," referring to both the act and its consequences.[5] Its antonym is זָכַר, "to remember." God does not forget those who cry out to him (Ps 9:13 [ET 9:12]; cf. Is 49:15) and he promises never to forget his covenant promises (e.g., Deut 4:31). For God to forget would, of course, be contrary to his omniscience, but he promises not to "remember" the sins of those whom he forgives (Is 43:25; cf. Ps 79:8). In contrast, the wicked presume in their heart that "God has for-

---

1 Cf. Niehaus, "Amos," 472.

2 Marti, *Das Dodekapropheton*, 217, translated by Wolff, *Joel and Amos*, 328, including n. 36.

3 Wolff, *Joel and Amos*, 328.

4 Andersen and Freedman, *Amos*, 693.

5 Cf. H. D. Preuss, "שָׁכַח," *TDOT* 14:671–77.

gotten" and does not see the evil they have done (Ps 10:11; cf. Job 8:13), but the sins of such impenitent people are not forgiven. Those who forget God go to Sheol (Ps 9:18 [ET 9:17]). The implication in Amos 8:7 is that Yahweh's pledge "to never forget" means that Israel will never be forgiven (7:8; 8:2).

8:8 הֲעַל זֹאת לֹא־תִרְגַּז הָאָרֶץ—The interrogative *he* is prefixed to the preposition עַל in the sense of "because, on account of." The verb רָגַז in the Qal means "to be agitated, tremble, quiver, and quake" and often expresses agitation growing out of some deeply rooted emotion (e.g., Ex 15:14; Deut 2:25; Is 32:10–11).[6] It can be used physically and poetically, as in Ps 18:8 (ET 18:7), where רָגַז describes the quaking of the foundations of the mountains before a storm marking Yahweh's advent.

וְאָבַל כָּל־יוֹשֵׁב בָּהּ—For אָבַל, "mourn," see the fourth textual note on 1:2. The feminine suffix on בָּהּ refers back to הָאָרֶץ in the preceding clause. Compare the similar plural phrase וְאָבְלוּ כָּל־יוֹשְׁבֵי בָהּ in 9:5.

וְעָלְתָה כָאֹר כֻּלָּהּ—The verb עָלָה, "to rise, go up," can refer to water flooding, as in, for example, Is 8:7; Jer 46:7–8; Amos 9:5. The "Nile" (יְאוֹר) with the preposition כְּ here has the article and is spelled doubly defectively, כָאֹר, for כַּיְאוֹר, the combination of יְאוֹר with הַ and כְּ. The plene spelling without the article, כִּיאוֹר (יְאוֹר with כְּ), occurs in the next clause. The singly defective spellings with the article, כַּיְאֹר, and without the article, כִּיאֹר, are used in 9:5. For the article with this proper name, see GKC, § 125 e.

As the most remarkable of the ancient world's river systems, the Nile formed an indispensable resource for Egypt.[7] In Egyptian literature, the term "Nile" is often followed by the adjective "great" to denote its central artery within its delta system.[8] Annually this river would inundate its flood plain and then recede. The dramatic, cyclic rise and fall of the Nile is used as a simile in Amos 8:8 and 9:5 for the quaking of the earth caused by Yahweh. Compare Is 19:5–9, where Yahweh desiccates the Nile.

וְנִגְרְשָׁה וְנִשְׁקְהָ כִּיאוֹר מִצְרָיִם׃—The Niphal of גָּרַשׁ means to "be driven, tossed about."[9] In Is 57:20 it describes the tossed sea. The Qere וְנִשְׁקְעָה is the Niphal of שָׁקַע. The Kethib, וְנִשְׁקָה, omits the *ayin* (ע), possibly due to an aural error. In both the Qal and the Niphal, the verb שָׁקַע means "to sink, subside" (e.g., the Qal in Jer 51:64). It appears in the Qal in Amos 9:5.

8:9 וְהָיָה ׀ בַּיּוֹם הַהוּא—The phrase "on that day" recalls the Day of Yahweh theme in 5:18–20. בַּיּוֹם הַהוּא was used in judgment contexts in 2:16 and 8:3, and it will be again in that way in 8:13. It will also be used in the Gospel promise of 9:11.

נְאֻם אֲדֹנָי יְהוִה—This will be repeated in 8:11. For נְאֻם יהוה, see the second textual note on 2:11.

וְהֵבֵאתִי הַשֶּׁמֶשׁ בַּצָּהֳרָיִם—The idiom for the sun setting normally employs the verb בּוֹא in the Qal (e.g., Judg 19:14). The Hiphil of בּוֹא here, וְהֵבֵאתִי, indicates that it is Yahweh who will cause the sun to set at midday, perhaps by a solar eclipse. The accent

---

6 Cf. G. Vanoni, "רָגַז," *TDOT* 13:304–8.

7 Cf. H. Eising and J. Bergman, "יְאֹר," *TDOT* 5:359–63.

8 J. R. Huddlestun, "Nile (Old Testament)," *ABD* 4:1108. For the Nile's course and hydrology, see B. R. Williams, "Nile (Geography)," *ABD* 4:1112–16.

9 Cf. H. Ringgren, "גָּרַשׁ," *TDOT* 3:68–69.

on וְהֵבֵאתִי is shifted to the ultima because the perfect has *waw* consecutive (GKC, § 49 l). In 5:8 Amos employs the Hiphil of חָשַׁךְ to speak of Yahweh as the one "who darkens day into night" (וְיוֹם לַיְלָה הֶחְשִׁיךְ). Later in chapter 5, he speaks of the Day of Yahweh as being "darkness and not light" (5:18, 20).

The noun צָהֳרָיִם refers to the highest point of the sun during the day.[10] The antithesis of making the sun go down at midday is in Josh 10:13, where Yahweh causes the sun to stand still to extend the daylight. In Joshua, Yahweh's power over the sun is a portent of victory for Israel; in Amos, it signals all-out disaster for Israel.

וְהַחֲשַׁכְתִּי לָאָרֶץ בְּיוֹם אוֹר׃—The Hiphil of חָשַׁךְ means "to darken, cause darkness," and is antonymous to both "day" (יוֹם) and "light" (אוֹר).

8:10 וְהָפַכְתִּי חַגֵּיכֶם לְאֵבֶל—The combination of the verb הָפַךְ with the preposition לְ frequently means "to turn [something] into [something else]," as in, for example, Ex 7:17 and 1 Sam 10:6. The verb does double duty for the next clause too. It was used in a different sense in 4:11; see the first textual note there.

The plural of the noun חַג with the same suffix (חַגֵּיכֶם) appeared also in 5:21; see the first textual note and the commentary there. "Your festivals" is a brief reference to northern Israel's perverted and syncretistic worship, which Yahweh condemns in 2:6–8; 3:14; 4:4–5; 5:5–6, 14, 21–27; 7:9–17. The noun אֵבֶל, "mourning," occurs twice in this verse and was also in 5:16. It is cognate to the verb אָבַל, "mourn," in 8:8 and 9:5.

וְכָל־שִׁירֵיכֶם לְקִינָה—The plural of the noun שִׁיר was used in the same sense for worship "songs" in 5:23; see the first textual note and the commentary there. For the noun קִינָה, "funeral dirge," see the second textual note on 5:1.

וְהַעֲלֵיתִי עַל־כָּל־מָתְנַיִם שָׂק—The Hiphil of עָלָה can mean "to clothe, put [clothing or ornaments] on [someone]" (see BDB, 4). The verb does double duty for the following clause too. The dual מָתְנַיִם refers to the "loins, waist."

The noun שַׂק, "sackcloth," the direct object of the verb, refers generally to loosely woven cloth, usually made from goat hair and thus black.[11] Its main use was for garments indicating that the person wearing them was in a state of grief or mourning (e.g., 1 Ki 21:27; Jer 48:37; Esth 4:1–4; Dan 9:3). Fasting and the donning of sackcloth often went together. For example, after Elijah pronounced judgment upon Ahab's house, Ahab put on sackcloth and began to fast (1 Ki 21:27). David instructed people to put on sackcloth and mourn after Abner's death (2 Sam 3:31). The people of Israel put on sackcloth and repented of their sins after hearing the Torah read by Ezra (Neh 9:1–4). The removal of sackcloth is equated with joy: "you have turned my mourning into dancing; you have loosened my sackcloth and girded me in joy [פִּתַּחְתָּ שַׂקִּי וַתְּאַזְּרֵנִי שִׂמְחָה]" (Ps 30:12 [ET 30:11]).

וְעַל־כָּל־רֹאשׁ קָרְחָה—קָרְחָה, "baldness, a bald spot," could be produced by shaving the head as a mourning rite, but this practice was prohibited for Israel in Lev 21:5 and Deut 14:1. Yet baldness as a sign of grief is inflicted by Yahweh in prophetic judgment oracles, for example, Is 22:12 and Ezek 7:18, both of which also have "sackcloth."

---

[10] Cf. H. Niehr, "צָהֳרַיִם," *TDOT* 12:264–66.

[11] Cf. W. Thiel, "שַׂק," *TDOT* 14:184–89.

וְשַׂמְתִּ֫יהָ כְּאֵ֣בֶל יָחִ֔יד וְאַחֲרִיתָ֖הּ כְּי֥וֹם מָֽר׃—The feminine suffixes on the verb וְשַׂמְתִּ֫יהָ, "I will place/make *it*," and on the noun וְאַחֲרִיתָ֖הּ, "*its* end," abstractly refer to the whole situation of disaster described previously (GKC, § 135 p).

The construct phrase כְּאֵ֣בֶל יָחִ֔יד has a genitive of advantage: "like mourning *for* an only son" (so Waltke-O'Connor, 9.5.2e, including example 13; GKC, § 128 h, and Joüon, § 129 e, consider it a kind of objective genitive). This phrase designates grief in its most intense form. The masculine adjective יָחִיד, "lone, sole," can mean "only son" (Gen 22:2, 12, 16; Prov 4:3).[12] In Judg 11:34 the feminine adjective refers to Jephthah's "only" daughter (הִ֣יא יְחִידָ֔ה), and it is reinforced by the words "he had beside her neither son nor daughter" (אֵֽין־ל֥וֹ מִמֶּ֛נּוּ בֵּ֖ן אוֹ־בַֽת). Grieving for an only son may signal Yahweh's eschatological Day of Judgment (Jer 6:26; Zech 12:10). This is what Amos means in this context. Compare Zech 12:10, where after God declares, "They shall look upon me whom they have pierced," there is lamentation over the יָחִיד in the prophecy of the Messiah, God's only Son, called μονογενής in Jn 1:14, 18; 3:16, 18.

The adjective "bitter" (מַר) modifies the nouns "mourning" (מִסְפֵּד) in Ezek 27:31 and "death" (הַמָּוֶת) in 1 Sam 15:32.[13] The "bitter day" (י֥וֹם מָֽר) of Amos 8:10 denotes the same "day" of judgment referred to elsewhere in the book.[a] In a similar vein, Zeph 1:14 announces that on "the Day of Yahweh," "a warrior there will be crying out bitterly" (מַ֥ר צֹרֵ֖חַ שָׁ֥ם גִּבּֽוֹר).

(a) Amos 1:14; 2:16; 3:14; 4:2; 6:3; 8:3, 9, 10, 11, 13

8:11 הִנֵּ֣ה ׀ יָמִ֣ים בָּאִ֗ים נְאֻם֙ אֲדֹנָ֣י יְהוִ֔ה—The "days" (יָמִים) that are "coming" (בָּאִים) continue the "day" of judgment theme from 8:10. הִנֵּה יָמִים בָּאִים was also in the judgment oracle of 4:2. But it will be repeated in the Gospel promise of 9:13.

וְהִשְׁלַחְתִּ֥י רָעָ֖ב בָּאָ֑רֶץ—The verb שָׁלַח, "to send," appears in the Hiphil only five times in the OT, all in judgment contexts, compared to around five hundred sixty attestations in the Qal and two hundred sixty in the Piel.[14] In the other four Hiphil uses of שָׁלַח, Yahweh sends swarms of flies against the Egyptians (Ex 8:17 [ET 8:21]), wild animals as a covenant curse (Lev 26:22), Rezin king of Aram and Pekah king of Israel against Judah (2 Ki 15:37), and a famine (Ezek 14:13).

The noun רָעָב appears twice in this verse and nowhere else in the book. It means "hunger" and/or "famine" and is used as an object only in clauses with Yahweh as the subject of the verb, as here.[15] רָעָב often appears in contexts of destruction, injury, and want (e.g., Is 5:13; Jer 14:18; Ezek 14:21). Amos describes a famine of food and a drought of water in his lists of plagues in 4:6–8. Whereas prior famines threatened physical life, the famine of hearing Yahweh's words jeopardizes Israel's spiritual and eternal life.

לֹֽא־רָעָ֤ב לַלֶּ֙חֶם֙ וְלֹֽא־צָמָ֣א לַמַּ֔יִם—In nominal clauses the use of לֹא instead of אֵין makes a more emphatic negative statement. This will not be a "famine" (רָעָב) "for food" (לַלֶּחֶם) nor a "thirst" (צָמָא) "for water" (לַמַּיִם).

---

[12] Cf. H.-J. Fabry, "יָחִיד," *TDOT* 6:46.

[13] Cf. H. Ringgren and H.-J. Fabry, "מרר," *TDOT* 9:15–19.

[14] Cf. F.-L. Hossfeld, F. van der Velden, and U. Dahmen, "שָׁלַח," *TDOT* 15:49–73.

[15] Cf. T. Seidl, "רָעָב," *TDOT* 13:538–43.

The noun צָמָא, "thirst," will recur in 8:13 in a literal sense as a cause of fainting. The noun is used metaphorically here for thirst caused by a spiritual drought: the absence of the life-giving, satisfying Word of Yahweh. It is used for a deadly lack of knowledge and faith in Yahweh in Is 5:13. The corresponding verb צָמֵא is used for being physically thirsty in Is 65:13.[16] In Ps 42:3 (ET 42:2) the psalmist's soul thirsts (צָמְאָ) for the living God. In Is 55:1 Yahweh freely offers spiritual food and drink to anyone who is "thirsty" (the related adjective צָמֵא), and he compares his efficacious Word to life-giving rain (Is 55:10–11).

כִּ֥י אִם־לִשְׁמֹ֔עַ אֵ֖ת דִּבְרֵ֥י יְהוָֽה׃—The combination כִּי אִם has the adversative sense "but rather, instead." The infinitive construct לִשְׁמֹ֔עַ, "to hear," is commonly translated as a verbal noun, a famine "of hearing." The plural construct phrase דִּבְרֵ֥י יְהוָֽה, "words of Yahweh," occurs only here in Amos. The singular construct phrase is in the judgment oracles of 7:16 and 8:12.

8:12 וְנָע֗וּ מִיָּ֥ם עַד־יָ֖ם וּמִצָּפ֣וֹן וְעַד־מִזְרָ֑ח—Amos describes the people's futile search. This bicolon uses the Qal of נוּעַ, which does double duty for both clauses. It describes an unsteady and staggering movement. See the first textual note on 4:8, where נוּעַ depicts the Israelites' wandering quest for water. It appears twice in other stems in 9:9.

The phrase מִיָּם עַד־יָם, "from sea to sea," may indicate traveling over the entire world (Zech 9:10; Ps 72:8).[17] Here, however, it probably indicates from the Mediterranean to the Dead Sea or vice versa. Joel 2:20 refers to "the eastern sea" (הַיָּם֙ הַקַּדְמֹנִ֔י, that is, the Dead Sea) and "the western sea" (הַיָּ֖ם הָאַחֲר֑וֹן, that is, the Mediterranean Sea). Or instead of the Dead Sea here, the southern boundary may be the Red Sea at the Gulf of Aqaba. Niehaus notes an Akkadian phrase and believes that מִיָּ֥ם עַד־יָ֖ם refers to the area between the Mediterranean Sea and the Persian Gulf, which is the full extent of the Assyrian Empire, the empire that would conquer and exile northern Israel.[18]

Parallel to "from sea to sea" is וּמִצָּפ֣וֹן וְעַד־מִזְרָ֑ח, "and from north to east." This is rather vague and again could indicate searching over vast areas. *BHS* disregards the Masoretic accents and includes the verb that heads the following clause, יְשׁוֹטְט֛וּ, with this second geographic merism. One translation that follows that rearrangement of the syntax is the NIV: "and wander from north to east." The translation above follows the MT syntax, as do most English versions.

יְשׁוֹטְט֛וּ לְבַקֵּ֥שׁ אֶת־דְּבַר־יְהוָ֖ה—The Polel of שׁוּט is parallel to the Qal of נוּעַ at the beginning of the verse. Both the Qal and the Polel of this second verb refer to wandering over vast areas.[19] The Qal describes the action of Israelites roaming over the desert looking for manna (Num 11:8; cf. the Qal in 2 Sam 24:2, 8; Job 1:7; 2:2). The Polel may have an intensive meaning, suggesting rapid and frantic roving to and fro (see

---

[16] Cf. D. Kellermann, "צָמֵא," *TDOT* 12:405–9.

[17] This is how Wolff understands its use in 8:12: the phrase designates "the uttermost boundaries of the earth" (*Joel and Amos*, 330–31).

[18] Niehaus, "Amos," 475. The Akkadian is *ultu tamti eliti adi tamti šapliti*, "from the upper sea to the lower sea." For the role of Assyria in fulfilling the prophecy of Amos, see further the excursus "The Assyrian Empire."

[19] Cf. E.-J. Waschke, "שׁוּט," *TDOT* 14:528–30.

Dan 12:4). The Polel is used for the eyes of Yahweh ranging over the entire earth (Zech 4:10; 2 Chr 16:9).

The Piel infinitive construct with preposition לְבַקֵּשׁ forms a purpose clause: "to seek, search for." בִּקֵּשׁ is in the same semantic field as דָּרַשׁ, "to seek" (Amos 5:4–6, 14).

וְלֹא יִמְצָאוּ׃—The chilling judgment is "but they will not find" the divine Word.

8:13 בַּיּוֹם הַהוּא תִּתְעַלַּפְנָה הַבְּתוּלֹת הַיָּפוֹת—The temporal phrase is repeated from 8:9. The verb עָלַף only appears three times in the OT in the Hithpael: here and Gen 38:14 and Jonah 4:8. For its form, see GKC, § 54 k. The Hithpael conveys the idea of swooning from weakness. It also appears three times in the Pual. The typical choice for translating both stems of עָלַף is "to faint," but this is not in the sense of a temporary loss of consciousness. In Amos 8:13 "fainting" is closer to a near-death experience than it is to merely feeling woozy.

The subject is the adjectival phrase הַבְּתוּלֹת הַיָּפוֹת, "the beautiful maidens." For the noun בְּתוּלָה, see the first textual note on 5:2.

Even though the Hithpael imperfect תִּתְעַלַּפְנָה is feminine plural to match its subject, the verb does double duty for the next clause, in which the subject is masculine plural (GKC, § 146 g; Joüon, § 150 q).

וְהַבַּחוּרִים בַּצָּמָא׃—The verb "will faint" is implied for "and the young men from thirst." For the noun בָּחוּר, see the first textual note on 2:11. For צָמָא, see the third textual note on 8:11.

8:14 הַנִּשְׁבָּעִים בְּאַשְׁמַת שֹׁמְרוֹן—The construction of the Niphal of שָׁבַע, "to swear," with the preposition בְּ attached to what is invoked to guarantee the oath also appears in 4:2; 6:8; and 8:7. See the first textual note on 4:2. The construct phrase אַשְׁמַת שֹׁמְרוֹן, literally, "the guilt of Samaria," must refer to some false deity; see the commentary. For שֹׁמְרוֹן, "Samaria," see the second textual note on 3:9.

The relative participle הַנִּשְׁבָּעִים is continued in the next clause by וְאָמְרוּ, a perfect with conjunctive *waw* (Waltke-O'Connor, § 37.7.2a, including example 9).

וְאָמְרוּ חֵי אֱלֹהֶיךָ דָּן—This clearly refers to a deity, called אֱלֹהֶיךָ, "your god." The phrase "as your god lives, Dan" is typical of an oath (e.g., Gen 42:15–16; 1 Sam 14:39). חֵי is the adjective חַי, "living, alive," probably in construct (see BDB). It (with the conjunction וְ) begins the next clause too. "Dan" (דָּן) was where Jeroboam ben Nebat established one of two syncretistic sanctuaries with a golden calf, which he declared was a representation of the god(s) who delivered Israel from Egypt (1 Ki 12:28–30).[20]

וְחֵי דֶּרֶךְ בְּאֵר־שָׁבַע—The final oath in 8:14 is "as lives the Way of Beersheba." It apparently refers to a god worshiped at the shrine in Beersheba.[21] דֶּרֶךְ, "way," often refers to a religious course of life, whether of faith, righteousness, and eternal life, or of unbelief, wickedness, and eternal perdition (see Psalm 1 and BDB, 5–6). The Ugaritic cognate *drkt* means "dominion, strength, might" and may also be used to describe a

---

[20] See A. Biran, "Dan (Place)," *ABD* 2:12–17, and King, *Amos, Hosea, Micah*, 101–2, for historical and archaeological information on Dan.

[21] For the details on the excavation at Beersheba, see D. W. Manor, "Beer-sheba," *ABD* 1:641–45.

deity.[22] In place of a word for "way," the LXX repeats ὁ θεός σου, "your god," from the preceding clause.

וְנָפְלוּ וְלֹא־יָקוּמוּ עוֹד׃—This exact wording for "and they will fall, and they will never rise again" occurs only here in the OT, but similar expressions appear in, for example, Is 24:20; Jer 25:27; and Amos 5:2. It connotes an ultimate disaster and eternal perdition.

Commentary

By Torah mandate, work was to cease on the Sabbath day (Ex 20:8–11; Deut 5:12–15).[23] The marketers during the time of Amos outwardly kept the Sabbath while inwardly they longed to return to their corrupt business practices and slave trafficking (Amos 8:4–6). For such injustice, Yahweh promises a day of punishment. This "day" resonates with the theme already established in the book (1:14; 2:16; 3:14; 4:2; 5:18–20; 6:3). "Days are coming" (8:11) when Israel's high flyers would be permanently grounded (8:9–10, 13–14).

Amos' preaching in chapters 5–6 warns about eschatological judgment on the Day of Yahweh (5:18–20), but God still implored the people to seek him and promised that if they did, they would live (5:4, 6, 14). Israel still had time to repent. In Amos' first two visions (7:1–3 and 7:4–6), Yahweh relented from executing the threatened judgments. But now the four eschatological markers in 8:7–14 ("day/days" in 8:9–11, 13) indicate that the clock has struck the midnight hour.[24] The finality of Amos' second pair of visions (7:7–9; 8:1–3) reverberates throughout the remainder of chapter 8.

Yahweh sought to expunge the Northern Kingdom's Canaanite fertility worship in King Ahab's day (874–853 BC)[25] through the ministry of Elijah (1 Kings 18) and subsequently through the eradication of Ahab's house, including his pagan wife, Jezebel, by Jehu (2 Kings 9–10). But 2 Ki 14:23–24 indicates that by following the ways of Jeroboam ben Nebat, Jeroboam ben Joash supported the apostate worship sites in Bethel and in Dan. Amos 2:7–8; 3:14; 4:4–5; and 8:14, for example, indicate that fertility worship was part of the north's religious life at this time.

By and large, the surviving Canaanites surrounding Israel in Amos' day were traders who bought and sold, who moved money and goods. The distinctive difference between Israelites and Canaanites was not territorial or linguistic. *It was spiritual and ethical.* The more Israel was involved in Canaanite worship, the more the nation adopted ruthless business practices. Amos connects the underhanded marketplace practices described in 8:4–6 with the worship life in 8:14 that introduces three Canaanite gods, "the Guilt of Samaria," "your

---

22 As noted by Smith, *Hosea, Amos, Micah*, 387; cf. Paul, *Amos*, 271, including nn. 29–30.

23 See the excursus "The Sabbath."

24 For a Gospel counterpart using "day" and "hour" language, describing the imminent parousia of Christ as the dawn of the day of salvation, see Rom 13:11–12.

25 These dates are from Thiele, *The Mysterious Numbers of the Hebrew Kings*, 94.

god … , Dan," and "the Way of Beersheba." 2 Ki 17:15 states the reason why Yahweh destroyed the Northern Kingdom: "they went after false gods, and they became false, and [they went] after the nations around them although Yahweh had ordered them not to act like them." They had strayed far from Yahweh and his promise to send the Messiah, who is "*the way* and the truth and the life" (Jn 14:6).

8:7 Much like he did in 4:2 and 6:8, the prophet again cites Yahweh's oath as a prelude to judgment. In previous oaths in the book of Amos, Yahweh swears "by his holiness" (4:2) and "by himself" (6:8). "Jacob" here indicates that Yahweh is Lord and Judge over both the Northern and Southern Kingdoms, since in Amos "Jacob" probably refers to both kingdoms.[26] Yahweh's solemn oath sets the tone for the rest of chapter 8. His declaration, literally, "I will not forget forever," is a more powerful way of saying, "I will always remember," and is similar to his repeated declaration "I will never again forgive" (7:8; 8:2). The prophet announces that the people's sins will be retained (cf. Jn 20:23).

8:8 This verse begins with a rhetorical question, a common literary device in Amos.[27] "On account of *this* … ?" connects Yahweh's judgment with the merchant's dishonest business dealings detailed in 8:4–6, which began with "hear *this*" (8:4).

Yahweh declared to Amos that the creational changes such as the plagues in 4:6–11 display the hand of God. Amos' reception of divine revelation (3:7) enabled him to accurately interpret what was happening in the world. The report in 1:1 of an earthquake two years after the close of his last oracle indicates that the shaking functions not only as a temporal marker, but also as a theological theme throughout the book (see also 3:15; 4:11; 9:1, 5). In 8:8 the massive quaking of the earth is likened to the Nile River, which annually floods and then subsides.[28] In 9:5 Yahweh strikes the earth (הַנּוֹגֵעַ בָּאָרֶץ, 9:5) so that it again heaves just like the Nile surges and falls.

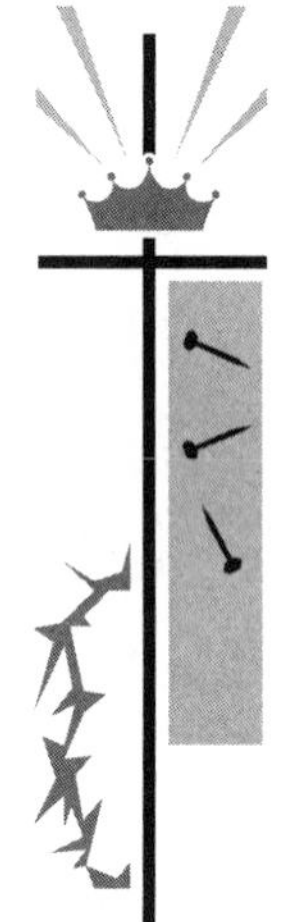

As a literary motif, the earthquake is one of the major thrusts of the book. As a theological theme, it announces "the removal of things shaken—the things having been made—in order that the things that cannot be shaken may remain" (Heb 12:27), that is, so that his new and everlasting creation may arise (Amos 9:11–15; cf. 2 Pet 3:10–13). In this new creation, all believers will receive "a kingdom that cannot be shaken" (Heb 12:28). The believing remnant will never be uprooted from the new land (Amos 9:15). The divinely caused earthquakes in, for example, Ex 19:18 and Hag 2:6–7, as well as Mt 27:51–53, where dead saints came to life, anticipate the final judgment and eschatological salvation of the faithful when Christ returns (e.g., Mt 24:29–30; Rev 1:7) and all the dead shall be raised—believers to eternal life (Dan 12:2–3; Rev 20:11–15).

---

[26] Andersen and Freedman, *Amos*, 121–22.

[27] For other rhetorical questions, see 2:11; 3:3–8; 5:18, 20, 25; 6:2, 12; 9:7.

[28] Jer 46:7–8 also employs the imagery of the rising of the Nile River, but in his case it describes the military might of Pharaoh Neco and his army.

8:9 While 8:8 describes the effects of Yahweh's judgment upon the earth, 8:9 envisions what will happen to the rest of the creation. Amos 8:8 describes *terrestrial* convulsion; in 8:9 the scene changes to the *celestial* world. Later in 8:10 the destruction will come upon people.

The events in 8:8–9 are connected to each other by means of the *waw* consecutive verbal formation (וְהָיָה) that begins 8:9. In this way, Amos uses merism to indicate that the entire cosmos will participate in Yahweh's judgment against unfaithful Israel. Joel 2:10 also combines the earth and the heavens in judgment: "before them [the army of locusts] the earth shakes, the heavens tremble [רָגְזָה אֶרֶץ רָעֲשׁוּ שָׁמָיִם], the sun and moon grow dark, and the stars no longer shine." Detailing his final advent, Jesus speaks in similar terms in his Olivet Discourse (e.g., Mt 24:29; Mk 13:24–25; Lk 21:25–26).

"The day" referred to in Amos 8:9 is the same day when the earthquake described in 8:8 begins to shake. The phrase בַּיּוֹם הַהוּא ("on that day") is the same day of judgment also described in 1:14; 2:16; 3:14; 4:2; 5:18–20; 6:3; 8:3, 10–11, 13. However, a new day is coming when wrath will give way to mercy because of Yahweh's promises to David (9:11, 13; cf. Ps 89:4–5, 21–30 [ET 89:3–4, 20–29]).

When Yahweh makes the sun set "at midday" so that there is "darkness for the earth in a day of light" (Amos 8:9), he is invoking the covenant curse described in Deut 28:29.[29] Yahweh is able to uncreate creation because he is the Creator, a fact described in Amos' three "creation" hymns (4:13; 5:8–9; 9:5–6).[30] The second hymn celebrates Yahweh who is "the one darkening day into night" (5:8).

Wiseman notes that a total solar eclipse occurred on June 15, 763 BC, during the reign of the Assyrian king Ashur-dan III (772–755 BC),[31] a contemporary of northern Israel's king Jeroboam ben Joash (793–753 BC),[32] during whose reign Amos ministered (1:1). Whether the darkness Amos describes should be connected with this eclipse in 763 BC or not, the darkness he portrays is reminiscent of his "Day of Yahweh" speech in 5:18–20, which indicates that that day will be "darkness and not light" (5:18, 20). The removal of light is a theme announced throughout prophetic texts.[b] The curse of darkness was also thrust against the Egyptians at the time of the exodus (Ex 10:21–29).[33] The shocking connection is this: Israel has become Yahweh's enemy! Israel also appears in Egypt's place in Amos 4:10 and 5:17. How the tables have turned!

(b) E.g., Is 5:30; 9:1 (ET 9:2); Jer 13:16; Ezek 34:12; Joel 2:10; Zeph 1:15

[29] For similar passages, see, for example, Is 59:10; Jer 15:8; Micah 3:6.

[30] These three doxologies or hymns are often called creation hymns but that title is inadequate because it ignores their additional content about special revelation, judgment, salvation, and eschatology. See the textual notes and the commentary on 4:13.

[31] Wiseman, "Jonah's Nineveh," 46.

[32] These dates for Jeroboam's reign are from Thiele, *The Mysterious Numbers of the Hebrew Kings*, 116.

[33] The darkening of the sun is also part of some theophanies; when Yahweh is present, it is a time of deep darkness (e.g., Ex 19:16; 1 Ki 8:12; Joel 2:2).

8:10 The events that will transpire on the earth (8:8) and in the heavenly bodies (8:9) will also impact people. Creation will revert to chaos; so will human society. "Social order and cosmic order are in fact deeply interrelated."[34]

Amos often employs the theme of reversal.[35] Here it will be from gladness to gloom.[36] Yahweh vows, "I will turn your festivals [חַגֵּיכֶם] into mourning and all of your songs [וְכָל־שִׁירֵיכֶם] into a funeral dirge [לְקִינָה]." Because Israel's elite were "turning" (the verb הָפַךְ in 5:7; 6:12) justice and righteousness into wormwood, Yahweh will change day into night (8:9) and "turn" (הָפַךְ in 8:10) joyful sounds into laments. The reversal in 8:10 depicts festive joy turned into deep sadness.[37] Sackcloth and a shaved head (the meaning of "baldness") are typical signs of mourning.

In 5:1–3 Amos takes up a lament for Israel. In 5:16–17 every place becomes a place of lament, while almost everyone is recruited to mourn. In 8:3 the prophet indicates there will be wailing at the king's palace in Samaria. Now the mourners will don sackcloth (שַׂק) and shave their heads bald (קָרְחָה). These are expressions of lament at times of calamity and disaster (e.g., Is 3:24; 15:2–3; Ezek 7:18). A festal robe may be replaced by a coarsely woven loin cloth draped around the hips, and hair may be shaved off of the head (as also in Jer 48:37). The sorrow will be so intense that Amos likens it to the weeping over the loss of an only son.[38] This is piercing sadness because at the death of an only son, the family's entire future is wiped out.

It is a "bitter day" (יוֹם מָר, 8:10) when the entire cosmos unravels (8:8–9), when joy turns to sorrow as when an only son dies (8:9–10). Because her husband and her two sons had died, Naomi spoke these words of anguish to the women in Bethlehem: "Do not call me Naomi; call me *Mara*" (Ruth 1:20), using a word related to the adjective "bitter" used in Amos 8:10. Israel's halcyon days of Jeroboam ben Joash were about to be turned into one big bitter day: the fall

---

34 Fretheim, *God and World in the Old Testament*, 171.

35 Besides 8:9–10, a dramatic reversal is present in 2:9; 3:1–2; 4:4–5; 5:18–20, 21–27; 6:1–7; 9:11–15.

36 This follows Paul, *Amos*, 263, n. 12. Great joy turned to extreme sorrow is a common theme in the prophets, classically stated in Jer 7:34: "I will bring an end to the sounds of joy and gladness and to the voices of bride and bridegroom in the towns of Judah and the streets of Jerusalem, for the land will become desolate" (cf. Jer 16:9; 25:10; Ezek 26:13; Lam 5:15).

37 The church father Lactantius equates this verse with the events that transpired on Good Friday:

> Suspended, then, and fastened to his cross Christ cried out to God the Father in a loud voice and willingly laid down his life. In that same hour there was an earthquake, and the veil of the temple that separated the two tabernacles was cut in two, and the sun was suddenly withdrawn, and from the sixth hour until the ninth hour there was darkness [Mk 15:33]. The prophet Amos bears witness to this. "And it shall come to pass in that day, says the Lord, that the sun shall go down at midday, and the day shall be darkened of light. And I will turn your feasts into mourning and all your songs into lamentation." (*Epitome of the Divine Institutes*, 4.19, quoted in Ferreiro, *The Twelve Prophets*, ACCS 14:112)

38 For similar expressions, see Jer 6:26 and Zech 12:10.

of northern Israel to Assyria in 722 BC.[39] This portended Good Friday and the final Judgment Day (see the commentary on 5:18–20 and 8:11).

In 8:7 Yahweh swears by the pride of Jacob that Israel's sins will never be forgotten. If this isn't bad enough, in 8:8–10 Yahweh adds cosmic undoing to these spiritual woes. The land will move up and down and its inhabitants will mourn, darkness will cover the land, joy will be replaced by lament, and baldness will stigmatize every head. This will indeed be a bitter day!

8:11 The refrain "days are coming," first stated in 4:2, is stated again in 8:11. In this way the eschatological focus of the chapter continues (see also 8:3, 9, 13). The eschatological day or days involved has several fulfillments: (1) 722 BC with the Assyrian destruction of northern Israel and its capital, Samaria; (2) the ultimate "mourning for an only son" (8:10) on Good Friday (Zech 12:10; Rom 8:32; see the fifth textual note on Amos 8:10); and (3) the Last Day, when the Son of Man will come with the clouds, "and every eye will see him, even those who pierced him, and all the tribes of the earth will mourn because of him" (Rev 1:7, alluding to Zech 12:10).

The idiom "behold, days are coming" (הִנֵּה יָמִים בָּאִים) reappears in 9:13. The phrase ties together three different phases in Amos' view of the last days:[40]

1. The famine for Yahweh's Word, involving the cessation of prophecy (8:11–12)
2. The judgment and destruction of the Northern and Southern Kingdoms (4:1–3)
3. The restoration of God's people, united from believing Israelites and believing Gentiles, in the new creation, the Edenic land (9:13–15)

In 8:8–9 Yahweh promises to bring about a cosmic upheaval that in turn will usher in a time of deep remorse (8:10). Whereas in 8:9–10 the sorrow is on account of Yahweh's *presence*, in 8:11–12 the tragedy is because of Yahweh's *absence*. No longer will the people experience the famine and drought brought about by the destruction of the natural world (e.g., 4:6). Rather, they will undergo an even harsher judgment: hunger and thirst will arise because of a famine of hearing no words from Yahweh. Without access to his words, Israel will be lost. Compare Jn 6:68, where the apostle Peter confesses to Jesus, "Lord, to whom shall we go? You have the words of eternal life."

No longer will the people of Israel hear from their God. In their deepest moment of need, they will finally seek Yahweh (unlike the stubbornness described in 4:6–11; cf. the invitation to "seek" him in 5:4, 6, 14), but in these future days Yahweh will offer no word. The divine silence will be deafening as well as destroying. Israel rejected Yahweh's words (2:11–12; 7:10–17). Now the punishment will fit the crime.

Luther uses the term *platz regen* to describe a local downpour of the Gospel that then moves on. The reformer writes:

---

[39] See the excursus "The Assyrian Empire."

[40] Cf. Andersen and Freedman, *Amos*, 403.

> Let us remember our former misery, and the darkness in which we dwelt. Germany, I am sure, has never before heard so much of God's word as it is hearing today; certainly we read nothing of it in history. If we let it just slip by without thanks and honor, I fear we shall suffer a still more dreadful darkness and plague. O my beloved Germans, buy while the market is at your door; gather in the harvest while there is sunshine and fair weather; make use of God's grace and word while it is there! For you should know that God's word and grace is like a passing shower of rain [*platz regen*] which does not return where it has once been [cf. Eccl 12:2]. It has been with the Jews, but when it's gone it's gone, and now they have nothing. Paul brought it to the Greeks; but again when it's gone it's gone, and now they have the Turk. Rome and the Latins also had it; but when it's gone it's gone, and now they have the pope. And you Germans need not think that you will have it forever, for ingratitude and contempt will not make it stay. Therefore, seize it and hold it fast, whoever can.[41]

Luther also writes:

> On the other hand, there is no more terrible disaster with which the wrath of God can afflict men than a famine of the hearing of his Word, as he says in Amos [8:11]. Likewise there is no greater mercy than when he sends forth his Word, as we read in Psalm 107[:20]: "He sent forth his word, and healed them, and delivered them from destruction."[42]

Yahweh's anger is sometimes demonstrated by his silence. Micah 3:4 says as much: "Then they will cry out to Yahweh, but he will not answer them, and he will hide his face from them at that time" (cf. Is 59:1–2; Ezek 7:26; 9:9; 11:22–23; Lam 2:9). In Judg 17:6; 18:1; 19:1; and 21:25, the historian says that "Israel had no king," and in Judg 17:6 and 21:25, he writes: "Everyone did what was right in his own eyes." The result was that "the Word of Yahweh was rare in those days; there were not many visions" (1 Sam 3:1). Yahweh's refusal to speak also occurs in 1 Sam 14:37: "So Saul inquired of God, 'Shall I go down after the Philistines? Will you give them into Israel's hand?' But he [God] did not answer him on that day" (cf. 1 Sam 28:6, 15–16). Those who would not listen to Yahweh's Word through the prophets (Amos 2:11–12; 7:10–17) or heed his judgment through disasters (4:6–11) will be completely cut off from his words. The conversation is over. Yahweh will now administer his just judgment.

Jesus gives this same warning to the church in Ephesus: "Repent. … If not, I will come to you and remove your lampstand from its place" (Rev 2:5). In this case, the "lampstand" indicates Christ's presence. His absence means silence and death.

Yahweh tested Israel and gave the people manna to show that "man does not live on bread alone, but man shall live on every word that proceeds from the mouth of Yahweh" (Deut 8:3), and Jesus cited these words during his temptation

---

[41] Luther, "To the Councilmen of All Cities in Germany: That They Establish and Maintain Christian Schools" (AE 45:352–53; WA 15.31–32).

[42] Luther, *The Freedom of a Christian* (AE 31:346).

after fasting forty days (Mt 4:4; Lk 4:4). In Jer 1:9 the prophet writes: "Yahweh ... said to me, 'Behold, I have put my words in your mouth.' " Fourteen chapters later Jeremiah says, "When your words came, I ate them; they were the joy and delight of my heart" (Jer 15:16; see also Ezek 3:1–4).[43] When this food is taken away, there can be only one result: death. The lack of access to Yahweh's Word is one of the curses of exile (e.g., Deut 4:28; 32:20). These curses, however, only envision a temporary famine of Yahweh's Word until his wrath reaches its limit (e.g., Lev 26:44–45; Deut 4:29–31; 30:1–3).

In the fullness of time (Gal 4:4), Yahweh would send his final Word, Jesus (Jn 1:14; Heb 1:1–2), who promises never to leave his baptized believers and never to forsake them (Heb 13:5; Mt 28:20). Those who hunger and thirst for this righteousness will be filled (Mt 5:6).

8:12 The distress of not hearing Yahweh's words is now depicted in terms of desperate seeking. The people described in this verse are those who had rejected the Word when God called to them in grace to seek him and live (5:4, 6, 14). Instead of seeking Yahweh through faithful hearing of his Word and visiting his holy temple in Jerusalem, they frequented idolatrous shrines (4:4; 5:5; 7:9; see also 8:14) and rejected his words spoken through his prophets (2:12; 7:10–12).

These are the ones who were trampling the destitute upon the dust (2:7; 8:4); storing away the rewards of lawless acts (3:10); oppressing the poor, crushing the needy, and saying to their husbands, "Bring that we may drink!" (4:1). They turned justice into wormwood (5:7; 6:12), longed for the Day of Yahweh because they wrongly thought it would bring them even greater prosperity (5:18–20); were complacent on Mount Zion and felt secure on Mount Samaria (6:1); brought near the evil day (6:3); lay on ivory beds and enjoyed the finest cuisine (6:4); improvised on the lyre, imagining that they were like King David the psalmist (6:5); profanely drank wine from sacred bowls (6:6); and said, "When will the New Moon be over so we may sell corn" (8:5) and "The evil will not overtake nor confront us" (9:10).

Four distinct classes in unfaithful Israel are part of this group called "all the sinners of my people" (9:10): the royal officials (3:9–15), the magistrates (5:10–12), the priests (7:10–17), and the merchants (2:6–8; 8:4–6). In principle, and eschatologically, all who reject the invitation to repent and believe God's Word of messianic salvation (9:11–15) will find themselves under this divine judgment of separation from his Word.

Wherever these people roam, they will not find Yahweh's Word. They will frantically run "from sea to sea and from north to east" (Amos 8:12). This refers

---

[43] The words "joy" (שִׂמְחָה) and "delight" (שָׂשׂוֹן) appear together four more times in Jeremiah, and each time they are paired with חָתָן, "bridegroom," and כַּלָּה, "bride" (Jer 7:34; 16:9; 25:10; 33:11). By means of this poetic word association, Jeremiah evokes the exuberance and ecstasy experienced by a bride and bridegroom. In Jer 15:16, he connects such joy and delight with eating Yahweh's Word.

to a search that would traverse vast expanses of the earth (see the first textual note on 8:12). There is no reference to traveling "south" because the Negev would offer neither food nor water. Or the omission of "south" may indicate that it would be futile for the Israelites to go south to Jerusalem, the place from which Lion Yahweh roars judgment for them (1:2; cf. 3:4, 8, 12; 5:19). Northern Israel had rejected the dynasty of David and the Solomonic temple in Jerusalem almost two hundred years earlier (ca. 920 BC) when Jeroboam ben Nebat, who had broken from King Rehoboam of Judah, erected the idolatrous substitute shrines at Bethel and Dan (1 Ki 12:26–33). To go south to Jerusalem would indicate the confession of that sin by means of a broken and contrite heart, but Israel's pride stood in the way of this return. Hungering for Yahweh's Word and never finding it means the *end* of Israel as God's people, which further defines the "end" judgment in the fourth vision (8:1–3).

This vain searching by apostate Israel is in contrast to Moses' earlier statement, later confirmed by St. Paul, that for believers no journey is necessary because "the word is very near you; it is in your mouth and in your heart" (Deut 30:14; Rom 10:8). The apostle explains that Christ has come down from heaven, suffered, died, and risen, so there is no need to attempt to search for him in heaven above nor in the abyss below (Rom 10:6–7). In Jesus Christ, the divine Word has become flesh (Jn 1:14), and he promises to be with his church through his Word and Sacraments to the close of the age (Mt 28:19–20).

8:13 "On that day"—that is to say, on the Day of Judgment—Israel's youngest, strongest, and most beautiful will faint away. The end of the most highly esteemed men and women in Israel's society is a theme in Amos (e.g., 2:14–16; 4:1–3), as well as in other prophetic laments (e.g., Lam 1:15, 18).

8:14 Amos 8:12 described the people as looking for Yahweh's Word in all the wrong places. This verse refers to their false belief in the possibility of life by means of other deities, which they imagine to be alive ("as your god lives … as lives …"). Life is what they seek; death is what they will experience ("they will fall, and they will never rise again"). Their three oaths by false gods in 8:14 are consistent with their attendance at the idolatrous shrines mentioned in 4:4; 5:5; 7:9, 10–13, all of which stand in contrast to "Zion … Jerusalem" (1:2) and "the tabernacle of David" (9:11).

Whereas Yahweh swears "by his holiness" (4:2), "by himself" (6:8), and "by the pride of Jacob" (8:7), the only other instance of swearing in the book is here, where the guilty swear using three different oath formulae. To take an oath in the name of a god "is thus to place oneself under the power of a god affirmed to be one who lives, thereby accounting for the oath formula 'as [your god] lives' (חַי)."[44] To swear by a god was to take that god as your own, yet there was no room for other gods in Israel's relationship with Yahweh (Ex 20:3; Deut 5:7).

[44] Wolff, *Joel and Amos*, 331.

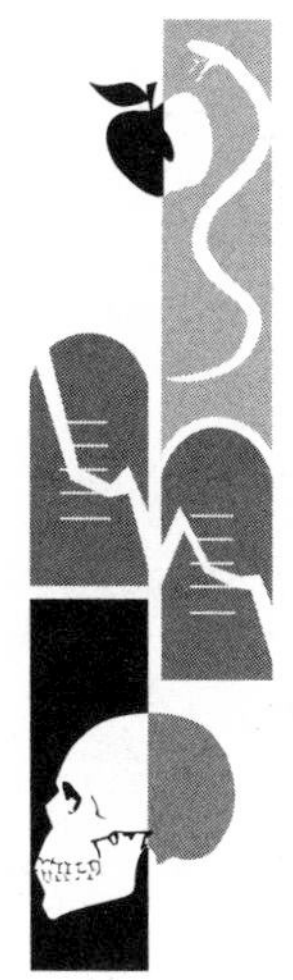

The first oath invokes "the Guilt of Samaria." This may refer to the worship of a golden calf erected almost two centuries earlier (1 Ki 12:28–30) at the Bethel sanctuary, which was the state shrine for the northern kingdom (Amos 7:13), whose capital was Samaria.[45] If this is the case, then Amos is employing a cacophemism,[46] inferring that Israel incurs guilt when the people worship at Bethel. Yahweh had implied this earlier: "go to Bethel and transgress" (4:4).

Another possibility is that the noun translated as "guilt," *ʾashmah*, refers to the Aramean deity אֲשִׁימָא, "Ashima," worshiped by the people of Hamath who were resettled in the Northern Kingdom by the Assyrians (2 Ki 17:29–30). This likely is the same as the fertility goddess Asherah, who was venerated by the Canaanites even before the Israelites conquered the promised land (cf. Deut 16:21) and who was an object of idolatrous worship in northern Israel (e.g., 1 Ki 16:33; 18:19) and apostate Judah (e.g., 1 Ki 15:13; 2 Ki 18:4; 21:3, 7; 23:4–15).[47] The deliberate distortion of her proper name into the common noun אַשְׁמָה, "guilt," would then be a polemic against this goddess, similar to the polemical mispronunciations "Sikkuth" and "Kiyyun" in Amos 5:26.[48]

Amos 2:7–8 describes sex in a cultic ritual setting, while 6:4–7 (and perhaps 4:1) portrays Israel's participation in a pagan *marzēaḥ* feast.[49] Hosea, the other eighth-century prophet besides Amos who addresses the Northern Kingdom, has much more to say about its spiritual and sexual adultery (e.g., Hosea 1–2; 4:10–19). Those verses may relate to Amos 8:14 if it indicates that Israel was enslaved in the fertility worship of Asherah and her consort, Baal, who could be one of the three deities mentioned in 8:14. Baal and Asherah are paired in some biblical texts (e.g., Judg 6:25–30; 1 Ki 18:19; 2 Ki 17:16). King Ahab had erected "an altar for Baal in the house of Baal that he built in Samaria. And Ahab made an Asherah" (1 Ki 16:32–33).

The second oath quoted in Amos 8:14 is "as your god lives, Dan." In all likelihood this refers to the image of a calf erected at Dan by Jeroboam ben Nebat (1 Ki 12:28–30).[50] The Canaanites often represented Baal by the image of a

---

[45] Compare the condemnation of the golden calf in Moses' day in Deut 9:21 and the idolatry of Samaria and northern Israel condemned by a rough contemporary of Amos, the eighth-century prophet Hosea (Hos 8:6; 10:8). "Samaria" appears five times in the book of Amos (3:9, 12; 4:1; 6:1; 8:14). These verses indicate that Samaria is guilty of infidelity, complacency, injustice, and idolatry.

[46] The prophet employs this same literary feature in 5:26 where the MT spelling of סִכּוּת and כִּיּוּן is artificial; the vowels are equivalent to the vowels that appear in גִּלּוּל ("idol") and/or שִׁקּוּץ ("detested thing").

[47] Cf. Andersen and Freedman, *Amos*, 709; Barstad, *The Religious Polemics of Amos*, 143–201.

[48] For a discussion of Asherah, see King, *Amos, Hosea, Micah*, 97–101, who says: "In Canaanite religion Asherah was a mother goddess, with emphasis on breasts, lactation, procreation, and fertility" (p. 98).

[49] See the second textual note and the commentary on 6:7.

[50] Archaeologists have unearthed the sanctuary area in Dan, but the remains are not sufficient enough to lead to any definitive conclusions about the religious beliefs of the worshipers at

bull, and so it is possible that in popular thought the golden calf at Dan came to be associated with Baal. Whatever its identity, Amos scornfully refers to it as *your* god, as opposed to *the* God, Yahweh. His subtle use of the form חֵי instead of חַי for "lives" confirms this interpretation: Yahweh uses the latter for himself ("as I live," in, e.g., Num 14:28; Is 49:18; Ezek 14:20), and people use it in the oath "as Yahweh lives" (e.g., Judg 8:19; 1 Sam 19:6; Ruth 3:13), while the former is used for all other oaths.[51]

The third oath is "as lives the Way of Beersheba." The exact meaning of this is quite uncertain. Paul suggests that it "may refer to the taking of an oath by the life of the 'way,' that is, by the 'pilgrimage to Beer-sheba.' "[52] On the other hand, a Ugaritic cognate to דֶּרֶךְ, "way," could support interpreting the phrase as a deity's name meaning "the strength/dominant one of Beersheba."[53]

From "Samaria" then farther north to "Dan" and then south to "Beersheba" in Judah, Yahweh uses a merism whereby both northern Israel and southern Judah are indicted for worshiping other gods. That Judah too was complicit in idolatry is the implication of "Beersheba" also in 5:5. Israel's calling was to live out its life in singular allegiance to Yahweh. Commenting on Deut 4:15–20, Wright aptly notes (see also Is 44:9–20; Pss 115:4–8; 135:15–18):

> Idols have "form" but do not speak. Yahweh has no "form," but he decisively speaks. Idols are visible but dumb. Yahweh is invisible but eloquent.[54]

A mute idol or image cannot substitute for the triune God, who speaks through his Word, which is living and powerful (Heb 4:12), in order to confront, rebuke, love, and forgive. "Idolatry … is fundamentally an escape from the living voice and commands of the living God."[55] Since Israel was invoking other gods, the people no longer heeded Yahweh's Word (cf. Amos 2:11–12; 7:10–17), who would become personally incarnate in Christ (Jn 1:1–18; Rev 19:13). Idolatry results in a community that defines success by accumulation rather than righteousness and justice. Going after worthlessness ends in worthlessness (2 Ki 17:15; Jer 2:5). The faithless Israelites had become like that which they worshiped (Hos 9:10).

Spiritually dead people often end up oppressing, abusing, and taking advantage of others (Amos 8:4–6). Yahweh's concluding sentence, "they will fall, and

---

this temple. See Biran, *Biblical Dan*, 159–233, and "An Israelite Horned Altar at Dan." See also J. R. Spencer, "Golden Calf," *ABD* 2:1065–69, which discusses Jeroboam's calves as well as the calf made by Aaron.

[51] See the use of חֵי in oaths invoking the life of a person in, for example, Gen 42:15–16; 1 Sam 1:26; 2 Ki 2:2, 4, 6. The only exception is Dan 12:7, where חֵי is used for the one true God, "him who lives forever." The speaker may be the preincarnate Christ, God the Son; see Steinmann, *Daniel*, 497–501, 568–69.

[52] Paul, *Amos*, 272.

[53] Andersen and Freedman, *Amos*, 709. They also mention the possibility that this deity could be Baal.

[54] Wright, *Deuteronomy*, 50–51.

[55] Wright, *Deuteronomy*, 71.

they will never rise again" (8:14), is similar to 5:2, which laments fallen Virgin Israel. It signifies death eternal. OT Israel's history has come to an end (8:2). Yet there is an eschatological future for a believing remnant gathered from Israel and the Gentiles (9:11–15). This new "Israel of God" (Gal 6:16) is defined by the apostle in Romans 9–11 as consisting of all believers in the Messiah from Israel (Rom 9:5), Jesus Christ.

Summary

Amos 8:7–14 contains these echoes from earlier sections of Amos:[56]

1. Lamentation (8:8–10; cf. 5:1–3, 23; 8:3)
2. Famine and drought (8:11–12; cf. 4:6–8)
3. Oaths (8:7, 14; cf. 4:2; 6:8)

These connections with earlier oracles indicate that 8:7–14 is a summary oracle before Amos' fifth and final vision in 9:1–4.

The book of Amos contains eight oracles with the formula "on that day" or "days are coming."[57] Six of these are in chapters 8 and 9 (8:3, 9, 11, 13; 9:11, 13). These chapters are therefore more eschatological in nature and a confirmation of earlier oracles. The first six of the eight are frightening oracles of judgment, but the final two promise eschatological days of messianic restoration and abundance (9:11, 13).

The desire of Israel's businessmen was to "take care of business, *every* day," so they despised the Sabbath and holy days (8:5–6). Yet 8:14 indicates that idol worship was the primary sin of the people. Regardless of the name of the deities who were worshiped—most likely syncretistically, alongside Yahweh—the worship was apostate. The Israelites had forsaken "the one thing … needful" (Lk 10:42). Is 55:6 says: "Seek Yahweh while he can be found; call on him while he is near." In apostate Israel's case, Yahweh would no longer be found; he would not be near. For the idolaters, gone are the days when Yahweh would be a "very present help in trouble" (Ps 46:2 [ET 46:1]). Yahweh's words will not be present for those who had rejected them; his mercies will come to an end (cf. Ps 77:9–10 [ET 77:8–9]). The other gods they invoked *could not* save, and now Yahweh *would not* save them. They have reached a dead end—literally.

Yet it need not be so for all who hear God's Word "today" (Heb 3:7–15; 4:6–7). In stark contrast to the final deity in 8:14, "the Way of Beersheba," in the NT, Jesus claims for himself the divine title ἡ ὁδός, "*the way*," as well as "the truth and the life," and explains that "the way" means that he alone leads to the Father (Jn 14:6). Moreover, "the Way" was also a title for the infant Christian church (e.g., Acts 9:2; 19:9, 23; cf. Acts 16:17; 18:25). This is the road to eternal life.

---

[56] Cf. Anderson and Freedman, *Amos*, 817.

[57] See "on that day" in 2:16; 8:3, 9, 13; 9:11, and "days are coming" in 4:2; 8:11; 9:13.

Amos 9:1–4

The Fifth Vision: Yahweh Topples the Temple

Translation

9 [1]I saw the Lord standing by the altar, and he said,
"Strike the capital [of the pillar]
so that the thresholds shake.
Cut off the head of all of them,
and the remainder of them with the sword I will slay.
Not one fugitive from them will flee,
and a survivor from them will not escape.
[2]"Even if they dig down to Sheol,
from there my hand will seize them.
And even if they ascend to heaven,
from there I will bring them down.
[3]And even if they hide themselves on the peak of Carmel,
from there I will search out, and I will seize them.
And even if they hide themselves from my eyes at the bottom of the sea,
from there I will command the serpent, and it will bite them.
[4]And even if they go into captivity before their enemies,
from there I will command the sword, and it will slay them.
And I will set my eye upon them for evil and not for good."

Textual Notes

9:1 רָאִיתִי אֶת־אֲדֹנָי נִצָּב עַל־הַמִּזְבֵּחַ—The first four visions each began with a Hiphil form of רָאָה, "to show." See the first textual note on 7:1. But this fifth and final vision begins with a Qal form, רָאִיתִי, "I saw." For נִצָּב עַל־, see the second textual note on 7:7. Most interpreters[1] agree that הַמִּזְבֵּחַ, with the definite article, refers to "the altar" at the idolatrous temple in Bethel erected by Jeroboam ben Nebat, king of northern Israel (1 Ki 12:26–33), not to the altar at the Jerusalem temple in Judah. Amos referred to "the altars of Bethel" in 3:14, and Bethel was the national shrine for northern Israel (7:13). The only other occurrence of מִזְבֵּחַ in Amos refers to altars in northern Israel that were the sites of drunken idolatry and immorality in the worship of other gods (2:8; see 1 Ki 12:31).

וַיֹּאמֶר הַךְ הַכַּפְתּוֹר וְיִרְעֲשׁוּ הַסִּפִּים—After the perfect רָאִיתִי in the preceding clause, the imperfect with *waw* consecutive, וַיֹּאמֶר, here refers in past time to a continuation of the same unique event (Waltke-O'Connor, § 33.3.1a, including example 9). The Hiphil

---

[1] E.g., Andersen and Freedman, *Amos*, 835; see also Paul, *Amos*, 274, including n. 3.

of נָכָה appeared also in 3:15; 4:9; and 6:11. See the first textual note on 3:15. With the singular imperative הַךְ, Yahweh apparently directs an individual to "strike"; see further the commentary.

Here כַּפְתּוֹר refers to the "capital" of a pillar (BDB, 1), the rounded knob at the top of a pillar supporting the temple's roof. In this case, the definite singular "the capital" collectively stands for all the capitals on all the pillars of the temple. Pillars were a major feature of Iron Age temples. In other contexts, the noun כַּפְתּוֹר can refer to a knob or bulb that was an ornament on the lampstand of the tabernacle. Probably the capital of the pillar had a similar shape or ornamented features.

The imperative הַךְ followed by the Qal imperfect with conjunctive *waw*, וְיִרְעֲשׁוּ, forms a purpose/result clause: "strike ... so that the thresholds shake" (GKC, § 109 f). The verb רָעַשׁ, "to shake, quake," is cognate to the noun רַעַשׁ, "earthquake," in 1:1. See the sixth textual note on 1:1.

The "thresholds" (הַסִּפִּים) of the temple probably were made of cut stone and rested in the ground. The noun סַף may indicate the "threshold" of a house (e.g., Judg 19:27; 1 Ki 14:17). It also may refer to the "threshold" of the Jerusalem temple (Is 6:4; 2 Chr 3:7; cf. Ezek 43:8). "Keeper(s)/guard(s) of the threshold" denotes priests or Levites who served at the entrance of the tabernacle (1 Chr 9:19) and at the entrance of the Jerusalem temple (2 Ki 12:10 [ET 12:9]; 22:4; 23:4; 25:18; Jer 35:4; 52:24; 2 Chr 34:9) as well as guards of the Persian palace (Esth 2:21; 6:2). The gates of the eschatological temple seen by Ezekiel have a "threshold" (Ezek 40:6–7; 41:16).

וּבְצַעַם בְּרֹאשׁ כֻּלָּם—The Qal imperative of בָּצַע, "to cut off, break off," has a proleptic or redundant plural suffix, the same suffix as on כֻּלָּם, literally, "cut off them by the head of all of them." This could refer to the tops of the pillars, but the following clause about Yahweh killing with the sword indicates that it refers to cutting off the heads of the Israelites, especially those worshiping at the idolatrous temple. בָּצַע can refer to the action of a weaver who "cuts off" a ready-woven piece of material.[2] Hezekiah's prayer conveys this meaning of the verb: "I have rolled up my life like a weaver; he cuts me off [יְבַצְּעֵנִי] from the loom; from day until night you finish me off" (Is 38:12). Compare the Niphal of גָּזַר, "be cut off," in Is 53:8; Ezek 37:11; and Ps 88:6 (ET 88:5).

וְאַחֲרִיתָם בַּחֶרֶב אֶהֱרֹג—The feminine noun אַחֲרִית here means the "rest, remainder" of a group of people. It has a similar meaning in Amos 4:2; see the fourth textual note there. It has a temporal meaning in 8:10.

Except for 1:11, in all other Amos passages with a "sword" (חֶרֶב), it is wielded by Yahweh himself (4:10; 7:9; 9:1) or by his agents who carry out his judgments (7:11, 17; 9:4, 10).

For the Qal of הָרַג, "kill, slay," which is repeated in 9:4, see the second textual note on 2:3. There it refers to Yahweh killing Moabites, enemies of his people. However, in all its other occurrences in Amos, it refers to Yahweh using the sword to kill people whom he had called to be his own but who turned against him: unfaithful Israelites (4:10; 9:1, 4).

---

[2] Cf. D. Kellermann, "בצע," *TDOT* 2:205–8.

לֹא־יָנ֤וּס לָהֶם֙ נָ֔ס וְלֹֽא־יִמָּלֵ֥ט לָהֶ֖ם פָּלִֽיט׃—These two clauses are in synonymous parallelism. For נוּס, "to flee," see the first textual note on 2:16. Its participle, נָס, "a fleeing person," is the subject of its imperfect, יָנוּס. In this construction, the participle can represent a vague subject, anyone, so this could be rendered "nobody will be able to flee" (Joüon, § 155 d; similarly GKC, § 144 e). In 2:14 the prophet used the cognate noun מָנוֹס.

The prepositional phrase לָהֶם is used in both clauses with לְ in the sense of possession (Joüon, § 130 g), "belonging to them," referring to people belonging to the group of those attacked by Yahweh. English idiom requires "from/of them."

The Niphal of מָלַט has an intransitive meaning, "to escape." The transitive Piel appears once in 2:14 and twice in 2:15; see the third textual note on 2:14. The noun פָּלִיט, derived from the verb פָּלַט, "to escape," may denote a survivor or escapee (e.g., Gen 14:13; Judg 12:4–5; Ezek 7:16; 24:26–27).

9:2 אִם־יַחְתְּר֣וּ בִשְׁא֔וֹל—The hypothetical particle אִם, "if," appears here and in 9:3–4 a total of five times.[3] Each time it is followed by an imperfect verb and then all but one time by a prepositional phrase (the second instance has an accusative of destination). In the first, second, and fourth instances, the construction expresses a contrary to fact condition; it "ironically represents an impossibility as possible" (GKC, § 159 r). The אִם clause is an unreal protasis, and then the apodosis affirms that judgment will come anyway. Only the third and fifth אִם clauses are not unreal: in the third one, some Israelites could hide on top of Mount Carmel (9:3a; cf. 1 Ki 18:42), and the fifth one is a true prediction of the imminent fate of northern Israel, which will "go into captivity before their enemies" (9:4a). In all five instances, אִם can be translated as "even though" (Joüon, § 171 d).

The Qal of חָתַר, "to burrow, hollow out, dig," can denote digging into or through an object: the heavy wall of the temple in a vision (Ezek 8:8) or the wall of a mud brick house (Ezek 12:5, 7, 12; Job 24:16). חָתַר is used metaphorically here to apply to people who will try to burrow into Sheol in order to escape from Yahweh's wrath. It would be humanly impossible for people to dig their way into Sheol and much less possible to escape divine wrath there.

Sheol (שְׁאוֹל) is a proper noun designating the gloomy underworld into which the spirits of departed unbelievers descend.[4] Because שְׁאוֹל is where the wicked go after death, the term is frequently translated as "hell" in the KJV (as here). The LXX renders the prepositional phrase here as εἰς ᾅδου, "into Hades." That same word for hell, ᾅδης, is used in such NT passages as Mt 11:23; 16:18; and Lk 16:23. Cognates to Sheol do not appear in other Semitic languages, although an equivalent in Akkadian is *Arallû*, the "Land of No Return."[5] The etymology of שְׁאוֹל is uncertain. It occurs sixty-six times in the OT[6] and always means the realm of the dead located deep in the earth. Synonyms

3 Other uses of pentads by Amos are the fivefold refrain "but you did not return to me" (4:6–11); the five visions (7:1–3; 7:4–6; 7:7–9; 8:1–3; 9:1–4); and the five curses in 7:17.

4 See, for example, Ezekiel 31–32 and the excursus "Sheol" in Lessing, *Jonah*, 249–55.

5 Bottéro, *Religion in Ancient Mesopotamia*, 204.

6 This includes Is 7:11, where most scholars and versions—ancient and modern—emend the MT to read "Sheol."

include אֲבַדּוֹן ("place of destruction"), קֶבֶר ("grave"), שַׁחַת ("corruption; pit"), בּוֹר ("pit"), and in some contexts אֶרֶץ ("earth," e.g., Ex 15:12; Jonah 2:7 [ET 2:6]).

Sheol represents separation from Yahweh, which in itself is a deplorable destiny (see, e.g., Is 38:18; Pss 88:5, 10–12 [ET 88:4, 9–11]; 115:17). Yet Amos 9:2 indicates that Sheol is not beyond Yahweh's reach and power (cf. Ps 139:8; Prov 15:11) since he saves his believers from going there. Yahweh's power over Sheol is climactically displayed in Jesus Christ, "who has destroyed death and has brought life and immortality to light through the Gospel" (2 Tim 1:10). In Peter's Pentecost sermon, he preaches the resurrection of Christ as the fulfillment of Ps 16:10: "you shall not abandon me to Sheol; you shall not let your holy one see corruption" (Acts 2:27, translating Sheol as ᾅδης, "Hades"). In Rev 1:18 the exalted Christ declares that he holds the keys "of death and Hades [ᾅδης]."

מִשָּׁם יָדִי תִקָּחֵם—The combination מִשָּׁם, the preposition מִן ("from") and the adverb שָׁם ("there"), begins the apodosis in all five of the hypothetical scenarios introduced with אִם. In each case, the apodosis states how Yahweh will retrieve or judge those who sought to escape. Here Yahweh declares, "From there my hand will seize them." Yahweh's hand is not too short to save—or to judge (Num 11:23; Is 50:2; 59:1).

וְאִם־יַעֲלוּ הַשָּׁמַיִם מִשָּׁם אוֹרִידֵם׃—It would be even more impossible for a person to transport himself into heaven. The Qal imperfect of עָלָה, "to ascend," takes an accusative of destination, הַשָּׁמַיִם. Yet even if people would ascend to heaven, Yahweh declares, "From there I will bring them down" (אוֹרִידֵם, the Hiphil imperfect of יָרַד with suffix).

9:3 וְאִם־יֵחָבְאוּ בְּרֹאשׁ הַכַּרְמֶל—The Niphal of חָבָא has the middle or reflexive meaning "hide oneself."[7] The Hithpael and Niphal of חָבָא appear in Gen 3:8, 10 to depict the activity of Adam and Eve trying to hide themselves from God in Eden. In twenty-five of its thirty-four times in the OT, חָבָא describes people hiding in fear of death and judgment. The Niphal of חָבָא is parallel and synonymous with the Niphal of סָתַר two clauses later in 9:3.

Amos employed the phrase רֹאשׁ הַכַּרְמֶל, "the top/peak of Carmel," in 1:2; see the fifth textual note there. It also occurs in 1 Ki 18:42, where Elijah ascends there.

מִשָּׁם אֲחַפֵּשׂ וּלְקַחְתִּים—The verb חָפַשׂ denotes "to search."[8] The Piel, used here (אֲחַפֵּשׂ), connotes diligent seeking (e.g., Zeph 1:12). After its imperfect, "I will search out," the perfect with *waw* consecutive וּלְקַחְתִּים refers to subsequent action: "and (then) I will take them" (Joüon, § 119 c; similarly, GKC, § 112 p).

וְאִם־יִסָּתְרוּ מִנֶּגֶד עֵינַי בְּקַרְקַע הַיָּם—The Niphal of סָתַר has a reflexive or middle meaning, "to hide oneself."[9] מִנֶּגֶד עֵינַי means, literally, "from before my [Yahweh's] eyes." The Niphal of סָתַר appears in a similar context in Jer 23:24. Yahweh's vision penetrates every barrier (Job 34:21) so that he sees evildoers; they are unable to find any hiding place (Job 34:22; see also Jer 16:17). Zeph 2:3 indicates that the righteous may

---

7 Cf. S. Wagner, "חָבָא," *TDOT* 4:165–71.

8 Cf. F. Maass and G. J. Botterweck, "חָפַשׂ," *TDOT* 5:112–13.

9 Cf. S. Wagner, "סָתַר," *TDOT* 10:362–72.

be hidden on the day of Yahweh's wrath, while in Ps 19:13 (ET 19:12), the righteous ask that even their hidden transgression be forgiven.

The noun קַרְקַע, "floor," normally denotes the floor of a building (Num 5:17; 1 Ki 6:15–16, 30; 7:7), but here it is the "floor/bottom" of "the sea" (הַיָּם).

מִשָּׁם אֲצַוֶּה אֶת־הַנָּחָשׁ וּנְשָׁכָם׃—Literally, "from there I will command the serpent, and it will bite them," this construction could be rendered as "I will command the serpent to bite them" (Joüon, § 177 j). The Piel imperfect אֲצַוֶּה, "I will command," recurs in 9:4. The definite noun הַנָּחָשׁ, "the serpent," is the subject of a suffixed Qal perfect of נָשַׁךְ, "to bite," also in 5:19, where too this action executed divine judgment. See the fourth textual note on 5:19. Other verses where a "serpent" (נָחָשׁ) "bites" (נָשַׁךְ) include Gen 49:17; Num 21:6, 9; Prov 23:32; Eccl 10:8, 11. According to Gen 3:15, the "serpent" (נָחָשׁ, Gen 3:1–2, 4, 13–14) will "crush" (the verb שׁוּף) the heel of the woman's Seed (the crucifixion of Christ executed God's judgment against the sin of fallen humanity), but the Seed will crush the serpent's head (Christ triumphs over Satan, sin, and death; cf. Rom 16:20; Gal 3:16–19, 29).

9:4 וְאִם־יֵלְכוּ בַשְּׁבִי לִפְנֵי אֹיְבֵיהֶם—The noun שְׁבִי, "captivity," appears in 4:10; see the third textual note there. לִפְנֵי אֹיְבֵיהֶם, "before their enemies," pictures a victory parade in which the captured people are forced to march in front while the victors drive them from behind.

מִשָּׁם אֲצַוֶּה אֶת־הַחֶרֶב וַהֲרָגָתַם—Instead of wielding the sword directly, as he does in 4:10; 7:9; 9:1, here Yahweh says, "From there I will command the sword." The noun חֶרֶב is feminine, hence it is the subject of the feminine Qal perfect of הָרַג, "kill, slay" (as in 9:1), with *waw* consecutive and suffix. In this context, וַהֲרָגָתַם could be rendered as a purpose/result clause: "so that it kills them."

וְשַׂמְתִּי עֵינִי עֲלֵיהֶם לְרָעָה וְלֹא לְטוֹבָה׃—The idiom of someone setting (שִׂים) his eyes (עֵינַיִם) upon (עַל) someone else usually conveys the meaning of watching out for the benefit of that person, as Yahweh does in Jer 24:6 and as other people do in Jer 39:12; 40:4 (cf. Gen 44:21). But here Yahweh again inverts Gospel language into Law[a] and turns the phrase into a description of his wrathful and destructive gaze: לְרָעָה וְלֹא לְטוֹבָה, "for evil and not for good." The adjective רַע appears in 5:13–15; see the second textual note on 5:13. The adjective טוֹב appears in 5:14–15; see the first textual note on 5:14. Feminine forms of both adjectives are used because Hebrew characteristically employs feminine forms to express abstract concepts, such as "good" and "evil."

(a) See also Amos 2:9–11; 3:1–2; 4:4–5, 12, 13; 5:8–9, 18–20; 7:8; 8:2; 9:1, 5–6, 7, 10

Commentary

The Structure of Amos 9:1–10

The hymnic doxology in 9:5–6 weaves together the preceding text of 9:1–4 and the following text of 9:7–10 and breaks 9:1–10 into three units:

1. 9:1–4: The inescapability from the divine judgment and the destruction of Bethel's temple.
2. 9:5–6: The cosmic Judge and the eternal temple.
3. 9:7–10: Reaffirmation of Yahweh's judgment.[10]

[10] Noble, "Amos' Absolute 'No,' " 331.

Although 9:1–10 contains three units, it exhibits an overall unity.[11] כַּפְתּוֹר, *kaphtor,* is a catchword and pun because in 9:1 it denotes the "capital(s)" of the temple pillars, while in 9:7 it denotes the island of "Caphtor" (Crete).[12] The two imperative commands uttered by Yahweh in 9:1, "strike" (הַךְ) and, literally, "and cut off them" (וּבְצַעַם), are balanced by him saying "I will command" (אֲצַוֶּה) in 9:3 and "behold, I am commanding" (הִנֵּה אָנֹכִי מְצַוֶּה) in 9:9. There are also several references to Egypt: 9:5 contains "Nile" and "Egypt," while 9:7 mentions both "the Cushites" and "Egypt." Additionally, Yahweh sets his eyes upon Israel for evil and not for good in 9:4 and 9:10; he slays them with the sword in 9:1, 4, 10; and he shakes the temple in 9:1 and the house of Israel in 9:9.

Moreover, the outer verses of 9:1–10 are bracketed by "on that day" sayings (8:13–14; 9:11–12), while the expression "they will fall, and they will never rise again" (8:14) is countered with the resurrection of the falling tabernacle of David (9:11).[13] A further outer ring of the composition are the "behold, days are coming" sayings (8:11–12; 9:13–15).[14]

Stuart summarizes the theological themes in 9:1–10: "It is fraught with images of universality in Yahweh's control of all spaces (vv 2–4), all nature (vv 5–6), and all nations (vv 7–10). He controls all and has total power; none can escape from his judgment."[15] Yet that judgment is not the final word; it prepares for the Gospel promise of messianic resurrection and the eschatological restoration of the new creation in the concluding passage of the book, 9:11–15.

Introduction to Amos 9:1–4

Amos' fifth and final vision brings to climactic conclusion the prior four visions and describes the enactment of the predictions of judgment in the third and fourth visions.[16] The distinctive beginning of the fifth vision report, "I saw the Lord standing by the altar," sets it apart from the other four.[17] Amos sees Yahweh. It was time for Israel to meet its God (4:12). Paul points out that Amos' five visions are tied together by a graduated development of severity:

> The punishment in the first vision is executed only against the agricultural land; in the second vision, the soil as well as the underground sources of water are desiccated; the sanctuaries and the "house" of Jeroboam are the targets of the threat in the third vision; and in the fourth vision, the entire nation is visited

---

[11] This paragraph follows Stuart, *Hosea–Jonah*, 390.

[12] Compare the pun on קֵץ, *qets,* "end," and קַיִץ, *qayits,* "summer fruit," in 8:1–2. See also the pun in 5:5: "Gilgal [הַגִּלְגָּל, *haggilgal*] surely will go into exile [גָּלֹה יִגְלֶה, *galoh yigleh*]."

[13] Limburg, *Hosea–Micah*, 125.

[14] Limburg, *Hosea–Micah*, 125.

[15] Stuart, *Hosea–Jonah*, 395.

[16] The five visions in the book of Amos may be categorized under three sub-groupings: the first two (7:1–3; 7:4–6); the third and fourth (7:7–9; 8:1–3); and the fifth (9:1–4).

[17] The other four began with "this is what the Lord Yahweh/he showed me." See the first textual note on 9:1.

with a devastating decimation, whose ultimate inescapability is dramatically portrayed in the final vision.[18]

As judgment in the visions waxes, interaction between Yahweh and Amos wanes. The first pair of visions (7:1–3; 7:4–6) included Yahweh's judgment, the prophet's petition as an intercessor, and Yahweh's change from Law to Gospel, so that he did not carry out the judgment. In the second pair (7:7–9; 8:1–3), Yahweh is not only the giver but also the interpreter of the visions. His mind is made up: "I will never again forgive him" (7:8; 8:2). By repeating this same verdict, but with different symbols (first a plumb line, then a basket of summer fruit), the third and fourth visions emphasize the certainty of Yahweh's decision. The fourth vision (8:1–3) states *that* "the end is coming," while the fifth vision states *how* the judgment will be enacted. It will be final, definitive, and decisive; nothing will be spared, nothing protected, nothing left. It promises a complete dismantling of the false temple at Bethel, its priesthood, and the Israelites who worshiped there.

In the fifth vision, there is no conversation between Yahweh and the prophet. Yahweh commands; Amos is silent. The veil is rent asunder and Amos sees the coming destruction with all of its gruesome details. He can say or do nothing. The prophet's role is diminished to the point that the only actor in the vision is Yahweh. Although Amos' fifth vision has some balance and symmetry, it has been called "prosaic more than poetic."[19] The counterfeit temple at Bethel is destroyed so that Yahweh's authentic temple may take center stage (9:6, 11). The human is replaced by the divine, and the idolatrous dynasty is thrown down by the eternal dynasty of Yahweh enacted through the Messiah from the line of David (9:11–15).

The effects of Yahweh shaking the earth are witnessed throughout the book of Amos. See 1:1; 3:15; 4:11; 8:8; 9:1, 5; and in a Gospel context, 9:13.[20] In the fifth vision, the destructive quaking reaches its climax. Apostate northern Israel considered the temple at Bethel to be "the house of the kingdom" (7:13), the sacrosanct center of the nation's life, the key to its political stability and economic prosperity. Its destruction sets off disorder and death that have far reaching effects (9:2–4). The chief agents who will shake northern Israel will be the Assyrian army, which will conquer it in 722 BC (fulfilling, e.g., 5:27; 6:14),[21] and Josiah, who will destroy the main altar and the Asherah at Bethel as well as other shrines (2 Ki 23:15–19). All this is triggered by Yahweh's Word (Amos 3:7–8).

This vision is the most devastating and dramatic. It is not an accident that it involves the temple and its attendants because Bethel was the center of the

---

[18] Paul, *Amos*, 223.

[19] Andersen and Freedman, *Amos*, 838.

[20] See the fourth textual note on 9:13.

[21] See the excursus "The Assyrian Empire."

problem. Apostasy was rampant, in part because Amaziah's priestly leadership at the temple was corrupt and directly opposed Yahweh's prophetic Word (7:10–17). The vision needs to be interpreted in light of 7:10–17, for after Amos' fiery confrontation with Amaziah, there could only be one destiny for the Bethel shrine: destruction. Bethel is the primary focus, but because Amos' preaching is directed at both the Northern and the Southern Kingdoms, Jerusalem may not be far from consideration. For that matter, worship sites at Gilgal (4:4; 5:5), Beersheba (5:5; 8:14), and Dan (8:14) have also been in Yahweh's purview. Therefore the vision may foresee the destruction of the temples in northern Israel as well as the Jerusalem temple and other shrines in Judah, since the beliefs and worship practices of both kingdoms became corrupt and syncretistic.[22] There are similarities between Amos' fifth vision and Ezekiel's vision of the destruction of the Jerusalem temple (Ezekiel 8–11), such as the imperative command to "strike" (the Hiphil imperative of נָכָה in Ezek 9:5; Amos 9:1) and the slaying of idolaters (Ezek 8:18–9:11; 11:13; Amos 9:1, 4).

Like the other visions in Amos, 9:1–4 combines the real with the transcendent. The altar, capitals, thresholds, and the Assyrian army are all real and earthly; Yahweh and his efficacious words are transcendent yet directly impact the persons, events, and buildings on earth.

9:1 Isaiah begins his prophetic call vision similarly by recording, "I saw the Lord" (וָאֶרְאֶה אֶת־אֲדֹנָי, Is 6:1). He then gives fuller details of his vision (Is 6:1–4) and responds, "Woe is me" (אוֹי־לִי, Is 6:5), that is, "I am as good as dead." In contrast, Amos quite matter of factly says, "I saw the Lord standing by the altar" (רָאִיתִי אֶת־אֲדֹנָי נִצָּב עַל־הַמִּזְבֵּחַ, Amos 9:1).

Referring to the apostle John's declaration that "no one has ever seen God, but the only-begotten God, who is in the bosom of the Father, has exegeted him" (Jn 1:18), the church father Chrysostom asks:

> Tell me, John, what do you mean when you say, "No one has ever seen God"? What shall we think about the prophets who say that they saw God? Isaiah said, "I saw the Lord sitting on a high exalted throne" [Is 6:1]. And, again, Daniel said, "I saw until the thrones were set, and the ancient of days sat" [Dan 7:9]. And Micaiah said, "I saw the God of Israel sitting on his throne" [1 Ki 22:19]. And again, another prophet said, "I saw the Lord standing on the altar, and he said unto me, 'Strike the mercy seat' " [LXX Amos 9:1]. And I can gather many similar passages to show you as witnesses of what I say.
>
> How is it, then, that John says, "No one has ever seen God"? He says this so that you may know that he is speaking of a clear knowledge and a perfect comprehension of God. All the cases cited were instances of God's condescension and accommodation. That no one of those prophets saw God's essence in its pure state is clear from the fact that each one saw him in a different way. God is a simple being; he is not composed of parts; he is without form or figure. But all these prophets saw different forms and figures. God proved this very thing through the mouth of another prophet. And he persuaded those

[22] Cf. Andersen and Freedman, *Amos*, 680.

> other prophets that they did not see his essence in its exact nature when he said, "I have multiplied visions, and by the ministries of the prophets I was presented" [LXX Hos 12:11 (MT 12:11; ET 12:10)]. What God was saying was, "I did not show my very essence, but I came down in condescension and accommodated myself to the weakness of their eyes."[23]

The vision seen by Amos here is not of the grace to be revealed fully in the incarnate Christ. Rather, it is one of inescapable judgment. Those impacted by this vision, as well as by all the events described throughout 9:1–10, are those whom God calls "all the sinners of my people" (9:10). In its broadest sense, the judgment applies to all unbelievers of all times. But more specifically in Amos, the "sinners" in OT Israel include the corrupt businessmen described in 2:6–8 and 8:4–6, the drunken wives in 4:1, the royal officials in 3:9–15, the magistrates in 5:10–12, and the apostate priests represented by Amaziah in 7:10–17. Andersen and Freedman believe that this vision echoes Yahweh's condemnation in 8:7, "I will never forget any of their deeds," with the result that the Israelites "will fall, and they will never rise again" (8:14).[24]

Jeroboam ben Nebat once "was standing by the altar" (1 Ki 13:1) and burning incense at the false shrine he had built at Bethel (1 Ki 12:26–33). Since then, "the whole thing [worship at Bethel] was a counterfeit: a counterfeit feast on a counterfeit altar to prop up a counterfeit monarchy" in northern Israel.[25] Now Yahweh, the real King, comes to tear it down. His presence at the altar at Bethel is not a sign of his favor; rather, as Yahweh does repeatedly in Amos, he uses language to express judgment that in other contexts has Gospel import.[26] The perceived blessing of Yahweh's presence is really to *destroy*. "Instead of providing security and hope, this temple will bring deadly panic."[27]

Who is commanded to "strike" (הַ֚ךְ) the altar at Bethel? It could be that the performative Word of Yahweh does the smiting (cf. Hos 6:5), while others[28] believe that possibly the destroying angel (Ex 12:23; 2 Sam 24:15–17; 2 Ki 19:35) is addressed. Mays suggests that the command to strike the capitals is a rhetorical device, "a way of saying with emphatic authority: 'Let the capitals be smitten,' "[29] as if God said something like, "Let it happen" (cf. Is 13:2; Jer

---

[23] Chrysostom, *Against the Anomoeans*, 4.18–19, quoted in Ferreiro, *The Twelve Prophets*, ACCS 14:115. For a discussion on what Chrysostom calls God's "condescension" as the presence of the second person of the Trinity, who appeared to prophets and others before the time of his incarnation of the Virgin Mary, see Gieschen, "The Real Presence of the Son before Christ."

[24] Andersen and Freedman, *Amos*, 838–39.

[25] Motyer, *The Message of Amos*, 194. Bethel is one of Yahweh's main targets throughout Amos (3:14; 4:4; 5:5–6; 7:10, 13).

[26] Yahweh changes Gospel language into Law also in 2:9–11; 3:1–2; 4:4–5, 12, 13; 5:8–9, 18–20; 7:8; 8:2; 9:4, 5–6, 7, 10.

[27] Smith, *Hosea, Amos, Micah*, 401.

[28] E.g., Niehaus, "Amos," 479.

[29] Mays, *Amos*, 153.

5:10; Amos 3:9). Similarly, it is unclear to whom the plural imperatives in Amos 3:13 are addressed. Andersen and Freedman think that the imperative in 9:1 is addressed to an "unnamed person [who is] one of the leaders of the heavenly host (perhaps the commander; cf. Josh 5:13–15)."[30] In any case, the emphasis is not on who will do the smiting, but the certainty of the smiting itself, as well as the fact that Yahweh is commanding the destruction.

Also unstated is the referent of the third masculine plural object suffix on the verb in וּבְצַעַם בְּרֹאשׁ, literally, "and cut off *them* by the head." On the one hand, it may refer to the capitals, or tops, of the pillars. If the pillars supported a roof, then cutting off their heads would cause the roof to collapse and destroy the contents of the temple, including any worshipers there. It is better, however, to understand the referent as the unfaithful Israelites, particularly the elite who were worshiping in the idolatrous sanctuary. Their heads are to be cut off.

The "capital(s)" (הַכַּפְתּוֹר), or tops, of the pillars and the "thresholds" (הַסִּפִּים) of the doorways represent the highest and lowest points of the temple. By means of this merism, the vision indicates that the entire edifice is going to be destroyed. The same is true in Zeph 2:14, which refers to the "capitals" and "threshold" of the city of Nineveh, which would be entirely demolished. It will be a top-to-bottom devastation, not unlike that of the Philistine temple of Dagon destroyed by Samson (Judg 16:25–30).

Lest the Israelites think that only those actually in the Bethel temple will be killed, Yahweh warns, "And the remainder of them with the sword I will slay" (Amos 9:1). The pronominal suffix "them" (attached to וְאַחֲרִיתָם) has the same referent as all of the third masculine plural suffixes from this point forward through 9:4: they are "all the sinners of my people" (9:10).[31] Once again Yahweh strikes a note of universal judgment (cf. 2:14–16; 5:18–20). There will be no escape. Ironically, finality is announced at the Bethel temple, the very place where these people gathered to celebrate the salvation of Israel; the first king of the Northern Kingdom had told them that their redemption had come through the god(s) whose image was there (1 Ki 12:28). But salvation was not found in apostate Israel's worship centers (Amos 4:4; 5:5; 8:14). Instead, they were places of death.

9:2 After the command to destroy the temple at Bethel, this next verse describes Yahweh's judgment of the worshipers who seek to escape his wrath.[32] This verse begins the series of five[33] conditional sentences that ends in 9:4. Each protasis begins with "even if" (אִם), and each apodosis begins with "from there"

---

[30] Andersen and Freedman, *Amos*, 680. They add that the smiter is "surely not the prophet, rather a member of the heavenly court, as commentators have recognized from early times to the present" (p. 835).

[31] Andersen and Freedmen, *Amos*, 836.

[32] For similar futile attempts to flee God's wrath, see Job 34:21–22; Lk 23:30; Rev 6:15–17.

[33] Other uses of pentads by Amos are as follows: the fivefold refrain "but you did not return to me" (4:6–11); the five visions (7:1–3; 7:4–6; 7:7–9; 8:1–3; 9:1–4); and the five curses in 7:17.

(מִשָּׁם). In Jer 23:24 Yahweh asks: " 'If a man hides himself in hiding places, will I not see him?' declares Yahweh. 'Do I not fill the heavens and the earth?' " Yahweh sees everything. All avenues of escape are closed. The Pentateuch and its curses indicate that there is no one who can save or deliver another out of Yahweh's hand (e.g., Deut 28:29; 32:39). There will be no detours, no alternate routes, and no off-road trails. It will be impossible for "all the sinners of my people" (9:10) to flee from Yahweh's judgment.

The first place the unfaithful people will seek reprieve will be in Sheol, but no matter how low this place of death may be, it is transparent to Yahweh (Prov 15:11). Indeed, he redeems and raises up his faithful people from Sheol (1 Sam 2:6; Hos 13:14; Ps 49:16 [ET 49:15]). But his fire pursues unbelievers down to Sheol. "A fire has been kindled by my anger, and it burns to lowest Sheol [עַד־שְׁאוֹל תַּחְתִּית]" (Deut 32:22). Yahweh will "take, seize" (לָקַח, Amos 9:2) those digging down to Sheol, and they will not escape.[34] Yahweh also "took, seized" (לָקַח) Amos to be his prophet (7:15), and likewise there was no way for him to do anything else (3:8). When someone is taken by Yahweh, resistance is in vain.

Yahweh establishes that there will be no escape anywhere in the universe, neither to hell ("Sheol") nor to "heaven." Amos 9:2 creates a merism with "ascend to heaven" (הַשָּׁמַיִם), which is the exact opposite of digging down to Sheol.[35] Elijah literally ascended into heaven when he was assumed (2 Ki 2:11), but here in Amos, the ascent to heaven is pretentious. In Obad 4 the prophet echoes the same judgment toward Edom: "Even if you could exalt (your nest) like the eagle, and even if among stars you could set your nest, from there I will bring you down—utterance of Yahweh."[36] A similar pretentious flight to heaven is described by Isaiah, who mocks the hubris of the pagan king, apparently as a type of Satan (Is 14:13; see also Jer 49:16).

9:3 Flight is marked by pairs of extremes, Sheol and heaven in 9:2 as well as Mount Carmel and the depths of the sea in 9:3. In this verse, Yahweh zeros in on where people may think there are safe places on earth, the high mountains and the deep sea. The point of these extremes is this: there is *nowhere* for unbelievers to flee in order to escape Yahweh's wrath.

Mount Carmel is 1,800 feet above sea level and has numerous forests and caves.[37] But even such a mighty fortress will not prevent Yahweh from executing his justice. During the ministry of Elijah (ca. 870 BC), about a century before

---

[34] See the excursus "Sheol" in Lessing, *Jonah*, 249–55.

[35] The merism of heaven and Sheol also appears in Ps 139:7–8 to indicate Yahweh's control over everything and everyone. These verses in Psalm 139 are the obverse of Amos 9:2–3.

[36] This translation is from Raabe, *Obadiah*, xxiii.

[37] Driver notes that Mount Carmel affords two possible hiding areas: (1) it has many limestone caves in which someone may hide, and (2) the summit is thickly wooded (*Joel and Amos*, 221–22). Niehaus writes: "Since the top of Carmel is mentioned, it is more likely that its dense forest is the intended hiding place" ("Amos," 481).

the time of Amos (ca. 760 BC), Yahweh had defeated and executed the prophets of Baal at Mount Carmel (1 Ki 18:19–40). For idolaters in Amos' day, trying to "hide themselves" (the Niphal of חָבָא) from Yahweh on the top of Mount Carmel is as futile as Adam as he shivers in the shrubbery and confesses, "I hid myself" (Niphal of חָבָא, Gen 3:10). Yahweh seeks those who had refused to repent in order to judge them, even as he seeks the lost in order to save them through repentance and faith (Lk 15:4–10; 19:10).

If there is no refuge in the heights of Carmel, there certainly will be no safe haven in the depths below. "Sheol" in Jonah 2:3 (ET 2:2) corresponds to that prophet's sinking toward the bottom of the sea, depicted in Jonah 2:6–7 (ET 2:5–6) as a place that is as far removed from human reach as possible. Yet Yahweh saved his prophet even there (Jonah 2:7, 10–11 [ET 2:6, 9–10]). But for the unbelievers condemned in Amos, even if they were to reach the depths of the sea, "from there" Yahweh "will command the serpent, and it will bite them." "Serpent" (נָחָשׁ) is the term used for the devil in Gen 3:1–14 and the serpents in Num 21:6–9, as well as the biting serpent that is the final slayer in Amos 5:19. Yahweh sent serpents to bite the Israelites to death in Num 21:6–7, yet those who looked to an impaled bronze serpent were healed and lived (Num 21:8–9), typifying that all who look to the Son of Man have eternal life (Jn 3:14–15).

Since sea snakes only live in shallow tropical waters, not the deep sea, the "serpent" here probably refers to a supernatural creature, a monster like Leviathan (Is 27:1; Job 40:25–41:26 [ET 41:1–34]). OT texts that build on Yahweh saving Israel in the exodus through the Red Sea describe Yahweh as slaying a sea monster, called Leviathan (Pss 74:13–14; cf. Ps 104:26) or Rahab (Ps 89:11 [ET 89:10]; Is 51:9). It is in the book of Job that Leviathan receives the most attention. This terrifying monster would overpower any person, but Yahweh puts a rope through his nose (Job 40:26 [ET 41:2]), making him like a harmless pet on a leash. Or he becomes like a fish in a bowl, since Yahweh has set limits for the sea (Job 38:8–11), his home. Leviathan is a personification of evil, rather than simply an earthly animal.[38] In Job 41:10–11 (ET 41:18–19), Leviathan breathes fire like a dragon (cf. Rev 12:3). He inhabits the sea (Job 41:23–24 [ET 41:31–32]), which can be symbolic of chaos and evil (Job 9:8; 26:12–13; 38:8–11). Job 41:25–26 (ET 41:33–34) says Leviathan rules over all the worldly "sons of pride" as their king, and "on earth is not his equal" (a description of the devil in stanza 1 of Luther's "A Mighty Fortress Is Our God").[39]

[38] Supporting the view that the creature has theological significance are extrabiblical texts in which a sea monster has religious significance. Several ancient Near Eastern mythologies contain a story about a god killing a creature or god of chaos and disorder called a dragon or serpent. Such a story is attested in the Babylonian Creation Epic, where Marduk kills Tiamat, a large sea creature. Similar accounts have been found at Ugarit, where the creature is called Lotan (*ltn*, cognate to Leviathan), and in Hittite literature.

[39] E.g., *LSB* 656:1.

The NT identifies Satan, the prince of the demons, as the ancient serpent and "dragon" (δράκων, Rev 12:3–13:11; 16:13; 20:2). Amos affirms that this serpent will "bite" or terrorize all unbelievers. However, the lake of fire is the eternal destiny of Satan and his hordes (Rev 20:10) and there will be no sea (nor sea monster) to threaten believers in the new heaven and new earth (Rev 21:1). Neither will the new Jerusalem contain anything evil, chaotic, or unclean (Rev 21:27). Everything will be made subject to Christ and then in turn to God the Father (1 Cor 15:24–28). The triune God controls, restrains, and ultimately defeats all evil (1 Jn 3:8).

9:4 In the previous verse, Yahweh uses a serpent to enact punishment; here he employs the sword.[40] After exhausting the vertical extremes in the universe as well as the earth, the possibility exists that perhaps someone might escape using a horizontal route—in this case the farthest distance abroad, captivity. One of the covenant curses includes this promise: "You will beget sons and daughters, but they will not be yours because they will go into captivity [יֵלְכוּ בַּשֶּׁבִי]" (Deut 28:41).[41] The impending exile is a theme in Amos.[42] Yet even in exile the sword will accomplish Yahweh's bidding.

In the grand finale of his fifth vision, Yahweh again takes time-honored Gospel language and stands it on its head so that it becomes a judgment.[43] The expression שִׂים עַיִן עַל, "to set an eye upon" someone, elsewhere in the OT is always used in a positive sense (Gen 44:21; Jer 24:6; 39:12; 40:4). Here, however, Yahweh says, "I will set my eye upon them *for evil* [לְרָעָה] and not for good."

This verse in Amos is different from almost every other OT text that mentions Israel's exile. In most passages of this sort, captivity is intended as punishment and refining (e.g., Is 6:12–13; 11:1; Jeremiah 24), not for annihilation. Both Jeremiah (e.g., Jer 24:5–7; 29:10–14) and Ezekiel (e.g., Ezek 37:1–14) indicate that Israel's theological future lay with the exiles in Babylon, who one day would return. But Amos offers no such hope; Israel's conquering enemies will not appear as their "savior." Instead of driving the exiles to repentance and renewed faith, the exile will be an occasion for Yahweh's final act of just judgment.

Josiah's demolition of the sanctuary at Bethel (2 Ki 23:15–20) in about 623 BC may be a partial fulfillment of Amos 9:1–4. The use of the verb זָבַח,

---

[40] Yahweh's "sword" is almost personified in Ezek 21:13–22 (ET 21:8–17) and also, for example, Is 34:5; Jer 47:6; Hos 11:6. Amos refers to "the sword" as a covenantal curse in 4:10; 7:9, 11, 17; and 9:1. "By metonymy of the adjunct, the sword is spoken of as slaying them, whereas it is actually the foe wielding the sword who will do it" (Niehaus, "Amos," 481).

[41] For the verb הָלַךְ and בַּשֶּׁבִי (or בַּשְּׁבִי) forming the clause "they will go into captivity," see also, for example, Jer 20:6; 22:22; Ezek 12:11; 30:17–18; Lam 1:18.

[42] Amos explicitly mentions the exile of northern Israel for the first time in 4:2–3. It is on ongoing theme in the rest of the book (5:5, 27; 6:7; 7:11, 17; 9:4).

[43] Yahweh does this also in 2:9–11; 3:1–2; 4:4–5, 12, 13; 5:8–9, 18–20; 7:8; 8:2; 9:1, 5–6, 7, 10.

"sacrifice," in 2 Ki 23:20 for Josiah's slaughter of Bethel's priests indicates that he understood his actions to be a ritual judgment against the priests, the altar, and the shrine. Josiah's destruction was so complete that excavations at Bethel have never uncovered any remains of the sanctuary.[44]

Amos' fifth vision points forward to the day when Christ will come again to judge the living and the dead. The Lutheran Confessions state:

> It is also taught among us that our Lord Jesus Christ will return on the last day for judgment and will raise up all the dead, to give eternal life and everlasting joy to believers and the elect but to condemn ungodly men and the devil to hell and eternal punishment (AC XVII).

There will be no escape on this Last Day either; "for we must all appear before the judgment seat of Christ" (2 Cor 5:10). Only those who through faith and sacramental union with Christ have had their robes washed white in the blood of the Lamb will inherit eternal life (cf. Rev 7:14–17).

Summary

What Amos sees in his fifth vision is a pentad that depicts a message of total judgment. In the vision Yahweh considers all of the possible ways of escape and then slams each door shut so that none of "all the sinners of my people" (9:10) are able to reach safety.[45] The vision begins with the words "I saw the *Lord*" (רָאִיתִי אֶת־אֲדֹנָי, 9:1).[46] Amos' use of "Lord" connects this vision with his third "creation" hymn[47] in 9:5–6, which begins "truly the Lord Yahweh of armies" (וַאדֹנָי יְהוִה הַצְּבָאוֹת). The one who commands the destruction in 9:1–4 is none other than the Creator of the universe depicted in 9:5–6.

Amos' fifth vision comes at a time of great security and abundance for Israel during the reign of Jeroboam ben Joash (1:1; 7:9–11). Economic growth and military might are both on the rise. But the capitals and thresholds of Bethel's temple will shake,[48] leading to its destruction and Yahweh's judgment against apostate Israel. Everything and everyone will be destroyed. Idolatrous Israel had many altars (2:8; 3:14), but "the altar" in 9:1 probably refers to the great altar at Bethel, which Jeroboam ben Nebat had constructed (1 Ki 12:32–33). This altar defined the nation's ongoing infidelity toward Yahweh.[49]

---

[44] As noted by Andersen and Freedman, *Amos*, 842.

[45] Cf. Smith, *Hosea, Amos, Micah*, 401.

[46] Laetsch suggests that Amos uses "Lord" rather than the covenant name Yahweh to denote "one possessing power, authority, designating God as the God of absolute authority and power to do as He pleases with His subjects" (*The Minor Prophets*, 183).

[47] The three doxologies or hymns in the book are 4:13; 5:8–9; and 9:5–6. They are often called creation hymns but that title is inadequate because it ignores their additional content about special revelation, judgment, salvation, and eschatology. See the textual notes and the commentary on 4:13.

[48] This is part of the theme throughout the book that Yahweh will cause the earth to quake. See 1:1; 3:15; 4:11; 8:8; 9:1, 5; and, in a Gospel context, 9:13.

[49] Noble states: "The sanctuary—and especially the altar, beside (or upon) which Amos sees Yahweh standing—was the focal point of communication between deity and people; thus,

Amos 9:1–4 lists seven divine actions,[50] and 9:2–4 has five conditional sentences.[51] These numbers add to the ominous nature of the vision as they unequivocally declare that all possible escape routes will be blocked off. The Israelites will have to face Yahweh (4:12) no matter where they attempt to hide; he will find them in Sheol, in heaven, in the thick forests and/or numerous caves on Mount Carmel, in the bottom of the sea, and even in a foreign land during their captivity.

Amos' fifth vision includes a cosmological merism with "Sheol" and "heaven" and an earthly merism by means of "Mount Carmel" and "the bottom of the sea." Some psalms employ this technique of merism in order to extol Yahweh for his universal power and presence. For example, Ps 95:3–5 praises Yahweh "in [whose] hands are the depths of the earth; the heights of the mountains are his also" (cf. Pss 103:11–12; 148:1, 7).[52] In structure and style, Amos 9:2–4 reflects this hymnic tradition of the OT, but it functions to stress the inescapability of Yahweh's judgment. Psalm 139 affirms Yahweh's presence in the midst of a vast and threatening world; Amos 9:2–4, on the other hand, is a guarantee of Yahweh's destructive dominion.[53] What other texts affirm as hopeful—Yahweh's dominion over the entire universe—is reason for the unbelievers to be utterly *hopeless*. Israel would fall, and the temple would be toppled. At the time of the prophet's ministry (ca. 760 BC) some forty years before Assyria would conquer northern Israel, the inhabitants did not think it could happen (6:3a; 9:10b), but it did. Everything turned to ashes.

While in the context of Amos, the toppled temple in 9:1 most likely is the one in Bethel, its demolition may also anticipate the later judgment inflicted on idolatrous Judah through Babylon in 587, when the Jerusalem temple was destroyed. Both of these judgments on unfaithful OT Israel foreshadowed the razing of the Herodian Jerusalem temple in AD 70 by the Romans, executing God's judgment on the Jewish nation for rejecting the Messiah. Yet Jesus himself interpreted that coming destruction of the temple as a sign of the universal

---

for God to be portrayed as destroying it is 'a way of saying that from his side Yahweh breaks off the intercourse through the cult' " ("Amos' Absolute 'No,' " 331, quoting Mays, *Amos*, 153).

[50] Limburg, "Sevenfold Structures in the Book of Amos," 221.

[51] Amos employs other heptads in 1:3–2:5; 2:6–8; 2:14–16; 3:3–6; 4:4–5; 4:6–11; 5:8–9; 5:21–23; 6:1–6. Amos' other pentads are the fivefold refrain "but you did not return to me" in 4:6–11; the five visions (7:1–3; 7:4–6; 7:7–9; 8:1–3; 9:1–4); and the five curses in 7:17.

[52] The hymns in Amos (4:13; 5:8–9; 9:5–6) contain similar poetic merisms. For example, 4:13 names Yahweh as the one "who forms mountains and who creates wind," a merism that asserts Yahweh's control over the most permanent and the most transient aspects of his creation. The doxology in 9:5–6 describes Yahweh with these words: "he is the one who builds his upper chambers in heaven; he founds his vault upon the earth." This merism indicates that Yahweh's temple fills heaven and earth.

[53] Commentators discuss this ironic use of Israel's hymnic tradition. Mays writes: "The hymnic theme is reversed" (*Amos*, 154). Soggin calls Amos 9:2–4 "a negative parallel to Ps. 139" (*The Prophet Amos*, 123).

judgment at the end of the world (Mt 23:30–25:46). Therefore no modern reader may presume that he somehow will avoid equal accountability to God the Judge. That presumption would contradict the teaching in Amos 9:1–4 of the inescapability of judgment. Rather, the proper response for all readers—Jewish and Gentile—is sincere repentance and genuine faith in Jesus, the risen tabernacle of David (9:11), the new and living temple who shall never fall. Yahweh's final words in the book are a Gospel promise of resurrection and restoration for the remnant of all who repent and believe in him (9:11–15).[54]

[54] See also the excursus "The Quotation from Amos 9 in Acts 15."

Amos 9:5–6

Yahweh Shakes the Earth

Translation

9 5 Truly the Lord Yahweh of armies is he who touches the earth and it shakes,
and all who dwell in it mourn,
and all of it rises like the Nile,
and it sinks again like the Nile of Egypt.
6 He is the one who builds his upper chambers in heaven;
he founds his vault upon the earth.
He is the one who calls for the waters of the sea
and pours them out upon the face of the earth—
Yahweh is his name.

Textual Notes

9:5 וַאדֹנָ֨י יְהוִ֜ה הַצְּבָא֗וֹת—The initial *waw* is emphatic with the nuance of affirmation (Joüon, § 177 n) and is rendered "truly." This full divine title, "the Lord Yahweh of (the) armies," occurs only here in Amos. It is a combination of two shorter titles, אֲדֹנָי יְהוִה, which occurs often in Amos (see the fifth textual note on 1:8), and יְהוִה הַצְּבָאוֹת, "Yahweh of (the) armies," which occurs in Amos only in 9:5. The second textual note and the commentary on 3:13 discuss the similar long divine title יהוה אֱלֹהֵי (הַ)צְּבָאוֹת.

הַנּוֹגֵ֤עַ בָּאָ֙רֶץ֙ וַתָּמ֔וֹג—Like the two previous hymns in Amos (4:13; 5:8–9), this one has participial divine titles.[1] All three titles in these two verses are Qal participles with the article: הַנּוֹגֵעַ, "he (is the one) who touches" (9:5), הַבּוֹנֶה, "he (is the one) who builds" (9:6), and הַקֹּרֵא, "he (is the one) who calls" (9:6). The first and third participles are continued by an imperfect with *waw* consecutive (הַנּוֹגֵעַ ... וַתָּמוֹג in 9:5 and הַקֹּרֵא ... וַיִּשְׁפְּכֵם in 9:6c–d); see Joüon, § 118 r. The second participle is continued by a perfect (הַבּוֹנֶה ... יְסָדָהּ in 9:6a–b). Both the participles and the finite verb forms have a timeless significance and are translated in English by the present tense.

The verb נָגַע, "to touch," often takes the preposition בְּ (here on בָּאָרֶץ, "the earth") on the thing touched. In this context, נָגַע indicates Yahweh's omnipotence to bring about worldwide upheavals in creation by a mere tap with his finger. Compare the power of God's "finger" in Ex 8:15 (ET 8:19) and Lk 11:20. This verb with Yahweh as the subject occurs in theophanies also in Pss 104:32 and 144:5.[2] Yahweh's touch (directly or through a heavenly messenger) is often beneficial, empowering people to serve him faithfully.[a] Jesus could heal and raise the dead by his touch (Mt 8:3, 15; Lk 7:14–15).

(a) Is 6:7; Jer 1:9; Dan 8:18; 10:10, 16, 18; cf. Ezek 3:14

---

[1] These hymns and other texts with participial titles for God are cited in Waltke–O'Connor, § 37.3d, note 28.

[2] Cf. L. Schwienhorst, "נָגַע," *TDOT* 9:204–5.

But God also touches the wicked with his righteous judgment (Gen 12:17; 1 Sam 6:9). Yahweh's touch is always authoritative and efficacious.

The Qal imperfect with *waw* consecutive וַתָּמוֹג could be translated as a purpose or result clause, "touches the earth *so that* it shakes." The verb is feminine to match its feminine subject, אֶרֶץ. The Qal of מוג may mean "to melt" in the intransitive sense in Ezek 21:20 (ET 21:15), where Yahweh's sword terrifies the unfaithful Israelites so that their hearts melt (or shake). The Qal might have the transitive meaning "to (cause something to) melt" in Is 64:6 (ET 64:7; see BDB, 2). The only other instance of the Qal is in Ps 46:7 (ET 46:6), where the earth "melts" or "shakes," as in Amos 9:5, but at the voice of Yahweh. Its Hithpolal in Amos 9:13 refers to the hills flowing with wine. In Nah 1:5 the Hithpolal is parallel to רָעַשׁ, "shake," the verb used in Amos 9:1. The Niphal of מוג in the context of Ps 75:4 (ET 75:3) most likely refers to the earth and its inhabitants shaking or quaking, rather than melting. Therefore the Qal in Amos 9:5 and Ps 46:7 (ET 46:6) probably means to "waver" (*HALOT*), "be moved, agitated" (BDB, addenda, s.v. מוג), or "shake."[3] Thus it is part of the earthquake theme in Amos; see also 1:1; 3:15; 4:11; 8:8; 9:1, and in a Gospel context, the last clause of 9:13.

וְאָבְלוּ כָּל־יוֹשְׁבֵי בָהּ—For אָבַל, "mourn," see the fourth textual note on 1:2. See the second textual note on 8:8 for the identical clause but with singular forms of the plural verb (וְאָבְלוּ) and plural participle in construct (יוֹשְׁבֵי) here.

וְעָלְתָה כַיְאֹר כֻּלָּהּ—See the third textual note on 8:8 for the identical clause, except for the singly defective spelling here of the proper noun "Nile" (יְאֹר) with the article and the preposition כְּ. The antecedent of the feminine suffix on כֻּלָּהּ and the implied subject of the feminine verbs וְעָלְתָה and, in the next clause, וְשָׁקְעָה is the feminine noun אֶרֶץ, the "earth," in 9:5a.

וְשָׁקְעָה כִּיאֹר מִצְרָיִם׃—See the fourth textual note on 8:8, which concludes with the identical last two words (except for the plene spelling there of יְאוֹר). The Qere there was a Niphal of שָׁקַע, while the Qal, וְשָׁקְעָה, occurs here, but both mean "to sink."

9:6 הַבּוֹנֶה בַשָּׁמַיִם מַעֲלוֹתָו—Literally, Yahweh is the one "who builds in the heavens his upper chambers." Ps 147:2 states: בּוֹנֵה יְרוּשָׁלַםִ יְהוָה, "the builder of Jerusalem is Yahweh."[4] Nothing can be built to stand unless Yahweh builds it (Ps 127:1). בָּנָה is in Ps 78:69, where Yahweh builds his sanctuary like the high heavens. No structure that people can build (בָּנָה) is sufficient to contain Yahweh (Is 66:1).

The Kethib is the plural noun מַעֲלוֹת with the form of suffix normally found on a singular noun, מַעֲלוֹתוֹ, which agrees with the form of suffix on the singular parallel word וַאֲגֻדָּתוֹ in the following clause. The Qere is the plural noun with the normal form of suffix, מַעֲלוֹתָיו. The noun מַעֲלָה usually refers to a "step, stair" of a temple (e.g., Ezek 40:6), an altar (Ex 20:26; Ezek 43:17), a throne (1 Ki 10:19–20), or a palace (2 Ki 20:9–11 || Is 38:8). However, it can have other meanings, and here it may refer to the "*stories* of

---

[3] Waltke–O'Connor, § 23.6.1a, discusses verbs with "middle" Niphal meanings that correspond to their intransitive Qal meanings. In § 23.6.1c, example 5a, Waltke–O'Connor cites Amos 9:5 but translates the Qal verb as "melts."

[4] Later, when the unfaithful Israelites had aroused his wrath, Yahweh refers to "the day they built it" (Jer 32:31). Cf. S. Wagner, "בָּנָה," *TDOT* 2:166–81.

heaven" (BDB, s.v. מַעֲלָה II, 3; similar is KJV). Many versions render it as "his upper chambers" (e.g., RSV, ESV, NASB), as does the translation above.

In the OT, Jacob's vision at Bethel contains a "ladder" or "ramp" (סֻלָּם, Gen 28:12) that extends from earth to heaven. Niehaus writes: "It seems likely, if we interpret this word [מַעֲלוֹתָו] against the background of God's total revelation, that the steps to his heavenly temple (Exod. 26:30; cf. Rev. 11:19) are intended as metonymy, that is, the part for the whole, so we may translate the phrase as 'his temple.' "[5] Sweeney notes that steps were a common feature in Mesopotamian ziggurats upon which temples were built.[6] Some propose emending to עֲלִיּוֹתָיו, the suffixed plural of עֲלִיָּה, "roof chamber," used in Ps 104:2–3, where Yahweh stretches out the heavens and lays the beams for "his roof chambers" on the waters.[7]

וַאֲגֻדָּתוֹ עַל־אֶרֶץ יְסָדָהּ— The redundant feminine suffix on the final verb, יְסָדָהּ, is retrospective, referring back to the feminine noun וַאֲגֻדָּתוֹ at the beginning of the clause. The syntax is, literally, "his vault, on the earth he founded it."

The noun אֲגֻדָּה appears only four times in the OT. It usually refers to something firmly held together: a "bunch" of hyssop (Ex 12:22), a "company" of soldiers (2 Sam 2:25), or the thongs of a yoke (Is 58:6). Here Amos employs the word to denote the sky as Yahweh's "vault."[8] This vault is elsewhere called the "firmament" (רָקִיעַ, e.g., Gen 1:6–8; Pss 19:2 [ET 19:1]; 150:1) or "the circle [חוּג] of the earth" (Is 40:22; see חוּג also in Job 22:14; Prov 8:27).

The verb יָסַד, "to establish, found," often refers to laying the foundation of a permanent building.[9] Amos uses יָסַד to depict Yahweh's action of erecting his temple that stretches from heaven to earth.

הַקֹּרֵא לְמֵי־הַיָּם וַיִּשְׁפְּכֵם עַל־פְּנֵי הָאָרֶץ—The identical wording was in 5:8. See the fourth textual note and the commentary on 5:8.

יְהוָה שְׁמוֹ׃—The identical affirmation was in 5:8. See the fifth textual note and the commentary on 5:8.

Commentary

Just as Samson destroyed the Philistine temple of the god Dagon along with its priests and worshipers (Judg 16:23–30), in like manner Amos 9:1–4 declared that Yahweh will annihilate the idolatrous temple erected at Bethel, which had been an ancient patriarchal site of proper worship. Whereas the Bethel sanctuary and its personnel will face Yahweh's sword of execution, the crucified and risen Christ himself will be the new temple "not built by human hands" (Mk 14:58; cf. 2 Cor 5:1; Heb 9:11) that will stand forever (Amos 9:11; cf. 9:6a).

---

5 Niehaus, "Amos," 483.

6 Sweeney, *The Twelve Prophets*, 270–71.

7 For the discussion, see Paul, *Amos*, 280, n. 75.

8 BDB, 4, and Paul, *Amos*, 280, including n. 77. Strangely *HALOT*, 4, gives the plural "vaults."

9 R. Mosis, "יָסַד," *TDOT* 6:110.

The fivefold series of conditional sentences in 9:2–4 indicates that Yahweh is the commander in chief who marshals his army of soldiers, including a serpent and a sword, who are at his beck and call to carry out his orders of destruction. It is appropriate, therefore, that the first word in the next verse (9:5) is וַאדֹנָי, "and/truly the Lord."[10] This ties 9:5–6 to 9:1–4, which begins with "I saw the Lord [אֲדֹנָי]." The hymn (9:5–6) also connects the judgment of 9:1–4 with Yahweh as the general of armies (יְהוִֹה הַצְּבָאוֹת, 9:5) and as the cosmic Creator and the Redeemer of the world.[11] Yahweh alone has the ability to bring about the events detailed in Amos' fifth vision (9:1–4) and to accomplish salvation for all peoples (9:7, 11–12).

Amos' three doxologies or hymns in are 4:13; 5:8–9; and 9:5–6. They are often called "creation hymns," but they involve more than just Yahweh as Creator.[12] When compared with the other two hymnic doxologies in 4:13 and 5:8–9, this third hymn reflects many of the earlier doxological themes that celebrate Yahweh's power in creation and through destructive nature. Amos 9:5–6 "has a central pivotal role just like the hymn in 5:8–9."[13] The vocabulary and theology of judgment and salvation in 9:5–6 are skillfully woven throughout the surrounding verses in 9:1–4 and 9:7–10.

Consequently the themes of the third hymn reverberate throughout 9:1–10. Yahweh is the divine builder of heaven and controller of the waters of the sea (9:6), so no one can hide in heaven (9:2) or in the bottom of the sea (9:3) nor escape through the sieve (9:9). How could they elude (9:2–4) the one whose upper chambers reach into the highest heavens, and whose vault is founded upon the earth (9:6)? Yahweh's touch is powerful enough to cause the earth to shake just as the Nile floods and recedes (9:5), just as he causes the thresholds of the temple to quake (9:1) and the sieve to shake in 9:9. General Yahweh (9:5) commands (the verb צִוָּה in 9:3–4, 9) the judgment so "the sword" (9:1, 4) will kill "all the sinners of my people" (9:10). Yahweh evaporates the waters of the sea and pours them out "upon the face of the earth" (9:6), and he will destroy the most sinful kingdom "from the face of the earth" (9:8).

9:5 This verse resembles others (Micah 1:4; Nah 1:5; Pss 46:7 [ET 46:6]; 75:4 [ET 75:3]) that depict the earth shaking at Yahweh's theophany. Yahweh is the commander over both heavenly and earthly armies (4:13; 5:8–9; 6:14) who has the destructive power to destroy the cosmos, and by implication, that

---

10 For the force of the conjunctive *waw*, see the first textual note on 9:5.

11 In the first two hymns (4:13; 5:8–9), Yahweh's name is invoked only at the end of the first verse (4:13; 5:8). In this last hymn, Yahweh's name is invoked at the start. This suggests at least two ideas: (1) "the Lord Yahweh of armies" (9:5) ties into the warfare theme of 9:1–4, and (2) the creational aspects of 9:6 lead into the claim of 9:7 (also affirmed in 9:12), namely, that Yahweh has a plan of redemption that involves Gentile nations as well as Israel. Cf. Story, "Amos—Prophet of Praise," 76.

12 See the textual notes and the commentary on 4:13.

13 Smith, *Amos*, 357.

same power will bring an end to Bethel's idolatrous temple (9:1–4) as well as "all the sinners of my people" (9:10).

The rising and falling of the Nile is a small-scale version of the universal flood in the time of Noah, which was an act of anti-creation (Gen 6:6–7) that anticipates the final incineration of the world (2 Pet 3:4–12). The earthquakes and shakings in Amos (1:1; 3:15; 4:11; 8:8; 9:1, 5) also make the creation totter as signs of the end of the world (Mk 13:8). As in Amos 8:8, the flooding and receding of the Nile River is a simile in 9:5 for the quaking of the earth. Disastrous historical events may trigger a reversion to primordial chaos (e.g., Ps 46:3–4 [ET Ps 46:2–3]; Matthew 24–25), and at the final judgment the present created heaven and earth shall pass away (2 Pet 3:4–12; Rev 21:1; cf. Rev 8:12; 16:20). Yet for all his redeemed, God promises "new heavens and a new earth in which righteousness dwells" (2 Pet 3:13; see Amos 9:13–15).

9:6 This last verse of the hymn announces that Yahweh's temple extends throughout creation and that he is able to control the waters of the world, and if needed, he may pour these waters out in judgment. This identical act is also celebrated in Amos' second creation hymn in 5:8.[14]

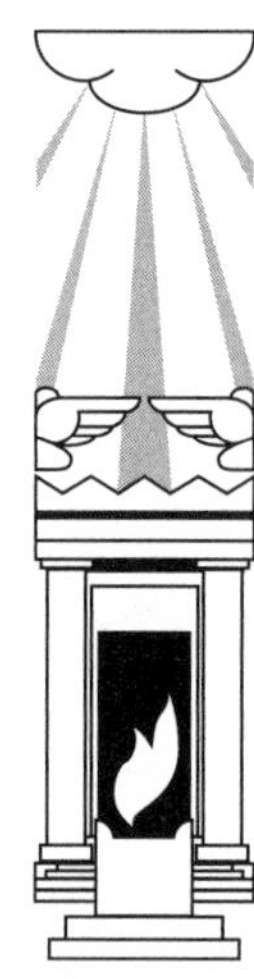

The cosmic temple Yahweh constructs in Amos 9:6 has several theological links with the original creation in Genesis 1–2 and with the building of the tabernacle in Exodus 25–31; 35–40.[15] The tabernacle and later Solomon's temple in Jerusalem were both intended to be microcosms of Eden and models of the universe restored (Pss 11:4; 78:69). They were the dwelling places of Yahweh's grace and glory (Ex 40:34; 1 Ki 8:10–11), and his glory is also on display in the world (Ps 19:2 [ET 19:1]). Yahweh is both the God of the heavens above and on the earth below (Deut 4:39; Josh 2:11; 1 Ki 8:23). The tabernacle and temple were the dwelling places of Yahweh's real presence, the locations from which he dispensed the forgiveness of sins and everlasting salvation in time and space.

Just as the tabernacle was modeled after the heavenly temple (Ex 25:9, 40; Heb 8:5),[16] so the building described by Amos is in the heavens while also having foundations upon the earth. Is 66:1, using the same imagery, indicates that

---

[14] See the commentary on 5:8.

[15] Fretheim explores these connections in *God and World in the Old Testament*, 128–31. Cf. also Levenson, who writes (*Creation and the Persistence of Evil*, 86):

> The function of these correspondences [between the original creation and the building of the tabernacle] is to underscore the depiction of the sanctuary as a world, that is, an ordered, supportive, and obedient environment, and the depiction of the world as a sanctuary, that is, a place in which the reign of God is visible and unchallenged, and his holiness is palpable, unthreatened, and pervasive.

[16] Moses was given a vision of the heavenly archetypal reality itself. The Hebrew word תַּבְנִית in Ex 25:9, 40 is usually translated as "pattern." LXX Ex 25:40 translates it as τύπος, "a type, exemplar." Heb 8:5 refers to Moses' construction of the tabernacle according to the heavenly τύπος, "type," and the service of the OT priests at the tabernacle, which was a ὑπόδειγμα, "copy." Heb 9:23–24 describes the earthly sanctuary and its appointments with the plurals ὑποδείγματα, "copies," and ἅγια … ἀντίτυπα, "holy places … antitypes." Delitzsch writes: "ὑπόδειγμα ["copy"] … is a visible image or pattern, whether as a foretype which is followed (iv. 11), or an after-copy (as here [8:5] and ix. 23] from an original. … The tabernacle

heaven is Yahweh's throne and the earth is his footstool.[17] In the OT, there is always a distinction between heaven, the place where Yahweh dwells, and the holy places where he appears, yet both places are closely related.

Yahweh has made the totality of creation for his home, while his intensified presence is both in heaven (e.g., Ps 2:4) and in Zion (e.g., Is 8:18b).[18] In this way, the building Amos depicts is similar to the vision Jacob has in Gen 28:12, as well as the great sanctuary described in Ex 15:17 and Ps 78:69.[19] In the OT era, even though God had not yet become incarnate in his Son, his usual noncorporeality and invisibility were not the same as absence. He was really present in these places.

These texts point to the fullness of time (Gal 4:4) when there would be a new temple (Jn 2:18–22). This temple is God's permanent dwelling place (Col 1:19; 2:9). The visible and the invisible worlds would be united in the glory and splendor of Yahweh made flesh in Jesus (Jn 1:14–18). Jesus Christ, both true God and true man, spans the abyss between the heavenly, eternal world and the historical world of time and space in this fallen world. The personal union of the two natures in Christ bridges the gap between this world and the celestial world, opening heaven to all who believe in him.

While the sanctuary in Bethel was destroyed (Amos 9:1), as also was the temple in Jerusalem built by Solomon and the one rebuilt after the exile,[20] the risen and exalted Christ stands forever (Rev 1:18). Perfect salvation comes now through this glorified mediator who has led the way from this world into the next, offering the all-sufficient sacrifice for salvation in the heavenly sanctuary (Heb 9:11–12). This salvation shall be consummated in the new Jerusalem in the new creation, where there shall be no need of any temple building, since God and the Lamb are her temple (Rev 21:22).

Cyril of Alexandria advocated a similar Christological interpretation of Amos 9:5–6:

> The statement *He who builds his ascension into heaven* could be a reference also to Christ, and rightly so; it is he who came from on high and from heaven, being born by nature God from God. … He made it [heaven] accessible to people on earth, ascending to the Father as "a forerunner on our behalf" [Heb 6:20]—and as the divinely inspired Paul writes, "he opened for us a new and living way" [Heb 10:20]—and appearing as man "on our behalf in

---

is for him [the author of Hebrews] the shadow of a heavenly substance, but not the shadow of another shadow" (*Hebrews*, 2:31–32, 34).

[17] A correspondence was even part of ancient pagan religions. Bruce writes: "As early as the Babylonian *Enuma elish* there is a heavenly *ubshukkinaku* or 'court of assembly' corresponding to the earthly temple" (*Hebrews*, 166, n. 30). He quotes Albright, who says that in Phoenician "it would seem that the words *bêtu*, 'house,' and *hêkalu*, 'temple,' refer both to a residence in heaven and to temples on earth" (*Archaeology and the Religion of Israel*, 88).

[18] Cf. Fretheim, *The Suffering of God*, 37–39.

[19] For a discussion, see Andersen and Freedman, *Amos*, 719.

[20] See "Summary" in the commentary on 9:1–4.

> the presence of the God" [Heb 9:24] and Father, who also "along with him raised us and seated us in the heavenly places" [Eph 2:6; cf. Eph 1:20]. You see, when Christ ascended, *he built* his own *ascension* also for us if what blessed Paul says is true: [Cyril then quotes 1 Thess 4:15–17].[21]

Summary

The last of Amos' three hymns verifies that behind the destructive agents in 9:1–4 is the cosmic Creator. Yahweh is not only Lord of the nations (1:3–2:16; 9:7, 12), he is Lord of all creation. Sheol is not beyond his reach; the heights of the heavens are his also (9:2, 6). The significance of 9:5–6 is singled out by its central position in 9:1–10. The hymn begins and ends with the name of Yahweh.[22] In this way it identifies the Lord of the creation as the divine commander and judge in the judgment (9:1–4, 7–10).

In the OT, the earthly tabernacle (later, the temple) was a type or replica of the one in heaven (Ex 25:9, 40). Because Yahweh was present in both, they interacted and intersected. "The upper structure in heaven and the lower structure on earth together represent the abiding place of the Most High."[23] In Amos 9:6, the emphasis is on Yahweh's heavenly sanctuary that touches the earth. The reconciliation of humanity to God by means of his real presence, first in Israel's tabernacle, then in Solomon's temple, is realized climactically in Jesus Christ.

---

[21] Cyril of Alexandria, *Commentary on the Twelve Prophets*, 2:123.

[22] The sacred name Yahweh (יהוה) frames the hymn because it is the second Hebrew word of 9:5 and second-to-last Hebrew word of 9:6.

[23] Andersen and Freedman, *Amos*, 845.

Amos 9:7–10

The Final Judgment

Translation

9 [7]**"Are not you like the children of the Cushites to me, O children of Israel?"**
declares Yahweh.
"Did not I bring up Israel from the land of Egypt
and the Philistines from Caphtor
and the Arameans from Kir?
[8]**Behold, the eyes of the Lord Yahweh are upon the most sinful kingdom,**
and I will destroy it from the face of the earth;
except I will never completely destroy the house of Jacob,"
declares Yahweh.
[9]**"For behold, I am commanding,**
and I will shake among all the nations the house of Israel,
as something is shaken in the sieve,
and rubbish will not fall to the ground.
[10]**By means of a sword all the sinners of my people will die,**
those who are saying, 'The evil will not overtake nor confront us.' "

Textual Notes

9:7 הֲלֹ֨וא כִבְנֵ֨י כֻשִׁיִּ֜ים אַתֶּ֥ם לִ֛י בְּנֵ֥י יִשְׂרָאֵ֖ל—The combination הֲלֹ֨וא, "is not?" sets up a question that expects an affirmative answer. Here it emphasizes that what Yahweh says, although shocking to the Israelites, is nevertheless true (GKC, § 150 e). The phrase "the children of the Cushites" (בְּנֵ֨י כֻשִׁיִּ֜ים) refers to a people who were closely associated with the Egyptians (see 2 Ki 19:9; Is 20:3–5). Cush is normally identified with Nubia rather than, as has sometimes been claimed, the modern country of Ethiopia.[1] Nubia was immediately south of Egypt, south of the first cataract of the Nile. The prepositional phrase לִ֛י means "in relation to me" (see BDB, s.v. לְ, 5 a (*d*)), indicating that God considers the relationship of the Cushites to himself to be the same (in some respects) as Israel's relationship to himself. Here בְּנֵ֥י יִשְׂרָאֵ֖ל is a vocative.

נְאֻם־יְהוָ֑ה—For "declares Yahweh," see the second textual note on 2:11. It recurs at the end of 9:8.

הֲלֹ֣וא אֶת־יִשְׂרָאֵ֗ל הֶעֱלֵ֙יתִי֙ מֵאֶ֣רֶץ מִצְרַ֔יִם—The Hiphil perfect הֶעֱלֵ֙יתִי֙, "I brought up," from עָלָה, does triple duty in this verse. First it has Israel as its direct object (אֶת־יִשְׂרָאֵ֗ל). In the next two lines, it is the implied verb with the Philistines and then Aram as its direct objects (see the next two textual notes). In all three cases, the preposition מִן is prefixed to the land or country "from" which Yahweh delivered the particular people.

---

[1] Cf. Andersen and Freedman, *Amos*, 869.

(a) See also, e.g., Gen 50:24; Ex 3:8, 17; Num 16:13; 1 Sam 8:8; 10:18; Jer 2:6; Micah 6:4; Ps 81:11 (ET 81:10); 1 Chr 17:5

The Hiphil of עָלָה with God as subject and Israel (e.g., "the children of Israel") as the stated or implied object occurs often in the OT referring to the exodus redemption, as in Amos 2:10; 3:1; 9:7.[a]

וּפְלִשְׁתִּיִּים מִכַּפְתּוֹר—The Philistines, whose ultimate country of origin is unknown, in all likelihood came to Canaan partly overland via Anatolia and partly by ship via Crete, or Caphtor.[2] They allied themselves with other Sea Peoples, but were defeated by Egypt in about 1190 BC. They settled in the towns of Gaza, Ashkelon, Ashdod, Ekron, and Gath. The Philistines accepted the worship of Canaanite deities. Scripture mentions that they had temples to Dagon in Gaza (Judg 16:21–23) and Ashdod (1 Sam 5:1–3) and a temple dedicated to Ashtaroth (Astarte) (1 Sam 31:10). The clashes between Philistines and Israelites are reflected in the books of Judges and Samuel.

Caphtor also appears in Deut 2:23 and in the last colon of Jer 47:4: שְׁאֵרִית אִי כַפְתּוֹר, "the remnant of the island of Caphtor." It is traditionally identified as the island of Crete.[3] The Philistines are called כְּרֵתִים, "Cretans," in Ezek 25:16 as well as in Zeph 2:5. In 1 Sam 30:14 the Philistine territory in Palestine is called נֶגֶב הַכְּרֵתִי, "the Negev of the Cretans."

וַאֲרָם מִקִּיר׃—As a nation Aram flourished from the eleventh century BC through the eighth century BC, during which Amos ministered.[4] Its capital was Damascus, named in Amos 1:3, 5; 5:27 (see the commentary on 1:3). The context indicates that the people of אֲרָם are meant, so the translation above uses "Arameans."

The region of Kir (קִיר) is mentioned three other times in the OT: 2 Ki 16:9; Is 22:6; Amos 1:5. On its location, see the fourth textual note on 1:5.

9:8 הִנֵּה עֵינֵי ׀ אֲדֹנָי יְהוִה בַּמַּמְלָכָה֮ הַחַטָּאָה— For the divine title אֲדֹנָי יְהוִה, "the Lord Yahweh," see the fifth textual note on 1:8. The noun מַמְלָכָה is cognate to מֶלֶךְ, "king," and is formed with the nominal preformative *mem.*[5] It means "kingdom." Its plural is in 6:2, and its singular is in the construct phrase referring to the state temple of northern Israel at Bethel (7:13). Since Israel was God's kingdom, it must have been shocking for the Israelites to hear themselves referred to as הַמַּמְלָכָה הַחַטָּאָה, "the sinful kingdom." The definite article on the two words indicates a superlative (see GKC, § 133 g; Joüon, § 141 j): Israel is "the *most* sinful kingdom." Israel appears to be the chief of sinners (cf. 1 Tim 1:15) as confirmed in Amos 2:6–16 and the rest of the book. חַטָּא can be an adjective, "sinful," its use here in 9:8, or a noun, "sinner," its use in 9:10, where again it refers to Israelites. Those are its only occurrences in Amos.

וְהִשְׁמַדְתִּי אֹתָהּ מֵעַל פְּנֵי הָאֲדָמָה—Yahweh used the identical Hiphil perfect (but without the *waw* consecutive as here) of שָׁמַד in 2:9 to state that "I destroyed/annihilated" the Amorites to enable Israel to possess the land. See the first textual note on 2:9. Shockingly here the object of his destruction is the kingdom of Israel, as also in the next clause, though it is restricted there. The feminine suffix on the direct object marker אֹתָהּ refers back to מַמְלָכָה in the preceding clause. The combination מֵעַל, "from upon,"

---

2 Cf. H. J. Katzenstein, "Philistines (History)," *ADB* 5:326–27.

3 R. S. Hess, "Caphtor," *ABD* 1:869–70 surveys the opinions about the identity of Caphtor and then concludes: "Thus the identification of Caphtor with Crete remains a probability."

4 Cf. W. T. Pitard, "Aram (Place)," *ABD* 1:338–41.

5 Cf. K. Seybold, "מַמְלָכָה," *TDOT* 8:359–60.

is also used in 7:11, 17 for Israel's exile from the land (see also 5:23), but פְּנֵי הָאֲדָמָה, "the face of the earth," occurs only here in Amos. הָאֲדָמָה has the sense of the whole "earth" also in 3:2.

אֶפֶס כִּי לֹא הַשְׁמֵיד אַשְׁמִיד אֶת־בֵּית יַעֲקֹב—The phrase אֶפֶס כִּי means "nevertheless" or "except." It restricts the preceding general statement and offers clarification. See Waltke-O'Connor, § 39.3.5e, including example 26, and Joüon, § 173 a.

When used with לֹא, an infinitive absolute usually precedes it, but here the word order is לֹא הַשְׁמֵיד אַשְׁמִיד. "The regular place of the negative is between the intensifying infinitive absolute and the finite verb. … Exceptions are Gn 3:4 … ; Am 9:8; Ps 49:8 [ET 49:7]" (GKC, § 113 v; see also Joüon, § 123 o). The Hiphil infinitive absolute הַשְׁמֵיד, spelled plene (with ֵי [see GKC, § 53 k]), functions adverbially in this context: "I will not *utterly* destroy" (GKC, § 113 n; see also Waltke-O'Connor, § 35.4). The nation of Israel will be destroyed, but its people will not be completely eradicated.[6]

נְאֻם־יְהוָה׃—See the second textual note on 2:11.

9:9 כִּי־הִנֵּה אָנֹכִי מְצַוֶּה וַהֲנִעוֹתִי בְכָל־הַגּוֹיִם אֶת־בֵּית יִשְׂרָאֵל—The construction with the pronoun אָנֹכִי, the participle מְצַוֶּה, and the finite verb וַהֲנִעוֹתִי, literally, "I am commanding and I will shake," could be rendered as "I am giving the command to shake." For similar constructions, see the first textual note on 6:11 and the fourth textual note on 9:3. The Qal of נוּעַ means "stagger, wander" in 4:8 and 8:12; see the first textual note on 4:8. It appears here in the Hiphil perfect with *waw* consecutive (וַהֲנִעוֹתִי) and in the next clause in the Niphal imperfect (יִנּוֹעַ). In the Hiphil, it frequently refers to shaking the head (e.g., 2 Ki 19:21; Ps 109:25). Only here is it employed to describe a shaking like that done with a sieve. The Niphal has the corresponding passive meaning, "be shaken." Amos 9:9 foretells the exile, when Yahweh will scatter Israel among the nations and kill most of the people (9:4, 8).

כַּאֲשֶׁר יִנּוֹעַ בַּכְּבָרָה—The passive Niphal יִנּוֹעַ has no subject, so the translation adds an indefinite one: "as *something* is shaken." The noun כְּבָרָה appears in the OT only in Amos 9:9, but its use in postbiblical Hebrew makes the meaning certain. In Rabbinic Hebrew it can refer to a "*basket* used as a *sieve* … a household sieve … [or] the large sieve of the threshing floor" (Jastrow, 2). Here it denotes a large mesh sieve, which lets fine grain get through, but catches stalks, pebbles, and other trash. Both Wolff and Paul point to Sirach 27:4:[7] "When a sieve is shaken, the refuse appears" (NRSV).

וְלֹא־יִפּוֹל צְרוֹר אָרֶץ׃—This noun צְרוֹר is often translated as "pebble" (BDB, s.v. צְרוֹר II, under the root צרר III; so also RSV, ESV). It appears only here and in 2 Sam 17:13. The LXX translates צְרוֹר with σύντριμμα, "ruin, destruction," in Amos 9:9 but with λίθος, "pebble, stone," in 2 Sam 17:13. 2 Sam 17:13 describes the demolition of a city as so complete that not even a צְרוֹר will remain. Niehaus first considers that צְרוֹר may refer to some kind of rubbish, then the possibility that it could be related to the homograph that means "bundle, parcel, pouch" (BDB, s.v. צְרוֹר I, under the root צרר I, to "bind, tie up"):

---

6 Paul, *Amos*, 285. Andersen and Freedman, *Amos*, 867, render the clause as "nevertheless, I shall not utterly destroy the house of Jacob."

7 Wolff, *Joel and Amos*, 349; Paul, *Amos*, 286, n. 39. See also Stuart, *Hosea–Jonah*, 394.

> If the metaphor involves grain, worthless rubbish remains in the sieve, but the good grain falls through to the ground. Thus, the good will make it through, the wicked will not. If, however, the material in the sieve is sand or gravel, then the compact material (צְרוֹר, anything that is compact, as in 2 Sam. 17:13) is preserved. In this view, God affirms that he will preserve a remnant throughout the devastation, for he intends to rebuild the "house of David," not let it terminate with the exile.[8]

The translation above follows Niehaus' first suggestion and translates the last phrase of 9:9, "rubbish will not fall to the ground." The refuse refers to the faithless Israelites described throughout the book of Amos.

In prose "to the ground" would normally be expressed by אֶרֶץ with locative *he* (אַ֫רְצָה) or with the preposition לְ, but the heightened poetic style here simply uses the accusative in pause, אָֽרֶץ.

9:10 בַּחֶ֫רֶב יָמ֫וּתוּ כֹּל חַטָּאֵי עַמִּ֑י—The noun חֶרֶב also appears in 1:11; 4:10; 7:9, 11, 17; 9:1, 4. See the second textual note on 7:11, which too has בַּחֶרֶב and the imperfect of מוּת.

The feminine of the adjective חַטָּא, "sinful," was in 9:8; see the first textual note there. Here the masculine plural in construct is used as a noun, "sinners." If the construct chain כֹּל חַטָּאֵי עַמִּ֑י, "all the sinners of my people," were an epexegetical genitive (cf. GKC, § 128 x), it would means that "all … my people" are "sinners" who will be slain. However, that would contradict the promise in 9:8 and the promise of a believing remnant, which becomes explicit in 9:11–12, where some Israelites and some Gentiles ("the remnant of Edom," 9:12) shall be saved by grace through faith. Therefore the construction must be a partitive genitive (cf. GKC, § 128 i and r): only those members of "my people" who are "sinners" and who are "saying" the following clause will be slain.

הָאֹמְרִ֗ים לֹֽא־תַגִּ֧ישׁ וְתַקְדִּ֛ים בַּעֲדֵ֖ינוּ הָרָעָֽה׃—This participial clause further describes those "sinners of my people" who will be killed by the sword. They are הָאֹמְרִ֗ים, "those who are saying …" They think they are immune from judgment. The feminine noun הָרָעָֽה, "the evil," is the subject of the two feminine verbs. The Hiphil of נָגַשׁ, "to bring near, present" was in 5:25 and 6:3, but here it must mean "to reach, overtake." BDB, *HALOT*, and some commentators propose emending תַּגִּישׁ to the Qal תִּגַּשׁ, which normally means "to draw near, approach." However, many Hiphil verbs can have an internally transitive meaning, equivalent to the usual meaning of a Qal verb. That also applies to the next verb, the Hiphil of קָדַם, which in the context here must literally mean "shall not come in front about us" (BDB, 1). The only other instance of the Hiphil of קָדַם in the OT is in Job 41:3 (ET 41:11).

Commentary

"The Most High gave the nations their inheritance, when he divided the children of men, he fixed the borders of the peoples" (Deut 32:8). Yahweh not only gave Canaan to Israel, but he was also responsible for bringing all of the nations into their inherited lands.

---

[8] Niehaus, "Amos," 487.

Amos 9:7 is not the first time in the book where Yahweh equates Israel with other peoples. In the oracles against the nations, he links unfaithful Judah (2:4–5) and Israel (2:6–16) with the pagan nations (1:3–2:3), while in 3:1–2 he announces that Israel is just a "clan," implying that it is not a nation per se, but a smaller part of the one nation comprised of all the peoples of the earth. Israel had no right to claim that she was number one among the nations (6:1). Just the opposite was true. The Israelites were "sinners" (9:10) just like everyone else (Rom 3:9–23).

In fact, Israel's status as Yahweh's chosen covenant people meant that they would receive a stricter judgment (2:6–16; 3:1–2; 9:8–10). But the judgment depicted in 9:8–10 is not wholesale. "All the sinners of my people" (9:10a) are those Israelites who are apostate. They engage in idolatry[b] and various kinds of infidelity. Among them are the oppressors of the poor (2:6–8; 4:1; 5:11–12; 8:4–6), the king (1:1; 7:9–11) and his officials (3:9–15), the malicious magistrates (5:10–12), the corrupt priesthood represented by Amaziah (7:10–17), and the dishonest merchants (2:6–8; 8:4–6). In contrast, the believers include "the righteous" (2:6; 5:12); the faithful poor, oppressed, and needy people (2:6–7; 4:1; 5:11–12; 8:4–6); and those who heed the call to seek Yahweh and live (5:4, 6, 14). They make up "the remnant of Joseph" (5:15). It is to such as these that Yahweh will give the inheritance of his everlasting kingdom (Amos 9:11–15; cf. Mt 25:34; 1 Cor 6:9–10).

(b) Amos 2:7–8; 3:14; 4:4–5; 5:5–6, 14, 21–27; 7:9–17; 8:5, 10, 14; 9:1

9:7 Yahweh's questions in this verse indicate that Israel did in fact know that her election was solely by grace (cf. Deut 7:7–8). He demands that Israel concede that he is concerned about all the nations and has performed great works for the benefit of other peoples. Israel was not unique in that respect.

True, Israel alone had received the redemptive exodus from Egypt as the paradigmatic OT act of divine salvation, as Yahweh affirms elsewhere in Amos (2:9–11; 3:1–2; 5:25). The migrations of the other peoples mentioned in 9:7 did not involve the giving of the Torah, the covenant of Moses, the forgiveness of sins through the tabernacle and its sacrificial system, and the promise that God would dwell among them in the land in which the Messiah would be born. Israel received salvation (as in the Second Article of the Creed), whereas the other peoples received good and providential gifts in creation (as in the First Article of the Creed). But God's plan involves other nations, as will become explicit when the future messianic kingdom through the resurrection of the tabernacle of David (9:11) will include believing Gentiles ("the remnant of Edom," 9:12). This plan comes to fruition on Pentecost and in Acts 15, as great numbers of Gentiles are incorporated into "the Israel of God" (Gal 6:16) through faith alone in the Christ apart from observing the Law of Moses (Rom 3:20–28; Phil 3:9).[9]

But in the OT era, Israel alone was given the credo "hear, O Israel, Yahweh your God, Yahweh is one" (Deut 6:4), and this also implied that Israel was his

[9] See further the excursus "The Quotation from Amos 9 in Acts 15."

one elect people. Yahweh had not sworn covenant faithfulness to any other people (Deut 7:7–8; Amos 3:2). But Israel had now abused Yahweh's grace and election. Yahweh therefore (again!) overturns a popular Israelite belief by turning Gospel language into Law condemnation.[10] In this case, Yahweh inverts the exodus theme. Since others experienced their own kinds of exoduses, Israel was not alone in that regard, and Israel had disinherited itself through its unfaithfulness.[11]

The arrogant Israelites believed they were eternally in a position of grace due to Yahweh's rescue of the nation from Egyptian bondage, so the people thought they were exempt from judgment (9:10b). This might be compared to a "once saved, always saved" theology. In their oppression of the poor and needy, the leaders were saying in effect: "Yahweh loves to forgive, and we love to sin—so let's continue to do what we love to do, so that Yahweh may continue to do what he loves to do: forgive us!" They would answer St. Paul's question "shall we continue in sin so that grace may abound?" (Rom 6:1) affirmatively. But grace and salvation are received through faith, and when people abandon that faith and live wantonly, they are no longer in God's kingdom of grace.

The first people to whom Yahweh compares Israel are the Cushites. In Num 12:1, Aaron and Miriam oppose Moses because of his Cushite wife. If the attitude of Moses' siblings reflects Israel's attitude toward Cush in general, then to equate Israel with the Cushites would be particularly humiliating and an affront to the people's conception of their identity as Yahweh's people. But Moses' marriage to this woman is a sign that all believers are to be welcomed into God's people.[12]

The land of Cush was south of Egypt. The oracle in Isaiah 18 against those "beyond the rivers of Cush" (Is 18:1) is about faraway people described as "tall and smooth" and "feared near and far" (Is 18:2, 7). In a similar way, Yahweh uses "Edom" in Amos 9:12 to represent all Gentile nations, and here his reference to the Cushites is about a people in the farthest reaches of the known lands.[13] Yahweh cites the Cushites as representing distant nations, beyond the territory of the eight closer nations under divine judgment in 1:3–2:16. The Cushites are not referred to because of the color of their skin (cf. Jer 13:23) or their status as slaves (cf. 2 Sam 18:21; Jer 38:7), but because they represent a

---

[10] Yahweh changes Gospel language into Law also in 2:9–11; 3:1–2; 4:4–5, 12, 13; 5:8–9, 18–20; 7:8; 8:2; 9:1, 4, 5–6, 10.

[11] Just as Yahweh is evenhanded in his governing of the nations (9:7), he is also just in condemning Judah (2:4–5) and Israel (2:6–16) alongside of the pagan nations condemned in 1:3–2:3.

[12] Compare the book of Ruth, where Boaz marries the Moabitess and she is incorporated into Israel through faith as well as by marriage. She even becomes an ancestress of King David and of Jesus Christ (Ruth 4:17, 22; Mt 1:5).

[13] In Isaiah 34 Edom is a cipher for all of the enemies of Israel and God. Likewise Ezekiel 38–39 is a universal oracle against all eschatological enemies of the church, subsumed in the title "Gog of the land of Magog" (Ezek 38:2).

distant land (cf. Esth 1:1; 8:9) and as such indicate that "even the most inaccessible nation is still under God's surveillance and sovereignty."[14] God has no prejudice or partiality ethnically, geographically, politically, or historically, as he will demonstrate when he shows St. Peter that Gentiles are equally welcome in his church through faith alone (Acts 10:34–35; see also Rom 2:11; Eph 6:9).[15]

The theme of Yahweh's protection and care even for those outside his covenant of grace is demonstrated, for example, throughout the book of Genesis. He delivers Hagar and Ishmael (Gen 16:6–14; 21:8–21) and is "with the boy" (Gen 21:20) even after he leaves the home of Abraham. After Abimelech returns Sarah to Abraham, Yahweh takes away the barrenness of the women in Abimelech's household (Gen 20:17–18). Joseph testifies that Yahweh used him to preserve life, especially the line of the patriarchs, who bore the messianic promise (Gen 45:4–9; 50:20), but through Joseph, Egypt also had enough to eat during the famine and Egypt was able to provide food for "the entire world" (Gen 41:57). Foundational to Yahweh's providential care and preservation of "outsiders" is his original creation of the world and the human race (Genesis 1–2) and his covenant with Noah and all flesh (Gen 9:9–17).

Yahweh is Lord over the Cushites, indeed over the entire world, and also over those who live within a closer proximity to Israel, in this case "the Philistines" and "the Arameans" (Amos 9:7). Yahweh compares Israel's exodus to the migrations of some of the nation's fiercest adversaries, the Philistines and Arameans.[16] The Philistine migration occurred during the general ancient Near Eastern upheaval that extended from the Late Bronze Age to the Early Iron Age. During this same time, the nation of Aram also grew. In this way, "Amos resituates Israel, Yahweh, and the nations by asserting that what is true concerning Yahweh cannot be contained or domesticated into Israel's favorite slogans, categories, or claims."[17] "The children of Israel" (9:7a, referring to all the Israelites in both Judah and Israel)[18] do not have exclusive rights to an exodus deliverance. Yahweh is the one who is one of a kind, and he delivers all people, by grace through faith (cf. Jn 3:16; 2 Cor 5:19; 1 Jn 2:2). The Sacrament of Christian Baptism is an "exodus" by which the baptized become heirs of God's promises and of the new promised land (Gal 3:26–29; cf. 1 Cor 10:2; Eph 5:26–27; Titus 3:5–6; 1 Pet 3:18–22).

The comparison of Israel to Cush, Philistia, and Aram is intended to subvert the Israelites' overconfidence and presumption that Yahweh's gift of the

---

[14] Paul, *Amos*, 282.

[15] Israel is often referred to as Yahweh's son (e.g., Ex 4:22; Hos 11:1), as well as his virgin bride (e.g., Jer 18:13; 31:4; cf. Eph 5:25–27). Eschatologically in Christ, other nations are also called Yahweh's people (e.g., Is 19:25).

[16] Heschel writes: "The nations chosen for this comparison were not distinguished for might and prestige—countries such as Egypt or Assyria—but rather, nations which were despised and disliked" (*The Prophets*, 33).

[17] Brueggemann, *Texts That Linger, Words That Explode*, 99.

[18] Andersen and Freedman, *Amos*, 98–99, 122.

exodus legitimized their self-importance, oppression of the poor, and autonomy. Hence the comparison "is not territorial or political or ethnic or linguistic. It is Yahwistic: alike to Yahweh."[19] Israel's apostasy and sinfulness (9:10) reduced their exodus to a mere geographical relocation, completely equivalent to the relocations of the Philistines and the Arameans.

Since the Israelites had chosen to serve other gods,[20] they forfeited the benefits of Yahweh's gracious act of salvation in the exodus. For the unbelieving Israelites, the exodus is therefore no different than Yahweh resettling the Cushites, Philistines, and Arameans.

Luther comments:

> Whoever has sinned will be guilty before the Lord, whether he be Israelite or Egyptian. Nothing will profit you, because you defend your own wickedness with the promises God has shown to you. But they have nothing to do with you, so long as you do not believe the Word of God but are wicked, as Peter says in Acts 10:34–35: "Truly I perceive that God shows no partiality, but in every nation anyone who fears Him and does what is right is acceptable to Him." It is as if he were saying: "He has respect for those who fear [Him] and keep His Word."[21]

God had entered into a covenantal relationship with Israel alone (Amos 3:2), but this did not only mean more privileges, but also more responsibilities. That is to say, in 3:2 election is associated with responsibility, while in 9:7 it is disassociated with a more privileged status than the other nations. Yahweh led the Arameans and the Philistines to their lands, but they will come under the judgment of divine fire (Amos 1:3–5, 6–8). Will Israel be immune from the fire? Amos has already answered that in 5:6 and 7:4. He will answer it again in the next verse.

9:8 Yahweh's judgmental gaze, expressed with one eye in 9:4, returns in this verse, but here both eyes are "upon the most sinful kingdom." This kingdom is unnamed, but the context indicates that it must be Israel. Irrespective of her salvation history, the faithless nation is going to face utter destruction. Two times in 2:9 Yahweh employs the Hiphil of שָׁמַד, "to destroy," to describe his annihilation of the Amorites. By using the same verb here, he equates apostate Israel with the wicked Amorites, who also came under judgment and were expelled from the promised land when Israel conquered it under Joshua.

Yahweh will not, however, completely destroy "the house of Jacob," which refers not just to northern Israel, but to all the Israelites.[22] There will be

---

[19] Brueggemann, *Texts That Linger, Words That Explode*, 94.

[20] For condemnations of Israel's syncretistic worship and idolatry, see the commentary on 2:7–8; 3:14; 4:4–5; 5:5–6, 14, 21–27; 7:9–17; 8:5, 10, 14; 9:1 (the Bethel temple). See also the excursus "The Prophets and Israel's Worship" in the commentary on chapter 5 and the excursus "The Sabbath" in the commentary on chapter 8.

[21] Luther, "Lectures on Amos" (AE 18:187).

[22] Andersen and Freedman, *Amos*, 98–99, 125. In commenting on 9:8, they write: "The way in which we resolve the apparent contradiction between the two statements of v 8 is to say that

a "remnant of Joseph" (5:15) consisting of the believers who are the objects of Yahweh's concern throughout the book, described as the righteous, the penitent, the poor, the needy, and the oppressed (2:6–8; 4:1; 5:11–12; 8:4–6). God's "little flock" (Lk 12:32; cf. Amos 7:2, 5) will one day receive the kingdom (Amos 9:11–15).

9:9 Amos 9:9–10 is joined together with 9:8 not only syntactically with the explanatory כִּי, "for," but also by the common theme of judgment. Amos 9:8–10 indicates that the "sinners" (9:10) in both northern Israel and southern Judah will be destroyed, as will the transgressors in the other six nations in 1:3–2:3. But with the resurrection of the tabernacle of David (9:11), a remnant from Israel (5:15) and the Gentile nations (9:12) will worship Yahweh, and the eschatological age will begin, to be consummated in the abundance of the new earth (9:13–15). Yahweh governs every nation, gives the peoples land (9:7), and judges them (chapters 1–2). He will restore a remnant of believers from all nations.

Other prophets also promise a remnant. For example, Isaiah names one of his children Shear-jashub, meaning "a remnant shall return" (e.g., Is 7:3). Micah 5:7 (ET 5:8) says: "a remnant from Jacob shall be among the nations … like a lion among the beasts of the forest." Nah 2:3 (ET 2:2) says: "for Yahweh is restoring the majesty of Jacob as the majesty of Israel." The restoration comes through Jesus. In Mk 1:15, Jesus says, "The time has been fulfilled, and the kingdom of God has come near." He has come to gather all of the dispersed people of God into his new Israel, the church (Lk 13:29). A remnant from among all the nations, saved by grace alone through faith, will one day gather before the Lamb in the new Jerusalem to give thanks to him forever (Revelation 7).

Amos' metaphor in 9:9 is another promise to this remnant (cf. 5:15). It indicates that Yahweh will separate the sinners from the righteous. The unrighteous, called here the "rubbish," will perish; the righteous will survive and thrive. The metaphor probably involves pouring a mixture with grain through a sieve so that worthless rubbish remains caught in the sieve while the good grain falls through to the ground, a process to which Jesus alludes in Lk 22:31. Those who persevere in righteousness will make it through, but the wicked will not.

In Deut 4:30–31, Moses says, "When you are in distress and all these things have happened to you, in the latter days you will return to Yahweh your God and listen to his voice. For Yahweh your God is a merciful God; he will not abandon or destroy you or forget the covenant with your forefathers, which he swore to them." The oath Moses refers to is in Gen 3:15; 12:2–3; 17:7 (and similar verses), which promise the defeat of the devil through Yahweh's everlasting covenant with Abraham and his Seed (see Gal 3:16, 29). This promise

---

the kingdoms of Israel and Judah will be destroyed from the face of the earth, but there will be survivors who can be identified with the house of Jacob, that is, with the combined entity" (p. 908).

is fulfilled in Jesus Christ who is the "yes" to everything Yahweh has promised in the OT (2 Cor 1:20).

The phrase "for behold" (כִּי־הִנֵּה) appears four times in Amos (4:2, 13; 6:11; 9:9; cf. 6:14). In every case, it introduces the irrevocability of forthcoming judgment.[23] This judgment is total for "all the sinners of my people" (9:10). Those who shall be caught in the sieve include apostate Israel's monarchy (7:9–11) and royal officials (3:9–15), magistrates (5:10–12), priesthood (7:10–17), and corrupt businessmen (2:6–8; 8:4–6). Put another way, the targets of destruction are those who trample the poor (2:7; 4:1; 8:4), those who stifle prophecy (2:12; 7:10–17), those "who are treasuring up violence and destruction" (3:10), those with false hope in the Day of Yahweh (5:18–20), "those who are complacent" (6:1), those who "are rejoicing about Lo-debar" (6:13), those longing for the Sabbath to be over so they might continue their extortion (8:5–6), and those who say, "The evil will not overtake nor confront us" (9:10).

9:10 The qualifying phrase "all the sinners of my people" does not indicate that all Israelites will be killed. It is true that since the fall (Genesis 3) all people are sinners; "all have sinned and fallen short of the glory of God" (Rom 3:23; see also Rom 5:12–14). But all sinners who believe are reckoned as righteous through faith (Gen 15:6; cf. Is 53:11–12; Hab 2:4; Rom 3:21–26). Contextually, the judgment here is against those who are faithless and impenitent, as shown by them saying, "The evil will not overtake nor confront us."[24]

Broadly speaking, therefore, there were two groups in Israel, the "sinners" (9:10) and those sinned against, which correspond to the unrighteous and the righteous and the faithless and the faithful believers, respectively (cf. the two categories of people in Psalm 1). The survivors of the drastic purging of fire (cf. 1 Pet 1:7) will be joined with the remnant of believers from the Gentile nations to form Yahweh's new people (Amos 9:11–12). After all the nations have been brought low (Amos 1–2), there will be resurrection, restoration, and renewal (9:11–15).[25]

Yahweh again employs the rhetorical strategy of incriminating Israel based upon the people's own words, which he quotes here: "the evil will not overtake

---

[23] Judgment is emphasized by an oath formula in 4:2; by a doxology of judgment in 4:13; and by the employment of a merism in 6:11—both the large and the small house shall be smitten to bits and splinters. The first four Hebrew words of 9:9 are almost identical to the first four in 6:11.

[24] In Amos the participle of אָמַר, "saying," occurs four times, and in each case it quotes Israelite unbelievers. In addition to 9:10, which has the masculine plural participle, the feminine plural participle occurs in 4:1, where "those who are saying" (הָאֹמְרֹת) describes "the cows of Bashan," and the masculine plural participle occurs in 6:13, where "those who are saying" (הָאֹמְרִים) describes the ones rejoicing in their own strength. "You who are saying" (אַתָּה אֹמֵר) in 7:16 describes Amaziah.

[25] This same dual theme is in Isaiah 2: in Is 2:1–5 the humble people are envisioned streaming to Zion, and in Is 2:6–22 the Day of Yahweh brings down everyone and everything that is high and lifted up. Like Amos 9:7–15, Zephaniah's prophecy includes the theme of universal judgment (Zeph 1:1–3, 18) and then goes on to describe Yahweh's promise of a remnant (Zeph 2:3, 9).

nor confront us" (9:10).[26] Their denials and protests of innocence serve only to accentuate their guilt and rebellion. In the days of Jeremiah, Judah remained just as defiant: "You say, 'Surely I am innocent; surely his [Yahweh's] anger has turned from me.' But I am entering into judgment with you because you have said, 'I have not sinned' " (Jer 2:35; cf. Jer 5:12; 23:17). As long as people are unrepentant, there can be no absolution, no forgiveness, and no restoration.[27]

The definite article on הָרָעָה, "the evil/calamity" (9:10), indicates a specific event. It is the same judgment referred to as "a day of war ... a day of tempest" (1:14), "on that day" (2:16; 8:3, 9, 13), "on the day" (3:14), "an evil time" (5:13), "the Day of Yahweh" (5:18, 20), "the evil day" (6:3), "a bitter day" (8:10), as well as "days are coming" (4:2; 8:11). "The evil" (9:10) that the people deny has already been decreed by Yahweh: "I will set my eye upon them for evil" (9:4; cf. 9:8). This day has multiple fulfillments: the fall of the Northern Kingdom in 722 BC; Babylon's final siege of Jerusalem in 587 BC; Good Friday, when God's judgment fell on his own Son; and the Last Day, when he will condemn all unbelievers.[28]

"It is a fearful thing to fall into the hands of the living God" (Heb 10:31). This is why the author of Hebrews is so adamant about not falling away from faith in the triune God. Though Israel was once part of Yahweh's kingdom, the nation's leaders helped it leave and become "the most sinful kingdom" (Amos 9:8). The Israelites abused their election and structured their lives more like Canaanites than like the chosen people. Consequently they forfeited their election and were condemned. The Formula of Concord describe the loss of election in this way:

> The cause of condemnation is that men either do not hear the Word of God at all but willfully despise it, harden their ears and their hearts, and thus bar the ordinary way for the Holy Spirit, so that he cannot work in them; or, if they do hear the Word, they cast it to the wind and pay no attention to it. The fault does not lie in God or his election, but in their own wickedness. (FC Ep XI 12)

---

[26] Yahweh quotes his opponents also in, for example, Is 5:19; 9:9 (ET 9:10); 28:14–15; Amos 2:12; 4:1; 6:13; 8:5–6, 14 (cf. 5:14). For a discussion of quoted dialogue in prophetic books, see Gitay, *Prophecy and Persuasion*, 74, and Wendland, *The Discourse Analysis of Hebrew Prophetic Literature*, 54–55, who notes that "the insertion of even a snatch of direct speech has an instant dramatizing effect which causes its contents to stand out." Cf. Graffy, *A Prophet Confronts His People*, and Murray, "The Rhetoric of Disputation: Re-examination of a Prophetic Genre."

[27] An arrogant statement similar to that in Amos 9:10 is in Micah 3:11: "Is not Yahweh in our midst? No evil [רָעָה] shall overtake us." In Deut 29:18–19 (ET 29:19–20), Moses warns: "When a man hears the words of this oath and blesses himself in his heart, saying, 'I will have peace even though I will walk in the stubbornness of my heart,' the result will be to sweep away the watered as well as the dry [cf. Ezek 21:3 (ET 20:47); Lk 23:31]. Yahweh will not be willing to forgive him." In Ezek 8:12, Yahweh points to idolaters who were deluding themselves, saying, "Yahweh does not see us," while in Zephaniah's time people were saying in their hearts, "Yahweh will not do good, nor will he do evil" (Zeph 1:12).

[28] See the commentary on 5:18–20. The same eschatology pertains to the earthquake theme in Amos (1:1; 3:15; 4:11; 8:8; 9:1, 5). See the sixth textual note and the commentary on 1:1.

These Israelites ignored Yahweh's will for his kingdom and lived like those kingdoms that had no faith. This is one reason why Yahweh treated them like the rest of the kingdoms of the world (Amos 9:7). "They are sinners, but they think nothing of the law of God before which they stand condemned nor of the grace of God by which they could be redeemed."[29]

"*All* the sinners" (9:10) will be punished for "*all* [their] iniquities" (3:2) by means of Yahweh's sword (also in 4:10; 7:9, 17; 9:1, 4). In these verses, "the sword" is a synecdoche—a part for the whole—and stands for a military invasion. "The sword" also reflects a covenant curse: in Lev 26:25, Yahweh warns, "I will bring a sword upon you" (see also Deut 32:24, 41–42).

Summary

This section makes the Israelites aware, for the last time in Amos, of the covenant curses they are about to experience. Yahweh has set his face against them (Lev 26:17). He will execute vengeance by the sword and scatter them among the nations (Lev 26:33–39). Their infidelity has for all practical purposes undone their exodus redemption and put them on par with all the other nations (Amos 9:7). Yahweh will judge them accordingly.

The close connections between Amos 9:1–4 and 9:7–10 are attested by the repetition of vocabulary and the continuation of the theme of judgment.[30] The following words are used in both sections: כַּפְתּוֹר, although with different meanings, "capital" in 9:1 and "Caphtor" or "Crete" in 9:7; חֶרֶב, "sword" (9:1, 4, 10); עָלָה, "ascend, go/bring up" (9:2, 7); עַיִן, "eye" (9:3–4, 8); צָוָה, "command" (9:3–4, 9); רָעָה, "evil" (9:4, 10); and אָמַר, "say" (9:1, 10). "The sword" (9:1, 4, 10) forms an inclusio around the two texts.

Amos 9:1–4 and 9:7–10 also go together theologically. Amos' fifth and final vision (9:1–4) proclaims the inescapability of Yahweh's judgment. The rhetorical questions (9:7), the repetition of נְאֻם־יְהוָה, "declares Yahweh" (9:7–8), and the הִנֵּה, "behold," clauses in 9:8–9 function to confirm Yahweh's judgment in the last vision. Israel's transgressors will be visited for all their sins precisely *because* of their exodus from Egypt (3:1–2; 9:7) and their status as Yahweh's people (9:10). Yahweh's wrathful gaze is upon his people (9:4, 8), who constitute "the most sinful kingdom" (9:8).

In Amos 1:3–2:5, Yahweh announces judgment upon the foreign nations and Judah and then climatically focuses upon his target: *Israel* (2:6–16). In 9:1–10 he proclaims judgment upon both Judah and Israel and then zeros in on "all the sinners of my people" (9:10). The repetition of כֹּל, "all," in 9:1, 5, 9–10, and לֹא, "no," in 9:1, 4, 7–10 announces an absolute *no* to *all* the apostates in both kingdoms.

In Deuteronomy 28, Moses urges the Israelites to listen and to trust Yahweh's words. If they do so, they will remain in the land, but if not, they will face exile

---

[29] Motyer, *The Message of Amos*, 199.

[30] Cf. Noble, "Amos' Absolutely 'No,' " 333.

and the loss of the land. "Just as Yahweh rejoiced over you to do good to you and to multiply you, so Yahweh will rejoice over you to make you perish and to destroy you. And you shall be plucked off from the land to which you are going to possess it" (Deut 28:63). Amos announces the fulfillment of that threat: Assyria will enact it against northern Israel in 722 BC, and Babylon will finish it against southern Judah in 587 BC.

But to the believing remnant, Yahweh proclaims the message of Davidic resurrection and eschatological restoration, the salvation oracle in Amos 9:11–15. Yahweh will not only be Israel's destroyer (9:1–4). He is also the heavenly temple's builder (9:6). This hope is confirmed in 9:11, where the resurrection of the tabernacle of David is the foundation for the future of God's people.

Amos 9:11–15

The Resurrection of David's Falling Tabernacle

Amos 9:11–15

The Resurrection of David's Falling Tabernacle

Translation

9 [11]“On that day I will raise up the falling tabernacle of David.
I will repair their breaches,
and his ruins I will raise up,
and I will rebuild it as in days of old,
[12]so that they will possess the remnant of Edom,
that is, all the nations over whom my name is called,”
declares Yahweh, who is doing this.
[13]“Behold, days are coming,”
declares Yahweh,
“when the plower will overtake the reaper,
and the treader of grapes [will overtake] the one sowing the seed.
The mountains will drip sweet wine,
and all the hills will wave [with grain].
[14]And I will restore the restoration of my people Israel,
and they will rebuild desolated cities and dwell in them,
and they will plant vineyards and drink their wine,
and they will work gardens and eat their fruit.
[15]And I will plant them in their soil,
and they will never again be uprooted from the soil that I have given to them,”
says Yahweh your God.

Textual Notes

9:11 בַּיּוֹם הַהוּא—For the formula “on that day,” see the first textual note and the commentary on 2:16. Amos uses the formula in 2:16 and 8:3, 9, 13 to introduce judgment. For the related “Day of Yahweh,” see the commentary on 5:18–20. Only here in Amos does the formula introduce an oracle of salvation, as does the plural phrase in 9:13 about coming “days.”

אָקִים אֶת־סֻכַּת דָּוִיד הַנֹּפֶלֶת—The Hiphil of קוּם often has the causative and physical meaning “cause to arise, raise up” (see BDB, 1), as twice in this verse and also in 5:2, where Virgin Israel was pictured as a lady who had fallen (נָפַל, as here) on the ground, and there was no one to raise her up. The noun סֻכָּה usually denotes a small shelter or “booth” constructed of natural materials, such as branches, to provide protection from the elements (e.g., Gen 33:17; 1 Ki 20:12).[1] The plural of סֻכָּה denotes the booths for the Feast of Booths (e.g., Lev 23:34, 42–43; Deut 16:13; Zech 14:16, 18–19; Neh 8:13–18).

---

1 Cf. T. Kronholm, “סֻכָּה,” *TDOT* 10:244–52.

Because this festival was to remind Israel of her semi-nomadic wanderings in the desert, the booth was intended to be temporary. Is 1:8 states: "Daughter Zion will be left like a shelter/booth [כְּסֻכָּה] in a vineyard, a shed in a cucumber patch," while Job 27:18 uses the term to epitomize endeavors that quickly pass away. But סֻכָּה does not always denote a flimsy artifice. The word is employed to describe Yahweh's heavenly pavilion (Pss 18:12 [ET 18:11]; 31:21 [ET 31:20]) and his canopy on Zion (Is 4:5–6).

Some argue that in Amos 9:11 סֻכַּת should be emended to סֻכּוֹת, the plural form that refers to the city of Succoth. Their reasoning is based in part on the assumption that normally a booth was "a flimsy structure" that "would hardly have served well as a figure of speech for a shelter that provided national security."[2] And such a structure would hardly, it is alleged, have "breaches" and "ruins" (see the next two textual notes).[3] One advocate of this proposal points to the fact that Succoth was associated with the military campaigns of Gideon (Judges 8).[4] In addition, advocates of this proposal argue that Succoth served as a key Transjordan military base during David's military campaigns.[5] Rebuilt *cities* are, additionally, what Amos promises in 9:14.

Succoth in the Transjordan lay on the route between Penuel (Peniel) on the east side of the Jordan River and Shechem on the west (Gen 32:31 [ET 32:30]; 33:17–18). It was assigned to the tribe of Gad (Josh 13:27–28). By 732 BC all of Gilead had been annexed by the Assyrians, and Succoth was forever lost to Israel. This, some argue, may account for the reason why later scribes understood the word as סֻכַּת and not סֻכּוֹת.[6] Earlier Hebrew orthography of Succoth probably lacked the *waw* as a *mater lectionis*, which was added later.[7]

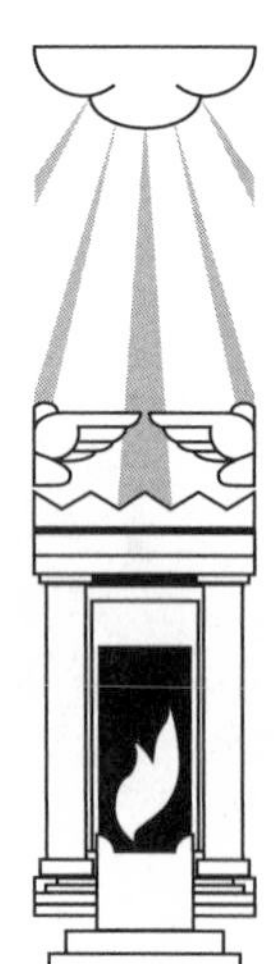

Yet this emendation of סֻכַּת to a plural city name, Succoth, is problematic. It has no textual support in the ancient versions and is contrary to the NT quotation in Acts 15:16, where James translates with τὴν σκηνὴν Δαυίδ, "the tent/tabernacle of David," which matches LXX Amos 9:11. In the LXX σκηνή is the word used to translate מִשְׁכָּן, the "tabernacle," frequently in Exodus 25–40; also in Lev 15:31; 17:4c; 2 Sam 7:6; and often in Numbers. In the LXX σκηνή also translates other words that refer to the tabernacle, including אֹהֶל often in Leviticus and יְרִיעָה in 2 Sam 7:2. Moreover, 1 Chr 15:1; 16:1; and 2 Chr 1:4 refer to *David* setting up a "tent" (LXX σκηνή; MT אֹהֶל) in Jerusalem for the ark of the covenant, which he moved there. (The LXX uses σκηνή for סֻכָּה in other passages too, for example, Gen 33:17, and in reference to the Feast of Booths or the booths constructed for that feast in Lev 23:34, 42–43; Deut 16:13; 2 Chr 8:13.) The Vulgate has *tabernaculum David* in both Amos 9:11 and Acts 15:16. The Targum has מַלְכוּתָא דְבֵית דָוִיד, "the kingdom of the house of David." The Peshitta has ܡܫܟܢܗ ܕܕܘܝܕ, "David's tabernacle/tent," with the noun ܡܫܟܢܐ, which can refer to the tabernacle and is cognate to the Hebrew מִשְׁכָּן, "tabernacle." Elsewhere in the OT,

[2] Richardson, "*SKT* (Amos 9:11)," 376.

[3] Stuart, *Hosea–Jonah*, 398.

[4] Stuart, *Hosea–Jonah*, 398.

[5] Richardson, "*SKT* (Amos 9:11)," 377–79, who understands סֻכּוֹת in 2 Sam 11:11 (as well as 1 Ki 20:12, 16) to refer to the city of Succoth, followed by Stuart, *Hosea–Jonah*, 398.

[6] Richardson, "*SKT* (Amos 9:11)," 377.

[7] Cf. Cross and Freedman, *Early Hebrew Orthography*, 56–57.

the city associated with the name of David is always Jerusalem, never Succoth in the Transjordan.

The LXX and the NT in Acts 7:43 (τὴν σκηνήν) and the Vulgate (*tabernaculum*) translate סִכּוּת, the false god "Sikkuth," in Amos 5:26 with a singular term for a tabernacle or tent. Probably they read their unvocalized Hebrew texts as סֻכַּת, the same form that is in 9:11.

The Qal active participle הַנֹּפֶלֶת (from נָפַל) is feminine singular (agreeing with סֻכַּת) in the attributive position. The time and aspect of such an attributive participle must be determined by context (GKC, § 116 d; Joüon, § 121 i). Within the nearer context of Amos and the larger context of the whole OT, the participle indicates that David's tabernacle began "falling" beginning with the division of the kingdom in 1 Kings 12, when the northern tribes ceded from the Davidic monarchy and the Jerusalem temple and Jeroboam ben Nebat set up alternative idolatrous shrines. The "falling" continued until the fall of Jerusalem in 587 BC and waves of exiles from Judah (the first of which was in 605 BC) were taken into Babylonian exile. Joüon, § 121 i, suggests the future perfect sense "which will have fallen."

וְגָדַרְתִּי אֶת־פִּרְצֵיהֶן—The verb גָּדַר only occurs in the Qal and usually has the literal meaning to "wall up … build a wall" (BDB). פֶּרֶץ, a "breach" in a city wall or other fortification, is sometimes associated with exile and/or captivity (e.g., Amos 4:3).

The triad of pronominal suffixes on פִּרְצֵיהֶן, "*their* [feminine plural] breaches," הֲרִסֹתָיו, "*his* [masculine singular] ruins," and בְנִיתִיהָ, "I will rebuild *it/her* [feminine singular]," all refer to David's tabernacle. As in "*their* breaches," the use of a feminine plural to modify a singular noun is common in Hebrew. "*His* ruins" may be a reference to David himself, while "I will rebuild *it/her*" is a reference back to the feminine singular noun סֻכָּה.[8]

וַהֲרִסֹתָיו אָקִים—The noun הֲרִיסָה, a "ruin," is a hapax legomenon, yet its cognate verb הָרַס, "tear down," appears in texts that describe the tearing down of cities (e.g., 2 Ki 3:25; Is 14:17) and walls (e.g., Jer 50:15; Prov 24:31). The verb אָקִים is repeated from the first clause of 9:11.

וּבְנִיתִיהָ כִּימֵי עוֹלָם׃—The verb בָּנָה, "build," here has its common physical nuance, as also in 5:11. It recurs in 9:14 with "cities" as its object. The phrase יְמֵי עוֹלָם can denote "any period more or less remote, for example, preexilic times (Mal. 3:4), the days of Moses (Isa. 63:9, 11; Mic. 7:14), or even the origin of the messianic shepherd (Mic. 5:1 [(ET 5:)2])."[9] For the plural construct of יוֹם with the preposition כְּ, see GKC, § 118 u. The phrase כִּימֵי עוֹלָם, "as in days of old," also appears in Micah 7:14 and Mal 3:4. Here it "is a nostalgic reflection upon the ideal period of the Davidic empire."[10]

9:12 לְמַעַן יִירְשׁוּ אֶת־שְׁאֵרִית אֱדוֹם—The combination לְמַעַן can indicate purpose or result or both, as here, when God carries out his purpose. The Qal of יָרַשׁ, "to inherit, take possession of," appears in 2:10, referring to Israel's conquest of the land; see the

---

[8] Cf. Nogalski, "The Problematic Suffixes of Amos IX 11," and Kaiser, "The Davidic Promise and the Inclusion of the Gentiles (Amos 9:9–15 and Acts 15:13–18)," 101–2.

[9] Niehaus, "Amos," 491.

[10] Paul, *Amos*, 290–91.

third textual note there. For the noun שְׁאֵרִית, "remnant," see the fourth textual note on 1:8, where it refers to a remnant of Philistines who perish, and the third textual note on 5:15, where it refers to a remnant of Israelites ("Joseph") whom God may graciously allow to endure.

The Gentile nation "Edom" is referred to earlier in 1:6, 9, 11; 2:1. Here in 9:12 the LXX translates אֱדוֹם with τῶν ἀνθρώπων, "of men, humankind," reading אָדָם instead of אֱדוֹם, "Edom." This fact, together with God's propensity to employ puns in Amos (e.g., 5:5; 7:7–8; 8:1–2), indicates that "Edom" here is probably a cipher or symbol for אָדָם, or all humanity, including Gentiles. In this way, אֱדוֹם stands for all the Gentile nations judged in 1:3–2:3 and, by analogy, for all of humankind. אֱדוֹם linguistically is therefore a synecdoche for the phrase "all the nations" (כָל־הַגּוֹיִם) in the next clause, which is parallel to it.[11]

וְכָל־הַגּוֹיִם אֲשֶׁר־נִקְרָא שְׁמִי עֲלֵיהֶם—The *waw* on the phrase וְכָל־הַגּוֹיִם is epexegetical: "that is." This clause further explains the people denoted by the proper noun אֱדוֹם, "Edom," in the preceding clause. The syntax is, literally, "all the nations whom my name is called over them." It can be rendered as "all the nations over whom my name is called" but usually is translated as "… who are called by my name." This means "whom I possess, claim as my own," and expresses gracious ownership. Similar expressions with שֵׁם, "name," and the Niphal of קָרָא, "be called," are used when God renames the patriarchs after giving them his gracious promises (Gen 17:5; 35:10) and in covenantal contexts when Israel is called by Yahweh's name (e.g., Deut 28:10; Is 48:1–2; Jer 14:9). The ark (2 Sam 6:2) and the temple (1 Ki 8:43; Jer 7:10–11, 14, 30), and Jerusalem (e.g., Jer 25:29; Dan 9:18–19) are called by Yahweh's name. Similar in outlook to Amos 9:12 is Is 43:6–7, which envisions a future people, called by Yahweh's name, who are gathered from many nations.

נְאֻם־יְהוָה עֹשֶׂה זֹּאת׃—For נְאֻם יְהוָה, which recurs in the next clause, see the second textual note on 2:11. The Qal relative participle עֹשֶׂה has the feminine singular demonstrative pronoun זֹאת as its object: "who is doing this." The feminine singular can refer to abstractions, here the entirety of the divine actions described in the surrounding verses. The LXX and Acts 15:17 translate with a plural, ποιῶν ταῦτα, "doing these things."

9:13 הִנֵּה יָמִים בָּאִים נְאֻם־יְהוָה—The identical phrase, "behold, days (are) coming," is in judgment oracles in 4:2 and 8:11. See the second textual note and the commentary on 4:2 and the first textual note and the commentary on 8:11. Here, however, it introduces the glorious Gospel promise of the fecund new creation.

וְנִגַּשׁ חוֹרֵשׁ בַּקֹּצֵר וְדֹרֵךְ עֲנָבִים בְּמֹשֵׁךְ הַזָּרַע—The Niphal perfect of נָגַשׁ with *waw* consecutive, וְנִגַּשׁ, "(and) will overtake," does double duty in these two clauses, since it is the implied verb in the second clause. Usually the Qal and Niphal of נָגַשׁ take the preposition אֶל, "approach to" someone or something. The Niphal here takes two prepositional phrases with בְּ (בַּקֹּצֵר … בְּמֹשֵׁךְ…) indicating that the subjects do not just "approach (near)" but actually reach and "overtake" the others. Each singular subject of

---

[11] Niehaus, "Amos," 491 writes: "The reading is a natural one, since אֱדוֹם is paralleled by כָּל־הַגּוֹיִם (all the nations)."

the verb includes a Qal participle, חֹורֵשׁ, "the plowing man," and וְדֹרֵךְ עֲנָבִים, "and the man treading grapes." The second subject is similar to דֹּרֵךְ בְּגַת, "the man treading in a winepress," in Is 63:2 (cf. Lam 1:15; Neh 13:15). These verses refer to one who presses grapes underfoot to extract their juice during the months of August and September.

The two prepositional phrases also each have a Qal participle. The first prepositional phrase, בַּקֹּצֵר, has the participle of קָצַר, "to reap, harvest," cognate to the noun קָצִיר, the "harvest," in 4:7. The second, בְּמֹשֵׁךְ הַזָּרַע, has the participle of מָשַׁךְ, which usually means "to pull, drag, draw." Only here in the OT does מָשַׁךְ mean something like to "*trail* seed" (BDB, 6), that is, to walk along and cast seed behind oneself, or "to go about with the bag of seed" (*HALOT*, 5). The participle with the object הַזֶּרַע (in pause, הַזָּרַע), "the seed," can be translated as "the one sowing the seed." The cognate noun מֶשֶׁךְ, perhaps meaning "*a trail* (of seed)" (BDB, 2) or "**leather pouch** … for seeds" (*HALOT*), occurs in the phrase נֹשֵׂא מֶשֶׁךְ־הַזָּרַע, "one bearing the seed bag(?)" in Ps 126:6. In the Palestinian agricultural cycle, the sower would commence his work in November or December.

וְהִטִּיפוּ הֶהָרִים עָסִיס—The sequence of the perfect with *waw* consecutive here, וְהִטִּיפוּ, "(and) will drip," followed by the imperfect in the next clause, תִּתְמוֹגַגְנָה, "will wave," indicates that the actions described in these clauses are in the same (eschatological future) time frame, not successive (Joüon, § 119 d). The same sequence of verb forms is in the first two clauses of 9:15.

Elsewhere in the OT, the Hiphil of נָטַף always means "to preach, prophesy"; see the third textual note on 7:16. In the Qal it normally refers to physical dripping. That must be the meaning of the Hiphil here, which likely is intransitive, the mountains will "drip" (BDB, Hiphil, 1), rather than transitive, "cause to drip, cause to flow" (*HALOT*, Hiphil, 1). The noun עָסִיס means "sweet wine" or "pressed out juice."[12] Probably it is an adverbial accusative: "drip (with) sweet wine."

The Gospel promise in Joel 4:18 (ET 3:18) has a clause that is identical but with the Qal imperfect of נָטַף instead of the Hiphil perfect with *waw* consecutive. Both verses are eschatological prophecies about the coming "day" (Joel 4:18 [ET 3:18]) or "days" (Amos 9:13) in the messianic new creation. The following clause in both Amos 9:13 and Joel 4:18 (ET 3:18) speaks of the "hills," but Joel promises that they "will flow with milk."

וְכָל־הַגְּבָעוֹת תִּתְמוֹגַגְנָה׃—In poetic texts, "hills" (גְּבָעוֹת) are often parallel to "mountains" (הָרִים), as also in, for example, Deut 33:15; Is 2:2; 40:12; Ps 72:3; Song 2:8.

The feminine plural הַגְּבָעוֹת is the subject of the corresponding Hithpolal imperfect תִּתְמוֹגַגְנָה. This rare conjugation of the middle *waw* verb מוּג has the -הִתְ prefix like a Hithpael and doubles (repeats) the final consonant (ג) like a Polal. Compare GKC, § 54 k, and Joüon, § 59, which, however, do not analyze this form. Usually מוּג means "to melt," although the Qal in 9:5 probably means "to shake, totter" (see the second textual note on 9:5). The Hithpolal of מוּג occurs elsewhere in Nah 1:5, referring to the hills (as here), but in a judgment context where it may mean "shake" or "melt," and in

---

12 Paul's translation "fresh wine" (*Amos*, 293) connotes that it is newly pressed out from the treading of grapes.

Ps 107:26, where it refers to hearts that "faint."[13] In the Gospel context here, after the mountains dripping with wine, the Hithpolal of מוּג usually is understood to mean to "flow" (BDB) with wine.

Paul understands it as "shall wave [with grain]," which is related to the meaning of the Qal ("shake") in 9:5. As Paul argues, this meaning also fits well within the chiastic structure of the verse:[14]

A Plowing and reaping grain (9:13c)
  B Treading grapes (9:13d)
  B' Dripping sweet wine (9:13e)
A' Waving with grain (9:13f)

9:14 וְשַׁבְתִּי֙ אֶת־שְׁב֣וּת עַמִּ֣י יִשְׂרָאֵ֔ל—The expression וְשַׁבְתִּי֙ אֶת־שְׁב֣וּת has the Qal perfect with *waw* consecutive of שׁוּב and what probably is its cognate accusative noun שְׁבוּת, "and I will restore the restoration," an emphatic expression meaning "and I will completely restore." Elsewhere in the OT, some similar clauses have as a Kethib or Qere variant what may be an alternate spelling of the same noun, שְׁבִית (e.g., Ezek 16:53; Zeph 2:7), whose form suggests that it could be from שָׁבָה, "take captive, take into exile," and the clause would then mean "and I will return/bring back the exile." Here in Amos 9:14, the LXX translates the clause as καὶ ἐπιστρέψω τὴν αἰχμαλωσίαν, "and I will return the captivity."

In either case, the idiom is an important prophetic expression of the promise of messianic redemption.[15] The idiom can be used for eschatological Israel, as here and in, for example, Ezek 39:25 and Ps 14:7, and expressly for converted Gentiles, as in Jer 48:47; 49:6, 39; Ezek 16:53; 29:14. Only in Job 42:10 is the expression used for an individual. Its usage in Job indicates that the phrase is not restricted to a return from captivity, but indicates God's reversal of misfortune and suffering into blessing and abundance.

"My people Israel" (עַמִּ֣י יִשְׂרָאֵ֔ל) was in judgment oracles in 7:8 and 8:2 but here refers to the eschatological people of God including believers from Israel and the Gentiles (9:11–12).

וּבָנ֞וּ עָרִ֤ים נְשַׁמּוֹת֙ וְיָשָׁ֔בוּ—Both verbs in these clauses (וּבָנ֞וּ ... וְיָשָׁ֔בוּ) and the verbs in the next two pairs of clauses (וְנָטְע֣וּ ... וְשָׁת֣וּ) and (וְעָשׂ֣וּ ... וְאָכְל֖וּ) are Qal third plural perfects with *waw* consecutive. In all cases there may be an implication of sequence: one would expect the rebuilding of the cities to precede their inhabitation, the planting of vineyards before the drinking of their wine, and the working of gardens before the eating of their fruit (cf. Joüon, § 119 f). בָּנָה, "to build," can mean "rebuild" (see BDB, Qal, 2 a). The feminine plural Niphal participle נְשַׁמּוֹת֙, "desolated," matches the gender and number of עָרִ֤ים, "cities." The Niphal of שָׁמֵם was used in a judgment oracle for the

---

[13] *HALOT*'s definition for the Hithpolal, "begin to move, come apart," fits in Nah 1:5 but not in the redemptive context of Amos 9:13.

[14] Paul, *Amos*, 293–94.

[15] See Hummel, *Ezekiel 1–20*, for a discussion of the philology (pp. 453–55) and of the theology (pp. 487–90) of the similar clauses in Ezek 16:53. See also Hummel, *Ezekiel 21–48*, for Christological expositions of Ezek 29:14 (pp. 873–74 and 888–89) and of Ezek 39:25 (pp. 1131–32 and 1143–44).

destruction of high places in 7:9; see the first textual note there. The phrase here presupposes the fulfillment of the judgment oracles before the restoration of the cities.

וְנָטְעוּ כְרָמִים וְשָׁתוּ אֶת־יֵינָם—These two clauses and the following two parallel clauses express the fulfillment of covenant blessings according to the Torah of Moses (e.g., Lev 26:3–4; Deut 28:1–5). In direct contrast, the antonymous last four clauses of 5:11 express a divine curse on Israel for violating the Sinai covenant. The verb נָטַע, "plant," appears in Amos only in 5:11 and 9:14–15. See the fourth textual note and the commentary on 5:11. Drinking (שָׁתָה) wine (יַיִן) was condemned in 2:8 and 6:6 because it was in contexts of idolatry, but the context here is divine blessing.

וְעָשׂוּ גַנּוֹת וְאָכְלוּ אֶת־פְּרִיהֶם׃—To make "gardens" (the plural of the feminine noun גַּנָּה) and "to eat" (אָכַל) their "fruit" (פְּרִי) recalls the Garden of Eden, whose description in Gen 2:8–3:24 has the same vocabulary for "eat" (אָכַל) and "fruit" (פְּרִי) with the corresponding masculine noun גַּן, "garden" (see also פְּרִי in Gen 1:11–12, 29). The verb נָטַע, "to plant," in the preceding and following lines also was used for God planting the Garden of Eden (Gen 2:8).

9:15 וּנְטַעְתִּים עַל־אַדְמָתָם—Agricultural language is used metaphorically in this verse for God's activities with his redeemed people. "And I will plant them" (וּנְטַעְתִּים) repeats the verb from 9:14. אַדְמָתָם is translated as "their soil" both here and in the next clause to convey the cultivation metaphor.

וְלֹא יִנָּתְשׁוּ עוֹד מֵעַל אַדְמָתָם אֲשֶׁר נָתַתִּי לָהֶם—The entire line looks to the future, as indicated by the opening imperfect. The Qal of נָתַשׁ, "uproot, pluck up," often refers to God exiling unfaithful Israel from the land, as in the covenant curse of Deut 29:27 (ET 29:28). See also 1 Ki 14:15; Jer 12:14; 2 Chr 7:20; and the Hophal in Ezek 19:12, where Israel is figuratively a vine. The negated Niphal here, וְלֹא יִנָּתְשׁוּ, literally, "and they will not be uprooted," ensures the longevity of God's planting in the preceding clause. The perfect נָתַתִּי is anterior, "the soil that I *have* given," referring to action that precedes the (unfulfilled) imperfect (see Joüon, § 112 i).

אָמַר יְהוָה אֱלֹהֶיךָ׃—This final formula serves as Yahweh's verbal signature, guaranteeing the veracity of the Gospel promise in 9:11–15, and indeed the veracity of the entire book. For signatory formulas in Amos, see the fifth textual note on 1:5. "Yahweh your God" appears often in covenantal texts with either the singular or plural pronominal suffix (e.g., Ex 8:24 [ET 8:28]; 15:26; 20:2; Lev 11:44; Deut 1:10). The only other appearances of אֱלֹהֶיךָ in Amos were in the judgment oracle of 4:12 and referring to the false god at Dan in 8:14. With the plural suffix, אֱלֹהֵיכֶם in 5:26 refers to other idols Israel had venerated. In the eschaton, all such idolatry will be a thing of the past (cf. 1 Jn 5:21; Rev 21:3; 22:3, 8–9).

Commentary

Amos 1:2–9:10 is intended to burn and bury the world of power politics and phony religion as these were known in Amos' day. Only after the killing message of the Law is the Gospel announced in 9:11–15. Pentateuchal covenant blessings promise a return from exile (e.g., Lev 26:44–45; Deut 4:29–31; 30:1–3; 32:36–43). There will be restoration for the believing remnant of Israel and the converted nations that will be beyond imagination (cf. Eph 3:20). Demolition is penultimate; salvation is *ultimate*. The "devouring fire who is a zealous God" (אֵשׁ אֹכְלָה הוּא אֵל קַנָּא) of Deut 4:24 is also the "merciful God" (אֵל רַחוּם) of Deut 4:31.

Amos 9:11–15 proclaims that the night of judgment (cf. 5:18–20) is over and the eschatological new "day" (9:11; cf. 9:13) is at hand. Salvation will burst forth, and there will be new life throbbing with hope. Yahweh has torn, but he will heal (Hos 6:1). He has killed but he will also make alive (Deut 32:39; 1 Sam 2:6; cf. 2 Ki 5:7). Yahweh has a plan for the entire created order, not just Israel. "The remnant of Edom" will be restored (Amos 9:12), the mountains will drip with new wine, and the hills will wave with grain (9:13).[16]

Just like other prophets, Amos is given the gift of peering into the future using the thought categories familiar to the OT covenant people: a risen Davidic tabernacle, creation restored, and Israel securely planted in the land forever. Isaiah for his part speaks about Yahweh's Branch (Is 4:2), the virgin birth of Immanuel (Is 7:14), the Prince of Peace on David's throne (Is 9:5–6 [ET 9:6–7]), and the Shoot from Jesse's stump (Is 11:1). Jeremiah envisions a new David who is "a righteous Branch, and he will reign as King and act wisely and accomplish justice and righteousness in the land" (Jer 23:5; see also Jer 23:6; 33:15). Micah promises a new David coming from Bethlehem who will be "ruler over Israel, whose origins are from of old, from eternity" (Micah 5:1 [ET 5:2]), and Ezekiel declares that in the coming age, Yahweh will set over his people "one Shepherd, my Servant David" (Ezek 34:23; cf. Ezek 34:24; 37:24–25). The poets speak of God's anointed Son (Psalm 2) and David's Lord enthroned at the right hand of Yahweh (Psalm 110).

These prophetic promises that cluster around Yahweh's promise to the house of David (2 Samuel 7; 1 Chronicles 17) are not confined to the Southern Kingdom. David made a covenant with the northern tribes (2 Sam 5:1–3). He must have been held dearly in the corporate memory of the faithful in the Northern Kingdom. When he returned to Jerusalem after Absalom's revolt, the northern tribes expressed a greater claim upon David than the people of Judah (2 Sam 19:44 [ET 19:43]). Even the northern prophet Hosea promises a return to Davidic splendor (Hos 3:5).[17] Hebrew prophets announce the coming of the Davidic Messiah who will reunite the Northern and Southern Kingdoms so that there will be one Israel, united forever (e.g., Ezek 37:15–28).

Because the few islands of hope in Amos 1:2–9:10 (e.g., 5:4, 14–15) are submerged in a tsunami of death, many doubt the authenticity of this last section in Amos. Wellhausen's remark regarding 9:11–15 is now classic: *Rosen*

---

[16] The interrelatedness between creation and God's people, under either his curse or his blessing, is expressed in, for example, Lev 26:32–43; Isaiah 11 and 65:17–25; Jer 4:23–28; Ezek 36:1–15; and Hos 4:1–3. In the NT, see Rom 8:18–23 and Revelation 21–22.

[17] Andersen and Freedman write: "Nostalgia for the great days of the united kingdom and the Golden Age of David and Solomon must have started early and increased steadily over the years" (*Amos*, 916).

und Lavendel statt Blut und Eisen ("roses and lavender instead of blood and iron").[18] The critical objection is that the promise of restoration in 9:11–15 is unthinkable in the context of the prophet's repeated threats of destruction. The section allegedly is anticlimactic because it fails to mention Amos' prominent words "justice" and "righteousness" (5:7, 15, 24; 6:12). It is additionally asserted that because similar optimistic ("all is well that ends well") endings were supposedly tacked onto other prophetic books, the same likelihood exists with 9:11–15.

The underlying assumption embraced by those who contend that 9:11–15 is not original with the prophet is that prophetic texts had to be continually reinterpreted.[19] A prophetic book purportedly was made more relevant by adding later material. Therefore, these critics hold, books like Amos grew over a lengthy period.[20] Amos is therefore seen as a collection of tradition and not the work of a single divinely inspired author.

Redaction critics term this editorial reshaping "routinization" (*Veralltäglichung*).[21] The supposed additions announce Yahweh's new word for a new community to implement in their lives. Because the language and themes of earlier texts were supposedly difficult for subsequent generations to grasp, the texts allegedly needed editing so they could speak to new situations. Weber's emphasis on updating and editing is assumed by redaction critics.[22] Carter writes of Weber: "A cursory look at his analysis of ancient Israel demonstrates its impact even on the most recent social science studies of the Hebrew Bible."[23]

---

[18] Wellhausen, *Die Kleinen Propheten*, 96 (trans. Paul, *Amos*, 288). Most scholars believe the majority of the sayings that comprise Amos are authentic, yet critics have questioned the following: the title (1:1), the oracle against Tyre (1:9–10), the oracle against Edom (1:11–12), the oracle against Judah (2:4–5), the confrontation between Amos and Amaziah (7:10–17), the hymnic sections (4:13; 5:8–9; 9:5–6), and the concluding oracle of salvation (9:11–15). Wolff's discussion on 9:11–15 is representative (*Joel and Amos*, 352–53). See further "Form Criticism" in the introduction.

[19] Steck writes: "Diachronic findings will show that prophetic books continually explain this aspect and present it anew in the transmission movement that these books include" (*The Prophetic Books and Their Theological Witness*, 58).

[20] Steck, *The Prophetic Books and Their Theological Witness*, 59.

[21] Clements ("Prophets, Editors, and Tradition," 447–49, including n. 10) adopts this term from Weber (*The Sociology of Religion*, 60–61). Clements writes: "If we are to look for some guidance as to the overall role which the editors of the prophetic literature adopted for themselves then we find some helpful guidelines in Max Weber's basic studies of prophetic tradition" ("Prophets, Editors, and Tradition," 447, including n. 10, citing Weber, *The Sociology of Religion*, 60–79, especially pp. 60–61). Clements also writes: "It is worth bearing in mind that Weber was not only very interested in, and attached to, the work of the Old Testament prophets, but was especially concerned to understand how fundamental changes take place in the structure, ideological ethos, and direction of human communities" (*Old Testament Prophecy*, 15). For Weber, see his books *The Sociology of Religion*, 60–79, and *Ancient Judaism*.

[22] Cf., e.g., Carter and Meyers, *Community, Identity, and Ideology: Social Science Approaches to the Hebrew Bible*.

[23] Carter, "Opening Windows onto Biblical Worlds: Applying the Social Sciences to Hebrew Scripture," 425.

Carroll develops Weber's ideas further when he explains that prophecy serves to legitimate developments within the community.[24] Carroll also leans on the work of Festinger and his colleagues,[25] who analyze "the responses shown by [modern] millennial prophetic movements to the experience of disappointed hopes."[26] The redactor's concern is assumed to be one of reinterpreting the prophet's work in order to bring about hope in the midst of despair. If one applies this theory to 9:11–15, the supposition is that editors added this oracle of hope to boost the morale of the despondent postexilic community of Persian Yehud.

But the objections to the authenticity of 9:11–15 are dubious for several reasons.[27] First, there is no reason to assume that the book should end "by means of a sword all the sinners of my people will die …" (9:10). Just as some other prophetic books end with eschatological visions of salvation for God's people,[28] it is fitting for Amos to conclude with Yahweh's resurrection of the fallen tabernacle of David and his planting of his new covenant people in the new creation. Second, all extant copies of Amos in Hebrew and the ancient translations include the full text of the book; there are no copies of shorter (allegedly earlier) versions of Amos, nor do any ancient interpreters refer to such versions.

Perhaps Greenberg marshals the best argument for the authenticity of 9:11–15 by deconstructing the presuppositions of those who doubt it:

> Doom oracles that end with a glimpse of a better future are declared composites on the ground of psychological improbability. Such prejudices are simply a prioris, an array of unproved (and unprovable) modern assumptions and conventions that confirm themselves through the results obtained by forcing them on the text and altering, reducing, and reordering it accordingly.[29]

---

[24] Carroll, "Ancient Israelite Prophecy and Dissonance Theory."

[25] Festinger et al., *When Prophecy Fails*.

[26] Clements, "Prophets, Editors, and Tradition," 446.

[27] Hasel lists those scholars who rightly believe Amos 9:11–15 derives from the eighth-century prophet Amos ("The Alleged 'No' of Amos and Amos' Eschatology," 15–16). He cites twenty-four authors between 1903 and 1970 and fourteen from 1970 until 1991 when his article was written.

[28] See, for example, Ezekiel 40–48; Joel 4:17–21 (ET 3:17–21), which has some specific parallels to Amos 9:11–15; Micah 7:18–20; Obad 19–21; Zeph 3:14–20; and Daniel 12.

[29] Greenberg, *Ezekiel*, 20. Hammershaimb, *Amos*, 135–38, argues for the authenticity of 9:11–15 based on ancient Egyptian parallels:

> The pattern of misfortune linked with good fortune has also been demonstrated in Egyptian oracles, e.g. in the prophecy of Neferrohu from *c.* 2000 B.C. Here the transition from prophecy of judgment to promise is quite as abrupt as in Amos. This has persuaded several commentators to change their minds and allow the possible authenticity of the promises in the prophets of the Old Testament. More generally, the change from misfortune to good fortune is found in Oriental dramas, in which both parts belong together to create the correct balance in life. Men of antiquity could therefore contain these contradictions in themselves. In the most recent scholarly work the view has been taken that the prophets took over this pattern from the cult.

The inspired prophets who wrote the words Yahweh spoke to and through them must not be forced to conform to a line of development theorized by modern interpreters.[30] Rearrangement of the sacred Scriptures of Israel in order to fit hypothetical editorial processes is not historically accurate, but an anachronism.[31] Neither is it theologically responsible.

Yahweh changed his course of action from executing judgment to showing mercy at least twice before in Amos (7:3, 6). Even though he issued irreversible judgments, declaring "I will not revoke it" (וְלֹא אֲשִׁיבֶנּוּ) eight times in chapters 1 and 2, he could, after carrying out those judgments, change his course from Law to Gospel *again*. Instead of the covenant curses, the repentant and believing remnant could instead receive God's blessings of grace. And this is exactly what 9:11–15 announces: repairing the "breaches" in 9:11 reverses the judgment that the city wall of Samaria would be broken with "breaches" through which the women would be taken captive (4:3).[32] The promises about rebuilding and planting in 9:14–15 reverse the earlier judgments in 5:11. The agricultural bounty in 9:13–14 restores the damage wrought by the drought in 1:2 and the plagues in 4:6–11. The people dwelling forever in the land in 9:15 reverses the warnings of exile in 5:5, 27; 6:7; 7:11, 17; 9:4.

Yahweh is "gracious and merciful, slow to anger, abounding in steadfast love, and relenting about disaster" (Joel 2:13).[a] Yahweh will restore his people (Amos 9:14). The dead will rise again (Is 25:8; 26:19; Dan 12:2–3)! The curse of Genesis 3 will be reversed!

(a) See also, e.g., Ex 34:6; 2 Ki 13:23; Jonah 4:2; Ps 145:8; Neh 9:17; cf. Amos 5:15

Deut 18:15–18 promises a successor for Moses, one who will be "a prophet from among your brothers," in whose mouth Yahweh will place his words and who will faithfully speak them. Amos is one fulfillment of this promise. Like Moses he helps form and shape a new community faithful to the Torah, that is, Yahweh's alternative to communities of disobedience, obdurateness, and oppression. And just as Moses led Israel out of Egypt to the brink of the promised land, Amos also straddles two worlds: a land behind him and a land in front of him. As a "new Moses," Amos announces the death of the one world (1:2–9:10) and the birth of another (9:11–15).

---

30 Albright, *From the Stone Age to Christianity*, 84, writing over a half century ago, points out the fallacy in critical methodology:

> In biblical research historicism has led to an exaggerated emphasis on the evolutionary principle in which unilinear schemes have become beds of Procrustes. All social, religious, or institutional phenomena must be made to fit into a given bed, regardless of the chronology or function which tradition accords them. If a phenomenon seems too advanced for its traditional phase it is assigned "on internal evidence" to a later stage; if it appears too primitive it is pushed back into an earlier phase, regardless of extrinsic evidence or lack of evidence.

31 Cf. Paul, *Amos*, 289–90, who expresses concerns with the redactional interpretation of these verses.

32 Similar is the promise in Is 58:12: "Some from you will rebuild the ancient ruins and will raise up the age-old foundations; you will be called a wall-builder of breaches [גֹּדֵר פֶּרֶץ], a restorer [מְשֹׁבֵב] of streets in which to dwell."

Moreover, Amos is like Moses in these ways: (1) both were shepherds (Ex 3:1; Amos 7:15); (2) both describe plagues that do not bring about the desired repentance (e.g., Ex 7:26–8:11 [ET 8:1–15]; Amos 4:6–11); and (3) both successfully intercede for Israel (Ex 32:11–14; Amos 7:1–6). Yet it is Jesus who is the ultimate fulfillment of the Torah promise of a prophet like Moses (Acts 3:12–26). He is the Good Shepherd (John 10), whose calls for repentance were often rebuffed (Lk 13:34), but who successfully interceded to bring God's mercy to sinners (Is 53:12; Lk 23:34; Rom 8:34; Hebrews 4–9).

9:11 "On that day" (9:11) and "behold, days are coming" (9:13) are eschatological Gospel phrases that refer to the time after the judgment. They follow "a day of war … a day of tempest" (1:14), which in Amos is equivalent to "the Day of Yahweh" (5:18–20), "the evil day" (6:3), "a bitter day" (8:10), as well as "that day" (2:16, 8:3, 9, 13), "the day" (3:14), "an evil time" (5:13), and "days [that] are coming" (4:2; 8:11). The last days (cf. Acts 2:17; Heb 1:1–2) are not worth comparing with the former days (cf. Rom 8:18). Yahweh's last days began in Jesus, whose love and life are the certain signs that "the kingdom of heaven is near" (Mt 4:17; Mk 1:15). On Good Friday Jesus endured God's wrath at the entirety of human sin, and because he suffered that day of judgment, all believers will be acquitted on Judgment Day. Because of his death and resurrection, the baptized are promised unutterable joy on the final day, when Jesus will complete the new creation he has already started (2 Cor 5:17; Gal 6:15; Phil 1:6) and usher his bride into the new heaven and the new earth (Rev 21:1).

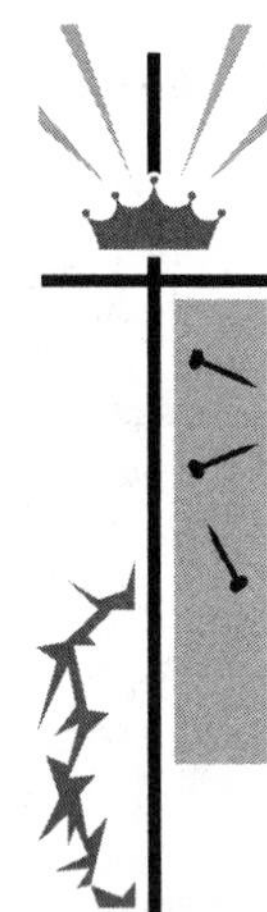

Yahweh declares, "I will raise up" (אָקִים, Amos 9:11), echoing his earlier gift of raising up prophets and Nazirites (וָאָקִים, "I raised up," 2:11), and fulfilling his promise made with the same Hebrew verb in Deut 18:18, "I will raise up a prophet" like Moses. All this suggests a personal prophetic identity for "the falling tabernacle of David." This phrase indicates "that David, his tabernacle, the kingdoms, and the people, are in substance one—that one stands and falls with the other."[33] Understood in this way, the resurrection of "the tabernacle of David" refers both to the bodily raising of the crucified Christ *and* the resurrection life given to all baptized members of his body, his church (e.g., Rom 6:1–4; Col 2:11–13).

The interpretation of this verse must begin with the Feast of Booths, which celebrated Yahweh's indwelling presence with Israel in the tabernacle. Later David erected a tent in Jerusalem and moved the ark of the covenant there.[34] As Cyril of Alexandria commented:

> *The tent of David* refers to the race of the Jews, or the house of Jacob. Now, it should be understood that when Cyrus released them from captivity, they then returned to Judea and rebuilt the Temple; they fortified the devastated cities, built houses in them, and dwelt in security, undergoing wars waged by some enemies, like Antiochus and Hadrian. …

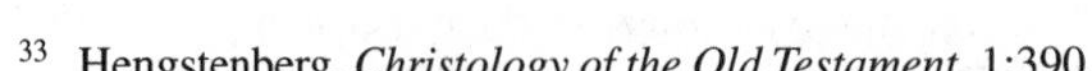

[33] Hengstenberg, *Christology of the Old Testament*, 1:390.

[34] See the second textual note on 9:11.

> While such is the factual reference in the passage, therefore, the deeper meaning closer to reality would be in Christ. You see, when the God and Father raised his *tent* that had *fallen* into death—that is, raised the flesh from the ground—and he came back to life, then it was that he restored all human things to their former condition, and imparted a fresh appearance to everything of ours that had been cast down. "Anyone who is in Christ is a new creation" [2 Cor 5:17].[35]

The raising of the "tabernacle," then, points forward to Christ as the Word made flesh, who "tented, tabernacled" among us (ἐσκήνωσεν, Jn 1:14). Because he is the new temple (Jn 2:18–22), the entire church, including Gentile believers, can be called the new temple as well (1 Cor 3:16–17; 6:19; 2 Cor 6:16; Eph 2:21). This churchly interpretation is confirmed by the quotation of Amos 9:11–12 in Acts 15:16–17 in reference to the inclusion of Gentiles in the church as the fulfillment of Amos' prophecy.[36]

David's military campaigns listed in 2 Samuel 8 end with his victory over Edom, his last enemy (2 Sam 8:13–14).[37] 2 Sam 8:15 states: "David was king over all Israel, and David was enacting justice and righteousness for all his people" (עֹשֶׂה מִשְׁפָּט וּצְדָקָה לְכָל־עַמּוֹ). The reign of the risen Son of David brings "justice … and righteousness like an ever-flowing wadi" (Amos 5:24) for *all* people incorporated into him. The central role of ethics in the book of Amos finds its clearest expression in this idea. Those BC hearers of Yahweh's promise in Amos 9:11 began anticipating the new David, and this hope enabled them to begin living in their present context in just and right ways.

NT believers place their trust in the new David, Jesus Christ (Lk 1:27; Rom 1:3). His gift of justice and righteousness for *all* people, simply through repentance and faith in him, was one of the defining marks of his ministry. The baptized rejoice in this love, even as they anticipate Christ's final coming again in glory. This anticipation creates in them the desire to make morally correct choices in life. John puts it this way: "Beloved, now [νῦν] we are children of God, and what we will be has not yet [οὔπω] been revealed. But we know that when he is revealed, we shall be like him, for we shall see him as he is. And everyone who has this hope in him purifies himself, just as he is pure" (1 Jn 3:2–3). The *now* of God's grace in Christ gives hope for the *not yet*, a hope that purifies the baptized to live in the present moment in just and right ways. These connections between ethics and eschatology are stated well by Childs, who

---

[35] Cyril of Alexandria, *Commentary on the Twelve Prophets*, 2:128.

[36] See the excursus "The Quotation from Amos 9 in Acts 15."

[37] Recently archaeologists have argued that at the time of the Davidic empire, Edom was not a state but merely a collection of loosely collected tribes and that the nation of Edom began in the eighth or seventh century BC. But one of the most recent excavations has pushed that date back to the twelfth to ninth centuries BC (see Levy and Najjar, "Edom and Copper," especially p. 33).

speaks of "an ethic of anticipation"[38] in which the hope for Christ's final coming proleptically manifests itself in the present moment for baptized believers.

Another connection with ethics is the promise that David's falling tabernacle will be raised up. This finds its ultimate fulfillment in the resurrection of Jesus on the third day, who said, "Destroy this temple [his body], and in three days I will raise it up" (Jn 2:19). Jesus "destroyed death and brought light and immortality to light through the Gospel" (2 Tim 1:10). He "was delivered over for our transgressions and raised for our justification" (Rom 4:25). Those who have been justified by grace through faith for Christ's sake are enabled in turn to display justice and righteousness. Forell states:

> Luther said that justification is the basis for all Christian ethics. There is no Christian ethics apart from Christian people; and only people justified by faith are Christian people. It was Luther who insisted that the person precedes the act, that ethics is always the ethics of people, and that one cannot have moral acts apart from moral people.[39]

King David's final victory was over Edom and this ushered in justice and righteousness for all the people under his reign. David's greater Son and Lord (Mt 22:44–45), Jesus, will come one more time to destroy "*the* last enemy" (1 Cor 15:26), death itself. On that day and in that place, perfect justice and righteousness will flow through the new city of Jerusalem (Revelation 21) as the baptized inherit the promises of Amos 9:11–15.

9:12 This verse further describes the evangelical result of the resurrection of "the tabernacle of David" (9:11).[40] From Amos' perspective the subject of the plural verb "they will possess/inherit" (יִירְשׁוּ) is implied to be the future restored and reunited kingdoms of north and south. The promise is that they will annex Edom, then the pledge is expanded to include "all the nations over whom my name is called."

Why is Edom singled out as representative of all the converted Gentile nations? First, "Edom" (אֱדוֹם) likely is a pun on "mankind, humanity" (אָדָם) and thus conveys Yahweh's gracious inclusion of believers from all peoples on earth (cf. Gen 12:3).[41] Second, of the six non-Israelite nations cited in 1:3–2:3, Edom is listed most often.[42] This may be interpreted to mean that Edom is a

---

[38] Childs, "Ethics and the Promise of God," 103.

[39] Forell, *Faith Active in Love*, 84, citing WA 17/2.166; WA 17/2.97–98; and *The Freedom of a Christian*, passim (see AE 31:327–77; see also AE 21:259–68).

[40] For an explanation of how the Gospel is expressed in the poetic parallelism of 9:12, see further in the excursus "Hebrew Poetry" in the commentary on Amos 1.

[41] Ezek 35:5–6 contains puns on the name of "Edom," אֱדוֹם, but in a judgment oracle against it. Ezek 35:5 employs the similar-sounding אֵיבָה, "enmity," and אֵידָם, "their calamity," and 35:6 has four occurrences of דָּם, "blood," whose two Hebrew consonants are at the end of "Edom," אֱדוֹם.

[42] In addition to the Edom oracle (1:11–12), the oracles against Gaza and Tyre (1:6, 9) implicate Edom for its trading of slaves, while the oracle against Moab speaks of burning the bones of the king of Edom to/for lime (2:1).

symbol for all the nations of the world.[43] Deut 30:7 indicates that after Israel's judgment, repentance, and restoration, it will have dominion over its enemies. The inheritance of Edom, therefore, signifies the end of all opposition to the kingdom of God as well as the incorporation of believers from all nations into the new David under his gracious reign. Jesus, Son of David and God the Son, was born to rule over "all the nations" (Rev 12:5, fulfilling Psalm 2).

To have Yahweh's name called over someone or something denotes Yahweh's ownership of that person or thing in a theological sense.[44] This language is most often used "in the context of covenant … and is used to denote Yahweh's ownership of his covenant people (e.g., Deut. 28:10; Jer. 14:9; of Jeremiah himself in 15:16), of Jerusalem (Jer. 25:29; Dan. 9:18), and of the temple (e.g., 1 Kings 8:43; Jer. 7:10–11, 14, 30)."[45] The implication of the phrase, therefore, is not only ownership by Yahweh, but the presence of Yahweh (Jer 14:9). The presence of Yahweh is implicit in the phrase in Jer 7:10–12, which describes the temple as the place where Yahweh's name dwells, and in Jer 7:14–15, where Jeremiah illustrates that being thrust away from Yahweh's presence is the antithesis of living as one upon whom Yahweh's name has been called. Those called by Yahweh's name are part of his kingdom, possession, and people; indeed, they are part of his spiritual temple.

Remarkably, Solomon's prayer at the dedication of the temple included the petition that even foreigners and aliens would direct their supplications toward the temple, which is called by Yahweh's name, and that as they would pray to Yahweh there in faith, he would graciously hear them (1 Ki 8:41–43). The inclusion of Gentile foreigners is also the thrust of Amos 9:12. In contrast, unbelief is characteristic of those who are not called by Yahweh's name (cf. Is 63:17–19). It is evident, therefore, that faith is the characteristic of those who are called by the name of Yahweh. In this context, those who belong to Yahweh—believers from both Israel and the nations—are the opposite of "all the sinners of my people"

---

43 Isaiah 34 also describes Edom as a cipher for all of Israel's enemies. Commenting on this chapter, Sweeney writes: "Edom serves as an example of YHWH's punishment against the nations" (*The Prophetic Literature*, 70). Hummel writes that Edom in Amos 9:12 is "a symbol and type of the kingdoms of this world" (*The Word Becoming Flesh*, 317). The relationship began as brothers, Esau and Jacob (Gen 25:26), but strained relations between them are already reflected in the Jacob-Esau narratives in Genesis (e.g., Gen 27:40–41). Although Edom was subjugated by the first kings of Israel (1 Sam 14:47; 2 Sam 8:13–14; see also 1 Ki 11:14–22; 22:48 [ET 22:47]), Edom attained independence during the time of Jehoram, king of Judah, in the mid-ninth century (2 Ki 8:20–22; 2 Chr 21:8–10). Edom became Israel's paradigmatic enemy in, for example, Obadiah and Ps 137:7. Isa 63:1–4 uses much of the same language as Isaiah 34, speaking of Edom and Bozrah in the context of "the day of vengeance." Woudstra gives further examples of where Edom appears to be a type of all the nations ("Edom and Israel in Ezekiel"). Raabe concludes: "When the prophets associate Edom closely with all the nations seen as an undifferentiated whole, Edom both represents itself and serves as a special illustration of all the nations" (*Obadiah*, 45). Raabe lists Amos 9 as one of the texts that illustrate this significance of Edom.

44 Cf. Stuart, *Hosea–Jonah*, 398.

45 Niehaus, "Amos," 492.

in Amos 9:10. These believers form "the remnant of Joseph" (5:15). Normally in the OT, only Israelite entities have Yahweh's name pronounced upon them, yet Amos declares that in the coming day(s), all who repent and believe (represented by "the remnant of Edom") will have equal status with Israel. The NT affirms that this promise has now been fulfilled in the church of Christ (e.g., Rom 1:16; 10:12; Gal 3:28; Col 3:11).

This is how James interprets the verse at the first apostolic council in Acts 15:17. In reiterating Peter, James states that in the new Christian community, God takes "from the Gentiles a people for himself" (Acts 15:14). Amos 9:11–12 thus refers to the believing remnant from Israel and Judah as well as the nations referred to in 1:3–2:3. Whereas all nations in Amos 1–2 came under Yahweh's judgment, now the promise is made that their faithful remnants will be restored by means of the new David. All of the nations owe their existence to Yahweh (9:7), and in the future some from each will repent and acknowledge him.[46] St. Paul puts it this way: "The Gentiles are coinheritors, members of the same body, and partakers of the promise in Christ Jesus through the Gospel" (Eph 3:6).

The last clause in the verse affirms that it is Yahweh "who is doing this." There are no obstacles that will prevent him from bestowing this gift in the new era. It will happen; Yahweh will see to it. The same participle, "doing," (עֹשֵׂה) appears in two of Amos' hymns, referring to Yahweh exerting his power in creation, judgment, and renewal (4:13; 5:8). Yahweh will enact the redemptive promises of 9:11–12 because he is the Creator and Redeemer. He has the power and authority both to destroy and to renew his creation.

9:13 After promising the rebirth of the Davidic kingdom, which includes the repentant remnant of the nations, this next section portrays the overwhelming abundance of the new creation, yielding bountiful blessings. During the Davidic and Solomonic reigns, Yahweh's blessings were often understood in agricultural terms, for example, 1 Ki 5:5 (ET 4:25): "Judah and Israel dwelled securely, each man under his own vine and under his own fig tree, from Dan even to Beersheba, all the days of Solomon." If the Feast of Sukkoth (whose name is the plural of the word for "tabernacle" in Amos 9:11) forms the background to this oracle, then its imagery fits well with these promises of harvest and abundance. Covenant blessings (e.g., Lev 26:3–5; Deut 30:9–10) indicate that when Yahweh reverses his curses, penitent and faithful Israel will experience agricultural bounty.[b]

(b) E.g., Is 29:17; 32:15–16; Jer 31:12–14; Ezek 34:26–27; 47:1–12; Hos 2:23–25 (ET 2:21–23); Joel 4:18 (ET 3:18); Micah 4:3–4; Zech 3:10; 8:12

[46] The same movement of the nations in Amos, from being under judgment to being under grace, occurs throughout the OT. This chapter switches from poetry to prose and from wrath to healing. In the prose section of Is 19:16–25, there are bold claims describing Egypt's conversion to the worship of Yahweh (e.g., Is 19:21). The prose section is broken into five "on that day" sections pointing to a future day of fruition, perhaps historical and certainly eschatological. The difference between the old Egypt and the new will be that the converts will know Yahweh and become a part of his people, as will also Assyrian believers. This second half of Isaiah 19 is a partial fulfillment of Isaiah's vision in Is 2:1–5, namely that all the nations will stream to Zion to worship at its glorified temple mount (Is 2:2; cf. "the tabernacle of David" in Amos 9:11).

The verse is structured chiastically (see the fourth textual note). The normal cycle of agriculture in Israel was as follows: plowing in autumn; sowing in winter; reaping in spring; and grape treading in summer. But in the days to come, the grain harvest will be so plentiful that the "plower" will be in the field at the same time as the "reaper," as if spring followed autumn and there was no winter. In like manner, the "treader of grapes" will be performing his work while the planting happens, as if there was no autumn. There will be double production in half the time.

Amos announces that Yahweh's restoration is not confined to people, but includes the entire creation, in harmony with Isaiah's depictions of the new earth (e.g., Is 11:6–9; 35:1–10; 41:18–20; 65:17–25). Such texts cannot be reduced to metaphorical musings. They are emblematic of Yahweh's plan to restore the entire created order (Rev 21:1–5).

Jesus' first miracle at Cana in Galilee, turning water into wine, is the announcement that these promises in Amos 9:13 are now present in him (Jn 2:1–11). Jesus creates the best wine for everyone at the wedding feast. His ministry has inaugurated the eschatological banquet (e.g., Mt 22:1–14; Lk 14:7–24; 15:23). The final feast (e.g., Mt 8:11; 25:1–13; Lk 13:29) includes all believers in a restored creation gathered around his table to enjoy the unending celebration of his redeeming love—the marriage supper of the Lamb (Revelation 19), of which the Lord's Supper is a foretaste (cf. Lk 22:16–18).

9:14 The message of Amos is an ongoing one of Law and Gospel. In Amos' first two visions (7:1–3 and 7:4–6), Yahweh changes his plans from judgment to mercy. In 9:14 too Yahweh announces a change from Law to Gospel. He promises to reverse his previous judgments. For the believing remnant, he will rebuild, replant, and remake all that had been lost.

The expression "I will restore the restoration" means that the faithful remnants of Israel (5:15) and the nations (9:12) will be restored to the former state of living as in Eden, only with greater enjoyment of Yahweh's blessings, fulfilling the covenantal blessing of Deut 30:3. Martens writes: "The expression was used to indicate recovery of loss sustained through economic depression or enemy incursion and then subsequent restoration to an earlier favorable position."[47] It appears in texts that issue eschatological hope for both Israel and Gentile nations (see the first textual note on Amos 9:14). Cyril of Alexandria follows the other possible meaning of the noun ("captivity" instead of "restoration") and explains: "The God of all also *turned back* our *captivity*; Christ proclaimed 'release to captives' [Lk 4:18; cf. Eph 4:8], and from the devil's oppression he rescued the earth under heaven."[48]

---

[47] Martens, *God's Design*, 301.

[48] Cyril of Alexandria, *Commentary on the Twelve Prophets*, 2:130.

The phrase "my people Israel" refers to God's people as a whole.[49] The vision of a restored "Israel" is consistent with the reference to its greatest king, "David," in Amos 9:11. "My people" (עַמִּי) indicates the communal nature of the messianic deliverance. This new state will not consist of isolated individuals but rather of a new community, "the communion of saints" (Apostles' Creed). Earlier in Amos, "my people" (7:8, 15; 8:2; 9:10) did not convey the endearing covenantal relationship (as it did in, e.g., Ex 7:4; Is 40:1). Through Amos, Yahweh mostly uses it to convey the shock of the people's present apostasy: for example, "the end is coming upon *my people*!" (8:2). But in 9:14, for the first time, Yahweh employs the wording with all of his deep affection and compassionate care. "These are *my* people!" "My people (Israel)" extends into the NT (e.g., Mt 2:6; Acts 18:10; 2 Cor 6:16) and reverberates into the eschaton ("his people," Rev 21:3).

The following three cola are emblematic of Yahweh's great reversal. The punishment levied on the magistrates earlier in Amos 5:11 was this: "houses of hewn stone you have built, but you will not live in them." In the coming days, however, the faithful remnant will enjoy the miraculously plentiful fruit of the land through their covenantal relationship with Yahweh. They will rebuild desolated cities and inhabit them (cf. Is 54:3; Jer 33:10–11). The theme of restoration picks up on the resurrection of David's falling tabernacle in 9:11. Because David's tabernacle will be restored, cities will likewise be rebuilt. This promise anticipates the fertile abundance in the city of God, the new Jerusalem (Rev 22:1–3). The baptized already are citizens of this place, and so they look eagerly for their Savior from there, Jesus Christ the Lord (Phil 3:20).

The second part of the futility curse in Amos 5:11 states: "choice vineyards you have planted, but you will not drink their wine" (cf. 4:9). But now Yahweh promises that his people will plant vineyards and drink the wine produced from them.[50] The restored community will live harmoniously with their God in the land so that it no longer mourns and withers (cf. 1:2; 4:6–11). Whereas the fall into sin brought death and the curse that the land would produce thorns and thistles (Gen 3:17–19), the new land will produce a harvest of everlasting abundance (cf. Jer 31:1–14; Ezek 36:8–12). The enjoyment of fruitful labor is a frequent prophetic way to express Yahweh's gracious blessing (e.g., Is 65:21–22; Jer 29:5, 28; Ezek 34:27; Zech 8:12).

9:15 Yahweh's restoring activity remains in focus. He is the one doing all of this (cf. Amos 9:12). Just as he first planted a garden in Eden (Gen 2:8), so he will plant his people in the new Eden. Foundational for this promise is 2 Samuel 7, the chapter where Yahweh issues the messianic pledge to David (cf. Amos 9:11) about his Son. Speaking through the prophet Nathan, Yahweh promises, "I will provide a place for my people Israel, and I will plant him, and

---

[49] Cf. Andersen and Freedman, *Amos*, 98–99, 125–26.

[50] Is 65:21; Ezek 28:26; and Ps 107:36–37 contain similar promises of rebuilding and planting.

he will dwell in place and no longer be disturbed" (2 Sam 7:10). The promise of Israel being planted in the land begins in the Song of the Sea in Ex 15:17: "you will bring them in and plant them" (תְּבִאֵמוֹ וְתִטָּעֵמוֹ), and continues in, for example, Is 65:21–22; Jer 24:6; 32:41; Ezek 28:26. While northern Israel was uprooted from its land in 722 BC and Judah in 587 BC, the prophets promise a new exodus when God's people will be redeemed and again planted in the land. In Is 37:31 (|| 2 Ki 19:30), the inhabitants of the house of Judah who survive the onslaught of Sennacherib's 701 BC invasion are promised that they will again take "root downward and bear fruit upward" (שֹׁרֶשׁ לְמָטָּה וְעָשָׂה פְרִי לְמָעְלָה). This is what Yahweh now promises for all believers, *forever*.

This promise does not merely proclaim a restoration of the first garden. The new order will not have the possibility of becoming undone by human sin. This cycle of the fall and redemption will never again be repeated. Guaranteeing this are the words "they will *never again* be uprooted." This recalls the description in Ps 1:3 of the righteous who is "like a tree transplanted by a canal of water that its yields its fruit in its season." By the grace of Yahweh, the remnant is passively plucked out of disaster and firmly transplanted in the soil. Yahweh's reference to soil is climatic. Instead of using the word אֶרֶץ, "land," he intentionally employs אֲדָמָה, "soil," which carries with it connotations of "all the nations" (כָּל־הַגּוֹיִם, Amos 9:12) descended from Adam (אָדָם), whose name recalls the soil (אֲדָמָה, *ʾadamah*) from which he was created (Gen 2:7; 3:19). This promise ends with Yahweh's "signature" as it were, guaranteeing the life to come: "says Yahweh your God."

New life in the original promised land was initially fulfilled by the remnant that returned from Babylonian captivity led by Sheshbazzar and David's descendant Zerubbabel (Ezra 1:1–11; 2:1–2; cf. Mt 1:12–13). Now those who are "in Christ" (Rom 6:11; 8:1; 1 Cor 1:30; cf. Eph 1:13) possess these promises (Gal 3:29) because they have a land inheritance that is "imperishable, unspoiled, and unfading" (1 Pet 1:4), which is the new heavens and the new earth (2 Pet 3:13). While they wait for the Savior to be revealed in his second advent, Jesus promises the baptized that they will never be plucked from his hand (Jn 10:28; Rom 8:37–39). At his second coming, all believers will inherit this kingdom and will reign with him forever (Rev 1:5–6) in the heavenly promised land. Stuart points out that "the referent for these promises is thus a continuum including all faithful believers from the exile through modern times and into the future—in some ways an amorphous group, but in every way the 'Israel of God' (Gal 6:16)."[51]

Summary

The book of Amos begins with a vision of Yahweh roaring like a lion, which causes the shepherds' pastures to mourn and the peak of Mount Carmel to wither (1:2). By the end of the book, this same voice of Yahweh promises that through

[51] Stuart, *Hosea–Jonah*, 400.

the Davidic line he will gather remnant groups of believers from Israel and the Gentile nations and plant them in an abundant land where the mountains will drip with sweet wine and the hills will wave with abundant grain (9:13). These promises point to the feast Jesus instituted in Holy Communion, in which the baptized are forgiven of all their sins and celebrate that death has been swallowed up in victory (Is 25:6–9; 1 Cor 15:54). This is a foretaste of the feast to come, when the church as Christ's bride will celebrate with her Bridegroom, Jesus, in the marriage feast of the Lamb, which will have no end (Rev 19:9).

These promises of the remnant's restoration require an explanation beyond that of scribal addition. Amos 9:11–15 builds on and is consistent with earlier divine promises (e.g., Amos 5:15). The "end" (8:2) did not mean the cessation of all Israelites nor the absence of hope for other nations. Yahweh would continue to act on behalf of his people. His promises to Abraham include an everlasting covenant (Gen 17:7). After the golden calf apostasy, Yahweh listened to Moses' intercessory prayers and offered Israel a new beginning (Ex 32:11–14) because he is a gracious and merciful God (Ex 34:5–6). The language of the Davidic covenant, moreover, includes the expectation that his kingdom will continue forever (2 Sam 7:13; cf. Is 9:5–6 [ET 9:6–7]). In Solomon's dedicatory prayer in 1 Ki 8:33–34, he prays that Yahweh would restore Israel to the land when the people would repent.

In Amos 9:11–15, Yahweh again surprises Israel with a new beginning. The nation's final chapter had appeared etched in stone. But Yahweh's restoration will happen even without any worthiness, virtue, or merit on the part of the people. Amos 9:12 proclaims that Yahweh is the one doing this. Divine monergism—that God alone is the one who initiates, accomplishes, and completes the work of salvation—lies at the heart of St. Paul's words: "while we were still enemies, we were reconciled to God through the death of his Son" (Rom 5:10).

Amos does not envision the temple and its worship as the foundation for the new future.[52] Nor are there priests in the restored community. Neither are there kings, military commanders, or armies. Gone are the royal officials of 3:9–15, the judges of 5:10–12, the revelers of 4:1–3 and 6:1–7, and the tradesmen of 2:6–8 and 8:4–6. The only people remaining are "the remnant of Joseph" (5:15) and "the remnant of Edom" (9:12), who are envisioned as workers planting their vineyards and tending their gardens (9:14), even as Amos himself had made his living off the land (1:1; 7:14–15). In Yahweh's future, the meek will inherit the earth (Mt 5:5).

But first, there will be no everlasting joy without temporary sorrow, no homecoming without exile and sojourn, no joyous victory without the scars of cross-bearing. The believing remnant will have to endure war, splintered

---

[52] Contrast the priestly prophet Ezekiel, who is given a vision of the eschaton patterned after the earthly temple and the original promised land. Yet the Christological reality foreseen by Ezekiel in chapters 40–48 is the same as that seen by Amos in 9:11–15 and by the apostle John in Revelation 21–22.

relationships, and a broken world before they live in a land where they will never be uprooted again. Law and Gospel work in Amos in marvelous and powerful ways, with the Gospel as the last word in the book.

Yahweh's final Word to humanity is Jesus (Jn 1:14; Heb 1:1–2), whose perfect life, atoning death, victorious resurrection, and promised second coming guarantee "the glory that will be revealed" (Rom 8:18), depicted in OT language in Amos 9:11–15. In the new heavens and the new earth, the old order of things, the devastation and destruction, the death and mourning, the crying and pain written on every page in the book of Amos will give way to the One who sits on the throne and says, "Behold, I am making all things new!" (Rev 21:5). Even so, come, Lord Jesus! (Rev 22:20).

Excursus

The Quotation from Amos 9 in Acts 15

The convening of the Jerusalem Council in Acts 15 is a pivotal point in the book of Acts and is a central event in the formative years of the Christian church. The reason the council is assembled is not to discuss if Gentiles can be saved, but if they can be saved if they continue living as Gentiles. The issue at hand is articulated as follows: "Unless you are circumcised according to the custom of Moses, you cannot be saved" (Acts 15:1; see also Acts 15:5). Circumcision is (for males) the necessary rite of incorporation into the covenant of Moses, and membership in this covenant requires obedience to the entire Torah. But Peter, Paul, and Barnabas testify that God has publicly confirmed the conversions of (uncircumcised) Gentile believers in Christ by giving them the Holy Spirit just as he has given this gift to the Jewish believers in Jesus (Acts 15:7–12; see also, e.g., Acts 10:44–48). The outpouring of this gift has already shown that salvation does not come by obedience to the Law of Moses, which is a "yoke" around the neck that, St. Peter admits, "neither our fathers nor we have been able to bear" (Acts 15:10). Rather, "we believe that we are saved by the grace of the Lord Jesus, in the same way as they [believing Gentiles] are" (Acts 15:11).

James, the half-brother of the Lord (Mt 13:55; Gal 1:19; cf. James 1:1), then addresses the issue by invoking Amos 9:11–12 (Acts 15:16–17). He appends to the Amos quotation the phrase γνωστὰ ἀπ' αἰῶνος, "made known of old," in Acts 15:18, based on Is 45:21 (cf. also Is 41:22; 42:9; 43:9; 48:6). This phrase reinforces that God's salvific actions in the infant church are fulfilling what he revealed long ago in his OT promises. By means of these words from Amos and Isaiah, James brings the various parties in the debate into agreement that the Gentiles are included in the Davidic promise of an eternal kingdom that has been ushered in through the life, death, and resurrection of Jesus. Both Jewish and Gentile believers are saved by grace alone, apart from works, apart from efforts to obey God's Law and the commands given through Moses. The counsel of James, based on the OT itself, is consistent with the fuller argumentation for justification through faith alone by the apostle Paul in, for example, Romans and Galatians. The doctrine of justification by grace alone and through faith alone remains the central article of the Christian faith (see AC IV and Ap IV), the *articulus stantis et cadentis ecclesiae*, "article by which the church stands or falls."

In several places, James' citation of the Amos verses in Greek diverges from both a literal translation of the MT (for which see the commentary) as well as from LXX Amos 9:11–12.[1] The conclusion of Niehaus is sound: "The Spirit, in his function as interpreter of the Old Testament, made use of a variant trans-

[1] For a thorough comparison, see Schart, "The Fifth Vision of Amos in Context," 65–68.

lation. And what he has said through James in fact only expands what appeared in the original words of Amos."[2]

Acts 15:16–18	**LXX Amos 9:11–12**
16 μετὰ ταῦτα ἀναστρέψω καὶ ἀνοικοδομήσω	11 ἐν τῇ ἡμέρᾳ ἐκείνῃ ἀναστήσω
τὴν σκηνὴν Δαυὶδ τὴν πεπτωκυῖαν	τὴν σκηνὴν Δαυιδ τὴν πεπτωκυῖαν
	καὶ ἀνοικοδομήσω τὰ πεπτωκότα αὐτῆς
καὶ τὰ κατεσκαμμένα αὐτῆς ἀνοικοδομήσω	καὶ τὰ κατεσκαμμένα αὐτῆς ἀναστήσω
καὶ ἀνορθώσω αὐτήν,	καὶ ἀνοικοδομήσω αὐτὴν
	καθὼς αἱ ἡμέραι τοῦ αἰῶνος,
17 ὅπως ἂν ἐκζητήσωσιν οἱ κατάλοιποι τῶν ἀνθρώπων τὸν κύριον	12 ὅπως ἐκζητήσωσιν οἱ κατάλοιποι τῶν ἀνθρώπων
καὶ πάντα τὰ ἔθνη ἐφ' οὓς ἐπικέκληται τὸ ὄνομά μου ἐπ' αὐτούς,	καὶ πάντα τὰ ἔθνη ἐφ' οὓς ἐπικέκληται τὸ ὄνομά μου ἐπ' αὐτούς,
λέγει κύριος ποιῶν ταῦτα	λέγει κύριος ὁ θεὸς ὁ ποιῶν ταῦτα.
18 γνωστὰ ἀπ' αἰῶνος.	

16 After these things I will return and rebuild	11 On that day I will resurrect
the tabernacle of David, which has fallen,	the tabernacle of David, which has fallen,
	and I will rebuild its fallen things,
and its destroyed things I will rebuild,	and its destroyed things I will resurrect,
and I will restore it,	and I will rebuild it,
	just as the days of old,
17 so that the remnants of men will seek the Lord, and all the nations over whom my name is called over them,	12 so that the remnants of men will seek, and all the nations over whom my name is called over them,
says the Lord, who is doing these things,	says the Lord God, who is doing these things.
18 made known from of old.	

Some of the variations may be accounted for if James is using a textual tradition for Amos that is slightly different than the versions preserved in the MT and the LXX.[3] He may be citing wording from a *testimonia* collection of OT prophecies of Christ, which may also have included Amos 5:25–27, since St. Stephen quotes it in Acts 7:42–43.[4] Or James may be translating the Hebrew (or citing the LXX) with some freedom in order to stress certain theological implications of the Gospel promise in Amos and its applications to the apostolic church.

The first modification in James' citation is that he gives the temporal setting of the promise not as ἐν τῇ ἡμέρᾳ ἐκείνῃ, "on that day," at the start of Amos

---

2 Niehaus, "Amos," 491.

3 Braun seeks to explain the variations by positing a Hebrew *Vorlage* different from and superior to the MT, in part because he believes James would not have quoted from a manuscript that was different from the original Hebrew ("James' Use of Amos at the Jerusalem Council," 117). Braun postulates harmonizing the MT with James by emending יִירְשׁוּ ("they will possess") to read יִדְרְשׁוּ ("they will seek"); אֵת to read אֶל, "to"; and אֱדוֹם ("Edom") to read אָדָם ("humankind"). He writes: "It is suggested that this emended reading was the wording of the *Vorlage* to James' testimonia read before the Jerusalem council."

4 See "The Message of Amos 5:21–27" in the commentary on 5:21–27.

9:11 in both the LXX and the MT, but as μετὰ ταῦτα, "after these things." The prior "things" would include Amos' fifth vision in 9:1–4, which involves the destruction of the temple (at Bethel). Thus James may be suggesting a parallel between the destruction of the temple in Amos 9:1–4 and the destruction of *the* temple—Jesus (e.g., Jn 2:18–22)—whose resurrection has ushered in the new age of the Holy Spirit (cf. Acts 2:17–21).

James also omits the phrase at the end of Amos 9:11 in both the MT and the LXX, where God states that he will rebuild the tabernacle of David καθὼς αἱ ἡμέραι τοῦ αἰῶνος, "just as the days of old." This may be due to his desire to accent discontinuity between David and Jesus. In this way, the resurrected "tabernacle of David" is not simply a return to the OT temple or the Davidic monarchy over Israel. Instead, the kingdom of God is now the church, consisting of all baptized believers, Jewish and Gentile, with the risen Son of David reigning at the right hand of the Father as King.[5]

James follows the LXX for the start of Amos 9:12 but as an object of the verb "they shall seek," he adds τὸν κύριον, "the Lord." In light of the context of passages such as Acts 1:21; 2:25, 34, as well as texts like Rom 10:13 (cf. Joel 3:5 [ET 2:32]), "Lord" here refers to Jesus. Indeed, in Rom 10:12, Paul writes that there is no difference between Jews and Greeks because they have "the same Lord." This is the gist of James' comments in Acts 15:19.

Finally, it is noteworthy that the long phrase that includes the emphatic repetitious prepositional phrase, καὶ πάντα τὰ ἔθνη ἐφ' οὓς ἐπικέκληται τὸ ὄνομά μου ἐπ' αὐτούς, "all the nations over whom my name is called over them," is exactly the same in both LXX Amos 9:12 and Acts 15:17. Within the context of Acts, the pronunciation of God's saving triune name (see Mt 28:19) over the peoples is fulfilled in God's salvific action in Christian Baptism (e.g., Acts 2:38–41; 8:36–38; 9:18; 10:48). Unlike circumcision, which was performed only on males, Christian Baptism is administered to "both men and women" (Acts 8:12), fulfilling the words of Joel (3:1–2 [ET 2:28–29]) about the outpouring of the Spirit on both men and women "in the last days" as quoted by Peter in Acts 2:17–18. In light of the preceding chapters in Acts, the wording takes on greater significance as it pertains to the sacrament of incorporation into the church, the body of the risen Christ. Other NT books portray Holy Baptism as union with Christ in both his death and in his resurrection (Rom 6:1–11), and as the antitype of circumcision (Col 2:11–13), confirming the apostolic con-

---

[5] Affirming the Christological interpretation of "the tabernacle of David," the codices Sinaiticus and Alexandrinus record "David" in Acts 15:16 (and in other verses) with a *nomen sacrum*. The Greek term for "David," spelled in full as Δαυίδ or Δαυείδ, appears in these manuscripts as ΔΑΔ ("DA—D," the first two letters and the last letter of the Greek name) with a line centered over it. The use of a *nomen sacrum* for "David" indicates that these manuscripts considered David to have messianic significance. On the *nomina sacra*, see Roberts, "*Nomina Sacra*: Origins and Significance," and Hurtado, "The Origin of the *Nomina Sacra*: A Proposal."

sensus that Gentiles need not be circumcised (Acts 15:19–21, 28–29; cf. Acts 15:1, 5).

Beyond the textual wordings, there are also issues of theology and eschatology involved in Acts 15:16–17. Premillennial dispensationalists use this passage as a proof text to support their understanding of the nature of God's kingdom, which involves two different plans of salvation, one for Gentiles and another for Jewish people.[6] *The Scofield Reference Bible* notes: "Dispensationally, this [Acts 15:13–18] is the most important passage in the N.T." It goes on to say: "The verses which follow in Amos describe the final regathering of Israel, which the other prophets invariably connect with the fulfillment of the Davidic Covenant."[7] According to this view, the ministry, death, and resurrection of Christ have not fully established the kingdom of God as promised in the OT prophets; there remains a future millennium during which Christ will reign on earth, a Jewish temple will be rebuilt, and animal sacrifices must be resumed there.

James does not begin his quotation with "on that day," as in Amos 9:11, but with μετὰ ταῦτα in Acts 15:16, translated as "after this" in KJV. *The New Scofield Reference Bible* states that "James introduced his quotation in such a way as to show what day Amos was talking about, namely, the time after the present world-wide witness (Acts 1:8), when Christ will return."[8] In other words, dispensationalists believe that Amos 9:11–15 is not about the rebuilding of God's people (Jewish and Gentile believers alike) through faith in the Gospel of Jesus Christ during the present church age, but instead looks ahead to the earthly millennial kingdom after the second coming of Christ. Since 1948, premillennial dispensationalists have understood the state of Israel (rather than the Gospel) to be the means for God's reunification of the Jewish people. According to this method of interpretation, OT prophecies that promise Israel's restoration to the land are literally fulfilled by the modern state of Israel. LaHaye and Jenkins call this the "super sign" of biblical prophecy.[9] Now, this view claims, the prophetic fuse has been relit, and history is racing toward the end with an accelerated pace. For this reason, the current events in the nation of Israel are of vital importance for premillennial dispensationalists.

But what will happen to the church? According to premillennial dispensationalists the church is God's alternate plan or a parenthesis. Christ established the church because Gentiles believed what the Jews rejected. This church age must end with the rapture before God can reestablish his primary work with the Jews and the culmination of history in Christ's thousand-year reign on earth.

---

6 Kaiser, *The Uses of the Old Testament in the New*, 177–94, analyzes the Amos quotation and evaluates dispensational views of it.

7 *The Scofield Reference Bible*, 1343, quoted by Kaiser, *The Uses of the Old Testament in the New*, 178, including n. 2.

8 *The New Scofield Reference Bible* (New York: Oxford University Press, 1967), note on Acts 15:16.

9 LaHaye and Jenkins, *Are We Living in the End Times?* 62.

However, this perspective ignores the fact that James is quoting from Amos and is citing the chronology as seen from Amos' perspective to explain what has happened since the time of Amos (the eighth century BC) until the death and resurrection of Christ and then the conversion of Cornelius and other Gentiles (Acts 10–11, 13–14), which caused such a stir (Acts 15:1–5). James appeals to the prophets to vindicate the Gospel of Christ crucified and risen as the one and only Gospel for all people, and to validate the Gentile mission as foreseen by the OT prophets. Premillennial dispensationalists often consider the interpretation that the text is fulfilled in the church as the kingdom of God as spiritualizing the OT text, but then they should acknowledge that it is James under the inspiration of the Holy Spirit who expresses this interpretation.

By using Amos 9:11–12 to teach a predetermined chronological plan for the future of ethnic descendants of Israel, dispensational premillennialism takes away the heart of the passage.[10] Christ's work on Calvary and his empty tomb are the foundation for the "the Israel of God" (Gal 6:16; cf. Romans 9–11), which consists of all baptized believers in Christ, who are heirs of God's OT promises (Gal 3:26–29). Jesus is the reason for Jewish people and Gentiles alike to turn to God, be called by his name, and be saved (Acts 4:12), as he announced long ago (Amos 9:11–15).

---

[10] LaRondelle, *The Israel of God in Prophecy*, 147–50, discusses James' quotation from Amos and rejects the dispensational interpretation of it.

Excursus

Preaching Like Amos

Introduction

God speaks through his Word to constitute his people and revitalize their relationship to him.[1] By means of his preached Word he creates in them repentance, renewed faith, and faithful living (see Is 55:10–11). But instead of believing and responding to the Word, people may over time grow weary of hearing it and dull their ears to its message. What was at one point surprising and remarkable is disregarded and ignored. When Yahweh's Word and his house of worship are taken for granted and twisted into commonplaces and slogans (e.g., Jer 7:4), the people's obduracy prevents God's means of grace from accomplishing the vital things that God intends through them: to judge and then to forgive sins, to grant new and everlasting life, to recreate lives, and to form and regulate human relationships.

God's Word and Sacraments serve as the glue that holds his people together in the community of their common faith in him. The Word also provides the sanctions that limit sinful people's abuse of each other. Spurning his Word creates a vacuum in which individual autonomy and selfishness emerge unchallenged and the community disintegrates.

The inhabitants and leaders of northern Israel had become deaf to Yahweh's Word. *Familiarity had tamed their awareness of roaring Lion Yahweh* (cf. Amos 1:2; 3:4, 8, 12; 5:19). People of means and ability found little to counter their own ambition and sense of entitlement. Oblivious to how they had become spiritually dead (e.g., 5:1–3), apathetic Israel became intoxicated with violence, bloodshed, and economic exploitation.

Yahweh commanded Amos to declare that it was all a lie, that the nation was sick and dying, and that people who refused to hear Yahweh's roar would soon be devoured (3:12; 5:19). To accomplish this goal, through Amos, Yahweh often takes Gospel language but uses it to express judgment[2] and warns that the ancient covenant curses in the Torah of Moses would be enacted.[3] Only after the people were moved to repentance would they be prepared to hear and believe the Gospel promise that God would resurrect the tabernacle of David so that

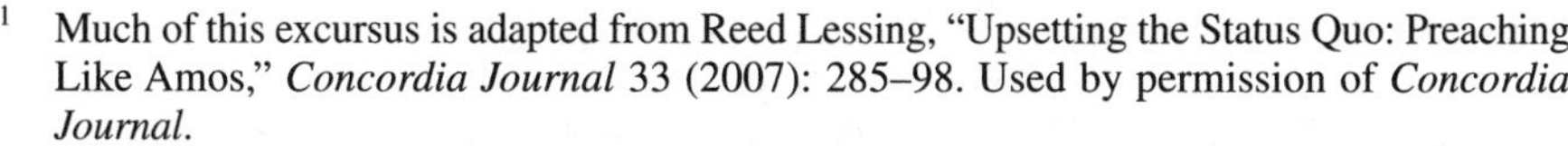

1 Much of this excursus is adapted from Reed Lessing, "Upsetting the Status Quo: Preaching Like Amos," *Concordia Journal* 33 (2007): 285–98. Used by permission of *Concordia Journal*.

2 Yahweh changes Gospel language into Law in 2:9–11; 3:1–2; 4:4–5, 12, 13; 5:8–9, 18–20; 7:8; 8:2; 9:1, 4, 5–6, 7, 10.

3 The application of the covenant *curses* (not the blessings) from the Torah of Moses to Israel is frequent in Amos. See, for example, 4:6–11; 7:4, 17.

all believers, including even Gentiles, might inherit everlasting life in the new creation (9:11–15).

Noted homiletician Eugene Lowry writes: "The first step in the presented sermon, then, is to upset the equilibrium of the listeners, and is analogous to the opening scene of a play or movie in which some kind of conflict or tension is introduced."[4] Saying what is unexpected causes listeners to stop in their tracks. They might think, "What's going on here? That's not the way I've heard it before!" Once the equilibrium is upset, the pastor has gained a hearing, and he may then proceed to the task of probing the problem and offering the solution in the Gospel of Jesus Christ.

One way to "upset the equilibrium of the listeners" is by employing the homiletical strategy of inversion.[5] By putting the cart before the horse, the pastor alters the expected sequence and thereby elicits people's attention. For example, preaching on the incarnation a pastor may state, "This is a *riches to rags* story." Literary critics call this use of language irony.[6] Irony involves "the perception or awareness of a discrepancy or incongruity between words and their meaning, … or between appearance and reality."[7]

By the first half of the eighth century BC, Israel had become *deaf* to its theological language.[8] Faced with this situation, Yahweh, speaking through the prophet Amos, employed homiletical inversions so as to upset the equilibrium of his listeners and move beyond the familiar, the expected, and what had become clichés for his audience. God did not call Amos simply to repeat words from the Pentateuch, but neither was he sent on a mission to jettison Israel's theological language. Andersen and Freedman write: "A judicious balance needs to be struck, one in which the prophet's role as conservator of ancient tradition is blended with that of radical critic of current behavior and intention."[9] Amos scholars often note the prophet's sophisticated appropriation of forms and tradi-

---

4 Lowry, *The Homiletical Plot*, 30–31.

5 Rossow discusses this homiletical strategy in *Preaching the Creative Gospel Creatively*, 137–40.

6 Alonso Schökel writes: "The Greek and Latin classics left us two basic forms of irony: rhetorical irony, which consists in saying the opposite of what one intends, but allowing this to be understood; and dramatic irony … , which consists in making a character say something which he does not understand or the implications of which he has not grasped" (*A Manual of Hebrew Poetics*, 157). The inversions in Amos come under Alonso Schökel's category of rhetorical irony. The classic study on irony in the OT is Good, *Irony in the Old Testament*.

7 Cuddon, *A Dictionary of Literary Terms and Literary Theory*, 460.

8 Through Isaiah, whose ministry began (ca. 740 BC) a couple of decades after that of Amos (ca. 760 BC), Yahweh indicates that Israel had ears but could not hear and eyes but could not see (see Is 6:9–10). Yahweh laments, "Who is blind but my servant and deaf like the messenger I send? Who is blind like the dedicated ones and blind like the servant of Yahweh?" (Is 42:19; see also Is 43:8; Mt 13:13; Mk 4:12). A century and a half later (in the sixth century BC), Yahweh describes the same problem through the exilic prophet Ezekiel (e.g., Ezek 3:4–7; 33:30–33).

9 Andersen and Freedman, *Amos*, 539.

tions as well as his carefully crafted language.[10] For example, Crenshaw argues that Amos uses liturgical texts and ideas throughout his book to make contact with his audience, only to turn the themes against Israel.[11] It is almost universally agreed that the book of Amos contains masterful inversions of earlier texts.[12]

Throughout Amos, Yahweh takes Israel's theological premises and reshapes them to awaken his listeners from their drunken stupor (2:8; 4:1; 6:6–7). He cites assumptions that his impenitent audience believed could not be contradicted *and contradicts them*! Amos peppers the nation's leaders with challenging "in your face" questions. What if Israel is *just like* the other nations (1:3–2:16)? What if the election of Israel means the people's *judgment* (3:1–2)? What if their worship is a *crime* (4:4–5)? What if the nation is not alive at all, but *dead* (5:1–17)? What if the Passover happened again, but this time *Israel* is the first-born of Egypt (5:17)? What if the Day of Yahweh turns out to be the *night* of Yahweh (5:18–20)? What if Yahweh's presence at the (Bethel) temple brings not a blessing but a *curse* (9:1–4)? And what if Yahweh had accomplished an exodus for *other nations* (9:7)? By relentlessly posing these unsettling inversions, he takes the people's language and turns it against them. These texts are now considered in greater detail.

Amos 1:3–2:16

The first example of inversion is in 1:3–2:16, which consists of the longest oracle against other nations in the Book of the Twelve. Whether in warfare, public lamentation, a court setting, or a worship setting, oracles against the nations either explicitly or implicitly always boded well for Israel (e.g., 1 Sam 15:2–3; Ezekiel 25–32, followed by the Gospel promises in Ezekiel 33–48). Amos inverts this genre and adapts it for his own purpose in order to make a stinging accusation against Israel's elite.

From 1:3 through 2:5 Amos' audience in all likelihood cheered and applauded after each neighboring nation was condemned. With the next judgment pointing to the Southern Kingdom of Judah (2:4–5), the number reaches seven. Seven is a number commonly used in the Bible to denote completeness,

---

[10] Among Amos commentators, there appears to be unanimous agreement on the prophet's literary skill. Wolff marvels that in the two dozen short oracles one finds a "wealth of rhetorical forms" (*Joel and Amos*, 91). Mays hails Amos as one who displays "remarkable skill at using all the devices of oral literature available in Israel's culture" (*Amos*, 6). Andersen and Freedman note that Amos is one of the most "versatile verbal craftsmen" among the prophets (*Amos*, 144). They are particularly fascinated by the structural and thematic dimensions that unify the whole book literarily (*Amos*, 17–18). Paul speaks of Amos' "distinctive literary style" (*Amos*, 7), as well as the way he uses literary traditions and conventions with "creative sophistication" (*Amos*, 4). The lone dissent seems to come from Hayes who claims that "there is nothing especially creative in Amos's preaching" (*Amos, the Eighth-Century Prophet*, 38).

[11] Crenshaw, "Amos and the Theophanic Tradition," 214.

[12] For example, Mays says that Amos "does seem to take up the themes of the theological tradition from his audience and use them in a way that was completely 'unorthodox' and unexpected" (*Amos*, 57).

making an eighth oracle unexpected. The people of northern Israel could then safely assume that the sermon had come to an end. But Yahweh's wrath was about to fall upon *Israel.*

Amos inverts the genre of oracles against the nations to announce Law to people expecting Gospel. The prophet upsets the equilibrium of those in his audience who were embracing the belief "come weal, come woe, our status is quo."

Amos 3:1–2

Amos begins this section with these words: "Hear this word that Yahweh has spoken concerning you, O children of Israel, concerning the entire clan that I brought up from the land of Egypt" (3:1). His audience might have concluded at the end of this verse that the exodus was a sign of Yahweh's ongoing and eternal favor; the exodus guaranteed Israel's "favored nation status" before Yahweh.

In the next verse, however, Amos flatly contradicts these expectations. He quotes Yahweh as saying, "You alone have I chosen from all the clans of the earth. Therefore I will visit upon you the punishment for all your iniquities" (3:2). Amos inverts the election verb יָדַע, "to know, choose." The shocking surprise in 3:1–2 is this: *because* of their closeness to Yahweh, the Israelites will, *all the more*, be punished. The inversion consists of making their status as the chosen people the basis for judgment. Just as he does in 1:3–2:16, the prophet takes a Gospel tradition and places it within the context of a judgment oracle. Amos employs earlier texts in totally new ways to reverse the expected conclusions of his audience to the end that they will awake from their spiritual slumber (cf. Eph 5:14).

Amos 4:4–5

In 4:4–5 Amos takes the genre of priestly Torah and turns it upside down. He imitates the priestly call to worship (see Psalms 81 and 95), then condemns Israel's worship at its idolatrous shrines, not only because that worship violated the Torah prescriptions for worship, but also because justice and righteousness were nonexistent in the land (Amos 5:7; 5:24; 6:12).

Imitating the call to worship, 4:4 begins with an imperative of בּוֹא. "Go [בֹּאוּ] to Bethel," Amos cries out. Then the other shoe drops. Instead of continuing with the theme of worship, kneeling, or bowing down, he says, "And transgress [וּפִשְׁעוּ]." Amos had employed the cognate noun פֶּשַׁע, "transgression," throughout 1:3–2:3 to denote "crimes against humanity." These crimes are as follows:

1. The Arameans used animals to drag flint-studded weighted pieces of wood back and forth across the prostrate Gileadites, skinning them alive (1:3–5).
2. In 1:6–8 Gaza/Philistia is ushered before Yahweh's judgment seat because of its practice of selling off conquered peoples as slaves.

3. The charge against Tyre (1:9–10) echoes the previous oracle against Gaza/Philistia, which is similarly accused of handing over an entire community to Edom (1:6). These two nations located on the Mediterranean coast are guilty of the same crime: slave trade.
4. Edom is accused of pursuing his brother with a sword and ripping open pregnant women (1:11–12). The use of "his brother" (אָחִיו) may refer to the kinship between Edom and Israel, as Esau and Jacob are often referred to as brothers (e.g., Gen 25:26; 27:40–41; Num 20:14; Obad 10, 12).
5. Ammon also ripped open the wombs of pregnant women, killing both the mothers and their unborn children, for the sake of expanding their border (1:13–15).
6. While Edomites and Ammonites are judged because they destroyed the future, that is, children in their mother's wombs (1:11, 13), Moabites fall under Yahweh's judgment because they destroyed the past: they burned a dead king's bones to use as plaster (2:1–3).

The shock in 4:4, therefore, is that Israel's worship life is placed on the same moral level as these crimes of the nations! The Israelites' syncretistic *worship* is a crime against Lion Yahweh!

Amos 5:1–17

The funerary lament in Amos 5:1–17 is similar to David's lament over the deaths of Saul and Jonathan (2 Sam 1:19–27). The similarities indicate that Amos is inverting still another genre to suit his rhetorical purposes. In this case, he is lamenting the death of a nation that is still very much physically alive!

Amos begins in 5:1 with the noun קִינָה, "funeral dirge," which denotes a mourning song for dead people. Those who heard 5:1 would naturally ask, "Who died?" The answer in 5:2 is this: "*you*, but you aren't aware of it yet!" People are being addressed as though they are unburied corpses!

Amos continues his strategy of inversion in 5:17. Yahweh's declaration "I will pass through your midst" (אֶעֱבֹר בְּקִרְבְּךָ) in this verse is very similar to Ex 12:12, 23. Just as Yahweh passed through Egypt and killed the firstborn of every family whose doorposts were not marked with the blood of the Passover lamb, so he will again launch an attack. But when Yahweh passes through this time, it will not be to destroy Israel's enemies, but rather to destroy his new enemy: *Israel!*

Amos 5:18–20

In 5:18–20 Amos employs a woe oracle, rhetorical questions, and a gripping simile to shock his audience out of their lukewarm state (cf. Rev 3:16).

The prophet begins this unit with the cry הוֹי, which is often translated as "woe," "ah," "alas," or something along these lines. Much like church bells in a small town tolling to announce a funeral, when a person cried out, הוֹי, one would immediately ask, "Who died?" In Amos' case, the answer would be this: "*you*" (cf. 1 Ki 13:30).

In his next inversion, Amos announces that the Day of Yahweh will actually be the *night* of Yahweh. Amos 5:18–20 suggests that the prophet was trying to refute a widely held view that "the Day of Yahweh" would usher in more of Yahweh's blessings.

The prophetic discourse once again takes a popular tradition that was positively understood and turns it upside down. Contrary to popular opinion, when Yahweh appears it will not be a day of national victory and celebration but a night of horrific disaster and defeat. Even if a person experiences several miraculous escapes, "peace at last" turns out to be a biting serpent (5:19; cf. 9:3).

Amos 9:1–4

In the grand finale of his series of five visions,[13] Amos again takes several time-honored ideas and inverts them. His first move is to employ a cosmological merism in 9:2–3 by means of "Sheol" and "heaven" (9:2) and "the peak of Carmel" and "the bottom of the sea" (9:3). Some psalms employ merism in order to extol Yahweh for his universal power and protecting presence. For example, Ps 95:3–5 praises Yahweh "in [whose] hands are the depths of the earth; the heights of the mountains are his also." However Amos uses the motif as a guarantee of Yahweh's *destructive* reach. What was normally affirmed as hopeful—Yahweh's dominion over the entire universe—is Israel's reason to abandon all hope of escaping judgment. The people are called to despair and repent (then hear the Gospel in 9:11–15).

The second inversion is in Yahweh's declaration "I will set my eye upon them" (וְשַׂמְתִּ֨י עֵינִ֧י עֲלֵיהֶ֛ם, 9:4; cf. 9:8). This idiom and similar ones are employed elsewhere in the OT in a positive sense (Gen 44:21; Jer 24:6; 39:12; 40:4), yet Yahweh continues, "I will set my eye upon them for *evil* [רָעָה] and *not* for good."

Amos 9:7

The impenitent Israelites believed they were eternally in a position of grace and goodness because of Yahweh's rescue of the nation from Egyptian bondage. It was as though they embraced a "once saved, always saved" theology. But the exodus did not automatically imply Yahweh's divine protection for the later generations that lapsed into idolatry. In 9:7 Amos records Yahweh as asking this:

> "Are not you like the children of the Cushites to me, O children of Israel?"
> declares Yahweh.
> "Did not I bring up Israel from the land of Egypt,
> and the Philistines from Caphtor,
> and the Arameans from Kir?"

The first people to whom Yahweh compares Israel are the far-away Cushites in Africa. Yahweh shows no favoritism ethnically, geographically, politically, or historically (see Acts 10:34–35; Rom 2:11; Eph 6:9). Yahweh is Lord over

---

[13] Amos' five visions are in 7:1–3; 7:4–6; 7:7–9; 8:1–3; 9:1–4.

the Cushites, indeed over the entire world, but also over those who live within a closer proximity to Israel, in this case also the Arameans and the Philistines, some of the nation's fiercest adversaries. Yahweh employs the same verb "to bring up" (עָלָה in the Hiphil) frequently used for the salvific exodus redemption (to "bring up" Israel from Egypt [e.g., Ex 3:8, 17]) but here applies it to Israel's *enemies*.

These comparisons indicate that in Yahweh's eyes unfaithful Israel is no better, but is *just like* Cush, Philistia, and Aram. One can almost hear the audience's reaction, "You have made them equal to us" (Mt 20:12).

Conclusions

Amos was sent to people who did not seem to notice, did not seem to care, and were unable to act. Their leader—Jeroboam ben Joash (1:1; 7:9–11)—fostered the nation's idolatry and closed his eyes to human needs, economic inequities, and broken social systems. The people sought gods at shrines other than Jerusalem[14] and boasted in horses and chariots rather than Yahweh (Ps 20:8 [ET 20:7]). They indulged in unbridled greed, brutality, and stinginess. Leadership in the Northern Kingdom was undisturbed and insensitive to these maladies. In this context, Amos would not have been effective if he had employed stereotyped language, because stereotyped language is a language of cliché. The immediate danger of cliché is the audience's indifference. This is what Homer meant when he spoke about the poet's creativity: "For men praise that song the most which comes the newest to their ears."[15] Through Amos, Yahweh inverted language and genres in order to gain a hearing from the people.

Jesus went even farther than Amos. He not only uttered subversive words, he is *the* subversive Word. In his antagonistic context (e.g., Mt 23:25–26; Mk 3:6; Lk 4:28–29; Jn 8:59), Jesus employed inversions. His best known reversals are in the Beatitudes (Mt 5:1–12; Lk 6:20–26). He also said, for example, the following: "For whoever wants to *save* his life will *lose* it, but whoever *loses* his life for my sake will *find* it" (Mt 16:25). "Many who are *first* will be *last*, and the *last* will be *first*" (Mt 19:30; cf. Mt 20:8). "Let the *greatest* among you become as the *youngest* and the *leader* as *one who serves*" (Lk 22:26). The most joyful Pauline inversion expresses what Luther called "the joyous exchange":[16] God "made him who knew *no sin* to *become sin* for us so that in him we might

---

14 See 2:7–8; 3:14; 4:4–5; 5:5–6, 14, 21–27; 7:9–17; 8:5, 10, 14; 9:1 (the Bethel temple).

15 Homer, *Odyssey*, 1.351–52, quoted by Gitay, "Reflections on the Study of the Prophetic Discourse," 213.

16 The phrase *der fröhlich Wechsel* ("the joyous exchange") appears in Luther's German version of *The Freedom of a Christian* (WA 7.25), a work he originally wrote in Latin. The Latin version is translated in AE 31:327–77 (see especially 31:351–52), and the German version is translated in Bertram Lee Woolf, trans., *Reformation Writings of Martin Luther* (London: Lutterworth, 1952), 1:349–79 (see especially 1:363–64). See also, for example, AE 26:172–79, 276–91 (the exchange is termed "this fortunate exchange" on 26:284); 30:225; 31:297–99; 48:12–13.

become the righteousness of God" (2 Cor 5:21). Indeed, inversion is more than an effective homiletical technique. The inversion that sinners are justified simply through faith in the sinless Christ is the very Gospel itself!

Pastors can learn from the rhetorical strategies in Amos in order to avoid letting their sermons become full of dull, conventional, and routinized speech. People slumber spiritually when they disregard theology as familiar jargon. One solution is to preach with adrenalin-laden inversions that push beyond the status quo. To be sure, the preaching of Law and Gospel requires language that is faithful to the text and in accord with sound doctrine. But at the same time it must shock sensitivity, call attention to what is not noticed, break the routine, and cause people to reconsider things that they have come to take for granted.

Amos offers more than just a *rhetoric* of preaching; he also teaches a *theology* of preaching. The prophet's audience apparently knew of Yahweh's past actions in the exodus and conquest (e.g., 2:4, 9–11) and longed for Yahweh's future action (e.g., 5:18–20). But despite their knowledge of the past and hope for the future, they lacked present faith, and they rejected the present Word from Yahweh (2:12; 7:10–17). They did everything they could to squelch the *viva vox Dei* ("living voice of God"). Their reasoning went something like this: "if we can successfully deny that Yahweh has any Word for us in the present moment, then we can remain 'religious' and still be free to do anything we want!" Amos' theological task, then, was to strip away the past and the future and confront Israel with Yahweh's *present* Word of Law and Gospel.

The well-known phrase *viva vox evangelii*, "the living voice of the Gospel," describes Luther's theology of preaching:

> Everything the apostles wrote is one Gospel. And the word "Gospel" signifies nothing else than a sermon or report concerning the grace and mercy of God merited and acquired through the Lord Jesus Christ with His death. Actually, the Gospel is not what one finds in books and what is written in letters of the alphabet; it is rather an oral sermon and a living Word, a voice that resounds throughout the world and is proclaimed publicly, so that one hears it everywhere. …
>
> Now he who preaches these facts [how Christ saves us through his work] and writes about them teaches the true Gospel, just as all the apostles, particularly St. Paul and St. Peter, do in their epistles.[17]

The reformer states that when a pastor steps down from the pulpit he should be able to say, "with St. Paul and all the apostles and prophets, … 'God himself has said this.' … Whoever cannot boast like that about his preaching, let him give up preaching."[18] Luther's theology of the Lord's Supper rightly emphasizes the doctrine of the real presence of the body and blood of Christ. Luther also rightly emphasizes the real presence of the voice of Jesus Christ in faithful proclamation. In this way, Luther follows in the footsteps of Paul, who placards

---

[17] AE 30:3.

[18] AE 41:216 (cf. Meuser, *Luther the Preacher*).

Christ before the eyes of his hearers (Gal 3:1) and brings people to repentance and faith at the present moment: "behold, *now* is the acceptable time; behold, *now* is the day of salvation" (2 Cor 6:2; cf. Rom 8:1). Although the ministries of Israel's prophets and the earthly ministry of Jesus Christ are finished, once-for-all-time events, they remain vitally current for people today. The Word of God "is living and active" (Heb 4:12); through it he confronts, converts, and claims people as his own. Preaching cites past history and future events to confront people in the present moment.

Yet if the past and future are the *only* focal points in preaching, then the error is not only rhetorical, it is theological. A sermon that focuses solely upon what God has done in the past or will do in the future neglects that preaching is the proclamation of the *viva vox Dei*. God always has a present Word for his people. Christ is not preached if he is not preached as condemning and absolving *now*.

Forde maintains that all too often the proclamation of the Gospel gets displaced by explanation, teaching, lecturing, and the like.[19] But Lutheran preaching—indeed prophetic and apostolic preaching—is to be "the direct declaration of the Word of God, that is, the Word *from* God."[20] This is opposed to preaching *about* God. Preaching like Amos means that pastors include present-tense verbs and first- and second-person pronouns. Just as the pastor absolves, baptizes, and distributes the Eucharist in the present tense, so the sermon is also God's present action, *his current mighty act.*

Moral chaos and unbridled exploitation will not change through more advanced church programs or better parish strategies, but rather by the bold and rhetorically charged proclamation of God's Word for the present moment. This word brings holiness back into history, lets justice and righteousness roll like a river (Amos 5:24), embraces suffering in a climate of complacency, voices hope in the midst of despair, and refuses brutality in the name of Christ and his kingdom.

Instructed by Amos and fired by the Holy Spirit, the employment of the homiletical strategy of inversion preaches Law and Gospel in order to awaken the church from what has grown ordinary and stale and routine. Following the lead of Amos, pastors will be better equipped to proclaim Yahweh's Word of Law that finally yields to the Gospel's greatest inversion of all—anticipated already in Amos 9:11: "Why do you look for the *living one* among the *dead*? He is not here, but he has *risen*!" (Lk 24:5–6).

---

[19] Forde, *Theology Is for Proclamation*, 1.

[20] Forde, *Theology Is for Proclamation*, 2.

Index of Subjects

Index of Passages

Apocrypha, Old Testament Pseudepigrapha, and Other Jewish Literature

Early Christian Literature

Ecumenical Creeds

Lutheran Confessions

Works of Martin Luther

Lutheran Hymnals

Ancient Near Eastern Literature

Classical Literature